St. James Guide to

NATIVE
NORTH AMERICAN
ARTISTS

St. James Guide to

NATIVE NORTH AMERICAN ARTISTS

With a Preface by
Rick Hill

And an Introduction by
W. Jackson Rushing

Editor
Roger Matuz

ST. JAMES PRESS

AN IMPRINT OF GALE

DETROIT • NEW YORK • TORONTO • LONDON

Metropolitan State University
Library Services
St. Paul, MN 55106

Roger Matuz, *Editor*

Nicolet V. Elert
Project Coordinator

Laura Standley Berger, Joann Cerrito, Dave Collins, Miranda Ferrara,
Kristin Hart, Janice Jorgensen, Margaret Mazurkiewicz, Michael J. Tyrkus,
St. James Press Staff

Peter M. Gareffa, *Managing Editor, St. James Press*

Mary Beth Trimper, *Production Director*
Shanna Heilveil, *Production Assistant*

Cynthia Baldwin, *Product Design Manager*
Pamela A. E. Galbreath, *Art Director*
Pamela A. Reed, *Photography Coordinator*
Randy Bassett, *Image Database Supervisor*
Mikal Ansari, Robert Duncan, *Imaging Specialists*

While every effort has been made to ensure the reliability of the information presented in this publication, St. James Press does not guarantee the accuracy of the data contained herein. St. James Press accepts no payment for listing; and inclusion of any organization, agency, institution, publication, service, or individual does not imply endorsement of the editors or publisher.

Errors brought to the attention of the publisher and verified to the satisfaction of the publisher will be corrected in future editions.

The paper used in this publication meets the minimum
requirements of American National Standard for Information Sciences—
Permanence Paper for Printed Library Materials, ANSI Z39.48-1984.

This publication is a creative work fully protected by all applicable copyright laws, as well as by misappropriation, trade secret, unfair competition, and other applicable laws. The authors and editors of this work have added value to the underlying factual material herein through one or more of the following: unique and original selection, coordination, expression, arrangement, and classification of the information.

All rights to this publication will be vigorously defended.

Copyright © 1998
St. James Press
835 Penobscot Building
Detroit, MI 48226

All rights reserved including the right of reproduction in whole or in part in any form.

Cover photo: *Tree of Life* diptych by Juane Quick-to-See Smith. Courtesy Steinbaum Krauss Gallery, New York, and Jan Cicero Gallery, Chicago.

St. James guide to native North American artists / with a preface by
Rick Hill ; and introduction by W. Jackson Rushing ; editor, Roger
Matuz.
   p. cm.
  Includes bibliographical references and indexes.
  ISBN 1-55862-221-7 (alk. paper)
  1. Indian artists United States. 2. Indian artists Canada.
I. Matuz, Roger.
E98.A7S8 1997
704.03'97--dc21
                                              97-18453
                                                   CIP

Printed in the United States of America

St. James Press is an imprint of Gale
10 9 8 7 6 5 4 3 2

CONTENTS

PREFACE

"Tradition is the enemy of progress. Progress is the enemy of tradition," stated Ric Glazer Danay, a Mohawk artist, explaining his philosophy about Indian art at a 1988 conference of Native artists in Lethbridge, Alberta. Danay, who grew up in New York City but teaches art at the University of California, pokes fun at the debates surrounding contemporary Indian art. In response to endless questions about cultural authenticity, maintaining tradition, and artist responsibility, Danay established the following "aesthetic realties," which give us an idea of how contemporary Indian art might function differently from native art in the past. First, the aesthetic prerogative of the Native artist is not to define art but to create art works. Secondly, it is manifest that the bulk of Native art is often overly decorative and that the bulk of decoration is not art. Thirdly, Native art is not for curators, not for directors of museums, and not for gallery owners. Lastly, Danay believes that art and Native aestheticism are characterized by discipline, restraint, and organization, as well as the abandonment of old forms for new ones. In his view, traditional aesthetics would not serve Indian culture if it did not possess a dignity of its own.

For Native Americans, artistic tradition runs deep with both community asethetics and social interaction. That tradition is often recalled by the leading contemporary artists as a source of their own inspiration, but they also note that this is a very different world from that of their ancestors. Therefore, their art must be more responsive to the circumstances of life today. It is interesting to note that the clear majority of these artists do not live in their ancestral communities. In fact, many of them have multiple cultural identities, a unique combination of tribal affiliations, racial backgrounds and an urbanized worldview. Do they still represent the cultural or spiritual thinking of their relatives on the reservation? What is the consequence to the native community of having the visionary thinkers of that community living somewhere else? Can an Indian artist who lives and breathes far away from the community have an impact on the quality of thinking of that community? Are the leading Native American artists creating a new vision for Indian nations, or simply a way to make a living for themselves?

As you may imagine, there are no easy answers to these questions. There are also many more questions that need to be asked. I choose to not focus on who is an Indian and why it is a bad idea to buy an Indian Vision from a non-Indian. That should be self-evident, and if it is not, there is no way I can explain it to you. What I want to look at are the visions offered by contemporary Indian artists of their own people. The artists of the past were never as far removed from their home communities as the Indian artists of today appear to be. I would like to know, in their own thinking, how the Indian artists view themselves.

"Indian artists are as important as our politicians," stated Dana Williams, a Potawatomi artist and associate curator of a 1992 Montreal exhibition on Native art (*New Territories: 350-500 Years After*, Ateliers Vision Planetaire). "We are the defenders of our culture and witness to many changes taking place within our world." Witnessing has become a popular notion in the arts of people of color. But is witnessing and recording enough to assure the survival of Native thinking? For Williams, art provides ways to communicate to non-Natives, ways to heal the racism that was evident in the armed conflict at Oka in 1990. "I like the idea of using art as therapy and as the ideal vehicle to use as an educational tool to assist us in reaching our target group—the non-Native Canadian. Because art is tangible, art is visible, and everyone from the very aged to the very young can appreciate a work of art."

While some artists may object to being measured by the impact they have on Indian communities instead of mainstream art circles, I feel that it is a legitimate concern. Certainly it is an underground discussion among Indians. Often times, artists are dismissed because of where they live, how they treat other Indians, their political views, whether or not they are tribally enrolled, whether or not they speak their own language, the source of their imagery, whether or not they went to art school. It seems that there is more discussion about artists than the impact of their work on Indians. I have never attended an Indian art conference where the issue of the connection of the artist to community, culture and religion has not been raised. In fact, it is part of the sales pitch for the art.

In the past, contemporary artists proposed that art provides a sacred connection to the past, that the contemporary artist has inherited a cultural legacy, and that it is a tradition that they maintain. Joanne Cardinal-Schubert, in the 1992 exhibition organized by Williams, stated that she interprets the world through the eyes of generations of Indians—how they have used art—and sees art as her way to defend the visions of her ancestors. "As artists our only weapon in this battle for survival," stated Cardinal-Schubert, "is our knowledge, responsibility and a commitment to share our worldview with others.... We determine what the future will be by our actions."

Among artists who do not want to be measured by their ancestral past there has been a growing feeling that they are artists who just happen to be Indian, and that they should be allowed artistic freedom to create anything they want. I do find it ironic that they seem to only gain acceptance in the art world because they are Indians and have not been accepted as mainstream Indian artists.

Polarization of the Camps

The various views of what is legitimate in Indian art may simply be opposing points of view among a very diverse group of artists. Imagine for a minute trying to define "white art" as if there were only one standard that applied to all European countries and their American descendants. Imagine trying to state that there could be no cross-cultural influences between the French, English or Italians in art. Imagine that American fine arts were measured against the work of Sunday artists and commercial craftspeople. You can then begin to understand how ludicrous some of the discussions about Indian art have been. There can certainly not be one standard of thought that applies to all Indians or all Indian artists. There never was, even before the word "art" was introduced to Indians.

For some Indian artists, maintaining the principles of their community aesthetic are important. They see their art functioning for the sake of the community. These artists tend to make things that are used in the family, in rituals, in community events. People who make dance clothing come to mind. Drums, rattles, bowls, cloth, carvings and all types of work are made for personal expression and communal belief at the same time. The primary motivation of these artists is to maintain traditions, and they are active participants in their traditional culture. The community could not function without these artists. We seldom hear from this group: they don't write essays, they don't demonstrate their work at museums, and they don't necessarily participate in the marketplace. Yet, where would the traditions be without them?

There are Indian artists who pride themselves on maintaining techniques and design motifs of their ancestors in their contemporary work. They have established a regional or national reputation for the quality of their work, have studied the artistic traditions of their community and often have learned their art from family members. These artists are well respected by their community for preserving the traditions of that community. Interestingly enough, they actually create the most innovations in the arts, because they take community norms and establish new ways to express them. Think of the evolution in beadwork, pottery and jewelry among Indians of the last three hundred years. Nearly every Indian community now considers beadwork to be "traditional," and yet each generation produces new styles of beadwork. Glass beads, although of European origin and often influenced by European patterns of use, have become one commonality in nearly ever Indian home in the country. Yet, much of the pottery and jewelry produced by Indians is sold to non-Indians, and these media have become respected art forms on their own. While we argue about how to label this work—art, craft, fine art, commercial art—we do not deny the beauty of the accomplishments.

Then there are Indian artists who produce work for the Indian market circuit, attending art shows, pow wows and cultural festivals to sell their work. This work covers the full range from moderately priced jewelry and beadwork to sculptures and prints. Pow wow crafts are often still connected to community traditions, but generally cater to preconceived ideas of Indianness in the eyes of the consumer. While there are many crafts made and sold at pow wows that are very well done and the pow wow market serves as a way for many Indians to acquire crafts that they will use in their own homes or rituals, there is a disturbing trend in this area of the arts. The emergence and wide diffusion of pan-Indian articles like the Dream Catcher shows that new trends can start and be elaborated upon, but they are often accompanied by distorted ideas of sacredness, and the craftspeople often make up their own stories about these items in order to make them more spiritually significant to the buyer. The origin and function of the Dream Catcher has been described in many different ways. In fact, you can now find Dream Catcher craft kits in stores across the country. You can see them hanging from car mirrors. You can see them at every pow wow. I have yet to see one over an Indian bed. Maybe Indians like bad dreams.

For some Indian artists, art is a form of cultural therapy, reconnecting the artist to ancestral beliefs, tribal histories and cultural heroes. These artists often work at the local level, receiving respect from their community because their work shows pride in the traditions of the past and honors those that fought hard to maintain that way of life. The strength of this work is in the imagery and emotions evoked, not necessarily in the exactness of the execution of the art. That the artist connects to sources of knowledge through the arts is of most importance. Art curators would generally dismiss this work as "bad art," but to the

Indians artists it serves a great need to keep awareness of traditions alive, to demonstrate a personal commitment to the traditions. It is the way by which most Indian visual artists begin to explore what art can do.

However, there is also a smaller group of Indian artists who seek recognition in fine art circles; they choose to exhibit their work in professional art galleries and often lecture on Indian arts. The clear majority of these artists resent having their work measured by a tribal aesthetic that they feel is no longer relevant to this generation. They have been the most vocal about seeing their work as fine art, not "Indian art," much in the mode of Fritz Scholder. Because of their high visibility in the Indian art press, these artists often receive the most attention in university exhibitions and conferences, serve more often as consultants to museum programs, write more often on the arts, curate more exhibitions and, therefore, have the most impact on public perception of Indian art among curators, collector and art patrons. As it turns out, they also have most likely been trained in the arts at a university and have advanced college degrees. They measure their own work by a different standard.

The Artists Speak

While it is difficult to capsulize artists' view on their art, and personal views change through time, I will try to use the words of artists themselves to make salient points. In a session of the 1987 Lethbridge symposium titled "Swimming the Mainstream: A Dialogue with Artists of Native Ancestry Who Are Receiving Recognition and Critical Acclaim," the artists Carl Beam, Jane Ash Poitras, Joanne Cardinal-Schubert and Bob Boyer led a discussion of their roles as artists who are Indians.

Carl Beam, an Ojibway painter and printmaker, sees no useful purpose in a dialogue about Native art: "I never consider myself as a proponent of Native art or those kinds of things. That's an art historical problem, an anthropological problem that other people deal with.... I just deal with the problems of art production.... It's hardly worth entertaining as a serious debate about what constitutes Native Art! That's not an important issue! The thing is, we have these tools, we use these tools, but what you want to say, ultimately, with these new tools is up to yourself. Our responsibility is to our art work. We're not going to a sort of *mind-control*, or *mind-Nazi,* about artistic decisions regarding art. What we do as artists is what we do as artists."

Freedom to express oneself has become the war cry of the contemporary artists, but Beam also realizes that social injustice impacts on that sense of freedom. When asked about social causes he supports, Beam replied: "There is kind of missionary zeal about changing everything in the world.... Being an artist, a painter, etc, it looked like a poor vehicle (medium) to do that in and I didn't join a lot of stuff that was happening at the time because possibly your strongest ultimate weapon for affecting change might be discipline in art, discipline and pursuing, paying attention to the craft of what you do and utilizing all that external stimulation wherever it happens in the world, as it pertains to Native people.... I, as a Native artist, have had to adopt everybody and consequently use everything that's happening in terms of stimulation as regards Native people, and give it back via the art work, somehow."

Is Beam's thinking that much different from that of Fred Benjamin, a Mille Lacs Ojibway elder who talks of the origin of Indian songs and indicates how Indians create art? "The way the Indian people, long ago, made their songs was by looking at what the Great Spirit gave them to understand in their minds...to make songs out of what they saw," stated Benjamin. "Like the leaves when the wind blows: they're shaking, they make a little noise. That's how they got the idea to put bells on their legs. And sometimes you see a fowl, like an eagle, an owl, a chickenhawk. The Indian people looked at them, the way they'd swing their wings, how they'd go down and up. That's how they'd make the pitch of their songs.... And everything they'd see; when they looked at the sky, the clouds, they'd make songs out of those. And they'd make words out of the clouds that they saw. And they'd think that there's a kind of a holy spirit going around, and that's how they'd make their songs." (From *Circle of Life: Cultural Continuity in Ojibwe Crafts*, St. Louis County Historical Society, Chisholm Museum and Duluth Art Institute, Minnesota, 1984.)

So it would make sense that if the Indians of today see a dead bird, killed by chemical contamination, a mushroom cloud that killed several hundred thousand people, or people who attempt to destroy their world, their artistic reaction would be different. The process is the same, only the subject of that observation and creativity has changed. Nature as a primary artistic inspiration is a commonly held idea about Indian art of the past, and still influences many of the artists of today. Duane Goodwin, an Ojibwe craftsperson, expressed his feeling about the importance of maintaining that connection through art. "In my beadwork, you've noticed, there's a lot of floral design. That comes from having a special caring feeling for the flowers, natural essence in nature. I think it's something beautiful enough to look at, to always get a lift from it when you look at it, even if it's for casual wear or everyday use. You can still adorn yourself with pretty shapes and colors.... If you like that sort of thing, if you like art, you can display it on your body. Your body can be like a wall to display artwork on."

Carl Beam reminds us that all forms of art can exist and that there can be very different, often contradictory, forms of art within the same community. He views the thinking tradition as being just as important as the spiritual tradition. He thinks of artists as being responsible only if they give a response to what they are confronted with in their life. However, that response cannot be a lie and must be based upon the real life experience of the artist and not a romantic view of their ancestral past. Indian realities, according to Beam, have changed: "But if you are looking for art done by a Native person and if you can't accept this as the reality of what's today, then that is your problem!... Paradoxes, in fact, do exist side by side in this world."

Sacred Sources

Sacred sources of knowledge can also be important artistic sources as well. Jane Ash Poitras is a Cree painter who was the first native woman to receive an M.F.A. in printmaking from Columbia University in New York City. She feels that art schools cannot make you into a good artist. "A master at art is born a master," said Poitras. "It's up to you to go out and seek good art.... Because this whole thing is about excellence. When we're in the field of art and we are representing ourselves as artists, we are a voice in the country, visually and in other ways too...and we have to give them the best." Of course this begs the question of who defines the "best" for Indians. Is it the same standards in the arts as defined by non-Indians?

Poitras also sees art as a form of sharing. She was a street kid, adopted by non-Indians in an era when there was a lot of shame associated with being an Indian. For her, art is a way of sharing real life experiences and the thoughts that those experiences inspire. Poitras had a significant turning point in her life when she was introduced to traditional thinking through the sweat lodge. "I went into the sweat lodge for very specific purposes, for healing purposes, and also to purify myself because I was full of a lot of venom, or something, and it worked! The belief is that when you see a Vision in a sweatlodge the person that enters the sweat lodge is never the same as the person who leaves, and I was never the same person after that.... I revealed my soul to the viewer. The overwhelming response of the viewer was so incredible, because then they could share partly with me what had happened to me and what I found out for myself. So, art is sharing. You do the art to understand yourself and, maybe also, to let the viewer help understand themselves."

By this interpretation, the artistic process is very much like that of the past. The vision seeker gains an understanding that is then interpreted through art. Others "read" the significance of that interpretation and can reflect on their own experiences. Among the Plains cultures of the past, the visions were translated onto a shield. Each was a different interpretation of the sharing power. One warrior could respect the vision and artistry of another's shield without having to know all of the details of that vision. The artist's job in those days was to find a powerful way to express the substance of that vision. Of course, in Poitras's case, the fact that she received her vision in the traditional process enriches the validity of this approach. But what about those Indians who do not go on their own vision quest? Is there art equally as valid with their realities?

In regard to being called an Indian artist, Poitras concludes: "In the end it didn't matter what classification or what label they put on me. In the end art speaks for itself and no matter where you go and what you do that's what counts. When it's good art, it's good and no matter what labels you put on it, it doesn't matter!"

Many Native artists have come to the conclusion that there are no conclusions. People change the way they live their lives. Beliefs change. Perspectives change. The art of any individual will therefore change over the years. In the past, archaeologists have tried to define the arts by their similarity over the years, rather than to accept the premise that Beam puts forth: change is actually traditional. Joanne Cardinal-Schubert, a Blackfeet painter and installation artist, calls for the consumer to be more informed and says that not every Indian makes a good artist: "I think that the danger is that you put up an umbrella that says *Native Art* on it and there's going to be an awful lot of people that are going to be jumping under it to get out of the rain, and they are not always going to be people that have the same integrity and qualitative processes of creation that a lot of artists have. We're in a profession!... Why is it that anybody that picks up something and makes 'marks' is all of a sudden an artist?"

Contemporary painters are often accused of being media stars and catering to Western notions of art—breaking traditional art rules, and even being less Indian than people who make jewelry, baskets or cloth. Bob Boyer, a Metis painter who teaches art at the Federated Indian College in Regina, recognized that there are conflicting notions of academic supremacy held by some of the artists themselves. "So there's a lot of people who (practice) sort of an *academic snobbery* who say, 'Gee, these guys aren't very good. They're selling to everybody!' And then on the other hand there's the flip of the coin where there's six of us up here who sort of run the game of playing so-called *academic excellence*: we get into these exhibitions. The critics write about us. All of the White writers write about us. All the right people put us in all the right books, the right exhibitions...it's a real dilemma! Artists tend to be very prima donna(ish), egotistical, ego-centric and so on. If they see anybody else getting a bigger chunk of the cake, then it just becomes a bigger problem."

How did Indians get themselves into such a corner of arguing over what it takes to be an artist? The answer is clouded in the very history of the clash of cultures brought about when European ideas of art and Indian ideas of art were oceans apart.

The Creation of an Indian Art Persona

"They are fond of painting, and practice it with considerable skill, considering that they have no rules of art," French Jesuit Father Gabriel Sagard wrote in 1632, as he traveled among the Huron Indians in what is now Quebec. Sagard could not see the Indian "rules" and instead judged their art by his own definition. Very early commentary, based upon Euro-centric ideas of culture, art and civilization, divided Indian art into various categories of curio, artifact, archeological specimen, folk art, primitive art, crafts and fine art. All of these definitions have come from the outside looking in, as various academic disciplines fought for prominence over the last 150 years. The rules were still being set by non-Indians.

At Bacone Junior College, an Indian school in Muskogee, Oklahoma, another approach was underway. In 1935 an art program was started that would be directed by now-famous Indian artists Acee Blue Eagle, Woody Crumbo and Dick West, Sr. Indian artists would now teach art to Indians. The likes of Archie Blackowl, Fred Beaver, Blackbear Bosin, and Jerome Tiger passed through Bacone and became celebrated artists. The Bacone program produced a school of art that honors the past, recalls the beauty of traditional culture and makes common scenes of the past very heroic and dramatic. The style, still popular in Oklahoma, focuses on the Plains Indian warrior, tribal oral histories, ceremonies and spiritual traditions. This style defined Indian art in Oklahoma and became the focus of the Philbrook Museum of Art in Tulsa, which sponsored annual competitions from 1946 to 1979.

In the important 1941 *Indian Art of the United States* exhibit at the Museum of Modern Art in New York, the curators, working with the Indian Arts and Crafts Board of the Department of the Interior, attempted to change the belief that Indian art must be frozen in time. They suggested that Indian objects should be seen as art rather than artifact. They dismissed the people who refused to recognize that Indians, like all other people, change. "There are people who have created for themselves a romantic picture of a glorious past that is often far from accurate," the curators wrote in the catalog to the exhibition. "They wish to see the living Indian return to an age that has long since passed and they resent any change in his art. But these people forget that any culture that is satisfied to copy the life of former generations has given up hope as well as life itself. The fact that we think of Navajo silversmithing as a typical Indian art and the horsemanship of the Plains tribes as a typical Indian characteristics proves sufficiently that those tribes were strong enough to make such foreign contributions entirely their own by adapting them to the pattern of their own traditions.... Invention or adaption of new forms does not necessarily mean repudiation of tradition but is often a source of its enrichment.... To rob a people of tradition is to rob it of inborn strength and identity. To rob a people of opportunity to grow through invention or through acquisition of values from other races is to rob it of its future."

To many this was a watershed, but it was also a time when Indian painting had been defined by the standards set at The Studio at the Santa Fe Indian School, through the tutoring of Dorothy Dunn. The style the studio promoted as "traditional" painting was a seen as a logical extension to the art of the past. The characteristic flat, two-dimensional style of that kind of painting was made justifiable. Indian art of the past had no visual perspective, no realism, no shadows. However, that strategy worked and the art consumers of the East began to patronize Indian artists in the West. This style of painting was the first real commercialization of Indian art, as it was produced entirely to be sold to non-Indians and therefore to cater to their tastes. Art was seen as a form of economic development as much as a way to keep disaffected Indians in school. As the years went on, the consumer demanded a sense of authenticity in the accuracy of the details and expected scenes of ritual and history. To do otherwise was considered an artistic sin. Curators, art juries and art sale organizers edited out the art did that did not fit the prescribed categories deemed appropriate for Indians.

Certainly the Indian students that Dorothy Dunn worked with at the studio would later have a great impact on the visual arts among Indians. Her students included Allan Houser, Oscar Howe, Fred Kabotie, Pablita Velarde, Pop Chalee, Joe Herrera, Ben Quintana, Quincy Tahoma, Andrew Tsinahjinnie, Gerald Nailor and Harrison Begay. What they learned in her studio classroom was to become known as "traditional Indian painting," a misnomer that still has a stranglehold on our understanding of Indian art. In reality it was a style that was taught in the Dunn classes, a style that benefitted from a longer tradition of Indian use of color, shape, line and flattened perspective. The Dunn style allowed for obvious connection to traditional forms of painting, inspired by kiva painting, hide painting and pictographic imagery. Her style was part of the larger-than-life heroic art that came out of that era, as a reaction to the Great Depression. That style of art helped the Indians feel good about being an Indian, helped to remind of the good old days when Indian life was noble.

In an article Dunn wrote for *National Geographic* (1955), she provided the most concise description of the style she promoted: "The Indian painter poses no models, follows no color theory, gauges no true perspective. He seldom rounds the subject by using light and shade. Often he leaves the background to the imagination.... By omitting nonessentials, he produces abstract symbols for plants, animals, earth, and sky. Yet he acutely senses life and movement and can convey mood or intense action with a few lines.... A typical Indian painting is, therefore, imaginative, symbolic, two-dimensional."

Not all Dunn''s students liked her approach to art. Allan Houser tells of his dissatisfaction with the "traditional" style of that era: "Dorothy Dunn told me that if I was going to do things that are realistic, then you better go on out and take the next bus home.... Everyone was encouraged to their own background for traditional things. That is all she permitted us to do. If you did a landscape or something, she wouldn't accept it.... My only objection to Dorothy Dunn was this: she trained us all the same way. 'You either paint like this, Mr. Houser, or it's not Indian art.' "

Oscar Howe, Allan Houser and Joe Herrera left the Santa Fe Indian School Studio and developed their own unique styles. I don't know how many times I heard Allan Houser say that contemporary Indian artists had to find their own unique style, had to study what was being done, and had to search for their own way to express themselves, and not copy someone else. Oscar Howe certainly found it difficult to gain acceptance for his own unique style.

In 1962, a unique experiment in Indian education was undertaken by the Bureau of Indian Affairs. A century of denying the value of the arts in Indian education was reversed with the establishment of the Institute of American Indian Arts, a high school in Santa Fe dedicated to development of the arts for Indians. The objectives of that experiment have evolved over time, with the Institute still growing and changing. The thinking that gave birth to this art experiment was a combination of evolving social attitudes towards Indians, changing federal politics and a social renewal among Indians who had suffered a generation of relocation and assimilation. The arts were thought to be both a way to help Indians through school and a way for Indians to express what it meant to be an Indian in the twentieth century.

IAIA taught that Indian art is rooted in the past, a past that was nature-centered, based upon ritual and ceremony. Art and religion were inseparable. Indian art was influenced by all aspects of the cosmos—the sun, wind, earth, rain, sky, lightning, water, moon, trees, and animals. Art by Indians was therefore a symbolic offering, seeking to favorably alter mystical forces for the sake of community well-being. The function of the arts in traditional Indian society was to draw the people in closer harmony with nature through music, dance, symbolic designs, and ceremonies that bring spiritual and mystical powers to attention. The seeds of traditional culture remained passionately alive over one thousand years. It was the Indian ability to adapt to a changing social, political and economic environment that allowed the culture to survive.

In its three decades of arts education, IAIA has seen nearly three thousand students pass through its studios and classrooms. The impact of IAIA is just beginning to be understood as the second generation of students—the children of the alumni—are now attending IAIA. There is no other model like IAIA in the art world. This single institution has influenced the majority of artists who are now leaders of the contemporary Indian art movement. IAIA has helped to produce many of America's most creative Indian and Alaska Native artists through instruction in the visual arts, the performing arts, creative writing and museum studies. The invigorating mixture of creative Indian faculty at IAIA combined with the political climate of a country that was beginning to rethink what Indians were all about fostered IAIA's role as a laboratory for the Indian art experiment.

Much of the new style of art was developed in reaction to the older forms that had come to be called "traditional"—where Indian painters were expected to paint a certain way, no matter what their tribal affiliation or their personal experiences. Allan Houser fought against that mold, as did several others in the early 1940s and 1950s. IAIA encouraged experimentation. The debate over what is traditional has raged ever since.

In the *First Annual Invitational Exhibition of American Indian Paintings* at the art gallery of the U.S. Department of Interior Building in Washington, D. C., in 1964, eighty-eight recent works were featured as contrasted to forty-four works made from 1930 to 1958. The catalog for the exhibition explained the significance of the IAIA artists: "The invitational section of the exhibition, which includes the work of several recent Institute students, vividly reflects the new spirit of experimentation and invention which has resulted in a wide latitude of styles and media now at the command of Native American artists....

Whatever latitude of present day expression, it is significant to note that, throughout the half century or more of the development of contemporary Native American art, regardless of the individual artist's personal form of expression, whether he chooses a realistic style for a literal depiction of ceremonial or social activity, or an abstract or experimental style to express a personal or universal vision or tribal myth or belief, the Native American artist's primary concern has remained directed toward the interpretation, or reinvention of the traditional beliefs and imagery of his people."

An underlying spirit of contemporary Indian art was expressed by Earl Biss, a Crow painter who gained much attention for the unique style he developed in representing the old days of his people. Biss created a series of circular paintings using free-flowing movement and color to attempt to illustrate what spiritual forces look like. These were like dreamscapes from within the soul, created to give a sense of the power of the life forces in the Crow universe. The circle is a common Indian symbol of life and unity and recalls the shape of the Plains Indian warrior's shield that would often be decorated with dream-inspired images. These in effect become shields for the modern warrior/artist. However, it is a view from within the spiritual power that was reflected in the symbolic designs of the older shields. In 1967, Biss said: "I feel that the inborn flair for art is due to my Indian background. I believe that my sense of balance and color was passed down by my ancestors and this sense cannot be lost, even though tradition is not portrayed in my work...and, therefore, though my painting is not materially related to Indian tradition, it is still basically Indian art."

"Color and design are determined by my response to actual process—application, spontaneity, and rhythm," explained Biss in 1973: "The process in itself is the 'art happening' with the completed piece the product. I do not restrict my works to outward imagery, but try to capture or illustrate those powers or forces of nature which play such an important part in reality. These are in many ways realistic paintings."

Many Ways of Seeing was the title of the twentieth anniversary exhibition of the Institute of American Indian Arts. The catalog for that exhibition predicted new directions for Native American artists beyond the period of the 1980s, which has been seen as a "renaissance of the Indian." Three areas of development were called for in that catalog. First, there would be a continuation of old forms by traditionalists whose lives remain tribally-rooted and to whom such expressions are natural and purposely tribal. Secondly, there would be a revival of old forms by certain people who are looking for cultural renewal and national recognition for Native Americans even though the forms are not useful nor do they perform any function in their lives or have any relationships to their lifestyles. Thirdly, there would be a search for new forms, led by Indian youth whose individualistic art impulses supplanted the tribally prescribed styles set by their ancestors.

These predictions of fourteen years ago have remained remarkably on target. Of the first group, traditional practitioners of rituals and ceremonies still require specific works for the exercise of their religion. This remains the smallest group of artists who continue to produce the articles needed for the spiritual expressions of each Indian nation. The second group is the largest, the art sellers, who create market demand and continue to evolve art forms that are commercially viable, from ceramics to textiles to crafts. These artists create for others and often do not use the art they create as part of their lifestyle. The last group are the Indian art world's explorers, who search through all media for new ways to express their personal feelings about being an Indian in this world.

New symbols have also emerged on the Indian art scene. The earth as mother has become an important inspirational aspect of the contemporary arts, yet there are very few references to the Mother Earth concept in the visual symbols of the past. Certainly there are references to the land, land forms and celestial bodies. But there are not many specific symbols that show the earth as mother. Mike MacDonald, a Native video artist from British Columbia, sees a new use in symbols: "We all have a responsibility to the earth and as artists we have a responsibility to take whatever symbols the earth gives us and try to use them to make this a better earth."

Can the artists remake the earth? That seems like a Creator-like job.

Contemporary Native American artists certainly draw upon their ancestral connections to animals, plants and earthforms as they seek a new kind of sacred imagery, one that does not violate pre-existing usage of sacred imagery, but recalls the sacred intent of image-making used by their relatives. The eagle, buffalo, bear, and wolf are often used as endangered sacred species in Indian art and serve as a metaphor for Indians themselves. What happens to the animals will eventually happen to us all. So animals become the most obvious symbols to recur in contemporary art.

But it is a confusing metaphor. How well have Native communities practiced their own environmental conservation? Some tribes use the lure of open hunting to attract tourist hunters. Others, in the Midwest, have established extensive fish conservation programs. However, there is an annual battle between Indians and conservation officers, as many Indians kill animals out of season, and bag more than their fair share. Among the Iroquois in upstate New York, whitetail deer are killed and sold to non-Indians on a regular basis. Indian violations of an Indian environmental ethic rarely make it into the Indian art world. Nor is there any sense that the environmental ethic is being carried today. Nearly all of the animal imagery in contemporary Indian art recalls ancient connections, as if the high-powered rifle, four-wheel drive or power boats were not used by Indians. How we relate to nature beyond the ritual is the real test to the validity of belief. Art should call those actions into question as much as it should remind us of ancient connections.

The most significant change in the area of "sacred" imagery is the emergence of an internal dialogue on restrictions that have been placed on the use of certain images in the visual arts. While other societies might label it as censorship, Indian artists are often more respectful of the wishes of the religious fundamentalists. There are some images that traditionalists feel are not appropriate to use in art for sale, or even art for non-ritual purposes. These would include the Katcina images of the Pueblo, medicine masks of the Iroquois, use of real eagle feathers, as well as visions of certain rituals considered too sacred to display. The irony is that these were actually the kind of images that were used to give birth to contemporary forms of painting, and now are considered taboo to the children of those who used them in the first place. In fact, "traditional" Indian painting has been defined by depiction of religious scenes. Accuracy in those depictions was considered one of the standards to measure quality such paintings.

Today is different. What our grandparents may have done in the arts might not have been proper, and our communities have reacted to what was created. Some believe that the economy has changed and that the older artist were forced to deal in imagery that would sell. It is only within the last three decades that communities have asked themselves what is appropriate to sell because of the emerging interest in Indian art. Yet, these questions of propriety often conflict with what the consumer wants. The very persona of contemporary Indian art was based upon ancient sacred connections that the contemporary art allowed the non-Indian viewer to share in.

Indian artists of today have been drawn into a defensive posture, forced to defend their art to patrons, curators and collectors. They still have to defend against outsider definition. They also have to defend their blood quantity, to prove that they are even Indian enough to make "Indian art."

Shared Visions, Different Realities

In 1972, an exhibition at the Winnipeg Art Gallery, *Treaty Numbers 23, 287, 1171—Three Indian Painters of the Plains,* presented the works of Jackson Beardy, Daphne Odjig, and Alex Janvier, three of the leading contemporary artists in Canada at that time. The digits in the title refer to their tribal enrollment numbers. Janvier, a Dene Indian, uses an abstract style combined with tribal symbols. He described his approach: "In my work, very often Indian terms and symbols appear and will continue to influence the art; it comes very naturally and it takes its own course. Some symbols are traditional and many are yet symbols ahead of their time."

Yet, Janvier has created his own style to which he has remained true to this very day. "I speak my language and I can say that to be proud like my ancestors I can never be, because to be as proud I must be free to live in harmony with nature and the Great Spirit, therefore my pride would never measure that of my grandfathers. However, I have done my best, since finding out the difference. I feel very true to my work; it is really my 'thing' and not carrying off a traditional Caucasian version of Indian perception."

Arthur Amiotte, Lakota artist and former Institute of American Indian Arts Regent, sees art as a combination of history and personality. "The American Indian has tenaciously held on to his arts," states Amiotte, "not in the sense of object alone, but rather as a fabric that binds and holds together many dimensions of his very existence. The arts are to him an expression of the integrated forces that tie together and unify all aspects of life.... [The Indian artist] is, therefore, the eyes, ears and voice of his own age. More than that, he has his personal record, which, to a culture without a written language, is the partial repository or encyclopedia of its oral tradition."

Contemporary Ojibway artist George Morrison, of Grand Portage, Michigan, describes his artistic search for reality as being "tied with the traditional Great Lakes Indian beliefs in 'the power of the rocks, the magic of the waters, the religion of the trees, the color of the wind and the enigma of the horizon.'" At the *Shared Visions* conference in Phoenix, Morrison, who was part of the mainstream abstract expressionist movement in New York City in the 1940s, explained that in the beginning he was "more interested in 'mechanics of painting' than Indian imagery." However, he began to use a horizon line in his landscape paintings and later in his sculptures. He does try to make it into an "Indian" thing. In fact other contemporary native artists at that conference, such as James Lavadour, Kay WalkingStick, and Truman Lowe, deal with landscape in their art. It is not solely an Indian characteristic, but their personal connection to nature is certainly inspired by their culture.

Lavadour, a Walla Walla painter from Oregon, has his own theory of the landscape that influences his art that is not much different from how traditional Indians would have related to and been inspired by the land. Lavadour believes the act of painting is an act of nature, and "for me, the event of nature is something that is a very profound thing, that within that event, there are many things to learn.... I've had to kind of go out and ask questions of rocks, and walk over mountains, and stick my feet in the stream, and that kind of thing, that is how I learned. And those things are what I've brought back and made my painting out of."

For Lavadour, art is a vital, organic force that has many characteristics and uses among Indians. But he also sees art as a way for Indians to benefit the world because, "It's a force.... It's a spirit. It's a light. I believe it's a light that is being generated in our community, that's got to illuminate many things in the world community.... It has to have an effect, because I see it all the time, because people are alienated from nature. You bring a landscape into the city, and people go 'Wow!' It's as if you're talking about some mythical thing, or something that does not exist."

WalkingStick, a Cherokee painter who teaches art at Cornell University, deals more directly with Indian thinking of the land as being sacred and her personal belief that land is what is truly sacred in her life, which is why she paints landscapes. "Waterfalls can be metaphors for life experiences of what is 'so beautiful and so bittersweet, it passes so quickly.'" By painting these things, she is trying to make the mythic relationships more real and more understandable. She often contrasts views of nature with images of herself to reflect moments in her life and how she finds identification with forces of nature.

Truman Lowe, a Winnebago sculptor from Wisconsin, takes direct inspiration from his woodland environment. "The trees, leaves and branches have particular forms and patterns that change as you walk around them." In his work, using wood is the first way to connect to that environment. Pattern and texture become the next level of recall to what the woods provide. "Streams become metaphors for life, a brief moment, then it moves on to disappear off in another place," according to Lowe. He sees Indian ancestors as having "a very eloquent visual language of symbols that is based upon ideas of simplicity, of what is spiritual and mythical." But most importantly, he sees that the most unique thing about Indians who make art is their real sense of self: "They know who they are when they are putting this image down. That's the contribution [they make to world civilization]."

To Lowe, the streams in his art are more than pro-environmental statements. The water is like tradition and can represent the history of art among Indians: "Most of us know that it came from someplace, and it's like standing on the banks of a stream—that you only see what comes into view, and eventually it disappears; you don't really know where it going, or where it will end up. But what it does is that you have this view for a very short period of your time, and it's a unique view, but it will always continue. It will continue for centuries."

Message Carriers

IAIA's most famous alumnus was T. C. Cannon, a Caddo/Kiowa painter. His work is considered to be the best from that generation of art students who struggled to redefine the function of art for Indians. Cannon met with an untimely death but left evidence of the thinking of the time that contradicts the notions of art as an elitist activity. "I dream of a great breadth of Indian art that ranges through the whole region of our past, present, and future," wrote Cannon (in an undated manuscript), "something that doesn't lack the ultimate power that we possess. From the poisons and passions of technology arises a great force with which we must deal as present-day painters. We are not prophets—we are merely potters, painters, and sculptors dealing with and living in the later twentieth century.... By the simple and beautiful virtue of being Native American, with the blood of mountain and bird motivation, we still have to be soldiers in our homeland."

Artists as soldiers. Who is the enemy? What is to be defended? When do you know you have won? Some of the new Indian artists see themselves as witnesses to the ever changing cultural landscape that Indians find themselves in. It is a very different landscape from their grandparents or parents, yet it is a landscape that they can share with two or three generations of their relatives. Edward Poitras, a Metis sculptor explains it this way: "I have assumed the role as witness/interpreter that my great-great grandfather had on Treaty Number 4. I am a Treaty Indian of Metis and Indian ancestry. The Indians have given me a claim to the land that goes back twenty thousand years, a language in nature and a world view that recognizes the cyclical nature of time. The Metis have given me their dreams of a mixed nation with recognition of difference and equality."

Perhaps it is this kind of duality, faced by most Indian artists in one form or another—born on a reservation but living in the city; raised by Indian parents, but married to a non-Indian; raised by Indian parents of two different tribes and having to choose one with which to identify; participating in both traditional and Christian ceremonies—that creates a different kind of person. This new person sees the world very differently. It should be expected that the message of their art should be a very different take on the ideas of the past as well as thinking never before explored by Indians in the past.

That duality of the Indian artist was described by Edward Castillo, a Cahuilla professor in Native American studies at Sonoma State University, in a 1993 catalog of California Indian art in which he saw the artists approach the form and content of their work from uniquely individual perspectives. "They share a deeply felt connection to their own tribal heritage and a keen awareness of being Native Americans in a predominately non-native culture." Castillo sees the dualities faced by Indian artists as "common experiences vs. individual perspectives, traditional themes vs. contemporary representations, indigenous cultures vs. 'mainstream' expectations."

Mary Lou Fox Radulovich, Director of the Ojibwe Cultural Foundation, gave a view of how art functions for Indians: "Indian people have no word for art. Art is a part of life, like hunting, fishing, growing food, marrying and having children. This is an art in the broadest sense...an object of daily usefulness, to be admired, respected, appreciated and used, the expression thereby nurturing the needs of both body and soul, thereby giving meaning to everything. "

In 1973, Cayuga Chief Jacob Thomas, a woodcarver and Longhouse ritualist, wrote a statement for an exhibition of Iroquois art that embodies the Iroquoian thinking about creative skills: "As we grow up we are pronounced and called in a particular line. We give thanks to the creator for our ability and talents which we proudly present to the people—we are never competing. We are showing what the human hands may do for our culture as it is the only thing we have left. This is the way we can express our minds to the world today so that our culture may be revived. Now, we the artists and craftspeople proudly present our ability which the creator has given us. We forever give thanks to our creator for what we are today."

Compare that kind of thinking to what Peter Jones, a Seneca/Onondaga ceramic artist who attended IAIA from 1963 to 1965, has said: "I don't like the term Indian art. I am an Indian who happened to choose art as a way of life. It suits the way I live and it allows me to be the kind of person I want to be. I work in clay because I like the immediacy of the material. It takes me from five to fourteen hours to complete a piece. I work directly with the material without sketches. I let the clay react to my direction. I want the finished piece to look like clay. My subject matter is usually about my people or of people who may affect my people. I believe that my people are natural beings and that they do not need to be romanticized as stoic, red, colorful, cultural oddities in twentieth-century America by art or artists, although they are."

Parker Boyiddle, Delaware/Kiowa painter and graduate of IAIA similarly explains the difference between his life and that of his ancestors: "What I am trying to do is reflect my environment and transcend a cultural gap. People can only idealize their ancestral past. My ancestors were Plains Indians—the Kiowa on my father's side and Delaware on my mother's; both hunted buffalo and were nomads. Today there is no way I could live that life, but I can exercise some of the customs, morals, and religion of my people and still function in this twentieth-century life."

Art can be many things to Indians. Indians can live many kinds of legitimate lives. However, it is becoming increasingly important that art reflect the real lives of the Indians of today and not reflect romanticized notions of a past never experienced. Perhaps Bob Haozous said it best and most simply in *The Submuloc Show/Columbus Wohs* exhibition in 1992: "Art should be a portrait of who people are."

—Rick Hill, Tuscarora

An earlier version of this essay appeared in *Indian Artist* magazine, Spring 1995. It appears here courtesy of the author and *Indian Artist*.

INTRODUCTION

The publication of the *St. James Guide to Native North American Artists* coincides, roughly, with the centennial of the ethnological research undertaken by Jesse Walter Fewkes at Hopi in 1899, which resulted in a landmark text, "Hopi Katcinas Drawn by Native Artists" (*Bureau of American Ethnology Report* 21, Washington, D.C., Government Printing Office, 1903). Trained as an art historian, I am accustomed to organize my understanding of and to produce a discourse about significant cultural artifacts using such cognitive categories as *fine art, period style,* and *prime objects.* Thus, I find the symmetry tantalizing: the modern period of American Indian art bracketed by twin *fin-de-siecle* sensibilities and a pair of historic publications. Fewkes's report was the first essay on aboriginal cultural symbolism based on works of art commissioned for the study of such symbols. *Native North American Artists* is an ambitious scholarly reflection on the last one hundred years of Indian art: over three hundred entries biographical and critical in nature and complete with exhibition histories and bibliographies.

Scope of Native North American Artists

Though its subjects range from near mythical figures, such as the Hopi-Tewa potter Nampeyo, whose career dated from the late nineteenth century, to Rebecca Belmore, a young but well-established Anishnabe conceptual and performance artist from Canada, this volume cannot be absolutely comprehensive, nor does it pretend to offer interpretive closure on any artist, period, or style. Like any reference work, it will surely have, for some reader at least, an intolerable lacuna—a cherished artist missing from its pages. However, its "short list" is, in fact, generously long, and the admittedly painful decisions about the inclusion and exclusion of artists were made by a fourteen-member multicultural advisory committee of archivists, artists, anthropologists, art historians, curators, and librarians. Virtually all media are represented, including, for example, wood sculpture (Willie Seaweed), beadwork (Marcus Amerman), and photography (Richard Ray Whitman). Similarly, dozens of Native American cultures, from the Atlantic to the Pacific, and from the Rio Grande to the Arctic, are represented in its pages by accomplished artists belonging to several generations, from the reservation period to the postmodern, or so-called post-colonial period. Distinctions between the traditional and the avant garde, and between fine art and crafts, have been held in abeyance, so that contemporary regional artists from the reservation appear alongside their university-educated urban peers.

What links these artists, aside from the fact that they all have worked in the twentieth century, is the shared colonial context, which often obliges professional aboriginal artists to enact the intersection of different aesthetic traditions. Furthermore, beyond considerations of ethnicity and cultural inheritance—which like class and gender are almost always valid ones—in this context Native American art, given its multiplicity and diversity, is "not an art category at all, but a shared sociopolitical situation, constituted by a devastating history" (Charlotte Townsend-Gault, "Having Voices and Using Them: First Nations Artists and 'Native Art,'" *Arts Magazine,* February 1991). Even so, all of the elements of an "art category" are present here, including among numerous others, provenance, patronage, iconography, stylistic development, and creative solutions to marketing and problems inherent in various media. In the essays in this book, however, these aspects of Native art history are not viewed through the lens of geography or medium (like Plateau beadwork), culture area or function (Woodlands tourist arts), or the problematic of assimilation and stylistic authenticity (the Studio style of modern painting). Instead, the myriad issues attendant upon twentieth-century Native art are organized here in histories of individual artists. The diachronic aspect of modern Indian art is realized here only collectively as the sum of autonomous but interrelated entries on specific individuals who are *social* beings nevertheless, their identities as artists formed in specific (multi)cultural circumstances.

Institutional Patronage and Native North American Art History

"Believing that a series of pictures made by the *cleverest* artists [my emphasis] among the Hopis would be a valuable means of studying the symbolism of the tribe," Fewkes hired Kutcahonauu (White Bear), aged thirty, to make "drawings of all the personations of the supernatural beings which appear in Hopi festivals." Recognizing a range of artistic ability among the individuals he encountered at Hopi, Fewkes made a qualitative evaluation: White Bear was the "ablest of all who were considered." In short, what is true elsewhere was reaffirmed at Hopi—some have artistic talent, many others do not. Indeed, Fewkes did not commission drawings indiscriminately, since he wanted only those Hopi men who were "competent to paint a collection of pictures of the kind desired." He reported, for example, that White Bear's uncle, Homovi, also "drew some of the best pictures." Provided with new materials (paper, pencils, brushes, and pigments), the artists returned in a few days with several paintings, which Fewkes "found to be so good that they were encouraged to continue the work." Notice his choice of words and the clear, if subtle, implications: Fewkes was perfectly able and willing to make distinctions about the representational skills of the "primitive" men at Hopi, some of whom obviously must have been not so clever, relatively incompetent, not as good as others, or certainly not the best.

Fewkes obviously had taste and expectations about quality in drawing and painting, and even though he wanted imagery "primarily to illustrate the symbols and symbolic paraphernalia," the resulting work showed "the ability of the Hopis in painting." Again, this statement indicates that Fewkes was confident he could recognize talent in painting, and even though we cannot and should not discount his sensitivity and intuition, it is worth noting that his acquisition of aesthetic criteria was part and parcel of his socialization and education.

Although Fewkes knew that he was dealing with individuals, the power of the social collective from which they emerged and its beliefs about the propriety of making images of Katcinas was made clear immediately:

> At first the collection was freely offered to all comers for inspection…until some person circulated a report that it was sorcery to make these pictures, and this gossip sorely troubled the painters and seriously hampered them in their work, but the author was able to persuade the artists and the more intelligent visitors that no harm would come to them on account of the collection.

Let us ignore, on this occasion, the disturbing ethnocentrism manifest in Fewkes's comment about the "more intelligent visitors," and focus instead on the complex social and cultural interchange revealed in this statement. Citizen Fewkes, as an individual, is the representative of the institution, the Smithsonian Institution alone, but also that more abstract entity: liberal / humanistic / imperial *Science*. Through the largesse of the particular institution and its "outreach" program, the Bureau of American Ethnology, Fewkes introduced both the concept and practice of remuneration for graphic representation (and, perhaps, collaboration with social science) to Hopi. White Bear, Homovi, and the others represent what we might call the fiction or illusion of artist as free agent. They derived, no doubt, personal satisfaction from engaging in creative acts related to their spirituality, acts that also resulted in validation and payment from their patron, who was a cultural outsider. This remarkable combination of rewarding stimuli must have encouraged them to resist the pressure put on them to discontinue the drawings. And yet, as individuals they were really no more autonomous than the rest of us, including Fewkes. They were husbands, sons, brothers, and uncles, who had relations and obligations at Hopi, and the Katcinas they pictorialized belonged both to their unique experience and to the society in which they were enculturated. Religion—art, idea, and practice—we are reminded, is paradoxically private *and* communal. The artists were "free," in an existential sense, to work for Fewkes only as long as they were willing to pay the "social price" for doing so. Fewkes's "less intelligent visitors," who are more properly understood as negative critics within the local audience, are cultural insiders, and they constitute the cautionary element that exists in any culture in a time of transition, often patrolling the boundaries of knowledge and propriety, using that most effective instrument—gossip. Despite the fear and friction generated at Hopi as a result of an awkward imbalance of power, Fewkes was able to persuade the artists to continue in the commoditization of (sacred) culture. I do not mean to imply here any value judgement about the conservative criticism of the drawings or the decision by White Bear and his colleagues to proceed in their collaboration with Fewkes. What interests me is that the historic muticultural exchange at Hopi at the end of the nineteenth century, which resulted in "Hopi Katcinas Drawn by Native Artists," was in essence a microcosm of Native American art in the twentieth century.

The Emergence of the Native American Art Market

In his cogent analysis of the emergence of a market for Native American art in the Southwest in the 1880s, Edwin L. Wade identified a "dynamically interactive form of cultural change, wherein native peoples, grasping for cultural legitimacy and survival in the industrialized West, accept the economic option of converting culture into commodity." ("The Ethnic Art Market in the Southwest, 1880-1980," in *History of Anthropology,* Vol. 3, 1996.) According to Wade, this form of exchange often resulted in a struggle within the Indian community, with "the preservation of 'traditional' aesthetic culture straining against the forces of community development and individual cultural creativity." Not only is this an accurate description of the situation at Hopi involving White Bear and the other artists in Fewkes's employ, but it also fits many, if not most, of the major developments in Native art in the ensuing decades. Although names, places, and certain issues changed in every decade of this century, we can certainly identify the following: 1) artists trying to reconcile their desire to be creative *individuals* (in the context of the Western paradigm of artistic freedom) with the need to be respected members of an aboriginal *community;* 2) elements in tribal culture resisting, with varying degrees of vigor, the introduction into Native America of such concepts and practices as avant gardeism and the secularization of creativity; 3) artists and their Native and non-Native audiences wrestling with the twin problems of authenticity and the shifting boundary between the sacred and the profane.

The fact that many of today's most critically and commercially successful Native artists were educated in university art schools and are at least partly "urban" in orientation has not diminished the intensity of this dilemma. On the contrary, many Indian "fine artists," who were nourished from the 1970s until recently by the solidarity they found in group exhibitions and in an informal national network of their peers, now question the ultimate usefulness of this version of Native collectivity. Wade also anticipated this turn of events when he wrote in 1985 that contemporary Indian artists "now seem forced to make a choice between isolation in a ghettoized ethnic art market and entry into the mainstream of 'fine art.'" The constant repetition of the trope "Indian artist *vs.* artist who is Indian" has become irritatingly tiresome, but it does not mean that anything like consensus on this issue has finally been achieved within the Native art world. Another, and to my mind more meaningful, way of casting this distinction is to ask what one seeks in art—revelations of an individual consciousness or a window onto the collective consciousness of a society?

Art and Art Criticism

Each of these questions has, broadly speaking, corresponding art-historical modes of inquiry. The first, which usually results in monographs or catalogs of solo exhibitions, focuses on the biography and, frequently, the psychology of the artist, stressing his or her uniqueness: formative inspiration (or trauma) and an attendant iconography of private myth; mastery of mediums; invention of new techniques; introduction of new subjects; and so on. The second emphasizes social and cultural contexts, resulting in thematic and more synthetic studies concerned with historical forces, such as religious institutions, the state, museums, mass media, and the marketplace, which construct—to use the current vernacular—a social agent, in this case, the artist.

The increasing acceptance since the 1960s in "progressive" discourses on art of the fragmentation or deconstruction of a unified self/artist (derived, in part, from Roland Bathes's concept of the "death of the author," as described in *Image-Music-Text*), has resulted in histories that are more contextual and take into account the creative role of the patron, critic, and audience. Unfortunately, this is too often accompanied by a loss of appropriate interest in the unique mental properties and technical achievements of the individual artists (as a self-defined creator or inventor of culture who makes specific choices). Conversely, biographical studies of individual artists are often too celebratory and blissfully naive about the artist's complicity in the creation and marketing of his/her public persona.

Concerning the history of twentieth-century Native art, to which this volume will make a substantial contribution, we safely assume that some practitioners of a socially oriented method often read the discourse on individual artists as a romantic valorization of genius that functions more or less like an advertisement, serving the needs of capitalist consumers who are increasingly hungry for ethnicity. And something like the reverse is no doubt also true: historians and critics who feel compelled to champion the individual creator, and who have more invested in process, quality, and objects, surely read the so-called New Art History as too theoretical and overly political, at the expense of a more traditional concern with aesthetic beauty. My sense is that both sets of criticism are valid.

Art history, as defined and developed in Western Europe and North America, has unjustifiably exaggerated the distinction between, and relative importance of, individual agency and the social collective in the creative process. They are inseparable, of course, and our study of art cannot neglect either one or the other without suffering a loss of validity and instrumentality. It seems awkward to have to state the obvious: individuals acquire the sense of self in relation to others, and a society is a group of cooperating individuals. But the recent animosity between advocates of the two aforementioned critical paradigms suggests that some plain talk, if not a truce, is in order. Native American art history, as I have witnessed it in recent years, is not yet riven with this factionalism. But the two discursive forms—call them biography and social history—are easily identifiable in the historiography of twentieth-century Indian art. At the risk of being prescriptive, I hope to see the scholarship on modern Indian art tease out more effectively, and thus reveal more fully, the complete interpenetration of impulses from the artist and his or her society within important works of art. Although *Native North American Artists* needs no apologia, it pleases me nonetheless to articulate what I hope is obvious. A collection of scholarly entries on individual indigenous artists cannot help but facilitate the kind of art history I envision. With apologies to Fewkes: surely the *cleverest* among us will use this volume to produce the kind of "collection" desired—a history of twentieth-century Native art in which the aesthetic accomplishments of individual artists illuminate cultural contexts, and vice versa.

—W. Jackson Rushing

EDITOR'S NOTE

"As soon as you can, find yourself, your own way of expressing what you want to say. Eventually it will come, and you will have your own identity then, and you will start creating things that you feel deeply about inside." —Allan Houser, to his students.

Native North American Artists presents information on leading artists in a wide variety of genres, from those who sustain traditions and introduce innovations, like potters of the Southwest and wood carvers of the Northwest, to painters blending methods and symbols from various cultures, to makers of masks and glassware, basketweavers, photographers, and others—in short, a plentiful sampling of arts practiced by Native Americans during the past one hundred years and on the terms defined by each artist. The contexts from which this book is drawn and in which it can be most useful are addressed by W. Jackson Rushing in his introduction.

Native American art is artwork created by Native Americans. This seems like a simple enough proposition, and it was indeed the tenet followed in preparing this volume, but, in fact, the issue is clouded by myriad definitions of and expectations about Indian art and artists from within and outside Native American communities. This theme and a historical overview of twentieth-century Native American art are addressed in Rick Hill's preface.

Their excellent essays are followed by over 350 entries on artists involved in creating works they feel deeply about.

This book was made possible by contributions from many talented individuals sharing a passion for artistic expression. An advisory board, consisting of curators, scholars, artists, librarians, and administrators, all of whom have some specialty in Native American culture, nominated and shaped the list of artists represented, with additional recommendations coming from many informed contributing essayists. The advisors and essayists are duly noted elsewhere in this publication, and with gratitude I salute their accomplishments.

Artists were selected to represent a broad range of art forms, and inclusion was based on their work having received significant attention within the art community through individual or group exhibitions and publications. Not all of the significant artists could be represented in a single publication with the breadth of information provided in these individual artist entries, particularly if we were unable to contact them or if information proved scarce. The editors certainly welcome commentary and materials that can help expand coverage for future editions.

It should be noted that with the assent of individual tribes, federal laws in the United States and Canada offer strict definitions for categorizing an individual as Native American and First Nations, respectively. If any questions arose about the authenticity of an artist's indigenous ethnic origin under those terms, editors and contributors made every attempt to contact the artist, tribal agencies, family, and other organizations to clearly establish ethnicity. If no conclusive documentation was made available, the artist was then omitted from this publication.

The arrangement of entries is alphabetical, based on the name—native or anglicized—with which the artist signed their work or was best known. The artist index cross-references native and anglicized names for individual artists to help facilitate locating particular individuals, and common variant spellings are noted in the biographical section of each entry, as appropriate, as are rough English translations of native names.

The editor wishes to express appreciation to advisory board members, who fashioned an outstanding list of representative artists and provided guidance during the long process of bringing this project to fruition. Deep thanks as well to the many contributing essayists, who labored to contact artists, perform research, compile information, and write essays on the artists and their works.

Additionally, a host of other people made significant contributions, provided leads, shared knowledge and information, and helped in no small way to make this publication possible. They include Michael Hice and the staff at *Indian Artist* magazine;

Research Archivist Jim Reynolds and the staff at the Heard Museum for making available their extensive artist files; Atlatl, the national service organization for Native American arts, for providing contact information on numerous artists; Edwin L. Wade, curator at the Museum of Northern Arizona; Rosemary Ellison, Chief Curator, Southern Plains Indian Museum and Craft Center; Ingo Hessel and Lori Cutler at the Canadian Inuit Art Information Centre; Doreen Vaillancourt and Barry Case at the Department of Indian and Northern Affairs Canada; Triscia Losher, Kathy Dauphinais, Julia Matuz, Sierra Matuz, Allison Jones, and Claire for their editorial and research assistance; and many others at museums, Native arts organizations, and galleries throughout North America.

Thanks, too, to the editors at St. James Press, particularly Nicolet Elert and Dave Collins, for their patience and diligence in seeing this massive project reach publication.

—Roger Matuz

ADVISERS

Margaret Archuleta
Curator of Fine Arts, Heard Museum, Phoenix, Arizona

Janet Catherine Berlo
Scholar, University of Rochester, New York

Duane Champagne
Director, American Indian Studies Center, University of California, Los Angeles

Janet Clark
Curator, Thunder Bay Art Gallery, Thunder Bay, Ontario

Colleen Cutschall
Artist, scholar, Brandon University, Brandon, Manitoba

Rick Hill
Assistant for the National Museum of the American Indian, Smithsonian Institution, Washington, D.C.

Odette Leroux
Curator of Inuit Art, Canadian Ethnology Service, Hull, Quebec

Gerald McMaster
Curator of Contemporary Indian Art, Canadian Museum of Civilization, Hull, Quebec

David Penney
Curator of Native American Art, Detroit Institute of Arts

Carla Roberts
Executive Director, Atlatl, a national service organization for Native American arts, Phoenix, Arizona

W. Jackson Rushing
Scholar, University of Missouri, St. Louis

Allan Schwartz
Head Librarian, Institute of American Indian Arts, Santa Fe, New Mexico

Jennifer Vigil
Scholar, University of Iowa, and curator.

Mary White
Head Librarian, American Indian Studies Center, University of California, Berkeley

Alfred Young Man
Artist, scholar, Native American Studies Department, University of Lethbridge, Alberta

CONTRIBUTORS

Larry Abbott
Craig Bates
Perry Bear
Janet Catherine Berlo
Bruce Bernstein
Deborah Burrett
James D. Campbell
Jennifer Complo
Lisa Cooley
Lori Cutler
Colleen Cutschall
Rebecca Dobkins
Margaret Dubin
Kate C. Duncan
Phoebe Farris
Louis Gagnon
Vesta Giles
Barbara Hager
Russell P. Hartman
Ingo Hessel
Rick Hill
Gerhard Hoffmann
Gisela Hoffmann

Marion E. Jackson
Marilee Jantzer-White
C. J. Laframboise
Christine Lalonde
Roger Matuz
Nancy Marie Mithlo
Ruth B. Phillips
Carol Podedworney
Kristin Potter
Marla Redcorn
Lisa Roberts
Abraham Rogatnick
Allan J. Ryan
Gregory Schaaf
Margot Blum Schevill
Kevin Smith
Bently Spang
Ann Storey
Charlotte Townsend-Gault
Amelia M. Trevelyan
Jennifer C. Vigil
John Anson Warner
Robin K. Wright
Leona M. Zastrow

St. James Guide to NATIVE NORTH AMERICAN ARTISTS

LIST OF ENTRANTS

Elizabeth Abeyta
Narciso Abeyta
Tony Abeyta
Larry Ahvakana
Norman Akers
Manasie Akpaliapik
Freddie Alexcee
Elsie Allen
Alvin Amason
Marcus Amerman
Arthur Amiotte
Ahmoo Angeconeb
Abraham Anghik
Luke Anguhadluq
Ruth Annaqtussi Tulurialik
Barnabus Arnasungaaq
Spencer Asah
Gilbert Atencio
Lorencita Atencio Bird
James Auchiah
Frank Austin
Marty Averett
Awa Tsireh
Mary Azbill

Amos Bad Heart Bull
Rebecca and Kenny Baird
Rick Bartow
Sara Bates
Carl Beam
Jackson Beardy
Beatien Yazz
Fred Beaver
Larry Beck
Harrison Begay
Lance Belanger
Dennis Belindo
Rebecca Belmore
William and Mary Benson
Carrie Bethel
Susie Bevins
Frank Big Bear
Big Lefthanded
Earl Biss
Archie Blackowl
George Blake
Acee Blue Eagle
Dempsey Bob
Vincent Bomberry
Blackbear Bosin
Bob Boyer
Parker Boyiddle

David Bradley
Bennic Buffalo
Jimalee Burton

T. C. Cannon
Douglas Cardinal
Joane Cardinal-Schubert
Sherman Chaddlesone
Jeffrey Chapman
Nellie Charlie
Tina Charlie
Robert Chee
Benjamin Chee Chee
Michael Chiago
Domingo Cisneros
Peter Clair
Corwin Clairmont
Dana Claxton
Lorenzo Clayton
Doug Coffin
Grey Cohoe
Helen Cordero
Jessie Cornplanter
Douglas Cranmer
Mirac Creepingbear
Woody Crumbo
Colleen Cutschall

Popovi Da
Tony Da
Joe David
Davidialuk Alasuaq Amittu
Robert Davidson
David Dawangyumptewa
Frank Day
Patricia Deadman
Blake Debassige
Mamie Deschillie
Patrick DesJarlait
Cecil Dick
The Dick Family
Freda Diesing
Preston Duwyenie

Charles Edenshaw
Mark Emerak

Joe Feddersen
Anita Fields
Jody Folwell
Harry Fonseca
William B. Franklin

Ted Garner
David General
Richard Glazer Danay
Rose Gonzales
Luis Gonzalez
Louise Goodman
Carl N. Gorman
R. C. Gorman
Dorothy Grant
Sharol Graves
Lela and Van Gutiérrez

Hachivi Edgar Heap of Birds
Vivien Hailstone
Minisa Crumbo Halsey
Bob Haozous
Helen Hardin
Walter Harris
James Havard
Faye HeavyShield
Joe Herrera
Velino Shije Herrera
Joan Hill
Rick Hill
Stan Hill
Jack Hokeah
Rance Hood
John Hoover
Robert Houle
Conrad House
Laurie Houseman-Whitehawk
Allan Houser
Oscar Howe
Richard Hunt
Tony Hunt
Wolf Robe Hunt
Douglas Hyde

Johnny Inukpuk

Edna Davis Jackson
Nathan Jackson
Alex Janvier
G. Peter Jemison
Tony Jojola
Ruthe Blalock Jones

Fred Kabotie
Michael Kabotie
Kai Sa
Goyce Kakegamic
Joshim Kakegamic
Helen Kalvak
Karoo Ashevak
Rod Kaskalla
John Kavik
Kenojuak Ashevak
Louisa Keyser
Ki-Ke-In
Yeffe Kimball

King Kuka
Zacharias Kunuk

Glen La Fontaine
Jean LaMarr
Frank LaPeña
Calvin Larvie
James Lavadour
Charlie Lee
Lucy Lewis
George Littlechild
Carm Little Turtle
Jim Logan
Charles Loloma
Otellie Loloma
Dan V. Lomahaftewa
Linda Lomahaftewa
Milland Dawa Lomakema
Joseph Lonewolf
George Longfish
Mary Longman
Albert Looking Elk
C. F. Lovato
Truman Lowe
James Luna

Mike MacDonald
Jack Malotte
Victoria Mamnguksualuk
Teresa Marshall
Bobby C. Martin
Mungo Martin
Crescencio Martínez
Julian and Maria Martínez
Mario Martínez
Glenna Matoush
Sarah Jim Mayo
Solomon McCombs
Christine McHorse
Mabel McKay
Gerald McMaster
Larry McNeil
Grace Medicine Flower
Rafael Medina
Trinidad Medina
Kay Miller
P. Y. Minthorn
Vicente Mirabal
Al Momaday
Preston Monongye
Geronima Cruz Montoya
Waldo Mootzka
Stephen Mopope
George Morrison
Norval Morrisseau

Raymond Naha
Gerald Nailor
Dan Namingha
Nampeyo

Nora Naranjo-Morse
David Neel
Lloyd Kiva New
Shelly Niro
Ron Noganosh
Joseph No Two Horns

Daphne Odjig
Melvin Olanna
Nathan Hale Olney, Jr.
Jessie Oonark

Oqwa Pi
Joanna Osburn-Bigfeather
Osuitok Ipeelee

David Chethlahe Paladin
John Pangnark
Josie Papialook
Julia Parker
Neil Parsons
Leonard Paul
Tonita Peña
Victor Pepion
David Ruben Piqtoukun
Pitseolak
Lillian Pitt
Susan Point
Edward Poitras
Jane Ash Poitras
Otis Polelonema
Tom Poolaw
Pop Chalee
Abraham Pov
Bill Powless
Charles Pratt
Bill Prokopiof
Pudlo
Charles Pushetonequa

Polingaysi Qoyawayma
Dextra Quotskuyva

Carl Ray
Herman Red Elk
Kevin Red Star
Bill Reid
Arthur Renwick
Leonard Riddles
Rick Rivet
Diego Romero
Mateo Romero
José D. Roybal

Ida Sahmie
Ramona Sakiestewa
Allen Sapp
Gary Schildt
Fritz Scholder
James Schoppert

Willie Seaweed
Joseph Senungetuk
Arthur Shilling
James Silverhorn
Luke Simon
Preston Singletary
Duane Slick
Ernest Smith
Jaune Quick-to-See Smith
Lois Smoky
Soqween
Bill Soza
Bently Spang
Ernest Spybuck
Standing Bear
Maxx Stevens
Kathryn Stewart
Susan Stewart
Patrick Swazo Hinds
Carl Sweezy
Roxanne Swentzell

Margaret Tafoya
Quincy Tahoma
Gerald Tailfeathers
Joe Talirunnilik
Lucy Telles
Charlene Teters
Roy Thomas
Art Thompson
Dana Tiger
Jerome Tiger
John Tiktak
Bruce Timeche
José Rey Toledo
Leanna Tom
Herman Toppah
Brian Tripp
Roger J. Tsabetsaye
Monroe Tsatoke
Andy Tsinahjinnie
Hulleah Tsinhnahjinnie
Faye Tso
Mark Tungilik
Ovilu Tunnillie
Lucy Tasseor Tutsweetok
Frank Tuttle
Marion Tuu'luuq

Judas Ullulaq

Pablita Velarde
Romando Vigil
Darren Vigil Grey

Joseph Waano-Gano
Lloyd Wadhams
Kay WalkingStick
Denise Wallace
Antowine Warrior

Wa Wa Chaw
Dick West
Gary White Deer
Emmi Whitehorse
Richard Ray Whitman
The Williams Family
Amanda Wilson
Lyle Wilson
Margaret Wood
Elizabeth Woody

Alfred Young Man
Yuxweluptun

Paul Zotom

ABEYTA, Elizabeth

Variant names: Nah-Glee-eh-bah
Tribal affiliations: Navajo
Ceramist and sculptor

Born: Gallup, New Mexico, 1956. **Education:** Attended Navajo Community College, Tsaile, Arizona, 1974; Institute of American Indian Arts, Santa Fe, 1976-78; studied ceramics at San Francisco Art Institute, 1980; University of Wyoming. **Career:** Began working as an artist in the 1970s. **Awards:** First place in sculpture, *Navajo Show*, Museum of Northern Arizona, Flagstaff, 1985; second place in sculpture, SWAIA, Indian Market, 1989; first place in sculpture, SWAIA, Indian Market, 1990; second place in sculpture, SWAIA, Indian Market, 1992.

Selected Group Exhibitions

1983   *12th Annual Trail of Tears*, Cherokee National Museum, Tahlequah, Oklahoma
1984   *13th Annual Trail of Tears*, Cherokee National Museum, Tahlequah, Oklahoma
1985   *Navajo Show*, Museum of Northern Arizona, Flagstaff
1986   *Navajo Show*, Museum of Northern Arizona, Flagstaff
       Intertribal Indian Ceremonial, Red Rock State Park, New Mexico
1987   *New Mexico Arts and Craft Fair*, Albuquerque
1988   *Earth, Hands and Life*, Heard Museum, Phoenix
       Traditions and Innovations, Institute of American Indian Arts, Santa Fe
1991   *Sherwoods, Spirit of America*, Second Annual Indian Market Award Winners Exhibition, Beverly Hills, California
1994   *Sisters of the Earth: Contemporary Native American Ceramics*, Bush Barn Art Center, Salem, Oregon
1995   *Tony Abeyta and Elizabeth Abeyta*, J. Cacciola Galleries, New York

Publications

On ABEYTA: Books—*Beyond Tradition: Contemporary Indian Art and Its Evolution* by Lois and Jerry Jacka, Flagstaff: Northland Publishing Co, 1988. **Articles**—"Ancient Traditions, New Horizons" by Lois Essary Jacka, *Arizona Highways*, 62, no. 5, May 1986; "Elizabeth Abeyta" by Catherine Rips, *Southwest Art*, vol. 20, June 1990.

*

Elizabeth Abeyta comments:

Art was always there (in my family life)—you never really thought about it. And each one of us picked something that was appealing to us—two-dimensional work or writing—and we always had that. I always thought of it as my sanity.

*   *   *

Elizabeth Abeyta began her career as an artist upon the suggestion of her father, artist Narciso Abeyta, also known as Ha-so-da, who had studied at the Santa Fe Indian School under Dorothy Dunn along with Allan Houser and Pablita Velarde. Her mother, Sylviann Shipley, whose family had owned the Shipley School for Girls near Philadelphia, embraced her husband's Navajo traditions as well as traditional Navajo arts. She encouraged her children to explore their creative impulses through the arts. "She's the one who got me interested in pottery," states Abeyta. "We had big buckets and washtubs in our yard of different clays. And we'd grind them through screens, to get the purest form. So we all grew up with access to lots of clay." Consequently, art was a part of Elizabeth Abeyta's daily life.

Although her artistic training began at home, she pursued formal instruction at the Navajo Community College in Tsaile, Arizona, in 1974. In 1976 she entered the Institute of American Indian Art in Santa Fe (IAIA). She describes her two years at IAIA as "somewhat restricting because of the emphasis upon staying in your tribal background and producing marketable art." Despite feeling constrained, she found the experience valuable: "In some ways I learned more from the students than the instructors, although I respected the instructors very much. Allan Houser, especially, was my hero." In 1980, before completing her degree at IAIA, she was accepted and enrolled in the San Francisco Art Institute, majoring in ceramics. She only stayed there a semester (working with Richard Shaw) before she felt the need to move on and break away.

Abeyta's ceramic sculpture comes out of a long figurative ceramic tradition in the Southwest. Her sculptures depict singers, dancers, mudheads, and kachinas and reflect the faces of the Navajo people. She describes her work as having strong traditional roots, "but I take them a step further. Most of my pieces are connected to some Indian mythology, but my finishes are very contemporary. I have my own method which is very unorthodox. When my figures are completed, I might look and think, 'warm colors.' I might start with red iron oxide wash, then fire the piece, then later airbrush it with a matte acrylic. I want to achieve earthtone finishes so my pieces resemble the rocks of the Southwest. In creating sculptural forms, I seek the female essence of clay, emphasizing the spiritual and universal strength of women."

Her work reflects the blending of the two disparate cultures of her parents: Navajo and French Canadian. Drawing on these various influences, Abeyta weaves humor and tradition into her dynamic sculptures. The *koshares* and mudheads, although not part of her Navajo background, are common subjects in her work as a result of their presence at the many Pueblo dances that she and her family attended as guests of her parents' friends. She is drawn to their symbolism. The elaborate embellishments on her sculptures enhance the dynamic nature of the work while bringing to life her figures. The sculptures at times become miniature installations with the various accoutrements. Items such as miniature bowls, Navajo rugs and baskets allow the viewer to create different arrangements and ultimately various stories. Storytelling is an important aspect of her work. *Two Sisters: After the Squaw Dance* is based on a Navajo tradition. Abeyta explains: "When young Navajo girls reach puberty, they have a big 'coming out' party in the summer—kind of like a debutante ball. It's a very social event with feasting, singing and dancing at night. The girls go through special rituals, including asking young men to dance. It's a way for the girls to let eligible men know who they like. Well, these two sisters have been to a Squaw dance and stayed too long. Now one sister is leading the other one home, creeping through the moonlight before dawn."

Ultimately her work reflects themes of strength, family, tradition and connectedness. Clay is the medium in which she expresses these important elements of her life. As clay connects her to the earth, her sculptures reinforce the connections between each of us.

—Jennifer Vigil

ABEYTA, Narciso

Variant names: Ha So Da
Tribal affiliations: Navajo
Painter

Born: Canoncito, New Mexico, 15 December 1918; full Hispanic name is Narciso Platero Abeyta; Navajo name means "Fiercely Ascending" and has also been spelled Ha-So-Da. **Education:** Santa Fe Indian School; Sumerset Art Institute, Williamsburg, Pennsylvania; University of New Mexico, B.F.A., 1952. **Military Service:** U.S. Army, World War II. **Career:** Illustrated *Ay-Chee, Son of the Desert,* when he was 16; poster artist; demonstrated painting, San Francisco World's Fair, late 1930s; State Employment Commission, Gallup, New Mexico, 1950s through 1960s; boxer, including Golden Gloves semifinalist, Chicago, 1953; muralist, including classroom at Santa Fe Indian School, 1934, and Maisel's Indian Trading Post, Albuquerque, New Mexico, 1939. **Awards:** Poster artist, Inter-Tribal Indian Ceremonial, 1938, and Golden Gate Exposition (second place, 1939); numerous honors at fairs and juried competitions, including Scottsdale National Indian Art Exhibition (1963), Inter-Tribal Indian Ceremonial (1975, 1979, 1982, 1987), and Philbrook Museum of Art.

Selected Group Exhibitions

1937   *American Indian Exposition and Congress*, Tulsa, Oklahoma
1939   *Golden Gate Exposition,* San Francisco
1955   *An Exhibition of American Indian Painters*, James Graham and Sons, New York
1955-56 European tour sponsored by the University of Oklahoma, Norman
1958-61 European tour sponsored by the University of Oklahoma, Norman
1959-60 *Contemporary American Indian Paintings,* New Jersey State Museum, Trenton

1965   Fine Arts Gallery, San Diego, California
1972   Cherokee National Museum, Tahlequah, Oklahoma
1978   *100 Years of Native American Painting,* Oklahoma Museum of Art, Oklahoma City
1984   *Indianascher Kunstler,* organized by the Philbrook Museum, Tulsa, Oklahoma (traveled in Germany through 1985)
1987   *Red Earth Festival,* Myriad Plaza, Oklahoma City
1991   *Shared Visions: Native American Painters and Sculptors in the Twentieth Century,* Heard Museum, Phoenix, Arizona
1994   *Translating Navajo Worlds: The Art of Narciso (HA-SO-DA) and Tony Abeyta,* Wheelwright Museum of the American Indian, Santa Fe, New Mexico
1996   *Drawn from Memory: James T. Bialac Collection of Native American Art,* Heard Museum, Phoenix, Arizona

Collections

Arizona State Museum, University of Arizona, Tucson; Elkus Collection, California Academy of Sciences, San Francisco, California; Museum of New Mexico, Santa Fe; Museum of Northern Arizona, Flagstaff; Philbrook Museum of Art, Tulsa, Oklahoma; Smithsonian Institution, Washington, D.C.; University of Oklahoma, Norman; Wheelright Museum of the American Indian, Santa Fe, New Mexico; Woolaroc Museum, Bartlesville, Oklahoma.

Publications

On ABEYTA: Books—*American Indian Painters,* by Oscar B. Jacobson and Jeanne D'Ucel, Nice, France, 1950; *American Indian Painting of the Southwest and Plains Areas*, by Dorothy Dunn, Albuquerque: University of New Mexico, 1968; *Indian Painters and White Patrons*, by J. J. Brody, Albuquerque: University of New Mexico Press, 1971; *Southwest Indian Painting: A Changing Art,* by Clara Lee Tanner, Tucson, 1973; *Images of American Indian Art,* New York, 1977; *100 Years of Native American Painting*, exhibition catalog by Arthur Silberman, Oklahoma Museum of Art, Oklahoma City, 1978; *American Indian Painting and Sculpture,* Patricia Broder, New York, 1981; *Indianascher Kunstler,* by Gerhard Hoffman, Munich, 1984; *Shared Visions: Native American Painters and Sculptors in the Twentieth Century,* by Margaret Archuleta and Dr. Rennard Strickland, New York: The New Press, 1991.

*   *   *

Abeyta developed a singular style that marked a departure from the stylized, flatstyle painting he learned at the Santa Fe Indian School, creating a kind of individualistic flair in the 1930s that foreshadowed developments in the 1960s, when several Native American artists were insistent and successful in redefining and recreating the terms in which their art would be recognized. In a more subtle fashion, Abeyta simply painted his own way, and his early work was well-regarded from 1934 through 1940; it did not, however, generate the kind of financial basis on which he could live—a common plight even more severe for Native artists at the time, and he painted more infrequently just prior to World War II; his career picked up again in the 1960s.

Abeyta's work is compared at times with that of his Santa Fe classmate, Andy Tsinahjinnie, for its panache within a somewhat recognizable Southwestern style, but Abeyta was less versatile in his approach and palette, perhaps reflecting interruptions in his career but more likely showing his preference for a focused range of themes and use of color. Abeyta's depictions of humans and animals are robust and lively. His early work features more open space and blocks of color than his more crowded paintings from the 1960s and onward. The advent of World War II, in which Abeyta fought, forsaking a scholarship to Stanford University, came at a critical time in his development, and he didn't paint consistently again until the late 1950s, due at least in part from lingering effects of shell shock. Abeyta's later work won several important awards, was exhibited consistently, and provides a rich illustration of Navajo life, ceremonies, and mythology. The verve and openness of his early work, for which he won early recognition, is not as apparent later on.

Abeyta began expressing himself artistically at an early age, drawing with charcoal on canyon walls. The colors surrounding him in the rocky landscape of western New Mexico and his familiarity with Navajo sand painting influenced the recurrence of brown, yellow, and red shades that pervade in his work. He had already developed a strong personal style by the time he entered the Santa Fe Indian School, as the school's art administrator, Dorothy Dunn, has noted. By the time Abeyta was sixteen, he was commissioned to illustrate a book, *Ay-Chee, Son of the Desert,* by Hoffman Birney. His poster, *The Sun Carrier,* was chosen to promote the Inter-Tribal Indian Ceremonial in 1938, and he also won second prize for a poster submitted for the Golden Gate Exposition in 1939. He demonstrated painting techniques at the San Francisco World's Fair in 1939. His work was exhibited and praised, but he painted more sparingly in the early 1940s while struggling to make ends meet. Abeyta won a scholarship to study at Stanford but instead served in World War II. Following the war, he painted infrequently, though prewar works won prizes at the New Mexico State Fair in 1947.

Abeyta entered the University of New Mexico in the late 1940s and graduated with a degree in fine arts in 1952. He had been working odd jobs after the war and was a skillful boxer, reaching the semifinals in the national Golden Gloves competition in Chicago in 1953. Upon his return to New Mexico, Abeyta took a civil service position that he maintained for the next two decades while he gradually eased back into painting.

Freshness and spontaneity are adjectives commonly used to describe Abeyta's early work. Jamake Highwater has compared Abeyta's individualistic approach to those of Oscar Howe, Fritz Scholder, and Norval Morrisseau, each of whom developed singular styles outside of more mainstream Native painting traditions, or what was expected or thought typical of Indian painting by the outside world. His work stresses mythological elements differently from general trends of artists from the Santa Fe School, where ceremonials were often depicted in a flat, realistic manner resulting from stylized figures and minute detail; from this very general base, many great artists introduced personal variations. Rather than beginning with strongly focused images, Abeyta retained a sense of the dynamic by rendering figures with muscular and slightly distorted features, like the long-legged animals of *Antelope Hunt* (1938); flourishes of vegetation and color contrasts, often black and white, play with the predominance of earth tones. These elements contribute a sense of energy, action and drama, with characters acting and responding to each other, and animals robust and vigorous. The Navajo ceremonial hunt depicted in a mural at Maisel's Indian Trading Post, Albuquerque, New Mexico, in 1939, is perhaps the best example, a sweeping vista of fleeing antelope, pursuing hunters, and a landscape alive with the mix of earth tones and vegetation.

Abeyta painted a wide range of works on Navajo themes, showing a quieter tone when appropriate to capture more routine activities in simple and beautiful compositions. His later work is more complex, at least in look, as central images are brought more into the foreground and less open space on the canvas makes the works busier in appearance. The sense of vitality and action remains as well, and a greater sense of mythological elements and subject matter pervades. In *Chicken Pull* (1972), the whirl of three muscular horses and designs that stand out on clothing combine to effect a spurt of activity seemingly caught at the height of action, and *Fire Dance* (1973) is almost overwhelming with its mix of dancers and clouds of smoke. These more intense and clotted paintings can be viewed as either a creative expansion of the more controlled vigor of his early work, or as less refined and and more labored expressions, but they contribute to a dynamic body of work that has generated renewed interest in the 1990s. This interest is furthered, in part, because of the ascension of Abeyta's son, Tony, as one of the brightest young artists, and is certainly based on the merits of Abeyta's accomplishments and uniqueness, early and late. Perhaps *Werewolf* (1970), with the openness and concentrated action of earlier work combined with the more intense, almost frenzied goings-on of his later paintings, bridges his career: in this painting there is legendary subject matter, blended images of animal, human, and vegetation, balanced contrasts between a dark horse and light werewolf, and dramatic action—in this case, a frightened woman attempting to flee the scene on horseback—all hallmarks of his best work.

—Perry Bear

ABEYTA, Tony
Variant names: Ha So De
Tribal affiliations: Navajo
Painter

Born: Antonio Abeyta, Gallup, New Mexico, 6 November 1965; Ha So De translates to Fierce Ascension. **Education:** Institute of American Indian Arts, AA, 1986; Maryland Institute, College of Art, BA, 1988; postgraduate work at the Chicago Art Institute and in southern France and Florence, Italy. **Awards:** SWAIA Indian Market, Santa Fe, 1989-96, poster artist, 1992; Inter-Tribal Indian Ceremonials, 1988, 1993. **Address:** c/o Tony Abeyta Gallery, #3 St. Francis Plaza, Ranchos de Taos, New Mexico, 87557.

Individual Exhibitions

1985	Institute of American Indian Arts Museum, Santa Fe, New Mexico
1986	Lacoste Ecole de Beaux Arts, Lacoste, France
1990	Tony Abeyta Gallery, Ranchos de Taos, New Mexico

Selected Group Exhibitions

1985	Governors Gallery Show, Santa Fe, New Mexico
	Kirkpatrick Museum Center, Oklahoma City, Oklahoma
	Pembroke State University, Native American Resource Center, Pembroke, North Carolina

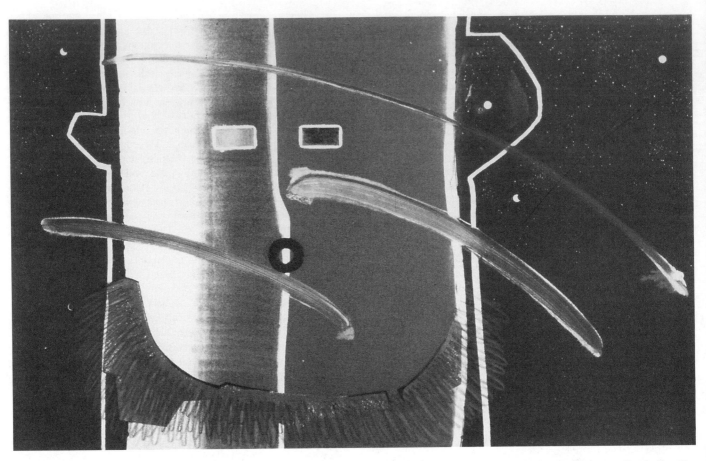

Tony Abeyta: *Cosmic Katchina.* **Photograph by Larry Phillips; courtesy Institute of American Indian Arts Museum, Santa Fe, New Mexico.**

1987-88 D'Aumell Collective Arts, Santa Fe, New Mexico
1988   *The Institute of American Indian Arts, Ink, Stones, Blocks and Plates,* Pueblo Grande Museum, Phoenix, Arizona
        Americana West Gallery, Washington, D.C., Chicago
        MICA Space Gallery, Baltimore, Maryland
1989   *6 from Santa Fe,* Gibbs Museum of Art, Charleston, South Carolina
1990   Southwest Collectibles, Palm Springs, California
        Sherwood's, Beverly Hills, California
1991   American West Gallery, Chicago, Illinois
1993   American Indian Community House Gallery, New York
1994   *Translating Navajo Worlds: The Art of Narciso (Ha-So-Da) and Tony Abeyta,* Wheelwright Museum of the American Indian, Santa Fe, New Mexico
        Crow Canyon Exhibition, Washington D.C.

Collections

Tony Abeyta Gallery, Ranchos de Taos, New Mexico; Institute of American Indian Arts Museum, Santa Fe, New Mexico; Wheelwright Museum of the American Indian, Santa Fe, New Mexico.

Publications

On ABEYTA: Books—*6 from Santa Fe: Contemporary Native American Art from Santa Fe,* by Charlotte Brailsford, Gibbs Mu-seum of Art, Charleston, South Carolina, 1989; *Translating Navajo Worlds: The Art of Narciso (Ha-So-Da) and Tony Abeyta,* by John Neary, Wheelwright Museum, Santa Fe, 1994. **Articles**—"Ink, Stones, Blocks and Plates," by Lynne Pyne, *Phoenix Gazette,* January 5, 1988; "Tony Abeyta: A Brash Young Artist," by Douglas Mann, *Santa Fe Reporter,* August 16, 1989; "The Path to Success," by K.C. Compton, *Focus,* Santa Fe, October/December 1993.

*   *   *

Of the contemporary Native American artists in the Southwest, young Tony Abeyta is among the most promising. The son of Narciso Abeyta, a pioneer of Native American painting, from child-hood Tony was exposed to his father's work, and the wish to be an artist himself came naturally and early on. His own painting style, however, is completely different from that of his father's and from what is regarded as traditional Native American art in general. One of the reasons may be an extensive and highly varied formal art training in the United States and abroad in southern France and Florence. He immersed himself in contemporary as well as histori-cal mainstream art and came to appreciate the masterpieces of such diverse artists as Picasso, Velasquez, and Rothko. The exploration of the universe of art became a process of self-discovery and strengthened his penchant for the abstract. Among the modern American painters, Mark Rothko had a decisive influence on him. However, Abeyta interprets Rothko's color field technique in his own characteristic way saying, "Rothko's work functions as religious device on the most basic level. If one stares hard into a bright purple field moving into dark purple field moving into blackness, there is a physical alteration of the eyes and senses which can produce a profound experience."

Abeyta's acquaintance with various expressions of art and different ways of living—he enjoyed his stay in Europe—also made him all the more aware of his Navajo heritage, as a man and an artist. He returned home to his native New Mexico and came to see himself as a contemporary American Indian painter.

Land is a source of inspiration for Abeyta. In Gallup, New Mexico (the place of his birth), Canyon de Chelly, and in the hills around there he finds inspiration, and new ideas for his paintings come during hiking and fishing, from walking among Anasazi ruins (Canyon de Chelly), and from looking at the cultural imprint his forefathers left on the land.

His cultural heritage is present in several features of his work. Themes relating to his images are based on religious concepts—Kachinas, spiritual mediators between gods and men, and mythical beings like Father Sky and Mother Earth appear again and again in his paintings. But contrary to the traditional painters, Abeyta does not use the images for documentary purposes; he sees the portrayal of deities as sacrilegious, and is more interested in the abstract, the idea of the deity rather than the deity itself. Furthermore, his pan-Indian inclination leads him to incorporate cross-cultural American Indian motifs.

Abeyta's Navajo heritage also influences his choice of aesthetic medium. He likes to experiment with surface textures, especially sand, because he likes the idea of incorporating something in his images that is part of the earth: "What the sand is really about is building up a surface that recalls a pictograph or cave painting." It also evokes the use of sand in Navajo healing ceremonies, but he denies that he is imitating the Navajo sand painting style.

There is a strong spiritual element in Abeyta's art, but also social and political commentary, which form a strong dichotomy, two very different ideas at play—pure spiritual force of Native American religion, and on the sociopolitical level, more Western ideas. But his social criticism is more discreet than obvious and may be expressed as subtle irony, rather than blunt teaching and preaching. In *Father Sky, Mother Earth Contemplating the Science of Spirituality* (1993), the triumph of the airplanes flying over the earth in the form of a Kachina mask is revealed as a deception and an expression of human hubris. When asked whether, as an artist, he wants to make people aware of the spiritual force inherent in all things, his answer was: "Who am I to tell someone what to believe? I merely want to raise questions."

—Gerhard and Gisela Hoffman

AHVAKANA, Larry (Ullaaq)

Tribal affiliations: Inupiat
Sculptor and mixed media artist

Born: Fairbanks, Alaska, 8 July 1946. **Education:** Institute of American Indian Arts, Santa Fe, 1966-1969; Cooper Union School of Arts, New York; BFA, Rhode Island School of Design, 1972. **Career:** Instructor, Institute of American Indian Arts, 1977-80, Pratt Art Center, 1980; Artist-in-the-Schools Program, Alaska, 1974; artist-in-residence, Barrow, Alaska, 1972-73, Anchorage, 1975; workshops and lectures in glassblowing, sculpture, and carving. Commissions include: Institute of American Indian Arts, 1970;

Alaska State Court Building, Anchorage, 1974; and commercial operations in Barrow and Anchorage.

Individual Exhibitions

1977	Alaska State Museum, Juneau, Alaska
	Anchorage Historical and Fine Arts Museum, Alaska
	Governor's Gallery, Juneau, Alaska
1984	Arctic Bay Trading Co., Carmel, California
1985	Van Grabill Fine Arts, Scottsdale, Arizona
1991	Lawrence Ahvakana, Legend Keeper, Stetter Gallery, Scottsdale, Arizona
1995	*Ahvakana, A Retrospective/New Work,* Anchorage Museum of History and Art, Anchorage, Alaska

Selected Group Exhibitions

1967	*Scottsdale National Indian Arts Exhibition,* Scottsdale, Arizona
1971	*American Art Show,* Brooklyn Fine Arts Museum, Brooklyn, New York
	American Art Gallery, New York
1974	*Earth Fire and Fibre Show,* Anchorage Historical and Fine Arts Museum, Anchorage, Alaska
	The Antique Gallery, Anchorage, Alaska
1977	*Survival: Life and Art of the Alaskan Eskimo,* Newark Museum, Newark, New Jersey
1978	*Alaskan Art,* Smithsonian Institution, Washington, D.C.
	Los Llanos Gallery, Santa Fe, New Mexico
	Institute of American Indian Arts, Santa Fe, New Mexico
	Via Gambara Gallery, Washington, D.C.
1981	Sacred Circle Gallery of American Indian Arts, Seattle, Washington
1982	*Uniquely American,* Art Train, Detroit, Michigan
1983	*Mask Show,* The Gathering Gallery, Ketchikan, Alaska
	Stonington Galleries, Anchorage, Alaska
1984	Antique, Ltd., Anchorage, Alaska
1985	*Mask Show,* Marianne Partlow Gallery, Olympia, Washington
	Contemporary Native American Artists of Washington, Washington State Arts Council Art Bank - Seattle Center, Seattle, Washington
1986	*Other Gods: Containers of Belief,* Everson Museum, Syracuse, New York; Contemporary Arts Center, New Orleans, Louisiana; Municipal Art Gallery, Los Angeles, California;
	Pilchuck: The Creative Fire, Washington State Museum, Olympia
1987	*Third Biennial Native American Fine Arts Invitation,* Heard Museum, Phoenix
1988	*Spiritual Imagery Multi-Media,* Eileen Kremen Gallery, Fullerton, California
	Artists Respond: A People in Peril, Visual Arts Center of Alaska
1990	*Bending Traditions,* University of Alaska Museum, Fairbanks
1991	*Legend Keeper,* Stetter Gallery, Scottsdale, Arizona
1992	*Decolonizing the Mind, End of a 500 Year Era,* Center on Contemporary Art, Seattle, Washington
	Documents Northwest, The Poncho Series 1492/1992, Seattle Art Museum, Seattle, Washington

Publications

On AHVAKANA: Books—*Survival: Life and Art of the Alaskan Eskimo,* by Barbara Lipton, Newark, New Jersey, 1977; *Aleut and Eskimo Art: Tradition and Innovation in North Alaska,* Seattle, 1977; *Contemporary Art from Alaska,* Washington, D.C., 1978; *Contemporary Art from Alaska from the Collection of the Anchorage Historical and Fine Arts Museum,* Anchorage, 1979; *Crossroads of Continents: Cultures of Siberia and Alaska,* by William W. Fitzhugh and Aron Crowell, Washington, D.C., 1988; *1492/1992* (The PONCHO Series), Seattle, Washington, 1992; *Decolonizing the Mind: End of a 500 Year Era,* Seattle, Washington, 1992; *Artists of the Pacific Northwest: A Biographical Dictionary, 1600-1970,* London, 1993. **Articles**—"Contemporary Indian Artists," by Lloyd E. Oxendine, *Art in America,* July-August 1972; "Contemporary Alaskan Eskimo Art," by R.L. Shalkop, *American Indian Art Magazine,* Winter 1978; "Larry Ahvakana" (interview), *Art Talk,* January 1991.

*

Larry Ahvakana comments:

I know my own culture and have a very personal view of the drastic changes that have occurred within my ancestral land of northern Alaska and the village of Utkiavikmutt. From one epidemic to the next, my people suffered but prevailed, adapting to the changes. Through oral history and culture ceremonies my people have kept their identity.

*   *   *

Larry Ahvakana is a meticulous craftsman who uses modern sculptural techniques and materials to affirm his native Inupiat heritage. In the spirit of a traditional artisan and reflecting his rigorous academic background, he painstakingly designs and sculpts his stone or wood pieces. Sensual yet elegant, his artworks are made to be touched and savored. While his emphasis on the sheer beauty and appropriateness of materials gives a profound aesthetic quality to his work, he also makes conceptual pieces that communicate on a deeper symbolic level.

Ahvakana personally interprets native Alaskan myth and ceremony, especially the ancestral songs and dances that accompany the hunt. Under this broader category of inspiration from his Inupiat heritage, he has created two consistent types of sculptural work. The first is massive stone or pottery figures engaged in traditional activities, such as drumming, dancing or fishing; the second includes more intricate conceptual pieces. The focus on mass, which predominates his figurative sculptures regardless of media, fully exploits their three-dimensionality; thus, even his small sculptures have a great deal of presence. His more conceptual works, on the other hand, are often quite linear—sophisticated bas-reliefs with complex allegorical narratives.

Ahvakana studied with Allan Houser at the Institute of American Indian Arts in Santa Fe. Some of his earliest works, *Drummer,* for example, look a great deal like Houser's *Muscular.* With bulging forms not yet completely realized, they are too much under the influence of the older master.

Soon, however, Ahvakana found his own expressive voice, and he has created an impressive body of work during the past quarter-century. The sculptor found this voice partly by evoking ancient religious beliefs in works using modern materials and design. In

Shaman Turning into Seal (1975, ivory and sterling silver), Ahvakana expresses the Inupiat belief that humans have a second self in the form of an animal. He also draws upon the close connection between human, animal, celestial and spirit worlds to create sardonic sculptures with an ecological message. In *Breaching Whale* (1992) Ahvakana protests drilling for oil in the Arctic Ocean. Shrewdly exploiting a fifty-five gallon oil drum, and thus offering a recycling as well as a critical message, he created a very sympathetic marine mammal with a human face. This is the customary way to represent the spirit of his people unified with that of the whale. His knowledge of the best possible use of materials amplifies his narrative and symbolic content.

The sculptor's works almost always contain social and political implications that support and reinforce the surface meaning. In *Have You Ever Danced for What You Eat?* (1971, marble and ivory), Ahvakana represents a traditional figure performing a ceremonial dance before the killing of a seal; however, the title also refers to the demeaning position in which native peoples have been placed since the conquest of the Americas.

Ahvakana's work of the 1990s combines his two proficiencies—linearity and mass, concept and beauty. *Walrus Man* (1992) is a self-portrait as a shaman. The sculptor has again made wonderful use of materials; this time they are industrial—concrete, aluminum, glass and copper. The tiny air bubbles in the concrete that make up the body of the walrus man cause it to look like fossilized whale bone, a traditional carving material; thus, there is a witty dialogue across the centuries. The aluminum hands are completely regular, interpreted as flat cut-outs with the thumbs so large they look like additional fingers, contradicting the toolmaker function of fingers with opposed thumb. Instead, they seem to be antennae that can receive electronic messages, or perhaps transmit power or light. Ahvakana is a modern shaman, urbanely negotiating the worlds of traditional past and electronic/industrial present.

Also evoking native beliefs and spirituality is *Qaluquq* (*Winter Whale Ceremony,* 1993; red and yellow cedar, acrylic paint, with bead work by Jim Stephans), in which Ahvakana interprets an Inupiat ceremony for returning the spirit of the whales taken during the previous hunting season to their sacred place. His design incorporates distinct figurative and symbolic areas bounded by elegant, planed wood surfaces. There is a stimulating formal play between the two- and three-dimensional shapes, between the unpainted wood and the polychromia, and between the smooth planar surfaces of the board and the jagged forms of the mountains. Sparse and elegant, this work again displays the sculptor's elegant choice and handling of materials.

Ahvakana's strong yet evocative work exemplifies the principle that growth and artistic adaptation mean life rather than death to a native culture. His excellent education and strong grounding in his native Inupiat culture bring together the best of both worlds.

—Ann Storey

AKERS, Norman

Tribal affiliations: Osage; Pawnee
Painter

Born: Fairfax, Oklahoma, 25 October 1958. **Education:** Kansas City Art Institute, BFA, 1982; Institute of American Indian Arts,

Santa Fe, New Mexico, Certificate of Museum Training, 1983; University of Illinois, Champaign-Urbana, MFA, 1991. **Career:** Intern, Museum of Fine Arts, Santa Fe, 1983; collections inventory, Institute of American Indian Arts Museum, Santa Fe, 1987; Gallery Nine, Champaign-Urbana, 1990; visiting assistant professor, School of Art and Design, University of Illinois, 1991-93; visiting artist, Institute of American Indian Arts, 1993; adjunct professor, Bacone College, Pawhuska, Oklahoma. **Awards:** Graduate Fellowship Award, University of Illinois, Champaign-Urbana, 1988-89; S.W.A.I.A. Indian Market, Santa Fe, New Mexico (first and third places, 1985; second and third, 1987; third, 1988), and first place, Scottsdale Indian Arts and Crafts Exhibition, Scottsdale, Arizona, 1987.

Selected Group Exhibitions

1983   Stables Art Center, Taos, New Mexico
1984   Institute of American Indian Arts Museum, Santa Fe, New Mexico
        PO AE PI Emergence Place for the Arts, Santa Fe, New Mexico
1985   Pembroke State University, Pembroke, North Carolina
        C.G. Rein Galleries, Santa Fe, New Mexico
        Governor's Gallery, State Capitol, Santa Fe, New Mexico
        San Juan Community College, Farmington, New Mexico
1986   Lubbock Arts Festival, Lubbock, Texas
        Southern Plains Indian Museum and Crafts Center, Anadarko, Oklahoma
1987   Scottsdale Indian Art Show and Crafts Exhibition, Scottsdale, Arizona
1988   Red Cloud Indian Art Show, Heritage Center, Pine Ridge, South Dakota
        Tribal Gallery, Los Angeles
        University of New Mexico, Albuquerque, New Mexico
        Pensacola Museum of Fine Art, Pensacola, Florida
1990   Milwaukee Institute of Art and Design, Milwaukee, Wisconsin
        Peace Museum, Maurice Spertus Museum of Judaica, Chicago
        Northern Indiana Arts Association, Munster, Indiana
1991   Beacon Street Gallery, Chicago
        Krannert Art Museum, Champaign-Urbana, Illinois
        University Galleries Illinois State University, Bloomington-Normal
1991-92 *Without Boundaries,* Jan Cicero Gallery, Chicago (traveling)
1992   Steensland Art Museum, St. Olaf College, Northfield, Minnesota
1993   *Pathology of Symbols: Recent Works by Osage Painters Norman Akers and Louis Ballard,* I space, Chicago
1994   *Eiteljorg Invitational: New Art of the West 4,* Eiteljorg Museum, Indianapolis, Indiana
1995   *From the Red Earth: IAIA Oklahoma Alumni,* Institute of American Indian Arts Museum, Santa Fe, New Mexico
        Contrasts, Jan Cicero Gallery, Chicago
        Contemporary Native American Prints, Goshen College of Art, Goshen, Indiana
        Gilcrease Native American Invitational, Gilcrease Museum, Tulsa, Oklahoma
1996-97 *Native Streams: Contemporary Native American Art,* Jan Cicero Gallery, Chicago, and Turman Art Gallery, Indiana State University, Terre Haute (traveling)

Collections

Department of Interior, Washington, D.C.; Thomas Gilcrease Museum, Tulsa, Oklahoma; Institute of American Indian Arts Museum, Santa Fe, New Mexico; Southern Plains Indian Museum and Crafts Center, Anadarko, Oklahoma; White Hair Memorial Resource Center, Hominy, Oklahoma.

Publications

By AKERS: Book—*Southern Plains Indian Museum and Crafts Center*, Anadarko, Oklahoma, 1986.

On AKERS: Books—*Lost and Found Traditions,* by Ralph T. Coe, Seattle, 1986; *Native Streams: Contemporary Native American Art,* Jan Cicero Gallery (Chicago)and Turman Art Gallery (Terre Haute), 1996. **Articles**—"Artists Seek Out the Spiritual Underpinnings of Life," by Deborah Phillips, *Pasatiempo Magazine, The New Mexican,* Santa Fe, New Mexico, April 20, 1984; "Governor's Gallery Goes American Indian," by John Arnold, *Albuquerque Journal,* Albuquerque, New Mexico, July 28, 1985; "Artist Says, Painting is a Performance," by Michael Roth, *The New Mexican,* Santa Fe, New Mexico, August 15, 1985; "Quality Marks Exhibition of Indian Artists' Work," by David Bell, *Journal North,* Albuquerque, New Mexico, August 14, 1986; "Gallery Nine Exhibit Offers Frenetic Art," by Gisele Atterberry, *News-Gazette,* Champaign-Urbana, Illinois, August 4, 1991.

*

Norman Akers comments (1996):
One of the common themes that can be discerned throughout my work is the experience of having to use a personal symbology to make sense out of the daily schisms between: old/new, Western/Osage, personal/cultural. Through the use of images and symbols, I work to define my thoughts, beliefs, memories, and traditions, which are an inherent part of my cultural and personal make-up. (from *Native Streams* catalog)

*   *   *

Norman Akers is known primarily for his work in oil on large canvases. He attended the Institute of American Indian Arts in Santa Fe in the early 1980s, then moved in 1988 to the University of Illinois to pursue an MFA in painting. There, he began creating his very personal "dreamscapes," in which he attempts to reconcile the dichotomies he sees in everyday reality. The paintings are expressionistic and contain a mingling of the abstract and the figurative. Akers feels that much of the impact of his work "depends upon the successful organization of various abstract and representational elements." The works have also been called surrealistic because images are presented naturalistically but within the context of subconscious, rather than naturalistic, relationships. *Collision of Heavenly Structures* (1990) illustrates the surrealistic aspect of Aker's works.

In his most personal and expressive pieces, Akers goes beyond an inquiry into the above mentioned dichotomies he calls "daily schisms." His works are autobiographical, perhaps autotherapeutic, in that he attempts to deal with personal concerns through the painting process. Indeed, Akers admits that he needs to be a bit troubled to feel he is on the right track with his work. For instance, he developed his personal symbology while in Illinois because the process helped him to deal with the growing disconnection he was feeling from the people, environment, and personal worldviews that were a part of his life in Oklahoma. The autobiographical characteristics of the works are the obvious and inevitable results of that process. Personal images appear in chaotic, yet choreographed, compositions reflecting his need to connect with family, environment and traditional tribal beliefs.

A series of icons make up what Akers calls a "personal symbology." Some refer to tribal tradition, others to entirely personal experience. Akers states, "The use of images and symbols from both Native American and Western sources works to create narratives in my painting, all of which define many of my beliefs and thoughts on self, culture, and spirituality." Some of the images Akers frequently uses appear in *I Hope You Got There* (1993). For instance, a lunch box that refers to an Osage funeral custom appears in this and in other works. Currently Akers is isolating individual images from his symbology, such as the lunch box, and placing them in less personal and more ordered contexts such as grids. He states, "You have to question whether something really has validity to you, true meaning to you in terms of a belief system. Things lose their meaning as you change and grow as a person and as an artist and you move on to new things. That's where I am now and I feel like being a little more impersonal now. I have been working with the same elements for five years and feel it's beginning to exhaust itself. The paintings have become so concrete and make almost too much sense to me." His creative exploration of the unknown is part of the artist's exploration of his own changing worldview. The most fundamental spiritual questions continue to be revealed and considered in the paintings.

—Kevin Smith

AKPALIAPIK, Manasie

Tribal affiliations: Inuit
Carver

Born: Manasie Paneloo Akpaliapik, Arctic Bay, Northwest Territories, 23 August 1955. **Education:** Taught to carve by grandparents Elisapee and Peter Ahlooloo, legendary carvers from Arctic Bay; schooled in Iqualuit, Winnipeg, and Greenland; returned to Arctic Bay in 1985 to learn drum dancing and kayak making in preparation for EXPO 86, where he demonstrated these skills at the N.W.T. Pavilion. **Family:** First wife died, 1979; two children from this marriage, both died, 1979; Geralyn Wraith, commonlaw wife from 1986 to separation in 1995; son from this union, Kiviuq Wraith-Akpaliapik. **Career:** Nomadic hunter and fisherman; moved to Montreal in 1979 and began carving professionally; demonstrated drum dancing and kayak making at EXPO 86, Vancouver; one of three Native artists commissioned to carve a coat of arms for the new Museum of Civilization, Hull, Quebec; performed the drum dances at an International Cultural Festival, Shiraoi, Japan, 1989; returned to the Northwest Territories in 1989 to learn and record stories and songs from elders in Arctic Bay, Igloolik, and Pond Inlet, sponsored by a Canada Council Grant. **Agent:** Tony Duguid.

Individual Exhibitions

1989	*Ivory Carvings by Manasie Akpaliapik*, Images Art Gallery, Toronto
1990	*Manasie: The Art of Manasie Akpaliapik*, Winnipeg Art Gallery
1996	*The Art of Manasie Akpaliapik*, Maslak Mcleod Gallery, Santa Fe
	In Harmony with Nature: Arctic Artistry, Hastings-on-Hudson, New York
	Into the Heart of a Legend, Native Art Gallery, Oakville, Ontario

Selected Group Exhibitions

1985	*Uumajut: Animal Imagery in Inuit Art*, Winnipeg Art Gallery
1986	*EXPO 86*, N.W.T. Pavilion, Vancouver
	Native Business Summit, Toronto
1988	*Building on Strengths: New Inuit Art from the Collection*, Winnipeg Art Gallery
	Arctic Forms: Inuit Sculpture, Arctic Inuit Art Gallery, Richmond, Virginia
1990	*Arctic Mirror*, Canadian Museum of Civilization, Hull, Quebec
1991	*Jawbone Sculpture*, Inuit Gallery of Eskimo Art, Toronto
	The Earth Spirit Festival, Harbour Front, Toronto
	The Hand: Images in Inuit Sculpture, Isaacs Inuit Gallery, Toronto
1992	*Inuit Art on the Mezzanine: New Acquisitions*, Winnipeg Art Gallery
	Inuit Art: Drawing and Recent Sculpture, National Gallery of Canada, Ottawa
	Salon International Europ'art 92, Galerie Saint Merri, Geneva, Switzerland
	New Territories, 350-500 Years After, Les Ateliers Vision Planetaire, Montreal
	Borealis: Inuit Images of Man and Animals, Freeport Art Museum and Cultural Center, Freeport, Illinois.
1993	*Multiple Realities: Inuit Images of Shamanic Transformation*, Winnipeg
	Sculpture Inuit et Retrospective, Pudlo Pudlat, Canadian Guild of Crafts - Quebec, Montreal
	The Inuit Imagination, Winnipeg Art Gallery, Winnipeg
1994	*Share the Vision: Philadelphians Collect Inuit Art*, Art Space Gallery, Philadelphia
	Inuit Art from the Canadian Arctic, Bayly Art Museum, University of Virginia, Charlottesville

Collections

Art Gallery of Nova Scotia, Halifax; Canadian Museum of Civilization, Hull, Quebec; National Gallery of Canada, Ottawa; Prince of Wales Northern Heritage Centre, Yellowknife, Northwest Territories; Sam Sarick Collection, Art Gallery of Ontario, Toronto; Winnipeg Art Gallery.

Publications

On AKPALIAPIK: Books—*Canadian Arctic Producers: Manasie Akpaliapik*, Canadian Arctic Producers Co-operative Ltd., 1985;

Manasie Akpaliapik: Carving. Courtesy of the artist and Tony Duguid.

UUMAJUT: Animal Imagery in Inuit Art by Bernadette Driscoll, Winnipeg Art Gallery, 1985; *The Art of Manasie Akpaliapik* by Darlene Wight, Winnipeg Art Gallery, 1990; *Vision Planetaire, Nouveaux Territoires: 350/500 Ans Apres: Une exposition d'art aborigene contemporain du Canada,* Montreal: Vision Planetaire, 1992; *The Inuit Imagination: Arctic Myth and Sculpture* by Harold Seidelman and James Turner, Vancouver and Toronto: Douglas & McIntyre, 1993. **Articles**—"UUMAJUT: Animal Imagery in Inuit Art" by Alison Gillmore, *Arts Manitoba*, vol. 4, no. 3, Summer 1985; "Building on Strengths: New Art from the Collection" by Darlene Wight, *Tableau*, vol. 1, no. 5, 1988; "Artist Perfects Balancing Act" by Randal McIlroy, *Winnipeg Free Press*, Winnipeg, Manitoba, 25 August 1990; "Drawings and Recent Sculpture at the National Gallery of Canada" by Maria Meuhlen, *Inuit Art Quarterly*, vol. 7, no. 3, Summer/Fall 1992; "Carving Is Healing to Me: An Interview with Manasie Akpaliapik" by John Ayre, *Inuit Art Quarterly*, vol. 8, no. 4, Winter 1993; "Manasie Akpaliapik" by Gary Allen Hood, *Indian Artist*, vol. II, no. 2, Spring 1996; "Sculpting from Polar Roots" by Deirdre Kelly, *The Toronto Globe and Mail*, 19 July 1996.

*   *   *

One of Canada's most eminent Inuit carvers, Manasie Akpaliapik began his life as a nomad. His family travelled three times per year as the arctic seasons changed, living the traditional way of their ancestors. At the age of 12 he was sent off to school and the life of movement he had known slipped from under his feet. Since then he has always remained a sort of nomad, only now he travels between cultures, restlessly moving to push back personal and social tragedies that have followed him since he left for school, and searching for the sense of home that came with those nearly lost traditional ways.

Akpaliapik is interested in taking the stories and legends he heard as a child while he watched his grandparents carve, and depicting them in his carvings. It is his way of ensuring that these important stories live on to inspire subsequent generations who will be pushed even further from their ancestral way of life. In addition to recounting these stories, Akpaliapik's pieces also probe into the social issues affecting aboriginal people. His own substance abuse problems and the alarming frequency of suicide in many native communities have both been explored in Akpaliapik's carvings.

What sets Akpaliapik's work apart from the Inuit carvings we see in airports and stores aimed at the tourist market is the personal element and vision he injects into both simple and complex forms. Taking recurring themes in his life, he transforms raw materials into complete thoughts, not static images. His use of organic elements as carving mediums has brought him much acclaim, and he is always exploring the possibility of new materials. As a result, his work expands the potential for empathy and understanding beyond boundaries of culture, race, or religion. Being a visionary artist in a class by himself has left Akpaliapik feeling limited, or restricted on occasion, by people's definitions of what Inuit art must be, as he pursues materials, textures, and colors not traditionally found in the Canadian Arctic.

Akpaliapik chooses his raw materials carefully, preferring muskox horn, caribou antler, whale bone, and even mastodon ivory over the more traditional soapstone. Organic materials, Akpaliapik believes, keep him closer to nature and the earth. He is drawn to the unique shapes and textures of the raw pieces and responds to them as he creates. The smooth ivory is often used for small, delicate images, many of which depict women. In contrast, the rugged and explosive power of whale bone, with its porous and rough consistency, inspires the creation of bizarre spirits and striking images of human and animal transformation. U.S. Customs restrictions regarding the import of endangered animal products have frustrated Akpaliapik, since it limits many of his most acclaimed works—his carvings in whale bone—to Canadian collections. He points out that only whales that have been dead for many years are suitable for use. All of his materials have come from whales and creatures that died in the wild.

Akpaliapik's stone works and combination pieces are also held in high regard in the Canadian art community. One of his most acclaimed pieces, from the collection of the National Gallery of Canada, is a dramatically sculpted portrait of a man, carved from whale bone, gripping his head in pain. The man's eyes are wild and rolled back. His open mouth appears to be a scream of agony frozen in time, with no end. From the top of the man's head sprouts a detailed wine bottle carved from brown soapstone, an indication of alcoholism that plagues many of the Inuit people, including Akpaliapik, who calls this piece a self portrait. It is interesting that the use of brown soapstone for the bottle implies a material not traditionally associated with Inuit carving, in the way that alcohol was a foreign substance to the traditional Inuit. It seems that working in stone may also be a responsive process for Manasie Akpaliapik.

Deeply concerned with social issues of the North, like alcoholism, Akpaliapik sees them more clearly by looking at them from the outside. He uses carvings to heighten awareness of these issues by telling traditional stories and legends and relating them to current issues. His work has touched on the tragedy of child abuse through the depiction of the traditional tale of Kautjajuk, a poorly treated orphan, in one of his carvings.

Within his carvings, Akpaliapik is also known for his masterful use of inlay techniques. He uses inlay to articulate eyes, or even to highlight and accent details within a piece. Inlay is one of the more tangible techniques he uses to create a complex system of balance within his carvings. Visual balance comes from his choice of materials and how they are used in concert, as well as individually. Balance also appears in the relationships between the characters being depicted, between his subject matter and the recurring themes they represent, and the shapes and textures they are expressed within.

Akpaliapik has been referred to in the press as "extreme." His pieces, filled with complex themes and fluid lines, are never stagnant. They can individually represent intense emotion or quiet beauty, or even both within the same piece. His carving is guided by his dreams, memories, and his creative flow.

—Vesta Giles

ALEXCEE, Freddie

Variant names: Wiksomnen
Tribal affiliations: Tsimshian; Iroquois
Painter and carver

Born: Wiksomnen (Great Deer Woman), in Port Simpson, British Columbia, Canada, c. 1857; baptized into Christianity as a youth and took the name Frederick; surname also spelled Alexee. **Education:** Apprenticed to Tsimshian carvers. **Career:** Wood carvings for Tsimshian social rites; painter in oil and watercolor; commissioned for paintings, c. 1900-25, and a series of glass lantern slides on Tsimshian history and legends, c. 1917-25; commissioned for curios and carvings on Native Christian themes at Fort Simpson, outlet of the Hudson Bay Company, in Port Simpson. **Died:** c. 1944.

Selected Group Exhibitions

1927   *West Coast Art: Native and Modern,* National Gallery of
            Canada, Victoria Memorial Building, Ottawa

Collections

Art Gallery of Ontario, Toronto; Thomas Burke Memorial, Washington State Museum, Seattle; Canadian Museum of Civilization, Hull, Quebec; Manitoba Museum of Man and Nature, Winnipeg, Manitoba; University of British Columbia Museum of Anthropology, Vancouver; Vancouver City Museum; Wellcome Institute for the History of Medicine, London, England.

Publications

On ALEXCEE: Books—*Exhibition of West Coast Art: Native and Modern,* by Marius Barbeau, Ottawa, National Gallery of Canada, 1927; *Tsimshian Clan and Society,* by Viola Garfield, Seattle, Uni-

versity of Washington Press, 1939; *Early Painters and Engravers in Canada*, by J. Russell Harper, Toronto, University of Toronto Press, 1970. **Articles**—*Canadian Review of Music and Art*, Vol. 3, nos. 11 & 12, 1945; "Old Port Simpson," by Marius Barbeau, *The Beaver*, Summer 1945; "Frederick Alexcee, Indian Artist," by Deidre Simmons, *The Journal of Canadian Art History,* Vol. XIV, 2, 1991.

*   *   *

Freddie Alexcee was among many Native artists caught between cultures, living in a social environment in which the traditions of his heritage were discouraged in a changing, Westernized society, leaving him without firm footing in either community. Alexcee created a small but remarkable body of paintings and carvings that provide images of Tsimshian history and also reflect a hybrid of Native and Western art forms. He was an artist who bridged the past and present, in the view of scholar Deidre Simmons.

Alexcee was born at Port Simpson, British Columbia, to a Tsimshian mother and Iroquois father. His mother was from the Gilndzano Tribe of the Tsimshian Nation. In the mid-nineteenth century, Alexcee's father arrived at Fort Simpson from the Northeast to work at that outpost of the Hudson Bay Company, and it was there that he met Alexcee's mother. As a youth, Alexcee converted to Christianity, probably based on his father's background, yet retained ties to traditional Tsimshian spirituality. When he was five, gold was discovered in the territory, bringing a flood of newcomers, and when he was nine, a smallpox epidemic broke out. A third of his Tsimshian Nation died from the dreaded disease.

Alexcee was mentored in traditional Tsimshian carving, including fashioning pieces and sacred masks for use in secret ceremonial rituals. In order to participate in this activity, he must have been initiated into secret rituals. However, since his carving never fully matched or realized the features of traditional Tsimshian art, it is assumed that his apprenticeship was interrupted, or that he was informally introduced to Western styles of representation and created works that form a synthesis of both styles. Perhaps he simply forged his own style, finding a place in the changed social environment of the Northwest and respecting the sacredness of Tsmishian art by not attempting to perfectly replicate subjects and forms for non-indigenous settlers. That traditional aboriginal ceremonies were banned by the Canadian government between 1884 and 1951 obviously played a role.

Alexcee's totem poles and model houses, as well as a canoe and carved figures, rely on painting for the most intricate details, a departure from typical Tsimshian art to that time, in which all features were carefully carved into the wood. His wide range of existing carvings, from curios to pieces based on Tsimshian and Christian themes, are only partly representative of Tsimshian art. Alexcee, then, was among the first artists to pursue forms that reflect an influence of Western art—a transitional artist—but the hybrid style he developed was uniquely of his own creation. For example, *Winged Angel Baptismal Font,* c. 1886, reputed to be the first carved Native depiction of an angel, reflects Tsimshian styles and Western images: the head takes the form of a Tsmishian mask, and the body relates to the form of Tsimshian totems, but the face has European features and the robe and wings are distinctly Western. Details are finely rendered, particularly the robe, which flows and creases in correlation with the grain of the wood.

Alexcee became a noted painter at Fort Simpson, creating works that depict scenes and activities involving fellow tribesmen, Tsimshian legends, and historical events, and he was especially proficient in land and seascapes. He was acclaimed enough locally to receive regular commissions from the Hudson Bay Company for paintings and carvings, including curios for the tourist trade. Alexcee was also commissioned for paintings by William Benyon, an agent for Sir Henry Wellcome, a noted British philanthropist and collector who founded the Wellcome Institute for the History of Medicine, in London. In addition to pieces on Tsimshian legends and historical incidents, Alexcee was employed around 1920 to paint a series of lantern slides illustrating local stories and legends that Wellcome used during lectures.

Alexcee's paintings show excellent skill with panoramic views and a less accomplished hand portraying people and action. Two of his paintings were displayed in a 1927 exhibition in Ottawa as examples of folk art. One of the paintings depicts a battle between Haidas and Tsimshian at Fort Simpson, with the bay and fort in the foreground and mountains beyond especially well-executed, while a second shows Fort Simpson in its earliest days, with totem poles still prominent. An untitled and undated piece in the Canadian Museum of Civilization collection provides a stunning aerial view of Fort Simpson that displays Alexcee's mastery of panoramas. From the edge of a bay dotted with boats, to the fort on a peninsula, to an expanse of water sweeping out to peaks in the horizon, he created a vivid, bird's-eye view of the area in a manner of photographic realism. Benyon commented on pieces like this in a 1944 letter to the folklorist Marius Barbeau, who had co-curated the 1927 exhibition in Ottawa that included Alexcee's work. Benyon stated: "Strange as it may seem, his paintings of landscapes were very much better than his works in native designs and carvings."

—Perry Bear

ALLEN, Elsie
Tribal affiliations: Pomo
Basketweaver

Born: Elsie Comanche Allen in Sonoma County, California, 22 September 1899. **Career:** Basketweaver; head of the basket committee for the Pomo Women's Club; taught basketry at the Mendocino Art Center and other California locations; commissioned for numerous demonstrations around the United States. **Awards:** Honorary Doctorate of Divinity as Pomo Sage, c. 1970; Outstanding Achiever Award, Women's Foundation of San Francisco, 1986; Elsie Allen High School is named after her. **Died:** 31 December 1990.

Selected Group Exhibitions

1948	Ukiah Chamber of Commerce Exhibit, Ukiah, California
	University of California, Berkeley
1949	Clubhouse, Todd Grove Park, Ukiah, California
c. 1960	12th District Fair, Ukiah, California
1974	Grace Hudson Museum, Ukiah, California
	Oakland Museum of California, Oakland, California
1976	Smithsonian Institution, Folklike Festival, Washington, D.C.
1980	Grace Hudson Museum, Ukiah, California
1991	*A Promise Kept*, Mendocino County Museum, Willits, California

Collections

Collection of Genevieve Allen Aguilar; Grace Hudson Museum, Ukiah, California; Lowie Museum, University of California, Berkeley; Mendocino County Museum, Mendocino, California; Museum of California, Oakland.

Publications

On ALLEN: Books—*Remember Your Relations: The Elsie Allen Baskets, Family and Friends* by Suzanne Abel-Vido, Dot Brovarney and Susan Billy, Berkeley, California, 1972, reprinted 1996; *Pomo Basketmaking—A Supreme Art for the Weaver*, Healdsburg, California: Naturegraph Publishers, 1972; *Lost and Found Traditions: Native American Art 1965-85* by Ralph T. Coe, Seattle: University of Washington Press, 1986. **Articles**—"Pomo Banded Baskets and Their Dau Marks" by Barbara Winter, *American Indian Art Magazine* vol. 10, no. 4, Autumn 1985; "The Grace Hudson Museum" by Lee Davis, *News from Native California*, November/December, 1988; "California Indian Women's Clubs: Past and Present" by Marsha Ann McGill, *News from Native California,* Spring 1990; "More about Dau Marks: Visiting Four Pomo Basket Makers" by Barbara Winter, *American Indian Art Magazine*, Autumn 1996. **Video**—*Pomo Basketry*, Berkeley: Lowie Museum, University of California, 1962.

*

Elsie Allen comments (1972):

Basketweaving needs dedication and interest and increasing skill and knowledge; it needs feeling and love and honor for the great weavers of the past who showed us the way. If you can rouse in yourself this interest, feeling and dedication, you also can create matchless beauty and help me renew something that should never be lost.

*   *   *

Allen was a gifted and outstanding weaver of "Happy Baskets," a more decorative form of traditional basketry that features colorful feathers and beads incorporated during the weaving process, rather than added on as adornments. Her success with the innovative Happy Baskets resulted in numerous invitations to demonstrate the craft of basketweaving, helping to perpetuate its practice within and outside Native communities. She also used her recognition as a means for improving community interests.

Allen's favorite gathering spots for materials were on the Navarro and Russian Rivers in northern California, where she found sedge root, an amber grass that grows along creek beds; bulrush root, a tule rush plant; and red bud, with thin succor stems two to three feet long. These natural materials were used to form the basket shells. The bulrush roots were dyed black, usually by soaking them in a pail with rusty nails. The polychrome weft materials were split into thirds with a graceful movement between hands and teeth. The pith is scraped off with a pen knife, a piece of broken glass, or obsidian. The material is split several times to form thin wefts, which expert weavers could sometimes sew in over 30 stitches per inch. The edges are carefully trimmed to create uniformity in surface texture. The baskets' inner rods were often made from willow, and one to three carefully-shaved willow rods compose the foundation. A metal tipped awl is poked through the foundation and the weft is sewn round and round.

Elsie Allen: Twined burden basket, c. 1920. Photograph by Seth Roffman; courtesy Dr. Gregory Schaaf collection.

Allen derived her distinctive and colorful utilitarian artwork by elaborating on the uniqueness of Pomo designs with the feathers and beads. Her "Feathered Jewel" baskets continued a 5,000-year-old basket making tradition. In making feather baskets, Allen twisted colorful bird feathers between her thumb and forefinger, precisely placing them under a stitch and then securing them by pulling tightly. Her favored feathers came from the iridescent green mallard duck, yellow meadowlark, redheaded woodpecker, bluebird, redwing blackbird, quail and pheasant. Allen's precise blending of design and color made her baskets much sought after.

The Pomo process of melding in objects during weaving was also practiced with beads. Pomo beaded baskets are distinguished from other regional baskets because Pomo weavers thread the sedge root through the beads, while others weave the basket first, then sew glass beads on one-by-one with cotton thread.

By the 1940s, Allen's reputation was secure, and she became more active in community service, including spreading and sharing the wealth of Pomo traditions. She was a founding member of the Pomo Women's Club, established in March 1940, and served as head of the club's basket committee. In this role she organized exhibits and activities, including a four-day showing of Pomo baskets with support from the Ukiah Chamber of Commerce. Allen also arranged exhibits and weaving demonstrations featuring seven Pomo craftspeople at the University of California at Berkeley. Museums, galleries and social clubs regularly requested talks and presentations. Allen also defended native rights throughout her life. She and the Pomo Women's Club supported a lawsuit against a local movie theater owner who ordered native children to sit in the

back of the hall. Their united effort resulted in a quick settlement and the establishment of equal rights for Indians throughout the area.

Like her mother, Annie Burke, Allen worked with linguists and historians to record and preserve the different local Pomo dialects. The Smithsonian Institution recognized her as an outstanding traditional weaver and invited her to demonstrate on several occasions at the Folklike Festival in Washington, D.C., including the bicentennial celebration in 1976.

—Gregory Schaaf

AMASON, Alvin

Tribal affiliations: Aleut
Painter, sculptor, and mixed media artist

Born: Alvin Eli Amason, Kodiak Island, Alaska, 1948. **Education:** Central Washington University, BA in 1973, MA in 1974; Arizona State University, MFA, 1976. **Career:** Fisherman; artist; lecturer, College of Great Falls, Montana, 1978, Institute of American Indian Art, 1978, Alaska State Council on the Arts Conference ("Seeing with the Native Eye"), 1981, University of Alaska, Fairbanks, 1984, Visual Arts Center of Alaska, 1989; Board Member, Alaska State Council of the Arts (Governor's appointment), 1978-80, and Institute of Alaska Native Arts, 1978-80; Chair, Department of Art, Navajo Community College, 1976-78; Director, Native Art Center of the University of Alaska, Fairbanks, 1992—. **Address:** c/o Suzanne Brown Gallery, 7160 Main Street, Scottsdale, Arizona 85251.

Selected Group Exhibitions

1972	Pacific Northwest Arts and Crafts Fair, Belview, Washington
1973	Washington State College (now Central Washington University), Ellensburg, Washington
1975	Four Corners State Biennial, Phoenix, Arizona
1980	*Across the Nation: Fine Art for Federal Buildings 1972-1979*, Hunter Museum of Art, Chattanooga, Tennessee
	Spirit of the Earth, Native American Center of Living Arts, Niagara Falls, New York
1981	*Magic Images*, Philbrook Art Center, Tulsa, Oklahoma
	Art of the States: Nine Alaskans, Alaska State Museum
1984	*50 States, 50 Artists*, Fuller Goldeen Gallery, San Francisco
	Innovations, Heard Museum, Phoenix, Arizona
	Uniquely American: The West Coast, Art Train, Detroit, Michigan
1985	Western States Prints Invitational, Portland Art Museum, Portland, Oregon
1985-87	*Alaska Native Heritage Festival*, Anchorage Museum of History and Art, Anchorage, Alaska
1989	*Multi-media Work*, Carnegie Art Center, Walla Walla, Washington
1990	*New Art of the West*, Eitelijorg Museum, Indianapolis, Indiana
	Russian America, Washington State Historical Society, Tacoma, Washington

Publications

On AMASON: Books—*The Place of Art in the World of Architecture* by Donald Thalacker, New York: Chelsea House, 1980; *Aleut and Eskimo Art* by Dorthy Jean Ray, University of Washington Press, 1981; *Crossroads of Continents* by William W. Fitzhugh and Aron Crowell, Smithsonian Institution Press, 1988; *Russian America, the Forgotten Frontier* by Barbara Sweetland Smith and Raymond J. Barnett, Washington State Historical Society, 1990. **Article**—"Alvin Amason," interview, *Institute of Alaskan Native Arts Newsletter*, July 1980.

Collections

Alaska State Museum, Juneau; Anchorage Museum of History and Art, Anchorage, Alaska; Baranov Museum, Kodiak, Alaska; Heard Museum, Phoenix, Arizona; Indian Arts and Crafts Board, Department of the Interior, Washington, D.C.; Kansas City Art Institute, Kansas City, Missouri; National Collection of Fine Arts, Smithsonian Institution, Washington, D.C.; Nordjyllands Kunstmuseum, Aalborg, Denmark; State of Alaska Art Bank, Anchorage, Alaska; U.S. Government Services Administration, Federal Building, Anchorage, Alaska.

*   *   *

Alvin Amason stands out as one of the small number of contemporary Aleut artists who has achieved commercial and critical success in the national Indian art world. Like Aleut sculptors John Hoover and Bill Prokopiof, as well as jeweler Denise Wallace, Amason integrates traditional subject matter with a highly personal style in primarily contemporary media. But unlike his peers, Amason's primary medium is oil paint on canvas.

Amason grew up with his grandfather, a bear guide, and still identifies with the native Aleut way of life. He learned how to fish and briefly considered making his living as a commercial fisherman. "I was going to be an engineer; before that a bush pilot; before that a fisherman. As I flunked my engineering exam ... I walked across the hall to the art room and [have been] there ever since," he recalled in a 1980 interview.

After completing his M.F.A. at Arizona State in 1976, Amason traveled throughout the Southwest for the next fifteen years, painting and teaching art. In 1992 he returned to his home state of Alaska, where he became director of the Native Art Center of the University of Alaska, Fairbanks. Since then he has focused his attention on teaching and lecturing on art and organizing state- and education-sponsored art activities.

In his paintings and occasional mixed-media sculpture, Amason depicts the natural elements of his home environment in a style that is thoroughly contemporary, and occasionally whimsical. Animals are captured at strange angles and features are exaggerated in Amason's interpretations. A walrus becomes a mass of tusks and hairy flesh when viewed from underneath and at close range. A polar bear is a mass of white paint, identified only by the small black flecks that serve as facial features, and a scrawled title, "polar bear." A small ice cream cone floats above the bear's head, reiterating its whiteness and creating a sensation of coldness.

Amason's keen imagination and his frequent use of text, which he calls "an ongoing conversation," lends a surreal character to his paintings. Words—sometimes painted directly on the canvas, in a casual, school-boy script, and sometimes captured in the title—

indicate a parallel vision, in which the beauty of nature complements ideas about the environment and personal identity. In *Ou Vous Allez Les Gars Pendant L'Hiver* (1983), an oil painting selected for inclusion in the first annual Heard Museum invitational exhibit (*Innovations: New Expressions in Native American Painting*, 1983-84), a bird's head in profile dominates the canvas, its sad eye the focal point. Large white circles indicate snow, while the words of the title are inscribed in the sky.

In the catalog accompanying the Heard exhibit, Amason explains his approach: "I am an Aleut. That is simply a fact, but I am not trying to carry on any ethnic tradition in my art. I am just using my background the way all painters use their background in their work." Ethnic identity is an aspect of the self and part of artistic inspiration, but not the sole reason for the creation of artworks.

Amason has received commissions to create paintings for public buildings in Alaska, including the Anchorage International Airport and the U.S. Federal Courthouse Building in Anchorage. His art also graces the walls of several Alaskan public schools. An active member of the native Alaskan art community, Amason has served as a board member for the Alaska State Council of the Arts and the Institute of Alaska Native Arts.

—Margaret Dubin

AMERMAN, Marcus

Tribal affiliations: Choctaw
Bead artist and painter

Born: Phoenix, Arizona, 10 September 1959. **Education:** Whitman College, Walla Walla, Washington, B.F.A., 1981; Institute of American Indian Arts, Santa Fe, New Mexico, 1982-1983; Anthropology Film Center, Santa Fe, 1983-1984. **Awards:** Santa Fe Indian Market, Innovative Use of Traditional Techniques, and Eight Northern Pueblos Council Arts and Crafts Show, Most Creative New Design, 1984; Santa Fe Indian Market, 1990.

Individual Exhibitions

1986   *Paintings by Marcus Amerman*, Southern Plains Indian Museum, Anadarko, Oklahoma

Selected Group Exhibitions

1986   *Pictorial Beadwork*, Southern Plains Indian Museum, Anadarko, Oklahoma

1987   *Contemporary Native American Artists*, Governor's Gallery, State Capitol Building, Santa Fe, New Mexico

1989   *Fourth Biennial Fine Arts Invitational*, Heard Museum, Phoenix, Arizona

1990   *Artifacts for the Seventh Generation*, American Indian Contemporary Arts, San Francisco

1991   *The Human Figure in American Indian Art: Cultural Reality or Sexual Fantasy?*, Institute of American Indian Arts Museum, Santa Fe, New Mexico

1992   *Visions from Native America: Contemporary Art for the Year of Indigenous Peoples*, U.S. Congress Rotunda, Washington D.C.

Marcus Amerman: *Big Bow, Kiowa,* **1986. Photograph by Larry McNeil; courtesy Institute of American Indian Arts Museum, Santa Fe, New Mexico.**

Creativity is our Tradition, Institute of American Indian Arts Museum, Santa Fe, New Mexico

Pathways of Tradition: Indian Insights into Indian Worlds, National Museum of the American Indians, Smithsonian Institution, U.S. Customs House, New York

1993 *Lollapalooza '93*, traveling, alternative rock festival

1994 *Indian Humor*, American Indian Contemporary Arts, San Francisco (traveling)

Native American: Reflecting Contemporary Realities, American Indian Contemporary Arts, San Francisco

1995 *The Native American Fine Arts Movement*, Henley Exhibition Center, Henley-on-Thomas, Oxfordshire, England

Connections to the Past, Morning Star Gallery, Santa Fe, New Mexico

Collections

Institute of American Indian Arts Museum, Santa Fe, New Mexico; Oklahoma Center for Science and Art, Kirkpatrick Center, Oklahoma City, Oklahoma; Southern Plains Indian Museum, Anadarko, Oklahoma; United States Department of the Interior, Washington, D.C.

Publications

On AMERMAN: Books—*Lost and Found Traditions,* by Ralph T. Coe, Seattle, 1986; *The New Beadwork,* by Kathlyn Moss and Alice Scherer, New York, 1992; *Creativity Is Our Tradition: Three Decades of Contemporary Indian Art at the Institute of American Indian Arts*, by Rick Hill, Santa Fe, 1992.

*

Marcus Amerman comments:

I'm always astounded by the whole notion of creating, taking the products of my imagination and manifesting them into physical form. Creating comes very naturally to me. I think it is in my nature to create, just like it's in a spider's nature to spin a web, or in a bird's nature to sing its song. My work is about the process of creating.

I don't think my work so much displays a style as it does reveal an attitude towards art and creating. It's like a warrior's attitude towards war, but instead of taking on opponents, I challenge myself with different techniques, materials, art forms and ideas. When I seek and find that new idea which is both beautiful and powerful, then I take it on, I confront it, fearlessly.

*   *   *

Marcus Amerman utilizes techniques from traditional Indian culture, specifically the use of beads to decorate or enhance a functional item, to create a new genre of beadworking—portraiture—which unites his interests in painting and beadwork. Amerman draws upon a wide range of influences to create strikingly original works that reflect his background: having lived in three different regions with strong artistic traditions, his academic introduction to pop art and social commentary, and his inventive explorations of the potential artistic forms and expressions through beadwork.

Amerman was raised in Oregon, where he became fascinated with the colorful beadwork of Columbia Plateau and Plains peoples.

When glass beads became widely available in the early nineteenth century, artists of the Columbia River area expanded on their traditional geometric patterning to include floral forms, and as smaller beads in more various colors reached the region by mid-century, animal images and human forms in action became more prominent design motifs. Amerman expands on this kind of representational imagery, which included symbols and even flags during the World Wars, in his own work, whether capturing the pride of great Native American leaders or creating humorous, and at times, audacious commentary on contemporary life. During summers spent in New Mexico during his youth, Amerman became acquainted with Southwest art traditions and landscape colors and patterns that had been recreated in art. When his family relocated to Oklahoma, Amerman was introduced to the peyote-stitch beadwork, bold geometric shapes, and vibrant coloring of Plains beadworkers.

Amerman returned to Washington to the Northwest at Whitman College in Washington, where he earned his B.A., and then enrolled at the Institute of American Indian Arts in Santa Fe. There he originally pursued his love of painting, but soon began transferring the art of beadwork onto the flat surface of the canvas. In *Big Bow Kiowa*, a piece he completed in 1979 while a student at the Institute, Amerman used colored beads as a medium for creating an image of the great Kiowa chief. Shadowing and background contribute depth and texture, with Amerman's skill evident in the blended colors and noble bearing of his subject. Amerman used photographs from which to model Big Bow, a practice he continued, in addition to relying on sketches and verbal descriptions, when making images of other Native American leaders, including Sitting Bull, Geronimo, and Chief Joseph.

Native peoples have for generations infused beauty into everyday functional items. Typically, items were meant to reflect and portray aspects of native culture, history and family descent.

Amerman has taken an established form of traditional native craft and innovated by applying it to the two dimensional art of painting. His repertoire has continually expanded, from applying his craft to such traditional items as pow wow clothing and cradleboards, to outlandish creations, such as tuxedos and clothing accessories. Amerman's new medium has incorporated elements of pop art, especially in portraits of contemporary music and film stars, and social commentary, usually through humor. This variety of skillful uses of beads has led to exhibitions in many different kinds of venues: official sites of state in Washington, D.C. and London; significant formal institutions such as the Southern Plains Indian Museum and the Heard Museum; showcases for contemporary trends in Native American art like American Indian Contemporary Arts of San Francisco; and the annual alternative traveling rock festival, *Lollapalooza.*

—C. J. Laframboise

AMIOTTE, Arthur

Variant names: Warpa Tanka Kuciyela; Wanbli Hocoka Waste
Tribal affiliations: Oglala Lakota
Painter, mixed media artist, and textile artist

Born: Arthur Douglas Amiotte, Pine Ridge, South Dakota, 25 March 1942; received native name Warpa Tanka Kuciyela (meaning Low

Arthur Amiotte: *The Visit,* 1995. Courtesy Buffalo Bill Historical Center, Cody, Wyoming; gift of Mrs. Cornelius Vanderbilt Whitney.

Black Bird), 1942; and Wanbli Hocoka Waste (Good Eagle Center), 1972. **Education:** Summer workshop with Oscar Howe, University of South Dakota at Vermillion, 1961; Northern State College, BS in Education, 1964; graduate course work at University of Oklahoma and University of South Dakota, art education at Pennsylvania State University, and study of southwest techniques and cultures at the Institute of American Indian Art, 1966-1970; mentored by Christina Standing Bear, Oglala Teton Sioux craftsperson and keeper of a sacred bundle, 1965-1979, and Peter Catches, Sr., Oglala Teton Sioux Shaman and Sun Dance priest, 1972-1976 (as novice apprentice) and 1977-1982 (as assistant); Master of Interdisciplinary Studies: Anthropology, Religion and Art, University of Montana, 1980-83. **Career:** Art instructor, 1964-1971; lecturer on art, Lakota history, religion and culture, 1969—; Director of Curriculum Development, U.S. Department of Interior, Aberdeen Area Office, 1971-1974; Lakota Studies instructor, 1975-1980; Lakota Studies Department Chairman, Standing Rock Community Col-

lege, Fort Yates, North Dakota, 1978-82; commissions for paintings, designs, logos, book covers, book illustrations, and posters, 1979—; Professor of Native Studies, Brandon University, 1982—; Consultant on Indian Cultures of the Northern Plains, White Horse Creek, Ltd., 1985-present; curator, including Plains Section, Museum of Natural History, Smithsonian Institution, 1991; commission appointments and board of directors, including National Native American Art Studies Association, Indian Arts and Crafts Board, National Foundation for the Advancement of Arts, Presidential Advisory Council for the Performing Arts, Council of Regents Institute of American Indian Arts, National Museum of the American Indian; board of trustees, Buffalo Bill Historical Center, Cody, Wyoming, 1992; member, commission for Indian Memorial, Little Big Horn, Montana (appointed by Secretary of the Interior), 1994, Indian Advisory Committee and consultant to architect, National Museum of the American Indian, 1995; fellowship, Artists at Giverny Program, 1997. **Awards:** Honorary Doctor of Law, Brandon University, 1994; "Outstanding Contribution to South Dakota History," Dakota History Conference and Center for Western Studies, Augustana College, 1992; Getty Foundation grant for art history research, 1993; Honorary Doctorate of Lakota Studies, Oglala Lakota College, Kyle, South Dakota, 1988; numerous fellowships and teaching honors.

Individual Exhibitions

1966   Waterloo Municipal Galleries, Waterloo, Iowa
1972   American Art Gallery, Wooster Street, New York
1973   Civic Fine Arts Center, Sioux Falls, South Dakota
1974   Galleria Del Sol Crafts Gallery, Santa Barbara, California
        Sheldon Memorial Art Center, University of Nebraska, Lincoln
1975   Fairtree Crafts Gallery, Madison Avenue, New York
1976   Hand and the Spirit Crafts Gallery, Fifth Avenue, Scottsdale, Arizona
1979   Via Gambaro Gallery, Washington, DC
1980-86 Mt. Rushmore National Monument Concession Building, Mt. Rushmore, South Dakota
1981   Fine Arts Gallery, University of Montana, Missoula
        Amiotte Wall Hangings, Colorado Springs Fine Art Center, Colorado Springs, Colorado; Fort Collins Fine Arts Center, Fort Collins, Colorado
1982   *Current Works from the Shamanic Tradition,* North Dakota State Historical Center, Bismarck, North Dakota; Dahl Fine Arts Center, Rapid City, South Dakota
1985   Brandon Allied Arts Center, Brandon, Manitoba
1986   *Amiotte Wall Hangings 1967-85,* Iowa State University, Ames
1988   *Amiotte Since 1963: The Last 25 Years, A Retrospective,* Oscar Howe Art Center, Mitchell, South Dakota
        Twenty-five selections from Amiotte 25 year Retrospective, Augustana College, Sioux Falls, South Dakota
1989   Huron Fine Arts Center, Huron, South Dakota
1990   Lincoln Galleries, Northern State University, Aberdeen, South Dakota

Selected Group Exhibitions

1961   *Five Man Show: Students of Oscar Howe,* W. H. Over Museum, University of South Dakota, Vermillion, South Dakota
1962-66 *Annual National Juried Indian Art Show,* Philbrook Art Center, Tulsa, Oklahoma
1967   *National Indian Art Show,* National Museum of Natural History, Smithsonian Institution, Washington, DC
1969-90 *Contemporary Sioux Painting,* National Touring Exhibition, U.S. Department of the Interior, IACB, Sioux Indian Museum, Rapid City, South Dakota
1970   *American Indian Art Today,* National Indian Art Show, Northern Virginia Fine Arts Association, Arlington, Virginia
1971   *Experiments in Collaboration,* Amiotte Family Show, U.S. Department of the Interior, IACB, Sioux Indian Museum, Rapid City, South Dakota; South Dakota Memorial Art Center, Brookings, South Dakota
1972   *Invitational National Indian Art Show,* Brooklyn Museum, Brooklyn, New York

1977   *National Invitational Indian Art Show,* Via Gambaro Gallery, Washington, DC
1978-79 *Five West River Artists,* Regional Traveling Exhibit, South Dakota Memorial Art Center, Brookings, South Dakota
1979   *The Real People,* National Art Show, International Native American Council on the Arts, Havana, Cuba and Niagara Falls, New York
1981   *American Indian Art in the 80s,* National Indian Art Show, Native American Center for the Living Arts, Niagara Falls, New York
1982   *Night of the First Americans,* Benefit for Amerindian Circle, National Indian Art Show, Kennedy Center, Washington, DC
        A Song for Our Ancestors, Gallery of the American Indian, New York; Community House, Taos, New Mexico
1982-83 *Contemporary North American Indian Art,* Museum of Natural History, Smithsonian Institution, Washington, DC
1982-84 *National Parks Touring Indian Art Show,* organized at National Parks Headquarters, Harpers Ferry, West Virginia
1983   *Students of Oscar Howe: A Retrospective,* U.S. Department of the Interior, IACB, Sioux Indian Museum, Rapid City, South Dakota; University of South Dakota, Vermillion
        Contemporary Lakota Arts, Creighton University Galleries, Omaha, Nebraska
1984   *Catching Shadows,* Photo portraits of Prominent Indian Artists by Stephen Gambaro shown with paintings by subjects, Gilcrease Museum, Tulsa, Oklahoma
1985   *Contemporary Plains Art* (five man show accompanying exhibit to international exhibit, *Circles of the World*), California Academy of Science, San Francisco
        Homecomings, North Dakota Museum of Art, Bismarck, North Dakota; Grand Forks, North Dakota
        Visions of the Earth, National Indian Art Show Benefit, Native American Rights Fund, Boulder, Colorado
1986   *Voices of Today: Cultural Expressions of Native People of North America,* American Indian Institute, Bozeman, Montana; Nippon Club Gallery, New York; The Triangle Native American Society, Duke University Museum of Art, Durham, North Carolina
1987-88 *Dream Catcher' Artists Guild,* Sioux Indian Museum, U.S. Department of the Interior, Rapid City, South Dakota; Freeman Gallery, San Marcos, California
1987-90 *Plains Indian Arts Continuity and Change,* organized by National Museum of Natural History, Smithsonian Institution Washington, D.C. (traveling)
1988   *Northern Plains Tribal Arts,* Sioux Falls, South Dakota
        Lakota Arts Continuum: One Hundred Years of the Art of the Oglalas and Their Relatives, South Dakota Centennial Exhibit, Red Cloud Heritage Center, Pine Ridge, South Dakota; Dahl Fine Arts Center, Rapid City, South Dakota
        The Dream Catcher's Guild, Dahl Fine Arts Center, Rapid City, South Dakota
1989   *Three Man Show,* Sierra Nevada Museum of Art, Reno, Nevada
        Fonseca, Lamarr and Amiotte: Three Person Show, Nevada State Historical Society, Las Vegas, Nevada

Pictographs, A Centennial Retrospective, Eastern Montana College, Billings, Montana

South Dakota Centennial Art Exhibition, Pierre, South Dakota

Center for Western Studies, Plains Art Exposition, Sioux Falls, South Dakota

Art for a New Century, Civic Fine Arts Center, Sioux Falls, South Dakota; South Dakota Art Museum, Brookings, South Dakota

Sioux Crafts Adaptations, U.S. Department of the Interior, Indian Arts and Crafts Board, Sioux Indian Museum, Rapid City, South Dakota

1990   *Red Cloud International Exhibitions and Competition,* Pine Ridge, South Dakota

Wounded Knee, High Plains Heritage Center, Spearfish, South Dakota

1990-91 *Vision of Hope,* Akta Lakota Museum, Chamberlain, South Dakota

1992   *Northern Plains Indian Art Exposition,* Sioux Falls, South Dakota

United Tribes Indian Art Exposition, Bismarck, North Dakota

Artists Who Are Indian, Northcutt Steele Gallery, Billings, Montana

1992-93 *Native America: Reflecting Contemporary Realities,* Los Angeles Craft and Folk Art Museum

Visions of the People, Minneapolis Institute of the Arts, Minneapolis, Minnesota

1993   *In Out of the Cold,* Center for the Arts at Yerba Buena Gardens, San Francisco

1993-96 *Spirit of American Indian Art,* American Indian Contemporary Art, San Francisco

1994   *American Indian Humor,* American Indian Contemporary Art, San Francisco

1994-95 *This Path We Travel,* National Museum of the American Indian, New York

Indian Times, Kunsthallen Brandts, Klaedafabrik, Odense, Denmark

Collections

Akta Lakota Museum, Chamberlain, South Dakota; Denver Art Museum, Colorado; Haffenreffer Museum, Bristol, Rhode Island; Hampton University, Hampton, Virginia; Heritage Center, Inc., Red Cloud Indian School, Pine Ridge, South Dakota; Oscar Howe Memorial Art Center, Mitchell, South Dakota; Institute of American Indian Arts Museum, Santa Fe, New Mexico; Minneapolis Art Institute, Minnesota; Museum of Natural History, Smithsonian Institution, Washington, D.C.; National Museum of the American Indian, New York; New York Port Authority, World Trade Center, New York City; Shelden Memorial Art Center, University of Nebraska, Lincoln; South Dakota Heritage Center, South Dakota State Capitol, Pierre; South Dakota Memorial Center, Brookings, South Dakota; U.S. National Park Service Offices, Denver, Colorado; Whitney Gallery of Western Art, Cody, Wyoming.

Publications

By AMIOTTE: Books—*Photographs and Poems by Sioux Children,* Rapid City, Sioux Indian Museum, 1971; "Foreword," *The Sacred Pipe: Black Elk's Account of the Seven Rites of the Ogala Sioux,* by Joseph Epes Brown, Norman, University of Oklahoma Press, 1983; "The Lakota Sun Dance: Historical and Contemporary Perspectives," in *Sioux Indian Religion,* Raymond DeMallie and Douglas Parks, editors, Norman, University of Oklahoma Press, 1985; "An Appraisal of Sioux Arts," in *An Illustrated History of the Arts of South Dakota,* Sioux Falls, Augustana College, Center for Western Studies, 1989; "Eagles Fly Over," "Our Other Selves," and "The Road to the Center," reprinted in *I Become Part of It,* D. M. Dooling and Paul Jordan, editors, New York: Parabola Books, 1989; "The Sun Dance," *Native American Dance: Ceremonies and Social Traditions,* Charlotte Heth, editor, Washington, D.C., Smithsonian Institution. **Articles**—"Our Other Selves: The Lakota Dream Experience," *Parabola,* Vol. 1, no. 3, 1983; "The Call to Remember," *Parabola,* August 1992.

On AMIOTTE: Books—*100 Years of Native American Painting,* exhibition catalog by Arthur Silberman, Oklahoma Museum of Art, Oklahoma City, 1978; *American Indian Painting and Sculpture,* Patricia Broder, New York, 1981; *This Path We Travel: Celebrations of Contemporary Native American Creativity,* Smithsonian Institution, Washington, D.C., 1994. **Articles**—"Arthur Amiotte's Banners," by Barbara Loeb, *American Indian Art Magazine* 10 (2), 1985; "Art that Spans Two Cultures," by Hattie Clark, *Christian Science Monitor,* August 11, 1987; "Inside Arthur Amiotte," by Marguerite Mullaney, *Inside the Black Hills,* Fall 1990. **Film**—*Somewhere, Sometime: Tribal Arts 1989,* South Dakota Public Television, 1989; *Lakota Sacred Traditions,* BBC, 1992; *Museum of Natural History* (interview), Smithsonian Institution, 1993.

*   *   *

Arthur Amiotte's career as a practicing artist, now in its fourth decade, has encompassed numerous media and styles of work. The most recent, his collage series, explores issues in Lakota history and art history, layered with a dose of social criticism as well.

Amiotte's early years were divided between his maternal grandparents' home in Manderson on the Pine Ridge Reservation and his mother's home in Custer, South Dakota. Amiotte graduated from Northern State University in Aberdeen, South Dakota, with a Bachelor's Degree in Art and Art Education. During the 1960s and 70s, Amiotte taught art at elementary school, junior high, and university levels and performed graduate work in studio art, anthropology, and art education. Perhaps the most influential of these educational experiences was the summer workshop at the University of South Dakota at Vermillion in 1961 with the great Lakota modernist, Oscar Howe. Amiotte recalls Howe's influence as having many dimensions:

> First of all, I was influenced by Oscar Howe's clear belief that he was an artist —that it was legitimate and possible for an Indian person to be a professional artist. Secondly, he taught us that it was acceptable to draw from our own cultural experience—to have Native content in our art.

Amiotte's paintings from the 1960s show the influence of Howe. Amiotte's traditional Lakota artistic and spiritual legacy has been an important source of inspiration as well. His mentors included Pete Catches, the great Lakota Shaman and Sun Dance priest, and Christina Standing Bear—Amiotte's grandmother—an expert in hide tanning, beadwork, and quillwork. His grandmother's guidance allowed Amiotte to move easily between the traditions of men's arts and women's arts; he is equally adept in media ranging from painting and drawing to hide work and textile arts. He also mixes these media, blurring the traditional distinctions between them. In the 1970s, for example, he produced quilts, banners, and other textile constructions that either followed Lakota traditions explicitly or else abstracted color and design principles from them in order to make works which resonated in both the Lakota and modernist traditions.

In the 1980s, Amiotte returned to a simpler, bolder graphic style, one that harkened back to Lakota work at the end of the nineteenth century and the beginning of the twentieth, including the work of his own great-grandfather, Standing Bear. Amiotte painted scenes of traditional Lakota life—idealized portraits of finely dressed figures engaged in dance and ceremony. In the *Shamanic Series* of that decade, he further pared down of his style and imagery to a bold pictography, painted on a large scale.

In 1988 Amiotte began a dramatic new direction, starting a collage series. Recalling the circumstances of the inauguration of this series, the artist states:

> The Oscar Howe Center in Mitchell, South Dakota, offered me a 25-year retrospective exhibit, and I needed to produce some new works. I was writing the chapter on Sioux art for a *History of Art in South Dakota* book, and trying to establish a chronology for Lakota art. I began to realize that there was a whole period left out by contemporary artists, who were either doing romanticized versions of pre-reservation life, or still working in the Oscar Howe style, or working in a contemporary pictographic style that was a replay of the hide painting and early ledger drawing style. But the period from the 1880s to the 1940s was being ignored—the whole reservation period and post-reservation period. This was a dynamic time. Indian people were exposed to magazines, pictures, photographs. Daily life was infused with this mixture of non-literate/literate. There were new technologies, and children going to school and bringing information back into their homes. It seemed to me that it was more honest to deal with all this in my art, rather than to create a fake hide painting, which many artists were doing in the 1980s and continue to do today.

In his collage series Amiotte seeks to show the historical realities of early twentieth-century Native life as a synthesis of multiple cultural pathways. This hybridity is transmitted in the work not only through the subject matter, but also through the media used. It encompasses nineteenth-century pictographs, twentieth-century family photographs, and imagery garnered from magazines and the discards of early modern culture, such as receipt books, ledgers, and advertising circulars. The artist pastes, overlays, and juxtaposes; he footnotes artists who came before him, such as Standing Bear, Bad Heart Bull, and the female beadwork artists who made the vests and dresses he draws. Amiotte inscribes his own narration upon this hybrid mix, imposing a sense of order and personal history. The canvases of Amiotte's Collage Series serve not only as pages in the artist's own cultural biography, they also provide a penetrating portrait of a century of Lakota history.

Amiotte was one of fifteen artists whose collaboration (1993-4) resulted in an installation at the National Museum of the American Indian in New York and a book, *This Path We Travel*. In the exhibit, Amiotte had major responsibility for the schoolroom installation, featuring 1940s-style desks, some with collaged imagery on the

desk tops. This installation reconstitutes a pan-Indian style of schoolroom common in the 1930s through 1950s in Native schools across the country. Amiotte completed two collaged desks for this room, one of which shows five generations of Standing Bear and Amiotte family scholars.

While visually chronicling twentieth-century education, the artist reminds us of the literate Lakota of the nineteenth century: literate in pictorial means, they left visual accounts of their names and histories. Because their histories are integral to Lakota identity at the end of the twentieth century, they are remembered and recorded by their artistic descendants as well. In all of its diverse manifestations, Amiotte's work focuses on the rich artistic and cultural legacy of Lakota people.

—Janet Catherine Berlo

ANGECONEB, Ahmoo
Tribal affiliations: Ojibway
Painter and printmaker

Born: Sioux Lookout, Ontario, in 1955. **Education:** Visual Arts, York University, Toronto, 1976-77; Dalhousie University, Halifax, Nova Scotia, 1985-89; B.F.A., Lakehead University, Thunder Bay, Ontario, 1993. **Career:** Taught native studies at Dalhousie University, visiting artist or artist-in-the-schools at a variety of educational and cultural venues; cultural ambassador representing Ojibway art in tribal, national, and personal capacities on an international basis.

Individual Exhibitions

1973-83 Centre d'Art, Baie St. Paul, Quebec
    Nishnawbe Arts, Toronto
    Houston North Gallery, Lunenberg, Nova Scotia
1984 Houston North Gallery, Lunenberg, Nova Scotia
    Centre d'Art, Baie St. Paul, Quebec
1985 Canadian Guild of Crafts, Montreal
    Kiva Gallery, Toronto
1986 The Guild Shop, Toronto
1987 Centre for Indian Art, Thunder Bay
1988 Institute of American Indian Art, Santa Fe
    Sacred Art Gallery, Seattle
1990 Northern Images, Winnipeg
1991 Feheley Fine Art, Toronto
1992 Atelier Sommering, Cologne
    Sandia Arts, Basel, Switzerland
    Galerie St. Merri, Paris
1994 Feheley Fine Arts, Toronto
    Franz Hitze Haus, Munster
1996 Inuit Gallery, London, Ontario
    Geronimo's Studio, Munich
    Sandia Arts, Basel

Selected Group Exhibitions

1972-83 Centennial Room, Sault Ste. Marie, Ontario
    Gallery of Native Art, Toronto

Tundra Gallery, Sault Ste. Marie, Ontario

The Public Gallery, Halifax, Nova Scotia

1984 *Arcs Sacra*, Halifax

1986 *Maritime Indian Artists*, Gallery One, Moncton, New Brunswick

1988 *Ascending Culture,* Discovery Centre, Fort Lauderdale

Contemporary Visions, National Conference Centre, Ottawa

1989 *Contemporary Art of the Anishnabe,* Thunder Bay Art Gallery, Ontario

1991 *First Nations Art,* Woodland Centre, Brantford, Ontario.

1993 *Native Canadian Art*, Galerie Im Alter Kloster, Cologne.

1994 *Three Generations of Anishnabe Art Creating,* Mari-1, Thunder Bay, Ontario

1995 *Art of the Matawa Nishnawbek*, Thunder Bay

1996 *The Art of the Anishnawbek: Three Perspectives*, Royal Ontario Museum, Toronto

Collections

Art Gallery of Nova Scotia, Halifax; Arts Centre Group, London, England; Confederation College, Thunder Bay; McMichael Canadian Collection, Kleinberg, Ontario; Museum Institute of American Indian Art, Santa Fe; National Museum of Civilization, Ottawa; Royal Ontario Museum, Toronto; Thunder Bay Art Gallery, Ontario; University of Osnabruck.

Publications

On ANGECONEB: Books—*Norval Morrisseau and the Emergence of the Image Makers,* by Tom Hill and Elizabeth McLuhan, Toronto, 1984; *The Sound of the Drum,* by Beth Southcott, Erin, Ontario, 1984; *Challenges Catalogus* (exhibition catalog), by Gerald McMaster, Amsterdam, 1985. **Articles**—"Indian Attitude," by Barry Sarah, *Commonwealth Art Links Review,* April/June, 1980; "Artist experiments with form and colour in pursuit of an individual style," by George Kenny, *Toronto Native Times,* April 1981; "In the Galleries," by Joanne Claus, *Evening Times Globe,* August 8, 1986; "Resistance or Seduction: The Art of Allen Angeconeb," by Astrid Brunner, *Arts Atlantic,* No. 2, 1988; "Arts Review: Ahmoo Angeconeb," by Vesa Peltonen, *Window Explorer*, March 1996.

*

Ahmoo Angeconeb comments (1987):

In October of 1980, I discovered more of myself. I knew that I came from the father's Caribou totem (the northern equivalent of the southern Ojibway's deer totem). To my amazement I came to the realization that my totem's tribal responsibility was that of an artist; the Caribou were the creative people.

It was then that I decided I should take a rest from painting for a while and try to explore other mediums. I decided that I should do more drawing and explore different forms of printmaking, especially etching and engraving. I had remembered seeing a lot of engravings while I was in Paris.

I started looking at drawing as a serious art medium, not just as a cartoon or a study for a painting, but as a work of art in itself...

In 1984, I made plans to create some small linoleum block prints in a series using four different images. These images were of different species of birds; birds that I was very familiar with. I designed and used two images of the same species emphasizing the number two. I feel the number two, or duality, is very significant: day/night; good/evil; male/female; sun/moon; the yin and the yang.

In the later months of 1984, I managed to get some zinc plates to do some etching. I just loved the feel of the line-making as I scratched the burin tool over the plate. I felt line would be the strongest element to be used in transferring my drawings over and creating a print. I thought to myself, "Etching is line and the line is etching."

One of my most successful prints with line, I personally feel, is the 1985 print, *Medicine Wheel.* This print is an example of a great marriage between the line and etching technique.

In the 1985 totem series of etchings, I wanted to use line again. With the help of metamorphic animal/human imagery, white lines on brown paper, I wanted to create the special relationship between the human and the animals they share the world with.

In the prints from 1985, 1986 and 1987, I kept in mind the teachings and the ideas of the "Traditionalists" of the Woodlands School. To maintain and continue to hold fast to tradition and yet still create using a different medium. All of these sets of prints ... in a series of four, represent an aspect of the traditional spiritual values and ideals of the Ojibway. These are in print form, and, as such, are prints for future generations to see—future Ojibways—to help understand and maintain their culture within their society and within themselves.

With these line prints some say I am now "reverting" compared to the art work that is done by the new generation of artists of native ancestry. Perhaps it is true. But I always believed and still believe that you are what you create. One sees the world as one has lived it and continues to live it. One sees the world as they want to create and recreate it, to interpret it and to reinterpret it.

I know one has to continually grow and create for one's sake in order to fulfill their own well-being, and to continue to grow intellectually, spiritually, and physically.

*   *   *

Prior to 1980, Ahmoo Angeconeb's paintings adhered to the formal and iconographic precepts of the New Woodland school, exhibiting such tendencies as blank background planes, undifferentiated areas of vibrant colour, x-ray perspectives, and linear determinatives. Eventually, Angeconeb's style grew away from these formal considerations while remaining committed to New Woodland's philosophical intent. Continuing to depict an Ojibway worldview, Angeconeb introduced stylistic elements foreign to the school's aesthetic vocabulary. For instance, the artist often adopted a figure-ground relationship and form lines of minute thinness and significant number, as well as a predominance for line over colour.

The changes in Angeconeb's formal aesthetic can be attributed not only to the artist's desire to achieve a personal visual interpretation distinct from the New Woodland school, but also to the artist's research into the art traditions of indigenous cultures worldwide. Angeconeb acquired first-hand knowledge of techniques and traditions during extensive travels around the world. Gaining an appreciation for the so-called primitive arts, Angeconeb became aware of similarities in their formal languages. He soon began working with imagery and techniques from a variety of sources.

Angeconeb's visual vocabulary has been expanded by the use of images from Western art history and from the traditional imagery of a number of world cultures: Pre-Columbian, African, American Southwest and Southeast, Inuit, Ojibway and North American Northwest Coast. Angeconeb's images feature a primarily narrative

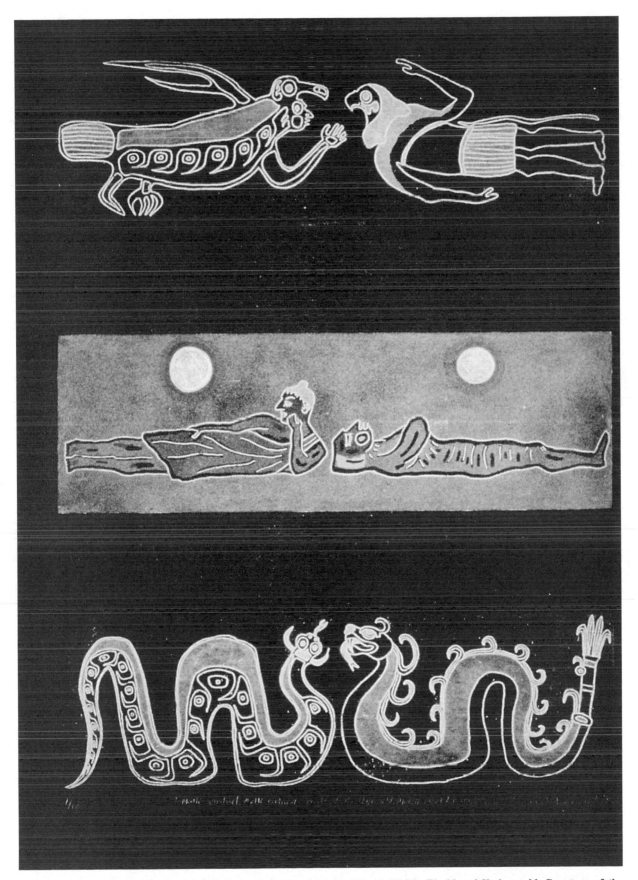

Ahmoo Angeconeb: *Multi-Spiritual, Multi-Cultural Spirits of the Sky World, Middle World and Underworld.* **Courtesy of the artist.**

format extracted from an earlier iconic base in which anthropomorphic and zoomorphic characters figure in great profusion. Thus, Angeconeb has used the aesthetic base of the New Woodland school as the point of departure for his personal aesthetic vision. Drawing on the example of Norval Morrisseau and the teachings of Carl Ray, Angeconeb has attempted to express what it means to him to be Ojibway and an artist.

Since 1988, Angeconeb has worked to develop an international market and understanding for the contemporary art of the First Nations. To this end, the artist has produced and toured exhibitions of his own works and those of his colleagues for dissemination throughout Europe and the United States. His role in this capacity—as cultural ambassador—has been important and equal to his contribution as a visual artist, continuing and expanding the legacy of the New Woodland school for future generations.

—Carol Podedworney

ANGHIK, Abraham (Apakark)

Variant names: Abe Ruben
Tribal affiliations: Inuit
Sculptor

Born: Paulatuk, Canada, 250 miles north of the Arctic Circle, 1951.
Education: Studied printmaking, silversmithing and sculpture under Ron Senungtuk at the University of Alaska. **Career:** Hunter, sculptor.

Individual Exhibitions

1973	Arctic Arts Gallery, Edmonton, Alberta
1975	Arctic Arts Gallery, Edmonton, Alberta
1976	Langlois Gallery, Yellowknife, Northwest Territories
1977	*Drawings and Sculpture,* Pollock Gallery, Toronto
1978	*Recent Sculpture,* Pollock Gallery, Toronto
1980	Bayard Gallery, New York
1981	Images for a Canadian Heritage, Vancouver
1991	*Spirit of my People,* Alaska Gallery of New York, New York

Selected Group Exhibitions

1974	University of Alaska, Fairbanks
1978	*The Coming and Going of the Shaman: Eskimo Shamanism and Art,* Winnipeg Art Gallery
1981	*The Inuit Sea Goddess,* Surrey Art Gallery, Vancouver
1982	*New Work by a New Generation,* University of Regina
1985	*Uumajut: Animal Imagery in Inuit Art,* Winnipeg Art Gallery
1990	*Arctic Mirror,* Canadian Museum of Civilization, Hull, Quebec
1992-93	*Borealis: Inuit Images of Man and Animals,* Freeport Art Museum and Cultural Centre, Freeport, Illinois
1993	*The Shaman's Drum - Echoes of the Past,* Images of the North, San Francisco
1994	*Inuit Art from the Canadian Arctic,* Bayly Art Museum, University of Virginia, Charlottesville
1995	*Keeping Our Stories Alive: An Exhibition of the Art and Crafts from Dene and Inuit of Canada,* Institute of American Indian Arts Museum, Santa Fe

Collections

Art Gallery of Ontario, Toronto; Canadian Museum of Civilization, Hull, Quebec; Inuit Cultural Institute, Rankin Inlet, Northwest Territories; McMaster University Art Gallery, Hamilton, Ontario; McMichael Canadian Art Collection, Kleinburg, Ontario; National Gallery of Canada, Ottawa; Prince of Wales Northern Heritage Centre, Yellowknife, Northwest Territories; Royal Ontario Museum, Toronto; Winnipeg Art Gallery.

Publications

On ANGHIK: Books—*The Coming and Going of the Shaman: Eskimo Shamanism and Art,* by Jean Blodgett, Winnipeg: Winnipeg Art Gallery, 1979; *Arctic Vision: Art of the Canadian Inuit,* by Barbara Lipton, Ottawa: Canadian Arctic Producers, 1984; *Out of Tradition: Abraham Anghik/David Ruben Piqtoukun: A Retrospective Exhibition,* by Darlene Wight, Winnipeg: Winnipeg Art Gallery, 1989. **Articles**—"Abe Anghik: Contemporary and Accomplished Canadian Artist," by Walter Austerer, *Arts & Culture of the North,* 5(2), 1981; "Sojourns to Nunavut: Contemporary Inuit Art from Canada," by Frank Vallee, *Inuit Art Quarterly,* 6(3), Summer 1991; "Indigena: Perspectives of indigenous peoples on five hundred years," by Marybelle Mitchell, *Inuit Art Quarterly,* vol. 7, no. 3, Summer/Fall, 1992; "Arts form the Arctic, a Celebratory Exhibition," by Jan Ingram, *Inuit Art Quarterly,* vol. 8, no. 3, Fall, 1993; "Multiple Realities: Inuit Images of Shamanic Transformation," by George Swinton, *Inuit Art Quarterly,* vol, 8, no. 4, Winter, 1993, pp. 43-47.

*   *   *

Some of the most innovative young Inuit artists since 1980 have emerged from the extreme western Canadian arctic, including Abraham Anghik and his brother, David Ruben Piqtoukun, from the community of Paulatuk. Anghik is one of fifteen children of a migratory hunting family who settled in Paulatuk in 1967. Their ancestry combined Bering Sea Inupiaq from Alaska and Mackenzie Delta Inuit from Canada. Anghik's early years included cultural initiation by learning to hunt with his community, followed by cultural deprivations endured in the harsh residential schooling system. Paradoxically, it is the synthesis of these two lifeways, Inuit traditions and Western-style education, that has forged his distinctive art style.

Anghik's pivotal influence as an artist is Ron Senungetuk, an Inupiaq Eskimo who was a professor at the Native Arts Center at the University of Alaska in Fairbanks. Anghik first met Senungetuk in 1971. Of this experience Anghik says, "For the first time in years I felt at home. Although I had none of the prerequisites for entry into the course, I had the good fortune of apprenticing under Professor Senungetuk in 1972." The primary focus of the Native Arts Center was to provide the serious student with instruction and study in combining traditional stories and imagery with contemporary forms. Students were encouraged to market their finished works, thus enabling them to integrate with the community and to ease the pain of social and academic acculturation.

After his studies in Alaska, Anghik returned to Canada, living and working in various southern cities before settling in the

Vancouver area, where he began to achieve success as a sculptor. Since the 1980s he has been prolific in his output, investigating the properties of whalebone, wood, Brazilian soapstone, limestone, and other materials.

Shamanic transformation is one of the key themes that Anghik repeatedly explores in his work, which often merges a traditional Inuit sculptural look with a sleek, abstract modernism. Having lived in Alaska and British Colombia, he has also studied the aesthetics of traditional Northwest Coast sculpture of the Haida, Kwakiutl and Tlingit peoples and incorporated some of their principles into his own work.

While Anghik has traditionally worked in small to medium-sized format (with most pieces smaller than a meter in size), since 1990 he has experimented with monumental sculpture. His 1991 commission for the Glaxo Corporation in Ontario, *Northern Myth, Northern Legend,* is nearly 5 meters tall. The theme, relevant to Glaxo's work as a pharmaceutical concern, is the mythological beginnings of medicine and the interrelationships of the sea goddess Sedna, the animals, the Inuit, and the shaman. Another large collaborative commission was done for the Calgary, Alberta, Stock Exchange in 1995.

—Janet Catherine Berlo

ANGUHADLUQ, Luke

Variant names: Anglosaglo; Young Bull Caribou
Tribal affiliations: Inuit
Sculptor

Born: Chantrey Inlet, Northwest Territories, Canada, 1895; last name also spelled Anguhalluq. **Career:** Hunter, carver. **Family:** Married artist Marion Tuu'luq; two of his children, Ruth Qualluaryuk and Mark Uqayuittaq (by adoption) are also artists. **Died:** 1982.

Luke Anguhadluq. Photograph by and courtesy of Marion Jackson.

Individual Exhibitions

1971   *Drawings by Anglosaglo,* Fleet Gallery, Winnipeg, Manitoba
1972   *Drawings by Anglosaglo of Baker Lake,* The Innuit Gallery of Eskimo Art, Toronto
1982   *Luke Anguhadluq: Prints and Drawings,* Gallery Moos, Calgary, Alberta
1988   *Luke Anguhadluq: Baker Lake Prints and Drawings 1970-1982,* The Upstairs Gallery, Winnipeg
1989   *The Drummer Stopped the Drumbeat,* Houston North Gallery, Lunenburg, Nova Scotia
1993-95 *From the Centre: The Drawings of Luke Anguhadluq,* Art Gallery of Ontario, Toronto (traveling)

Selected Group Exhibitions

1972   Winnipeg Art Gallery, Manitoba
        Hugh Moss Gallery, London
1973   *Three Artist from Baker Lake,* Mazelow Gallery, Toronto
1974   *Eskimo Art,* Queens Museum, Flushing, New York

1976   *The People Within—Art from Baker Lake,* Art Gallery of Ontario, Toronto
1977   *Angohadluq and Esa - Drawings,* Artemus, Montreal
1977-82 *The Inuit Print/L'estampe inuit* (international traveling exhibition)
1978   *Inuit Games and Contests: The Clifford E. Lee Collection of Prints,* University of Alberta, Edmonton
        Polar Vision: Canadian Eskimo Graphics, Jerusalem Artists' House Museum, Israel
1979   *Spirits and Dreams - Arts of the Inuit of Baker Lake,* Department of Indian Affairs and Northern Development, Ottawa
1980   *Inuit Master Artists of the 1970s,* Inuit Gallery of Vancouver, British Columbia
1981   *Eskimo Games: Graphics and Sculpture/Giuochi Eschimesi: grafiche e sculture,* National Gallery of Modern Art, Rome
1983   *The Arctic/L'Artique,* UNESCO, Paris
        Inuit Masterworks: Selections from the Collection of Indian and Northern Affairs Canada, McMichael Canadian Collection, Kleinburg, Ontario

1984   *Gjoa Haven Sculpture/Wallhangings,* Atlantic Galleries,
        Fredericton, New Brunswick
        Die Kunst aus der Arktis, University of Siegen at Villa
        Waldrich, Siegen, Germany
1985   *Baker Lake Prints 1985,* The Innuit Gallery of Eskimo
        Art, Toronto
1987   *I Am Always Thinking About the Animals,* Houston North
        Gallery, Lunenburg, Nova Scotia
1988   *The World Around Me,* University of Lethbridge Art
        Gallery, Lethbridge, Alberta
1989   *Spoken in Stone: An Exhibition of Inuit Art,* Whyte Mu-
        seum of the Canadian Rockies, Banff, Alberta
1991   *Soujourns to Nunavut: Contemporary Inuit Art from
        Canada,* Bunkamura Art Gallery, Tokyo (traveling)
1994   *Arctic Spirit, 35 Years of Canadian Inuit Art,* Frye Art
        Museum, Seattle

Collections

Agnes Etherington Art Center, Queen's University, Kingston,
Ontario; Amon Carter Museum of Western Art, Fort Worth, Texas,
U.S.A.; Art Gallery of Greater Victoria, British Columbia; Art Gal-
lery of Nova Scotia, Halifax; Art Gallery of Windsor, Ontario;
Canada Council Art Bank, Ottawa; Canadian Guild of Crafts
Montreal; Canadian Museum of Civilization, Hull, Quebec; Clifford
E. Lee Collection, University of Alberta, Edmonton; Dennos Mu-
seum Center, Northwestern Michigan College, Traverse City;
Edmonton Art Gallery, Alberta; Klamer Family Collection, Art
Gallery of Ontario, Toronto; Macdonald Stewart Art Centre, Guelph,
Ontario; McMaster Univesity Art Gallery, Hamilton, Ontario;
McMichael Canadian Art Collection, Kleinburg, Ontario; Mendel
Art Gallery, Saskatoon, Saskatchewan; Musee des beaux-arts de
Montreal, Quebec; Museum of Anthropology, University of Brit-
ish Columbia, Vancouver; National Gallery of Canada, Ottawa;
Prince of Wales Northern Heritage Centre, Yellowknife, Northwest
Territories; Simon Fraser Gallery, Simon Fraser University, Burnaby,
British Columbia; University of Alberta, Edmonton; University of
Lethbridge Art Gallery, Lethbridge, Alberta; Victoria and Albert
Museum, London; Whyte Museum of the Canadian Rockies, Banff,
Alberta; Winnipeg Art Gallery, Manitoba.

Publications

On ANGUHADLUQ: **Books**—*Arts of the Eskimo: Prints,* Patrick
Furneaux and Leo Rosshandler, eds., Montreal: Signum Press in
association with Oxford University Press, Toronto, 1974. **Ar-
ticles**—"Eskimo Art Reconsidered," by George Swinton,
Artscanada, vol. 27, no. 6, December-January, 1971-72; "Anguhadluq's
Art: Memories of the Utkuhikhalingmiut," by Charles H. Moore,
Etudes/Inuit/Studies, vol. 2, no. 2, 1978; "Uumajut: Animal Imagery in
Inuit Art," by Alison Gillmore, *Arts Manitoba,* vol. 4, no. 3, Summer,
1985; "The Inuit Phenomenon in Art-Historical Context," by Hal
Opperman, *Inuit Art Quarterly* 1(2), 1986; "From the Centre: An
Examination of the Drawings of Luke Anguhadluq," by Cynthia Cook,
Inuit Art Quarterly 10(1), Spring, 1995.

*   *   *

The life of Luke Anguhadluq spanned most of the twentieth
century and his experience epitomized the cultural and physical
dislocations faced by most Inuit of his generation. Born near the
Back River in one of the most isolated regions of the North Ameri-

can Arctic, Anguhadluq (whose name means "young bull caribou"
in his native Inuktitut language) grew to maturity hunting caribou,
fishing, and learning the traditional skills and ways of his culture. It
was not until Anguhadluq was in his teenage years that the rifle
became available in the Back River area, and he was most likely an
adult before he had his first actual encounter with a white man,
which may have been with the Danish explorer, Knud Rasmussen,
who traveled the North American Arctic in the 1920s and spent
several days in Back River in 1923. Rasmussen recorded in his Fifth
Thule Expedition Report a meeting there with a tall and broad-
shouldered young man later identified as Anguhadluq.

Physically strong and tall in stature, Anguhadluq became a successful hunter and respected camp leader for a large extended family
group. A drastic decline in the caribou herds in the Central Arctic in
the 1950s, however, led to widespread hunger and starvation among
the inland Inuit and impinged drastically on Anguhadluq's life. With
the depletion of the caribou herds and his own advancing age, it
became increasingly difficult for Anguhadluq to sustain himself and
his family by hunting. Finally, in 1961, when Anguhadluq was 65,
he and his wife, Marion Tuu'luq, reluctantly gave up the traditional
hunting lifestyle of the Inuit and moved to the newly established
settlement of Baker Lake.

In Baker Lake Anguhadluq and Tuu'luq continued to live in a
tent and approximate as much as they could their style of living on
the land, finally moving into a small frame house only in 1967. In
Baker Lake they also encountered scores of other relocated Inuit
and government workers providing medical and social services and
aiding the sick and hungry Inuit in the resettlement process. Arts
and crafts projects were introduced by federal officers and arts
advisors in an effort to enable relocated Inuit to develop new means
of economic independence when they could no longer rely on hunting. Anguhadluq and his wife participated in some of these early
efforts and drew on their traditional cultural skills. Anguhadluq
made soapstone carvings and traditional hunting instruments, and
Tuu'luq participated in sewing projects, making fur mitts and boots
and other traditional garments and accessories.

In 1970 the Baker Lake arts and crafts projects gained new momentum with the arrival of Sheila and Jack Butler in the community
of artists. Under the Butlers' guidance, fledgling efforts to establish
a printmaking program in Baker Lake realized success, and
Anguhadluq and Tuu'luq both became actively involved in making
drawings for the new printmaking program. Prints based on
Anguhadluq's drawings appeared in the 1972 annual Baker Lake
print collection and every year following until his death in 1982.

Anguhadluq's drawings and prints are identifiable by a distinctive personal style in which he isolates his lively figures of humans
and animals on a blank white background and separates his figures
from one another without overlap. His subject matter is inspired by his
long experience on the land. Images of men and women in traditional
dress, traveling scenes with dogteams or kayaks, hunting and fishing
scenes, and caribou—either singly or in herds—are common in
Anguhadluq's work. The traditional drum dance is another theme that
Anguhadluq repeatedly explored, usually positioning a vitally active
drummer in the center of the page and surrounding the drummer with a
group of figures oriented to the four different edges of the paper.

Anguhadluq's flexibility in the orientation of figures was a function, in part, of his drawing method. He frequently made his drawings while sitting on the floor with the drawing paper between his
outstretched legs. Turning the paper as he worked, he would orient
figures to the edge of the paper closest to him in each subsequent
turn of the page. For this same reason, Anguhadluq's syllabic signa-

ture often appears on his drawing oriented in a direction inconsistent with the groundline or positioning of major figures of the work.

Although he became a recognized artist only in the final decade of his life, Anguhadluq's contribution to twentieth century Canadian art is significant. His drawings and prints have been included in more than 70 group shows of Inuit art, including the major international touring exhibition, *The Inuit Print/L'estampe inuit* (1977-1982). Anguhadluq's drawings were featured in a major solo exhibition, *From the Centre: The Drawings of Luke Anguhadluq*, organized by Cynthia Waye Cook for the Art Gallery of Ontario in 1993. Anguhadluq's colorful, lively images give access to the experience and thinking patterns of a traditional Inuit hunter for whom art became a vehicle of expression in the final decade of a long and productive life.

—Marion E. Jackson

ANNAQTUSSI TULURIALIK, Ruth

Tribal affiliations: Inuit
Painter

Born: Kazan River, Northwest Territories, Canada, 1934; name also transliterated as Annaqtusii, Annuktoshe, Annaqtuusi, Anaktose. **Family:** Married Hugh Tulurialik: children Barbara Qulaut, Marianne Paunngat, and Casey Unurniq; her sisters, Nancy Kangeryuaq and Winnie Owingayak, are artists. **Career:** Interpreter, odd jobs, artist.

Individual Exhibitions

1986   *The Vital Vision: Drawings by Ruth Annaqtussi Tulurialik.* Art Gallery of Windsor, Ontario (traveling)

Selected Group Exhibitions

1973-74 *Baker Lake Prints and Drawings,* Winnipeg Art Gallery, Winnipeg, Manitoba (traveling)
1977   National Museum of Man, Ottawa
1978   *The Zazelenchuk Collection of Eskimo Art,* Winnipeg Art Gallery, Winnipeg, Manitoba
1979   Agnes Etherington Art Centre, Kingston, Ontario
1980   *The Inuit Amautik: I Like My Hood to be Full,* Winnipeg Art Gallery, Winnipeg, Manitoba (traveling)
1982   *Shamans and Spirits: Myths and Medical Symbolism in Eskimo Art,* National Museum of Man, Ottawa
         Inuit Myths, Legends and Songs, Winnipeg Art Gallery, Winnipeg, Manitoba
1983-84 *Contemporary Indian and Inuit Art of Canada,* organized by Indian and Northern Affairs Canada, United Nations General Assembly Building, New York
1987-89 *Contemporary Inuit Drawings,* Macdonald Stewart Art Centre, Guelph, Ontario (traveling)

Publications

By ANNAQTUSSI TULURIALIK: Book—*Qikaaluktut: Images of Inuit Life,* with David F. Pelly, 1986.

On ANNAQTUSSI TULURIALIK: Books—*The Coming and Going of the Shaman* by Jean Blodgett, Winnipeg, Winnipeg Art Gallery, 1978; *Inuit Art in the '70s* by Marie Routledge, Kingston, Agnes Etheringron ArtCentre, 1979; *The Inuit Amautik: I Like My Hood to be Full,* Lauren J. Woodhouse, editor, Winnipeg, Winnipeg Art Gallery, 1980; *Inuit Myths, Legends, and Songs,* Winnipeg, Winnipeg Art Gallery, 1982; *The Vital Vision: Drawings by Ruth Annaqtussi Tulurialik* by Marion E. Jackson and David Pelly, Windsor, Ontario, 1986; *Contemporary Inuit Drawings* by Marion E. Jackson and Judith M. Nasby, Guelph, Ontario, 1987.

*   *   *

A highly-original self-taught artist, Ruth Annaqtussi Tulurialik is best known for her exuberant, boldly colored drawings, which record the stories and experiences of the traditional Inuit culture. Her mature drawings abound with lively vignettes of shamans in performance, spirit helpers, Inuit in traditional dress, hunting and fishing scenes, children playing, kayakers, and Arctic birds and animals. She combines generalized depictions of traditional Inuit culture with references to well-known Inuit legends and/or historical events, including such significant happenings as the coming of Christian missionaries and interactions between Inuit and White traders.

Annaqtussi Tulurialik herself has been positioned throughout her own life at the intersection of cultures, one foot in the traditional culture of her Inuit ancestors and the other in the culture of Euro-Canadians who recently established permanent residence in the Arctic. As an infant only a few months old, Annaqtussi Tulurialik was adopted by her uncle, a respected Anglican catechist named Thomas Tapatai, who took her from her birthplace along the Kazan River to the Anglican mission at Baker Lake, where she was raised by Tapatai and his wife Elisapee. Growing up around the mission and trading post at Baker Lake, Annaqtussi Tulurialik absorbed the teachings of the Anglican church and also gained a rudimentary understanding of English while retaining her own Inuktitut language and her strong identification with Inuit traditions.

Annaqtussi Tulurialik's favorite times as a child were those when Inuit from the camps on the land would come into Baker Lake for religious holidays and for trade. During those times, she would visit the tents of the elders, including her natural mother, Martha Talerook, and would listen intently to them conversing through the night, passing on the experiences and wisdom of their lives and the traditional legends of the Inuit culture. In later years Annaqtussi Tulurialik would remember these stories and life experiences and record them in her drawings, crowding her pages full with buoyant figures and vividly imagined details.

As Annaqtussi Tulurialik grew to adulthood, she witnessed Baker Lake grow from an isolated mission and trade site to a community of more than a thousand people. The settlement grew rapidly during the 1960s, as Inuit suffering from starvation and disease moved from remote camps to Baker Lake for government health and social service programs that were then being established in northern communities. Because Annaqtussi Tulurialik spoke Inuktitut and could understand some English, she was able to facilitate communication between the relocated Inuit and the new government workers. This ability led to her employment as an interpreter at the new government nursing station. In that position and in later in jobs at the coffee shop and local hotel, Annaqtussi Tulurialik established financial independence and also continued her role of facilitating communication between cultures.

During the period of resettlement at Baker Lake in the 1960s, the Canadian federal government supported experimental efforts to

Ruth Annaqtussi Tulurialik. Photograph by Marion Jackson.

develop arts and crafts programs to provide new economic opportunities for relocated Inuit. Annaqtussi Tulurialik became involved in some of these early projects, trying her hand at sewing garments. These projects gained momentum in the 1970s under the guidance of artistic advisors, Sheila and Jack Butler, who lived in the community in the early-1970s and helped to establish the Sanavik Co-operative. The Butlers emphasized collaboration and collective decision-making. They encouraged a large number of Inuit to draw and also trained those interested to translate the drawings into stonecut and stencil prints. Annaqtussi Tulurialik was one of the Baker Lake

Inuit to make drawings and become actively involved in the co-op effort. The 1972 Baker Lake stonecut and stencil print entitled *The Flood*, based on a drawing by Annaqtussi Tulurialik, is exemplary of the high level of artistic energy and technical competence that characterized the productions of the Sanavik Co-operative in those formative years.

Because of their technical complexity, Annaqtussi Tulurialik's drawings proved to be a challenge to the printmakers, however. She constructs her drawings by overlaying gestural strokes of different colors to create a lively surface, and printmakers found it difficult to translate her drawings into stonecut or stencil print images without sacrificing the spontaneity and energy of the original drawing. For this reason, relatively few of Annaqtussi Tulurialik's drawings have been translated as prints, and she is primarily known for her drawn images.

Annaqtussi Tulurialik's drawings were featured in a 1986-87 touring exhibition, *The Vital Vision - Drawings by Ruth Annaqtuusi Tulurialik,* organized by the Art Gallery of Windsor, Ontario. Her drawings also formed the basis for a book, *Qikaaluktut: Images of Inuit Life,* which she produced in 1986 in collaboration with writer and friend, David F. Pelly. In her drawings, as in her life, Ruth Annaqtussi Turlurialik strives to record, preserve and pass on the stories—both lived and imagined—that reflect the strength and vitality of the Inuit culture. Annaqtussi Tulurialik's drawings have become her form of storytelling and an avenue for cross-culture communication. Through her drawings, she passes on the legacy of her culture to her children and future generations of Inuit and gives access to the Inuit culture to those of other cultural backgrounds as well.

—Marion E. Jackson

ARNASUNGAAQ, Barnabus

Tribal affiliations: Inuit
Career

Born: Kazan River area of the Northwest Territories, 1924; surname also transliterated as Akkanashoonark, Akkanarshoonak, Arngrnasungaaq, Arnasungnaaq, Arknasungark. **Family:** Married graphic artist and carver Fanny Arngnakik; their sons David and Norman are carvers as well. **Career:** Began carving after moving his family to Baker Lake, Northwest Territories.

Individual Exhibitions

1976   *Stone Sculpture by Akkanashoonark of Baker Lake,* Inuit Gallery of Eskimo Art, Toronto
1979   *Recent Sculpture by Barnabus Argrnasungaaq (Akkanashoonark) of Baker Lake,* Upstairs Gallery, Winnipeg
        Barnabus Arnasungnaaq: Recent Sculpture, Gallery One, Toronto
1981   Inuit Galerie, Mannheim, Germany
1992   Inuit Galerie, Mannheim, Germany

Selected Group Exhibitions

1964   *Eskimo Carvers of Keewatin, N.W.T.,* Winnipeg Art Gallery
1977   *Sheokju of Cape Dorset & Eleven Sculptors of Baker Lake,* Victor Waddington Gallery, London
1980   *La déesse inuite de la mer/The Inuit Sea Goddess,* Musée des Beaux Arts de Montreal, Quebec (traveling)
1983   *An Enduring Tradition II: Inuit Carving from the Northwest Territories,* Inuit Gallery of Vancouver
1987   *Inuk, Inuit: Art et tradition chez les esquimaux d'hier et d'aujourd'hui,* Musée des Beaux Arts d'Arras, France
1988   *Arctic Forms: Inuit Sculpture,* Arctic Inuit Art Gallery, Richmond, Virginia

1989   *Art Inuit, la Sculpture des esquimaux du Canada,* presented by l'Iglou Art Esquimau, Douai at Les Chiroux, Centre Culturel de la Walloni, Liege, Belgium
1990   *Art Inuit, la Sculpture des Esquimaux du Canada,* presented by l'Iglou Art Esquimau, Douai at Centre d'Action Culturelle du Bassin Houllier, Lorrain, Saint Avold, France
        Art Inuit, presented by l'Iglou Art Esquimau, Douai at Galerie Ombre et Lumiere, Ensisheim, France
        Granville Island Canadian Inuit Sculpture Exhibition, Vancouver Inuit Art Society
        Inuit Sculpture: Displayed in Conjunction with the 1991 Cape Dorset Annual Graphics Collection, Muscarelle Museum of Art, Williamsburg, Virginia
1992   *Salon International Europ'art '92,* presented by Galerie Saint Merri, Geneva, Switzerland
1993   *The Treasured Monument,* Marion Scott Gallery, Vancouver
1994   *Arctic Spirit: 35 Years of Canadian Inuit Art,* Frye Art Museum, Seattle
1995   *Keeping Our Stories Alive: An Exhibition of the Art and Crafts from Dene and Inuit of Canada,* Institute of American Indian Arts Museum, Santa Fe

Collections

Art Gallery of Ontario, Toronto; Canadian Museum of Civilization, Hull, Quebec; Dennos Museum Center, Northwestern Michigan College, Traverse City; Eskimo Museum, Churchill, Manitoba; Glenbow Museum, Calgary, Alberta; Inuit Cultural Institute, Rankin Inlet, Northwest Territories; Macmillan-Bloedel Limited, Vancouver; McMichael Canadian Art Collection, Kleinburg, Ontario, Museum of Anthropology, University of British Columbia, Vancouver; National Gallery of Canada, Ottawa; Prince of Wales Northern Heritage Centre, Yellowknife, Northwest Territories; Sarick Collection, Art Gallery of Ontario, Toronto; University of Lethbridge Art Gallery, Lethbridge, Alberta; Winnipeg Art Gallery.

Publications

On ARNASUNGAAQ: Books—*Sculpture of the Eskimo* by George Swinton, Toronto: McClelland and Stewart, 1972; *Stone Sculpture by Akkanashoonark of Baker Lake,* Toronto: Innuit Gallery of Eskimo Art, 1976; *The Inuit Imagination: Arctic Myth and Sculpture* by Harold Seidelman and James Turner, Vancouver/ Toronto: Douglas & McIntyre, 1993. **Articles—**"A Talent to Carve" by Helen Burgess, *North,* vol. 12, 1965; "My Uncle Went to the Moon" by K. J. Butler, *artscanada,* vol. 30, nos. 5 and 6, December/January, 1973; "The Inuit Collection of the Winnipeg Art Gallery" by Bernadette Driscoll, *Canadian Antiques & Art Review,* vol. 2, no. 17, April 1981.

*   *   *

Barnabus Arnasungaaq was born and raised out on the land in the Kazan River area of the Northwest Territories. He began carving after moving his own young family into the nearby community of Baker Lake, where his children could begin school. After first experimenting with caribou antler, he began working with stone in 1960. In the years since, his name has become internationally known and his work has come to epitomize what George Swinton in *Sculp-*

ture of the Inuit refers to as the "distinctively bulging Baker Lake style." Arnasungaaq's talent was recognized almost immediately, and in 1964 he travelled to Winnipeg to attend the *Eskimo Carvers of Keewatin* exhibition featuring the best of the region's sculpture.

Known for its hardness, the dark, matte stone of the Baker Lake area becomes almost malleable in the hands of Arnasungaaq. The smooth, massive, rounded forms seem more likely to have been worked from clay than chipped from stone. The unforgiving reputation of the local black or grey stone is practically imperceptible in the ample curves, flowing lines and inviting texture of these carvings. The dull luster of an Arnasungaaq finished piece is so alluring that one almost expects it to be warm to the touch—not a quality one generally anticipates as a product of the work of axes and files. Although the hardness of the stone affords little in the way of detail, Arnasungaaq's rotund subjects are always discernable. His sculpture is not intended to be abstract, but the minimal detail and simplicity of form might initially challenge our notion of realism.

Arnasungaaq's most common subjects, human figures and musk-ox, are favoured by the artists of Baker Lake mainly because they are so familiar. He once said, "I always see men so therefore it is a lot easier for me to work on them. I hardly see the musk-ox or other animals and my memory fades very quickly so that is why I make men." His treatment of these subjects often results in a monumentality or heroic quality, no doubt a reflection of his own sentiments. Clearly, Arnasungaaq's carving style and subject matter complement each other very well. In particular, the musk-ox, an animal of massive proportions, is presented as a noble, powerful beast. A somewhat cumbersome figure, its enormous body rests on short sturdy legs, and what little detail is evident defines the long hairy coat resting like a giant blanket over its back. In some instances the coat is incised with long vertical lines or short scratches that describe the hairy texture.

Similarly, on carvings of hunters, family groups or mother and child figures, the surfaces are not refined and are only as smooth as the material allows. The beauty and clarity of Arnasungaaq's basic forms eliminates the need for further detail or explanation. Much of the strength of his sculpture is subtley conveyed by an absence of negative space, or the flowing outline of a parka and the very simply rendered faces.

In addition to his career as a stone carver, Arnasungaaq also participated in a 1965 experimental graphics workshop, producing prints and drawings. Although the Baker Lake Graphic Collections of later years were very successful, Arnasungaaq had turned his attention back to sculpture. His work has been the subject of five solo shows in Toronto, Winnipeg and Mannheim, Germany. His biography lists eighty-five group exhibitions to date in North America and Europe. The Canadian Museum of Civilization, the National Gallery of Canada, the Glenbow Museum and the Museum of Anthropology at the University of British Columbia include Arnasungaaq's sculpture in their collections.

—Lori Cutler

ASAH, Spencer

Variant names: Lallo
Tribal affiliations: Kiowa
Painter

Born: Near Carnegie, Oklahoma, c. 1905. **Education:** St. Patrick's Mission School, Anadarko, Oklahoma; clandestine art classes; University of Oklahoma, 1926-29; studied mural painting under Olle Nordmark, Fort Sill Indian School, 1938. **Career:** Farmer, traditional dancer, painter; commissioned for murals by the University of Oklahoma, Fort Sill Indian School, and others, including a series of murals at St. Patrick's Mission, 1929; art instructor, Fort Sill Indian School. **Died:** 1954, in Norman, Oklahoma.

Selected Group Exhibitions

1928   *Five Kiowas*, traveling exhibition arranged by Oscar Brousse Jacobson
        Five Kiowas, First International Art Exposition, Prague, Czechoslovakia
1930   *Southwest States Indian Art Show*, Santa Fe
1931-33 *Exposition of Indian Tribal Arts,* Grand Central Galleries, New York
1937   *American Indian Exposition and Congress*, Tulsa, Oklahoma
1955-56 European tour sponsored by the University of Oklahoma, Norman
1958-61 European tour sponsored by the University of Oklahoma, Norman
1972   *Contemporary Southern Plains Indian Painting*, tour organized by the Southern Plains Indian Museum and Oklahoma Indian Arts and Crafts Cooperative, Anadarko, Oklahoma
1978   *100 Years of Native American Painting,* Oklahoma Museum of Art, Oklahoma City
1979   *Sharing Our Wealth,* Oklahoma Historical Society, Oklahoma City
1981-83 *Native American Painting*, Amarillo Art Center, Amarillo, Texas (traveling)
1984-85 *Indianascher Kunstler* (traveling, Germany), organized by the Philbrook Museum, Tulsa, Oklahoma
1985   *Native American Fine Arts*, Heard Museum, Phoenix, Arizona
1990   *American Indian Artists: The Avery Collection and the McNay Permanent Collection,* Marion Koogler McNay Art Museum, San Antonio, Texas
1991   *Kiowa Murals,* The Southern Plains Indian Museum and Crafts Center, Anadarko, Oklahoma
1991-96 *Shared Visions: Native American Painters and Sculptors in the Twentieth Century,* Heard Museum, Phoenix, Arizona

Collections

Anadarko City Museum, Oklahoma; Denver Art Museum, Denver, Colorado; Thomas Gilcrease Institute of American History and Art, Tulsa, Oklahoma; Heard Museum, Phoenix, Arizona; Indian Arts and Crafts Board, Department of the Interior, Washington, D.C.; Fred Jones, Jr., Museum of Art, University of Oklahoma, Norman; Marion Koogler McNay Art Museum, San Antonio Texas; Museum of the Great Plains, Lawton, Oklahoma; Museum of Northern Arizona, Flagstaff; Oklahoma Historical Society Museum, Oklahoma City; Philbrook Art Museum, Tulsa, Oklahoma; Woolaroc Museum, Bartlesville, Oklahoma.

Publications

On ASAH: Books—*Kiowa Indian Art*, by O. B. Jacobson, Nice, France, 1929; *Indian Painters and White Patrons*, by J. J. Brody,

Albuquerque: University of New Mexico Press, 1971; *Song from the Earth, American Indian Painting,* by Jamake Highwater, Boston: New York Graphic Society, 1976; *100 Years of Native American Painting,* by Arthur Silberman, Oklahoma City: Oklahoma Museum of Art, 1978; *Kiowa Voices: Ceremonial Dance Ritual and Song* (1981) and *Kiowa Voices: Myths, Legends, and Folktales* (1983), by Maurice Boyd, Ft. Worth: Texas Christian University Press; *Native American Painting: Selections from the Museum of the American Indian,* by David M. Fawcett and Lee A. Callander, New York: Museum of the American Indian, 1982; *American Indian Artists: The Avery Collection and the McNay Permanent Collection,* by Jean Sherrod Williams, San Antonio: Marion Koogler McNay Art Museum, 1990; *Kiowa Murals,* Anardarko, Oklahoma: Southern Plains Indian Museum & Crafts Center, 1991; *Shared Visions: Native American Painters and Sculptors in the Twentieth Century,* by Margaret Archuleta and Dr. Rennard Strickland, Phoenix: Heard Museum, 1991; *Artists and Craftspeople,* by Arlene Hershfelder, New York: Facts on File, Inc., 1994. **Articles**— "American Inter-Tribal Indian Art," by Rose V. S. Berry, *Art and Archeology XXXII,* November-December, 1931; "Indian Arts Fund Collection of Paintings," by Clara Lee Tanner and Anne Forbes, *El Palacio,* December, 1948; "The Development of Modern American Indian Painting in the Southwest and Plains Areas," by Dorothy Dunn, *El Palacio,* November, 1951; "Kiowa Indian Art, A Pochoir Portfolio," by Maybelle Mann, *American Art & Antiques,* January-February, 1979; "The Kiowa Five," by W. K. Stratton, *Oklahoma Today,* November-December, 1990.

*   *   *

Spencer Asah was one of the original "Kiowa Five" artists who established the "flat style" of modern painting in the Southern Plains region. Asah's work exemplified the now classic Oklahoma paradigm, featuring flat colors, clear outlines, sinuous curves, and an emphasis on line, which is used to separate discrete color areas. The paintings of Asah and the Kiowa Five are called flat style because they are decidedly two-dimensional in their appearance insofar as they lack such European features of perspective. The Kiowa Five artists, including Asah, James Auchiah, Jack Hokeah, Stephen Mopope, and Monroe Tsatoke, have become famous for their pioneering of what is now regarded as "classic" or "traditional" Southern Plains painting in Oklahoma.

There was a fair amount of similarity (both in style and content) of the paintings of the Kiowa Five. In speaking of the traits of the art of this group, the preeminent authority on the subject, the late Arthur Silberman, has offered the following analysis:

> The paintings of the Kiowa school are unique and instantly recognizable. The treatment is often broad, the use of color is bold and employs strong contrasts. In these paintings, with their strong decorative feeling, and flamboyant use of color, one can find sensitivity and depth. The paintings have a tendency to be of single figures or small groups. The dance figures echo the character of Plains dancing—virtuoso effects emphasizing the individual rather than the ceremonial. A wide range of subject matter is used: dances of all kinds, portraiture, humor, lyricism and mysticism. At times, there is true realism with subjects shrewdly observed and deftly characterized.

Several of the members of the Kiowa Five group were descendants of notable tribal leaders, warriors, and medicine people. This was certainly true of Asah, who was the son of a buffalo medicine man and was raised in a milieu of traditional Indian values. As well, Asah was fortunate to be educated at the St. Patrick's Mission School in Anadarko. Along with Hokeah, Auchiah, and Mopope, Asah was the beneficiary of the ministrations of Father Isidore Ricklin, O.S.B., who was interested in the religious and educational well-being of his students. Because Asah and Hokeah were orphaned at a young age, they were enrolled as boarding students and therefore spent a longer period of time at St. Patrick's than did Auchiah and Mopope. In any case, Sister Olivia Taylor (of Choctaw Indian heritage) was the first art teacher for these students. She provided her students with elementary art education in terms of proportions, depth, and horizon.

In 1916 Mrs. Susan (Susie) Ryan Peters arrived in Anadarko to work as a Field Matron in the Indian Service. She was impressed with what she regarded as the inherent artistic talents of several of the Kiowas in the Anadarko region and felt that they needed meaningful encouragement. In 1918 Peters organized art classes for several Kiowas, including Asah, Tsatoke, Mopope, Auchiah, and Hokeah, with Mrs. Willie Blaze Lane of Chickasha as instructor. These classes were more or less clandestine since the Bureau of Indian Affairs (BIA) at the time did not approve of art courses that would encourage students to pursue topics relevant to their traditional tribal cultures. Instead the BIA hoped Indian students would lose all traces of their cultural heritage in order for them to assimilate into the dominant white culture. Nonetheless, Peters persevered in her efforts to encourage her proteges and to persuade the staff at St. Patrick's School to continue their art education program.

Peters arranged for three of the Kiowas, Asah, Hokeah, and Tsatoke, to enroll in special art classes at the University of Oklahoma in 1926. They were joined later by Mopope and in 1927 by Auchiah. Asah, Hokeah, and Mopope lived together on campus as single students, while Auchiah and Tsatoke (who were married) lived in apartments off campus. The Kiowas received formal art training from Professor Edith Mahier who, according to art historian Rosemary Ellison, encouraged her charges to express their own native artistic approach to design and composition. The Director of the School of Art, Dr. Oscar Brousse Jacobson, became interested in the Kiowa art students and did much to encourage and facilitate their studies. To help finance their second year, Peter and Jacobson, along with Lewis Ware—a member of the state legislature—sought and obtained financial aid for the Kiowas from L. H. Wentz of Ponca City, Oklahoma. Hence, the experience of special classes for the Kiowa students went from 1926 to 1929.

In their experience under the mentoring of Mahier and Jacobson, the Kiowas were able to have access to excellent materials and they had the freedom to learn to use them as seemed appropriate to them. While they had a special room in the art department for their work, they were also encouraged to mix informally with the other students and thereby to share experiences and knowledge. Much has been made by J. J. Brody (1971) that Jacobson had some artistic influence over the Kiowas in terms of his own orientation towards the "art deco" style, a popular illustrative approach in the 1920s. While this may be true, it can also be pointed out that art deco is a style that is not at all incompatible with what the Kiowa artists were working out on their own. The fact that they might have been influenced to some degree by this paradigm of the era is something they could take in stride.

In the spring of 1929, Asah, along with Mopope, Hokeah, and Auchiah, worked on a series of murals at St. Patrick's Mission to memorialize the life and work of Father Isidore. These murals were placed in Father Isidore's Memorial Chapel where they remained until 1968 when the building was demolished. Today they are the protective possession of the Indian Arts and Crafts Board's Southern Plains Indian Museum & Crafts Center in Anadarko.

Asah, along with Hokeah and Mopope, was considered to be an outstanding Indian dancer and frequently performed at pow-wows and special events in that capacity; Auchiah and Tsatoke were skilled singers and drummers who often accompanied them. In addition, Asah studied the secco and fresco techniques of mural painting under the famed Swedish artist, Olle Nordmark, at the Fort Sill Indian School near Lawton. Mopope and Auchiah were fellow students (along with others) of Asah. In 1939 Asah became an art instructor at the Fort Sill Indian School.

—John Anson Warner

ATENCIO, Gilbert

Variant names: Wah Peen
Tribal affiliations: San Ildefonso Pueblo
Painter

Born: Gilbert Benjamin Atencio, 1930, Greeley, Colorado; Wah Peen means Mountain of the Sacred Wind. **Education:** Self-taught artist; graduated from Santa Fe Indian School in 1947. **Military Service:** U.S. Marine Corps. **Career:** Painter, ceramist, and illustrator; governor of San Ildefonso, beginning in the mid-1960s. **Awards:** Honors from various fairs and exhibitions, including the Heard Museum Guild Indian Fair and Market, Phoenix; Inter-Tribal Indian Ceremonies, Gallup, New Mexico; Museum of New Mexico, Santa Fe; Philbrook Museum of Art, Tulsa, Oklahoma; and the Scottsdale National Indian Arts Exhibition, Arizona. **Died:** April 1995.

Selected Group Exhibitions

1952   *Southwest Indian Paintings*, Heard Museum, Phoenix, Arizona
          National Gallery of Art, Washington, D.C.
1955   DeYoung Museum, San Francisco
          An Exhibition of American Indian Painters, James Graham and Sons, New York
1955-56 European tour, sponsored by the University of Oklahoma, Norman
1958-61 European tour, sponsored by the University of Oklahoma, Norman
1961-62 Philbrook Art Center, Tulsa, Oklahoma
1964-65 *First Annual Invitational Exhibition of American Indian Paintings*, United States Department of the Interior, Washington, D.C.
1965   *Selected Works of Indian Artists Represented in the Butler Collection*, Heard Museum, Phoenix, Arizona
1969   Heard Museum, Phoenix, Arizona
1973   *An Exhibition of American Indian Art, 1920-1972*, The Art Center, Hastings College, Hastings, Nebraska

1978   *100 Years of Native American Painting*, Oklahoma Museum of Art, Oklahoma City, Oklahoma
1979-80 *Native American Paintings*, organized by the Joslyn Art Museum, Omaha, Nebraska (traveling)
1981   Philbrook Museum of Art, Tulsa, Oklahoma
1984-85 *Indianascher Kunstler* (traveling, Germany), organized by the Philbrook Museum, Tulsa, Oklahoma
1988   Ecomnomos Works of Art, Santa Fe, New Mexico
          When the Rainbow Touches Down, Heard Museum, Phoenix, Arizona
1989   Jean Seth Gallery, Santa Fe, New Mexico
1990   *American Indian Artists: The Avery Collection and the McNay Art Museum*, Marion Koogler McNay Art Museum, San Antonio, Texas
1990-91 *One with the Earth*, organized by the Institute of American Indian Arts and Alaska Culture and Arts Development, Santa Fe, (traveling)
1991-96 *Shared Visions: Native American Painters and Sculptors of the Twentieth Century*, Heard Museum, Phoenix, Arizona

Collections

Amerind Foundation, Dragoon, Arizona; Bureau of Indian Affairs, Department of the Interior, Washington, D.C.; Denver Art Museum, Colorado; M.H. De Young Memorial Museum, San Francisco; Thomas Gilcrease Museum of American History and Art, Tulsa, Oklahoma; Heard Museum, Phoenix, Arizona; Indian Arts and Crafts Board, Denman Collection, United States Department of the Interior, Washington, D.C.; Institute of American Indian Arts Museum, Santa Fe, New Mexico; Museum of New Mexico, Santa Fe; Museum of Northern Arizona, Flagstaff; Philbrook Museum of Art, Tulsa, Oklahoma; School of American Research, Santa Fe, New Mexico; Southwest Museum, Los Angeles.

Publications

On ATENCIO: Books—*American Indian Painting of the Southwest and Plains Area*, by Dorothy Dunn, Albuquerque, 1968; *Southwestern Indian Ceremonials*, by Tom Bahti, Flagstaff, 1970; *Indian Painters and White Patrons*, by J.J. Brody, Albuquerque, 1971; *Southwest Indian Painting: A Changing Art*, by Clara Lee Tanner, Tucson, 1973; *American Indian Painting and Sculpture*, by P. J. Border, New York, 1981; *Shared Visions: Native American Painters and Sculptors of the Twentieth Century*, by Margaret Archuleta and Rennard Strickland, Phoenix, The Heard Museum, 1991. **Articles**—"Selected Works of Indian Artists Represented in Butler Collection," by Joan Bucklew, *Arizona Republic*, December 12, 1965.

*		*		*

The pueblo of San Ildefonso in New Mexico may well be called the cradle of modern Indian painting in the Southwest. Here Crescencio Martinez drew his first pictures of Native American ceremonial dancers for Dr. Edgar L. Hewett, Director of the School of American Research in Santa Fe, and left an impressive record at his untimely death in 1918. Awa Tsireh, Julian Martinez and others followed in his footsteps and brought about a renaissance in Southwest Indian art.

Gilbert Atencio, nephew of Maria Martinez, continued the art tradition not only of his pueblo but also of his family, who have

Gilbert Atencio: Depiction of a shinney game (with self-portrait at center of painting), c. 1950. Courtesy Museum of Indian Arts and Culture, Santa Fe, Dorothy Dunn Kramer Collection.

brought forth painters like Crescencio and Julian Martinez, Popovi and Tony Da, and the famous potter Maria. Atencio had some kind of a formal art training at the Indian School in Santa Fe and distinguished himself as a talented draughtsman early on, selling his first pictures before his graduation in 1947.

Initially, Atencio was especially interested in portrait painting. An early portrait of Maria and Julian Martinez, with Julian showing a pot to Maria, who is seated, became famous. Apart from the fact that the picture is neatly done, both people were easily recognized by those who knew them—remarkable considering that until the 1960s portraits done by Indian artists were practically nonexistent. The painting reveals some of the features that distinguish Atencio's work, especially his meticulous attention to detail in clothes, hairstyle, and personal adornment.

Atencio is a traditionalist. During his whole career as a painter, scenes of everyday life and the rituals of his pueblo, especially the dances, remained his main theme. In this respect he is similar to Hopi painter Fred Kabotie, who was active for a time in Santa Fe and whose influence spread to the Rio Grande Valley. Like Kabotie, and unlike artists of the Studio at Santa Fe Indian School, Atencio strove for a realistic, three-dimensional rendering of his subject matter, at least in some phases of his career. In the 1950s, for instance, he depicted a San Ildefonso women's dance with the plaza for its setting and houses in the background. He rendered perspective by diminishing the distant figures and objects and showed an

unusual love of detail and authenticity. Not only are the dancers' costumes minutely rendered, but even the flowered curtains of the windows and the potted plants on the window-sills are represented.

Realistic pictures like this early pueblo dance scene are a sharp contrast to such paintings of the 1960s as *Pueblo Mother and Child* and *San Ildefonso Potters*. The figures here are highly stylized, two-dimensional and silhouetted against a decorative background, with abstract motifs of clouds, rain, and corn of the Hopi universe.

A third variant of Atencio's painting style is represented by *Ceremonial Water Carriers* (1979), which was chosen as the official poster for the Gallup Inter-Tribal Indian Ceremonials, the largest annual gathering of Native Americans in the United States. The picture combines realistic traits with stylizations in a new manner, depicting three female members of a cult society bringing water from sacred lakes for ceremonial use. The three figures are stylized to suggest the natural forms of the body, and their faces have prominent cheekbones and slightly sunken eyes, attempts at three dimensionality. Their earnest, faraway expression, however, have no individuality and, together with the festive robes and rich jewelry, emphasize the women's roles rather than their personalities. In this way the ritual character of the act is pointedly emphasized. Atencio has dispensed in this picture with any kind of background: there is neither a suggestion of landscape as in his "realistic" images, nor a decorative design that may emphasize the stylized character of a picture. The decorative element is here restricted to the huge vases on the women's heads, which identify them as Pueblo Indians. The absence of personal and individualistic traits in this picture contributes to the impression of tranquility and dignity appropriate to the theme of a ritual act.

Atencio developed his style over the years. While he initially had painted in the traditional manner of Pueblo painters, using realistic and skillfully drafted figures, in the 1960s he increasingly began to add decorative elements in the background and to stylize and simplify his figures. From the 1970s on one notices a combination of realistic forms with certain stylized elements. Atencio's traditional character as a painter had its parallel in his lifestyle. A one time governor of San Ildefonso Pueblo, he had a strong sense of family and tribal responsibility and seldom ventured from his native pueblo.

—Gerhard and Gisela Hoffmann

ATENCIO BIRD, Lorencita

Variant names: To Pove
Tribal affiliations: San Juan Pueblo
Weaver and painter

Born: San Juan Pueblo, New Mexico, 1916; following her marriage, her name was Lorencita Atencio Bird. **Education:** The Studio, Santa Fe Indian School, and Albuquerque Indian School. **Career:** Arts and crafts practitioner; instructor, San Juan Co-op, San Juan Pueblo; craft demonstrator (weaving and embroidery), Bandelier National Monument and Pecos National Monument, New Mexico. **Awards:** Honors for her mantas at San Juan Pueblo (1945) and Santa Clara Pueblo (1974, 1985) fairs, Heard Museum Guild Indian Fair and Market (1984), Wheelwright Museum of the American Indian (1992). **Died:** 4 May 1995.

Selected Group Exhibitions

Exhibited most frequently at Santa Fe Indian Market and fashion shows at the Indian Cultural Center and the Country Club of Santa Fe.

1955-56 European tour, sponsored by the University of Oklahoma, Norman
1957 National Gallery of Art, Washington, D.C.
1958-61 European tour. sponsored by the University of Oklahoma, Norman
1994-95 *Timeless Impressions,* Heard Museum, Phoenix, Arizona

Collections

Heard Museum, Phoenix, Arizona; Philbrook Museum of Art, Tulsa, Oklahoma; Wheelwright Museum of the American Indian, Santa Fe, New Mexico.

Lorencita Atencio Bird: *Matachinas Dance,* **1937. Courtesy Museum of Indian Arts and Culture, Santa Fe, Margretta Dietrich Collection.**

Publications

On ATENCIO BIRD: Books——*The American Indian,* by Oliver LaFarge, New York, 1960; *American Indian Painting of the Southwest and Plains Area,* by Dorothy Dunn, Albuquerque, 1968; *Indian Painters and White Patrons,* by J.J. Brody, Albuquerque, 1971; *Modern by Tradition,* by Bruce Bernstein and W. Jackson Rushing, Santa Fe, 1995.

*   *   *

Lorencita Atencio Bird was a gifted artist of San Juan Pueblo, especially renowned for her mantas and other clothing items, but talented as well as a painter. In many ways her vocational and avocational interests blended seamlessly, as she focused on raising a family, applied her talents to creating ceremonial, decorative, and utilitarian clothing, and taught Pueblo children and adults in the arts of weaving, sewing and design. It has been said that she gave up art to focus more attention on her family, and while she did indeed stop painting in the 1950s, her weaving and embroidery were always part of her life. Officially, recognition came in the form of prizes, from consistent honors during the 1940s to more sporadic awards during the following decades, which reflects her more infrequent participation in fairs and juried competitions rather than peaks and valleys in her artistic development. In the pueblos around Santa Fe, her creations were sought for ceremonial dances and weddings and for more everyday use, including such popular accessories as tote bags, sashes and belts.

Atencio Bird's work first drew notice while she attended the Indian Schools at Santa Fe and Albuquerque. It was at this time, during her teens, that she started experimenting with the raised diamond design of embroidery that would become her trademark. Her embroidery and her watercolor paintings were purchased regularly enough for her to earn a living during the 1930s and 1940s, supplemented by stints where she demonstrated weaving and embroidery for the National Parks Service at Bandelier National Monument and Pecos National Monument. Two of her paintings were purchased by the Philbrook Museum of Art (then the Philbrook Art Center) in the 1940s and remain in the institution's permanent collection. Even as she returned to live full time at San Juan Pueblo in the 1950s, her work was shown in major exhibitions, one at the National Gallery of Washington, and twice on tours of Europe organized by the University of Oklahoma.

Atencio Bird's weaving and embroidery of mantas were her most excellent creations and reflect her deftness for planning and design, as well as her artistry. She never repeated the same design, and added further uniqueness to individual pieces by infusing them with various colors and elements of personal and communal symbolism. For example, many designs included openings in the embroidery through which spirits could pass easily, with the effortless passage and pleasant design helping to encourage them to bring good fortune. She often blended in the color gold, representing sunshine, and occasionally mixed in red with the gold "because sometimes life does not always go smooth." Butterflies, in addition to offering a pleasing and light image, represented everlasting life, and a checkerboard pattern illustrated that life can be secure. More traditional symbols, such as stacked triangles to represent mountains, or diamonds linked together with small lines to represent togetherness in a village, were also frequent design elements.

Atencio Bird applied this same approach to her many other creations, including white brocade sashes, rain sashes with corn husk balls, floated warp weave sashes that usually combined either red, black, and green, or red, white and green, crocheted or knitted leggings, shirts, skirts, and dance outfits. Atencio Bird often made ceremonial regalia, and with her daughter designed clothing for entire wedding parties. Her fame as a clothes designer was well known in the area, leading to commissions from local pueblos of Santo Domingo, Jemez, San Felipe, and Santa Clara.

Atencio Bird's ceremonial work was also based on a symbolism. White predominated on mantas made for weddings, the Buffalo Dance of the Water Clan, and the Basket Dance. Black was more evident for outfits worn during the Cloud Dance and the Buffalo Dance of the Summer Clan. Such care and concern for all aspects of creativity informed all of her work, and her life as well, for an artist whose life and "career" blended seamlessly.

—Perry Bear

AUCHIAH, James
Tribal affiliations: Kiowa
Painter

Born: Oklahoma (near the current site of Medicine Park), 1906. **Education:** St. Patrick's Mission School, Anadarko, Oklahoma; University of Oklahoma, special art classes with Spencer Asah, Monroe Tsatoke, Jack Hokeah, and Stephen Mopope, collectively known as the "five Kiowas," 1927-29, study under Olle Nordmark, Fort Sill Indian School, 1938. **Military Service:** U.S. Coast Guard, World War II. **Career:** Wrote English captions for Kiowa tribal calendar counts, 1918-25; muralist, St. Patrick's Mission School, Department of the Interior Building, Washington, D.C., U.S. Post Office, Anadarko, Oklahoma, 1930s; artist, teacher and museum curator. **Died:** 28 December 1974.

Selected Group Exhibitions

1928   *Five Kiowas*, traveling exhibition arranged by Oscar Brousse Jacobson
        Five Kiowas, First International Art Exposition, Prague, Czechoslovakia
1930   Southwest States Indian Art Show, Santa Fe
1947-65 *American Indian Paintings from the Permanent Collection*, Philbrook Art Center, Tulsa, Oklahoma (traveling)
1955-56 European tour sponsored by the University of Oklahoma, Norman
1958-61 European tour sponsored by the University of Oklahoma, Norman
1972   *Contemporary Southern Plains Indian Painting*, traveling exhibition organized by the Southern Plains Indian Museum and Oklahoma Indian Arts and Crafts Cooperative, Anadarko, Oklahoma
1978   *100 Years of Native American Painting*, Oklahoma Museum of Art, Oklahoma City
1979   *Sharing Our Wealth*, Oklahoma Historical Society, Oklahoma City
        Abstract Illusionism, Museum of Fine Arts, Springfield, and Danforth Museum, Framingham, Massachusetts

1980   *Plains Indian Paintings*, Museum of Art, University of
           Oklahoma, Norman (traveling)
1981-83 *Native American Painting*, Amarillo Art Center, Ama-
           rillo, Texas (traveling)
1982   *Native American Painting: Selections from the Museum
           of the American Indian,* Heard Museum, Phoenix
1990   *American Indian Artists: The Avery Collection and the
           McNay Permanent Collection,* Marion Koogler McNay
           Art Museum, San Antonio, Texas
1991   *Kiowa Murals,* Southern Plains Indian Museum and
           Crafts Center, Anadarko, Oklahoma
          *Shared Visions: Native American Painters and Sculp-
           tors in the Twentieth Century,* Heard Museum, Phoe-
           nix

Publications

On AUCHIAH: Books—*Kiowa Indian Art* by Oscar B. Jacobson,
Nice, France, 1929; *American Indian Painters* by Oscar B. Jacobson
and Jeanne d'Ucel, Nice, France, 1950; *American Indian Painting of
the Southwest and Plains Areas* by Dorothy Dunn, Albuquerque,
New Mexico, 1968; *Indian Painters and White Patrons* by J. J.
Brody, Albuquerque, New Mexico, 1971; *Song from the Earth:
American Indian Painting* by Jamake Highwater, Boston, 1976;
100 Years of Native American Art, exhibition catalog by Arthur
Silberman, Oklahoma City, 1978; *Kiowa Voices: Ceremonial Dance,
Ritual and Song* by Maurice Boyd, Fort Worth, Texas, 1981; *Native
American Painting,* exhibition catalog by Jeanne Snodgrass King,
Amarillo, Texas, 1981; *Native American Painting: Selections from
the Museum of the American Indian*, New York, 1982; *Shared Vi-
sions* by Margaret Archuleta and Rennard Strickland, Phoenix, 1991.
Articles—"The Development of Modern American Indian Paint-
ing in the Southwest and Plains Area" by Dorothy Dunn, *El Palacio*
LVIII, November 1951; "Kiowa Indian Art" by Maybelle Mann,
American Art and Antiques, January-February, 1979.

*   *   *

James Auchiah was a member of the important group of "Kiowa
Five" artists who established the "flat style" (or two-dimensional)
approach to painting on the Southern Plains. Along with Spencer
Asah, Jack Hokeah, Stephen Mopope, and Monroe Tsatoke,
Auchiah was one of the fathers of the school that has proven semi-
nal in twentieth-century Native American arts.

Like several of the other Kiowa Five artists, Auchiah came from
a distinguished family. His grandfather was the famous Kiowa chief,
Satanta, and his father, Mark Auchiah, was one of General Hugh
Scott's Fort Sill Indian scouts. Auchiah took an interest in art and
the cultural heritage of the Kiowa people at an early age. As a boy
he slipped past the guard in front of a Ghost Dance tipi and saw
sacred paintings being made. His grandmother was there at work
because she was a noted medicine woman and "color mixer" for the
Kiowa. She, indeed, was a major influence in Auchiah's life. In the
period 1918 to 1925, Auchiah was one of several helpers who
supplied English captions for a new calendar count started by the
daughter of Dohasan (famous keeper of one of the earlier Kiowa
tribal calendars). Indeed, Auchiah came to see his art as a record
preserving traditional Kiowa lore and history.

Auchiah received art instruction from Sister Olivia Taylor
(Choctaw heritage) at St. Patrick's Mission School in Anadarko. In
1918, when Susan (Susie) Ryan Peters organized a fine arts class in

her home and invited Mrs. Willie Baze Lane from Chickasaw to
offer lessons, Auchiah was a participant along with Tsatoke,
Mopope, Asah, and Hokeah. However, when his four friends and
colleagues went to the University of Oklahoma in Norman for
special art classes under Edith Mahier and Oscar Brousse Jacobson,
Auchiah did not join them until 1927. Both Auchiah and Tsatoke
were married when they attended the university and therefore lived
in apartments with their wives, while the other three artists stayed
on campus. Nevertheless, once Auchiah joined the group in 1927,
the Kiowa Five artists came into existence as a distinctive entity.

Greatly impressed with their art, Jacobson organized a traveling
exhibition of art by the Five Kiowas in 1928. This collection was
sent to the First International Art Exposition in Prague, where it
received great acclaim. In 1929, a portfolio edition of prints by the
five artists (plus Lois Smokey), *Kiowa Indian Art*, was published
in Nice, France. This was the first time that international recognition had come to the artists, and it was an auspicious occasion. This
portfolio is now a collector's item.

After his fruitful experience at the University of Oklahoma from
1927 to 1929, Auchiah joined with three of his associates (Asah,
Mopope, and Hokeah) to paint several murals honoring the memory
of Father Isidore Ricklin, the founder of St. Patrick's Mission School
in Anadarko, where the boys had studied. These murals were situated in Father Isidore's Memorial Chapel until 1968 when the building was razed. The murals are now in the safekeeping of the Indian
Arts and Crafts Board's Southern Plains Indian Museum & Crafts
Center in Anadarko.

Auchiah apparently liked to do mural work since he painted
quite a few over his lifetime. In fact, mural painting was a popular
artistic activity during the 1930s, as much of it was subsidized as a
method of depression-relief for beleaguered painters. In 1936 and
1937, Auchiah and Mopope painted murals in the new Post Office
Building in Anadarko; the murals are still there today to greet patrons. In 1938, Auchiah studied mural painting with the Swedish
master, Olle Nordmark, at the Fort Sill Indian School in Lawton and
received instruction in both secco (dry plaster) and fresco (wet
plaster) techniques. Nordmark's project had been instigated by
Oscar Jacobson, who continued to be helpful to Native American
art students throughout this period.

During the 1930s Auchiah painted a number of different murals
in various public buildings. One of his most notable commissions
was a very large work (8 ft. x 50 ft.) for the Department of the
Interior building's cafeteria in Washington, D.C. The subject matter
is the Harvest Dance.

In 1943, during wartime, Auchiah served in the Coast Guard and
received special permission to visit Fort Marion in St. Augustine,
Florida, where many Oklahoma warriors had been imprisoned from
1870 to 1875, and where some Native Americans earned incomes
by producing pictures for white patrons. The artwork of the best of
these painters (including many Kiowas) went beyond the conventions of ledger art by featuring more in the way of personal expression. Some of these artists, who made their appearance in the late
1920s, were the precursors of the Kiowa Five. Auchiah studied the
pictographs carved on the walls by the artist-prisoners and also
examined the museum's Indian documents.

It is important to note that Auchiah, along with Tsatoke, was a
leader in the Native American Church (peyote ritual). As both a
tribal historian and a religious leader, Auchiah enjoyed great respect
in the Kiowa community.

—John Anson Warner

AUSTIN, Frank

Variant names: Bahah Zhonie
Tribal affiliations: Navajo
Textile artist and designer

Born: Tsegi Canyon, near Tonalea, Arizona, 10 April 1938; Bahah Zhonie means Laughing Boy. **Education:** Arizona State University, University of Arizona, "Southwestern Indian Art Project" scholarship. **Family:** Married Rose L. Adajie, 1960; children Carmellia Rose, 1961, and Dwayne, 1964. **Career:** Silk screen designer, textile painter, fabric manufacturer, store owner (Cortez, Colorado), and watercolor painter. **Awards:** American Institute of Interior Designers, International Design Award, 1962; Scottsdale National Indian Art Exhibition, Scottsdale, Arizona, seven honors from 1962-72, including Grand Award.

Selected Group Exhibitions

1962-72 *Scottsdale National Indian Art Exhibition*, Scottsdale, Arizona
1963-65 *Inter-Tribal Indian Ceremonial*, Gallup, New Mexico
1964 *American Indian Art Exposition*, Wayne State University, Detroit, Michigan
1968 *James T. Bialac Collection of Southwest Indian Paintings*, Arizona State Museum, Tucson
1970 *Annual American Indian Artists Exhibition*, Philbrook Art Center, Tulsa, Oklahoma
1971 Laguna Gloria Art Museum, Austin, Texas
1972 Colorado Indian Market

Collections

Arizona State Museum, Tucson; Indian Arts and Crafts Board, United States Department of the Interior, Washington, D.C.; National Museum of the American Indian, Washington, D.C.

Publications

On AUSTIN: Books—*Indian Painters and White Patrons*, J. J. Brody, Albuquerque, University of New Mexico Press, 1971; *Southwest Indian Painting: A Changing Art*, Clara Lee Tanner, Tucson, University of Arizona Press.

*   *   *

Austin exhibited frequently for a decade covering the early 1960s through the early 1970s at art fairs and small galleries in the Southwest, then established and settled into a print studio and retail shop in Cortez, Colorado, focusing on individual clients and custom design. He had developed a strong reputation at fairs, winning several awards, and was honored in 1962 by the American Institute of Interior Designers with their International Design Award.

Austin was born into a traditional Navajo family at Tsegi Canyon, near Tonalea, Arizona, a place known in the Dené language as Tó Nehilííh, "Where the Water Flows to a Point and Forms a Pond or Lake." In his mid-teens, Austin was encouraged by Lloyd Kiva New, later Director of the Institute of American Indian Arts, to pursue his artistic talents, and he soon worked for New as a designer and printer. By the time he was twenty-four, Austin won

recognition as a silk screen designer and began exhibiting at fairs. His silk screen designs on fabric ranged from solid colors to multiple varieties, which he achieved through careful screen separations. As a textile painter, he also used special mixtures of colored pigments suspended through a medium on the textile.

Austin tired of the fair circuit by the late 1960s and began concentrating on establishing an outlet from which he could work, sell his designs, and tailor his work for specific clients, allowing him to broaden further into interior decoration. His original textile designs are available through the store and through distributors.

Spider Woman is recognized by tradition as having taught the Navajos how to weave, while Spider Boy designed the loom. While Austin's artistic career was formulating, Navajo weavers in his area were innovating the "Raised Outline" style. Austin applied this method and an array of silkscreen, paint, and design transfer techniques to his pieces. Austin's textile work and his use of watercolors carry on both traditional and modern Navajo practices.

—Gregory Schaaf

AVERETT, Marty

Tribal affiliations: Coushatta; Choctaw; Cherokee
Painter

Born: Dallas, Texas, 26 June 1942 **Education:** University of Texas, Arlington, 1960-63, San Francisco Art Institute, BFA, 1966, MFA, 1968. **Career:** Carpenter; professor of painting, drawing, and design, Oklahoma State University, Stillwater, 1969—, artist-in-residence, University of Lancaster, England, 1973-1974. **Awards:** State Arts Council of Oklahoma grant, 1992, Washington State Art in Public Places purchase.

Individual Exhibitions

1970 Gallery of the Fine Arts Department, University of Texas, Arlington
Whitehurst Gallery, Stillwater, Oklahoma
1971 Whitesitt Gallery, Kansas State College, Pittsburg, Kansas
East Central State College, Department of Art, Ada, Oklahoma
1975 Town and Gown Theatre Gallery, Stillwater, Oklahoma
Museum of Art, University of Oklahoma, Norman
East Central State College, Department of Art, Ada, Oklahoma
1983 *Marty Averett. Paintings*, C. N. Gorman Museum, University of California, Davis, California
1984 *Paintings by Marty Averett*, Southern Plains Indian Museum and Crafts Center
1985 *Marty Averett, Recent Paintings*, Amarillo Art Center, Amarillo, Texas
1988 Galeria San Miguel II, San Miguel de Allende, Guanajuato, Mexico
1989 Oklahoma Art Center, Oklahoma City, Oklahoma
1991 *Paintings by Marty Averett*, C. N. Gorman Museum, University of California, Davis, California
1992 *Marty Averett: Recent Work*, Hulsey Gallery, Norick Art Center, Oklahoma City, Oklahoma

Marty Averett: *Calvario Series #168.* Courtesy of the artist.

Selected Group Exhibitions

1961-63 Dallas County Annual Drawing, Painting, and Sculpture Exhibition, Dallas Museum of Fine Art, Texas

1965-66 *Spring Exhibition*, San Francisco Art Institute

1967 *Graduate Show*, Gallery of the San Francisco Art Institute

Contemporary Ceramics, Gardiner Art Gallery, Oklahoma State University, Stillwater

1973 *Group Show*, Great Hall, Lancaster University, Lancaster, England

1974 Exeter University Exhibition Hall, Exeter, England

Lancaster University, Lancaster, England

Palace of Nations, United Nations, Geneva, Switzerland

1978 Museum of Art, University of Oklahoma, Norman

1979 Mid-America Art Exhibition, Owensboro Museum of Fine Art, Owensboro, Kentucky

1980 Grover Cleveland Art Institute, Oklahoma City

1981 Ponca City Art Center, Ponca, Oklahoma

1985 *The New Native American Aesthetic*, Marilyn Butler Fine Art, Santa Fe

Beyond Blue Mountains, organized by the Seattle Center House, Seattle, Washington (traveling)

1986 *Color, Form, Emergence,* American Indian Contemporary Arts, San Francisco,

1990 *Tradition and Spirit*, Maryhill Museum of Art, Goldendale, Washington

1991 *Our Land/Our Selves: American Indian Contemporary Artists*, University Art Gallery, State University of New York, Albany

1992 *We, The Human Beings*, College of Wooster Art Museum, Wooster, Ohio

Decolonizing the Mind, Center on Contemporary Art, Seattle Washington

1993 Sacred Circle Gallery of American Indian Art, Seattle, Washington

Hulsey Gallery, Norick Art Center, Oklahoma City, Oklahoma

1994 Brenau College, Gainesville, Georgia

Collections

El Paso Museum of Art, El Paso, Texas; Gates Gallery, Port Arthur, Texas; Museum of Art, University of Oklahoma, Norman; Oklahoma Arts & Humanities Council, Art Center, Oklahoma City; San

Francisco Art Institute; University of Lancaster, Lancaster, England; University of Southern Illinois, Carbondale; Washington State Arts Commission, Olympia.

Publications

On AVERETT: Books—*Tradition and Spirit,* by Lynette Miller, Goldendale, Washington, 1990; "The Color of the Wind," by Lucy Lippard in *Our Land/Ourselves,* Albany, New York, 1990; *Decolonizing the Mind,* Seattle: Center on Contemporary Art, 1992; *We the Human Beings: 27 Contemporary Native American Artists,* Wooster, Ohio, 1992. **Articles**—"Boxes of Infinite Variety, by Judy Consden, *Fulcrum* (Lancaster, England), June 1974; "Marty Averett," by Peggy C. Gardner, *Art Voices South,* September/October, 1980; "The Second Biennial Native American Fine Arts Invitational," by Erin Younger and Robert Bruenig, *American Indian Art,* January 1985; "Beside and Beyond the Mainstream," by Victoria Beaudin, *Artweek,* November 2, 1985; "Reviews: Marty Averett and Richard Bivins," by Betty Ann Sisson, *Crosscurrents,* March/April 1994.

*

Marty Averett comments:

Formally my concerns have to do with spatial illusion, light and its quality, color and surface. I would classify myself as a colorist who is trying to arrive at a kind of personal truth about the image he makes.

Natural phenomena, the mysterious and enigmatic characteristics in nature that developed a special curiosity in me as a child are the things that continue to interest me most as an artist.

*   *   *

Born in Dallas, Texas, to a Coushatta mother and a Choctaw/Cherokee father, Averett grew up in a family that had been isolated from its tribal homeland for several generations. Yet, distinctive lifeways and values were imparted, which Averett only later recognized were part of his tribal legacy—foods the family ate, a respect for nature, even certain superstitions or taboos. "My father and grandfather taught me to see," the artist stated, referring to the formative experience of patiently observing the natural world under their guidance. This threesome is often represented in Averett's paintings with a group of three dots.

It is this personal symbolism and intense awareness of his surroundings that characterizes Averett's work. The artist's iconography is a highly abbreviated vocabulary. Despite (or perhaps because of) his careful scrutiny of the natural and human-made objects surrounding him in Stillwater, Oklahoma, where he makes his home, and of the things he has seen during his travels to Europe and Mexico, Averett relies on a small group of symbols. He views the artist as a visual poet, condensing the world's information into meaningful forms of simple elegance. The significance of Averett's idiosyncratic, hieroglyphic-like symbols is not always universally evident. Serving as the "Rosetta stone" of his own paintings, the artist translates the abstracted tobacco leaf as a representation of Native American culture, and the form of a hand as himself.

Since 1988 Averett has been developing the *Calvario Series,* in which a dichotomous scheme of new symbols was introduced. During a sabbatical year spent in Mexico, the artist was fascinated with the forms of the *calvario* shrines—small, Moorish-style buildings dedicated to Christ—and their function in colonized Mexico. To Averett they represent a loss of indigenous knowledge and history in the face of Catholicism. The *calvario*'s symbolic counterpart is a triangular form, evocative of Mayan and Aztec temples and the Egyptian pyramids, which represents the power of ancient indigenous culture. The layering and placement of the two symbols often creates an oppositional tension that increases their individual meanings exponentially. Indeed, it is this masterful relating of formal and symbolic elements that allows Averett to thrive with such a limited repertoire of images.

Averett's observations do not result in a mere extraction of symbols from their natural environment. He is as interested in the peculiarities of light and color surrounding an object as he is in the object's potential symbolism. Layering paint and symbols, the artist creates (or, as he prefers, "reveals") atmospheric phenomena of surrealistic depth. Lifting symbols and their attendant ambiance from different times, places, and perspectives, Averett will often section his painting, developing a dichotomous scheme of light/dark, day/night, hot/cold, and known/unknown. Sometimes integrated into this dualistic sectioning is a contrast of decorative surface designs with spatial illusionism. Repeating dots rendered in brilliant color may recall the decorative patterns of T. C. Cannon but are more likely to be observed directly from nature. Averett is a superb draughtsman, laying down and developing calligraphic marks that invite comparison with the *trompe-l'oeil* techniques of James Havard and the graceful scrawls of Cy Twombly. The diversity of influences on this art is consistent with the way he positions himself professionally—as a painter who happens to be of Indian descent. A professor of art at Oklahoma State University, Averett moves freely and comfortably through the mainstream art world, exhibitions of Native art, and the pan-Indian pow-wow community of Oklahoma.

—Lisa Cooley

AWA TSIREH

Variant names: Alfonso Roybal; Cattail Bird
Tribal affiliations: San Ildefonso Pueblo
Painter, potter, and silversmith

Born: San Ildefonso Pueblo, 1 February 1898. **Education:** School of American Research (painting daily with Fred Kabotie and Velino Shije Herrera). **Family:** Son of potter Alfonsita Martínez and Juan Estebán Roybal; nephew of painter Crescencio Martínez; cousin of painter José D. Roybal. **Career:** Farmer, potter, painter, museum employee, and silversmith. **Awards:** French Government, Palmes d'Académiques, 1954. **Died:** May 1955.

Individual Exhibitions

1918	Society of Independent Arts, New York
1925	Newberry Library, Chicago

Selected Group Exhibitions

1925	*Exhibition of American Indian Paintings and Applied Arts,* Arts Club of Chicago
1931	Exposition of Indian Tribal Arts, The College Art Association (international tour)

c. 1950   American Indian Art, University of Oklahoma (international tour)
1955   National Museum, Hall of Ethnology, Memorial Exhibition Group
          An Exposition of American Indian Painters, James Graham and Sons, New York
1979   *Native American Paintings*, Joslyn Art Museum
1984   *Indianischer Indian Art Show*, West Germany, organized by Philbrook Museum of Art, Tulsa, Oklahoma
1985   *The Hunt and the Harvest*, Gallery Association of New York State
1986   When the Rainbow Touches Down, Heard Museum, Phoenix (traveling)
1991   *Shared Visions: Native American Painters and Sculptors in the Twentieth Century*, Heard Museum, Phoenix

Collections

Amerind Foundation, Dragoon, Arizona; Berne Museum, Switzerland; Bank of America, Phoenix; Cincinnati Art Museum, Ohio; Corcoran Gallery of Art, Washington, D.C.; Columbus Gallery of Fine Arts, Ohio; Cranbrook Institute of Science, Bloomfield Hills, Michigan; Cleveland Museum of Art, Ohio; Denver Art Museum, Colorado; Dartmouth College Collection, Hanover, New Hampshire; Indian Arts & Crafts Board, Department of the Interior, Washington, D.C.; Joslyn Art Museum, Omaha, Nebraska; National Museum of the American Indian, Washington, D.C.; Montclair Art Museum, Montclair, New Jersey; Nelson-Atkins Museum of Art, Kansas City, Missouri; Mitchell Indian Museum, Kendall College, Evanston, Illinois; Museum of Modern Art, New York; Museum of Northern Arizona, Katheryn Harvey Collection, Flagstaff, Arizona; American Museum of Natural History, New York; Museum of New Mexico, Santa Fe; Millicent Rogers Foundation Museum, Taos, New Mexico; Museum of Art, Univeristy of Oklahoma, Norman; Philbrook Art Center, Tulsa, Oklahoma; Smithsonian Institution, Washington, D.C.; Southwest Museum, Los Angeles; Woolaroc Museum, Bartlesville, Oklahoma; Wheelright Museum of the American Indian, Santa Fe.

Publications

On AWA TSIREH: Books—*Introduction to American Indian Art.* 2 vols., by John Sloan and Oliver La Farge, New York: The Exposition of Indian Tribal Arts, Inc., 1931; *American Indian Painting of the Southwest and Plains Areas*, by Dorothy Dunn, Albuquerque: University of New Mexico, 1968; *Indian Painters and White Patrons*, by J.J. Brody, Albuquerque: University of New Mexico Press, 1971; *100 Years of Native American Painting* (exhibition catalog), by Arthur Silberman, Oklahoma Museum of Art, Oklahoma City, 1978; *Whenthe Rainbow Touches Down* (exhibition catalog), Seattle and London: University of Washington Press, 1988; *Shared Visions: Native American Painters and Sculptors in the Twentieth Century*, by Margaret Archuleta, and Dr. Rennard Strickland, New York: The New Press, 1991. **Articles**—"A Boy Painter Among the Pueblos," by Alice Henderson, *New York Times*, September 4, 1925; "American Indian Water Colors," by C. Norris Millington, *The American Magazine of Art.* 25, 2, August 1932; "America's First Painters," by Dorothy Dunn, *National Geographic Magazine*, March 1955; "Awa Tsireh: Painter of San Ildefonso," by Dorothy Dunn, *El Palacio*, April 1956.

*   *   *

The year 1918 marked the first time Pueblo Indian watercolors were displayed as art alongside non-Indian paintings in the annual exhibit of the *Society of Independent Artists* in New York City. Organized by American artist John Sloan, this exhibit included the work of Awa Tsireh, also known as Alfonso Roybal. Although Awa Tsireh is part of the greater Southwest Painting Movement (1910-1962), he and other artists from San Ildefonso, including Julian Martínez and Crescencio Martínez, were among the first Pueblo Indian painters to work in the watercolor medium. These artists produced stylistically similar works of art depicting genre scenes, ceremonial dances and dancers, and stylized compositions of animals and landscapes. As a group they developed a distinct style characterized by blocks of outlined color with little modeling, considerable detailing of costume, and little use of backgrounds, groundlines, and three-dimensional perspective. Together these artists helped define what came to be know as "traditional" Indian painting.

Awa Tsireh, the oldest of six children, was born into an artistic family: as a boy he helped paint his mother's pottery; his sister, Santana, painted the ceramics of her famous mother-in-law, Maria Martínez; and his uncle, Crescencio Martínez, with whom Awa Tsireh also worked, is credited with being the first San Ildefonsoan painter. Crescencio was hired in 1917 by Dr. Edgar Lee Hewett, director of the Museum of New Mexico, to produce a series of paintings depicting San Ildefonso ceremonies.

According to Awa Tsireh's sister, Santana Martínez, he began drawing as early as 1910: "he used to do sketches of dances and animals even before he went to school ... not very good, but then he was just starting." Awa Tsireh is often referred to as being self-taught, having received little or no artistic training. He did, however, receive formal education through the primary grades at the San Ildefonso Day School, where a teacher by the name of Elizabeth Richards provided Awa Tsireh and the other students with drawing supplies.

By 1917, the Santa Fe poet Alice Corbin Henderson had begun to commission and collect paintings from Awa Tsireh. At the same time, Elizabeth De Huff, wife of the superintendent to the Santa Fe Indian Boarding School, started to hold informal art sessions in her living room with several students from the school, notably Fred Kabotie, Otis Polelonema, and Velino Shije Herrera. Unlike his contemporaries Awa Tsireh did not attend this school. Except for trips to Santa Fe to sell his artwork, Awa Tsireh seldom journeyed far from his native pueblo. During one of his trips to Santa Fe, Awa Tsireh saw paintings by Kabotie, Polelonema and Herrera on display at the Museum of New Mexico and subsequently brought in his own artwork to show the museum's staff that he could do the same. Impressed with his artistic talent, Dr. Edgar Hewett hired Awa Tsireh to paint at the School of American Research along with Kabotie and Herrera during the 1920s.

More than a decade later, Awa Tsireh's paintings were included in the first major exhibition of American Indian art, the 1931 *Exposition of Indian Tribal Arts*, which toured the United States and Europe under the sponsorship of the College Art Association. Organized by American Indian art supporters and Santa Fe residents, the exhibit, along with a scholarly catalog, promoted all Native American artforms. One of Awa Tsireh's most famous works, *Corn Dance #1*, was part of the Exposition. Awa Tsireh's paintings continued to be exhibited in galleries and museums, including such venues as the American Museum of Natural History, The Arts Club of Chicago, the Museum of New Mexico, and Corcoran Gallery in Washington, D.C. Under the guidance of the painter Olive Rush, Awa Tsireh painted murals and large, mural-sized canvases in 1932-33.

Today, Awa Tsireh is considered one of the most innovative and influential painters associated with the early Pueblo Indian watercolor tradition. His artwork includes a variety of artistic approaches, including naturalistic representations of women making pottery, stylized renderings of dancers, and stylized depictions of animals in landscape settings. As an accomplished painter, potter, and silversmith, Awa Tsireh influenced his peers and succeeding generations of artists, including his nephew, J.D. Roybal.

—Lisa Roberts

AZBILL, Mary

Variant names: Mele Ke'a'a'la; Mary Kelly; Mary Clements
Tribal affiliations: Concow Maidu
Basketweaver

Born: Taiyum Koyo near Oroville, Butte County, California, 24 December 1854. **Education:** Data not available, but her ability to read and write in English and Hawaiian (and to converse in French and Spanish) indicates that she probably attended schools in California and/or Hawaii. **Family:** Married 1) George Clements, c. 1887 (divorced, c. 1892); one daughter (died as infant); 2) John Azbill, 1894; two sons, three daughters. **Career:** Personal Kahilibearer for King Kalakaua of Hawaii, 1881-1887; lady-in-waiting to Princess Liliuokalani, 1887; personal attendant in transport of King Kalakaua's body to Hawaii from San Francisco in 1892; representative for the Republic of Hawaii at the San Francisco Midwinter Fair, 1894-95; field hand in Sacramento Valley, c. 1895-1918; active basket weaver c. 1864-1932. **Died:** Chico, California, September 1932.

Individual Exhibitions

Exhibition data during the artist's lifetime is not available; the artist kept no known records. Exhibition of her baskets after her death includes numerous shows organized by her son, Henry Ke'a'a'la Azbill (1896-1973). Baskets by Azbill have been exhibited without being identified as such at the Bidwell Mansion State Historic Site, Chico, California, c. 1960.

Mary Azbill and son Henry with coiled baskets, c. 1904. Courtesy Craig D. Bates.

Collections

The Chico Museum, Chico, California; The Oakland Museum, Oakland, California; The Brooklyn Museum, Brooklyn, New York; Bidwell State Historic Park, Chico, California.

Publications

On **AZBILL: Book**—*Objects of Myth and Memory* by Diana Fane et al., New York 1991. **Articles**—"Collecting Among the Chico Maidu: The Stewart Culin Collection at the Brooklyn Museum" by Craig D. Bates and Brian Bibby, *American Indian Art Magazine* 8(4):46-53, 1983; "Regional Variation in Coiled Maidu Basketry: Materials and Technology" by Craig D. Bates and Bruce Bernstein, *Journal of California and Great Basin Anthropology* 4(2):187-202, 1982.

*   *   *

Of the many traditional Concow Maidu basket weavers, Mary Azbill stands out for her attention to detail and fine design sense. By the age of ten Azbill was weaving fine coiled baskets and using designs that she would continue to use for the next 68 years.

Azbill preferred using plants found in the Sacramento Valley for her basket materials, notably sedge root (buff-colored sewing material) and briar root (for black design elements). She wove a great number of presentation baskets, which were more finely stitched (approximately twelve stitches and three coils per inch) and had more complex pattern combinations than baskets made for culinary use. Like those made by Amanda Wilson, Azbill's baskets differ from those of her contemporaries in their flawlessly executed and evenly spaced designs. She made a number of truncated-cone shaped baskets averaging twelve inches in diameter and smaller, globular-shaped baskets that used complex patterning and fine stitching.

Azbill excelled in the creation of feather-covered baskets. She used feathers from male mallard duck scalps and from acorn and pileated woodpeckers to cover baskets. The baskets' rims were ornamented with white glass beads or with a unique combination of white glass beads, clamshell disc beads, and woodpecker feathers. Feathered baskets collected from the Maiduan peoples are uncommon, but during the 1970s there were extant at least three baskets and a pair of feathered-basketry disc earrings, all documented as made by Mary Azbill. Azbill's son, Henry, recalled that his mother had made other such earrings and baskets, but she had them buried with deceased friends and family members.

Azbill also created utilitarian baskets that were somewhat more coarsely stitched and had less precise design placement. She made these baskets for culinary purposes, such as preparing acorn mush and other native foods. Azbill made and used a bowl-shaped basket with a flat basketry lid for storing her ceremonial dance headpiece. Her son thought this innovative use may have been inspired by his mother's Hawaiian background, as carved wooden or basketry containers were used in the Hawaiian Royal Palace to store feathered leis.

Azbill's baskets were widely prized among the Native Californian community; they were treasured not only by her Indian neighbors of Bidwell's Rancho Chico, but also by more distant Maiduan, Nomlaki, Patwin, and Pomoan peoples. Many of Azbill's finest basket creations, however, including presentation baskets, feathered baskets, and feathered basketry earrings, were burned at annual mourning ceremonies in which Azbill participated, in addition to being buried with deceased Native people.

At the turn of the century, Azbill's baskets were sought after by non-Indian basket collectors. The field notes of collectors and curators such as Carroll S. Hartman, John Hudson, and others, make reference to her work. Brooklyn Museum Curator Stewart Culin purchased several baskets from Azbill on his trip to Chico in 1908.

Mary Azbill brought a new fineness and elegance to the basketry style of her people during her lifetime, yet her refinements were made within the established Native ideas of good taste. She recognized that she was practicing her art as basket-making traditions were ending among the Maidu people at Chico. At the time of her death there were no younger women of her village learning to weave. The centuries-long continuum of basket weaving died out at Chico not long after Azbill's death.

—Craig Bates

BAD HEART BULL, Amos

Variant names: Tatanka Cante Sice
Tribal affiliations: Oglala Lakota
Draftsman

Born: 1869. **Career:** Warrior, artist, tribal historian and policeman. **Died:** 1913.

Publications

On BAD HEART BULL: Books—*Sioux Indian Painting* by Hartley Burr Alexander, Nice, France: C. Szwedzicki, 1938; *A Pictographic History of the Oglala Sioux* by Helen Blish, Lincoln: University of Nebraska Press, 1967. **Articles**—"The Bad Heart Buffalo Manuscript," *Theatre Arts Monthly* 16, 1932; "Material on Short Bull" by Wilhelm Wildhage, *European Review of Native American Studies* 4, no. 1, 1990; "Short Bull: Lakota Visionary, Historian, and Artist" by Ronald McCoy, *American Indian Art Magazine* 17, no. 3, 1992.

* * *

Between 1890-1913, Amos Bad Heart Bull systematically drew in a large ledger he had purchased for that purpose. By the time of his death, he had completed some 408 drawings, ranging from early history of the Lakota and a record of their traditional regalia to chronicles of the Battle of Little Big Horn, the Ghost Dance, the murder of Sitting Bull, and the massacre at Wounded Knee.

While the original work is no longer available for study, having been buried with the artist's sister in 1947, Helen Blish's publication, *A Pictographic History of the Oglala Sioux,* thoroughly documents the drawing book, based on her own study of the book between 1927-1940 and interviews with the artist's relatives. According to them, prior to beginning this epic work, Bad Heart Bull had executed a winter count (the traditional mnemonic means of recording tribal history by a pictorial symbol for a significant event of each "winter" or year). In Blish's words, it was while working on that endeavor that the artist "realized the quantity of materials that was being left untouched—the battles, rituals, ceremonies, and various activities and interests that were not being recorded and yet were vitally significant in the life of the people."

Bad Heart Bull rendered a panoptic view of Lakota life, with details painstakingly conveyed both artistically and in inscriptions written in Lakota (with an occasional name written in English.) As Blish points out, it is significant that Bad Heart Bull did not undertake this epic work for any tribal archive or for tribal elders; this was not an "official" Lakota history. Moreover, it was not made at the behest of any anthropologist, collector, or other outsider who desired a record of Lakota life. It was a personal achievement that satisfied Bad Heart Bull's own vision of what it meant to be an artist and historian. It may be noteworthy that Bad Heart Bull's uncle, Short Bull, was himself a noted artist and historian who moved to Pine Ridge in 1890, the year that Bad Heart Bull commenced his magnum opus. Perhaps Short Bull played some role in inspiring Bad Heart Bull to undertake this ambitious pictorial narrative.

In terms of his artistic capabilities, Bad Heart Bull moved easily from large-scale epic scenes of warfare to miniature, map-like renderings, to intimate depictions of courtship and ceremony. He chronicles warfare between Lakotas and Crows from the 1850s to 1870s, as well as their adaptation to farming and ranching in the 1880s and 1890s. Bad Heart Bull freely experiments with new modes of representation, fearlessly tackling three-dimensional, back and three-quarter views, and aerial perspective. His work is dynamic and vigorous. Bold in its conception of the sweep and detail of Lakota history, it stands as an unparalleled achievement in the history of Native American art.

While art historians may mourn the loss of this unique art object, burial is an appropriately Lakota way of dealing with such a powerful and personal item. Customarily, one's most cherished possessions are either buried with the deceased or burned. Despite the loss of the original manuscript, the publication of some of Bad Heart Bull's drawings in the 1930s and the complete corpus three decades later had a profound effect on subsequent generations of Lakota artists, including Arthur Amiotte and Colleen Cutschall.

—Janet Catherine Berlo

BAIRD, Rebecca and Kenny

Tribal affiliations: Cree
Sculptor and painter (Rebecca); video artist (Kenny); and installation artists

REBECCA. Born: Rebecca Gloria-Jean Baird, Edmonton, Alberta, October 1954. **Family:** Sister of Kenny Baird. **Career:** Artist and lecturer; artist-in-residence, Canadian Museum of Civilization, Hull, and University of Toronto, Scarborough Campus, 1993. Member of Toronto Arts Council Visual Arts Committee; Board of Directors, Mercer Union and Women's Art Resource Centre. **Awards:** Canada Council honor, 1983-84; Canada Council Grant, 1986-90; Ontario Council Grant, 1988-89; Juno Award, Best Album Design for *Lost Together* (recorded by Blue Rodeo), 1992.

KENNY. Born: Kenneth Alvin Baird, Kirkland Lake, Ontario, Canada, 1956. **Career:** Illustrator, wig designer for the film *Amadeus* (1982); set designer, including 13 episodes of *Pee-Wee's Playhouse* (1987) and The Rolling Stones's Voodoo Lounge Tour interviews (1994); video director, including Leonard Cohen's "Future" and Blue Rodeo's "Hasn't Hit Me Yet"; interior and installation de-

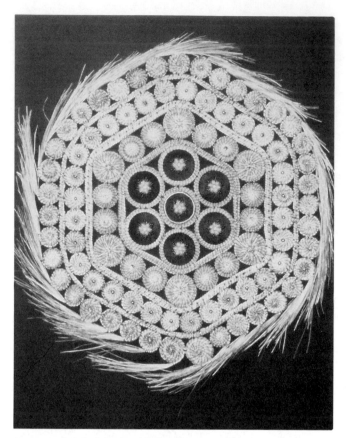

Rebecca Baird: *Memory Claim #1*

signer. **Awards:** Variety of honors from both the Canada Council and the Ontario Arts Council; Much Music Video of the Year award for "Hasn't Hit Me Yet" by Blue Rodeo, 1994.

Individual Exhibitions

Rebecca:

1983	*The Funnel*, Gallop Exit, Toronto
1985	*Trouble Rides a Fast Horse*, Garnet Press, Toronto
1986	*Stay Here With Us*, Thunder Bay Art Gallery, Thunder Bay, Ontario
1987	*A Certain Cowboy*, Garnet Press, Toronto
1988	*Selected Works*, N.I.I.P.A. Gallery, Hamilton, Ontario
1992	*Selected Works*, The White Water Gallery, North Bay
	Recent Work, The Lindsay Gallery, Lindsay
1993	*Selected Works*, The Station Gallery, Whitby
	A Time Within a Memory, Museum of Civilization, Hull, Quebec
1994	*Elements*, Thunder Bay Art Gallery, Thunder Bay, Ontario
1995	*Ground for Belief*, Koffler Gallery, Toronto
	Selected Works, Chatham Art Gallery, Chatham, Ontario

Selected Group Exhibitions

Rebecca and Kenny:

1989	*Don Quixote,* Garnet Press, Toronto
1990	*Mixed,* Garnet Press, Toronto

1991	*Thirst,* Garnet Press, Toronto
	Mixed, Temiskaming Art Gallery, Haileybury

Rebecca:

1983	*Chromaliving*, Chromazone, Toronto
1984	*Chromaloffing*, Grunwald Gallery, Tornoto
1985	*Private Image/Public Myth*, Public Image Gallery, New York
	Electro Graphics, Gallery '76, Tornoto
	Lariat du Jour with Handsome Ned, Idee Gallery, Toronto
1986	*The Snow Show*, Idee Gallery, Toronto
	Best Presents, Garnet Gallery, Toronto
1987	*From Sea to Shining Sea*, The Power Plant, Toronto
1988	*Ode'min*, Laurentian Museum & Gallery, Sudbury, Ontario (traveling)
1989	*The Art of the First Peoples*, York Quay Gallery, Toronto
	The Salvage Paradigm, Wynick/Tuck, Toronto
1991	*Memory and Subjectivity*, Garnet Press, Toronto, (traveling)
1992	*Beyond 1992: Experiments in Cross-Cultural Collaborations*, A Space, Toronto
	New Territories, Les Ateliers de Planetaire Inc., Montreal, Quebec City
	C(o)vert, The Station Gallery, Whitby, Ontatio
	Indigina, Museum of Civilization, Hull, Quebec
1992-93	*Canada's First People*, Syncrude Corporation, Toronto (traveled through Canada and Japan)
1993	*Re-Mapping: Tales of Desire*, A Space, Toronto
	The Power of Place, Legislative Building, Toronto
1994	*A Love of the Land*, The Homer Watson Gallery, Kitchener, Ontario
	RE—PUBLIC Installation, Sternberk Symposium, Czech Republic
	Fetish and the Shaman, Indianapolis Art League, Indiana
1995	*Basket, Bead & Quill*, Thunder Bay Art Gallery, Ontario
1996	*Women and Medicine*, Niagara Arts Company, St. Catharines
	Altered States: Rituals of Exchange, Walter Phillips Gallery, Banff
	Material Bliss, Justina M. Barnike Gallery, Toronto

Kenny:

1983	*Snow Show*, Idee Gallery, Toronto
1990	*First Nations Art '90*, Woodland Cultural Centre, Brantford, Ontario
1991	*First Nations Art '91*, Woodland Cultural Centre, Brantford, Ontario
1992	*New Territories—350/500 Years After*, Vision Planetaire, Montreal (traveling)
	Selected Works, Natura Cultura, Italy, Belgium, Denmark, Switzerland
	Indigena, Museum of Civilization, Hull, Quebec
1993	*The Memorial Project*, A Space, Toronto
1996	*Altered States: Rituals of Exchange*, Walter Phillips Gallery, Banff

Collections

Rebecca: The Canada Council Art Bank, Toronto; Canadian Museum of Civilization, Hull, Quebec; Canadian Native Arts Foundation, Ottawa; Chatham Cultural Centre, Chatam, Ontario; Royal Ontario Museum, Toronto; Thunder Bay Art Gallery, Thunder Bay, Ontario; Winnipeg Art Gallery, Winnipeg, Manitoba. **Kenny:** Canadian Museum of Civilization, Hull, Quebec; Department of Foreign Affairs, Ottawa.

Publications

On Rebecca BAIRD: Articles—"The Female Changing Direction: A New Perspective on Native Women's Art," by Susan Crean, *Canadian Art,* Spring 1989; "Cereal Art Aims to Feed Minds," by Lynn Pyne, *The Phoenix Gazette,* September 23, 1994; "Rebecca Baird's self-discovery enriches mixed-media art," by Dierdre Hanna, *Now Magazine,* September 1995; "Confrontation and Redemption: Three First Nation Artists," by Debbie O'Rourke, *Espace,* Fall 1995.

On Kenny BAIRD: Articles—"Artist's Profile," by Kelly Rude, *Canadian Art,* Fall 1991; "Brother and Sister unveil an eloquent exhibition," *Toronto Star,* February 20, 1990; "Blood is thicker than ego," by Donna Lypchuk, *Metropolis,* 1990.

*　　*　　*

Rebecca Baird began her early artistic work in Toronto in the company of artists associated with the influential Canadian collectives *Chromaliving* and Fast Wurms. Subsequently, Baird has worked both as an independent visual artist and in a collaborative relationship with her brother, Kenny Baird.

Kenny Baird's art practice originated in the media industry, where he produces images for use on album covers and within magazines, is involved in hair and costume design, and designs sets for film, television, night clubs and restaurants as well as providing artistic direction for various music videos.

In 1981, along with Fast Wurms member Napo B, Rebecca Baird travelled to Arizona and New Mexico. The trip encouraged Baird to examine the history and value systems of a culture with which she had close ties. Baird became better aware of the history of treaty-breaking, genocide and acculturation, atrocities that were inflicted on a culture whose life values praise unity and peace. Baird eventually turned to an exploration of her Cree ancestors and found that in Canada the story was the same. She responded with art to redress the inaccuracies of history. Similarily, Kenny, principally in association with Rebecca, has produced a body of work marked by an exploring interest in the roots of Native North American cultures and in the effects of colonization on these cultures.

Rebecca Baird's independent work has covered a variety of media: painting on hide, installation work, intimate personal constructions of found objects, and, more recently, elaborate works of braided sweetgrass decorated in traditional quillwork. The work that Baird has produced collaboratively with her brother is principally installation and is distinguished by its largesse in terms of size and theme, being at once both theatrical and historical. Rebecca's contribution to the collaborative work is principally reflected in the works' attention to detail, in the sensual juxtaposition of texturally rich materials, such as velvet, glass, and sweetgrass, and thematically, in terms of the initially required research phase of production. Kenny's presence has been articulated in the sheer size of the works, which mimic the scale and grandeur of set design, in the theatrical ambience of the work, and in a flair for the sensual use of materials.

—Carol Podedworny

BARTOW, Rick
Tribal affiliations: Yurok
Carver, mask maker, and painter

Born: Richard E. Bartow in Newport, Oregon, 1946. **Education:** B.A. in Secondary Art Education, Western Oregon State College, Monmouth, Oregon, 1969. **Military Service:** Served in the Vietnam War for thirteen months between 1970-71. **Family:** Wife, Julie; son Booker Crow born in 1985. **Career:** Maintenance man, bartender, blues guitarist 1971-77; worked with handicapped children in Oregon, late 1970s; teacher, late 1970s-1980s; professional artist. **Awards:** Art in Public Places, Washington State Arts Commission; Oregon Arts Commission Fellowship in Visual Arts; Brandywine Visiting Artist Fellowship, Philadelphia, Pennsylvania; Betty Bowen Special Recognition Award, PONCHO, Seattle Art Museum; Washington State Arts Commission, "Who We Are: Autobiographies in Art"; Print commissioned for Oregon Corrections Division by the Oregon Arts Commission; Governor's Arts Awards, Newport, Oregon (chosen to create awards presented to recipients). **Address:** c/o Froelick Adelhart Gallery, 817 S. W. Second Avenue, Portland, Oregon, 97204.

Selected Group Exhibitions

1985   Jamison Thomas Gallery, Portland, Oregon
        Masks, Marianne Partlow Gallery, Olympia, Washington
1986   Jamison Thomas Gallery, Portland, Oregon
        Sacred Circle Gallery, Seattle, Washington
1987   *Man in a Box,* Jamison Thomas Gallery, Portland, Oregon and Marianne Partlow Gallery, Olympia, Washington
        Jamison Thomas Gallery, New York
        American Indian Contemporary Art Gallery, San Francisco
1988   *Works on Paper,* Jamison Thomas Gallery, Portland, Oregon, and New York City
1989   *Recent Drawings and Sculpture,* Jamison Thomas Gallery, New York
        Recent Work, Salishan Lodge, Gleneden Beach, Oregon
        Drawings, Susan Cummins Gallery, Mill Valley, California
1990   *Drawings and Dance Masks,* Rutgers Barclay Gallery, Santa Fe, New Mexico; Jamison Thomas Gallery, Portland, Oregon
        Drawings, Chase Gallery at City Hall, Spokane, Washington; Fairbanks Gallery, Oregon State University, Corvallis, Oregon
1991   *Stories,* Jamison Thomas Gallery, Portland, Oregon
1992   *Wings and Sweat,* Jamison Thomas Gallery, Portland, Oregon
        Oregon Spotlight '92, Coos Art Museum, Coos Bay, Oregon
        Drawings, Paintings, and Masks, Sun Valley Arts and Humanities Center, Sun Valley, Idaho
1993   *Truth Abandoned,* Gallery of Tribal Art, Vancouver, British Columbia.
        Visiting Artist Series, Clatsop Community College, Astoria, Oregon
        Art in the Governor's Office, State Capitol, Salem, Oregon

1994   *My Eye, Your Eye*, Jamison Thomas Gallery, Portland, Oregon

Questions of Belief, Yanagisawa Gallery, Tokyo, Japan

The Oar of the Boat, Peiper-Riegraf Gallery, Frankfurt, Germany

Circles and Shadows, Francine Seders Gallery, Seattle, Washington

Four Songs to Sing, Gallery of Tribal Art, Vancouver, British Columbia.

1995   *Four Winds*, Froelick Adelhart Gallery, Portland, Oregon

Maude Kerns Art Center, Eugene, Oregon

1996   Gallery of Tribal Art, Vancouver, British Columbia.

Salamander Gallery, The Arts Center, Christchurch, New Zealand

1997   *Sensing the Root*, Gallery of Tribal Art, Vancouver, British Columbia

Dirt and Bone, Froelick Adelhart Gallery, Portland, Oregon

Yanigasawa Gallery, Tokyo, Japan

1998   Dorothee Peiper-Riegraf Gallery, Frankfurt, Germany

Selected Group Exhibitions

1983   *Newport Jazz and Arts Festival*, Newport, Oregon

1985   *Indian Artists of Washington and Oregon Show*, American Indian Contemporary Arts Gallery, San Francisco

1986   *Governor's Indian Art Exhibition*, Salem, Oregon

Native American Art: Our Contemporary Visions, Read Stremmel Gallery, San Antonio, Texas

Masks: New Expressions in Transformation and Obscurity, Oregon School of Arts and Crafts, Portland

1987   *The Artist and the Myth*, Monterey Peninsula Museum of Art, Monterey, California

Oregon Biennial, Portland Art Museum, Portland, Oregon

Oregon, Washington Juried Exhibition of Art, Maryhill Museum, Goldendale, Washington

Schneider Museum of Art, Southern Oregon College, Ashland, Oregon

Innerskins/Outerskins: Guts and Fishskin, Craft and Folk Art Museum, San Francisco

New Directions Northwest: Contemporary Native American Art, Portland Art Museum, Portland, Oregon

Contemporary Visions: Fifteen Native American Artists, Read Stremmel Gallery, San Antonio, Texas

1988   Kenneth Banks Gallery, Oakland, California

Birds and Flight: Various Interpretations, Francine Seders Gallery, Seattle, Washington

Native American Art of California and Nevada, Jerome Evans Gallery, Sacramento, California

The Coyote as Mythological Figure, Wentz Gallery, Oregon Art Institute, Portland, Oregon

Masks, Masques, Maxs, Arizona Commission of the Arts, (traveling)

A Midsummer Night's Dream: Dreams as Personal Mythology, Blackfish Gallery, Portland, Oregon

1989   *First Impressions: Northwest Monotypes*, Seattle Art Museum, Seattle, Washington

Oregon Arts Commission Fellowship Recipient Show, A. N. Bush Gallery, Salem Art Association, Salem, Oregon

Masks and Works on Paper, Francine Seders Gallery, Seattle, Washington

New Masks, Marianne Partlow Gallery, Olympia, Washington

Animal Imagery, Susan Cummins Gallery, Mill Valley, California

1990   *Wotazootoo!*, Joan Robey Gallery, Denver, Colorado

A Spirit Reigns, Marianne Partlow Gallery, Olympia, Washington

Native Proof, American Indian Community House Gallery, New York

1991   *Drawings*, Joan Robey Gallery, Denver, Colorado

Without Boundaries: Contemporary Native American Art, Jan Cicero Gallery, Chicago

Oregon Biennial, Portland Art Museum, Portland, Oregon

The Artist in the Art: Self Portraits, Bumbershoot, The Seattle Arts Festival, Seattle, Washington

Shared Visions: Native American Painters and Sculptors in the Twentieth Century, Heard Museum, Phoenix, Arizona (traveling)

A Moveable Feast, Marianne Partlow Gallery, Olympia, Washington

Big Sky Indian Market, Native American Cultural Institute of Montana, Billings, Montana

A Panoply of Masks, Marianne Partlow Gallery, Olympia, Washington

The Sacred Bear, In Two Worlds, Missoula Art Museum, Missoula, Montana

25th Anniversary Exhibitions, Francine Seders Gallery, Seattle, Washington

Earth Fire Water, Clatsop Community College, Astoria, Oregon

Sum of the Parts, Jamison Thomas Gallery, New York

The River, Benton County Historical Society and Museum, Philomath, Oregon

1992   *The Betty Bowen Legacy: Fourteen Years of Award Winning Art*, Security Pacific Gallery, Seattle, Washington

Artists Who Are Indian, Northcutt Steele Gallery, Eastern Montana College, Billings, Montana

The Spiritual World of the Native American, Oguni-Machi, Ogunitown, Shizuoka City, Japan

The Submuloc/Columbus Wohs, Atlatl, Phoenix, Arizona, (traveling)

Who We Are: Autobiographies in Art, Washington State Arts Commission, Olympia, Washington

Spirit of the West: A Celebration of the Arts, West One Bank, (traveling)

The Corrections Print Project: Prints by 20 Oregon Artists, Maveety Gallery, Salishan Oregon

Native Iconography, A. N. Bush Gallery, Bush Barn Art Center, Salem, Oregon

Face of the Soul: An Exhibition of Masks, 1078 Gallery, Chico, California

Transformed Traditions: An Exhibit of Contemporary American Indian Art, Art Gallery, Santa Rosa Junior College, Santa Rosa, California

1993   *Small Figurative Sculpture*, Susan Cummins Gallery, Mill Valley, California

Native America: Reflecting Contemporary Realities, Craft and Folk Art Museum, Los Angeles

Rick Bartow: *Deer Spirit,* 1994. Courtesy Froelick Adelhart Gallery, Portland, Oregon.

Crosscut: The Oregon Biennial, Portland Art Museum, Portland, Oregon

Contemporary Icons, A.N. Bush Gallery, Bush Barn Art Center, Salem, Oregon

Northwest Native American and First Nations People's Art, Western Gallery, Western Washington University, Bellingham, Washington

A Kindred Spirit: Contemporary Painting, Prints and Sculpture by Eight Native American Artists, Bedford Gallery/Regional Center for the Arts, Walnut Creek, California

1994   *Only the Shadow Knows: Revelations from the Unconscious*, Art Access Gallery, Salt Lake City, Utah

Earth, Fire, Water, Oregon School of Arts and Crafts, Portland, Oregon, Jamison Thomas Gallery, Portland, Oregon

New Work by Gallery Artists, Jamison Thomas Gallery, Portland, Oregon

Oregon Invitational Drawing Exhibition, Lane Community College, Eugene, Oregon

Public Encounters, Bush Barn Art Center, Salem, Oregon

Artists Who are Indian, The Denver Art Museum, Denver, Colorado

1995   *Art Without Frontiers: Rick Bartow, John Bevin-Ford, Lillian Pitt,* Memorial Union Art Gallery, University of California, Davis

Fifteen Years, Jamison Thomas Gallery, Portland, Oregon

New Western Art, The Benton County Historical Museum, Philomath, Oregon

Bridges and Boundaries/Brucken und Abgrenaungen, The Peiper-Riegraf Collection, Frankfurt Bonn, Haus an der Redoute, Germany; sponsored by the American Embassy and the City of Bonn

Contemporary Totems, Bush Barn Art Center, Salem, Oregon

The Flower Show, Jamison Thomas Gallery, Portland, Oregon

1996   *Brucken und Abgrenzungen,* Zeitgenossische Indianische Kunst, Frankfurt, Germany

Seen and Unforeseen, Bush Barn Art Center, Salem, Oregon

Rick Bartow and Lillian Pitt, Sunbird Gallery, Bend, Oregon

In Bloom, The Heathman Hotel, Portland, Oregon

I Stand in the Center of Good, American Indian Community House, New York

Pacific Dragons ... The Art of Protest and Promise, Uxbridge Gallery, Howick, New Zealand

1997   *Washington Remembers: A Conference on Life, Loss and Traditional Rituals of Grief,* Washington State History Museum, Tacoma

Collections

Heard Museum, Phoenix, Arizona; Knight Library, University of Oregon, Eugene; Metropolitan Arts Commission, Portland, Oregon; Oregon Health Sciences University, Portland; Portland Art Museum, Portland, Oregon; Washington State Arts Commission, Olympia; Washington County Public Services Building, Hillsboro, Oregon; Willamette University, Salem, Oregon.

Publications

On BARTOW: Catalogs—*Fedora*, Oregon Arts Commission and Committee for the Humanities, 1980-82; "R. E. Bartow," in *Portfolio: American Indian Contemporary Arts*, 1986; "Rick Bartow," *Who We Are: Autobiographies in Art,* Washington State Arts Commission, 1991; "Wings and Sweat: The Visionary Art of Rick Bartow 1986-1992," exhibition catalog, essay by David P. Becker, Jamison Thomas Gallery, Portland, Oregon, 1992; "Rick Bartow," by Lois Allen, *Craftsman House Publishers*, Australia, 1995.. **Articles** — "Sweat Lodge and Inspiration," by Roberta Ulrich, *The Oregonian*, October, 4, 1985; "R. E. Bartow," by Abby Wasserman, *Native Vision* III no. 2, May/June 1986; "Isolationism," *Northwest Artpaper*, August 15, 1986; "Man Behind the Mask," by Doug Marx, *Oregon Magazine*, March/April 1988; "Out of the Darkness: The Transformations of R. E. Bartow," by Timothy White, *Shaman's Drum,* Summer 1988; "Connecting Past and Present," by Abby Wasserman, *Artweek,* April 15, 1989; "Indian Market: Santa Fe's Show of Shows," *The Santa Fe New Mexican Pasatiempo*, August, 17 1990; "Art by the Saks-full," *The Oregonian,* Aug., 24, 1990; "Rick Bartow's Ecstasy and Obsession," by Randy Gragg, *The Oregonian,* Dec. 27, 1991; "Profiles: Rick Bartow," by Cheryl Hartup, *Visions,* Winter 1993; "Truth and Transformations," *The Weekend Sun,* July 1993, Vancouver, British Columbia; "Artists Who Are Indian," *On and Off the Wall,* The Denver Art Museum Newsletter, January/February 1994; "Indian Arts for a Contemporary World," *The Christian Science Monitor,* February, 7, 1994; "Bartow Steps Out," by Randy Gragg, *The Oregonian,* March 2, 1994; "Bartow Steps Out," by Randy Gragg, *The Oregonian,* March 2, 1994; "Self Examination," *Artweek,* October, 6, 1994; "Von Kojoten Und Menschen: Der Indianerkunstler Rick Bartow in Frankfurt," *Frankfurter Allgemeine Sonnstagszeitung,* October 23, 1994, Frankfurt Germany; "Bartow: Conversations with an Artist," *Inkfish Magazine,* 1994.

*

Rick Bartow comments:

Beneath the surface of each drawing are numerous drawings. If we peel back the layers of onion-like skins we arrive at a gestural mark, the bone.

The dirt is the dry pastel, the bones are the marks under the skin of color, the wood of the pencil.

The dirt is the land, the bones are chisels.

The dirt is the flesh of the bones in the end.

It is the multi-colored garment for our bones, our final robe, the one we shall wear to return to from whence we came. The chisel of bone, tooth or antler to hew and hack at the root and branch to create images and forms from annual rings and branchy knobs. Summers, falls and winter written indelibly in the living flesh of the forest.

Under the dirt lie the bones in their proper place—foundations for a lineage of peoples to the land. We become the place through out contributions of the family to the dirt. Gradually ... gradually it becomes us as we nourish it.

A song about people and the land, memories, tears, dirt and bones.

*   *   *

A deer bound within a gesturing human figure, a singer provoking his own avian metamorphosis, a defiant blue bear whose body roughly dissolves into a pale human ghost: these partially abstracted figures are what the Yurok artist Rick Bartow describes as "transformational images," through which he seeks to investigate the profound and redemptive relationship between the human and animal realms.

The energies and erasures that characterize Bartow's artistic vision are evident in his vehement application of materials. Working primarily in graphite, charcoal and pastel, Bartow often retains his initial gesture, while in other instances fields of pure color result. This highly emotive style is tempered with Bartow's delicate sense of draftsmanship. Frequently reworked in the later stages of pictorial development, line is used to indicate and subtly reorient rather than contain Bartow's compositions.

Bartow's artistic influences consist of an eclectic group, including Marc Chagall, Drake Deknatel, Jim Dine, Joe Feddersen, Lillian Pitt, Larry Rivers and Fritz Scholder. Commonly contextualized within an even wider range of artistic production, Bartow's work has been directly compared to that of Kathe Kollwitz (expressionism) and Odilon Redon (symbolism). While this associative strategy places Bartow within an art-historical context, it is also indicative of how his images elicit multiple—and ostensibly incongruous—interpretations, because they can be just as deeply troubling and confrontational as they are restorative and calming.

The binary between the diagnostic and the curative, and the process of creation that involves both, is fundamental to Bartow's artistic philosophy. As he has frequently noted, his work is integral to a greater therapeutic process of healing and renewal. Since the late 1970s, when he created a series of self-exploratory images in charcoal on newsprint, art-making has enabled Bartow to work through his memories of the Vietnam War, deal with his addiction to alcohol, and fulfill the demanding roles of husband and father. Much of this success can also be attributed to his decision to return to his childhood home of Newport, Oregon, in the early 1970s. Having rediscovered his family heritage, Bartow speaks with admiration of his grandfather, who moved from California to Oregon homesteaded land in 1928. Likewise, he is appreciative of living in the house he grew up in because it provides him with an intimate sense of familial continuity.

Concerning his Yurok ancestry and the related question of "authenticity" in Native American art, Bartow quotes Chagall, who once said, "let us try to discover what is authentic in our lives." While many perceive a direct correlation between traditional/authentic, and non-traditional/inauthentic, Bartow dismisses such simplifications because he believes that authenticity ultimately resides within the individual experience. Consequently, although he did not grow up on the Mad River reservation in northern California, as do many others of Yurok descent, this fact neither lessens the sincerity nor compromises the meaning of Bartow's work. Whereas his emphasis on self-exploration in art-making is potentially self-indulgent, Bartow has not lost sight of the broader communities (art and otherwise) within which he moves. This is evident in his approach towards mask making. Interested in the creative process as well as the power and meaning of masking, Bartow began carving masks in the early 1980s. While he was inspired by Northwest Coast masks, he was also aware of the social codes associated with their creation and, as an outsider, was weary of infringing on established traditions. Consequently, while Bartow acknowledges his indebtedness to Northwest Coast carvers (particularly for their tools), his masks are very much derived from his own experience.

Similarly, Bartow maintains respect for Native religious practices while integrating aspects of them into his work, which is rich in shamanic undercurrents. Drawing on his experience with the animals around his home and his knowledge of their mythological roles, Bartow provides glimpses of the raven, the coyote, the crow and others amidst interaction or transformation. While the use of spiritually imbued subject matter has a potential for cliché, by favoring a suggestive over a depictive style, Bartow avoids this danger, for he understands that the mythical aspect of his own existence is, in part, indeterminate and abstract.

Continuing to integrate his personal and cultural experiences, Bartow's recent body of works, beginning in 1995, were inspired by a trip to Japan. This series consists of tentative, self-contained studies in which he combines various images with fragments of the Japanese syllabary. Although they are less emotionally charged than his earlier works, these images are evidence of Bartow's ongoing faith in image-making as a means of generating meaning and tranquillity in his life.

Bartow's ongoing faith in artmaking as a means for generating healing and creating tranquility in one's life is evidenced in a 28 ft. cedar pole carved in bas relief. Commissioned specifically for installation on a greenway of a newly expanded boulevard in Newport, Oregon, Bartow's pole provides a tangible means of reestablishing a sense of community amidst loss of land in the name of progress. Bartow cites a variety of sources, including his work with John Bevan Ford (a Maori elder and master carver), as his inspiration for this piece, which incorporates abstracted, interlaced ribbons of water that form the "body" of a wide-eyed archaic visage. Although he assigns no particular provenance to the design of the head, which appears both protective and omniscient, it vaguely resembles an ancient Wishram figure known in translation as "she who watches." This visual correspondence serves as an appropriate, if unintended, allegory to the enduring divinity of the natural world despite devastation brought about through human error and expansion.

—Kristin Potter

BATES, Sara
Tribal affiliations: Cherokee
Installation artist

Born: Muskogee, Oklahoma, 1944. **Education:** Fine Art/Studio and Women Studies, California State University, Bakersfield, BA, 1987; Sculpture and Painting/Intermedia, University of California, Santa Barbara, MFA, 1989. **Career:** Director of Media Services, Westcor, Phoenix, Arizonal; National Media Services Director, Hahn Property Management, San Diego, California; Marketing Director, Cousins Properties, Atlanta, California, 1973-82. Graduate Teaching Assistant, University of California, Santa Barbara, California, 1987-89; Cherokee Nation Artist in Residence, Department of Education, Cherokee Nation, Tahlequah, Oklahoma, developing summer arts program as well as courses for children, 1988-90; Artist in Residence/Instructor, UCLA Artsreach, Los Angeles, California, 1989-90; Director of Exhibitions and Programs/Curator, American Indian Contemporary Arts, San Francisco, California, 1990-95; Artist in Residence, Headlands Center for the Arts, Marin Headlands, Sausalito, California, 1992-93; Instructor, Native American Studies, Contemporary Native American Art, San Francisco State University, 1995-96; Instructor, University of California, Berkeley Extension, San Francisco, 1996; Artist Committee, San Francisco Art Institute, 1993-1995, Board of Trustees, 1995; Curatorial Advisor, Cherokee National Museum, 1996; member, College Art Association, New York; lecturer, juror, panelist, workshop leader at numerous conferences, fairs, and universities; Curator, numerous exhibits at American Indian Contemporary Arts, San Francisco, and touring exhibits, including *Indian Humor* (1993-95) and *The Spirit of Native America* (1994-96). **Awards:** Public Art Program commission for three "Honoring" circles and installation, lecture, and discussion, San Francisco Arts Commission, 1997.

Individual Exhibitions

1990   San Francisco College of Oriental Medicine, San Francisco, California

Selected Group Exhibitions

1971   Delgado Museum, New Orleans, Louisiana
1986   *Artist as Shaman,* The Women's Building, Los Angeles
1988   UCEN Gallery, University of California, Santa Barbara
1989   *MFA Thesis Exhibition,* University of California Art Museum, Santa Barbara
1991   *Spirit as Source*, Bade Museum, Pacific School of Religion, Berkeley, California

Honoring Series Installations

1992   *Migration of Meaning*, INTAR Gallery, New York
        Hillwood Art Museum, C.W. Post/Long Island University, New York
        Pittsburgh Center for the Arts, Pittsburgh, Pennsylvania
        Lehigh Art Galleries, Bethlehem, Pennsylvania
        North American Land Issues, Pro Arts Gallery, Oakland, California
        Material Dimensions, Richmond Art Center, Richmond, California
1993   *A Kindred Spirit*, Bedford Gallery/Regional Center for the Arts, Walnut Creek, California
        Utopian Dialogues, Los Angeles County Municipal Gallery, California
        We Are Related, Center for the Arts at Yerba Buena Gardens, San Francisco
        Headlands Center for the Arts, Sausalito, California
        Toi te Aotearoa World Celebration of Indigenous Art and History, Te Taumata Gallery, Auckland, New Zealand
1994   *In the Spirit of Nature: Coming Home*, San Jose Museum, San Jose, California
        Plaza delle Esposizioni, Rome, Italy
1995-96 *Experiencing into Art*, Crocker Art Museum, Sacramento, California (traveling)
1996   *Native Streams "Honoring" Series Installation,* Jan Cicero Gallery, Chicago; Holter Museum of Art, Helena, Montana
        Eiteljorg Museum of American Indian and Western Art, Indianapolis, Indiana
        Spirit as Source, Sienna Heights College, Adrian, Michigan
        Beyond the 95th Meridian: Indian Territory 1996, University of Tulsa, Oklahoma

1997   *Affinities and Influences*, Neuberger Museum of Art, State University of New York, Purchase (organized by Montclair Museum, Montclair, New Jersey)

Collections

Whittier Graphics, Inc., Whittier, California.

Publications

By BATES: Books—Editor, *The Spirit of Native America,* San Francisco, 1993; Editor, *Indian Humor* (catalog), San Francisco, 1995; Editor, *Dancing Across Time: Images of the Southwest* (catalog). San Francisco, 1995; Essay, *20th Century Native American Art: Essays on History and Criticism,* W. Jackson Rushing, editor, London, 1997.

On BATES: Books—*The Migration of Meaning: A Source Book,* Intar Gallery, New York, 1992; *Toi te Ao: Aotearoa World Celebration of Indigenous Art,* Wellington, New Zealand, 1993; *Native Streams: Contemporary Native American Art,* Jan Cicero Gallery, Chicago, and Truman Art Gallery, Indiana State University, Terre Haute, 1996; *New Art,* Margaret Chase, editor, New York, 1997. **Articles**—"Contradictory Natures," by Sally McQuaid, *Artweek*, August 23, 1992; "The Independent Voice of the Visual Arts," by John Kissick, *New Art Examiner,* March 1993; "Sense of Place," by Jean Robertson, *Surface,* Vol. 21, no. 4, Summer 1997.

*

Sara Bates comments:

In order to understand the visual dialogue found in this series of artworks called "Honoring," and to access the "forms" used to create this exchange, it is necessary to understand that Native American people, in general, perceive the environment as an aware, conscious entity permeated with spiritual power. Our traditional belief systems teach us to respect the environment because it holds the order and structure of things.

This relationship between the natural world and Human Beings is sacred, reciprocal and mutually dependent. Interactions with the environment are a respectful and spiritual exchange; we know the presence of Human Beings affects the interplay of nature's forces. The concept of being in harmony with this interplay requires very careful attention to life's pathways and processes.

It is important to honor events and experiential knowledge. The "Honoring" pieces I create center on the traditional worldview of my tribe, the Cherokee. They represent how I, as one Cherokee, incorporate traditional views in my everyday life. I connect and honor these fluid relationships with the natural world by participating in gathering from the natural environment. Forms are then created which express this process through the infusion of tribally-specific symbols and other, personally developed symbols that are more than a representation of concept or phenomenon, or simply an emotionally-charged icon; many times, the symbols become part of the symbolized reality itself. Symbols reveal the accumulation of knowledge and wisdom.

My lived experience and my traditional values tell me this information is sacred. I have been gathering from the natural world and participating in this process for eighteen years. All that I have gathered will fit into four small boxes, 15" x 22" x 12". I recycle everything I honor. When an exhibition is complete, I pick up all

Sara Bates: *Honoring* (one of a series), installed at the Los Angeles Municipal Art Gallery, 1993. Courtesy of the artist.

materials in the "Honoring" and recycle them into a new form. I continually create these forms in my studio, whether anyone sees them or not. I gather only in small amounts, asking permission through prayer for what I take from the Earth and follow the natural cycle of the seasons. Some things I borrow and return to the natural place where I found them. My relationship to the natural world is complex and healing. I believe this information is vital to understanding what it means to be a Human Being.

*   *   *

Sara Bates is part of an influential group of Native American fine artists that have enveloped elements of their cultural background with European artistic traditions. This group of artists exhibit together based on philosophical ideals, rather than a common style or technique. Bates is important as an artist and curator in this movement. In the early 1990s, as the Director of Exhibitions and Programs for American Indian Contemporary Arts, San Francisco, California, Bates perpetuated the momentum of the contemporary Native American fine arts movement by developing and touring numerous exhibitions that deal with important social and philosophical issues faced by the American Indians living today. Such

exhibitions as *Native America, Reflecting Contemporary Realities,* have helped to explain these cultural concerns to the general public.

Bates was trained was as a painter and sculptor, but her *Honoring Series* circles, for which she is best known, are best described as installation pieces. Measuring from 8 to 12 feet in diameter, these works embody the spiritual and aesthetic sense of the Cherokee culture realized as modern abstraction. They are constructed on the floor and combine thousands of natural elements, such as sand, pebbles, pine cones and dried flowers, in elaborate patterns and rhythms that reflect her cultural and contemporary sense of expression. This dual aesthetic is constantly repeated throughout the work. It is found in the reverence for nature, expressed through the use and reuse of natural elements. On some occasions natural elements used in the works are returned to their original environment. This directly reflects the Cherokee way of revering and caring for the earth, which in turn cares for human beings. The reuse of material can also be described in more contemporary terms as recycling. Here again is the message that humans must care for the earth, but this interpretation refers to a more secular or environmental view that the earth cannot withstand constant consumption.

The *Honoring* installations have an awe-inspiring sense of meditative power and appeal, primarily from the contradiction of delicacy in massive and precise forms. Bates's strict and personal geometry combine and contrast with the organic materials in an unexpectedly natural fashion. The effect is to draw in the viewer to examine the individual elements of the work, which creates a closeness with the piece. This closeness may symbolize a closeness to nature. Historically, the concept of owning land or parts of nature is foreign to many Native American cultures. It is an interesting attitude to explore with regard to Bates's Honoring Series, since they may not be owned by an institution or individual. Each individual piece is site-specific, drawing on indigenous natural materials. The work cannot be handled or manipulated. They are, in essence, phantom works of art that are dispersed at the end of each exhibition. Once the piece is disembodied it ceases to exist, except in memory. This may symbolize the delicate balance of nature and the consequences of upsetting that balance.

Sara Bates is able to combine the aesthetics of her cultural background and the modern world in order to give the viewer a multi-level visual and intellectual experience. Her work exemplifies the notion that Native American art, artists and their cultures are alive and well. They are living, working and evolving in ways that challenge commonly held notions about Native American art and its ability to compete in the contemporary art world.

—Jennifer Complo

BEAM, Carl

Tribal affiliations: Ojibway
Mixed media artist, sculptor, printmaker, and painter

Born: West Bay, Manitoulin Island, Ontario, 1943. **Education:** Kootenay School of Art; University of Victoria, British Columbia, BFA, 1975; University of Alberta, graduate studies. **Career:** Various jobs, including logger, construction worker, millwright operator, and ironworker; full-time artist since mid-1970s; commission for multimedia construction (*Exorcism*, 7 ft. x 20 ft.), Thunder Bay National Exhibition Centre and Centre for Indian Art; artist in residence, Artspace, Peterborough, Ontario, 1988. **Awards:** Artist's grant, Council Canada, 1984.

Individual Exhibitions

1977   Eagle Down Gallery, Edmonton, Alberta
1979   Maxwell Museum, University of New Mexico, Albuquerque
1980   Thompson Gallery, Toronto
1981   Gallery 480, Elora, Ontario
1982   *Two Sides to All Stories: Carl Beam, Important Art for the 1980s,* Scharf Gallery, Santa Fe, New Mexico
        Laurentian University Museum and Arts Centre, Sudbury, Ontario
1984   *Altered Egos: The Multimedia Work of Carl Beam,* Thunder Bay National Exhibition Centre and Centre for Indian Art
1985   Brignall Gallery, Toronto
        The Art Gallery of York University, Toronto
1989   *A Piece of My Life: Prints by Carl Beam,* Agnes Etherington Art Centre, Kingston, Ontario
        The Columbus Project, Artspace, Peterborough, Ontario

1993   *Italian Exhibitions of the Columbus Boat,* Arnold Gottlieb Gallery, Toronto (traveled in Italy)

Selected Group Exhibitions

1975   Emily Carr Centre, Victoria, British Columbia
1976   Graphic 5 Art Gallery, Edmonton, Alberta
1977   Eagle Down Gallery, Edmonton, Alberta
1978   Tundra Gallery, Sault Ste. Marie, Ontario
1979   Emily Carr Centre, Victoria, British Columbia
        Ojibwe Cultural Foundation, West Bay, Ontario
        University of New Mexico, Albuquerque
1980   *Woodland Art,* The Art Gallery of Brant, Brantford, Ontario
        Anishnawbe Mee-kun, Ojibwe Cultural Foundation, West Bay, Ontario
1981   *At the Edge of the Woods,* Native American Center for the Living Arts, Niagara Falls, New York
        Viewpoint, Art Gallery of Hamilton, Ontario
        Confluences of Tradition and Change, C. N. Gorman Museum and Richard L. Nelson Gallery, Davis, California
1982   *Renewal: Masterworks of Contemporary Indian Art from the Canadian Museum of Civilization,* Thunder Bay National Exhibition Centre and Centre for Indian Art, Thunder Bay, Ontario
        Lutz-Bergerson Gallery, Taos, New Mexico
        New Work by a New Generation, Norman Mackenzie Art Gallery, Regina, Saskatchewan
        Paintings on Pottery by Ann and Carl Beam, Maxwell Museum, University of New Mexico, Albuquerque
1983   *Directions: An Exhibition of Masterworks,* Northwestern National Exhibition Centres, Hazelton, British Columbia
        New Directions: 8 Indian Artists, Gallery 10, New York
        New Growth from Ancestral Roots, The Koffer Gallery, Toronto
1983-84 Laurentian University Museum & Arts Centre, Sudbury, Ontario
1983-85 *Contemporary Indian and Inuit Art of Canada,* organized by the Department of Indian and Northern Affairs (traveling)
1984   Meervart Gallery, Amsterdam, The Netherlands
1985   *Zeitgenossische Kunst der Indianer und Eskimos in Kanada,* Canadian Museum of Civilization, Ottawa, Ontario; opened in Dortmund, Germany and toured Canada
        Multicultural Celebration of the Arts, Northern Crafts Gallery, Manitoulin Island, Ontario
        Challenges, organized by the Canadian Museum of Civilization, Ottawa, Ontario, for the Holland Festival, DeMeervaart Centre, Amsterdam, The Netherlands
1986   Tom Thomson Memorial Gallery, Owen Sound, Ontario
1987   Beckett Gallery, Hamilton, Ontario
        Southwest Museum, Los Angeles
1989   *Political Landscapes,* Tom Thomson Memorial Gallery, Owen Sound, Ontario
        Beyond History, Vancouver Art Gallery, Vancouver, British Columbia
        In the Shadow of the Sun, organized by the Canadian Museum of Civilization, Ottawa (traveling)

Carl Beam: *Columbus and Bees* (from the *Columbus Suite*), c. late 1980s/early 1990s. Courtesy of Amelia Trevelyan.

1991   *Art of the First Nation,* Woodland Indian Cultural Centre, Brantford, Ontario

        Solidarity: Art After Oka, Saw Gallery, Ottawa, Ontario

1992   *Contemporary First Nations Art,* Ufundi Gallery, Ottawa, Ontario

        Land, Spirit, Power, National Gallery of Canada, Ottawa, Ontario

1993   *Seeing a New World: the Works of Carl Beam and Frederic Remington,* Gettysburg College Art Gallery, Gettysburg, Pennsylvania

1996   *The Helen Band Collection,* Thunder Bay Art Gallery, Thunder Bay, Ontario

1997   *Transitions: Contemporary Canadian Indian and Inuit Art,* organized by Indian and Northern Affairs Canada and Department of Foreign Affairs and International Trade, Paris, France (traveling in Canada and France)

Collections

Albright-Knox Gallery, Buffalo, New York; Art Gallery of Hamilton, Hamilton, Ontario; Canadian Museum of Civilization, Hull, Quebec; The City of Buffalo, New York; The City of Revelstoke, British Columbia; The City of Sudbury, Ontario; Department of Indian and Northern Affairs - Canada, Ottawa, Ontario; Gallery 480, Elora, Ontario; Government of Ontario Art Collection, Sudbury, Ontario; Heard Museum, Phoenix, Arizona; Laurentian University, Museum and Arts Centre, Sudbury, Ontario; McMichael Canadian Collection, Kleinburg, Ontario; New College, University of Toronto, Ontario; Ojibwa Cultural Foundation, West Bay, Ontario; Thunder Bay Art Gallery, Thunder Bay, Ontario; Wilfred Laurier University, Waterloo, Ontario; Woodland Indian Cultural Educational Centre, Brantford, Ontario.

Publications

On BEAM: Books—*The Sound of the Drum: The Sacred Art of the Anishnabec,* by Mary E. Southcott, Erin, Ontario, 1984; *Altered Egos: The Multimedia Work of Carl Beam* (catalog), by Elizabeth McLuhan, Thunder Bay, 1984; *Manitoulin Island: The Third Layer,* exhibition catalog by Berhhard Cinander, Thunder Bay Art Gallery, Thunder Bay, Ontario, 1987; *Carl Beam: the Columbus Boat,* exhibition catalog, by Richard Rhoades, The Power Plant, Toronto, Ontario, 1992; *In the Shadow of the Sun,* exhibition catalog, Canadian Museum of Civilization, Hull, Quebec, 1993; *Seeing a New World: the Works of Carl Beam and Frederic Remington,* exhibition catalog, by Amelia Trevelyan, Gettysburg College Art Gallery, Gettysburg, Pennsylvania, 1993. **Articles**—"Native Art Notions: Free-thinking Carl Chooses to Digress from the Morrisseau Cliche," by Trish Wilson, *Kitchener-Waterloo Record,* May 13, 1981; "Carl Beam: No More Walden," by T, M. Collins, *Artlines,* January 1982; "Renewal 2," by Robert Reid, *The Art Post,* August-September 1985; "Carl Beam," *Parachute,* September-October, 1985; "Making Missins, Remarking History: The Columbus Project of Carl Beam, *Artscraft,* Summer 1990; "Carl Beam: The Columbus Project," *Parallelogramme,* Vol. 17, no. 4, 1992; "Trilling Us Softly, by Alison Gilmor, *Border Crossings,* Summer 1993.

*   *   *

The paintings, prints and constructions of Carl Beam stand at the cutting edge of contemporary art and push insistently at its boundaries. The autobiographical cast of his work and his use of personal, commercial, and classic imagery from the histories of art and photography offer complexities of style and content that place this work within the vanguard of Post Modernism and its self-conscious deconstruction of tradition, both historic and aesthetic. Presented with a gallery full of Beam's work, one is reminded vaguely of Joseph Cornell, of his boxes—as though exploded and then examined through a microscope—or of Rauchenberg, albeit with a more complex exploration of issues and a far more personal irony.

Beam offers his audience much more than a deconstruction of certain aspects of modernism, however, although these elements alone give his work a stature and sophistication equal to any of his contemporaries. In addition, there is a rich undercurrent of meaning flowing in and around the Post Modern content of his creations. That extra dimension proceeds from Beam's self-conscious response to his own background as a Native American, living within and between two cultures. Beyond the examination of Post Modern aesthetic and contextual issues, his work explores the nature, implications and results of cultural interaction, the very fabric of contemporary reality.

As such, his work always presents a vision of things that fits very clearly into contemporary Euro-American culture, yet outside of it in many ways. This added ingredient gives the work a depth and richness that is rare in much of art today. He accomplishes this most often by examining socio-political myths and icons of European tradition and playing them off against equally potent, but fundamentally different, myth and symbol from Native culture. Through repetition and reversal of a few central images, Beam compares the two traditions and the cultural baggage each includes. Through this subtle and carefully crafted process he calmly unravels the texts commonly attached to these images. Then he weaves them together once again in a complex Post Modern tapestry of symbol and meaning governed by a new and broader vision.

Carl Beam began life quite literally as the product of two cultures: his mother is Ojibway, his father Euro-American. Thus, he is contemporary artist, Canadian citizen, and a member of the Ojibway, or Anishnabe, as well as Anglo communities. He explores and unfolds these multiple identities in his work, resulting in his unique vision. From within this multi-layered identity, he sees and interprets the world from many, often divergent, perspectives. His scrupulous honesty in this process prevents his ignoring or privileging any of the realities he lives. The result is a clear, often stark, vision of the world, of the composite nature of culture and the universal imperative of responsibility, regardless of the content or medium in which he works.

He is obsessed by an urge to create, to contribute, to interpret, to do whatever is most needed, most significant in today's world, and scrupulous and self-conscious honesty permeates everything he does. Therein lies the nature of his genius as well as its source. His personal history as human and artist is a veritable odyssey of exploration and explication guided by these obsessions. It began as he built his own life experience working and traveling all across the North American continent, from his teens onward. He began the search in West Bay, an Ojibway reserve on Manitoulin Island in southern Ontario. His searchings have come full circle today as he lives and works there once again.

Beam found his artist calling in British Columbia, dabbling in oil painting during years as a logger and ironworker. This passing interest soon became the focus of his life, and he went quickly from high school drop-out to degree candidate, first in commercial art at

Kootenay School of Art and then at the University of Victoria where he completed a BFA. In the late 1970s, he left an MFA program at the University of Alberta to become a full time artist. In subsequent years he has continued to travel far and wide, both geographically and in terms of artistic media, driven by his sense of message and mission. He always chafed at the limitations faced by Native artists in Canada—the need to be "Indian" and at the same time "contemporary," to be a part of mainstream developments in the art world, but not at the expense of one's "indianness," and, thereby, subject to the charge of being less than authentic. Although he maintained contact with artists and family in West Bay, in 1980 Beam avoided these issues for a time by moving to the more congenial artistic atmosphere of New Mexico, exploring Native media there and redefining and reinterpreting them in contemporary terms.

In the New Mexico years, Beam became an accomplished potter, exploring ancient forms and, at the same time, enlarging the scope of his work to incorporate international events and imagery. By this time, his use of media also included large scale work in watercolor, painting on canvas and plexiglass, and various mixed media constructions. Subject matter increasingly combined autobiographical references and considerable political content, usually of international significance. In these works, both personal and political references can be read in individualized imagery designed to call up more generalized truths, and vice versa. That is, he may also utilize universally familiar imagery to elucidate individual need and experience. Generally, one kind of reference predominates and the others bleed through, both intellectually and literally, as individual works are explored. Text, both hand written and stenciled, sometimes cryptically brief, sometimes exhaustively detailed, often accompanies the images. Media imagery, both historic and contemporary, as well as historic and personal photographs, become increasingly important, too, as do references to the fine art of the past.

The results are intensely personal, yet curiously universal. He identifies and exploits the expressive dissonance between those disparate elements. The juxtaposition makes demands on the viewer. One has to think, to reconcile the contradictions or remain ignorant in the face of what is obviously a powerful statement. He carefully selects and combines potent and familiar signs. Through that combination (and with the added incentive of his own, often lengthy, inscriptions) Beam encourages the viewer to read those familiar images and interpret them anew. The result is a crumbling of the cliched familiarity that surrounds the imagery. They are given new life, a restoration of earlier significance as well as new strength within the context of present reality, as Beam has put it, "looking at the world as it is, not how we'd like it to be."

It is never merely a matter of content, either. The power of Beam's work resides as well in the aesthetics of what he creates. Color, form and texture deliver powerful messages on their own, inexorably linked to the imagery, but operating independently, as well. Some knowledge of the imagery used enhances the experience of this work, particularly on intellectual levels, but formal content is equally potent. The results are often wonderfully ironic, delivering an aesthetic message that is fully as powerful as that available intellectually, but often a mirror image reversal of the imagery itself. *The Unexplained*, from the *Columbus Suite*, is an apt example. Those unfamiliar with the role of the Gan in Apache tradition tend to assume that the two hooded figures are the victims of torture, the racially-based degradation of individuals by those invoking fundamentalist religious views as a rationalization for their violent acts. Their combination with the Avignon Pieta brings to mind the role of torture and sacrifice in Christian tradition and the relationship be-

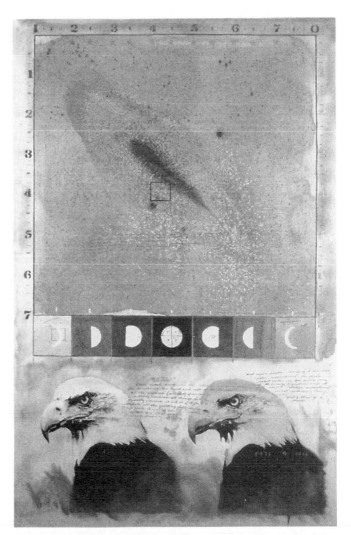

Carl Beam: *Stellar Association,* **1980. Photograph by Rick Hill.**

tween those elements, the teachings of Jesus and the violence done throughout history in the name of Christianity. The nasty, bloody drips that run down the entire surface of the print and the general degradation of the surface reinforce these impressions. Even without knowledge of the Christian subject matter, the human content of the lower image, mourning the torture and death of a loved one, calls up ideas about man's inhumanity to man and the disjunction between humanity's capacity for compassion and cruelty. The specific comparison of traditional native and Christian ideas and practice of religion would be lost, in this case, but the larger, universal nature of the work's content bleeds through regardless of the background information the viewer brings to the image.

Since returning to Ontario, Beam has moved through yet more media: wood sculpture, video and, currently, adobe and rammed earth architecture. Throughout his career, he has refused to allow his vision to be limited by media concerns. He employs whatever medium he feels will be most effective in presenting content. Content is always the privileged element in his work. His most recent work involves a return to the New Mexico experience, the re-invention of adobe architecture.

Early in the 1990s he set out to build his own home, using traditional southwestern adobe technology adapted to the soil and climate of Ontario. The transition from two-dimensional gallery fare to supremely practical architecture was a perfectly natural one for Beam. Honest evaluation of the needs of his community, expanded by a characteristic vision of the most pressing needs of the world at large, has led him to explore and develop low cost housing, first for himself and then for the world. The pattern is a familiar one, played out again and again in Beam's life as an artist. Each phase of his career has pushed him logically and inevitably to the next.

—Amelia Trevelyan

BEARDY, Jackson

Tribal affiliations: Cree; Ojibway
Painter and illustrator

Born: Garden Hill Reserve, Island Lake, Manitoba, 24 July 1944. **Education:** Technical Vocational School, Winnipeg, Manitoba, 1963-1964; School of Fine Arts, University of Manitoba, Winnipeg, 1966. **Career:** Commercial artist, Band Council member for the Garden Hill Band, Island Lake, Manitoba (elected), teacher, lecturer, field researcher; founding member, The Group of Seven, and the associated Native Artists Inc.; art advisor and cultural consultant, Manitoba Museum of Man and Nature, Department of Native Studies, Brandon University, and the Department of Indian Affairs and Northern Development, Ottawa. Member, National Indian Arts Council, Ottawa; Manitoba Arts Council, Winnipeg; Prison Arts Foundation, Ottawa; Canadian Artists' Representation, Ottawa; Canadian Indian Artist Association. Commissioned by the Canadian Catholic Conference of Bishops, 1975, St. John's College, University of Manitoba, mural, 1976, Manitoba Museum of Man and Nature, mural (*The Great Chain of Being*), 1978, City of Winnipeg, coin design, 1978, Province of Manitoba, painting presented to Queen Elizabeth II, 1979, City of Winnipeg, 1979, International Association for the History of Religion, painting presented to Crown Prince of Japan, 1980, Winnipeg Women's O.R.T. (*Loons '81*), painting, 1981. **Awards:** Canada Centennial Award, 1967; Canada Council Grant, 1982; Board of Directors, Manitoba Arts Council. **Died:** 1984.

Individual Exhibitions

1965   University of Winnipeg, Manitoba
1967   United College, Winnipeg, Manitoba
1969   Royal Bank of Canada, Winnipeg, Manitoba
1970   National Arts Centre, Ottawa, Ontario
1976   Pollock Gallery, Toronto, Ontario
1977   *Images for a Canadian Heritage*, Vancouver, British Columbia
        Robertson Galleries, Ottawa, Ontario
1978   Fort Garry Trust, Winnipeg, Manitoba
1979   Gallery One, Toronto, Ontario
        Galerie Martal, Montreal, Quebec
        Children of the Raven Gallery, Vancouver, British Columbia
1980   The Raven Gallery, Minneapolis, Minnesota
        Robertson Galleries, Ottawa, Ontario
        Eaton's Fine Art Gallery, Winnipeg, Manitoba

1981   Images Gallery, Vancouver, British Columbia
1982   Rothwell Galleries, Ottawa, Ontario
1995   *Jackson Beardy: A Life's Work*, Thunder Bay Art Gallery, Ontario

Selected Group Exhibitions

1967   Indian of Canada Pavilion, Expo '67, Montreal
1970   *Manitoba Days*, National Arts Centre, Ottawa
1972   *Treaty Numbers: No. 23, 287, 1171*, Winnipeg Art Gallery
1974   *Canadian Indian Art '74*, Royal Ontario Museum, Toronto
        Gallery Anthropas, London
        Merritt College, Oakland, California
1975   Wallack Galleries, Ottawa
1976   *Contemporary Native Art of Canada: The Woodland Indians*, Royal Ontario Museum, Toronto (traveled to England and Germany)
        Wells Gallery, Ottawa
1977   *Native Graphics*, Winnipeg Art Gallery
        Contemporary Indian Art: The Trail from the Past to the Future, MacKenzie Gallery and Native Studies Programme, Trent University, Peterborough, Ontario
        Links to a Tradition, Department of Indian and Northern Affairs for the Canadian Embassy in Brazil
1978   Merton Gallery, Toronto
1979   *Indian Art '79*, Woodland Indian Cultural Educational Centre, Brantford, Ontario
1980   *Manitou Citizens' Bursary Fund for Native Peoples Show*, Winnipeg
        Graphics Gallery, Ottawa
1982   *Five Woodland Indian Artists*, Raven Gallery, Minneapolis
        Renewal: Masterworks of Contemporary Indian Art from the National Museum of Man, Thunder Bay, Ontario
        Contemporary Indian Art at Rideau Hall, Ottawa
1983-85 *Contemporary Indian and Inuit Art of Canada*, organized by the Department of Indian and Northern Affairs (traveling)

Collections

Canadian Museum of Civilization, Ottawa; Department of Indian and Northern Affairs, Ottawa; Department of Justice, Supreme Court, Ottawa; Glenbow-Alberta Institute, Calgary; Manitoba Museum of Man and Nature, Winnipeg; McMichael Canadian Collection, Kleinburg, Ontario; Mother Theresa's Hospital, Calcutta, India; Royal Ontario Museum, Toronto; Simon Fraser University, Burnsby, British Columbia; University of British Columbia, Vancouver; University of Wellington, New Zealand; Winnipeg Art Gallery; Windsor Castle, London.

Publications

By BEARDY: Publications illustrated—*When the Morning Stars Sang Together* by John Morgan, Toronto, 1974; *Almighty Voice* by Leonard Peterson, Winnipeg, 1976; *Ojibway Heritage* by Basil Johnston, Toronto, 1976; *The Canadian Journal of Native Studies,* Vol. 4, no. 1, Winter 1983. **Film—***The Making of the Thunderbirds,* Sesame Street Productions, Canadian Broadcasting Corporation, 1979.

On BEARDY: Books—*Contemporary Native Art of Canada: The Woodland Indians,* Royal Ontario Museum, Toronto, 1976; *The Sweetgrass Lives On: Fifty Contemporary North American Indian Artists,* Jamake Highwater, New York, 1980; *Woodlands: Contemporary Art of the Anishnabe,* exhibition catalog by Carol Podedworny, Thunder Bay, 1989. **Articles**—"Treaty Numbers 23, 287, 1171," *ArtsCanada,* early autumn, 1972, "The Canadian Influence in Paris," *Artsmagazine,* October-November, 1977; "The Life and Art of Jackson Beardy," *Arts Manitoba,* Vol. 1, No. 1, 1977; "Contemporary Algonkian Legend Painting," *American Indian Art Magazine,* Vol. 3, No. 3, 1978; "Jackson Beardy: The Art and the Artist," *Canadian Dimensions,* Vol. 12, No. 6, 1979; "Contemporary Canadian Indian Art," by John Anson Warner, *Masterkey,* Vol. 58, No. 4, 1984. **Film**—*Jackson Beardy, The Making of an Artist,* Canadian Broadcasting Corporation, 1977.

*   *   *

Jackson Beardy was a leading Native figure in the late 1960s and 1970s, advocating both politically and artistically for the rights of the peoples of the First Nations in Canada. As a founding member of the New Woodland School and as a community representative on various cultural and political organizations, Beardy forged a path and created a legacy of activism for those who followed. Beardy's influence on the revitalization of Woodland culture and the policies and methods of Canadian institutions handling and interpreting art treasures of First Nations has been an important contribution to the development and history of the art of the First Nations.

Treaty Numbers 23, 287, 1171 was one of the first exhibitions in Canada to address First Nations art within an aesthetic as opposed to anthropological framework. The exhibition was curated by the late Jacqueline Fry for the Winnipeg Art Gallery in 1972 and included the work of Daphne Odjig, Alex Janvier, and Jackson Beardy. Appropriately, these artists would become associated with a move toward the application of new methodological approaches to native art in the 1970s that would continue to be refined and developed throughout the 1980s.

In the early 1970s, Odjig, Janvier, and Beardy actively advocated for the rights of Native artists through their formation of what was popularly called the Group of Seven with artists Norval Morrisseau, Carl Ray, Eddy Cobiness and Joseph Sanchez. Through their association—professionally known as Native Artists, Inc.—these artists provided a much-needed informal but focused forum for criticism amongst artists. They organized exhibitions, worked toward the development of a scholarship program, developed strategies to inform the public about their work, and worked to control the production and marketing of their art. The Group of Seven hoped to encourage Native control of Native interests; separate their work from the established Indian art marketing program, which emphasized "Indianness"; and dispense with art-world arguments regarding the artistic versus anthropological significance of works of art by Native artists.

For Beardy, the Group of Seven was only the beginning. He would subsequently augment his career as an artist with the role of cultural activist, serving as art advisor and cultural consultant to the Manitoba Museum of Man and Nature, the Department of Native Studies at Brandon University, and the Department of Indian Affairs and Northern Development in Ottawa. He was also an active member of the National Indian Arts Council, the Manitoba Arts Council, the Prison Arts Foundation, Canadian Artists' Represen-

tation, Canadian Indian Artist Association, and a council member for the Garden Hill Band of Island Lake, Manitoba.

As a visual artist Beardy was a pivotal figure during his lifetime and has become emblematic of a style, period, and movement. As one of the founding members of the New Woodland School, and as part of the founding generation of modern Native artists in Canada, Beardy was one of the first to wed Ojibway tradition with European notions of fine art. His art is representative of the New Woodland School style: iconic figures, an undifferentiated background, systems of linear determinatives, x-ray perspectives, and vibrant unmixed hues. With cultural specificity, it reflects his search for "a visual symbolic language that would convey a cohesive world view," as Colleen Cutschall described it in 1994. Beardy created an art of profound cultural change—steeped both in a traditional heritage and a contemporary reality and relevance. His work is powerful in its historical, cultural and political significances.

Throughout his lifetime, Jackson Beardy's social work traversed cultures, instigated change, marked the combined aesthetic/political intersection that would ensure the activity of a second generation of Native "modernists." In 1972, Jackson Beardy was awarded the Canadian Centennial Medal, and in 1984 his memorial service was the first ever held in the Blue Room of the Manitoba Legislative Buildings. Here federal, provincial, and civic leaders joined Beardy's family and Native leaders and elders in mourning Beardy and paying tribute to his life and work.

—Carol Podedworny

BEATIEN YAZZ

Variant names: Jimmy Toddy; Little No Shirt
Tribal affiliations: Navajo
Painter and illustrator

Born: James Toddy near Wide Ruins, Arizona, 5 March 1928. **Education:** Sherman Institute, a government Indian school in Riverside, California; Stewart Indian School, Carson City, Nevada; Mills College, Oakland, California (studied under Yasuo Kuniyoshi), 1947; Art Institute of Chicago. **Military Service:** U.S. Marine Corps during World War II, serving as one of the "code talkers" using the Navajo language to relay coded messages. **Career:** Policeman, Navajo Police Department, Fort Defiance, Arizona; art instructor, Carson Indian School; book illustrator; and painter. **Awards:** First place, Heard Museum Fair Guild and Indian Market, 1978; nine awards, Inter-Tribal Indian Ceremonies, 1968-87; honors, Philbrook Museum of Art Annual Indian Art Exhibition, 1968-72; Red Cloud Indian Art Show, 1976.

Individual Exhibitions

1940   Illinois State Museum, Springfield, Illinois
1941   La Jolla Gallery of Art, La Jolla, California
1979   Heard Museum, Phoenix
1985   Southwest Museum, Los Angeles

Selected Group Exhibitions

1958   *Southwest Indian Arts,* Palace of the Legion of Honor
           Museum, San Francisco

Beatien Yazz: *Warriors on Horseback,* c. 1960. Photograph by Dong Lin; courtesy California Academy of Sciences, Elkus Collection.

1966	*Southwest Indian Arts II,* Palace of the Legion of Honor Museum, San Francisco
1968	*The James T. Bialac Collection of Southwest Indian Paintings,* Arizona State Museum, University of Arizona, Tucson
1976	*The Elkus Collection of Southwestern Indian Art,* California Academy of Sciences, San Francisco
1978	*100 Years of Native American Painting,* Oklahoma Museum of Art, Oklahoma City
1980	*The Toddy Family,* Navajo Nation Museum, Window Rock, Arizona
1981-83	*Native American Painting,* Amarillo Art Center, Amarillo, Texas (traveling)
1986-90	*When the Rainbow Touches Down,* Heard Museum, Phoenix, Arizona (traveling)
1991-96	*Shared Visions: Native American Painters and Sculptors in the Twentieth Century,* Heard Museum, Phoenix, Arizona (international traveling exhibit)
1995-96	*With a View to the Southwest: Dorothy Dunn,* Museum of Indian Arts & Culture, Museum of New Mexico, Santa Fe
1996	Mitchell Indian Museum, Evanston, Illinois

Collections

Albuquerque Museum, New Mexico; Arizona State Museum, University of Arizona, Tucson; California Academy of Sciences, Elkus Collection, San Francisco; Bern Museum, Switzerland; Children's Museum of Indianapolis, Indiana; Cincinnati Museum of Natural History, Ohio; Denver Art Museum, Colorado; Heard Museum, Phoenix, Arizona; Heritage Center, Red Cloud Indian School, Pine Ridge, South Dakota; Indian Arts and Crafts Board, U.S. Department of the Interior, Washington, D.C.; Museum of Indian Arts and Culture, Museum of New Mexico, Santa Fe; Museum of Man, San Diego, California; Museum of Northern Arizona, Flagstaff; National Museum of the American Indian, Smithsonian Institution, Washington, D.C.; Navajo Nation Museum, Arizona; Philbrook Art Center, Tulsa, Oklahoma; Roswell Museum and Art Center, Roswell, New Mexico; School of American Research, Santa Fe, New Mexico; Southwest Museum, Los Angeles; Thomas Gilcrease Institute of American History and Art, Tulsa, Oklahoma; Wheelwright Museum of the American Indian, Santa Fe, New Mexico; Woolaroc Museum, Bartlesville, Oklahoma.

Publications

By BEATIEN YAZZ: Books—*The Last Horse* by Stan Steiner (illustrated by Beatien Yazz), New York: Macmillan, 1961; *Yazz, Navajo Painter* with Sallie R. Wagner and J. J. Brody (also illustrated by Beatien Yazz), Flagstaff, Arizona: Northland Press, 1983.

On BEATIEN YAZZ: Books—*Spin a Silver Dollar* by Alberta Hannum (illustrated by Beatien Yazz), New York: The Viking Co., 1945; *American Indian Painters* by Oscar Jacobson and Jeanne d'Ucel, Nice, France: C. Szwedzicki, 1950; *Paint the Wind* by Alberta Hannum (illustrated by Beatien Yazz), New York: The Viking Co., 1958; *American Indian Painting of the Southwest and Plains Areas* by Dorothy Dunn, Albuquerque, New Mexico: University of New Mexico Press, 1968; *The James T. Bialac Collection of Southwest Indian Paintings*, exhibition catalog, by Clara Lee Tanner, Tucson, Arizona: University of Arizona Press, 1968; *Indian Painters & White Patrons* by J. J. Brody, Albuquerque, New Mexico: University of New Mexico Press, 1971; *Southwest Indian Painting, a Changing Art* by Clara Lee Tanner, Tucson, Arizona: University of Arizona Press, 1973; *100 Years of Native American Art*, exhibition catalog, by Arthur Silberman, Oklahoma City, Oklahoma: Oklahoma Museum of Art, 1978; *American Indian Painting & Sculpture* by Patricia Janis Broder, New York: Abbeville Press 1981; *Native American Painting*, exhibition catalog, by Jeanne Snodgrass King, Amarillo, Texas: Amarillo Art Center, 1981; *Navajo Painting,* by Katherin Chase, Flagstaff, Arizona: Museum of Northern Arizona Press, 1983; *The Elkus Collection, Southwestern Indian Art*, edited by Dorothy K. Washburn, San Francisco: California Academy of Sciences, 1984; *When the Rainbow Touches Down*, exhibition catalog, by Tryntje Van Ness Seymour, Phoenix, Arizona: The Heard Museum, 1988; *Shared Visions, Native American Painters and Sculptors in the Twentieth Century*, exhibition catalog, by Margaret Archuleta and Rennard Strickland, Phoenix, Arizona: The Heard Museum, 1990. **Articles**—"Modern Navajo Water Color Painting," by Linzee King Davis, *Arizona Highways* 32 (7), July 1956.

*   *   *

Beatien Yazz is known primarily for his Pan-Indian illustrative painting style, derived, in part, from the Santa Fe Studio Style introduced in the 1930s by Dorothy Dunn at the Santa Fe Indian School. Beatien Yazz was born and grew up on the Navajo Reservation at Wide Ruins, Arizona, and gained artistic notoriety while still a youth, under the guidance and patronage of Bill and Sallie Lippincott, who operated the local trading post and supplied the young artist with supplies. In 1940, when Beatien Yazz was only 12 years old, his work was exhibited at the Illinois State Museum. Another exhibit followed in 1941 at the La Jolla Gallery of Art in La Jolla, California. With the publication of the immensely popular *Spin a Silver Dollar* in 1945 (a sequel, *Paint the Wind*, was published in 1958), Beatien Yazz's career was solidly launched.

Beatien Yazz is mostly self-taught, without any extended formal art education, but a number of factors and experiences have influenced his work. As a youth, he was exposed to art through books and magazines and by artist friends of the Lippincotts who visited during the summers and sometimes offered him limited instruction.

During World War II, Beatien Yazz was inducted into the Marines and served with the Navajo Code Talkers, a secret all-Navajo unit whose members transmitted military messages in a specially-developed code based on the Navajo language. He served in the Pacific arena and later with the occupation forces in China, experiences that would later influence his art. Upon returning to the states, he enrolled at the Sherman Institute, a government Indian school in Riverside, California, and later transferred to the Stewart Indian School at Carson City, Nevada. A friendship with Chicago artist Jimmie Swann, who visited the Lippincotts at Wide Ruins, resulted in a visit to Swann's studio in Chicago in 1947. There Beatien Yazz studied Swann's copper etchings and with only a rudimentary explanation of the process involved, successfully executed several etchings himself. Also in 1947, through the interces-

sion of the Lippincotts, Beatien Yazz was admitted to a summer class at Mills College in Oakland, California, to study under Japanese artist, Yasuo Kuniyoshi.

Partly because of these many influences, the artist's work is not always easily characterized. He is one of the best known and most prolific of twentieth-century Navajo artists with a very large body of work to his credit, and like many self-taught artists, particularly Native Americans, he first drew and painted subjects that he saw around him, rendering them in a flat but generally realistic style, with little if any perspective or surrounding context. This was in keeping with the Navajo sense that drawings should be largely representational.

Through practice, Beatien Yazz became a more skillful illustrator and increasingly listened to, but did not necessarily follow, advice from the Lippincotts and others as to what constituted "good art." As early as 1940, he visited the Santa Fe Studio, and several paintings completed over the next several years include Studio-style conventions that he observed there. His adoption of the Studio Style, however, was gradual and never whole-hearted, as he responded to various influences in his life and blended many different styles. Of the year he later spent at Santa Fe as a student, he remembers learning how to mix colors together and how to draw human and animal forms.

In a career that spans more than 50 years, Beatien Yazz has worked mostly in casein and tempera. In the 1970s and 1980s, he often worked in acrylics, as well. Most of his work has been in the traditional style, but he has also experimented with the abstract. A common thread in all his paintings is a desire to depict traditional stories told by his grandfather and other elders, or scenes he remembers from his own youth. In this sense, his work chronicles a lifestyle that today's Navajo youth will never experience.

Beatien Yazz skillfully blends colors to create moods or suggest movement in his work. Few other Navajo artists painting in the traditional style have mastered this skill better. Beatien Yazz's personal philosophy about painting is that one learns by doing, and that is how his own painting improved. He has developed a keen memory for details and he taps into that reserve whenever he works. Details of dress and movement at ceremonies have to be carefully memorized to ensure accuracy when later painted.

The artist has gone through several phases in his career. A failed first marriage, isolation for many years from his children from that marriage, and alcoholism all influenced his work, in both good and bad ways. Frustration sometimes challenged him to convey great depth of feeling in his work, while at other times it resulted in repetitive, uninspired work. But through all the trials, Beatien Yazz has persevered in his artistic quest. He has served as a role model for many younger Navajo artists, most especially his three oldest sons, Irving, Marvin, and Calvin, each of whom is an accomplished artist. Sadly, failing eyesight has prevented Beatien Yazz from producing much work in recent years.

—Russell P. Hartman

BEAVER, Fred

Variant names: Eka La Nee
Tribal affiliations: Creek
Painter

Born: Eufala, Oklahoma, 2 July 1911; Eka La Nee translates as Brown Head. **Education:** Bacone College, 1931; Haskell Indian

School, 1935. **Military Service:** U.S. Air Force during World War II. **Career:** Bureau of Indian Affairs, Field Service, 1935-60 (except for years of military service); artist, 1960-80; restored Acee Blue Eagle's mural at the Coalgate, Oklahoma, Post Office, 1965; commissioned for murals, paintings (State of Oklahoma, for the Governor's gallery; Oklahoma Republican Committee, gift for President Eisenhower), and designs (Franklin Mint for three Bicentennial medallions, 1976). **Awards:** Designated as Master Artist, Five Civilized Tribes, 1973; honors at major festivals and juried competitions, including All-American Indian Days, Inter-Tribal Indian Ceremonials, Five Civilized Tribes Competitive and Masters shows, Philbrook Art Center annuals, and Southwestern Association on Indian Arts Annual Market. **Died:** 18 August 1980.

Selected Group Exhibitions

1960   *Philbrook Annual Indian Art Exhibition*, Philbrook Museum, Tulsa, Oklahoma
1962-65 *American Indian Paintings from the Permanent Collection*, Philbrook Museum, Tulsa, Oklahoma (traveling)
1963   *Bismark National Indian Art Show*, sponsored by the Chamber of Commerce and Bismark Art Association, Bismark, North Dakota
              Contemporary American Indian Art, United States Department of State, Washington, D.C. (traveling)
1964-65 First Annual Invitational Exhibition of American Indian Paintings, United States Department of the Interior, Washington, D.C.
1978   *100 Years of Native American Painting,* Oklahoma Museum of Art, Oklahoma City, Oklahoma
1981-83 *Native American Painting*, Amarillo Art Center, Amarillo, Texas (traveling)
1984-85 *Indianascher Kunstler* (traveling, Germany), organized by the Philbrook Museum, Tulsa, Oklahoma
1991-96 *Shared Visions: Native American Painters and Sculptors in the Twentieth Century,* The Heard Museum, Phoenix, Arizona

Collections

Bureau of Indian Affairs, United States Department of the Interior, Washington, D.C.; Center for Great Plains Studies, University of Nebraska, Lincoln; Denver Art Museum, Colorado; Eiteljorg Museum, Indianapolis, Indiana; Five Civilized Tribes Museum, Muskogee, Oklahoma; Thomas Gilcrease Institute of American History and Art, Tulsa, Oklahoma; Heritage Center, Inc., Collection, Pine Ridge, South Dakota; Indian Arts and Crafts Board, United States Department of the Interior, Washington, D.C.; Kiva Museum of the Koshare Indian, Boy Scouts of America, La Junta, Colorado; National Museum of the American Indian, Smithsonian Institution, Washington, D.C.; Museum of Northern Arizona, Flagstaff; National Park Service Collection, United States Department of the Interior, Washington, D.C.; Oklahoma State Art Collection, Oklahoma City; Philbrook Museum, Tulsa, Oklahoma; Roswell Museum and Art Center, Roswell, New Mexico; Woolaroc Museum, Bartlesville, Oklahoma.

Publications

On BEAVER: Books—*American Indian Painting of the Southwest and Plains Areas*, by Dorothy Dunn, Albuquerque, University of

New Mexico Press, 1968; *The American Indian Speaks,* John R. Milton, editor, Vermillion, Dakota Press, 1969; *American Indian Painting*, by Jamake Highwater, New York Graphic Society, 1976; *American Indian Painting and Sculpture*, by Patricia Janis Broder, New York, Abbeville Press, 1981; *Indianische Kunst im 20 Jahrhundert*, by Gerhard Hoffman, et al., Münich, Germany, 1984; *Shared Visions: Native American Painters and Sculptors of the Twentieth Century,* by Margaret Archuleta and Rennard Strickland, Phoenix, The Heard Museum, 1991; *Visions of the People: A Pictorial History of Plains Indian Life*, by Evan M. Maurer, Minneapolis Institute of Arts, 1992.

*   *   *

Fred Beaver was a Muskogee (Creek) artist who became one of the best known flat style painters from Oklahoma. He was known primarily, however, for his depiction of Seminole, rather than Muskogee, subjects. Beaver did not initially consider art a career option and took a position with the Indian Service in 1935. In 1945 he was encouraged by Acee Blue Eagle to paint professionally. He submitted entries to Philbrook's first Indian Annual in 1946, then entered more competitions, participated in exhibits, and eventually considered painting his main pursuit. He resigned from his position with the Indian Service in 1960 to devote full time to his art.

Beaver was a self-taught artist. He began drawing before starting school as a child, and although he later attended Bacone College, where he studied art, he was only there a few weeks. Beaver taught himself by looking at books and prints and paintings of other Indian artists. The early Kiowas were especially influential in his own development, and Beaver related his own self-training and independence to theirs:

> As far as I'm concerned this tradition of Indian art, at least here in Oklahoma, was created by people who trained themselves and didn't have very much influence from European art and knew almost nothing about it. The paints and the papers, sure, that came from the whites. But the way we paint, that came from us. Just like I taught myself to paint, so did Mopope and Tsatoke and all those Kiowa boys. I really knew those very first Kiowa boys and I know that [their art teacher] Miss Peters pretty much let them do what they wanted to do. Their art was their own, all the way. That was *true* Indian art.

In the evenings after work, he painted and eventually developed a distinctive style. His paintings are highly decorative yet they also are serious attempts at historical documentation and cultural preservation. Beaver gave attention to authentic detail; well-researched designs became the elements of composition. For instance, in *Florida Seminole Family* (1953), the tribal designs on the family members' clothing become the design focus of the composition itself. This concern for both decorative design and content led to works that are formal and colorful, yet static and relatively without expression. *Florida Seminole Women-Daily Life* (1962) is pleasing to the eye because of harmonious color and interesting pattern. It is an engaging piece also because of its depiction of traditional activities in a Seminole village. It does not, however, contain dramatic action or emotional expression. Beaver was not as concerned with eliciting emotion or drama as he was with accurately portraying tribal culture in aesthetically pleasing paintings.

Fred Beaver: *Seminole Family.* Courtesy Gilcrease Museum, Tulsa, Oklahoma.

For his subjects, he usually chose Creek and Seminole families engaged in either everyday or ceremonial activities. He began painting Seminole subjects upon entering the Philbrook Annual in the 1940s. He was trying to avoid repeating the "feathered Indian" paintings that so many Indian artists seemed to be doing at the time. Portrayal of traditional Seminole life became his central focus, and he researched the tribe and often visited the Florida Seminoles. Paintings such as *Alligator Hunt* (1948) and *Seminoles Bringing in Supplies* (1952) feature tribal dress unique to the Seminoles and refer to everyday tribal activities. Paintings of Creek subjects were often of ceremonial activities, such as in *Creek Women's Ribbon Dance* (1949) and *Sing Ceremony-Eve of the Creek Stickball Game* (1951). Beaver sought to preserve the ways of his people in such paintings. He painted scenes from his childhood and legends told to him by his parents and grandparents. Beaver was one of the few early flat-style painters who brought a focus to the Woodland traditions through easel painting. His success with popularizing Seminole and Creek subjects broadened the range of accepted Native American painting during the 1940s and 1950s.

—Kevin Smith

BECK, Larry

Tribal affiliations: Norton Sound Yupik
Sculptor and mask maker

Born: Lawrence James Beck, Seattle, Washington, 20 May 1938, of Norton Sound Yupik, Norwegian, and English descent. **Education:** Burnley School of Professional Art, Seattle 1960-61; University of Washington, BA in painting, 1964; MFA in sculpture, 1965. **Family:** Married three times, three children. **Career:** Graphic illustrator, Boeing Company; instructor, University of Oregon, Eugene 1966-67, Fidalgo Art Institute, La Conner, Washington, 1969-70, Highline Community College, Midway, Washington, 1971, California State University, Humboldt, 1973-74, Evergreen State College, Olympia, Washington, 1986; Visiting Fine Arts Fellow, University of Southampton, England, 1967-68. **Awards:** First prize, Arts and Architecture Pavilion Show, University of Washington, 1965; First Award, Art in Public Places, Statewide Tactile Arts Competition, 1971; Award for Sculpture, Pacific Northwest Annual, Seattle Art Museum, 1973; National Endowment for the Arts, Artist Trust grant, 1993. Public art commissions include Golden Gardens Park, Seattle; Highline Community College, Midway, Washington; King County International Airport, Seattle; several public sculptures in Seattle. **Died:** 27 March 1994 in Seattle, Washington.

Individual Exhibitions

1965   *Master of Fine Arts Thesis Exhibition,* University of Washington School of Art, Seattle
1973   *Inukshuk Series, Twelve New Sculptures by Lawrence Beck,* Polly Friedlander Gallery, Seattle
1982   Alaska Native Arts and Crafts, Anchorage, Alaska
1985   *The Walrus Provides,* Alaska Native Arts and Crafts, Anchorage, Alaska
1993   *Larry Beck: Masks,* Whatcom Museum of History and Art, Bellingham, Washington

Selected Group Exhibitions

1964   *Pacific Northwest Arts and Crafts,* Bellevue, Washington
        Northwest Annual, Seattle Art Museum, Seattle, Washington
1967   *Reed College Invitational Summer Exhibition,* Portland, Oregon
        Northwest 1967, Seattle Art Museum Pavilion
1968   Studio Open Mouth, University of Southampton, England
        Pacific Northwest Arts and Crafts Invitational Sculpture Exhibition, Bellevue, Washington
1971   *Arts of the Eskimo,* Thomas Burke Museum, University of Washington, Seattle
1972   *Northwest Annual,* Seattle Art Museum Pavilion
1973   *Northwest Annual,* Seattle Art Museum Pavilion
1974   *Skagit Valley Artists,* Seattle Art Museum Pavilion
1975   *The Governor's Invitational Exhibition,* Olympia, Washington
        Northwest Invitational Sculpture Exhibit, Washington State University, Pullman
        The City of Seattle Selects, Henry Gallery, University of Washington, Seattle
1977   *Celebration 1977,* Spokane Invitational Sculpture Exhibit
        Northwest 1977, Seattle Art Museum
        Invitational Group Show, Alaska Visual Arts Center, Anchorage
1979   *Lawrence Beck/Sculpture, Paul Heald/Paintings,* The Henry Gallery, University of Washington, Seattle
1981   *The First Annual December Mask Show,* Sacred Circle Gallery of American Indian Art, Seattle
1982   *The Second Annual December Mask Show,* Sacred Circle Gallery of American Indian Art, Seattle
        Sylvia Lark (Paintings), Lawrence Beck (Sculpture), Sacred Circle Gallery of American Indian Art, Seattle,
1983   *Contemporary Native American Art,* Western Washington University, Bellingham
1984   *Hidden Faces,* Alaska Native Arts and Crafts, Anchorage
        No Beads, No Trinkets, Palais de Nations, United Nations, Geneva, Switzerland
1985   *Visage Transcended: Contemporary Native American Masks,* American Indian Contemporary Arts Gallery, San Francisco
        Beyond Blue Mountains, The Public Art Space, Seattle Center
        Spectrum: Art by Native Americans, Evergreen State University, Olympia, Washington
        Washington/Oregon Artists, American Indian Contemporary Arts Gallery, San Francisco
1986   *Fantasy on Wheels,* Bellevue Art Museum, Washington
        Rick Bartow and Larry Beck, Evergreen State College, Olympia, Washington
        What Is Native American Art?, Philbrook Art Center, Tulsa, Oklahoma
        Alaskamute '86, Institute of Alaska Native Arts, Fairbanks (traveling)
1987   *Seattle Sculpture: 1927-1987,* Bumberbiennial, Seattle Arts Festival
        Double Take, Fine Arts Gallery, Federal Reserve Bank of Kansas City, Missouri
        Masks Facing the World, Whatcom Museum of History and Art, Bellingham, Washington

3rd Biennial Native American Fine Arts Invitational, Heard Museum, Phoenix, Arizona

Masterworks of North American Indian Art, Philbrook Museum of Art, Tulsa, Oklahoma (traveling)

New Directions North West: Contemporary Native American Art, Portland Art Museum, Oregon (traveling)

1987-89 *The Eloquent Object: The Evolution of American Art in Craft Media Since 1945,* Philbrook Museum of Art, Tulsa, Oklahoma (international traveling exhibition)

1988-95 *Artists Respond: A People in Peril,* Visual Art Center of Alaska, Anchorage (traveling)

Crossroads of Continents: Cultures of Siberia and Alaska, Smithsonian Institution, Washington, D.C.

1989 *Crossed Cultures,* Documents Northwest, the PONCHO Series, Seattle Art Museum

1991 *Carriers of the Fire,* American Indian Community House, New York

1993 *Native America: Reflecting Contemporary Realities,* American Indian Contemporary Arts, San Francisco

1994 *Arts from the Arctic, an Exhibition of Circumpolar Art,* Anchorage Museum of History and Art

Collections

Anchorage Museum of History and Fine Art; Bellevue Art Museum, Bellevue, Washington; Caslista Corporation, Anchorage. Alaska; Heard Museum, Phoenix, Arizona; Indian Arts and Crafts Board, U.S. Department of Interior, Washington D.C.; Seattle City Light Gallery; University of Alaska Museum, Fairbanks; Washington State Arts Commission, Olympia.

Publications

On BECK: Books—"Larry Beck," *The Eloquent Object: The Evolution of American Art in Craft Media Since 1945,* Philbrook Museum of Art, Tulsa, Oklahoma, 1987, (reprinted in L. Lippard, *Mixed Blessings,* New York, 1990); "Lawrence Beck," *Artists Respond: A People in Peril,* Visual Art Center of Alaska, Anchorage, 1988; "Larry J. Beck," *Crossroads of Continents: Cultures of Siberia and Alaska,* 1988. Articles—"The Pacific Northwest Today," *Art in America,* October-December, 1968; "Larry Beck," *Journal of Alaska Native Arts,* September-October, 1983; "Larry Beck," *Native Views,* July-August 1986; "After the Art Boom, What? Alaskan and Inuit Art: A Resurgence," *Inuit Art,* vol. 7, no. 1, 1992; "Seattle," *Sculpture Magazine,* July-August, 1994; "Larry Beck," *American Indian Art Magazine,* vol. 12, no. 1, 1995.

*

Larry Beck comments:

When I begin a piece of work—a sculpture or a mask—I want this work to have a certain magic or power.... When my art is working, I have connected with this *tunghat,* or powerful spirit, through the shade of the particular piece. Finding and refining this connection is the essence of my work.

*　　*　　*

Sculptor Larry Beck translated traditional Eskimo approaches to the creation of three-dimensional images into a contemporary idiom, like many late twentieth-century Native artists, reclaiming ancient sensibilities through his own experience as an urban Native. His witty masks and sculptures constructed of car parts and kitchen utensils caught the fancy of public and critics alike and restored an essential Eskimo means of connection between artist, materials, spirit and image. To date, no artists of Alaskan heritage have explored the use of found objects in the way Beck did.

Beck grew up in Seattle. During his university training in the 1970s his work was large scale, free standing and formalist. Angular planes, or flowing parallel bands of cast metals, fabricated steel, or fiberglass, were often titled simultaneously in Yupik and English. One series, which he called *Inukshuks,* meaning presence, sought to capture essential gestures of the *Olrowok Inua* (Spirit of Falling Sideways) or the *Talutak Inua* (Spirit of Curtain).

In the late 1970s, Beck saw a growing interest in Eskimo masks at museums and exhibitions, leading him into experimentation on a smaller, more intimate scale. In a moment of recognition while searching for car parts in a Skagit Valley wrecking yard he saw in them the inspiration for masks of his own. He scavenged junk yards, kitchen shops, and the Boeing surplus warehouse, extracting car mirrors and tires, kitchen utensils, and discarded materials, which suggested the forms and surface qualities of nineteenth century Bering Strait Yupik Eskimo masks. Eskimo artists in generations past created masks of found objects from the village beach after a private experience of awareness, in which a creature revealed its true inner spirit and image, its *inua.* Like his Yupik ancestors, Beck saw new potential in old things, and through them experienced his own inspiration—turning over the chrome mirror of a 1969 Oldsmobile Cutlass to find the reflective orb of a spirit face.

Beck's Wal-ruses hang on the wall—witty allusions to nineteenth-century masks of driftwood that reference the *inuas* of the animals on which the Eskimo were traditionally dependent for survival. Made of the found objects of his twentieth-century American world, Beck's creatures, constructed from oil cans, hubcaps, rivets and tire parts, inspire laughter at their ingenuity, then a shock of recognition. These are fabrications about oil; the influence of the oil industry is displacing the Eskimo subsistence economy and centuries-old connection with the *inua* of the walrus and other animals.

Like those of several Alaskan artists (Tlingit James Schoppert among them) who became aware of Eskimo masks in the 1970s, especially through those pictured in the National Gallery catalog, *The Far North,* Beck's masks sometimes referenced the form of published examples rather closely. Clever, bold and sassy, his masks, such as *Punk Nanuk Inua* (Punk Bear Spirit) and *Ooger Uk Inua* (Punk Walrus Inua), and herds of walruses, showed at scores of public and commercial galleries in the United States and abroad. Some were more exploratory than others, and some images occasionally became redundant, but most contained a visual power to grab the attention of the viewer and generate awareness about the nature of inspiration and its visual manifestation, as well as to amuse. Beck was just beginning to work in a new direction when he died in 1994.

—Kate Duncan

BEGAY, Harrison

Variant names: Haskay Yah Ne Yah
Tribal affiliations: Navajo
Painter and illustrator

Born: White Cone, Arizona, 15 November 1917; Navajo name means Warrior Who Walked Up to His Enemy. **Education:** Fort

Wingate, 1927; self-taught, 1927-34; Santa Fe Indian School, 1934-39; studied architecture at Black Mountain College, North Carolina, 1941-42. **Military Service:** U. S. Army during World War II. **Career:** Farmer; muralist for the Works Projects Administration; painter, 1946—; cofounder, Tewa Enterprises, silkscreen operation. **Awards:** Inter-Tribal Indian Ceremonials 8-time Grand Award; Palmes d'Academiques, 1945.

Individual Exhibitions

1967   *The Sacred Mountains of the Navajo: Four Paintings by Harrison Begay,* Museum of Northern Arizona, Flagstaff
1989   Gumna, Japan

Selected Group Exhibitions

1947-65   *American Indian Paintings from the Permanent Collection,* Philbrook Art Center, Tulsa, Oklahoma (traveling)
1955-56   European tour sponsored by the University of Oklahoma, Norman
1958-61   European tour sponsored by the University of Oklahoma, Norman
1959-60   *Contemporary American Indian Paintings,* New Jersey State Museum, Trenton
1962   Philbrook Art Center, Tulsa, Oklahoma
1963   *Bismark National Indian Art Show,* sponsored by the Chamber of Commerce and Bismark Art Association, Bismark, North Dakota
1964   Read Mullan Gallery of Western Art, Phoenix, Arizona
1964-65   First Annual Invitational Exhibition of American Indian Paintings, United States Department of the Interior, Washington, D.C.
1968   *James T. Bialac Collection of Southwest Indian Paintings,* Arizona State Museum, University of Arizona, Tucson
1973   *American Indian Art, 1920-1972,* The Art Center, Hastings College, Hastings, Nebraska
1975   Heard Museum, Phoenix, Arizona
1978   *100 Years of Native American Painting,* Oklahoma Museum of Art, Oklahoma City, Oklahoma
1979-80   *Native American Paintings,* organized by the Joslyn Art Museum, Omaha, Nebraska (traveling)
1980   *Native American Art at the Philbrook,* Philbrook Museum of Art, Tulsa, Oklahoma
1981-83   *Native American Painting,* Amarillo Art Center, Amarillo, Texas (traveling)
1982   *Native American Painting: Selections from the Museum of the American Indian,* Heard Museum, Phoenix, Arizona
1984-85   *Indianascher Kunstler* (traveling, Germany), organized by the Philbrook Museum, Tulsa, Oklahoma
1986   *When the Rainbow Touches Down,* Heard Museum, Phoenix, Arizona (traveling)
1990   *American Indian Artists in the Avery Collection and the McNay Permanent Collection,* Koogler McNay Art Museum, San Antonio, Texas
1991-92   *Shared Visions: Native American Painters and Sculptors in the Twentieth Century,* The Heard Museum, Phoenix, Arizona

1996   *Drawn from Memory: James T. Bialac Collection of Native American Art,* Heard Museum, Phoenix, Arizona

Collections

Amerind Foundation, Dragoon, Arizona; Arizona State Museum, University of Arizona, Tucson; Center for Great Plains Studies, University of Nebraska, Lincoln; Denver Art Museum, Denver, Colorado; Eiteljorg Museum of American Indians and Western Art, Indianapolis, Indiana; Thomas Gilcrease Institute of American History and Art, Tulsa, Oklahoma; Heard Museum, Phoenix, Arizona; Heritage Center, Inc., Collection, Red Cloud Indian School, Pine Ridge, South Dakota; Joslyn Art Museum, Omaha, Nebraska; Koogler McNay Art Museum, San Antonio, Texas; Montclair Art Museum, Montclair, New Jersey; Museum of New Mexico, Santa Fe; Museum of Northern Arizona, Flagstaff; Philbrook Museum of Art, Tulsa, Oklahoma; Millicent Rogers Foundation Museum, Taos, New Mexico; School of American Research, Santa Fe, New Mexico; Smithsonian Institution, Washington, D.C.; Southeast Museum of the North American Indian, Marathon, Florida; Southwest Museum, Los Angeles; University of Oklahoma, Norman; Wheelwright Museum of the American Indian, Santa Fe, New Mexico; Woolaroc Museum, Bartlesville, Oklahoma.

Publications

By BEGAY: Books illustrated—*Little Indian Basket Maker,* by Ann Nolan Clark, Los Angeles, 1957.

On BEGAY: Books—*American Indian Painters,* by Oscar B. Jacobson and Jeanne D'Ucel, Nice, France, 1950; *A Pictorial History of the American Indian,* by Oliver LaFarge, New York, 1956; *Indian Art in America: The Arts and Crafts of the North American Indian,* by Frederick J. Dockstader, Greenwich, Connecticut, 1962; *American Indian Painting of the Southwest and Plains Areas,* by Dorothy Dunn, Albuquerque: University of New Mexico, 1968; *Indian Painters and White Patrons,* by J. J. Brody, Albuquerque: University of New Mexico Press, 1971; *Song from the Earth: American Indian Painting,* by Jamake Highwater, Boston, 1976; *100 Years of Native American Painting,* exhibition catalog by Arthur Silberman, Oklahoma Museum of Art, Oklahoma City, 1978; *American Indian Painting and Sculpture,* Patricia Broder, New York, 1981; *Indianascher Kunstler,* by Gerhard Hoffman, Munich, 1984; *The Arts of the North American Indian: Native Traditions in Evolution,* Edwin L. Wade, ed., New York: Hudson Hills Press in association with Philbrook Art Center, Tulsa, Oklahoma, 1986; *When the Rainbow Touches Down,* exhibition catalog by Tryntje Van Ness Seymour, Heard Museum, University of Washington Press, 1988; *Beyond Tradition: Native American Art and Its Evolution,* by Jerry and Lois Jacka, Flagstaff, Arizona, 1988; *American Indian Artists in the Avery Collection and the McNay Permanent Collection,* Jean Sherrod Williams, editor, San Antonio, 1990; *Shared Visions: Native American Painters and Sculptors in the Twentieth Century,* by Margaret Archuleta and Dr. Rennard Strickland, New York: The New Press, 1991. **Articles**—"Modern Navajo Water Color Painting," by Linzie W. King Davis, *Arizona Highways,* July 1956; "Navajo Painting," by Katherine Chase, *Plateau,* Vol. 54, No. 1, 1982.

*   *   *

Harrison Begay: *Rounding Up Wild Horses,* 1938. Courtesy Museum of Indian Arts and Culture, Santa Fe.

Harrison Begay was born at White Cone, Arizona, in 1917 and went to school in 1927 at Fort Wingate, staying only a single year. He apparently then schooled himself while living at home and helping with the family's homestead. Begay re-entered school in 1934, at the Santa Fe Indian School, graduating in 1939 as the class salutatorian. He was a student of Dorothy Dunn's Studio—with such classmates as Alan Houser, Andy Tsinajinnie, and Pop Chalee—and studied architecture at Black Mountain College in North Carolina. Begay served three years in the U. S. Army during World War II and since that time has been a full time painter.

Begay is noted for finely detailed paintings based on Navajo life and culture as well as nature. Through the use of a subdued and harmonious palette of hues, he creates lively scenes that are at once calm and beautiful. Begay's hunting paintings, for example, depict the moment at which the hunter and prey are one—the animal serenely grazing, and the hunter's bow pulled and poised for the release. He preferred to paint real life scenes, rather than mythological themes. Friend and teacher Geronima Montoya said of Begay, "He focussed more on the landscape, the red rocks and the mountains and the cliffs, and just Navajo life" (*When the Rainbow Touches Down,* 1988).

In the 1950s Begay cofounded Tewa Enterprises in Santa Fe to sell silkscreen reproductions of his work. Other Native American artists, including Allan Houser, Pop Chalee, and Gerald Nailor sold reproductions through Tewa Enterprises. At the time, this was a bold step, but the continued success of Begay's reproductions and Tewa Enterprises demonstrates his foresight and business acumen.

Begay was awarded the French Palmes d'Académiques in 1954, is included in almost every exhibition and publication on Indian painting, is an internationally-recognized artist, and has been a seminal influence for Navajo painters.

—Bruce Bernstein

BELANGER, Lance
Tribal affiliations: Maliseet
Installation artist

Born: Near the Tobique Reserve in New Brunswick, 1956. **Education:** Manitou Community College, Lamacaza, Quebec, 1976; University of Regina, Saskatchewan, 1977-78. **Career:** Full-time artist, 1982—; artist-in-residence, Banff School of Fine Arts, Banff, Alberta.

Individual Exhibitions

1984	Ottawa City Hall
1985	Vik Gallery, Edmonton
1986	Ottawa City Hall
	Saskatchewan Cultural Exchange Society, Regina
1988	Piewonski Gallery, Santo Domingo, Dominican Republic
1992	Definitely Superior, Thunder Bay, Ontario
1993	*Maliseet Artist Lance Belanger with Lithic Spheres*, Gallery Connexion, Fredricton, New Brunswick
	New Works by Lance Bellanger, Gallery Connexion, Fredricton, New Brunswick
	Neo Lithic Tango, Mercer Union, Toronto
1995	*Tango,* Arts Court, Ottawa
	Burdett Coutts Gallery, Toronto
	Tango, Oakville Art Gallery, Oakville, Ontario
1996	*Tango,* Thunder Bay Art Gallery, Thunder Bay, Ontario
1997	*The Tango in Costa Rica,* National Museum of Costa Rica, San Jose

Selected Group Exhibitions

1982	World Assembly of First Nations, Assinabioa Gallery, Regina, Saskatchewan
1983	*Indian Social Realities,* American Indian Community House Gallery, New York
1984	*Four Aboriginal Artists,* Galerie D'Art, Moncton, New Brunswick
	Points of View, The Community Gallery, New York
1985	Manuge Gallery, Halifax, Nova Scotia
1987	Gallery 1898, Annapolis Valley, Nova Scotia
	Gallery 101, Ottawa
1989	*Indian Art '89,* Woodland Cultural Centre, Brantford, Ontario
	Decelebration, Saw Gallery, Ottawa
1990	*Le Salon de Jeune Peinture,* Le Grand Palais
	Esthetica Diffusa, International Multimedia Centre, Salerno, Italy
	Storie Naturali, Museo d'Arte Contemporanea di Villa Croce, Genoa
1991	Museum of Modern Art, Tampere, Finland
	Andrea Demedtshuis, Saint-Baafs-Vivje, Belgium
	Visions of Power, Leo Kamen Gallery, Toronto
	Fourth Havana Biennial, National Museum of Fine Arts, Havana
	Kwa'nu'te, Micmac and Maliseet Artists, Atlantic Centre, New Brunswick
	Solidarity: Art After Oka, Saw Gallery, Ottawa
1992	*New Territories,* Visions Planetaire, Montreal
	Indigena, Canadian Museum of Civilization, Ottawa
1992-93	*Neolithic Tango,* Mercer Union, Toronto
1993	*Pe'l A'tukwey: Recent Works by Mi'kmaq and Maliseet Artists,* Art Gallery of Nova Scotia, Halifax
	Kulturele Dienst, Gemeentehuis Rijksweg, Belgium
1994	Brandts Klaedefabrik, Odense, Denmark

Collections

Alberta Heritage Collection, Calgary; Canadian Museum of Civilization, Ottawa; Carleton University, Ottawa; Department of Northern and Indian Affairs, Ottawa; Moncton City Hall, New Brunswick; Piewonski Gallery, Santo Domingo; Tranaeker International Sculpture Gardens, Odense, Denmark; Trent University, Trent, Ontario; University of New Brunswick, Halifax; University of Moncton, New Brunswick; Vik Gallery, Edmonton, Alberta; Woodland Cultural Institute, Brantford, Ontario.

Publications

By BELANGER: Article—"Canada to Host International Symposium of Indigenous Artists," *Culture Plus—Unesco,* 1990.

On BELANGER: Books—*Pintor Canadiense Expondria,* Santo Domingo, Dominican Republic, 1988; *Decelebration,* exhibition catalog by Jacqueline Fry and Brian Maracle, Ottawa, 1989; *Indian Art '89,* (exhibition catalog by Tom Hill, Brantford, Ontario, 1989; *Le Salon de Jeune Peinture,* exhibition catalog by Marie Mauze, Paris, 1990. **Articles—**"The Art of the Native Americans" by Jean Sheppard, *New York Daily News,* 4 November 1983; "Native Intelligence" by Lucy R. Lippard, *The Village Voice,* 27 December 1983; "Indigenous Artists of Canada Exhibit" by Diana Hallett, *Ottawa Review,* 11-15 March 1983; "Belanger Indifferent to the Conventional" by Jeff Bear, *AMMSA* (Edmonton), 1983; "Decking the Halls in Lower Midtown" by Diana Freedman, *Artspeak Gallery Review* (New York), Vol. VI, no. 8, 1984; "Imagery Is Challenging, Haunting: Lance Belanger at the Vik Gallery," by Phylis Matousak, *Edmonton Journal,* 28 September 1985; "The Vision Takes Wing" by Mary Ann Smyths, *Artscraft* (Ottawa), Winter 1988; "Dark Reflections" by Glen Allen, *Maclean's Magazine,* 4 May 1992; "Native Artists Seize..." by John Bentley Mays, *Toronto Globe and Mail,* 17 May 1992; "Indigena" by Gerald McMaster, *Art Journal,* Fall 1992; "Indigena" by Robert Powell, *MUSE* (Ottawa), Winter 1993; "Lance Belanger: Tango" by Pat Durr, *ARTSatlantic* 52, Spring/Summer, 1995; "Dancing in from the Margin" by Marcia Kubacki, *ARTSatlantic* 52, Spring/Summer 1995.

*   *   *

Lance Belanger is part of a generation of First Nations artists in Canada who have had the benefit of approximately 40 years of contemporary mainstream activity. From the relative obscurity of the generation of George Clutesi, through the struggles and gains of the likes of the generation of Norval Morrisseau (among the traditionalists) and Robert Houle (among the modernists), Belanger and others have found themselves part of a lively and energized debate regarding the exhibition, interpretation, and collection of the art of the First Nations in Canada. Often this latter generation has represented itself through installation work that concerns itself with current socio-political and cultural issues affecting Native artists and their communities.

Belanger's mature work has been distinguished by an interest in the reproduction and interpretation of the giant stone balls of Costa Rica. The stone balls are Pre-Columbian artifacts found among the ruins of the Taino people—the first people of the new world that Columbus encountered. When Belanger first began his stone ball work around 1990, the project was very much concerned with the

Lance Belanger: Installation, Yukon Art Centre, 1996. Courtesy of the artist.

reclamation of indigenous territories—physical, intellectual, and aesthetic in scope. The artist planted spheres around the globe: in Finland, Cuba, and various sites in the United States and Canada. The artist's intention was, in part, to question the anthropological methodologies historically applied to the interpretation of historic—and until recently—contemporary indigenous art and artifacts.

Subsequently, Belanger's research and interaction with the stone balls and those who study them has led him to the production of a body of installation work concerned with *interpretation*. Using the tango as metaphor, Belanger has initiated a relationship between art and science,

old and new, that recognizes the tensions inherent in the project and searches for alternative foundations in which to view aboriginal art. As Belanger has stated, "the only resolution is to work with the positive elements of the science [of anthropology], positive people in the science and try something different." Belanger's installation work for the project has been the melding of various media (found-objects, sculpture, and video), time periods, and methodologies (art historical, anthropological, and historio-cultural).

Belanger's work is part of a recent and conscious move to reclaim and rewrite history from an indigenous perspective. For the artist, the stone balls of Costa Rica have provided "a cultural and intellectual foundation for the continued emergence and participation of contemporary Aboriginal cultures of the western hemisphere in modern societies." When the present is recalled years from now, the process of indigenous reclamations in art and society will define the intellectual activity of this period. Belanger and his work will be remembered as important within this context.

—Carol Podedworney

BELINDO, Dennis

Variant names: Aun-So-Te
Tribal affiliations: Kiowa; Navajo
Painter

Born: Phoenix, Arizona, 12 December 1938; enrolled member of the Kiowa tribe; Kiowa name, which belonged to his maternal grandfather, translates as "foot." **Education:** Bacone College, 1956-58; BFA, University of Oklahoma, 1962; University of New Mexico, MBA, 1973-74. **Career:** Social activist for Native Americans, President of the Bay Area Native American Council in San Francisco, and negotiator with Native Americans who occupied Alcatraz Island; between officials of the Bureau of Indian Affairs (BIA) and the leaders of the American Indian Movement (AIM) when AIM occupied the Bureau's offices in Washington, D.C.; and when AIM occupied Wounded Knee on the Pine Ridge Indian Reservation in South Dakota. Educator and curriculum consultant, Art/Native American culture awareness, in various public schools and colleges in Oklahoma and California; and painter. **Awards:** First Award, Plains Division, Philbrook Art Indian Annual, Tulsa, Oklahoma, 1960; First place, Poster Division, 1965, and Purchase Award, 1981, Inter-Tribal Indian Ceremonials, Gallup, New Mexico; Merit Award, Trail of Tears Annual, Tahlequah, Oklahoma, 1984; completed a painted tipi utilizing family traditional designs that was presented by the State of Oklahoma to the Prefecturate Government of Kyoto, Japan, by Governor Bellmon and the artist, 1987.

Individual Exhibitions

1967   Heard Museum, Phoenix, Arizona
1981   The Galleria, Norman, Oklahoma
1983   Museum of the Southern Plains Indian, Anadarko, Oklahoma

Selected Group Exhibitions

1965   *Second Annual Invitational Exhibition of American Indian Paintings,* United States Department of the Interior, Washington, D.C.
1967   Northern Plains Indian Museum, Rapid City, South Dakota
1968   Amarillo Art Center, Amarillo, Texas
        Millicent Rogers Museum, Taos, New Mexico
        Abilene Fine Arts Museum, Abilene, Texas
        Museum of Texas Tech University, Lubbock, Texas
1972   *Contemporary Southern Plains Indian Painting,* sponsored by the Southern Plains Indian Museum and the Oklahoma Indian Arts Co-operative, Anadarko, Oklahoma (traveling)

1980   Oklahoma Art Center, Oklahoma City, Oklahoma
1981   Smithsonian Institution, Washington, D.C.
        American Indian Art in the 1980s, Native American Center for the Living Arts, Niagara Falls, New York
1982   Kennedy Center for the Performing Arts, Washington, D.C.
1983   Indian Paint Brush Gallery, Siloam Springs, Arkansas
1984-85 *20 Jahrhundert Hans am Waldese,* Berlin, Germany
        Indianischer Kunstler, organized by Philbrook Museum of Art, Tulsa, Oklahoma (traveling, West Germany)
1985   Martin von Wagner Museum, Wurzburg, Germany
        Jahrhunderthalle Hochst, Frankfurt, Germany
        Von der Heydt Museum, Wuppertal, Germany
        Kunstverein, Mannheim, Germany
        Kunstraum, Hamburg, Germany
1986   Center of the American Indian, Kirkpatrick Center, Oklahoma City, Oklahoma
1989   Center of the American Indian, Kirkpatrick Center, Oklahoma City, Oklahoma
1990-91 Red Earth Indian Center, Oklahoma City, Oklahoma
1991   Center of the American Indian, Kirkpatrick Center, Oklahoma City, Oklahoma
1992   Franco-American Institute Exhibit, Rennes, France
1993   Red Earth Indian Center, Oklahoma City, Oklahoma

Collections

Inter-Tribal Ceremonial Association, Gallup, New Mexico; Robb Moore collection, Oklahoma City, Oklahoma; Oklahoma Historical Society, Oklahoma City; Fred Schonwald Collection, Oklahoma City.

Publications

On BELINDO: Books—*Indian Painters and White Patrons,* by J. J. Brody, Albuquerque, University of New Mexico Press, 1971; *Contemporary Southern Plains Indian Painting,* catalog by Rosemary Ellison, Anadarko, Oklahoma, 1972; *Kiowa Voices:* Vol. 1 (*Ceremonial Dance, Ritual, and Song,* 1981) and Vol. 2 (*Myths, Legends, and Folktales,* 1983), by Maurice Boyd, Fort Worth, Texas; *American Indian Art in the 1980s,* exhibition catalog by Lloyd Kiva New, Niagara Falls, New York, 1981.

*

Dennis Belindo comments (1983):

I am one of several contemporary Kiowa artists who acknowledge an indebtedness to those who have gone before. My artistic contribution to today's society is an extension of my ancestor's gift to me. I consider myself a neo-traditionalist. I employ the traditional Indian painting technique of using form, line and color to record in pictorial narrative the history and material culture of our people. I add to the traditional approach a high degree of self-expression, which is a reflection of me as an individual and encompasses my influences, my training and my experiences. I am fascinated by form, movement, color and tension within the picture plane, however tension which is quieted by balance, harmony, feeling and emotion.

*   *   *

Dennis Belindo: *Kiowa Pow-Wow Dancer.* **Courtesy private collection of John Warner.**

Dennis Belindo is a Kiowa/Navajo painter whose artistic career has been situated primarily in Oklahoma. Belindo executes many paintings featuring Kiowa dancers and members of Kiowa men's societies engaged in various sorts of ceremonial activities. His work is bold, dynamic, and highly expressive. Belindo loves brilliant color juxtapositions and the art public appreciates his bold creations, which are clearly executed with a consummate sense of craftsmanship. Even when he paints a more gentle and mystical scene, his work is still poignant and stirring. In a sense, one might say that his paintings are eloquent.

Belindo's art can be categorized as "transitional modernism." While Belindo's pictures always possess a definite sort of Kiowa subject matter, symbolism, iconography, themes, and motifs, he nevertheless simultaneously employs a distinctive modernist approach and technique. Belindo appears to have one foot in the world of the Kiowa Five flat style and the other foot in the world of modernist expression.

When asked about influences on his art, Belindo cited the examples of Stephen Mopope (Kiowa), Dick West (Cheyenne), and Oscar Howe (Yankton Sioux). Those three sources of inspiration can be seen in Belindo's work, and Quincy Tahoma (Navajo) and Blackbear Bosin (Kiowa/Comanche) can be added as well. West, Howe, Tahoma, and Bosin were post-World War II artists who went beyond the confines of the Santa Fe Studio/Kiowa Five paradigmatic limits, pioneering modernist forms of expression for a subject matter still rooted in tradition (i.e., transitional modernism). Tahoma and Bosin painted pictures that still featured realistic figures but did so with a new flair, drama, theatricality, and Dionysian presence. West, although remaining essentially traditionalist in his own work, used to teach his students to be open to new influences but to retain the superlative craftsmanlike skills that had always characterized the best kinds of Indian art. And Howe, of course, searched out abstraction and European variants of cubism in order to portray subject matter with different planes of geometric shapes and abstractions. Belindo has been influenced by all of these mentors (consciously or unconsciously) and has produced a hybrid, transitional modernist art of his own.

Belindo seems to especially enjoy the subject matter of dancers and Kiowa warrior society activities. For example, in his 1983 one-man exhibition at the Southern Plains Indian Museum & Crafts Center in Anadarko, five paintings are illustrated in the accompanying brochure. The titles of these paintings illuminate Belindo's substantive focus: *Gourd Clan Dancers* (1968), *Eagle Dancer* (1981), *Ohoma Dancers* (1981), *Keepers of the Shields* (1982), and *Medicine Man* (1966). *Medicine Man* is similar to Bosin's work, while in the other four pictures the geometric planes and abstraction of Howe are structurally in evidence. The sense of fidelity, accuracy, and craftsmanship is everywhere to be experienced, as West counseled his students at Bacone College in Muskogee, Oklahoma. Belindo studied at Bacone Junior College in Muskogee (1956-1958) under the guidance of Dick West.

In addition to being a professional painter, Belindo has worked from time to time in art education/Native American culture awareness in various public schools and institutions of higher learning in both Oklahoma and California. He has had an extremely variegated career, including two interesting positions in the 1970s that involved his negotiating skills: As President of the Bay Area Native American Council in San Francisco, he was called upon to assist in negotiations with Indians occupying Alcatraz, and he assisted in negotiations between officials of the Bureau of Indian Affairs (BIA) and the leaders of the American Indian Movement (AIM) when

they occupied the Bureau's offices in Washington, D.C., and later at Wounded Knee. In general, it can be said that Belindo has worked in a variety of civic an educational organizations relevant to Indian affairs over the years. However, since 1978 Belindo has sought to devote ever increasing amounts of time to his painting activities.

—John Anson Warner

BELMORE, Rebecca

Tribal affiliations: Ojibway
Performance artist and installation artist

Born: Upsala, Ontario, 1960. **Education:** Ontario College of Art. **Career:** Artist. **Awards:** Several grants from the Ontario Arts Council.

Individual Exhibitions

1988	*Artifact #671B*, Thunder Bay, Ontario
	Crazy Old Woman Child, Indian Friendship Centre, Thunder Bay
	I'm a High-Tech Teepee Trauma Mama, Native Student Council, Lakehead University, Thunder Bay
	Mushkegokwe/Swampwoman, Women Against Military Madness, Minneapolis
1989	*Nah-doe-tah-moe-win*, Galerie Saw, Ottawa
1992	*Ayumee-aawach Oomama-Mowan: Speaking to Their Mother* (with Marjorie Beaucage), XYZ, Toronto
1993	*Wana-na-wang-ong*, Contemporary Art Gallery, Vancouver
1995	*Tourist Act #1*, Institute of American Indian Art, Santa Fe

Selected Group Exhibitions

1988	*Souvenir from the Northern Front*, Mayworks, Toronto
	See Jane Sew Strontium, Definitely Superior, Thunder Bay
	The New Traditionalists, Definitely Superior, Thunder Bay
1989	*Changers: A Spiritual Renaissance*, National Arts and Crafts Corporation, Ottawa
	Broadcast, Definitely Superior, Thunder Bay
1990	*Biennale d'art actuel*, Quebec City
	Multi-Media Works: A Native Perspective, AKA, Saskatoon
	Telling Things, Art Metropole, Toronto
	Young Contemporaries 90, London Regional Art Gallery
1991	*Bienal de la Habana*, Havana, Cuba
	Okanata, A Space, Toronto
	Between Views, Walter Phillips Gallery, Banff
	Interrogating Identity, Grey Art Gallery, New York
	A Likeness, Agnes Etherington Art Centre, Kingston
1992	*Enduring Strength*, Intermedia Arts and Two Rivers Gallery, Minneapolis
	Land, Spirit, Power, National Gallery of Canada, Ottawa
	Princesses, Indiennes et Cowgirls: Stereotypes de la Frontiere, Oboro, Montreal

1993   *Stand*, Erie, Pennsylvania
        Margins of Memory, Art Gallery of Windsor, Ontario
1994   *Rencontre internationale d'art performance de Quebec*,
            Le Lieu, Quebec City
        Sixth Native American Fine Arts Invitational, The Heard
            Museum, Phoenix
        Faret Tachikawa Art Project, Tokyo
1995   *Longing and Belonging: From the Faraway Nearby*, Santa Fe
        History 101: The Re-Search for Family, St. Louis, Missouri
1996   *Liaisons*, The Power Plant, Toronto
        Metissages, Galerie Optica, Montreal

Publications

By BELMORE: Article—"Autonomous Aboriginal High-Tech Tee-pee Trauma Mama," *Canadian Theatre Review*, No. 68 (Fall 1991).

On BELMORE: Articles—"Changing Directions: A New Perspective on Native Women's Art," by Susan Crean, *Canadian Art*, 1989; "Having Voices and Using Them," by Charlotte Townsend-Gault, *Arts Magazine*, 1991; "Interrogating Identity," by Rachel Weiss, *High Performance*, 1991; "Woodlands Indian Souvenir Art as Visual Text: Reinventing Iconology in the Post-Colonial Age," by Ruth Phillips *Texts 8*, 1992; "Contingent Histories, Aesthetic Politics," by W. Jackson Rushing, *New Art Examiner,* 1993; "Whose Nation?" by Scott Watson, *Canadian Art*, 1993; "Rebecca Belmore: Wana na wang ong," by Robin Laurence, *Canadian Art*, 1994; "Rebecca Belmore," by Charlotte Townsend-Gault, *Parachute*, 1994; "Introducing SITE Santa Fe," by Charles Dee Mitchell, *Art in America*, 1995; "Longing and Belonging: From the Faraway Nearby," by Kathleen Fleming, *Parachute* 1996.

*   *   *

Rebecca Belmore belongs to a generation of First Nations artists in eastern Canada whose work grows out of their awareness of the complexity of their cultural position. A graduate of the Ontario College of Art, Belmore professes an ambivalence toward the art scene—following its international developments, but also drawn to the world of her grandparents' generation and the Anishinabe world view, to which she responds simply by saying: "It is crucial that we speak about our connection to the land." It is this predicament of trans-cultural identity, in conjunction with a belief in the efficacy of hybrid forms of cultural expression, that marks the real difference between her performances and installations and the paintings of Norval Morrisseau and his followers in the Woodland School that emerged in the 1960s from the first shock of the encounter between modern art and a linear style extracted from traditional Ojibway forms.

At a time when the apparent certainties against which modernism chafed have evaporated, so that postmodernism appears to have grown from arbitrariness, Belmore's certainties come from being Ojibway. In part, the effect of her earliest performance works depended, as she intended, on her nativeness to get a hearing. For example, the riotous *I'm a High-Tech Teepee Trauma Mama* has Belmore and her sisters wailing, fraught by ironic contradictions with which they must live; the refrain runs, "I'm a plastic replica of Mother Earth." In *Artifact #671B* she presented herself as a living, labelled and boxed artifact at the side of a road along which the Olympic torch was carried to the 1988 Winter Games in Calgary. It was in dramatic support of the Lubicon and their boycott of *The Spirit Sings*, the exhibition in Calgary for which some of the greatest

Rebecca Belmore: *Rising to the Occasion*. **Photograph by Michael Beynon.**

native art had been retrieved from its international diaspora. The Olympic exhibition was sponsored by Shell Oil, with whom the Lubicon were locked in dispute over use of resources on their land.

These works also show Belmore's early awareness, evident in all her subsequent work, that there are different audiences for art. For this artist, moving away from the defining frame of an art gallery was not only a manoeuvre that recurs for the 20th century avant-garde, and one for which Canadian artists seem to have a particular affinity, but also a move to reach a variety of social groups.

The most spectacular example of this strategy is *Ayumee-aawach Oomama-Mowan: Speaking to Their Mother,* which combines her reach for audiences beyond those normally associated with art and her concern to give voice to the silenced and marginalised. It is a huge and beautifully constructed wooden megaphone designed to be set up out of doors and allowing people to speak directly to Mother Earth—a metaphor for the expression of anguish, anger and concern over what is also referred to as "the environment." Since its first exposure in the Rocky Mountains near Banff in 1991, the work has travelled with Belmore to more than ten sites in First Nations communities, urban and reservation. The Assembly of First Nations used the megaphone to voice their formal Aboriginal Peoples Protest at the exclusion of their representatives from the First Ministers Conference held in Ottawa in June, 1996. It enabled the expression of anger at this persistence of official doublethink, first outside the Prime Minister's residence during the conference dinner, later outside the External Affairs Building. The intent at the second location was not to be ironic but to make a historical point about the distinction between aboriginal nations and the nation called Canada. This move into an overtly political context was the megaphone's ultimate vindication. Belmore comments: "Perhaps I have moved this artwork into a different place by allowing it to enter into an official political realm. Hopefully, it insists and continues to echo: 'we are of this land.'"

Two installations made for specific art galleries show Belmore working within the exclusively art context. They demonstrate her confidence that an Anishinabekwe sensibility informs everything she does, and that labels are not required. *Wana-na-wang-ong* was a transposition of the native name for a place in Ontario where she played as a child, which translates as "curve" and "something beautiful." These ideas she rendered in sand on the gallery floor and in immense curved hangings woven entirely from spruce roots. They are also intended as renderings of the conventions of greenish-brown-painted rectangles to which the Group of Seven's landscape convention could, irreverently, be reduced. *Temple*, made for the Power Plant Gallery situated where the city of Toronto meets the shore of Lake Ontario, is really a temple for the invocation of impurity. More than two thousand plastic bags filled with water, water from a "dead" lake included, are piled into a great geometric cascade—simultaneously beautiful and horrifying. Nearby, a telescope piercing the gallery wall allows another kind of concentrated view of dead water.

A strong idea is often the only link between some very disparate elements in Belmore's works. The genres to which she subscribes reject the classical unities and compositional values; her success with them depends therefore on her ability to blend form with conviction. *New Wilderness*, a piece made for the international exhibition, *Longing and Belonging: From the Faraway Nearby* in 1995, concretises what Belmore described as "a crazy road trip from Sioux Lookout to Santa Fe—lots of Walmart shopping, airport gift shops and weird little places. The Oklahoma City bomb-site was a significant must-see stop." At each of 168 sites (the number of people who died in the bombing) she bought a mug, usually decorated with some goofy native or nature image, and filled it with the local soil. Upon arrival in Santa Fe the mugs were shattered, their shards becoming a mural and the earth forms arranged on metal spikes. The formal devices relate Belmore to the work of British sculptors such as Richard Long and Tony Cragg. She is using an international sculptural idiom to convey her feeling that North America has become a "human wilderness," overlaying "fear and violence" on the land that she treasures.

Belmore does not welcome special treatment for her work as "native," but if it is possible to identify determination and sensibility as native in general, or as Anishinabe in particular, then Belmore's work makes that case with conviction.

—Charlotte Townsend-Gault

BENSON, William and Mary

Tribal affiliations: Pomo
Jewelry designer (William) and basketweavers

WILLIAM. Born: 1862, on a ranch near Kelseyville, California. **Family:** Married 1) a Yokaya Pomo woman; 2) Pomo basketweaver Mary Knight. **Career:** Basketweaver, craftsman, and consultant for Pomo ethnologists; demonstrated basketweaving at various sites around the United States. **Died:** 1937.

MARY. Born: Mary Knight, c. 1879, near Ukiah, California. **Career:** Basketweaver; demonstrated basketweaving at various sites around the United States. **Died:** 4 June 1930.

Selected Group Exhibitions

1904   Louisiana Purchase Exposition, St. Louis World's Fair, St. Louis, Missouri
1979   Museum of the American Indian, New York
1996   Crocker Art Museum, Sacramento, California

Collections

British Museum, London, England; Brooklyn Museum, Brooklyn, New York; Denver Art Museum, Denver, Colorado; Phoebe Apperson Hearst Museum of Anthropology, University of California, Berkeley; Grace Hudson Museum, Ukiah, California; Museum of the American Indian, Washington, D.C.; Peabody Museum, Harvard University, Cambridge, Massachusetts; Smithsonian Institution, Washington, D.C.

Publications

On the BENSONS: Books—"The Basketmaker: The Pomoans of California," by Sally McLendon and Brenda Holland, *The Ancestors: Native Artisans of the Americas*, Anna C. Roosevelt and James G. E. Smith, editors, New York, Museum of the American Indian, 1979; *Objects of Myth and Memory: American Indian Art at The Brooklyn Museum*, by Diana Fane, Ira Jacknix, Lise M. Breen, Brooklyn, The Brooklyn Museum and University of Washington Press, 1991; *The Fine Art of California Indian Basketry*, by Brian Bibby, Sacramento, Crocker Art Museum and Heyday Books, 1996. **Articles**—"Ethnographic Museum Collections and Their Use by Anthropologists," by Bruce Bernstein, *Museum Anthropology*, Vol 13, no. 1, 1989; "Pomo Baskets: The Legacy of William and Mary Benson," by Sally McLendon, *Native Peoples* v. 4, n. 1, 1990.

*   *   *

William Benson created remarkable coiled basketry and ceremonial pieces, including feathered hairpins and belts and finely incised elk horn daggers. Mary Knight, who became William's wife, was also was an exceptional weaver, and by the time she and William married late in the nineteenth century, Mary had developed a distinct, austere style of basketmaking that made her works far exceed utilitarian purposes. Their work captured the attention of collectors, including Dr. John Hudson, Grace Nicholson, and Stewart Culin. Nicholson, a Pasadena art dealer with ties to museums and collectors throughout the United States, became a patron and maintained an inventory of the Bensons' works ("List of Indian Baskets Made by Mary and William Benson, Pomo Tribe," Museum of the American Indian Archives).

Mary Benson was raised in a traditional, Pomo-speaking community that purchased their land late in the nineteenth century and were able to sustain customs, maintaining an above-ground ceremonial house and a traditional, semisubterranean sweat house, for example. She learned

Mary Benson: Boat basket, c. 1900. Photograph by Seth Roffman; courtesy Dr. Gregory Schaaf collection.

to weave baskets for utilitarian purposes but created such perfect, harmonious designs that the baskets became prized by collectors by the time she reached her early twenties and married William. In traditional fashion, Mary gathered her materials: sedge root from a grass that grows along creek banks, which gave the baskets a tan shade; redbud, with thin succor stems two to three feet long; and bulrush roots, often dyed black. These materials were used to form the shell, and the baskets' inner rods were often made from willow, with one to three carefully-shaved willow rods composing the foundation. A metal tipped awl is poked through the foundation and the weft is sewn round and round. Sally McClendon (*Native Peoples*, 1990) characterized Mary Benson's style: "The design compositions of Mary Benson's baskets have a certain austere beauty. . . Mary Benson was clearly producing art objects—museum material and no longer the stuff of everyday life."

William made ceremonial pieces and commercial products, including ear ornaments, beads, and pendants. For ceremonial use he created dance dress accessories, such as ear ornaments made with bone or wood and adorned with colorful feathers from quail, red woodpecker, and goldfinch. Mary and William also made feather baskets, weaving the feathers into the design as opposed to adding them on. Clamshells and abalone shells (with their light rainbow glaze) were among the materials William used in creating jewelry. The couple's baskets and ornaments extended and expanded upon centuries-old practices, and the success they enjoyed provided a steady source of income. They shared their crafts with fellow Pomo, helping to keep traditions alive during a time of forced cultural assimilation into American society. Both of the Bensons died in the 1930s, at a time when Pomo basketry sadly was experiencing a decline.

However, William and Mary traveled across the country during the first two decades of the twentieth century, demonstrating their remarkable skills. In 1904, for example, Dr. Hudson commissioned

them to exhibit their pieces and demonstrate their methods at the Louisiana Purchase Exposition in St. Louis, where they both won prizes. In 1907, the Bensons met Culin, who represented the Brooklyn Museum and commissioned a number of Pomo ethnographic items. While many of these items are representative of Pomoan tradition, the Bensons' creations were often quite innovative and individualistic. An excellent example is a micro-mini basket (1/8" x 3/8") that William wove around a faceted garnet on a gold stick pin, a remarkable manipulation of materials and craftsmanship on such a minute scale. California Native artist Frank Tuttle pointed out:

> The notion that it was somehow built around that stone in there is just amazing, almost unbelievable. Baskets have this sort of historical sense about them.... We think of the making of baskets as being sort of limited—technique-wise, material-wise—in order to fit into certain criteria. And then here's this beautiful pin, this obvious example of manipulation of materials and technical wizardry, and we want to attribute it to a more recent time, because we're more familiar with micro-chips and other types of small things. Given all those decades ago, it's quite a creation.

—Gregory Schaaf

BETHEL, Carrie

Tribal affiliations: Mono Lake Paiute
Basketweaver

Born: Carrie McGowan in Lee Vining, California, 4 July 1898.
Family: Married 1) an unidentified Paiute man (divorced); 2) Harry

Carrie Bethel: Coiled basket, 1933. Courtesy National Park Service, Yosemite Museum, Yosemite National Park, California.

Bethel (divorced prior to 1960). **Career:** Completed first three-rod coiled basket in 1910. Worked as a cook for road crews and at a variety of domestic jobs throughout her adult life. **Died:** 24 February 1974.

Individual Exhibitions

Exhibition data is incomplete. The artist is not known to have kept records of exhibits, and all of her personal papers were destroyed in a fire c. 1970. The following list is derived from a variety of sources:

1926	Indian Field Days, Yosemite Valley, California
1929	Indian Field Days, Yosemite Valley, California
	June Lake Field Days, June Lake, California
1939	Golden Gate International Exhibition, Treasure Island, San Francisco
1973-96	Yosemite Museum, Yosemite National Park, California
1996	The Old Schoolhouse Museum, Lee Vining, California

Selected Group Exhibitions

1994-95	*Revivals: Diverse Traditions: 1920-1945*, American Craft Museum, New York
1996	*The Fine Art of California Basketry*; Crocker Art Museum, Sacramento

Collections

The Old Schoolhouse Museum, Lee Vining, California; Yosemite Museum, National Park Service, Yosemite National Park, California.

Publications

On BETHEL: Books—*The Story of Early Mono County* by Ella M. Cain, San Francisco 1961; *Tradition and Innovation: A Basket History of the Indians of the Yosemite-Mono Lake Area* by Craig D. Bates and Martha J. Lee, Yosemite, 1990; *The Fine Art of California Basketry* by Brian Bibby, Sacramento 1996. **Articles**—

"Miwok-Paiute Basketry 1920-1928: Genesis of an Art Form," by Craig Bates, *American Indian Art Magazine* 4(4):54-59, 1979; "Made For Sale: Baskets from the Yosemite-Mono Lake Region of California," by Craig Bates, *Moccasin Tracks* 7:4, 1981; "Ethnographic Collections at Yosemite National Park," by Craig Bates, *American Indian Art Magazine* 7(32):28-35, 1982; "Yosemite Miwok-Paiute Basketry: A Study in Cultural Change," by Craig Bates, *American Indian Basketry Magazine* II(4):23-29, 1982; "Yosemite: A Melting Pot for Indian People and Their Baskets," by Craig Bates and Martha J. Lee in *Strands of Time: Yokuts, Mono and Miwok Basketmakers*, Fresno 1988.

*   *   *

Carrie Bethel, whose career as a weaver spanned the first three-quarters of the twentieth century, was perhaps the most innovative of all the weavers of the Yosemite-Mono Lake region. At the time of her death she was the last weaver making the fancy-style baskets for which the Yosemite-Mono Lake region was known.

Bethel learned to weave baskets as a child. Her first completed basket in 1910 was made in three-rod technique with a split willow background. It had an unusual redbud and bracken fern root design of ducks and flowers that was copied from a crochet book. By the 1920s Bethel was an accomplished weaver and a prominent competitor in the Yosemite and June Lake Indian Field Days celebrations. She enjoyed a special artist-patron relationship with basket collector James Schwabacher, who purchased most of her larger baskets. In 1929 Bethel demonstrated at the Indian Exhibition of the Golden Gate International Exposition, held on Treasure Island near San Francisco, and her baskets were sold at the trading post there. Although she derived part of her income from selling her baskets, she also worked in a variety of domestic jobs throughout her life, including cooking for road crews and doing laundry at hotels.

Bethel made baskets in three techniques throughout her career: her twined, single-rod coiled, and three-rod coiled baskets were all consistently well executed. Her baskets show a characteristic attention to careful trimming of materials, design placement and stitching. By the 1920s Bethel was well known for her neat, new-style, three-rod baskets with complex red and black patterns, and, with few changes, she produced these baskets into the 1960s. In her later years there was less demand for large (more expensive) new-style baskets, and between 1950 and 1970 she produced many beaded, twined, spaced-stitched three-rod, single rod, and small new-style coiled baskets. One of her finest new-style baskets, a large globular coiled basket with ornate red-and-black patterning in the Field Days style, was completed, however, in about 1960.

By the 1930s Bethel was producing a unique style of miniature beaded basket that she would continue to create until her death. These were all of a similar size, about two inches in diameter and three-quarter inches in height, and were neatly and evenly executed in a variety of complex patterns with small, multi-colored glass beads. In addition to the miniature baskets, Bethel also produced larger beaded baskets, some of which had fitted, beaded lids.

Carrie Bethel's work exemplified the finest weaving of the Yosemite-Mono Lake region. Free from the constraints of traditional patterns and of baskets made for native use, Bethel took basket weaving into a new dimension of creativity. It is unfortunate that she was the last producer of this weaving style.

—Craig Bates

BEVINS, Susie
Tribal affiliations: Inupiat
Mask maker and carver

Born: Prudhoe Bay, Alaska, 1941; surnames have been Ericsen, Qimmiqsak, Beechie, and Beechey. **Education:** Atlanta School of Art, Atlanta, Georgia, 1968-69; Anchorage Community College, Anchorage, Alaska, 1970-71. **Career:** Commissioner, Anchorage Museum of History and Art; Board of Trustees, Anchorage Advisory Arts Commission, Institute of Alaska Native Arts; Second Circle Board, Atlatl, Panelist, Municipality of Anchorage One-Percent For Art; Co-Chair, Arts from the Arctic UNESCO Project; Board of Directors 1987-90, Visual Arts Center of Alaska, Director/Coordinator 1985-86, VACANAW Native Artists Workshop Symposium; Native Arts Panelist 1989-90, Alaska State Council on the Arts. Artist-in-residence, Visual Arts Center, Anchorage, Alaska, 1980-87; guest lecturer at University of Alaska, Alaska Pacific University, Anchorage Museum of History and Art; guest instructor, Anchorage School District, Indian Cultural Program. **Awards:** Research Grant, Institute of Alaska Native Arts, 1985; Travel Grants, Alaska State Council on the Arts, 1987-88; Arts Endowment, Alaska Native Heritage Park Art Auction, Cook Inlet Region Foundation, Inc., 1990.

Individual Exhibitions

1983	*Transition*, A.N.A.C. Gallery, Anchorage, Alaska
1984	*Praise to the Father Spirit*, Visual Arts Center of Alaska, Anchorage, Alaska
	Reflections of a Time Past, Alaska Gallery, New York
1988	*Artists Respond: A People in Peril*, Visual Arts Center of Alaska, Anchorage
1989	*Crossed Cultures*, Seattle Art Museum, Seattle, Washington
	As In Her Vision, American Indian Contemporary Arts, San Francisco, California

Selected Group Exhibitions

1982	University of Oregon Museum of Art, Eugene, Oregon
1983	*Earth, Fire, Fiber*, Anchorage Museum of History and Art, Anchorage, Alaska
1984	Alaska Gallery, New York
1985	*Traditions/Innovations*, Stonington Gallery, Seattle, Washington
	Native American Traveling Show to Japan, Emerald Visions Gallery, Eugene Oregon
1986	*Midnight Dream Mask*, Pegasus Gallery, Corvallis, Oregon
	Alaska/New York Dialogue, A.R.C.O. Gallery, Anchorage, Alaska
1987	*New Directions Northwest*, Portland Art Museum, Portland, Oregon
1988	*Artists Respond: A People in Peril*, Visual Arts Center of Alaska, Anchorage, Alaska
1989	*Crossed Cultures*, Seattle Art Museum, Seattle, Washington
	As In Her Vision, American Indian Contemporary Arts, San Francisco

1990   *XIII All Alaska Juried Art Exhibition*, Anchorage Museum of History and Art, Anchorage, Alaska
1992   The 5th Biennial Native American Fine Art Invitational, The Heard Museum, Phoenix, Arizona
        Portfolio III: Ten Native American Artists, American Indian Contemporary Arts, San Francisco
        Decolonizing the Mind, Center for Contemporary Art, Seattle, Washington
1992-94 *The Submuloc Show/Columbus Whos*, organized by Atlatl, Phoenix, Arizona (traveling)
1993   *Native America: Reflecting on Contemporary Realities*, American Indian Contemporary Arts, San Francisco

Collections

Anchorage Museum of History and Art, Anchorage, Alaska; Municipality of Anchorage, Alaska; Portland Art Museum, Portland, Oregon; State of Alaska 1% For Art in Public Places, Juneau.

Publications

On BEVINS: Books—*Contemporary American Women Sculptors*, by Virginia Watson-Jones, New York, 1986. **Articles**—"Sculptor Catches Soul in Stone," *Alaska Woman* Magazine, August, 1983; "I am Qimmiqsak: A Rebirth of Cultural Pride," in *Alaska Native News* Magazine, Fall 1985; "Sound Sculpture in the North," by Jan Ingram, *Art Week*, January, 1986; "Transitions," by Carol Phillips, *Alaska Horizons,* November, 1986; "Art Resolves Conflict for Women," by Judy Stone in *San Francisco Chronicle,* 1988.

*   *   *

Susie Bevins was born in 1941 at Prudhoe Bay, a remote community on the northern coast of Alaska, to an elderly English trader and his Norwegian-Eskimo wife. Her father died while Bevins was still an infant, and her mother took her to live at Point Barrow and soon remarried. At the age of eleven, Bevins and her family again relocated, this time to Anchorage. As a young woman Bevins studied the fine arts in Anchorage, Georgia, and Italy and is currently one of the most well known contemporary Eskimo artists.

Bevins's personal history and experiences are the primary focus of her mixed-media work: "My artistic expression draws from childhood memories, interpersonal relationships and spiritual faith, together with values, emotions and conflicts derived from my cross-cultural experiences." Yet this was not always so. Early in her career Bevins encountered narrow expectations concerning what she, as a female Eskimo artist, should produce. While Eskimos are generally known for their small ivory sculptures, Eskimo women are recognized for their sewing, and at one point it was suggested to Bevins that she make traditional objects, such as parkas. Although her early work consists of "images I have seen somewhere and attempt(ed) to copy," Bevins felt profoundly conflicted with this mode of artistic expression. Despite her "traditional" upbringing, Bevins never felt totally at ease with the greater Eskimo community. Her mixed ancestry, which is evident in her fair coloring, has long complicated her search for cultural and individual identity. Also, having studied a wide variety of artistic traditions and processes, Bevins did not care to be "bound by tradition."

An important event in her personal life that profoundly affected her artistic career was a journey Bevins made in the early 1970s to Beechey Point. On family lands, she and her mother set up camp for three weeks and hunted caribou. During this time in isolation, through personal contemplation, Bevins made peace with herself concerning her mixed heritage and realized that art—both the process and product—is a vehicle in which to creatively explore and express her concerns.

Bevins has also found guidance and support in other Native artists, such as the late James Schoppert, with whom she studied at the University of Anchorage. Throughout his career Schoppert (an artist of Tlingit/Tahltan ancestry) sought to integrate his personal style with his cultural traditions and was extremely articulate on the subject of artistic integrity as a Native artist living in the late twentieth century. Contemporary Native artists often risk rejection because their work is neither traditional enough for one's community nor stereotypical enough for the art market. Consequently, Bevins thinks it is important for Native artists to support each other in their endeavors and has developed friendships with other "non-traditional" Native artists, including Joe Feddersen and John Hoover.

Bevins's work is explicit in both content and form. For example the mask, *Split Personality*, consists of two halves that are cubistically divided and slightly askew. One half of the visage bears a lip labret, a traditional adornment of the Eskimo, while this ethnic signifier is conspicuously absent on the other half of the mask. In *People in Peril*, Bevins presents four human figures with their internal viscera exposed. While the "x-ray" representation of internal anatomy is an ancient Eskimo stylistic trait, she unites this with her own concerns to create a visually provocative commentary on the devastating influence of alcoholism in the north. The thematic nature of Bevins oeuvre is evident in her expressive titles, like *Grieving Spirit, Bound by Tradition,* and *Divided Heritage*.

Bevins is now a well known and respected member of the greater Alaskan art community. As an artist in residence, Bevins shares her knowledge and experience as a teacher and lecturer and has been an active member of the Visual Arts Center of Alaska for several years. Her desire to unite artists has been manifested in her participation in workshops, symposiums, and numerous group shows.

—Kristin Potter

BIG BEAR, Frank

Tribal affiliations: Anishnabe
Painter

Born: Frank Big Bear, Jr., White Earth reservation, Minnesota, 8 July 1953. **Education:** University of Minnesota, studying with George Morrison in Studio Arts. **Career:** Artist in residence at Heart of the Earth School in Minneapolis, Minnesota, 1973. **Awards:** Grants from the Jerome Foundation (1982), the Bush Foundation (1986 and 1992), and the McKnight Foundation (1992).

Individual Exhibitions

1984   Breams Gallery, St. Paul, Minnesota
1985   Bockley Gallery, New York and Minneapolis (annual through 1989)
1987   North Dakota Museum of Art, Grand Forks, North Dakota

Plains Art Museum, Moorehead, Minnesota

1989   Bethel College and Seminary, St. Paul, Minnesota

1991   Rochester Art Center, Rochester, Minnesota

1992   *Works on Paper 1984-1991*, Two Rivers Gallery, Minneapolis

1994   *Out of the North*, Institute of American Indian Arts Museum, Santa Fe

Bockley Gallery, Minneapolis

1996   Johnson Heritage Post Art Gallery, Grand Marais, Minnesota

1997   The Jacobson Foundation, Norman, Oklahoma

Selected Group Exhibitions

1983   Gallery 10, New York

Project Studios One, New York

1985   *Homecomings: Native American Artists,* North Dakota Museum of Art, Grand Forks

Jewels of the Desert, Philadelphia Museum of Art

1987   *The Drawing Show,* Katherine Nash Gallery, University of Minnesota, Minneapolis

1989   *Heard Biennial,* Heard Museum, Phoenix, Arizona

1990   *Metaphorical Fish,* University Gallery, University of Minnesota, Minneapolis

Artists Conceptions: How We See Our Past, Minnesota Historical Society, St. Paul

Endangered: Visual Art by Men of Color, Intermedia Arts Gallery, Minneapolis

1991   *Paper Dreams on Fire,* Minnesota Artists Exhibition Program, Minneapolis Institute of Arts

1992   The Ojibwe Art Expo

Centered Margins: Contemporary Art of the Americas Toward a Post-Colonial Culture, Bowling Green State University, Bowling Green, Ohio

Enduring Strength, Two Rivers Gallery and Intermedia Arts Gallery, Minneapolis

1993   *Six McKnight Artists,* MCAD Gallery, Minneapolis College of Art and Design, Steensland Art Museum, Northfield, Minnesota, St. Mary's College, Winona, Minnesota

Collections

Dayton Hudson Collection, Minneapolis; General Mills, Minneapolis; Minneapolis Institute of the Arts; Minnesota Historical Society, St. Paul; Minnesota Museum of American Art, St. Paul; Plains Art Museum, Moorehead, Minnesota; North Dakota Museum of Art, Grand Forks; St. Cloud University, St. Cloud, Minnesota; St. Paul Companies, Minnesota; Walker Art Center, Minneapolis; Frederick R. Wiseman Art Museum, Minneapolis.

Publications

On BIG BEAR: Books—*Song From the Earth: American Indian Painting* by Jamake Highwater, Boston, 1976; *Tradition and Innovation,* exhibition catalog, Plains Art Museum, 1988; *Mixed Blessings: New Art in a Multicultural America* by Lucy Lippard, New York 1990; *Metaphorical Fish,* exhibition catalog, University of Minnesota Art Museum, 1990. **Articles**—"The Traditional Present," *Artpaper,* December 1986; "The Odd and Lovely Line We Call Line," *Artpaper,* May 1987; "Frank Bigbear Jr.," *Artforum,* 1987; "People to Watch: Frank Big Bear, Jr.," *Minnesota Monthly,* June 1989; "Frank Big Bear, Jr.," *American Indian Art Magazine,* Winter 1989.

*

Frank Big Bear comments:

I see things. One time [during my early years] I was alone in the farmhouse; I heard a voice upstairs, and I saw these bears coming down. I was afraid they were going to kill me. Maybe that's why I'm an artist now, because of my imagination.

*   *   *

An unnerving complicity links Frank Big Bear's eye with the world, but deducing the nature of that complicity can be a tricky business. Frequently intensely personal, Big Bear's seemingly chaotic imagery demands intense scrutiny if one is to decipher its wider themes. Although often compared with the cataclysmic turmoil depicted by Netherlands painter Hieronymus Bosch, Big Bear's portrayals speak more of survival than damnation. For his visual vocabulary Big Bear cites lived experience and, in an ironic turnabout, Picasso—well known for his cultural appropriations. While cubism overturned prevailing traditions in European art, Big Bear's abstraction challenges representations that claim to depict Native American realities.

Big Bear is a storyteller. Rendered in Prisma color pencils and/or paint, his stories reflect the sense of immanence that is the strength of tribal stories. Themes of survival abound. From his earliest childhood drawings executed on brown paper bags, Big Bear's art has provided an outlet for a rich imagination. Imagination and the images through which it is realized defy their paper boundaries, spilling over the edges to eschew physical constraints of time and space.

Although it is tempting to seek parallels between Big Bear's images and Surrealism's allusions to the unconscious, his visions and images have physical manifestations, are therefore social, and thus a social force. Big Bear's creativity transcends representative processes that would delimit and contain the meanings of Indian identity.

A number of compelling works from the 1980s hint at Big Bear's aesthetic strategies. In *Urban Spirits* and *Red Boy,* Big Bear harnesses the energy of colors simultaneously violent and joyful to the force of vigorous lines. In *Urban Spirits,* color and line define the decay of an urban ghetto in which a mirror reflects the ravaging effects of alcohol. *Red Boy's* display of color draws the viewer into a world dominated by a grotesquely twisted, yet paradoxically triumphant, figure who is holding aloft a mirror. *Playful Evening Spirits* introduces a warrior shown contemplating his pale and dark reflection. Big Bear's subject matter is frequently concerned with perception and its tools, such as mirrors. Abstraction, like the humor in oral stories, has the capacity to liberate while preserving ego and deflecting hostility. Aesthetically and philosophically, identity is neither essentialized nor cast in self-identical terms, but emerges as a cumulative history of human relations marked by relocation, alcoholism and poverty.

Again in later works, such as *Broken Hearts/Broken Dreams* from 1992, style and content collaborate with color. Burnt orange, acidic green, fuschia and blue clash, imbuing the bar-room scene with an aura of unreality. Cubism skews the physiognomy of the faces of several Native Americans gathered around a table. Outside and in the distance stands a twisted, barren tree. Paradoxically, the table's beer bottles and pack of Marlboros stand out in sharp relief. The image overflows with contradictions, a sense of natural reason turned awry.

Big Bear's mode of abstraction appears to be quite central to his art. Resistance to fixing the subject is essential in interplays between style and content. His art testifies to the extraordinary impact of Western urbanity and consumerism on Native Americans. Yet Big Bear's images are more than prevailing metaphors for acts of human consciousness. They are citational acts that serve as critical resources for rethinking the formation of identity. As such they are performative in nature. And it is through these images, his art, that Big Bear, an Indian artist working in an urban setting, identifies himself as Anishnabe.

—Marilee Jantzer-White

BIG LEFTHANDED

Variant names: Klah Tso; Old Hostin Claw
Tribal affiliations: Navajo
Painter

Career: All paintings attributed to Big Lefthanded are dated between 1905-1912 by scholars and were composed around Indian Wells and Tuba City, Arizona.

Collections

Museum of Northern Arizona, Katherine Harvey Collection, Flagstaff, Arizona; Smithsonian Institution, Washington, D.C.

Publications

On BIG LEFTHANDED: Books—*Navaho Indian Painting: Symbolism, Artistry, and Psychology,* by Leland C. Wyman, Boston, 1959; *Indian Painters and White Patrons*, by J. J. Brody, Albuquerque, 1971. **Articles**—"Big Lefthanded: Pioneer Navajo Artist," by Leland C. Wyman, *Plateau,* Summer 1967.

*　*　*

Big Lefthanded is credited with five secular paintings, including one of a village scene, and 28 reproductions of Navajo sacred ceremonies, which he produced for Matthew M. Murphy, a trader and Navajo agent. These works are generally dated from 1905 to 1910, though some sources have listed them as having been started as early as 1902 and completed as late as 1913. Big Lefthanded, a Navajo singer and performer of rites, was among the first southwestern artists recorded by white people to engage in commissioned and secular art and to use commercial watercolors as part of his repertoire.

Two other Navajo artists, Choh and Apie-Begay, along with Big Lefthanded, are grouped as the earliest Navajo artists recorded in history by non-Native Americans. Choh and Big Lefthanded were considered by some sources to be the same person, but scholarship since the mid-1960s distinguishes between them. In 1889, ethnographer Robert Wilson Shufeldt published a drawing of a locomotive and credited the artist as "Choh," who was known to have been

born in the mid-1850s and was a nephew of Navajo Chief, Mariano. Shufeldt first encountered Choh drawing with colored pencils on paper in the late 1880s at Fort Wingate, in Arizona territory. Shufeldt recorded, "The first time I overlooked Choh to see what he was about he was laboring away at a gaudily dressed chief riding at full tilt upon his Indian steed. His work was rather above that of the average Indian artist." This is probably the first published piece of Western art criticism on a Navajo artist, with standards established outside the community. Apie Begay produced a sketch of Ye'i (supernatural beings) for Dr. Kenneth Chapman around 1902, and about that same time, Matthew M. Murphy, a trader and agent who worked among the Navajo, commissioned Big Lefthanded for a series of paintings that were rendered with the common pigments and adhesives used by Native artists as well as opaque commercial watercolors and commercial oils. The Smithsonian Institution owns all but one, which is held by the Museum of Northern Arizona, depicting two dancers performing in the Mountainway—a ceremonial with nine all-night performances, dances and chants; the Mountainway is a dwelling place of mythical figures, and the nine-night chant, perfomed between the first frost of autumn and the first thunderstorm of spring, is enacted for healing purposes, as the infirm are central figures during the ceremonies, assisted by ritual performers who help them receive cures for their maladies.

The Smithsonian pieces offer further glimpses at the Mountainway and Nightway ceremonies. One piece shows god-impersonators about ready to perform, preparing to be sprinkled with corn meal by the chanter, who reaches for a basket carried by an ill person; details in the scene include a hogan, the chanter, the patient and basket, a talking God, six male and female gods, a person who sprinkles water, and a dressing area; the male gods hold rattles and feather sprigs, while the females only hold feather sprigs. Another painting illustrates the Navajo Feather Dance, featuring two dancers each within a personal space represented by a ground line.

Of the five secular paintings attributed to Big Lefthanded in the Smithsonian collection, one shows galloping horses raising a cloud of dust: the action and the attitudes of the riders "make this one of the loveliest known early American Indian paintings," according to Leland C. Wyman. As in all of Big Lefthanded's work, proportions are non-naturalistic; dancers have elongated bodies, short limbs and small heads; space is not defined, except for occassional ground lines; and viewpoints are combined. The separate ground lines seem less important for realistic purposes than for the symbolic importance attributed to the figure depicted. Big Lefthanded's paintings are finely executed, from costumes and sequences to particular roles and approaches, offering fascinating glimpses of significant cultural rituals.

—Roger Matuz

BISS, Earl

Variant names: Meadow Lark Boy; Spotted Horse
Tribal affiliations: Crow; Chippewa
Painter

Born: Renton, Washington, 29 September 1947; Meadow Lark Boy was his name as a child, Spotted Horse is his name as a man. **Education:** Institute of American Indian Arts, 1966; San Francisco

Art Institute, 1966-72, BA; independent study, The Netherlands, Greece, and France, 1973.

Individual Exhibitions

1969	Yakima Regional Library, Yakima, Washington
	Collectors Gallery, Seattle, Washington
1972	Britton Gallery, San Francisco, California
	Museum of the Plains Indian, Browning, Montana
1974	Jaid Gallery, Richland, Washington
1975	Institute of American Indian Arts Museum, Santa Fe, New Mexico
	Sun Spirits Gallery, Santa Fe, New Mexico
1975-77	Elaine Horwitch Gallery, Scottsdale, Arizona
1978	Museum of the American Indian, Wichita, Kansas
	Linda McAdoo Gallery, Scottsdale, Arizona
	The Squash Blossom Gallery, Chicago
	The Jamison Galleries, Santa Fe, New Mexico

Selected Group Exhibitions

1965	*Young American Indian Artists,* Riverside Museum, New York
	New Mexico Museum of Fine Art, Santa Fe, New Mexico
	Institute of Contemporary Indian Art, Washington, D.C.
1966	Edinburgh Festival, Edinburgh, Scotland
	Berlin Festival, West Berlin, Germany
1967	Center for the Arts of Indian America, Washington, D.C.
	Alaskan Centennial, Anchorage, Alaska
1968	American Indian Historical Society, San Francisco
	Spring Show, San Francisco Art Institute
1970	World's Fair, Osaka, Japan
1971	San Jose Museum of Fine Art, San Jose, California
1972	Central Washington State College, Ellensburgh, Washington
1973	Capricorn Asunder Gallery, San Francisco
	Amon Carter Institute of American Indian Arts, Fort Worth, Texas (traveling)
1973-74	*New Directions,* Institute of American Indian Arts, Santa Fe (traveling)
1974	New Mexico Museum of Fine Art, Santa Fe, New Mexico
	Institute of American Indian Arts Alumni Exhibition, Amon Carter Museum of Western Art, Fort Worth, Texas
1975	Crimson Cliffs Gallery, Sedona, Arizona
	Sculpture, Heard Museum, Phoenix, Arizona
	Thompson and Son Gallery, Aspen, Colorado
	Frisco Gallery, San Francisco, California
	Sun Spirits Gallery, Santa Fe, New Mexico
	Janus Gallery, Santa Fe, New Mexico
	Elaine Horwitch Gallery, Scottsdale, Arizona
1978	Wheelwright Museum of the American Indian, Santa Fe, New Mexico
1979	*The Real People,* International Native American Council of Arts, Casa de las Americas, Havana, Cuba
1981	Buffalo Bill Historical Center, Cody, Wyoming
1982	Buscaglia-Castelani Art Gallery, Niagara University, Niagara Falls, New York
1983	Heard Museum, Phoenix, Arizona
1984-85	*Indianascher Kunstler* (traveling, Germany), organized by the Philbrook Museum, Tulsa, Oklahoma
1987	San Jose State College, San Jose, California
1989	*Paint, Bronze and Stone,* Mitchell Indian Museum, Kendall College, Evanston, Illinois
1991	*One With the Earth,* organized by the Institute of American Indian Arts and Alaska Culture and Arts Development, Santa Fe, New Mexico
1992	*Creativity Is Our Tradition,* Institute of American Indian Arts Museum, Santa Fe, New Mexico

Publications

On BISS: Books—*Institute of American Indian Arts Alumni Exhibition,* by Lloyd Kiva New, Fort Worth, Texas, 1974; *Song from the Earth: American Indian Painting,* by Jamake Highwater, Boston, 1976; *Magic Images: Contemporary Native American Art,* by Edwin L. Wade and Rennard Strickland, Norman, Oklahoma, 1981; *Indianascher Kunstler,* by Gerhard Hoffman, Munich, 1984; *The Arts of the North American Indian: Native Traditions in Evolution,* Edwin L. Wade, ed., New York: Hudson Hills Press in association with Philbrook Art Center, Tulsa, Oklahoma, 1986; *Creativity Is Our Tradition,* by Rick Hill, Santa Fe, 1992. **Articles**—"Biss," by Gwen Battle Horne, *Southwest Art* magazine, Winter 1977-78; "Earl Biss Paints a Perfect Dream: Windows to Another Tie and Place," and interview, *SunStorm* magazine, December 1989.

*

Earl Biss comments (December 1989):

I believe my work was most influenced by the works of the European masters, the violent translucent skies of Turner, the impressionistic brush work of Monet ... I also have a great admiration for the stark emotional statements of Edvard Munch and Kokoschka. I was much taken by the landscapes of Albert Pinkham Ryer and the garish color schemes of the Fauve movement. I believe that my work projects these admirations with obvious awareness of the freedom of Pollock, de Kooning and the action of the fifties. (From *SunStorm* magazine.)

*　　*　　*

Earl Biss could be called a cosmopolitan among the Indian painters, not only because he has lived and travelled in several European countries and various parts of the American West, but also because, as an artist, he was exposed to and influenced by a great many diverse art styles, old and new. Having spent his childhood in the Northwest, he studied under the guidance of Fritz Scholder at the Institute of American Indian Arts in Santa Fe, New Mexico, and completed his studies, together with T.C. Cannon, at the San Francisco Art Institute in California. He then travelled in Europe for a year of independent study, painting in the Netherlands and immersing himself in the works of Old Dutch Masters; getting deeply involved with French impressionists, especially Monet, at the museums in Paris; and staying on the Isle of Corfu, Greece, painting the Mediterranean light and inhaling its atmosphere.

During the years of his studies Biss discovered his own style and subject matter. After being exposed to the influence of Abstract Expressionism in America and Pop Art at the IAIA, he decided in Europe that abstraction was not important to him any more. Instead, he became caught up in the moody atmosphere of the great Dutch painters. Then, in Paris he was intrigued with the lighter colors of the works of the French Impressionists, which after 1973

Earl Biss: *Winter War Party*, 1975. Photograph by Rick Hill.

lightened up his palette and also strengthened his interest in landscape painting.

Biss draws subject matter from his Indian background, from "the rich cultural background of my people ... people with a spirituality built upon a oneness with the earth and the elements. A lore immersed in natural powers, the ability to conjure direction from the Gods, which are one with every being whether it be live or inanimate" (*SunStorm* magazine, December 1989). He discovered that his main interest was depicting groups of Indians, landscapes, and changes in the seasons. Highly acclaimed are the more than 30 versions of his *Snowstorm* series, which show his indebtedness to impressionism and his strong interest in conveying atmosphere and mood.

His inclination toward landscape painting is deeply rooted in personal experience. He likes to recreate on his canvases the idyllic Snoqualmie Valley of Washington, where he grew up. He strives to capture the timelessness of life and nature inherent in idyllic scenes to stir the mood of the observer. He stated, "I choose to portray calm, alluring scenes, void of anguish that annoys the serenity I feel we all would much rather have ... The world that I would have us all live in and experience is a world that perhaps only the imagination will allow us" (*Southwest Art* magazine, December 1977).

—Gerhard and Gisela Hoffman

BLACKOWL, Archie

Variant names: Mis Ta Moo To Va
Tribal affiliations: Cheyenne
Painter

Born: Weatherford, Oklahoma, 23 November 1911; Mis Ta Moo To Va translates as Flying Hawk. **Education:** Fort Sill Indian School, University of Kansas, Art Institute of Chicago. **Career:** Teacher; muralist (Philbrook Museum of Art, Tulsa; Palmer House, Chicago; Fort Sill Indian School, Oklahoma; Riverside Indian School, Oklahoma; Kiowa Hospital, Oklahoma); civil service; industrial painter; Walt Disney Studios; and artist. **Awards:** Several at fairs in Oklahoma; Inter-Tribal Indian Ceremonials, Gallup, New Mexico, and American Indian Art Exhibition, Wayne State University, Detroit, Michigan. **Died:** September 1992.

Selected Group Exhibitions

1947-65 *American Indian Paintings from the Permanent Collection*, Philbrook Art Center, Tulsa, Oklahoma (traveling)

1963 *Contemporary American Indian Art*, United States Department of State, Washington, D.C. (traveling)

1967   Oklahoma Art Center Gallery, Oklahoma City
1972   *Contemporary Southern Plains Indian Painting*, tour organized by the Southern Plains Indian Museum and Oklahoma Indian Arts and Crafts Cooperative, Anadarko, Oklahoma
        Trail of Tears Art Show, Cherokee National Museum, Tahlequah, Oklahoma
1978   *100 Years of Native American Painting*, Oklahoma Museum of Art, Oklahoma City
1979-80 *Native American Paintings*, organized by the Joslyn Art Museum, Omaha, Nebraska (traveling)
1980   *Plains Indian Paintings*, Museum of Art, University of Oklahoma, Norman (traveling)
        Midwest Professional Artists Benefit Show, Tulsa Garden Center, Tulsa, Oklahoma
1981   *Mayfest International Festival*, Winston-Salem, North Carolina
        Views and Visions: The Symbolic Imagery of the Native American Church, Southern Plains Indian Museum, Anadarko, Oklahoma
1981-83 *Native American Painting*, Amarillo Art Center, Amarillo, Texas (traveling)
1984-85 *Indianascher Kunstler* (traveling, Germany), organized by the Philbrook Museum, Tulsa, Oklahoma
1990   Creighton Preparatory School, Omaha, Nebraska

Collections

Anadarko City Museum, Anadarko, Oklahoma; Thomas Gilcrease Institute of American History and Art, Tulsa, Oklahoma; Heritage Center, Inc., Collection, Red Cloud Indian School, Pine Ridge, South Dakota; Indian Arts and Crafts Board, Department of the Interior, Washington, D.C.; Kiva Museum of the Koshare Indian, Boy Scouts of America, La Junta, Colorado; Laguna Gloria Art Museum, Austin, Texas; Museum of Northern Arizona, Flagstaff; Oklahoma Historical Society Museum, Oklahoma City; Oklahoma State Art Collection, Oklahoma City; Philbrook Museum of Art, Tulsa, Oklahoma; Millicent Rogers Foundation Museum, Taos, New Mexico; Smithsonian Institution, Washington, D.C.; Southern Plains Indian Museum, Anadarko, Oklahoma.

Publications

On BLACKOWL: Books—*American Indian Painters,* by Oscar B. Jacobson and Jeanne d'Ucel, Nice, France, 1950; *Indian Artists from Oklahoma,* by Oscar B. Jacobson, Norman, 1964; *American Indian Painting of the Southwest and Plains Areas,* by Dorothy Dunn, Albuquerque, New Mexico, 1968; *Indian Painters and White Patrons,* by J. J. Brody, Albuquerque, New Mexico, 1971; *Song from the Earth: American Indian Painting,* by Jamake Highwater, Boston, 1976; *100 Years of Native American Art* (exhibition catalog), by Arthur Silberman, Oklahoma City, 1978; *American Indian Painting and Sculpture,* by Patricia Broder, New York, 1981.

*   *   *

Archie Blackowl was one of the early twentieth century Native American easel painters who knew many older tribal traditions and documented them through art. Blackowl also depicted more recent tribal ceremonies, such as those of the Native American Church. His paintings were authentic because of his first-hand experience;

for example, he was a member of the Sun Dance Clan. His experience directly affected his painting style and treatment of subject matter. *Sunrise Dance of the Sun Dance* (1945) was boldly composed by an artist confident in his knowledge of the subject matter. The figures are displayed with authentic detail indicating their place in the ceremonial. Blackowl began to experiment in the early 1950s, eventually arriving at a more complex style that he used successfully in later paintings.

Blackowl's paintings of the 1940s were strong because of their singular focus on authentic subjects within simple, but powerful, flatstyle compositions. *Cheyenne Burial,* a mural painted for the Philbrook Museum in 1945, demonstrates the parallel simplicity of subject and composition. The overall composition is basic: a scaffold is placed directly in the center of the piece and forward; mourners are at either side; in the distance, fellow tribal members on horseback are leaving the scene; two horses await the return of their riders—the placement of the figures provides a basic symmetrical balance. Clarity is strengthened by the omission of peripheral information. A horizon line, some distant peaks, and a very few clumps of vegetation and rocks are all that suggest foreground and background. Most of the painting surface is one uniform background color. Although these compositional devices are common in flatstyle paintings, their value is especially noticeable in works with straightforward subjects, like *Cheyenne Burial*. The simplicity of the composition mirrors the simplicity of the subject matter and makes it easily readable.

Blackowl experimented as his style developed, and his later paintings did not always contain the uncomplicated compositional characteristics of *Cheyenne Burial*. A similar painting done in 1952 is in marked contrast to *Cheyenne Burial*, although both paintings are of the same subject and bear the same title. The 1952 painting loses simplicity and clarity in a number of ways. For example, the scaffold is placed upon what may, or may not, be a natural rise in the earth. It consists of horizontal layers of colors that get darker closer to the top. This gives the platform a man-made, pyramidal appearance. The viewer is left to question the form. There are other problems that divert attention from the main subject. The background is filled with a very dark sky, yet the foreground and figures appear to be in daylight. In the sky above the scaffold is an outline drawing of a hunter on horseback chasing a buffalo. Blackowl also put more detail in the foreground and background than in earlier pieces. Clothing is somewhat stylized, containing non-traditional designs. All of these competing compositional elements do not make the painting less compelling. They do, however, cause it to have less clarity and integrity than earlier works. Such experimentation eventually led to the development of a style that was more successful when used in paintings of Native American Church ceremonies. Here, the subject was itself more complicated and so a more complex treatment was appropriate. Blackowl's Native American Church scenes often contain representational portrayals of ceremonial activities combined with more abstract depiction of experiences related to the ceremony. *Mother's Prayer* (1974) is a complex but highly successful composition. Blackowl balanced contrasting design elements, such as the bright halo around the peyote and the dark values in the painting, and achieved a balance of both literal and implied meanings in layering representational images of altar, ceremonial objects, and human figures within the overall, more abstract, fan design. In these later paintings, Blackowl rediscovers an artistic integrity equal to that found in his earlier works.

—Kevin Smith

BLAKE, George

Tribal affiliations: Hupa; Yurok
Ceramist, painter, and carver

Born: Hoopa Reservation, California, 1944. **Family:** Married Annabelle Sylvia, a distinguished artist who specializes in traditional Yurok cradle baskets. **Education:** Two years as a missionary for the Indian Shaker faith; College of the Redwoods, Eureka, California; University of California, Davis. **Career:** Director, Hoopa Tribal Museum, 1980-84; instructor, crafting of dance regalia and other ceremonial and utilitarian objects; co-curator of the exhibition, *Carving Traditions of Northwest California*, Phoebe Apperson Hearst Museum of Anthropology, Berkeley, California, 1995. **Awards:** National Heritage Fellowship, Folk Arts Program; National Endowment for the Arts, 1991.

Individual Exhibitions

1980   *The Artistry of George Blake,* Museum of the Plains Indian and Craft Center, Browning, Montana

Selected Group Exhibitions

1974   *Redwood Art Association 16th Annual Exhibition*, Redwood, California
1975   *I Am The People*, Sacramento, California (traveling)
1978   *Indian Arts and Crafts,* Heard Museum, Phoenix, Arizona
        American Indian Art Now, Wheelwright Museum of the American Indian, Santa Fe, New Mexico
1979   *California Indian Artists*, California State University, Long Beach
1980   *Spirit of the Earth,* Buscaglia Castelani Art Gallery, Niagara University, Niagara Falls, New York
1984   *American Indian Ceramic Art: Yesterday, Today, and Tomorrow,* Sacred Circle Gallery of American Indian Art, Seattle, Washington
        America 1984, Smith Anderson Gallery, Palo Alto, California
1985   *Visage Transcended*, American Indian Contemporary Arts, San Francisco
        The Extension of Tradition, Crocker Art Museum, Sacramento, California
1986   *Native Visions*, N.I.E.A. Conference, Bally Hotel, Reno, Nevada
1987   *Contemporary Visions*, Read Stremmel Gallery, San Antonio, Texas
1988   *Red Cloud Indian Show*, The Heritage Center, Pine Ridge, South Dakota
1990   Heard Museum, Phoenix, Arizona
        Recent Work by Five Northern California Indian Artists: George Blake, Jean LaMarr, Frank LaPeña, Brian Tripp & Frank Tuttle, Gallery Route One, Pt. Reyes Station, California
1991   *A Dialogue with Tradition*, Brooklyn Museum, New York
1993   Heard Museum, Phoenix, Arizona
1995   *Carving Traditions of Northwest California,* Phoebe Apperson Hearst Museum of Anthropology, Berkeley, California

Publications

On BLAKE: Books—*Lost and Found Traditions: Native American Art 1965-1985*, by Ralph T. Coe, Seattle, 1986; *Carving Traditions of Northwest California*, by Ira Jacknis, Berkeley, 1995. **Articles**—"Northern California Events," by Linda Yamane, *News from Native California*, Berkeley, Spring 1990; "George Blake: A Traditional/Contemporary Artist," by Bev Ortiz, *News from Native California*, Berkeley, California, Autumn 1995; "The Carver's Art of the Indian of Northwestern California: An Exhibition at the Phoebe Hearst Museum of Anthropology," by Ira Jacknis, *American Indian Art Magazine*, Autumn 1995.

*

George Blake comments (1993):

I was in high school when my aunt started making baskets and they needed acorn spoons for the feasts. That's how I got started making acorn spoons, and that's how I got started in art work.

I went to Homer Cooper, an old Indian guy, and began to really delve into the culture.... This old guy Homer Cooper was an amazing man. His house was like a museum when I went there.

Homer... told me things, and how things were made. If I was interested enough to try it on my own, and if I failed, he'd show me. I could always remember the way he did this: I would be making a string for a bow, and he was telling me to spin it, and I said, 'spin it?' And then I went and I tried it, and I came back and I was so frustrated. And when he showed me, he laid it in the palm of his hand, and he just took two batches and he began to twist them with eighty-two-year-old knobby knuckles and feeble hands. And it was so easy, when I got the principle down. I just couldn't believe it, before my eyes I could see string just emerging so easy and then I knew. But that's the way he taught me.

*   *   *

George Blake has helped revitalize traditional arts and crafts in Northern California through his efforts as an artist, instructor, and participant in ongoing ceremonies, all of which fuse into his day-to-day lifestyle. At the same time, Blake expands traditions through his individual touches, which include humorous and ironic views as well as social commentary. Blake's wide range of artwork includes ceramics, paintings, canoes, bow and arrow sets, elk horn purses, and ceremonial featherwork. He also instructs members of the Hupa, Yurok, Karuk, and Wiyot tribes and promotes Northern California Native art in local venues and national exhibitions. Additionally, Annabelle Blake, his wife, specializes in traditional baby cradle baskets; like their ancestors, Annabelle gathers hazel sticks for the frame and willow or spruce roots for the wrapping. The baby fits snugly into the cradle basket and is carried on the mother's back. A strap from the cradle basket secures around mother's forehead.

For thousands of years, the Pacific coastline has been a major North-South trade route for native peoples and those who came much later. The diversity of original roots is reflected in the different languages spoken in the region. Blake's Hupa people speak Athabascan, which has a geographic range that extends from the Dené in British Columbia to the Navajo and Apache in the Southwest. Blake's Yurok "Down River" people speak Algonquin, one of the most dispersed language families, ranging from the Cree and Anishinabe in Canada, Blackfeet on the Plateau, Cheyenne and Arapaho on the Great Plains, Kickapoo in Mexico, and Delaware,

George Blake: Carved wooden spoon, 1980. Photograph by Seth Roffman; courtesy Dr. Gregory Schaaf collection.

bols popular in basketry, including a snake's nose and stacked wood, with all design motifs balanced in the middle of the piece. Blake explains that he wants "to keep these designs alive." The piece was made in 1991 for another exhibition, *A Dialogue with Tradition*, held at the Brooklyn Museum, New York.

The second example of Blake's art is a life-sized baby in a basketry cradle carved out of Port Orford cedar with abalone shell and glass trade bead decorations. This piece is one-of-a-kind, started in 1974, set aside and finished in 1987. A third example, *Cigar Store White Man, No. 1* (1995) is reflective of the social commentary, bold satire in this case, that frequents his work. Blake is poking fun at old stereotypical images of Cigar Store Indians carved in nineteenth- and early twentieth-century Euro-American folk art. Anthropologist Ira Jacknis noted that Blake "modeled the face after popular singer Mel Tormé and the hands after a Balinese carving. His brother-in-law, who had fashion experience, helped with the plaid jacket. The first in a projected series, this was meant to be a maquette version [41 3/4" high] for a full-size figure.

These examples indicate that Blake is not only helping preserve his culture, he also is going beyond tradition by making his own unique artistic statements. In his culture, an artist must earn the right to innovate new designs and forms. Blake has earned that right.

Blake also instructs locals on the making of ceremonial regalia and utilitarian tools and other objects, and he participates in community rituals. For example, he has continued the tradition of carving a redwood canoe, usually from a single redwood log, to be used in the "Boat Dance," part of the White Deerskin ceremonial held biannually along the Klamath and Trinity rivers. Blake explains that his goal is to "give the Indian community a chance to look at the wealth of things that were . . . from the area . . . and a chance to actually just look and research by looking at it. There's a real interest in carving right now, and a document of these things back into the community could only help. I want to bring that excitement back to the people."

—Gregory Schaaf

Pequot and Wampanoag on the Atlantic seaboard. The Karuk or "Upstream" people speak Hokan, one of California's most ancient languages also spoken by the Pomo, Washoe, Chumash, Mojave, Ipai and Tipai southward into Baja California.

Although the Hupa, Yurok and Karuk speak different languages, they share a rich culture. The women are honored as the makers of finely twined basketry caps, cylindrical purses, beargrass skirts, trays and bowls. The men are most recognized for finely carved wooden canoes, elkhorn purses, elkhorn and maplewood spoons, as well as elaborate feathered headdresses and regalia.

George Blake grew up during the "Termination Era," when federal Indian policy sought to assimilate native peoples into mainstream American society, which resulted in human suffering and loss of cultural identity. Blake responded by searching out the elders who retained traditional knowledge while encouraging people his own age and younger to get involved in their culture. The results are a successful model for cultural revival efforts being made throughout the Western Hemisphere and by indigenous peoples around the world.

Three of Blake's carvings that were part of a major exhibition he helped curate, *Carving Traditions of Northwest California*, illustrate his artistic concerns. An upright elkhorn purse, used to hold valuable dentellium shell necklaces, has designs that feature sym-

BLUE EAGLE, Acee

Variant names: Che Bon Ah Bula
Tribal affiliations: Creek; Pawnee
Painter, sculptor, and ceramist

Born: Alex C. McIntosh, Wichita Reservation, Oklahoma, 17 August 1909 (also listed 1907 and as 9 August 1909 and 1911); took the name Blue Eagle from his paternal grandfather; Che Bon Ah Bula translates as Laughing Boy. **Education:** Riverside Indian School, Bacone College, University of Oklahoma, and commercial art classes, Oklahoma State University, 1951-52. **Military Service:** U.S. Army Air Corps, World War II. **Career:** Represented Oklahoma Boy Scouts, European tour, 1929; lectured at Oxford University and toured Europe, introducing American Indian Art, 1935; founded and headed Art Department at Bacone College, 1935-38; murals throughout Oklahoma, including federal buildings in Colgate and Seminole, Muskogee Public Library and Veteran's Administration Hospital, Muskogee, and a mural for the U.S.S. Oklahoma, a ship lost at Pearl Harbor; taught art at Oklahoma State University and the Technological School in Okmulgee, Oklahoma, after World

War II; lectured on children's television, early 1950s, and hosted a children's television show in Tulsa, Oklahoma, 1954-55; artist and dancer. **Awards:** Numerous at fairs, ceremonials, and juried competitions, including American Indian Exposition, Denver Art Museum, International Art Exhibition of Sports Subjects (held in conjunction with the 1932 Olympic Games in Los Angeles), Inter-Tribal Indian Ceremonials, and Philbrook Annual Indian Art Exhibition; medal, National Art Museum of Ethiopia, presented by Emperor Haile Selassie, 1952; named Outstanding Indian in United States, American Indian Exposition at Anadarko, Oklahoma, 1958; Resolution for Service to the State, Oklahoma Legislature, 1959; Acee Blue Eagle Building, Haskell Indian Nations University, named in his honor. **Died:** 18 June 1959.

Individual Exhibitions

1934   Young Galleries, Chicago
1936   Washington, D. C., Arts Club, Washington, D. C.
1952   National Art Museum of Ethiopia, Addis Ababa
1953   Thomas Gilcrease Institute of American History and Art, Tulsa, Oklahoma
1957   Philbrook Museum of Art, Tulsa, Oklahoma
1959   Thomas Gilcrease Institute of American History and Art, Tulsa, Oklahoma
1969   *Blue Eagle: A Retrospective Exhibition*, Philbrook Museum of Art, Tulsa, Oklahoma

Selected Group Exhibitions

1930   Art Exposition, Prague, Czechoslovakia
1931-33 *Exposition of Indian Tribal Arts*, Grand Central Art Galleries, New York
1932   *International Art Exhibition of Sports Subjects*, Los Angeles, California
1934   Chicago Century of Progress, Chicago, Illinois
1936   Rockefeller Center, New York
1937   *American Indian Exposition and Congress*, Tulsa, Oklahoma
1941   Museum of Modern Art, New York
1944   *Northwest Art Exhibition*, Spokane, Washington
1947-65 *American Indian Paintings from the Permanent Collection*, Philbrook Museum of Art, Tulsa, Oklahoma (traveling)
1951   Denver Art Museum, Denver, Colorado
1955   *An Exhibition of American Indian Painters*, James Graham and Sons, New York
1963   *Contemporary Indian Art*, U.S. Department of State, Washington, D.C.
1978   *100 Years of Native American Painting*, Oklahoma Museum of Art, Oklahoma City, Oklahoma
1980   *Native American Art at the Philbrook*, Philbrook Museum of Art, Tulsa, Oklahoma
1984-85 *Indianascher Kunstler* (traveling, Germany), organized by the Philbrook Museum, Tulsa, Oklahoma
1990   *American Indian Artists in the Avery Collection and the McNay Permanent Collection*, Koogler McNay Art Museum, San Antonio, Texas
1991-96 *Shared Visions: Native American Painters and Sculptors in the Twentieth Century*, The Heard Museum, Phoenix, Arizona (traveling)

1996   *Drawn from Memory: James T. Bialac Collection of Native American Art*, Heard Museum, Phoenix, Arizona

Collections

Bacone College, Bacone, Oklahoma; Bureau of Indian Affairs, Washington, D.C.; Creek Indian House and Museum, Okmulgee, Oklahoma; Denver Art Museum, Denver, Colorado; Fine Arts Museum, Museum of New Mexico, Santa Fe; Thomas Gilcrease Institute of American History and Art, Tulsa, Oklahoma; Institute of American Indian Arts Museum, Santa Fe, New Mexico; Kiva Museum of the Koshare Indian, La Junta, Colorado; Museum of Northern Arizona, Flagstaff; National Museum of Ethiopia, Addis Ababa; Oklahoma Historical Society Museum, Oklahoma City; Philbrook Museum of Art, Tulsa, Oklahoma; Millicent Rogers Foundation Museum, Taos, New Mexico; Seminole Public Library, Seminole, Oklahoma; University of Oklahoma, Museum of Art, Norman.

Publications

By BLUE EAGLE: Book—*Oklahoma Indian Painting, Poetry,* Tulsa, 1959.

On BLUE EAGLE: Books—*American Indian Painters,* by Oscar B. Jacobson and Jeanne d'Ucel, Nice, France, 1950; *Indian Artists from Oklahoma,* by Oscar B. Jacobson, Norman, 1964; *American Indian Painting of the Southwest and Plains Areas,* by Dorothy Dunn, Albuquerque, New Mexico, 1968; *Indian Painters and White Patrons,* by J. J. Brody, Albuquerque, New Mexico, 1971; *Song from the Earth: American Indian Painting,* by Jamake Highwater, Boston, 1976; *Great North American Indians: Profiles in Life and Leadership,* by Frederick J. Dockstader, New York, 1977; *100 Years of Native American Art* (exhibition catalog), by Arthur Silberman, Oklahoma City, 1978; *Native American Art at the Philbrook,* by John T. Mahey, Tulsa, 1980; *American Indian Painting and Sculpture*, by Patricia Janis Broder, New York, 1981; *Native American Painting* (exhibition catalog), by Jeanne Snodgrass King, Amarillo, Texas, 1981; *Indianascher Kunstler,* by Gerhard Hoffman, Munich, 1984; *The Arts of the North American Indian: Native Traditions in Evolution*, Edwin L. Wade, ed., New York, 1986; *American Indian Artists in the Avery Collection and the McNay Permanent Collection,* Jean Sherrod Williams, editor, San Antonio, 1990; *Shared Visions: Native American Painters and Sculptors in the Twentieth Century,* by Margaret Archuleta and Dr. Rennard Strickland, New York: The New Press, 1991; *Shared Visions,* by Margaret Archuleta and Rennard Strickland, Phoenix, 1991. **Articles**—"Indian Artists," *American Magazine,* April 1937; "Vigorous Revival of Indian Art Forms," by Beatrice Levin, *El Palacio,* February 1953.

*   *   *

In addition to being a prolific painter and an artist who worked within various forms, including ceramics, leather, and silversmithing, Acee Blue Eagle was a tireless promoter of Native American art and culture. He established and directed the art department at Bacone College, an institution in which many noted Native American artists have honed their skills; lectured throughout the United States, as well as Europe and Africa, on Native American culture; and collected artwork and encouraged artists to pursue their craft. His own work is emblematic of the flatstyle painting of the Plains, showing ceremonies, animals, and scenes of everyday life, and his murals depict important symbols, such as the Thunderbird (whose flapping wings brought thunder and rain), and activities, including the buffalo hunt. The pictorial realism and authenticity in his renderings of clothing and artifacts, which reflects extensive material and field research and discussions with elders, makes his works significant as historical documents as well as vibrant artistic expressions. A central subject usually dominates his paintings, with spare groundline or setting, and little, if any, background, and his images ranged from quiet moments of interaction among humans and with nature, to active depictions of ceremonial dances, to high drama of hunts on the Plains.

Blue Eagle was born Alex C. McIntosh to a Scottish father and Creek/Pawnee mother. Both of his parents died when he was young, and he lived with his grandparents, who also passed away during his childhood; W. R. Thompson, of Henryetta, Oklahoma, was appointed his legal guardian and helped Blue Eagle pursue his education. Blue Eagle took the name of his maternal grandfather, and Acee comes from having been called "Ah Say" since he was a child and reflects the initials of his first and middle name.

Artistic ability and affability were traits Blue Eagle displayed early on: drawing with sticks in dried out creek beds and using crayons and pencils on paper as his early media, he also began painting by imitating the flatstyle drawings and ledger art on hides practiced by his ancestors. His affability (as reflected in his Creek name—Che Bon Ah Bula, Laughing Boy), combined with his knowledge and studies of Native American culture, led to important positions in the art world. He had represented Oklahoma Boy Scouts during a European tour in 1929 and returned there as an artist in 1935, studying and lecturing at Oxford University and touring Europe to introduce programs and exhibitions on American Indian art. He was associated with leading instructors, artists (including the Kiowa Five painters, James Auchiah, Stephen Mopope, Spencer Asah, Jack Hokeah, and Monroe Tsatoke), and art collectors in Oklahoma, such as Oscar B. Jacobson, a professor at the University of Oklahoma who organized important exhibitions of Native American art in the United States and Europe, and Thomas Gilcrease, who bequeathed the Gilcrease Museum in Tulsa. Blue Eagle was instrumental in founding and developing the renowned art department at Bacone College, which has contributed greatly to the preservation and expansion of Native American art. Following service in World War II and an earlier mural commission of a buffalo hunt for the U.S.S. Oklahoma, a ship sunk at the raid on Pearl Harbor, Blue Eagle resumed his active career as a lecturer for schools and civic groups around the United States and as an instructor at Oklahoma State University Technical School in Okmulgee. He died in 1959, after delaying a hospital visit in order to finish up a booklet on the early Indian art of Oklahoma. An Indian burial ceremony was held on the grounds of the Gilcrease Museum in his honor.

As an exemplary practitioner of flatstyle painting, Blue Eagle captured moments in which his detailing of figures—from coiffure, to dress, to objects—are of primary importance. The patterns, colors and symbols on a woman's dress, belt and boots, for example, form decorative patterns in the center of *Woman and Faun* (c. 1945), with a flowing sash contrasting the more geometric shapes on the clothing. Various paintings of buffalo hunts are similarly vivid and informational in their depiction of regalia and weaponry, as are portraits of dancers performing ceremonies in full costume. The play of natural colors and exquisite detailing in Blue Eagle's paintings, as well as the authenticity in the scenes he depicted, put him at the forefront of Native American painting in the middle of the twentieth century.

This same kind of authenticity appears in his leatherwork, beadmaking, silversmithing, sculpture and silk screening. Blue Eagle contributed to a revival of sculpture, which derived from his studies of artifacts. He reproduced small-scale sculptures of fetishes used for personal protection, ritualistic sculptures on ceremonial staffs, and everyday utensils and bowls. His leatherwork transposes traditional Native American symbols into this media, and, like all of his work, reflects his concern for preserving cultural traditions through authentic, non-stereotypical images adapted to newer art forms. Cultural messages persist as new media are explored and used to relay the outstanding attributes of communities of the Plains.

—Perry Bear

BOB, Dempsey
Tribal affiliations: Tlingit
Carver

Born: Telegraph Creek, British Columbia, 1948. **Education:** Traditional training from parents and grandparents; Kitanmax School of Northwest Coast Art Ksan, Hazelton, British Columbia (studied with Freda Diesing), 1972-74.

Individual Exhibitions

1989   *Dempsey Bob: Tahltan-Tlingit, Carver of the Wolf Clan*, Grace Gallery, Vancouver, British Columbia
1993   *Dempsey Bob: Myth Maker and Transformer*, Vancouver Museum, Vancouver, British Columbia

Selected Group Exhibitions

1974   *In Praise of Hands*, First World's Craft Exhibition, Ontario Science Centre, Toronto
1980   *The Legacy,* Edinburgh International Festival, Edinburgh, Scotland (organized by the British Columbia Provincial Museum)
1981   *Arts of the Salmon People*, Museum of Northern British Columbia, Prince Rupert, British Columbia
1982   *Northern Comforts*, Potlatch Art Gallery, Vancouver, British Columbia
1983   *National Native Indian Artists Symposium*, Northwestern National Exhibition Centre, Hazelton, British Columbia
1986   *Robes of Power: Totem Poles on Cloth,* Museum of Anthropology, University of British Columbia, Vancouver, British Columbia
1987   *Pacific Northwest Coast Masks: From the Collection of the Museum of Anthropology,* University of British Columbia, Canada House Cultural Centre Gallery, London, England
        Hands of Creation: An Exhibition of Northwest Coast Native Art, Inuit Art Gallery, Vancouver, British Columbia
        Eloquent Objects, The Philbrook Museum of Art, Tulsa, Oklahoma

1988   *Lost and Found Traditions: Native American Art 1965-
        1985*, Renwick Gallery of the National Museum of
        American Art, Smithsonian Institution, Washington,
        DC (traveling)
1989   *Northwest Native Art*, Osaka, Japan
        Beyond the Revival: Contemporary Northwest Native Art,
        Charles H. Scott Gallery, British Columbia
1990   *Wolves and Humans,* Vancouver Museum, Vancouver,
        British Columbia
        Out of the Cedar Came ..., Museum of Northern British
        Columbia, Prince Rupert, British Columbia
        Northwest Coast Contemporary Native Show, Prince
        Rupert, British Columbia
1992   *Land, Spirit, Power: First Nations at the National Gallery
        of Canada*, National Gallery of Canada, Ottawa, Ontario
        (traveling)
        *Sharing the Culture: The Port Edward Group, North Port
        Edward*, British Columbia, Rockskilde Festival,
        Rockskilde, Denmark
        New Territories: 350/500 Years After, Vision Planetaire,
        Montreal, Quebec
1994   *Multiplicity: A New Cultural Strategy*, Museum of An-
        thropology, University of British Columbia, Vancouver,
        British Columbia
1995   *Opening of the Motherland Gallery*, Fukuoka, Japan
1996   *Topographies: Aspects of Recent British Columbia Art*,
        Vancouver Art Gallery, Vancouver, British Columbia
        Remembering the Way, American Indian Contemporary
        Arts, San Francisco

Collections

British Columbia House, London, England; Canada House, Lon-
don, England; Canadian Museum of Civilization, Hull, Quebec;
Centennial Museum, Ketchikan, Alaska; Department of Indian
and Northern Affairs, Ottawa, Ontario; Hamburgisches Mu-
seum fur Volkerskunde, Hamburg, Germany; City of Ketchikan,
Alaska; Museum of British Columbia, University of British
Columbia, Vancouver; Museum of Ethnology, Osaka, Japan;
Museum of Northern British Columbia, Prince Rupert, British
Columbia; Owase Community Cultural Centre, Owase, Japan;
Ridley Island Coal Terminal, Prince Rupert, British Columbia;
Ridley Island Grain Terminal, Prince Rupert, British Columbia;
Royal British Columbia Museum, Victoria, British Columbia;
Saxman Tribal House, Saxman, Alaska; Smithsonian Institution,
Washington, D.C.

Publications

On BOB: Books—*Indian Artists at Work*, by Uilli Steltzer,
Vancouver: J.J. Douglas, 1976; *The Legacy: Continuing Traditions
of Canadian Northwest Coast Indian Art*, by Peter Macnair, Alan
Hoover and Kevin Neary, Victoria: British Columbia Provincial
Museum, 1980. **Articles**—"Native Art Past and Present," by Sam
Middleton, *The Edmonton Sun*, April 24, 1981; "Carver Speaks
through Art," by Kathleen Logan, *Prince Rupert News*, May 20,
1983; "Northwest Indians Find Their Roots—Way Above Ground,"
by Alan Bayless, *The Wall Street Journal,* August 22, 1983; "Renowned Carver to Give Lessons," *Whitehorse Star* (Yukon), September 26, 1984; "The Sky is the Limit: Conversations with First
Nations Artists," by Robert Enright, *Border Crossings*, 1992; "The

Big Money in Northwest Coast Native Art," by Alan Bayless,
Financial Times, August, 28, 1993.

*   *   *

A conservative tradition, Northwest Coast Indian art is highly
distinctive and easily identifiable, whether expressed in a ceremonial mask, a wooden spoon, or a silver bracelet. Moreover, there is
great similarity between precontact, postcontact and contemporary work because of explicit rules governing almost every aspect
of expression, including the design, composition, iconography, and
color choice. Due to this, many of those who venture too far from
the standard are looked upon with derision and derogatorily labeled
"clever." Yet for them, to make strictly traditional art is to reinforce
static perceptions and erroneous stereotypes, and to deny the complex multicultural experiences that inform their artistic vision. The
Tlingit/Tahltan artist Dempsey Bob is well aware of these issues.

Although he has worked with other materials and processes, Bob
prefers wood carving and is well known for his bowls, masks,
panels, and sculptures. While his carvings exemplify a great affinity with work of the past, this is not in conflict with his status as a
contemporary artist. According to Bob, the creation of art firmly
based in tradition is central to his identity as an artist and individual
as well as a profound means of integrating the past with the present.

Concerning the issue of innovation vs. tradition in Northwest
coast art, Bob believes that an individual must first commit to
intense study in which they fully internalize the rules of expression. This manner of learning provides a structure for discipline and
knowledge essential to the creation of art that requires a high degree
of technical and conceptual skill. According to Bob, it is only after
such study that an artist can build on or stray from tradition in a
significant and valid way. In clarification of his own intentions, Bob
states: "I'm not trying to re-create the past, but you have to have a
base understanding from which to innovate ... you have to go back
to go ahead."

When he started carving in the late 1960s, Bob found it difficult
to "go back" because there were few elders from which to learn.
Because Northwest Coast art has long played a profound part in
ceremonies, the lack of producing artists was indicative of a greater
cultural dilemma at the time, that of ceremonies on the demise.
However, due to the current cultural revival of ceremonies, Bob's
work is in high demand within the greater Northwest native communities and he is regularly commissioned to create frontlets, leggings and other regalia.

Bob's work is also well known nationally and internationally. In
the deftly carved wooden mask, *The Smart One!* (1989), Bob presents his interpretation of a Northwest Coast storyteller. The thick
black eyebrows, carefully graded curves, and successful integration
of three dimensional form and two dimensional design are exemplary of the Northwest coast style. However, Bob's individual
talent is evident in his sophisticated interpretation of physiognomy, in which stylized elements (such as the broad curve of the
mouth) and naturalistic elements (such as cheekbones) are united to
produce a visually compelling piece.

Having himself mastered the rules of aesthetic expression, in
such works as *Raven's Panel* (1989), Bob risks radical innovation.
While creating this bas relief, Bob found out about the Exxon Valdez
oil spill that polluted hundreds of miles of water and killed a variety
of wildlife off the coast of Alaska. In response Bob used blue
(rather than black) for the formline around the raven, colored the
salmon and water black, augmented some of the oval shapes, and

included a mirror in this image. While he acknowledges that this panel may not be fully accepted by his community, he felt it necessary to make such changes.

In addition to his woodwork, Bob makes button blankets, over seventy of which have been distributed among the Tlingit. However, this enormous accomplishment cannot be accredited to Bob alone. In addition to his career as an artist, Bob is also an educator and teaches the children in his community how to make these blankets. Grounded in the past, active in the present, and optimistic about the future, Bob himself is a "Smart One"—a visual storyteller—whose art and influence attest to the ongoing vitality and richness of his Northwest coast heritage.

—Kristin Potter

BOMBERRY, Vincent

Tribal affiliations: Six Nations
Sculptor

Born: Six Nations, Ontario, 26 August 1958; member of the Six Nations, Cayuga (Wolf Clan). **Family:** Married; two daughters, Valarie and Pauline, two sons, Siryl and Dennis.

Selected Group Exhibitions

1980   *At the Edge of the Woods*, The Turtle, Niagara Falls, New York
        Beckett Galery, Hamilton, Ontario
        Contemporary Art of the Iroquoia, McDonald Gallery, Toronto
1981   *Native Art Auction,* Native Canadian Centre, Toronto
        Indian Art '81, Woodland Indian Cultural Educational Centre, Brantford, Ontario
1983   *Contemporary Indian and Inuit Art of Canada*, United Nations, New York (traveling)
1985   *From Masks to Maquettes*, McIntosh Gallery, London, Ontario
1986   *Contrasts*, The Gallery, Brock Centre for the Arts, St. Catherines, Ontario
        Iroquoia, Two Turtle Indian Art Gallery, Oshweken, Ontario
        New Beginnings, Native Business Summit, Toronto
        Ascending Culture, Terrasses de la Chaudiere, Hull, Quebec
1987   *A Celebration of Contemporary Canadian Native Art*, Woodland Indian Cultural Educational Centre, Brantford, Ontario (traveled to Southwest Museum, Los Angeles)
1988   *A Native Experience,* Beckett Gallery, Hamilton, Ontario
        Shadow of the Sun, Museum of Civilization, Ottawa (international traveling exhibit)
        Indian Art '88, Woodland Cultural Centre, Brantford, Ontario
1989   *Indian Art '89*, Woodland Cultural Centre, Brantford, Ontario
        Gallery Indigena, Stratford, Ontario
        Manfred Gallery, Toronto

1990   Beckett Gallery, Hamilton, Ontario
1991   *Five From the Land*, Adams Art Gallery, Dunkirk, New York
1991-96 *First Nations Art* (annual), Woodland Cultural Centre, Brantford, Ontario

Collections

Canadian Museum of Civilization, Ottawa; Department of Indian and Northern Affairs, Ottawa; Thunder Bay National Exhibition Centre and Centre for Indian Art, Thunder Bay, Ontario; Woodland Cultural Centre, Brantford, Ontario.

Publications

On BOMBERRY: Books—*From Masks to Maquettes,* exhibition catalog by Norma Dinniwell, McIntosh Gallery, London, Ontario, 1985; *Carrying the Message: An Introduction to Iroquois Stone Sculpture* by Wolfgang Prudek, Dundas, Ontario, 1986. **Articles**—"First Impressions," *Native Arts West*, November 1981; "Art from Six Nations," by Linda Bramble, *Enroute* 15, no. 9, September 1987.

*

Vincent Bomberry comments:
Through my work I am trying to express my views as a Native living in today's society in regards to cultural indifference, similarities, prejudices, environmental issues and political and industrial issues which effect the future of the people and the world.

My desire is to work and create monumental size stone and steel sculpture that will have a greater impact on the viewer. I want to inspire the younger generation to also create art and make all people who see my work aware that there is more to Native art than just traditional crafts.

*   *   *

Bomberry's pieces frequently exhibit a duality masked in abstraction. The end result is powerful sculptures that stir the viewer into a state of reaction and question. His stone figures seem to be in a perpetual state of transformation, with the appearance of moving, writhing, and pushing their way out of a limiting prison of stone. His pieces often display cycles of tension within his subjects on both an internal and personal level as well as on a broader global scale.

A number of Bomberry's images have been appropriately described as aggressive and can even appear violent in the same ferocious manner of seasonal weather changes and intense emotion. The figures in his pieces are never settled, static or even comfortable. Elements within these striking sculptures are often represented in dualities, each of which appears dependent on the other in order to define itself. An oscillation or cycling of energy moves between the two sides, regardless of what portion of the human condition they represent. These elements appear to react to each other, creating a vicious circle that cannot be broken.

Added to these strong artistic elements, Bomberry's style of using mythology as a vehicle for bringing to light recurring themes of social tension is unique. The duality is further exhibited in the

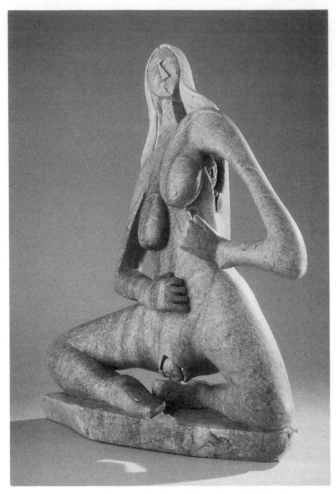

Vincent Bomberry: *The Birth of Good and Evil.* Courtesy Canadian Museum of Civilization.

manner in which Bomberry's sculptural style appears both primal and abstractly modern at the same time.

One of Vincent Bomberry's signature pieces, *The Birth of Good and Evil,* from the collection of the Canadian Museum of Civilization in Ottawa, powerfully demonstrates his distinct style. This stone carving, created in 1982, depicts the Iroquoian legend of the great birth of the Primal Twins as they emerge from the Earth—their mother. The first twin, the Sky Holder, representing good, pushes down from the birth canal of the mother. In opposition, the evil twin, also known as Flint, or Tawiskaron, contrastingly pushes his way into the world from below the arm of the "mother," becoming the powerful ruler of the underworld. The balance of good and evil as opposing forces creates a tangible tension that grips the piece in a moment of metamorphosis.

Many of Bomberry's other works take on a layered feel of cubism with a central image apearing repeatedly, each time removed from the original interpretation. And just as his pieces are in continual states of transformation, so is his personal style, which is constantly moving and pushes tangible feelings into the mind of the viewer, leaving lasting impressions of passion, conflict, and connection.

—Vesta Giles

BOSIN, Blackbear
Variant names: Tsate Kongia
Tribal affiliations: Kiowa; Comanche
Painter

Born: Francis Blackbear Bosin near Anadarko, Oklahoma, 5 June 1921. **Education:** High School; turned down university scholarships to work on family farm; no formal artistic training, but studied on his own at St. Patrick's Mission School in Anadarko. **Military Service:** U.S. Marine Corps, World War II. **Career:** Farmer, artist, illustrator, commerical artist, gallery owner, and platemaker. **Awards:** Numerous, including mural commissions for McConnell Air Force Base and high schools in Wichita, Kansas, sculpture (*Keeper of the Plains*) for the City of Wichita, 1967, and painting series, Indian Arts and Crafts Board, Department of the Interior, Washington, D.C.; U.S. Chamber of Commerce, Civil Servant Award, 1959, Indian Arts and Crafts Board, Certificate of Appreciation, 1966, Waite Phillips Trophy for Outstanding Contributions to American Indian Art, Philbrook Museum, Tulsa, Oklahoma, 1967. **Died:** 9 August 1980.

Individual Exhibitions

1971   Southern Plains Indian Museum and Craft Center, Indian Arts and Crafts Board, United States Department of the Interior, Anadarko, Oklahoma

Selected Group Exhibitions

1947-65 *American Indian Paintings From the Permanent Collection,* Philbrook Art Center, Tulsa, Oklahoma (traveling)
1955   *An Exhibition of American Indian Painters,* James Graham and Sons, New York
1964   Read Mullan Gallery of Western Art, Phoenix
1965   *White House Festival of the Arts,* Washington, D.C.
1970   Museum of the Plains Indian, Browning, Montana
1972   *Contemporary Southern Plains Indian Painting,* Southern Plains Indian Museum and the Oklahoma Indian Arts and Crafts Co-Operative, Anadarko, Oklahoma (traveling)
1978   *100 Years of Native American Art,* Oklahoma Museum, Oklahoma City (traveling)
1979-80 *Native American Paintings,* Joslyn Art Museum, Omaha, Nebraska (traveling)
1980   *Midwest Professional Artists Benefit Art Show,* Tulsa Garden Center, Oklahoma
        Plains Indian Paintings, Museum of Art, University of Oklahoma, Norman (traveling)
        Native American Art at the Philbrook, Philbrook Museum, Tulsa, Oklahoma
1984-85 *Indianischer Kunstler* West Germany (traveling)
1991-92 *Shared Visions: Native American Painters and Sculptors in the Twentieth Century,* Heard Museum, Phoenix, Arizona (traveling)
1992   *Visions of the People,* Minneapolis Institute of Arts (traveling)

Blackbear Bosin: *Winter Hunt.* Courtesy Gilcrease Museum, Tulsa, Oklahoma.

Collections

Bureau of Indian Affairs, United States Department of the Interior, Washington, D.C.; Denver Art Museum; Eiteljorg Museum, Indianapolis; Thomas Gilcrease Institute of American History and Art, Tulsa, Oklahoma; Heard Museum, Phoenix; Indian Arts and Crafts Board, United States Department of the Interior, Washington, D.C.; Philbrook Art Center, Tulsa, Oklahoma; Wichita Art Association Gallery, Wichita, Kansas; Wichita Art Museum, Kansas.

Publications

On BOSIN: Books—*A Pictorial History of the American Indian* by Oliver LaFarge, New York, 1956; *The American Indian* by Oliver LaFarge, New York, 1960; *Contemporary Southern Plains Indian Painting* by Myles Libhart, Anadarko, Oklahoma, 1972; *Song from the Earth: American Indian Painting* by Jamake Highwater, Boston, 1976; *100 Years of Native American Art* by Arthur Silberman, Oklahoma City, 1978; *Native American Painting: Selections from the Museum of the American Indian* by David M. Fawcett and Lee A. Callander, New York, 1982; *The Arts of the North American Indian: Native Traditions in Evolution* edited by Edwin L. Wade, New York, 1986; *Shared Visions* by Margaret Archuleta and Rennard Strickland, Phoenix, 1991; *The Native Americans: An Illustrated History* by Betty and Ian Ballantine, Atlanta, 1993. **Articles**—"America's First Painters" by Dorothy Dunn, *National Geographic Magazine*, vol. CVII, no. 3, March 1955.

* * *

Blackbear Bosin was essentially self-taught and absorbed artistic influences on his own, eventually creating a unique style. During the 1940s he attended St. Patrick's Mission School, where he had the opportunity to peruse books on European and American art and view a collection that contained works by Kiowa artists who had studied under Oscar Jacobson at the University of Oklahoma. He was impressed by the works, particularly the artists' use of color and their simple composition. Bosin's early period of serious painting was influenced by these Kiowa artists, particularly Stephen Mopope, Monroe Tsatoke and James Auchiah.

Throughout his career, Bosin would maintain some manner of the Kiowa flat style, in part to sustain visionary qualities that would be lost in stricter adherence to realism. His use of the flat style design was, according to Bosin, a continuation of traditional Indian thinking, looking for the representation of the essence of something, rather than the literal representation of its outward appearance. Yet Bosin pushed the boundaries of this style of Native American painting. He experimented with mainstream modern movements of twentieth century, to which he was exposed through his independent studies. He stated that there were similarities between European Surrealism and Native American flat style in that both

Bob Boyer: *Moctezuma's Nightmare,* 1996. Courtesy of the artist.

rejected realism and both required painstaking control and clarity of detail. His experimentation in combining flat style with Surrealism is seen in such works as *Green Corn Dance.*

Bosin was also interested in European illusionist style, even though flat-style remained dominant in his compositions. He began experimenting in the early 1950s by gradually adding background and foreground elements, as in *Winter Hunt.* The eventual incorporation of European perspective, illusionism, and complete backgrounds and foregrounds in otherwise flat style works contributes to the uniqueness of his painting. Bosin consciously tested the boundaries of flat style painting and opened new possibilities by adding transparent watercolor background to an otherwise opaque, flat painting. This experimentation provided possibilities for dramatic narrative action in his compositions. This was to serve his admitted preference for emotional impact. Initially, Bosin simply added background and foreground in early works such as *Winter Hunt* to add to the "storyline." This is seen also in *Death Bird.* By the mid-1950s, both Bosin's dramatic narrative and his technique had become more sophisticated. *And They Moved without Him* shows increased use of transparent wash, more action in lines and gestures, gradation of values, a horizon line and European perspective. All of this heightens the dramatic effect and adds sophistication to the piece, which successfully retains flat style elements.

The two most notable examples of this style from Bosin's mature period are in the collection of the Philbrook Museum. *Prairie*

Fire and *Wind Spirit* each feature central figures and other compositional elements in flat style, yet employ the European techniques. Because of the narrative action, the focus of these paintings is on the composition as a whole, rather than on the central figures as is common in the flat style. In Bosin's works of dramatic action, traditional European techniques are used to imply movement and action within a static, flat form. Bosin used flowing and repetitive lines in the direction of movement, causing the viewer's eye to be led in the direction of the action, and to imply movement beyond the edge of the painting. Placement of people, animals, horses, etc. within compositions often serves the narrative priority over formal considerations. In *Prairie Fire,* for instance, the placement of wild animals next to humans and horses heightens the drama of the story. In *Wind Sprit,* the inclusion of a baby adds even a melodramatic, yet believable element. The Philbrook paintings serve as an example of the dramatic and effective combination of realism and flat style that make Bosin's work particularly unique for the time.

In his later years, Bosin viewed the traditional flat style as somewhat of a hindrance to Indian artists, a limitation imposed by the non-Indian market. Bosin's own innovations overcame such external limitations while retaining flat style elements. Some of his later works move farther from flat style. *From Whence Comes All Life,* a mural for a Wichita, Kansas, bank, includes narrative elements, references to early tribal designs, and Miro-like composition and forms. His 44-foot-high steel sculpture,

Keeper of the Plains, combines his sense of the dramatic with a cubist styling and sense of history. His command of European techniques and flat style, combined with his talent for depicting narrative drama make Bosin's work stand apart from that of his contemporaries.

—Kevin Smith

BOYER, Bob

Tribal affiliations: Métis
Painter and installation artist

Born: Prince Albert, Saskatchewan, 1948. **Education:** University of Saskatchewan, Bachelors of Education, 1971. **Career:** Community program officer, Norman Mackenzie Art Gallery, Regina, Saskatchewan, 1973-75; program supervisor, Northern Continuing Education, Buffalo Narrows, Saskatchewan, 1975-76; personnel officer, Department of Northern Sasakatchewan, La Ronge, Sasakatchewan; assistant professor and consultant in Indian art, 1978-80, department head, associate professor, 1980—, Saskatchewan Federated Indian College, Regina; chairperson, Society of Canadian Artists of Native Ancestry; traditional dancer; artist; curator.

Individual Exhibitions

1973   Art Department Gallery, University of Saskatchewan, Saskatoon
1980   Splash Gallery, Ottawa
1985   Woltjen/Udell Gallery, Edmonton, Alberta
1986   *Bob Boyer's Recent Blankets,* Brignall Gallery, Toronto
        Recent Watercolors, Club Gallery, Regina, Saskatchewan
1988   *A Blanket Statement,* Museum of Anthropology, University of British Columbia (traveling)
1989   *Summer Dreams,* Mountain Prayers, Ufundi Gallery, Ottawa
        New Works on Paper, Canvas, and Blanket, Assiniboia Gallery, Regina, Saskatchewan
1990   *New Work,* Canadian Art Gallery, Calgary, Alberta
        New Paintings on Flannel and Paper, Galerie Dresdnere, Toronto
1991   *Shades of Difference: The Art of Bob Boyer,* Edmonton Art Gallery, Edmonton, Alberta
1992   *Works from Summer 92,* Norman Mackenzie Art Gallery, Regina, Saskatchewan
1994   *New Blankets,* Galerie Dresdnere, Toronto
        Bob Boyer: A Survey, Keyano College Gallery, Fort McMurray, Alberta

Selected Group Exhibitions

1971   *Three Students,* Campion College, University of Regina, Regina, Saskatchewan
        Funk Three, Burnaby Art Gallery, Burnaby, British Columbia
1973   *C.A.R.: Saskatchewan North,* Saskatoon Public Library, Saskatchewan

1979   *Former Art Students,* Mackenzie Art Gallery, Regina, Saskatchewan
1980   *Contemporary Indian Art of Saskatchewan,* Rosemont Art Gallery, Regina, Saskatchewan
1981   *Art Amerindian '81,* National Arts Centre, Ottawa
1982   *Seven Canadian Artists,* The Foundry, Washington, D.C.
        Artists of the Church Gallery, Ottawa
1983-65 *Contemporary Inuit and Indian Art of Canada,* (traveling in the United States and South America)
1984   *Horses Fly Too,* Mackenzie Art Gallery, Regina, Saskatchewan
1985-87 *The Métis Show,* Glenbow Museum, Calgary, Alberta
        Two Worlds, Mackenzie Art Gallery, Saskatchewan (traveling)
1986   *Sapp, Lonechild, Boyer and Beaudry,* Organization of Saskatchewan Arts Councils (traveling)
        A Celebration of Contemporary Native Art; Part I, Canadian Consulate, Los Angeles
        Cross Cultural Views, National Gallery of Canada, Ottawa
        New Beginnings: Native Business Summit, Toronto Convention Centre, Ontario
        Ascending Culture, Terrasses de la Chaudiere, Hull, Quebec
1987   *Eight from the Prairies,* Thunder Bay Art Gallery, Thunder Bay, Ontario
        Out of Saskatchewan, Vancouver Art Gallery, British Columbia; B.B. Mendel Art Gallery, Saskatoon, Saskatchewan; Rosemont Art Gallery, Regina, Saskatchewan
        A Celebration of Contemporary Canadian Art, Part II, Southwest Museum, Los Angeles
1988-90 *In The Shadow of The Sun,* National Museum, Ottawa (traveling in Canada and Germany)
1989   *Curators Choose,* Art Gallery of Ontario, Toronto
        Indian Art, Beaux Arts Galerie, Paris
        Selections from the Permanent Collection of the Regina Public Library, Regina, Saskatchewan
1990   *Found Objects,* Mendel Art Gallery, Saskatoon, Saskatchewan
        Seeing Red, Agnes Etherington Gallery, Kingston, Ontario
        Contemporary Rituals, 3-Person Show, Whitewater Gallery, North Bay, Ontario (traveling)
        Travel and Identity, Mackenzie Art Gallery, Regina, Saskatchewan
1991   *Myth and Magic in America: The Eighties,* Museo Contemporaneo de Monterrey, Mexico
1992   *Reconstructed Symbols Deconstructed Meaning,* Cleveland Art Centre, Ohio
1994   Museum of Textiles, Toronto (traveling)
1995   *First Nation Perspective,* Mendel Gallery (traveling)
1995   *Who Speaks for the Rivers?,* Derek Simpkins Gallery of Tribal Art, Vancouver, British Columbia
1996   *Recent Acquisitions,* Thunder Bay Art Gallery, Thunder Bay, Ontario

Collections

Ben Gurion University, Israel; Canada Council Art Bank, Ottawa, City of Regina Art Collection, Regina, Saskatchewan; Federation of Saskatchewan Indian Nations, Regina, Saskatchewan; Glenbow

Bob Boyer: *Where You Been?,* 1996. Courtesy of the artist.

Museum/Art Gallery, Calgary, Alberta; Indian and Northern Affairs Canada, Ottawa, Ontario; Interprovincial Pipe and Steel Corporation, Regina, Saskatchewan; Kamloops Art Gallery, Kamloops, British Columbia; McMichael Canadian Collection, Kleinburg, Ontario; Mendel Art Gallery, Saskatoon, Saskatchewan; National Gallery of Canada, Ottawa; National Museum of Man, Ottawa; Native Canadian Centre of Toronto, Toronto; Regina Public Library Art Collection, Regina, Saskatchewan; Saskatchewan Arts Board, Regina; Saskatchewan Museum of Natural History, Regina; Thunder Bay Art Gallery, Thunder Bay, Ontario; Winnipeg Art Gallery, Winnipeg, Manitoba.

Publications

On BOYER: Books—*The Permanent Collection: Thunder Bay Art Gallery,* exhibition catalog edited by Marcy Menitove, Thunder Bay, Ontario, 1986; *In the Shadow of the Sun* by Gerald McMaster, Hull,

Quebec, 1993. **Articles**—"Where To Go From Here," *Artscraft,* Summer 1990; "The Sky Is the Limit: Conversations with First Nations Artists," *Border Crossings,* 1992; "Crossovers: Relative History" by Meeka Walsh, *Border Crossings,* 1992; "Bob Boyer, Saskatchewan's Artist's Wonderfully Witty Blanket Paintings Weave Modern with Tradition," *Now* (Toronto), 10-16 November 1994.

*   *   *

Boyer began exhibiting as a professional artist in 1970, his work being included in numerous ground-breaking exhibitions across Canada over the next 25 years. His career developed during a period distinguished by struggle, innovation, and change, and Boyer has been pivotal to the Native art, or "First Nations" art movement and its manifestation in visual cultural productions.

The first works of Boyer's to receive critical acclaim were his paintings on (Hudson Bay) blankets. Rich metaphors for the artist's articulation of the assaults against the Native peoples in Canada by colonizers, Boyer's blankets are testaments to cultural persistence. The concept for the blankets came during a trip Boyer made to Japan, where political banners caught his eye and his imagination. Amalgamating the banner idea to a statement regarding First Peoples in Canada seemed more than appropriate, as many of the First Peoples had been decimated by the distribution of blankets infected with smallpox. Stylistically, the blankets combine the abstract decorative motifs and symbols of traditional Native design along with the western attributes of easel painting defined through the form of late modernist abstraction. Subsequently, Boyer's work would be significantly positioned within a new generation of modernist Indian artists.

In the late 1980s, Boyer began to experiment with installation as a form of visual expression. The work he created in this genre continued the critical commentary on the colonizing actions against Native Peoples. Oftentimes using biting political satire and punning as a means to express his anger and frustration, Boyer has distinguished himself as one of the first modernists to use humour as an expressive means to define the Native American experience. Subsequently, a generation of Native artists in Canada, among them Theresa Marshall and Lawrence Paul, have found humour to be a profoundly effective means of articulating a perspective often positioned in opposition to that of a controlling mainstream.

Since the early 1990s, Boyer has returned to the blanket as the support for his painterly vision, producing works that are rich in visual expression. Recent works by the artist continue his practice of recalling symbolic and visual traditions rooted in an indigenous heritage, and revealing the contemporary manifestation of that ancestry's future. As both an educator and an artist, Boyer maintains an important role in Canada, instructing and influencing many art historians and artists in this country. Boyer has also curated a number of exhibitions, among them the important *100 Years of Saskatchewan Indian Art (1830-1930)* (1975), *New Works by a New Generation* (co-curated, 1982), and *Allen Sapp: A Retrospective* (1994).

—Carol Podedworny

BOYIDDLE, Parker
Tribal affiliations: Kiowa; Delaware
Painter and sculptor

Born: Parker Boyiddle, Jr., Chickasha, Oklahoma, 21 July 1947. **Education:** Institute of American Indian Arts, Santa Fe, 1964-66; work-study with sculptor John Chamberlain, 1965; Pima Community College, Tucson, Arizona, 1972-73. **Military Service:** U.S. Air Force, 1967-71. **Career:** Sculptor and painter; muralist, including Kiowa Tribal Complex, Carnegie, Oklahoma; artist in residence, Institute of American Indian Arts Museum, 1995; member, American Indian and Cowboy Artist Association. **Awards:** American Indian and Cowboy Artist Association, first place painting, 1977, 1980, 1984; George Phippen Memorial Award, sculpture, 1977; Philbrook Museum of Art, Grand Award (Painting), 1978; Colorado Indian Market, 1986; Red Earth Festival, 1987; Cherokee National Museum, 1977, 1984, 1989, 1991-92.

Individual Exhibitions

1978-79 *Paintings and Lithographs by Parker Boyiddle*, Southern Plains Indian Museum, Anadarko, Oklahoma

Selected Group Exhibitions

1965-66 *Young American Indian Artists*, Riverside Museum, New York
1977 Cherokee National Museum, Tahlequah, Oklahoma
1978 Phippen Museum of Western Art, Prescott, Arizona
1979 Pierre Cardin Espace Gallery, Paris, France
1980 *Pintura Amerinda Contemporanea*, Museo del Instituto Artes, Amerindos, Chile (traveling in South America)
1984 Cherokee National Museum, Tahlequah, Oklahoma
      Museum of Man, San Diego, California
1985 *Eye of My Mind: Contemporary American Indian Art*, Museum of Man, San Diego, California
1992 *Aspen/Snowmass Celebration for the American Indian*, Aspen, Colorado (sponsored by the National Museum of the American Indian, Smithsonian Institution, Washington, D.C.)
1993 *Native Peoples: Our Ways Shall Continue*, Denver Art Museum, Denver, Colorado
1994 *Moving Murals of Oklahoma: Contemporary Native American Painting*, organized by the Jacobson Foundation, Norman, Oklahoma (traveling)
1995 *Art from the Red Earth: The IAIA Oklahoma Alumni Association*, Institute of American Indian Arts Museum, Santa Fe, New Mexico
1996 Institute of American Indian Arts Museum, Santa Fe, New Mexico
      Kiowa Masters, Tribes Gallery, Norman, Oklahoma

Collections

Institute of American Indian Arts Museum, Santa Fe, New Mexico; Kiowa Tribal Museum, Carnegie, Oklahoma; Southern Plains Indian Museum, Anadarko, Oklahoma.

Publications

On BOYIDDLE: Articles—"Kiowa Murals," by Joan Frederick Denton, *Southwest Art*, July 1987; "Finding Rainy Mountain," *Oklahoma Today*, June 1990; "Rock Stars," *Oklahoma Today*, May/June 1994. **Film**—*Windrunner*, Indian Health Service, Albuquerque, New Mexico, 1990.

*

Parker Boyiddle comments:

What I am trying to do is reflect my environment and transcend a cultural gap. People can only idealize their ancestral past. My ancestors were Plains Indians—the Kiowa on my father's side and Western Delaware on my mother's side: both hunted buffalo and were nomads. Today there is no way I could live that life, but I can exercise some of the customs, morals, and religion of my people and still function in this twentieth century life.

*   *   *

Parker Boyiddle: *Offering to the Sun.* **Courtesy of the artist.**

Parker Boyiddle emerges from a rich tradition of Kiowa, Plains, and Oklahoma art. His paintings display the same careful attention to detail that characterizes the work of the Kiowa Five artists. Subjects are chosen for their invocation of Plains tribal history. Like fellow Oklahomans Acee Blue Eagle, Blackbear Bosin, and Rance Hood, Boyiddle often infuses his subjects with high drama. And yet this artist is equally at ease creating sculptural forms of abstract elegance.

The artist considers himself first a sculptor. He did not begin painting until he attended the Institute of American Indian Arts in the 1960s. However, the two modes of working each impact the other. The musculature of Boyiddle's painted figures, for example, seem almost chiseled, and his distinctive use of color, light and shadow reinforces the sculptural effect of the two-dimensional image. In *Offering to the Sun,* the figures appear to be rendered in bronze. Likewise, the bronze and stone works often rely on painterly surface effects such as patinas, differing levels of polish, and contrasting textures.

Boyiddle's work has been called theatrical. In creating his striking paintings, the artist takes on roles similar to those in theatrical productions, bathing his subject with the saturated color of stage lighting, costuming figures in historically accurate dress, directing action across his dynamic compositions. Human and animal figures are often fused or superimposed, suggesting the powerful daily connection with the natural world that characterized Kiowa and Plains tribal life. Boyiddle has no illusions about the role of such historical representations: "People can only idealize their ancestral past," he stated bluntly. Yet the artist believes that these portrayals fulfill a very real need for a generation of young people "trying to identify with themselves and connect with their history."

Boyiddle's sculpture is strongly influenced by the work of Allan Houser, who was an instructor at the Institute of American Indian Arts when Boyiddle attended the school. Like his mentor, Boyiddle displays great stylistic breadth—from a historically accurate and highly detailed pair of pipe carrier figures, to a Rodinesque study of a hand, to elegantly abstracted eagle forms. Perhaps most significant, and certainly most unique, is the limited-edition bronze, *New Life,* commemorating the birth of the artist's son in 1979. The sculpture depicts a woman with her newborn in the moment following childbirth. The new mother is still in a squatting, birthing position. The child is balanced precariously on her hand. The as-yet uncut umbilical cord still joins the two. Boyiddle describes the scene as the "encapsulation of being"—that transitory moment when a woman is face to face with a part of herself. Unlike most of the artist's human figures, this one offers few clues to her identity. The non-descript tunic has no cultural reference. The figure's knee, which is sinking into the earth implied beneath it, reminds us that as one life begins, another is a step closer to its end. By emphasizing the cyclical nature of birth and death, the sculpture transcends temporal and cultural boundaries. The treatment of the subject is unusual and has met with a share of resistance in the Indian art world. Yet the theme of childbirth can be traced to pre-contact petroglyphs, where it was presented with equal candor.

Boyiddle is a regular participant in some of the best-known Indian art events. He is often an award winner at the Red Earth Festival in Oklahoma City and at the Santa Fe Indian Market. In 1984, he was commissioned, along with Mirac Creepingbear and Sherman Chaddlesone, to create a series of murals for the Kiowa tribal complex in Carnegie, Oklahoma. Boyiddle is working on a

Parker Boyiddle. Photograph by Sanford Mauldin; courtesy of the artist.

collaborative sculpture project to be unveiled in 1998 at Walt Disney World in Florida.

—Lisa Cooley

BRADLEY, David

Tribal affiliations: Chippewa; Sioux
Painter, printmaker, and sculptor

Born: David Paul Bradley, Eureka, California, 1954; enrolled member of the Minnesota Chippewa tribe. **Education:** Coursework at the College of St. Thomas, St. Paul, Minnesota, 1972-73, and University of Arizona 1974; Institute of American Indian Art, A.F.A, 1977-79; College of Santa Fe, B.F.A., 1980. **Career:** Peace Corps volunteer, 1975-76; professional artist and book illustrator, 1979—; studio artist, Elaine Horwitch Galleries, 1980-89; lecturer and panelist at several universities; vice-president and co-founder, Native American Artists Association; committee member, New Mexico Indian Arts and Crafts Task Force and the New Mexico Commission on Indian Affairs; board member, Southwest Association on Indian Art; member of the Artist Planning Committee for the Smithsonian Institution's National Museum of the American Indian; visiting artist/professor, Institute of American Indian Arts, 1991-93. **Awards:** Valedictorian, Class of 1979, Institute of American Indian Art; Minnesota Chippewa Tribe, Award of merit in Art, 1979; Southwestern Association for Indian Art Santa Fe Indian Market, only artist to ever have won first prize in both sculpture and painting.

Individual Exhibitions

1979-80 Institute of American Indian Art, Santa Fe
1980-81 Judith Stern Gallery, Minneapolis, Minnesota
1981-90 Elaine Horwitch Gallery, Santa Fe
1991 *Restless Native: David Bradley,* Plains Art Museum, Fargo, North Dakota, and Moorehead, Minnesota
1993 Wheelwright Museum of the American Indian, Santa Fe
1996 Wheelwright Museum of the American Indian, Santa Fe

Selected Group Exhibitions

1979 Ojibwe Art Expo, University of Minnesota Gallery, Minneapolis
1980 *Pintura Amerinda Contemporanea,* Museo del Instituto Artes, Amerindos, Chile
      Heard Museum, Phoenix
      Five Man Sculpture Show, Wheelwright Museum of the American Indian, Santa Fe
1981 *Nine from New Mexico,* Foundation Gallery, New York
      Walk in Beauty, National Invitational Indian Art Show, Santa Fe
      The Sweet Grass Lives On, University of California, Davis
      National American Indian Art Show, Turtle Center, Niagara Falls, New York
      Indian and Hispanic Invitational Art Show, Institute of American Indian Arts Museum, Santa Fe
      American Indian Art Invitational, Lima, Peru
1981-92 *Confluences of Tradition and Change: 24 American Indian Artists,* R.L. Nelson Gallery and C.N. Gorman Museum, Davis, California (traveling)
1982 *Contemporary North American Art,* National Museum of Natural History, Smithsonian Institution, Washington, D.C.
      Night of First Americans, John F. Kennedy Center for the Performing Arts, Washington, D.C.
      Eight Native Minnesota Artists, Minneapolis Institute of Arts
      Native American Pictoral Traditions, Aspen Institute, Creston, Colorado
1983 *Visions of the Earth,* Boulder, Colorado
      Wild West Show, Alberta College of Art Gallery
      Indian Self Rule, Sun Valley Center for the Arts, Sun Valley, Idaho
1984 *Contemporary Native American Art,* Museum of Fine Arts, Santa Fe
      Innovations: New Expressions in Native American Painting, Heard Museum, Phoenix
1984-85 *Indianischer Kuntsler,* Philbrook Museum of Art, Tulsa, Oklahoma
1985 *Eight Artists,* The Southwest Museum, Los Angeles
      Homecomings: Native American Artists, North Dakota Museum of Art, Grand Forks
      Signale, Amerika Haus, Stuttgart, West Germany (traveling)

1986 *Contemporary Native American Artists,* Governor's Gallery, Capitol Building, Santa Fe
1987 *Traditions and Innovations: 7 American Artists,* Plains Art Museum, Moorehead, Minnesota
      Recent Generations: 20 Years of Native American Art, Heard Museum, Phoenix
      Statements 87, New Mexico Arts Invitational, Albuquerque
      Plains Indian Art Invitational, Plains Indian Museum, Buffalo Bill Historical Center, Cody, Wyoming
1988 *Common Ground,* Albuquerque Museum, Albuquerque, New Mexico
      Works on Paper, Rio Grande Institute Group Show, San Antonio, Texas
1989 *Glyphs of New Mexico: New Interpretations,* Governor's Gallery, New Mexico State Capitol Building, Santa Fe
      Contemporary Indian Art, Stables Art Center, Taos, New Mexico
1990 *Artists and Advocates,* Boulder, Colorado (traveling)
      Creations of the Four Directions, Institute of American Indian Arts Museum, Santa Fe
      Appropriation/Transformation, University of New Mexico Art Museum, Johnson Gallery, Albuquerque, New Mexico
      Radicals and Renegades, Institute of American Indian Arts Museum, Santa Fe (national traveling exhibition)
      Artists of the Southwest, Eiteljorg Museum, Indianapolis, Indiana
1990-91 *One With the Earth,* exhibit and tour arranged by the Institute of American Indian and Alaska Culture and Art Development, Santa Fe
1991 *After 5 PM ... and on weekends,* Institute of American Indian Arts Faculty Exhibition, Institute of American Indian Arts Museum, Santa Fe
1993-96 Series of exhibitions throughout Europe

Collections

Albuquerque Museum, New Mexico; Buffalo Bill Historical Center, Cody, Wyoming; Denver Art Museum; Gilcrease Museum, Tulsa, Oklahoma; Heard Museum, Phoenix, Arizona; Institute of American Indian Arts Museum, Santa Fe, New Mexico; Joslyn Art Museum, Omaha, Nebraska; Norman Mackenzie Art Museum, University of Regina, Saskatchewan; Museum of the American Indian, New York City; Museum of Mankind, Vienna, Austria; National Museum of American Art, Washington, D.C.; Museum of Fine Arts, Santa Fe; Plains Art Museum, Fargo, North Dakota, and Moorehead, Minnesota; Millicent Rogers Museum, Taos, New Mexico; Stamford Museum, Stamford, Connecticut; United States Embassy, Oslo, Norway; Wheelwright Museum of the American Indian, Santa Fe.

Publications

On BRADLEY: Books—*Confluences of Tradition and Change: 24 American Indian Artists,* exhibition catalog, L. Price Amerson, Jr., editor, Davis, California: Richard L. Nelson Gallery, University of California, 1981; *American Indian Art in the 1980s,* exhibition catalog by Lloyd Kiva New, Niagara Falls, New York: Native American Center for the Living Arts, 1981; *American Artists,* Santa Fe: Krantz, 1984; *The Arts of the North American Indian: Traditions in Evolu-*

David Bradley: *Indian Country Today,* **1996. Courtesy of the artist.**

tion, Tulsa: Philbrook Art Center, 1986; *The Arts of the North American Indian: Native Traditions in Evolution,* Edwin L. Wade and Rennard Strickland, editors, New York: Hudson Hills Press, 1986; *Creativity Is Our Tradition: Three Decades of Contemporary Indian Art* by Rick Hill, Santa Fe: Institute of American Indian and Alaska Native Culture and Arts Development, 1992. **Articles—** "Outside the Pueblo," by Katherine Smith, *Portfolio: The Magazine of Fine Arts,* July-August, 1982; "Frames of Reference: Native American Art in the Context of Modern and Post-Modern Art," by Gerhard Hoffman, *Southwestern Contemporary Arts Quarterly,* Spring 1987; "'Fake' Indian Artists Challenged," *Santa Fe Reporter,* August 10, 1988; "Three Political Artists," *Southwest Profile Magazine,* September 1990; "Indian/Non-Indian," *Albuquerque Journal,* March 25, 1991.

*

David Bradley comments:

I have always been an artist. Art is about freedom and with that freedom comes responsibility. Social responsibility has always been a big issue for me and that is reflected in my work. For me Art has never been about stuffing one's pockets. To be an artist is to seek Truth.

*   *   *

Bradley blends a keen sense of social responsibility with mastery of the techniques of sculpture and painting. Early pieces reflect his interest in folk art, through which he honed his craft and gradually worked in weighty commentary with wit and arresting images. From more singular statements and stark works, Bradley has evolved figurative and abstract sculpture and painting with increasing depths of allegory, satire, and humor. These developments reflect restless creativity as well as personal evolution and application of various approaches for presenting events from a Native American point of view. For example, some of Bradley's paintings are rendered in a semi-realistic, flat style, while others are more abstract and painted thickly. He can combine principles of traditional pueblo painting with Renaissance techniques, demonstrating knowledge of Western art and a deep understanding of "being part of modern Indian life."

Bradley's artistic talents were evident in childhood, and his early life experiences inform the socio-political views he expresses. Enduring a difficult childhood in a large and poor family, he was shuttled among various foster homes and had an unsuccessful adoption with a white family before being reunited in his mid-teens with his family. The Indian Child Welfare Act subsequently reformed the ways in which states approach such sitations. Bradley attended the College of St. Thomas in St. Paul, Minnesota, but after two semesters, restlessness led him to travel in the Southwest and Mexico. He briefly resumed his studies at the University of Arizona in 1974, then continued traveling before joining the Peace Corps in 1975.

His experience in the Peace Corps in Central America and the Caribbean helped forge Bradley's political and artistic concerns. In Haiti, reputed to be the poorest country at that time in the Western Hemisphere, Bradley witnessed a revival in folk painting, and then a similar revival in Guatemala, where he lived among Mayans. Upon his return to the United States, Bradley entered the Institute of American Indian Arts, developing his artistic talents, graduating at the head of his class, and becoming involved in Institute affairs as the student representative on the Board of Regents.

Bradley had intended to ease into a professional artistic career, and he enjoyed a steady income, particlarly through his association with Elaine Horwitch Galleries, but he also became acutely aware of corruption in the art industry; this included exploitation of Native artists by museums and galleries of the Southwest, Indian *poseurs*, and commercialization of art that returns nothing to Native American communities, which led him to political activisim as a voice in Native arts organizations and state boards of art in the Southwest.

Though this experience made him realize that "Indians are, by definition, political beings," socio-political awareness had always informed Bradley's art. His sculpture, *Indian Affected by Anti-Indian Backlash*, 1979, was an early commentary on contemporary experience. The alabaster sculpture presents a slumping Indian resting on his left elbow and peering through his fingers, which are covering his eyes in an expression of someone facing yet another test of endurance. Representative of his early work, this sculpture harkens to the folk-art style of the Southwest and Central America, while exhibiting clean and classical lines.

Bradley enlarged upon this base by experiementing with a wide range of styles, from Pueblo painting, to developing a semi-realistic and flat presentation, to imitating masters of the Renaissance and other Western traditions. Satire and humor also became more evident, as in a series of paintings that parody major works of art to depict events from a Native American point of view. *The Last Supper*, for example, presents a traditional pueblo feast day in the manner of Da Vinci's painting, and *American Gothic Ghost Dancers* and *Homage to Crow King* satirize of the colonization of Indians. Using familiar images of Western civilization and peopling them with images of Native American experience forces the viewer to consider the historical experience of Native America. More recently, Bradley's art has ranged from landscapes to abstract collages while keeping social issues in the forefront and inspiring the viewer to consider them while admiring the artist's technique and presentation.

—Leona Zastrow

BUFFALO, Bennie

Variant names: Going South
Tribal affiliations: Cheyenne
Painter

Born: Clinton, Oklahoma, 39 January 1948. **Education:** Institute of American Indian Arts, Santa Fe, 1963-67; San Francisco Art Institute, 1970-72; Southwestern State College, Weatherford, Oklahoma, 1972-73; University of Oklahoma, Norman, 1975-76, majoring in filmmaking. **Military Service:** U.S. Army, 1967-70, served in Vietnam. **Awards:** Scottsdale National Indian Arts Exhibition, 1967; American Indian Exposition, Anadarko, Oklahoma, 1971 and 1974; Philbrook Museum Annual Indian Art Exhibition (juried), 1974-75; Trail of Tears Art Show, Cherokee National Museum, Tahlequah, Oklahoma, 1986. **Died:** 1994.

Individual Exhibitions

1980   *Paintings by Benjamin Buffalo*, Southern Plains Indian Museum and Craft Center, Anadarko, Oklahoma

Bennie Buffalo: *Red & Blue Blanket on a Pendleton,* 1968. Photograph by Larry McNeil; courtesy Institute of American Indian Arts Museum, Santa Fe, New Mexico.

Selected Group Exhibitions

1972   *Contemporary Southern Plains Indian Painting,* sponsored by the Southern Plains Indian Museum and Oklahoma Indian Arts Cooperative (traveling)

1973   Cherokee National Museum, Tahlequah, Oklahoma

1973-74 *New Directions,* Institute of American Indian Arts Museum, Santa Fe (traveling)

1974   *The Institute of American Indian Arts Alumni Show,* Amon Carter Museum of Western Art, Fort Worth, Texas

1975-80 *Pinturas Amerindas Contemporanes/E.U.A.,* sponsored by United States Department of State and International Communications Agency, Washington, D.C. (traveling, South America)

1980-81 The Galleria, Norman, Oklahoma

1981   *Views and Visions: The Symbolic Imagery of the Native American Church,* Southern Indian Plains Museum, Anadarko, Oklahoma

1984-85 *Indianascher Kunstler* (traveling, Germany), organized by the Philbrook Museum, Tulsa, Oklahoma

1987   *Red Earth Festival,* Myriad Art Plaza, Oklahoma City, Oklahoma

1991   *Aspen/Snowmass Celebration for the American Indian,* sponsored by the National Museum of the American Indian, Smithsonian Institution, Aspen, Colorado

       One With the Earth, organized by the Institute of American Indian Arts and Alaska Culture and Arts Development, Santa Fe, New Mexico

1992   *Creativity is Our Tradition: Three Decades of Contemporary Indian Art at the Institute of American Indian Arts,* Institute of American Indian Arts Museum, Santa Fe, New Mexico

Collections

Institute of American Indian Arts Museum, Santa Fe, New Mexico; Southern Plains Indian Museum, Anadarko, Oklahoma.

Publications

On BUFFALO: Books—*The Institute of American Indian Arts Alumni Show,* by Lloyd Kiva New, catalog, Fort Worth, Texas, 1974; *Song from the Earth: American Indian Painting,* by Jamake Highwater, Boston, 1976; *Pinturas Amerindas Contemporanes/E.U.A.,* Phoenix, 1979; *The Sweet Grass Lives On,* by Jamake Highwater, New York, 1980; *Paintings by Benjamin Buffalo: Exhibition Guide,* Southern Plains Indian Museum and Craft Center, Anadarko, Oklahoma, 1980; *Magic Images: Contemporary Native American Art,* by Edwin L. Wade and Rennard Strickland, Norman, Oklahoma, 1981; *Indianascher Kunstler,* by Gerhard Hoffman, Munich, 1984; *Creativity is Our Tradition: Three Decades of Contemporary Indian Art at the Institute of American Indian Arts,* by Rick Hill, Santa Fe, 1992.

*

Bennie Buffalo comments (1992):

From abstraction to realism I am trying to relate my art to free thinking.... I am attempting to create a synthesis of the pure, unexplainable, abstract thought processes that occur in every mind, every day. The feeling that music can create for the soul, so also does reality award us the visual stimuli that gave our people beauty. (From *Creativity Is Our Tradition*)

*   *   *

Bennie Buffalo underwent an extensive, ten-year formal art training, which started with his enrollment at the Institute of American Indian Arts in Santa Fe in 1963. After an interruption from 1967 to 1970—he served in the U.S. Army and was sent to Vietnam—he continued his studies at the San Francisco Art Institute, followed by a year of study at the Southwestern State College in Weatherford, Oklahoma, and, finally, from 1975-76 he majored in filmmaking at the University of Oklahoma in Norman. The experiences of these years, greatly varied in character, were a decisive factor in shaping his very distinctive painting style.

At the IAIA, the greatest influence was exerted by fellow students Earl Biss, T.C. Cannon, and Kevin Red Star. Strongly individualistic as these artists are, they incorporated different reactions to Native American traditions and Western influences in the arts. In San Francisco in the 1970s, the Anglo painter Richard Lindner was a major influence on the art scene, and, at the University of Oklahoma, Buffalo's experience with the art of filmmaking, together with his interest in photography, broadened his tendency towards realism in painting.

The stylistic change that occurred during the formative years is best summed up in Buffalo's statement from 1980: "I wanted to get away from the traditional, two-dimensional type of work. I'm trying to express the realism of our American Indians by photographic exactness instead of depicting things that are too detailed" (*Paintings by Benjamin Buffalo: Exhibition Guide*). This statement seems to imply that his subject matter is Indian whereas his style is that of Western photorealism. A closer view, however, reveals that his photorealism is permeated with un-realistic, "abstract" elements that can be traced to the Native American feeling of life and Indian spirituality. He does not fully embrace the method of photorealism, but enjoys "a sort of abstractness": "The different areas of the painting all come together to make the whole more realistic. And then, different areas of the painting are abstract, such as the skin tones, hair treatment, clothing, etc."

An example of this seemingly strange combination of photorealism and abstractness is *Canadian Cree Straight Dancer*. The figure of the dancer seems to be painted perfectly realistically, but the colors—of the body, the face, and the blue garment—are slightly blurred, and there is an almost imperceptible play of flicker effects that brings about a certain "abstractness" and lends the dancer a slightly surreal or even mystical aura. A similar effect is achieved through the almost obtrusively loud red of the background, evoking the hallucinatory color effects of a peyote dream. Thus, we find in this, for a painting seemingly so atypical of "pure" photorealism, a typically Indian expansion of the concept of reality, embracing the representation of the inner life, the psyche, and mystical experiences. The dance motif, with its ceremonial and religious connotations, moreover, transforms photorealism's expressive concentration on the surface of things by summoning up the spiritual dimension of the Indian's feeling for life.

As to his treatment of the Indian subject matter, Bennie Buffalo has certain traits in common with T.C. Cannon, Kevin Red Star and others who express with their paintings their deep concern about the Native American's situation in our times. *Rodeo Queen*, for instance, shows Native culture has entered the stage of advertising, marketing, and consumption, with the Indian making himself a part of the Wild West myth. In other cases, like *Girl in Elk Tooth Dress*, Buffalo uses the Western tradition of portrait painting to reveal discrepancies that derive from inconsistencies in accommodation of the Native and white worlds. Through his selection and interpretation, the so-called photorealism becomes in his paintings a means of

a personal commentary on the Native American situation as a hybrid between two cultures. Again, it is in accordance with other modern Indian painters, David Bradley for instance, that he does not render this inconclusive state from a tragic perspective, but employs the ironic distance of the well-meaning observer who registers facts and translates them into artistic forms.

—Gerhard and Gisela Hoffman

BURTON, Jimalee

Variant names: Ho Chee Nee
Tribal affiliations: Creek; Cherokee
Painter

Born: Jimalee Chitwood in El Reno, Oklahoma, 23 January 1906; Native name translates as Leader. **Family:** Married Dan A. Burton, 1933 (died, 1954). **Education:** Indian schools in Colony, Geary, and Weatherford, Oklahoma; Southwestern Teachers College; University of Tulsa. **Career:** Radio program supervisor and host in Oklahoma, 1930s to early 1940s; editor of *The Native Voice* newspaper; songwriter, poet, and writer; artist. **Awards:** National Penwoman Association Award for her short story, "Indian Legend of Creation"; 1947 Purchase Award, Philbrook Museum of Art.

Selected Group Exhibitions

1947	Philbrook Museum of Art, Tulsa, Oklahoma
1961	University of Florida, Sarasota
1963	University of Georgia, Athens
1964-65	*First Annual Invitational Exhibition of American Indian Paintings,* United States Department of the Interior, Washington, D.C.
1965	El Centro Gallery, Miami, Florida
1966	Five Civilized Tribes Museum, Muskogee, Oklahoma
1967	Glenbow Museum, Calgary, Alberta
1968	M.H. De Young Memorial Museum, Fine Arts Museums of San Francisco
	Oakland College of Arts and Crafts, Oakland, California
1971	Galveston Art Center, Galveston, Texas
1974	Denver Art Museum, Denver, Colorado
1977	Lowe Gallery, Miami, Florida

Collections

Thomas Gilcrease Institute of American History and Art, Tulsa, Oklahoma; Philbrook Museum of Art, Tulsa, Oklahoma.

Publications

By BURTON: Books—*Indian Heritage, Indian Pride*, Norman, University of Oklahoma Press, 1973. **Film**—*Indian Legends of Ho Chee Nee*, 1963.

On BURTON: Books—*American Indian Painting of the Southwest and Plains Areas*, by Dorothy Dunn, Albuquerque, Museum of New Mexico Press, 1968; *Indian Painters and White Patrons*, by J. J. Brody, Albuquerque, University of New Mexico Press, 1971;

That's What She Said: An Anthology of Contemporary Native American Women, Rayna Green, editor, Bloomington, Indian University Press, 1984. **Articles**—"Sarasota Art," Elihu Edelson, *News* (Sarasota, Florida), October 1, 1961.

*   *   *

Jimalee Burton enjoyed an active career in a variety of media through which she addressed issues and celebrated the cultural heritage of her people in Oklahoma, where she lived for most of the first fifty years of her life, and Florida, where she relocated following her husband's death in 1954. Airwaves, newspapers, film, books, and paintings were media through which Burton expressed herself and provided opportunities for others to share their views and experiences. She was a ground breaker in some respects, becoming the first Native American woman, for example, to have paintings exhibited at the Philbrook Museum of Art, which occurred in 1947.

Burton maintained an extremely active life, as befits her Native name, Ho Chee Nee, which translates as Leader. She was eager to promote education for Native Americans and to share the wealth of her cultural heritage, from its Florida roots to forced resettlement in Oklahoma. Burton had originally intended to become a teacher, but found numerous other outlets for educating through various media. Beginning in the 1930s, Burton hosted a radio program that ran for ten years and featured news, information, and cultural activities, including readings of her original poetry and prose, which often recounted Indian legends. She also began editing *The Native Voice,* an intertribal newspaper published out of Vancouver, British Columbia. Later, after having established herself as an artist, Burton was commissioned to help in a film project; the resulting documentary, *Indian Legends of Ho Chee Nee,* was released in 1963. A prolific period of writing followed, with poetry and prose published by small presses and journals, culminating with *Indian Heritage, Indian Pride: Stories That Touched My Life,* published in 1973. All the while, Burton undertook extensive research in Indian lore, traveling throughout North and South America, in a sense as a cultural ambassador, but also intent on piecing together elements of her mixed Creek and Cherokee background as well indigenous people in general. The results of this research are evident in her writings and paintings, which she began focusing on more exclusively in the 1960s and 1970s.

Burton studied sculpture at the University of Tulsa late in the 1930s, followed by instruction in painting at the University of Mexico with Carlos Merida. She proved more adept at painting, particularly for presenting themes and motifs relating to Native American culture. Of special interest in Burton's paintings are her feminine interpretations of the ceremonies and daily experiences of women. This much-needed perspective was originally a novelty and strength in her early paintings, but as her talent matured her renderings of these topics and this perspective began to receive equal acclaim. Her work during the 1960s offered new interpretations of subject matter that had been addressed by countless artists; through dramatic close-ups and greater sense of color and background, which added to mood and action, Burton discovered new ways of illuminating her explorations of myths and legends and, in a sense, arrived as a contemporary artist. This maturation is evident in increased exhibitions, including such important shows as the one held at the University of Florida, Sarasota (1961), an exhibition that was in many ways a breakthrough for Burton, garnering her the respect and confidence that rewarded her perseverance; the *First Annual Invitational Exhibition of American Indian Paintings,* Washington, D.C. (1964-65); and the exhibition at the Five Civilized Tribes Museum, Muskogee, Oklahoma (1966), which emphasized how far her talent had ripened in terms of liveliness, color, and background, since her first show at the Philbrook in 1947.

—Gregory Schaaf

CANNON, T. C.

Variant names: Pai-doung-u-day
Tribal affiliations: Caddo; Choctaw; Kiowa
Painter

Born: Thomas Wayne Cannon, Lawton, Oklahoma, 27 September 1946, to a Caddo/Choctaw/French mother and a Kiowa/Scotch-Irish father; Pai-doung-u-day means "One who Stands in the Sun." **Education:** Institute of American Indian Arts, Santa Fe, New Mexico, 1965-66; San Francisco Art Institute, 1966-67; College of Santa Fe, 1970-71; Central State University, Edmond, Oklahoma, 1971-74. **Military Service:** U.S. Army, 101st Air Cavalry, 1967-69; served in Vietnam. **Career:** Artist, writer, musician, composer; Artist-in-Residence, Dartmouth College, Colorado State University, National Park Service. **Awards:** American Indian Exposition, Anadarko, Oklahoma, 1964; Scottsdale National Indian Arts Exhibition, 1966; National Hall of Fame for Famous American Indians, 1988; commissions, including a mural for the Daybreak Star Indian Cultural Education Center in Seattle, Washington, 1976, and *A Remembered Muse*, commissioned by the Santa Fe Opera, 1978.

Individual Exhibitions

1971   *Paintings and Graphics by T. C. Cannon*, Southern Plains Museum, Anadarko, Oklahoma
1975   Beaumont-May Gallery at Hopkins Center, Dartmouth College, New Hampshire
1976   Wheelwright Museum of the American Indian, Santa Fe, New Mexico
1979   *T. C. Cannon Memorial Exhibition*, Aberbach Fine Art, New York
1990-91   *T. C. Cannon, Native American: A New View of the West*, National Cowboy Hall of Fame and Western Heritage Center, Oklahoma City, Oklahoma (traveling)

Selected Group Exhibitions

1965   *Second Annual Invitational Exhibition of American Indian Paintings*, United States Department of the Interior, Washington, D.C.
1968   *Cultural Olympics*, Mexico City, Mexico
1972   *Two American Painters* (Cannon and Fritz Scholder), National Collection of Fine Art, Smithsonian Institution, Washington, D.C. (international traveling exhibition)
        Contemporary Southern Indians Plains Paintings, Southern Plains Museum, Anadarko, Oklahoma
        Edinburgh International Art Festival, Scotland
1973-74   *New Directions,* Institute of American Indian Arts Museum, Santa Fe, New Mexico (traveling)

1974   *Institute of American Indian Arts Alumni Exhibition*, Amon Carter Museum of Western Art, Fort Worth, Texas Buffalo Bill Historical Center, Cody, Wyoming
1980   *Walk in Beauty: A National Invitational Native American Art Show*, Santa Fe Festival of the Arts, Santa Fe, New Mexico
1984   *Indianische Kunst im 20 Jahrhundert*, Munich, Germany (traveling)
1990-91   *One With the Earth*, organized by the Insitute of American Indian Arts and Alaska Culture and Arts Development (traveling)
1991-96   *Shared Visions: Native American Painters and Sculptors of the Twentieth Century,* Heard Museum, Phoenix, Arizona (traveling)
1992   *Creativity is our Tradition*, Institute of American Indian Arts Museum, Santa Fe, New Mexico

Collections

Central State University Museum of Art, Edmonds, Oklahoma; Eitlejorg Museum, Indianapolis, Indiana; Heard Museum, Phoenix, Arizona; Institute of American Indian Arts, Santa Fe, New Mexico; National Collection of Fine Art, Smithsonian Institution, Washington, D.C.; Philbrook Museum, Tulsa, Oklahoma; Seattle Arts Commission, Seattle, Washington; Southern Plains Indian Museum, Anadarko Oklahoma; Wheelwright Museum of the American Indian, Santa Fe, New Mexico.

Publications

On CANNON: Books—*Institute of American Indian Arts Alumni Exhibition*, by Lloyd Kiva New, Amon Carter Museum of Western Art, Fort Worth, Texas, 1974; *American Indian Painting and Sculpture,* by Patricia Janis Broder, New York, 1981; *Indianische Kunst im 20 Jahrhundert*, by Gerhard Hoffman, Munich, Germany, 1984; *The Arts of the North American Indian: Native Traditions in Evolution,* Edwin L. Wade and Rennard Strickland, editors, New York: Hudson Hills Press, 1986; *T. C. Cannon, Native American: A New View of the West,* by William Wallo and John Pickard, Oklahoma City, 1990; *Shared Visions: Native American Painting and Sculpture of the Twentieth Century,* Margaret Archueleta and Rennard Strickland, editors, Heard Museum, Phoenix, Arizona, 1992; *Creativity Is Our Tradition: Three Decades of Contemporary Indian Art,* by Rick Hill, Santa Fe: Institute of American Indian and Alaska Native Culture and Arts Development, 1992; *Native American Arts and Folklore,* David Campbell, editor, Grenwich, Connecticut, 1993.

*   *   *

T. C. Cannon was the single most important artist to emerge from the Bureau of Indian Affairs school in the arts for Indians in Santa

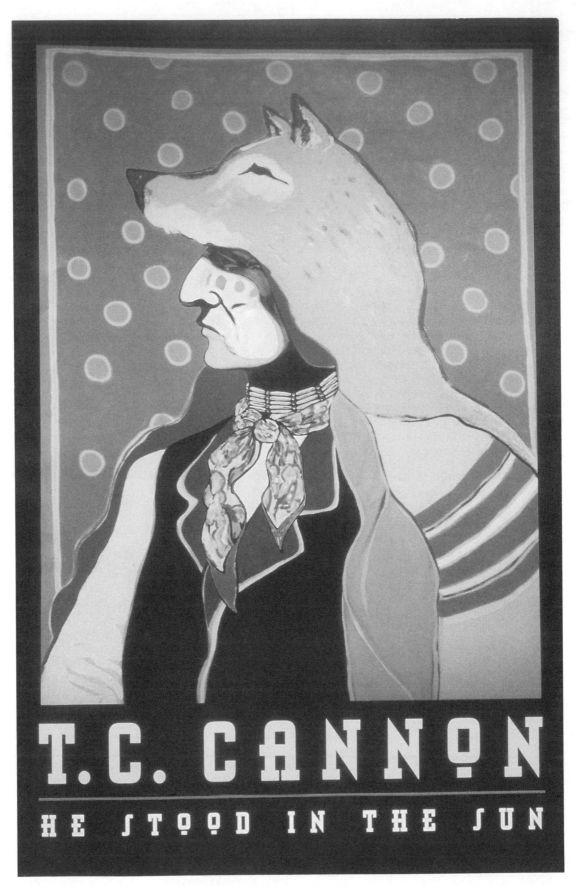

T. C. Cannon: *He Stood in the Sun,* 1970. Photograph by Seth Roffman; Fox Fine Art Collection, courtesy Cannon Estate.

Fe. His work as a student lead the way for other students as well as his instructors, who included Fritz Scholder. At Institute of American Indian Arts, Cannon experimented with imagery and styles that gave birth to the modernistic movement among Native American artists toward abstraction, satire and social commentary.

Many factors combined to allow Cannon to explore artistic options and create a new way of presenting the Indian in his art. He was 19 years old when he entered IAIA, which had the most creative staff of artists and educators ever assembled to teach art to Indians. He is said to have developed a good relationship with Fritz Scholder, an instructor at IAIA, and they were more like equals than student and teacher; both were exploring new ways of seeing. He also was fortunate to have fellow students such as Bill Soza and Alfred Young Man, who challenged each other; their creative energy influenced the direction of Cannon's work. The political and social climate of those times also presented Cannon with issues that he dealt with in his art, and a unique picture emerges of what the life of contemporary Indians was like.

It is his early work at IAIA that has the most vitality, and this is best seen in *Mama and Papa Have the Going Back to Shiprock Blues*, made before 1966. It has become the pivotal painting for the era because it was about contemporary Indians caught in a real moment, not the romanticized images of the past that had invaded Indian art. This work was featured in the only exhibition of contemporary Indian art to ever be held at the Smithsonian's National Collection of Fine Art in Washington, D.C.: *Two American Painters* brought the work of both Cannon and his former teacher, Fritz Scholder, to a new audience in 1972, a critical time in Indian history, as the country was rethinking attitudes and policies towards Indians. The exhibition curator, Robert Ewing, then Director of the New Mexico Museum of Fine Art, intentionally wanted their work presented as fine art, rather than "Indian art," because of the negative connotations that the term represented in the minds of fine art aficionados.

Cannon enlisted in the U.S. Army during the Vietnam War era (1967-69) and served in the 101st Air Cavalry, earning two Bronze star for valor during the Tet Offensive; however, deeper insight into military affairs affected his art for the next ten years before his untimely death in a car accident while he was a professional artist in Santa Fe. This is most evident in 20 foot mural he painted in 1977, *Epic in Plains History: Mother Earth, Father Sky and the Children Themselves*, for the Daybreak Star Cultural Center in Seattle, Washington. In this work he shows the history of his people and the importance of the underlying belief system that still unites the cultures of the Plains Indians. In the center of the mural, Cannon places his own hand prints in red and yellow below a scene of a warrior on horseback killing a U.S. Soldier. A Gourd Dancer, as a representative of the older warrior societies, sings on the edge the canvas to represent life today. Cannon intentionally made him appear to moving off the canvas, to show that life goes on for the Plains people.

In 1972, Cannon completed *Village with Bomb*, showing a Plains Indian woman holding a baby in a decorated cradle board. Behind them a huge orange mushroom cloud rises, recalling televised and photograph images of the bombing of villages in Vietnam, but also saying that same process was involved in the killing of Indians in this country. The image of the atomic bomb explosion was a sub-theme to much of Cannon's work, as were scenes from the fight between cavalry and Indians, which is especially ironic in that Cannon would join the contemporary version of that calvary and attack people in their native land.

Cannon's early success was felt by many of the graduates of IAIA at the time, but Cannon was one of to first to reach out beyond Santa Fe. Often overlooked is the fact that Cannon was influenced by another mentor, William Wallo, a non-Indian, while at Central State University in Oklahoma, a year before the D.C. exhibition and then two years after. In 1975 Cannon served as artist-in-residence at Dartmouth College and his commercial success was growing. Much of the work he did as a professional artist focused on rethinking images of the past. He would take historic photos of Indians and re-animate them with colorful feelings of life and movement, but also with a sense of hostility felt by his generation. Yet his sketch books and lesser known works continue to show a satirical wit in dealing with images, ideas and icons of both Indians and attitudes towards Indians.

Cannon has been described as shy, sensitive and erudite. His friends tell of his joy of music. He left behind many poems and writings that reveal a very different persona than much of his art would tell. It is through his writings that we find what was on his mind, the questions about art, about women, about war. His pen searched his soul deeper than his paint brush could. We also see a pain that was so deeply felt—that his death, while tragic, may have also been a release from the emotional realities that Cannon, and many of the Indian of his generation, faced with trepidation.

—Rick Hill

CARDINAL, Douglas

Tribal affiliations: Métis
Architect

Born: Douglas Joseph Cardinal, Calgary, Alberta, 7 March 1934. **Education:** University of British Columbia, Vancouver, 1953-54; University of Texas, Austin, 1956-63, B.Arch. 1963. **Career:** Design Architect, Bissell and Holman, Red Deer, Alberta, 1963-67; Principal, Douglas J. Cardinal Architect, Red Deer, Alberta, 1964-67, and Edmonton, Alberta 1967-76; Douglas J. Cardinal Architect, Edmonton, Alberta, since 1976. **Awards:** Honor Award, Alberta Association of Architects, 1968; Honor Award 1969 and Award of Excellence, 1978, City of Red Deer, Alberta; Award of Excellence, *Canadian Architect*, 1972; Achievement of Excellence Award in Architecture, Province of Alberta, 1974; Canada Council Molson Prize for the Arts, 1993; Banff Centre National Arts Award, 1990; Aboriginal Achievement Award, 1995; honorary doctorates, University of Windsor, Ontario, University of Calgary, Alberta; member, Royal Canadian Academy of Arts, 1974; fellow, Royal Architectural Institute of Canada, 1983. **Address:** Douglas J. Cardinal Architect Ltd., 10160 112th Street, Edmonton, Alberta T5K 2L6.

Building Designs

1967	Guloien House, Sylvan Lake, Alberta
	St. Mary's Church, Red Deer, Alberta
1970	Alberta Indian Education Centre, master plan, Edmonton
1971	Stettler Municipal Hospital, Alberta
1972	Hay River High School, Northwest Territories
	Provost Provincial Building, Alberta
	St. Michael's School, Bow Island, Alberta
	Grande Prairie Regional College and Theatre, Alberta

1975   Kehewen School, Alberta
1976   Ile La Crosse School, Alberta
        Bonnyville Rehabilitation Centre, Alberta
1977   La Ronge Elementary School, Saskatchewan
        Alberta Government Services Centre, Ponoka
1978   Slave Lake Senior Citizens Residence, Alberta
        Slave Lake Drop-In Centre, Alberta
        Community Development Studies (James Smith, Onion
            Lake, Thunderchild, Saddle Lake, and Cold Lake)
1979   Grotski House, Edmonton, Alberta
1980   Spruce Grove Composite High School, Alberta
1981   Spruce Grove Multi-Use Building, Alberta
        Space Sciences Centre, Edmonton, Alberta
1983   Churchill High School, Manitoba
1984   Holy Trinity Catholic High School, Edmonton, Alberta
        St. Albert Place, Leighton Colony, Banff, Alberta
1985   National Museum of Man, Hull, Quebec
1989   Canadian Museum of Civilisation, Hull, Quebec
1990   Saskatchewan Federated Indian College, master plan and
            concept design for expansion, Regina
1993   Institute of American Indian Arts, master plan, Santa Fe,
            New Mexico
        National Museum of the American Indian, Smithsonian
            Institution, Washington, D.C. (scheduled for comple-
            tion in 2001)
1996   Tatsikiisaapo'p, Kainai Middle School, Lethbridge,
            Alberta

Exhibitions

1978   University of Alberta, Edmonton
        Burnaby Art Gallery, British Columbia
1979   *Transformations in Modern Architecture*, Museum of
            Modern Art, New York (traveling)

Publications

By CARDINAL: Book—*Of the Spirit : Writings by Douglas Cardinal*, Edmonton, Alberta 1977. Article—"In Harmony with the Land," *Habitat* (Ottawa), no. 3/4, 1977.

On CARDINAL: Books—*A Decade of Canadian Architecture*, by Carol Moore Ede, Toronto 1971; *Explore Canada*, by George Ronald, Toronto 1974; *Building with Words: Canadian Architects on Architecture*, W. Bernstein and R. Cawker, editors, Toronto 1981. Articles—"Alberta Indian Education Centre," by R. Gretton, *Canadian Architect* (Toronto), September 1970; "The Work of Douglas Cardinal," by Abraham Rogatnick and A. Balkind, *Artscanada* (Toronto), October 1976; "Two Buildings by Douglas Cardinal," *Canadian Architect* (Toronto), February 1978; "Doug Cardinal," by Suzanne Zwarun, *En Route* (Weston, Ontario), November 1983; "Preview : National Gallery and Museum of Man," *Canadian Architect* (Toronto), February 1984; "The Cardinal Rule," by Lynda Ashley, *Alberta Construction* (Edmonton), March/April 1984; "Streets are in at this Museum," by George MacDonald, *Canadian Heritage* (Toronto), December 1984; "Building Canada's Museum of Man: An Interprofessional Dialogue," by George MacDonald, *Museum* (Paris), vol. 38 no. 1, 1986; "Canadian Museum of Civilisation, Hull, Quebec," by Martin Bressani, *Canadian Architect* (Don Mills, Ontario), November 1989; "Canadian Museum of

Civilisation," by Anupam Banerji, *Architecture + Urbanism* (Tokyo), July 1990.

*

Douglas Cardinal comments:

In my profession and in my daily living, I have always maintained that the endeavours of all Canadians should be towards a betterment of the human condition. Therefore, in my role as a planner and architect, as the coordinator of technologists, I see tremendous opportunity to petition the needs of the individual and to reinstate our humanness as the most important element in all our efforts.

Learn from your body. Solve the problem organically. You have a brain, a stomach, a mouth, a heart, a pair of lungs. You think, eat, talk, feel, breathe. Build around what you are and want to be. I have found that placing the needs of the human being before the systems created by modern man ensures that man is indeed served by these systems rather than becoming a slave to them.

*   *   *

Douglas Cardinal's aim has been to give architectural expression to a synthesis of the indigenous culture of Native North Americans and Euro-American culture. Although his ancestry is largely Native American, he has had to take deliberate steps in his adulthood to learn and absorb Indian lore and philosophy, an effort that, coming after his study of architecture, inexorably influenced his philosophy of architecture as profoundly as it influenced his philosophy of life.

It is mainly the culture of the Plains Indians of Central Canada and the North-Central United States that Cardinal has studied and, to a considerable extent, practices. Since the Plains Indians are not noted for a strong building tradition, the impression of their culture on the work of an architect would be assumed to be slight. However, in Cardinal's case, the lack of dominating structural techniques or architectural stylistic details as base ingredients has been irrelevant. It is the Indian attitude toward life, toward nature, toward humankind and toward collective and private functions that Cardinal is most interested in utilizing, expressing and practising. Formal influences do indeed enter, however, since Cardinal believes that the Indian way is based on certain spatial conceptions that pervade Indian thought, which, when taken into account, result in superior architectural solutions, as well as superior solutions to the problems of life itself.

This is reflected in his emphasis on the circle and on curvilinearity, which, in Cardinal's view, tend to facilitate the most natural physical as well as symbolic functions of man. The circle symbolizes, but also facilitates, the double function of face-to-face group contact, as well as the communication, radiation and dissemination of ideas from a central point, and of the double need of the individual to face toward the company of society and also to face away into the loneliness of the wider world.

Cardinal's emphasis on curvilinearity is inspired on the one hand by a positive response to the notion of humankind and their works as constituting an integral part of nature, a nature that seems to favor curvilinear forms flowing easily and felicitously in and out, to and from, every direction at once. On the other hand, there is also a kind of negative defiance in Cardinal's use of curves, which in his mind contradicts rectilinearity, rigid sequential thinking, and straight lacedness of the culture that he feels the Europeans brought to and imposed upon the western hemisphere with an arrogant and erroneous conviction of its superiority over indigenous cultures.

Cardinal's reflections on ancient Indian conceptions of life and nature have been complemented by his interest in utilising the most advanced techniques available to execute the unusual and complex forms of his designs. For one of his earliest works, St. Mary's Church in Red Deer, Alberta (1967) he relied on computerised calculations to realize both the structure and form of the reinforced concrete roof. Since then, Cardinal has furthered his dependence on computer assistance in the design of the Space Services Centre in Edmonton (1981) and the spectacular Canadian Museum of Civilization in Hull, Quebec (1989), across the river from the Ottawa Parliament Buildings. Other significant projects include Grand Prairie Regional College (1972), master plan and concept design for the expansion of the Saskatchewan Federated Indian College in Regina (completion due 1997), master plan for the campus of the Institute of American Indian Arts at Santa Fe (1993), and the principal design for the National Museum of the American Indian, Smithsonian Institution in Washington, D.C., due to open in 2001.

According to Cardinal, an Indian view has deeply affected every aspect of his architectural practice and he has placed great emphasis on patiently fostering group decision-making on the part of his clients and on an open-minded, honest response to these decisions on the part of the architect. This practice is perhaps best exemplified in preparations for the National Museum of the American Indian, where an advisory board consisting of several Native American artists and leaders are consultants on the project.

—Abraham Rogatnick/Roger Matuz

CARDINAL-SCHUBERT, Joane

Tribal affiliations: Peigan
Painter, printmaker, and installation artist

Born: Red Deer, Alberta, 22 August 1942. **Education:** Alberta College of Art, certificate program, 1968; University of Calgary, B.F.A., 1977; Management Development for Arts Administrators, Banff Centre, certificate in cultural resources management, 1983. **Career:** Assistant curator, University of Calgary Art Gallery, 1978; assistant curator, publications and exhibition installation, Nickel Art Museum, University of Calgary, 1979-85; Native art activist, Society of Canadian Artists, including lobbying Canadian arts institutions to represent contemporary works of Native artists; curator, lecturer, poet; member of Alumni Board, University of Calgary, beginning 1984. **Awards:** Scholarships and grants, including Queen Elizabeth Scholarship Award, 1976, Alberta Culture Assistance Award, 1974-76, Canadian Museums Association Bursary, 1983, Banff Centre Scholarship, 1983 Alberta Travel Grant, 1984; Olson's Juried Canadian Publications and Purchase Award, 1985; member, Royal Canadian Academy of Arts, 1986.

Individual Exhibitions

1978   Muttart Gallery, Calgary, Alberta
       Canadian Heroes, Red Deer Museum, Red Deer, Alberta
1979   Peter Whyte Gallery, Banff, Alberta
1981-82   Masters Gallery, Calgary, Alberta

1983   *New Beginnings*, Masters Gallery, Calgary, Alberta
1984   *Homage to Smallboy*, Vik Gallery, Calgary, Alberta
1985   *Something New*, Delta Bow Valley Conservatory, Calgary, Alberta
       This Is My History, Thunder Bay Art Gallery, Thunder Bay, Ontario
       Genesis of a Vision, Ufundi Gallery, Ottawa, Ontario
1986   *Genesis of a Vision—The Warshirt Series*, Masters Gallery, Calgary, Alberta
       Red Deer and District Museum and Archives, Red Deer, Alberta
1987   Ottawa School of Art Gallery, Ottawa, Ontario
1988   Gulf Canada Gallery, Calgary, Alberta
1990   *Lesson*, Art Tribe, Articule Gallery, Montreal, Quebec
1993   *Keepers "Counting Coup,"* Gallery of Tribal Art, Vancouver, British Columbia
1995   *Dream Beds*, Gallery of Tribal Art, Vancouver, British Columbia
       The Lesson, Central Michigan University, Mount Pleasant

Selected Group Exhibitions

1967   Alberta College of Art, Calgary, Alberta
1968   SUB Art Gallery, University of Alberta, Edmonton
1974   *Contemporary Artists*, Festival Calgary, Calgary, Alberta
1975   *Royal Horses Mouthpiece*, Dandelion Gallery, Calgary, Alberta
1975-76   *Images of Light*, Dandelion Gallery, Calgary, Alberta
1978   *Cardinal-Schubert, McAvity, Wheeler*, University of Calgary Art Gallery, Calgary, Alberta
1982   White Village Fine Art, Edmonton, Alberta
1983   *International Art Exhibition*, Stockholm, Sweden
       Alberta House, London, England
1984   *Homage to Smallboy: Environmental Sculpture*, Gleichen Park, Gleichen, Alberta
       Sharing Visions, touring Japan and Korea
1986   *Expo '86*, Alberta Pavilions, Vancouver, British Columbia
       Four Canadian Artists, Brignell Gallery, Toronto, Ontario
       Visions from the Other Side of the Mountain, Harrison Hot Springs, Alberta
1987   Agnes Etherington Art Centre, Kingston, Ontario
1988   Southwest Museum, Los Angeles, California
1989   *Why Do You Call Us Indians?*, Gettysburg College Art Gallery, Gettysburg, Pennsylvania
       Preservation of a Species: This Is My History, Meridian Gallery, San Francisco, California
       Beyond History, Vancouver Art Gallery, Vancouver, British Columbia
1990   *Preservation of a Species. Cultural Currency, Spill, Burial Platform, The Lesson, Art Tribe*, Articule Gallerie, Montreal, Quebec
1991   *Art for All*, Edmonton Art Gallery, Edmonton, Alberta
1992   *Preservation of a Species: Letters to Emily*, Essen, Germany
       Looking and Seeing, Gallery of Tribal Art, Vancouver, British Columbia
       New Territories, 350/500 Years After, Vision Planetaire, Montreal, Quebec
1993   *Indigena*, Canadian Museum of Civilization, Hull, Quebec (traveling)
       Canadian Art, Palais Gallerie, Prague, Czechoslovakia
1993-94   *First Ladies*, A Space Gallery, Toronto, Ontario

Collections

Alberta Art Foundation, Calgary; Alberta Historical Resources Foundation, Calgary; Board of Education, Regina, Saskatchewan; Canadian Embassy, New York, and Stockholm, Sweden; Canadian Museum of Civilization, Hull, Quebec; Department of Indian and Northern Affairs, Canada, Ottawa, Ontario; Native Secretariat, Edmonton, Alberta; Thunder Bay Art Gallery, Thunder Bay, Ontario; University of Lethbridge, Lethbridge, Alberta.

Publications

By CARDINAL-SCHUBERT: Catalogs—*This Is My History,* by Joane Cardinal-Schubert and Deborah Godin, Thunder Bay, 1985; *Time for Dialogue,* Calgary, 1992.

On CARDINAL-SCHUBERT: Books—*New Territories: 350/500 Years After*, Ateliers Vision Planetaire; Tétrault/Williams, Montreal, 1992; *Indigena: Contemporary Native Perspectives*, Gerald McMaster, editor, Vancouver/Toronto, 1992.

*   *   *

Throughout her career as a visual artist Joane Cardinal-Schubert has consistently credited her ancestors, their experiences and philosophies, and her personal history and experiences within that family as the guiding and reflective sources of her imagery and articulation of that imagery. Her works provide an honest and open dialogue with herself and her viewers about the reality of growing up and living in a society that categorized First Nations as "other." Her works are seen as provocative primarily because they represent a candid, internal discourse on many of the issues prevalent in Canadian society, such as systemic racism and colonialism still perpetuated in the latter half of the twentieth century.

While many artists face hardships and challenges in pursuing academic training, Cardinal-Schubert made her viewers aware that for her and for other Native people, this act alone was fraught with politicization. The failure of North American educational systems in regard to First Nations was a well known fact among Native educators, sociologists, anthropologists, and many other professional fields that dealt directly with Native people. There has been an acceptance of this failure by both the educational systems and by a general public whose knowledge and awareness was continually anesthetized. Cardinal-Schubert would spend her life examining, creating, and reviewing these issues and presenting them to unsuspecting viewers with increasing irony, parody, humor, revelation and confidence.

Early on, Cardinal-Schubert's father, Joe, recognized the importance of a formal academic education for his children and had Joane enroll at the Alberta College of Art, in which she completed a certificate program in 1968. Later, in 1977, Cardinal-Schubert would complete her B.F.A. at the University of Calgary in printmaking and painting. During these years Cardinal-Schubert was already beginning to formulate the dialogue and imagery that would begin to reverse the status quo view of Native people and of Native art and artists. In spite of being introduced to all the styles and techniques of the Western and Canadian art world, Cardinal-Schubert would only selectively choose from among these formal choices to incorporate in her own imagery. Her early works are centered on the players of Canadian Native history both past and present at a time when these political and spiritual leaders had never been acknowl-

edged in the history of nations. Having been more influenced by her enormously talented and creative family than by the previous inter-tribal styles so prevalent in the United States from the 1920s up to the mid 1960s, Cardinal-Schubert was able to pursue her revisionist histories through large mural-size works, such as *Riel's Rebellion.* Parallel to the first decade of exhibiting, Cardinal-Schubert worked at the Nickel Art Museum at the University of Calgary, gaining firsthand experience as a curator in both publication writing and exhibition installation, while working continually among and with many professional artists. The deconstructivist theories of the 1980s, which Cardinal-Schubert became adept at illustrating in her own work, provided her with a method for addressing the corruptness she experienced in the lives of those she calls "The People."

Alberta pictographs, medicine wheels, ethnoastronomy and Native sacred sites would begin to dominate her imagery in the late 1980s and early 1990s. She would also look to indigenous knowledge everywhere, to appreciate the achievements of First Nations and to increase her understanding of the socio-political and cultural issues of her time. Museums as a resource for objectifying or subjectifying Native art and as a cultural business would come under sharp scrutiny through installation works, such as *Preservation of a Species* and *Is This My Mother's?,* exhibited in *Beyond History* at the Vancouver Art Gallery, 1989. No longer was the painting medium sufficient to express the convoluted notions of Indianess as defined by colonialist institutions. Cardinal-Schubert's work had began to combine sculpture, text, painting, photography, and performance into compelling and provocative environments. As a Native art activist, Cardinal-Schubert, with other Native artists through the Society of Canadian Artists of Native Ancestry, was responsible for lobbying Canadian arts institutions to begin representing the contemporary works of Native artists. Her work is included in the seminal exhibition of the latter part of the twentieth century, called *Indigena* (1992), a quincenntennial exhibition that responded angrily and honestly to five hundred years of colonialism and was sponsored by the Canadian Museum of Civilization. In this exhibition she continued the series on *Preservation of a Species*, adding the work, *Deconstructivists*. Several walls of text and peepholes allowed audiences to read about a Native's response to the most common of circumstances and to see themselves in relation or indifference to First Nations. Audiences had to struggle physically to get at the peepholes, which were not at normal adult heights. She forces audiences to dig deeper and struggle to understand why First Nations people feel and see as they do and to get beyond the romantic ideals imposed on them.

Another installation, *The Lesson* (1994), exhibited in the *First Ladies* group exhibition at A Space in Toronto and in 1995 at Central Michigan University, recreates a classroom setting with "The Lesson" written on the blackboard chalk. *The Lesson* recalls how First Nations gave up their families, education, religion, values, culture, and laws only to be given a new set of families, education, values, culture, and laws that were supposed to be for everybody. This lesson goes on to explain the resulting damage and how artists of this century gave them back their spirit.

On the other wall are the names of many Native people who were engaged in the struggle for freedom and equality. Their names are struck out with a line across them, not so they will be forgotten, but because they gave their lives. Cardinal-Schubert would have First Nations students participate in a performance in which she was the teacher and the students read "The Lesson," line by line, in chorus. When she paused, a student would stand and give their memory of their school experience. The performance was a purifying agent for those who participated and enabled viewers to review the historical whitewashing that Native children have been subjected to in this century. This work is an important contribution to the postmodern critique that has allowed voices of people of color to be heard and seen in public institutions in North America.

Joane Cardinal-Schubert's art is insightful, emotionally direct, and critical of all ideals that allowed Native history and culture to be overwritten and wiped clean from the memories of the dominant society. The pain and anger that has festered emotionally and psychologically from quick fixes on these issues is carefully opened by her work and redressed, by dealing with the issues and their complexities and by targeting the values and philosophies that contribute to the ignorance that creates the problems. Her work is articulate in text and imagery, with purposeful control. She engages her audiences intellectually and rivets them emotionally with the realization of shared experience.

—Colleen Cutschall

CHADDLESONE, Sherman

Tribal affiliations: Kiowa
Painter

Born: Lawton, Oklahoma, 2 June 1947. **Education:** Received early training in art from his father, John, in anatomy, portraiture, pencil sketching, and serigaphy; Institute of American Indian Art, Santa Fe, New Mexico, late 1960s; Central State University, Edmonds, Oklahoma, 1972-73. **Military Service:** U.S. Army; served in Vietnam. **Career:** Director, Indian Arts Workshop of the Neighborhood Arts Program, San Francisco, 1970-71; administrative manager, Kalispel Indian Reservation, Washington, beginning late 1970s; full-time artist beginning in the early 1980s; member, Kiowa Gourd Clan and Kiowa Black Leggins Society; commissions, including National Hall of Fame for Famous American Indians, Anadarko, Oklahoma, for busts of Santana (White Bear) and T. C. Cannon, and Kiowa Tribal Complex, Carnegie, Oklahoma, mural, with Parker Boyiddle and Mirac Creepingbear; artist-in-residence, Eiteljorg Museum, Indianapolis, Indiana. **Awards:** Numerous at fairs and juried competitions, including Scottsdale National Indian Arts Exhibition, 1967; Oklahomans for Indian Opportunity, 1982, Best of Show; American Indian Exposition, 1983, 1985, 1992; Trail of Tears Annual Art Show, 1984-85; Red Earth Festival, 1987.

Individual Exhibitions

1981   *Paintings by Sherman Chaddlesone,* Southern Plains Museum and Crafts Center, Anadarko, Oklahoma
1992   Southern Plains Museum and Crafts Center, Anadarko, Oklahoma

Selected Group Exhibitions

1967   Institute of American Indian Arts Museum, Santa Fe, New Mexico
1971   The Heritage Center, Inc., Pine Ridge, South Dakota
1973   *New Directions,* Institute of American Indian Arts Museum, Santa Fe, New Mexico (traveling)

1974   Amon Carter Museum of Art, Fort Worth, Texas
1975   *Pintura Amerindia Contemporanea/E. U. A.,* sponsored by the U.S. Department of State and International Communications Agency, Washington, D.C. (traveled to Bolivia, Chile, Columbia, Ecuador, and Peru, through 1979)
1982   Galleria, Norman, Oklahoma
1984   Cherokee National Museum, Tahlequah, Oklahoma
1985   Cherokee National Museum, Tahlequah, Oklahoma
1986   Museum of New Mexico, Santa Fe
1987   American Indian Contemporary Arts, San Francisco, California
         Myriad Plaza, Oklahoma City, Oklahoma
1990   *New Art of the West,* Eiteljorg Museum, Indianapolis, Indiana
1992   Kiowa Tribal Museum, Carnegie, Oklahoma
         Institute of American Indian Arts Museum, Santa Fe, New Mexico
1993   Philbrook Museum of Art, Tulsa, Oklahoma
1994   *Moving Murals of Oklahoma: Contemporary Native American Painting,* organized by the Jacobson Foundation, Norman, Oklahoma (traveling)
1996   *Visions and Voices: Native American Painting from the Philbrook Museum of Art,* Tulsa, Oklahoma

Collections

Institute of American Indian Arts, Santa Fe, New Mexico; Southern Plains Museum and Crafts Center, Anadarko, Oklahoma.

Publications

On CHADDLESONE: Books—*The Institute of American Indian Arts Alumni Exhibition,* by Lloyd Kiva New, Fort Worth, Texas, 1974; *Pinturas Amerindas Contemporanes/ E.U.A.,* by Lloyd Kiva New, Chile, 1979; *Kiowa Voices: Ceremonial Dance, Ritual and Song,* by Maurice Boyd, Fort Worth, Texas, 1981; *New Art of the West,* by Thomas Gentry, et al, Indianapolis, 1990; *Creativity Is Our Tradition,* by Richard Hill, Santa Fe, 1992.

*

Sherman Chaddlesone comments:

My primary concerns with the interaction of color and light persist and are evident today as, say, in 1973. Realism, especially photo-realism, has been of great interest to me lately... but those subliminal nuances which identify my Kiowa psyche will remain in my work. (From *Creativity Is Our Tradition*)

*   *   *

Noted for his versatility in exploring different styles of Native American painting and sculpture, Sherman Chaddlesone has successfully worked in many of the great stylistic movements within Native American art. Chaddlesone has an almost chameleon-like ability to slip into different styles, including ledger art, photo-realism, and abstract painting, influenced by friendships he made with T. C. Cannon and Benny Buffalo as a student at the Institute of American Indian Arts. Chaddlesone is forthright and generous with crediting those who have influenced his work. In Joan Frederick's *T. C. Cannon: He Stood in the Sun,* Chaddlesone explained, "I always wanted to do what he was doing in his art. I tried to keep tabs on his development, projects, and shows, his inspiration, and any information I might be able to follow. We were as tight as you can be."

His ability to absorb various styles into his own artistic sensibilities keeps Chaddlesone's work innovative and fresh. Although there is no obvious evolutionary development in his body of work— as he has often commented—one can note common stylistic themes throughout. Most of his works have strong graphic tendencies produced by dramatic color contrasts, as in *White Bear*, a 1973 acrylic on canvas. This work and others reveal Chaddlesone as an exceptional colorist working in pure primaries and reminiscent of the graphite colors of late-nineteenth-century ledger work.

Chaddlesone's figures in his painting and sculpture are often icons of Kiowa culture possessing a classic sense of timelessness and dignity. Oftentimes, the design of the figure's clothing becomes a subject in itself. Chaddlesone represents the aesthetic beauty of beadwork designs and makes clear the relationship between the figure and the design: the designs bring forth strength and power to the wearer.

Chaddlesone's ledger art works, his most popular and successful endeavors, demonstrate his ability to fuse an earlier Kiowa painting tradition with his personal artistic vision. Viewing *A Delegation of Kiowa Warriors,* an acrylic on canvas, is like stepping back in time. This powerful work by Chaddlesone is not an appropriation of a stylistic tradition, but rather a tribute to the Old Masters with whom Chaddlesone shares his artistic tradition. It demonstrates his love for earlier ledger painting and his knowledge and eye for the graphic and decorative line in the figures—Chaddlesone's elegant line is often created by brush rather than pen. Twelve warriors stand as heroic figures of Kiowa culture. In profiled, ledger style, these personas are silhouetted against a marbleized canvas background.

Chaddlesone treats his painting surface by either marbleizing the canvas or aging the paper carefully by ripping the edge. When Chaddlesone magnifies a ledger work to a 30 x 50 canvas, he rarely loses the delicacy of line and detail that make ledger art so exquisite. Repetition of form, graphic images created by interplay with color contrasts, and expertly detailed lines are characteristic of Chaddlesone's ledger work.

—Marla Redcorn

CHAPMAN, Jeffrey

Tribal affiliations: Anishnabe
Painter and sculptor

Born: Minneapolis, Minnesota, 14 September 1958. **Education:** Attended Minneapolis public schools, graduating from Minneapolis South High School 1976; attended Minneapolis Community college in 1978; Minneapolis College of Art and Design, B.F.A. 1984. **Family:** Married. **Career:** Member of planning committee for Minneapolis Indian Art Market, 1991-92; lecturer at St. Cloud State University, Apple Valley Middle School, and Mankato State University, 1992; lecturer at Burnsville High School, 1993; Hamline University, annually; Buffalo Intermediate School, 1993; advisory committee, Minneapolis Institute of Art, Arts of the Americas Gallery, 1993; community outreach task force, Minnesota Orchestra, 1993; artist mentor, Intermedia Arts of Minneapolis Emerging

Artist's Program, 1993; Apple Valley Middle School, 1992; Richfield Intermediate School, 1994; instructor of American Indian Art History, part-time, Minneapolis Community College, 1993-95. **Awards:** Honorable Mention Invitational Plains Art Exhibition, 1987; Minnesota Ojibway Art Expo, First Place in Water Color Painting in 1985 and 1987, First Place in Graphics in 1979 and 1980; Second Place in Graphics, 1981 and 1983, First and Third place in Stone Sculpture (pipestone) in 1985; Certificate of Merit in Graphic Arts Awards Competition, Painting Industries of America Inc., 1990; Graphic Arts Award for "Bears, Imagination, and Reality" Poster for Science Museum of Minnesota.

Individual Exhibitions

1984	Raven Gallery, Minneapolis
1986	Blandin Foundation, Grand Rapids, Minnesota
1986	*Paintings by Jeffrey Chapman*, U.S. Department of the Interior, Indian Arts and Crafts Board, Southern Plains Museum, Anadarko, Oklahoma
1986	Raven Gallery, Minneapolis

Selected Group Exhibitions

1985	*Artists in Residence*, University of Minnesota and Minneapolis Indian Center
	Emerging Artists, Minneapolis Indian Center
	Homecomings, North Dakota Museum of Art, Bismarck
1986	*Two Man Exhibition*, Minneapolis Indian Center
1987	*Invitational Plains Indian Art Exhibition*, Buffalo Bill Historical Center, Cody, Wyoming
	Group Exhibition, Penthouse of the Science Museum of St. Paul, Minnesota
	Traditions and Innovations, Seven Native American Artists, Plains Art Museum, Moorehead, Minnesota
1988	*Group Show,* Howard University, Alexandria, Virginia Colorado Indian Market, Denver
1989	*The Elders Show*, Bell Museum, University of Minnesota, Minneapolis
	Native American Expressions of Surrealism, Sacred Circle Gallery, Seattle
1990	*Gallery Artists Show*, Raven Gallery, Minneapolis
	Our Land Ourselves, Native American Contemporary Artists, Gallery Association of New York State, New York
1991	*From the Earth*, American Indian Contemporary Arts, San Francisco
	Without Boundaries, Contemporary Native American Art, Jan Cicero Gallery, Chicago
	The Fifth Biennial, Heard Museum, Phoenix
1992	*Contemporary Tribal Art, Old Forms New Ways,* Two Rivers Gallery, Minneapolis Indian Center, Minnesota
	Artists of the Circle, Paul Whitney Larson Gallery, University of Minnesota, St. Paul
	We the Human Beings: Twenty-Seven Native American Artists, College of Wooster, Wooster, Ohio
	For the Seventh Generation: Native Artists Counter the Quincentenary, Columbus, New York, Golden Artist Colors Gallery, Columbus, New York
	Enduring Strength, Contemporary Work by Northern Plains and Woodland Artists, Two Rivers Gallery and Intermedia Arts Gallery, Minneapolis

1993   *Myth and Memory*, First People's Gallery, Minneapolis
The American Hand, Minnesota Museum of Art, Landmark Center, Minneapolis
Visions Returned, Mahto Sapa Gallery, Mystic Lake Casino, Prior Lake, Minnesota
1995   *Indian Humor*, American Indian Contemporary Arts, San Francisco (traveling)
1996   *Native Streams*, Jan Cicero Gallery, Chicago (traveling)

Collections

Blandin Foundation, Grand Rapids, Minnesota; Bemis Corporation, Minneapolis; Buffalo Bill Historical Center, Cody, Wyoming; Gallo Corporation, Modesto, California; Minneapolis Target Center, Minnesota; Minnesota Chippewa Tribe, Fond du Lac Reservation, Cloquet; Minnesota Historical Society, St. Paul; North Dakota Museum of Art, Bismarck; Science Museum of Minnesota, St. Paul; U.S. Department of the Interior, Southern Plains Museum, Anadarko, Oklahoma.

Publications

On CHAPMAN: Articles—Eardrums Program, Artist's interview on Fresh Air Radio, Minnesota Public Radio, 1986; *Winds of Change Magazine*, 1989.

*   *   *

From an art historical perspective, Jeff Chapman's paintings suggest a postmodernist stance. Playing upon the contradictions of presence and absence, Chapman's ironies strike to the heart of survival. A native of south Minneapolis, Chapman's personal approach focuses on Native American issues, in particular, those addressing dual identity. Chapman's work is informed by a potent self-representation that both licenses his identity-based art practices, and distinguishes him as a native artist who deals explicitly with socio-political considerations of voice and power.

Chapman is both a painter who works with water color and airbrush, and a sculptor who recreates traditional wood courting flutes. Influenced by the avant-garde program at the Minneapolis College of Art and Design, where he received his B.F.A. degree, Chapman quickly revealed a conceptually sophisticated art that was replete with paradoxes. Animals cast shadows that belonged to different species while, elsewhere, partially revealed humans peered out from behind the edges of open doors and windows. Such artistic strategies interrupt the viewing process by subverting the observer's ground, and simultaneously afford subject positions to the shadowy figures that people Chapman's canvases. In his art, themes of visibility and invisibility take on unmistakably human dimensions in footprints that leave traces which lack any physical counterpart. Chapman's paintings employ transitional spaces as a point of departure. By shifting time and space, his images play with notions of fixity, coercing us into focusing on the slippery—and contradictory—nature of perspective, that of both viewer and artist. One way Chapman achieves this is through his ubiquitous use of windows and doorways. As spatial delineations, doubling as boundaries and zones of passage, they provide powerful metaphors for the projective elaboration of identity. They both demarcate and provide access, serving as a means for refracting contemporary Native American reality. Subtle doses of humor charge this work, mitigating the alienation that haunts doorways and windows, which obscure as often as they clarify the artist's intent.

Of his art, Chapman has stated, "Most of my work involves interlacing contemporary icons and images with traditional images, [and] in some fashion putting them together. All of my work involves symbology and cross symbology. Art as a whole is about communication." Yet this communication frequently turns on incongruity and paradox. For many Anishinabe, turtle spirits occupy a significant place. Chapman invests heavily in turtle imagery. At his most potent, Chapman, playing upon the turtle's poor eyesight, casts turtles in roles of seekers. When queried regarding his turtle symbology, he suggests that in Indian culture, many are looking for what has been lost. His turtles function as mnemonic devices, similar to the visual records inscribed on birch-bark, and traditionally used for recording history. Turtles bridge past and present, reservation and urban, ancient world views and modern realities.

What resonates in Chapman's images, what holds our attention, are the half-revealed figures that fix us—their viewers—in place. Chapman casts identity as a site of converging interarticulations, yet makes no attempt to fully describe those who such categories purport to represent. We are confronted with visibility and invisibility in terms of human relationships, and the different ways that we, as humans, express those relationships with the world.

—Marilee Jantzer-White

CHARLIE, Nellie

Tribal affiliations: Mono Lake Paiute
Basketweaver

Born: Nellie Jim in Lee Vining, California, summer 1867. **Family:** Married Young Charlie, a Miwok man from Yosemite, c. 1880s; divorced 1925. **Career:** Midwife; maker of baskets for her own use, for sale, and for use by other Native people; produced fancy, three-rod baskets by 1903 and was a major weaver and producer of fancy baskets for the non-Indian market from the 1920s until her death. **Died:** 21 July 1965.

Individual Exhibitions

Exhibition data is incomplete; the artist is not known to have kept records. The following is reconstructed from various sources:

1924   Indian Field Days, Yosemite Valley, California
1925   Indian Field Days, Yosemite Valley, California
1973-96 Yosemite Museum, Yosemite National Park, California
1996   Old Schoolhouse Museum, Lee Vining, California

Collections

Old Schoolhouse Museum, Lee Vining, California; Yosemite Museum, National Park Service, Yosemite National Park.

Publications

On CHARLIE: Books—*Tradition and Innovation: A Basket History of the Indians of the Yosemite-Mono Lake Area*, by Craig Bates and Martha J. Lee, Yosemite 1990. **Articles**—"Miwok-Paiute Bas-

Nellie Charlie: Coiled basket, 1924. Courtesy National Park Service, Yosemite Museum, Yosemite National Park, California.

ketry 1920-1928: Genesis of an Art Form," by Craig Bates, *American Indian Art Magazine* 4(4):54-59, 1979; "Made For Sale: Baskets from the Yosemite-Mono Lake Region of California," by Craig Bates, *Moccasin Tracks* 7:4 1981; "Ethnographic Collections at Yosemite National Park," by Craig Bates, *American Indian Art Magazine* 7(32):28-35, 1982; "Yosemite Miwok-Paiute Basketry: A Study in Cultural Change," by Craig Bates, *American Indian Basketry Magazine* II(4):23-29, 1982; "Yosemite: A Melting Pot for Indian People and Their Baskets," by Craig Bates and Martha J. Lee, in *Strands of Time: Yokuts, Mono and Miwok Basketmakers*, Fresno 1988.

* * *

Nellie Charlie was a prolific, versatile weaver of baskets; she made both traditional twined and coiled baskets for Native use, as well as fancy new-style baskets. Unique among basketry makers of her people, she incorporated patriotic motifs into the designs of some of her baskets. She also created a new style of utilitarian basketry for use in the modern homes of her grandchildren and non-Indians. Both Nellie Charlie and her sister Tina were married to the same man (a not uncommon

practice among the Mono Lake Paiute), and they lived together for most of their lives, undoubtedly influencing each other's weaving.

Charlie's earliest documented baskets were purchased from her in 1903 by C. Hart Merriam, a collector and naturalist. These included several utilitarian baskets as well as a finely woven basket with an arrowhead motif. Charlie told Merriam that in making the basket she had tried to see how fine a basket she could weave. The arrowhead patterning was inspired by designs in beadwork. By the 1920s, Charlie had developed a variety of distinctive and innovative designs for her baskets.

Nellie Charlie was a regular competitor in basketry competitions at the Yosemite Indian Field Days. The baskets she entered were primarily finely stitched and highly patterned. In 1924 her display of baskets won third prize and included both a new-style coiled basket with red and black patterns and a traditional twined mush boiler. She may have been the only weaver from the Yosemite-Mono Lake region to use patriotic symbols, such as a Union Shield and an American eagle clutching arrows, on her baskets. She also made a number of beaded baskets, utilizing a wide variety of designs, including horizontal bands, arrows, isolated geometric motifs, and vertically oriented zigzags.

In a further blending of old and new, Charlie adapted basketry forms and patterns to twentieth-century uses. She produced coiled, cylindrical baskets for holding knitting materials and baskets to be used as bassinets, for holding laundry, fruit bowls, hot pads and coasters. Some of these baskets had a stylized pattern which her daughters said was an "Indian H," for "Hess," the married surname of two of her daughters.

Nearly 100 years old at the time of her death, Nellie Charlie was an active weaver and beadworker through her final years. She, her sister Tina, and Leanna Tom were the last Yosemite-Mono Lake women born in the mid-nineteenth century who continued to weave until the mid-twentieth century.

—Craig Bates

CHARLIE, Tina

Tribal affiliations: Mono Lake Paiute
Basketweaver

Born: Tina Jim in Mono Lake, California, 16 August 1869. **Family:** Married Young Charlie, a Miwok man from Yosemite c. 1880s.

Career: Midwife; maker of baskets for her own use, for sale, and for other Native people; by the 1920s she was making fancy, three-rod baskets, and she continued to be a foremost producer of baskets for the non-Indian market until her death. **Died:** 1962.

Individual Exhibitions

Exhibition data is incomplete; the artist is not known to have kept records. The following is reconstructed from various sources:

1916   Bishop Harvest Days, Bishop, California
1925   Indian Field Days, Yosemite Valley, California
1926   Indian Field Days, Yosemite Valley, California
1929   Indian Field Days, Yosemite Valley, California
1930s   Wai-Pai-Shone Trading Post, Stewart, Nevada
1970-88 Mono County Museum, Bridgeport, California
1973-96 Yosemite Museum, Yosemite National Park, California

Collections

Redding Museum and Art Center, Redding, California; Yosemite Museum, National Park Service, Yosemite National Park.

Tina Charlie: Coiled basket, c. 1920s. Courtesy National Park Service, Yosemite Museum, Yosemite National Park, California.

Publications

On CHARLIE: Books—*Tradition and Innovation: A Basket History of the Indians of the Yosemite-Mono Lake Area,* by Craig D. Bates and Martha J. Lee, Yosemite 1990. **Articles**—"Miwok-Paiute Basketry 1920-1928: Genesis of an Art Form," by Craig Bates, *American Indian Art Magazine* 4:4, 1979; "Made For Sale: Baskets from the Yosemite-Mono Lake Region of California," Craig Bates, in *Moccasin Tracks* 7:4, 1981; "Ethnographic Collections at Yosemite National Park," Craig Bates, in *American Indian Art Magazine* 7(32):28-35, 1982; "Yosemite Miwok-Paiute Basketry: A Study in Cultural Change," by Craig Bates, *American Indian Basketry Magazine* II(4):23-29, 1982; "Yosemite: A Melting Pot for Indian People and Their Baskets," by Craig D. Bates and Martha J. Lee, in *Strands of Time: Yokuts, Mono and Miwok Basketmakers*, Fresno 1988.

*   *   *

Tina Charlie was an innovative weaver who excelled in the creation of very large, new-style fancy baskets and baskets with negative patterning. She was one of the foremost producers of Mono Lake Paiute new-style coiled baskets in the 1920s; several innovations in that style are directly attributable to her. She was married to the same man as her sister, Nellie (a common practice among Mono Lake Paiute people), and she lived with her sister for much of her life; as both women were weavers, they probably influenced each other's weaving styles.

Like her sister, Tina was a regular competitor in the Yosemite Indian Field Days basketry competitions. In both the 1925 and 1926 competitions she entered a basket with a black background, perhaps the earliest documentation of a negatively patterned basket in the Yosemite-Mono Lake region. She used black-dyed bracken fern root as the primary sewing material and worked the pattern in buff-colored sedge root and red-brown split redbud. Tina Charlie was perhaps one of only two weavers to attempt a basket of this type with a black background; fern root is a weaker sewing material than other materials used by the Mono Lake Paiute, and thus much more care was required in order to create a basket using bracken fern as the primary sewing strand.

While most of Charlie's contemporaries created new basket patterns derived from beadwork or their own imaginations, Charlie was unique in adapting patterns copied from Maiduan peoples. She used a variation of a traditional Maidu quail-plume motif on a basket that she completed in about 1929. It was one of at least four large (over twenty inches in diameter) finely made new-style baskets that she produced.

Tina Charlie made both coiled and twined baskets similar to her sister Nellie's, and she was noted for her excellent traditional utilitarian baskets. Charlie was a prolific and innovative weaver until her death in 1962.

—Craig Bates

CHEE, Robert
Variant names: Hashke-Yil-E-Cale
Tribal affiliations: Navajo
Painter

Born: 1938. **Education:** Commercial art instruction at Intermountain Indian School in Utah, under Apache artist/sculptor Allan Houser. **Military Service:** 1958-61. **Career:** Artist. **Awards:** Honors at the Scottsdale National Indian Arts Exhibition (1962), American Indian Art Exhibition (1964), and Annual Indian Arts Exhibition (Philbrook Museum, 1979), and multiple awards at the Navajo Nation Fair and the Gallup Inter-Tribal Indian Ceremonial. **Died:** 1981.

Selected Group Exhibitions

1962-64   Scottsdale National Indian Arts Exhibition, Arizona
1964   American Indian Art Exhibition, Wayne State University, Detroit
1964-65   First Annual Invitational Exhibition of American Indian Paintings, U.S. Department of Interior, Washington, D.C.
1968   *James T. Bialac Collection of Southwest Indian Paintings,* Arizona State Museum, University of Arizona, Tucson
1979-80   *Native American Paintings,* exhibit tour arranged by Josylyn Art Museum, Omaha, Nebraska
1979   *Annual Indian Art Exhibition,* Philbrook Museum of Art, Tulsa, Oklahoma
1981   *Hard Lines,* Navajo Tribal Museum, Window Rock, Arizona
          Native American Painting, organized by Amarillo Art Center, Amarillo, Texas (traveled through 1983)
1985   *Indianischer Kunstler,* organized by the Philbrook Museum, Tulsa, Oklahoma (traveled in West Germany)

Collections

Arizona State Museum, University of Arizona, Tucson; California Academy of Sciences, San Francisco; Beloit College Museum of Indian Arts and Culture; Children's Museum of Indianapolis; Cincinnati Museum of Natural History; Denver Art Museum; Heard Museum, Phoenix; Heritage Center, Red Cloud Indian School, Pine Ridge, South Dakota; Museum of New Mexico, Santa Fe; Museum of Northern Arizona, Flagstaff; National Museum of the American Indian, Smithsonian Institution, Washington, D.C.; Navajo Nation Museum; Philbrook Museum of Art, Tulsa, Oklahoma; Roswell Museum and Art Center, Roswell, New Mexico; Wheelwright Museum of the American Indian, Santa Fe.

Publications

On CHEE: Books—*American Indian Painting of the Southwest and Plains Areas* by Dorothy Dunn, University of New Mexico Press, 1968; *The James T. Bialac Collection of Southwest Indian Paintings*, exhibition catalog by Clara Lee Tanner, University of Arizona Press, 1968; *Southwest Indian Painting: A Changing Art* by Clara Lee Tanner, University of Arizona Press, 1973; *Navajo Painting* by Katherin Chase, Museum of Northern Arizona Press, 1983; *The Elkus Collection, Southwestern Indian Art,* edited by Dorothy K. Washburn, California Academy of Sciences, 1984.

*   *   *

Robert Chee never studied at the Santa Fe Indian School, but his work exemplifies the degree to which the Studio Style, introduced by Dorothy Dunn in the early 1930s at the school, defined Navajo

Robert Chee: *The Navajo Riders,* c. 1960. Photograph by Dong Lin; courtesy California Academy of Sciences, Elkus Collection.

painting until the early 1960s. During a rather short career from the mid-1950s until 1971, Chee produced an impressive body of work that chronicles Navajo ceremonies and daily life during the trading post era and the mid-twentieth century.

Except for two years of commercial art instruction at Intermountain Indian School in Utah, under Apache artist Allan Houser, Chee seems to have had little formal training. His early works, even more than later ones, are more in the form of caricatures than carefully composed paintings, often lacking in overall composition and attention to detail. Without any indication of a grounding surface or sense of perspective, his human subjects and plants and animals seemingly floated on the paper. Nonetheless, through continual practice and keen observance of work by other Studio-style artists, Chee established his own recognizable style within the Studio Style by the late 1950s.

Chee's Navajo subjects are always very thin and have very prominent cheekbones and lips that project slightly forward, much in the manner Navajos use their lips to indicate a direction. His men dress in blue jeans, while women wear long, layered and fully gathered skirts. Everyone walks in very long strides and more often than not, they seem to be half-smiling. Other conventions typical of the Studio style include highly stylized plants and clouds suggested by sweeping, scalloped lines that sometimes extend from the ground and frame the entire sky. Ceremonial or mythological elements in

the space above the main subjects, such as deity figures, sometimes arching across the sky like meteors, were another frequent device used by Chee. Especially in his earlier paintings, these decorative devices were sometimes more carefully executed than the main subject of a painting.

By the late 1950s and throughout the 1960s, Chee was among the most active of Navajo painters. He entered work in nearly every competition open to him and captured many awards at the Navajo Nation Fair, the Gallup Inter-Tribal Indian Ceremonial, the Scottsdale National shows, and the Philbrook competitions. His sense of overall design and composition improved as a result, but was never entirely consistent.

Chee worked mostly in water-based paints and casein on mat board, like most Studio-style painters. But whereas most other Navajo artists painted on lighter colors of matboard, Chee preferred dark blue and black matboards for his canvases. These were especially effective in portraying night scenes. His choices of colors was also somewhat limited, but his brushwork was bold and confident and never strayed far from the precepts of the Studio. In at least one painting, anthropologist L. C. Wyman commissioned Chee to depict a Navajo ceremony the artist had never witnessed. With the aid of photographs, Chee filled in the details, rendered in the conventionalized Studio manner. The completed painting is certainly ethnographically accurate in every detail, but it exemplifies the decorative style of Studio painting more than it conveys Chee's impression of a particular ceremony.

By the end of the 1960s, Chee's penchant for dark mat boards increasingly gave way to lighter boards and even his palette mellowed. Although his subject matter remained the same, Chee began to pay more attention to a work's composition. These changes were encouraging, but whatever direction Chee's work might have taken was abruptly ended when the artist died in a tragic accident.

—Russell Hartman

CHEE CHEE, Benjamin

Tribal affiliations: Ojibway
Painter

Born: Bear Island, Temagami Reserve, Ontario, 1944. **Commissions:** National Indian Brotherhood Calendar, 1975. **Died:** Ottawa, Ontario, 1977.

Individual Exhibitions

1973   University of Ottawa, Ottawa
        Nicholas Gallery, Ottawa
1974   Doma II Art Gallery, Waterloo, Ontario
1976   Evans Gallery, Toronto
        The Sea Chest, Halifax, Nova Scotia
1977   Marion Scott Galleries, Vancouver
1982   Glebe Community Centre, Ottawa
1983   Thunder Bay National Exhibition Centre and Centre for
        Indian Art, Thunder Bay, Ontario

Selected Group Exhibitions

1974   *Canadian Indian Art '74,* Royal Ontario Museum, Toronto
1976   Evans Gallery, Toronto
        Inukshuk Gallery, Waterloo, Ontario
        The Sea Chest, Halifax, Nova Scotia
1977   *Links to a Tradition,* Department of Indian Affairs and
        Northern Development (traveled in Brazil)
1982   *Renewal: Masterworks of Contemporary Indian Art from
        the National Museum of Man,* Thunder Bay National
        Exhibition Centre and Centre for Indian Art, Thunder
        Bay, Ontario
1983   *Contemporary Indian Art at Rideau Hall,* Department of
        Indian Affairs and Northern Development, Ottawa

Collections

Canadian Museum of Civilization, Ottawa; Department of Indian and Northern Affairs, Ottawa; McMichael Canadian Collection, Kleinburg, Ontario; Royal Ontario Museum, Toronto; Thunder Bay National Exhibition Centre and Centre for Indian Art, Thunder Bay, Ontario; Woodland Indian Cultural Educational Centre, Brantford, Ontario.

Publications

On CHEE CHEE: Books—*Benjamin Chee Chee: Paintings and Prints in the Collection of the Thunder Bay NEC/CIA,* exhibition

catalog with text by Elizabeth McLuhan, Thunder Bay, 1984; *The Sound of the Drum: The Secret Art of the Anishnabec* by Mary E. Southcott, Erin, Ontario, 1984; *The Permanent Collection: Thunder Bay Art Gallery,* exhibition catalog edited by Marcy Menditove, Thunder Bay, 1986; *Benjamin Chee Chee: The Black Geese Portfolio, and Other Works,* exhibition catalog with text by Janet Clark and Robert Houle, Thunder Bay Art Gallery 1991; *The Benjamin Chee Chee Elegies* by Patrick White, Toronto, 1992. **Articles—** "Ojibway Artist: Selling Beads Back to the White Man" by Catherine Jutras, *Tawow* (Ottawa), Vol. 4, No. 1, 1973; "The Search of Benjamin Chee Chee" by Robert McKeown, *Weekend Magazine,* 11 January 1975; "The Dying of Chee Chee" by Wayne Edmonstone, *Vancouver Sun,* 1 April 1977; "Inquest Likely in Jail Death," *Ottawa Citizen,* 28 April 1977; "Benjamin Chee Chee"by Ernie Bies, *Arts West,* Vol. 5, No. 7, November/December 1980; "Success of Ojibwa Painter Underlines Haunting Legacy" by Rudy Platiel, *Globe and Mail* (Toronto), 30 October 1981.

*   *   *

Benjamin Chee Chee came to national recognition and prominence in the early 1970s, a period which also saw the artists associated with the New Woodland School—Norval Morrisseau, Daphne Odjig, and Blake Debassige, among others—similarly gaining popular acceptance with a nationalistic Canadian audience, if not with the mainstream Canadian art world. Chee Chee's *oeuvre,* however, was distinct from that of the so-called legend painters.

For much of his short, four-year career as an artist, Chee Chee worked in two distinct styles: large abstract paintings, and smaller line drawings. The former were often created by applying stamping techniques with a wood block the artist had carved. Later, Chee Chee would experiment with stencilling, sponging, stippling, and feathering techniques as well. The abstract paintings were generally untitled, and referenced natural phenomena and biomorphic forms. The large oil on canvas *Migration* (1973) exemplifies one of Chee Chee's major aims in these works—to elicit the essence of the form and movement of Canadian Geese, or *nekug* in the Ojibway language.

Chee Chee's line drawings were also concerned with geese but were done in a representational style. With outlines suggesting the lyrical movement and graceful forms of geese, the style was culturally and historically important as well. Robert Houle has suggested that Chee Chee's outline and later solid black form images of geese, "reaffirmed the rigours of structural minimalism inherent in traditional Ojibway art, i.e. rock paintings, petroglyphs, and birch bark scrolls."

Chee Chee's last works, delivered by the artist to Canadian Indian Marketing Services in Ottawa just four hours before his arrest and two days before his untimely death by self-inflicted hanging, are known as *The Black Geese Portfolio.* These works combine the elegant lines of the outline paintings with the solidity evident in the artist's early abstract paintings. The portfolio comprises eighteen images that, like a series of film stills, capture the movement of a bird in flight. The portfolio also serves to establish a visual narrative that records the goose as icon in sweeping brushstrokes and a dynamic interplay of positive and negative space.

Geese are a culturally specific symbol to both the Ojibway and Canadians in general, and certainly this must have contributed to the popularity of Chee Chee's work, and to the artist's meteoric rise to national acclaim. Yet what is perhaps most important in the brief but significant life of Benjamin Chee Chee is the power of his work to function as cultural testament. First Nations artist and curator Robert Houle has noted: "The art of Benjamin Chee Chee is an affirmation of his imagination to perceive the world in terms of Ojibway imagery. [*The Black Geese Portfolio*] works have always been fascinating. Their economy of line and form create an image whose singularity is common to the Anishnabec and their neighbours, and it is this commonality that earned him his success in communicating biculturally.... He has left a legacy to a cultural symbol-system and to a country much in need of a commonality."

—Carol Podedworny

CHIAGO, Michael

Tribal affiliations: Tohono O'odham
Painter and illustrator

Born: Kohate Village, Tohono O'odham Reservation, 6 April 1946.
Education: Maricopa Community College. **Military Service:** U.S. Marine Corps; served in Vietnam. **Career:** Professional dancer, touring to demonstrate Native dances; barber; commercial dancer; full-time artist since 1980. **Awards:** Murals, including Sky Harbor International Airport Terminal (1990), Heard Museum (for its Rain exhibit, 1993-95), and Phoenix City Hall (1996). Posters for O'odham Tash (nine times), Casa Grande, Arizona; Heard Museum, Phoenix; and for the innaugural ceremonies for Arizona governor, 1991.

Selected Group Exhibitions

1981	O'odham Tash, Casa Grande, Arizona
1983	West Fest Art Exhibition, Houston, Texas
1984	Historical Society Museum, New York
1987	Scottsdale Native American Indian Cultural Foundation Arts and Crafts Competition, Scottsdale, Arizona (annually through 1991)
1990	Heard Museum Guild Indian Fair and Market, Phoenix
1991	Westfest Art Exhibition, Houston
1993	Heard Museum, Phoenix
1996	British Museum of Mankind, London
	Adobe Artes Gallery, Long Island, New York
1997	Arizona State Historical Museum, University of Arizona, Tucson

Collections

Gila River Arts and Crafts Center, Sacaton, Arizona; Heard Museum, Phoenix; Hoo-Hoogam Ki Museum, Scottsdale, Arizona.

Publications

By CHIAGO: Books illustrated—*Rainhouse and Ocean: Speeches for the Papago Year* by Ruth M. Underhill, Flagstaff, 1979.

*   *   *

Michael Chiago is an enrolled member of the Tohono O'odham (Desert People), who live in the Sonoran Desert, southern Arizona. Born to a Tohono O'odham mother (and basketmaker) and a Pima/

Maricopa father, Chiago was raised in the Phoenix area. Chiago attended St. John's Indian School, Laveen, Arizona, and graduated from high school in 1964. One of his major interests at St. John's was traditional Indian fancy dancing. He joined the school's dance group and spent summers traveling the United States and the world to demonstrate Indian dancing, including a performance at the 1964 New York World's Fair. He gives much credit to these dance experiences for his inspirations for his paintings. As he danced, he pictured figures on paper and began to paint such figures as hoop dancers and Kachinas.

After high school, Chiago attended barber school, then joined the Marine Corps and served in Vietnam. Returning to Phoenix after the war, he attended Maricopa Community College in Phoenix to study commerical art. Chiago worked for a magazine as a commercial artist during the day and created paintings about the traditions of his own people after work. His paintings were not sought after by collectors, so he sold many of them through trading posts and curio shops.

Chiago was discovered by the art world in 1980 when his painting, *The Sun Supplies All Life,* was reproduced by *Arizona Highways* magazine in an issue about solar energy. The large international readership of this magazine led to calls from readers, some of whom requested paintings. Chiago followed through and his career blossomed to the degree that he needed to quit his job and concentrate on his creative paintings.

Chiago works in watercolor and paints in a realistic style. His subject is traditional life among the Tohono O'odham as they work and live in the desert. For example, *Basket and Still Life Group* displays traditional basket materials, designs and tools of his people. His other paintings of basket themes, which includes depicting weavers practicing their craft, resulted from watching his mother and aunts weave baskets. Along with still lifes and captured moments of people at work and interacting, Chiago paints vibrant Indian dancing scenes that are less strictly representational and splashier in color and action. *Indian Dancer* and *Dancer in Full Costume* pay meticulous attention to detail while displaying the flair and dynamism of Tohono O'odham ceremonies.

—Leona Zastrow

CISNEROS, Domingo

Tribal affiliations: Tepehuane
Installation artist and mixed media artist

Born: Monterrey, Mexico, 25 January 1942. **Education:** Studied art, architecture, and cinematography during the 1960s at the University of Nuevo Leon, Monterrey, and the National Autonomous University of Mexico, Mexico City. **Career:** Editor of *La Rabia*, a poetry review, in Mexico, 1962; editor of *Cine-Estudio*, Mexico, 1964-65; taught Native arts and communication at Manitou College, La Macaza, Quebec, from 1974 to 1976; lived and worked at La Macaza, 1974-96; moved to Montreal in 1996; curated exhibitions in Canada, the United States, Cuba, Italy, and Norway; contributed to numerous symposia and conferences in Canada, the United States, Cuba, Poland, and Italy; artist-in-residence at the Vancouver Art Gallery, the McMichael Gallery (Kleinburg, Ontario), the Western Front (Vancouver), the Banff Centre for the Arts, and in Fort McMurray (Alberta), as well as in France and the

Dominican Republic; art jurist in Canada and the United States; created numerous mixed-media sculptures, installation works, site-specific projects, and videos. Minister of Cultural Affairs, Quebec, 1978, 1987, and 1988.

Individual Exhibitions

1975 *Requiem for Sarain Stump*, Windham College, Putney, Vermont

1978-79 *Homage to Manitou*, Galeria de Art Mexicano & Galeria Miro, Mexico City/Monterrey

1981-82 *Deathwatch/Veillee de Mort*, Charles H. Scott Gallery, Emily Carr College of Art, Vancouver

1983 *Cronica Boreal*, Saidye Bronfman Centre, Montreal

1988-89 *Laurentian Bestiary*, National Exhibition Centre, Thunder Bay, Ontario (travelled to Brantford, Ontario and Quebec City, St. Jerome, Sherbrooke, and Mt. Laurier, Quebec)

1989 *Potlatch*, Labyrinth Gallery, Lublin, Poland

1993 *Sky Bones*, Mendel Gallery, Saskatoon, Saskatchewan

1994 *Chichimeca Project*, Carrillo Gil Museum, Mexico City

Selected Group Exhibitions

1975 Manitou College, La Macaza, Quebec

1982 *New Work by a New Generation*, Norman Mackenzie Art Gallery, University of Regina, Saskatchewan

1985-87 *Zone of Silence*, Quebec Museum Art Gallery, Quebec; Ottawa School of Art; Mt. Laurier Exposition Centre; Museum of Anthropology, Durango, Mexico

1986-87 *Other Gods: Containers of Belief*, Everson Museum of Art, Syracuse (traveled to Washington, New Orleans and Los Angeles)

1988 *Aumento di Temperatura*, Neon Gallery, Bologna, Italy

  Facts of Imagination, Museum of Art, Washington State University

1989 *Estetica Difusa, Natura ad Arte*, International Multimedia Centre, Castello de Arechi, Salerno, Italy

  Beyond History, Art Gallery of Vancouver

1990 *Les Points Cardinaux*, Centre d'Exposition de la Gare, L'Annonciation, Quebec

  Exportacion, Casa de la Cultura, Havana, Cuba

  Interscope Installation and Performance Festival, Varsovie, Lublin, Poland

  Savoir Vivre, Savoir Faire, Savoir Etre, Centre International d'Art Contemporain, Montreal

1991 *Projet Ecart*, Centre d'Exposition de la Gare, L'Annonciation, Quebec (traveled to France, Norway, and Italy)

  Okanata, Workscene Gallery and A Space, Toronto

  A Force de Terre, Galerie Circa, Montreal

  Solidarity: Art After Oka, SAW Gallery, Ottawa

  Visions of Power, Earth Spirit Festival, Toronto

  Taiteilijaryhma Kanadasta, Museum of Modern Art, Tampere, Finland

  Fourth Biennial of Havana, Cuba

1992 *Nouveaux Territoires, 350/500 Ans Apres*, Maison de la Culture Mercier, Montreal

  Territori Interroti, Galeria Le Arie del Tempo, Genoa, Italy

  Land, Spirit, Power, National Gallery of Canada, Ottawa (traveled to Regina, Saskatchewan, and Houston, Texas)

  Indigena, Canadian Museum of Civilization, Ottawa (traveled to Halifax, Nova Scotia; Windsor, Ontario; Phoenix, Arizona; and Oklahoma)

1993 *L'Art Prend l'Air*, Musée des Beaux-Arts, Montreal (toured Quebec, Ontario, and Saskatchewan)

1994 *Kluane Expedition*, Yukon Arts Centre, Whitehorse

1995 *Collectif*, Centre International d'Art contemporain, Montreal

  Zone du Silence, Dix Ans Après, Chateau de Montgirous, Mayenne, France

  Seconde Nature, Centre d'Exposition de Baie St-Paul, Quebec

1997 *Breaking Borders*, St. Norbert, Winnipeg

Site-Specific Works

1984 *Chichimeca Resurrection*, Zone of Silence Project, Mexico

1988 *Cantata Laurentienne*, L'Annonciation, Vallée de la Rouge, Quebec

  Workshop, Vancouver Art Gallery, beaches, valleys, and mountains surrounding Vancouver

1989 *Deadlines ca Presse*, Preston Lake and Lake Champlain, Vermont and Quebec

Domingo Cisneros: *A force de terre I,* **1991. Courtesy of the artist.**

1990   *Ecart, Art-Aventure*, Lac Mitchinamecus, Hautes-Laurentides, Quebec

Loupes des Glaces, Lac Macaza, Hautes-Laurentides, Quebec

1991   *Installation Grop Marka*, Grop Marka Mountains, Norway

1992   *Celebrations*, Nakoda Nation Reserve and Peyto Glacier, Smithsonian Institution

1993   *A Thousand Bones of Mother Earth*, Mendel Art Gallery, Saskatoon

Kluane Expedition, Kluane Mountains, Canadian Art Odyssey's Society, Yukon

Present, Maradalen Glacier, Commission of the Lillehammer Olympic Games, Norway

1994   *Chichimeca Project*, Durango, Mexico

Installations d'Alcorceber, beach and hermitage, Alcorceber, Valencia, Spain

1995   *Zone of Silence Ten Years Later*, Desert of the Zone of Silence, Mexico

Collections

Thunder Bay Centre for Indian Art, Thunder Bay, Ontario; Indian Art Centre, Department of Indian and Northern Affairs, Ottawa, Ontario.

Publications

By CISNEROS: Books—*Macaza Cycle*, with Jeanne Fabb, Schenectady, New York, 1979; *Deathwatch*, Vancouver 1981 (published in French, Spanish, Italian, Polish, and Flemish); *Cronique Boreale*, Montreal 1983; *Laurentian Bestiary*, Thunder Bay 1988; *Mitchi*, Quebec 1990; *On the Trail*, London, England 1992; *Lac Boivin*, Quebec 1994; *Priere pour convoquer l'inspiration*, Belgium 1994; *Le Bestiaire Laurentien*, Quebec 1995. **Articles**—*La Zone du Silence*, special edition of *Intervention*, Quebec 1984; *Les Lieux Sauvages*, Nos. 17-18 of *Urgences*, Rimouski 1987; "Aimouk," *Natura Cultura*, Salerno, Italy 1988; "Ars Magna," *Inter*, Quebec 1990.

On CISNEROS: Books—*Laurentian Bestiary*, exhibition catalog by Anne-Marie Blouin, with essay by Carol Podedworny, Thunder Bay 1988; *Facts of Imagination*, exhibition catalog by Susanna Finell, Washington 1988; *Beyond History*, exhibition catalog by Tom Hill and Karen Duffek, Vancouver 1989; *Natura Mater*, exhibition catalog by Sergio Iagulli and Giancarlo Cavallo, Italy 1990-91; *Towards a Political History of Native Art*, by Alfred Young Man, Toronto 1991; *Matka toiseen todellisuuteen*, by Jacqueline Fry, Ottawa 1991; *Cuarta Bienal de la Habana*, exhibition catalog by Lilliane Llanes Godoy, Cuba 1991; *Themes of Immanence*, exhibition catalog by Anne West, Toronto 1992; *Renaissance*, exhibition catalog by Claire Gravel, Montreal 1992; *Land Spirit Power*, exhibition catalog by Diana Nemiroff, Robert Houle, and Charlotte Townsend-Gault, Ottawa, 1992; *Indigena*, exhibition catalog by Gerald McMaster and Lee-Ann Martin, Hull 1992. **Articles**—"Art, Geography and Resistance," by Alexander Wilson, *Massachusetts Review* (Boston) 1990; "Cisneros: Native Artist," by Kelly Cartwright, *Phoenix* (Montreal) 1990; "Festiwal Sztuki," by Bozena Kowalska, *Projekt* (Varsovie) 1990; "Los Nuevos Pintores de Leyenda," by Bartolome Ferrando, *Marina d'Art* (Valencia) 1990; "Avant de Faire de l'Art, l'Artiste Doit Etre un Chaman," by Claire

Gravel in *Le Devoir* (Montreal) 1990; "Earth's Bare Bones," by Marian MacNair, the *Montreal Mirror*, 1990; "Art Contemporain 90," by Jocelyne Lepage, *La Presse* (Montreal) 1990; "Native Artists Are Central to Savoir Vivre Exhibit," by Ann Duncan, *Gazette* (Montreal) 1990; "Ecart Ovvero Isolamento," by Eliana Quattrini, *Ex Arte* (Genoa) 1990; "Cent Jours," by Monique Brunet-Weinman, *Contemporanea* (New York) 1990; "Art Actuel et Ecologie, une Difficile Ecosophie," by Claire Gravel, *Vie des Arts* (Montreal) 1990; "Eco-logique, Eco-politique: Savoir-vivre, Savoir-faire, Savoir-etre," by Annie Molin-Vasseur in *ETC* (Montreal) 1990; "1990 ou le Defile des Grandes Expositions," by Claire Gravel, *Le Devoir* (Montreal) 1990; "Natura Mater Verzoent Kunst Met de Natuur," by F.L. Wielsbeke, *Het Volk* (Belgium) 1991; "Ecart: Art-Aventure," by Jean Dumont, *Le Devoir* (Montreal) 1991; "Interscope," by Grzegorz Borkowski, *Credo* (Varsovie) 1991; "A force de se taire," by Maire-Michele Cron, *Le Devoir* (Montreal) 1991; "Le Discours Ecologique Prend Forme d'Art," by Raymond Benatchez, *La Presse* (Montreal) 1991; "Visiteurs a L'Annonciation," by Jean Dumont, *Le Devoir* (Montreal) 1991; "I am a cultural warrior," by Ingrid Blekastad, *Oslo,* 1991; "Kunst og Natur," by Tor Erik Pettersen, *Nytt om Navn* (Lillehammer) 1991; "Karju saapui Tampereelle," by Eino Nieminen, *Aamulehti* (Tampere, Finland) 1991; "Les Dernieres Forces de la Terre," by Sylvie Olivier, *Vie des Arts* (Montreal) 1992; "Art Ecolo ou Ecolo Artistes?," by Veronique Robert, *L'Actualite* (Montreal) 1992; "Domingo Cisneros, un Tribut Subversif a la Terre Mere," by S. Royer, *Le Soleil* (Quebec) 1992; "Native Artists Seize the Moment to Display Anger Against History," by John Bentley Mays, the *Globe and Mail* (Toronto) 1992; "Le Juste Usage de la Rarete a Sept-Iles," by Lise Bissonnette, *Le Devoir* (Montreal) 1992; "Indigena and Land Spirit Power," by Carol Podedworny, *C* (Toronto 1993); "Des Chamans aux Guerriers de l'Art," by Guy Sioui Durand, *Inter* (Quebec) 1993; "L'Esprit du College Manitou et Boreal Multimedia: Nature Vive," by Felix Atencio, *Terres en vue/Land Insight*, 1993; "L'Art se Jette a l'Eau," by Mona Hakim, *Le Devoir* (Montreal) 1994; "De Chichimecas, Inventos del Sol y Espacios Intervenidos," by Arturo Mendoza Mocino, *Reforma* (Mexico) 1994; "El Proyecto Chichimeca de Domingo Cisneros, Algo Salido del Norte," by Merry MacMasters, *El Nacional* (Mexico) 1994; "La Diversidad Tecnica de Cisneros," by Cesar Octavio Larrana Carrasco, *Uno mas Uno* (Mexico) 1994; "Nouveaux Regards sur la Nature," by Dany Quine, *Le Soleil* (Quebec) June 1995; "La Macaza Veut Creer un Territoire culturel," in *Le Devoir* (Montreal), May 1995; "L'Art Reflechit, l'Eau Refracte," by Jacqueline Bouchard, *Esse* (Montreal) 1995; "L'Art et l'Eau," by Jacqueline Bouchard, *Espace 30,* Winter 1995. **Film**—*Skin and Bones*, documentary by Mariella Nitoslawska, Oko Productions, Concordian University, and the National Film Board of Canada.

*

Domingo Cisneros comments:

Here is a bone for your lost *nagual*. You already have the spruce roots, the wolf tail, the brains of the bear. A heart of bone as a third eye, so you would have it. Drink of the clouds and sleep with flowers. Give thanks. Summon your powers. Love your garden of materials. Draw positive energy even from the macabre and the funereal. Transform yourself into a raven, a vulture. Purge the forest of its daily massacre. Gather the slaughtered bodies, the strangled ones, the drowned. It is not true that they are dead. Drive off putrefaction with cedar. Burn it. Tend your paradise, master your hell. Your creations are axe blows. They will speak in every tongue, penetrating to the heart, fighting decadence, disenchantment. There are no regrets. The only cure is an art that is exorcist and warrior. (From *Deathwatch,* 1981.)

*   *   *

For over twenty years, Domingo Cisneros has been single-mindedly following an approach to art that seeks to rediscover and re-animate the fundamental inter-connectedness of humanity and nature. His is an art that seeks to heal the rupture between intellect and spirit, perhaps even between culture and nature, that he believes is the result of the imposition of Euro-American instrumental rationality—the mentality that sets humans above and in opposition to nature and views the environment as a collection of exploitable resources and solvable problems. To counter this mentality, to challenge its self-assurance, Cisneros creates perplexing, often disquieting assemblages and installations using materials such as the bones, teeth, claws, hooves, furs and skins of animals, the bark and roots of trees, feathers, hair, etc. —materials gathered and prepared in the forests of Quebec's Laurentian mountains, where he has chosen to live and work. His approach to art is the outcome of a journey that has taken him from leftist political activism in Mexico to the exploration of his Native identity, but in a place several thousand miles removed from the home of his Tepehuane ancestors.

Cisneros, of part Tepehuane descent, was born in Monterrey, Mexico, in 1942 and grew up in an urban environment in the towns of Nuevo Leon and Durango. During his years as a university student in Nuevo Leon and Mexico City, he was drawn to the literature of the Beat generation, and while editing a poetry review (1962), a film journal (1964-5), and working for film companies, he also wrote fiction influenced by such artists as Céline, Henry Miller, and Jack Kerouac. This came to an end in 1968 when the Mexican government responded to mounting leftist demonstrations by killing thousands of students in what came to be known as the Massacre of Tlatelolco. Cisneros became politicized and began to engage in activities that brought him to the authorities' attention and led to jail and beatings. He chose to leave Mexico and ultimately arrived in Canada, where he became a landed immigrant in 1969.

Disenchanted with both existentialist non-engagement and the possibilities of political action, Cisneros embarked on several years of travel throughout Latin America, Europe, and the South Pacific, pursuing a growing interest in the relationships between art, mythology, and ritual. It was during this period that his identification with his own Native heritage seems to have become definitive. On his return to Canada in 1974 he became part of an important experiment in Native education at Manitou College in La Macaza, Quebec (a small town in the Laurentians, 85 miles north of Montreal). This was the first college in Canada run for and by Natives, and attracted Indian, Metis, and Inuit students from across the country. Cisneros taught Native arts and communication until the college was closed by the government in 1976.

It was here that his own art began to take shape. Cisneros had been visiting elders on reserves and studying objects in museums, trying to learn traditional techniques in the hope that these could be used to create a vital, contemporary art. He was disappointed, however, by the insistence of many of his students that he was stressing empty repetition of traditional forms. At the same time he was working with students on such problems as drug addiction; he led students into the forest to learn to survive without the artificial supports of the city and reintroduce them to the relationships between traditional rituals, respect for nature, and respect for themselves as part of nature. He came to believe that the wounds caused

by cultural loss and spiritual death could only be healed by a process that attempted to reconnect body, spirit, and nature, and he began to explore the potential of art to be such a process. Rather than mimic the forms of the past, his art has become an attempt to recover the fundamental motivation of what he sees as the most powerful art of traditional Native cultures, art that sought to bring human experience into harmony with the forces of nature.

His is not, however, a bucolic or in any way sentimental view of nature. His art grows out of an unflinching meditation on the presence of death at the heart of existence. Indeed, his method of working is itself an engagement with the central, necessary fact of death— salvaging materials from animals he has hunted for food and scouring the forest for the remains of others that have died or been killed, cleaning and preserving these materials, becoming familiar with their properties, their potential, and seeking the conjunction of elements that will convey at least a glimpse of the unpredictable complexities and powers of the nature from which Western culture has worked so hard to insulate itself.

Despite his choice of materials and methods, Cisneros rejects the suggestion that his work is in any way "primitivist" or "ethnic." He writes: "The origins of all of us, physical and artistic, lie in nature. I think a bear, or a bird, is as contemporary and as cross-cultural as an automobile (*Macaza Cycle,* 1979)." It is in order to reach those origins that Cisneros rejects both nostalgia and narrow definitions of Native art.

And although there may be similarities to some environmental, process, or even performance art, Cisneros' work also attempts to break with most European art traditions and what he sees as their limited and impotent concepts of creativity. Instead, he seeks to create new forms that will have the power to at least begin to restore the unity of art, spirit, and nature rejected by Western culture and broken in Native culture by European colonization. In this sense, his work has an undeniably political intention. Indeed, it can be seen as the effort to create a radical practice that is at once spiritual, ecological, and political.

Whether installed in the confines of a contemporary art gallery or situated on the land in response to a particular environment, Cisneros' art asserts its disturbing, quietly subversive presence, challenging viewers—both Native and non-Native—to confront their alienation and loss of spiritual power.

—Deborah Burrett

CLAIR, Peter

Variant names: Biel
Tribal affiliations: Micmac
Basketweaver and installation artist

Born: Big Cove, New Brunswick, c. 1950. **Education:** Learned wood and basketweaving techniques from his parents.

Selected Group Exhibitions

1983   *Mactaquac Festival,* New Brunswick
1985   *Annual Craft Festival,* Toronto, Ontario
           Oyster Bay Festival, Long Island, New York
           Clement Cormier Gallery, Moncton, New Brunswick
1986   Regent Gallery, Fredericton, New Brunswick

Collections

Canadian Museum of Civilization, Ottawa, Ontario.

Publications

On CLAIR: Catalogs—*Braided Spirit*, University of New Brunswick Art Centre, 1993; *Pe'l A'tukwey: Let me tell a story— Recent Work by Mi'kmaq and Maliseet Artists*, Art Gallery of Nova Scotia, 1993; *Epogan: Recent Work by Peter J. Clair,* by Janet Clark, Thunder Bay Art Gallery, Thunder Bay, Ontario, 1997.

*   *   *

Peter Clair is a renowned maritime basket sculptor working in contemporary styles that simultaneously reach back to his rich Micmac ancestry and stretch far forward, beyond the parameters of basket making as they are usually defined. In fact, his work is often called wood weaving, as opposed to basketweaving, reflecting his use of tree bark layers. He is a master of the traditional functional and fancy forms of basketry and is a pioneer in the realm of basketry as sculpture. Using traditional techniques and patterning passed on by his parents ("this old, old design" his mother called it), Clair blends concerns for form and structure, respect for the natural world, and cultural statements. In *Apapi* (1996), for example, strips of yellow lines used by police form the weft of the basket, which is inverted and becomes cagelike, noted Janet Clark in the catalog, *Epogan: Recent Work by Peter J. Clair*.

Through his basket sculptures, Clair actively challenges his viewers and the art establishment to include perceptions of art and culture from the First Nations perspective, and the effect has been years of meticulously thought-out pieces constructed with un-

Peter Clair and some of his works. Photograph by Shirley Bear; courtesy of the artist.

matched care and detail. One of Clair's most shown and talked about pieces is the 1993 installation, *Cusp*, first exhibited at the University of New Brunswick Art Centre. This remarkable installation involves both traditional basketry, using ash splints, as well as more contemporary sculptural elements and incorporates woven fabric and music. *Cusp* consists of seven standing figures isolated from each other by suspended vertical cloth banners. Each of these figures represents one of the seven sacred directions: east, south, west, north, father sky, mother earth, and the self. The tall figures are woven from strips of cloth as cloth is a traditional offering to the creator. In the centre of the installation, grounding the focus of the viewer, is the central figure in the piece—the ash splint basket drum, stretched tight with a tanned rawhide skin. Around this drum, the characters of the piece are anchored to a thought, a dream, or a memory that travels outward, absorbing, and purifying. In the center of the installation, the drum acts much like a cog in a wheel of a larger woven piece that encompasses the seven figures, the viewer, the physical space and even sounds of distant chanting and drumbeats.

Weaving itself is a metaphor on many levels, from the continuation of ancient traditions to the creation of new forms that challenge preconceptions. The *Epogan* exhibition of 1997, for example, features a series of works he completed during a year, with design motifs shared in all of the pieces, which differ in size, forming a series of experimentations with pattern, technique, and material. *Ogtjipesg* (1995) features an image of the artist's daughter on a large basket set on a tripod of willow sticks. Through such autobiographical references, as well as political commentary, concern for the natural world in selecting, gathering, handling, and making the material into art, as well as leaving some designs unfinished or irregular, Clair introduces several layers of meaning and invigorates an ancient craft with new possibilities. "When speaking about his work," noted Clark, "Peter Clair makes reference to pattern without break, without a beginning or end. This is the pattern that flows around and through his large woven baskets, just as in essence it flows through the artist himself."

—Vesta Giles

CLAIRMONT, Corwin

Tribal affiliations: Salish; Kootenai
Photographer, printmaker, painter, and mixed media artist

Born: St. Ignatius, Montana, 1947. **Education:** University of Montana, 1966-67; Montana State University, B.A., 1967-70; California State University, Los Angeles, M.A., 1970-71; San Fernando State University, 1971. **Career:** Salish Kootenai College since 1970s: assistant vice-president, coordinator of job corps educational enhancement programs, campus coordinator of pilot B.A. program; curator, including *Contemporary and Traditional Montana Indian Art*, Big Fork Cultural Center (1992) and *Treaty Times Past/Present/Future*, Missoula Museum of the Arts (1991); juror for art exhibits; member of advisory committee, Montana Arts & English Aesthetic Curriculum and Montana Arts Council; artist-in-residence, including Eiteljorg Museum, Indianapolis, and University of Washington, 1995; lecturer and panelist, various conferences and seminars; member, Confederated Salish and Kootenai Museum Site Committee, Montana Alliance for Art Education (treasurer), American Indian Research Opportunities (advisory board), Montana American Indian Committee for Higher Education, and Montana

Indian Contemporary Arts. **Awards:** Grants, Ford Foundation, 1977, National Endowment for the Arts, 1979, Colorado Dance Festival/Helena Film Society, 1990, Montana Arts Council, 1991.

Selected Group Exhibitions

1988   Centro Cultural de la Taza, Balboa Park, San Diego, California
1988-89 *Four Sacred Mountains: Color, Form and Abstraction*, Arizona Commission on the Arts, Phoenix (traveling)
1989   *Circle Way: Art of Native Americans*, Cambridge Multicultural Arts Center, Cambridge, Massachusetts (traveling)
1990   *Hammer, Nail, Brush Exhibit*, Beall Park Art Center, Bozeman, Montana
               Introductions: Contemporary American Indian Art and Emerging Artists, Montana State University, Bozeman (traveling)
1990-92 *Our Land/Ourselves*, University Art Gallery, Albany New York (traveling)
1992   *We the Human Beings*, College of Wooster Art Museum, Wooster, Ohio
1992-93 *Sublumoc Show/Columbus Wohs*, Evergreen Gallery, Washington (traveling)
1993   Park Gibson Square Art Center, Great Falls, Montana
1994   Hockeday Art Center, Klaspell, Montana
               Montana Indian Art Exhibit, Billings
1995   *Contemporary Indian Art*, Denver Art Museum, Denver, Colorado
1995   Sand Piper Gallery, Polson, Montana
1996   *Cultural Patterns*, Contemporary Crafts Gallery, Portland, Oregon
               Art of the West, Eiteljorg Museum, Indianapolis, Indiana

Collections

Beall Park Art Center, Bozeman, Montana; Eiteljorg Museum, Indianapolis, Indiana; Hockeday Art Center, Klaspell, Montana.

Publications

On CLAIRMONT: Books—*Etching*, by Leonard Edmonson, New York, 1973; *Our Land/Ourselves*, exhibition catalog by Deborah Ward, Albany, 1990; *The Sublumoc Show/Columbus Wohs*, exhibition catalog by Carla Roberts, Phoenix, Atlatl, 1992; *We the Human Beings*, exhibition catalog, Wooster, Ohio, 1996; *Art of the West*, Eiteljorg Museum, Indianapolis, 1996. **Articles**—"A Habit of Spirit," *West Coast Art Week*, Oakland, October 1990; "A Powerful and Moving Exhibit," *Village Herald Art Review* (Stony Brook) 17 July 1991; "Bridging Old and New Traditions," *New York Times*, 28 July 1991.

*   *   *

Corwin Clairmont is among an important group of Native American fine artists who have chosen to use elements of their cultural background in combination with European artistic traditions to make a political statement. In this way, Clairmont's work is akin to that of Jaune Quick-to-See Smith and Edgar Heap of Birds. Quick-To-See Smith uses a traditional painting on canvas format with elements of collage. Heap of Birds works with language and myriad animated and

Corwin Clairmont: *Narrow-Curves-Snow & Ice-River Near-the Pipe Line Trucks, with the Threat of Disaster, Run On #7,* 1995. Courtesy of the artist.

non-animated formats in his conceptual pieces. All three artists have in common overt political messages expressed in their art work.

Clairmont uses elements of printmaking, photography and language in a collage format to create his images. These images give sharp attention to governmental and environmental injustices as imposed on the Native American community. One would expect such content to render harsh images. Though the message is strong, the delivery is fairly subtle. The viewer must approach the work and examine its many photographic and literary images in order to understand its social and political commentary. Essentially, the viewer must have an intimate encounter with the piece in order to fully appreciate the message. To have a casual relationship with Clairmont's work is to miss the meaning, significance, and irony of the work.

In Clairmont's 1995 works, *The Yellowstone Pipeline Series,* he addresses the environmental ramifications of the Yellowstone Pipeline and the oil trucks that travel through the Confederated Salish and Kootenai Reservation. The controversy lies in the negotiation of a new lease for the Yellowstone Pipeline and the route used by the trucking company when transporting the oil. This conflict served as the inspiration for Clairmont's ominous collage images. In order to create swirling and colliding images, he photographed oil trucks on their routes through the reservation and then tore these photographs into pieces. The photographic pieces are affixed to monoprint in a chaotic fashion over the monotype swirl of primary colors. Consequently, the viewer can see only portions, or flashes of the surrounding mountains and portions of the trucks and other vehicles on the highway. This gives the halting sensation of falling or tumbling through two different environments. One environment is the highly realistic photograph medium, the other is the bold and surreal mat finish of the background color. This may symbolize two realities, or two ways of seeing the issues and the environment. It may also be the expression of the collision of those realities.

Clairmont creates and is interested in printmaking and photography due, in part, to its ability to be reproduced in multiples. He believes art should be accessible to all people and that the marketplace should not determine an artist's content. Clairmont is not concerned that a work sell to a popular audience, he is instead dedicated to promoting Native American art and artists and ensuring opportunities for their self expression. To this end, Clairmont has spent the last 15 years at the Salish Kootenai College in Ronan, Montana. He has served as professor and administrator as well as mentor for many young artists and non-artists alike. His advocacy for American Indian people is expressed in his lifestyle as well as his art work.

—Jennifer Complo

CLAXTON, Dana

Tribal affiliations: Lakota Sioux
Performance artist and filmmaker

Born: Yorkton, Saskatchewan, 1959. **Education:** General Studies (part-time), Simon Fraser University. **Career:** Photographer, filmmaker, illustrator, and performance artist.

Performances and Screenings

1991   *Ten Little Poems*, Neo-Nativist Pitt Gallery, Vancouver
1993   *Tree of Consumption*, Grunt Gallery, Vancouver
1994   *SA (revisited),* Treaty 4, Standing Buffalo, Saskatchewan
       Bench Remarks, Public Art on Bus Benches, Society for Non Commercial Art, Vancouver
       Twentieth Anniversary Screenings, Video In, Vancouver; Video Screenings, EM Video, Calgary
       Racing Thru Space, Artspeak, Vancouver
       Walking with the Ancients, Museum of Modern Art, New York
1995   *New View 95*, Media Arts Centre, Columbia, South Carolina; Herland Festival, Calgary Status of Women; Women's International Film and Video Festival, Winnipeg
1996   *Reviewing Canadian Video*, Open Space, Victoria
       Urban Fictions, Presentation House, North Vancouver
       Topographies, (film installation) Vancouver Art Gallery

Dana Claxton: Production still from *The Red Paper.* **Photograph by Cliff Andstein; courtesy of the artist.**

Publications

On CLAXTON: Book—*Topographies: Aspects of Recent B.C. Art,* exhibition catalog by Grant Arnold, Monika Kin Gagnon, Doreen Jensen; Vancouver Art Gallery, 1996.

* * *

Claxton represents a generation of young native artists, many of them women, whose work is not easily separated from their social concerns and their community roles. Their work is as likely to be made for audiences in shopping malls, on public transit or on television as in an art gallery, for they are concerned to break down the distinctions between high and popular art forms, perceived as one of the legacies of a hierarchical colonial system.

Claxton's work in film and video is distinguished by its reliance on visual symbols and metaphors. Her target is the greed and hypocrisy inseparable from the words of the colonisers. Where text occurs it tends to be a formal and expressive device in itself, or to be parodic. For example, the native protagonists in *The Red Paper* speak a stylised, faux Elizabethan English, to match their clothes. This reversal of cultural roles, speech and costume serves to highlight the hypocrisy of so-called "civilized" values. The title makes reference to the 1969 Statement of the Government of Canada on Indian Policy (the infamous "white paper policy") that proposed assimilation as a solution to the country's 'Indian problem.' The 25-minute film tells through reversed roles, in mock-heroic manner, the conflicting values of sixteenth-century European explorers and their discoveries. The film is projected into an elaborate, gilded picture frame and viewed by an audience sitting on gilded, salon chairs—an installation that emphasises Eurocentric views of the Indian as a confection.

However, *The Red Paper,* with its complex but underdeveloped symbolism, does not reach its target with the same assurance as shorter videos, such as *I Want to Know Why*. Here images of Indians are taken from the architectural decoration of the Manhattan Savings Bank in New York. These computer-manipulated stone images come and go, filling the screen, while pulsating music and a voice-over tell again and again of the premature deaths of her mother and grandmother, and screaming the demand to know why. The brutal reality of these women's lives is in counterpoint to the idealised Indians who were at the same time decorating the monuments of capitalism that expropriated and destroyed their way of life. The effect is successful because there can be no argument.

The Shirt (1994) suggests that European dress-codes were a form of strait-jacketing, while *Tree of Consumption* (1994) uses environmental devastation as a metaphor for a society ravaged by the disease of consumerism. In *Buffalo Bone China,* which looks at the gentility that was one of the by-products of the extermination of the buffalo, Claxton has found a potent symbol of the way in which one social system preys upon and profits from another. With a film planned on Lawrence Paul Yuxweluptun, whose paintings also are aimed at a wide audience, it is clear that advocacy of First Nations' rights and causes is the driving force behind Claxton's work.

—Charlotte Townsend-Gault

CLAYTON, Lorenzo
Variant names: Chorti
Tribal affiliations: Navajo
Painter

Born: Canconcito, New Mexico, 29 April 1951; Navajo name means Shortest Distance from Mind to Hand. **Education:** California College of Arts and Crafts, 1972-74; Cooper Union, 1974-77, B.F.A. **Military Service:** U.S. Army, 1969-72. **Career:** Artist; displays, Navajo Museum of Ceremonial Arts, Santa Fe, New Mexico, 1974; art supplies distribution, 1977-79; lithographer, Handworks and Maurel Studio, New York, 1979-84; technician and lithography instructor, Parsons School of Design and Cooper Union, both New York; visiting artist, Museum of the American Indian, New York, 1982; commission, Jane Vorhees Zimmerli Art Museum, Rutgers University. **Awards:** New Jersey State Arts Council Grant, 1983, Pollock-Krasner Foundation Award, 1986.

Individual Exhibitions

1983   Gallery 6, New York
1987   Morris Museum, Morristown, New Jersey
1996   Barrett House Galleries, Poughkeepsie, New York

Selected Group Exhibitions

1982   Institute of Humanistic Studies, Aspen, Colorado
        American Indian Community House, New York
1983   *Modern Native American Abstraction*, Philadelphia Art Alliance, Philadelphia, Pennsylvania, and American Indian Community House, New York
        Marilyn Butler Gallery of Fine Art, Scottsdale, Arizona
        Department of Fine Art, University of Oklahoma, Stillwater
        Galleria del Cavallino, Venice, Italy
        Gallery Ten, New York City
        Heard Museum, Phoenix, Arizona
1984   *Director's Choice,* American Indian Community House, New York
        University Art Galllery, California State University, Carson
        The New Native American Aesthetic, Marilyn Butler Gallery of Fine Art, Scottsdale, Arizona
        Seattle Center for the Arts, Seattle, Washington
        Museum of the Rockies, Montana State University, Bozeman
        No Beads, No Trinkets, Palais des Nations, Geneva, Switzerland
        Queens Art Gallery, Sackville, New Brunswick
        Pratt Institute Manhattan Gallery, New York
1985   Pratt Institute Gallery, Brooklyn, New York
        Grolier Club, New York
        Jane Vorhees Zimmerli Art Museum, Rutherford, New Jersey
        Sacred Circle Gallery, Seattle, Washington
        Hutchins Gallery, Long Island University, Brookville, New York
        Aurora Gallery, Closter, New Jersey
        Dome Gallery, New York
        Jersey City Museum, Jersey City, New Jersey

1990   Artworks, Trenton, New Jersey
1992   Heard Museum, Phoenix, Arizona
1993   Museum of Northern Arizona, Flagstaff
1994   *Osaka Triennial Print Show,* Osaka, Japan
        Hudson Guild Exhibition, New York
1995   Museum of Northern Arizona, Flagstaff
        Barrett Hough, Poughkeepsie, New York
        Museum of Northern Arizona, Flagstaff
1996   M.B. Modern Gallery, New York

Collections

Arizona State Museum, University of Arizona, Tucson; Heard Museum, Phoenix, Arizona; Morris Museum, Morristown, New Jersey; Newark Museum, Newark, New Jersey; Jane Vorhees Zimmerli Art Museum, Rutgers University, New Jersey.

Publications

On CLAYTON: Books—*Modern Native American Abstraction,* exhibition catalog by Edgar Heap of Birds, Philadelphia Art Alliance, 1983. **Articles**—"Native Intelligence," by Lucy Lippard, *Village Voice,* 27 December 1983; "Modern Works of American Indians," by Grace Glueck, *New York Times,* 30 November 1984; "Review," Grace Glueck, *New York Times,* 30 October 1988.

*   *   *

As a child, Lorenzo Clayton left the Navajo reservation with his family and received education in "white" institutions like St. Michael's High School in Santa Fe, New Mexico, followed by three years' service in the U.S. Army. Discovery of his artistic inclinations led him to the California College of Arts and Crafts, in Oakland, and he completed his training in the East, at Cooper Union, New York, graduating with a B.F.A. in 1977. At that time he "decided to cut his artistic ties with the past and be an 'American' painter and printmaker" (catalog of the exhibition, *Modern Native American Abstraction,* 1983). New York City (and vicinity) became his home for the next few years, as he worked in various art-related jobs and as an artist.

Using a wide range of materials and artistic media, including oils and acrylic paint, chalk, silk screen transfer and even adhesive tape, he created bold works that began winning consistent acclaim in the early 1980s. In spite of his long-time absence from his native area and his decision to be an "American" painter, Clayton never severed his ties with his Native heritage. He was visiting artist at the Museum of the American Indian, New York, in the fall of 1982, and exhibited repeatedly with other well-known Native artists, including Fritz Scholder, Jaune Quick-to-See Smith, and James Havard. Edgar Heap of Birds, an activist for Native American art and artists, credited Clayton with developing "one of the most ambitious and individualistic visual languages in Native painting."

It is small wonder, then, that in 1991 Clayton returned to his Navajo homeland and came to realize, as he told author and museum curator Edwin Wade (Museum of Northern Arizona) that "the gift of ancestors is not to be taken lightly, but rather to be cherished and used in new creations"; he discovered that "there is something about the reservation that does not die when you leave: the smell of earth after rain, the sun projected on clouds turning them into a rainbow of color, the burning cedar in the hogan to purify the air, the taste of posole and pork cooked on an open fire." These feelings have continually inspired his work, which is both abstract and rich in mysterious imagery. When more concrete, his images may make powerful statements highlighting the situation of the Native in the twentieth century. In the recent series, *Come Across,* for example, we see the long-lost cartoon friends and toys of a Navajo child caught between two worlds, and we see the question forming as to whether the values of one society can co-exist with the other.

—Gerhard and Gisela Hoffmann

COFFIN, Doug
Tribal affiliations: Potawatomi; Creek
Sculptor and mixed media artist

Born: Lawrence, Kansas, 1946. **Education:** University of Kansas, Lawrence, B.F.A.; Cranbrook Academy of Art, Bloomfield Hills, Michigan, M.F.A. in metalworking, 1975; Fort Wright College, Spokane, Washington, teaching fellowship, 1975; University of Saskatchewan, Saskatoon, sculpture studies, 1977. **Military Service:** Marine Corps. **Career:** Instructor, College of Santa Fe and Institute of American Indian Arts; erected totems in New Mexico, Arizona, New York, New Jersey, Pennsylvania, Florida, Colorado and Kenya, Africa. **Address:** c/o Elaine Horwitch Galleries, 129 W. Palace Ave., Santa Fe, New Mexico 87501.

Selected Group Exhibitions

1979   *5th Annual Outdoor Sculpture Show*, Shidoni Gallery, Tesueque, New Mexico
1980   *Festival of the Arts*, Santa Fe, New Mexico
1981   Albright Knox Art Gallery, Buffalo, New York
1982   *New Works by a New Generation*, Norman McKenzie Art Gallery, Regina, Saskatchewan
        Contemporary Southwest Art, Grand Palais, Salon d'Automne, Paris
1991   Canadian Museum of Civilization, Ottawa, Ontario
1992-97 Various gallery exhibitions arranged by his representatives, Elaine Horwitch Gallery and Copeland/ Rutherford Fine Art, Ltd.

Collections

Heard Museum, Phoenix, Arizona; Institute of American Indian Arts, Santa Fe, New Mexico; Native American Center for the Living Arts, Niagara Falls, New York; Wheelwright Museum, Santa Fe, New Mexico.

*   *   *

Coffin and his brothers, Barry and Tom, are all artists. Their father was a coach at Haskell Institute, a junior college for Indians in Kansas. Coffin credits his parents with giving him a sense that life is meant to be explored to its fullest, and for the Coffins art offered that opportunity and sense of freedom. At one time

Doug Coffin at work on one of his sculptures, Niagara Falls, New York, 1980. Photograph by Rick Hill.

they were all settled as artists in Santa Fe. Coffin went to art school, earning his B.F.A. at the University of Kansas, and his M.F.A. in metalworking at the Cranbrook Academy of Art in 1975. In between he was in the Marine Corps. He received a national teaching fellowship at Fort Wright College in Spokane in 1975.

Coffin's studies had focused on jewelry making, but he became engrossed with sculpture after studying with Anthony Caro at the University of Saskatchewan in Canada in 1977. Since the late 1970s, Coffin has concentrated on monumental sculpture, liking the sense of power that the large works offer. Coffin created a series of major installations of "totem" sculptures, large painted wood and metal sculptures that first appear like the totem poles of the northwest coast. However, Coffin has created his own visual language upon these poles, a language that seeks a more universal feeling, relying less on a narrative storyline, and more on powerful design metaphors. He seeks to reach the commonalty of all cultures rather than being representative of any single native cultural worldview. They rise from 12 to 37 feet and usually have a single wood pole upon which is added a crowning arrangement of shapes, colors and design forms that give a bold abstract declaration of a powerful spirit-being. He draws inspiration from the Plains Indian shields to create the top designs of the totems. He has erected such totems in New

Mexico, where he still maintains his studio, Arizona, New York, New Jersey, Pennsylvania, Florida, Colorado and Kenya, Africa.

To Coffin, good art is the excellence that an artist achieves by the creative combination of ideas, techniques and a masterful execution of both. In his smaller works, he creates phallic-looking wood figures that he either paints or covers with rawhide, adding other natural or man-made materials to create a feeling of internal tension and inner strength. He seeks to create a manifestation of universal spirits, powerful and soothing at the same time. Animal bones, horse hair, and rawhide are used to give a sense of antiquity. Aluminum, glass, brass tacks and colorful paint are used to push the figure into the future. The hard-edge forms are contrasted with the sensuous shapes and tactile materials he uses.

To some, Coffin's works may appear to be the typical abstract "Santa Fe style;" as a result, his work is often overlooked in major Indian art exhibitions. Yet, much of what he does deserves more attention because Coffin as been able to draw from his cultural base and from that of other indigenous cultures to create a new metaphor. His works show us that the power of object-making is timeless and that given the time to reflect upon it, most people can draw their own sense of strength from his creations. His monumental works will stand the test of time.

—Rick Hill

COHOE, Grey

Tribal affiliations: Navajo
Painter

Born: Tocito, New Mexico, 1944. **Education:** Phoenix Indian High School; Institute of American Indian Arts, 1966-67; coursework at College of Santa Fe, 1967, Fort Lewis College, Durango, Colorado, 1968, Haystack Mountain School of Crafts, Deer Isle, Maine, 1967; University of Arizona, 1967-71, B.F.A., and 1972-74, M.F.A. **Career:** Artist and writer (fiction and poetry); art instructor, Navajo Tribe, Tocito, New Mexico, 1965; graduate teaching assistant, University of Arizona, 1973-74; instructor, Institute of American Indian Arts, 1975-early 1980s; workshop instructor, Haystack Mountain School of Crafts, 1976; poetry readings and lectures, mid 1970s-mid 1980s; book illustrator; designed emblem for New Mexico Parks & Recreation, 1967. **Awards:** Honors at juried competitions, including Arizona State University, Heard Museum Guild Indian Fair and Market, and Scottsdale National Indian Arts Exhibition; National Indian Short Story Contest (Third Place), 1973. **Died:** 2 November 1991.

Individual Exhibitions

1969   East Gallery, Farmington, New Mexico

Selected Group Exhibitions

1966   American Indian Heritage Art Exhibition, Oklahoma City, Oklahoma
1967   Smithsonian Institution, Washington, D.C.
        Biennial Exhibition of American Indian Arts and Crafts, Center of the Arts of Indian America, Washington, D.C.
1968   Arizona State Museum, University of Arizona, Tucson
        Olympic Pavilion, Mexico City
1972   Navajo Community College, Many Farms, Arizona
1973   *United States Information Agency Exhibitions*, international touring: Suva, Fiji Islands; Accra, Ghana; Asuncion, Paraguay; Bamako, Mali; Dacca, Bangladesh; Fort Lamy, Chad; Montevideo, Uruguay; Nicosia, Cyprus; Mogadiscio, Somali; Niamey, Niger
        New Directions, Institute of American Indian Arts Museum, Santa Fe
1974   *MFA Thesis Exhibition*, University of Arizona Exhibition Hall, Tucson
1975   Desert Designs, Vienna, Virginia
        Wall Gallery, Phoenix, Arizona
        Print Collector's Gallery, Santa Fe, New Mexico
        Institute of American Indian Arts Museum, Santa Fe, New Mexico
1975   *Pinturas Amerindas Contemporanes/E.U. A.,* sponsored by United States Department of State and International Communications Agency, Washington, D.C. (toured South America through 1980)
1976   *Southwest Fine Arts Biennial,* Santa Fe, New Mexico
        Artist's Co-op Gallery, Santa Fe, New Mexico
        Sioux Indian Arts and Crafts Center, Rapid City, South Dakota
        Anderson-Hopkins Gallery, Arlington, Virginia
        Centennial House Gallery, Deer Isle, Maine
1978   Native American Center for the Living Arts, Niagara Falls, New York

Grey Cohoe: *Spirit Dance of the Sun and the Moon.* **Photograph by Larry Phillips; courtesy Institute of American Indian Arts Museum, Santa Fe, New Mexico.**

1982-86 Los Llanos Gallery, Santa Fe, New Mexico
1984   *Indianascher Kunstler*, organized by the Philbrook Museum, Tulsa, Oklahoma (traveled in Germany through 1985)
1991   *One with the Earth,* organized by the Institute of American Indian Arts and Alaska Culture and Arts Development, Santa Fe, New Mexico (traveled through 1992)
1992   *Creativity Is Our Tradition: Three Decades of Contemporary Indian Art at the Institute of American Indian Arts,* Institute of American Indian Arts Museum, Santa Fe, New Mexico

Collections

Arizona State Museum, University of Arizona, Tucson; Institute of American Indian Arts Museum, Santa Fe; Philbrook Museum of Art, Tulsa, Oklahoma.

Publications

By COHOE: Books illustrated—*The King of the Thousand Islands,* by Claude Aubry, Garden City, New York, 1971; *National*

Congress of the American Indian (program), Washington, D.C. 1975. **Prose and poetry collected**—*Design for Good Reading*, New York, 1969; *South Dakota Review*, Summer 1969 and Summer 1971; *Pembroke Magazine*, Summer 1972 and Autumn 1973; *Nimrod*, Spring/Summer 1972; *The Whispering Wind*, Terry Allen, editor, New York, 1972; *Myths and Motifs in Literature*, New York, 1973; *Ethnic American Short Stories*, New York, 1975.

On COHOE: Books—*Southwest Indian Painting: A Changing Art*, by Clara Lee Tanner, Tucson, 1973; *Song from the Earth: American Indian Painting*, by Jamake Highwater, Boston, 1976; *Pinturas Amerindas Contemporanes/E.U. A.*, Phoenix, 1979; *Indianascher Kunstler*, by Gerhard Hoffman, Munich, 1984; *The Arts of the North American Indian: Native Traditions in Evolution*, Edwin L. Wade, ed., New York: Hudson Hills Press in association with Philbrook Art Center, Tulsa, Oklahoma, 1986. **Articles**—"Friends Say Man Found Dead in Alley Was Artist with Alcohol Problems," by Steve Terrell, *The New Mexican*, 3 November 1991; "The Passing of Grey Cohoe," by Rick Hill, *Santa Fe Reporter*, 13-19 November 1991.

*   *   *

After Grey Cohoe's untimely death, which came as a shock to the Indian community in Santa Fe, Rick Hill, director of the IAA Museum and a long-time friend, drew a verbal portrait of the artist in a local newspaper. He described him as "one of Santa Fe's best 'unknown' artists." Once a rising star on the Indian art horizon, whose work had been exhibited in nearly twenty countries, Cohoe never received the critical acclaim, the financial success or the honor bestowed upon his contemporaries. Cohoe's addiction to alcohol and gradual decline is more than a personal tragedy and must be seen in the larger context of an Indian experience of being caught between two worlds, and not belonging to either one.

This duality became the central theme in Cohoe's work and contributed to his style. He combined images of traditional Navajo life with elements of contemporary Anglo-American culture, displaying the discrepancies with a bitter undertone and even a satiric bite. In *Rite for Autumn Harvest*, for example, he takes up the central motif of traditional Indian painting, the ceremonial dance. But in Cohoe's image, the dance no longer occupies the center of attention—the dancers being rather small, their figures blurred to a mass and removed to the lower left. Huge crosses on the mountains indicate the powerful presence of Christian religion, which Cohoe saw as a destructive force to the "Navajo way." The image seems to suggest the loss of the old contact of the Indians with the spiritual sphere beyond in a world that is dominated by other forces, and this tension gives the picture its modern quality.

Another means of expressing the Indian's predicament in modern society is Cohoe's surrealistic rendering of his figures, who often have empty faces with no eyes, thus being "invisible" to their surroundings. They point to the basic problem in his world: that communication and harmony between the differing worlds of Indians and whites are practically impossible. In his own life, Cohoe experienced a rigid boarding school, where Navajo language and food were forbidden; he subsequently felt alienated in the Anglo world and out of touch with the traditions of Navajo culture. Cohoe exemplifies his belief by taking his themes from everyday life and creating a realistic basis for his pictures. With clearly autobiographical references, he frequently paints everyday events in the life of Tocito, his birthplace, in New Mexico. Sometimes the social-

critical aspect is hidden, as in the seemingly harmonious *Summer Day at Tocito*, and sometimes it is only part of the "message," as in *The Battle of the Butterflies at Tocito*. The "battle-scene" in the barroom, with its suggestion of violence, destruction, and death intends to make an existential statement that includes social criticism, but, going beyond that, has as its theme the alienation of man, his inability to communicate, and his brutality in dealing with his fellows.

While living between two cultures proved disastrous for Grey Cohoe, he greatly benefited as a painter from combining Native themes, motifs and pictorial ideas in his art with Western styles and modes of painting. His images are influenced by pop art, with its destruction of customary contexts, color field painting, with its clear demarcation and balancing of color zones as "pure" painting; and surrealistic tendencies, which manifest themselves in the estrangement of his figures. Apart from these general trends in his images, Cohoe's hallmark as a painter is his rich coloration—the bold combination of unexpected colors and ample use of negative space, his predilection for the decorative, and his love for the play with patterns and designs. With all that he had his audience in mind. He once said in an interview that he wanted people to enjoy his work—the paint elements, the design, the composition, the color statements, as well as the messages. "I do want them to enjoy it. It's like, in my work, I'm offering people a party they're never going to forget."

—Gerhard and Gisela Hoffmann

CORDERO, Helen

Tribal affiliations: Cochití Pueblo
Painter

Born: Helen Quintana Cordero, Cochití Pueblo, New Mexico, 1915. **Career:** Taught pottery in Bernalillo, near Albuquerque, New Mexico; demonstrated Storyteller ceramic process regularly at Peco National Monument, New Mexico, and around the U.S. **Awards:** Numerous, including First, Second, and Third prizes, New Mexico State Fair, 1964, and First Place, Santa Fe Indian Market, 1965; First Place, "Traditional Pottery, Painted, Miscellaneous," 1971; New Mexico Governor's Award for Pottery, 1982. **Died:** 24 July 1994.

Individual Exhibitions

1981-82 *Tales for All Seasons*, Wheelwright Museum of the American Indian, Santa Fe, New Mexico

Selected Group Exhibitions

c. 1960 Santo Domingo Feast Day, Santo Domingo Pueblo, New Mexico
1973 *What Is Folk Art?*, Museum of International Folk Art, Santa Fe
1974 *World Crafts Exhibit*, Toronto, Ontario
1979 *One Space, Three Visions*, Albuquerque Museum, New Mexico
Storyteller Show (annually through 1982), Adobe Gallery, Albuquerque, New Mexico

1981   *American Indian Art in the 1980s,* Native American Center for the Living Arts, Niagara Falls, New York
        Heard Museum, Phoenix, Arizona

Collections

Museum of International Folk Art, Santa Fe, New Mexico; Museum of New Mexico, Santa Fe.

Publications

On CORDERO: Books—*Pueblo Pottery of the New Mexico Indians,* by Betty Toulouse, Santa Fe, 1977; *Nacimientos: Nativity Scenes by Southwest Indian Artists,* by Guy and Doris Monthan, Flagstaff, 1979; *The Pueblo Storyteller,* by Barbara A. Babcock, Tucson, 1986; *Lost and Found Traditions: Native American Art, 1965-1985,* by Ralph T. Coe, Seattle, 1986; *Talking with Clay: The Art of Pueblo Indian Pottery,* by Stephen Trimble, Santa Fe, 1987; *American Indian Art: The Collecting Experience,* by Beverly Gordon, Madison, 1988. **Articles**—"Clay Changes: Helen Cordero and the Pueblo Storyteller," by Barbara A. Babcock, *American Indian Art Magazine,* Spring 1983.

*

Helen Cordero comments (1983):

Today everything's easy. Buy their clay, their paint, take them to big ovens in Albuquerque. Grandma Clay doesn't like it and a lot of them don't even know about Grandma Clay. To make good potteries, you have to do it the right way, the old way, and you have to have a special happy feeling inside. All my potteries come out of my heart. I talk to them. They're my little people. Not just pretty things that I make for money. (From *American Indian Art Magazine.*)

*   *   *

Born in 1915 in the Rio Grande pueblo of Cochití, which is known for its pottery, Helen Cordero became one of its most famous inhabitants. She introduced the Storyteller figurine as a new and very successful genre in pueblo pottery.

Cordero's beginnings as an artist were all but promising. After an unsuccessful start at bead and leather work, she was encouraged by Juanita Arquero, a relative and life-long friend (and an accomplished potter), to try her hand at ashtrays, bowls and vessels, which they sold at the Crazy Horse Store in Old Town, Albuquerque. But whereas Juanita made beautiful vessels, Helen's did not turn out right. The turning point in her career came when the two women began teaching pottery at a school in Bernalillo near Albuquerque. One of the teachers mentioned to them figurines made in the past in Cochití, and when Juanita suggested that Helen should try to make such pieces, Helen jumped at the idea and thus started making the figurines with which she was to become famous.

Cordero did not invent figurative pottery in Cochití, as is often claimed, she rather reinvented it. Puebloan Indians had formed ceramic images of themselves, their gods and the animals around them for at least 1600 years. When, however, Spanish missionaries appeared on the scene they regarded the figurines, which were sometimes used in ceremonies, as idols and discouraged the Puebloans from making them. Thus, the figurative tradition was interrupted for a long time. Nevertheless, the art of making clay images sur-

vived and thrived again when tourism began flourishing in the late nineteenth century in the West. Tourists were delighted with what they regarded as "curios" and asked for more. This development, which was furthered by Indian traders, met with the disgust of serious students and scholars of native handicraft; an 1889 article in *American Anthropologist,* by William H. Holmes, was titled "The Debasement of Pueblo Art." Such scholars feared that Indian art by going commercial would lose its original character, as well as its quality. And, indeed, between 1915 and 1960, the quality of the drummers, dancers, "singing mothers," and others declined and for a long time pottery was silent in the pueblo.

When Helen Cordero introduced to the general public her first Storyteller in 1964, she was following the ceramic tradition of the "singing mother," who had been a favorite subject among potters and buyers alike. Helen modified the motif, however, by exchanging the mother for a male figure, the grandfather. She said later that she had envisioned her own grandfather, Santiago Quintana, when she made the figure. He had been an excellent storyteller, and children loved him and loved listening to his stories. She portrayed him as he would sit, with his eyes closed and his mouth open while he was telling his story. She also modified the motif by giving her storyteller a great number of children, instead of just one, and all were listening to his tale, spellbound.

One of the first scholars to realize that Helen had broken new ground was folk art collector Alexander Girard, who around 1960, saw her first pieces at a feast in Santo Domingo. He bought all he could get and commissioned a Nativity scene, thus encouraging Cordero to enlarge her repertoire and try new themes. In the following years, Helen did a lot of experimenting, created different forms of singing mothers and storytellers, and introduced new characters and themes: a drummer, because her husband was a fine drummer; a pueblo father, a water carrier, a nightcryer; various animals, like owls and turtles; and a Hopi maiden, as well as nativity scenes and variations on the children's hour. The storyteller, however, remained her favorite subject and established her fame.

Since Helen Cordero's invention of the Storyteller figure, a great many potters have followed in her footsteps. Today, the typical storytellers are female, and they vary from each other in many ways with more and more children crawling over them or crowding around them. The children are rendered in various postures and may be engaged in many activities—holding a lamb for instance or playing with a hobby horse. Thus, Helen Cordero has prepared a field of great creativity and has set an example in quality and good craftsmanship. Moreover, she has led the way from tourist attraction to serious folk art.

—Gerhard and Gisela Hoffmann

CORNPLANTER, Jessie

Tribal affiliations: Seneca
Illustrator, painter, and carver

Born: Cattaraugus Reservation, New York, 1889; from the Snipe Clan of the Seneca Nation. **Military Service:** Served in World War I; received a Purple Heart. **Career:** Commissioned at age nine by the State of New York for sketches relating to the life of the Long House people; instructor, carver, author, singer at tribal ceremonies, and painter; served as ritual chief of the Long House. **Died:** 1957.

Jessie Cornplanter: *Lacrosse Player,* 1908. Photograph by Rick Hill; collection of New York State Museum, Albany.

Selected Group Exhibitions

1982   *Native American Painting,* Museum of the American Indian (traveling)

Collections

National Museum of the American Indian, Washington, D.C.; New York State Museum, Albany; Rochester Museum of Arts and Sciences, Rochester, New York.

Publications

By CORNPLANTER: Books—*Iroquois Indian Games and Dances,* (text and illustrations) Chicago: Starr, 1913; *Legends of the Longhouse,* (text and illustrations), Philadelphia: J.B. Lippincott, 1938. **Books Illustrated**—*Iroquois Uses of Maize and Other Food Plants,* by Arthur C. Parker, Albany: New York State Museum, 1910; *The Code of Handsome Lake, the Seneca Prophet,* by Arthur C. Parker, Albany: New York State Museum, 1910; *Cry of the Thunderbird: The American Indian's Own Story,* Charles Hamilton, editor, New York: McMillan, 1950.

On CORNPLANTER: Books—*Indian Painters and White Patrons,* by J. J. Brody, Albuquerque, University of New Mexico Press, 1971; *Handbook of North American Indians: Northeast,* edited by Bruce G.Trigger, Washington, D.C.: Smithsonian Institution Press, 1978; *Native American Painting: Selections from the Museum of the American Indian,* by David M. Fawcett and Lee A. Callander, New York: Museum of the American Indian, 1982. **Articles**—"The Meanings of Native American Art," by William C. Sturtevant, *The Arts of the North American Indians,* Edwin L. Wade, editor, New York: Hudson Hills Press and Philbrook Art Center, 1986; *In the Shadow of the Sun,* by Gerald McMaster, Canadian Museum of Civilization, Hull, Quebec, 1993.

*   *   *

Jessie Cornplanter was a child prodigy. At the age of nine, in 1898, he completed sketches of life among the Long House people, commissioned by the state of New York, and in 1901 Cornplanter drew a 7" x 10" complex composition, with forty-three figures and enlivened with watercolors. This work, *Indian New Year: Fourth Day on Jan. 25th. 1901,* depicts the ritual of the Midwinter Ceremony, which involves masked healers on the Cattaraugus Reservation who are called the "Friends" by the People of the Longhouse. Young Cornplanter recorded the event with amazingly sharp, expressive, and complex details. At fourteen, he published his first illustrated book, *Iroquois Indian Games and Dances,* and soon after illustrated Arthur Parker's *Iroquois Uses of Maize and Other Food Plants* (1910) and *The Code of Handsome Lake, the Seneca Prophet* (1913).

The Code of Handsome Lake is a treatise on a spiritual movement that inspired followers of a visionary to organize and live according to a code of ethical principles. In the late eighteenth century, Handsome Lake had a vision and unified groups of people with positive ideas. The code he established compliments the "Great Law of Peace," the ancient treatise delivered by the Great Peacemaker, establishing participatory democracies in a united confederation of five Iroquoian nations (later joined by a sixth, the

Tuscarora). Jessie's nation, the Seneca, are addressed as "Elder Brothers" along with the Mohawk, and together they form the "Upper House," similar to the U.S. Senate; indeed, Senate Resolution 76 (1982) recognizes that the Great Law of Peace of the Iroquois Confederacy served as a model for the three-part system of American government. The philosophy of "peace" as a way of life influenced Cornplanter's world view.

Cornplanter grew up to become an important member of the Seneca Nation, as a singer in tribal ceremonies, ritual chief of the Long House, and chief of New Town, the Indian village of the Snipe Clan. As an artist he preserved tribal history by sketching scenes from the past recounted through oral histories, illustrating myths, and recreating scenes of everyday Seneca life.

These drawings were part of a great legacy Cornplanter contributed on the cultural traditions of the Seneca. He toured as a dancer and singer and recited verse in his native language and in English, which he continued to learn after leaving school following the fifth grade. Through his drawing, performances, and letters, he left a vast body of knowledge that serves as an excellent source for the history, traditions, and legends of the Seneca people. He was frequently interviewed by anthropologists and corresponded with several of them. William C. Sturtevant, editor and writer of the distinguished Smithsonian Institution series, *Handbook of North American Indians,* places Cornplanter in historical and ethnographic perspective: "His earliest known drawings are lively and accurate depictions of scenes of reservation life, especially ritual subjects. Quite soon, he introduced reconstructions—the poses and activities being ones he had observed, but the clothing and architecture remained those of an earlier day. Later, he drew illustrations of myths." Cornplanter accomplished this "with no formal training and no known informal artistic influences, but with great and widely recognized talent."

Jesse Cornplanter was a direct descendant of Cornplanter, the great nineteenth-century Seneca tribal leader, who pursued a policy of balancing the adoption of U.S. agricultural practices and government among the Iroquois with an emphasis on maintaining cultural traditions, a practice that his descendant pursued as well. The elder Cornplanter was a half-brother to Handsome Lake.

—Gregory Schaaf

CRANMER, Douglas
Tribal affiliations: Kwakiutl
Carver

Born: Alert Bay, British Columbia, 1927. **Education:** Apprenticed in carving with Mungo Martin (carver-in-residence, British Columbia Provincial Museum) and Bill Reid, whom he assisted in a commission by the UBC Museum of Anthropology to recreate the primary elements of a nineteenth century Haida village. **Career:** Worked as a commercial fisherman and lumberjack; UBC commission with Bill Reid, 1957-62; managed an Indian-owned art shop, the Talking Stick, early 1960s; member of the foundation faculty, Kitanmax School of Northwest Coast Indian Art, Hazelton, British Columbia; instructor, Vancouver Centennial Museum, 1973 and in Alert Bay, beginning in 1977; founding member, U'mista Cultural Centre, Alert Bay.

Selected Group Exhibitions

1971   *The Legacy,* British Columbia Provincial Museum, Victoria, British Columbia (traveled internationally through 1981)

1993   *In the Shadow of the Sun,* Canadian Museum of Civilization, Hull, Quebec (traveling)

Publications

On CRANMER: Books—*The Legacy: Tradition and Innovation in Northwest Coast Indian Art,* by Peter L. Macnair, Alan L. Hoover, and Kevin Neary, Vancouver and Seattle, Douglas & McIntyre/ University of Washington Press, 1984.

*   *   *

Douglas Cranmer, a Southern Kwakiutl (Kwakwaka'wakw) from the Nimpkish band of Alert Bay, is a revered artist in British Columbia now regarded as a "senior statesman" in the field. Cranmer synthesized the three-dimensional qualities of the "Central Style" of the Southern Kwakiutl with the two-dimensional formline features of the "Northern Style" in order to produce a kind of hybrid art both distinctive and modernist. In addition, Cranmer is one of the few living connections between the historic Southern Kwakiutl artists and the present generation. Although he has not been as prolific as some artists, his work is much admired and he is held in high esteem.

When Cranmer was a boy growing up in Alert Bay, he was able to observe such talented older-generation artists at work as Arthur Shaughnessy and Frank Walker. But as a young man Cranmer did not immediately decide to become an artist and therefore, like most others of his age, worked in the fishery and forest industries. It is said that in his forestry work he was able to develop a knowledge of and appreciation for wood that was to have salient effect later on when he decided to pursue the carving arts.

When Cranmer came south in the 1950s he was to have the exceptional experience of apprenticing with two of the most noted artists of the day, Mungo Martin (Southern Kwakiutl) and Bill Reid (Haida). In his work with Martin (who was his step-grandfather), Cranmer was able to thoroughly learn and absorb the principles of the three-dimensional Southern Kwakiutl art (sometimes called the "Central Style"). From approximately 1952 to 1962 (when he died), Martin was the carver-in-residence at the British Columbia Provincial Museum in Victoria. Given his tribal background and cultural heritage, this experience was naturally seminal for Cranmer.

However, Cranmer also came to assist Reid in his commission with the UBC Museum of Anthropology to recreate the primary elements of a nineteenth-century Haida village: six totems and a memorial figure, along with a plank house winter dwelling and a mortuary house. In this project, Cranmer learned a great deal about the "Northern Style," with its formlines, ovoids, U-forms, and S-forms. Moreover, the Northern Style of the Haida was a restrained, aristocratic, elegant, and formal art that featured inner tensions within its flat (or two-dimensional) figures. Greatly impressed, Cranmer was to incorporate many of the lessons he learned from Reid into his own personally distinctive style. Cranmer worked with Reid for almost three and a half years during the period from 1957 to 1962.

According to museum curator Peter L. Macnair, although the two-dimensional Northern Style approach is evident in Cranmer's art, his work is still basically Southern Kwakiutl, albeit distinctively personal. Such a contention is borne out, Macnair feels, in an analysis of Cranmer's work. In his curatorship at the Royal British Columbia Museum in Victoria, Macnair was one of those who helped to assemble a magnificent collection of contemporary Northwest Coast Indian art by some of the leading Canadian practitioners in the province. Called "The Legacy," the collection has been exhibited at various times and places in North America and Europe since it was first organized in 1970-71. There are three pieces by Cranmer. One of them is a laminated red cedar panel featuring a monster halibut and the Thunderbird in a transformation scene. Although it is definitely Southern Kwakiutl in character, the approach employed by Cranmer is two-dimensional.

Also according to Macnair, in the mid-1970s Cranmer began experimenting with two-dimensional design in a more uninhibited and abstract manner. Such innovative art was usually executed as a painting or in silkscreen print form. Included in *The Legacy* collection are two examples of this avant-garde Northwest Coast art by Cranmer, *Killer Whales* (1976) and *Canoe* (1978), which are unquestionably abstract in nature. Nevertheless, the figurative elements are identifiable images from Southern Kwakiutl art. When he produced works like these, Cranmer earned a reputation as an inno-

Douglas Cranmer: Detail of panel from *Tsonoqua,* U'mista Cultural Centre, Alert Bay, British Columbia. Photograph by J. A Warner.

vative artist interested to push Northwest Coast Indian art into more contemporary and abstract modes of expression. Indeed, his reputation as an "artistic progressive" has been vouchsafed ever since the 1970s.

In addition to his creative work, Cranmer also earned some attention in the early 1960s for his work in helping to operate an Indian owned and controlled art shop, the Talking Stick. Even more importantly, Cranmer has served as a teacher, perpetuating the tradition of master / apprentice. Notably, he was one of the "foundation faculty"—along with Tony Hunt, Robert Davidson, Duane Pasco, and others—at the Kitanmax School of Northwest Coast Indian Art in Hazelton, British Columbia. This school was associated with the 'Ksan village project, which is a recreated Gitksan community centered around the revival of that tribe's artistic traditions. The training program at 'Ksan has been important and Cranmer was one of those who helped train the first generation of 'Ksan artists in 1970. Also, Cranmer has taught in such locales as the Vancouver Centennial Museum in 1973 and Alert Bay, beginning in 1977.

Cranmer participated in the creation of the U'mista Cultural Centre in Alert Bay. In 1980 the Southern Kwakiutl were able to get back the so-called "Potlatch Collection" from Canadian governmental authorities. In 1921 Dan Cranmer held an illegal potlatch and as a result of a government crack-down, many Kwakiutl families had to surrender precious ceremonial items (including masks, screens, rattles, and so on) to the Canadian government for pathetically low fees. After years of agitation and negotiations, the Alert Bay (Nimpkish) Southern Kwakiutl were able to recover their lost items and to ensconce them in a museum of their own. A giant plank house-like museum was built overlooking the waterfront at the northern edge of Alert Bay. Cranmer helped to appropriately decorate the facade of the new structure: on the front of the building facing the water he recreated a giant painting of *Thunderbird with Killer Whale*, executed in the same manner as a nineteenth-century plank house front painting in Alert Bay. And along the side of the building (the actual entranceway for visitors), he created a series of two-dimensional panels, depicting Southern Kwakiutl crest figures, flanking the left side of the doors.

—John Anson Warner

CREEPINGBEAR, Mirac

Variant names: Aun-So-Bea
Tribal affiliations: Kiowa; Pawnee; Arapaho
Painter

Born: Mirac Lee Creepingbear (a clerk registering birth certificates misread his mother's spelling of Miracle), Lawton, Oklahoma, 8 September 1947; native name translates as Big Foot. **Education:** South Community College, Oklahoma City, Oklahoma. **Career:** Electric company employee; full-time artist beginning mid-1970s; painted mural at the Kiowa Tribal Museum, Carnegie, Oklahoma, with Parker Boyiddle and Sherman Chaddlesone. **Awards:** Numerous at fairs and juried competitions, including Philbrook Museum of Art, 1979; Inter-Tribal Indian Ceremonial, 1979-80; Cherokee National Museum, 1982, 1984; American Indian Exposition, 1982, 1985; Red Earth Festival, 1989. **Died:** 28 October 1990.

Individual Exhibitions

1981   Southern Plains Indian Museum and Crafts Center, Anadarko, Oklahoma
1984   Jacobson House, Norman, Oklahoma
1992   Southern Plains Indian Museum and Crafts Center, Anadarko, Oklahoma
1993   Red Earth Indian Center, Oklahoma City

Selected Group Exhibitions

1979-85 *Oklahomans for Indian Opportunity*, The Galleria, Norman, Oklahoma
1981-83 *Native American Painting*, Amarillo Art Center, Amarillo, Texas (traveling)
1982   *Night of the First Americans*, John F. Kennedy Center for the Performing Arts, Washington, D.C.
1983   Native American Center for the Living Arts, Niagara Falls, New York
1984   Philbrook Museum of Art, Tulsa, Oklahoma
         Heritage Center, Inc., Pine Ridge, South Dakota
1985   Institute of American Indian Arts Museum, Santa Fe, New Mexico
1986   Cherokee National Museum, Tahlequah, Oklahoma
1987   Kiowa Tribal Museum, Carnegie, Oklahoma
1992   Kiowa Tribal Museum, Carnegie, Oklahoma
1996   *Visions and Voices: Native American Painting from the Philbrook Museum of Art*, Tulsa, Oklahoma

Collections

Heritage Center, Inc., Pine Ridge, South Dakota; Institute of American Indian Arts Museum, Santa Fe, New Mexico; Kiowa Tribal Museum, Carnegie, Oklahoma.

Publications

On CREEPINGBEAR: Books—*Native American Painting*, by Jeanne Snodgrass King, Amarillo, Texas, 1981; *Vision and Voices: Native American Painting from the Philbrook Museum of Art*, Lydia Wyckoff, editor, Tulsa, 1996. **Articles**—"Mirac Creepingbear," *Southwest Art,* September 1992.

*   *   *

Mirac Creepingbear often expresses a single moment in the exchange between God and humans in his paintings. In some works, it might be an internal personal contemplation of God's strength and force, while in others the dynamic and thunderous manifestation of God's greatness. His intimate and personal portrayal of these themes is the foundation of most all his works. With his individualistic interpretation, grounded in a painting tradition yet set apart, Creepingbear realized a new direction for the stylized and fluid lines of the peyote visionary painters who include his maternal uncle, Herman Toppah, Woody Big Bow, Al Momaday and Lee Monette Tsatoke. As works from these painters were often decorative and occasionally static, Creepingbear liberated the line with his spontaneous brushwork. Contoured plane and line unified in an innovative way, breathing life and form into his figures. His resulting style yields a vitality that recalls the spiritual force often found in the "Kiowa Five" pieces nearly forty years earlier.

Creepingbear once said that he did not theorize about the structural makeup of a painting but worked spontaneously instead. His free-hand brush strokes moving in and out of the painting, like *His Father's Society*, reflects this approach. The power of his work embodies a knowing of things seen and unseen, as the Spirit moves into many of his paintings, through them, and flows out again. As the Spirit moves through the scene you can see its path in a wave of swirling lines. The figures in the painting conform to and are effected by its path; even the details of hair and fringe yield to its force, forming the unifying vehicle that ties the composition together.

His Father's Society illustrates the manifestation of God's strong presence to a group, occurring in an electrifying moment with sur-realistic elements. Past and present are fused together with a sym-bolic layering of buffaloes, pictographs and a procession of ances-tors walking to the heavens. The painting is illuminated with a profusion of iridescent colors of orange, blue and purple hues, the colors of the sunset.

Kiowa Sun Dancer, set within a sun dance arbor, captures a more contemplative and individual exchange between God and human. The cold and dank arbor is especially suggestive, as God, the breath of life, moves into the painting with a motion of light and air and has entered the sun dance figure, illustrated in high tones of greens and blues—the force of the Spirit, and man and God become one. This exchange is juxtaposed with the dark figures huddled in a circle in the brush arbor.

Towards the end of his life in the late 1980s, Creepingbear em-barked on yet another style, different from *Kiowa Sun Dancer* and *His Father's Society*. These later works show a world of infinite space where the figure is part of a different realm, with little or no connection to the earth as we know it. Perhaps it is Creepingbear's symbolic vision of where the spirit of his people live, a place where the inner vision or spirit is realized in complete. Figures are pre-sented in a black background with dots of stars, and colors range from deep crimson to an almost blood-red shade. Faces are painted in a shiny blackish-blue, illuminated from a mysterious source.

The artist's mother, Rita Creepingbear, recalled how he began to visualize historical stories. She once told him to go into his imagina-tion: "If you lay flat on your back and meditate, you can almost see things... If you're up and around your mind's not thinking right, so you have to lay down an meditate and it'll come back to you." Creepingbear's imagination, combined with his profound knowl-edge of Kiowas, inhabited that realm. His elusive figures are inte-grated into an expansive and mysterious world. Though Creepingbear's expressionistic style was new, his message was time-less—an exchange between God and man.

—Marla Redcorn

CRUMBO, Woody

Tribal affiliations: Potawatomi
Painter and printmaker

Born: Woodrow Wilson Crumbo, Lexington, Oklahoma, 21 January 1912. **Education:** Tutored in Native American traditions by Belo Cozad (Kiowa), including crafting and playing flutes, and by Susie Peters in basic painting; studied watercolors with Clayton Henri Staples, Ameri-can Indian Institute, 1931-33; studied painting and drawing with Oscar Jacobson, University of Wichita, 1933-36; studied murals with Olaf Nordmark, University of Oklahoma, 1936-38. **Career:** Led a Native dance troupe on a U.S. tour, early 1930s; director, art department, Bacone College, 1938-41; painted numerous murals at such places as the Philbrook Art center, Tulsa, Oklahoma, the United States Depart-ment of the Interior, and the Fort Sill Indian school, among others; community activist, working with and advising Thomas Gilcrease, founder of the Gilcrease Museum, Tulsa, promoting Indian art, includ-ing founding a print studio in Taos, New Mexico, and assisting the Tiguas in their efforts to become an officially recognized tribe, among many social activities; served on the Oklahoma State Arts Council, 1978-84. **Awards:** Numerous, including scholarships and fellowships; valedictorian, American Indian Institute; national dance contest win-ner, 1935; Native American Rights Fund, Featured Artist, 1987. **Died:** 4 April 1989.

Selected Group Exhibitions

1937   *American Indian Exposition and Congress*, Tulsa, Oklahoma
        McCombs Gallery, Bacone College, Bacone, Oklahoma

1947-65 *American Indian Paintings from the Permanent Collec-tion*, Philbrook Art Center, exhibit and tour

1955-56 University of Oklahoma European Tour

1958-61 University of Oklahoma European Tour

1972   *Contemporary Southern Plains Indian Painting*, South-ern Plains Indian Museum and Oklahoma Indian Arts and Crafts Cooperative, Anadarko, Oklahoma

1978   *100 Years of Native American Painting*, Oklahoma Mu-seum of Art, Oklahoma City

1979   *Sharing Our Wealth*, Oklahoma Historical Society, Okla-homa City

1979-80 *Native American Paintings*, Mid-America Arts Alliance Project, organized by the Josylyn Art Museum, Omaha, Nebraska, (traveling)
        Native American Art at the Philbrook, Tulsa, Oklahoma

1980   *Plains Indian Paintings*, Museum of Art, University of Oklahoma, Norman (traveling)

1981-83 *Native American Painting*, Amarillo Art Center, Ama-rillo, Texas (traveling)

1982   *Native American Painting: Selections from the Museum of the American Indian*, The Heard Museum, Phoenix

1984   *Indianischer Kunstler*, organized by Philbrook Museum of Art, Tulsa, Oklahoma (traveled in West Germany through 1985)

1987   Native American Rights Fund, Inc., Boulder, Colorado
        Cherokee National Museum, Tahlequah, Oklahoma

1990   Koogler McNay Art Museum, San Antonio, Texas
        American Indian Artists: The Avery Collection and the McNay Permanent Collection, Marion Koogler McNay Art Museum, San Antonio, Texas

1991   *Mayfest International Festival*, Winston-Salem, North Carolina

1991-92 *Shared Visions: Native American Painters and Sculptors in the Twentieth Century*, Heard Museum, Phoenix

1994   Center for Great Plains Studies, University of Nebraska, Lincoln

Collections

Bureau of Indian Affairs, United States Department of the Interior, Washington, D.C.; Center for the Great Plains Studies, University of Nebraska, Lincoln; Cleveland Museum of Art, Ohio; Creek In-dian Council House and Museum, Okmulgee, Oklahoma; Eiteljorg

Museum, Indianapolis, Indiana; Thomas Gilcrease Institute of American History and Art, Tulsa, Oklahoma; Indian Arts and Crafts Board, United States Department of the Interior, Washington, D.C.; Joslyn Art Museum, Omaha, Nebraska; Kiva Museum of the Koshare Indian, Boy Scouts of America, La Junta, Colorado; National Museum of the American Indian, Smithsonian Institution, Washington, D.C.; Minneapolis Institute of Arts, Minnesota; Museum of Northern Arizona, Katherine Harvey Collection, Flagstaff; Oklahoma Museum of Natural History, Norman; Philbrook Museum of Art, Tulsa, Oklahoma; San Francisco Museum of Modern Art, California; Sioux Indian Museum and Craft Center, Indian Arts and Crafts Board, United States Department of the Interior, Rapid City, South Dakota; Southwest Museum, Los Angeles; Wichita Art Museum, Kansas.

Publications

On CRUMBO: Books—*A Pictorial History of the American Indian* by Oliver LaFarge, New York, 1956; *American Indian Painting of the Southwest and Plains Areas* by Dorothy Dunn, Albuquerque: University of New Mexico Press, 1968; *Song from the Earth: American Indian Painting* by Jamake Highwater, Boston: New York Graphic Society, 1976; *100 Years of Native American Art* by Arthur Silberman, Oklahoma City, 1978; *American Indian Painting and Sculpture* by Patricia Janis Broder, New York: Abbeville Press, 1981; *Native American Painting: Selections from the Museum of the American Indian* by David M. Fawcett and Lee A. Callander, New York: Museum of the American Indian, 1982; *Kiowa Voices: Ceremonial Dance, Ritual and Song* by Maurice Boyd, Fort Worth, Texas Christian University Press, 1981; *Kiowa Voices: Myths, Legends, and Folktales* by Maurice Boyd, Forth Worth, Texas Christian University, 1983; *Indianische Kunst im 20 Jahrhundert* by Gerhard Hoffman, et al., Münich, Germany, 1984; *The Arts of the North American Indian: Native Traditions in Evolution*, Edwin L. Wade, editor, New York: Hudson Hills Press, 1986; *Shared Visions* by Margaret Archuleta and Renard Strickland, Phoenix: Heard Museum, 1991; *The Native Americans: An Illustrated History* by Betty and Ian Ballantine, Atlanta, Turner Publishing, 1993.

*   *   *

Woodrow Wilson (Woody) Crumbo contributed to the evolution of Native American painting as an artist and as a promoter of Native American art. His own art reflected a love for Native American tradition as well as a deep concern for the social and political issues affecting Indian people. Crumbo's art was inextricably tied to his convictions and is best appreciated not only through its intrinsic qualities but also within the context of his efforts on behalf of Native Americans.

Crumbo's mature style, seen chiefly in painting and print-making, was the result of the same traditional and modern influences that shaped his life. Throughout his early childhood during the 1920s, Crumbo was influenced by close relationships with members of tribal groups in Oklahoma. He was tutored in Native American traditions by Belo Cozad, a Kiowa who passed to Crumbo the honor of flute making and playing. In the early 1930s Crumbo led a dance troupe in a government-sponsored tour throughout the U.S. that brought him into contact with a variety of dance traditions. These first-hand experiences lend an authenticity to his depiction of dancers, and ceremonies. As a result of his travels, he was also influenced by painters from the Southwest who worked in the Studio Style. In the 1930s he studied watercolor at Wichita State University in Kansas. He then studied drawing and painting at the University of Oklahoma with Oscar Jacobson from 1936 to 1938. He also learned mural technique from Olof Nordmark from 1939 to 1941.

Crumbo originally painted in the Oklahoma Kiowa style, due to his association with some of those artists during his youth and his own early tutelage under Susie Peters. By the end of the 1930s, Crumbo had successfully incorporated elements of the Studio Style in his paintings. He eventually developed a composite style in which the figures are founded in the Kiowa style and detail and overall composition are borrowed from the Studio Style, European influence, and original ideas. Formal training strengthened Crumbo's basic skills and left stylistic impressions on his work. Art Deco influence is seen in his Peyote birds, "spirit horses," and other figures. In these works there is a particular affinity with Parisian Deco artists. Art Deco style blended well, formally, with both the Kiowa and Studio styles in Crumbo's works dominated by design. This composite style provided works with compelling design for the expression of content.

In the early and mid-1940s, Crumbo personalized his style, making his compositions more original and adding his own details, such as his signature lines of dots. This is seen particularly in the numerous works of that period depicting peyote meetings. The flat, broad areas of color reminiscent of the Kiowa style remain, particularly in figures. *Singers for the Dance,* from the Gilcrease collection, is a good example. By the end of the 1940s, the content of works sometimes took an overtly social and political tone, particularly focusing on issues that affected Native Americans. The best known example is *Land of Enchantment* from the Philbrook collection, which examines social inequality within the context of the southwest Native American art market. Crumbo also created works that more subtly pointed to his social concerns. An example is *Scaffold Burial,* from the Gilcrease collection. The American flag in the painting acknowledges contemporary Native American patriotism, a contribution that was noticeably overlooked in America following World War II. Crumbo was clearly before his time in such efforts, expressing intellectually challenging ideas decades before Native American artists from the Institute of American Indian Arts.

Crumbo's concern for the welfare of his fellow Native Americans, artists in particular, was also expressed through his teaching. In 1938, he took the position of director of the Bacone College art department in Muskogee. He held the position until 1941. Crumbo took satisfaction in providing personal mentorship and support to young artists. His interest in the careers of fellow artists continued after Bacone. In the mid-1940s, Crumbo began an association with Thomas Gilcrease, founder of Gilcrease Museum. As an advisor to Mr. Gilcrease, Crumbo successfully encouraged the purchase of Native American art and suggested exhibitions for artists. He also lobbied Mr. Gilcrease to pay increased stipends to Native American artists-in-residence at the museum. Crumbo also promoted Indian art through the founding of a print studio in Taos that employed Native people. Efforts on behalf of Native Americans included assisting the Tiguas in their efforts to become an officially recognized tribe. He also publicly sought understanding for peyotists. Crumbo stated some of his goals early in his career. He wished to assist Native American artists, to help create a market for their work and to make Native American art more accessible to the general public. Crumbo's art and actions reveal his dedication to those goals and his success in achieving them.

—Kevin Smith

CUTSCHALL, Colleen

Tribal affiliations: Oglala Lakota
Painter and installation artist

Born: Pine Ridge, South Dakota, 3 August 1951. **Education:** Indian Art Workshops under Oscar Howe, 1967-68; Barat College, Lake Forest, Illinois, B.F.A., 1973; Black Hills State College, Spearfish, South Dakota, South Dakota Secondary Teaching Certification, 1975; Black Hills State College, M.S. Ed., 1976; Women Artists Workshop, Oregon State University, 1979; Mayan Art and Archaeology tour of Guatemala, 1988; Asian Religious Art and African Religion, Brandon University, Brandon, Manitoba. **Career:** Teacher/advisor, Indian Education Project, Rapid City, South Dakota, 1973-75; Lakota resource teacher, Rapid City Public Schools, 1975-78; bilingual bicultural education training specialist,

Colleen Cutschall: *The Pregnant Grandfather*, 1988. Photograph by Ken Frazer; collection of Manitoba Arts Council; courtesy of the artist.

Delta Bilingual Bicultural Training Resource Center, University of Utah, Salt Lake City, Utah 1977-78; teacher orientation associate, Northwest Regional Educational Laboratory, Northwest Indian Reading Program, Portland, Oregon, 1978-1980; curriculum developer, Standing Rock Community College, FIPSE Integrated Cultural Curriculum and Research Program, Fort Yates, North Dakota, 1981-82; gallery manager, Northern Lights Gallery, Deadwood, South Dakota, 1982-84; program management specialist, Northern Plains Resource and Evaluation Center II, United Tribes, Bismark, North Dakota 1984-85; associate professor and coordinator of visual arts, Brandon University, Brandon, Manitoba 1984-present. **Awards:** Brandon University Board of Governors Award for Excellence in Community Service, 1992.

Individual Exhibitions

1980   Sioux Indian Museum and Crafts Center, U.S. Department of Interior, Indian Arts and Crafts Board, Rapid City, South Dakota
1985   *Encore*, Artmain Gallery, Minot, North Dakota
1990   *Voice in the Blood*, Art Gallery of Southwestern Manitoba, Brandon (traveled through 1995)
1993   *Catching the Sun's Tail*, permanent installation, Brandon University, Brandon, Manitoba
1995   *Sister Wolf in Her Moon*, Thunder Bay Art Gallery, Thunder Bay, Ontario
1996   *House Made of Stars*, Winnipeg Art Gallery, Winnipeg, Manitoba

Selected Group Exhibitions

1992   *Enduring Strength*, Intermedia Arts and Two Rivers Gallery, Minneapolis, Minnesota (traveled through 1994)
1993   *Cloisters*, Mentoring Artists for Women's Art and St. Norbert's Art and Cultural Center, St. Norbert, Manitoba
1994   *Selected Manitoba Artists*, Ace Art, Winnipeg, Manitoba (traveled to Guadalajara, Mexico)
1995   *Across Backgrounds and Traditions*, Central Michigan University Art Gallery, Mount Pleasant, Michigan
        Bead, Basket and Quill, Thunder Bay Art Gallery, Thundery Bay, Ontario (traveling)
1996   *The Arch in Patriarch*, St. Norbert's Art and Cultural Center, Winnipeg, Manitoba
        Blowing on the Mud: Art of the First People, Kenderdine Gallery, University of Saskatchewan, Saskatoon, Saskatchewan

Collections

Government of Manitoba, Winnipeg; Oscar Howe Art Center, Mitchell, South Dakota; Indian and Northern Affairs Art Bank, Ottawa; Kenderdine Gallery, University of Saskatchewan, Saskatoon, Saskatchewan; MacKenzie Art Gallery, Winnipeg, Manitoba; Sioux Indian Museum and Craft Center, Indian Arts and Crafts Board, U.S. Department of the Interior, Rapid City, South Dakota; Winnipeg Art Gallery, Manitoba.

Publications

By CUTSCHALL—"Myth and Ceremony," paper delivered at the University Art Association Conference, Montreal, Quebec,

1990; "How Native People Represent Their Own Art Histories," paper presented at the Native American Art Studies Association Conference, Sante Fe, New Mexico; "Jackson Beardy: Ambassador, Alchemist, Artist," *Jackson Beardy: A Life's Work,* Winnipeg Art Gallery, Winnipeg, Manitoba, 1994; "Voice in the Blood: Suffering and Compassion, Readings in Aboriginal Studies," *World View* (Brandon, Manitoba) 3, 1995; "A Commentary: Teaching and Learning Native American Art," paper delivered at the Native American Art Studies Conference, Tulsa, Oklahoma, 1995; *Garden of the Evening Star,* exhibition catalog for *Arch in Patriarch,* St. Norbert's Art and Culture Center, Winnipeg, Manitoba, 1996; "Commentary on Works of W. Boneshirt," *Plains Indian Drawings 1865-1935: Pages from a Visual History*, Drawing Center and the American Federation of Arts, New York, 1996.

On CUTSCHALL: Book—*House Made of Stars*, with essays by Alan J. Ryan and Ruth B. Phillips, Winnipeg Art Gallery, Winnipeg, Manitoba, 1996. **Articles**—"The Sky Is the Limit: Conversations with First Nations—The Educated Ceremonialist," by Robert Enright, *Border Crossings* 1, no. 4, 1992; "Ritualizing Ritual's Rituals," by Charlotte Townsend-Gault, *Art Journal*, 1992.

*   *   *

Colleen Cutschall's paintings and installation pieces translate intricate ethereal fibres of Lakota story, myth and cosmology into images that can be absorbed and understood on a global scale. *Voices in the Blood*, Cutschall's 1990 series of paintings, brought Lakota cosmology to light in a manner that had never been seen before. She drew extensively on the writings of James Riley Walker, a doctor working on the Oglala Sioux reservation at Pine Ridge, South Dakota, from 1896 to 1914. He had collaborated with Lakota storyteller George Sword, and was permitted to record the sacred stories of the Lakota holy men in order to preserve them for future generations of Lakota. Many of these pieces, like Walker's writings, have a distinct narrative quality to them. It was in this series that Cutschall also perfected her unique painting technique that recreates intricate styles of beading.

Much of Cutschall's work acts to educate and inspire the viewer. One of her goals is to reintroduce her own people to their own cosmological systems. Her paintings and installations emphasize recurring themes of mythology merged with current native issues, actively promoting understanding between native and non-native communities.

One of the most powerful themes approached by Cutschall centres around the use and near loss of rituals in native and non-native societies. In *Catching the Sun's Tail* (1993), for example, Cutschall probes the depths of ritual in traditional and contemporary society. This installation piece pays deep respect to her Lakota roots. In keeping with its ritualistic themes, *Catching the Sun's Tail* opened at Brandon University on the winter solstice, with a ritualistic ceremony that involved opening a ring of stone circles to signify the opening of the show and burning a ceremonial smudge with smoke to purify the site.

This piece combines elements of nature—earth, rocks, animal bones, and feathers—with modern technological representations, like recycled parachutes and halogen lights, linking past, present and even the future. Here Cutschall offers viewers the medicine wheel as an anchor or focus for the re-emergence of spirituality in native communities. *Catching the Sun's Tail* is a strong reminder that not only is native culture an essential element to our collective past, and to our current lives, but is also vital to the future of all races.

Cutschall's more recent installation piece, *Sisterwolf In Her Moon* (1996), focuses further on human need for ritual by addressing menstruation—a topic feared in some cultures, sacred in some, and even reviled in others. Sisterwolf deals with women re-discovering themselves as sacred beings. Sisterwolf is a metaphorical woman sitting isolated in the middle of a room as she menstruates, and is undergoing a deep and mysterious connection with the cosmos as a result. In this symbolic moon lodge the menstruating woman is indeed sacred, and somewhat mysterious to outsiders.

Sisterwolf's head is a willow basket and her hair is a fringed blue and black shawl. Around her are protective herbs and items of great symbolism. She sits meditating on a wolf hide and wears a beaded wolf pendant around her neck. Benevolent animal spirits hover in the room to guide and protect her. As she meditates, Sisterwolf focuses on a giant silver spider web before her. The web connects many things with nearly invisible lines. In front of Sisterwolf are four baskets, each of which rests on its own blanket. These baskets can be seen as offerings. One basket sits on an old Pendleton Blanket, originally belonging to Cutschall's Grandmother. The basket contains skulls, a copy of *Bury My Heart at Wounded Knee*, and newspaper articles recounting cultural genocide in South America. Other baskets highlight addiction and other concerns Sisterwolf may take an active interest in pointing out.

With Sisterwolf, Cutschall has created a complete character, with a past, preferences, and a unique personality that is at the same time both an alter ego and a metaphor for the journey of all women, conscious of it or not. The piece has pushed even further beyond the visual elements and into narrative, now creating such a vivid character that it is difficult to consider her as simply a work of art. She has a life. She is like a memory, or a thought or idea that can't quite be grasped if you look directly at it. Sisterwolf inspires and even gently demands her viewers look with all the senses.

The pieces from her most recent exhibit, *House Made of Stars*, a multi-media series of celestial paintings, sculptures, and installations, form an ambitious series that illuminates the manner in which First Nations people of the plains have traditionally looked to their extensive knowledge of the stars and the heavens as a cultural plan or map. Within this map lie the foundations of ritual and living itself.

The quality of the shaman or priestess pervades Cutschall's work, which consistently reaches out to all people, drawing them into her circle. Through her artwork she reflects events, stereotypes, and controversies in a manner that is straightforward and respectful, through the powerful medium of Lakota symbolism, achieving one of her goals by educating people who view her work.

—Vesta Giles

DA, Popovi

Tribal affiliations: San Ildefonso Pueblo
Potter

Born: Anthony Martinez, Pueblo of San Ildefonso, New Mexico, 10 April 1923; legally changed his name to Popovi Da during the 1940s, and also known as Squash-Flower-Colored-Fox. **Education:** Santa Fe Indian School, where he was a student of Dorothy Dunn and Geronima Montoya. **Military Service:** U.S. Army, World War II. **Career:** Founded and operated Popovi Da Studio, Pueblo of San Ildefonso, 1948, with his wife, Anita Da, and promoted and served as a representative of Pueblo art at national and international conferences; governor, San Ildefonso Pueblo, 1952-60; Chairman, All-Indian Pueblo Council; muralist, including Maisal's Indian Trading Post, Albuquerque, New Mexico. **Died:** 17 October 1971.

Selected Group Exhibitions

1967	*Three Generations Show* (Maria, Popovi Da, and Tony Da), United States Department of Interior, Washington, D.C., and Institute of American Indian Arts, Santa Fe, New Mexico
1981	Native American Center for the Living Arts, Niagara Falls, New York
1986	*When the Rainbow Touches Down,* Heard Museum, Phoenix, Arizona (traveling)
1990	*American Indian Artists in the Avery Collection and the McNay Permanent Collection,* Koogler McNay Art Museum, San Antonio, Texas
1990-91	*One with the Earth,* organized by the Institute of American Indian Arts and Alaska Culture and Arts Development, Santa Fe, New Mexico
1991-92	*Shared Visions: Native American Painters and Sculptors in the Twentieth Century,* Heard Museum, Phoenix, Arizona
1996	*Drawn from Memory: James T. Bialac Collection of Native American Art,* Heard Museum, Phoenix, Arizona

Collections

Eiteljorg Museum of American Indians and Western Art, Indianapolis, Indiana; Thomas Gilcrease Institute of American History and Art, Tulsa, Oklahoma; Indian Arts and Crafts Board, Department of the Interior, Washington, D.C.; Museum of New Mexico, Santa Fe; Museum of Northern Arizona, Flagstaff; Museum of the Rockies, Browning, Montana; Millicent Rogers Foundation Museum, Taos, New Mexico; Smithsonian Institution, Washington, D.C.

Publications

On DA: Books—*American Indian Painting of the Southwest and Plains Areas,* by Dorothy Dunn, Albuquerque: University of New Mexico, 1968; *Southwest Indian Painting: A Changing Art,* by Clara Lee Tanner, Tucson, 1973; *Great North American Indians: Profiles in Life and Leadership,* New York, 1977; *American Indian Art in the 1980s,* by Lloyd Kiva New, Niagara Falls, 1981; *One Thousand Years of Southwestern Indian Ceramic Art,* by Patrick T. Houlihan, New York, 1981; *Talking with Clay: The Art of Pueblo Pottery,* Santa Fe, 1987; *When the Rainbow Touches Down,* exhibition catalog by Tryntje Van Ness Seymour, Heard Museum, University of Washington Press, 1988; *American Indian Artists in the Avery Collection and the McNay Permanent Collection,* Jean Sherrod Williams, editor, San Antonio, 1990; *Shared Visions: Native American Painters and Sculptors in the Twentieth Century,* by Margaret Archuleta and Dr. Rennard Strickland, New York: New Press, 1991.

*　　*　　*

Anthony Martinez was born in 1921 to Maria and Julian Martinez. In the 1940s, he legally changed his name to Popovi Da, his Tewa name. In contrast to many other successful Tewa potters, Popovi Da was a male as well as of a younger generation, who grew up accepting tourists as part of the daily reality of Pueblo life. Pottery was made almost exclusively for non-Indians, and English—not Spanish—was the second language. Furthermore, he attended the Santa Fe Indian School and was a student in Dorothy Dunn's and Geronima Montoya's painting classes, producing paintings exclusively for sale to Anglo patrons. Although all four of the Martinez boys attempted to be potters and painters, only "Popovi Da, like Maria, was a born artist" (all quotations are through the courtesy of Anita Da, who graciously agreed to be interviewed in 1993 about her late husband, their business, her mother-in-law, and her life). Popovi Da died in 1971, a man caught between the Pueblo world of accommodation and community and the Anglo world of individuality and competition.

Da helped change the commercial production relationship and, in contrast to Kenneth Chapman, Edgar Lee Hewett, and the Santa Fe museums, promoted his mother as an artist of extraordinary vision and talent—as she was and had always been. Popovi Da could speak for his mother and was comfortable traveling and doing business in the Anglo world. Maria had not been able to promote herself because of cultural barriers. Popovi Da also possessed tremendous technical skills and creative artistic talent, so that promotion of his mother worked to his advantage as well. He helped the public recognize the singularity of his and his mother's work.

Maria and Julian Martinez's legacy liberated Popovi Da of some of the shackling traditions of Pueblo pottery making. In addition to becoming acquainted and used to a steady stream of visitors to his parents home, growing up in the 1930s and 1940s provided Da with opportunities for travel and interaction with many Anglos.

These changes in San Ildefonso resulted in his being more comfortable with the American language and world. In addition, as part of the next generation of potters, he was freer to experiment because both the Anglo and Pueblo world had by the 1950s been working within the same, familiar formula for Pueblo pottery making and marketing since the 1920s.

In 1948, he and his wife opened the Popovi Da Studio in the Pueblo of San Ildefonso. They were the first Indian people to obtain a loan from a Santa Fe bank: $3000 helped them renovate a building on the west side of the San Ildefonso plaza. "Popovi was a wonderful spokesman, people appealed to him," noted Anita Da. "He had a strong personality ... he was dynamic." His enthusiasm for pottery was infectious and he was promoter, yet, "he never wanted to be famous, it just happened—all he had to do was open his mouth or put his hands to work." His mother too, had a vibrant and contagious personality, her smile warm and genuine, with a willingness to talk to everyone. "Maria was much like Popovi, except she never had Po's ability to speak English and communicate with White people." In addition, Maria possessed a traditional Pueblo woman's humility; she was a woman of her generation, reluctant to call attention to herself and always willing to accommodate others. She had been able to keep the outside world away from the pueblo. "As far as Indians were concerned, Maria was just another person; of course the outside world knew about her."

The 1920s and 1930s artistic formulas were broken by Popovi Da. Beginning in the late 1960s, customers desired an individual artist's pot, demanding that all pieces were signed to authenticate the pot as art—not curio or souvenir. The marketing of Pueblo pottery too was changed. With the increase in demand for pottery, the artists had more ability to control the access and therefore the price of pottery. Moreover, the promotion of individual potters became more common as gallery showings increased. Buyers were more inclined to buy pots directly from the artist. These were all techniques created and first used by Popovi Da, helping shape the world of Indian Arts as we know it today.

While he was a truly visionary artist of unsurpassed technical skill and creativity, we, nonetheless, also need to evaluate his influence in the marketing of Pueblo art. His gallery was the first gallery to promote the work of individual Pueblo artists. Anita and Popovi Da displayed objects as individual works in dramatic art settings, not on the floor or on tables or mixed in with animal skins, Navajo rugs, and cheap souvenir pottery. Rather, they were placed on glass shelves free of dust and the bric-a-brac of the Indian trader business.

Within Da's own lifetime, others recognized his talents as a ceramicist. In 1955, at the onset of his potting career, a teacup sized bowl sold for $6.50; in 1965 the same sized piece sold for $55, and in 1975 for $1000. In 1970, pieces of Maria's and Po's work were selling for as much as $4000; within a year of Da's death, his pottery pieces were selling for $12,000.

Money is a hollow way to measure an artist's life. A truer assessment of his success is his remarkable influence on the work of subsequent generations of potters. All of the "innovations" in use among Pueblo potters today originated in Popovi Da's work—duotone, scraffito, inlaid heshi and turquoise, and the polychrome revival, as well as the gun metal finish, which no one has been able to duplicate. Popovi Da's work empowered both worlds to broaden their understanding of Pueblo pottery's potential. Finally, Popovi Da emphasized the singular artistry of his own and Maria Martinez's work by adding a date to the signature on the base of the pot.

—Bruce Bernstein

DA, Tony
Tribal affiliations: San Ildefonso Pueblo
Painter and potter

Born: Anthony Da, San Ildefonso Pueblo, New Mexico, 1 April 1940. **Family:** Son of Popovi Da and Anita Montoya, grandson of Maria and Julian Martinez. **Military Service:** U.S. Navy. **Awards:** All-State High School Award, New Mexico; numerous from fairs and juried competitons, including those organized by the Heard Museum, Museum of New Mexcio, Philbrook Museum of Art, the Smithsonian Institution, and the Inter-Tribal Indian Ceremonial, Santa Fe Indian Market, and Scottsdale National Indian Art Exhibition.

Selected Group Exhibitions

1959   Museum of New Mexico, Santa Fe
1967   *America Discovers Indian Art,* Smithsonian Institution, Washington, D.C.
      Three Generations Show (Maria, Popovi Da, and Tony Da), United States Department of Interior, Washington, D.C., and Institute of American Indian Arts, Santa Fe, New Mexico
      Center for the Arts of Indian America, Art Gallery of the Department of the Interior, Washington, D.C.
1978   *100 Years of Native American Painting,* Oklahoma Museum of Art, Oklahoma City, Oklahoma
1978   Renwick Gallery, National Collection of Fine Arts, Washington, D.C.
1981   *Indian Art of the 1980s*, Native American Center for the Living Arts, Niagara Falls, New York
1981   *Native American Painting,* Amarillo Art Center, Amarillo, Texas (traveled through 1983)
1982   *Native American Painting: Selections from the Museum of the American Indian*, Heard Museum, Phoenix, Arizona
1984   *Indianischer Kunstler*, organized by the Philbrook Museum, Tulsa, Oklahoma (traveled in Germany through 1985)
1988   *When the Raibow Touches Down,* Heard Museum, Phoenix, Arizona (traveling)
1990   *American Indian Artists in the Avery Collection and the McNay Permanent Collection,* Koogler McNay Art Museum, San Antonio, Texas
1996   *Drawn from Memory: James T. Bialac Collection of Native American Art,* Heard Museum, Phoenix, Arizona

Collections

Heard Museum, Phoenix, Arizona; Museum of the American Indian, Washington, D.C.; Mitchell Indian Museum, Kendall College, Evanston, Illinois; Museum of New Mexico, Santa Fe.

Publications

On DA: Books—*Southwest Indian Painting: A Changing Art,* by Clara Lee Tanner, Tucson, 1973; *Seven Families in Pueblo Pottery,* by Rick Dillingham, Albuquerque, 1974; *Art and Indian Individualists,* by Guy Monthan and Doris Monthan, Flagstaff,

Arizona, Northland Press, 1975; *Songs from the Earth: American Indian Painting,* by Jamake Highwater, Boston, 1976; *Pueblo Pottery of the New Mexico Indians,* by Betty Toulouse, Santa Fe, 1977; *100 Years of Native American Painting,* by Arthur Silberman, Oklahoma Museum of Art, Oklahoma City, Oklahoma; *American Indian Art in the 1980s,* by Lloyd Kiva New, Niagara Falls, 1981; *One Thousand Years of Southwestern Indian Ceramic Art,* by Patrick T. Houlihan, New York, 1981; *Native American Painting: Selections from the Museum of the American Indian,* by David M. Fawcett and Lee A. Callander, New York, 1982; *Talking with Clay: The Art of Pueblo Pottery,* Santa Fe, 1987; *When the Rainbow Touches Down,* exhibition catalog by Tryntje Van Ness Seymour, Heard Museum, University of Washington Press, 1988; *Beyond Tradition: Contemporary Indian Art and its Evolution,* Flagstaff, 1988; *American Indian Artists in the Avery Collection and the McNay Permanent Collection,* Jean Sherrod Williams, editor, San Antonio, 1990. **Articles**—"The Beauty Collectors," by Barbara Cortright, *Arizona Highways,* May 1974.

*   *   *

Tony Da is a member of the famed Martinez family of potters and painters. His father was Popovi Da (who changed his legal name from Martinez to Da in the 1940s) and his grandparents were Maria and Julian Martinez. Like his father, Tony Da excelled as both a painter and potter, winning recognition as a painter beginning in his mid-teens and becoming a more expert craftsman through the tutelage of his grandmother while in his mid-twenties. Tony Da became so intrigued by making pottery, in which he incorporated traditional methods and designs while introducing more contemporary flourishes, that he began concentrating less on painting by the early 1970s; his artistic production was curtailed when he suffered a motorcycle accident that left him debilitated.

Tony Da, like his grandfather, who died when Tony was three, and his father, showed early enthusiasm and skill for painting. When he was in grade school, his father and mother opened the Popovi Da Studio in the Pueblo of San Ildefonso, through which they began marketing and promoting pottery made by family members as well as the larger community of San Ildefonso. Along with drawing on the artistic expertise readily available around him, Tony Da began expressing a personal style, favoring watercolors and often painting what he observed in the pueblo. At fifteen, he won a regional competition sponsored by the Smithsonian institution, and his work was exhibited at the Museum of New Mexico before he turned twenty.

After returning from the Navy in the mid-1960s, Da lived with his grandmother, who taught him traditional methods for making pottery and shared her innovations. This included controlling the firing process, which had allowed her and her husband to develop their famed black-on-black style around 1920, and the inventive finishes—gun metal, sienna, and duo-tone—that she and Popovi introduced during the 1950s and 1960s. Tony quickly perfected the techniques and took part in the *Three Generations Show* (Maria, Popovi Da, and Tony Da), which exhibited at the United States Department of Interior, Washington, D.C., and Institute of American Indian Arts in Santa Fe. That year he also won major prizes for ceramics at the Inter-Tribal Indian Ceremonial. From this period through the mid-1970s, Da won awards at all the major art competitions in the southwest. However, the early 1970s was a difficult period as well: his father died in 1971, and Maria Martinez, likely in her eighties, stopped making pottery in 1972.

Tony Da's pottery blends the sophisticated technique and design and the polished look of the Martinez/Da tradition with a personal, contemporary approach. He used such decorative elements as turquoise, mother of pearl, and coral shells. Ancient symbols and designs that characterized the works of his predecessors remained strong, balanced by the introduction of slight adornments. Da's paintings continued to receive attention as well and were included in several important exhibitions, even after he stopped painting on a consistent basis. In addition to works that feature images of pueblo life, Da created stylized pieces in which the images were abstracted against a background of design motifs, usually featuring muted earth tones and themes and symbols relating to the pueblos of the Southwest. *Symbols of the Southwest* (1970), in which designs from art forms of pottery, textiles, sandpainting, and architecture are blended with symbols from pueblos, is an example of these various motifs, colors, and patterns arranged in a single piece.

—Perry Bear

DAVID, Joe

Variant names: Ka-Ka-win-chealth
Tribal affiliations: Nuu-Chah-Nulth
Carver and printmaker

Born: Opitsaht Village, Clayoquot Sound, Vancouver Island, British Columbia, 1946; his name, Ka-Ka-win-chealth, which he received from his father when he was twenty-three years old, translates roughly to Supernatural White Wolf Transforming into Whale. **Education:** Commercial art program, Camosun College; apprenticed in carving to Duane Pasco, Frank Charlie, and Russell Spatz; studied graphic design under Bill Holm. **Career:** Commercial artist; mentor to apprentice carvers, including Art Thompson; helped found Northwest Coast Indian Artists Guild, 1977; commissioned for totem poles, including *Expo '74,* Vancouver, and city of Spokane, Washington.

Selected Group Exhibitions

1971	*The Legacy,* organized by the Royal British Columbia Museum, Vancouver (traveled through 1980)
1980	British Columbia Provincial Museum, Victoria
1979	Field Museum of Natural History, Chicago
1980	*Group Show* (with Robert Davidson and Norman Tait), Heard Museum, Phoenix, Arizona
1987	National Museum of Greece, Athens
1989	Museum of Ethnology, University of Zurich, Switzerland
1992	Strathern Centre, Montreal, Quebec
1993	Inuit Gallery of Vancouver, British Columbia
	University of British Columbia, Museum of Anthropology, Vancouver
	In the Shadow of the Sun, Canadian Museum of Civilization, Hull, Quebec (traveled)

Collections

Alberni Valley Museum, Alberni, British Columbia; Campbell River Museum, Campbell River, British Columbia; City of Seattle, Washington; City of Vancouver, British Columbia; Heritage Center, Inc., Collection, Pine Ridge Indian School, Pine Ridge, South Dakota; Indian and Northern Affairs Canada, Ottawa, Ontario; Museum of Anthropology, University of British Columbia, Vancouver; National Museum of Canada, Ottawa, Ontario; Riveredge Foundation, Devonian Group, Calgary, Alberta; Royal British Columbia Museum, Victoria; Vancouver City Museum, British Columbia.

Publications

On DAVID: Books—*Looking at Indian Art of the Northwest Coast,* by Hillary Stewart, Seattle, 1979; *The Legacy: Continuing Traditions of Canadian Northwest Coast Art,* by Peter MacNair, Alan Hoover, and Kevin Neary, Victoria, 1980; *Northwest Coast Indian Graphics,* by Edwin Hall, Margaret Blackman, and Vincent Rickard, Seattle, 1981; *Susan Point, Joe David, Lawrence Paul: Native Artists from the Northwest Coast,* Zurich, Switzerland, 1989; *In the Shadow of the Sun,* by Gerald McMaster, et al, Ottawa, 1993.

*   *   *

The Native American artists of Canada's Northwest Coast have worked for centuries in wood, mainly cedar, producing huge totem poles and impressive masks, decorated objects for daily use, and religious paraphernalia. They carved and painted intricate designs on house fronts and canoes, on totem poles and masks, on bowls, boxes, and chests. After a time of decline in the nineteenth and early twentieth centuries, including the outlawing of some cultural traditions, a dramatic revival of Native art tradition has been taking place since the 1960s, and it is in this context that Joe David's work must be seen.

David is a printmaker, jeweler, and carver and has been at the forefront of the renaissance in Northwest coast Indian art. He works in a variety of different cultural styles, combining the fluid line characteristic of the old Westcoast style with design elements from other Northwest coast traditions. By merging traditional forms and non-conventional imagery he has created his own individual expression.

An accomplished carver, David is well-known especially for his various masks, among which the Wolf mask is one of his favorites. He has a personal relationship to this mask since his name, Ka-Ka-win-chealth, which he received from his father when he was twenty-three years old, means "supernatural white wolf transforming into whale." In Westcoast mythology the wolf is linked to the whale, and in Westcoast legend a supernatural white wolf transformed itself into a killer whale, which explains the white markings characteristic of that species of whale.

David's wolf masks are headdresses of the typically Westcoast flat-sided, boxy style. They are made of red cedar and colored with acrylic paint. The wolf is distinguished by its long snout and flared nostrils, large teeth and prominent ears. Unlike many contemporary wolf headdresses, which are made of a number of boards glued together, David's are as a rule carved from one piece of wood according to the earliest method of manufacture.

Printmaking is a relatively new art form on the Northwest Coast dating from the 1950s, and serigraphy is the most important graphics technique adopted by Northwest Coast Indian artists. The content of prints may be personal or traditional, including ancient crests or mythological figures. As to form, the artists are designing in the traditional styles of their forebears, of which vibrant colors

and the traditional s-shapes, u-forms, and ovoids are the distinguishing marks. An inspiration for later artists has been Mungo Martin who created the first important paper designs. Among those who followed his example are Henry Speck, Roy Vickers, Tony Hunt, and Robert Davidson.

In 1977 a number of Northwest Coast native artists founded the Northwest Coast Indian Artists Guild with the intent to gain international recognition for Northwest Coast art. Joe David was among them. His *Eats-quin* was one of prints to be included in the first annual catalog. Eats-quin, a mouse who inhabits Meares Island where Joe David lives, is rendered in the form of a merman, a mythological figure of the Northwest Coast. Wrapped around him is his house, the earth, and above his head is the sky and the universe. He has a grain of rice in the palm of each hand. David says, "I bring to him rice and grain and fruits for which, in exchange, he allows me to roam the beaches and forests of his little island world." There is a perfect balance of realistic and abstract imagery in this print. The artist has used thin lines to accentuate various parts of the body, in contrast to the bold, geometric framing elements. The curving lines of arms and hands and the turned head suggest the quick movements a mouse would make in peering out of its home in the earth.

Other well-known serigraphs are *Memorial Canoe* and *Memorial Rainbow Drum,* both printed by Joe David for his 1977 potlatch, a traditional Northwest Coast feast, in memory of his father, Hyacinth David. In *Memorial Canoe,* the vessel represents motherhood, while the floating paddle in the rear stands for fatherhood and is detached because his father is dead. The rest of the paddles symbolize the fourteen children. The stars above the paddle were Hyacinth David's crest and the forms below the canoe represent the ocean and the earth. This partial framing of the composition is reminiscent of old Westcoast technique.

The figures in *Memorial Rainbow Drum* represent a man transforming into a raven. While driving home after his father's death, the artist saw a vision of a raven beneath a double rainbow. The rainbow is in many cultures a symbol of the transition between life and death; Raven is the Transformer in Northwest Coast mythology, and he created the world. The image was painted on a drum used at the memorial potlatch and later made into a silk screen design, which was sold to finance the feast.

—Gerhard and Gisela Hoffmann

DAVIDIALUK Alasuaq Amittu
Tribal affiliations: Inuit
Sculptor and printmaker

Born: In an igloo, Nunagiirniraq, Quebec, 1910; name also transliterated as Davidealuk, Davidialu, and Davidiulu. **Family:** Second child and first son of Samuili Amittuq and Aalasi Aqpatuq; married Maina Aquttuq Arsaapaaq; 7 children and one adopted son. **Career:** Hunter and fisherman; demonstrated carving, Inuit sculpture exhibition, Montreal, 1965; attended the opening of Inuit exhibition at the National Museum, Copenhagen, Denmark, 1972. **Awards:** Best in Show, for a batik in the exhibit *Crafts from Arctic Canada,* organized by the Canadian Eskimo Arts Council, 1975. **Died:** 3 August 1976.

Individual Exhibitions

1976   *Sculpture by Davidialuk,* Fleet Gallery, Winnipeg, Manitoba

1977   *Davidialuk Memorial Exhibition,* The Guild Shop, Toronto, Ontario

1978   *A Memorial Show of Prints by Davidialuk,* Snow Goose Associates, Seattle, Washington

1979   *La Vie et l'Oeuvre de Davidialuk Alasuaq,* Musée du Quebec, Quebec City

1983-84   *Davidialuk Alasuaq: Inuit Artist of Northern Quebec,* Ministere des affaires culturelles du Quebec, Quebec City (traveling)

Selected Group Exhibitions

1965   *Arctic Values '65,* New Brunswick Museum with the cooperation of the Department of Indian and Northern Affairs, St. John, New Brunswick

1971   *The Art of the Eskimo,* Simon Fraser Gallery, Simon Fraser University, Burnaby, British Columbia

1974   *Oral Tradition,* National Museum of Man, Ottawa, Ontario

1978   *The Coming and Going of the Shaman: Eskimo Shamanism and Art,* Winnipeg Art Gallery, Winnipeg, Manitoba

1979   *Eskimo Narrative,* Winnipeg Art Gallery, Winnipeg, Manitoba (traveling)

        Inuit Art in the 1970s, Agnes Etherington Art Centre, Kingston, Ontario

1980   *Inuit Graphics from the Collection of the Montreal Museum of Fine Arts,* Musée des Beaux-Arts de Montreal

        The Inuit Amautik: I Like My Hood to Be Full, Winnipeg Art Gallery, Winnipeg, Manitoba

1981   *Spirits and Shamans/Esprits et chamans,* Department of Indian Affairs and Northern Development, Ottawa, Ontario

1982   *Inuit Myths, Legends and Songs,* Winnipeg Art Gallery, Winnipeg, Manitoba

1983   *Grasp Tight the Old Ways: Selections from the Klamer Family Collection of Inuit Art,* Art Gallery of Ontario, Toronto (traveling through 1985)

1986   *The Spirit of the Land,* Koffler Gallery, Toronto, Ontario

        Daivdee Alasuaq: Artiste Inuit du Nouveau-Quebec, Tuttavik, Mississauga, Ontario

1987   *Contemporary Inuit Art Drawings,* Macdonald Stewart Art Centre, Guelph, Ontario

1989   *Spoken in Stone: An Exhibition of Inuit Art,* Whyte Museum of the Canadian Rockies, Banff, Alberta (traveling)

1990   *Arctic Mirror,* Canadian Museum of Civilization, Hull, Quebec

        Inuit Drawings, Inuit Gallery of Vancouver, British Columbia

1991   *Soujourns to Nunavut: Contemporary Inuit Art from Canada,* Bunkamura Art Gallery, Tokyo (traveling)

1993   *Multiple Realities: Inuit Images of Shamanic Transformation,* Winnipeg Art Gallery, Winnipeg, Manitoba

        In the Shadow of the Sun, Canadian Museum of Civilization, Hull, Quebec (traveling)

1994   *Arctic Spirit: 35 Years of Canadian Inuit Art,* Frye Art Museum, Seattle, Washington

1995   *Immaginario Inuit, Arte e cultura degli esquimesi canadesi,* Galleria d'Arte Moderna e Contemporanea, Verona, Italy

Collections

Art Gallery of Greater Victoria, Victoria, British Columbia; Art Gallery of Ontario, Toronto; Art Gallery of York University, Downsview, Ontario; Avataq Cultural Institute, Montreal, Quebec; Canadian Guild of Crafts Quebec, Montreal; Canadian Museum of Civilization, Hull, Quebec; Dennos Museum Center, Northwestern Michigan College, Traverse City, Michigan; Eskimo Museum, Churchill, Manitoba; Agnes Etherington Art Centre, Queen's University, Kingston, Ontario; Glenbow Museum, Calgary, Alberta; Indiana University of Pennsylvania, Indian, Pennsylvania; Inuit Cultural Institute, Rankin Inlet, Northwest Territories; Macdonald Stewart Art Centre, Guelph, Ontario; McMichael Canadian Art Collection, Kleinburg, Ontario; Musée d'Art Contemporain de Montreal, Quebec; Musée du Quebec, Quebec City; Museum of Anthropology, University of British Columbia, Vancouver; National Gallery of Canada, Ottawa, Ontario; New Brunswick Museum, St. John, New Brunswick; Royal Ontario Museum, Toronto; Saputik Museum, Povungnituk, Quebec; Whyte Museum of the Canadian Rockies, Banff, Alberta; Winnipeg Art Gallery, Winnipeg, Manitoba; York University, Toronto.

Publications

On DAVIDIALUK: Books—*The Coming and Going of the Shaman: Eskimo Shamanism and Art,* by Jean Blodgett, Winnipeg, 1978; *Contemporary Inuit Art Drawings,* by Marion Jackson and Judith Nasby, Guelph, Ontario, 1987; *The Inuit Imagination: Arctic Myth and Sculpture,* by Harold Seidelman and James Turner, Vancouver/Toronto: Douglas & McIntyre, 1993; *In the Shadow of the Sun,* by Gerald McMaster, et al, Hull, Quebec, 1993. **Articles**—"Two Inuit Artists in Copenhagen," by Barry Gunn, *Inuttituut,* Autumn, 1972; "Davidialuk's Work: A Living History," by Harold Seidelman, *Arts & Culture of the North,* Fall 1980; "Davidialuk's Unique Talents Are Viewed on 'Home' Ground," by Sandra B. Barz, *Arts and Culture of the North* 7(1), New York, 1984; "Mythmakers: Davidialuk and Talirunili," by Darlene Wight, *Tableau* 1(5), 1988; "Inuit Art: Tradition and Regeneration: At the Canadian Museum of Civilization, Hull, Quebec," by Nancy Gautsche, *Inuit Art Quarterly* 8(2), 1993.

*   *   *

Davidialuk Alasuaq Amittu was among the most eminent Inuit artists of this century, recognized for his talents as a storyteller and fabulis, transforming the power of the word into stone to become the archetypal carver of Nunavik. He visually conveyed stories, fables, and legends, drawing on the rich Inuit oral tradition and his own experiences as a nomadic hunter. His sculptures, prints, and even batik have given witness to the difficult life of old, a traditional life he knew well, of a nomad moving regularly in quest of new game and according to the dispensation of natural resources. The works of Davidialuk are veritable icons of modern Inuit art from Nunavik and correspond to the phase of maturity, roughly 1960 to 1975, of this new art.

Davidialuk was a talented storyteller: his work reveals the inmost Inuit thoughts, pragmatic and imaginative. And when not creating narratives, his representations of animals are quasi documentaries, capturing singular attitudes that characterize various animals—a beluga, for example, gently guiding her young with a pectoral fin, or a female osprey transporting her young on her back. Dramatic intensity and often tragic situations are relayed in his work, suggesting a fatalistic outlook with prisoners of destiny in a demanding world. His human characters are often victims of voracious animals or other human beings; supernatural forces also provoke eerie situations. Transformation scenes occur as well, recalling shamanism and Inuit magic. Indeed, it is astonishing to consider the number of horrific visions Davidialuk created. However, from another perspective, the scenes do not appear as scary because it is the references that render them horrible: thus, the importance of verbal narrating in the works of Davidialuk.

His sculptures usually include a base carved in the mass of stone that often serves as a strip of ground or a similar abstraction as a foundation for the scene. Contrary to practices by other Inuit sculptors, who include knives and harpoons in ivory or the tine of Caribou antler, materials less fragile than soapstone, one rarely encounters accessories in Davidialuk's sculptures. Davidialuk defies the stone and proves his ingenuity in disengaging the slightest accessory in the block of his sculpture. The malleable soapstone serves audacious volumes through thinning—a sail represented in the tale of two "ghosts," Maqijuq and Nuvalingaq, for example, or the aurora borealis symbolized by a thick cylindrical spiral revolving in the air. The richness of his invention is equally manifested in his celebrated representations of a young mermaid as well as mythical creatures possessing heads and legs without a body to show the Kajjutajuit (noisy flying heads) and the Tunnituarruit (small, tattooed spirits) that he created as motifs in his sculptures.

In the sculptures of Davidialuk, one finds numerous perforated parts, deriving from his original utilization of the expressive power of "gaps" and hollows that skillfully focus the most significant elements in the scenes represented. This is noticeable in scenes of open space, as in area surrounding the head of a barnacle-goose looking out above its nest in a protective pose. In other pieces, an arm or a leg juts out in a defensive posture, sometimes oversized and assuming the character of an active force. Among other expressive mechanisms employed by Davidialuk are forms representing abridgements, spatial compressions evident in the short and sturdy limbs of his figures.

Volumes are massive and protuberances are principally functional, strongly expressive and stripped of all elegance in Davidialuk's sculptures. Strokes imprinted on his polished sculptures make precise the sense of size he attributed to the volume and remain for certain reasons. Most often, these details illustrate such aspects as the warbling of a bird, claws of animals, or the texture of fur. When presenting the whites of eyes, however, Davidialuk proceeds by scraping the area, a technique that also serves on occasion to signify the ornamental border of traditional clothing, or whiteness on a wild goose. Even with these details, Davidialuk's finished work has little elaboration and his pieces permit the traces of his tools to be visible. He willingly adapted knives, files, hatchets and other tools for his use as a sculptor. It should be noted that his second wife, Maina Aquttuq, as well as their son, Aisa Aviliajuk Amittu, regularly contributed to the polishing of finished pieces. Yet, the forms retain a coarse aspect, and an astonishing force is released in the rawness that expresses spontaneity, a sense of urgency, and expressive strength.

Combined with narrative values, Davidialuk's works contributed to an emancipation and certainly affirmed the identity of the Inuits of Nunavik. In some cases Davidialuk imprints words and even texts under the base of his sculptures, as well as in drawings and prints. However, by working on several pieces simultaneously, Davidialuk occasionally imprinted erroneous narratives where themes and allusions are completely different from the subject represented.

The graphic works of Davidialuk were among the first to be included in the workshop engravings of Puvirnituq. The 1962 publication has three of his engravings, and a total of 87 were published during his career with several more not cataloged.

The themes he explored in these engravings are essentially inspired by the oral tradition of Inuit life of the past. His rendering of the themes was enhanced by his ability to place them visually in a Nordic environment. These settings do more than enrich the tales: they become pretexts to detail the material culture, customs, and beliefs of his people, which make Davidialuk's prints of great interest from an ethnographic viewpoint.

His prints are mostly monochromes—black, bluemarine, gray, green, turquoise, or brown on white paper—except for five works showing two or four colors published in 1973 and a commemorative series of seven prints published after his death. Davidialuk almost always engraved his name accompanied by themes elaborated directly on his molds. He was resourceful with other techniques to create textural effects: to represent hair he juxtaposes tight rows of short, wide strokes, or pierces holes in the surfaces of molds, or binds lines. He also includes small rectangles and trapezoid forms to signify blocks of an igloo. Realized most often on large white paper or drawing tablets, he drew vibrant, contour lines colored-in with markers or crayons; by retaining strokes (rather than blending them into solid blocks of color), changing the direction of crayon stokes, or wiping the colors to overflow the lines, he further animated the presentation.

In his drawings one can recognize the same themes present in his sculptures and prints. Other consistencies are observable: the faces of his figures are always shown in profile or full-face, but never at three-quarters; limbs are generally short and practically deprived of articulation at the elbows and wrists, but legs show much more flexibility. His figures very often float on the background of white paper, but perspective and gradation provide the effects of depth.

It remains difficult to advance hypotheses on the evolution of Davidialuk's art, but it is acceptable to say that by the end of the 1950s his works attained a fair level of complexity, particularly in illustrating a tale. During the final months up to his death, "the Great Davidialuk," as he was called in Inuit, had a new spark of creativity, reducing details while preserving the tone—quasi caricature—of his manner for presenting coarse bulk minimally defined. At the same time, his sculptures are shined with wax or blackened with shoe polish. He also began sculpting wood.

For the benefit of his and future generations, Davidialuk has materialized the life, myth, and beliefs of his people while reinventing, as needed, traditional stories that relay the days of old that haunted him through the years.

—Louis Gagnon

DAVIDSON, Robert

Tribal affiliations: Haida
Carver, jewelry designer, and printmaker

Born: Hydaburg, Alaska, 4 November 1946. **Education:** Apprenticeship with Bill Reid; Vancouver School of Art 1967-68, 1969-70.

Career: Instructed carving with 'Ksan Project in Hazelton, British Columbia, 1968; sponsored by Air Canada to demonstrate carving in Bern, Switzerland, 1972; worked on totem pole with Bill Reid, adzed beams for the Haida Long House at the B.C. Provincial Museum in Victoria, 1973; commissioned by the Canadian Broadcasting Corporation to carve Cedar Dance Screen, 1976; founding member of the Northwest Coast Indian Artist Guild, 1977, commissioned by Historic Sites of Canada to create a monument to Charles Edenshaw for his contributions to the arts of Canada, and assisted Bill Reid on a totem pole in Skidegate, Haida Gwaii, 1977; hosted "Tribute to Living Haida" potlatch and celebration in Massett, British Columbia, formed "Rainbow Creek Dancers," which performs traditional and contemporary Haida songs and dances, and assisted brother Reg Davidson in carving a 30-foot totem pole, Tamagawa University in Tokyo, Japan, 1980; hosted "Children of the Good People" potlatch, Massett, British Columbia, and keynote speaker, Arts Conference, Fairbanks, 1981; mural commission, Southwest Museum, Los Angeles, 1983; taught advanced Northwest Coast totem design, Ketchikan, Alaska, 1984; *Raven Bringing Light into the World* used on album cover, *Waiting for a Miracle*, Bruce Cockburn, 1984; hosted "Every Year the Salmon Come Back," two-day celebration, Massett, British Columbia, 1987; co-host, "Urban Feast," bringing Haida Culture to the Urban Haidas 1993-94; maintains comprehensive apprenticeship programs in wood carving and jewelry. **Awards:** Honorary Doctor of Fine Arts, University of Victoria, 1992; honoris causa, Doctor of Laws, Simon Fraser University, 1994; National Aboriginal Achievement Award for Art and Culture and Order of British Columbia, 1995; Order of Canada, 1996.

Individual Exhibitions

1971   Vancouver Museum and Planetarium, Vancouver, British Columbia
1978   Bent Box Gallery, Vancouver, British Columbia
1979   *Cycles: The Graphic Art of Robert Davidson*, University of British Columbia Museum of Anthropology, Vancouver, British Columbia
1983   Faschwerk Gallery, Bad Salzuflen, West Germany
        Maple Ridge Art Gallery, Maple Ridge, British Columbia
1989   Inuit Gallery, Vancouver, British Columbia
        Eagle Song, Derek Simpkins Gallery of Tribal Art, Vancouver, British Columbia
1990-91 *Selected Prints, from 1982 to 1990*, Watcom Museum, Bellingham, Washington
1992   *Robert Davidson: Recollections*, Arthur Ross Gallery, University of Philadelphia, Pennsylvania
        Derek Simpkins Gallery of Tribal Art, Vancouver, British Columbia
1993   *Eagle of the Dawn* (major retrospective exhibition), Vancouver Art Gallery, Vancouver, British Columbia; Canadian Museum of Civilization, Hull, Quebec

Selected Group Exhibitions

1971   *Legacy: Contemporary B.C. Indian Art*, Royal British Columbia Museum, Victoria, British Columbia
1980   *Group Show* (with Joe David and Norman Tait), Heard Museum, Phoenix, Arizona

1983   *B.C. Arts and Artists, 1931-1983*, Vancouver Art Gallery, Vancouver, British Columbia
        B.C. Printmakers, Victoria Art Gallery, Victoria, British Columbia
1987   *Hands of Creation*, Inuit Gallery, Vancouver, British Columbia
1989   *Collector's Vision*, Barrie Art Gallery, Barrie, Ontario
        Masks, Inuit Gallery, Vancouver, British Columbia
1990   Meridian Gallery, San Francisco, California

Collections

City of Montreal, Quebec; Community of Massett, British Columbia; Government of Ireland, Dublin; MacLean Hunter Building, Toronto, Ontario; Museum of Anthropology, University of British Columbia, Vancouver; Museum of Civilization, Hull, Quebec; National Gallery of Canada, Ottawa, Ontario; The Vatican, Vatican City, Italy.

Publications

On DAVIDSON: Books—*Robert Davidson: Haida Printmaker*, by Hillary Stewart, Vancouver, 1979; *A Haida Potlatch*, by Ulli Steltzer, Seattle, 1982; *Robert Davidson, Eagle of the Dawn,* edited by Ian Thom, Vancouver, 1993; "In Search of Things Past, Remembered, Retraced, and Reinvented," by Martine Reid, *In the Shadow of the Sun: Perspectives on Contemporary Native Art*, Hull, Quebec, 1993, *Eagle Transforming: The Art of Robert Davidson,* edited by Sacko Usukawa, Vancouver, 1995. **Articles**—*Tawow,* Vol. 2, No. 2, 1971; "Cycles: The Graphic Art of Robert Davidson," by Marjorie Halpin, *Museum Note #7*, U.B.C. Museum of Anthropology, 1979; "An Art Reborn," by Eve Johnson, *Vancouver Sun,* 25 October 1986; "Noblest Eagle of Them All," by Terry Glavin, *Vancouver Sun*, 9 May 1988; "Return of the Salmon Eaters," by Ann Mayhew, *Beautiful British Columbia Magazine,* Fall 1990; "Taking Hold of the Reins," by Lisa Fitterman, 21 November 1992; "On the Cutting Edge: Robert Davidson Leads a Haida Renaissance," by Patricia Hulchy, *Macleans,* August 1992; "Art of the Healing Eagle," by Robin Lawrence, *The Georgia Straight*, 2-9 June 1993; "Haida Artist Taps Healing Power of Art," by Chris Dafoe, *Globe and Mail* (Toronto), 3 July 1993; "The Spirited Masks of Robert Davidson," by Aldona Jonaitis, *Shaman's Drum*, Fall/Winter 1993; "On the Edge of a Knife," by Carol Orff, *Canadian Art*, Vol. 11, No. 1, Spring 1994; "Giving New Life to Haida Art and the Culture it Expresses," *Smithsonian*, January 1995.

*

Robert Davidson comments:

The purpose of my art is to express the contemporary life and meaning of my ancestral culture, that of the Haida people of Haida Gwaii (Queen Charlotte Islands). From the time I raised the first totem pole in this century in my home village of Massett, I have been committed to the use of cultural knowledge in order to celebrate the present as well as the past. As a bicultural Haida-Canadian artist, I draw upon my own experience of life to give personal and collective meaning to my work. "The challenge is to create images that we can all relate to," I mentioned when discussing my first major commission for a public location, *The Three Watchmen*, a three-totem pole sculpture at the Maclean-Hunter Building in Toronto. The same intention is evident in my four-foot bronze,

Robert Davidson: *After He Has Seen the Spirit*. Photograph by
William McLennan; courtesy UBC Museum of Anthropology.

aven bringing light to the world, commissioned by the Canadian
Museum of Civilization in Hull, as well as a second three-pole
sculpture and a three-foot bronze frog commissioned by Pepsico
for its Sculpture Garden in New York State.

I return frequently to Haida Gwaii to renew my spirits. Fishing is an
annual event in our lives and it really slows me down to the natural
cycles of life, such as the tides and the return of the salmon, and makes
me realize how fragile our whole existence is. Also, in the cultural realm,
every time we have a potlatch it is a way of expressing Haida knowledge, and there are always new people speaking and taking the responsibility for carrying it forward into the future.

*   *   *

Along with the eminent Bill Reid, Robert Davidson is the most
famous and celebrated Northwest Coast Indian artist active today.
His reputation rests upon two major foundations: he is considered
to be an accomplished carver and highly innovative in silver and
gold jewelry design, serigraphy, and sculpture. He is a lineal descendant of perhaps the greatest Haida artist, Charles Edenshaw
(1839-1920).

An analysis of Davidson's art must first take into account the
fact that in the decades preceding Davidson's activity, Haida art

was moribund. While a few artists on the Queen Charlotte Islands imperfectly carved argillite for the tourist market, there
were virtually no practicing artists after the death of Edenshaw
in the 1920s. Thus, unlike contemporary Kwakiutl artists, who
are connected with a continuing tradition of at least a few artists
active during this difficult period (from the 1920s through the
1950s or so), Reid and Davidson encountered no master artists
with whom they could apprentice. In the specific case of
Davidson, however, this younger artist had the example and
tutelage of Reid to assist him in the process of learning the
principles of Haida art. Reid had engaged in research and a redis-
covery process concerning Haida art in the 1950s, and by the
1960s he was a sufficiently mature artist to serve as a master
teacher for the younger Davidson. Both of them studied pieces
from museum collections and discussed technical and stylistic
issues with their curators. At first, Reid and Davidson tended to
copy Haida works from the past, but as learning and experience
increased, both of them were able to develop more personal
styles.

Reid and Davidson were heavily reliant upon the academic study
of older Haida art in order to acquire the requisite knowledge about
this style. Museum collections, photographs, and books played a
prominent role in their learning process. Perhaps no book was more
important to them, and to countless other aspiring Northwest Coast
Indian artists, than Bill Holm's *Northwest Coast Indian Art: An
Analysis of Form*, which was first published in 1965. Although the
book is generically titled, Holm focused almost exclusively upon
the "Northern Style" of the Haida, Tsimshian/Gitksan/Nishga, and
Tlingit peoples. Holm exhaustively analyzed the northern art style
in terms of its basic structure—the formline foundation of designs
(appearing in the usual black/primary, red/secondary, and tertiary
colors), which took such shapes as the ovoid, U-form, S-form, and
salmon-trout s-head. His rigorous and systematic analysis (accompanied by many meticulous illustrations) became a virtual textbook
on the subject for collectors, students of Indian art, and active or
would-be Indian artists.

In the mid-1960s Davidson was just about ready for the "Northwest Coast Indian Art Renewal," which was announced with such
fanfare in the 1967 centennial exhibition, *Arts of the Raven* (with an
exhibition catalog co-authored by Wilson Duff, Bill Holm, and Bill
Reid), at the Vancouver Art Gallery. In the early 1970s Davidson
made a prediction about the course of his career that was to prove
prescient: he stated that his initial goal was to achieve the artistic
standards of the old carvers, and once that had been achieved, he
wanted to reinterpret Haida art in contemporary forms and to help
educate others about the excellence of Northwest Coast art. That is
exactly what he has been able to achieve.

Davidson has worked successfully in almost every medium: wood
carving, silver and gold jewelry, argillite, metal sculpture, and print
making. However, Davidson's fame rests most solidly on his many
wood carvings, which exhibit a high degree of craftsmanship and a
thorough understanding of traditional design. His sheer confidence
and panache in working with wood is evident in almost every piece.
As one example, *Three Variations on Killer Whale Myths*, comprising three totem poles he carved (with the assistance of his younger
brother, Reg Davidson, and Glen Rabbena) for the Pepsicola Sculptural Garden in Purchase, New York, are superb examples of contemporary, classic Haida style. Martine Reid noted that "Davidson
works within a strict convention, exploring and refining it with
subtle variations, preserving a certain conservative austerity, and
sacrificing movement and expression for unity and form. However,

the artist's talent and his sense of design transcend the potential risk of rigidity as the poles radiate their eloquence with a remarkable, restrained strength."

Davidson has established a formidable reputation for innovation in his art. As with several other contemporary Northwest Coast Indian artists, he finds the media of gold and silver jewelry, metal sculptures, and silkscreen prints to be most compatible for his explorative ideas. Davidson has made a large number of silkscreen prints and these have proved to be very popular on the art market. Beginning in the 1970s, Davidson began to produce graphics that pushed Haida designs into new realms of abstract expression. His two-dimensional graphic art has sought out new ways to relate Haida design to the total space available, as well as to negative space. Yet, no matter how abstract his silkscreen prints can be, he still employs Haida iconography throughout his work.

Davidson is also one of those artists who has sought to relate his art career to his home community. Like some others, he has returned to Masset in order to employ his art to affirm his own status prerogatives in the social structure and to promote a sense of "cultural renewal" among the Haida people. This is an important legitimizing activity among artists who do not want their work to be understood as intended for white consumers only. As early as 1969, Davidson returned to Masset to carve and erect a forty-foot totem pole (the first to be raised in that community for some ninety years). In 1977-78 he carved the Charles Edenshaw Memorial Housefront & Houseposts (assisted by Reg Davidson and Gerry Marks) in order to honor his esteemed predecessor. He has also given several potlatches. Davidson is not only an active artist who sought to make his work culturally relevant to his Haida community, he has also reintroduced the practice of the master/apprentice relationship to train younger persons as artists. Hardly out of an apprenticeship program himself with Bill Reid in 1969-70, Davidson went to the newly established Kitanmax School of Northwest Coast Indian Art at 'Ksan, near Hazelton, British Columbia, to instruct students there in the principles of the 'Northern Style' (along with other distinguished faculty).

—John Anson Warner

DAWANGYUMPTEWA, David

Tribal affiliations: Hopi; Navajo.
Painter

Born: Near Flagstaff, Arizona, 17 October 1957. **Education:** Institute of American Indian Arts, A.F.A., museum studies, 1976; Haskell Indian Junior College, 1979-80; University of Northern Arizona, A.F.A. 1983, B.F.A. 1986; Northern Arizona Institute of Technology, 1989-90. **Career:** Counselor and consultant; National Park Service seasonal technician; coordinator and poster artist for the *Festival of Native American Arts,* Flagstaff, Arizona, with the Cococino Center for the Arts and the Museum of Northern Arizona; Board of Directors, Cococino Center for the Arts; panelist, Arizona Commission for the Arts, painter and printmaker. **Awards:** *Festival of Native American Arts,* Flagstaff, Arizona, various awards from 1979 to 1990; Santa Fe Indian Market, including first place, 1981-84, and the Patrick Swazo Hinds Award, 1983; Indian Arts and Crafts Association, Santa Fe, New Mexico, 1994.

Individual Exhibitions

1984	Wheelright Museum of the American Indian, Santa Fe, New Mexico
1989-94	Gallery of the Republic, Austin, Texas
1993	Southwest Museum, Los Angeles

Selected Group Exhibitions

1979	Festival of Native American Arts, Cococino Center for the Arts, Flagstaff, Arizona
1981	Institute of American Indian Arts Museum, Santa Fe
1982	*Night of the First Americans*, John F. Kennedy Center for the Performing Arts, Washington, D.C.
1984	Museum of New Mexico, Santa Fe
1986	*Zeitgenossische Indianische Kunst*, Germany (traveling)
1987	*Four Sacred Mountains: Color, Form and Abstraction*, Navajo Community College, Tuba City, Arizona
1988	*Four Sacred Mountains: Color, Form and Abstraction*, Arizona Commission on the Arts, Phoenix (traveling through 1989)
1989	*Zeitgenossische Indianische Kunst*, Germany (traveling)
1990	Festival of Native American Arts, Cococino Center for the Arts, sponsored by Museum of Northern Arizona, Flagstaff, Arizona
	American Indian Artists in the Avery Collection and the McNay Permanent Collection, Marion Koogler McNay Art Museum, San Antonio, Texas
	One with the Earth, organized by Institute of American Indian and Alaska Culture and Arts Development, Santa Fe (traveling through 1991)
1991	Rhode Island School of Design, Providence, Rhode Island
	Museum of Northern Arizona, Flagstaff, Arizona
1992	Arizona State Capitol Building, Phoenix, Arizona
1993	*Aspen/Snowmass Celebration for the American Indian*, Aspen, Colorado, sponsored by the National Museum of the American Indian, Smithsonian Institution, Washington, D.C.
1994	Institute for American Indian Arts, Santa Fe
1995	Mathes Cultural Center Gallery, San Francisco, California
1996	San Diego Museum of Man, San Diego, California

Collections

Haskell Indian School, Lawrence, Kansas; Heard Museum, Phoenix, Arizona; Indian Arts and Crafts Board, United States Department of the Interior, Washington, D.C.; Institute of American Indian Arts Museum, Santa Fe; Museum of Northern Arizona, Flagstaff, Arizona; University of Kansas, Lawrence, Kansas; Wheelright Museum of the American Indian, Santa Fe.

Publications

On DAWANGYUMPTEWA: Books—*Beyond Tradition: Contemorary Indian Art and Its Evolution*, by Jerry and Lois Essary Jacka, Flagstaff: Northland Publishing Co., 1988; *American Indian Artists in the Avery Collection and the McNay Permanent Collection,* exhibition catalog by Jean Sherrod Williams, San Antonio, 1990. **Articles**—*Indian Market Magazine*, 1996

*   *   *

Metropolitan State University
Library Services
St. Paul, MN 55106

Dawangyumptewa was born of two major Southwest Native American traditions, Hopi and Navajo, and draws from both rich ancestries, creating elegant, stylized images and vibrant colors. Themes are drawn from his background as well—the Hopi Water Clan on his mother's side and the Navajo Bitter Water Clan of his father—resulting in mythical and spiritual subjects and frequent layered images of stars, baskets, dragonflies, water maidens, and other related symbols and ceremonial designs. Water is recurrent in his work, and Dawangyumptewa himself is a member of the Water (Patki) Clan. His paintings are distinguished by rich color and active elements, often displaying a shimmering quality. *Butterfly Dance at the Zoomorph Plaza*, on handmade paper with gouache and 23-karat gold leaf, for example, includes traditional triangle motifs at the edges, with butterflies and dragonflies, reeds and water plants hovering over a darkening green watery background.

Dawangyumptewa was raised in remote areas on the Hopi and Navajo reservations, where he became steeped in the traditions of his family heritage and developed his unique style free from outside influences. His talent drew the attention of a high school teacher, who suggested that he apply for admission at the Institute of American Indian Arts. At the IAIA, Dawangyumptewa focused on museum studies and took a few courses in painting and drawing, graduating in 1976. Increasing interest in painting led him to Haskell Indian Junior College, where he majored in fine art and learned the techniques of Plains Indian paintings; elements of the flat style and its more common contemporary variations appear in background sections of Dawangyumptewa's paintings, with dynamic colors and swirling figures in the forefront.

Many of Dawangyumptewa's recurring motifs are evident in *Turtle Sounds*, which abstracts natural forms. For example, turquoise clusters represent turtle shells seen through a watery surface. The otherworldly quality of the painting and its inviting blend of soft colors is pleasing and rewards deeper reflection: turtle shell rattles are among the instruments used by kachina dancers to create sounds in a spiritual appeal for rain. Other water elements are present in the painting as well: a misting sky, a Patki water maiden with lines of rain streaming on her face toward her corn earrings, blue bubbles rising, and floating turtles are more obvious hints. Symbolic and mythic elements include an embroidered Kachina cape with a stacked triangle design symbolic of rain clouds, and a blanketed figure in the center of the painting is most likely a water carrier. Tall grasses and huge blossoms add a sense of elegance and contribute to the flow of the images. As in many of his works, a woman is present in this painting, perhaps reflecting his upbringing among sisters and aunts as well as representing female roles in Water Clan activities.

Dawangyumptewa's work has proven tremendously popular at a fairs and markets, where he regulary wins awards, allowing him to sell his art directly. He became involved with administration of fairs in northern Arizona, serving on the Board of Directors of the Cococino Center for the Arts, as a member on the Commission on the Arts and Sciences, and as a panelist on the Arizona Commission for the Arts. With his fluid layering of images, swirling figures, subtle use of shapes familiar in Navajo and Hopi art, and his lulling, reflective pools of color, Dawangyumptewa is creating a rich body of work to complement his important involvement in the contemporary art scene of the southwest.

—Perry Bear

DAY, Frank

Variant names: Ly-dam-lilly
Tribal affiliations: Concow Maidu
Painter

Born: Frank Leverall Day, Berry Creek, California, 25 February 1902; Native name means Fading Morning Star. **Family:** Married Marian Katherine Hermann in 1944, with whom he adopted a son, Billy, in 1944; divorced Hermann in 1961; married Florence Stubblefield in 1964. **Education:** Attended Greenville Indian Boarding School, 1908-16, and public school in Berry Creek. **Career:** Agricultural worker and lumberman most of his adult life; after a disabling accident in 1960, took up oil painting as an aspect of his recovery. **Died:** Sacramento, California, 13 August 1976.

Individual Exhibitions

1963	American River College, Sacramento, California
1964	*Maidu Tales in Oil,* American Indian Historical Society, San Francisco, California
1976	Crocker Art Gallery, Sacramento, California
1986	*Frank Day: Paintings of Maidu Life and Legends,* Sacramento History Center, Sacramento, California
1997	*Memory and Imagination: The Legacy of Maidu Indian Artist Frank Day,* Oakland Museum, Oakland, California

Selected Group Exhibitions

1973-75	Pacific Western Traders, Folsom, California
1980	*Two Views of California: Maidu Paintings by Frank Day and Harry Fonseca,* Heard Museum, Phoenix, Arizona
1981	*American Indian Art in the 1980s,* Native American Center for the Living Arts, Niagara Falls, New York
1984	*Pioneers in Paradise: Folk and Outsider Artists of the West Coast,* Long Beach, California
1985	*The Extension of Tradition: Contemporary Northern California Native American Art in Cultural Perspective,* Crocker Art Museum, Sacramento, California
1986	*Cat and a Ball on a Waterfall: 200 Years of California Folk Painting and Sculpture,* Oakland Museum, Oakland, California
1991	*Sacred Spaces, Spirit Places: The Worldview Imagery of Five North Central California Native Artists, 1958-1991,* Memorial Union Gallery, University of California at Davis
	The Human Figure in American Indian Art: Cultural Reality, or Sexual Fantasy?, Institute of American Indian Arts, Santa Fe, New Mexico
1991-96	*Shared Visions: Native American Painters and Sculptors of the Twentieth Century,* Heard Museum, Phoenix, Arizona

Collections

Crocker Museum, Sacramento, California; C.N. Gorman Museum, University of California, Davis; Heard Museum, Phoenix, Arizona; Institute of American Indian Arts Museum, Santa Fe; Maidu Heritage Foundation, Sacramento, California; Museum of Anthropology, California State University, Sacramento; United States Department of the Interior, Indian Arts and Crafts Board, Washington, D.C.

Publications

On DAY: Books—*Maidu Tales in Oil,* exhibition catalog, American Indian Historical Society, San Francisco, 1967; *Native American Painting: Selections from the Museum of the American Indian,* New York, 1982; "A Tribute to Native Survival," by George Longfish in *The Extension of Tradition,* edited by Janice Driesbach and Frank LaPena, Sacramento, 1985; *Cat and a Ball on a Waterfall: 200 Years of California Folk Painting and Sculpture,* exhibition catalog by Harvey Jones, Oakland, 1986; *Shared Visions: Native American Painters and Sculptors in the Twentieth Century,* by Margaret Archuleta and Rennard Strickland, Phoenix, 1991; *Modern by Tradition: American Indian Painting in the Studio Style,* Santa Fe, 1995; *Memory and Imagination: The Legacy of Maidu Indian Artist Frank Day* by Rebecca J. Dobkins with Carey Caldwell and Frank R. LaPena, Oakland 1997.

*

Frank Day comments (1975):

[Once] in a while I take up color and paint a little bit because if I do not do this, all things will be forgotten. It's good enough all right to sing and talk and explain things on these broadcasts here or especially on tape recording or on records, but it's also nice to have someone who's able to print this or illustrate by color upon a chart and then it would remain that way. You cannot change it then. And then you've got to be honest and true about it. And not copying from anybody else. But just translating the language, the Maidu language, and putting it up on a chart. And this shows exactly how the Maidu people had been doing before the coming of the white man. (From a 1975 tape recording, LA186 series, tape 9, University of California Language Laboratory.)

*   *   *

Frank Day was the first self-taught Native American painter in northern California to depict the customs of his tribe, and is considered by many to be one of the key elders in California Indian art history. By taking these first steps toward visual self-representation, he offered an empowering precedent for many contemporary California Indian artists. His visionary paintings are characterized by bold color, strong composition, and a distinctly self-taught style.

Growing up in Butte County, California, Day belonged to the Concow Maidu tribe, whose territory includes the upper Sacramento Valley and Sierra Nevada foothills. Day's father, said to have been born before the 1848-49 Gold Rush, was one of the last traditional leaders of his band. From his father and other elders, Day learned the language, myths, legends, songs, and traditions of his people. However, Day never became a leader like his father, and it wasn't until 1960 that he began to use painting to communicate and record his cultural knowledge.

While working as an agricultural laborer in 1959 or 1960, Day had a serious accident in which he broke both knees. He spent weeks recuperating in a hospital, where he took up art as an aspect of his rehabilitation. Day's first efforts included still lifes, landscapes, pictures copied from art books, autobiographical subjects,

and a hospital scene. During this early period, Day's work had little explicitly "Indian" content or style. Much of his initial work was relatively rudimentary in comparison to paintings dated just two or three years later, though Day apparently quickly learned to draw with the brush and adopted oil as his life-long medium.

The chronology of events leading to Day's embrace of Maidu subject matter in his artwork is not completely clear. It is known that soon after he began painting, Day made the acquaintance of anthropologists. Beginning in 1961, one anthropologist in particular, Donald Jewell of Sacramento, became Day's primary patron and interlocutor. Jewell encouraged Day to paint specific aspects of Maidu folklore and culture and began to record Day's descriptions of his paintings, eventually taping at least 40 hours of recordings Day continued this practice of documenting his artwork through tape recordings and written notes throughout his career.

From the early days of his career to its end, Day painted subjects that fall into four primary categories: 1) autobiographical topics, portraying personal experiences; 2) historical subjects, depicting events Day said had been recounted to him by his elders; 3) ethnographic subjects, portraying customary activities in the everyday lives of precontact Maidu; and 4) subjects from Maidu myth, legend, and ritual. Frank Day himself described his art as a translation of the Maidu language, which he believed was "the basis...of what the Maidu people are."

Day's "translation" metaphor emphasizes not only the communicative dimension of his art, but also the cross-cultural nature of that communication. He viewed his work as visual translations through which he sought to make the Maidu people and their past better understood by others.

Regardless of his or others' claims for the ethnographic accuracy of his work, Day's paintings should not be understood as merely, or exclusively, documentary. Though many paintings indeed illustrate factual aspects of Maidu culture, Day's work is better understood as visionary, rather than ethnographic. Day's painting, *E-nom-oe, or Dancing Girl and Whirling Snake* (1973), a dramatic image of a snake coiled about a naked young woman and set in a surrealistic landscape, is an example of the creative tension in Day's art between vision and realism. In notes made about this painting, Day stressed the truthfulness of the image, yet to accept Day's invitation to scrutinize his images for their "truth" content is to risk overlooking their freedom and wonder.

In 1973, Day's work came to the attention of Herb and Peggy Puffer, the owners of Pacific Western Traders, a Folsom, California, gallery and trading post specializing in Native American art. This institution was to play a critical role in the last years of Day's career by providing him with a broader audience that included other Native American artists as well as art patrons. Day's storytelling sessions at Pacific Western Traders became performance events and gave his audiences the chance to see and hear the cross-cultural translation he intended his art to be. Day achieved some of his best work under the Puffers' patronage, including *Toto at Bloomer Hill* (1973), an animated image of a Maidu deer dancer. During this period Day made the acquaintance of artists Harry Fonseca and Frank LaPena, and instructed the group, now known as the "Maidu Dancers and Traditionalists," captained by LaPena, in the art of Maidu dance.

While Day's oeuvre can be thought of as a celebration of Maidu traditions and history, his bold visionary compositions go beyond the strictly documentary. Day's art challenges the notion that the value of Native American art is to be found in the degree to which it adheres to a standard of ethnographic authenticity. Frank Day is

one of relatively few Native American artists who have been readily embraced by those interested in "outsider art," in part for the very qualities that disturb those who expect documentary accuracy in his work. These qualities, common to much outsider art, include the depiction of worlds very real to the artist but otherwise inaccessible to the viewer. Much of Day's work remains a mystery, not solved, but shared with the viewer.

—Rebecca Dobkins

DEADMAN, Patricia

Tribal affiliations: Mohawk
Photographer

Born: Oshweken, Ontario, 24 April 1961. **Education:** Fanshawe College, London, Ontario, diploma in fine art, 1986; University of Windsor, B.F.A., 1988; attended Photography Studio at Banff Centre for the Arts in Alberta, 1991. **Career:** Professional photographer since the late 1980s; member of NIIPA, the Native Indian/Inuit Photographers Association.

Individual Exhibitions

1989   *Recent Works,* NIIPA, Hamilton, Ontario

Patricia Deadman: Photo quintet—*preserve, conserve, reserve, self-serve, deserve,* 1994. Courtesy of the artist.

1990   *Fringe Momentum,* Thunder Bay Art Gallery, Thunder
        Bay, Ontario
        A Moment in Time, NIIPA, Hamilton, Ontario

Selected Group Exhibitions

1985   *Encer Studies,* Woodstock, Ontario
        Woodstock Art Gallery, Woodstock, Ontario
1987   *Indian Art '87,* Woodland Cultural Centre, Brantford,
        Ontario
1988   *Artistic Views,* NIIPA, Hamilton, Ontario
        Group Show, City Market, Windsor, Ontario
        Three Sisters, NIIPA, Hamilton, Ontario
        Indian Art '88, Woodland Cultural Centre, Brantford,
        Ontario
        Buffalo State College, NIIPA, Buffalo, New York
1989   *Contemplations,* Niroquois Gallery, Brantford, Ontario
        Art of the First Peoples, Queens Quay Gallery,
        Harbourfront, Toronto, Ontario
        First Annual Native Art Show, NIIPA, Hamilton,
        Ontario
        The Ten of Us, Niroquois Gallery, Brantford, Ontario
1990   *You Asked For It,* Niroquois Gallery, Brantford, Ontario
        Art of the First Nations, Woodland Cultural Centre,
        Brantford, Ontario
        Through the Lens, Compas Gallery, Heard Museum, Phoenix
        Telling Pictures, Kingston Artist Association, Inc.,
        Kingston, Ontario

        The Shawl, Discovery Gallery, Royal Ontario Museum,
        Toronto
        Arts Hamilton Exhibition, Hamilton, Ontario
        Figures, Niroquois Gallery, Brantford, Ontario
1991   *No Borders,* NIIPA, Hamilton, Ontario
        Springtales, Niroquois Gallery, Brantford, Ontario
        Visions of Power, Earth Spirit Festival, Leo Kamen Gal-
        lery, Toronto, Ontario
        Through an Eagle's Eye, Gallery Lambton, Sarnia, Ontario
1992   *If the Spirit Moves You,* Saw Gallery, Ottawa
1993   *Contemporary Camera,* Red Head Gallery, Toronto
1994   *From Icebergs to Iced Tea,* Thunder Bay Art Gallery
1995   *Alternative,* McMichael Canadian Art Collection,
        Kleinberg, Ontario

Collections

Department of Indian and Northern Affairs, Hull, Quebec; Thunder Bay Art Gallery, Thunder Bay, Ontario.

Publications

On DEADMAN: Catalogs—*Fringe Momentum,* Thunder Bay Art
Gallery, 1990; *Visions of Power,* Earth Spirit Festival, Toronto,
1991; *First Nations Art, '86-'91,* Woodland Cultural Centre,
Brantford, 1991.

❉   ❉   ❉

Deadman is part of a second generation of NIIPA (Native Indian/Inuit Photographers Association) photographers. Following in the footsteps of the likes of Rick Hill, Jeffrey Thomas, and Tim Johnson, Deadman and her colleagues entered the world of Native-produced photography during a period when it was gaining significant ground. Institutions like NIIPA in Canada have begun the task of rewriting history, researching, and presenting the work of a generation of photographers nearly lost—artists such as George Johnston and Murray McKenzie. For Deadman and other Native photographers of her generation, this history has made a significant impact on their work in terms of both how it is produced and what it says.

Deadman has been exhibiting professionally since the late 1980s. Her work has been marked particularly by an experimentation into the manipulated camera image as well as by a number of profoundly intuitive and intense images in black-and-white. Deadman has also produced a selection of photo-based artist's bookworks.

Deadman is recognized for her colourful Pow Wow images, each marked by the movement and delight of the dance, by the significance of the contemporary event within the construction of traditional Native cultures. Subsequent to the production of her dance-inspired photocollages, Deadman produced a number of black-and-white series that take as their theme the natural environment. These images take the form of both standard single image works, as well as of images of diverse size and format presented in complex, multi-media bookworks.

Work such as *Ice Views* and the *Serve* series suggest that Deadman's recent work has become more overtly issue-oriented, often with the inclusion of text overlays that proclaim the subtext of the photographic images. Acutely engineering a reading of the land and a structuring of the viewer's gaze, the artist constructs works that position icons, cliches, values and beliefs in relationships that reframe commonly held notions. In this regard, Deadman's photographs continue the tradition in Native photographic work to rethink representation and history.

—Carol Podedworny

DEBASSIGE, Blake

Tribal affiliations: Ojibway
Painter, graphic artist, carver, and printmaker

Born: Manitoulin Island, Ontario, 22 June 1956. **Education:** Attended public schools on Manitoulin Island; the Manitou Arts Foundation Summer School; and Laurentian University. **Family:** Married to Cree dramatist, painter and writer and storyteller Shirley Cheechoo, one son. **Career:** Professional artist—painting, printmaking (etching and serigraphs), wood carving—with commissions from public agencies for posters, murals and other work; served on art selection juries and co-curated several exhibitions; theatre designer for productions of the De-ba-jeh-mu-jig Theatre Group based on Manitoulin Island, which he helped found; has owned and operated the Kasheese Studios Art Gallery at West Bay, Manitoulin, since the early 1980s. **Awards:** Honorary Doctorate in the Arts, Laurentian University, 1995.

Individual Exhibitions

1973   Ontario Institute for Studies in Education, Toronto
        Samuel Zacks Gallery, Toronto
        Gallery 103, Toronto

1974   Gallery 103, Toronto
1979   Walter Engel Gallery, Toronto
1982   Nancy Pooles's Studio, Toronto
1984   Nancy Pooles's Studio, Toronto
1985   Thunder Bay Art Gallery, Thunder Bay, Ontario
        Ontario North Now Pavilion, Ontario Place, Toronto
1987   Nancy Pooles's Studio, Toronto
1988   Canada House, London, England
1996   Geronimo's Studio, Munich

Selected Group Exhibitions

1973   Chinquacousy Library Gallery, Bramalea, Ontario
1974   Oakville Centennial Gallery, Oakville, Ontario
        Canadian Indian Art, Royal Ontario Museum, Toronto
1975   Aviva Art Show and Auction, Toronto
        Indian Art '75, Woodland Cultural Centre, Brantford, Ontario
        McMichael Canadian Collection, Kleinburg, Ontario
1976   *Contemporary Native Art of Canada*, Royal Ontario Museum (traveling)
        Laurentian Museum and Arts Centre, Sudbury, Ontario
        McMichael Canadian Collection, Kleinburg, Ontario
        Indian Art '76, Woodland Cultural Centre, Brantford, Ontario
1978   Aviva Art Show and Auction, Toronto
        Royal Ontario Museum, Toronto
        McMichael Canadian Collection, Kleinberg, Ontario
        Hart House Gallery, University of Toronto
        Galleria d'Arte Contemporanea, Rome
1979   Gallery of the American Indian, New York City
        McMichael Canadian Collection
        Aviva Art Show and Auction, Toronto
1980   Aviva Art Show and Auction, Toronto
1981   National Arts Centre, Ottawa
        Native Art Auction, Native Canadian Centre, Toronto
1982   Native Art Auction, Native Canadian Centre, Toronto
1983   Royal Ontario Museum, Toronto
        McMichael Canadian Collection, Kleinburg, Ontario
        Laurentian University Museum and Arts Centre, Sudbury, Ontario
        Woodland Indian Cultural Centre, Brantford, Ontario
        Contemporary Indian and Inuit Art of Canada, United Nations Art Gallery, New York (traveling)
1984   *Norval Morrisseau and the Emergence of the Image Makers*, Art Gallery of Ontario (traveling)
        Toronto Art Mosaic '84, Ukrainian Canadian Art Foundation
1985   Heard Museum, Phoenix
        McMaster University Art Gallery, Hamilton, Ontario
        Indian Art '85, Woodland Cultural Centre, Brantford, Ontario
        Science North, Sudbury, Ontario
        Gallery 815, Le Conseil des Arts de Hearst, Hearst, Ontario
1986   Native Business Summit, Toronto Convention Centre
        Department of Indian and Northern Affairs, Hull, Quebec
1987   *Indian Art '87*, Woodland Cultural Centre, Brantford, Ontario
        Southwest Museum, Los Angeles
        Thunder Bay Art Gallery, Thunder Bay, Ontario

1988	*In the Shadow of the Sun*, Canadian Museum of Civilization (traveling)
1989	Americas Society, New York
	Ontario Native Arts Conference, Ontario College of Art, Toronto
	Ontario Indian Art '89, Woodland Cultural Centre, Brantford, Ontario
1990	*Indian Art '90*, Woodland Cultural Centre, Brantford, Ontario
1991	*Manitou Minissing: Art from the Island of the Spirits*, University Museum, Indiana University of Pennsylvania, Indian
	Tom Thompson Memorial Art Gallery, Owen Sound, Ontario
	Ojibwe Cultural Foundation, West Bay, Ontario
	Sarnia Public Art Gallery, Sarnia, Ontario
	Indigenous People's Conference, King's College, London, Ontario
1992	*Eclectica*, Heard Museum, Phoenix
	First Nations Art '92, Woodlands Cultural Centre, Brantford, Ontario
	Birthtales, A Space Gallery, Toronto
	Two Row Wampum Project, Niagara Falls Art Gallery
1993	University of Osnabruck, Germany
	For the Love of It, Heard Museum, Phoenix
	Distinctly Canadian, McMichael Canadian Collection, Kleinburg, Ontario
	Budapest Ethnographic Museum
1994	Sudbury Theatre Centre, Sudbury, Ontario
	Thunder Bay Art Gallery, Thunder Bay, Ontario
	Woodland Cultural Centre, Brantford, Ontario
	Province of Ontario, Legislative Building, Toronto
1995	Laurentian University Museum and Arts Centre, Sudbury, Ontario
	Basket, Bead and Quill, Thunder Bay Art Gallery, Thunder Bay, Ontario
	Riverwest Art Centre, Milwaukee, Wisconsin
1996	*The Art of the Anishnawbek*, Royal Ontario Museum, Toronto
	Rodman Hall Arts Centre, St. Catherines, Ontario
	Grimsby Public Art Gallery, Grimsby, Ontario

Collections

Anishinabe Spiritual Centre, Espanola, Ontario; Art Gallery of London, London, Ontario; Assembly of First Nations, Ottawa, Ontario; Canadian Museum of Civilization, Hull, Quebec; Department of Indian and Northern Affairs, Hull, Quebec; Glenhurst Arts Council, Brantford, Ontario; Government of Ontario, Ottawa; Heard Museum, Phoenix, Arizona; Hospital for Sick Children, Toronto; Laurentian Museum and Arts Centre, Sudbury, Ontario; London Regional Art Gallery, London, Ontario; McMichael Canadian Collection, Kleinburg, Ontario; New College, University of Toronto; Ojibwe Cultural Foundation, West Bay, Ontario; Ontario Northland Railway, North Bay, Ontario; Petro Canada Collection, Calgary, Alberta; Royal Ontario Museum, Toronto; Statens Etnografiska Museet, Stockholm, Sweden; Tom Thomson Memorial Gallery, Owen Sound, Ontario; Thunder Bay Art Gallery, Thunder Bay, Ontario; Woodland Cultural Centre, Brantford, Ontario.

Publications

By DEBASSIGE: Books—*The Art of the Anishnabek: Three Perspectives,* with Ahmoo Angeconeb and Roy Thomas, Royal Ontario Museum, Toronto, 1996. **Articles**—"Dualism: The Physical and the Spiritual," in *Blake Debassige and Stephen Hogbin, Political Landscapes #2: Sacred and Secular Sites,* Tom Thomson Memorial Art Gallery, Owen Sound, Ontario, 1991; "Beyond the Woodlands: Four Manitoulin Painters Speak Their Minds," by Theresa S. Smith with Blake Debassige, Shirley Cheechoo, James Simon Mishibinijima and Leland Bell, in *American Indian Quarterly*, 18(1), 1994.

On DEBASSIGE: Books—*ROM: Contemporary Native Art of Canada, Manitoulin Island,* Toronto, 1978; *Norval Morrisseau and the Emergence of the Image Makers,* by Elizabeth McLuhan and Tom Hill, Toronto: Art Gallery of Ontario and Methuen Publications, 1984; *The Sound of the Drum: The Sacred Art of the Anishnabec,* by Mary E. Southcott, Erie, Ontario: Boston Mills Press, 1984; *Debosegai,* Thunder Bay Art Gallery, Thunder Bay, 1985; *Im Shatten der Sonne: Zeitgenossische Kunst der Indianer und Eskimos in Kanada [In the Shadow of the Sun: Contemporary Indian and Inuit Art of Canada],* edited by Gerhard Hoffmann, Edition Cantz and Canadian Museum of Civilization, Ottawa, 1988. **Article**—"If it's Not Shamanic, Is it Sham?," by Valda Blundell and Ruth B. Phillips, *Anthropologica* 25, no. 1, 1986. **Film**—*Spirit Speaking Through*, Canadian Broadcasting Corporation, television documentary, 1985.

*   *   *

Blake Debassige became an artist in the mid 1970s while still in high school and began showing his work in public exhibitions before he was twenty. This early entry into the art world is evidence of the hothouse atmosphere that existed at that time in relation to the emerging pictorial art of Woodlands Indian artists. Like other young Native artists of the time, he was inspired by the spectacular successes of such older Woodlands artists as Norval Morrisseau, Carl Ray, Jackson Beardy and Daphne Odjig during the preceding decade and by the deeply felt need of his generation to preserve indigenous knowledge that seemed to be rapidly passing from memory. Visual art presented itself as a way back to the aboriginal world view and values that the assimilationist policies of church and state had sought to supress on Manitoulin Island for over a century. Debassige's project, like those of his associates, has involved both attentive apprenticeship to elders and independent historical research.

As a group these artists are often called the "Woodlands School." Debassige himself objects to this term because it has tended to present the group as a homogenous movement rather than a collection of individuals who have worked with common purpose but in artistically diverse ways. Perhaps more than any other member of the group, Debassige has succeeded in fusing traditional graphic traditions, expressed in such media as rock art and birch bark incising, with Western traditions of figuration and with modernist pictorial space.

Debassige was first drawn to the new Anishnaabe art work while still a student, when Carl Ray, a prominent member of the Woodlands School, visited his high school. From Ray, from his teachers at the summer art institutes organized by the Manitou Arts Foundation at Schreiber Island, from Anishnaabe artist Isidore Wadow, and from his own rigorous study of Anishnaabe art traditions

Debassige developed a highly individual graphic style. He has spoken of how, during this period of self-education, he trained his hand to draw in the manner of his ancestors by copying reproductions of rock art from a pamphlet distributed by the Ontario Ministry of Natural Resources. The elements of his mature style appeared early. They include a flat, modernist pictorial space; a rigorous structuring of the pictorial elements to produce stable, balanced compositions; clean, economical and slightly geometricized form lines to describe his figures; and a refined interpretation of the "x-ray" style—a traditional Anishnaabe graphic convention in which internal organs and skeletal elements are depicted to indicate the spiritual empowerment of an animal or a human.

Debassige's paintings and graphics frequently investigate traditional Anishnaabe teachings about the nature of cosmic order, the cycles of the seasons, the interdependence of animal, plant and human life and the common principles at work in the world's great spiritual systems. He frequently relates these themes to highly contemporary problems such as the destruction of the environment, the alienation of Native youth, or family breakdown. His most famous single early work, *Tree of Life*, painted for a Catholic spiritual centre near his home, engages many of these themes at the same time that it constitutes a serious, intellectual investigation into the underlying commonalities of Christianity and Anishnaabe spirituality. In it, the artist conflates the crucified body of Christ on the Anishnaabe world tree, the great axis of the cosmos that acts as a channel of spiritual communication. Together these structures organize and align all the forms of life—animals and birds, human beings and plants—revealing a harmony and a moral order that, according to both religions, is inscribed by the Creation.

Despite the enthusiastic reception of art by Woodlands artists during the 1960s and 1970s, and the large number of exhibitions held during that period in Canadian cities, Woodlands School art has since suffered a decrease in popularity. None of the large comprehensive exhibitions of contemporary Native art mounted by major Canadian museums during the 1990s included this art, featuring instead the work of art-school trained artists working in more fashionable postmodern and postcolonial modes. The commercial market, too, fell off and, not surprisingly, many younger Woodlands School artists stopped making art.

The continuing commitment of Debassige and his close associates, Leland Bell and James Simon Mishibinijima, is an outstanding exception to this pattern. These artists have become increasingly vocal in their opposition to what they regard as the domination of the major art venues by a postmodern aesthetic and a system of privilege that are alien to the lives of most reserve Indians. In 1991 Debassige wrote of his unhappiness with the "registered intellectuals" (most of them Native products of white art schools) who exert a "God-like power" in deciding what is and is not art. Yet Debassige has himself also experimented recently with more conceptual and experimental modes. In his co-curated exhibition of 1991, *Political Landscapes #2: Sacred and Secular Sites,* he displayed an uncharacteristically text-based and conceptual work, *Minidowin,* a large painted map of Manitoulin Island with stencilled names of sacred Anishnaabe sites in the mode of Jasper Johns or Robert Houle. In 1996, at the Royal Ontario Museum's exhibition *Three Anishnabe Artists,* he presented *Ahmoo,* and *Walking Man,* two life-sized plywood cut-out figures of aboriginal men that were in part a gently satirical take-off on the well known *Walking Woman* series of eminent Canadian conceptual artist Michael Snow.

—Ruth B. Phillips

DESCHILLIE, Mamie

Tribal affiliations: Navajo
Ceramist

Born: Mamie Bedon, in Burnham, Navajo Nation, New Mexico, 27 July 1920. **Career:** Sheperd; folk artist; active with a local senior citizens association; volunteer student monitor.

Selected Group Exhibitions

1983   Wheelwright Museum of the American Indian, Santa Fe
1986   *Lost and Found Traditions: Native American Art 1965-1985*, traveling exhibit organized by the American Federation of the Arts, New York
1988   *anii ánáádaalyaa'íí: Continuity and Innovation in Recent Navajo Art*, Wheelwright Museum of the American Indian, Santa Fe
1990   Museum of Northern Arizona, Flagstaff
        The Cutting Edge, organized by the Museum of American Folk Art; traveled to New Britain Museum of American Art, New Britain, Connecticut, Laguna Art Museum, Laguna Beach, California; Telfair Museum, Savannah, Georgia; Tampa Museum of Art, Tampa, Florida; Whatcom Museum, Bellingham, Washington
1993   *Made in USA*, Collection de l'Art Brut, Lausanne, Switzerland
        Leets'aa bi Diné Dáályé: It Is Called Navajo Pottery, Hearst Museum of Anthropology, University of California, Berkeley
1994   *Contemporary Art of the Navajo Nation*, organized by Cedar Rapids Museum of Art, Iowa; traveled to Albuquerque Museum; University Art Museum, State University of New York, Albany; Museum of the Southwest, Midland, Texas
1996   *Adaptations*, Museum of Indian Arts and Culture, Museum of New Mexico, Santa Fe

Collections

Children's Museum of Indianapolis; Natural History Museum of Los Angeles County; Navajo Nation Museum, Window Rock, Arizona; Hearst Museum of Anthropology, University of California, Berkeley; Wheelwright Museum of the American Indian, Santa Fe.

Publications

On DESCHILLIE: Books—*Lost and Found Traditons: Native American Art 1965-1985*, exhibition catalog by Ralph T. Coe, New York: The American Federation of the Arts, 1986; *Folk Art of the People: Navajo Works*, exhibition catalog by Charles Rosenak, St. Louis: Craft Alliance Gallery, 1987; *anii ánáádaalyaa'íí: Continuity and Innovation in Recent Navajo Art*, exhibition catalog by Bruce Bernstein and Susan McGreevy, Santa Fe: Wheelwright Museum, 1988; *Museum of American Folk Art Encyclopedia of Twentieth-Century American Folk Art and Artists* by Chuck and Jan Rosenak, New York: Abbeville Press, 1990; *The People Speak: Navajo Folk Art,* by Chuck and Jan Rosenak, Flagstaff, Northland Publishing Co., 1994; *Trading Post Guidebook* by Patrick Eddington and Susan Makov, Flagstaff, Northland Publishing Co., 1995; *Southwest-*

Mamie Deschillie: *Brown and White Cow,* 1985. Photograph by Chuck Rosenak; courtesy of the Chuck and Jan Rosenak collection.

ern Pottery: Anasazi to Zuni by Allan Hayes and John Blom, Flagstaff, Northland Publishing Co., 1996. **Articles**—"Navajo Mud Toys" by Scott Sandlin, *New Mexico Magazine*, December 1984; "Mamie Deschillie," *Folk Art Finder*, March 1986.

*   *   *

Mamie Deschillie is regarded by many as the founder of the Navajo Folk Art Movement. Whether or not she was the very first to produce whimsical, unfired clay figurines around 1980, since then she has been at the forefront of a movement that has spread to every corner of the Navajo homeland, attracting artists who now work in a wide range of media. Deschillie herself has become internationally famous for her creative and amusing creations fashioned from the simplest of natural and recycled materials.

Born in northwestern New Mexico on the Navajo Reservation, where she still resides, Deschillie was raised very traditionally. She attended school only through the second grade and speaks only a few words of English. As a child, she spent many hours herding the

family's sheep and goats, and when asked around 1980 by trader, Jack Beasley, to make something she remembered from her childhood, she thought of clay animals and other figurines that her mother used to make while they were out herding. Similar figurines had been made by the Navajo since the late 1800s, but because of the ephemeral nature of the pieces, very few survived, and the tradition has never received more than passing notice from the outside world.

Deschillie's first "mud" toys, or figurines, were decorated with a variety of found and recycled materials, such as bits of cloth, pieces of string, tufts of horse hair or sheep's wool, and pieces cut from corrugated cardboard boxes. Several other Navajo folk artists began producing similar figurines at about the same, but Deschillie's can usually be distinguished on the basis of the whimsical modeled or painted facial features and the eclectic accessories she gives each one.

Dressing her figurines in bits of clothing and other materials was Deschillie's innovation. The resulting individual personality of each figurine is what collectors find so appealing. Deschillie has made her share of animals familiar to her, including sheep, goats, and cows, as well as Navajo men and women on horseback. She has even made a Navajo-style nativity set of mud figurines. But she also produces animals she has only seen in pictures, such as elephants and other circus animals.

In 1987, Mamie Deschillie set off in a slightly different artistic direction and began making figures cut from corrugated cardboard boxes. She calls these "cutouts," or "cardboards." Like her mud figurines, which she still continues to make, her "cutouts" are accessorized with recycled clothing and other found materials. Additional details are painted. Animals and people are her favorite subjects and they appear as individual figures or as groups. Sometimes the two are combined and in unexpected forms, such as a child riding a giant rabbit.

Because the cardboard figures are made of more durable materials and are much larger than the mud toys, sometimes measuring up to six feet, they afford Deschillie considerably more artistic freedom. She uses a sewing machine to sew cloth remnants and pieces of discarded clothing into new clothing for her figurines. Cows are dressed in discarded long-johns and cast-off shirts, while sheep and goats might sport coats of natural wool. Her cutouts of Navajo people are dressed exactly as their real-life models, with women wearing long calico or velveteen skirts and men dressed in jeans and western shirts. Jewelry and other accessories are suggested with beads, sequins, and yarn.

Deschillie has been called an ambassador of goodwill for Navajo culture and a superstar of Navajo folk art. Both titles are accurate. This proud matriarch who has never had an art lesson in her life has become an internationally famous folk artist. Her work has been shown in museums throughout the United States and as far as Switzerland, and is sold in posh art galleries and museum shops. Despite these accolades and the notoriety brought by her work, Deschillie's life has not noticeably changed. She is still active with the local senior citizens association and she still volunteers to accompany students on the school bus. Her art is inspired by her life and surroundings and is her way of sharing the joy and pride she derives from them. Her art has inspired many other Navajo people, also without formal art training, to express themselves in a wide range of media, including wood and stone carving, beadwork, weaving, and pottery. All of these crafts have long traditions among the Navajo, but the number of contemporary practitioners and the freedom of expression displayed in their work is at a high, in large part because of the public's response to Deschillie's free-spirited, whimsical creations.

—Russell P. Hartman

DesJARLAIT, Patrick

Variant names: Magawbo
Tribal affiliations: Chippewa
Painter

Born: Red Lake reservation, Minnesota, 1 March 1921; native name means "Boy in the Woods." **Education:** Attended federal boarding schools at Red Lake and Pipestone, Minnesota; graduated Red Lake Senior High School; attended Arizona State College (now University) in Phoenix; studied mural painting at Phoenix Indian School with Olle Nordmark. **Military Service:** U.S. Navy, San Diego, California, 1942-45. **Family:** Married Eleanor Luther in

1942, marriage dissolved in 1945; married Ramona Needham in 1946. **Career:** Art director at the Japanese Relocation Center, Poston, Arizona 1941; during WW II, served as commercial artist specializing in training films for Visual Aids department, San Diego naval base; commercial artist in Minnesota for Reid Ray Films (now Campbell Mithun Esty), Brown and Bigelow, and Northern Ordinance. **Awards:** Campbell-Mithun Advertising Agency art competition, 1954; Walter Bimson Grand Award, Arizona National Indian Arts Exhibition, 1963; Elkus Memorial Award, Inter-Tribal Indian Ceremonials, Gallup, New Mexico, 1964; Scottsdale National Indian Art Exhibition Special Award, 1968; Carlos Beuf Silver Cup Award, Sheridan Wyoming, 1968; Philbrook Museum of Art Award, 1969; representation at the Center for Arts of Indian America in Washington, D.C., 1969; Minnesota State Fair Award, 1969. **Died:** November 1972.

Individual Exhibitions

1945 Fine Arts Gallery, San Diego
1946 St. Paul Gallery and School of Art (now the Minnesota Museum of American Art)
1972 *Memorial Exhibition*, American Indian Center, Minneapolis
1995-97 *Patrick DesJarlait Touring Exhibition*, multiple venues in Minnesota

Selected Group Exhibitions

1963 *Arizona National Indian Arts Exhibition*
1964 *Inter-Tribal Indian Ceremonials*, Gallup, New Mexico
1968 *Scottsdale National Indian Art Exhibition*
   All-American Indian Days, Sheridan, Wyoming
1969 Philbrook Museum of Art, Tulsa, Oklahoma
1994 *Patrick DesJarlait and the Ojibwe Tradition*, Minnesota Museum of American Art, St. Paul

Collections

Campbell Mithun Esty; Heard Museum, Phoenix; Minnesota Historical Society; Philbrook Museum of Art, Tulsa, Oklahoma; U.S. Department of the Interior, Washington, D.C.

Publications

On DesJARLAIT: Books—*American Indian Painting of the Southwest and Plains Areas* by Dorothy Dunn, Albuquerque, New Mexico, 1968; *Patrick DesJarlait: Conversations with a Native American Artist*, as recorded by Neva Williams, Minneapolis, Minnesota, 1975; *American Indian Painting and Sculpture* by Patricia Janis Broder, New York, 1981; "Controversy in Native American Art," by Jamake Highwater, in *The Arts of the North American Indian*, 1986; *Shared Visions: Native American Painters and Sculptors in the Twentieth Century*, exhibition catalog by Margaret Archuleta, Heard Museum, Phoenix, 1991; *Patrick DesJarlait and the Ojibwe Tradition*, exhibition catalog, Minnesota Museum of American Art, 1995.

* * *

As early as 1936, Patrick DesJarlait's painting, *Red Lake Powwow*, reveals his intense interest in generating a new way of seeing. Very possibly the earliest Indian modernist, DesJarlait married the

Peter DesJarlait. Courtesy San Diego Historical Society Photograph Collection.

flatness of mural painting with cubism to create an abstract yet personal perspective on modernism. Although superficially his images appear to follow in the tradition of Diego Rivera, DesJarlait denied any such influence. On a philosophical level, he rejected Rivera's socialistic and universalizing stance, finding more affinity with van Gogh, whose early works probed the world of Dutch peasantry.

In a similar fashion, DesJarlait detailed the quotidian in modern life at Red Lake. *Red Lake Fisherman,* from 1946, part of a three piece series later dated 1961 by DesJarlait, illustrates an engagement with modernism that cuts to the heart of nature versus culture debates within the humanities. Indeed, in *Red Lake Fisherman* and throughout his *oeuvre* DesJarlait faced no such dilemmas, consistently rendering relationships between Anishinaabe and Red Lake in terms of reciprocal mutuality rather than mastery.

DesJarlait's visual environments orchestrate what is significant through the establishment of frameworks of legibility. These frameworks provide cues as to how his art might be reckoned with both by individuals and the larger population. Using mediums of oil and watercolors, DesJarlait employed art as a critical resource to articulate the very terms of symbolic and political legitimacy for Anishinaabe from his native Red Lake reservation.

World War II exerted a formative influence on DesJarlait's artistic directions. At the beginning of the war, he served as art director at the Japanese relocation camp in Poston, Arizona. DesJarlait shared with the camp's Japanese students experience with the realities of dispossession that created a bond that he later openly acknowledged. Henceforth, the notion of place would play a vital role in DesJarlait's work.

Both aesthetically and psychologically, the curved line figures predominantly in DesJarlait's art and attests to the inseparable relationship between Anishinaabe and Red Lake. To further these associations, DesJarlait employs triangular compositional techniques that imbue his images with a stability that works, on a subconscious level, to intertwine past and present. In paintings that portray inexorable processes of change, DesJarlait depicts change to emphasize the resilience of Anishinaabe lifeways. His genius resides in an ability to reaffirm traditional perspectives and document their specific historicity, while capitalizing on western artistic techniques. In the process, he created a modernist breakthrough in Native American art.

From an art historical perspective, DesJarlait occupies a pivotal place. DesJarlait made a conceptual leap that, in breaking with traditional mediums facilitated his attempts to illustrate Anishinaabe modernity. DesJarlait rendered legible interpretations of modernity that, in their prescience, anticipated key issues of the seventies. Contextualized within modern modes of artistic portrayal, DesJarlait gave the Anishinaabe present an enormous presence, while working to free its representations from stereotyping and aesthetic fetishization. These artistic and philosophical strategies parallel larger cultural issues at stake in modernism, while clearly situating DesJarlait's work within art history's modernist traditions.

—Marilee Jantzer-White

DICK, Cecil

Variant names: Da'-Ga-Dah'-Ga
Tribal affiliations: Cherokee
Painter

Born: Near Rose Prairie, Oklahoma, 16 September 1915; native name means Standing Alone. **Education:** Bacone College, Bacone, Oklahoma; Santa Fe Indian School. **Awards:** Cherokee Nation of Oklahoma, Heritage Award, or Sequoyah Medal, 1983; Five Civilized Tribes Museum, Master of Heritage Award, 1988; Cecil Dick Master of Heritage Award established in his honor.

Individual Exhibitions

1983   *Cecil Dick: 50 Year Retrospective,* Cherokee Nation Museum, Tahlequah, Oklahoma

Selected Group Exhibitions

1937   *American Indian Exposition and Congress,* Tulsa, Oklahoma
1939   Bacone College, Bacone, Oklahoma
1947-65 *American Indian Paintings from the Permanent Collection,* Philbrook Museum of Art, Tulsa, Oklahoma (traveling)
1972   Five Civilized Tribes Museum, Muskogee, Oklahoma
1984   *The Bacone Indian Art Retrospective,* Bacone College, Bacone, Oklahoma
1987   *Red Earth Festival,* Myriad Plaza, Oklahoma City
1991   *Shared Visions: Native American Painters and Sculptors of the Twentieth Century,* Heard Museum, Phoenix, Arizona (traveling through 1992)

Collections

Five Civilized Tribes Museum, Muskogee Oklahoma; Thomas Gilcrease Institute of American History and Art, Tulsa, Oklahoma; Heard Museum, Phoenix, Arizona; National Museum of the American Indian, Smithsonian Institution, Washington, D.C.; Philbrook Museum of Art, Tulsa, Oklahoma.

Publications

On DICK: Books—*American Indian Painters,* by Oscar B. Jacobson and Jeanne d'Ucel, Nice, France: C. Szwedzicki 1950; *American Indian Painting of the Southwest and Plains Areas,* by Dorothy Dunn, Albuquerque: University of New Mexico Press 1968; *Indian Painters and White Patrons,* by J. J. Brody, Albuquerque: University of New Mexico Press, 1971; *Song from the Earth: American Indian Painting,* by Jamake Highwater, Boston: New York Graphic Society, 1976; *American Indian Painting and Sculpture,* by Patricia Janis Broder, New York: Abbeville Press, 1981; *The Bacone Indian Art Retrospective: A Half Century of Native American Art,* by Rennard Strickland, Bacone College, 1984; *Shared Visions: Native American Painters and Sculptors of the Twentieth Century,* by Margaret Archuleta and Rennard Strickland, Phoenix: The Heard Museum, 1991.

*   *   *

Cecil Dick is known as the twentieth-century Cherokee painter most committed to the accurate depiction of the history and culture of his tribe. He also has been noted for his use of unusual and original stylized images within the context of flat-style painting. Both characteristics appeared more frequently in his work as he matured as an artist. Dick first worked predominantly in the Woodland style typical of many Native American art students from Bacone College. He also attended the Studio School in Santa Fe, and his early paintings show the influence of both the Bacone and Studio traditions. Early paintings are simple with few figures, little background and minimal detail. These simple compositions bear witness to the legacy of the Kiowa painting style at Bacone. Dick's colors were often subtle and his palette was limited in early as well as mid-career compositions like *The Deer Hunter* (Gilcrease Museum). Some works also contain elements of pan-Indian art, which was common for Woodland painters from Bacone.

As his painting style developed, the background and foreground became more complete, figures became more detailed, and innovative designs emerged. Bold colors began to appear, as in such pieces as *Cherokee Medicine Man* (Gilcrease Museum). The painting is dominated by highly saturated hues of purple and violet. Small areas of warm color provide interest and balance. At first glance, the piece seems to contain the basic composition and technique of many flat-style paintings from Bacone and the Studio. Closer examination reveals some of the unique changes that Dick incorporated into the flat-style format. For example, the bands of outline on the medicine man figure have become so varied in thickness as to be considered areas of shading. The sky is filled with brush strokes that create short, repetitive, horizontal areas of purple that are darker than the purple underneath. The effect is to add movement and agitation to the painting. It is a technique reminiscent of the painterly post-impressionist styles. It is certainly not in keeping with flat-style tradition.

But it is the images of the mythical creatures surrounded by the medicine man's smoke that are the most unusual for Woodland painting. Those stylized images show why some suggest Art Deco influenced Cecil Dick's more mature work. Certainly it has been established that twentieth century Native American painting was indeed influenced by mainstream Art Deco style. In Dick's case, however, it is unclear whether or not his stylization derived from Art Deco; the figures in *Cherokee Medicine Man* are also similar to images from meso-America and Mexico. Out of necessity, Dick devised ways of portraying certain Cherokee mythical beings that had no precedent in visual representation. These figures, then, should not be considered as anything other than original until evidence of influence has been shown.

Throughout his career, Dick focused on painting accurate portrayals of Cherokee history. He used careful research and his life-long experiences with Cherokee culture as his sources. Dick's status as a traditionalist is evidenced by the comments of his contemporaries, such as the sculptor Willard Stone, who praised Dick as knowing more about Cherokee history and tradition than anyone living. Dick's respect by his peers is further evidenced by his receiving the Heritage Award or, Sequoyah Medal, from the Cherokee Nation of Oklahoma in 1983. The award had only been conferred twice before in the tribe's history, the first honoree being Sequoyah, the inventor of the Cherokee syllabary.

—Kevin Smith

DICK Family, The

Tribal affiliations: Piaute; Washoe
Basketweavers

MINNIE DICK. Born: Coleville, Antelope Valley, California, c. 1875, of Piaute descent. **Family:** Married Washoe Dick; son, Levi. **Died.**

TOOTSIE DICK SAM. Born: Coleville, Antelope Valley, California, c. 1880. **Family:** Sister of Minnie Dick; married Sam. **Died:** 1928.

LENA FRANK DICK. Born: Coleville, Antelope Valley, California, c. 1889. **Family:** Daughter of Charley and Lucy Frank; sister of Lillie Frank James and Jessie Wade, also basketweavers; married 1) George Emm; one daughter, Juanita; 2) Levi Dick, son of Minnie and Washoe Dick. **Died:** 1965.

LILLIE FRANK JAMES. Born: Coleville, Antelope Valley, California, c. 1885. **Family:** Daughter of Charley and Lucy Frank; sister of Lena Dick and Jessie Wade, who also were basket weavers; married Willie James; two children. **Died:** 1948.

Selected Group Exhibitions

1915   Panama Pacific Exposition, San Francisco, California (Tootsie Dick)
1996   *The Fine Art of California Indian Basketry*, Crocker Museum of Art, Sacramento, California
        Albrecht-Kemper Museum of Art, St. Joseph, Missouri

Collections

California State Indian Museum, Sacramento, California; Field Museum of Natural History, Chicago, Illinois; C. Hart Merriam Collection, University of California, Davis; Heard Museum, Phoenix, Arizona; Phoebe Hearst Museum of Anthropology, University of California, Berkeley; Nevada State Museum, Carson City, Nevada; Peabody Museum, Harvard University; University Museum, University of Pennsylvania; Yosemite National Park, National Park Service, Yosemite, California.

Publications

On the DICK Family: Books—*California Indian Basketry: An Artistic Overview*, by Arthur Silva and William Cain, Cypress, California, 1976; *Degikup: Washoe Fancy Basketry 1895-1935*, by Marvin Cohadas, Vancouver, 1979; "Washoe Innovators and Their Patrons," by Marvin Cohodas, *Arts of the North American Indian: Native Traditions in Evolution*, edited by Edwin L. Wade, New York, 1986; *Indian Baskets,* by Sarah and William Turnbaugh, Westchester, Pennsylvania, 1986; *Native American Basketry of Central California*, by Christopher Moser, Riverside, California, 1987; *Tradition and Innovation: A Basket History of the Indian of the Yosemite-Mono Lake Region*, by Craig Bates and Martha Lee, Yosemite National Park, 1990; *Native American Basketry: The Hartman Collection*, by Bruce Bernstein, St. Joseph, Missouri, Albrecht-Kemper Museum of Art, 1996; *The Fine Art of California Indian Basketry*, by Brian Bibby, Sacramento, Crocker Art Museum, 1996. **Articles**—"The Washoe Florescence: 1895-1935," by Marvin Cohadas, *Vanguard,* Vol. 8, no. 5, 1979; "Lena Frank Dick: An Outstanding Washoe Basket Weaver," by Marvin Cohadas, *American Indian Art Magazine,* Autumn 1979.

*   *   *

The extended family of basketweavers that included Minnie, Tootsie, and Lena Dick and Lillie Frank James were major contribu-

The Dick Family: Polychrome degikup basket by Lillie James, c. 1920. Photograph by Seth Roffman; courtesy Dr. Gregory Schaaf collection.

tors to the excellence of Washoe basketmaking from roughly 1910, when Minnie Dick began selling her wares through the general store in Colville, California, through the mid-1930s. Minnie, Tootsie, and Lena Dick each introduced innovations and expanded on the artistry of basketmaking, and Lillie James, while less innovative, was an expert weaver. Like other Washoe weavers, including the renowned Louisa Keyser and Sarah Jim Mayo, Minnie, Tootsie, Lena, and Lillie depended on the tourist trade around Lake Tahoe as steady consumers for their works. Unlike their famous contemporaries, however, the Dick clan did not benefit as much from patronage and direct access to Carson City, Nevada, where entrepreneur Abe Cohn established the most noted center for selling baskets. Minnie and Tootsie were sisters; Lena (nee Frank) married Minnie's son, Levi Dick, and Lillie was Lena's sister.

Minnie first began selling through the Coleville general store around 1910, followed by Tootsie around 1913, and Lena in 1916. Minnie was the first in her area to introduce the characteristics of fancy design that had been popularized by Louisa Keyser and Sarah Jim Mayo. Minnie's works featured alternating motifs integrated through the similarity in configuration, blended-in through smaller motifs to create an overall pattern. Combined with her development of a more spherical degikup shape than Louisa Keyser had popularized, Minnie began a spirit of innovation taken further by Tootsie and Lena.

Tootsie became the most popular weaver outside of Carson City, improving on Minnie's innovations by employing more sophisticated designs, including some drawn from beadwork as well as bird and butterfly motifs, which suggest the influence of works by Sarah Jim Mayo. Tootsie excelled with bush and stalk patterns and originated a more subtle zig-zag design, achieving representational and geometric elements, often with two alternating designs. In addition to being influenced by Mayo's basket designs, Tootsie became familiar with Louisa Keyser, who used her connections with the Cohns to help Tootsie sell baskets in Carson City. Nevertheless, the large majority of Tootsie's works were sold through the Emporium, the general store in Colville. For the next decade, Tootsie enjoyed consistent sales as she continued to tinker, experiment and innovate, until a personal tragedy left her emotionally drained. Tootsie committed suicide in 1928 following the death of her six-year-old daughter from spiral meningitis.

An early example of Tootsie's basketry survives in the Wilma and Edward Hartman Collection, first exhibited at the 1915 Panama Pacific Exposition in San Francisco. The materials in the basket include sun-bleached willow for white color, dyed bracken fern roots for black, and split redbud shoots for red. The design on the Hartman basket is a complex of diamonds, triangles and chevrons. Moving from right to left, the direction of the coiling process, a red, vertically-elongated diamond with black serrated edges appears with stacks of small, red-bordered black diamonds leading to a black and red diamond pinnacle. Black bars are adjacent, flanked by inward pointed red chevrons. The next design is composed of two upper rows of red diamonds outlined in black. Below these appear a red hourglass and black triangle pointing upward. The design elements are larger in the middle and smaller on the top and bottom, giving the basket a monumental effect. To the left appears a white diamond outlined in black, surmounted by a black "U" shape topped with a red and black "V" form. The central diamond is flanked by red, inward-pointing chevrons. Below the central white diamond appears three smaller black and white diamonds.

The uniformity of the spherical form gives this basket a grand appearance. Tootsie Dick achieved this effect by carefully shaping the inner rods and applying consistent pressure to these warps while weaving the globular shape. She achieved a refined quality by carefully shaping wefts in a uniform width. This requires hours and hours of shaping each sewing strand with a sharp knife to create perfect, ribbon-like wefts.

After Louisa Keyser died in 1925 and Tootsie's death in 1928, Lena Dick, and her sisters, Lillie James and Jessie Wade, are acknowledged as the foremost Washoe basketweavers during a general period of decline. By the mid-1930s Abe Cohn had died, few younger weavers were carrying on the tradition of basketmaking, and as Lena Dick's eyesight began failing, she increasingly concentrated on purely utilitarian baskets. Lena and Lillie shared a patron in Fred Settlemyer, but most of their works were sold through a local store run by Cordelia Hardy. Lillie James was a shy sister who contributed a majority of the finished products, and Lena gradually became more dynamic. Expanding on Tootsie's design elements, Lena juxtaposed red and black variations, including patterns that gradually grow larger moving toward the top. Lena's works can be said to display the tautness and precision of baskets by Louisa Keyser and the bolder designs of Mayo.

However, Lena's baskets often were mistaken for those of her more noted contemporaries, whose baskets sometimes sold for over $1,000. Marvin Cohadas, a scholar of Washoe basketry, deserves recognition for bringing Lena out of obscurity in 1979 with an important article in *American Indian Art Magazine*. Cohadas learned much of Lena's life through interviews with her granddaughter, Marjorie. For example, as a young woman Lena loved to ski, and when she had married and settled, Lena served as midwife for many Antelope Valley women. When her daughter Juanita, whom Lena bore while still a young teenager, was young, Lena hid her in the mountains whenever officers came to take Indian children to the boarding school in Stewart, Nevada. Lena followed Washoe tradition and even in the late 1940s performed traditional Washoe puberty ceremonies for Marjorie.

Cohadas described the influence of Lena's married life: "Lena and Levi spent their married life primarily in Coleville. During her years of active weaving, around 1920-1935, Lena's sister Lillie and her husband Willie James lived nearby.... Lena and Levi also joined the Native American Church, whose peyote rituals were designed to draw Indians away from alcohol and give them a renewed sense of responsibility and community."

During the first part of the Great Depression, Lena wove under the patronage of a San Francisco orthodontist, Roscoe A. Day. His agent, local rancher Fred Settlemyer, commissioned both Lena and her sister Lillie. However, neither the patron, Day, nor the agent, Settlemyer, ever met Lena Dick, and the decline in consumer interest in and promotion of baskets led to a quickly disappearing mar-

ket at about the time Lena Dick began having trouble with her eyesight. Many of her works were not properly attributed until after her death in 1965.

Lillie Frank James's baskets feature butterfly, swastika, flame, serrated chevrons and stacked triangle designs. Her most prominent type of basket was the three-rod, polychrome degikup, a spherical shaped bowl. Her weaving was fine, averaging about 25 stitches per inch, and most of her baskets were under 12 inches in diameter. One of her unique techniques was her method of running different colored stitches along the coil, instead of the standard method of clipping with each change in color. She often used an oval start in making a round basket, an approach common among Washoe weavers. Lillie's evolution of basketmaking included an early emphasis on globular, degikup baskets, resembling the other leading Washo basket weavers, Dat So La Lee, Lena Dick and Maggie James. The shape of Lillie's degikup baskets changed during the mid 1910s, becoming more rounded while her compositions continued to be arranged in a distinctive horizontal zig-zag layout. During the 1920s Lillie's baskets developed a higher shoulder and a wide orifice, with large and bold design elements that gave way later to more delicate features. Through the mid 1930s, she compressed her shapes, lowering the height in relationship to the width. The baskets' shoulders are still high with a wide orifice.

—Gregory Schaaf and Perry Bear

DIESING, Freda

Tribal affiliations: Haida
Carver, jewelry designer, printmaker, and button designer

Born: Prince Rupert, British Columbia, 1925, in the Sadsugohilanes Clan of the Haida. **Education:** Vancouver School of Art, British Columbia; Kitanmax School of Northwest Coast Indian Art, 'Ksan, British Columbia, under Robert Davidson and Bill Holm. **Career:** Instructor, 'Ksan Indian Art School, Hazleton, British Columbia, and in Prince Rupert and Terrace, British Columbia; teaches annual carving seminar in Ketchikan, Alaska; commissioned for relief wall mural, Prince Rupert General Hospital.

Selected Group Exhibitions

1972	*'KSan, Breath of our Grandfathers*, National Museum of Civilization, Hull, Quebec
1974	*Canadian Indian Art '74*, Royal Ontario Art Museum, Toronto, Ontario
1977	*Links to Tradition*, organized by Department of Indian Affairs and Northern Development for touring Brazil
1980	Heritage House, Vancouver, British Columbia
	The Legacy, British Columbia Provincial Museum, Victoria, British Columbia
1981	*Art of the Salmon People*, Prince Rupert, British Columbia
1982	*Renewal: Masterworks of Contemporary Indian Art from the National Museum of Civilization*, Thunder Bay Art Gallery, Ontario
1993	*Art of the Mask: Works from the Peacock Collection*, Thunder Bay Art Gallery, Ontario

Frieda Diesing: Cormorant Headdress, 1987. Photograph by Kenji Nagai; courtesy Inuit Gallery of Vancouver.

1994   *Spirit Faces*, Vancouver Inuit Art Gallery, British Columbia

1995   *Contemporary Indian and Inuit Art of Canada*, organized by the Department of Indian and Northern Affairs, traveling in the United States and Canada through 1996

1996   *Topographies: Aspects of BC Art*, Vancouver Art Gallery, British Columbia

Collections

City of Prince Rupert, Prince Rupert, British Columbia; Department of Indian and Northern Affairs, Ottawa, Ontario; National Museum of Civilization, Hull, Quebec; Royal Ontario Museum, Toronto, Ontario.

Publications

On DIESING: Books—*Indian Artists at Work,* by Ulli Stelzer, Vancouver, 1976; *The Legacy: Continuing Traditions of Canadian Northwest Coast Indian Art*, by Peter L. Macnair, Alan L. Hoover, and Kevin Neary, Victoria: The British Columbia Provincial Museum, 1980; *Northwest Coast Indian Graphics: An Introduction to Silk Screen Prints*, by Edwin S. Hall, Jr., Margaret B. Blackman, and Vincent Rickard, Seattle: University of Washington Press, 1981; *Totem Poles of Prince Rupert*, by Dawn Hassett, and F. W. M. Drew, Prince Rupert, Museum of Northern British Columbia, 1982*; Robes of Power: Totem Poles on Cloth*, by Doreen Jensen, and Polly Sargent, Vancouver: The University of British Columbia Press, 1986; *Hands of Creation: An Exhibition of Northwest Coast Native Art,* Inuit Gallery of Vancouver, 1987; *Northwest Coast: Native American Art,* by Barbara Loeb, St. Louis: Craft Alliance Gallery, 1989. **Articles**—"Indian Artifacts at NAC" and "'Ksan Means

Skeena in Hazleton, British Columbia," by Alixe Carter, *Ottawa Journal,* 2 November 1972; "'Ksan's Frieda Diesing," *Tawow,* Vol. 3, Spring 1972; "A Long Way to Go," by Kim Pemberton, *Prince Rupert News,* August 6, 1982; "Faces at an Exhibition," by Brian Johnson, *Maclean's*, 5 December 1994.

*   *   *

Freda Diesing is an artist whose work bridges male and female traditions. Her work closely conforms to the traditional style of her ethnic group, the Haida of British Columbia, yet as a woman who works in wood, paint, and cloth, she breaks down traditional gender barriers in Northwest Coast art.

Among the most well-known women working in the Northwest Coast art style today, Diesing is equally celebrated for her role as an influential art teacher. She has been active in the regeneration of Northwest Coast artistic traditions that has occurred during the last thirty years. Among most Northwest Coast groups, the great totem poles, house posts, dance screens, ceremonial masks, and textiles of the nineteenth century had become almost lost arts by the mid-twentieth century. But recent decades have seen the vigorous reemergence of these traditions, both for use in community ceremonies and for sale in the international art market.

Diesing credits her maternal grandmother with sparking her interest in both art and Haida traditions: "I was always interested in the past because that was the life my grandmother had been born into," (interview with essayist). Diesing spent much of her childhood living in her grandmother's household. Her earliest artistic memories concern her grandmother's carved spoons made out of mountain goat horn, and the spruce root baskets her grandmother wove.

The first Northwest Coast style carving Diesing performed was in 1967, when she was already 42 years old. In the previous decade she had briefly attended the Vancouver School of Art, where she studied painting. For British Columbia's centennial year, she wanted to do a project commemorating the Native traditions of the province. She carved a model Haida village out of balsa wood to commemorate the fact that her grandmother had lived in such a village. The following year Diesing carved her first cedar mask. She studied under several famous carvers, both Native and non-Native, including Tony Hunt, Henry Hunt, Bill Holm, Robert Davidson, and Duane Pasco. In turn, she herself became a notable teacher. From her carving and design classes have emerged a number of well-known members of the younger generation of artists, including Dempsey Bob, Norman Tait, Donnie Yeomans, and Gerry Marks. Diesing has taught at the 'Ksan Indian art school in Hazleton, British Columbia, as well as in Prince Rupert and in her home town of Terrace. Since 1974 she has often taught an annual carving seminar in Ketchikan, Alaska as well, extending her sphere of influence even wider.

Diesing is an unusual artist in several respects. She is the best known contemporary female carver; most other carvers—like their nineteenth-century predecessors—are male. She has designed and executed a number of totem poles that stand in Prince Rupert, Terrace, and Kitsam Kalem village in the Canadian province of British Columbia. Some of these poles are original designs, while others, like the Eagle Chief's Pole erected in Prince Rupert, recreate nineteenth-century poles. This was carved by Diesing and her colleague, Josiah Tate, in 1975.

Freda Diesing is perhaps best known for her portrait masks, which she calls "imaginary persons." They are seldom specific portraits, but rather are semi-realistic, with facial and decorative stylizations typical of Northwest Coast carving. They often depict women, recognizable by the labret, or decorative plug, worn in the lower lip. Life-size, these masks can be worn in ceremonial dances, though most are sold to non-Indian collectors. Diesing says, "It sometimes comes out different than what you expect. As I refine it, it might lose certain characteristics—become young rather than old. It comes out like *it* wants to." She does no preliminary sketches, but carves right into the block of wood. Though her masks conform to Northwest Coast stylistic conventions, the artist points out that they are not copies; each is an original interpretation.

Just as Diesing is unusual as a female carver, she is also one of few women who have participated in the male-dominated silk-screen printmaking enterprise that began in the 1970s; indeed, the best known book on this art form includes only two women—one of them Diesing—among some fifty artists discussed. Diesing seldom makes prints anymore, and does not like to teach printmaking because of her sensitivity to the chemicals involved. But many of the students in her Northwest Coast design classes execute their work in the silk-screen print medium.

Though she is best known for her work in the male-dominated arts of sculpture and printmaking, Diesing has occasionally worked in women's textile arts as well. Her 1985 eagle crest button blanket was featured in an important publication on this art form. As a well-known artist in the traditional formline design system of the Northwest Coast, since 1970 she has designed many button blankets for others to sew. The 1985 eagle robe was the first one she designed, cut, *and* sewed herself. Diesing, as a member of the eagle clan, has hereditary rights to display, carve, and wear these emblems.

Freda Diesing's art remains closely tied to the traditional styles and forms of her people. Yet at the same time, she breaks down these traditions by transgressing the gender barriers that in earlier

times prevented women from carving wood. Her fluency in all media, and her work as a teacher of carving and formline design make her an important force in the contemporary art scene of the last twenty years on the Northwest Coast.

—Janet Catherine Berlo

DUWYENIE, Preston

Variant names: Loma-I'-Quil-Va-A
Tribal affiliations: Hopi
Potter and jewelry designer

Born: Preston Virgil Duwyenie, Hotevilla, Third Mesa, Arizona, 6 September 1951. **Education:** Institute of American Indian Arts, 1980-82; Colorado State University, B.F.A., Metalsmithing (with a minor in ceramics), 1982-84; Colorado State University, M.F.A. program. **Career:** Instructor, including graduate teaching assistant, metalsmithing and jewelry, Colorado State University, 1986-88, professor of traditional pottery, jewelry, design, Institute of American Indian Arts, 1988-92, professor of jewelry, University of New Mexico, 1992-present; workshops and lectures, including Boward Community College, Davie, Florida, 1988, Winter Market Seminar, Southwestern Association for Indian Affairs, Santa Fe, New Mexico, 1989, Chapparal Elementary School, Santa Fe, New Mexico, 1990,

Preston Duweynie: *Earth in Balance* storage jar. Courtesy of the artist.

Mexico, 1990, Canadian tour (on behalf of the United States Information Service-Arts in America Program), 1994, and numerous workshops and lectures at the Museum of Fine Arts, Santa Fe, New Mexico; curator, including Colorado State University and the Institute of American Indian Arts; panelist, grant application review, New Mexico Commission on the Arts, 1991. **Awards:** Numerous, from the Santa Fe Indian Market, Inter-Tribal Indian Ceremonial, and New Mexico State Fair beginning in 1980, ENIPC Artist and Craftsman Show, San Ildefonso Pueblo beginning in 1982, Colorado Indian Market beginning in 1985, Hopi Show, Museum of Northern Arizona beginning in 1989, Heard Museum Guild beginning in 1991, Southwest Museum, beginning 1992, and Red Earth festival beginning in 1993.

Selected Group Exhibitions

Exhibits regularly at annual art fairs and markets throughout the southwest, 1980s and 1990s, including Creative Arts Symposium, Fort Collins, Colorado, Colorado Indian Market, Denver, Eight Northern Pueblos Council Arts and Crafts Show, San Ildefonso Pueblo, Native American Festival, Houston, Texas, and the Red Earth Festival, Oklahoma City, Oklahoma, as well as museum-sponsored annual fairs at Coconino Center for the Arts, Flagstaff, Arizona, Heard Museum, Phoenix, Arizona, Northern Arizona Museum, "Hopi Show," Flagstaff, Arizona, and the Southwest Museum, Los Angeles, California. Frequently exhibited as well during the 1980s and 1990s at Institute of American Indian Arts Museum, Santa Fe, New Mexico, Lincoln Center for the Arts, New York, New York, National Center for Atmospheric Research, Boulder, Colorado, Native Americans Rights Fund Art Benefit Show, Boulder, Colorado, Taylor Museum, Colorado Springs, Colorado, and Turtle Museum, Niagara Falls, New York.

Collections

Denver Art Museum, Colorado; Heard Museum, Phoenix, Arizona; Institute of American Indian Arts Museum, Santa Fe, New Mexico; Museum of Fine Arts, Museum of New Mexico, Santa Fe; Millicent Rogers Foundation Museum, Taos, New Mexico.

*

Preston Duwyenie comments:

Although my art has broadened through educational opportunities, I have not lost the ambition to represent my heritage. The Hopi people have produced some of the finest aesthetics of the country, thus, this background to a great extent motivates what I do. In my art, my aim is to bring the best from my multi-cultural influences into this society. I would like to help others gain an appreciation of Native American culture and at the same time expose Native Americans to the non-native. I feel the need to challenge the established world of art and eventually to contribute to it as a goal. Above all to establish cultural innovations offering alternatives in artistic expression with experimentation in various techniques and mediums.

*   *   *

Preston Duwyenie has distinguished himself as a modern master of traditional Hopi pottery techniques. In addition to his work as a potter, he has created a considerable body of fine jewelry. In both art forms he has demonstrated a unique contemporary style that is respectful, seamless, original and highly innovative.

Born at Hotevilla, Third Mesa, Arizona, Duwyenie comes from a family of working artists where virtually everyone practices some form of traditional arts. His father carved, and his mother was a painter, drawer and basketmaker. Duwyenie acknowledges his earliest work was sheer imitation. At the age of 15 he completed his first three-dimensional kachina carvings. Shortly thereafter he expanded into other types of metal, wood, and stone sculpture.

Duwyenie's pursuit of a full-time career in the arts began after a chance trip to Santa Fe's Indian Market in the summer of 1978, where he was introduced to the possibility of attending the Institute of American Indian Arts (IAIA). He began classes there in the fall of 1979. At IAIA he was introduced to three-dimensional arts and began to explore the integration of metalwork and ceramics in finished pieces. He also credits IAIA for exposing him to various firing methods, including Japanese raku firing and the gas and electric kiln. At IAIA he also benefitted from instruction in the traditional pottery firing methods of the Santa Clara Pueblo, renowned for their black pottery.

After IAIA, Duwyenie attended and graduated from Colorado State University, Fort Collins, with a Bachelor of Fine Arts in metalsmithing and a minor in ceramics in 1984. In 1988 he returned to IAIA as a Professor of Contemporary Ceramics. An important part of the artist's maturation came from his teaching experience, which helped him to better understand and reinforce techniques in order that he could teach them to other people. Like many of his peers, he draws inspiration and knowledge from a strong, established cultural tradition. Utilizing this as both source and foundation, Duwyenie has taken traditional Hopi pottery practices and adapted new techniques to create pieces that are less functional and more decorative. Duwyenie's pieces are clearly dictated by the clay sources. He gathers clay in the traditional manner and follows traditional preparation techniques. He uses the firing process as a tool of refinement. In this stage, some of his pieces take on a drastic change. For instance, yellow clay brought in from Hopi may fire red. His work is also influenced by historic pots found at Sikatki, a Hopi word for yellow house.

Duwyenie's career features three specific series of work in both clay and jewelry. His *Earth in Balance* series begun in 1983 was inspired by the Hopi legend of Gatayo, a huge serpent that lives beneath the Earth and is held in check by the twin grandsons of the great Spiderwoman. He worked at this particular series for a number of years using the same motif and design elements, with only a minor degree of experimentation in the firing process. The finished pieces feature a wavy line on the surface representing Gayato and an asymmetrical rim representing the Earth.

These pieces were followed by some two-dimensional work and sculptures that were part of his *Clouds* series. One piece, *Cloud Stone*, now in the collection at the Denver Art Museum, is an excellent example of Duwyenie's integration of jewelry into his pottery pieces. Made out of alabaster and copper, the piece stands about three-and-a-half feet high and is primarily composed of 400 pounds of black-and-white alabaster coarsely textured on all sides except for one. The odd side is polished and features a zig zag design made out of copper, fashioned after abstract patterns of clouds from the Hopi people. The brown copper is capped off on both ends with white copper made out of tubing. Highly phallic in appearance, *Cloud Stone* is meant to represent the Hopi people's belief in the maleness of the upper atmosphere.

Duwyenie continues working on pottery and jewelry in the *Shifting Sands* series, where he draws from nature as an inspiration. The clay works follow the female aspects of the universe. The pottery forms are egg-shaped, fashioned on the form of a pregnant woman. In other recent works Duwyenie continues to introduce and rework ancient designs, maintaining the integrity of the designs while innovatively incorporating them in his own modern pieces.

—C. J. Laframboise

EDENSHAW, Charles

Variant names: Da.axiigang
Tribal affiliations: Haida
Carver

Born: Da.axiigang, Skidegate, Haida Gwaii (Queen Charlotte Islands, British Columbia), c. 1839. **Family:** Married K'woiyang, c. 1873, 11 children; the couple were baptised into Christianity in 1885, taking the names Charles and Isabella; became chief Itinsaw, c. 1885, which is most commonly anglicized as Edenshaw, and also as Edensaw and Edenso. **Died:** 1920, Old Massett, Haida Gwaii (Queen Charlotte Islands, British Columbia).

Individual Exhibitions

1967   *Arts of the Raven,* Vancouver Art Gallery, British Columbia

Selected Group Exhibitions

1927   *Exhibition of Canadian West Coast Art—Native and Modern,* National Gallery of Canada, Ottawa, Ontario

Collections

American Museum of Natural History, New York; Thomas Burke Memorial Washington State Museum, Seattle; Canadian Museum of Civilization, Hull, Quebec; Field Museum of Natural History, Chicago; Pitt Rivers Museum, Oxford, England; Royal British Columbia Museum, Victoria, British Columbia; Seattle Art Museum, Washington; University of British Columbia Museum of Anthropology, Vancouver; Vancouver City Museum, British Columbia.

Publications

On EDENSHAW: Books—*Exhibition of Canadian West Coast Art,* National Gallery of Canada, Ottawa, 1927, *Haida Carvers in Argillite,* by C. Marius Barbeau, Ottawa, 1957; *Art of the Raven,* by Wilson Duff, Bill Holm, and Bill Reid, Vancouver, 1967; "Charles Edenshaw (1839-1924)," *Great North American Indians: Profiles on Life and Leadership,* by Frederick Dockstader, New York, 1977; "Will the Real Charles Edenshaw Please Stand Up?," by Bill Holm, *The World Is as Sharp as a Knife: An Anthology in Honour of Wilson Duff,* edited by Donald Abbott, Victoria, 1981; *During My Time: Florence Edenshaw Davidson, a Haida Woman,* by Margaret B. Blackman, Seattle, 1985; "Franz Boas, John Swanton, and the New Haida Sculpture at the American Museum of Natural History," by Aldona Jonaitis in *The Early Years of Native American Art History,* edited by Janet Catherine Berlo, Seattle and Vancouver, 1992; "Hlga.S7agaa: Haida Argillite," *The Spirit Within: Northwest Coast Native Art from the John H. Hauberg Collection,* edited by

Steven C. Brown, New York and Seattle, 1995. **Articles**—"Life and Art of Charlie Edenshaw," by F.M. Appleton, *Canadian Geographic Journal,* July 1970, "Charles Edenshaw and the Creation of Human Beings," by Alan L. Hoover, *American Indian Art Magazine,* Summer 1983; "Charles Edenshaw: His Art and Audience," by Alan L. Hoover, *American Indian Art Magazine,* Summer 1995.

*   *   *

Charles Edenshaw was known by his Haida name, Da.axiigang, until 1885, when he and his wife, K'woiyang, were baptised and took names of European royalty, Charles and Isabella. At this time he was also given the chiefly name, Itinsaw, which was Anglicized as Edenshaw, by his maternal uncle, Albert Edward Edenshaw, head of the Sdaast'aas Eagle lineage. During his lifetime, Charles Edenshaw was recognized by the Haida people as being one of their best artists, and anthropologists Franz Boas and John Swanton as well as such collectors as Charles F. Newcombe, James G. Swan, and George T. Emmons sought him out as a source of art and cultural information during the late nineteenth and early twentieth centuries.

Edenshaw was born during a period when Haida culture was experiencing an economic and artistic flowering, spurred by increased wealth brought by European and Euro-American trade; he survived the devastating small pox epidemic of 1862 and later missionization and colonization by Euro-Canadians. By the time he took the chiefly name Itinsaw in 1885, potlatching had been outlawed in Canada and much of the social and ceremonial life that had fostered the production of Haida art in the past had been forbidden and suppressed by missionaries and government agents. Edenshaw, along with a handful of other Haida artists, was able to preserve haida culture and traditions through work made for sale to outsiders, carving wooden and argillite (black stone) bowls, chests, model poles and houses, wooden frontlets and masks, engraving silver jewelry and cane ferules with carved ivory handles, and painting basketry objects made by his wife, Isabella. Though much of what he produced was made for sale to outsiders, in his youth he had made full-sized totem poles and house posts, and he continued to make functional settees, cradles and jewelry for Haida people and his own family's use. Though totem poles were no longer raised after the 1880s, Edenshaw designed crest images for Christian tombstones, which replaced memorial totem poles.

Little is known of his early artwork, though it is believed that Edenshaw started carving argillite and silver in Skidegate when he was about fourteen. When he came of age in the late 1850s, he moved to Kung and later to Massett to live with his maternal uncle, Albert Edenshaw, as was the Haida custom. During the 1860s and 70s, he was probably trained as a totem pole carver by Albert Edenshaw. At least three poles from Skidegate have been attributed to him. By the time Charles and Isabella moved to Massett in the 1880s, Edenshaw's art style was fully developed, and he was earning his entire income from his art, not needing to supplement it like other Haida artists though fishing and hunting. Edenshaw's personal style is renowned for its originality and innovative narrative forms and acclaimed as well for its adherence to the sophisticated formline design principles that characterize Haida art. His model poles and houses documented historical houses and family crest poles that identified the lineage owner, while his argillite platters often illustrated elaborate narratives from the Raven origin stories, the most important legends of the Haida people.

Exhibition of the Canadian West Coast Art, Native and Modern, mounted by the National Gallery of Canada in 1927, seven years after Edenshaw's death, was the first to show his work as "fine art" along with the work of other Canadian artists, including Emily Carr, Paul Kane, and A.Y. Jackson. However, the small catalog for this exhibit doesn't attribute the individual pieces by Haida artists, but lists only "No. 112, Slate Carvings," and the text reports, "many of the best pieces of this kind are the work of the famous Haida chief, Edenshaw." Since none of Edenshaw's carvings were signed by him, the attribution of his work has been based on a few well documented collections, such as Swanton's at the American Museum of Natural History, by stylistic comparison and speculation. This, along with the fame of the Edenshaw name, has resulted in many pieces being attributed to Charles Edenshaw over the years that were actually made by other artists.

During the mid-twentieth century, Marius Barbeau was principally responsible for bringing argillite carving to the attention of the outside world through his publications, *Haida Carvers* and *Haida Masks.* These books are important for being the first to record the biographies of Haida artists and identify individual Haida artists with their work at a time when no other serious scholars were doing so. Unfortunately, many of Baribeau's attributions, particularly those for Charles Edenshaw, are incorrect. More recently much work has been done to clarify the record, starting with the 1967 exhibit, *Arts of the Raven,* held at the Vancouver Art Gallery, which featured an entire gallery (66 objects) devoted to the work of Charles Edenshaw. Bill Holm's *Will the Real Charles Edenshaw Please Stand Up?,* the most detailed analysis of Charles Edenshaw's art to date, was the first attempt to analyze a progression in Edenshaw's style through time, and also to differentiate it from several other Haida artists whose work had been confused with his, such as John Robson, Tom Price, John Cross, and Gwaitehl.

Charles Edenshaw's eyesight and health declined after 1910, and his art production probably tapered off during the last ten years of his life, although he is said to have carved until his death. His career remains remarkable for the quality and range of objects produced over his lifetime, as well as its stylistic and narrative innovation that expanded traditional Haida style beyond its previous boundaries. Charles Edenshaw's work continues to inspire his descendants, including Robert and Reg Davidson, his great-grandsons, and Jim Hart, his great-great grandson.

—Robin K. Wright

EMERAK, Mark

Tribal affiliations: Inuit
Printmaker

Born: Prince Albert Peninsula, Northwest Territories, Canada, 1901.
Career: Hunter, fisherman, artist. **Died:** 23 March 1983.

Selected Group Exhibitions

1968 Holman Prints (annual collection)
1977 *The Inuit Print/L'estampe inuit,* National Museum of Man, Ottawa (traveled through 1982)
1978 *Inuit Games and Contests: The Clifford E. Lee Collection of Prints,* University of Alberta, Edmonton
   Polar Vision: Canadian Eskimo Graphics, Jerusalem Artists' House Museum, Jerusalem
1980 *The Inuit Amautik: I Like My Hood to Be Full,* Winnipeg Art Gallery
1981 *The Moveable Feast,* Arts and Learning Services Foundation, Minneapolis (traveled through 1983)
1982 *The Beat of the Drum,* Arctic Circle, Los Angeles
1983 *The Way We Were—Traditional Eskimo Life,* Snow Goose Associates, Seattle, Washington
1984 *The Story Tellers of Holman Island: A Retrospective Exhibition of Rare Stonecut Prints from 1968-1979,* Arctic Circle, Los Angeles
   50 Inuit Prints, Simpson's, Toronto
   Visions of Rare Spirit: 20 Years of Holman Prints, Port Colborne Libray, Ontario
   Arctic Vision: Art of the Canadian Inuit, Department of Indian Affairs and Northern Development and Canadian Arctic Producers, Ottawa (traveled through 1986)
1985 *Chisel and Brush/Le ciseau et la brosse,* Department of Indian Affairs and Northern Development, Ottawa (traveled through 1987)
1986 *Inuit Graphics through the Years: Rare Prints from the Arctic,* Arctic Artistry, Scarsdale, New York
1987 *Inuit Graphics from the Past,* Arctic Artistry, Scarsdale, New York
   1987 Eskimo Art, Franz Bader Gallery, Washington, D.C.
   Contemporary Inuit Drawings, Macdonald Stewart Art Centre, Guelph, Ontario
1988 *In the Shadow of the Sun: Contemporary Indian and Inuit Art in Canada,* Canadian Museum of Civilization, Ottawa (traveling)
1990 *Arctic Mirror,* Canadian Museum of Civilization, Hull, Quebec
1992 *Inuit Art on the Mezzanine: New Acquisitions,* Winnipeg Art Gallery
   Inuit Art: Drawings and Recent Sculpture, National Gallery of Canada, Ottawa
1993 *The Prints Never Seen: Holman, 1977-1987,* Albers Gallery of Inuit Art, San Francisco
   Contemporary Inuit Drawings, Muscarelle Museum of Art, Williamsburg, Virginia
1994 *Arctic Spirit: 35 Years of Canadian Inuit Art,* Frye Art Museum, Seattle
1995 *Exhibition of Inuit Art,* Harbourfront Centre, Toronto
1996 *Works on Paper from the Permanent Collection of Inuit Art,* Canadian Guild of Craft Quebec, Montreal
   Exhibition of Inuit Art, Glenhyrst Art Gallery, Brantford, Ontario

Collections

Canadian Guild of Crafts Quebec, Montreal; Canadian Museum of Civilization, Hull, Quebec; Glenbow Museum, Calgary, Alberta;

Inuit Cultural Institute, Rankin Inlet, Northwest Territories; Clifford E. Lee Collection, University of Alberta, Edmonton, Alberta; McMichael Canadian Art Collection, Kleinberg, Ontario; Musée des Beaux Arts de Montreal; National Gallery of Canada, Ottawa; Prince of Wales Northern Heritage Centre, Yellowknife, Northwest Territories; University of Alberta, Edmonton; Winnipeg Art Gallery.

Publications

On EMERAK: Books—*Art of the Eskimo: Prints,* edited by Ernst Roch, Toronto, 1974; *John Kavik/Mark Emerak,* Winnipeg, 1981; *Arctic Vision: Art of the Canadian Inuit* by Barbara Lipton, Ottawa, 1984; *Contemporary Inuit Drawings* by Marion E. Jackson, Guelph, Ontario 1987; *Kalvak/Emerak Memorial Catalog* by Bernadette Driscoll, Holman, N.W.T., 1987; *Contemporary Inuit Drawings: The Gift Collection of Frederick and Lucy S. Herman,* Williamsburg, 1993. **Articles**—"Christianity and Inuit Art" by Jean Blodgett, *The Beaver,* Autumn, 1984; "Maps as Metaphor: One Hundred Years of Inuit Cartography" by Robin McGrath, *Inuit Art Quarterly,* Spring 1988; "Drawing and Printmaking at Holman" by Janet Catherine Berlo, *Inuit Art Quarterly,* Fall 1995.

*   *   *

For most of his life on Victoria Island in Canada's Northwest Territories, Emerak led a traditional, nomadic existence, seal hunting on the sea ice in winter, fishing and polar bear hunting in the spring, and caribou hunting in the late summer and autumn. Only in his later years did he settle in the village of Holman on Victoria Island and begin a career as an artist, which ultimately brought him international acclaim. Holman is one of several communities in the Canadian arctic (and the only one in the Western arctic) with a print-making program. During most years since 1966, Holman has published its own catalog of limited-edition prints.

Like fellow local artist Helen Kalvak, Emerak began to draw under the encouragement of Father Henri Tardy, a French missionary who did much to encourage the development of the art cooperative at Holman. The first appearance of Emerak's work in the Holman corpus of prints was in 1968, with his stonecut print, *Women's Clothes.* The irregular angles of the stone echo the angular lines of the traditional skin garments Emerak has so deftly depicted.

Themes of acculturation are prominent in two of his best-known prints, *First White Man's Ship* (1982) and *Simon of Cyrene* (1983). Yet non-Inuit themes actually are rare in Emerak's work. Fewer than a half-dozen of the 900 Emerak pieces in the Inuit drawing archive at the Holman Eskimo Co-operative depict southern implements or subjects—a pair of scissors or a pocket watch makes an occasional appearance.

Hunting Caribou When I Was Young (1980-81) is a popular Emerak lithograph quite characteristic of his main thematic concerns. In this print, the litho crayon accurately captures the tentative line of this elderly artist, for whom subject matter was always more important than style. At the bottom of the image, three figures hunt caribou with bows and arrows. Each reaches the mark. Three hulking polar bears look on, each vividly rendered in bright yellow and enclosed in an oval. This work displays the mixing of spatial perspectives that is common in Inuit drawings done by artists of Emerak's generation. As he worked, the artist turned the paper to draw the hunters at right angles to their prey. Two of the

hunters are male. The third, a female, holds a baby in the hood of her large parka (many Inuit women are hunters). The absence of groundline and the vast expanse of unmarked white paper read as a snowy landscape.

In numerous other drawings of the late 1960s and 1970s, Emerak reenacts Copper Inuit hunting practices. Incidents of butchering caribou, the ceremonial partitioning of meat after a successful hunt, and the harpooning of seals are all given new life through the pencil of this skilled hunter. His work provides late twentieth-century Inuit and non-Inuit people a window into the demanding way of life lived by Inuit hunters for countless generations before the mid-twentieth century.

—Janet Catherine Berlo

FEDDERSEN, Joe

Tribal affiliations: Colville; Okanagan
Sculptor, mask maker, and photographer

Born: Omak, Washington, 1953. **Education:** Wenatchee Valley College, Washington, 1979; University of Washington, Seattle, B.F.A. in printmaking, 1983; University of Wisconsin, Madison, M.F.A., 1989. **Career:** Assisted in the teaching of printmaking, Institute of Alaska Native Arts, University of Alaska, Fairbanks, and Mount Hood Community College, Portland; art instructor, Evergreen State College, 1989- ; curator, consultant, and juror; member, board of directors, Colville Confederated Tribal Arts and Humanities Board.

Individual Exhibitions

1984   Sacred Circle Gallery, Seattle
1985   Sacred Circle Gallery, Seattle
1986   C. N. Gorman Museum, University of California, Davis
1987   *Photographs: Joe Feddersen,* Y Galleria Posada, Sacramento, California
       Dazzlers, Elizabeth Leach Gallery, Portland, Oregon
1988   *Computer Graphics,* Lynn McAllister Gallery, Seattle
       Works on Paper, American Indian Contemporary Arts, San Francisco
       Fractured Spaces, Lynn McAllister Gallery
1990   Elizabeth Leach Gallery, Portland, Oregon
1993   Elizabeth Leach Gallery, Portland, Oregon
       Evergreen Galleries, Evergreen State College, Olympia, Washington
1994   *Archives,* (with Elizabeth Woody) Tula Foundation, Atlanta, Georgia

Selected Group Exhibitions

1982   *Group Show,* Galerie AKMAK, Berlin
       Sacred Circle Gallery, Seattle
       Modern Artists in a Rural Community, W. V. C., Wenatchee, Washington
1983   Sacred Circle Gallery, Seattle
       Contemporary Native American Art, University of Oklahoma at Stillwater (traveled through 1985)

1984 *No Beads, No Trinkets,* Palais des Nations, Geneva, Switzerland

Native American Artists—California and the West Coast, Mission Cultural Center, San Francisco

Landscape, Landbase, Environment, New York

Native American Aesthetics, Marilyn Butler Gallery, Santa Fe

Ancient Visions in Contemporary Art, Willamette University, Salem, Oregon

Contemporary Native Art, Touchstone Gallery, Spokane, Washington

Signale Indianischer Kunstler, Gallerie AKMAK, Berlin, Germany (traveled)

1985 *The Photograph and the American Indian,* Princeton University, Princeton, New Jersey

Beyond Blue Mountains, Seattle Center

New Ideas from Old Traditions: Contemporary Native Art, Yellowstone Art Center, Billings, Montana

Washington/Oregon Artists, American Indian Contemporary Arts, San Francisco

Pacific State Print and Drawing Exhibition, Hilo, Hawaii

1986 *Providence Hospital Print Project, Visions of Alaska,* Anchorage, Alaska

Visage Transcended: Contemporary Native American Masks, American Indian Contemporary Arts, San Francisco (traveled)

New Directions/Northwest, Portland Art Museum, Portland, Oregon (traveled through 1988)

1987 *Lowe/Feddersen,* Wright Museum, Beloit, Illinois

Third Biennial, Heard Museum, Phoenix

Traditions in a New Age, Museum of the Rockies, Bozeman, Montana

Our Contemporary Visions, Stremmel Galleries, Reno, Nevada

Contemporary Native American Photography, Atlatl, Phoenix, Arizona (traveled through 1989)

1988 *Feddersen/Beck,* Stemmel Gallery, Reno, Nevada

Prints, American Indian Community House, New York

1989 *Tremblay, Parsons, Feddersen,* Evergreen State College, Olympia, Washington

Native Art, Multi-Cultural Center, Cambridge, Massachusetts

Alumni/Faculty Exhibit, Gallery '76, Wenatchee, Washington

Contemporary Native Art, N.A.U. Art Gallery, Flagstaff, Arizona

Prints, American Indian Contemporary Arts, San Francisco

Introductions, Montana Indian Art and Culture Association (traveled through 1991)

1990 *Artist Made Prints,* Jan Cicero Gallery, Chicago

Governors Invitational Exhibition, Capital Museum, Olympia, Washington

Contemporary Native Art, Maryhill Museum, Maryhill, Washington

Eleven Stories, Sacred Circle Gallery, Seattle

Pan American Exhibition, Wind Horse Gallery, Seattle

We Are Part of the Earth: Contemporary Works on Paper, Centro Cultural De La Raza, San Diego

Native Proof, American Indian Community House, New York

1991 *Without Boundaries,* Jan Cicero Gallery, Chicago

Living Room Pow Wow, Helio Gallery, New York

10th Anniversary Show, Elizabeth Leach Gallery, Portland, Oregon

Works on Paper, N.A.U., Flagstaff, Arizona

Our Land/ Ourselves, University Art Gallery, State University of New York at Albany

1992 *Shamans, Saints, Heroes, and King/Contemporary Icons,* Gallery, Bend, Oregon

Latent Image, Seattle Central Community College

Contemporary Northwest Native American Art, Columbia Art Gallery, Hood River, Oregon

We, the Human Beings/27 Contemporary Native American Artists, College of Wooster Art Museum, Wooster, Ohio

The Sublumoc/ Columbus Show (with Elizabeth Woody) organized by Atlatl, Phoenix, Arizona (traveled)

1993 *For the Seventh Generation* (with Elizabeth Woody), Art in General, New York

The Spirit of Native America, US Information Agency Arts American Program Latin American Tour

Northwest Native American and First Nations People's Art, Western Gallery, Western Washington University, Bellingham

Rhythms of Vision, Renshaw Gallery, Linfield College, McMinnville, Oregon

Annual National Invitational Drawing Exhibition, Eppink Art Gallery, Emporia, Kansas

1994 *Artist Handmade Books* (with Elizabeth Woody), American Indian Community House, New York

Artists Who Are Indian, Denver Art Museum, Denver, Colorado

Visions, American Indian Contemporary Arts, San Francisco (traveled through 1997)

1995 *La Jeune Gravure Contemporaine,* Salle de Fête de la Marie du Vieme, Paris

Native Survival, American Indian Community House, New York

The Land, Tacoma Art Museum, Washington

Landscape, Jan Cicero Gallery, Chicago

1996 *Native Streams,* Jan Cicero Gallery, Chicago (traveling)

The West Seattle Trail (with Quick-To-See-Smith and Don Fels), Public Art, Seattle

Collections

Department of Interior, Indian Arts and Crafts Board, Washington, D.C.; Kings County Art Commission, Seattle, Washington; MicroSoft Collection, Heywood, Washington; Portland Art Museum, Oregon; Seattle Art Museum, Washington; University of Hawaii, Hilo; Washington State Art Commission, Olympia.

Publications

On FEDDERSEN: Books—*Maske Und Regenbild, Moderne Indianerkunst in der Galerie Akmak,* exhibition catalog by Rolf Brokschmidt, Gallery AKMAK, Berlin, 1982; *Signale, Indianischer Kunstler,* exhibition catalog by Katrina Hartje, Galerie AKMAK, Berlin, 1984; *Visions of Alaska,* exhibition catalog, Providence Hospital, Anchorage, Alaska, 1986; *Portfolio: Eleven Indian Artists,* American Indian Contemporary Arts, San Francisco, 1986; *Mixed*

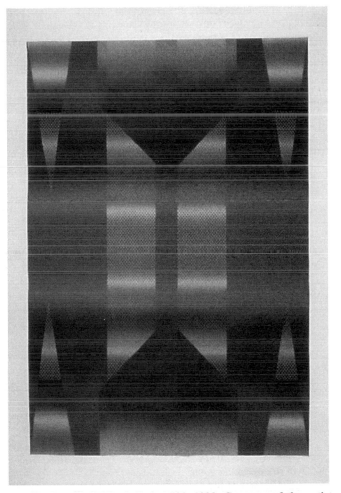

Joe Fedderson: *Indian Blanket #20,* 1993. Courtesy of the artist.

Blessings: New Art in a Multi-Cultural Media by Lucy R. Lippard, New York, 1990; *Contemporary Native American Art* by David Penney and George Longfish, Seattle, 1994. **Articles**—"Indian Artists: Imagery is Abstract, Powerful" by D. Tarzan, *Seattle Times,* 10 September 1983; "Indian Photography, Going Out Guide," *New York Times,* 26 April 1984; "Photographing Ourselves," *Artspace,* Fall 1985; "Elegant Expressionism" by Victoria Dalkey, *Sacramento Bee,* 31 May 1987; "Continuing the Dialogue" by Lucia Enriquez, *Reflex,* November/December 1990; "Joe Fedderson," *Northwest Art and Artists,* May/June 1991; "Contested Ground" by W. Jackson Rushing, *New Art Examiner,* November 1991; "Native American Art in the Postmodern Era" by Kay WalkingStick, *Art Journal,* Fall 1992; "Matched Media" by Lois Allan, *Art Week,* 4 October 1993; "Words of Humor, Words of Rage" by Victoria Josslin, *Reflex,* November/December 1993.

*   *   *

The prints and mixed media of Colville/Okanagan artist Joe Fedderson are wrought with subtle tension. Unified yet inherently incomplete, Fedderson's work is about *process,* and simultaneously engages the viewer in the dissolution and materialization of form and energy. While individual pieces stand on their own, his preference for working in a series format allows him to proceed organically by oscillating between coherence and gradual evolution.

Fedderson's most widely known suite of prints, *Rainscapes,* of the mid 1980s, consist of dense yet transparent abstractions that bespeak the elemental forces of nature. In these prints Fedderson creates a rich fusion of color and form through the use of multiple printing plates. This is further enhanced by the addition of acrylic paint and reflective materials such as staples, pins, and mirrors. Despite an emphasis on the planar surface of these images, at a distance tactility dissolves in the luminous depths that both elude and engulf the viewer. Beyond the purely visual, his *Rainscapes* induce a synaesthetic response and are known to invoke the memory of a cool drench on ones skin, the smell of rain, as well as the crisp and improvisational sounds of jazz music.

For Fedderson the creation of art is part of the greater process of self-discovery in relation to his environment. A silhouetted figure commonly occurring in his work that is, at once, integrated within yet distinct from the richly woven patterns. While the interpenetration of geometric and figurative is a visual analogy between artist/context, this reoccurring shadow also serves as an extension of the viewer and invites intimate interaction with the work itself. According to the artist, his goal is "to create a dialogue that conveys statements originating from personal experiences."

While his work is not superficially loaded with ethnic signifiers, he is greatly inspired by Native American artistic traditions and cultural values. In his *Blanket Series* (early 1990s), for example, Fedderson created richly colored monotypes based on Plains Indian and Pendelton blanket designs. The hard-edged abstraction of these prints is offset by the bands of color that gradually swell and diminish in intensity and hue. Attracted to a Northwest coast fishing story in which "one is able to gain strength from their traditions to overcome outside influences," Fedderson created the relief print, *Grandmother's Mountain* (1992). At times native influences are so fully embedded within the images they are almost imperceptible. Images such as *Gold Web,* which is about the accumulation of material wealth, contains a chevron pattern based on indigenous basketry designs.

Fedderson has recently expanded his artistic range to encompass more politically strident works. In collaboration with the poet/artist Elizabeth Woody, Fedderson created *Histories Are Open to Interpretation* for the Submuloc Wohs/Columbus Show (1992), which includes two poems composed by Woody. While "Sun," printed in bold black font, is suspended on a bier-like transparent screen, "Gold" is submerged in a pool of water underneath. Strategic placement of light casts shadows of the words from above onto the surface of the water below. Despite the radically different materials and message, Fedderson's aesthetic is apparent in the multiple layers (creating a clever yet somber metaphor for the term "subtext"), and the interplay of light, depth and translucence. Again, attention is paid to the viewer as participant, and it is the conceptually rich yet physically sparse nature of this piece that invites personal contemplation.

Fedderson's latest series, *Plateau Geometrics* (1996), consists of hard-edged abstractions in which he integrates his immediate experience of natural and cultural elements. While the grid-like pattern upon which these images are based is derived from traditional plateau bags, the textures and colors allude to the land, light, and seasons of the Northwest. In contrast to his earlier "melodic" works, this series is indicative of his maturing *poetic* vision.

While both methodical and steady in his approach to art making, Fedderson is also highly experimental and innovative and has ventured into sculpting, mask-making, and photography. Due to this, some have noted with slight dismay the incongruity of his oeuvre.

However, rather than cling to a banal concept of consistency, Feddersen has accepted a more difficult pursuit, that of making imagery that reflects his growth and struggles as a contemporary artist.

—Kristin Potter

FIELDS, Anita

Tribal affiliations: Osage; Creek
Ceramist, sculptor, and mixed media artist

Born: 1951. **Education:** Northeastern Oklahoma State University, 1980; Oklahoma State University, B.F.A., 1991. **Awards:** Best of Division/Diversified Art Forms, 1994, Red Earth Festival.

Selected Group Exhibitions

1988   *Earth, Hands and Life,* Heard Museum, Phoenix
1990   *Indian Summer,* Bartlesville, Oklahoma
        Oklahoma Indian Market, Okmulgee, Oklahoma
        Osage Museum, Pawhuska, Oklahoma
        Tsa-La-Gi Cherokee Cultural Center, Tahlequah, Oklahoma
1991   *Red Earth,* Oklahoma City, Oklahoma
        Lawrence Indian Art Show, Lawrence, Kansas
        Museum of Anthropology, University of Kansas, Lawrence
1992   Indian Market, Sante Fe
        United States Ambassador's Show, Rabat, Morocco
1993   Institute of American Indian Arts, Sante Fe
1994   Gentle Tzi-Shu Gallery, Pawhuska, Oklahoma
        Henry Roan Horse Gallery, Sante Fe, New Mexico, and Tahlequah, Oklahoma
        Gardiner Art Gallery, Oklahoma State University, Stillwater
1995   Galleria, Norman, Oklahoma
        Turtle Island Gallery, Bethesda, Maryland

Collections

Institute of American Indian Arts Museum, Sante Fe; Southern Plains Museum, Anadarko, Oklahoma.

Publications

On FIELDS: Book—*Sisters of the Earth: Contemporary Native American Ceramics,* Bush Barn Art Center, Salem, Oregon. **Article**—"Dancing Clay" by Diane Berna-Heath, *Southwest Art,* March 1994.

*   *   *

Anita Fields uses dresses, boxes, feminine figures and window structures to convey her attitude about being a Native American woman today. Empty dress forms act as metaphors reflecting relationships that shape and direct our individual and communal identities. Clothing as symbols of status and affiliation stand alone, figureless in Fields' work. Fields is able to create motion with the flowing ceramic garments—capturing moments in larger narratives. The simplicity and elegance of the clothing forms are somewhat nostalgic while also relaying a sense of pride. *Plains Dress,* from 1994, appears to capture a woman dancing. The viewer is left to construct the identity of the wearer. There is a dynamic quality in the posturing of the dress that also conveys a sense of timelessness—possibly representing someone from a pow-wow today or from a dance or ceremony from years earlier. Fields' works suggest a connection and continuity with the past—with her heritage. This connection also reflects an interest in exploring identity and the complexity of Native women's identity in the twentieth century.

Her most recent work has focused on medium-sized slab and coil constructed forms that are narrative in nature. She describes these pieces as "employing symbolic elements that reflect human emotions and sensibilities." *Turtle Woman's Purse,* from 1994, illustrates her interest in connecting narrative and issues of identity. A slab constructed clay basket holds personal items that would have belonged to a woman. The combination and arrangement of the objects in the basket suggest the narrative. The viewer is challenged to "create the story"—solve the mystery of the person who owned these objects. As the title suggests, this is Turtle Woman's purse, with each object acting as a piece of the puzzle giving the viewer another glimpse at the larger picture. A mirror and several pouches are just some of the objects in the purse. A turtle amulet, made to hold an infant's umbilical cord, symbolizes Turtle Woman's connection to her family and community as well spiritual protection.

Ultimately, Fields feels her work relates "how we communicate with ourselves and the world around us. In my work I honor spiritual strength, courage and survival of Native American women."

The field of sculpture has traditionally been dominated by men. Consequently, Fields' choice to create ceramic sculpture attests to her own strength and courage. Ceramics or pottery has traditionally been seen as part of women's art production in Native communities. So on another level, Fields' work is challenging viewers to rethink the categories and roles they have previously assigned to Native American women artists.

—Jennifer C. Vigil

FOLWELL, Jody

Tribal affiliations: Santa Clara Pueblo
Potter

Born: Espanola, Santa Clara Pueblo, New Mexico, 4 August 1942. **Education:** Taught how to make traditional Santa Clara pottery as a child by her mother, Rose Naranjo; College of Santa Fe; University of New Mexico, B.A. and M.A. **Career:** Educator, early 1960s through mid 1970s; lecturer; full-time potter beginning 1974. **Awards:** Numerous, in ceramics, including First Prize, Heard Museum Guild Show, 1979, and Best of Show, Santa Fe Indian Market, 1985.

Selected Group Exhibitions

1981   *American Indian Art in the 1980s,* Native American Center for the Living Arts, Niagara Falls, New York

1987   *Eight Indian Artists, II*, Southwest Museum, Los Angeles

Collections

Heard Museum, Phoenix, Arizona.

Publications

On FOLWELL: Books—*Beyond Tradition: Contemporary American Indian Art and Its Evolution*, by Jerry and Lois Jacka, Flagstaff, 1988. **Articles**—"Courage: Her Greatest Asset," by Barbara Perlman, *Arizona Arts and Lifestyle*, Summer, 1980; "Jody Folwell, Potter," by Barbara Cortright, *Artspace*, Summer, 1982; "The Evolution of a Craft Tradition," by Grace Lichtenstein, *Ms. Magazine*, April 1983; "Eight Artists II: Contemporary Indian Art at the Southwest Museum," by Suzanne Kenagy, *American Indian Art Magazine*, Winter 1987; "Expressionist Pottery from Native America," by Ron McCoy, *Southwest Profile*, November-January, 1991-92; "Jody Folwell," by Sally Eauclaire, *Southwest Art*, August 1992. **Film**—"Jody Folwell," *American Indian Artists II*, Public Broadcasting System, 1992.

*   *   *

Jody Folwell comes from a leading family of Santa Clara potters known for their innovation. Her mother, Rose Naranjo, taught Folwell how to make traditional Santa Clara pottery as a child. Although she uses traditional materials and techniques, Folwell's work is a departure from the blackware pottery characteristic of Santa Clara Pueblo. Folwell's imagery is innovative and often controversial, as her pots become a canvas on which she incises and carves images that address social and political issues. Her work has a strong narrative quality that gives depth and power to her imagery.

Folwell embraces the limitless potential of pottery, while addressing non-traditional themes, including the equal rights amendment, premenstrual stress, and marriage difficulties. *Flight of the Dog*, where Folwell refers to rape, represents such concerns. This particular piece references an encounter Folwell had with two drunken men who tried to chase her as she jogged one day through the arroyos near Santa Clara. Her innovation expands beyond imagery to the very form of her pottery. She has introduced many unusual shapes in her work, some of which she leaves plain while others are embellished with her provocative imagery.

Folwell does not like to be thought of as a craftsperson, believing that skills can be perfected but that creativity cannot. She does not view her work aesthetically, but rather in terms of how it challenges the viewer to explore the issues woven into the imagery. To this end, she continually experiments with new shapes, styles and colors. Part of her effort to challenge herself and her work has led her to collaborate with artists such as Bob Haozous.

Initially, Folwell's work was not readily accepted. It did not fit the traditional image of southwestern pottery. As a result of a series of successful exhibitions and awards from juried shows such as Santa Fe Indian Market, Folwell has gained recognition as one of the leading contemporary Native American potters. Continuity and tradition are maintained as she encourages and passes on her skills to her daughter Polly Rose.

—Jennifer C. Vigil

FONSECA, Harry

Tribal affiliations: Maidu
Painter and mixed media artist

Born: Sacramento, California, 5 January 1946, of Maidu, Hawaiian and Portugese descent. **Education:** Studied at Sacramento City College and California State University, Sacramento. **Career:** Professional artist and lecturer. **Awards:** Best of Show Award, *Indian Art Now*, Wheelwright Museum, 1979; fellowship, Southwestern Association on Indian Affairs, 1980; board member, Wheelwright Museum, 1993-95.

Individual Exhibitions

1976   *Paintings by Harry Fonseca*, Museum of the Plains Indian, Browning, Montana
1977   *So That's the Beginning*, Quail Plume Studio, Sacramento, California
1978   *The Maidu Creation Story*, Gorman Museum, University of California, Davis
1980   *Two Views of California: Frank Day and Harry Fonseca*, Heard Museum, Phoenix
1983   *In Search of Coyote: The Paintings and Works on Paper by Harry Fonseca*, Wheelwright Museum, Santa Fe
1984   *Swan Lake*, October Art, New York
1986   *Coyote: A Myth in the Making*, National Museum of Natural History, Smithsonian Institution, Washington, D.C.
1987   *Coyote Comes to Market Street*, American Indian Contemporary Arts, San Francisco
        Coyote's Wild and Woolly West, Elaine Horwitch Gallery, Santa Fe
1989   *Stone Poems: New Paintings by Harry Fonseca*, Southwest Museum, Los Angeles
1990   *Coyote Steps Out*, Santa Barbara Museum of Natural History
        Harry Fonseca: New Paintings, Meridian Gallery, San Francisco
1991   *Stone Poems: Recent Paintings by Harry Fonseca*, American Indian Community House Gallery, New York
1992   *The Discovery of Gold and Souls in California*, Crocker Art Museum, Sacramento
        Galerie Calumet, Heidelberg, Germany
        A Gift from California: The Maidu Creation Story, Meridian Gallery, San Francisco
1993   *Stone Poems*, East Hawaii Cultural Center Gallery, Hilo
1996   Cline LewAllen Contemporary, Santa Fe
        Earth, Wind, and Fire, Wheelwright Museum, Santa Fe
1997   Galerie Calumet, Heidelberg, Germany

Selected Group Exhibitions

1982   *Night of the First Americans*, John F. Kennedy Center for the Performing Arts, Washington, D.C.
1985   *The Extension of Tradition*, Crocker Art Museum, Sacramento
1986   *Eight Artists*, Southwest Museum, Los Angeles
1989   *An Exhibition of Contemporary Native American Art*, Northern Arizona University Art Gallery, Flagstaff
1990   *Artifacts for the Seventh Generation*, American Indian Contemporary Arts, San Francisco, California

Harry Fonseca in his studio. Courtesy of the artist.

Art Hamburg, Hamburg, Germany

1991   *Portfolio III: Ten Native American Artists*, American Indian Contemporary Arts, San Francisco

Our Land/Ourselves, University Art Gallery, State University of New York, Albany

Shared Visions, Heard Museum, Phoenix

1992   *We, the Human Beings*, College of Wooster Art Museum, Wooster, Ohio

Decolonizing the Mind: End of a 500-Year Era, Center for Contemporary Art, Seattle

The Spiritual World of the Native American, Oguni Exhibition Hall, Oguni, Japan

Photographs of Edward S. Curtis and Five Contemporary Native American Artists, Shizuoka City Gallery, Japan

A Collection of Contemporary American Indian Paintings, Amerika Haus Frankfurt, Frankfurt, Germany

The Alcove Show, Museum of Fine Arts, Santa Fe

1993   *Visions and Voices: Contemporary Native American Artists*, Museums at Blackhawk, University of California, Danville

The Spirit of Native America, American Indian Contemporary Arts, San Francisco

1995   *Indian Humor*, American Indian Contemporary Arts, San Francisco

Cultural Connections, Austral Gallery, St. Louis, Missouri

Collections

California State Indian Museum, Sacramento, California; Crocker Art Museum, Sacramento, California; Heard Museum, Phoenix, Arizona; Hood Museum, Dartmouth College, Hanover, New Hampshire; Linden Museum, Stuttgart, Germany; Monterrey Fine Arts Museum, Monterrey, California; Museum Fur Volkerkunde, Berlin; Museum of New Mexico, Albuquerque; Museum of Fine Arts, Albuquerque; Oguni Museum, Oguni, Japan; University Art Museum, Berkeley, California; Washington State Arts Museum, Olympia; Wheelwright Museum, Santa Fe.

Publications

By FONSECA: Articles—"Artist's Statement," *Portfolio III*, American Indian Contemporary Arts, San Francisco, California, 1991; "Artist's Statement," *We, The Human Beings*, College of Wooster Art Museum, Wooster, Ohio, 1992; "Artist's Statement,"

The Spirit of Native America, American Indian Contemporary Arts, San Francisco, California, 1993; "Artist's Statement," *Indian Humor,* American Indian Contemporary Arts, San Francisco, California, 1995.

On FONSECA: Books—*Coyote: A Myth in the Making* by Margaret Archuleta, National History Museum Foundation, Washington, D.C., 1986; *Earth, Wind, and Fire,* Wheelwright Museum, Santa Fe, 1996. **Articles**—"Harry Fonseca" in *The Sweet Grass Lives On* by Jamake Highwater, New York: Lippincott and Crowell, 1980; "Harry Fonseca" in *The Extension of Tradition* edited by Frank LaPena and Janice Driesbach, Crocker Art Museum, Sacramento, 1985; "Modern Rock Drawings: Harry Fonseca Paintings at Southwest Museum" by Nancy Ann Jones, *Artweek* 20, No. 42, 14 December 1989; "Coyote: An Interview with Harry Fonseca" with Lorenzo Baca, *News from Native California* 4, No. 3, Spring 1990; "Harry Fonseca" by Rick Hill in *Half-Indian, Half-Artist,* Museum of Fine Arts, Santa Fe, 1992; "Choice" by Frank LaPena, *News from Native California* 7, No. 2 Spring 1992; "Harry Fonseca" by Darryl Wilson, *News from Native California* 7, No. 1, Winter 1992; "Contemporary Northern California Native American Art" by Frank LaPena, *California History* LXXI, No. 3, Fall 1992; "Giving Visual Form to Myth: Interview with Maidu Artist Harry Fonseca" with Larry Abbott, *Akwe:kon* X, No. 2, Summer 1993; "Harry Fonseca: Earth, Wind, Fire," *The Messenger,* Fall-Winter 1996-97.

*

Harry Fonseca comments:

So often our dissatisfaction runs pale to those that came before. History does not lessen our concerns and feelings, but has the potential to amplify the elegance of our struggle. Once the stones are tossed, we become part of the intertwining ripples and in that, WE ARE GLAD TO BE HERE; to embrace the wonder and movement of this miraculous mystery called living.

*   *   *

In his twenty-year career Fonseca has explored diverse imagery, from tribal myths to rock art to the figure of Saint Francis, but the one constant has been his openness to new influences and sources of inspiration. Fonseca's earliest pieces drew from his Maidu heritage, and included transformations of basketry designs and dance regalia. The creation myth of the Maidu, as recounted by his uncle, Henry Azbill, became the source of a major 1977 work, *Creation Story.* This piece visually renders the embodiment of Maidu culture, Helinmaideh, the Maidu Big Man, or God. Helinmaideh appears in the center of the canvas on a raft with Turtle. This myth continues to inspire Fonseca, as his 1991 *The Maidu Creation Story* shows. The basic imagery of this painting suggests petroglyphic symbols of the Coso Range in California, and although less figurative than the 1977 work, continues to give visual form to myth. Fonseca does not replicate his past imagery but looks for new ways of connecting to tradition through the transformation of imagery.

The *Coyote* series, which Fonseca began in 1979 (and which, after a few years' hiatus, he has started again), also deals with transformation, this time in the figure of Coyote, the trickster and transformer. Fonseca places Coyote in contemporary settings, such as San Francisco's Mission District. Coyote can become an updated and sneaker-wearing Rousseau, holding his palette on a Parisian quay (*Rousseau Revisited,* 1986), or headdress-clad and sneakered (*Coyote in Front of Studio,* 1983). Fonseca filters his vision

Harry Fonseca: *Discovery of ...* Courtesy of the artist.

of the artist and the Indian in society through Coyote. One of Fonseca's recent works in this style, *Saint Coyote* (1993), follows the unique stylization that is the hallmark of the series with the addition of angelic, flying Coyotes in leather jackets. This work is a comment on the attempt to canonize Junipero Serra, who is identified with the missionization of California. The original title of the piece was *Sorry, Father Serra, Only the Best Coyotes Will Do.* Fonseca contends that if anyone deserves sainthood it should be Coyote.

Fonseca's ongoing interest in petroglyphs and pictographs led him to develop the *Stone Poems,* an extended series of works begun in 1988 exploring the imagery of rock art, not only from California but throughout the West and Southwest, especially Utah. The *Stone Poems* are not meant to be an interpretive recording of rock images but a way of self-exploration. The canvases, some as large as 6' by 12', suggest the size and scope of petroglyphic panels *in situ.* Generally, one image anchors the piece with other images peripheral to the central image, creating a sense of depth. Fonseca has also used petroglyph imagery on his *Magic Box* pieces (1990)—shipping crates adorned with sheep, spirals, and other figures. Newer works based on the petroglyphs of flute players just outside of Santa Fe are on paper rather than canvas and are smaller and more concerned with design elements and with the apparent simplicity of the images. For example, one work depicts a figure with its hands over its head and its feet together, creating an upper and lower circle. The viewer's careful observation brings the image to life.

Fonseca's work took a more political turn in 1992 with the *Discovery of Gold and Souls in California* series. These 160 mixed-media pieces measure about 15" by 11" and offer subtle variations on the image of a black cross surrounded by gold leaf and partially covered with red oxide. The subject of this series is the genocide—physical, emotional and spiritual—of the Native people of California. The paintings concern the rise of the mission system and the later discovery of gold in Northern California. These two invasions fractured the integrity of tribal life and devastated communities throughout California.

Fonseca's responsiveness to new sources for his art led to the 1995 collaboration with Australian aboriginal artist Judy Watson. The collaboration began when Fonseca met Watson in New Zealand as part of a gathering of some eighty artists from the Pacific Rim, the Pacific Northwest, and other regions. Fonseca observed her technique of placing canvases on the grass, pouring water on them, and staining and rubbing them with dirt. They subsequently collaborated on one painting at the gathering in New Zealand. Watson then came to Santa Fe and worked with Fonseca at his studio for a day, completing some eight paintings. One of these paintings, *blue/black figure* (1995), depicts a cocoon-like form partially enveloped in white, suggesting a mysterious figure emerging or receding into space. Other collaborative images use the single figure with two snakes running the length of both sides of the canvas. Fonseca continued to develop similar paintings along this line, such as the series *In the Silence of Dusk He Began to Shed His Skin, with the Dawn He Would Never Be the Same* (1995). These works, like others of Fonseca's, are about metamorphosis and change, growth and rebirth.

The collaboration led in large measure to Fonseca's most recent work focusing on the transformative meanings of the the Maidu deer dancer, Icarus, and Saint Francis. Similar in structure and design, these works depict their subjects centered on the canvas. Fonseca focused on these specific subjects because the earlier works were, to him, somewhat too ethereal, and he desired to anchor the viewer in a more recognizable image. The deer dancers are not literal depictions, but dark silhouetted figures. The images of Icarus and Saint Francis arose from Fonseca's desire to pursue the same style of painting while focusing on a specific individual. The former were actually interpretations of rock art images in Utah, while Fonseca's interest in Saint Francis generated the latter. In these works Fonseca places Saint Francis in an active environment, but the figure is secure and solid. The suite of six paintings is about a man who had and followed a vision, not about the Catholic Church. The paintings suggest the need to test the self and to take risks and go against social and religious norms. They are about struggle and flight. From his earliest work, Fonseca has been engaged with the multi-dimensional images of cultural myth and history. From the visual representations of Maidu creation to transformations of the rock art legacy of those who came before, to meditations on history and the meaning of the individual in society, Fonseca uses his art to explore his relationship to the past and his place in the present. Whether of Coyote, Icarus, or Saint Francis, his images embody the universality of human experience.

—Larry Abbott

FRANKLIN, William B.

Tribal affiliations: Navajo
Painter

Born: Ganado, Arizona, 17 May 1947. **Education:** Galileo High School, San Francisco; Northern Arizona University, Flagstaff, 1972-76, majoring in sociology and minoring in art (silversmithing and stone sculpting, dabbled with painting). **Career:** Sociologist and energy planner, 1976-80; full time artist since 1980; commissioned by Sacred Lands Project, Washington, D.C. for illustration (*Cry the Sacred Ground*), 1986. **Awards:** SWAIA Santa Fe Indian Market, First Place, 1981, 1984-86, Hardin Award, 1979, Poster Artist, 1994; Museum of Northern Arizona, Flagstaff, First Place, 1974, 1981, 1984-86; Inter Tribal Indian Ceremonials, 1994.

Individual Exhibitions

1994   ' Wheelwright Museum of the American Indian, Santa Fe, New Mexico

Selected Group Exhibitions

1974   Navajo Show, Museum of Northern Arizona, Flagstaff, Arizona
1985   Gallery Capistrano, San Juan Capistrano
1989   *Paths Beyond Tradition: Contemporary American Indian Art Show,* San Diego Museum of Man
1990   Tokyo Book Fair, Tokyo, Japan
1991   Heard Museum, Phoenix, Arizona
         Coconino Center for the Arts, Flagstaff, Arizona
1993   San Diego Museum of Man
1994   Art Trek Gallery, Flagstaff, Arizona
         Old Town Gallery, Flagstaff, Arizona
         San Diego Museum of Man
         Coconino Center for the Arts, Flagstaff, Arizona

Collections

Coconino Center for the Arts, Flagstaff, Arizona; Museum of Northern Arizona, Flagstaff; Wheelwright Museum of the American Indian, Santa Fe, New Mexico.

Publications

On FRANKLIN: Books—*Beyond Tradition: Contemporary Indian Art and its Evolution,* by Jerry and Lois Jacka, Flagstaff, 1988; *Cry the Sacred Ground,* by Anita Parlow, Washington, D.C., 1989; *Enduring Traditions: Art of the Navajo,* by Jerry and Lois Jacka, Flagstaff, 1994. **Articles**—"American Indian Fine Art," *Arizona Highways,* May 1986.

*   *   *

William B. Franklin, whose work is well-known in the Southwest and beyond, with collectors from New York to San Francisco, never received formal art training. Born in Ganado, Arizona, on the Navajo Reservation at a time when the Navajo way of life and thinking was still very traditional, he helped his great grandmother herd sheep as a small child and watched his grandmother weaving and silversmithing. The impressions of those days, still vivid in his memory, together with the stories he heard as a child and the spiritual atmosphere in which he grew up had an important impact on his imagination as an artist and became a source of inspiration for his painting.

Franklin realized his serious interest in art relatively late in life, at age 25. Upon leaving high school one of his biggest problems was not knowing what kind of vocation he was suited for. In 1972 a prayer ceremony was done for his family, and it was then that he asked permission to be an artist. His request was granted and he enrolled at Northern Arizona University, where he studied from 1972 to 1976, majoring in sociology and minoring in art, focusing on silversmithing and stone sculpting and dabbling with painting.

It was only after he had started to work full-time in 1976 that Franklin began to concentrate on painting in his spare time. He rented a studio in Flagstaff, where he painted at night and over the weekends, teaching himself various techniques and styles. Though familiar with a number of artists through his art classes, museums, and books, there was no one in particular whom he emulated. It is with a certain pride that Franklin describes himself as self taught and as being fortunate to maintain the inner drive and commitment to keep on painting.

The year 1980 marked a turning point in Franklin's career. Painting became his profession. He rented a larger studio with space for more pieces and larger canvases, and began participating in exhibitions and regularly at fairs, where he started marketing his work. Since then he has been an (almost) annual contributor to the prestigious Santa Fe Indian Market, where he makes most of his sales and has been awarded many prizes and awards, including the Hinds Memorial Award and the Helen Hardin Award. In 1994, his painting, *Red Dream: The Return from the Long Walk*, was chosen as that year's poster image.

By 1980 Franklin had developed various techniques and compositional ideas as well as a number of themes and motifs drawn, to a large extent, from his native background. He continually experiments, reflecting his preference for spontaneity over rules. His media, accordingly, are numerous: oil, acrylics, watercolor, pencil, pen and ink, pastel, and prints. He likes acrylic washes and sometimes draws on paint stains and strokes to create intermingling designs and impressionistic imagery. All of his paintings are rich in color and reminiscent of natural colors of the Southwest, and range from semi-realistic representations, some of which are narratives, to highly stylized designs filled with native and sometimes hidden imagery. An example of the latter is *Corn Spirit Conversations*: at first glance resembling a Navajo pictorial rug design, a hint at Franklin's Navajo heritage, his image turns out to be a highly detailed combination of abstract forms with realistic elements. The parallel vertical forms represent the corn spirits as mediators between the world of the humans below (at the bottom of the picture) and the spirit world above. Thus, the abstract all-over design can be interpreted as an abbreviation of the Navajo universe. At the same time, the balance between form and meaning, abstract and realistic elements, is kept intact. The contrasting spheres of humans and spirits are integrated as decorative bands on top and at bottom into the pattern and symmetrical arrangement of the whole. Franklin has found his own way of combining realism and abstraction, representative and decorative, elements in Indian art.

—Gerhard and Gisela Hoffmann

GARNER, Ted

Variant names: Kangi Yotaka
Tribal affiliations: Standing Rock Sioux
Sculptor and mixed media artist

Born: Seattle, Washington, 10 February 1957, of Sihasapa/ Miniconjou Lakota heritage; native name means "Sitting Crow"). **Education:** Assistant to sculptors Jerry Peart, John Henry, and Mark di Suvero, 1974-78; Kansas City Art Institute, B.F.A., 1982. **Award:** Award of Merit, Mid-Four Annual Juried Art Exhibit, Nelson-Atkins Museum, Kansas City, Missouri, 1981; Site Works Grant, 39th Arts Festival of Atlanta, 1992; Martin and Doris Rosen Award, *Sixth Rosen Outdoor Sculpture Competition and Exhibition,* Appalachian State University, Boone, North Carolina, 1992; Purchase Award, *New Art of the West 5,* Eiteljorg Museum of American Indian and Western Art, Indianapolis, Indiana, 1996. **Address:** c/o Jan Cicero Gallery, 221 West Erie St., Chicago, Illinois, 60610, (312)440-1904.

Individual Exhibitions

1978   C.N. Gorman Museum, University of California, Davis

Selected Group Exhibitions

1977   Walter Kelly Gallery, Chicago
1979   *5th Regional Undergraduate Show,* University of Missouri, Kansas City
1981   *Confluences of Tradition and Change: 24 American Indian Artists,* Richard L. Nelson Gallery, University of California, Davis, and Museum of the Southwest, Midland, Texas
      Mid-Four Annual Juried Art Exhibit, Nelson-Atkins Museum, Kansas City, Missouri
1982   *28th Annual Drawing & Small Sculpture Show,* Ball State University, Muncie, Indiana
1983   *Contemporary Native American Art,* Gardner Art Gallery, Oklahoma State University, Stillwater
      Grayson Gallery, Chicago
1987   *New Directions Northwest: Contemporary Native American Art,* Portland Art Museum, Oregon
1990   *New Horizons in Art: 21st Exhibition of Illinois Artists,* North Shore Art League, Winnetka, Illinois
      40th Annual Quad State Juried Art Show, Quincy Arts Club, Quincy, Illinois
1991   *Juried Sculpture Competition,* Elgin Community College, Elgin, Illinois
1992   *39th Arts Festival of Atlanta,* Georgia
      We, The Human Beings: 27 Contemporary Native American Artists, College of Wooster Art Museum, Ohio

      Showcase: Bi-State, Davenport Museum of Art, Iowa
      Sixth Rosen Outdoor Sculpture Competition and Exhibition, Appalachian State University, Boone, North Carolina
      New Horizons in Art: 22nd Exhibition of Illinois Artists, North Shore Art League, Winnetka, Illinois
1993   *Abstract Chicago 1993,* Klein Art Works, Chicago
      Minnetonka Center for the Arts, Wayzata, Minnesota
1994   Jan Cicero Gallery, Chicago
      Three Chicago Sculptors, Klein Art Works, Chicago
      44th Annual Quad-State Juried Exhibition, Quincy Art Center, Quincy, Illinois
      52nd Annual Juried Exhibition, Sioux City Art Center, Sioux City, Iowa
1995   Socrates Sculpture Park, City of New York Department of Parks and Recreation
      Sculpture 95, Sacred Circle Gallery of American Indian Art, Seattle
      Tribal and Western Art of the Great Plains, Oscar Howe Art Center, Mitchell, South Dakota
1996   *New Art of the West 5,* Eiteljorg Museum of American Indian and Western Art, Indianapolis, Indiana
      Glass, Fiber, Wood: The Kindred Eye, Rockford Art Museum, Rockford, Illinois
      Native Streams: Contemporary Native American Artists, Jan Cicero Gallery, Chicago, and Turman Art Gallery, Indiana State University, Terre Haute
      Movements: Contemporary Native American Art, Penelec Art Gallery, Allegheny College, Meadville, Pennsylvania

Collections

Brunnier Art Gallery, Iowa State University, Ames; Chicago Children's Museum; Elgin Community College, Elgin, Illinois; Field Museum of Natural History, Chicago; Washington State Arts Commission, Olympia.

Publications

On GARNER: Exhibition catalogs—*Confluences of Tradition and Change: 24 American Indian Artists,* Richard L. Nelson Gallery, University of California at Davis and the Museum of the Southwest, Midland, 1981; *Contemporary Native American Art,* Gardiner Art Gallery, Oklahoma State University, 1983; *New Directions Northwest,* Portland Art Museum, 1987; *39th Arts Festival of Atlanta Visual Arts Catalog,* Arts Festival of Atlanta, 1992; *Sixth Rosen Outdoor Sculpture Competition and Exhibition,* Catherine J. Smith Gallery, Appalachian State University, Boone, North Carolina, 1992; *We, The Human Beings: 27 Contemporary Native American Artists,* College of Wooster Art Museum, 1992; *Seventh Annual*

Rosen Outdoor Sculpture Competition and Exhibition, Catherine J. Smith Gallery, Appalachian State University, Boone, North Carolina, 1993; *Abstract: Chicago 1993,* Klein Art Works, Chicago, 1993; *1994 North American Sculpture Exhibition,* Foothills Art Center, Golden, Colorado; *Native Streams: Contemporary Native American Art,* Jan Cicero Gallery, Chicago, and the Turman Art Gallery, Indiana State University, Terre Haute, Indiana, 1995; *New Art of the West 5,* Eiteljorg Museum of American Indian and Western Art, 1996. **Articles**—"Egalitarian Sculptor" by Douglas Davies, *Newsweek,* 27 October 1975; "It Must Be Something," *The New Yorker,* 3 November 1975; "'Supersculpture' Turns City into Canvas" by Steve Diamond, *Artworks,* 1976; "Ted Garner: Icarus Flies Again" by Valerie Alexander, *Magazine of the Kansas City Art Institute,* Spring 1982; "Art Galleries" by Alan G. Artner, *Chicago Tribune,* 24 June 1983; "Art: Modern Works of American Art" by Grace Glueck, *New York Times,* 30 November 1984; "Sculptor Shapes New Highlight for Aurora" by Steve Lord, *Aurora Beacon-News* (Aurora, Illinois), 18 November 1987; "Art in the Park" by John Dziekan, *Chicago Tribune,* 20 November 1987; "Artwork Is Going Places" by David Mannweiler, *Indianapolis News,* 19 October 1988; "Fest Sculptures" by Catherine Fox, *Atlanta Journal & Constitution,* 23 September 1992; "Subtlety Marks Show" by Jacqueline Hall, *Columbus Dispatch,* 7 February 1993; "Art in the Park" by Jerel Harris, *Kansas City Star,* 10 June 1993; "Jaune Quick-to-See Smith/Ted Garner" by Olga Zdanovics, *New Art Examiner,* December 1994; "'Sculpture '95' Exhibit Highlights the Singularity of the Sacred Circle" by Regina Hackett, *Seattle Post-Intelligencer,* 21 July 1995; "Mundane and Mystical" by Janet I-Chin Tu, *Seattle Times,* 24 August 1995; "Native Traditions, Values, Ideas" by John Boylan, *Reflex,* September 1995; "The Heart of the West" by S. L. Berry, *Indianapolis Star,* 21 July 1996; "*Native Streams* Exhibit at Dahl Fine Arts Center," *Indian Country Today,* 22 July 1996.

*

Ted Garner comments:

My aim in making art is to combine the power and aesthetics of my Native American heritage with modern techniques, materials and art history. Currently, I am attempting in my smaller pieces to marry my long standing interests in sculpture and painting by making intricate wood sculptures, then painting them with watercolors and applying covering coats of lacquer to protect and to provide "depth."

I have for some time also been building larger sculptures that incorporate seating and play areas for children.

*   *   *

As a contemporary sculptor, Ted Garner takes current social and political concerns from the native community and presents them with wit, humor, and poignancy, blending the art of irony with truth. Garner's numerous sculptures invite extended reactions ranging from laughter to shock and deep reflection. *Deer Heart,* a sculpture consisting of a large wooden heart shape sprouting deer antlers from out the top, is a classic example of Garner's ability to take a concept with strong associations to visual stereotypes and place them in an ironic context. *Deer Heart* is straightforward and uncomplicated in appearance, but it shatters romantic images brought to mind by the related phrase, "Dear Heart," through a sharp sense of simple irony.

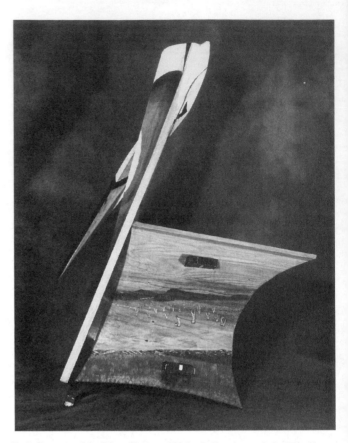

Ted Garner: *My Blue Heron,* 1996. Collection of the Eiteljorg Museum of American Indians and Western Art; courtesy of the artist.

Garner's art reflects his upbringing, during which he experienced common American popular culture outside of a home environment influenced by his parents, both of whom worked as anthropologists; Garner draws from contemporary methods and influences, particularly the surreal and abstract, to present native issues that are often timeless. Using wood, metal, bright watercolors and lacquer for his smaller sculptures, Garner addresses issues such as media manipulation, heavy-handed government, and the paradoxes of power. One piece, *Spin Doctor,* explores the construction of the media and how information is systematically manipulated, shaped, and eventually packaged in order to present a predetermined impression for the public. His 1992 piece, *Pentagon Dunce,* shows Garner's recognition and mockery of the motivations behind war, greed, and cruelty. Money is represented by two detached semicircles coated in bills, with camouflage—a perfect symbol for deception—rockets, and what appears to be a pentagon shaped megahorn filled with arabic symbols, perhaps representing the voice and culture of the Middle East. From all of these alarming metaphors fall simple wooden tears.

Hail to the Chief, 1993, is another powerful and typical Garner piece, reflecting his simulateous thematic approach to various social and cultural issues. A small wood sculpture with associations to gambling (it is mounted on a disk suggesting a roulette wheel), presidential elections and patriotism (as suggested by the multi-associative title and images of major candidates in the 1992 election viewed through a slot machine window), with the abstract figure's arm falling forward in what seems like the "tomahawk chop," a rallying cry by fans of sports teams such as the Seminoles and the Braves. The wealth of associations the viewer can detect and build on reflects the wit and depth of Garner's work.

—Vesta Giles

GENERAL, David
Tribal affiliations: Oneida
Sculptor

Born: Oshweken, Ontario, 31 May 1950. **Education:** Wilfred Laurier University, Waterloo, Ontario; Hamilton Teacher's College, Ontario; self-taught sculptor. **Family:** Wife, Mary, and children, Miles, Aisha, Sara, Megan. **Career:** Steel worker, elementary school teacher; senior cultural development officer, Department of Indian and Northern Affairs, Ottawa, Ontario; advisory committee member, National Indian Artist Symposium; co-founder and past chairman, Society of Canadian Artists of Native Ancestry; Board of Trustees, McMichael Canadian Collection, Kleinburg, Ontario. **Awards:** Cultural Grant, Department of Indian and Northern Affairs, Ontario Arts Council Grant, sculpting.

Individual Exhibitions

1983	*Transformation: The Art of David General*, Woodland Indian Cultural Education Centre, Brantford, Ontario
1984	*Transformation: The Art of David General*, Thunder Bay National Exhibition Centre and Centre for Indian Art, Thunder Bay, Ontario
1986	*Maquettes, Concepts and Designs for Monumental Sculpture*, Brock University, St. Catharines, Ontario
1988	*In Seclusion: Recent Works by David General*, Intuit Gallery, London, Ontario
1993	*Modern Eagle, Modern Vision*, Koffler Gallery, North York, Ontario

Selected Group Exhibitions

1976	*Indian Art '76*, Woodland Indian Cultural Educational Centre, Brantford, Ontario
	Art Gallery of Brant, Brantford, Ontario
	Seneca Art '76, Woodland Indian Cultural Education Centre, Brantford, Ontario
1977	*Links to a Tradition*, Indian and Northern Affairs, Brasilia Sao Paulo, and Bahai, Brazil
1980	*Wood Transformed*, Ontario Crafts Council, Toronto
	Contemporary Art of Iroquoia, MacDonald Gallery, Government of Ontario, Toronto
	First Man Gallery, Calgary, Alberta
1981	*Native Art Auction*, Native Canadian Centre of Toronto
1982	*Second National Native Art Auction*, Native Canadian Centre of Toronto
	The Buckhorn Wild Life Festival, Buckhorn, Ontario
	Contemporary Images of the Woodland Artist, Leslie Ross Gallery, Brantford, Ontario
	Renewal, Thunder Bay National Exhibition Centre and Centre for Indian Art, Thunder Bay, Ontario

David General: *Hawk Woman*, 1995. Photograph by D. M. General; private collection.

1983	*Directions: An Exhibition of Masterworks*, Northwestern National Exhibition Centre, Hazelton, British Columbia
1984	*Common Heritage: Contemporary Iroquois Artists*, Queen's Museum, New York
1986	*Contrasts*, Brock Centre for the Arts, St. Catharines, Ontario
	From Masks to Maquettes, Tom Thompson Gallery, Owen Sound, Ontario; Thunder Bay National Exhibition Centre and Centre for Indian Art, Thunder Bay, Ontario; McMichael Canadian Collection, Kleinburg, Ontario
	Indian Art '86, Woodland Indian Cultural Education Centre, Brantford, Ontario
1987	*A Celebration of Contemporary Native Art*, Southwest Museum, Los Angeles, California
	A Native Experience, Beckett Gallery, Hamilton, Ontario
1988	*Indian Art '88*, Woodland Indian Cultural Educational Centre, Brantford, Ontario
	The Object Is the Object, Interim Gallery, Georgian College, School of Design and Visual Arts, Barrie, Ontario
	In the Shadow of the Sun: Contemporary Canadian Indian and Inuit Art, Mount St. Vincent, Halifax, Nova Scotia; Rijks Museum voor Volkenhunde, Steen Straat, Lerden, Netherlands (through 1990)

1991   *Okanata,* A Space, Toronto, Ontario
        The Very Breath of the Americas: Works by David Gen-
            eral and John Boyle, University of Waterloo Gallery,
            Waterloo, Ontario
1995   *The Kluane Expedition,* McMichael Canada Art Collec-
            tion, Kleinburg, Ontario

Collections

Blackburn Group, London Free Press, London, Ontario; Canadian Museum of Civilization, Hull, Quebec; Canadian Pacific Forest Products, Montreal, Quebec; Canadian Standards Association, Rexdale, Ontario; Carleton University, Ottawa, Ontario; Department of Indian and Northern Affairs, Ottawa, Ontario; Digital Equipment Ltd., Toronto, Ontario; Dunlop Art Gallery, Regina Saskatchewan; W. Ross MacDonald School, Brantford, Ontario; Maritime Paper Products, Halifax, Nova Scotia; McIntosh Gallery, University of Western Ontario, London; McMichael Canadian Art Collection, Kleinburg, Ontario; North American Indian Travelling College, Cornwall, Ontario; Ontario Crafts Council, Toronto; St. John Shipbuilding Limited, St. John, New Brunswick; Thunder Bay National Exhibition Centre and Centre for Indian Art, Thunder Bay, Ontario; Warner-Lambert Canada Inc., Scarborough, Ontario; Woodland Cultural Educational Centre, Brantford, Ontario; Yukon Permanent Art Collection, Whitehorse, Yukon.

Publications

By GENERAL: Books—*Indian Art '76,* Woodland Indian Cultural Educational Centre, Brantford, Ontario, 1976; *Contemporary Art of Iroquoia,* MacDonald Gallery, Ministry of Intergovernmental Affairs, Ottawa, 1980. **Articles**—"Indian Artist or Artists Who are Indian?," and "Artist Bill Reid Maintains Classic Haida Heritage," *The Native Perspective,* Vol. 3, no. 2, 1978; "Survival of the Iroquois Snowsnake Game," *The Native Perspective,* Vol. 2, no. 9, 1978; "Swimming in the Mainstream: Networking," *Proceedings from the National Native Indian Artists' Symposium IV,* University of Lethbridge, Lethbridge, Alberta, 1987; "Would it Carry More Weight if it Were Written in Stone?," and "Reach out and Touch Someone," *Artscrafts Magazine,* National Indian Arts and Crafts Corporation, Ottawa, Ontario, 1989; "After Oka," *Artscrafts Magazine,* National Indian Arts and Crafts Corporation, Ottawa, Ontario, 1990.

On GENERAL: Books—*Transformation: The Art of David General,* by Norma Dinniwell and Tom Hill, Woodland Indian Cultural Education Centre, Brantford, Ontario, 1982; *From Masks to Maquettes,* by Norma Dinniwell, McIntosh Gallery, University of Western Ontario, London, 1982; *Challenges,* by Gerald McMaster, Museum of Civilization, Ottawa, Ontario, 1987; *Networking: Proceedings from the National Native Artists Symposium IV,* by Alfred Youngman, 1987; *Modern Eagle, Modern Vision,* by Gloria Hickey, Koffler Gallery, North York, Ontario, 1987. **Articles**—"David General: Exploring Avenues," by Melissa Lazore, *The Native Perspective,* Vol. 3, no. 2, 1978; "General's Exhibition Title Appropriate," by Laura Ramsay, *The Brantford Expositor,* 19 September 1982; "General Is an Artist, Not an Indian Artist," *Sherbrooke Record,* Quebec, 2 April 1986; "General Escapes Bonds of 'Native Art,'" Rose Simone, *Brantford Expositor,* 7 March 1987. **Film**—*Kluane Art Expedition,* produced by Vic Ischenko, N.N.B.Y. Whitehorse, Yukon, 1993; *Lacrosse, The Creator's Game,* Ken Murch Produc-

tion, London, Ontario, 1993; *David General: New Imageries,* Sunday Arts Entertainment, Carol Moore-Ede (Executive Producer), CBC Television, Toronto, 1994.

*

David General comments:

Modernist sculpture searched for essence and vitality and found it in the artworks of numerous indigenous cultures, throughout the world. I searched for a presentation for the imagery and inspiration that my indigenous heritage provides me and found it in modernist sculpture. My outlook on art is very simple: don't do what everybody else is doing. There are very few First Nations artists working in bronze and even fewer working in marble. Why fight your way through a pack, if you don't have to? Classic materials, a distinctive imagery, an honest response to life and all it can provide—sounds like a formula for happiness to me.

*   *   *

David General is that rare breed of artist who combines a powerful kinaesthetic sense of energy and spirit with an inquisitive and intelligent thought process. Evolving out of a successful career as a painter in the early 1970s, his sculptures of today resonate in both the spiritual and intellectual realms, giving the viewer of his artwork a sense that reaches beyond visual stimulation.

General's sculptures show a probing interest in abstract relationships between animate and inanimate objects. His work demonstrates his preference for reproducing in three dimensional form the untouchable elements of ethereal energy that forms the core of a subject, rather than the physical likeness and outward details of that subject. General's stone masks are acclaimed for the haunting and eerie quality of the simple faces, particularly the eyes, which are gentle and piercing. General makes only one mask per year, and he is quick to stress that his masks are not ceremonial or functional.

General's inquisitive nature has led him to study various sources of stylistic inspiration. He has most notably studied the careers of Henry Moore, Norval Morisseau, and Haida carver Bill Reid. It was meeting Reid, and General's consequent extensive examination of Northwest Coast art forms and particularly the intricate transformation masks, that directed him to the sculptural and mask work we see today. General also cites Iroquoian legends and myths, as well as Mayan art and monumental Egyptian art as sources of inspiration.

The subjects in David General's work are never harsh or angry. His pieces carry an overriding sense of peace and serenity, yet they are not necessarily happy or content. For the most part, his forms are organic and personified with intricate character traits, and many pieces explore themes of transformation. General's symbolism is clear through the abstraction of his style. The mystery and energy of women, the elements, and eagles turn up again and again in his sculptures.

Through his choice in materials and subject matter, General accomplishes many layers of implication and meaning within each piece. He pays close attention to the way in which light reacts with the materials, giving the sculptures further mystery and texture. His choice of alabaster, a stone that is somewhat translucent, in his mask, *Moon's Reflection on the Ice* (1985), gives the viewer a sensation of something not quite of this earth, or manmade. The patterns on the stone also create the effect of clouds, or the lines on the surface of the moon, resting on the forehead of the mask, which furthers the effect.

Although General's pieces lean heavily into abstraction, he carefully titles each one, as if endowing them with specific and purposeful character traits. *Women with Spirit* (1982) is a piece that swings, pulses, and even seems to breathe and sigh. It captures the ingredients of women with spirit, as the title indicates. Another piece honoring the feminine spirit is *She Obscures My Vision* (1983), a particularly breathtaking work carved in Carrara Marble. The swirling layers of smooth whiteness in a gentle and expressive face is a pristine visual homage to General's mother, wife, and daughter. The lines are soft and undulating, the expression of the piece is serene, yet active, carrying an energy of all things sensuous and knowing. On a broader scale it highlights the unique and mysterious role of all women in society.

Other pieces by David General, like *The Encampment* (1983), speak of relationships. With three similar yet non-identical figures, he creates unique personalities in an intricate relationship. The figures carry the outward semblances of an intimate conversation. There is obvious give and take, and a slight struggle for power. Overall one is struck with the vital role each figure plays in balancing the overall effect of the piece. Now exploring monumentally sized pieces, General's art is moving to an even grander scale.

—Vesta Giles

GLAZER DANAY, Richard

Tribal affiliations: Mohawk
Sculptor and painter

Born: Richard Alan Danay at Coney Island, New York, 12 August 1942; mother divorced and remarried when he was young, and his name changed to Richard Glazer, but he has been known as Richard Glazer Danay since the 1960s. **Education:** California State University, Northridge, B.A., 1970; California State University, Chico, M.A., 1972; University of California, Davis, M.F.A., 1978. **Career:** Ironworker, 1960-63, 1967; United States Army Reserves, 1961-65; consultant, U.S. Office of Education, Office of Indian Education, 1974-79, U.S. Forest Service, Civil Rights Compliance, 1974-75, National Endowment for the Humanities, 1979; member, National Indian Education Association, College Art Association, Great Lakes Inter-Tribal Education Committee; board of directors, Educational Opportunity Center, Oneida Tribe of Wisconsin; lecturer and conference/panel participant on curriculum, art, and opportunity issues; instructor/coordinator, American Indian Studies, California State University, Chico, 1972-77; instructor, Native American studies and acting director, C. N. Gorman Museum, University of California, Davis, 1979-80; coordinator, American-Intercultural Programs/American Indian Studies, University of Wisconsin, Green Bay, 1980-85; California State University, Long Beach, 1985—; chair of American Indian history, University of California, Riverside, 1991-93; commissioner, Indian Arts and Crafts Board, U.S. Department of the Interior.

Individual Exhibitions

1970   Gallery II, San Fernando Valley State College, Northridge, California
1971   Jon Morehead Gallery, Chico, California
1976   C. N. Gorman Museum, University of California, Davis

Selected Group Exhibitions

1970   *Art for Peace,* Capitol Mall, Washington, D.C.
1973   *Fritz Scholder, Richard Danay, and Dick West,* Utah Fine Arts Museum, University of Utah, Salt Lake City
1974   *Northern Sierra Valley Art Show,* Redding, California
1975   *I Am These People,* State Capitol Building, Sacramento, California
1976   *In-Din-Art-I-Facs,* Humboldt Cultural Center, Eureka, California
        Harbor Gallery of Fine Arts, Harbor College, Los Angeles
        New Horizons in American Indian Art, Southwest Museum, Los Angeles
        Indian Images, organized by the University of North Dakota (traveling through 1977)
1977   Petrified Forest Museum, Petrified Forest, Arizona
        Center for International Arts, New York
        Letter Art Exhibit, Utrecht, Holland
1978   *Contemporary Indian Art,* California State University, Long Beach
        Last Intergalctic Postal Art Show, Richland, Washington
        Art Fiera '78, Bologna, Italy
        Aesthetics of Graffiti, San Francisco Museum of Art, California
1980   Aich Gallery, New York
        International Art and Poetry Show in Opposition to WW III, San Francisco, California
1981   *Erotic Art Exhibit,* New Vistas Gallery, Vista, California
        Native American Art '81, Philbrook Museum, Tulsa, Oklahoma
        American Indian Art of the 1980s, Native American Center for the Living Arts, Niagara Falls, New York
        The Return to the Central Fire, Oswego Art Center Gallery, Oswego, new York
        Changing Myths: The Evolution of Tradition, Sacred Circle Art Gallery, Seattle, Washington
1981   *Confluences of Tradition and Change,* R. L. Nelson Gallery, University of California, Davis (traveling through 1992)
1982   *American Indian International Art and Film Festival,* De Quincey University, California
        Visions of the Earth, Native American Rights Fund Center, Boulder, Colorado
        Contemporary American Indian Art, Susan B. Anthony Gallery, University of Wisconsin, Madison
        Night of the First Americans, John F. Kennedy Center for the Performing Arts, Washington, D.C.
        Affiches Indiennes d'Amerique du Nord, Musée de l'Homme, Paris
        Walk in Beauty, Sweeny Convention Center, Santa Fe, New Mexico
1984   Milwaukee Public Museum, Milwaukee, Wisconsin
        No Beads, No Trinkets, Palais des Nations, Geneva, Switzerland
        Indianascher Kunstler, organized by the Philbrook Museum, Tulsa, Oklahoma (traveled in Germany through 1985)
1985   *Red Cloud Indian Art Show,* Heritage Center, Red Cloud Indian School, Pine Ridge, South Dakota
1986-88 *What Is Native American Art?,* Philbrook Museum of Art, Tulsa (traveling)

Richard Glazer Danay: *What Goes Around,* 1993. Courtesy of the artist.

1989	British Museum, London, England
1990	Museum fur Volkerkunde, Vienna, Austria
1991	Southern Plains Indian Museum, Anadarko, Oklahoma
	Shared Visions: Native American Painters and Sculptors of the Twentieth Century, Heard Museum, Phoenix, Arizona (traveling through 1996)
1992	British Museum, London, England
	University of California, Long Beach

Collections

British Museum, London, England; Heard Museum, Phoenix, Arizona; Museum fur Volkerkunde, Vienna, Austria; Native American Center for the Living Arts, Niagara Falls, New York; Philbrook Museum of Art, Tulsa, Oklahoma; San Diego Museum of Man, San Diego, California; Seneca Iroquois National Museum, Salmanca, New York; Southwest Museum, Los Angeles, California; United States Department of the Interior, Washington, D.C.; University of Lethbridge, Lethbridge, Alberta; Washington State Art Collection, Olympia, Washington.

Publications

On GLAZER DANAY: Books—*Aesthetics of Graffiti,* by Rolando Castellon, San Francisco Museum of Art, 1978; *The Sweetgrass Lives On,* by Jamake Highwater, New York, 1980; *Confluences of Tradition and Change,* L. Price Amerson, Jr., editor, University of California, Davis, 1981; *Magic Images,* by Edwin L. Wade and Rennard Strickland, University of Oklahoma Press and the Philbrook Museum, 1982; *Indianische Kunst im 20 Jahrhundert,* by Gerhard Hoffman, et al., Münich, Germany, 1984; *The Arts of the North American Indian: Native Traditions in Evolution,* Edwin L. Wade and Rennard Strickland, editors, New York: Hudson Hills Press, 1986; *Mixed Blessings: New Art in a Multicultural Media,* by Lucy Lippard, New York, 1990; *Shared Visions: Native American Painters and Sculptors of the Twentieth Century,* by Margaret Archuleta and Rennard Strickland, Phoenix, Heard Museum, 1991; *I Stand in the Center of Good,* by Lawrence Abbott, University of Nebraska Press, 1994. **Articles**— "Review," by Charles Johnson, *Sacramento Bee,* January 10, 1976; "At the Edge of the Woods," by Rick Hill, *Turtle Quarterly,* Winter 1982; "New Ways of Old Visions," by Joan Randall and George Longfish, *Artspace,* Summer 1982.

*

Richard Glazer Danay comments (1992):
    HEAR ME MY COLLECTORS. I am tired of exhibition. Our artists are killed. Harden is dead. Loloma is dead. The old artists are all dead. It is the young men who say yes or no; T. C. Cannon who led the young men is dead. It is cold and we have no canvas. The collectors are freezing their funds. The artists, some of them, have

run away to the hills and have no brushes, no paint; no one knows where they are—perhaps working for the B.I.A. I want to have time to work at my creations and see how many of them I can find. Maybe I shall find them among the museums. Hear me, my collectors. I am tired; my brush is worn and bent. From where the easel now stands, I will see my creations no more forever.

*   *   *

Richard Glazer Danay comes from a dual heritage in that he is a Mohawk from the Caughnawaga Reserve near Montreal, and Jewish. His art is derived from both "Pop" and postmodernist art movements, and he employs a wry and ironic sense of humor in his interpretation of Indian themes and the status of women in modern American life. He is both a painter and a sculptor who can combine these media in the same work. In the words of University of California/Riverside Professor of Art, William Bradshaw, Glazer Danay can create "constructions of outstanding boldness and power. The work is bright, witty, satirical, and very strong in form and content." In a word, he is unique: no one is doing work quite like his. Glazer Danay is influential in the American art world for his art as well as for his role as a prominent educator and as a member of the U.S. Department of the Interior Indian Arts and Crafts Board.

Glazer Danay's compound name reflects his Mohawk and Jewish heritage. This background is sometimes reflected in his sense of dualities in his art. On the one hand, he is a Mohawk Indian from a people famed as high-steel workers on the skyscrapers of Manhattan. His father and other relatives worked in this profession, as did Glazer Danay himself for a period of time, which explains his birth on Coney Island. After his parents' divorce, his white mother remarried into a prominent Jewish family; his step-uncle was Nathan Glazer, the famed Harvard sociologist. Glazer Danay is not a traditionalist artist who is steeped in the "spirituality" and "mysticism" of the Indian past. As he puts it: "You have to find out who you are. I have a wry sense of humor, and I see a lot of bizarre humor in things. I figure why should I paint in a mystical style? I did that for years. I'd say, 'I'm going to try and paint this mysterious, mystical painting.' But I'm not the least inclined towards mysticism or spiritualism. I'm a cynic, and I may as well paint like a cynic."

Although Glazer Danay admits that he was not a very motivated student in his younger days, he did manage to acquire a B.A. from California State University/Northridge (1970), an M.A. from California State University/Chico (1972), and an M.F.A. from the University of California, Davis (1978). Consequently, Glazer Danay has always tried to find his home base or sense of employment security within the bureaucratic confines of academe.

Glazer Danay's art frequently features "constructions" that are painted in obtrusive and even "eye-pounding" colors that can shock viewers, such as the brilliantly decorated "hard hats" for which he became well known. No one can explain the use of such colors better than Glazer Danay himself:

> One of the biggest things other artists accuse me of is using garish colors. And it's true. I'm a good colorist when I have to be, but it got to the point where I found all those lovely tubes and why should I dilute it with the next color? I think my whole mentality grew up with Disneyland and Hollywood. As a kid, I moved from Coney Island to West Hollywood. The first time I went to Las Vegas, I felt right at home. This is a place I understood, a lot of garish color — big, busy nudes flashing on and off in neon.

Sometimes Glazer Danay's proclivity for "big, busty nudes," coupled with his preference to use Playboy nudes as models, has caused controversy. One gallery director in Binghamton, New York, removed one of his paintings, *Buffalo Girl with Boots*, from a contemporary Indian art exhibition in 1986. Apart from the fact that a female was shown nude, adorned only with a buffalo head and boots, the collage included several rear views of nude figures and two people engaged in love play. As one Binghamton wit commented, "The nudity doesn't bother me and there's no problem with the buffalo head. But those cowboy boots..."

More recently, Glazer Danay has experienced either a mid-life crisis or a heightening of his feelings of alienation from the bourgeois art marketplace. In 1992, he decided to withdraw from all commercial activities related to art galleries (with their consumer ethos and hype), doing so by issuing a statement (see the artist's comment above) that parodies the famous speech made by the Nez Perce Chief Joseph in his surrender to American troops in the Bear Paw Mountains of Montana in 1877.

No more forever? Well, at least for now. According to Glazer Danay, his most recent work does not much involve Indian themes or iconography. However, he states that he is planning a series of works on Manhattan Island called, *I'll Take Manhattan*—which he calls "big *map* paintings ... like topographical maps."

—John Anson Warner

GONZALES, Rose
Tribal affiliations: San Juan Pueblo
Potter

Born: Rose Cata, San Juan Pueblo, New Mexico, c. 1900. **Family:** Married Robert Gonzales, 1920, and moved to his native San Ildefonso Pueblo. **Education:** Santa Fe Indian School; learned pottery from her mother-in-law, Ramona Sanchez Gonzales. **Career:** Potter since the 1920s; demonstrated and taught potterymaking at San Ildefonso. **Died:** 1989

Selected Group Exhibitions

1974   Maxwell Museum of Anthropology, Albuquerque, New Mexico
1978   Renwick Gallery, National Collection of Fine Arts, Washington, D.C.

Collections

Heard Museum, Phoenix, Arizona; Maxwell Museum of Anthropology, Albuquerque, New Mexico; Museum of New Mexico, Santa Fe, New Mexico; School of American Research, Santa Fe, New Mexico; Texas Tech Museum, Lubbock, Texas.

Publications

On GONZALES: Books—*Southwest Indian Craft Arts*, by Clara Lee Tanner, Tucson, University of Arizona Press, 1968, reprinted 1975; *Seven Families in Pueblo Pottery,* Maxwell Museum of Anthropology, Albuquerque: University of New Mexico Press, 1974;

Rose Gonzales: Redware ceramic vessel, c. 1940. Courtesy Museum of Indian Arts and Culture, Santa Fe.

Southwestern Indian Arts and Crafts, by Ray Manly, Tucson, Ray Manly Photography, 1975; *Pottery Treasures: The Splendor of Southwest Indian Art*, by Jerry Jacks with text by Spencer Gill, Portland, Graphic Arts Center, 1976; *Generations in Clay: Pueblo Pottery of the American Southwest,* by Alfred E. Deterred and Fred PLO, Flagstaff, Northland Press, 1980; *Fourteen Families in Pueblo Pottery,* by Rick Dillingham, Santa Fe, 1994. **Articles**—"Rose Gonzales," by Nancy Fox, *American Indian Art Magazine,* Autumn 1977.

*   *   *

Rose Gonzales is among the great twentieth-century potterymakers of the Pueblos, contributing to the revitalization of the art, introducing innovations, and beginning a family tradition that was continued by the excellent work of her son, Tse-Pe. Although not as well known and celebrated as some of her contemporaries, like Maria Martinez, Gonzales helped broaden the range of styles offered during a crucial stage of what has since been termed the "San Ildefonso Renaissance." Her work was eagerly sought during her lifetime and maintains high value, reflecting her significant contribution.

Gonzales was born in San Juan Pueblo around the turn of the century, probably in the early 1900s. She met and married Robert Gonzales and settled with him in his native San Ildefonso Pueblo. Just a few months before Gonzales moved to San Ildefonso, Maria and Julian Martinez had perfected a new style of pottery, called at first "two-blacks," and today internationally known as black-on-black. By 1925, Maria and Julian had revitalized the pottery traditions of San Ildefonso and helped generate an artistic flowering that made San Ildefonso an arts center. During the first half of the twentieth-century, waves of artistic invention and accomplishment were occurring, as they were in neighboring communities, and several noted painters and potters emerged from the Pueblo, including pot-

ters and such painters as Crescencio and Julian Martinez, Oqwa Pi, and Romando Vigil, followed by mid-century artists like Gilbert Atencio, Popovi Da, and Jose D. Roybal, and on to flourishing artists of the final quarter of the century, who include Tony Da and Jody Folwell.

Gonzales was taught potterymaking by her mother-in-law, Ramona Sanchez Gonzales, and became adept during the early stages of San Ildefonso's burgeoning arts renaissance. Gonzales introduced her own design innovations, which added to the variety of excellent wares being produced at the Pueblo. The Martinez's and other potters applied paint to their pieces for design elements, but Gonzales carved her designs into the blackware, providing a contrast and complement and spinning off a new style that became popular and well-regarded.

Carving pots for decorative elements had been practiced in several of the Pueblos. These incisions usually ran deep and were smoothed off to form neat grooves. Gonzales favored a slighter incision and ran her lines along rounded edges, also a distinctive trait of her pottery, creating her own style within the wave of works being produced at the Pueblo, a form of innovation on innovation that reflects the creative environment of San Ildefonso.

Carved and polished, black-on-black wares proved especially beautiful. Gonzales most frequently designed her bowls, pots, canteens, and other pieces with recognizable patterns of the Southwest, including the serpent, Awanyu, the Thunderbird, clouds and lightning ("Kiva Steps"), and triangular shapes. Her works were exhibited in museums and she showed regularly at fairs in the southwest, winning awards consistently. Gonzales was active in the cultural and administrative affairs of the Pueblo and began instructing young potters, just as she had been instructed in the arts by her mother-in-law. Her most acclaimed student was her son, Tse-Pe, who not only mastered the carving technique and helps sustain the revitalized tradition, but also experimented freely with colors and shapes of pottery. Tse-Pe and his first wife, Dora, also taught by Gonzales, were among the first to be successful with inlays, particularly turquoise, and with multiple firings that create variations in color. These developments, especially inlaid pottery, became a regular part of the repertoire of contemporary potters exhibited at fairs of the Southwest.

—Perry Bear

GONZALEZ, Luis

Variant names: Wo Peen
Tribal affiliations: San Ildefonso Pueblo
Painter

Born: San Ildefonso Pueblo, New Mexico, 10 September 1907; Wo Peen means "Medicine Mountain." **Education:** Santa Fe Indian School. **Career:** Ceremonial singer and dancer; governor, San Ildefonso Pueblo, 1944-45; muralist, including Lodge of Seven Fires, YMCA, Springfield, Massachusetts; painter; farmer.

Selected Group Exhibitions

1925   *Exhibition of American Indian Paintings and Applied Arts*, Arts Club of Chicago, Chicago, Illinois
        Robert Lowie Museum of Anthropology, University of California, Berkeley

Luis Gonzalez: *Horse,* c. 1950. Courtesy Museum of Indian Arts and Culture, Santa Fe, Dorothy Dunn Kramer Collection.

Collections

Denver Art Museum, Denver, Colorado; Eiteljorg Museum, India-
napolis, Indiana; Kiva Museum of the Koshare Indian, La Junta,
Colorado; Museum of the American Indian, New York; Museum of
New Mexico, Santa Fe; Museum of Northern Arizona, Flagstaff;
Philbrook Museum of Art, Tulsa, Oklahoma; Millicent Rogers
Foundation Museum, Taos, New Mexico; School of American Re-
search, Santa Fe, New Mexico; University of California, Berkeley;
University of Oklahoma, Norman; Woolaroc Museum, Bartlesville,
Oklahoma.

On GONZALEZ: Books—*Pueblo Indian Painting,* by Hartley
Burr Alexander, Nice, France, 1932; *American Indian Painting of
the Southwest and Plains Areas,* by Dorothy Dunn, Albuquerque,
1968; *Southwest Indian Painting: A Changing Art,* by Clara Lee
Tanner, Tucson, 1973; *Native American Painting: Selections from
the Museum of the American Indian,* by David M. Fawcett and Lee
A. Callendar, New York, 1982.

*   *   *

Luis Gonzalez (Wo Peen) was among the numerous watercolorists to emerge in San Ildefonso during the first three decades of the

twentieth century. These artists, who included Crescencio and Julian Martinez, Awa Tsireh (Alphonso Roybal), Tonita Peña, and Encarnacion Peña (Soqween), produced stylistically similar works depicting ceremonial dances and stylized compositions of animals and landscapes. As a group they developed a distinct style characterized by blocks of outlined color with little modeling, considerable detailing of costume, and little use of backgrounds, groundlines, and three-dimensional perspective. These artists helped define what came to be known as "traditional" Indian painting, or more particularly, Pueblo painting.

Gonzalez is a less-heralded member of this grouping of painters, but his work was among the most widely exhibited in the years prior to World War II. By the time he was thirty, Gonzalez had works exhibited in major venues in the east (New York and Boston), midwest (Chicago), and far west (the San Francisco Bay area), as well as the Southwest and Southern Plains. During this period he also painted seven murals for a YMCA-sponsored collegiate camp in Springfield, Massachusetts, that featured Pueblo symbols and designs, serpents and thunderbirds. Gonzalez's output after World War II was sparse. Continually active in his Pueblo as a ceremonial singer and dancer as well as an administrator, serving as governor in 1945-46, he concentrated on farming and earning more stable wages and later lost his right hand in a hunting accident. By the late 1950s he began painting more regularly, focusing on animals, particularly horses, that were rounded, muscular, and active. As in all of his works, these paintings are dominated by a single or few figures sharply sketched and painted in the two-dimensional, flatstyle manner with little background and occasional symbols for rainclouds, kivas, mountains, and other southwestern scenes. While his works are excellent examples of early Pueblo painting, the plainness of his designs and uses of color as well as his acute stylization, although particularly effective in rendering robust shapes in human and animal forms to contrast with the more geometric designs of his symbols, are most responsible for his lesser status as an artist. Nevertheless, Gonzalez's work shows outstanding talent in outlining, fine brushwork, and balance among his central figures and estoteric symbols.

—Perry Bear

GOODMAN, Louise

Tribal affiliations: Navajo
Potter

Born: Louise Rose Goodman in Arizona, 25 December 1937. **Career:** Began making pottery in the early 1970s.

Selected Group Exhibitions

1988   *anii ánáádaalyaa'íí ; Continuity and Innovation in Recent Navajo Art*, Wheelwright Museum of the American Indian, Santa Fe, New Mexico
1989   *Navajo Junction: Where Navajo Potteries Meet*, Arizona State Museum, University of Arizona, Tucson
1993   *Leets'aa bi Diné Dáályé: It Is Called Navajo Pottery*, Phoebe A. Hearst Museum of Anthropology, University of California, Berkeley, California

1994   *Contemporary Art of the Navajo Nation*, traveling exhibit organized by Cedar Rapids Museum of Art; Venues: Albuquerque Museum, Albuquerque, New Mexico; the University Art Museum, State University of New York, Albany; Museum of the Southwest, Midland, Texas

Collections

Amerind Foundation, Dragoon, Arizona; Arizona State Museum, University of Arizona, Tucson; Denver Art Museum, Colorado; P. A. Hearst Museum of Anthropology, University of California, Berkeley; Museum of Northern Arizona, Flagstaff; Navajo Nation Museum, Window Rock, Arizona; Wheelwright Museum of the American Indian, Santa Fe, New Mexico.

Publications

On GOODMAN: Books—*Navajo Pottery: Traditions and Innovations*, by Russell P. Hartman, Flagstaff, Northland Press, 1987; *anii ánáádaalyaa'íí ; Continuity and Innovation in Recent Navajo Art*, exhibition catalog by Bruce Bernstein and Susan McGreevy, Santa Fe, Wheelwright Museum, 1988; *The People Speak: Navajo Folk Art,* by Chuck and Jan Rosenak, Flagstaff, Northland Publishing Co., 1994; *Trading Post Guidebook*, by Patrick Eddington and Susan Makov, Flagstaff, Northland Publishing Co., 1995; *Southwestern Pottery: Anasazi to Zuni*, by Allan Hayes and John Blom, Flagstaff, Northland Publishing Co., 1996. **Articles**—"Techniques in Navajo Pottery Making," by Jan Bell, *Plateau* 58, no. 2, 1987; " ̄   ̄s and Their Work," by H. Diane Wright and Jan Bell, *Plateau* 58, no. 2, 1987; "Navajo Pottery: Contemporary Trends in a Traditional Craft," by H. Diane Wright, *American Indian Art* 12, no. 2, 1987.

*   *   *

Louise Goodman is one of the most prolific among current Navajo pottery makers in the Shonto-Cow Springs region of the Navajo Reservation in northern Arizona. She began making pottery around 1970 after learning the craft from her husband's sister, Lorena Bartlett. Her overall body of work could be described as eclectic, innovative, amusing, trendy, but most importantly, distinctive. Like many other Navajo potters, Goodman produces work firmly rooted in traditions several hundred years old which is at the same time very modern and appealing to contemporary craft collectors.

Early in her career, Goodman experimented with various vessel forms to determine what would sell best. This was the early period of the current revival of Navajo pottery, when public interest in Navajo wares was somewhat limited, as were the wares themselves. Over the years, she has made effigy vessels and figurines depicting virtually every domestic animal known to the Navajo, including sheep, goats, chickens, dogs, horses, cows, and mules. Wild animals include buffalo, bears, squirrels, and turtles. And like other folk artists, she has also produced more than one fanciful animal whose identity is left to the viewer's imagination.

Multi-spouted vessels also were an early experiment that underwent many transformations. The ever-popular double-spouted "wedding vase" is widely known, but Goodman and other potters also produced jars, pitchers, and vases with three, four, and even five openings or spouts. Some of these functioned as vases or pencil holders, while others were completely non-functional.

Goodman still makes a wide range of vessels, but by the early

Louise Goodman: Navajo pitch-coated jar (1993) and bear figurine (c. 1989). Photograph by Dong Lin; courtesy the collections of Russell P. Hartman (jar) and Ruth K. Belicove (bear).

1980s, she had begun to establish her own niche in the marketplace by specializing in several forms that grew out of her early experiments. In the seventeenth and eighteenth centuries, when Navajo women cooked exclusively in pottery vessels, they produced bullet-shaped jars with pointed bases. This shape reflected its function, as it stood upright in nothing more than a shallow depression dug in the sandy bottom of a firepit and its tall, cylindrical shape provided greater body surface for readily conducting heat during cooking. Goodman is still one of the few potters who reproduces

these historic vessels, and many of them have been placed in museum collections.

Like most southwestern Indian pottery, Navajo wares are made by the coiling technique, in which coils of clay are stacked atop one another and scraped smooth before the next coil is added. Ancient Anasazi potters throughout the Four Corners area made utilitarian wares in which they smoothed only the interior of a vessel; exterior clay coils were simply pressed down and pinched, producing what is known as corrugated wares. Perhaps inspired by shards of these ancient wares found throughout the Navajo Reservation, Louise Goodman introduced pots that were scraped smooth only on the interior. She makes some vessels entirely in this manner, using a board to tap down each succeeding coil as she builds up a vessel's walls. In other pieces, she uses this technique only on the upper or lower part of a vessel. Other potters have tried to copy Louise's work by simply drawing incised lines around a pot in a spiral from base to top. But because Louise builds her coils up one at a time, the lines between adjacent coils do not spiral. The random pattern of fireclouds and the shimmer of piñon pine pitch on a finished vessel make these some of the most attractive examples of contemporary Navajo pottery.

The third vessel form for which Goodman is especially well known is the standing bear figurine. Ranging in height from 6 to 24 inches, the early examples of these were almost always in the form of coin banks, with slots cut out on their backs. More and more, however, these figurines are now made without the coin slot. The figurines themselves often have whimsical facial expressions and come in all body shapes, giving each one its own personality.

—Russell P. Hartman

GORMAN, Carl N.

Variant names: Kinyeonny Beyeh
Tribal affiliations: Navajo
Painter

Born: Carl Nelson Gorman, Chinle, Arizona, 5 October 1907; Navajo name means "Son of the Towering House People." **Education:** Otis Art Institute, 1947-51. **Military Service:** U.S. Marine Corps, Navajo Code Talker, World War II. **Career:** Technical illustrator, Douglas Aircraft, 1951-61; headed Navajo Arts and Crafts Guild, a tribally owned and operated crafts cooperative, 1962-66; instructor of Native American art, University of California at Davis, 1969-1972; Head, Navajo Health Authority, 1972-77; instructor, Navajo Community College, 1977-1980. **Awards:** Numerous art fair honors; commissions for ceremonial designs for the Los Angeles Indian Center and the Los Angeles Navajo Club; honorary doctorate, University of New Mexico; C. N. Gorman Museum, University of California at Davis, named in his honor.

Individual Exhibitions

1955	Gallup Public Library, Gallup, New Mexico
1956	Gallup Indian Center, Gallup, New Mexico
1964	University of the Pacific, Stockton, California
1972	C. N. Gorman Museum, University of California, Davis
1975	Philbrook Museum of Art, Tulsa, Oklahoma
1977	Navajo Community College, Tsaile, Arizona
1979	Navajo Tribal Museum, Window Rock, Arizona
1988	Museum of Northern Arizona, Flagstaff
1990	Heard Museum, Phoenix, Arizona
1997	C. N. Gorman Museum, University of California, Davis

Selected Group Exhibitions

1957	M. H. de Young Memorial Museum, San Francisco
1962	*Scottsdale National Indian Art Exhibition*, Scottsdale, Arizona
1963	Museum of Northern Arizona, Flagstaff, Arizona
	Sedona Arts Center, Sedona, Arizona
1964	Arizona State University Art Museum, Tempe, Arizona
	New Directions in American Indian Art, (father-son exhibit) Philbrook Museum of Art, Tulsa, Oklahoma
	First Annual Invitational Exhibition of American Indian Paintings, United States Department of the Interior, Washington, D.C.
1965	Heard Museum, Phoenix, Arizona
	Museum of New Mexico, Santa Fe, New Mexico
1967	American Indian Historical Society, San Francisco
1968	*James T. Bialac Collection of Southwest Indian Paintings*, Arizona State Museum, University of Arizona, Tucson
1972	C. N. Gorman Museum, University of California, Davis
1981	*Carl and R. C. Gorman*, Navajo Tribal Museum, Window Rock, Arizona
1983	Museum of Texas Tech University, Lubbock, Texas
1984	C. N. Gorman Museum, University of California, Davis
1985	Navajo Tribal Museum, Window Rock, Arizona
1996	*Drawn from Memory: James T. Bialac Collection of Native American Art*, Heard Museum, Phoenix, Arizona

Publications

By GORMAN: Books—"Foreword" in *Warriors: Navajo Code Talkers*, by Kenji Kawano, Flagstaff, Northland Publishing Co., 1990.

On GORMAN: Books—*The James T. Bialac Collection of Southwest Indian Paintings*, exhibition catalog, by Clara Lee Tanner, Tucson, University of Arizona Press, 1968; *The Navajo Code Talkers*, by Doris A. Paul, Pittsburgh, Dorrance Publishing Co., 1973; *Southwest Indian Painting: A Changing Art*, by Clara Lee Tanner, Tucson, University of Arizona Press, 1973; *Carl Gorman's World*, by Henry and Georgia Greenberg, Albuquerque, University of New Mexico Press, 1984.

Collections

C. N. Gorman Museum, University of California, Davis; Heard Museum, Phoenix, Arizona; Indian Arts and Crafts Board, U. S. Dept. of the Interior, Washington, D.C.; Museum of Northern Arizona, Flagstaff; Navajo Nation Museum, Window Rock, Arizona; Millicent Rogers Foundation Museum, Taos, New Mexico; Roswell Museum and Art Center, Roswell, New Mexico; Southwest Museum, Los Angeles.

*   *   *

Carl N. Gorman was among the first Native American artists to break from what was regarded as traditional painting. Without intending to do so, he played a large role in the fledgling contemporary Native American art movement. Born in 1907 and raised in the Navajo tradition, Gorman showed artistic inclinations while still a young boy, but his father steered him toward something that would earn him a living. Consequently, Gorman held a number of jobs as a young man and served in the U. S. Marines during World War II as a Navajo Code Talker. Following the war, he enrolled at the Otis Art Institute in 1947 to pursue his dream. Having no foundation in art, he spent his first year there studying design, composition, and

Carl N. Gorman: *Yeibichai*, 1985. Photograph by Dong Lin; courtesy the collection of Russell P. Hartman.

color. When his GI Bill benefits expired after four years, he accepted a technical illustrator's position with Douglas Aircraft (a position he held for more than 10 years) and continued taking evening classes at Otis for three more years. His zest for learning was boundless.

At Otis, Gorman drew any subject he wanted, and often carried a sketch pad while going about other activities, just to perfect his technique. During those years of study, he knew clearly that he wanted to succeed as an artist, but he wanted to succeed as a Navajo artist. He was proud of his heritage and wanted to share it with others, but he also wanted to interpret it in his own way, not in the flat style that others had determined was the "traditional" and only proper way for Indians to paint.

Gorman learned to paint in oils, watercolors and casein at Otis. He also studied sculpture and ceramics. When he painted, he wanted his subjects to come alive to appeal to the viewer on an emotional level. Some of his works during this period, more so than later, delivered a real message. None is more pointed or poignant that *Not Allowed*, in which an Indian veteran on crutches returns from war, only to be refused service in a bar because of social discrimination.

Showings of his work throughout southern California during the 1950s met with increasing success and notoriety. In his native Southwest, however, acceptance of his work was harder to achieve. There, the leading Native American art competitions operated under very narrow definitions of what was or wasn't genuine Native American art. Artists like Gorman, who painted outside those definitions, were more or less locked out of those competitions. That was to change in 1962 with the first Scottsdale National Indian Art Exhibit, where innovation was actually encouraged. Gorman entered three pieces, one of which won a Second Place award.

In 1962, Gorman and his wife, Mary, returned to the Navajo reservation where Gorman accepted an offer to head the Navajo Arts and Crafts Guild, a tribally owned and operated crafts cooperative. This was the first of several positions Gorman held after returning to his homeland, all of them aimed at helping his Navajo people attain a better life in a rapidly changing world.

In 1966, Gorman's nine-year-old son Kee was killed in an automobile accident. Kee was a promising artist in his own right, and his death paralyzed his father artistically. For four years Gorman was unable to even pick up a brush. During part of that time, he headed a project that recorded hundreds of hours of interviews with tradi-

tional Navajo healers and medicine men, speaking at great length about Navajo culture, history, and teachings. From these, he gained an incredibly deep understanding of his own roots, an understanding that would provide endless inspiration in later years.

In 1969, he joined the faculty at the University of California at Davis as an instructor of Native American art. His students represented many different tribes and Gorman instilled in them a sense of Indian heritage and pride. In return, they instilled in him the confidence to return to painting. Upon his leaving in 1972, the university honored him by establishing a museum dedicated to the creative expressions of Native American artists. The museum was named the C. N. Gorman Museum.

Gorman returned again to the Navajo Reservation to head the Navajo Health Authority, whose mandate was to identify and catalog the hundreds of medicinal plants used by the Navajo, and to foster better cooperation and understanding of each other between native Navajo healers and non-native doctors working on the reservation. This was yet another learning experience for Gorman. In 1977, he accepted another teaching position, at Navajo Community College.

By 1980, Gorman had given up classroom teaching and turned more and more to painting. Although he painted sporadically after leaving UC Davis in 1972, his many other commitments always prevented him from assembling a large body of work. In the 1980s, however, he had as much time as he wanted to paint, and his output during that decade was impressive. He returned often to his favorite subject of horses, trying to capture their essence in as few strokes as possible. Some of his works are reminiscent of the cave paintings in France in their simplicity. He also continued to depict scenes of Navajo life and culture, still playing the role of educator.

Gorman's long artistic career has been a series of peaks and valleys. Through much of his work, he has tried to teach the world about the Navajo world in its infinite variety. Thus, many of his paintings have no deep social message, but rather a softer, underlying message of understanding and appreciation for another cultural viewpoint. Gorman's greatest legacy, perhaps, is the inspiration he has shown to others, both artist and non-artist. His whole life has served as a model of individuality and personal pride.

—Russell P. Hartman

GORMAN, R. C.

Tribal affiliations: Navajo
Painter, sculptor, and ceramist

Born: Rudolph Carl Gorman, 26 July 1932, Chinle, Arizona; son of Carl N. Gorman. **Education:** Mexico City College; Northern Arizona University; University of the Americas; San Francisco State College. **Military Service:** U.S. Navy. **Career:** Artist since mid 1950s; purchased a Taos gallery,1968, and renamed it the Navajo Gallery, which served as his studio and home (1964-74) and remains a showplace for Gorman's work; associated with Tamarind Institute, Albuquerque, 1971-76; Houston Fine Art Press, 1979; board member, College of Granado, Arizona, Music at Angel Fire, New Mexico, Pacific Northwest Indian Center, Gonzaga University, Seattle, Taos Festival of Music, New Mexico, and Wheelwright Museum of the American Indian, Santa Fe; fellow, Kellog Fellowship Screening Committee, Navajo Heath Authority; standards committee member and juror, New Mexico Arts and Crafts Fair. **Awards:** Honorary doctorates, College of Grandado, Arizona (1978), Eastern New Mexico University, Portales (1980), Northern Arizona University, Flagstaff (1990); Humanitarian Award in Fine Art, Harvard University, 1986; Key to the City, El Paso, San Antonio, and Houston, Texas, Scottsdale, Arizona; R.C. Gorman Day, State of New Mexico, 8 January 1979, and San Francisco, 18 March 1986; numerous at fairs and juried competitions, including All-American Indian Days, Heard Museum Guild Indian Arts and Crafts Show, National Cowboy Hall of Fame, Philbrook Indian Art Exhibition, Scottsdale National Indian Arts Exhibition, and Tanner's All-Invitational Pottery and Painting Show; Governor's Award, State of New Mexico, 1989.

Individual Exhibitions

1963   Coffee Gallery, San Francisco, California
1965   Manchester Gallery, Taos, New Mexico
1966   Manchester Gallery, Taos, New Mexico
        Museum of Indian Arts, San Francisco, California
1967   Heard Museum, Phoenix, Arizona
1968   Manchester Gallery, Taos, New Mexico
1969   Suzanne Brown Art Wagon Gallery, Scottsdale, Arizona
1970   Navajo Community College, Many Farms, Arizona
        Northern Arizona University Art Gallery, Flagstaff, Arizona
1971   Suzanne Brown Art Wagon Gallery, Scottsdale, Arizona
        Gallery of Modern Art, Scottsdale, Arizona
1972   Julian Garcia, Albuquerque, New Mexico
        Jamison Gallery, Santa Fe, New Mexico
1973   Mary Livingston Gallery, Santa Ana, California
        Stables Gallery, Taos, New Mexico
        Western Art Gallery, Albuquerque, New Mexico
        Suzanne Brown Art Wagon Gallery, Scottsdale, Arizona
        Aspen Gallery of Art, Aspen, Colorado
1974   Baylor University, Waco, Texas
        Wartburg College, Waverly, Iowa
1975   Museum of the American Indian, New York
        Albuquerque Museum, New Mexico
        Wheelwright Museum of the American Indian, Santa Fe, New Mexico
        Stables Gallery, Taos, New Mexico

        Navajo Nation Museum, Window Rock, Arizona
1976   Freeman-Anacker Gallery, New Orleans, Louisiana
        Gallery of New Mexico, Santa Fe
        von Straaten Gallery, Chicago
1976-83 White Buffalo Gallery, Wichita, Kansas
1977   Stables Gallery, Taos, New Mexico
        Clarke-Benton Gallery, Santa Fe, New Mexico
        Clay Gallery, New York
        Tiger Indian Reservation, El Paso, Texas
        Walton Gilbert Gallery, San Francisco, California
1978   Julian Garcia, Albuquerque, New Mexico
        Kansas State University, Manhattan, Kansas
        Millicent Rogers Foundation Museum, Taos, New Mexico
        Gallery Mack, Seattle, Washington
1979   Bayard Gallery, Dallas, Texas
        Musée Municipal, St. Paul de Vence, France
1980   Navajo Turquoise Gallery, Paris
1981   Four Winds Gallery, Pittsburgh, Pennsylvania
        Ken Phillips Gallery, Denver, Colorado
        Now and Then Gallery, East Meadow, New York
        Westwood Gallery, Portland, Oregon
1982   *Gorman in Deutschland*, Galerie Pueblo, Neustadt, West Germany
        Gallery Hawaii, Maui
1983   Millicent Rogers Foundation Museum, Taos, New Mexico
        Now and Then Gallery, East Meadow, New York
        Galeria Capistrano, San Juan, Capistrano, California
1983   American West Gallery, Chicago
1986   Galerie Calumet, Heidelberg, Germany
1987   Galeria Capistrano, San Juan, Capistrano, California
        Grycner Gallery, Lahaina, Maui, Hawaii
1988   *R. C. Gorman, Chinle to Taos*, Millicent Rogers Museum, Taos, New Mexico
        Galerie Calumet, Heidelberg, Germany
1989-92 Galeria Capistrano, San Juan, Capistrano, California
        Rio Grande Gallery, Santa Fe, New Mexico
1990-97 Navajo Gallery, Taos, New Mexico

Selected Group Exhibitions

1964   Philbrook Art Center, Tulsa, Oklahoma
1965   Heard Museum, Phoenix, Arizona
1967   American Indian Historical Society, San Francisco, California
1968   *James T. Bialac Collection of Southwest Indian Paintings*, Arizona State Museum, University of Arizona, Tucson
1973   *American Indian Art*, Metropolitan Museum of Art, New York
        Gorman/Scholder Exhibit, Museum of Fine Arts, Santa Fe, New Mexico
1977   Heard Museum, Phoenix, Arizona
1978   *100 Years of Native American Painting*, Oklahoma Museum of Art, Oklahoma City
1981   *Carl and R. C. Gorman*, Navajo Tribal Museum, Window Rock, Arizona
1984   C. N. Gorman Museum, University of California, Davis, California
1984   *Indianascher Kunstler*, organized by the Philbrook Museum, Tulsa, Oklahoma (traveled in Germany through 1985)

R. C. Gorman: *Mother and Child*, 1960. Photograph by Dong Lin; courtesy California Academy of Sciences, Elkus Collection.

1991-96 *Shared Visions: Native American Painters and Sculptors in the Twentieth Century,* organized and premiered by the Heard Museum, Phoenix, Arizona (traveling in the U.S., Canada, and New Zealand)

Collections

Albuquerque Museum, New Mexico; Amerind Foundation, Dragoon, Arizona; California Academy of Sciences, Elkus Collection, San Francisco; Denver Art Museum, Colorado; El Paso Museum of Art, Texas; Gonzaga University, Spokane, Washington; C. N. Gorman Museum, University of California, Davis; Heard Museum, Phoenix; Heritage Center, Red Cloud Indian School, Pine Ridge, South Dakota; Indian Arts and Crafts Board, U.S. Department of the Interior, Washington, D.C.; Indianapolis Museum of Art, Indiana; Metropolitan Museum of Art, New York; Museum of Fine Arts, Museum of New Mexico, Santa Fe; Museum of Northern Arizona, Flagstaff; National Museum of the American Indian, Smithsonian Institution, Washington, D.C.; Navajo Nation Museum, Window Rock, Arizona; Northern Arizona University, Flagstaff; Pacific Northwest Indian Center, Gonzaga University, Spokane, Washington; Palm Springs Desert Museum, California; Jesse Peter Native American Art Museum, Santa Rosa Junior College, Santa Rosa, California; Philbrook Museum, Tulsa, Oklahoma; Millicent Rogers Museum, Taos New Mexico; Roswell Museum and Art Center, Roswell, New Mexico; Southwest Museum, Los Angeles, California; Wheelwright Museum of the American Indian, Santa Fe, New Mexico.

Publications

By GORMAN: Book—*The Man to Send Rain Clouds: Contemporary Stories by American Indians,* Kenneth Rosen, editor, illustrations and a story by Gorman, Viking Press, New York, 1974; *Radiance of My People,* Albuquerque, 1992.

On GORMAN: Books—*The James T. Bialac Collection of Southwest Indian Paintings,* exhibition catalog by Clara Lee Tanner, Tucson, University of Arizona Press, 1968; *Indian Painters and White Patrons* by J. J. Brody, Albuquerque: University of New Mexico Press, 1971; *Southwest Indian Painting: A Changing Art* by Clara Lee Tanner, Tucson, University of Arizona Press, 1973; *Masterworks from the Museum of the American Indian,* New York: Metropolitan Museum of Art, 1973; *Art and Indian Individualists* by Guy and Doris Monthan, Flagstaff, Northland Press, 1975; *R. C. Gorman: The Lithographs* by Doris Monthan, Flagstaff, Northland Press, 1978; *100 Years of Native American Painting* by Arthur Silberman, Oklahoma City, Oklahoma Museum of Art, 1978; *The Posters* by Patricia Hurst, Flagstaff, Northland Press, 1980; *The Sweet Grass Lives On: Fifty Contemporary North American Indian Artists* by Jamake Highwater, New York, Lippincott & Crowell, 1980; *Nudes & Foods, Gorman Goes Gourmet* by Virginia Dooley, Flagstaff, Northland Press, 1981; *The Drawings* by Mary Beth Green, Flagstaff, Northland Press, 1982; *Navajo Painting* by Katherin Chase, Flagstaff, Museum of Northern Arizona Press, 1983; *R. C. Gorman: A Portrait* by Chuck Henningsen, Boston, Little, Brown & Co., 1983; *The Elkus Collection, Southwestern Indian Art,* edited by Dorothy K. Washburn, San Francisco, California Academy of Sciences, 1984; *R. C. Gorman: Chinle to Taos* by Virginia Dooley, Taos, Millicent Rogers Museum, 1988; *R. C. Gorman: The Complete Graphics* by Ben Q. Adams and Richard Newlin, Albuquerque, Taos Editions, 1988. **Articles**—"R. C. Gorman: The Two Worlds of a Navajo Artist" by Ronald Leal, *Mankind* 2, no. 9, 1970; "An Indian and His Art: This Is Gorman" by Robert A. Ewing, *New Mexico Magazine,* Spring 1971; "R. C. Gorman : Fun Loving Indian Artist" by Martha Buddecke, *Southwest Art,* September 1972; "A Man For All Mediums" by Linda Durham, *Southwest Art,* June 1978; "The Unpredictable R. C. Gorman" by Guy and Doris Monthan, *American Indian Art* 3, no. 3, 1978; "R. C. Gorman: The Spirit of Changing Woman" by Catherine Wheeler-Orr, *Four Winds Magazine* 2, no. 2, 1981. **Films**—*R. C. Gorman,* PBS, KAET TV, Phoenix, Arizona, 1976; *Navajo Artist R. C. Gorman,* by Harold Joe Waldrum, Heese/ Waldrum Studios, 1987.

*   *   *

R. C. (Rudolph Carl) Gorman has to be counted among the founders of the contemporary Indian art movement. Certainly he was among the first contemporary Native American artists to establish an international following. The son of noted Navajo artist, Carl N. Gorman, the younger Gorman was raised on the Navajo Reservation and educated at mission schools. It was there he received his first art instruction.

Following high school and a tour of duty in the U. S. Navy, Gorman enrolled at Arizona State College (now Northern Arizona University), majoring in American Literature. A 1958 visit to Mexico introduced him to the works of the great Mexican muralists, Rivera, Orozco, Zuniga, Siqueiros, and Tamayo. Gorman identified with the human element captured in their works and set a goal for himself to depict his own people in that same spirit. The Navajo Nation awarded him a scholarship to study art at Mexico City College (now the University of the Americas), making him the first Navajo to study at a foreign university.

After a year's study, Gorman moved to San Francisco where he immersed himself in painting, experimenting with many different styles. During the day he worked as an artist's model, allowing him to attend the lectures without enrolling in the classes. Until the 1960s, Indian art was defined by what was taught at governmental Indian schools and only those artists who adopted traditional styles were accepted. Gorman's collection of his own works includes several pieces in this style, completed when he was very young. For the most part, however, Gorman has always been an individualist. Without any ties to these schools or to their descendant, the Institute of American Indian Arts in Santa Fe, he rejected limitations imposed by government school art programs. Instead, he developed his own style and painted whatever subjects he chose. A series of small gallery shows in the San Francisco Bay area in the late 1950s and early 1960s brought him some fame and allowed him to continue his personal quest.

In 1964, Gorman visited Taos, New Mexico, and showed his work to a gallery owner who offered him a solo show the following summer. In 1968, Gorman bought that same gallery and renamed it the Navajo Gallery. It has remained his base of operations ever since, serving also as his studio and home for more than 10 years. Today it remains a showplace for Gorman's own work as well as that of other Native American artists whom Gorman has taken under his wings. The artist once said, "Taos has magic . . . is magic."

Throughout his career, Gorman has worked in a variety of media. During the 1960s and 1970s he produced many drawings using acrylics, oils, oil pastels and mixed media. In some of these, the subject is engaged in a routine activity, seemingly unaware of being watched. In every instance, however, all hint of a background is removed, to focus the viewer's eye only on the subject. Contextual background was unnecessary in Gorman's philosophy of that period; only a person's physical presence and spiritual bearing mattered. Regardless of the medium, Gorman relied (and still does) upon very loose and broad strokes to merely suggest the shapes of his human subjects with a few carefully chosen lines. The face, hands, and feet are presented in more detail, because they can tell so much about a person. Women, especially, have been Gorman's favorite subjects, reflecting Navajo respect for women in general, as well as Gorman's own ties to his mother and to his aunts, as well as his fascination for the infinite variety in womanhood. But he has also featured male subjects from time to time, as well as Navajo rugs and themes based on Navajo teachings.

By the early 1960s, Gorman had already produced several linocuts, and in 1966, he produced his first lithograph in Mexico. In so doing, he discovered the medium he had been searching for, one that would allow him to reach a broader audience but still afford him the freedom and spontaneity of drawing. His first lithographs were only one color and although they were well received, they did not catapult Gorman to fame. In 1971, he began working with the renowned Tamarind Institute in Albuquerque, where over the next few years he produced five lithographic suites and eight individual lithographs, showing a variety of subject matter and techniques.

Throughout the 1970s, Gorman continued to work in lithography, mastering more complex techniques. He also produced a few etchings and serigraphs, but found that neither suited him. Instead, he worked at many different lithographic workshops and with many respected printers. His work became more and more complex, although as in his earlier drawings, emphasis remained on line and form. A grueling schedule of solo gallery shows in the late 1970s and phenomenal commercial success went hand in hand, leading to inquiries from foreign galleries. Gorman responded by producing lithographs in France, Japan, and Spain.

In 1979, Gorman began working with a new workshop, Houston Fine Art Press. The resulting lithographs were truly "full color." Gorman's style had gradually evolved to include more and more background details in a drawing, such as architecture, landscapes, and sky. The flowing lines of his unmistakable women were and are still there but now they are balanced against rich backgrounds that only add to the beauty.

During the 1980s, Gorman also ventured increasingly into the realms of bronze sculpture, ceramics, cast paper, and even etched glass. Lithography will always remain his medium of choice, but he never seems to tire of exploring new avenues. His life has been one of continual learning, yet few living artists are as prolific as Gorman. In his lifetime, he has produced more than 500 lithographs alone. His work has often been criticized as being repetitive and uninspired. Other rumors claim that Gorman himself offers little creative input into his work, instead delegating each step of the lithographic printing process to others. Lithography is necessarily a collaborative process, and while a few lithographs are clearly derived from historic photographs, no artist could produce such a consistently themed body of work as Gorman has done without completely involving himself. Success will always beget detractors, but Gorman's role in the history of Native American art is secure and without parallel.

—Russell P. Hartman

GRANT, Dorothy

Variant names: El Ski Di
Tribal affiliations: Kaigani Haida
Weaver, designer, and button designer

Born: Hydaburg, Alaska, 14 March 1955. **Education:** Graduated from high school in Seattle, Washington; two years of college from 1975 to 1977; received fashion design diploma from the Helen Lefeaux School of Fashion Design in Vancouver in 1987; informal apprentice with acclaimed Haida elder Florence Davidson in spruce root weaving. **Family:** Married Robert Davidson 1986, divorced 1996. **Career:** President of Dorothy Grant Ltd., (fashion design) and owner of the Galleria Boutique in Vancouver. **Awards:** *Winds of Change* Award as top First Nations fashion designer in Canada, 1993. **E-mail Address:** dgrant@cyberstore.ca

Individual Exhibitions

1983   *Quiet Wealth*, Vancouver
1989   Derek Simpkins Gallery of Tribal Art, Vancouver

Selected Group Exhibitions

1982   *Northwest Coast Art*, Stonington Gallery, Seattle

Dorothy Grant. Courtesy of the artist.

Dorothy Grant: *Raven Creation Tunic,* **collaborative piece with Robert Davidson. Photograph by Sam Short; courtesy Museum of Civilization, Ottawa.**

Collections

Canadian Museum of Civilization, Ottawa; DeYoung Museum, San Francisco; National Gallery of Canada, Ottawa; University of British Columbia Museum of Anthropology, Vancouver; Vancouver Museum.

Publications

On GRANT: Books—*A Haida Potlatch*, by Ulli Steltzer, Douglas & McIntyre: Vancouver, 1985; *Robes of Power: Totem Poles on Cloth*, edited by Doreen Jensen and Polly Sargent, University of British Columbia Press: Vancouver, 1986. **Article**—"Feastwear: Haida Art Goes Couture," *American Indian Art Magazine*, Autumn 1992.

*

Dorothy Grant comments:

There are many influences in my life as a traditional artist and as a fashion designer. Foremost influences have been my maternal grandmothers and aunties from Alaska and Haida Gwaii, and those before them. Their sense of strength and identity as Haida women has impressed me since I was a little girl. They each had something uniquely different in what they taught me—more than the techniques of Haida art, but also endurance and discipline. I have great respect for my traditional art form, for it has survived through many generations of artists, who have kept the form and integrity of the principles behind it. I believe that what I am doing with my work, in a style sense, is moving it, is making it pliable on garments. Art is not stoic. Good art must evolve to survive. My grandmothers would agree.

*   *   *

It is part of the perceived duty of any artist to evolve, create challenges for themselves in order to explore all possibilities of solutions and test the limitations of form, medium, structure, and even function. Dorothy Grant, artist of fashion, does all of this while remaining deeply rooted in her ancestral traditions.

Like totem poles and great canoes, elaborate button blankets and finely woven spruce root hats are a hallmark of the legendary Haida artistic traditions. Special songs and dances were created to show off the finest of button blankets. Grant learned the skills of making them from elders who carried on traditions passed on for hundreds and thousands of years. From the ground up, literally, Grant learned the entire process of creating a blanket, basket or traditional hat of the highest quality. She has pushed the traditional form against common distinctions between fashion and art, and the result has been a classic yet innovative line of *haute couture* fashion called Feastwear, which is based firmly on the first "feastwear" pieces that were the great button blankets of her ancestors.

The button blankets, in particular, provided the root of the pieces Grant creates today. These blankets, often referred to as "totem poles on cloth," are traditionally worn at potlatches, ceremonies, and other feasts and celebrations among the coastal peoples. Blankets are worn to proudly identify the wearer by the prominent display of hereditary crests. But as her skills for cutting the blanket designs, which can be likened to the brush strokes of a painter, gained her much recognition, Grant began exploring the idea that the strict rules of Haida formline design might be translated to contemporary clothing—that which we wear to our celebrations and ceremonies now. Thus, her acclaimed Feastwear line was born out of her curiosity and urge to reach beyond the blanket style she had by this time mastered.

The new territory Grant was exploring brought some unexpected criticism, with claims that fashion is not an art form but rather limited expression of popular culture. Grant puts into question limiting beliefs regarding the medium through which art is expressed. Her pieces create a soft bridge between an accepted ancestral art form—the button blanket, which was linked to specific functions proclaiming one's lineage and identity with pride and confidence through the wearing of ceremonial regalia—and a contemporary interpretation of those same ideas.

Grant set out intentionally to experiment with Haida formline design applied to the flexible and moving medium of cloth, using the shapes and natural drapery of the cloth as part of her expression of the art form. As she states in an essay from *Robes of Power*, "When I'm working on button blankets, I feel that I'm 'sculpting on cloth,' my scissors being like a chisel and hammer to a sculptor, defining every line with a precise cut." She knows well the strict rules of the Haida design language, in which characters and parts of characters are primary or secondary, and how the curved lines must balance traditional shapes such as the ovoid and the U, and all play their pre-ordained role in the overall design. The type of clothing itself is often also derived from the history of the Haida people. Many Feastwear coats, in particular, follow closely the style of Russian long coat worn by traders in the 1800s. Another dress, the *Hummingbird Copper Dress*, forms the shape of the traditional "copper" of the Coastal people as it wraps around the wearer. This dress, as in the button blankets, can be hung for display from doweling—a feature of many Feastwear pieces.

The *Raven Creation Tunic*, one of her first creations, is a direct descendent of the long appliquéd vests worn by the Northwest Coast people for ceremonies. The images tell the story of the Haida raven myth of creation. This piece is now prized in the permanent collection of the Canadian Museum of Civilization.

For all of these items in the Feastwear collection, Grant uses materials employed by her grandmother and teacher. She seeks out fine woolen fabrics for the base, using traditional contrasting colours of black and red, red and blue, and even experimenting with black and blue, and black and brown. As with the original blankets, Grant appliqués the designs onto the base piece of fabric and adds beads and mother-of-pearl button accents to highlight the shapes. Grant's trademark blanket borders, which set her apart from other artists in the medium, appear at times as well.

Grant doesn't subscribe to the notion that fashion is a seasonal concept where an item is discarded at the end of a year. She wants her pieces, like the great button blankets they pay homage to, to last forever. She rejects the idea that fashion cannot be considered art, and with her feastwear pieces scattered through the collections of the National Gallery of Canada and other notable institutions and private collections, her point seems to be made. This is art that one interacts with in a very personal way.

—Vesta Giles

GRAVES, Sharol
Tribal affiliations: Shawnee
Painter and mixed media artist

Born: Portland, Oregon, 1953. **Education:** Institute of American Indian Arts, Santa Fe, 1970; Mills College, Oakland, California, B.A. 1977; Master's Institute, Santa Clara, California, drafting and printed-circuit design; University of California at Berkeley Extension, San Francisco, graphic design; California College of Arts and Crafts, Oakland, life drawing; Computer Arts Institute, San Francisco, desktop publishing and multi-media; American Animation Institute, North Hollywood, animation. **Career:** Artist, illustrator.

Individual Exhibitions

1996   *One Woman Show*, Gallery Southwest, Tigard, Oregon

Selected Group Exhibitions

1977   *American Indian Artists*, American Indian Center, San Francisco
1978   *American Indian Art Show*, Mission Cultural Center Art Gallery, San Francisco
1980   *Corporate Show*, Datapoint Corporation, Sunnyvale, California
1982   *Group Show*, Telesensory Systems, Palo Alto, California
1984   *American Indian Art Show*, San Jose Indian Center, San Jose, California
1986   *The Computer as Art*, Southwest Museum of Science and Technology, Dallas, Texas
1987   *Red Cloud Indian Art Show*, Heritage Center, Pine Ridge, South Dakota
        Art from the Computer, California College of Arts and Crafts, Oakland
        Pandora's Box: Computer Generated Art, Southwestern University, Georgetown, Texas
        Computer Art Exhibition, University of the Pacific, Stockton, California
1988   *Bill Glass, Sharol Graves, and Bill Harjo*, Hapanyi Fine Arts, Santa Barbara, California
        Southwest Indian Art Association Indian Market, Santa Fe Plaza, New Mexico
        Contemporary Indian Art Show, Kenneth Banks, Oakland, California
1989   *Lawrence Indian Arts Show*, University of Kansas Museum of Anthropology, Lawrence
        Native Tricksters, Western Digital Imaging, Mountain View, California

In Her Vision: Fifteen Indian Women Artists, American Indian Contemporary Arts, San Francisco
1990   *Sharol Graves and Eric Mattila*, C. N. Gorman Museum, University of California, Davis
        Power of Process, American Indian Contemporary Arts, San Francisco
        Ancestors Known and Unknown, Art in General, New York
        Native Proof, American Indian Contemporary Arts, San Francisco, and American Indian Community House Gallery, New York
1991   *Native American Artists*, Contemporary Art Southwest Museum, Los Angeles
1992   *Ancestral Memories*, Falkirk Cultural Center, Marin, California
        Four Directions, Pro-Arts/Taller Sin Fronteras, Oakland, California
        Portfolio II, American Indian Contemporary Arts, San Francisco
1993   *Kindred Spirits: Eight Native American Artists*, Bedford Gallery, Walnut Creek, California
        Southwest Museum Benefit Art Auction, Southwest Museum, Los Angeles
        Through the Native Lens, Indian Market Photography Exhibition, Institute of American Indian Arts, Santa Fe
        Native American Awareness, Hewlett-Packard Corporation, Mountain View, California
1994   *Indian Humor*, American Indian Contemporary Arts, San Francisco
1995   *Fugitive Colors*, Luna Sea Gallery, San Francisco
1996   *Mother Earth One People*, Native American Month, B.P.A., Portland, Oregon
        Synchronized Spirits, Institute of American Indian Arts Triennial Exhibition, Santa Fe
        Ancestral Memories, Falkirk Cultural Museum, Marin, California
        National Museum of the American Indian, Smithsonian Institute, Washington, D.C.
        Ink People Center for the Arts, Eureka, California
        Trinity County Arts Council, Weaverville, California
        Del Norte Association for Cultural Awareness, Crescent City, California
1997   *Indian Humor*, Autry Western Museum, Los Angeles

Publications

By GRAVES: Books Illustratred—*The People Shall Continue* by Simon Ortiz, Children's Book Press, 1977; *Through Indian Eyes* by Beverly Slapin and Doris Seale, Oyate, 1992; *Fugitive Colors* by Chrystos, Cleveland State University Poetry Center, 1994.

On GRAVES: Exhibition catalogs—*Ancestral Memories*, Falkirk Cultural Center, 1992; *Portfolio II*, American Indian Contemporary Arts, 1992; *Indian Humor*, American Indian Contemporary Arts, 1994. **Articles**—"On Being Technically Creative" by Larry McNeil, *Alaska Native Magazine*, 1987; "Indian Artists Paint Dynamic Cultural Picture" by Joan Crowder, *Santa Barbara News Press*, 11 November 1988.

*   *   *

Sharol Graves: *Sacred Stones,* 1990. Courtesy of the artist.

One of the primary concerns of Native artists today is the issue of "tradition" and the degree to which identity, both individual and cultural, is expressed in one's work. While the preservation of indigenous artistic traditions is, for some, an inherent responsibility, others consider this to be an infringement on their autonomy as contemporary artists. Fortunately, individuals such as the Shawnee artist Sharol Graves have sought a balance wherein artistic integrity, personal experience, and cultural heritage are united in thoughtfully conceived works of art.

While Graves's interest in the arts developed prior to her enrollment at the Institute of American Indian Arts in 1968, it was there that she was introduced to the diverse legacy of Native American art; "The IAIA was an incredible fountain of artistic talent, and was in its 'heyday.' I saw Indians as creative people, potters, dancers, jewelers, actors, painters, sculptors, photographers, singers. Through my friends from different tribes I learned Native legends and spiritual beliefs. I became quite Indian-identified, and found great inspiration in my native heritage." In these surroundings she also became aware of the restrictive labels placed on native art and artists, as well as the expectations imposed by the markets for Native American art.

Determined not to reinforce stereotypes by satisfying the demand for tourist art, Graves utilizes unorthodox media, such as computers and computer generated imagery. After working in the computer industry of Silicon Valley in the mid 1980s, she became interested in the intricate visual patterning of computer boards. Paintings such as *Buffalo Dance* (1986) and *Indian Circuit* (1986) consist of well-known Native American signifiers, such as moccasins and buffaloes, which are located within a hard-edged technological design. By juxtaposing native culture and modern context in these images Graves interrogates erroneous conceptions of "the Indian mind." While these paintings are not traditional, per se (and in fact poke fun at the very notion in the clever verbal punning of the titles), Graves maintains that native people have always integrated outside objects and influences into their art. In fact, as she notes, there are stylistic affinities between computer-based design and Native American artistic traditions, such as beadwork and weaving.

In addition to her computer-based imagery, Graves has explored her heritage in an abstract series based on parfleche designs. Parfleche, French for "to parry an arrow," are rawhide containers that were primarily used by Plains cultures to carry personal belongings. These objects usually have a brightly colored geometric pattern that is repeated on the top and bottom of the bag. Because they are both durable and lightweight, parfleches became increasingly common with the horse culture of the nineteenth century and were popular gifts. While cultural styles have been identified, design elements usually had private significance known only to the artist.

Personal meaning is playfully hinted at in *Funky Joy Boy* (1990), a title of one of her parfleche-inspired paintings, in which the colors evoke associations with the desert sun, minerals, and a late summer bloom. As in this image, Graves often builds up layers of paint and scrapes it away to reveal the underlying hue, much like the early rare incised parfleches (believed to have been influenced by the creation of birchbark containers). In this playful yet delicate composition, the eye is given room to roam yet caught, for example, in the blustery field of buff-white bound and divided by fragile lines of crimson and ultramarine. In contrast, images such as *Sacred Stones* (1990) are much more reticent, brooding and complex. In this image a greater emphasis is placed on the tactility of the surface in which three stones wrapped in copper wire constitute the central composition. While she initially utilized light earthtones in this series, her darker images came about as a consequence of personal loss and spiritual growth.

Graves's interest in abstraction as a form of artistic expression developed out of her study of dance and the performing arts. Although she attended IAIA for graphics, she also studied dance, and later pursued a double major in art and dance at Mills College. Her experience with dance led to her experiments with figurative drawing, and the expressive potential inherent in the depiction of the human form. Because she wanted to more fully integrate her emotional and spiritual experiences into her art, Graves eventually developed an abstract style. Consequently, the Plains parfleche is a befitting inspiration as it provides her with a means in which to express her cultural, personal, and artistic concerns. Moreover, Graves's parfleche images are compelling evidence of the vitality and ongoing evolution of Native American artistic traditions.

—Kristin Potter

GUTIÉRREZ, Lela and Van

Tribal affiliations: Santa Clara Pueblo
Potters

LELA. Born: 1874. **Family:** Married Van Gutiérrez c. 1905: seven children. **Died:** 1969.

VAN. Born: Evangelio Van Gutiérrez, c. 1870. **Died:** 1956.

Selected Group Exhibitions

1974   *Seven Families in Pueblo Pottery,* Maxwell Museum, Albuquerque, New Mexico

Collections

Indian Arts Research Center, School of American Research, Santa Fe, New Mexico; Museum of Indian Arts and Cultures, Santa Fe, New Mexico.

Publications

On Lela and Van GUTIÉRREZ: Books—*Seven Families in Pueblo Pottery*, by Rick Dillingham, Albuquerque, University of New Mexico Press, 1974; *Santa Clara Pottery Today*, by Betty LeFree, Albuquerque, University of New Mexico Press, 1975; *Fourteen Families in Pueblo Pottery*, by Rick Dillingham, Albuquerque, University of New Mexico Press, 1994; *Southwestern Pottery: Anasazi to Zuni*, by Allan Hayes and John Blom, Flagstaff, Northland Publishing, 1996.

*   *   *

Lela and Van Gutiérrez, among the most famous potters from Santa Clara Pueblo, northwest of Santa Fe, New Mexico, are especially noted for excellent polychrome wares. In addition to their impec-

Lela and Van Gutiérrez: *Lightning, Rain and Kiva Steps* polychrome pot, c. 1950. Photograph by Seth Roffman. Courtesy Dick Howard Collection.

cable craftsmanship, the Gutiérrezes introduced many different colors of clay, glazes and paints, creating a rich variety of wares. Like Maria and Julian Martinez, the most famous of all Pueblo potters, Lela and Van worked as a pottery-making team. Lela formed the pots, while Van created innovative designs and processed the clay.

Lela began making pottery in the 1890s and started working with Van around the turn of the century, shortly before their marriage in 1905. Pueblo pottery specialist Rick Dillingham speculated that they introduced polychrome, or multi-colored pottery by 1910, but Betty LaFree, in *Santa Clara Pottery Today*, moved the date back to a more conservative 1930. Lela and Van produced pottery together for almost half a century, until 1949. Their most popular designs featured Avanyu, the plumed water snake who is said to live within the "bosom of Mother Earth."

Van stopped potterymaking in 1949; he was then in his late seventies, and he died in 1956. Lela made pots with her son, Luther, from 1949 to 1966. Lela and Van's children, Margaret and Luther, formed a pottery-making team beginning in the mid-1960s, and the tradition is being carried on by Luther's son, Paul Gutiérrez, along with Paul's wife, Dorothy, and their son, Gary. They are known for small animal figurines called animalitos, with a repertoire that includes bears, coyotes, dogs, turtles, crocodiles, beavers, owls, donkeys, giraffes and many other animals.

Speaking on their family heritage, Margaret explained: "Our pottery has come down to us through three generations. Our great-great grandfather, Ta-Key-Sane, was the one who created and started this kind of pottery, a long time ago. Most of the pottery he made was for his own use, like kitchen utensils that the ladies use nowadays, or for ceremonies. From what we can gather, our great-great grandfather was very artistic in making pottery and also in designing. Then, my great grandfather took over the making and designing of the pottery. He also was very artistic, only he tried to improve it by adding more colors and making the pottery in more different sizes; big ones and small ones, also figures and animals."

Lela and Van Gutiérrez made improvements in quality and design, respectively, and were able to receive steady incomes through sales and bartering. The pottery was and continues to be handmade, with no commercial products used. Much of the pottery of Lela and Van Gutiérrez is brick red or light brown, with multicolored areas of designs in green, blue, black, white and varying shades of red. The surface is semi-glossy, from polishing with a cloth; other Santa Clara potters produce a high gloss by polishing with smooth river stones. The descriptive term for Gutiérrez family pottery is "Buff Polychrome Ware."

Van learned potterymaking by age ten from his father, beginning when he was old enough to accompany him into the hills and mountains to hunt game for food; at the same time they searched for clay of different colors and flowers and roots for paints that would turn into different colors when fired. Soon, he was helping to design and make pottery, and introduced improvements on design while trying different colors, or slips. Van, in turn, took Luther, his son, into the mountains to show him the locations of different colors of clay. The father then taught his son how to mix the clays, encouraging experimentation of different combinations. The exact locations where the family gathers their colorful clays reportedly are "closely guarded secrets."

Lela taught her daughter, Margaret, to make pottery starting at age twelve. After Luther's death, Margaret created pottery on her own. She travels throughout the southwest to obtain certain rare colors of clay.

—Gregory Schaaf

HACHIVI Edgar Heap of Birds

Variant names: Edgar Heap of Birds
Tribal affiliations: Cheyenne; Arapaho
Printmaker, painter, and video artist

Born: Wichita, Kansas, 22 November 1954. **Education:** California College of Arts and Crafts; B.F.A., University of Kansas, 1976; M.F.A., Tyler School of Art, Temple University, 1979; studied at Royal College of Art, London, 1976-77. **Career:** Associate professor, department of art, University of Oklahoma; curator; international lecturer on Native art.

Individual Exhibitions

1979   *Lizards*, Tyler Gallery, Tyler School of Art, Philadelphia
1980   *Move Towards the Mound*, Balch Institute for Ethnic Studies, Philadelphia
1982   *Foreign Bodies*, Southern Plains Indian Museum and Crafts Center, Anadarko, Oklahoma

Hachivi Edgar Heap of Birds. Photograph by the artist.

1983   *In Our Language*, C. N. Gorman Museum, University of
        California, Davis
1984   *Full Blooded*, Center of the American Indian, Kirkpatrick
        Center, Oklahoma City, Oklahoma
1986   *Sharp Rocks*, CEPA Gallery, Buffalo, New York
        Born from Sharp Rocks: Edgar Heap of Birds, New
        Museum of Contemporary Art, New York
1987   *Heh No Wah Maun Stun He Dun/What Makes a Man*,
        American Indian Community House Gallery, New York
1988   *American Policy*, Orchard Gallery, Derry, Northern Ire-
        land
1990   *Claim Your Color*, Exit Art, New York
        Blood Beat, Mexic-Arte Museum, Austin, Texas
        Makers, Allen Chapman Activity Center Gallery, Uni-
        versity of Tulsa, Oklahoma
1991   *Dig the Mix*, University of Colorado Art Galleries, Boul-
        der
        Hard Weed, Artspeak Gallery, Vancouver, British Co-
        lumbia, and Definitely Superior, Thunder Bay, Ontario
1992   *Is What Is*, University of California Art Museum, Berke-
        ley, and Wexner Center for the Arts, Ohio State Uni-
        versity, Columbus
        Hachivi Edgar Heap of Birds, Sena Gallery, Santa Fe
        Words/Spirits, C. N. Gorman Museum, University of
        California, Davis
        Animals Trees Weather People, University of Arizona
        Museum of Art, Tucson
1993   *Public Art Works and Drawings*, Art Awareness, Lexing-
        ton, New York
1994   *Drawings, Paintings, and Sign Works*, Art Gallery, Pem-
        broke Pines, Florida
        New Work, Jan Cicero Gallery, Chicago
        Tell Your Self, Art Gallery of New South Wales, Sydney,
        Australia

Selected Group Exhibitions

1976   *30 Miles of Art*, Nelson-Atkins Museum, Kansas City,
        Missouri
1977   *Recent Works*, New 57 Gallery, Edinburgh, Scotland
1981   *Confluences of Tradition and Change*, C. N. Gorman
        Museum and the Richard L. Nelson Gallery, Univer-
        sity of California, Davis
1983   *Modern Native American Abstraction*, Philadelphia Art
        Alliance, Pennsylvania
1984   *No Beads—No Trinkets*, United Nations, Geneva, Swit-
        zerland
1986   *Liberty and Justice*, Alternative Museum, New York
        We Are Always Turning Around on Purpose, Amelie A.
        Wallace Gallery, State University of New York, Old
        Westbury
1987   *Eight Native American Artists*, Fort Wayne Museum of
        Art, Indiana
        Committed to Print, Museum of Modern Art, New York
        *Documenta 8/In Memory of Native Americans, In Memory
        of Jews—Relocate Destroy*, Kassel, Germany
1989   *Mid-America Biennial*, Nelson-Atkins Museum of Art,
        Kansas City, Missouri
1990   *In the Public Eye, Beyond the Statue in the Park*, Euphrat
        Gallery, DeAnza College, DeAnza, California
1991   *Lost Illusions*, Vancouver Art Gallery, British Columbia

        Border Issues: Negotiations and Identity, Center for Re-
        search in Contemporary Art, University of Texas at
        Arlington
        Words + Numbers, Museum of Contemporary Art,
        Wright State University, Dayton, Ohio
        Lost Illusions, Vancouver Art Gallery, Vancouver, British
        Columbia
        The Un-Making of Nature, Whitney Museum of Ameri-
        can Art, Stamford, Connecticut
        Bad Politics, Greg Kucera Gallery, Seattle
1992   *Green Acres: Neo-Colonialism in the U.S.*, Washington
        University Gallery of Art, St. Louis, Missouri
        *Land, Spirit, Power: First Nations at the National Gallery
        of Canada*, National Gallery of Canada, Ottawa, Ontario
        The People ... Themselves, Los Angeles Photography
        Center, Los Angeles
1993   *Death, Reverence, and the Struggle for Equality in America*,
        Betty Rymer Gallery, School of the Art Institute of
        Chicago
        Will/Power, Wexner Center for the Arts, Ohio State Uni-
        versity, Columbus
        American Indian Art in the Twentieth Century, Denver Art
        Museum
        Indigenous Investigations, University of North Texas Art
        Gallery, Denton
1993-96 *Keepers of the Western Door*, Center for Exploratory and
        Perceptual Art, Buffalo, New York
1994   *Stand: Four Artists Interpret the Native American Experi-
        ence*, Bruce Gallery, Edinboro University of Pennsyl-
        vania, Edinboro, Pennsylvania, and Erie Art Museum,
        Erie, Pennsylvania
        *Localities of Desire: Contemporary Art in an Interna-
        tional World*, Museum of Contemporary Art, Sydney,
        Australia
        Narratives, Painted Bride Art Center, Philadelphia
1995   *16 Songs/Issues of Personal Assessment and Indigenous
        Renewal*, University of North Texas Art Gallery,
        Denton
        *Hachivi Edgar Heap of Birds and Artists of Tandanya
        and Boomalli*, St. Louis Art Museum, Missouri
        Deterritorialization, Centro Cultural de la Raza, San Di-
        ego
        Native American Invitational and Masters Exhibition,
        Gilcrease Museum, Tulsa, Oklahoma
        Face Forward: Self-Portraiture in Contemporary Art, John
        Michael Kohler Arts Center, Sheboygan, Wisconsin
1996   *Gifts of the Spirit: Works by Nineteenth-Century and Con-
        temporary Native American Artists*, Peabody Essex
        Museum, Salem, Massachusetts
        Native Streams: Contemporary Native American Art, Jan
        Cicero Gallery, Chicago, and Turman Art Gallery, In-
        diana State University, Terre Haute (through 1997)

Publications

By HACHIVI: Articles—"Edgar Heap of Birds," in *We Are Al-
ways Turning Around on Purpose*, Old Westbury, New York: Amelie
A. Wallace Gallery, State University of New York, 1986; *Sharp
Rocks*, Buffalo, New York: CEPA Gallery, 1986. "Insurgent Mes-
sages for America," in *Afterimage 14*, No. 3, 1986; "Old Man Sat
Calm Near the Heat," in *Makers* (ed. by Heap of Birds), Point

Hachivi Edgar Heap of Birds: *American Leagues* billboard, 1996. Courtesy of the artist.

Riders Press, Cottonwood Arts Foundation, Norman, Oklahoma, 1988; "In Honor of Rain Forest," *Caliban*, No. 8, 1990; "American Policy," in *Reimaging America: The Arts of Social Change*, New Society Publishers, Philadelphia, Pennsylvania, 1990; "Statement by the Artist," in *Hachivi Edgar Heap of Birds: Matrix 131*, Wadsworth Atheneum, Hartford, Connecticut, 1996; "Of Circularity and Linearity in the Work of Bear's Heart," in *Plains Indian Drawings 1865-1935: Pages from a Visual History*, Drawing Center and American Federation of Arts, New York, 1996. **Videos—** *Insurgent Messages for America—Sharp Rocks*, co-produced with Pierre Lobstein, 1987; *What Follows . . .*, Visiting Artist Interview Series, Department of Fine Arts, University of Colorado, Boulder, 1991; "Sharp Rocks," co-produced with Pierre Lobstein, for the PBS series *American Flashcards,* 1992; *16 Songs*, consultant/interviewer, University of North Texas, Denton, Texas, 1995.

On HACHIVI: Books—*Claim Your Color*, texts by Papo Colo, Jean Fisher, Lowery Stokes Sims, and Edgar Heap of Birds, New York: Exit Art, 1990; *Building Minnesota*, by Joan Rothfuss, Minneapolis: Walker Art Center, 1990; "Hachivi Edgar Heap of Birds," in *Border Issues: Negotiations and Identity,* Arlington, Texas: Center for Research in Contemporary Art, University of Texas at Arlington, 1991; *Is What Is*, by Lawrence Rinder, Berkeley, California: University Art Museum/Pacific Film Archive 1992; "Street Chiefs and Native Hosts: Richard Ray (Whitman) and Hachivi Edgar Heap of Birds Defend the Homeland," by W. Jackson Rushing, in *Green Acres: Neo-Colonialism in the U.S.*, St.Louis: Washington University Gallery of Art, 1992; "Resonances Are Observed," by Joe Dale Tate Nevaquaya, and "A Conversation with Hachivi Edgar

Heap of Birds," by Larry Abbott, in *Will/Power*, Columbus, Ohio: Wexner Center for the Arts, Ohio State University, 1993; "Interview," with Sara-Jayne Parsons, in *Indigenous Investigations*, Denton, Texas: University of North Texas Art Gallery, 1993; "Hachivi Edgar Heap of Birds," in *I Stand in the Center of the Good*, edited by Lawrence Abbott, Lincoln, Nebraska: University of Nebraska Press, 1994; *Tell Your Self*, by Susan Snodgrass, Sydney, Australia: Art Gallery of New South Wales, 1995; *16 Songs*, by Jacquelyn Lewis-Harris, St. Louis Museum of Art, 1995. **Articles—**"Territorial Imperatives," by Maureen Sherlock, in *New Art Examiner 17*, No. 2, 1989; "Fighting Language with Language," by Lydia Matthews, in *Artweek 21*, No. 41, 1989; "Native Host: Hachivi Edgar Heap of Birds," by Phyllis Price, in *Front*, November-December, 1991. **Video—***Five Portraits*, produced by Pierre Lobstein (includes Bob Haozous, Edgar Heap of Birds, Dan Lomahaftewa, Emmi Whitehorse, and Richard Ray Whitman), 1988.

*

Hachivi Edgar Heap of Birds comments:
The native arrow points of the past were worked and formed to become sharp and strong weapons. These sharp rocks were responsible for the defense and welfare of the tribe. As weapons of war the sharp rocks of the Tsistsistas (Cheyenne) people were used for two separate purposes, as defense of attack weapons against man and as tools of preservation through hunting game animals. At this time the manifestation of our battle has changed. The white man shall always project himself into our lives using information that is provided by learning institutions and the elec-

tronic and print media. Through these experiences the non-Indian will decide to accept or reject that the Native Americans are a unique and separate people with the mandate to maintain and strengthen indigenous rights and beliefs. Therefore we find that the survival of our people is based upon our use of expressive forms of modern communication. The insurgent messages within these forms of modern communication must serve as our present day combative tactics.

*   *   *

Hachivi Edgar Heap of Birds' work can be situated in four separate but related areas: public commissions; typeset and printed messages, usually focusing on issues; drawings with words ("wall lyrics"); and paintings. Language is central to much of his work. He examines not only politics, history and the meaning of language itself, but explores and responds to his own experience.

Heap of Birds uses diverse venues and formats for the display of his site-specific public commissions, such as signs placed in public spaces and billboards. *Native Hosts* (1988) was comprised of twelve 18" x 36" enamel on metal signs installed in City Hall Park in New York City: an example is "NEW YORK [printed backwards] TODAY YOUR HOST IS SHINNECOCK." These signs refer to the various original inhabitants of New York State, but Heap of Birds' reversal of "NEW YORK" disrupts the viewer's processing of the information, thus foregrouning the problems of language manifest in the very process of naming and highlighting the gulf between Native and non-Native views of the world. *Native Hosts* have also appeared in other cities with tribal names specific to that region. The reversal of letters to draw attention to issues is also used in *Apartheid Oklahoma* (1989), a series of five billboards sponsored by the Indian Youth Project and placed in Oklahoma City and Norman. This billboard reads "SOONERS [backwards] RUN OVER INDIAN NATIONS APARTHEID OKLAHOMA" and alludes to the appropriation of Native lands begun in 1889.

Building Minnesota (1990) was another series of site-specific signs; installed along the banks of the Mississippi River in Minneapolis, each of the forty red-lettered metal signs (also 18" x 36") was mounted on steel poles and faced a roadway and path. The signs refer to forty Dakotas who were executed in 1862 and 1865 for their participation in the 1862 Dakota Conflict. (The forty who were hanged were part of a group of 303 men who were sentenced to death after a military tribunal. The others had their sentences commuted by Abraham Lincoln). The Dakota Conflict erupted as a result of white settlements in the Minnesota River Valley. The signs call upon the viewer to honor the lives of those executed, like Wa-kan-o-zha-zha (Medicine Bottle), Wa-hi'-na (I Came), and Na-pe'-sni (Fearless).

In addition to other stationary signs (*Day/Night*, 1991, in Pioneer Square in Seattle) and billboards (*Imperial Canada*, 1988, at the Winter Olympics in Calgary, and *South African Homelands*, 1986, at Cleveland State University) Heap of Birds has placed his signs on the sides of public buses. *Mission Gifts* (1991) was installed on the sides of San Jose and South Bay (California) transit buses. Like the irony of the title *Building Minnesota*, where Minnesota was literally built on the lands and bodies of Native people, *Mission Gifts* refers to the dubious "gifts" bestowed on the indigenous inhabitants of California through the Missionization process. The signs read: "SYPHILIS/SMALL POX/FORCED BAPTISMS/MISSION GIFTS/ENDING NATIVE LIVES."

Heap of Birds also uses language in his screenprints and statements that he issues to accompany exhibitions. These focus on political issues and are often responses to contemporary events. For the journal *Caliban* Heap of Birds published a number of these pieces as part of a series titled, *In Honor of Rain Forest* (1989). Individual works include such messages as "Burning Debt Burning Burgers," "Food for the Brick Prick," and "The Lizard Feeds U.S." *In Telling Many Magpies, Telling Black Wolf, Telling Hachivi* (1989) Heap of Birds focuses on the issue of using Indian names and images as mascots ("We Don't Want Indians/Just Their Names/ . . ."). Heap of Birds also uses stat photographs for his language pieces, as in the 1989 *For China* ("Don't Believe Miss Liberty") and the three-part *Public Enemy Care For Youth* ("The Brutality Which Is America"/"Raises Mad Dogs"/"That Were Once Beautiful Children").

Where the public art and the messages reveal little of the artist and are more politically oriented, the ongoing "wall lyrics," usually pastel on rag paper, are more gestural and personal, focusing on aspects of the artist's life and family. Done while the artist listens to music, the wall lyrics create a sense of colorful dance-like movement, in opposition to the starkness of the other language pieces. Using words in groups of twos and threes, the wall lyrics come out of the artist's direct experiences. They are not random free associations but specific thoughts that represent moments in the artist's perception of what is around him. In works like *Pretty in the Face* (1992, 15 drawings, each 22" x 30") and the *What Makes a Man* suite (*Tribal Warrior*; *Sexual*; *Self*; *Boy, Woman, Family*; 1987, four sets of 15 drawings, each 22" x 30") Heap of Birds uses language as the most direct method for expressing and communicating to a pluralistic audience.

Heap of Birds orchestrates the placement and sense of movement of the words to heighten communication. The wall lyrics have evolved into works using black marker on rag paper to most directly communicate to the audience what Heap of Birds calls "coded messages." Where the pastel wall lyrics were made up of separate panels, works like *Young Look* (1994), *The Allure* (1994), and *Sun to Sullen* (1995) are done in one-piece large formats of roughly 80" x 145". In these works Heap of Birds uses words and phrases of different sizes as visual anchors and to create a sense of circularity on the drawing surface. In *The Allure* the word "Vacant" is placed at the center and surrounded by other words and phrases, such as "Money Will Do It," "Yes They Shop," and "Don't Speak Without Idea + Mission."

These works resonate with a ledger drawing attributed to Heap of Birds' ancestor, Little Chief. The drawing, *Cheyenne Medicine Lodge* (dated c. 1876-78), depicts a medicine lodge nearly in the center encircled by groups of people in the fore- and midground, while in the background a plain with horses gives way to hills. The design of the work, with the movement of the figures around the lodge, is analogous to the image that Heap of Birds creates in his large-scale marker drawings.

Heap of Birds' continuing series of paintings, the *Neuf Series* ("neuf" is the number four in the Cheyenne language), have also undergone transformation. Appearing abstract, these paintings are Heap of Birds' most personal work. They focus on aspects of nature, like the red-earth canyon land around his ancestral home in Oklahoma and the various trees, plants and animals of which it is comprised. The movement of the shapes represents the contours of the land and the breaks in the canyon. The variegated interlocking leaf-shaped forms suggest the connections and the unity among all forms of life. Some of the paintings take on ceremonial or mythical associations, as in *Old Man Sat Calm Near the Heat* (1987). Because of his travels to Australia, New Zealand, New Guinea and other Pacific countries, the *Neuf Series* now depicts "oceanscapes" and the fish found in the Great Barrier Reef and throughout the Pacific. These untitled pieces from 1995 are larger (78" x 108") but similar in color and structure to the earlier *Neuf Series* works and take on new meanings in the context of Heap of Birds' ongoing experience.

Heap of Birds' recent collaborations with Australian aboriginal artists of Tandanya and Boomalli resulted in *16 Songs/Issues of Personal Assessment and Indigenous Renewal.* The sixteen words, or songs (for example, "four," "green," "resistance," "trees," "patience," "awareness"), which form the foundation of the exhibition, were written by Heap of Birds and were derived from his participation in Cheyenne Earth Renewal ceremonies held in Oklahoma. When Heap of Birds went to Australia he offered these sixteen words to the sixteen collaborating artists, who themselves created work based on their acknowledgment of the concepts inherent in the words. Thematically, the work generated by such artists as Fiona Foley, Judy Watson, Brenda L. Croft, Mark Blackman, and Gordon Hookey, explores such issues as individual and tribal identity and sovereignty, tribal relationships to the dominant culture, the influence of the global economy on indigenous communities, and the process of tribal endurance and renewal.

In addition to the marker on rag paper and the *Neuf Series* works, Heap of Birds created billboards which presented the words in groups of four in a manner reminiscent of his earlier signs. In his twenty-year career Heap of Birds has used his art as a way of exploring not only the political relationships of Native America to the dominant culture but also his own experiences as a Cheyenne-Arapaho individual. His art is a reflection of the continual growth and development of Native art.

—Larry Abbott

HAILSTONE, Vivien

Variant names: Cutcha
Tribal affiliations: Yurok; Karok
Basketweaver and jewelry designer

Born: Vivien Geneva Risling, village of Moreck, California, 16 October 1913, member of Hupa Tribe. **Education:** Primary education at public school; 1½ yrs at boarding school in Hoopa; educated in tribal ways by great-grandmother and elder relatives; mother taught her how to weave; De Quincey University, California, A.A. in art, 1983; also attended College of the Redwoods, Shasta College, and continues attending college. **Family:** Married to Albert Hailstone, 1940 (died 1979); two sons, Albert, and Damon (deceased). **Career:** Teacher and lecturer, artist-media basketry and jewelry, filmmaker, community activist; bookkeeper, cook, restaurant operator, welder, store manager, service station manager, sawmill operator, and gift-shop owner. **Awards:** Woman of the Year, 1979, University Women, Redding, California.; Golden Bear Award, California State Parks and Recreation Commission; Shasta Lake Union School District Honored Elder, 1989; Indian Advisory Council, State of California Parks and Recreation, 1970s; Blue Ribbon Planning Committee, Turtle Bay Museum Park, Redding, California; committee member, Watchful Eyes, Heard Museum, Phoenix, Ari-

Vivian Hailstone: Jewelry. Courtesy of the artist.

zona; Board of Directors, L.I.F.E.; advisor, lecturer, and panelist to *The Fine Art of California Basketry,* at the Crocker Art Museum, Sacramento, California; several prizes at State of California Indian Days, Heard Museum, Phoenix, Arizona, and Art Show of Eureka, California.

Selected Group Exhibitions

1965   College of the Redwoods
1996-97 *The Fine Art of California Basketry,* Crocker Art Museum, Sacramento (traveling)

Collections

Crocker Art Museum, Sacramento, California.

Publications

By HAILSTONE: Article—"The Past Is but the Beginning of the Beginning," *News from Native California,* Winter, 1992-93; "Is it Authentic, Indian Made, or Real Indian?," *News from Native California,* Spring 1996.

On HAILSTONE: Book—*The Fine Art of California Basketry,* by Brian Bibby, Berkeley: Heyday Books, 1996.

*

Vivien Hailstone comments:

I am a basket maker, as was my mother, great grandmothers, and all of the women in my family before them. I use the same method of weaving that they did and for baskets the material has always been the same. There was a time when some basket makers tried using Rit dye instead of the traditional alder bark. Unfortunately, dyed material faded or was too red. Some have tried making baskets with materials that are easier to use. But what works best is still the old material. For me the joy of making a basket includes gathering the materials. Sometimes a beautiful basket can take up to a year to make (if) you include the preparation time.

We also know that what was authentic two hundred years ago has evolved and changed just as we have evolved as a people. Examples would be beadwork, flag designs, and baskets made around bottles. Two hundred years from now people will be looking at what we make today and saying it is authentic. The yarn dance regalia and sequins we see at Pow Wows today will be the authentic....

The most important thing to remember as we try to define what is real or authentic is that definitions must not become set in concrete. We as Indian people should be allowed to define for ourselves what is authentic and we must be allowed to develop our art forms with the talent the Great Creator gave us.

*   *   *

Vivien Hailstone is a weaver of fine baskets, a collector, and a teacher of traditional Yurok-Karuk basketry. She has been instrumental in efforts to continue these traditions throughout northern California. She was one of fifteen California Indians who participated as a consultant to the exhibition and publication, *The Fine Art of California Indian Basketry*, in the fall of 1996. Revered as an elder and accomplished artist, her comments on the baskets to be exhibited are included, along with those of the other consultants.

Along with basketry, Indian rights are integral to the life and artistry of Vivien Hailstone. She has been a fighter, like her father, who was instrumental in changing the Indian boarding school to a day school. In conversations, she talks of basket weaving and then quickly moves to community activities, how basketry classes were looked down on in the past, the importance of the California Indian Basketweaver's Association, and more. At 83, she is full of ideas, plans, and projects and only finds time to weave late at night. In addition to teaching, she had a gift store at Hoopa for twenty-five years. She is on an advisory committee to a shop in Shasta Lake City, Indian Art and Design, which has works on consignment and offers classes too under the auspices of L.I.F.E. (Local Indians for Education, which was formed in 1970 and incorporated in 1978).

The basics of basket weaving were taught to Hailstone by her mother. During World War II, Hailstone became a welder and worked in Eureka. She later operated a saw mill with her brother for ten years, and had a gift stop from the late 1940s to the 1970s. Because old weavers were dying and the younger people were not too interested in the old ways, Hailstone tried to get the faculty at College of the Redwoods interested in having a basketry class, and by the 1960s, basketry classes were being taught in the extension of the College of the Redwoods by Ella Johnson, with Hailstone as her assistant. After learning to make pottery Hailstone and local women formed a pottery guild, with their own building and kiln, but the flood of 1964 destroyed or swept away, including her house, shop, and materials.

All the while in her spare time, Hailstone continued weaving baskets, and her work, along with other weavers, finally was shown at a big event she helped to organize in the 1960s, which was sponsored by the local P.T.A. To make sure the event was a success, she utilized tactics such as mail and telephone calls to organize the community.

Innovative in her art, Hailstone has also created jewelry that integrates abalone, dentallia, pine nuts, with finely woven medal-

lions. In 1970 she moved to Redding, where she still lives and exhibits at local fairs. Basketry is alive and well with California Indian weavers, thanks to people like Vivien Risling Hailstone.

—Margot Blum Schevill

HALSEY, Minisa Crumbo
Tribal affiliations: Creek; Potawatomi
Painter

Born: Minisa Crumbo, Tulsa, Oklahoma, September 1942; daughter of artist Woody Crumbo and Lillian Hogue. **Education:** Wasatch Academy, Mt. Pleasant, Utah; University of Texas, El Paso; Taos Academy of Fine Art, 1972-74; Contemporary School of Visual Art, New York, 1974-75. **Career:** Teacher (in Kansas, California and Tennessee, 1980s), art gallery owner, muralist (State of New Mexico, murals in public buildings series). **Awards:** Philbrook Museum of Art, graphics and painting awards, 1974; New Mexico art commission; Distinguished Service Award, Baker University, Baldwin, Kansas, 1982.

Individual Exhibitions

1975   Potawatomi Agency and Cultural Center, Shawnee, Oklahoma
1988   Museum of Ethnology, Budapest, Hungary
1989   Tennessee State University, Nashville, Tennessee
1992   Thomas Gilcrease Institute of American History and Art, Tulsa, Oklahoma

Selected Group Exhibitions

1975   Philbrook Museum of Art
        University of Nevada, Las Vegas
        University of Oregon
1978   Puskin Museum of Art, Moscow (traveled through 1979)
1987   Museum of Ethnology, Budapest, Hungary
        Museum of Ethnology, Zagreb, Yugoslavia
        Museum of National Literature, Prague, Czechoslovakia
1988   Tennessee State Museum, Nashville
1991   *Mayfest International Festival*, Winston-Salem, North Carolina
1993   Thomas Gilcrease Institute of American History and Art, Tulsa, Oklahoma

Collections

Thomas Gilcrease Institute of American History and Art, Tulsa, Oklahoma; Heard Museum, Phoenix, Arizona; Kansas Museum of History, Kansas State Historical Society, Topeka; Philbrook Museum of Art, Tulsa, Oklahoma; Puskin Museum of Art, Moscow, Russia.

*   *   *

Minisa Crumbo's growth as a professional artist is inextricably tied to her personal growth. While this may be said of other artists,

Minisa Crumbo Halsey. Photograph by Sabina Kuckelmann; courtesy of the artist.

Crumbo has repeatedly and consciously informed her work with her experiences of personal and spiritual growth. Her drawings and paintings document her emerging self-awareness, her initiation into tribal ceremonial ways, and her attainment of a personal vision that guides her artistic efforts and her personal life. Crumbo did not begin seriously considering herself an artist until the early 1970s, when she studied at the Taos Academy of Fine Arts with Ray Vinella. She focused for two years on draftsmanship and portraiture. Crumbo's portraits were commercially and critically successful. *Sun Hawk-Taos* was entered in the Philbrook annual in 1974 and remains one of her most accomplished portraits. Vinella encouraged his students not only to focus on public acceptance, but also to be sure they followed their own, personal vision. For Crumbo, portraiture was very personally satisfying. It brought her in close contact with native peoples from whom she learned a great deal about traditional life and various native world views. And through seeking to sensitively portray their personal and tribal identities, she aroused an awareness of her own self-identity. However, she was beginning to take Vinella's advice to consider a different focus, when he decided to leave Taos. He had become an important mentor to her and she recognized his leaving as a crisis in her continued artistic development. She sought a new direction and applied to the School of Visual Arts in New York.

In New York, Crumbo suddenly became responsible for her own growth. She was alone and without the mentor who had been so supportive in Taos. For the first time, she was compelled to exercise her independence as an artist and to take responsibility for making decisions that would affect her development. Crumbo set aside portraiture and opened herself to new ideas: she became intensely focused on figure studies and anatomy, learned a multitude of new skills and techniques, including silverpoint and sculpture, and was exposed to many influences that broadened both her personal and artistic awareness. She had the benefit of learning from many teachers, guest artists and lecturers; she learned about galleries and the professional art world, and became acquainted with many members of the New York City area Native American community. Most of the art she produced during this period was study work. Although it had been a time of learning and not exhibiting, she gained a new self-confidence and matured artistically.

When she returned from her studies, Crumbo tried to do portraits again but no longer found it satisfying. She had grown and needed new forms of expression to reflect that growth. Previously, she had always worked from life, whether painting portraits, florals, or landscapes, but she now began to experiment by no longer allowing herself to use models. Her decision forced her to find new direction and to draw from more personal resources. She began to focus on subject matter reflective of her spiritual life. For example, in the 1970s, she had participated in Native American Church meetings. *Peyote Water Drum* is a direct result of that participation. Upon returning from New York, she continued in medicine ways and made more paintings and drawings that represent spiritual world views.

In the early 1980s, Crumbo's spiritual growth became more precisely focused. Her medicine experiences and her growing interest in the significance of women in traditional Native American societies synthesized into a personal vision. Her new focus on "women's ways in the context of the natural world" initially compelled her to teach about this world view for eight years in California and Nashville. Since her energy was focused on teaching, she was less productive in the studio. But she was, in fact, crystallizing the concepts that would inform her later works. She began in the early 1990s creating paintings that are explorations of those concepts, including iconic women figures placed in symbolic compositions that may have reference to the relationship between women and the cosmos, to the feminine power in nature, or to the dependence on fertility to complete seasonal cycles. Her portrayal of these universal themes are informed by her years of personal spiritual growth, often in Native American cultural contexts, and by her maturity in both portraiture and unique expressionism.

—Kevin Smith

HAOZOUS, Bob

Tribal affiliations: Chiricahua Apache
Sculptor, mixed media artist, and installation artist

Born: Santa Fe, New Mexico, 1 April 1943. **Education:** California College of Arts and Crafts, B.F.A., 1971. **Career:** Artist-in-residence, Dartmouth College, 1989, City of Frankfurt, Germany, 1992; visiting artist, Te Waka Toi Maori tribe, New Zealand, 1991; mural commissions, including Daybreak Star Art Center, Seattle, Washington, 1978; sculpture commissions, including New York City Business Committee for the Arts (annual achievement award design, 1983), Heard Museum (1983), City of Philadelphia (William Penn Treaty Park, 1988), City of Phoenix (1990, Sky Harbor Airport); juror, Heard Museum Guild Arts and Crafts Invitational

(1979); lecturer, panelist (National Endowment for the Humanities Visual Arts Grant, 1993); presented anti-racist award to filmmaker and writer, Eric Bye, Antirasistisk Senter, Oslo, Norway, 1994; consultant, National Museum of the American Indian, 1995. **Awards:** Numerous from fairs and juried competitions, including those at the Philbrook Museum of Art (1972), Heard Museum (1973-75), and Santa Fe Indian Market (1976, 1984—collaborative work with Jody Folwell).

Individual Exhibitions

1979   Daybreak Star Arts Center, Seattle, Washington
1980   Heydt-Bair Gallery, Santa Fe, New Mexico
1982-83 Dewey-Kofron Gallery, Santa Fe, New Mexico
1983   Ron Hall Gallery, Fort Worth, Texas
1983-84 ACA Gallery, New York
1984-86 Four Winds Gallery, Pittsburgh, Pennsylvania
1985-88 Retig y Martinez Gallery, Santa Fe, New Mexico
1987   Taylor Museum, Colorado Springs Fine Arts Center, Colorado Springs, Colorado
1987-88 *Haozous Does Cats,* Wheelwright Museum of the American Indian, Santa Fe, New Mexico
1988   Prairie Lee Gallery, Chicago
1989   Hood Museum of American Art, Dartmouth College, Hanover, New Hampshire
1990   *Sacred Images to Go*, Retig y Martinez Gallery, Santa Fe, New Mexico
        Muerte/Amor, Galeria Universitaria Aristos, Universidad Nacional Autonoma de Mexico, Mexico City
1992   *Mayfest*, Tulsa, Oklahoma
        Apfelbaum-Sacred Images, Peiper-Riegraf Gallery, Frankfurt, Germany
        Vanishing White Man, Retig y Martinez Gallery, Santa Fe, New Mexico
1993   Fine Arts Center, Popejoy Hall, University of New Mexico, Albuquerque
        Vanishing Buffalo Herd, Retig y Martinez Gallery, Santa Fe, New Mexico
1994   *Steelhenge*, College of Santa Fe, New Mexico
        Haozous Does Chickens, Retig y Martinez Gallery, Santa Fe, New Mexico
1995   Allan Houser Sculpture Park, Institute of American Indian Arts Museum, Santa Fe
        Site Haozous, Wheelwright Museum of the American Indian, Santa Fe, New Mexico

Selected Group Exhibitions

1970   *The American Indian in California*, Oakland Museum, Oakland, California
1974   Graphic House Gallery, Santa Fe, New Mexico
1976   *Indian Images*, University of North Dakota (traveling)
        Allan Houser and Bob Haozous, Wheelwright Museum of the American Indian, Santa Fe, New Mexico
1977   Armory for the Arts, Santa Fe, New Mexico
1978   *Charlie Bird, Gail Bird, Bob Haozous, Yazzie Johnson, Harold Littlebird*, Treece Gallery, Evergreen, Colorado
1979   *Sweeney Center Installation*, Santa Fe Festival of the Arts, Santa Fe, New Mexico
        Contemporary Indian Art, Wheelwright Museum of the American Indian, Santa Fe, New Mexico

        Elaine Horwitch Galleries, Santa Fe, New Mexico
1980   *Santa Fe Salon Show*, Santa Fe Festival of the Arts, Santa Fe, New Mexico
        Cowboys and Indians: The Western Experience in Painting, Film, Photography, and Literature, Arvada Center for the Arts and Humanities, Arvada, Colorado
1981   *Walk in Beauty*, Santa Fe Festival of the Arts, Santa Fe, New Mexico
        Native American Arts '81, Philbrook Museum of Art, Santa Fe, New Mexico
        American Indian Art in the 1980s, Turtle Exhibition and Performing Arts Center, Niagara Falls, New York
        Heydt-Bair Gallery, Santa Fe, New Mexico
        American Indian Art Exposition, Cultural Center for the American Indian, Houston, Texas
        Houser and Haozous: A Sculptural Retrospective, Heard Museum, Phoenix, Arizona
1984   Sullivan Bisenius Gallery, Denver, Colorado
        Confluences of Tradition and Change: Twenty American Indian Artists, American Indian Community House, New York
        Icons and Iconoclasts: New York-New Mexico, Sarah Campbell Blaffer Gallery, University of Houston, Texas
        Indianische Kunst Im 20. Jahrundert, West Germany (traveling)
1985   Shidoni Gallery, Tesuque, New Mexico
        Native American Art Exhibition, Grand Palais, Paris, France
        No Beads, No Trinkets, Palais de Nations, Geneva, Switzerland
        Walking Westward, Mongerson Wunderlich Galleries, Chicago
        Heard Museum, Phoenix, Arizona
        Gallery 10, Scottsdale, Arizona
        What Is Native American Art?, Philbrook Museum of Art, Tulsa, Oklahoma
1986   *Neo-Humorists,* Armory for the Arts, Santa Fe, New Mexico
        New Mexico Sculpture, Albuquerque Spring Arts Festival
        Contemporary Indian Art, Governor's Gallery, State Capitol Building, Santa Fe, New Mexico
1987   Prairie Lee Gallery, Chicago
        Eight Artists II, Southwest Museum, Los Angeles
1988   Rettig Y Martinez Gallery, Santa Fe, New Mexico
        Galeria Expositum, Mexico City
1991   *Southwest Biennial and Singular Visions*, Museum of Fine Arts, Museum of New Mexico, Santa Fe
        Drawings by Sculptors, Sena Galleries, Santa Fe, New Mexico
        The Appropriated Object and Aesthetically Correct/Aesthetically Incorrect, Jonson Gallery of the University of New Mexico Art Museum, Albuquerque
        Shared Visions: Native American Painters and Sculptors of the Twentieth Century, Heard Museum, Phoenix, Arizona (traveled through 1992)
1992   *Sublomoc Show/Columbus Wohs*, organized by Atlatl, Phoenix, Arizona (traveled)
        Visions from Native America: Contemporary Art for the Year of the Indigenous Peoples, Morning Star Foundation, Washington, D.C.

Bob Haozous: *Cultural Crossroads of the Americas,* 1996. Courtesy of the artist.

Quincentennial Perspective: Artists Discover Columbus, Castillo Cultural Center, New York

1993 *Blue Skies Over New Mexico,* Governor's Gallery, State Capital Building, Santa Fe, New Mexico
Variety, Trondheim Sjofartsmuseum, Trodheim, Norway
Signals in Sculpture, Institute of American Indian Arts Museum, Santa Fe, New Mexico

1994 *1994 Sculpture Project,* College of Santa Fe, New Mexico
Self Portraits, Rettig y Martinez Gallery, Santa Fe, New Mexico
Shidoni Gallery, Tesuque, New Mexico
Socrates Park Sculpture Garden, Long Island, New York

1995 Monothon, College of Santa Fe, New Mexico
Museum of Northern Arizona, Flagstaff, Arizona
Center for Contemporary Arts, Santa Fe, New Mexico
Erotica Show, Copeland-Rutherford Gallery, Santa Fe, New Mexico

1996 Greythorne Gallery, Scottsdale, Arizona
Art from the Birthplace of the Atomic Bomb—New Mexico, USA, Albuquerque United Artists (traveled to Tokyo, Hiroshima and Nagasaki, Japan)
Peace Art Show: Atomic Synthesis & Social Fallout from New Mexico, USA, Albuquerque United Artists, South Broadway Cultural Center, Albuquerque, New Mexico

Curatorial Selections, Museum of Fine Arts, Museum of New Mexico, Santa Fe
Magnifico!, Albuquerque Festival of the Arts, Albuquerque, New Mexico

Collections

Albuquerque Museum, New Mexico; Arizona State University, Glendale, Arizona; Business Committee for the Arts, New York; City of Tulsa, Oklahoma; Dresdner Bank, Stuttgart, Germany; Heard Museum, Phoenix, Arizona; Hood Museum of Art, Dartmouth University, Hanover, New Hampshire; Josylyn Art Museum, Omaha, Nebraska; Museum of Fine Arts, Museum of New Mexico, Santa Fe; Museum of Indian Arts and Culture, Museum of New Mexico, Santa Fe; Phoenix College of Performing Arts, Phoenix, Arizona; Philbrook Museum of Art, Tulsa, Oklahoma; Millicent Rogers Foundation Museum, Taos, New Mexico; Sky Harbor Airport, City of Phoenix, Arizona; Southwest Plains Indian Museum, Anadarko, Oklahoma; Southwest Museum, Los Angeles; Trondheim Sjofartsmuseum, Trondheim, Norway; Stadmuseum Munster, Munster, Germany; Universidad Nacional Autonama de Mexico, Mexico City; University of Kentucky, Lexington; University of New Mexico, Albuquerque; Wheelwright Museum of the American Indian, Santa Fe, New Mexico.

Publications

On HAOZOUS: Books—*Art and Indian Individualists,* by Guy and Doris Monthan, Flagstaff, 1975; *Magic Images: Contemporary Native American Art,* Edwin L. Wade and Rennard Strickland, editors, Norman, Oklahoma, 1981; *Indianishe Kunst,* by Gerhard Hoffmann, Munich, 1984; *Bob Haozous—The Dartmouth Exhibition Catalog,* by William David Rettig, Hanover, New Hampshire, 1989; *Mixed Blessings: New Art in Multicultural America,* by Lucy Lippard, New York, 1990; *Appropriation and Transformation,* by Joseph Traugott, Albuquerque, 1990; *Shared Visions: Native American Painters and Sculptors of the Twentieth Century,* by Margaret Archuleta and Rennard Strickland, Phoenix, 1991; *Singular Visions,* by Sandy Ballatore, Santa Fe, 1991; Articles—"Interview: Bob Haozous," with Claire Wolf Krantz, *Art Papers,* March/April 1989; "Bob Haozous," *American Indian Art,* by Suzanne Kenagy, Summer 1990; "Native American Art: Pride and Prejudice," by Robin Cemblast, *Artnews,* February 1992; "Bob Haozous," *Southwest Art,* by Joy Waldron, August 1992; "Visions from Native America: Contemporary Art for the Year of the Indigenous Peoples," by Suzan Shown Harjo, *Encounters,* Fall 1992; "A Visit to Site Haozous," by Kathleen McLoud, *Pasatiempo, The New Mexican,* 29 September 1995; "Battling Bureaucracy," by Charlene Teters, *Indian Artist* magazine, Spring 1997. Films—"Allan Houser and Bob Haozous," *Sunday Morning with Charles Kuralt,* CBS, 1984; "Bob Haozous," *Colores,* #124, KNME/PBS, 1990; *Bob Haozous: American Artist,* Cinebar Video Productions, Barbara Frost, producer, 1992; *The Search for Mangas Coloradas,* Norwegian Public Broadcasting, Eric Bye, producer, Odd Avid Stromstad, director, 1993.

*

Bob Haozous comments:

All I offer are clues, no conclusions. My conclusion is to present the contradictions ... I love contradictions.

*   *   *

Over the past twenty-five years Warm Springs Chiricahua Apache artist Bob Haozous has created a substantive body of sculpture, executed in a variety of media, that presents in stunningly original fashion many of the contradictions that circumscribe contemporary existence on this planet, not only for Native Americans but for all peoples. Like few others, Haozous challenges viewers to re-evaluate their relationships to each other and to their respective living environments. Eschewing easy answers, he raises complex, often disturbing questions that demand considered and thoughtful responses. Ever hopeful of affecting change in public attitudes, behavior and even official policy, Haozous invests his work with equal parts compassion and critique, tempering each piece with a disarming measure of serious whimsy. It is a remarkably potent combination, reflecting an equally potent artistic vision that is no less radical nor innovative (for its time) than that of his late father, the acclaimed Apache sculptor, Allan Houser.

From his earliest carvings in walnut and marble to more recent creations in acid-sprayed steel, Haozous has sustained a consistent and passionate vision, shaped by traditional Apache and Navajo tribal values and a more universal concern for the well-being of humanity. The issues addressed and the subjects commemorated in his work are both culturally specific and globally inclusive, ranging from the racist and historical injustices perpetrated against Native Americans (and the subsequent erosion of their cultural identities), to the corrupting nature of wealth and power and the human capacity for greed. In recent years Haozous has devoted much of his time and energy to creating large-scale sculptures that foreground the grievous consequences of continued industrial waste, technological abuse and exploitation of the environment. "Bigger is better when there is a statement behind it," he says. Statements, of course, are seldom free of controversy.

Haozous does not take his role as an artist lightly. It is, for him, akin to a sacred calling, with a built-in cultural responsibility to create reality-based works derived from personal experience and present-day events, and not from romanticized notions of the past. Understandably, such sentiments do not endear him to those fellow members of the Indian arts community who still ply their trade on the streets of Santa Fe, catering to the whims and nostalgic fantasies of tourists.

Many of the contradictions that inform Haozous's art spring from the seeming incompatibility of Euro-American and Native American world views. The tension implicit in the strained relationship of these competing cultural perspectives is most frequently expressed by Haozous through the bold and ironic juxtaposition of simple shapes and silhouettes that have been infused with layered cultural reference. Over the years, Haozous has employed stylized images of bears, bisons, coyotes and fluffy clouds to symbolize the Native American cultural landscape, and airplanes, automobiles, tank traps and smokestacks as symbols of technological intrusion. It is, of course, in the artist's skilful combination and playful patterning of these elements that they acquire their aesthetic and political power.

In the 1970s, Haozous fashioned several finely detailed human figures and torsos from black walnut and other woods. A memorable piece from this period is the wickedly satirical *Totem Princess* (1977), a statuesque, 11-foot carving of a slender befeathered young woman in beauty pageant attire literally perched on a display pedestal. The word "Indian" appears at her feet. The entire sculpture is embellished with small white wooden balls like so many billboard lightbulbs. In similar fashion, Haozous appended several shiny metal balls to the surface of his pink marble effigy of Mother Earth, *Lady with a Necklace* (1979). Like giant ball-bearings randomly tossed, these polished spheres proclaim a technological presence both ominous and appealing. Aesthetically, they at once complement and disturb the pattern of madly swirling airplanes incised upon the figure's ample evening gown.

The early 1980s saw Haozous create a number of painted limestone figures that deconstructed with surprising sensitivity such myths as the frontier cowboy (*Neophyte Cowboy,* 1981) and the fearless Apache warrior (*Last Great American Hero,* 1980). Their colorful veneer is a poignant counterpoint to the pervading mood of melancholy.

By the mid-1980s Haozous had begun to explore the design and construction possibilities of forged steel. Plated, painted or plain, it promised unlimited opportunities for aesthetic expression and experimentation. The prospect of making large-scale sculptures was especially attractive. Over the last decade Haozous has worked almost exclusively in this medium, creating numerous pieces ranging in size from the modest to the massive and the truly monumental. Throughout, his themes have remained remarkably consistent: *Apache Pull Toy* (1989), his bullet-riddled gunfighter on wheels, wryly recalls his earlier cowboy pieces; a clearly distressed *Ozone Madonna* (1989) personifies the threatened South American tropical rainforest; the seven-story *Artificial Cloud* (1992), erected in downtown Tulsa, Oklahoma, pays mute testimony to the ultimate impact of pollution.

In late 1993, eleven of Haozous's most imposing steel sculptures were gathered together in a circle on the grounds of the College of Santa Fe for the exhibition, *Steelhenge*. A mini-retrospective of works created since 1987, it served to highlight the parallels between Native American thought and ancient European earth-centred religion. A celebration of healing and cross-cultural sharing was held in conjunction with the show at the time of the winter solstice.

A final note concerns the controversy surrounding Haozous's billboard-sized steel sculpture, *Cultural Crossroads of the Americas*, erected in the fall of 1996 in the University of New Mexico's Yale Park. According to the chair of the University committee that selected Haozous's design, the "unauthorized" addition of a coil of razor wire to the top of the finished piece constituted a significant departure from the approved design, and therefore a breach of contract. In a move that smacked of blatant intimidation and bureaucratic censorship, the university refused to pay its portion of the artist's fee until the wire or the entire sculpture was removed. Unquestionably, the razor wire adds political force to the cultural encounter portrayed in the piece—the wire is in fact the same "security tape" that helps define the Mexican/American border—but for Haozous and his many supporters in the recently formed Borderlines Coalition group, the issue is not (nor was it ever) about the addition of razor wire, but the violation of artistic integrity and the attempted suppression of freedom of expression. These are issues of concern far beyond the borders of the Indian art world.

—Allan J. Ryan

HARDIN, Helen

Variant names: Tsa-Sah-Wee-Eh
Tribal affiliations: Santa Clara Pueblo
Painter

Born: Helen Hardin (a month after her birth at the Santa Clara Pueblo reservation, a naming ceremony was held and she was given the name Tsa-Sah-Wee-Eh ("Little Standing Spruce"), Albuquerque, New Mexico, 28 May 1943. **Education:** Attended predominantly white schools, including a Catholic high school; spent the summer of her junior year in the Southwest Indian Art Project for Native American students at the University of Arizona (1960); University of New Mexico, 1961-62. **Family:** Daughter of artist Pablita Velarde; daughter Margarete born, 1964; married Cradoc Bagshaw, 1973. **Career:** Commissioned paintings and lectures for the Enchanted Mesa Gallery, Albuquerque, New Mexico, 1960s through early 1970s; worked independently as a studio artist from the mid-1970s until her death. **Awards:** Honors at the Santa Fe Indian Market, Scottsdale National Arts Exhibition, The Heard Museum in Phoenix, Arizona, and the Philbrook Art Center in Tulsa, Oklahoma. **Died:** 4 June 1984 in New Mexico.

Individual Exhibitions

1962   Coronado Monument, Albuquerque, New Mexico
1964   Enchanted Mesa Gallery, Albuquerque, New Mexico

1968   U.S. Embassy, Bogota, Columbia
1971   U.S. Embassy, Guatemala
1977   Kansas State University, Manhattan, Kansas
1978   Forrest Fenn Gallery, Santa Fe
1979   Tanner's Indian Arts, La Jolla, California
1980   California State University at Long Beach
        Galeria Capistrano, San Juan Capistrano
1981   Squash Blossom Gallery, Aspen, Colorado
1983   Western Images Gallery, Chester, New Jersey
1984   Institute of American Indian Art, Santa Fe
1989   Wheelwright Museum, Santa Fe
1991-94 Silver Sun Gallery, Santa Fe
1994   *Passing on the Spirit: Helen Hardin*, Institute of American Indian Art, Santa Fe

Selected Group Exhibitions

1973   May D&F, Denver
1974   Heard Museum, Phoenix
1975   Ashton Gallery, Scottsdale, Arizona
1977   Halls Plaza, Kansas City, Missouri
        Philbrook Art Center, Tulsa, Oklahoma
1979   *National Women in the Arts Show*, Springfield, Illinois
        Native American Paintings, Mid-America Arts Alliance Project, Joslyn Art Museum, Omaha, Nebraska (traveling through 1980)
1980   *American Indian Woman's Spring Art Festival*, Indian Pueblo Cultural Center, Albuquerque, New Mexico
        Whitney Gallery, Taos, New Mexico
1981   Sugar Creek Country Club, Houston
        Salon d'Automne, Grand Palais, Paris
1982   National Museum of Natural History, Smithsonian Institution, Washington, D.C.
        County College of Morris, Morristown, New Jersey
1984   *Indianischer Kunstler*, organized by Philbrook Museum of Art, Tulsa, Oklahoma (traveling in Germany through 1985)
1989   *Paint, Bronze, and Stone*, Mitchell Indian Museum, Kendall College, Evanston, Illinois
1991   *Shared Visions: Native American Painters and Sculptors in the Twentieth Century*, Heard Museum, Phoenix (traveling through 1992)

Publications

On HARDIN: Book—*Changing Woman: The Life and Art of Helen Hardin* by Jay Scott, Flagstaff, Arizona, 1989. **Articles**—"Helen Hardin: Tsa-sah-wee-eh Does Her Thing," by Walter Briggs, *New Mexico Magazine*, March/April 1970; "Helen Hardin: A Retrospective," by Lou Ann Farris Culley, *American Indian Art Magazine*, Summer 1979; "Allegory and Metaphor in the Art of Helen Hardin," by Lou Ann Farris Culley, *Helicon Nine*, Fall 1981; "Artist Helen Hardin Exhibit at CMM," by Shelia Lacouture, *The Bernardsville, New Jersey News*, 7 October 1982; "Helen Hardin (1943–1984): Casting Her Own Shadow," by Karen Shane, *Southwest Art*, June 1985; "Helen Hardin," by Gary Allen Hood, *Native Peoples*, Summer 1994. **Film**—*American Indian Artists I*, Public Broadcasting System documentary, 1974.

*

Helen Hardin: *Bear Fetishes*, **1978. Photograph by Rick Hill.**

Helen Hardin comments (1976):

I think the reason I don't fear death is because I know that I'll always be here through my paintings. I have a lifetime, no matter how long or how short, to do it in, and I want to be good at what I'm doing. I want to make it complete. It's the reward of living and the reward I have to give to those who survive me. It's the only thing I can give that's really me.

*   *   *

Hardin successfully combined the imagery, composition, and color common among traditional Indian painters with a geometric abstraction of shapes, colors, and composition. The influence of her mother, the artist Pablita Velarde, was a constant in her life. Hardin attributed her sense of detail to her mother's teachings and Hardin's early work was influenced by the cultural heritage displayed in Pablita Velarde's work. But Hardin's work also had an inventiveness, confidence, and uniqueness. Not wanting to be labeled a traditional Indian painter, she went beyond tradition. Hardin resisted the realism of her forebears and produced paintings in which geometric details became the prominent elements.

Hardin's mastery of abstraction proved that she could do something different. The transition in her art from realism to abstraction occurred after a 1968 visit to her father in Bogota, Columbia. In an exhibition at the U.S. embassy where she sold 27 paintings, Hardin received recognition as an individual artist, separate from her mother's fame. Her change to abstraction was also the result of being introduced to drafting tools, such as compasses, protractors, and plastic curves. Geometry gave her linear structure and a method of investigating light, space, and color.

In 1975 Hardin was the only woman artist in a PBS film series about Native American artists. By 1976 her role as a leader in contemporary Native American art was being recognized. Her work grew in depth and complexity. The influence of anthropology began to permeate her art as she studied the ancient designs of the Hohokam, Mogollon, Anasazi, and Mimbres cultures (300 B.C.-1300 A.D.). Hardin wanted to personalize the impersonal inventory of ancient Native American iconography and to de-tribalize and de-mystify it. Hardin worked on her Kachina series through the 1970s and into the 1980s. Considering Kachinas (intermediaries responsible for rain, corn and fecundity) to be her spiritual forebears, Hardin painted them as Cloud People. With her *Woman* series in 1980, the connection between Kachinas, humanity and herself as an individual is clarified.

The painting, *Metamorphis* (1981), represents a definitive example of Hardin's art in the early 1980s. It is a masklike face, bisected and composed of airbrushed rectangles and symbolic material derived from Kachina masks worn during sacred ceremonies conducted by Hopi Indians in Arizona. The upper right quadrant resembles the Hopi Sun Kachina. Saw-toothed structures and geometric designs are adapted from pre-historic pottery, and the figures' hairstyles resembles those common among Hopi, Pueblo, and Navajo peoples. This painting, like all of Hardin's work, consists of many varnished layers of acrylic paint applied with atomizers, brushes, pens, and household sponges. Hardin's art merged archaeology and tribalism with the contemporary and personal and sought a return to ancient realms by modern means. Hardin called *Metamorphis* a self-portrait.

In the early 1980s, Hardin also experimented with printmaking, specifically etching. In 1980 she produced four prints, *Fireside Prayers, Bountiful Mother, The Healers,* and *Messenger of the Sun.*

Fireside Prayers portrays robed figures gathered in a smoky semi-circle; *The Healers* depicts fetish bears with healing properties; *Messenger of the Sun* is an exploration of the eagle; and *Bountiful Mother* is a dramatic figure dressed in a white robe parted across pale blue corn kernels that make up the body. *Changing Woman* (1981) is considered one of her most ambitious etchings —a self-portrait of the artist as a young woman and ageless Kachina. Hardin also reproduced the image in a painting with brighter hues, *Changing Woman* (1981).

Hardin embarked on a series of paintings with themes relating to women: these include *Medicine Woman* (1981), *Listening Woman* (1982), *Winter Woman* (1982), and *Creative Woman* (1982). According to Hardin, her female imagery represents woman's intellectual, emotional, and sensitive characteristics, as opposed to the physical traits most often evident in images of women by male artists.

In 1981 Hardin was diagnosed with cancer. Although suffering from the disease, she continued when possible to paint, and at her death she left uncompleted her final work, *Last Dance of the Mimbres* (1984). She died at home with her daughter and her husband by her side in 1984. A posthumous exhibit was held in 1984 at the Institute of American Indian Arts Museum in Santa Fe, New Mexico.

—Phoebe Farris

HARRIS, Walter

Tribal affiliations: Tsimshian
Carver, printmaker, jewelry designer, graphic artist, and painter

Born: Kispiox, British Columbia, 1931; member of the Gitksan people, who with the Coast Tsimshian and Nishga are subdivisions of the Tsimshian. **Education:** Kitanmax School of Northwest Coast Indian Art, 'Ksan, British Columbia, studying under Jack Layland (jewelry making), Duane Pasco and Doug Cranmer (woodcarving), and Bill Holm (Northwest Coast graphic design), 1969. **Career:** Given his uncle's hereditary name of Geel, designating him as a recognized leader of Kispiox among the chiefs of the nation, 1957; instructor, Kitanmax School of Northwest Coast Indian Art; artist. **Awards:** Numerous commissions, including stone relief sculpture, House of Commons, Parliament Building, Ottawa; wall panel mural, Canadian Embassy, Paris; wall panel mural, Royal Centre, Vancouver, British Columbia.

Selected Group Exhibitions

1980   *The Legacy,* Edinburgh International Festival
1995   *Who Speaks for the Rivers?,* Derek Simpkins Gallery of Art, Vancouver
1996   *Topographies: Aspects of Recent BC Art,* Vancouver Art Gallery

Collections

British Columbia Provincial Museum, Victoria; Canadian Embassy, Paris; Department of Indian and Northern Affairs, Ottawa; First Nations House of Learning, University of British Columbia,

Walter Harris: *Killer Whale,* **1996. Courtesy of the artist.**

Vancouver; Golden Gate Park, San Francisco; House of Commons, Ottawa; 'Ksan Village, Hazelton, British Columbia; Museum of Anthropology, University of British Columbia, Vancouver; National Museum of Civilization, Ottawa.

Publications

On HARRIS: Books—*Indian Artists at Work* by Uilli Steltzer, Vancouver: J. J. Douglas, 1976; *In the Shadow of the Sun: Perspectives on Contemporary Native Art*, Canadian Ethnology Service, Mercury Series Paper 124, Hull, Quebec: Canadian Museum of Civilization, 1993. Articles—"Walter Harris and Sun Mask," *Gazette* (Canadian Museums Association), vol. 6, nos. 5 and 6, 1973; "Totem Art of the Northwest Coast," *Sunset Magazine*, May 1973; "Inheritance and Innovation: Northwest Coast Artist Today" by Peter Macnair, *ArtsCanada*, Nos. 184-87, December/January 1973; "Indian Affairs Gets Touch of Class," *Indian News*, vol. 19, no. 4, 1978; "Walter Harris," *The Narrative Perspective*, vol. 3, no. 2, 1978; "Four Carvers of Ksan" by Keith Watt, *Western Living*, October 1980. Films—*Spread Your Wings*, Sunrise Films, Toronto, Ontario, 1980.

*   *   *

Walter Harris is a Gitksan artist from the village of Kispiox near Hazelton, British Columbia. The Gitksan—along with the Coast Tsimshian and Nishga—are a subdivision of the Tsimshian peoples. The Gitksan have lived for centuries along the banks of the Skeena River. Harris is one of the best known artists of this tribe, having established a reputation for excellence in the areas of carving, jewelry making, graphic arts, murals, and painting. In addition to these achievements, he is a revered teacher at the Kitanmax School of Northwest Coast Indian Art. Perhaps his name and reputation will always indelibly be associated with the founding of 'Ksan, a reconstructed historical Indian village at the junction of the Skeena and Bulkley Rivers.

'Ksan is an important symbol of the revival or renewal of Northwest Coast Indian arts in the postwar era. By the 1960s it was evident that the Gitksan had lost much knowledge about their historical arts and it was also evident that the tribe needed some kind of renewal in economic and cultural terms. 'Ksan materialized as a result of the concerted efforts by the Gitksan themselves as well as outside financial support from the provincial and federal governments. Consequently, in 1970 'Ksan was formally opened as a cultural center that took the form of a replica of a nineteenth-century Gitksan village. It is intended not only to preserve precious artifacts and ancient ways, but also to renew and pass on Gitksan art and culture to future generations. There are seven major structures in the village: Frog House; Wolf House; Fireweed House; Gift Shop; Studio; Workshop; and Museum Exhibition Centre.

Some of the traditional house fronts of the cedar plank buildings are painted and there are several totem poles standing on the premises—most are free-standing poles, while one is a house front pole. There is a 'Ksan performing arts group famed for its authentic costumes and its performances of Gitksan dances and songs in a program called, "Breath of Our Grandfathers."

Very importantly, associated with the 'Ksan project is the Kitanmax School of Northwest Coast Indian Art. Since the old apprenticeship system for creating new artists was moribund, several instructors from the "outside"—including Duane Pasco, Douglas Cranmer, Robert Davidson, and Tony Hunt, among others—were brought in to teach the first groups of students. Walter Harris and Earl Muldoe were among the first graduates of the school, which actually started in 1969. Harris studied jewelry making under Jack Layland, wood carving under Duane Pasco and Douglas Cranmer, and graphic design under Bill Holm. Harris was so talented that he soon became an instructor there himself and taught at the institution for many years.

Tsimshian arts had always possessed a refined and sensitive character; wood carvings, in particular, featured a stylized sense of realism. Talented students like Harris learned the distinctive traits of Tsimshian art and went on to develop a personal style of their own. One of the features of the wooden carvings by 'Ksan artists is that oftentimes they will refrain from painting the image (whether it is a model totem pole, a panel, a mask, or a piece of sculpture) in order to let the natural color of the wood and the beauty of the wood grain manifest themselves. The Tsimshian always used color sparingly (oftentimes just black and red). In many of their contemporary works, therefore, this tendency is carried forward into a complete naturalism. A good example of this trait can be found in a recent carving by Harris, a killer whale sculpture made on commission for the Vancouver Art Gallery.

'Ksan also has produced a distinctive variety of silkscreen graphic arts that bear—with their emanating figurations suggesting motion—the hallmarks of Duane Pasco's approach and guidance. Harris has produced silkscreen prints, one of the ways by which he has garnered popular fame. Obviously, when instructors outside the culture were initially used in the training school, it is natural that some eclectic and hybrid forms would emerge. After all, a living art is always changing due to influences from various sources.

Before he attended the Kitanmax School, Harris was destined to play a major leadership role among the Gitksan people in his home village of Kispiox. In 1957 he was given his uncle's hereditary name of *Geel*, which conferred upon Harris the responsibilities of a recognized leader of Kispiox among the chiefs of the nation. After his experience at Kitanmax, he carved and raised a totem pole in Kispiox in 1971. As Karen Duffek has observed, "His involvement with the renewal of Gitksan ceremony shows that 'Ksan's positive impact on the community has surpassed the original goals set for the programme."

Harris has enjoyed a successful career due to the high quality of his work. In particular, he has created (either in solo activity or in association with other Tsimshian colleagues) many monumental works on commission. For instance, many visitors to the UBC Museum of Anthropology in Vancouver are greeted by "The 'Ksan Doors" at the entrance, which were created by Harris (working with Earl Muldoe, Vernon Stephens, and Art Sterritt). The two doors and adjoining side panels, when closed, form a rectangular structure, inspired, according to a museum brochure, by the Northwest Coast bent box that symbolizes culture as the container of the meaning of human life. Among some of his other masterpieces are the following works: a high relief stone sculpture located above the entry to the Canadian House of Commons in Ottawa, Ontario; wall-sized panel murals at the Canadian Embassy in Paris and the Royal Centre in Vancouver, British Columbia; totem poles raised at 'Ksan Village, Hull, Quebec, Rochester, New York, Baltimore, Maryland, San Francisco, Saint Jean Port Joli, Quebec, and Japan.

Despite the fact that he has had some bouts of poor health in the past few years, Harris still works daily in his workshop, called "The Hiding Place," in Kispiox.

—John Anson Warner

HAVARD, James

Tribal affiliations: Chippewa; Choctaw
Painter

Born: Galveston, Texas, 1937. **Education:** Sam Houston State College, Huntsville, Texas, B.S., 1959; Pennsylvania Academy of Fine Arts, Philadelphia, 1965.

Individual Exhibitions

1974	Galerie Ahler, Stockholm, Sweden
	Galleries Fabian Carlsson, Goteberg, Sweden
	Galleries Krakeslatt, Bromolla, Sweden
	Marian Locks Gallery, Philadelphia, Pennsylvania
1976	Delahunty Gallery, Dallas, Texas
1980	Tolarno Galleries, Victoria, Australia
1981	Louis K. Meisel Gallery, New York
1983	Hokin/Kaufman Gallery, Chicago
1984	Janus Gallery, Los Angeles
1986	Lavignes-Bastille, Paris
1988	Marian Locks Gallery, Philadelphia, Pennsylvania
	Elaine Horwitch Gallery, Santa Fe, New Mexico
1991	Alan Stone Gallery, New York
	Marian Locks Gallery, Philadelphia, Pennsylvania
1993	Hokin Gallery, Palm Beach, Florida
1996	Alan Stone Gallery, New York

Selected Group Exhibitions

1965	Long Beach Museum of Art, Long Beach, California
	University of Massachusetts, Amherst,
	National Collection of Fine Arts, Washington, D.C.
1970	M. H. DeYoung Memorial Museum, San Francisco
	Museum of Fine Arts, Houston, Texas
	Seattle Art Museum, Washington
1971	Smithsonian Institution, Washington, D.C.
1975	Nordjyllands Kunstmuseum, Aalborg, Denmark
	Baltimore Museum of Fine Art, Maryland
1976	Indianapolis Museum of Art, Indiana
	Fort Wayne Museum of Art, Indiana
1977	Solomon Guggenheim Museum, New York
1978	Amerika Haus, Frankfurt, Germany
1979	*Abstract Illusionism,* Danforth Museum of Art, Framingham, Massachusetts
	Museum of Fine Arts, Springfield, Massachusetts, Phoenix Art Museum, Phoenix, Arizona
	Reality of Illusionism, Denver Art Museum, Colorado, and University of Southern California, Los Angeles
1980	Albright Knox Museum, Buffalo, New York
1981	Museum of the Southwest, Midland, Texas
	Confluences of Tradition and Change: 24 American Indian Artists, organized by R. L. Nelson Gallery and C. N. Gorman Museum, Davis, California
1984	*Indianascher Kunstler*, organized by the Philbrook Museum, Tulsa, Oklahoma (traveled in Germany through 1985)
1985	*50 Artists, 50 Printers,* Tamarind Institute, Albuquerque, New Mexico
1988	*Riders with No Horses,* C. W. Post College, Brookville, New York

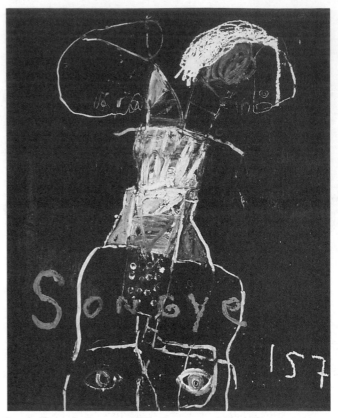

James Havard: *Songye,* 1996. Courtesy of the artist and Allan Stone Gallery, New York City.

1989	*Los Angeles Art Fair*
1990	*Chicago International Art Exposition*
1991	*Directions,* Marian Locks Gallery, Philadelphia, Pennsylvania
	Tokyo Art Fair
1992	Butler Institute of American Art, Youngstown, Ohio
	Cooper-Hewitt Museum of Art, New York
1993	High Museum of Art, Atlanta, Georgia
1995	Taft Museum, Cincinnati, Ohio
1996	Toledo Art Museum, Toledo, Ohio

Collections

Solomon Guggenheim Museum, New York; Heard Museum, Phoenix, Arizona; Los Angeles County Museum; Metropolitan Museum of Art, New York; Museum of Modern Art, Stockholm, Sweden; National Collection of the Smithsonian Institution, Washington, D.C.; New York University, New York; Oklahoma Art Center, Oklahoma City; Pennsylvania Academy of Fine Arts, Philadelphia; Philadelphia Museum of Art, Pennsylvania; Toledo Art Museum, Toledo, Ohio; Wheelwright Museum of the American Indian, Santa Fe, New Mexico.

Publications

On HAVARD: Books—*The Sweet Grass Lives On,* by Jamake Highwater, New York, 1980; *Confluences of Tradition and Change: 24 American Indian Artists,* L. Price Amerson, Jr., editor, Davis, California, 1981; *Magic Images: Contemporary Native American*

Art, by Edwin L. Wade and Rennard Strickland, Norman, Oklahoma, 1981; *Arts of the Indian Americas,* by Jamake Highwater, New York, 1983; *Indianascher Kunstler,* by Gerhard Hoffmann, Munich, 1984; *The Arts of the North American Indian,* by Edwin L. Wade, New York, 1986.

*   *   *

James Havard is an important painter who has made his home in Santa Fe for many years. In his more recent works, he explores his ancestral roots in paintings redolent with symbology of Native American cultures. These paintings have all the raw authenticity of art brut and folk art, ancient cave paintings, the work of Jean Dubuffet, and the primordial mythos that provides their true underpinnings.

There is a phenomenal vigor in their execution, with the implicit suggestion that the painter is struggling mightily to inveigle a numinous truth out of brute pigment and form. The semi-abstracted totemic figures that populate his recent paintings thus possess an inward vitality and an atavistic life that invariably renders them invigorating and even haunting.

Fragments of text and scattered signs, embryonic or fully realized but roughly delineated figures, unfettered pigment and the detritus of the mark-making itself gel in compositions that articulate the folklore of the moment wherein Havard finds himself. Mounted in ornate sculpted frames that complement them, the primitivistic images are captivating.

Havard was born in Galveston, Texas, and lived in New York for many years, where he earned international recognition as a pioneer of abstract illusionism, a form in which he used trompe l'ocil techniques to suggest abstract signs hovering as on a pane of clear glass installed over a deeper backdrop. He became a well-known abstract artist concerned with the dynamics of surface manipulation, and yet the floating illusionism in his paintings often drew upon symbols relating to his Native American heritage. An acknowledged master of this form of abstract illusionism, Havard has created a style wholly and distinctly his own.

His work evolved into a more purely—and somewhat more conventional—abstraction, with an action painting emphasis (as in de Kooning). Havard, who has always been experimental with his materials, then investigated collage with paint in his series called *Membres.* These works would reach their epitome in paintings in an exhibition at the Hokin Gallery in Palm Beach, Florida.

After recovering from a life-threatening illness, Havard has moved on to an even more arresting personal iconography. The quest for the primordial origins of his people surely inspired these works, rife as they are with symbols and images relating to his heritage.

These figural works were the subject of a solo exhibition mounted at the Allan Stone Gallery in New York. Principally figurative studies, the primitive figures refer to the symbology of specific North American Indian and also African tribes. This is true of the painting *Songye* (1996, oil and wax on wood), which references the Basongye tribe of Zaire, the art of which includes the famous striated Kifwebe masks and magical community fetish figures that Havard alludes to. But if he were just elliptically referring to these tribes, his work would be much less interesting. Instead, his work evokes their very spirit. He privileges a mark-making that is as authentic and arresting as it is open-ended and allusive.

These works have something of the authenticity of the cave paintings at Lascaux, a hard-won figurative integrity with abstract elements—one which speaks of the painter's own origins, and the origins of the life-world itself. Spidery tendrils of paint, roughly outlined, delineate atavistic figures that enjoy a certain universality. They have a very fetish-like quality. These paintings relate to the previous illusionistic abstraction more closely than one might at first think, for they are, in effect, flip side. The painter's career-long fascination with signs yields here to an obsession with figurative signs. The figure here is a distressed sign that nonetheless endures the ravages of time. It is nothing more or less than a stand-in for the self: a self redeemed from the deep well of time; a self abstracted, perhaps, from the context of cosmogonic mythos that permeates the iconography of Native North Americans. These paintings must count among the strongest, toughest, and most compelling works Havard has executed in his ongoing struggle to wrest human meanings from mute form. They herald a fruitful new phase in this remarkable artist's career.

—James D. Campbell

HEAVYSHIELD, Faye

Tribal affiliations: Blackfoot
Sculptor, installation artist, and mixed media artist

Born: Standoff, Blood Reserve, Alberta, 1953. **Education:** Alberta College of Art, Calgary, 1980-85; University of Calgary, 1985-86. **Awards:** Various grants, including Asum Mena, Culfrobe Memorial, and H.J. Heinz scholarships, and Canada Council "B" grant.

Individual Exhibitions

1993 *Heart, Hoof, Horn,* Glenbow-Alberta Institute, Calgary, Alberta (traveling)
1994 *Into the Garden of Angels,* Power Plant, Toronto

Selected Group Exhibitions

1986 *Canadian Native Business Summit,* Toronto, Ontario
1986-90 *Asum Mena,* Front Gallery, Edmonton, Alberta
1987 *Alberta Inspirations,* Nova Gallery, Calgary, Alberta
    Contemporary American Indian Art, Amherst, Massachussetts
1988 *Contemporary Native Art from Alberta,* Dartmouth, New Hampshire
1989 *Heard Museum 4th Biennial Invitational,* Phoenix, Arizona
1989-91 *Changers: A Spiritual Renaissance,* NIACC (traveling)
1992 *Time to Dialogue,* Triangle Gallery, Calgary, Alberta
    Ufundi Gallery, Ottawa, Ontario
    Canada's First People, Syncrude Canada (traveling)
    New Territories, 350/500 Years After, Vision Planetaire, Montreal, Quebec
    Land, Spirit, Power, National Gallery, Ottawa, Ontario (traveling)
1993 *Yesterday, Today, Tomorrow,* Triangle Gallery, Calgary, Alberta
    Local Stories, Edmonton, Alberta
1994 *She: A Roomful of Women,* Thunder Bay Art Gallery, Thunder Bay, Ontario

Feminist Works from the Permanent Collection, Glenbow Museum, Calgary, Alberta
The Heart As, Pitt Gallery, Vancouver, British Columbia
Sisters, Feminist Spin Forum, Calgary, Alberta
1996   *Faye HeavyShield, Shelley Niro, Eric Robertson*, Contemporary Art Gallery, Vancouver, British Columbia

Collections

Alberta Art Foundation, Edmonton; Glenbow Museum, Calgary, Alberta; Heard Museum, Phoenix, Arizona; India Art Centre, Department of Northern and Indian Affairs, Ottawa, Ontario; National Gallery of Canada, Ottawa.

Publications

On HEAVYSHIELD: Articles—"4th Biennial Native American Fine Arts Invitational at the Heard Museum," by Margaret Archuleta, *American Indian Art*, Winter 1989; "*Land, Spirit, Power*, Art of First Nations at National Gallery," by Nancy Beale, *Montreal Gazette*, October 1992; "*Land, Spirit, Power*," by Maryanne Barkhouse, *Matriart*, Vol. 3, no. 2, 1992;"Bone Things: The Art of Faye HeavyShield," by Robert Enright, *Border Crossings,* Fall 1992; "Contingent Histories, Aesthetic Politics," by W. Jackson Rushing, *New Art Examiner,* March 1993; "Whose Nation? First Nations Art in the Past and Present," by Scott Watson, *Canadian Art*, Spring 1993; "Intuition...," by Mike Murphy, *Artichoke,* Fall 1993; "Heart, Hoof, Horn," by Nancy Tousley, *Canadian Art*, Fall 1993; "Artist Creates from Experiences," by Nancy Beale, *Ottawa Citizen*, 13 April 1994; "Faye HeavyShield: An Intuitive Voice," by Robert Houle, *Aboriginal Voices,* Fall 1994; "Nations in Urban Landscapes," by Robin Laurence, *Border Crossings,* February 1996.

* * *

Faye HeavyShield has achieved an enviable reputation for her ability to invest minimalistic structures with inordinate expressive force. A sculptor of distinction, she has always chosen an esthetic of simplicity over complexity in her work.

HeavyShield was raised on the Blood Reserve in the prairie province of Alberta. She studied at the University of Calgary and later at the Alberta College of Art. This was a formative learning experience where she first came to recognize the exigencies of her own creative voice. She is known for using minimal material expressions and investigating the textural qualities of objects. The content of her work stems from her own memories, as she herself avers, and the memories of her people. This mnemonic reservoir, with its roots in her own childhood, lends her work a highly convincing auratic life.

HeavyShield's work deals with Native issues, but the works themselves are always open to multiple interpretations. They discourage taxonomy and leave ample room for our own projected meanings. Noted for her minimalist style, she uses the bare minimum of materials to express a maximal aesthetic experience in which our own feelings, memories, and imaginative acts are all put in play. Using simplified geometric forms made from wood and fiberglass and fabric with a low-key use of color, she plays on an unusually rich register of meanings. "Vaguely familiar objects are abstracted by the stretch of imagination and memory with the focus on texture and substance," she has said of her own work.

There is a phenomenal delicacy in this work that betrays a rare sense of communion with her materials and what they may say.

The most minimal structures have a suggestive power made all the more so by virtue of this delicacy. They form powerful networks of feeling in which we are invariably enmeshed.

One such work, the important *Like Thanks for the Blanket* (1989), is accessible on several levels. Here, a tall, vertical, triangular shape suggests the betrayal of a people, an icon for dwelling as well as an anthropormorph. The simple fiberglass housing is raised off the floor on wooden stilts. Most importantly, HeavyShield is here making a metaphorical comment on the reaction of Native North Americans to the discovery that the "gift" blankets distributed to them during the first winters of incarceration after the Indian Wars of the 1800s were infested with the smallpox virus. The fiberglass, cloak-like shape is intended to symbolize the "gift" blankets. The small, sharp barbs are meant to express the smallpox pustules on the skin. Her works lend an immense yet quiet dignity to the voice of the Native people and to their emotions in the wake of that discovery.

The triangular shape raised on stilts also has a powerfully anthropormorphic suggestion, reminding us of the enduring strength of the Native people and the fact of their survival in adverse circumstances. The shape further echoes the tipi-form dwellings so redolent of the Plains cultures. HeavyShield has said appropos of this work: "I was remembering a time when living in a tipi meant you could just pick up and go. It was a description of oneself."

HeavyShield always pares away anything that might be extraneous in her work. She hones her pieces incessantly, subtracting anything that might impede communication of a deeply felt situation. This is the reductive ethic of her vision. In all her work, HeavyShield tackles difficult issues uncompromisingly an with a real economy of form. A deft, humanizing touch, an advanced degree of stoicism and deliberate simplicity are always present in this haunting art of memory.

—James D. Campbell

HERRERA, Joe
Variant names: See Ru
Tribal affiliations: Cochití
Painter

Born: Joe Hilario Herrera, Cochití Pueblo, New Mexico, 17 May 1923; See Ru translates as "Blue Bird." **Education:** Santa Fe Indian School; University of New Mexico, B.A., 1953; University of New Mexico, M.A., Education, 1962. **Career:** Professional artist; director of Indian education, New Mexico State Department of Education; governor, Cochití Pueblo; instructor, Southwest Indian Art Project, University of Arizona; secretary, All-Indian Pueblo Council; chairman, Annual Governors Inter-State Indian Council. **Awards:** Les Palmes d'Academiques, 1954.

Selected Group Exhibitions

1937   American Indian Exposition and Congress, Tulsa, Oklahoma
1952   Museum of New Mexico, Santa Fe, New Mexico
        Museum of Modern Art, New York, New York
1975   *Pintura Amerindia Contemporanea*, United States Department of State, Washington, D.C. (toured South America through 1980)

1979   *Native American Paintings*, Joslyn Art Museum, Omaha, Nebraska

1982   *Native American Painting: Selections from the Museum of the American Indian*, Museum of the American Indian, New York, New York

1984   *Indianischer Kunstler*, Philbrook Museum of Art (toured West Germany)

1988   *When the Rainbow Touches Down*, Heard Museum, Phoenix, Arizona

1991   *Shared Visions: Native American Painters and Sculptors of the Twentieth Century*, Heard Museum, Phoenix, Arizona

Collections

Amerind Foundation, Dragoon, Arizona; Center for Great Plains Studies, University of Nebraska, Lincoln, Nebraska; Colorado Springs Fine Arts Center, Colorado Springs, Colorado; Denver Art Museum, Denver, Colorado; Thomas Gilcrease Institute of American Art and History, Tulsa, Oklahoma; Indian Arts and Crafts Board, Washington, D.C.; Museum of New Mexico, Santa Fe, New Mexico; Museum of Northern Arizona, Flagstaff, Arizona; National Museum of the American Indian, Smithsonian Institution, Washington, D.C.; Philbrook Art Center, Tulsa, Oklahoma; Millicent Rogers Museum, Taos, New Mexico; San Diego Museum of Man, San Diego, California; Tweed Museum of Art, Duluth, Minnesota.

Publications

On HERRERA: Books—*Contemporary American Indian Painting*, by David E. Finley, H.K. Press, Washington, D.C., 1953; *American Indian Painting of the Southwest and Plains Areas*, by Dorothy Dunn, University of New Mexico Press, Albuquerque, New Mexico, 1968; *Indian Painters and White Patrons*, by J. J. Brody, University of New Mexico Press, Albuquerque, New Mexico, 1971; *Southwest Indian Painting: A Changing Art*, by Clara Lee Tanner, University of Arizona Press, Tucson, Arizona, 1973; *Song from the Earth*, by Jamake Highwater, New York Graphic Society, Boston, Massachusetts, 1976; *American Indian Painting and Sculpture*, by Patricia Janis Broder, Abbeville Press, New York, 1981; *Native American Painting: Selections from the Museum of the American Indian*, by David M. Fawcett and Lee A. Callander, Museum of the American Indian, New York, 1982; *Lost and Found Traditions: Native American Art 1965-1985*, by Ralph T. Coe, University of Washington Press, Seattle, 1986; *When the Rainbow Touches Down*, by Tryntje Van Ness Seymour, Heard Museum, Phoenix, 1988; *Aesthetically Correct/Aesthetically Incorrect*, by Joseph Traugott, Jonson Gallery, University of New Mexico, Albuquerque, 1991; *Native American Art and the New York Avant-Garde*, by W. Jackson Rushing, University of Texas Press, Austin, 1995; *Modern by Tradition: American Indian Painting in the Studio Style*, by Bruce Bernstein and W. Jackson Rushing, Museum of New Mexico Press, Santa Fe, 1995. **Articles**—"Dancing Indians Are His Subject," by W. Thetford LeViness, *Desert Magazine*, August 1949; "The Art of Joe Herrera," by Dorothy Dunn, *El Palacio* 59, no. 12, December 1952; "America's First Painters," by Dorothy Dunn, *National Geographic Magazine* CVII, no. 3, March 1955; "Indian Art Comes of Age," by Ina Sizer Cassidy, *New Mexico Magazine* 35, no. 2, February 1957; "American Indian Painting," by Jean Snodgrass, *Southwestern Art* 2, no. 1, November 1967; "In the Name of Progress, Is History Being Repeated?," by Jean Snodgrass-King, *American Indian Art Magazine*, Spring 1985; "Tribute Honors N.M. Catalyst," by Simone Ellis," *Albuquerque Journal*, 4 April 1993; "The Battle Over Tradition," by Richard W. Hill, Sr., *Indian Artist*, vol. 1, no. 1, Spring 1995.

*

Joe Herrera comments:

As far as my own work is concerned, I developed some traits which are reflected in my art. One was where there are perfectly delineated single and group figures with two-dimensional colors of flat areas. The other is an abstract style utilizing native designs. The style is somewhat conservative and decorative. The antiquity of the brush goes without saying. An atomizer is used to spray the painting. Spatter technique is suggested as is done in Awatovi painting. Adapting Cubism in my shared vision, I condensed a variety of sources and experiences into each final composition. I added colors to the symbols where none existed originally. The importance of this is to give focus to the placing and balancing of the total picture.

*   *   *

In the work of Joe Herrera one witnesses the development and evolution of contemporary Native art. From the earliest influences of his mother, Tonita Pena (Quah Ah, 1895-1949), and others at San Ildefonso, such as Alfonso Roybal (Awa Tsireh) and Maria and Julian Martinez, to his Studio paintings of the 1930s, to his study at the University of New Mexico in the early 1950s and experiments with modernistic techniques under the influence of Raymond Jonson and the creation of "Pueblo modernism," Herrera's art reflects the movement from a codified style promulgated by Dorothy Dunn to the emergence of a contemporary individual style utilizing both traditional imagery and abstraction. In the early 1950s Herrera explored and photographed many sites throughout the Southwest, such as the Galisteo Basin in New Mexico, and subsequently used these images in his own work. His interest in the excavated kiva murals at Awatovi also inspired him. As early as 1950, Herrera's style was evolving from imagery reminiscent of the Studio to new imagery based on petroglyphs.

Herrera began his career observing his mother's painting activities, and she assisted him when he began his own work in earnest. His formal training led to the Studio in Santa Fe, where he was enrolled from 1936 to 1940, although he never studied with Dorothy Dunn. However, his work from this period is typical of the two-dimensional flat imagery that was produced at this time. *Cochiti Deer Dancer* (c. 1936-40), *Men's Arrow Dance* (1938), and even the later *Koshare* (c. 1945-50) and *Elk Dance* (1947) reveal the stylistic markers of the Studio. Each of these works depict individual or groupings of ceremonial figures, with close attention to details of color, regalia, and the posture of the dancer. The intent of these works was to reproduce iconographic cultural figures. This attention to detail, especially in works done after 1940, was honed by Herrera's employment at the Laboratory of Anthropology in Santa Fe doing illustrations for Dr. Kenneth Chapman.

When Herrera entered the University of New Mexico in 1950 he had been exposed to the cultural and religious ceremonies of Cochiti, and through his connection to the artists from San Ildefonso he also had knowledge of the symbolic dimensions of Pueblo imagery that appeared in the work of the Martinez's and to a degree in that of Roybal. At the university a number of strands came together for Herrera: he began to study the work of Cubism and such European modernists as Paul Klee and Wassily Kandinsky, and he was encouraged by Raymond Jonson to continue his study of rock art. In his work based on petroglyphs and kiva murals, Herrera used spraying and spattering of paint and incorporated symbolic designs. Even before such works as *Altar Pictograph* (c. 1951-55), *Petroglyph: Parrot Dancers* (c. 1951-1955), and *Hunting Ceremonial* (c. 1951-55), however, some of Herrera's work was taking on an abstract cast and revealing interlocking shapes and forms that most likely were applied to more "recognizable" petroglyphic imagery a year or so later. For example, *Design* (1950) is one of Herrera's most abstract works with little or no petroglyphic resonance. It seems more reflective of Raymond Jonson's series of seventeen paintings, *Pictographic Compositions*, from 1946-47. However, the non-representational works in this series were Jonson's translations of petroglyphs, so the "petroglyphic resonance" of Herrera's *Design* emerges in much more symbolic ways than in the later work.

One might see the 1951 *Untitled* as a transitional piece that anticipates Herrera's painting throughout the 1950s; indeed, Herrera's influence on artists like Helen Hardin might be traced to works of this type. In this work, a series of arcs, possibly delineating the underworld, the earth, and the sky, contain such forms as gradated circles (perhaps a waxing moon with curved lines of connection to the earth), clouds shapes, and a line that runs from the bottom left to the top right of the painting. What could be called the central image is an abstract bird or feather pattern. There is a clear suggestion of Pueblo imagery, as the work bridges the abstraction of *Design* and the aforementioned more representational works from the early 1950s. This is not to say that these works do not utilize symbolic elements, only that the symbols are more recognizable. *Altar Pictograph* depicts the water serpent (avanyu), clouds, rainbows, and falling rain; *Petroglyph: Parrot Dancers* portrays a line of four dancers with Kokopelli and two other figures surrounded by images representing the moon, a snake, the earth, rain, and clouds; *Hunting Ceremonial* compresses numerous scenes into one panel and can be read as a diagram of the universe, with the rain clouds, sun and hunters on a trail on the top of the painting to images of the underworld on the bottom.

Beginning in the late 1950s Herrera basically took a hiatus from painting, as he became involved with other activities, including acting as secretary of the All-Indian Pueblo Council for twelve years, Director of Indian Education for the New Mexico State Department of Education, and in 1974 working as the governor of Cochití. Herrera also hosted a radio program based at Cochití. In 1960 Herrera was an instructor in the Southwest Indian Art Project held at the University of Arizona. There he influenced numerous young students, including the Hopi artist Mike Kabotie, son of Fred Kabotie.

After his retirement from public life in the early 1980s Herrera returned to painting on a more regular basis. In *Spring Ceremony for Owah* (1983) he uses the image of dancers in a kiva setting. Here, Herrera employs his signature spatter technique for a rather straightforward depiction of two lines of dancers in regalia. In a pair of acrylics from the late 1980s (both titled *Untitled*) Herrera depicts ceremonially clad figures in a geometrical space. The figures are not recapitulations of the figures in his 1940s work, but they are also not quite as abstract an image as that in *Hunter* (1954). Rather, they are visual ciphers of myth and ritual. Regrettably, declining health over the past few years has not allowed Herrera to continue with his painting.

Herrera was criticized by many in the Indian art world, including his mother, when he broke with the Studio-style imagery of the 1930s. Some said that his work was no longer "Indian art." However, Herrera's place in the history of Indian art is based on his reconciliation of supposed opposites: traditional Native symbols and modernistic art techniques. Herrera was able to blend the symbolic content of petroglyphs and murals with the contemporary impetus toward abstraction.

—Larry Abbott

HERRERA, Velino Shije

Variant names: Ma Pe Wi
Tribal affiliations: Zia Pueblo
Painter

Born: Zia Pueblo, 22 October 1902. **Education:** Santa Fe Indian Boarding School, and after school painting sessions. **Career:** Rancher; educator in painting at the Albuquerque Indian School; illustrator, bookbinder, laborer on archeological digs, painter for the School of American Research, Santa Fe. **Awards:** Commissioned to paint 2,200 feet of murals, U.S. Department of the Interior Building, Washington D.C., 1939; Grand Award, Inter-Tribal Indian Ceremonials, 1948; Palmes d'Academiques, France, 1954. **Died:** 30 January 1973.

Selected Group Exhibitions

1919	Museum of New Mexico, Santa Fe
1927	Corona Mundi International Center, New York
1928	Newbery Library, Chicago
1931	*Exposition of Tribal Indian Arts*, sponsored by the College Art Association (toured the United States and Europe through 1933)
1932	Corcoran Gallery of Art, Washington, D.C.
1937	*American Indian Exposition and Congress*, Tulsa, Oklahoma
1947-65	*American Indian Paintings from the Permanent Collection,* Philbrook Art Center, Tulsa, Oklahoma
1955	*An Exhibition of American Indian Painters,* James Graham and Sons, New York
1955-56	European tour, organized by the University of Oklahoma, Norman
1958-61	European tour, organized by the University of Oklahoma, Norman
1964	Read Mullan Gallery, Phoenix, Arizona
1978	*100 Years of Native American Painting*, Oklahoma Museum of Art, Oklahoma City, Oklahoma
1984	*Indianascher Kunstler,* organized by Philbrook Museum, Tulsa, Oklahoma (traveled in Germany through 1985)
1986	*When the Rainbow Touches Down,* Heard Museum, Phoenix (traveling)

Collections

Amon Carter Museum of Art, Fort Worth, Texas; Cincinnati Art Museum, Ohio; City Art Museum, St. Louis, Missouri; Cleveland Museum of Art, Ohio; Denver Art Museum; Columbus Gallery of Fine Arts, Columbus, Ohio; Corcoran Gallery of Art, Washington,

Velino Shije Herrera: *Nature Worship.* Gift of Lillian Henkel Haass; courtesy Detroit Institute of Arts.

D.C.; Thomas Gilcrease Institute of American History and Art, Tulsa, Oklahoma; Heard Museum, Phoenix, Arizona; Indian Arts and Crafts Board, United States Department of the Interior, Washington, D.C.; Millicent Rogers Foundation Museum, Taos, New Mexico; Montclair Art Museum, Montclair, New Jersey; Museum of Northern Arizona, Flagstaff; Philbrook Art Center, Tulsa, Oklahoma; San Diego Museum of Man, California; School of American Research, Santa Fe; Southwest Museum, Los Angeles; Wilmington Society of Fine Arts, Wilmington, Delaware; Wheelwright Museum of the American Indian, Santa Fe; Woolarc Museum, Bartlesville, Oklahoma.

Publications

On HERRERA: Books—*Introduction to American Indian Art* by Oliver La Farge and John Sloan, New York, 1931; *American Indian Painting of the Southwest and Plains Areas* by Dorothy Dunn, Albuquerque, 1968; *Indian Painters and White Patrons*, by J. J. Brody, Albuquerque, 1971; *100 Years of Native American Painting* by Arthur Silberman, exhibition catalog, Oklahoma Museum of Art, Oklahoma City, 1978; *When the Rainbow Touches Down* by Seymour Tryntje Van Ness, exhibition catalog, Seattle & London, 1988; *Shared Visions: Native American Painters and Sculptors in* the Twentieth Century by Margaret Archuleta and Dr. Rennard Strickland, New York, 1991. **Articles**—"American Indian Water Colors" by C. Norris Millington, *The American Magazine of Art*, 25, no. 2, August 1932; "America's First Painters" by Dorothy Dunn, *National Geographic Magazine*, CVII, no. 3, March 1955.

* * *

Velino Shije Herrera, later called Ma Pe Wi, was part of the original group of early Pueblo Indian easel painters (1910-1930). Members from this first group, Herrera, Fred Kabotie, Alfonso Roybal, and Tonita Peña, to name a few, depicted scenes from the social and religious life of their respective pueblo communities using watercolors and paper. When compared to historic painted art forms such as pottery and kiva murals, these secular paintings marked a distinct change in both subject matter and medium. Pueblo Indian watercolor paintings were championed as a new art form and were marketed primarily for sale to white patrons.

As a teenager, Herrera attended the Santa Fe Indian Boarding School, where he and a few other students, Kabotie, Otis Polelonema, and Roybal, were invited to paint after school at the home of Elizabeth De Huff, wife of the school's superintendent. Despite the Bureau of Indian Affairs ban prohibiting arts training De Huff provided the students with art supplies during these informal art sessions and encouraged them to draw and paint.

At the time when Herrera began easel painting, it was not considered a viable profession for American Indians by many native and non-native people. Some of the painters found it difficult to work at home due to negative attitudes in their pueblo communities towards this type of secular painting, especially if it involved the depiction of ceremonial dances. In fact Herrera was later ostracized by the elders of his pueblo for his painting activities. Nevertheless he continued to paint kachinas and dance ceremonies, stating, "I have danced in the ceremonies. I feel it is important to record these costumes."

In 1919 the paintings that came out of the De Huff art sessions were exhibited for the first time at the Museum of New Mexico, where they caught the attention of Dr. Edgar L. Hewett, then director of the museum. Of his start in painting Herrera recalled, "Dr. Hewett selected a few he thought had talent and started us to painting. I was one. I have been painting ever since." Along with Kabotie and Roybal, Herrera was hired by Hewett as a bookbinder, a laborer on archeological digs, and as an artist painting for the School of American Research.

No doubt Herrera and his contemporaries influenced one another. Their works of art share certain characteristic traits, like the use of outlined forms, paint applied in blocks of color, extensive detailing of clothing, and use of non-specific space. Despite this each artist developed their own particular area of specialization. For Kabotie it was his detailed representations of ceremonial dances and dancers, while Peña is distinguished for her images of women working or dancing. Herrera is most noted for his sensitive handling of landscapes and hunting scenes. Herrera utilized a stylized treatment of the land and its inhabitants. Although not like the European-American concepts of landscape, Herrera's representation of the natural world is indicative of his pueblo world view where key elements are singled out for attention and contemplation.

Throughout the 1920s and 1930s Herrera's paintings were exhibited nationally in New York, Chicago and Washington D.C. His paintings were also included in the *Exposition of Tribal Indian Arts*, which toured the United States and Europe from 1931 to 1933, promoting all forms of American Indian art. Herrera maintained a studio in Santa Fe and taught painting at the Albuquerque Indian School in 1936. In 1939 Herrera and five other artists were commissioned to paint 2,200 feet of murals for the new U.S. Department of the Interior Building in Washington D.C. Herrera also illustrated numerous books by Ruth Underhill. Further recognition of his artistic talents came in 1954 when he received the French *Palmes d'Academiques* award. Unfortunately, Herrera did little painting after a 1956 auto accident in which he was injured and his wife was killed.

—Lisa Roberts

HILL, Joan
Variant names: Chea-Se-Quah
Tribal affiliations: Creek; Cherokee
Painter and illustrator

Born: Muskogee, Oklahoma; Native name means "Red Bird." **Education:** Northeastern State College, B.A., 1952; figure drawing classes at Philbrook Art Center, mid-1950s; Bacone College, special study of Indian art with Dick West, 1958-63. **Career:** Instructor of art, Tulsa Secondary Public Schools, 1952-56; instructor of art and adult art education, and Muskogee Art Guild consultant, 1959-60; American Association of University Women, 1962-63; board of directors, T. H. Hewitt Painting Workshops, 1965-78; Youth & Art Advisory Board, Oklahomans for Indian Opportunity, 1973-82; Member, National League of American Penwomen, Inc.; Commission on the Status of Women, appointed by Governor of Oklahoma, 1989; Bacone Alumni Hall of Fame, 1991. **Awards:** Over 250 honors, including 13 Grand Awards and five Special Trophies in juried fairs; Commemorative Medal from Great Britain, the "Oscar d' Italia 1985," from Academis Italia, Cremona, Italy, and the Waite Phillips Special Artist's Trophy for Lifetime Achievement from the Philbrook Art Center; numerous commissions, including University of Central Oklahoma, 1990 (installed permanently), State of Oklahoma's Governor's Commission on the Status of Women, for Women's Day at the Capitol, 1990, Cherokee Nation, 1990, and Oklahoma Institute of Indian Heritage for its Spirit of the People, 1991.

Individual Exhibitions

1979   Lang Institute, Beijing, People's Republic of China (traveling)
1993   *Paintings by Joan Hill*, Southern Plains Indian Museum and Crafts Center, Anadarko, Oklahoma

Selected Group Exhibitions

1964   *First Annual Invitational Exhibition of American Indian Paintings,* Department of the Interior, Washington, D.C.
1965   *American Embassies Overseas*, Department of the Interior, traveling
1967   *America Discovers Indian Art*, Smithsonian Institution, Washington, D.C.

Center for American Indian Arts, Department of the Interior, Washington, D.C. (annually through 1970)

1976   *One with the Earth*, Institute of American Indian Arts, Santa Fe, New Mexico (traveling)

U.S. Military Museum, Smithsonian Institution, Washington, D.C. (traveling exhibition to military bases)

1978   *100 Years of Native American Painting*, Oklahoma Museum of Art, Oklahoma City

1980   *Native American Art at Philbrook*, Philbrook Museum, Tulsa, Oklahoma

Naiwas: National American Indian Women's Association Show, Via Gambaro Studio-Gallery, Washington, D.C.

Centennial Touring Art Exhibit, Bacone College, Bacone, Oklahoma

1982   *Night of the First Americans*, Kennedy Center for Performing Arts, Washington, D.C.

Contemporary North American Indian Art, National Museum of Natural History, Smithsonian Institution, Washington, D.C.

1988   *Southeast American Indian Art Show*, Marietta-Cobb Fine Arts Center, Marietta, Georgia

Contemporary Southeastern Indian Artists: Keepers of Culture, Anniston Museum of Natural History, Anniston, Alabama

1990   *New Art of the West*, Eiteljorg Museum of American Indian and Western Art, Indianapolis, Indiana

Artists and Advocates, Native American Rights Fund, Boulder, Colorado (traveling through 1993)

1991   *Shared Visions: Native American Painters and Sculptors in the Twentieth Century*, Heard Museum, Phoenix, Arizona

1993   *Moving the Fire: The Removal of Indian Nations to Oklahoma*, organized by the Philbrook Museum of Art, premier at International Monetary Fund Visitors Center, Washington, D.C., as part of the Inaugural activities (traveling)

1994   *Watchful Eyes: Native American Women Artists*, Heard Museum, Phoenix (traveling)

1995   *Native American Invitational & Master Exhibit Celebrates Oklahoma Art*, Thomas Gilcrease Institute of American History and Art, Tulsa, Oklahoma

1996   *Visions & Voices: Native American Painting from Philbrook Museum of Art*, Philbrook Museum, Tulsa, Oklahoma

Oklahoma, Spirit of the People, Zenith Gallery and Adams National Bank, Washington, D.C.

Collections

Central State University, Edmond, Oklahoma; Fine Arts Museum, Santa Fe, New Mexico; Five Civilized Tribes Museum, Muskogee, Oklahoma; Heard Museum, Phoenix, Arizona; Heritage Center, Inc., Red Cloud Indian School, Pine Ridge, South Dakota; McCombs Gallery, Bacone College, Bacone, Oklahoma; Museum of the American Indian, Heye Foundation, New York; Museum of New Mexico, Santa Fe; Museum of Northern Arizona, Flagstaff; Philbrook Art Center Museum, Tulsa, Oklahoma; Southern Plains Indian Museum, Anadarko, Oklahoma; United States Center for Military History, Smithsonian Institution, Washington, D.C.; United States Department of the Interior in Washington, D.C.

Publications

On HILL: Books—*Indian Painters and White Patrons*, by J. J. Brody, Albuquerque, 1971; *Songs from the Earth: American Indian Painting*, by Jamake Highwater, Boston, 1976; *100 Years of Native American Painting*, by Arthur Silberman, exhibition catalog, Oklahoma Museum of Art, Oklahoma City, 1978; *The Sweet Grass Lives On*, by Jamake Highwater, New York, 1980; *Centennial Touring Art Exhibit*, by Donald Humphrey and Jeanne Snodgrass King, Muskogee, 1980; *Native American Art at the Philbrook*, exhibition catalog by John Mahey, et al, Tulsa, 1980; *American Indian Painting and Sculpture*, by Patricia Janis Broder, New York, 1981; *New Art of the West*, by Thomas gentry, et. al, Indianapolis, 1990; *Shared Visions: Native American Painters and Sculptors in the Twentieth Century*, by Margaret Archuleta and Dr. Rennard Strickland, New York, 1991; *Native American Art and Folklore,* David Campbell, editor, Greenwich, Connecticut, 1993.

*   *   *

Joan Hill's work has long received favorable attention for a number of reasons. Her painting style was initially noteworthy, in part, for staying within standard definitions of the flat style, yet was so obviously modern. Her elegantly simple draftsmanship produces highly formal and idealized figures, while Hill is a colorist; her mother remarked on her unusual choice of colors even during her childhood, when she made yellow skies and blue trees. Throughout the various stages of her artistic development, the non-traditional use of color has remained constant.

Hill's first formal training was at Northeastern State University. She majored in education and her classes focused more on teaching methods than studio art. After graduation, she obtained a teaching position with the Tulsa Public Schools. While in Tulsa, she took figure drawing classes at Philbrook Art Center. Hill determined to quit her teaching job and focus full time on painting. She began taking classes from Dick West, director of the art school at Bacone College. West noticed her focus on color and pointed out how each Indian artist seems to choose a particular color for human figures. At that time, she tended to use a deeply saturated red. Her use of color became part of her stylistic signature and is a vital element of many of her best known paintings, including *The First Ceremony: Mother and Child* (1979) and *Sacred Ceremony of the Temple Mound* (1989).

Dick West encouraged her to try Indian art, but she felt at first that she had not been raised traditionally and therefore was not qualified. At the time, she had a backlist of over 30 portrait commissions, and was painting landscapes as well. West encouraged her to do research, focusing on her own tribal heritage, and Hill was surprised by the depth of Native tradition within in her family. Her father and other family members responded by accommodating her interest in ceremonial activities and recalling tribal and family history. She began creating paintings that featured her own colorist style on Native American subjects.

From 1964 to 1980, Hill traveled to over thirty-six foreign countries while attending painting workshops. She was exposed to many teachers, artists' studios, and museum collections throughout the world. Of these experiences, Hill was most effected by studying in person the art of Paul Gaugin and the Fauves. Indeed, Hill claims that Gaugin is the artist whose work has most affected her own. It is easy to draw parallels between the two in their simplification of both form and color, and emphasis on non-traditional color placement. Their motivations are similar also in their attempts to create, through less naturalistic style, more personal and powerful visions. Hill had already long been interested in "interpreting the way (she) felt, not what a camera would record." Her exposure to Gaugin and the Fauves did not alter her art, but simply enhanced an already existing interest.

Hill used the workshops as opportunities to work with new subject matter to inspire her growth. Teachers and other students sometimes considered her color choice remarkable. She responded by saying that the colors mirrored the way she felt and that it seemed natural to use them. In Venice, while other artists in the workshop painted the water as it appeared, Hill painted the water and the sky with yellows.

The workshop trips occurred about twice a year. When back in Oklahoma, Hill continued Native American paintings that were increasingly informed by both her experiences abroad and her participation in her tribal heritage at home. *Moon of the Dance of the Wolf* (1969), for example, combines Native American theme with highly expressive warm colors. More recent works, such as *Baptism on the Trail* (1991) and *The Water Dwellers* (1992), also contain Native American subjects, but are ultimately studies of the relationships between colors. Yet, Hill has not placed interest in style over content. *Women's Voices at the Council* (1990) is an example of her continuing commitment to keep tribal history in the forefront of much of her recent work.

—Kevin Smith

HILL, Rick

Tribal affiliations: Tuscarora
Painter, carver, photographer, and basketweaver

Born: Richard Hill in Buffalo, New York, 1950. **Education:** Art Institute of Chicago, 1968-70; State University of New York, Buffalo, M.A., 1980. **Career:** Iron and construction worker, mid-1960s to 1971; educator and writer; museum positions, including Buffalo Historical Society, Buffalo, New York, and the Turtle (an Iroquois cultural center), Niagara Falls, New York, mid-1970s; managed Indian art collections and exhibitions, Department of Northern Affairs, Ottawa, Canada, 1982-85; director, Institute of American Indian Arts Museum, Santa Fe, New Mexico, 1990-94 (opened 1992, absorbing and expanding the collection of the Institute of American Indian Arts); consultant, Museum of the American Indian, Smithsonian Institution, Washington, D. C., since late 1980s; curator, including *Creativity Is Our Tradition,* Institute of American Indian Arts Museum, 1992, and *Gifts of the Spirit*, Peabody Essex Museum, Salem, Massachusetts, 1996. **Awards:** Fellowships, including New York State Historical Society (photography, 1971), America the Beautiful Fund (painting, 1973), and Creative Artists Public Service, (painting, 1976); photography award, America the Beautiful Fund, 1972.

Individual Exhibitions

1973   Buffalo Museum of Science, Buffalo, New York
1975   Museum of the Hudson Highlands, Hudson, New York
1977   American Indian Art Collection, Shawnee, Oklahoma

1978   Four Corners Gallery, Miami, Florida
1982   Siena College, Loudenville, New York
1983   Museum of the American Indian, New York
1986   *Portraits: Paintings and Photographs by Rick Hill,* Thunder Bay Art Gallery, Thunder Bay, Ontario

Selected Group Exhibitions

1973   Everson Museum of Art, Syracuse, New York
1974   University Museum, Philadelphia, Pennsylvania
1976   Artist's Committee Gallery, Buffalo, New York
1977   Philbrook Museum of Art, Tulsa, Oklahoma
1978   Woodland Indian Cultural Education Center, Brantford, Ontario
       Denver Art Museum, Denver, Colorado
       Arnot Art Gallery, Elmira, New York
1979   *The Real People,* International Native-American Council of Arts, Casa de las Americas, Havana, Cuba
       American Indian Art Gallery, New York
1980   Woodland Indian Cultural Education Center, Brantford, Ontario
       Buscaglia-Castellani Art Gallery, Niagara Falls, New York
1981   Oswego Art Guild, Oswego, New York
       Via Gambaro Gallery, Washington, D. C.
1982   C. N. Gorman Gallery, University of California, Davis
       Cleveland Museum of Natural History, Cleveland, Ohio
       Sienna College, Loudonville, New York
       Night of the First Americans, John F. Kennedy Center for the Performing Arts, Washington, D. C.
1983   Niagara Community College, Sanborn, New York
       Lowe Art Gallery, Syracuse, New York
       Queens Museum, Queens, New York
       The Other America, New Society of Fine Arts, Berlin, Germany (traveled in Europe through 1984)
1984   *Canoe Festival,* Ottawa, Ontario
       Fondo del Sol, Washington, D. C.
       Woodland Indian Cultural Education Center, Brantford, Ontario
       Southern Plains Indian Museum, Anadarko, Oklahoma
1985   *Visions,* Photo Union Gallery, Hamilton, Ontario
1986   Ottawa School of Art, Ontario
1986-89   Woodland Indian Cultural Education Center, Brantford, Ontario
1990   Tower Fine Arts Gallery, State University of New York, Brockport
1992   Natural History Museum, Smithsonian Institution, Washington, D. C.
1996   *Visions + Voices*, Philbrook Museum of Art, Tulsa, Oklahoma
1997   American Indian Contemporary Arts, San Francisco, California

Collections

Canadian Museum of Civilization, Ottawa, Ontario; Cleveland Museum of Natural History, Cleveland, Ohio; Department of Indian and Northern Affairs, Ottawa, Ontario; Indian Arts and Crafts Board, U. S. Department of the Interior, Washington, D. C.; Institute of American Indian Arts Museum, Santa Fe, New Mexico; International Center of Photography, New York; Native American Center for the Living Arts, Niagara Falls, New York; Philbrook

Museum of Art, Tulsa, Oklahoma; Seneca-Iroquois National Museum, Salamanca, New York; Southern Plains Indian Museum, Anadarko, Oklahoma; Woodland Indian Cultural Education Center, Brantford, Ontario.

Publications

By HILL: Books—*Creativity Is Our Tradition,* Santa Fe, Institute of American Indian Arts Museum, 1992; *Creations Journey: Native American Identity and Belief,* by Rick Hill and Tom Hill, Washington, D. C., Smithsonian Institution Press, 1994; *Gifts of the Spirit,* Peabody Essex Museum, Salem, Massachusetts, 1997. **Articles**—"The Battle Over Tradition," *Indian Artist* magazine, Spring 1995.

On HILL: Books—*I Stand in the Center of Good,* by Lawrence Abbott, Lincoln, University of Nebraska Press, 1994. *Visions + Voices: Native American Painting from the Philbook Museum of Art,* Lydia Wyckoff, editor, Tulsa, 1996. **Articles**—"New Directions in Iroquois Photography," by Tim Johnson, *Turtle,* Winter 1983; "The Native American Artist: Caught Between Culture and Commerce," by Zoe Tolone, *New Times,* 20 July 1983; "Indian Art through Indian Eyes," by Rowena Dickerson, *Santa Fe Reporter,* 15 August 1990; "Indian Art—Indian Voices," by William Clark, *Albuquerque Journal,* 19 August 1990; "Museum Directions: Reclaiming Authority," interview with Jacqueline M. Pontello, *Southwest Art,* June 1992.

*

Rick Hill comments (1990):

I am an Indian, and I am an Indian nationalist. I really believe in Indians. I believe in the power of our traditions, culture, art and ingenuity to overcome anything we set our minds to. For this reason, I like Indian art. It represents the Indian mind at work trying to resolve a problem, offering an alternative, or commenting on the times....

Every generation has to define for itself what it means to be an Indian. Just as our grandfathers did things that cultural anthropologists refer to as assimilation or acculturation, we do things today that our grandparents could never have conceived of doing. So, it is a continuum that is constantly changing.

Being an Indian is to do something about what you think it means. I have chosen art, for in its expressions it promises a future. (From "Indian Art through Indian Eyes," *Santa Fe Reporter,* 15 August.)

*   *   *

As a member of the contemporary Native North American art movement and the Iroquois Nation, Richard W. "Rick" Hill speaks with two voices in his work—not to be confused with a "forked tongue," the characteristic that pseudo Indians in the old western movies attributed to the white man's duplicitous speech. Quite to the contrary, Hill strives to speak the truth about Native culture. Hill's voices are visual and literary, and in both he seeks to counter the forked tongue, non-Native definitions of Native culture and its art that have been perpetuated since the late 1400s. His work in both realms has placed him among the contemporary Native art movement's leaders in the current focus on self-definition.

While not all information gathered by non-Indian culture about Indians is wrong or necessarily de-humanizing, a significant amount is, and it is that information that has most often shaped the understanding of Native peoples on this continent. Existing stereotypes and misconceptions that arise from this misinformation consistently place Indian people in a romantic time period somewhere between the 1700s and 1900s, ignoring the continued existence of Native culture beyond that time period and up to the present. Imagery of Native people created by non-Natives throughout the history of the U.S. has run the gamut from large scale historical paintings of a "Noble Savage" to the photographic documentation of a vanishing race. In the interim, imagery falsely depicted Native people as a bloodthirsty menace to society, in what amounted to a calculated attempt by the U.S. government to influence the public to support the genocide of Indian people and ensure completion of the westward expansion.

This imagery has so permeated the collective consciousness of this country that the "Indian on the Hill" stereotype, as I refer to it, is often the only definition of Indian culture that contemporary society will accept. It has become the definitive Indian art form and even contemporary Indian artists are expected not to deviate from it. When an Indian artist speaks in the present tense, as most contemporary Indian artists do, he or she taps into the stream of unresolved guilt feelings this country harbors about its past treatment of Indian people. It is easier to deal with Indian people in romantic terms rather than day to day realistic terms. Hill's work consciously embraces reality.

Hill's visual art can be seen not only as a way of personally honoring his people, but also as a way of directly responding to the influence of non-Native imagery of the past on definitions of Native culture. In terms of responding to the offending imagery, the artist is decidedly proactive. Using the basic structure of the imagery as a foundation, he reconstructs visual tableaus that counter the misinformation with sometimes elegant, sometimes intentionally crude results.

The artist's paintings from the 1970s, early in his career, appear to target historical paintings, like those created by George Catlin, for reconstruction. *George and Hubert Buck,* a polished, realistic watercolor, is a classic example of the artist's stance during this time period. The elderly Buck brothers, in traditional Iroquois regalia, are placed in the foreground of the picture plane. Two white tail "buck" deer are observing the brothers in close proximity in the background of the work. In the view the artist gives us, the brothers' forms are each naturally superimposed over one of the two deer in the background, the elder brother over the older deer and the younger brother over the younger deer. The younger of the Buck brothers is drumming and singing what one, by their traditional dress, could assume is a traditional Iroquois song, while the older brother shakes a rattle in time to the song. The hard realism and upper torso view of the Native subjects of the painting is certainly in keeping with the Catlinesque requirements of the Noble Savage portrait. As well, the painting incorporates the requisite Indian-in-traditional-dress-in-the-woods formula. However, Hill subverts the formula by depicting these particular Indians as real people. Elderly and a bit overweight, these are not the svelte, hard-muscled, "Wind in the Head" warriors pop culture loves to conjure, a characterization that has grown out of Catlin's works and those of other historical painters. They are not icons or mythological figures either. Rather, they are most likely people from Hill's own community, perhaps blood or clan relatives. On another level, they are people that anyone, regardless of cultural background, might know.

Rick Hill: *Shades and Braids: Warrior as Ironworker,* 1984. Courtesy of the artist.

They are someone's father, grandfather or uncle and, as the Buck brothers, they are Native people who are firmly rooted in contemporary existence (see the ribbon shirt, the close cropped hair). Attend any one of the hundreds of pow wows held across the country and you will find men like these in various types of traditional regalia, seated in lawn chairs around the dance arbor, visiting with their relatives and eating Indian tacos.

In the painting, Hill also shows us that, though they are contemporary Native men, the brothers are still very much connected to their cultural past, as many contemporary Native people are. The singing, drumming and rattling are ritual activities that connect the men to thousands of years of prior Iroquois existence and which lead them, ultimately, to the natural world. In the painting the artist reveals this connection to the natural world in the attentive stare of the deer and in their fearless proximity to the brothers. It is as if the brothers are speaking directly to the deer with their song, re-engaging a conversation that has occurred countless times over the millennia. In fact, in most tribes today, as in the past, there exist certain people who are designated to carry on these very real conversations with the natural world: they are referred to as medicine people.

Because he is a contemporary Iroquois, Hill's accounting of the modern Iroquois experience in his artwork has powerful implications. In so doing, he is assuming the societal role his ancestral predecessors held. These artists of the past, like Hill, defined a living culture using materials from within Native culture and without. Rather than perpetuating the Indian-on-the-Hill stereotype, he chooses to reveal the multiple connections that still exist between the past of Native culture and the present—a continuum of existence. His work functions as a re-writing of the history of Native culture, specifically Iroquois culture, adding a deeper degree of complexity to an often oversimplified existence. Examining Hill's entire oeuvre, one sees that he has always been very conscious of the possible implications of his work. These early works of the 1970s were his time to develop and refine a visual and literary dialogue, an even louder voice that has come to be his trademark.

The 1980s saw a marked change in the artist's painting style, as well as an injection of humor and satire into decidedly more pointed reconstructive images. His most notable pieces during this period directly reference the Indian portrait genre that started with Catlin's paintings and continued through Edward Curtis' photographs of the "vanishing" Native American. Hill uses areas of rich, mostly valueless color to fashion upper torso portraits of modern day Native Americans, Curtis-like images of vanished Indians, and reverse anthropological portraits of notable non-Natives. The resulting images possess a crude, cartoonish quality that helps deliver the artist's satirical message.

Hill's painting, *He Died of Measles,* is a Curtis-like portrait that strips away the hazy, romantic, vanishing-noble-savage veneer that Curtis and other portraiteers applied to their representations, to reveal what really lies beneath: a way of life altered forever by non-Indian presence. The image is of an Iroquois warrior in brightly striped traditional regalia with all the trimmings. The painted over eyes, dark and hollow, and the unhealthy complexion contradict the bright regalia and romantic subject matter, casting a pall over the otherwise idyllic image. What remains is a haunting physical presence, a specter-like figure that tells the story behind the story.

The artist's portraits of contemporary Indian males feature a consistent sunglasses-worn-indoors motif, a reservation community phenomenon and Indian inside joke. The well-known Native writer Vine Deloria once said the best thing the white man ever brought to Indian culture was Ray Ban sunglasses: they go a long way toward restoring the dignity (see "cool") of the Indian male and, when worn indoors, are usually accompanied by a vigorous head nod greeting.

Hill uses the motif most effectively in the painting *Seeker of Red Dots,* which depicts a sunglasses-clad, aspiring contemporary Indian artist posed between two of his abstract paintings hanging on a gallery wall. His position between the two paintings suggests the transition of the young artist's career. He is a contemporary Indian warrior battling the elements of the mainstream non-Native artworld—warnings about ghettoization, misconceptions, stereotypes, the devaluation of Indian art by western culture, and his sunglasses are like mirrors on the regalia of his ancestors: they deflect the bad medicine, the warnings, and turn it back on the sender.

This battle of the contemporary Indian artist is one that Hill is all too familiar with and one that he fights on his own terms. His most effective weapons in the battle have been his lived experience as a contemporary Indian and artist, and the written word. In his various roles as curator, museum director, educator, and critical writer, his voice has helped shape the foundation of self-definition now forming within the contemporary Native arts movement. His approach to dealing with the critical issues facing contemporary Indian art and culture has been a pragmatic one. He chooses to deal with the entire spectrum of Native art, from the ancient work on up, as a way of showing that all Native art is part of an uninterrupted continuum of making that is centuries old. In addressing the Native art spectrum, Hill's overriding concern is that it be examined by, and that definitions emerge from, primarily the Native perspective.

Hill has applied this philosophy in his various capacities within the museum world. He has curated and co-curated numerous Native art exhibitions both at the national level and within the Native community, implementing his philosophy through exhibition design, thematic focus, and the catalog essay. In a recent curatorial endeavor, he teamed with Suzan Shown Harjo, Southern Cheyenne curator/poet/Native activist, and Richard Conn, former Native arts curator at the Denver Art Museum, to produce an exhibition, *Gifts of the Spirit,* at the Peabody Essex Museum in Salem, Massachusetts. The exhibition featured historical works from the Peabody Essex's extensive Native collection combined with the contemporary work of living Native artists. The design of the exhibition was a radical departure from the typical anthropological format of dividing Native art work into geographic regions. To better illustrate the connections between the work of artists of the past and the contemporary Indian artists of today, the curatorial team decided to juxtapose historical pieces alongside contemporary works without regard to geographic origin. The works were allowed to speak on their own terms, providing valuable new insights into the depth and breadth of the Native continuum of art making. The success of the exhibition was due in great measure to the inclusion of the Native perspective in all aspects of the planning and implementation of the exhibition, a key element in Hill's philosophy. As successful as Rick Hill's exhibitions have been, they are ultimately transitory vehicles for change. His most profound and enduring contributions in the critical realm have been his written works, which have appeared as catalog essays, journal essays, and magazine articles. His articles have addressed the critical issues facing Native artists and Native culture in general, and how those same issues manifest themselves within his own Iroquois Nation. His writing style mirrors his visual style, as he deals with similar issues in the same thoughtful, humorous, and introspective fashion. The true power of his writing lies in his ability, and willingness, to articulate his personal experience as it relates to the issues he is discussing. In this way he is helping to build a solid foundation of self-definition based on his lived experience as a Native person, an act that establishes the Native perspective as the primary source from which definitions of Native culture and art can emerge.

One of the most potent examples of Hill's writing style is the catalog essay he wrote for the *Gifts of the Spirit* exhibition. In it he chronicles the history of beadwork within the Iroquois Nation from contact forward. It is a compelling account. Even more compelling, though, is the account of his own experience as a contemporary beadworker, a little known component of his oeuvre. He eloquently reveals the personal significance of creating traditional beaded outfits for his children, which were used in ceremony and social pow wows, and the personal loss he felt when those items were stolen in 1992. Though they were retrieved intact shortly thereafter, Hill's expression of the deep emotion he felt at the time of their loss reveals a deep connection to the ancestral past not often articulated. His feeling of loss is the same loss Native people of the past must have felt as they watched their villages—full of the same items made with love and imbued with the same essence of the maker—being burned and looted by non-Indian soldiers. And, it is that same emotion that Native people today feel when they see these items in museum collections: a palpable sense of loss similar to the loss of a loved one.

The overall strength of both Hill's visual and literary work lies in his ability to tell a good story. He is able to capture the essence of storytelling, of the oral tradition, in his work in much the same way an Indian elder does. Rather than answering an entreaty directly, an elder will often present the questioner with a story and allow them to find their own answer within the story. Hill's ability to make these connections with the past, to pull information and technique forward in time, is invaluable to the contemporary Native North American art movement and Indian culture in general. His willingness to expend his energy in a multitude of directions for the better of Indian artists and the Indian community has affected this generation profoundly and will affect many generations to come.

—Bently Spang

HILL, Stan

Tribal affiliations: Tuscarora; Mohawk
Carver

Born: Stanley R. Hill, Six Nations Reserve, Ohsweken, Ontario, 16 November 1921, to a Tuscarora father and a Mohawk mother: by tradition, the Iroquois adopt the tribal affiliation of their mother, so Hill considers himself a Mohawk; however, the Canadian government categorizes Indians according to their father's tribe, so he is listed as a Tuscarora on the tribal enrollment for the Six Nations Band. **Education:** Oshweken, Ontario schools and Metalsmith School, Boston, Massachusetts. **Military Service:** U.S. Navy, World War II. **Career:** Construction and iron worker for thirty-three years, including twelve as co-owner of a steel construction company; field laborer; full-time artist since the mid 1960s. **Awards:**

Stan Hill: *Corn Spirit,* **1990. Photograph by Stan Metz; courtesy of Rick Hill.**

Over 50, including Northern Arts and Crafts Show in Buffalo, New York, First Place, 1975; Scottsdale Annual Indian Art Exhibition, Third Place in Sculpture, 1976; 32nd Annual American Indian Artist Exhibition, Philbrook Art Center in Tulsa, Oklahoma, First Place Award in Sculpture, 1977; Heard Museum Guild Annual Indian Art Show, Phoenix, Arizona, First Place in Sculpture, 1980.

Individual Exhibitions

1977   *Bone Carvings by Stanley Hill,* Sioux Indian Museum and Crafts Center, Rapid City, South Dakota
1982   Niwodihi Gallery, Scottsdale, Arizona
1984   *Stan Hill: Iroquois Art,* Schoharie Museum of the Iroquois Indian, Schoharie, New York

Selected Group Exhibitions

1985   *Lost and Found Traditions: Native American Art 1965-1985,* national touring exhibition through 1987
1989   Ganondagan State Historical Site, New York

Collections

Bolle Museum, Paris; Canadian Museum of Civilization, Ottawa, Ontario; Eitlejorg Museum, Indianapolis, Indiana; Indian Art Centre, Government of Canada, Ottawa, Ontario; Indian Arts and Crafts Board, Department of the Interior, Washington, D.C.; McMichael

Canadian Collection, Kleinberg, Ontario; Miccosukee Museum, Tamiami Trail, Florida; Museum of the Iroquois Indian, Schoharie, New York; Rochester Museum and Science Museum, Rochester, New York; Royal Ontario Museum, Toronto, Ontario; Seneca Iroquois Museum, Salamanca, New York; Woodland Indian Cultural Education Center, Brantford, Ontario.

Publications

On HILL: Books—*American Indian Lives: Artists and Craftspeople,* by Arlene Hirschfelder, New York, 1994. **Articles**— "Iron and Antler: The Art of Stan Hill," by G. Peter Jemison, *Northeast Indian Quarterly,* Winter 1990; "Stanley Hill and Lost Art of Carving," *The Indian Trader,* March 1982; "Iroquois Sculptors," *American Indian Art Magazine,* Spring 1990.

*

Stan Hill comments (1977):

I did not plan to be an artist; therefore, working with bones and antlers was quite accidental.

After doing a few carvings, the antlers and bones seemed to come alive. A whole new world opened to me. It appeared that any discarded bone or antler could be transformed into a life-like object of beauty.

I am an instinctive carver. Every piece is a challenge. It has always been amazing to me to see my carvings slowly come alive with my inner feelings. It gives me great satisfaction to be able to give life to some animal that has lived his life upon this earth and the remains discarded and thrown away.

My work makes me fully realize that life is a circle. Even though we cannot see life, does not mean it isn't there. (From the catalog *Bone Carvings* by Stanley Hill.)

*   *   *

Stan Hill was raised on a farm on the largest reservation in Canada, where he gained a respect for the annual cycles of nature, the sustenance given by the ripening crops, and the importance of animals. While he did not grow up within the traditional rituals of his people, his real life experiences paralleled that of his ancestors, who were noted farmers, hunters and warriors. Hill left the reserve and worked on fruit farms and in construction in the Lewiston, New York, area, where he met his wife Alma, a Tuscarora Indian. He then became an ironworker, like many other Mohawk men in his era, and was drafted into the American Navy during the World War II, where he served as a deep sea diver in the South Pacific to locate and repair ships. After the war he returned to Buffalo, New York, and resumed his career as an ironworker.

The tragic death of one of his four sons in a car accident changed Stan's life. He became more introspective and turned to art for consolation. He started by carving rings out of stainless steel nuts he would pick up on the job site. His first works were of animals and images of ironworking. On a mountain-climbing trip in Alaska, he saw an eagle for the first time in his life and watched as it swooped down and captured a fish. Upon returning home, he was given a piece of bone and encouraged to carve that eagle by his brother-in-law, Duffy Wilson, himself a stone sculptor. When he did, a whole new life was begun, at the age of 55. Hill decided to sell his construction business and take up carving full time. "For 33 years I worked in the construction business, up there in the sky

with the high steel," explained Stan. "It was a dangerous job, very hard work. I was good at it. But there's more to a man than making a living."

Hill is a self-taught artist, carving moose and deer antler, animals bones and ivory. His work recalls traditional beliefs, but it is truly unique in that he taught himself how to carve, how to craft the images he wants, and how to market his work. In fact, he did not have much schooling at all, but worked hard to make his life significant to himself, his family as well as the others he meets through his art. He is proud of his accomplishments but is not comfortable calling himself an artist, as he views the process of making art as a gift from a higher power. He believes that the power to think about the meaning of life is enhanced by the discipline that art requires. The hours it takes to carve allow him to think about the things that matter to him and to work his way through what he was taught, what he used to believe, and to seek a more enlightened understanding. In this way, Hill believes that one of the functions of art for Indians is the meditative process: the creative energy of making art feeds the creative thinking about meaning.

Since the mid-1970s, Hill has used his art as his way to make a difference. He works for change, as he says: "So there's nothing I could say that would make you understand my feelings. The feelings of an Indian. That's why sometimes, I guess, the artist tries to get his feelings into his work, hoping that the white man can understand it." Sometimes the recognition he receives amazes him, other times it confuses him, as he can remember a more racist time when Indians were looked down upon; now, people will pay for what he has to say as an Indian.

Hill lived with the belief that life without struggles is no life. His own struggles have enriched his life. With each success he grew more thankful for the gift of art. Through his antler and bone carvings he grew more sensitive to the ways of his ancestors. His work shows the eagles, deer, bear, turtles, beaver, herons, hawks and wolves that animate the oral history of his people, as well as the legendary spirit of corn, beans and squash that he experienced as a young boy planting seeds, hoeing the fields and harvesting the fruits of the earth.

To see his work today, you would think that he was a born carver, that he spent his whole life perfecting his skill and vision. Yet, Stan is a self-taught artist and single-handedly revived bone carving, one of the most ancient American Indian art forms. There were no rules for him to break, no blueprints to follow, no instruction manual to read for what he has done. It is his sheer self-determination that has allowed the beauty of his work to come forth. He works diligently to find the right tools, the right techniques, the right feelings that he wants to project. Over the last 30 years, Hill has remade himself through his art, becoming more in tune with his ancestors, and his experience proves that art has power to transform the artist.

—Rick Hill

HOKEAH, Jack
Tribal affiliations: Kiowa
Painter

Born: Western Oklahoma, 1902. **Education:** Special art course, 1926, and classes 1927-29, University of Oklahoma. **Career:** Produced memorial murals at St. Patrick's Mission School, 1929, and the Santa Fe Indian School, 1932; artist and dancer.

Individual Exhibitions

1928   *Five Kiowas*, traveling exhibition arranged by Oscar Brousse Jacobson
1930   Southwest States Indian Art Show, Santa Fe
1931-33 *Exposition of Indian Tribal Arts*, tour organized by the College Art Association
1955-56 European tour sponsored by the University of Oklahoma, Norman
1958-61 European tour sponsored by the University of Oklahoma, Norman
1966   Southern Plains Indian Museum and Craft Center, Indian Arts and Crafts Board, Anadarko, Oklahoma
1978   *100 Years of Native American Art*, Oklahoma Museum of Art, Oklahoma City (traveling)
1979-80 *Native American Paintings*, Mid-America Arts Alliance, Joslyn Art Museum, Omaha, Nebraska (traveling)
1980   *Plains Indians Paintings*, Museum of Art, University of Oklahoma (traveling)
1984-85 *Indianascher Kunstler*, organized by the Philbrook Museum, Tulsa, Oklahoma (touring West Germany)
1991   *Mayfest International Festival*, Charlotte, North Carolina
1991-92 *Shared Visions: Native American Painters and Sculptors of the Twentieth Century*, Heard Museum, Phoenix, Arizona

Collections

Anadarko City Museum, Oklahoma; Cleveland Museum of Art, Ohio; Denver Art Museum, Colorado; Thomas Gilcrease Institute of American History and Art, Tulsa, Oklahoma; Indian Arts and Crafts Board, Department of the Interior, Washington, D.C.; Joslyn Art Museum, Omaha, Nebraska; Marion Koogler McNay Art Museum, San Antonio Texas; Museum of Art, University of Oklahoma, Norman; Museum of New Mexico, Santa Fe; Philbrook Art Museum, Tulsa, Oklahoma; Millicent Rogers Foundation Museum, Taos, New Mexico.

Publications

On HOKEAH: Books—*Kiowa Indian Art,* by Oscar B. Jacobson, Nice, France, 1929; *American Indian Painters,* by Oscar B. Jacobson and Jeanne d'Ucel, Nice, France, 1950; *American Indian Painting of the Southwest and Plains Areas,* by Dorothy Dunn, Albuquerque, New Mexico, 1968; *Indian Painters and White Patrons,* by J. J. Brody, Albuquerque, New Mexico, 1971; *Song from the Earth: American Indian Painting,* by Jamake Highwater, Boston, 1976; *100 Years of Native American Art,* exhibition catalog by Arthur Silberman, Oklahoma City, 1978; *Kiowa Voices: Ceremonial Dance, Ritual and Song,* by Maurice Boyd, Fort Worth, Texas, 1981; *Native American Painting,* exhibition catalog by Jeanne Snodgrass King, Amarillo, Texas, 1981; *Native American Painting: Selections from the Museum of the American Indian,* New York, 1982; *Shared Visions,* by Margaret Archuleta and Rennard Strickland, Phoenix, 1991.

*   *   *

Jack Hokeah was one of the "Kiowa Five" artists who were the founders of the traditional, or classical "flat style" of Indian painting on the Southern Plains. Like the other members of the Kiowa Five—Spencer Asah, James Auchiah, Monroe Tsatoke, and Stephen Mopope—Hokeah painted ceremonial dances, hunting parties, events from legend and ritual, and musicians and singers. Hokeah was an excellent dancer with a large repertoire, and many of his works are based on and recreate dances.

Up to a point, the story of Hokeah is similar to that of the other Kiowa Five painters. He received his early education at St. Patrick's Mission School in Anadarko, was orphaned at an early age (like Spencer Asah) and became a boarding student. He received art instruction from Sister Olivia Taylor, who was of Choctaw heritage. Like his four comrades, Hokeah also enjoyed the benefit of the art classes organized by Susan (Susie) Ryan Peters at her home in 1918, and later registered for the special art course with Asah and Tsatoke at the University of Oklahoma in 1926. Later joined by Auchiah and Mopope, Hokeah enjoyed his years (1926-1929) at that institution, receiving instruction and encouragement from faculty member Edith Mahier and University of Oklahoma School of Art director, Oscar Brousse Jacobson. Additionally, Hokeah's work was included in the traveling exhibition put together by Jacobson that traveled to Prague, Czechoslovakia, for the First International Art Exposition. Some of Hokeah's art was reproduced in the folio, *Kiowa Indian Art,* published in Nice, France, in 1929. Finally, Hokeah worked with three of his friends—Asah, Mopope, and Auchiah—to produce the memorial murals at St. Patrick's Mission School commemorating the life of Father Isidore Ricklin.

However, around 1930 Hokeah's path began to depart from those of the other Kiowa Five. It was in 1930 that Susan Peters began to organize trips for the Kiowa Five artists to appear at the Gallup Inter-Tribal Ceremonials in New Mexico. These trips generally served two purposes: the artists' appearances promoted their art to new consumers, and four of the five (Asah, Mopope, Hokeah, and Auchiah) performed as dancers, while Tsatoke (his health already failing) contented himself with singing. In 1930, Hokeah went from Gallup to Santa Fe to attend a fiesta, where he met the famous potter, Maria Martinez, of San Ildefonso Pueblo. Hokeah stayed with her as an adopted son for ten years. In 1932, while in Santa Fe, Hokeah participated in an inter-tribal group to create murals for a new arts and crafts building at the U.S. Indian School in Santa Fe. According to art historian Rosemary Ellison, school officials were so pleased with the process and results of this project that they resolved to initiate an art department in the school. Thus was born "The Studio," which opened in the fall of 1932 under the auspices of Miss Dorothy Dunn.

Some art historians have been critical of Hokeah's work, as evidenced in the remarks of Jamake Highwater: "Hokeah tended to paint rather stiffly, so much so that his work has been compared to the bold line and simplicity of detail of Mexican codices. The rigidity of this style verges on stenciled monotony, which is startlingly ornate at its best, and brashly decorative at its worst." On the other hand, Arthur Silberman is rather more positive: "What his bold and theatrical painting of dancers may have lacked in delicacy and sensitivity was made up by the exuberance with which he endowed these powerful and arresting figures." Hokeah's reputation is secure as one of the Kiowa Five, though he had effectively retired from his painting career by the end of the 1930s.

—John Anson Warner

HOOD, Rance

Variant names: Au Tup Ta
Tribal affiliations: Comanche
Painter, sculptor, and illustrator

Born: Near Lawton, Oklahoma, 3 February 1941; Comanche name means "Yellow Hair." **Career:** Odd jobs (mills and oil fields); sculptor and painter. **Awards:** Numerous, at American Indian Exposition, Anadarko, Oklahoma (1967-72, including Grand Awards in 1969 and 1972), and the Philbrook Art Center annual (1968-70, including First Place, 1970); for book cover illustration (1985, best Western genre), poster art (American Artists Lithograph Competition), and sculpture (American Indian Film Festival).

Selected Group Exhibitions

1972   *Contemporary Southern Plains Indian Painting,* organized by the Southern Plains Indian Museum and the Oklahoma Indian Arts and Crafts Co-operative (traveling)

1978   *100 Years of Native American Art,* Oklahoma Museum of Art, Oklahoma City (traveling)

1979   *Native American Paintings,* Mid-America Arts Alliance, Joslyn Art Museum, Omaha, Nebraska (traveling)

1980   *Plains Indians Paintings,* Museum of Art, University of Oklahoma (traveling)

1981   *Views and Visions: The Symbolic Imagery of the Native American Church,* Southern Plains Indian Museum, Anadarko, Oklahoma

       Native American Painting, Amarillo Art Center Exhibition, Amarillo, Texas (traveling)

1984   *Indianascher Kunstler,* organized by the Philbrook Museum, Tulsa, Oklahoma (traveled in Germany through 1985)

1992   *Franco-American Institute Exhibit,* Rennes, France

Collections

Eiteljorg Museum, Indianapolis, Indiana; Thomas Gilcrease Institute of American History and Art, Tulsa, Oklahoma; New Britain Museum of American Art, New Britain, Connecticut; Oklahoma State Art Collection, Oklahoma City; Philbrook Art Museum, Tulsa, Oklahoma; Smithsonian Museum, Washington, D.C.; Southern Plains Indian Museum, Anadarko, Oklahoma.

Rance Hood in his studio, 1994. Photograph by Joan Frederick; from the Frederick Collection, Western History Collections, University of Oklahoma.

Publications

On HOOD: Books—*Song from the Earth: American Indian Painting,* by Jamake Highwater, Boston, 1976; *100 Years of Native American Art,* exhibition catalog by Arthur Silberman, Oklahoma City, 1978; *Native American Painting,* exhibition catalog by Jeanne Snodgrass King, Amarillo, Texas, 1981; *Magic Images: Contemporary Native American Indian Art,* Norman, Oklahoma, 1981; *Indianasche Kunst im 20 Jahrhundert,* by Gerhard Hoffman, et al, Munich, 1984. **Article**—"Storm Center: Rance Hood," by Carol Dickinson, *Southwest Art,* November 1985.

*

Rance Hood comments:

To understand my paintings you must attempt to understand the Indian way of vision: You must understand that a painting is only a symbol of something very powerful, something that happens inside you that is influenced by voices of visions in another world. The Indian knows this power as Medicine: it is the voice, the sight and the strength of the spirit and the soul.

*   *   *

Rance Hood is best classified as a traditionalist (or neo-traditionalist) active in the fields of painting, stone and bronze sculpture, and prints. He is the preeminent representative of the traditional flat style of painting first originated in easel art form by the noted Kiowa Five artists. However, Hood has not been content to rest with this legacy. He has developed the style into a more dramatic and forceful mode that can be termed neo-traditionalism. His technique and sense of color are stunning—traits that become all the more remarkable when one realizes that Hood is a self-taught artist.

Hood was raised on allotted land by his grandparents near Lawton, Oklahoma. His grandfather was a leader of the Native American Church (peyote cult) in the area and served as the "Road Man," or the individual who prepared the peyote altar for ceremonies. It was from his grandparents that Hood acquired his strong religious and spiritual orientation towards the peyote ritual, which is often featured prominently in his paintings. When his grandparents died, Hood quit school and eventually ended up staying with a brother in Los Angeles. It was during his sojourn in Southern California that Hood became most aware of Indian art. He saw a painting (*Eagle Dancer*) by Woody Crumbo and states that, "It blew my mind. We went into a dime store and my brother bought some cheap water colors and one brush. I painted two months and finally sold two paintings to friends for a few dollars. That assured me enough to go on."

Hood returned to Oklahoma in the 1960s and did a great deal to inform himself about Indian art in general and Comanche culture in particular. He visited Plains Indian art exhibitions and talked to many Comanche elders in order to garner their recollections. It was during this time, too, that Hood worked on his skills and technique in painting. He remembers that Lee Monnett Tsatoke (son of Monroe Tsatoke of the Kiowa Five fame) and others helped him out with useful tips: "I learned to keep everything very clean, to use casein and tempera. I developed confidence with watercolor and with my own conceptions. I don't use models. When I do, the figures came out stiff. Tsatoke and others taught me shortcuts involving flipping a toothbrush loaded with white to make a snowstorm or swinging an aerosol can of white acrylic to create a gust of wind." (Dickinson, 1985)

Hood's art reflects his Comanche heritage, visionary and spiritual life, and mysticism. Many of his paintings feature the Comanche ideal that a male should try to be a successful hunter and warrior: such a role incorporates spiritual strength and a mystical awareness of life's essences. Hood's males are indeed "mystic warriors of the Plains." There is a Dionysian sense to his paintings as can be discerned in some of his titles: *Thunder on the Plains, Crazy Dog Warrior, His Death Song, Forbidden Hunting Ground,* and *Sun Dance Vision.* In paintings where males are depicted in hunting and warfare activities, a sense of turbulent motion is often evident. Horses and men are rendered in heroic style featuring wildly active poses. Most often his figures are placed on a simple ground line against a plain or brooding sky (with maybe a few clouds or birds to accentuate a mood).

When Hood turns his attention to more spiritual topics and those having to do with interpersonal relationships, the mood is often one of reverence, stillness, and tenderness, as can be seen in works like *Love Song, To Father Sky & Mother Earth, Morning Blessing,* and *Medicine Way.* Given the fact that he can be a versatile artist who is well aware of other approaches in Indian art, he can also produce works in the Mexican-cum-southwestern mode reminiscent of the work of R. C. Gorman (Navajo), such as *Pueblo Woman.* And sometimes he can demonstrate his sense of humor to good effect in a painting like *Indian Bar Scene,* where an Indian woman is peering through a bar windowpane searching for her errant man, who is inside and seated at the bar with a beer in his hand.

When Hood traces his artistic roots back to seminal influences, he credits two persons in particular - Monroe Tsatoke and Woody Crumbo. Both of these figures were consummate painters who demonstrated a great deal of technical prowess and artistic integrity. Also, he professes a great deal of respect for Jerome Tiger and Blackbear Bosin, two deceased colleagues in the Oklahoma Plains traditionalist movement. This seems a logical association since both Tiger and Bosin added new directions and themes to Oklahoma Indian painting in the post-World War II period. In particular, both of them, like Hood, were not afraid to infuse their work with a deeper sense of emotion, feeling, and drama.

—John Anson Warner

HOOVER, John

Tribal affiliations: Aleut
Sculptor

Born: Cordova, Alaska, 1919. **Education:** Leon Derbyshire School of Fine Arts, Seattle, Washington; Institute of American Indian Arts, studying under Allan Houser. **Career:** Professional sculptor since the 1960s; artist in residence, Institute of American Indian Arts; judge for sculpture, Santa Fe Indian Market, 1990. **Awards:** Numerous, including first place, Heard Museum Guild Indian Fair and Market and Philbrook Art Center.

Individual Exhibitions

1975   *Sculpture by John Hoover,* Museum of the Plains Indian
          and Crafts Center, Browning, Montana

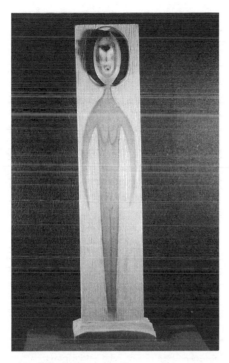

John Hoover: *Famine Woman*. Photograph by Larry Phillips; courtesy of the Institute of American Indian Arts Museum, Santa Fe, New Mexico.

Selected Group Exhibitions

1974	Stonington Gallery, Anchorage, Alaska
1979	Anchorage Historical and Fine Arts Museum, Alaska
1984	Native American Center for the Living Arts, Niagara Falls, New York
	Indianische Kunst, organized by the Philbrook Museum, Tulsa, Oklahoma (traveled in Germany through 1985)
1986	*Portfolio,* American Indian Contemporary Arts Gallery, San Francisco
1987	*New Directions Northwest,* Evergreen State College, Olympia, Washington
1988	*Crossroads of Continents: Cultures of Siberia and Alaska,* Smithsonian Institution, Washington, D.C.
1990	Glen Green Gallery, Santa Fe
1991-96	*Shared Visions: Native American Painters and Sculptors in the Twentieth Century,* Heard Museum, Phoenix, Arizona
1992	Stonington Gallery, Anchorage, Alaska
1994	Quintana Gallery, Portland, Oregon

Collections

Anchorage Historical and Fine Arts Museum, Alaska; Heard Museum, Phoenix, Arizona; Institute of American Indian Arts, Santa Fe, New Mexico; Smithsonian Institution, Washington, D.C.

Publications

On HOOVER: Books—*Sculpture by John Hoover,* Museum of the Plains Indian and Crafts Center, Browning, Montana, 1975;

Contemporary Native Art of Alaska from the Collection of the Anchorage Historical and Fine Arts Museum, Anchorage Historical and Fine Arts Museum, 1979; *The Sweet Grass Lives On: 50 Contemporary North American Indian Artists,* by Jamake Highwater, New York: Lippincott and Crowell, 1980; *This Song Remembers: Self-Portraits of Native Americans in the Arts,* Jane B. Katz, editor, Boston: Houghton Mifflin Co., 1980; *Aleut and Eskimo Art: Tradition and Innovation in South Alaska,* Dorothy Jean Ray, Seattle: University of Washington Press, 1981; *Aleut Art: unangam aguqaadangin, unangan of the Aleutian Archipelago,* by Lydia Black, Anchorage, Alaska: Aang Angagin Press, 1982; *Magic Images: Contemporary Native American Art,* by Edwin L. Wade and Rennard Strickland, Norman: University of Oklahoma Press and Philbrook Art Center, 1982; *American Indian Art in the 1980s,* Niagara Falls, Native American Center for the Living Arts, 1984; *Indianische Kunst im 20, Jahrhundert: Malerei, Keramik und Kachina figuren: indianischer Kunstler in den USA,* Munich: Prestel-Verlag, 1985; *Portfolio,* San Francisco, American Indian Contemporary Arts Gallery, 1986; *New Directions Northwest,* Olympia, Washington, Evergreen State College, 1987; *Crossroads of Continents: Cultures of Siberia and Alaska,* by William W. Fitzhugh and Aron Crowell, Washington, D.C.: Smithsonian Institution Press, 1988; *Shared Visions: Native American Painters and Sculptors in the Twentieth Century,* by Margaret Archuleta and Rennard Strickland, Phoenix, Arizona: Heard Museum, 1991; *Artists of the Pacific Northwest: A Biographical Dictionary, 1600s-1970,* by Maria Sharylen, Jefferson, North Carolina and London, McFarland & Company, Inc., 1993. **Articles**—"Department of Interior Buys Art by Edmonds Couple," by Bob Lane, *Seattle Times,* 31 March 1967; "Contemporary Indian Artists," by Lloyd E. Oxendine, *Art in America,* July-August, 1972; "John Hoover," by Guy and Doris Monthan, *American Indian Art,* Winter 1978.

*   *   *

John Hoover, like the shamans who inspire him, mediates between two worlds, understanding that the artist, in bringing forms to life, serves as a link between the material and spiritual realms. An innovative sculptor in wood, bronze, and stone, he creates personal interpretations of Inuit and Northwest Coast mythology and folktales. Through original forms that express his deep reverence for the natural world, his imaginative sculptures represent the mystery and inner spirit of the Pacific Coast with its interdependence of bird, animal, marine and human life.

Hoover's earliest works were landscape and seascape oil paintings. These were not as creative nor as personal as his subsequent three-dimensional works. An interest in woodcarving led to an exploration of the techniques and subject matter of traditional Northwest coast sculpture; however, he found that they were too structurally rigid for his expressive purposes.

In his later work Hoover has become technically proficient. Some pieces from the early 1970s, such as *Otter Woman* and *Heron Spirit* are less polished in design and execution than subsequent sculptures. He had studied with Allan Houser at the Institute of American Indian Arts in Santa Fe and eventually developed his personal style to match his improving technique.

Hoover values stories about people who have relationships with animals; the idea of transformation is a leitmotif in his work. *Man Who Married an Eagle* (1972, polychromed cedar) has a basis in folktale, yet the narrative elements do not overwhelm the formal qualities. Deeply evocative of spirituality that retains mystery while communicating visually, the piece amalgamates spirit and bird forms and represents the process of metamorphosis.

In a later piece, *Winter Loon Dance* (1977-78, polychromed cedar), Hoover created a new type of sculptural ensemble, a monumental circular form so finely balanced and impeccably proportioned that the viewer can feel the movement of the loons in water. Elongated shapes seem to rise out of the sea. Bird forms intermingle with delicately indicated faces, breasts and thighs. Belying its large height and breadth (97 ½" x 57 ½"), the sculpture appears light, sensual and airy. A new interpretation of the *Dance of Life*, it conveys a feeling of freedom that could be a woman dancing or a bird flying. On the other hand, if the work were smaller in scale, it could be a crown for a nature goddess. The haunting faces that appear in this and many of his sculptures were probably inspired by the ancient Alaskan Okvik figurines, which symbolize fertility and maternity.

Researching his ancestral Aleut heritage, Hoover began to develop a personal style that was influenced by concepts about shamanism and access to both the natural and supernatural worlds. *Loon and Shaman* (1984, polychromed cedar) is a triptych having the form of two addorsed loons on the exterior and four mirrored loons on the interior, which flank a mysterious shamanic face that looks to past and the future, reality and the imagination, and an inner and outer vision. It functions on both a narrative and aesthetic level, with its layering impression reinforcing the shamanic concept of negotiation between domains. The closed and open forms stimulate a sense of unfolding over time. The loon, a recurring image in Inuit culture, was believed to have created the earth and is a special helper to shamans in their healing functions. Thus, Hoover draws upon his ancestral heritage, while he also feels free to modify it for new expressive purposes. In an analogous way, his triptychs have been influenced by both Northwest Coast transformation masks and Russian multi-paneled altarpieces.

Hoover uses traditional tools on cedar four to five hundred years old and likes to leave the chisel marks on his finished bas-relief work. He accents his sculpture with polychromia in customary Northwest coast colors—washes of sienna, red, cerulean blue and yellow ochre. Since Hoover prefers pale hues, he mixes his pigments with white and thins them with linseed oil and turpentine. His technical means have been very consistent for the past twenty-five years; the overall aesthetic effect of his oeuvre as soon as it reached its maturity is decorative and curvilinear, yet elegant and restrained.

Self-taught, working alone, and researching his Aleut heritage through books, oral histories and government documents, Hoover is reclaiming a tragically devastated cultural heritage. Furthermore, he is bringing it to life in a creative and personal way with evocative works of art that will continue to communicate and carry the tradition into the future.

—Ann Storey

HOULE, Robert

Tribal affiliations: Saulteau; Ojibway
Installation artist, mixed-media artist, and painter

Born: St. Boniface, Manitoba, 1947. **Education:** University of Manitoba, Winnipeg, B.A., 1972; International Summer Academy of Fine Arts, Salzburg, Austria, summer 1972; McGill University, Montreal, Quebec, B.Ed., 1975. **Career:** Curator, including *Early Watercolors by Alex,* Canadian Museum of Civilization, 1980, *New Works by a New Generation,* Norman McKenzie Art Gallery, 1982, *New Beginnings: A Celebration of Native Expression at the First Native Business Summit,* Toronto, 1986, *Benjamin Chee Chee,* Thunder Bay Art Gallery, 1991, *Land, Spirit, Power,* National Gallery of Canada, 1992-94, and *Multiplicity: A New Cultural Strategy,* University of British Columbia Museum of Anthropology, 1993-94; artist in residence, Winnipeg Art Gallery, 1989, and McMichael Canadian Art Collection, 1989; member, board of directors, Association for Native Development in the Performing and Visual Arts, Toronto, 1993-94, Native Canadian Centre of Canada, Toronto, 1993-94, and Power Plant, Toronto, 1994-96, advisory committee, Centre for Contemporary Art, Toronto, 1994, visual arts committee, Toronto Arts Council, 1994; consultant, urban design, City of Toronto, 1994-95; instructor of Native studies, Ontario College of Art, 1990-97. **Awards:** Canada Council grants, 1985 and 1994-95; Janet Braid Award, Queen's University, for the catalog *Land, Spirit, Power,* 1993.

Individual Exhibitions

1975	*Faculty of Education,* McGill University, Montreal, Quebec
1976	Galerie Andre George, Montreal, Quebec
1980	Pollock Gallery, Toronto, Ontario
1981	Pollock Gallery, Toronto, Ontario
	Robertson Galleries, Ottawa, Ontario
1983	Soho Mercer Gallery, Toronto, Ontario
1984	St. Michael's College, University of Toronto, Ontario
1985	Brignall Gallery, Toronto, Ontario
1988	Ufundi Gallery, Ottawa, Ontario
1989	McMichael Canadian Art Collection, Kleinburg, Ontario
	Lost Tribes, Winnipeg Art Gallery, Winnipeg, Manitoba
1990	*Indians from A to Z,* Winnipeg Art Gallery, Winnipeg, Manitoba (traveling)
1991	Thunder Bay Art Gallery, Thunder Bay, Ontario
	Ufundi Gallery, Ottawa, Ontario
	Lost Tribes, Hood College, Frederick, Maryland
	Whyte Museum of the Canadian Rockies, Banff, Alberta
	Mackenzie Art Gallery, Regina, Saskatchewan
	Glenbow-Alberta Institute, Calgary, Alberta
	Canadian Museum of Civilization, Hull, Quebec
1992	*Zero Hour* (multimedia installation), Agnes Etherington Art Centre, Kingston, Ontario
	The Divas, Ufundi Gallery, Ottawa, Ontario
	Warpaint Portraits, Russell Gallery of Fine Art, Lindsay, Ontario
	Hochelega, Articule, Montreal, Quebec (traveled to XYZ Gallery, Toronto, Ontario; North Bay Arts Centre, Ontario; and New Gallery, Calgary, Alberta through 1993)
1993	*Kanata, Robert Houle's Histories,* Carleton University Art Gallery, Ottawa, Ontario
	Kennedy Gallery, North Bay, Ontario
	Anishnabe Walker Court (three-part installation), Art Gallery of Ontario, Toronto
1994	*Premises for Self Rule,* Garnet Press Gallery, Toronto, Ontario

1996 *Pontiac's Conspiracy,* Garnet Press Gallery, Toronto, Ontario

Selected Group Exhibitions

1974 *Canadian Art '74,* Royal Ontario Museum, Toronto
1976 *Art Education Graduates,* McGill University, Montreal, Quebec
1978 *Beyond Tradition,* Pollock Gallery, Toronto, Ontario
1981 *Works on Paper,* Galerie Sarah McCutcheon, Montreal, Quebec
1982 *New Works by a New Generation,* Norman McKenzie Art Gallery, Regina, Saskatchewan
1984 *Contemporary Native American Art,* Pratt Institute Gallery, Brooklyn, New York
   No Beads, No Trinkets, Allied Arts of Seattle, Washington, and Palais des Nations, Geneva, Switzerland
   Innovations: New Expressions in Native American Painting, Marilyn Butler Fine Art, Santa Fe, New Mexico
   Contemporary Native American Art, Gardiner Art Gallery, Oklahoma State University, Stillwater, Oklahoma
   New Growth from Ancestral Roots, Koffler Gallery, Toronto, Ontario
1985 *Challenges,* DeMeervaart Amsterdam, Netherlands
1986 *Cross Cultural Views,* National Gallery of Canada, Ottawa, Ontario
   Journey through Time, Brignall Gallery, Toronto, Ontario
1987 *Eight Artists II,* Southwest Museum, Los Angeles
   Recent Generations: Native American Art from 1950 to 1987, Heard Museum, Phoenix, Arizona
   Eight from the Prairies, Thunder Bay Art Gallery, Thunder Bay, Canada
   Elaine Horwitch Galleries, Santa Fe, New Mexico
1988 *Ode'Min,* Laurentian University Museum and Art Centre, Sudbury, Ontario
1989 *Beyond History,* Vancouver Art Gallery, Vancouver, British Columbia
   Indian Art '89, Woodland Cultural Centre, Brantford, Ontario
1989-90 Ufundi Gallery, Ottawa, Ontario
1990 *Numbers,* Art Gallery of Hamilton, Ontario
   Hood College, Frederick, Maryland
   Two Rivers Gallery, Minneapolis Art Centre, Minneapolis, Minnesota
   Why Do You Call Us Indians?, Gettysburg College Art Gallery, Gettysburg, Pennsylvania
1990-91 Art Gallery of South Okanagan, Peniction, British Columbia
   White Water Gallery, North Bank, Ontario
   Forest City Gallery, London, Ontario
   Definitely Superior, Thunder Bay, Ontario
   Confederation Centre for the Arts, Charlottetown, Prince Edward Island
   Contemporary Rituals, Memorial University Art Gallery, St. John's Newfoundland
1991 *Okanata,* A Space, Toronto, Ontario
   Submuloc Show/Columbus Wohs, Evergreen State College, Olympia, Washington (traveling)
1992 *Symbols & Meaning: Five Native American Artists,* McIntosh Gallery, London, Ontario
   Rethinking History, Mercer Union, Toronto, Ontario

Robert Houle: *A Warrior Shield for the Lubicon.* **Courtesy of the artist.**

1992-93 *Reconstructing Symbols, Deconstructing Meanings,* Howard Yezushi Gallery, Boston, Massachusetts
   Cleveland Center for Contemporary Art, Cleveland, Ohio
1993-94 *Trajectories of Meaning,* Garnet Press Gallery, Toronto, Ontario, and Art Gallery of Algoma, Sault Ste. Marie, Ontario
1994 *Hidden Values,* National Gallery of Canada, Ottawa, Ontario (traveling)
1995 *Notion of Conflict,* Stedelijk Museum, Amsterdam, Netherlands
   Displaced Histories, Canadian Museum of Contemporary Photography, Ottawa, Ontario
1996 *Where Is Canada? Real Fictions,* Museum of Contemporary Art, Sydney, Australia
   ReGrouping, McMichael Art Gallery, Kleinburg, Ontario
1997 *Ghostwriter 2,* Mercer Union, Toronto, Ontario
   Cultural Imprints: Contemporary Works by First Nations Artists, Burnaby Art Gallery, Burnaby, British Columbia

Collections

Art Gallery of Hamilton, Ontario; Art Gallery of Ontario, Toronto; Art Gallery of Windsor, Ontario; Artinvest, Toronto, Ontario; Canada Council Art Bank, Ottawa, Ontario; Burnaby Art Gallery, Burnaby, British Columbia; Canadian Museum of Civilization, Hull, Quebec; Canadian Native Arts Foundation, Toronto, Ontario; Carleton University Art Gallery, Ottawa, Ontario; Agnes Etherington Art Centre, Kingston, Ontario; Heard Museum, Phoenix, Arizona; Indian and Northern Affairs Canada, Ottawa, Ontario; Laurentian University Museum and Arts Centre, Sudbury, Ontario; McGill University, Montreal, Quebec; McMichael Canadian Art Collection, Kleinburg, Ontario; National Gallery of Canada, Ottawa, Ontario; Native Canadian Arts Foundation, Toronto, Ontario;

Native Canadian Centre of Toronto, Ontario; Nickle Art Gallery, Calgary, Alberta; North York Performing Arts Centre Art Gallery, North York, Ontario; Owens Art Gallery, Sackville, New Brunswick; Royal Ontario Museum, Toronto; Sandra Ainsley Artforms, Toronto, Ontario; Sandy Bay Educational Board, Marius, Manitoba; Southwest Museum, Los Angeles, California; Thunder Bay Art Gallery, Thunder Bay, Ontario; University of British Columbia, Museum of Anthropology, Vancouver, British Columbia; Winnipeg Art Gallery, Winnipeg, Manitoba; Woodland, Cultural Centre, Brantford, Ontario.

Publications

By HOULE: Catalogs—*New Works by a New Generation,* Regina, Norman MacKenzie Art Gallery, 1982; *Land, Spirit, Power,* Ottawa, National Gallery of Canada, 1992. **Articles**—"Sovereignty over Subjectivity," *C* magazine, Summer 1991; "The Deconstruction of the Columbus Indian," *Artichoke,* Fall 1992; "Anishnabe Walker Court," *C* magazine, Fall 1993; "A Mandate for the Thunder Bay Art Gallery," with Carol Podedworny, Thunder Bay, 1994.

On HOULE: Books—*Eight from the Prairies: Part Two,* by Carol Podedworny, Thunder Bay, Ontario, Thunder Bay Art Gallery, 1987; *Numbers,* by Ihor Holibitzky, Art Gallery of Hamilton, 1990; *Why Do You Call Us Indians?,* by Amelia M. Trevelyan, Gettysburg College Gallery, 1990; *Indians from A to Z*, Carol Phillips, et al, Winnipeg Art Gallery, 1990; *Lost Tribes,* by Amelia M. Trevelyan, Frederick, Maryland, Hood College, 1991; *Hochelaga,* by Curtis J. Collins, Montreal, Articule, 1992; *Kanata, Robert Houle's Histories,* by Michael Bell, Carleton University Art Gallery, 1993; *Future Traditions,* by Robert Swain, North York, Ontario, North York Performing Arts Centre Art Gallery, 1994; *Notion of Conflict: A Selection of Contemporary Canadian Art*, by Dorine Mignot, Amsterdam, Stedelijk Museum, 1995; *Real Fictions,* Clara Hargitay, et al, Sydney, Australia, Museum of Contemporary Art, 1996. *Articles*—"I Lost it at the Trading Post: Indian Art is Dead, Long Live 'Art by Indians,'" by Jay Scott, *Canadian Art,* Winter 1985; "New Visions in Canadian Plains Painting," by John Anson Warner, *American Indian Art Magazine,* Spring 1985; "Beyond Cultural Apartheid," by Carol Corbeil, *Globe and Mail,* 19 April 1986; "Eight Artists II: Contemporary Indian Art at the Southwest Museum," *American Indian Art Magazine,* Winter 1987; "Robert Houle: Daring *Hochelaga* Exhibit Raises Disturbing Issues about Native Sovereignty and Quebec," *Now* magazine, 19 November 1992; "Indegena and *Land, Spirit, Power,*" by Carol Podedworny, *C* magazine, Winter 1993; "Robert Houle at Garnet Press Gallery," *Artforum,* November 1994; "An Activist Recedes, an Artist Emerges," by Christopher Hume, *Toronto Star,* 11 July 1996.

*   *   *

The work of Robert Houle is sophisticated, erudite and almost always elegant. He has produced art objects in a host of different media with a clear exploration of each one's aesthetic potential as well as its ability to express and enhance content. Site-specific installations have been important elements within his oeuvre. In short, Houle's work has the look and range of interests that characterize much of mainstream contemporary art.

Houle's alter egos as art historian and curator, activist and teacher, emerge frequently throughout his work, especially in the intellectual sophistication of a series like *Lost Tribes,* created in the early

1990s. These works incorporated computer graphics as well as more traditional media, evidence of another of Houle's interests in technique as well as content: staying abreast of the latest developments in electronic media and other aspects of contemporary technology.

Despite its erudite and elegant quality and the technological sophistication of so much of Houle's work, the content is almost always recognizably native and distinctly political in its focus. Issues of exploitation and extinction, of agency and voice, abound, as well as exploration of relationships between Native and Euro-American definitions of power. However, unlike most artists who explore similar content (regardless of ethnicity) Houle approaches those issues in such subtle and aesthetically exquisite ways that one is impressed first by the striking formal qualities of each work, rather than being slapped in the face by its content. The layers of clear and often starkly political content are apparent but impress themselves only gradually upon the viewer's sensibilities. Houle's Indianness is unmistakable and any political agenda is always clear, but both are presented with an exquisite subtlety.

This sophistication may be attributed only in part to his extensive formal training in the art traditions of the western world, first at the University of Manitoba and, subsequently, at McGill in Quebec. That kind of educational background is not uncommon, in some degree, among many contemporary native artists. Nor is his earlier background unique. Houle grew up on the Sandy Bay Reserve in Southern Manitoba. Like several mainstream contemporary native artists, his interest in issues of personal and ethnic identity had its origin in the residential schools established and staffed by Indian Affairs. The effect of this experience, often excruciating for native children, is reflected in Houle's comment in the early 1990s: "I'm always conscious that what I do will be seen as an outcome of the colonized and conquered."

This self-conscious apprehension of audience response to his work, however unconscious that response might be, is not uncommon among contemporary native artists. But, once again, the subtle elegance of the work created is. Houle's complex deconstruction of the nature of contemporary reality for native Americans is often as exquisitely beautiful as it is relentless. His *Warrior Shield for the Lubicon* from the late 1980s is a powerful case in point. In this work and many others, Houle combines recognizably traditional forms with contemporary modes and media. This process constitutes a significant element of continuity between Houle's twentieth-century creative mode and native approaches to the creation of art works for millennia.

Traditionally, the native artists of North America inevitably combined affirmations of ancient tradition with a clear-eyed vision of present reality. The sophisticated and deconstructive elements in all of Houle's work bear witness to his understanding of and participation in the most up-to-date aspects of today's contemporary art scene. Yet, the combination of postmodern elements with ancient imagery and symbolism drawn from the rich art traditions of his ancestors, places him firmly within that longstanding tradition, as well. In fact, if his work did not involve a complex integration of postmodern, Euro-American style and content with ancient forms and symbols, his position within native art traditions would be less authentic.

Furthermore, standing at the intersection of two cultures, Houle brings to his art a full understanding of the significance of the forms and symbols he uses, whether native or Euro-American. In doing so, he has "turned on its head" the approach of non-native artists that incorporate tribal imagery into their work, whether earlier in this century or today. Unlike them, Houle is not appropriating decontextualized symbol and form to lend vitality to a moribund tradition. Nor is his work merely a nostalgic or even ironic reinterpretation of native motifs. Rather, he combines the stark and familiar forms of contemporary symbolism as well as native elements to elucidate the complex and often tragic realities of native history since the arrival of Europeans.

A remarkable depth of meaning is the result, proceeding not only from his extraordinary ability as an artist, per se, but from his simultaneous existence within two cultures and full participation in the artistic traditions of both.

—Amelia M. Trevelyan

HOUSE, Conrad

Tribal affiliations: Navajo
Mixed media artist and installation artist

Born: Rehoboth, New Mexico, 29 November 1956. **Education:** Fulton-Montgomery Junior College, Johnstown, New York; State University of New York, Johnstown; University of New Mexico, B.F.A., 1980; University of Oregon; Philchurch Glass Studio, Stanwood, Washington, 1986-90. **Awards:** Philchurch Glass School Scholarship, Southwestern Association on Indian Arts Fellowship Award, International Studies Grant, University of New Mexico; Inter-Tribal Indian Ceremonials, 1987, Southwestern Association on Indian Arts Annual Market, 1990.

Individual Exhibitions

1991   *Conrad House, A Survey: Ceramics, Drawings, Collage and Glassworks*, Sacred Circle Gallery, Seattle, Washington
1993   American Indian Contemporary Arts, San Francisco

Selected Group Exhibitions

1978   Albuquerque Museum Plaza Gallery, New Mexico
1979   Ken Phillips Gallery, Denver, Colorado
        Upstairs Gallery, Berkeley, California
1980   *The Grey Canyon Artists*, Wheelwright Museum, Santa Fe, New Mexico (traveling)
        Richard L. Nelson Gallery, University of California, Davis
1983   Portland Art Museum, Oregon
1984   Palais des Nations, Geneva, Switzerland
1986-88 *What Is Native American Indian Art?*, organized by the Philbrook Museum, Tulsa, Oklahoma (traveling)
1987   *Four Sacred Mountains Contemporary Indian Arts Festival*, Tuba City, Arizona
1988   *Portfolio II: Eleven American Indian Artists*, American Contemporary Indian Art, San Francisco, California
1991   *Aspen/Snowmass Celebration for the American Indian*, Aspen, Colorado organized by the National Museum of the American Indian, Smithsonian Institution, Washington, D.C.
1991-93 *Our Land, Ourselves*, University Art Gallery, Albany, New York (traveling)

1992-93 *The Submuloc Show/Columbus Wohs*, Phoenix, Arizona (traveling)
1993   Sacred Circle Gallery of American Indian Art, Seattle, Washington
1996-97 *Gifts of the Spirit: Works by Nineteenth Century and Contemporary Native American Artists*, Peabody-Essex Museum, Salem, Massachusetts

Collections

Heard Museum, Phoenix, Arizona; Indian Arts and Crafts Board, Department of the Interior, Washington, D.C.; Museum of the Plains Indian, Browning, Montana; Southern Plains Indian Museum, Anadarko, Oklahoma; University Art Museum, University of New Mexico, Albuquerque, New Mexico.

Publications

On HOUSE: Books—*The Arts of the North American Indian: Native Traditions in Evolution*, Edwin L. Wade and Rennard Strickland, editors, New York: Hudson Hills Press, 1986; *Beyond Tradition: Contemporary Indian Art and its Evolution*, Flagstaff, 1988; *Portfolio II: Eleven American Indian Artists*, San Francisco, 1988; *Our Land/Ourselves: American Indian Contemporary Artists*, exhibition catalog by Deborah Ward, Albany, 1990; *The Submuloc Show/Columbus Wohs*, exhibition catalog, Phoenix, 1992.

*   *   *

House has a very unusual education, combining fine arts and political science; he attained his M.F.A. from the University of Oregon in 1983 and has also has received training at the Philchuk Glass Studio in Stanwood, Washington.

Conrad House is a true artist in the sense that he is willing to explore many ideas and media in his search for meaning and balance in his life. He uses ceramics, textiles, painting, sculpture, or beadwork to express things about himself and his Navajo (Dine) culture. He prefers to call himself a multimedia artist, because, in addition to the visual arts, he is also a singer and dancer. House sees art as a process by which native communities can regain their own sense of self. Art is a living, viable part of the daily life of the Navajo and includes the philosophy, rituals and conduct of the people as much as the visual manifestations of belief, according to House. He firmly believes that some things are meant to stay secret among the people, not to be exploited by the visual artists.

In the 1980s House joined the Grey Canyon Group, along with fellow Navajo artists Emmi Whitehorse, Lorezo Clayton and Larry Emerson. By the late 1980s his worked focused on crayon and colored pencil on black paper, creating a very powerful optical effect, layering images that recall pottery designs, weaving symbols and animal representations. The turtle, wolf and bear images often folded into his designs are personal symbols that show his identification with his Oneida family clans from upstate New York. At the same time, he must respect the very powerful Navajo traditions about bear symbolism. House has traveled extensively and has studied museum collections in search of inspiration. He freely borrows ideas, color combinations and design forms from other tribal groups, from the Haida to the Seminole, but is respectful to try and learn their sensibility toward color, shape and technique so that he can adapt it to his own work.

In 1988 House won the Best of Division Award for his painting at the Indian Market in Santa Fe, New Mexico, followed by a fellowship from the Southwest Association on Indian Affairs. In 1994, House was one of several Native Americans who selected and commented on historic objects from the National Museum of the American Indian in New York City. His thoughts on Navajo culture, the role of the arts and personal artistic responsibilities formed part of interactive components for *All Roads Are Good: Native Voices on Life and Culture*, in which he shows a healthy respect for the traditions of his people, but reminds us that contemporary art will have different forms of expression. If artists are raised within their culture, House notes, their art will hold and sustain traditional beliefs, because "ours is an ongoing, living culture."

—Rick Hill

HOUSEMAN-WHITEHAWK, Laurie

Variant names: Wakan'-Je-Pe-Wein-Gah
Tribal affiliations: Winnebago; Santee Sioux
Painter, draftsman, and photographer

Born: Laurie Jay White in Omaha, Nebraska, 17 November 1952. **Education:** Johnson Community College, 1971-73; Kansas State Teachers College, 1974-76; Institute of American Indian Arts, 1976-77; Kansas City Art Institute, 1978; Haskell Indian Junior College, 1979-81. **Career:** Artist; instructor; artist-in-residence, lecturer and workshop leader, Native American arts and social programs, 1990- ; Founder and spokesperson for the Kansas Indian Artists Association. **Awards:** Numerous honors in juried shows from 1983.

Individual Exhibitions

1980	Institute of American Indian Arts Museum, Santa Fe
1981	Riley County Historical Museum, Manhattan, Kansas
1983	Pen & Ink Gallery, Lawrence, Kansas
1984	Southern Plains Indian Museum, Anadarko, Oklahoma
1985	Avanyu Gallery, Minneapolis
1989	Amer-Indian Gallery, Steamboat Springs, Colorado
1990	Plains Gallery, Omaha, Nebraska
1991	Siza Gallery, Chicago
1993	Mount Marty College, Yankton, South Dakota
	Powers of the 6 Directions, Native Creations Gallery, Lawrence, Kansas
	Tribal Expressions Gallery, Arlington Heights, Illinois
	Retrospective, Center for Great Plains Studies, University of Nebraska, Lincoln
1994	Freemont Art Gallery, Freemont, Nebraska
1996	Native American Art Center, Abilene, Kansas

Selected Group Exhibitions

1981	Institute of American Indian Arts traveling exhibit
1981-84	*Contemporary Plains Indian Artists*, Wichita Art Museum (traveling)
1983	Native American Rights Fund Headquarters, Boulder, Colorado

1987	Mittie Cooper Gallery, Oklahoma City, Oklahoma
1990	Smoky Hill Museum, Salina, Kansas
1991	Ellsworth Gallery, Ellsworth, Kansas
1992	Great Plains Indian Gallery, Lincoln, Nebraska
	Minnetrista Cultural Center, Muncie, Indiana
1993	Bacone College, Olkmulgee, Oklahoma
1994	Lincoln Indian Center Art Gallery, Lincoln, Nebraska

Publications

By HOUSEMAN-WHITEHAWK: Article—"Walking in Two Worlds," *Nebraska Humanities,* Vol. IV, No. 1, Spring 1994.

*

Laurie Houseman-Whitehawk comments:
I try to capture the mystical feelings that are such an important part of Native American rituals and lifestyle. These are spiritual powers, magical feelings, which cannot always be spoken but only seen and experienced by the viewer. I hope to bring the American Indian culture, both past and present, together for others to be able to relate to, not just exclusive for the American Indian, but for everyone. This is a Spiritual Message. I hope to dispell a lot of misunderstandings, and I feel that an image will speak louder than words.

*   *   *

Born on the Winnebago reservation in Nebraska in 1952, Laurie Houseman-Whitehawk reflects in her work the mixed traditions of the Nebraska Winnebagos, combining both Great Plains and Great Lakes imagery. In 1865, the Winnebago were removed, by treaty, from their home in Wisconsin to the plains of Nebraska, where the neighboring tribes are Plains groups whose traditions include beadwork and quillwork. Yet, as Houseman-Whitehawk's imagery shows, Winnebago women still maintain their distinctive art of ribbonwork, more commonly found among the groups who still reside near the Great Lakes.

Houseman-Whitchawk's cducation in art included courses at Haskell Indian Junior College in Lawrence, Kansas, the Institute of American Indian Arts in Santa Fe, Kansas State College, and the Kansas City Art Institute. Among these, she ranks the two Indian schools as the most significant. At Haskell, in the 1970s, she learned about the rich legacy of Indian painting styles of the last 100 years. In Santa Fe, she learned how to be a precise and careful draftsperson, and found important role models who showed, through personal example, that it is possible to be a successful Indian artist.

Houseman-Whitehawk's work is unique among contemporary American Indian painters, both in its technique and its subject matter. All of her works are done in *gouache*, an opaque watercolor medium that demands exacting technical standards. To fine watercolors from tubes she adds a great deal of white, rendering them opaque. Colors are painted next to, not on top of, each other. Gouache is an unforgiving medium, for unlike oil or acrylic paint, the artist can not rework or paint over an unsatisfactory section. She must discard the entire work and begin again. This technique, though not a popular one today, has a significant history in the development of twentieth-century American Indian painting. It was used by many of her male predecessors in the 1920s and 1930s, who were trying to establish a tradition of modern Indian painting. Like their work, Houseman-Whitehawk's art is characterized by its flat colors, decorative surface, and sinuous line.

Houseman-Whitehawk often focuses on Indian women, particularly women from her own Winnebago tribe. This was not always the case, however. For many years she imitated the male artists, like Woody Crumbo and Dr. Richard West, from previous generations whom she admired, and about whom she had learned in her course on Indian painting at Haskell Indian Junior College. Around the age of 30, Houseman-Whitehawk began to establish her characteristic imagery, when she began to focus more on Indian dancers, and then on women in particular. "I got tired of romanticizing the past," she says. "Sometimes as Indian artists we stereotype ourselves; it's not just a problem of whites stereotyping us." She began going to Indian powwows, where she photographed the dancers and other participants. Back in her studio, she would work from these photos to build up a body of works that celebrate Indian people as they are today. In one sense, she sees this as building on the nineteenth-century tradition of Curtis, Catlin, and Bodmer, who recorded the splendor of Indian costume and ceremonial behavior. And yet, for an Indian woman *herself* to do this, to wrest the acts of naming, seeing, and interpreting away from the white male, is an act of self-definition and empowerment.

At these powwows she eventually began to aim her camera at women rather than men. The results were impressive. *Sioux Woman*, from 1984, was one of her first experiments with female subject matter. The artist presents a tough, self-possessed woman who confronts the camera yet maintains her privacy behind sun glasses. Her buckskin dress, feather fan, fringed shawl, and beaded bag all recall the past. Yet her pose and her sunglasses emphatically proclaim her modernity. This image marked Houseman-Whitehawk's move into a new phase of her career. At around the same time she painted a Navajo woman on a horse. An idle comment by a viewer— "You're Winnebago! Why are you painting Navajo women?"— caused her to rethink her subject matter yet again. She began to focus more on Winnebago women. Out of this decision has come some of her strongest and most imposing images. A triptych completed in 1989 depicts a series of five Winnebago women in dance regalia. The individuality of each face, each blouse and ribbonwork skirt is rendered in careful detail. The vivid reds and blues of the clothing stand out against the strong greens and blues of a bright Nebraska summer's day—evocative of just the kind of July day when Winnebago powwows are held.

Housemany

yn-Whitehawk's works contain multiple levels of homage and celebration. Her technique pays tribute to the studio-trained, Indian male painters of the 1920s and 1930s who eased the way for contemporary Native artists. Her subject matter pays homage to previous generations of Native women artists, whose ribbonwork and beadwork she so lovingly depicts.

—Janet Catherine Berlo

HOUSER, Allan
Variant names: Haozous
Tribal affiliations: Chiricahua; Warm Springs Apache
Painter and sculptor

Born: Allan Capron Haozous, Apache, Oklahoma, 30 June 1914; Haozous translates as "The Sound of Pulling." **Education:** Boone School, Apache, Oklahoma; Santa Fe Indian School, studying under Dorothy Dunn; mural instruction under Olle Nordmark. **Family:** Son of Blossom and Sam Haozous, grand uncle was Geronimo; married Anna Marie Callegos (Navajo), five children: Roy, Lon, Robert, Phillip, Stephen. **Career:** Pipe fitter, boxer; commissioned with Gerald Nailor to paint murals, Department of the Interior Building, Washington, D.C.; commissioned for a monumental marble sculpture, *Comrade in Mourning*, honoring Native Americans who died in World War II, by the Haskell Institute (dedicated in 1948); commissioned to illustrate nine children's books on southwest Indian tribes, 1952-58; artist-in-residence and instructor, Inter-Mountain Indian School, Brigham City, Utah, 1951-62; instructor (and later head of sculpture department), Institute of American Indian Arts, Santa Fe, New Mexico, 1962-75; full-time sculptor after 1975; Heard Museum, National Advisory Board, 1980; dedication of *The Future (Chiricahua Apache Family)*, Fort Sill Apache Tribal Center (honors the memory of his parents and commemorates the 70th anniversary of the release of Apache Prisoners of War at Fort Sill), 1983; *Offering of the Sacred Pipe*, a monumental bronze, United States Mission to the United Nations; bronze bust of Geronimo, commemorating the 100th anniversary of the surrender of the Chiricahua Apaches, presented to the Fort Sill Apache Tribal Center, and the cast was presented to the National Portrait Gallery, Washington, D.C., 1986; Allan Houser Park, a sculpture garden, opened at the Institute of American Indian Arts, 1993. **Awards:** John Simon Guggenheim Scholarship for Sculpture and Painting, 1948; Palmes d'Académiques from the French government, 1954; Oklahoma Cultural Ambassador, 1984; University of Maine, Honorary Doctorate of Fine Arts, 1987; American Indian Distinguished Achievement Award and Lifetime Achievement Award, American Indian Resources Institute, Washington, D.C., 1989; National Medal of Arts (first Native American recipient), National Council on the Arts and President of the United States, National Medal of Arts 1992; Ellis Island Medal of Honor, May 1993; Art and Cultural Achievement Award, National Museum of the American Indian, Washington, D.C., 1994; numerous honors in juried fairs, including Heard Museum Guild Indian Fair and Market, Inter-Tribal Indian Ceremonial, National Academy of Western Art, Philbrook Museum of Art, Scottsdale National Indian Art Exhibition; Waite Phillips Trophy, Philbrook Museum of Art, 1969; Governor's Award for the Visual Arts, State of New Mexico, 1980, 1983-84; Oklahoma Hall of Fame, inducted 1985; Lifetime Achievement Award (inaugural), Southwestern Association for Indian Arts, Santa Fe, New Mexico, 1995. **Died:** 22 August 1994.

Individual Exhibitions

1976	Governor's Gallery, State Capitol, Santa Fe, New Mexico
1979	Hopkins Center, Dartmouth College, Hanover, New Hampshire
1983	*Allan Houser Retrospective*, Heard Museum, Santa Fe, New Mexico
1984	Wheelwright Museum of the American Indian, Santa Fe, New Mexico
1985	United States Mission to the United Nations, New York
1991-94	*Allan Houser: A Life in Art*, Museum of Fine Arts, Santa Fe, New Mexico (traveling)
1993	Eiteljorg Museum, Indianapolis, Indian
1996	*The Studio of Allan Houser*, Wheelwright Museum of the American Indian, Santa Fe, New Mexico

Allan Houser with *Full Moon,* 1984. Photograph by M. Tincher; courtesy Allan Houser, Inc.

Allan Houser Retrospective, Mongerson Wunderlich Galleries, Chicago, Illinois
Allan Houser: The Abstract Works, Niman Fine Art, Santa Fe, New Mexico

Selected Group Exhibitions

1939   *New York World's Fair,* New York
       Golden Gate International Exposition, San Francisco
       National Gallery of Art, Washington, D.C.
       Art Institute of Chicago
1955   *An Exposition of American Indian Painters,* James Graham and Sons, New York
1964   Blair House, Washington, D.C.
1970   Heard Museum, Phoenix, Arizona
1971   Philbrook Museum of Art, Tulsa, Oklahoma
1977   Sacred Circles Indian Art Exhibition, Kansas City, Missouri
1979   *Native American Paintings*, Joslyn Art Museum, Omaha, Nebraska
1980   *Contemporary Amerindian Painting,* Kennedy Center for the Performing Arts and Museum of Natural History, Smithsonian Institution, Washington, D.C.; traveled to Chile, Peru, Colombia, Ecuador, and Argentina
1981   *Salon d'Automne,* Grand Palais, Paris
       Native American Center for the Living Arts, Niagara Falls, New York
1983   *FIAC International Exhibit*, Salon d'Automne, Grand Palais, Paris
       Amerika Haus, Berlin, Germany (traveled to Hanover, Stuttgart, Heidelberg, Frankfurt, Hamburg, Nuremburg, and Munich
1984   Kunstlerhaus Wien, Vienna, Austria (traveled to Yugoslavia, Czechoslovakia, Romania, and Bulgaria through 1986)

1986   *When the Rainbow Touches Down*, Heard Museum, Phoenix, Arizona
1989   Gilcrease Museum, Tulsa, Oklahoma
       Gibbes Museum of Art, Charleston, South Carolina
1991   *A New Mexico Tradition: Southwestern Realism,* Taiwan Museum of Art, Taichung, Taiwan Republic of China
1991-96   *Shared Visions: Native American Painters and Sculptors in the Twentieth Century*, Heard Museum, Phoenix, Arizona

Collections

Amerind Foundation, Dragoon, Arizona; Arizona State Capitol, Phoenix; British Royal Collection, London; Centre Georges Pompidou, Paris; Dahlem Skuplturensammlung, Staatliche Museen Zu Berlin, Berlin, Germany; Denver Art Museum, Denver, Colorado; Thomas Gilcrease Institute of American History and Art, Tulsa, Oklahoma; Heard Museum, Phoenix, Arizona; Joslyn Art Museum, Omaha, Nebraska; Museum of Fine Arts, Museum of New Mexico, Santa Fe; Museum of Northern Arizona, Flagstaff; Museum of Art, University of Oklahoma, Norman; National Museum of the American Indian, Washington, D.C.; National Portrait Gallery, Washington, D.C.; Philbrook Museum of Art, Tulsa, Oklahoma; San Diego Museum of Man, San Diego, California; Scottsdale Center for the Arts, Scottsdale, Arizona; Southwest Museum, Los Angeles; Wheelwright Museum of the American Indian, Santa Fe, New Mexico; White House, Washington, D.C.

Publications

On HOUSER: Books—*American Indian Painters*, by Oscar B. Jacobson and Jeanne d'Ucel, Nice, France, 1950; *American Indian Painting of the Southwest and Plains Areas*, by Dorothy Dunn, Albuquerque, 1968; *Song from the Earth: American Indian Paint-*

ing, by Jamake Highwater, Boston, 1976; *Bronzes of the American West*, by Patricia Broder, New York, 1977; *100 Years of Native American Painting*, exhibition catalog by Arthur Silberman, Oklahoma Museum of Art, Oklahoma City, 1978; *This Song Remembers*, by Jane B. Katz, New York, 1980; *American Indian Painting and Sculpture*, by Patricia Broder, New York, 1981; *Indianascher Kunstler*, by Gerhard Hoffman, Munich, 1984; *The Arts of the North American Indian: Native Traditions in Evolution*, edited by Edwin L. Wade, New York: Hudson Hills Press in association with Philbrook Art Center, Tulsa, Oklahoma, 1986; *Allan Houser (Ha-o-zous)*, by Barbara Perlman, New York, 1987; *When the Rainbow Touches Down*, exhibition catalog by Tryntje Van Ness Seymour, Heard Museum, University of Washington Press, 1988; *Shared Visions: Native American Painters and Sculptors in the Twentieth Century*, by Margaret Archuleta and Dr. Rennard Strickland, New York: The New Press, 1991. **Articles**—"Show by Ha-oz-ous, Apache Indian, at Art Museum Is Recommended by Reviewer," by Dorothy Dunn, *Santa Fe New Mexican*, 18 March 1937; "Allan Houser, American Indian Artist," by Marjel de Laurer, *Arizona Highways*, August 1976; "The Timeless Sculpture of a Plain and Happy Man," by Barbara Perlman, *ARTnews*, December 1979; "Allan Houser, Grand Master Apache Sculpture," by Mary Carroll Nelson, *American Artist*, November 1980; "Allan Houser at 70," by Daniel Gibson, *Southwest Profile*, August 1984; "Exhibit Shows Allan Houser's Path to Perfection," by Diana Sandoval, *Masters of Indian Market Exhibition Guide*, supplement in the *New Mexican*, 22 May 1996; "Allan Houser: The Legacy of a Chiricahua Apache Sculptor," by Sally Eauclaire,

Indian Artist, Summer 1997. **Films**—*Allan Houser: Working Sculptor*, Public Broadcasting System, 1976; *Artist Between Worlds*, German television documentary, 1985; *Allan Houser: A Lasting Vision*, co-produced by Joanelle Nadine Romero, Phillip Haozous, Spirit World Productions, and Allan Houser, Inc., 1995.

*   *   *

Allan Houser became a legend during his lifetime, hailed as the patriarch of Native American sculptors, with honors heaped upon him. His sculpture, *Offering of the Sacred Pipe*, for the United States Mission to the United Nations in New York, has become the peace symbol of the world.

It was relatively late in life that he turned to sculpting, however, and as a boy he had not even dreamed of being an artist. He was already twenty when, in 1934, he started painting in Dorothy Dunn's Studio in the Santa Fe Indian School. In the studio he became a first-rate draftsman who achieved expressive effects through skillful lineation. In retrospect, Houser regarded his experience in Santa Fe as a mixed blessing. He had become frustrated with the old-style, flat Indian painting, even though he mastered it.

As a painter, Houser learned a lot by observing other artists, including Quincy Tahoma, Andy Tsinajinnie, and Gerald Nailor; with Nailor he opened a studio in Santa Fe in the late 1930s and collaborated on murals for the Department of the Interior Building in Washington. By observing these artists, Houser developed his compositional skill and the depiction of energy and strength, in which Tahoma excelled. Houser's paintings of hunting, fighting, and warfare, as well as ceremonial dances, bear witness to his ability to dynamize the motif and have the viewer experience a concentration of strength, vitality and aggressiveness. At the same time, these pictures document the life of his ancestors, the people of Geronimo, for whom he feels pride and with whom he identifies. He shows his respect for them by striving for authenticity down to the last detail: "Whenever I do something related to Indians in my work it's authentic."

Houser differs from Native American heroic painters by evoking in his paintings, among other things, the pain, death, and sorrow involved in fighting and war. Paintings like *Ill-Fated War Party's Return*, for instance, convey the depth of these themes by including lamenting women and, compositionally, by contrasting motion and overall stillness. Indeed, Houser's particular humanity lies in his readiness to accept and render weakness and frailty, as well as pride and dignity.

Houser never gave up painting completely, even when he turned to sculpture as his primary medium. The transition was gradual and came over the years. In 1940, when studying Italian fresco technique at Fort Sill, his instructor, Olle Nordmark, noticed the sculptural quality of his drawings. Houser's financial situation, however, made training in sculpting impossible. He again learned from observing others and from books. A milestone in his development as a sculptor was the commission of his first big monument, *Comrade in Mourning*, for the Haskell Institute in Lawrence, Kansas. A Guggenheim Fellowship in sculpture and painting followed, and from 1962 until his retirement in 1975, he was a sculpture instructor at the Institute of American Indian Art in Santa Fe.

As a sculptor, Houser was inspired by such modern artists as Henry Moore, Jean Arp, and Constantin Brancusi, and among the older ones, he admired Michelangelo. Moore's example stimulated him to work with negative space and abstract forms and confirmed him in his striving for a combination of grandeur and simplicity.

Allan Houser: *Apache Man*, 1985. Photograph by M. Tincher; courtesy Allan Houser, Inc.

These influences and his own vision and background combined for inspired and prolific work of great beauty, reflected in such works as *Earth Song,* the statue of an Apache singer, *Chiricahua Apache Family*, or *Prayer Song*, a kneeling Indian with feather bonnet and regalia. He rendered peaceful people "tending the flock," "heading home," or singing a song as well as spirited Apache warriors and vivid Mountain Spirit dancers, motifs he has also depicted in his paintings. Again and again he was inspired by the female form and the theme of maternity. His Native maidens and madonnas bear witness to his experimentation with forms and document the development of his sculpture, from realism to increasing abstractness. However, as he noted, "even if I use an abstract approach, the finished piece still has a relation to the Indian."

Houser's materials were stone and bronze and sometimes wood. He liked ebony and black walnut because it acquires a bronze-like finish after it is oiled, "which seems to me well suited to an Indian subject matter." Most of his stones were imported, but he also searched the mountains and mesas of New Mexico for stones with unusual shapes or textures. For sculptures of mothers and children, his favorite materials were limestone and marble; metal and darker stones he preferred for action studies. Several sites, including the Institute of American Indian Arts Museum, in Santa Fe, have permanent exhibits—sculpture gardens—of his work, and many others, including the Museum of New Mexico and the Wheelwright Museum of the American Indian, have sculptures in outdoor settings that provide a thematic emblem for the museum.

Houser's sculptures, to a greater extent than his paintings, convey the spirit of peace and harmony, of balance, of unity and timelessness. These were the values he believed in and were part of his Native heritage, as he saw it. He said late in his life that he did not work just for himself, but to honor the American Indian. "I hope to draw the attention to century-old Indian values, especially concepts of living in harmony with nature that can benefit all people."

—Gerhard and Gisela Hoffmann

HOWE, Oscar

Variant names: Mazuha Hokshina
Tribal affiliations: Yankton Sioux
Painter

Born: Joe Creek, South Dakota, on the Crow Creek Indian Reservation, 13 May 1915; Mazuha Hokshina means "Trader Boy." **Education:** The Studio, Santa Fe Indian School, 1935-38 (graduation salutarian); Dakota Wesleyan University, B.A., 1952; University of Oklahoma, M.F.A., 1953; studied mural techniques with Olaf Nordmark at the Indian Arts Center, Lawton, Oklahoma. **Military Service:** United States Army, World War II, European theatre, 1942-45. **Career:** Art instructor, Pierre Indian School; director of art, Pierre High School; professor of fine arts, State University of South Dakota; artist in residence, Dakota Wesleyan University and State University of South Dakota; served on various boards, including Institute of Indian Studies, State University of South Dakota; muralist, including Carnegie Library and Corn Palace, Mitchell, South Dakota; lecturer to the Near East and South Asia, U.S. Department of State. **Awards:** Numerous juried competitions, including those sponsored by the Denver Art Museum, Museum of New Mexico, Santa Fe, Philbrook Art Center, Tulsa, Oklahoma, and the National Indian Art Exhibition, Bismark, North Dakota; honorary doctorates from South Dakota State University, Dakota Wesleyan University, Haline University; Artist Laureate of South Dakota, 1952; elected fellow, International Institute of Arts and Letters, Geneva, Switzerland, 1960; Award of Recognition, Foundation for North American Indian Culture, Bismark, North Dakota, 1964; Oscar Howe Center, Mitchell, South Dakota, opened 1972; State of South Dakota, first annual Governor's Award, 1973; Oscar Howe Day proclaimed 19 September 1981, by the governor of South Dakota. **Died:** 7 October 1983.

Individual Exhibitions

1956   Philbrook Museum of Art, Tulsa, Oklahoma
        Fort Dodge, Iowa
1957   Museum of New Mexico, Santa Fe
1958   Denver Art Museum
        Philbrook Art Center, Tulsa, Oklahoma
1959   Joslyn Art Museum, Omaha, Nebraska
1960   Lucien Labaudt Gallery, San Francisco
        South Dakota State University, Brookings
        Sioux City Art Center, South Dakota
1961   University of Wisconsin, Madison
        Southwestern University, Memphis, Tennessee
        Civic Fine Arts Center, Sioux Falls, South Dakota
1962   Indian Arts and Crafts Center, Rapid City, South Dakota
1963   Dakota Wesleyan University, Mitchell, South Dakota
        Illinois State Museum, Springfield
1964   Theodore Lyman Wright Art Center, Beloit, Wisconsin
        Chaney Cowles Memorial Museum, Eastern Washington
            State Historical Society, Spokane, Washington
        Heard Museum, Phoenix, Arizona
        University of South Dakota, Vermillion, South Dakota
        Philbrook Museum of Art, Tulsa, Oklahoma
1965   Albert Lea Art Center, Albert Lea, Minnesota
        Butler County Historical Society, Grand Island, Nebraska
        Sioux Indian Museum and Crafts Center, Rapid City,
            South Dakota
1966   Evansville College, Evansville, Indiana
1967   Joslyn Art Museum, Omaha, Nebraska
        American Indian Arts, Center, New York
1969   Augustana College, Sioux Falls, South Dakota
1971   Heard Museum, Phoenix, Arizona
1972   South Dakota Memorial Art Center, Brookings, South
            Dakota
1973   Oscar Howe Art Center, Mitchell, South Dakota
1980   Oscar Howe Art Center, Mitchell, South Dakota
1981   Dacotah Prairie Museum, Aberdeen, South Dakota
        Oscar Howe Art Center, Mitchell, South Dakota
        Wyoming State Archives Museum, Cheyenne, Wyoming
1982   Dahl Fine Arts Center, Rapid City, South Dakota
        Brunnier Gallery, Ames, Iowa
        Oscar Howe Retrospective Exhibition, University of South
            Dakota, Vermillion (traveling through 1984)
1988   Northern Plains Tribal Art, Sioux Falls, South Dakota

Selected Group Exhibitions

1936   International tour, Paris and London

1947   *American Indian Paintings from the Permanent Collection*, Philbrook Art Center, Tulsa, Oklahoma (traveling through 1965)

1955-56 European tour sponsored by the University of Oklahoma, Norman

1958-61 European tour sponsored by the University of Oklahoma, Norman

1963   *Bismark National Indian Art Show*, sponsored by the Chamber of Commerce and Bismark Art Association, Bismark, North Dakota

        Contemporary American Indian Art, United States Department of State, Washington, D.C. (traveling)

        Denver Art Museum, Denver, Colorado

1965   *Second Annual Invitational Exhibition of American Indian Paintings*, United States Department of the Interior, Washington, D.C.

1966   *Fifty Artists from Fifty States*, American Federation of Artists (traveling through 1968)

1970   *Contemporary Sioux Painting*, Sioux Indian Museum and Crafts Center, Rapid City, South Dakota

1975   *Art Train*, United States bicentennial tour through 1976

        Pintura Amerindia Contemporanea/E. U. A., sponsored by the United States Departments of State and International Communications Agency, Washington, D.C. (traveling in South America through 1980)

1978   *100 Years of Native American Painting*, Oklahoma Museum of Art, Oklahoma City

1979   *Native American Paintings*, Joslyn Art Museum, Omaha, Nebraska (cosponsored by Mid-American Art Alliance Project; traveling through 1980)

1980   *Plains Indians Paintings*, organized by the Philbrook Museum, Tulsa (traveling)

1981   *A Plains Indian Art Festival*, Haffenreffer Nauseam of Anthropology, Brown University, Bristol, Rhode Island

        Philbrook Museum of Art, Tulsa, Oklahoma

        Contemporary Sioux Arts, Sioux Indian Museum and Crafts Center, Rapid City, South Dakota

1984   *Indianischer Kunstler*, organized by Philbrook Museum of Art, Tulsa, Oklahoma (traveled in Germany through 1985)

1991   *Shared Visions: Twentieth Century Native American Painting and Sculpture*, Heard Museum, Phoenix, Arizona (traveled internationally through 1992)

1992   *Visions of the People*, Minneapolis Institute of Arts, Minneapolis, Minnesota (traveling)

Collections

Bureau of Indian Affairs, United States Department of the Interior, Washington, D.C.; Center for Great Plains Studies, University of Nebraska, Lincoln, Nebraska; Civic Fine Arts Center, Sioux Falls, South Dakota; Dahl Fine Arts Center, Rapid City, South Dakota; Denver Art Museum, Denver, Colorado; Eisenhower Library, Abilene, Kansas; Evansville Museum, Evansville, Indiana; Heard Museum, Phoenix, Arizona; Heritage Center Inc. Collection, Red Cloud Indian School, Pine Ridge, South Dakota; Oscar Howe Art Center, Mitchell, South Dakota; Indian Arts and Crafts Board, United States Department of the Interior, Washington, D.C.; Joslyn Art Museum, Omaha, Nebraska; Museum of the American Indian, Heye Foundation, New York; Montclair Art Museum, Montclair,

New Jersey; Museum of New Mexico, Santa Fe, New Mexico; Museum of Northern Arizona, Flagstaff, Arizona; Nelson-Atkins Museum of Art, Kansas City, Missouri; Oklahoma Museum of Natural History, Norman; Philbrook Museum of Art, Tulsa, Oklahoma; Robinson Museum, Pierre, South Dakota; Sioux City Art Center, Sioux City, Iowa; Sioux Indian Museum and Craft Center, Indian Arts and Crafts Board, United States Department of the Interior, Rapid City, South Dakota; South Dakota Memorial Art Center, Brookings, South Dakota; Southwest Museum, Los Angeles; University of South Dakota, Vermillion.

Publications

On HOWE: Books—*Indian Art of the United States*, by Frederic Douglas and Rene D'Harnoncourt, New York, Museum of Modern Art, 1941; *A Pictorial History of the American Indian*, by Oliver LaFarge, New York, Crown Publishers, 1956; *Arts of the United States*, William H. Pierson, Jr., and Martha Davidson, New York, McGraw-Hill, 1960; *Oscar Howe: Artist of the Sioux*, by Robert Pennington, Sioux Falls, Dakota Territorial Centennial Commission, 1961; *American Indian Painting of the Southwest and Plains Areas*, by Dorothy Dunn, Albuquerque, University of New Mexico Press, 1968; *Howling Wolf*, Karen Daniels Peterson, editor, Palo Alto, American West Publishing Co., 1968; *Oscar Howe, Artist Laureate of the Middle Border*, by Mildred Soloday, Mitchell, Mitchell Printing Co. 1968; *The American Indian Speaks*, John R. Milton, editor, Vermillion, Dakota Press, 1969; *Contemporary Sioux Painting*, exhibition catalog by Myles Libhart, Rapid City, Tipi Shop, Inc., 1970; *Song from the Earth: American Indian Painting*, by Jamake Highwater, New York Graphic Society, 1976; *Pinturas Amerindas Contemporánes/E.U.A.*, by Lloyd Kiva New, Museo del Instituto de Artes Amerindios, 1979; *American Indian Painting and Sculpture*, by Patricia Janis Broder, New York, Abbeville Press, 1981; *Indianische Kunst im 20 Jahrhundert*, by Gerhard Hoffman, et al., Münich, Germany, 1984; *The Arts of the North American Indian: Native Traditions in Evolution*, edited by Edwin L. Wade, New York, Hudson Hills Press, 1986; *Shared Visions: Native American Painters and Sculptors of the Twentieth Century*, by Margaret Archuleta and Renard Strickland, Phoenix, Heard Museum, 1991; *Visions of the People: A Pictorial History of Plains Indian Life*, by Evan M. Maurer, Minneapolis Institute of Arts, 1992. **Film**—*The Sioux Painter*, 1973.

*   *   *

Oscar Howe created original works that remain startlingly modern, vital and innovative even in the proliferation of diverse styles of contemporary Native American art. Howe's development of a unique style seemed to be based on mainstream modern art and caused significant controversy and excitement. He was compelled to defend his new painting style when one of his entries was rejected by the annual Philbrook juried Indian art competition in 1958. By publicly defending his art, Howe helped achieve a form of liberation for Native American fine art. His struggle to overcome restricting definitions by a largely non-Indian public and leading art institutions of his day is now seen as a milestone in the claiming of the right to self-definition by Native American artists.

Howe attended the Santa Fe Studio in the mid-1930s and was instructed by Dorothy Dunn. Dunn was not always pleased with Howe's work, some of which seemed to foreshadow the stylistic developments that would occur later in his career. For instance, in

Sioux Riders (1936) one can see the emphasis on using the flat planes within figures bordered by line in an attempt to create action. The horses are positioned as if to represent the progressive stages in the movement of one horse. Howe's later style especially focuses on the action of figures by linear and plane emphasis reminiscent of cubism. Howe absorbed teachings and influences during his schooling in Santa Fe and eventually became a master of the Studio Style. *Dakota Duck Hunt* (1945) is a strong example of Howe's mature Studio Style and is one of the most well-known and reproduced images within the flatstyle genre. The painting is typical of the Studio Style in its use of traditional subject matter. It features two hunters crouching behind high reedy grass and observing approaching ducks. The composition is symmetrical, with the sky formally divided by an implied geometrical grouping of the flying birds. Foreground is stylized and background is minimal.

Two other paintings, *Dakota Teaching* (1951) and *Sioux Teacher* (1952), which both feature children gathered around an elder and receiving instruction, are also balance compositions rendered in the flat style with minimal background (a nearby tipi). *Dakota Duck Hunt*, *Dakota Teaching*, and *Sioux Teacher* represent the content and the style of painting that was encouraged by patrons. The paintings are of traditional activities and contain essentially static figures. Although they are highly accomplished and finely executed, many similar works were done equally well by other artists.

Howe's remarkable innovation is seen almost exclusively in paintings which portray dynamic motion. The most successful of these works began appearing in the late 1940s and early 1950s. *Sun Dance* (1949) and *Dance of the Double Woman* (1950) both have such degrees of action that they contrast easily with Howe's other work. For instance, in *Sun Dance*, even the action of a few falling objects is more dynamic than all of the flying birds in *Dakota Duck Hunt*. While figures are placed in more expressive and dynamic poses, they are still painted as representational. However, as Howe progressed in his technique, paintings became more abstracted, with figures becoming only partially recognizable and bodies deconstructed from a naturalistic point of view and reformed as geometric shapes and interacting colors. The most famous early example is *Victory Dance* (1954). In this work, only the very upper and lower portions of the dancer are clearly visible. Recognition of the body becomes less important than recognition of action in the abstract shapes of varied value and hues. Howe later used such abstraction to express the dynamism of the inner world, as in Sioux *Seed Player* (1974).

Howe did not give credence to the statement by some that his abstractions derived from European cubism, contending that his style was founded in the abstract art of his Yanktonai Dakota tradition and in his own personal conception. The innovative work of Oscar Howe is remarkable for its originality and its expression through dynamic abstraction. His style gave new vitality to cultural subjects that were in danger of becoming simply nostalgic. The obvious and compelling power of Howe's work made the debate over its acceptance all the more urgent. New questions of authenticity, identity and control indicated that the twentieth-century Native American art movement was experiencing the turmoil of growth and change. Native American artists continue to challenge the definitions and conventions of curators, art historians and patrons. Few have done so with works as vital and dynamic as those by Oscar Howe.

—Kevin Smith

HUNT, Richard
Variant names: Gwe-la-yo-gwe-la-gya-les
Tribal affiliations: Kwakiutl
Carver, mask maker, painter, and jewelry designer

Born: Alert Bay, British Columbia, 1951; Native name, Gwe-la-yo-gwe-la-gya-les, means "a man who travels around the world is giving." **Education:** Apprentice carver to his father, Henry Hunt, Royal British Columbia Museum at Thunderbird Park, 1973; studied jewelry making at Camosun College. **Career:** Chief carver, Thunderbird Park, 1974-86; owns and operates Kwa-Gulth Arts Ltd. of Victoria, British Columbia. **Awards:** Numerous commissions; Order of British Columbia, 1991; Order of Canada for Visual Arts, 1994.

Individual Exhibitions

1990	Vancouver, British Columbia
1995	*Richard Hunt Kwa-Giulth Sku Kingdom*, Derek Simpkins Gallery of Tribal Art, Vancouver

Selected Group Exhibitions

1971	*The Legacy*, British Columbia Provincial Museum, Victoria (traveled through 1980)
1986	*Expo '86*, Vancouver
1988	Canadian Pavillion, Expo '88, Brisbane, Australia
1992	*Chiefly Feasts*, British Columbia Provincial Museum, Victoria

Permanent Public Installations

1976	Museum of Ethnology, Osaka, Japan
1978	Captain Cook Museum, Middleborough, England
1979	British Columbia Provincial Museum, Victoria Canadian Cultural Centre, Paris
1980	City of Arts Centre in Edinburgh, Scotland
1982	CBC Headquarters, Vancouver
1983	Memorial Totem Pole (to the memory of chief Freddie Williams), Hopetown, British Columbia
1984	City of Liverpool, England
1985	Windsor Great Park, London, England
1986	Southwest Museum, Los Angeles
1987	City of Duncan, British Columbia (world's largest-in-diameter totem pole)
1989	National Museum, Ottawa St. Paul Science Centre, St. Paul, Minnesota (bear transformation mask)
1992	First Peoples' Language and Culture Council, Ottawa (12' x 4' table) American Museum of Natural History, New York (12' totem)

Collections

American Federation of Arts, New York; American Museum of Natural History, New York; Canadian Museum of Civilization, Hull, Quebec; Department of Indian and Northern Affairs, Ottawa; Royal British Columbia Museum, Victoria; University Museum, Philadelphia; University Museum, Philadelphia.

Richard Hunt: *Sun Mask.* Courtesy of the artist.

Publications

On HUNT: Books—*Indian Artists at Work* by Ulli Steltzer, Vancouver: J. J. Douglas, 1976; *Looking at Indian Art of the Northwest Coast* by Hillary Stewart, Seattle: University of Washington Press, 1979. **Articles**—"Richard Hunt: Renowned Native Carver" by Leslie Campbell, *Focus on Women*, June 1993; "Carving the Culture of a People" by Gery Lemon, *Victoria's Business Report*, vol. 12, no. 8, August 1994; "The Master's Touch" by R. Ashwell, *Westworld*, January/February 1973; "What's Fake or Genuine in Native Art? It Can Be Poles Apart" by Lon Wood, *Victoria Times Colonist*, 1994.

*   *   *

Richard Hunt is the son of Henry Hunt, grandson of Mungo Martin, and younger brother of Tony Hunt—all of which means that he comes from a distinguished and celebrated family of Kwakiutl artists. Hunt is a superbly skilled and prolific artist whose work is regarded by connoisseurs as among the finest Kwakiutl art available. Unlike some others, Hunt prefers to work exclusively within the Kwakiutl artistic tradition. His Indian name is Gwe-la-yo-gwe-la-gya-les ("a man who travels around the world is giving"), appropriate since he and his work have been seen all over the planet.

Hunt has lived most of his life in Victoria, British Columbia. In 1973 he began working for the Royal British Columbia Museum as an apprentice carver to his father, at Thunderbird Park. Upon his father's retirement, Hunt took over the position of chief carver at the park (from 1974 to 1986). In 1976 he worked on his first pole, which is now on exhibit at the National Museum of Ethnology in Osaka, Japan. In 1986 Hunt decided to leave his museum position in order to operate his own arts business, Kwa-Gulth Arts Ltd. of Victoria.

Hunt employs designs that come from his family and his cultural heritage. He has inherited two "wild man" images and a Kulus (young Thunderbird) image from his family. Also in relationship to his Kwakiutl background, Hunt is an experienced ritualist and dancer who has performed at many potlatches, feasts, and public performances. One indication of his high status is that he possesses the Hamatsa (Cannibal Bird) Dance among his ceremonial prerogatives. The Hamatsa ritual is the highest ranked of the Kwakiutl winter ceremonial dances, and Richard Hunt "owns" it two times over.

As a master of the Kwakiutl art style, Hunt has thoroughly internalized its principles. Kwakiutl art is more sculptural and three-dimensional than the arts of the northern peoples. It can be flamboyant and assertive in its demeanor and is usually more colorful than its northern counterparts; in addition to black and red, the Kwakiutl can also employ hues of yellow, brown, green, and orange in order to achieve greater coloristic effects. While many connoisseurs may prefer the discipline and aristocratic elegance of the Northern style, there is much to be said for the characterful and expressive arts of the Kwakiutl—its sensuous beauty and the kaleidoscopic colors, especially the Southern Kwakiutl to which the Hunt family belong.

Hunt produces art (such as masks) for patrons and for ceremonial use in potlatch/winter ceremonial contexts. As museum curator Peter L. Macnair noted, "While today the art is doing much to support the [potlatch] system, the potlatch is in turn being preserved by the entry of young people, particularly artists, who gain admittance through such arts as carving, painting, song, or dance." Some of the revival of traditional cultural life (including the potlatch/winter ceremonial system) is a consequence of various artists who can both rise in the social system and legitimize their art through participation in cultural revival events.

Two of Hunt's works, *Sun Mask* and *Sculpin Mask*, are ensconced in the Legacy collection of the Royal British Columbia Museum in Victoria. The *Sun Mask* shows that Hunt sometimes employs color in a relatively more reserved manner, typical of nineteenth-century Kwakiutl works; at other times, as in the *Sculpin Mask*, he will recapture the more flamboyant and even baroque sense of coloration once utilized by Willie Seaweed and others from the Blunden Harbor/Smith Inlet area. Seaweed and his cohorts used brightly colored enamel paints in their heyday of the 1920s to the 1940s (even Ellen Neel in the postwar era used them).

Hunt states that he is not disposed to create art derived from other tribal traditions since he is deeply committed to his own Kwakiutl heritage. In a similar vein, he is not enthusiastic about non-Indians creating Northwest Coast Indian art because these images do not belong to them and he feels it is legitimate to have a proprietary feeling about these designs: "I only do what belongs to my people....Every time I do something I am reclaiming my rights. Do I exploit my culture? Yes, in that it's mine to exploit."

In his current output Hunt's primary forte is in the field of woodcarvings. His ability to work with wood and his sense of it are nonpareil. Nonetheless, he also produces a fair number of silkscreen prints (frequently issued through the auspices of Pacific Editions Limited in Victoria). While most of his prints feature traditional Kwakiutl imagery, one work produced in 1993, *O Canada*, is particularly novel—symbolically portraying four Indians from tribes of the province of British Columbia. Hunt has described this atypical work:

> The top figure represents a Kwagulth Native wearing a Thunderbird headdress with cedar bark. To the left is our Westcoast brother wearing a Wolf headdress which also represents a hair hat. To the right is our Salish brother wearing a Wolf headdress with twisted wool down the back. The middle figure represents a visitor from the Kootenays wearing a war bonnet. The figures have been arranged in this specific order to show the Kwagulth from the northern tip of Vancouver Island, the Westcoast to the left, the Salish on the inside of the Island, and our visitor from the Kootenays.

Despite his preference for working with wood (especially red cedar), Hunt recently studied jewelry making at Camosun College.

He is now producing gold and silver works utilizing Kwakiutl designs. In 1988 he carved the world's largest-in-diameter totem pole for the city of Duncan, British Columbia. The pole stands twenty-four feet high and has a diameter of seven feet at the top. The technical and aesthetic challenges were successfully met.

—John Anson Warner

HUNT, Tony

Tribal affiliations: Kwakiutl
Carver, printmaker, mask maker, and jewelry designer

Born: Fort Rupert, Vancouver Island, British Columbia, 1942. **Education:** Traditional; apprentice to famous carver Mungo Martin. **Career:** Hereditary chief of the Prince Rupert Kwakiutl of British Columbia; apprenticed with Mungo Martin, 1952-1962; British Columbia Provincial Museum, 1962-1972; founded his own gallery, Arts of the Raven, 1970, in downtown Victoria; established an apprenticeship program at Arts of the Raven and arranged for sponsorship with the British Columbia Indian Arts and Crafts Society, where he is a board member; instructor, Kitanamax School of Northwest Coast Indian Art; numerous commissions for totem poles, including Alert Bay, British Columbia; B.C. Provincial Museum, Victoria, British Columbia; Buenos Aires, Argentina; Confederation Park, Hamilton, Ontario; Expo '67, Montreal, Quebec; Expo '67, Osaka, Japan; Field Museum of Natural History, Chicago; Heard Museum, Phoenix, Arizona; Horseshoe Bay, British Columbia; Mexico City, Mexico; Morioka, Japan; Park and Tilford Gardens, Vancouver, British Columbia; Peace Arch, Blaine, Washington; Thunderbird Park, Victoria, British Columbia; Royal Ontario Museum, Toronto, Ontario; University of British Columbia, Vancouver; University of Victoria, British Columbia.

Selected Group Exhibitions

1967	Gallery Libre, Montreal, Quebec
1968	Denver Art Museum, Denver, Colorado
1970	*Expo '70*, Osaka, Japan
1971	*Tony Hunt/Nathan Jackson,* Alaska State Museum, Juneau
1971-80	*The Legacy,* British Columbia Provincial Museum, Victoria, British Columbia
1972	Montreal Guild of Crafts, Montreal, Quebec
	First People Gallery, Chicago
1973	University of Philadelphia, Pennsylvania
	Heard Museum, Phoenix, Arizona
	Gallery Wall, Phoenix, Arizona
	Montreal Guild of Crafts, Montreal, Quebec
1973-75	Canadian National Exhibition, Toronto, Ontario
1974	*Canadian Indian Art,* Royal Ontario Museum, Toronto
1975	*Children of the Raven,* National Museum of Man, Ottawa, Ontario
	The Renaissance, Centennial Museum, Vancouver, British Columbia
	American Indian Arts and Crafts Show, Oakland, California; Seattle, Washington; Scottsdale, Arizona
1976	Canadian Catholic Conference Art Collection, Ottawa, Ontario

1977   Heard Museum, Phoenix, Arizona
1978   *Form and Freedom*, De Young Museum, San Francisco
1979   *Donnervogel and Ravival*, Hamburg Museum of Anthropology, Hamburg, Germany
        Gallery Hennermann, Bonn, Germany
1981   Daybreak Star Arts Centre, Seattle, Washington
        Hunt Family Heritage, National Museum of Man, Ottawa, Ontario
        International Trade Show, Frankfurt, Germany
1982   International Trade Show, Tokyo, Japan
        Maritime People of the Arctic and Northwest Coast, Chicago
        The Fall Trade Show, Toronto, Ontario
1989   *Expanding Traditions: Three Visions of Northwest Coast Indian Art*, Seattle, Washington
1991   *The Northwest Coast: A Collector's Vision*, Thunder Bay Art Gallery, Ontario
1992   Stonington Gallery, Seattle, Washington
        Nexus '92, Vancouver, British Columbia

Collections

Canadian Catholic Conference Art Collection, Ottawa, Ontario; Canadian Embassy, Mexico City, Mexico; Confederation Park, Hamilton, Ontario; Department of External Affairs, Bonn, Germany; Department of Indian and Northern Affairs, Ottawa, Ontario; Field Museum of Natural History, Chicago; Government House, Victoria, British Columbia; Hamburg Anthropology Museum, Hamburg, Germany; Heard Museum, Phoenix, Arizona; National Museum of Japan, Osaka, Japan; National Museum of Man, Ottawa, Ontario; Park and Tilford Gardens, North Vancouver, British Columbia; Parks Canada, Friendly Cove, British Columbia; Royal Ontario Museum, Toronto, Ontario; Stadpark, Canadian Forces Europe, Lahr, Germany; Museum of Anthropology, University of British Columbia, Vancouver, British Columbia.

Publications

On HUNT: Books—*Looking at Indian Art of the Northwest Coast*, by Hillary Stewart, Seattle, University of Washington Press, 1979. **Articles**—"Focus on Tony Hunt," by G. Schultz, *The Craftsman*, Vol. 6, No. 2, 1973; "Northwest Coast Indian Art from 1950 to the Present," by Karen Duffek, in *In the Shadow of the Sun: Perspectives on Contemporary Native Art*, Canadian Museum of Civilization, Canadian Ethnology Service, Mercury Series Paper 124, Hull, 1993; "The Big Money in West Coast Native Art," by Alan Bayless, *Financial Times*, 28 August 1994; "Faces at an Exhibition," by Brian Johnson, *MacLean's* magazine, 5 December 1995; "Totem Sways in the Winds and Council Support," by Jim Gibson, *Times-Colonist* (Victoria, British Columbia), 18 March 1995.

*   *   *

Tony Hunt is a Kwakiutl (Kwakwaka'wakw) from Fort Rupert on the northern coast of Vancouver Island in British Columbia, especially significant since he is not only a talented and productive artist but a hereditary leader of his Kwakiutl people. He has been active in both capacities for many years in British Columbia and is a fixture in the Northwest Coast Indian art revival of the province. It is important to emphasize that Tony Hunt has a perception of his art as closely related to the traditional social structure and culture of the Kwakiutl.

Hunt comes from one of the most famous and distinguished families on the Northwest Coast. One of his progenitors was the acclaimed George Hunt of Fort Rupert. A white man who was married to a Tlingit woman of high rank from Alaska, George Hunt served as a valued assistant and informant to the scholar Franz Boas. In fact, George Hunt is credited with being the seminal source of much of Boas' scholarship and research on the Kwakiutl; without George Hunt, Boas quite possibly could not have accomplished what he did in terms of documenting Kwakiutl life, history, culture, and language at the turn of the century. Equally important is the fact that Tony Hunt is organically connected to the great tradition of Kwakiutl artists who kept the tribal cultural heritage alive during the difficult years when the potlatch was outlawed (1884 to 1951). Hunt, along with his father, the noted artist Henry Hunt, apprenticed with Mungo Martin when the old master worked at Thunderbird Park/ Royal British Columbia Museum in Victoria. As Martin worked to restore old poles or to carve new ones, in addition to ultimately creating the Mungo Martin House at the park, Henry Hunt (plus Doug Cranmer) assisted him and learned the techniques and styles of Kwakiutl art. Thus, Tony Hunt's connection with tradition is real and well established.

Closely associated with the actuality of growing up in a traditional artistic/dance/potlatch milieu is the fact that Tony Hunt is now a hereditary chief of the Prince Rupert Kwakiutl of British Columbia. As a leader he has often dealt with public bodies on behalf of several projects that would aid the sense of cultural pride among the Kwakiutl people. In terms of relating his art to the wellbeing of his people, Tony Hunt and his father carved and raised two totem poles in Alert Bay in the early 1970s to honor the memory of his two grandfathers, Mungo Martin and Jonathan Hunt. Moreover, Tony Hunt has potlatched to legitimize the ceremonial names and privileges which his lineage claims.

Hunt's family first moved to Victoria in 1952 and as a young person he apprenticed with Mungo Martin. Upon Martin's death in 1962, he joined his father at the British Columbia Provincial Museum. However, in 1970 Hunt founded his own gallery in downtown Victoria, The Arts of the Raven, and in 1972 he resigned from his museum position in order to devote full time to making the gallery a success. For over fifteen years Hunt operated his gallery to provide the public and various organizations with high quality arts and crafts. As an integral part of his gallery's activities, Hunt established an apprenticeship program where aspiring young artists could come in order to learn from a master artist Hunt arranged for sponsorship of this apprenticeship program with the British Columbia Indian Arts and Crafts Society.

The success of Hunt's gallery and his teaching program for young artists helped to make him a major force in the Northwest Coast Indian art revival. Hunt and his apprentices fulfilled commissions from major organizations all over the world. One of these projects involved creating a huge totemic sculpture for permanent exhibition at the National Museum of Ethnology in Osaka, Japan. The quasi-totem pole is about fourteen feet high and features a Wolf holding a sculpin in its mouth. The work is unpainted and rendered in the Tsimshian/Gitksan style. The fact that a Kwakiutl administered gallery (with many Kwakiutl students) would create a Northern Style work reflects one of the traits evident in the revival: many artists from the Southern and Central-style backgrounds can create works in several tribal styles. Some experts in the field are going so far as to suggest that it would be wiser to label pieces according to "tribal style" (as opposed to simply denoting the tribal background of the artist), since this phenomenon is becoming more common.

The particular piece carved for Osaka included the work of several young artists who worked under Tony Hunt's supervision: Frank Nelson, Stan Hunt, John Livingston, Nelson Leeson, Dwayne Simeon, and Ross Hunt.

Hunt can work in several mediums and his preference is to produce art directly related to his Kwakiutl heritage. In particular, he is well-known for his wood carvings (including masks and totem poles), jewelry, and silkscreen prints. He possesses a superb technique as can be seen in two of his mask carvings that are a part of *The Legacy* collection of the Royal British Columbia Museum in Victoria. The "Bee Mask" was carved as a result of Hunt gaining the right to this image from a potlatch given by Mungo Martin; another mask in the collection, *Sea Raven Mask*, is a transformation piece, where the outside bird's image can part in order to reveal a moon in humanoid face. Visitors to the Victoria museum can also see a nearly full-sized recreation of the house of Jonathan Hunt of Fort Rupert, replete with painted facade and carvings, that was produced through the collaborative efforts of Henry and Tony Hunt.

Hunt also enjoys some fame as a pioneer in the creation of silkscreen prints. He started producing images on paper for silkscreen reproduction as early as 1960, although they do not seem to have become a major part of his output until the 1970s, when strict control over signed and numbered works was de rigueur. Silkscreen prints (along with jewelry and sculpture) lend themselves quite naturally to any innovative needs on the part of the artist, and Tony Hunt has tried out new ideas in this medium. According to Karen Duffek, Hunt has "introduced new subjects and new ways of depicting ancient themes. The "transformation" images, in particular, explore the Northwest Coast belief in the interchangeability of the two states of being: human-animal and natural-supernatural. Hunt uses a sexual metaphor to show the creatures interlocked as they penetrate each other during the instant of transformation.

It is notable that Hunt was asked to be one of the first teachers (in carving arts) at the Kitanamax School of Northwest Coast Indian Art when it started in 1969 at 'Ksan near Hazelton, British Columbia. Certainly there is ample evidence that Tony Hunt is one of the most distinguished artists now active in the Northwest Coast Indian art revival.

—John Anson Warner

HUNT, Wolf Robe

Variant names: Kewa
Tribal affiliations: Acoma Pueblo
Painter and jewelry designer

Born: Acoma Pueblo, New Mexico, 14 October 1905; also known as Wayne Henry Hunt and Kewa ("Growing Plant"). **Education:** Albuquerque High School; private study with Carl Redin and Frank Von Der Laucken; University of Chicago. **Career:** Operated several galleries in Oklahoma beginning in 1937 that sold leatherwork, jewelry, paintings, and other works; author, painter, and lecturer; dancer and dance troupe leader; interpreter; represented Native Americans at Hamburg, Germany, food exhibition, 1964. **Awards:** Scholarship, University of Chicago, Department of Anthropology; Oklahoma Indian of the Year, Council of American Indians, 1973; Waite Phillips Trophy, Philbrook Museum of Art, 1974. **Died:** 10 December 1977.

Individual Exhibitions

1967   Philbrook Museum of Art, Tulsa, Oklahoma
1980   Heard Museum, Phoenix, Arizona

Selected Group Exhibitions

1935   *American Indian Exposition*, Tulsa, Oklahoma
1964   *First Annual National American Indian Art Exposition*, Charlotte, North Carolina
1965   *Second Annual Invitational Exhibition of American Indian Paintings,* United States Department of the Interior, Washington, D.C.
1980   *Native American Art at the Philbrook*, Tulsa, Oklahoma (traveling)
        Native American Painting, Kansas City, Missouri (traveling)
1991   *Mayfest International Festival*, Winston-Salem, North Carolina

Publications

By HUNT: Books—*Dancing Horses of the Acoma,* by Helen Rushmore and Wolf Robe Hunt, Cleveland, 1963.

On HUNT: Books—*Indian Painters and White Patrons*, by J. J. Brody, Albuquerque, University of New Mexico Press, 1971; *Southwest Indian Painting: A Changing Art,* by Clara Lee Tanner, Tucson, University of Arizona Press, 1973; *Native American Art at the Philbrook*, by John Mahey, et al, Tulsa, 1980; *Native American Painting*, Kansas City, Mid-America Art Alliance, 1980. **Articles**— *The Tulsa World,* 5 May and 10 December 1977.

*   *   *

Wolf Robe Hunt was born at Acoma Pueblo in New Mexico in 1905 and moved to Tulsa, Oklahoma, in 1932. Many of Hunt's works, such as *Dancing with Snakes* (1967), bear witness to his Pueblo origins. This work, done in flat-style and containing no background or foreground, also illustrates some characteristics of Hunt's paintings. The entire work consists of three dancers and their ceremonial clothing, ritual objects and the snakes that they are holding. While action is indicated by the body position of the dancers, there is little drama to their movement and they are rather stiff. The figures appear very similar to one another, as if made from the same drawing, with only slight variation. A close look at the contour lines reveals that they consist of a series of alternating straight lines and sharp curves. Hunt uses this technique to create turns and curves in a figure, rather than a smooth, curvilinear line most often found in drawings. This unusual drawing style causes the eye to make quick movements when viewing the contour of figures, adding the sense of movement, but it is not certain as to whether or not that was the artist's intent. It is, however, seen in many of his paintings and helps to make his work identifiable.

Other works that indicate Hunt's Pueblo background contain design elements reminiscent of the pottery painting of the Southwest. Hunt used to paint Pueblo designs on pottery made by his mother, Morning Star. He stated, "At home we were always interested in art because my mother used to make pottery. And we [would paint] the scroll-work and all of that." *First Horse Comes to Acoma* (1976) serves as an example, with a flat-style horse in the center of the painting as the only figurative element of the composition. In fact, even the horse has a painted heartline, typical of animal design on certain Pueblo pottery. The entire background of the piece is filled with designs similar to that seen on pottery, such as the diagonal diamond shape composed of somewhat curved lines. Across the top of the piece, Hunt placed a row of a motif similar to, though necessarily representative of, the various tail-feather designs found on Hano polychrome ceramics.

In 1937, Hunt established the first of a number of galleries that he would open in and around Tulsa. At his galleries, Hunt sold his leatherwork, jewelry, paintings, and other works. Hunt stated, "We did everything you [need to do to] make a living. We did leatherwork, we did featherwork, we did silverwork. I already knew how to do silverwork. I'm still doing it today. So I was probably the first silversmith in Oklahoma. I'm sure I was the first one to establish my own place." Wolf Robe Hunt, like fellow artist Woody Crumbo, was also interested in opening the market up for other Native American artists. Accordingly, his galleries provided important outlets for other Native American artists, which became his primary interest following World War II.

—Kevin Smith

HYDE, Douglas
Tribal affiliations: Nez Percé; Assiniboine; Chippewa
Sculptor

Born: Hermiston, Oregon, 1946. **Education:** Institute of American Indian Arts, Santa Fe, New Mexico, 1962-63; San Francisco Art Institute, 1969-71. **Military Service:** U.S. Army, 1968-69; served in Vietnam. **Career:** Artist and instructor, Institute of American Indian Arts, 1971-74. **Awards:** Several at juried shows, including those sponsored by the Heard Museum, Phoenix, Arizona, Philbrook Art Center, Tulsa, Oklahoma, and the Scottsdale National Indian Art Exhibition; Santa Fe Rotary Foundation's Distinguished Artist of the Year Award, 1996; numerous commissions, including memorial tombstone for Josiah Redwolf, Nez Percé (1971), bust of Taza, Apache leader, for the American Indian Society, Washington, D.C. (1973), *Agua Caliente Women,* bronze (1994) for the Palm Springs Art Commission, and *Tribute to Navajo Code Talkers*, Phoenix, Arizona.

Individual Exhibitions

1968   Institute of American Indian Arts, Santa Fe, New Mexico

Selected Group Exhibitions

1963   Institute of American Indian Arts, Santa Fe, New Mexico
1965   *Second Annual Invitational Exhibition of American Indian Paintings*, United States Department of the Interior, Washington, D.C.
         Philbrook Art Center, Tulsa, Oklahoma
1966   Edinburgh Festival, Scotland
         Berlin Festival, Berlin, West Germany
         Alaska Centennial Exhibition, Anchorage, Alaska
1967   Institute of American Indian Arts Museum, Santa Fe, New Mexico

1968   *Cultural Olympics*, Mexico City
1971   Nez Percé Community, Lapwai, Idaho
         Contemporary Indian Artists—Montana, Wyoming, Idaho, Museum of the Plains Indian, Browning, Montana
1972   *Night of First Americans*, Kennedy Center for the Performing Arts, Washington, D.C.
         Heard Museum, Phoenix, Arizona
1973   *New Directions*, Institute of American Indian Arts Museum, Santa Fe, New Mexico (traveling through 1974)
1974   *Institute of American Indian Arts Alumni Exhibition*, Amon Carter Museum of Western Art, Fort Worth, Texas
         Buffalo Bill Historical Center, Cody, Wyoming
         Grand Salon, Paris, France
         Amon Carter Museum, Fort Worth, Texas
1981   *American Indian Art in the 1980s*, Native American Center for the Living Arts, Niagara Falls, New York
         Buffalo Bill Historical Center, Cody, Wyoming
         Historical Society Museum, Denver, Colorado
1986   Heard Museum, Phoenix, Arizona
1990   *Creativity is Our Tradition: Three Decades of Contemporary Art at the Institute of American Indian Art*, Santa Fe, New Mexico
1991   *Sapatq'ayn: Twentieth-Century Nez Percé Artists*, sponsored by the Idaho Humanities Council, Idaho Commission on the Arts, National Park Service, Nez Percé Tribe, and Northwest Interpretive Association (touring Washington, Idaho, Montana, and Wyoming)
1992   *Creativity Is Our Tradition: Three Decades of Contemporary Indian Art,* Institute of American Indian Arts Museum, Santa Fe, New Mexico

Collections

Amon Carter Museum, Ft. Worth, Texas; Department of the Interior, Washington, D.C.; Heard Museum, Phoenix, Arizona; Institute of American Indian Arts Museum, Santa Fe, New Mexico; Southwest Museum, Los Angeles.

Publications

On HYDE: Books—*The Sweetgrass Lives On,* by Jamake Highwater, New York, 1980; *American Indian Painting and Sculpture,* by Patricia Janis Broder, New York, 1981; *The Arts of the North American Indian: Native Traditions in Evolution,* edited by Edwin L. Wade and Rennard Strickland, New York: Hudson Hills Press, 1986; *Sapatq'ayn: Twentieth Century Nez Percé Art,* (introduction by Minthorn), Lewiston, Idaho: Northwest Interpretive Association and Confluence Press, 1991; *Creativity Is Our Tradition: Three Decades of Contemporary Indian Art,* by Rick Hill, Santa Fe: Institute of American Indian and Alaska Native Culture and Arts Development, 1992.

*   *   *

Douglas Hyde emerged from being one of the artistic disciples of Allan Houser, his former teacher, to a leading figure in the field of monumental sculpture. Three events changed his life and added a dimension to his work that is still driving his sculpture. First, Hyde had wanted to be a painter, but upon meeting Houser at the Institute of American Indian Arts as a senior student in their high school arts program, he was turned on to the idea that he could express

Doug Hyde: *The Singers,* **1973. Photograph by Larry Phillips; courtesy of the Institute of American Indian Arts Museum, Santa Fe, New Mexico.**

something about his ancestry through sculpture. Houser at first thought that Hyde should stick with painting after viewing his first sculpture, but they became good friends. Hyde's early work combined his sense of human form with ornamentation inspired by African tribal sculptures. *Sun & Moon Gods* (1967) shows the combination of the native American spirit figure, painted decoration and the use of nails, metal screens and staple that were used to empower African icons. He sought artistic/spiritual connections to ancestral voices.

The second major influence was Hyde's tour of duty in Vietnam in 1968-69, where he was wounded by a hand grenade thrown at him by his own troops. He was in the military police of the 198th Light Infantry Brigade and was chasing a suspect when the suspect unleashed the grenade and severely wounded Hyde. He returned from overseas and spent a year recuperating at home at the Nez Percé reservation, where he worked at making tombstones, which introduced him to the use of power tools and rekindled his personal interest in sculpture. Hyde began to look at the warrior figure in native cultures in a new way, and perhaps saw even more nobility in the elemental nature of native lives, as a contrast to what he saw during the Vietnam war.

Thirdly, Hyde returned to IAIA in 1971 and spent three years there to prepare himself for a career in the arts, and he also taught sculpture, taking over for Houser, who had retired. During this period he received two major commissions, one for a memorial for Taza, son of Cacaos, and one for Josiah Red Wolf for the Nez Percé Tribe. By the time he left IAIA, Lloyd Kiva New, the director of the Institute, felt that Hyde was imaginative, experimental and dedicated to his discipline. Hyde had grown to prefer the feel of stone and the physicalness of sculpture during the process and as a completed object. Most of his works are figurative, and he feels they each have their own personality: "Each piece is a separate person, an individual that has its own moods." His sense of self was renewed, his direction was set and his pride and determination carried him forward.

In 1973, Hyde won the best sculpture award at Santa Fe Indian Market and became connected with the Forest Fein Gallery, one of the most prestigious art dealers in Santa Fe. This was followed by a major award at the Heard Museum's Invitational competition in sculpture. He was commissioned to produce one of the largest pieces of public art ever made by a Native American, *Tribute to Navajo Code Talkers,* installed in Phoenix, Arizona. In 1996, Hyde was the recipient of the Santa Fe Rotary Foundation's Distinguished Artist of the Year Award.

No matter what the medium—wood, stone, bronze—Hyde continues to craft a style that has its own unique character, but one that honors the American Indian of the past and the present. Some may find his work derivative and stuck in the modernistic school of the southwest, but if you understand where Hyde has come from, what he has endured in his life, his art is a personification of his belief in himself as an individual who is an Indian. Each of his "people" are an extension of some aspect of his life, and in fact, a reconciliation, a tribute, to what has sustained him.

—Rick Hill

I-J

INUKPUK, Johnny
Tribal affiliations: Inuit
Carver

Born: Johnny Manumi Inukpuk, Kuujjuaq (northern Quebec), c. 1911; names also transliterated as Innukpuk, Inukpak, Jaani, Johnnie, Yani. **Family:** Four children with his first wife, Alicie Kuannanaaq Alakkariallak, ten children with his second wife, Mary Ukuujaq Saumik. **Career:** Traditional nomadic hunting, trapping and fishing existence; began carving while still living out on the land; moved his family into the Inukjuak settlement in the early 1950s; leader in his community and a highly respected artist. **Awards:** Elected member of Royal Canadian Academy of Art, 1973.

Individual Exhibitions

1980   *Johnny Inukpuk of Inoucdjouac,* Cottage Craft Gifts and Fine Arts Ltd., Calgary, Alberta
1984   *Later Works of Johnny Inukpuk,* Arctic Artistry, Hartsdale, New York
1987   *Johnny Inukpuk R.C.A.,* Galerie Le Chariot, Montreal, Quebec

Selected Group Exhibitions

1953   *Eskimo Carvings: Coronation Exhibition,* Gimpel Fils, London
1955   *Eskimo Sculpture,* National Gallery of Canada, Ottawa, Ontario
1971   *The Art of the Eskimo,* Simon Fraser Gallery, Burnaby, British Columbia
         Sculpture/Inuit: Masterworks of the Canadian Arctic, Canadian Eskimo Arts Council, Ottawa, Ontario (traveling through 1973)
1974   *Eskimo Art,* Queens Museum, Flushing, New York
1975   *We Lived by Animals/Nous Vivions des Animaux,* Department of Indian Affairs and Northern Development in cooperation with the Department of External Affairs, Ottawa, Ontario (traveling through 1979)
1980   *Eskimo Sculpture and Art Exhibit,* Yerkes International Galleries, Dobbs Ferry, New York
         Things Made by Inuit, La Federation des Cooperatives du Nouveau-Quebec, Montreal, Quebec (traveling through 1981)
1981   *Inuit Art: A Selection of Inuit Art* from the Collection of the National Museum of Man, Ottawa, and the Rothmans Permanent Collection of Inuit Sculpture, Canada National Museum of Man, Ottawa and Rothmans of Pall Mall Canada Ltd., Toronto, Ontario (traveling through 1982)
1983   *The Arctic/L'Artique,* UNESCO, Paris
         Artist of Arctic Quebec, Inuit Gallery of Vancouver, Vancouver, British Columbia
1985   *Masterwork Sculpture 1985,* Inuit Gallery of Vancouver, Vancouver, British Columbia
1986   *The Spirit of the Land,* Koffler Gallery, Toronto, Ontario
         Inukpuk Family Sculpture, Arctic Artistry, Harsdale, New York
1988-90 *Stories in Stone: Soapstone Sculptures from Northern Quebec and Kenya,* La Federation des Cooperatives du Nouveau-Quebec, Montreal, Quebec (traveling)
1990   *Arctic Mirror,* Canadian Museum of Civilization, Hull, Quebec
         Traditions and Innovations in Inuit Art, Sculpture in Stone, Images of the North, San Francisco
1991   *Mother and Child: Sculpture and Prints,* Albers Gallery, San Francisco
1992   *Hudson's Bay Company Collection of Inuit Art,* Winnipeg Art Gallery, Winnipeg, Manitoba
1995   *Immaginario Inuit, Arte e cultura degli esquimesi canadesi,* Galleria d'Arte Moderna e Contemporanea, Verona, Italy

Collections

Art Gallery of Greater Victoria, British Columbia; Art Gallery of Ontario, Toronto; Art Gallery of York University, Downsview, Ontario; Canadian Museum of Civilization, Hull, Quebec; Confederation Centre of the Arts, Charlottetown, Prince Edward Island; Dennos Museum Center, Northwestern Michigan College, Traverse City, Michigan; Agnes Etherington Art Centre, Queen's University, Kingston, Ontario; Glenbow Museum, Calgary, Alberta; Hudson Bay Permanent Collection, Winnipeg, Manitoba; Metropolitan Museum of Art, New York; Musée des Beaux-Arts de Montreal, Montreal, Quebec; Museum of Anthropology, University of British Columbia, Vancouver; National Gallery of Canada, Ottawa, Ontario; Prince of Wales Northern Heritage Centre, Yellowknife, Northwest Territories; Rothmans Permanent Collection of Eskimo Sculpture, Toronto, Ontario; Winnipeg Art Gallery, Winnipeg, Manitoba.

Publications

On INUKPUK: Books—*Sculpture of the Eskimo,* by George Swinton, Toronto, 1972, *The Inuit Imagination: Arctic Myth and Sculpture,* by Harold Seidelman and James Turner, Vancouver/Toronto: Douglas & McIntyre, 1993. **Articles**—"Johnny Innukpuk, Story in Stone," *The Beaver,* Winter 1963; "Johnny Inukpuk, A Great Artist," by Lucie Dumas, *Rencontre,* vol. 10, no. 1, September 1988; *Inuit Art Quarterly,* Summer 1990.

*   *   *

In 1973, Johnny Inukpuk was honored as the first Inuit artist elected to the Royal Candian Academy of Arts. However, he lived the majority of his life far from such fashionable society. As a chief of encampments for his nomadic people, he followed in the footsteps of his father, Old Inukpuk, whose oratory skills were a great part of his leadership qualities.

Johnny Inukpuk recalls that he was already sculpting small objects to exchange with seasonal visitors from the food supply ship, *Nascopie,* before the arrival in 1948 of James Houston, who influenced and promoted Inuit art and did much to bring it to Western attention. In addition to trading his artwork, Inukpuk sold furs to the trading post of the Revillon Freres Company and to agents of the Hudson Bay Company.

According to Inukpuk, he started sculpting regularly around 1953, a time when he lived in the vicinity of the Nauligaqvik River, north of Inunjuak. His first pieces were representations of nordic animals. He attests that his early human figures, though not documented, focused on traditional male activities, based directly on his experiences. To represent Inuit women, however, Inukpuk relates that he had to observe them a great while and took particular pleasure in attempting to penetrate their puzzling secrets. Eventually, the first sculpture that brought a good price had as its subject an Inuit woman caring for a child. It seems today that his view of the market and his desire to capture the feminine experience accounts for a great part of his motivation for assiduously pursuing this theme. Thus, during the first half of the 1950s, his most remarkable works are without a doubt his representations of women.

The bodies of women represented in Inukpuk's sculptures are exaggerated in mass, literally swollen; they constitute an enormous mass of circularity or enter into a rectangular prism with angles considerably rounded. The immense volume undulates, as if spreading. Additionally, the women's bodies often have one or two projecting heads—the larger head being the mother's and often facing a minuscule child's head, which she intends to nurse. Carved in magnificent soapstone, dark green or marbled, the pieces are carefully polished and have subtle details. Particularly startling are exquisitely notched designs that suggest garments. Moreover, the eyes and teeth are sometimes heightened in effect with inlaid ivory. However, Inukpuk would forsake the fastidious practice of inlaying, encouraged by the Qallunaat dislike for embellishments that are fragile and can be broken during the transportation of completed artworks to the south.

At the beginning of the 1960s and perhaps a little before, the style of Inukpuk's work is unified. The sculptor adds to his representations a socle simply suggested by a relief extricated at the very base of the sculpture. This contrivance assures more equilibrium to his works in which the lower part of the subject is narrower than the upper parts. This choice in the disposition of volume serves as a means for virtually elongating the subject. The socle, or portion of ground, isolates the subject in a reduced environment that foregrounds his figures and deemphasizes the natural world. Yet, Inukpuk always suggests the texture of small knolls, most often by leaving coarse traces on the rough shape of the base to symbolize the anarchic character of nature. In other cases, he will engrave small parallelograms on this portion of unpolished stone, a graphic element he multiplies until the surface is completely filled and appears in disorder. He also uses this effect combined with neat polishing to represent the hirsuteness of characters.

During this period as well, Inukpuk had a marked tendency for ornamentation of clothing, including a design serial that will hence-forth characterize his sculptures—a frontlet constituted of upright segments in relief to adorn the lower border of parkas, for example, and triangular forms of too small kamiiks at the feet of his figures, who are always dressed in the traditional manner.

At the same time, the articulation is done less smoothly. The volumes become complicated and offer a larger variety of designs, while becoming more bloated and less elegant. Still, faces are more elaborately rendered and gain in individuality. Hands and heads grow larger while the trunk of the body is shortened. By this deformation of volumes, Inukpuk reinforces the expressive character of bodily parts, which can be attributed to his will to better personalize each piece. In fact, he has asserted that he had already been told that the Qallunaat loved the sculptures done with a little exaggeration and did not like models done too realistically, and Inukpuk, himself, prefers sculptures with big heads on small bodies.

One can observe that the groove beneath the nose on the faces of some of his figures is very prominent and can suggest a harelip. Inukpuk confirmed this notion by stating that he once observed such an anomaly on a woman and that it pleased him. Notwithstanding this declaration, one must not believe that all of his human representations are necessarily grotesque because of physical defect, which he seemingly found satisfying. Another such example is his inclination to represent people with a flat nose, turned up with clearly viewed nasal passages.

The intense expressiveness of his work of the 1960s is superseded little by little by a loosening of dramatic tension and oriented toward an exploration, quasi caricature, of his subjects. In the 1970s, the forms are tightened and schematized. One also notes a significant reduction of detail, which coincides with the creation of smaller and less refined works. Even as he continued to explore various themes, he instilled an expression of childlike innocence and naivete. The disproportion of the head and hands, for example, is reminiscent of the proportions of a newborn and, by extension, those of dolls for young children, resulting in the feeling of being in the presence of a young child living in the body of an adult.

In 1974, the artist completed his only print, *A True Story of Johnny Being Attacked by Three Polar Bears While in His Igloo.* One report tells that the people of his community incited him to commemorate this story in mythic ways. If so, the result reflects the presence of ritual, where the witness in the experience materializes his vision, beyond using words, for the benefit of the community.

Surprisingly, Inukpuk has been included rarely in group exhibitions and only a few publications display his works. The enthusiasm with which George Swinton described his works, in particular *Mother Feeding Child* (1962), in *Sculpture of the Eskimo* (1972), contributed greatly to Inukpuk's renown.

Inukpuk continues to sculpt in his mid-80s. Even if he has reduced his activities, the Qallunaat continue to order his sculptures. It is a joy for him that people are still interested in his work, but he prefers to be told precisely what is desired because he needs at least three or four days to produce a sculpture representing a person. He is also very happy to see his works reproduced in books, feeling that his sculptures might be of use for educational purposes, since all of his work relates to real life. They were inspired by experiences and personal observations and convey everyday life.

—Louis Gagnon

JACKSON, Edna Davis

Tribal affiliations: Tlingit
Mixed media artist, textile artist, basketweaver, and sculptor

Born: Petersburg, Alaska, 1950. **Education:** University of Alaska, B.F.A., 1970; Oregon State University, 1980; University of Washington, M.F.A., 1983.

Individual Exhibitions

1988   Maude Kerns Art Center, Eugene, Oregon
        Ollantay Center for the Arts, New York

Selected Group Exhibitions

1980   Oregon State University, Corvallis, Oregon
1982   Portland Art Museum, Oregon
        Sacred Circle Gallery of American Indian Art, Seattle
1983   University of Washington, Seattle
1984   Anchorage Museum of History and Fine Arts, Alaska
1985   *Women of Sweetgrass, Cedar and Sage*, Gallery of the
        American Indian Community House, New York (traveling)
        Institute of Alaska Native Arts, Fairbanks
1986   *Eleven American Indian Artists*, American Indian Contemporary Arts Gallery, San Francisco
1987   *New Directions Northwest*, Evergreen State College, Olympia, Washington
        Southwest Museum, Los Angeles
1988   San Diego Museum of Man, California
1989   *Crossed Cultures,* Seattle Art Museum, Washington (traveling)
1991   Alaska State Museum, Juneau
        North Dakota Museum of Fine Arts, Fargo
1992   American Indian Contemporary Arts, San Francisco
1995   Sacred Circle Gallery of American Indian Art, Seattle

Collections

Alaska State Museum, Juneau; Anchorage Performing Arts Center, Alaska; Heard Museum, Phoenix, Arizona; Seattle Arts Commission, Washington.

Publications

On JACKSON: Books—*Gathering Ground: New Writing and Art by Northwest Women of Color,* Jo Cochran, J. T. Stewart, and Mayumi Tsutakawa, editors, Seattle, Seal Press, 1984; *Women of Sweetgrass, Cedar and Sage*, by Harmony Hammond and Juane Quick-to-See Smith, New York, Gallery of the American Indian, 1985; *Portfolio: Eleven American Indian Artists*, by Kenneth Banks and Abby Wasserman, San Francisco, American Indian Contemporary Arts Gallery, 1986; *New Directions Northwest*, Olympia, Evergreen State College, 1987; *Crossroads of Continents: Cultures of Siberia and Alaska*, by William W. Fitzhugh and Aron Crowell, Washington, D.C., Smithsonian Institution Press, 1988; *Crossed Cultures,* by Patterson Sims, Seattle Art Museum, 1989; *Mixed Blessings: New Art in a Multicultural America*, by Lucy R. Lippard, New York, Pantheon Books, 1990. **Articles**—"Edna Davis Jackson," *Journal of Alaska Native Arts*, (March/April, 1985); "Eight Artists II: Contemporary Indian Art at the Southwest Museum (Los Angeles)," by Suzanne G. Kenagy, *American Indian Art* magazine, vol. 13, Winter 1987.

*   *   *

Edna Davis Jackson's handmade paper works are embedded in the seasonal life of nature and the quotidian life of a woman and her community. While she incorporates Tlingit symbols, legends and materials into her mixed-media work, she also feels free to modify these elements to make them more suitable for her narrative and expressive ends. Her importance lies in her union of technical and artistic innovation with respect for ancient traditions; thus, she has succeeded in pushing the boundaries of the media of papermaking, textiles and basket making, just as she has achieved a linking of the Tlingit heritage with contemporary forms.

A synthesis of sculpture and collage, her work blends imagery of the Northwest Coast tribes, such as eagle, salmon and raven forms, with narrative content from her own life and that of her community. Masks and button blankets have been inspirational, and her sculptures are also analogous to traditional totem poles through their function of recording; they act as personal, family and community memory.

Jackson's mother was her first teacher, instructing her in sewing techniques that are still evident in her artwork today. In a process that goes back hundreds of years and connects her with even more ancient native women's work, she gathers red and yellow cedar bark in the spring from trees where women long ago came to get their bark for weaving. This requisite time in the forest gathering materials makes for a holistic creative process, which she values.

First exhibiting in 1980, Jackson experimented during her early period when she reworked standard textile and papermaking techniques and learned Tlingit and Salish mask-making. Since her Northwest coast masks attempted to duplicate traditional forms and styles, they were less successful than her later pieces. When her sculptures began to unify her skills with both textiles and papermaking as well as making use of the inherent qualities of cedar as a medium, they became more compelling. Continuing her experimentation with textiles, she has explored quilting, weaving, stitching and wrapping techniques. In investigating the limits of papermaking, she tears, cuts, distorts, laminates and casts the pulp over sculpted clay forms. She often combines the two media by weaving her handmade paper, as in *Spirit Mask* (1986), which consists of cast faces and a woven cedar paper torso.

Jackson's willingness to experiment is a particular strength. She sometimes imbeds yarn, lace and fabric in the paper pulp before casting and then makes an assemblage from this cast paper incorporating bits of feathers and bone. She has also used traditional geometric basket designs to create large pieces of relief sculpture. Often working at home in her kitchen or living room, Jackson is inspired by domestic occasions, such as the anniversary of her marriage, or her daughter's coming into puberty. Rarer are pieces that have political motivation or express ecological concerns, although these are themes which she has occasionally explored. *Cedar Woman Spirit (For All the Trees We've Logged*, 1988, cast cedar paper, wooden dowels, acrylic on canvas) is an example.

Jackson has united personal themes with both Tlingit and Western references to create a larger cultural framework. In *Ka-oosh and the Coho Salmon* (1981-83, cedar paper, linen, copper and acrylic), she painted extracts of salmon formline imagery on cedar paper masks portraying her husband. These abbreviated forms are visually comparable with Western-style musical notation, as well as an echo of the ceremonial face-painting that traditionally took place during potlatches; thus they function as deft visual puns. In this way she creates new legends by using her artwork to tell stories drawn from her life and the lives of friends and family.

Jackson's works are deeply grounded in traditional native artistic expression, yet they bring this heritage into the present through her creation of new forms and subject matter. While personal, her themes are not parochial, since she is well-educated and sophisticated in her expressive abilities. Although Jackson's wealth of personal references make her work evocative, they also cause it to be somewhat subjective and self-referential, thus requiring a discerning viewer. Jackson has expanded the technical limits and expressive possibilities of the medium of handmade paper, just as she has extended the boundaries of contemporary art to include the outstanding legacy of the Northwest Coast formline design. By returning home to Alaska after her graduate work and unabashedly using themes from her own life, she reinforces the postmodern realization that the familiar, resonant with authenticity, is fitting material for creative expression.

—Ann Storey

JACKSON, Nathan

Tribal affiliations: Tlingit
Carver

Born: Tenekee Springs, near Haines, Alaska, 1938; member of the Raven Clan. **Education:** Institute of American Indian Arts, Santa Fe, 1962-64. **Military Service:** U.S. Army. **Career:** Fisherman; dancer and ceremonial performer; active as an artist in the Southwest, 1962-67; returned to Alaska in 1967 to focus on classic Tlingit art and to teach apprentice carvers.

Individual Exhibitions

1988   University of Alaska, Fairbanks

Selected Group Exhibitions

1964   World's Fair, New York
1967   Folk Festival, Smithsonian Institution, Washington, D.C.
1971   *Tony Hunt and Nathan Jackson*, Hazelton, Alaska
1981   Centennial Hall, Juneau, Alaska

Nathan Jackson: Detail of *Raven Screen,* Ketchikan International Airport. Photograph by J. A. Warner.

1986   *Alaskameut '86: An Exhibit of Contemporary Alaska
         Native Masks,* Institute of Alaska Native Arts,
         Fairbanks

Selected Totem Sites

Angoon, Admiralty Island, Alaska; Harvard University, Cambridge, Massachusetts; Ketchikan Airport, Ketchikan, Alaska; Kobe, Japan; London, England; Naa Kahidi Theater, Sealaska Cultural Arts Park, Juneau, Alaska; New York City, New York; Salt Lake City, Utah; Seattle, Washington; Sitka National Historical Park, Sitka, Alaska; University of Alaska Museum, Fairbanks; Washington, D.C.

Publications

On JACKSON: Books—*Alaskameut '86: An Exhibit of Contemporary Alaska Native Masks,* Jan Steinbright, editor, Fairbanks, 1986; *Indians of the Northwest Coast,* by Maximilien Bruggmann and Peter Gerber, Seattle, 1989. **Articles**—"Family Trees: The Towering Richness of Indian Heritage Live on in Nathan Jackson's Totem Poles," by Jim Leveque, *Philip Morris* magazine, January-February, 1989; "Towering Totems: Nathan Jackson's Wolf Pole Rises to the Occasion," by Leslie Barber Noyes, *Southwest Art,* October 1991.

*   *   *

Nathan Jackson's work is encountered not only in Alaska, where he is among the best known and most highly regarded Tlingit artists now active in the panhandle, but throughout the world in places like New York, London, and Kobe, Japan. Jackson is a leader in the revival or renewal of Tlingit art and has produced a variety of items, including totem poles, bentwood boxes, masks, and house fronts.

Jackson was born into the matrilineal salmon clan of the raven moiety, and he recalls that he learned much about the lore of his people from his uncle and grandfather. After service in the American armed forces, he went to the Institute of American Indian Arts (IAIA) in Santa Fe, New Mexico, from 1962 to 1964, focusing his studies on graphics, design, and silkscreen making. Jackson returned to Alaska in 1967 in order to pursue his central vocation of creating works of art in the classic Tlingit tradition.

The Northwest Coast art revival in British Columbia, Canada, has received a great deal of attention from Canadian-based scholars and many of the artists active in that province are well known. Events and artists in Alaska are less understood and appreciated, partly because the revival of traditional arts is a more limited phenomenon there and the region is far from urban art markets. As a result, Tlingit art is less understood among collectors than Haida or Tsimshian creations. Historically, Tlingit art has always been regarded as sophisticated and elegant, distinctive but integral with the Northern Style of the Haida and Tsimshian / Gitksan / Nishga. In discussing Tlingit totem poles, for example, Edward Malin (*Totem Poles of the Pacific Northwest Coast*) alludes to their special traits:

> A major point of difference is the heavier reliance the Tlingit placed on the use of paints, together with the more extensive palette of employed colors. The artists greatly elaborated the details on wings and body parts of the subjects depicted. Little of the natural wood was allowed to show through, revealing a distinct difference from Haida and

Nathan Jackson in his carving shed. Photograph by J. A. Warner.

Tsimshian models. Notice also the Tlingit utilized appendages much more frequently to enhance the size of the figures.

In this regard, then, Tlingit art has sometimes been described as a "baroque" incarnation of the Northern Style. What is most distinctive, perhaps, is the characteristic use of a blue-green color on many Tlingit carvings. Employing these principles, Jackson has spent almost thirty years producing authentic Tlingit art works.

Jackson has a carving shed outside of Ketchikan in the Saxman Tlingit Indian village, just south of town. Saxman is a Tongass Tlingit community to which a great many historic Tlingit totem poles have been removed and are on display. In such a milieu, Jackson works on commissions and mentors apprentice carvers, including his son.

Among some of his more notable commissions, he created two 40-foot totem poles outside the Centennial Hall in Juneau. Also, because he sees a relationship between his art and the well-being of the culture of the Tlingit, he carved two large poles for the community of Angoon, a Tlingit village on Admiralty Island (where in early days few, if any, poles had been erected due to its northerly latitude). As well, he designed and supervised the painting of the raven and eagle motifs (the two Tlingit moieties) for the Naa Kahidi

Theater in the Sealaska Cultural Arts Park in Juneau, and he has several poles there that he either restored or reproduced at the Sitka National Historical Park.

Jackson's poles display his excellent skill with sharp, rounded-off features, especially evident in his ravens. Totems are read from top to bottom and the top figure usually identifies the clan to which the pole belongs. They tell stories of lineage, rites of passage, honor a great person, and can serve as wooden gravestones. Using primarily handmade tools, Jackson roughs out patterns from large trunks then uses smaller tools to carve fine details. Paint is applied to help outline features and enhance details, and Jackson uses the three primary colors of Tlinget totems—bluish green, brownish-red, and black. Formlines are used to delineate figures and such features as eyes and mouths, and emergent lines appear where carved planes meet, often emphasized by change of color. A distinctive feature of Tlinget art is the use of ovals, and a piece is often judged by the skill with which ovals are carved. Jackson is recognized as a master of the oval.

—John Anson Warner

JANVIER, Alex

Tribal affiliations: Chippewa
Painter

Born: Alexandre Simeon Janvier, Le Goff Reserve, Cold Lake First Nations, Alberta, 28 February 1935. **Education:** Southern Alberta Institute of Technology and Art (now the Alberta College of Art), Calgary. **Career:** Art instructor, University of Alberta Extension Department, 1961-63; commercial designer for Alberta Newstart Inc., 1969; incorporates Janvier Murals and Fine Arts, 1972; Arts and Crafts Consultant, Department of Indian Affairs, Ottawa, 1965; cultural advisor for the Indians of Canada Pavilion, *Expo '67,* and formed aboriginal advisory group, which included Jackson Beardy, George Clutesi, Tom Hill, Norval Morrisseau, Duke Redbird, Bill Reid, and Gerald Tailfeathers; Indian Association of Alberta, 1970; Professional Native Indian Artists, Incorporated, or the "Indian Group of Seven," 1973-75 with Daphne Odjig, Jackson Beardy, Eddy Cobiness, George Morrisseau, Carl Ray and Joseph Sanchez; National Indian Arts and Crafts Corporation, 1975-77; represented Canada with artists Betty Goodwin and Chris Reed in a cultural exchange with the Peoples Republic of China, 1985; advisor, and claims disputes in Alberta; numerous commissions, including Indians of Canada of Canada Pavilion, *Expo '67,* Montreal, Quebec, 1967, and National Museum of Man, Ottawa, Ontario, 1978-81. **Awards:** Royal Canadian Academic of Art, 1993.

Individual Exhibitions

1964   Jacox Gallery, Edmonton, Alberta
1966   *Cultural Activities,* Department of Indian and Northern
          Development, Ottawa, Ontario
1970   Framecraft Gallery, Edmonton, Alberta
          Winnipeg Art Gallery, Winnipeg, Manitoba
1973   Edmonton Art Gallery, Edmonton, Alberta
          Pollock Gallery, Toronto, Ontario
          Downstairs Gallery, Edmonton, Alberta

1974   Canue, Edmonton, Alberta
          Framecraft Gallery, Edmonton, Alberta
1975   Calgary Galleries, Calgary, Alberta
1976   Framework Gallery, Edmonton, Alberta
          Johnson Gallery, Edmonton, Alberta
1977   Gallery Moos, Toronto, Ontario
          *Alex Janvier: A New Dialogue Between Native Sensibility
            and Western Tradition,* National Museum of Man, Ottawa, Ontario
          Gallery Stenusgarden, Linkoping, Sweden
1978   *Contemporary Native Art of Canada: Alex Janvier,* Royal
            Ontario Museum, Toronto, Ontario
          West End Gallery, Calgary, Alberta
1979-82 Gallery Moos, Toronto, Ontario
          Hampton Galleries, Pontiac, Michigan
1979-81 Robertson Gallery, Ottawa, Ontario
1981-83 West End Gallery, Edmonton, Alberta
1983   *The Seasons,* National Arts Centre, Ottawa, Ontario
          Soho Mercer Gallery, Ottawa, Ontario
1984-85 Gallery Moos, Toronto, Ontario
          West End Gallery, Edmonton, Alberta
1987   West End Gallery, Edmonton, Alberta
1989   Gallery Moos, Toronto, Ontario
          Apple World, West End Gallery, Edmonton, Alberta
1990   *Inter-tribal Indians Unlimited,* Wallace Galleries, Calgary,
            Alberta
1991   West End Gallery, Edmonton, Alberta
          Classics, Wallace Galleries, Calgary, Alberta
          Gallery 1450, Victoria, British Columbia
1992   Robertson Galleries, Ottawa, Ontario
          Unique Gallery, Grande Praire, Alberta
1993   Yukon Gallery, Yukon, Whitehorse
          *The Art of Alex Janvier: His First Thirty Years, 1960-
            1990,* traveled to Woodland Cultural Centre in
            Brantford, Ontario; Canadian Museum of Civiliza-
            tion, Hull, Quebec; Edmonton Art Gallery,
            Edmonton, Alberta; Mendel Art Gallery, Saskatoon,
            Saskatchewan; Thunder Bay Art Gallery, Thunder
            Bay, Ontario

Selected Group Exhibitions

1950   International Vatican Exhibition, Rome
1965   Jacox Gallery, Edmonton, Alberta
1967   Indian Pavilion, *Expo '67,* Montreal, Quebec
1968   *Contemporary Indian Artists,* organized by the Glenbow
            Museum, Calgary, to tour western Canada
1970   McIntosh Memorial Art Gallery, University of Western
            Ontario, London, Ontario
1972   *Treaty Numbers 23, 287, 1171,* Winnipeg Art Gallery,
            Winnipeg, Manitoba
          Framecraft Gallery, Edmonton, Alberta
1973   Edmonton Art Gallery, Edmonton, Alberta
1974   *Uni-Art,* Edmonton, Alberta
          Gallery Athropos, London, England
          Inukshuk Gallery, Waterloo, Ontario
          Glenbow Institution of Art, Calgary, Alberta
          National Museum of Civilization, Ottawa, Ontario
1975   Traveling exhibition to London, Brussels, Paris, New
            York, Montreal, Toronto
          Dominion Gallery, Montreal, Quebec

Wallack Gallery, Ottawa, Ontario
Art Emporium, Vancouver, British Columbia
1976   *Cinader Collection*, Trent University, Peterborough, Ontario
Glenbow Institute of Art, Calgary, Alberta
1977   *Links to a Tradition*, Indian Affairs and Northern Development, travelling exhibition to Brazil
Contemporary Indian Art: The Trail from the Past to the Future, Mackenzie Gallery and Native Studies Programme, Trent University, Peterborough, Ontario
1982   *Tailfeathers/Sapp/Janvier*, Thunder Bay National Exhibition Centre and Centre for Indian Art, Thunder Bay, Ontario
Renewal: Masterworks of Contemporary Indian Art from the National Museum of Man, Thunder Bay National Exhibition Centre and Centre for Indian Art, Thunder Bay, Ontario
1983   *Contemporary Indian Art at Rideau Hall*, from the collection of the Department of Indian Affairs and Northern Development, Rideau Hall, Ottawa, Ontario
Contemporary Indian and Inuit Art of Canada, travelling exhibition to the United States, opened at the United Nations General Assembly Building, New York
Universiade '83 Kaleidoscope, Edmonton, Alberta
1985   *Two Worlds*, Mackenzie Art Gallery, Regina, Saskatchewan
Challenges, Holland Festival, Amsterdam
1986   West End Gallery, Edmonton, Alberta
New Beginnings, Native Business Summit, Toronto, Ontario
1987   *A Celebration of Contemporary Indian Art*, Southwest Museum, Los Angeles
Eight from the Prairies, Thunder Bay Art Gallery, Thunder Bay, Ontario
Museum of Man, San Diego
1988   *The Spirit of Lubicon*, Wallace Galleries, Calgary, Alberta
Modern Echoes of Ancient Dreams, ArtsCourt, Ottawa, Ontario
Gallery Moos, Toronto, Ontario
1989   *In the Shadow of the Sun*, Canadian Museum of Civilization, Hull, Quebec
1990   Wallace Galleries, Calgary, Alberta
1991   Triangle Gallery, Calgary, Alberta
West End Gallery, Edmonton, Alberta
1992   *The Mentors*, New Gallery, Calgary, Alberta
Land, Spirit, Power: First Nations Art at the National Gallery of Canada, Ottawa, Ontario
Alberts's First Nations: From the Four Directions, Provincial Museum, Edmonton, Alberta
1996   *Recent Acquisitions*, Thunder Bay Art Gallery, Thunder Bay, Ontario

Collections

Alberta Art Foundation, Government of Alberta, Edmonton; Helen E. Band Collection, Toronto, Ontario; Saidye & Samuel Bronfman Memorial Collection, Montreal, Quebec; Canada Council Art Bank, Ottawa, Ontario; Canadian Museum of Civilization, Hull, Quebec; Cinader Collection, Toronto, Ontario; Department of Indian Affairs and Northern Development, Hull, Quebec; Glenbow Museum, Calgary, Alberta; McMichael Canadian Art Collection, Kleinburg,

Ontario; Mendel Art Gallery, Saskatoon, Saskatchewan; Montreal Museum of Fine Art, Quebec; National Museum of Civilization, Ottawa, Ontario; Lester B. Pearson Collection, Ottawa, Ontario; Thunder Bay Art Gallery, Thunder Bay, Ontario; Winnipeg Art Gallery, Winnipeg, Manitoba.

Publications

On JANVIER: Books—*Indian Arts in Canada*, by Olive Dickason, Ottawa, 1972; *Treaty Numbers 23, 287, 1117: Three Indian Painters on the Prairie*, Edmonton, 1972; *Alex Janvier*, Royal Ontario Museum, Toronto, 1978; *The Art of Alex Janvier: His First Thirty Years: 1960-1990*, Thunder Bay Art Gallery, 1993; *In the Shadow of the Sun*, by Gerald McMaster, et al, Hull, Quebec, 1993. **Articles**—"Le Jeune Alex Janvier revele des beaux talents de peintre," by Dollard Morin, *Le Petit Journal*, 1953; "Janvier," *Artwest*, March/April, 1978; "China's Art Touches Janvier," by Phylis Matousek, *The Edmonton Journal*, 17 September 1985; "Alex Janvier," by Jacqueline Fry, *Art Canada*, Vol. XXIX, Autumn 1972; "It's Death and Rebirth," by Tom Hill, *Art Magazine*, Vol. 5, No. 18, Summer 1974; "Alex Janvier: 20th Century Symbols and Images," by Robert Houle, *Native Perspective*, Vol. 2, No. 9, 1978. **Films**—*Canadian Indian Canvas*, Henning Jacobsen Productions, Toronto, Ontario, 1973; *Colours of Pride*, National Film Board of Canada, 1973; *Alex Janvier: The Native Artist*, Alberta Native Communications Society, 1973; *Our Native Land: Alex Janvier*, CBC/CBO, 1983; *Seeing It Our Way: Alex Janvier*, CBC Edmonton, 1984; *Investment in Art*, Alberta Art Foundation, 1991.

*   *   *

Alexandre Simeon Janvier was born on the Le Goff Reserve, Cold Lake First Nations, Alberta. His father, Harry, was one of the last hereditary chiefs on the reserve (until he was deposed by the electoral system in 1947). Alex Janvier was raised in the Chipewyan tradition, speaking the Dene language until he attended the Blue Quill Residential School near St. Paul, Alberta.

In 1956, Janvier began formal art instruction at the Southern Alberta Institute of Technology and Art (now the Alberta College of Art) in Calgary. He graduated, after having won many of the college's awards, in 1960. The artist's formal education in the fine arts was, at the time, the exception rather than the rule. Most of his Native compatriots would be either self-taught or would have received either informal art classes or instruction in commercial art and design.

Following graduation, Janvier accepted a position as an art instructor with the University of Alberta Extension Department that he held for two years. In 1969, he worked for a year as a commercial designer for Alberta Newstart Inc. In 1972, he incorporated Janvier Murals and Fine Arts in an effort to assist the growth of his reputation and activities as an artist.

Subsequent to his work as an art teacher, Janvier held many positions and involved himself with various aboriginal organizations wherein the focus of his efforts would meld the artistic and cultural heritage of the First Nations in Canada. In 1965, Janvier became the arts and crafts consultant at the Department of Indian Affairs in Ottawa. Also in 1965, Janvier was chosen to be the cultural advisor for the Indians of Canada Pavilion, *Expo '67*, Montreal. He pulled together an aboriginal advisory group that included Jackson Beardy, George Clutesi, Tom Hill, Norval Morrisseau, Duke Redbird, Bill Reid, and Gerald Tailfeathers. In

1970, Janvier worked for the Indian Association of Alberta. Some years later, Janvier was invited by Daphne Odjig, Jackson Beardy, and Eddy Cobiness to join in their informal discussions about the future interpretations, marketing, and production of Native art. The group formalized themselves in 1973 as the Professional Native Indian Artists Incorporated, or the "Indian Group of Seven." Morrisseau, Carl Ray and Joseph Sanchez joined Odjig, Beardy, Cobiness and Janvier to organize exhibitions, develop proposals for the establishment of a scholarship program, control the marketing of their work, and develop a strategy to educate the public about their work. The group disbanded in 1975. That same year, the Department of Indian Affairs created the National Indian Arts and Crafts Corporation to assist in the marketing of Native art. Janvier was asked to become a member of its advisory committee. Following much controversy between the federal government and the artist members over the procedures recommended by the government to mass-produce Native art, the group disbanded in 1977. Today, Janvier works in Alberta, helping to settle land claims disputes in the province.

In recognition of his politicization, Janvier spent much of his career—from 1961 through 1977—signing his paintings with his treaty number only. The activity was ceased when Janvier felt it was no longer having any effect on the bureaucracy he was fighting against.

Throughout Janvier's artistic career, his work has seldom wavered from his commitment to produce work that uses an abstract vocabulary. It has been said that the basis of this work is a combined interest in his ancestral roots—in his knowledge of traditional abstraction in bead and quillwork, and in his formal (Western) art training—from which Janvier gained a knowledge of modernist abstraction and automatic painting by observing the work of Wassily Kandinsky, Paul Klee, and Joan Miro. In the last few years, particularly in works dating from 1990 and under the collective title the *Apple* series, however, the artist has begun to reintroduce a representational element similar to that evident in his some of his paintings from the early 1960s. Regardless of genre, line has remained the principal compositional element in Janvier's oeuvre. The artist has used line dually to articulate both form and content, to be both expressive and stabilizing.

The content of Janvier's paintings have changed and metamorphosized over the years, often reflecting the social and political interests and concerns of Janvier at the time of their production. Art mimicking life. In the 1960s, Janvier's work focused on images of rodeos, pow wows, the landscape, government politics and reserve communities. By the 1970s, however, following the politicization of Canadian society at the time, Janvier's work revealed growing political insights. The paintings often commented on the relationship between the First Nations peoples and federal and provincial government practices in Canada. By the late 1970s and throughout the 1980s, Janvier would increasingly address environmental, political, and religious issues.

In 1985, Janvier was chosen, along with artists Betty Goodwin and Chris Reed, to represent Canada in a cultural exchange with the Peoples Republic of China. Martin has noted that the trip profoundly affected Janvier's subsequent production. The artist's experience in the Peoples Republic precipitated a breakthrough in terms of both form and content that informs the artist's work to this day. In terms of themes, Janvier began to celebrate the reawakening of aboriginal culture. In terms of form, Janvier's compositions began to exhibit a looser gesture, freer forms, and a melding of colour areas.

Throughout his long and illustrious career in the Canadian art world and in association with aboriginal political and cultural organizations, Janvier has remained true to a personal philosophy he articulated in 1965 when he was arts and crafts consultant to the Department of Indian Affairs: "take pride in individual achievements; combine new techniques with older traditions; and do not allow the works to become exploited and mass-produced." Following these ideals, Janvier has become ensconced in the Canadian art world as an innovator and mentor. As Saulteaux artist and curator Robert Houle remarked on the occasion of Janvier's 1993 Retrospective exhibition, "Alex Janvier is a member of the Dene Nation, whose nomadic nobility is linguistically related to the Athapaskan speaking Navajo of the American southwest. From the land of the Dene, the strangers of the western subarctic, Janvier has brought the ambiguity of immaterial forces: light and shadow, fragility and strength, life and death, destructive power and transformative forces. These dual energies are not mystic; they are the materiality with which art is current, strategic, and political. This is the Janvier legacy."

—Carol Podedworny

JEMISON, G. Peter
Tribal affiliations: Seneca
Painter

Born: Gerald Peter Jemison, Silver Creek, New York, 18 January 1945. **Education:** University of Siena, Siena, Italy, 1964; State University of New York, Buffalo, B.S. in art education, 1967. **Career:** Site manager, Ganondagan, a restored Seneca town that thrived in the seventeenth century; director, American Indian Community House, New York; curator, including *Women of Sweetgrass, Cedar, and Sage*; lecturer; conference participant and panelist; President of the Council of Regents, Institute of American Indian Arts.

Individual Exhibitions

1973	American Art, New York
1976	*INCA Exhibition*, Native American Center for the Living Arts, Niagara Falls, New York
1982	Philadelphia Art Alliance, Philadelphia, Pennsylvania
1984	C. N. Gorman Museum, University of California, Davis
1985	Sacred Circle Gallery, Seattle, Washington
1987	*Mid-Career Retrospective: G. Peter Jemison*, Museum of the Plains Indian, Browning, Montana
	East West Shop, Victor, New York

Selected Group Exhibitions

1964	Annotecca Siena, Italy
1965	Albright-Knox Art Gallery, Buffalo, New York
1968	Tibor de Nagy Gallery, New York
1969	State University of New York, Buffalo
1971	*Contemporary American Indian Art*, Museum of the American Indian, New York
1972	Brooklyn Museum, Brooklyn, New York
1975	St. Bonaventure University, Olean, New York

1977   *Iroquois Art,* Dortmund, Germany; Arnot Art Museum, Elmira, New York

1979   *Resurgence,* Morris Museum, Morristown, New Jersey
        American Indian Community House, New York
        The Real People, Casa de los Americanos, Havana, Cuba

1980   Via Gambaro Gallery, Washington, D.C.
        Iroquois/Orenda/Vision, American Indian Community House Gallery, New York
        Dialogues, Just above Midtown Gallery, New York

1981   *Confluence of Tradition and Change,* C. N. Gorman Museum, University of California, Davis (traveling)
        American Indian Art of the '80s, Native American Center for the Living Arts, Niagara Falls, New York
        Sacred Circle Gallery, Seattle, Washington

1982   Pennsylvania State Museum, Harrisburg

1983   *6 Nations 7,* Emily and Joe Lowe Gallery, Syracuse University, New York
        Friends of Philbrook, Philbrook Museum of Art, Tulsa, Oklahoma
        Marilyn Butler Gallery, Santa Fe, New Mexico
        New Directions, Gallery 10, New York
        Janet Fleisher Gallery, Philadelphia, Pennsylvania

1984   *New Native American Aesthetic,* Marilyn Butler Gallery, Santa Fe, New Mexico
        C. N. Gorman Museum, University of California, Davis
        Common Heritage: Contemporary Iroquois Artists, Queens Museum, Flushing, New York
        Art Against Apartheid, Henry Street Settlement, New York
        No Beads, No Trinkets, Palais des Nations, Geneva, Switzerland
        Museum of Fine Arts, Santa Fe, New Mexico

1985   *New Ideas from Old Traditions,* Yellowstone Art Center, Santa Fe, New Mexico
        Southwest Museum, Los Angeles, California
        Four Native American Painters, Wooster Art Museum, Wooster, Ohio
        Cowboys and Indians, Common Ground, Boca Raton Museum of Art and Loch Haven Art Center, Orlando, Florida

1986   *The Arts of the North American Indian: Native Traditions in Evolution,* Philbrook Museum of Art, Tulsa, Oklahoma (traveling)
        We are always turning around on purpose, traveling in New York, Massachusetts, and Oklahoma

1987   *Double Take,* Fine Art Gallery, Kansas City, Missouri
        Portrait of Buffalo II, Bethune Gallery, Buffalo, New York
        We the People, Artists Space, New York

1988   *Indian Art '88,* Woodland Indian Cultural Education Center, Brantford, Ontario

1990   *Our Land/Ourselves,* University Art Gallery, State University of New York, Albany (traveling through 1991)

1992   *The Sublumoc Show/Columbus Wohs,* organized by Atlatl, Phoenix, Arizona (traveling)
        Shared Visions: Native American Painters and Sculptors of the Twentieth Century, Heard Museum, Phoenix, Arizona

1994   *Volume I, Book Arts by Native American Artists,* American Indian Community House Gallery, New York
        The Artist as Native, Babcock Galleries, New York

1995   *Native Survival: Responses to HIV/AIDS,* American Indian Community House Gallery/Museum, New York
        Members Gallery, Albright Knox Art Gallery, Buffalo, New York

1996   *Native Streams: Contemporary Native American Art,* Jan Cicero Gallery, Chicago, and Turman Art Gallery, Indiana State University, Terre Haute (traveling through 1997)

Collections

American Indian Community House Museum, New York; Heard Museum, Phoenix, Arizona; Museum of the Plains Indian, Browning, Montana; Schoharie Museum of the Iroquois Indian, Schoharie, New York.

Publications

On JEMISON: Books—*Confluences of Tradition and Change,* edited by L. Price Amerson, University of California, Davis, 1980; *The Sweet Grass Lives On,* by Jamake Highwater, New York, 1980; "Frames of Reference: Native American Art in the Context of Modern and Postmodern Art," by Gerhard Hoffmann; *The Arts of the North American Indian: Native Traditions in Evolution,* edited by Edwin L. Wade, New York, 1986; *Indian Art '88,* by Tom Hill, Woodland Indian Cultural Education Center, Brantford, Ontario, 1988; *Our Land/Ourselves,* edited by Deborah Ward, Albany, 1990; *Shared Visions: Native American Painters and Sculptors in the Twentieth Century,* by Margaret Archuleta and Dr. Rennard Strickland, New York, New Press, 1991; *The Sublumoc Show/Columbus Wohs,* edited by Carla Roberts, Atlatl, Phoenix, 1992; *I Stand in the Center of Good,* by Lawrence Abbott, Lincoln, Nebraska, 1994; *Native Streams: Contemporary Native American Art,* Jan Cicero Gallery, Chicago, and Turman Art Gallery, Indiana State University, Terre Haute, 1996. **Articles**—"23 Contemporary Artists," by Lloyd Oxendine, *Art in America,* Summer 1972; "Review," by Kay Larson, *Village Voice,* 22 October 1980; "Common Ground," by Kay Larson, *New York Magazine,* 20 June 1983; "Native Intelligence," by Lucy Lippard, *Village Voice,* 27 December 1983; "One Man's Grocery Bag Is Another Man's Canvas," by Robert A. Masallo, *The Sacramento Bee,* 19 February 1984; "Modern Works of American Indians," by Grace Glueck, *New York Times,* 30 November 1984.

*   *   *

Many of the contemporary American Indian artists see their work no longer simply as a work of art or themselves as artists with purely aesthetic concerns. They feel the necessity of finding and defining their identity as Indian artists before making statements through their art. G. Peter Jemison belongs in this category of Native American artists in search of their communal bases. Having been raised on the Cattaraugus Seneca Indian Reservation in New York State and having studied at the State University of New York at Buffalo, as well as the University of Siena, Italy, Jemison has lived in different worlds with different cultures. He has experienced reservation life and life in big cities, he is familiar with the old masters as well as with modern Western artists (Rauschenberg, Schwitters in particular) and he has learned from traditional as well as modern American Indian painters. Nevertheless, for some time he had the feeling that something was missing and that he had to go back to the roots of his Senecan tradition for a spiritual renewance and a sense of community.

Returning home from New York City was, in his own words, "a redemption by nature," and it was to nature that he turned now for

G. Peter Jemison: *Turtle Island Bag.* Photograph by Rick Hill.

inspiration and with a renewed feeling of responsibility. His art-work became more concerned with the natural world, which he no longer depicted from photographs but from the personal experience of being there within it. Moreover, he became conscious of the waste of natural resources, the number of trees it takes to produce paper bags, which are carelessly thrown away as refuse, and so he decided to make a statement through art by painting on ordinary shopping bags that he had made from handmade paper or paper that he had found. This was the beginning of his well-known *Bag Series*. Bags appealed to Jemison also because of the broader impli-cations associated with them. They were, on the one hand, humor-ous and temporal and they could also be made to carry a message. One piece, *Hunger on Reservations While Children in Africa Starve* (1981), was made from a grocery bag and was intended to remind people of the existence of misery in a world of plenty.

Much of Jemison's work has a political implications. Even though he insists that he is not an activist, he also agrees that he is politi-cally involved in the wider sense that the very act of making Indian art is political. Life on the reservation is an important issue for Jemison, and through his images he wants to make a comment on what is happening there. In a montage of 1990, *Buffalo Road III—Choices*, a huge painted buffalo is the backdrop for about twenty smaller images, some of them photographs, that are icons of the past as well as present day life on and off the reservation. This work, according to the artist, grew out of what happened on the Mohawk territories that year and was meant to reflect "the choices that seemed to be presented to us at this point in time. The issue of gambling casinos on our reservations versus a traditional way of life, the issue of the sovereignty of our nations, and ... all the mate-rial trappings" (from *I Stand in the Center of Good,* 1994). Such images are meant to make people understand that they are living in a critical time.

Jemison understands art as a way of communicating. He has a great respect and reverence for Indian painters before him—Dick West, Allan Houser, Fred Kabotie. These artists, he feels, commu-nicated more about Native Americans through their works than all the books that were written about them. The problem at the present is, as Jemison sees it, that Native art is being ignored or misunder-stood by white Americans who don't see Indians as what they are. Indian art, therefore, is not an end in itself; it is an important mani-festation of the Indian people and their way of thinking.

—Gerhard and Gisela Hoffmann

JOJOLA, Tony
Tribal affiliations: Isleta Pueblo
Glassblower

Born: Anthony T. Jojola, Albuquerque, New Mexico, 11 August 1958. **Education:** Haystack Mountain School of Crafts, Maine, 1977; Institute of American Indian Arts in Santa Fe, New Mexico, 1978; Pilchuck Glass School, Seattle, Washington, 1978, 1980-81, 1985-86; summer workshops, apprenticeship/internship to Dale Chihuly; College of Santa Fe, New Mexico, B.F.A., 1983; work-shop with Lino Tagliapiltra, Marseille, France, 1991. **Career:** Art-ist-in-Residence, Haystack Mountain School of Crafts, 1981; as-sistant to Dale Chihuly and William Morris; instructor, Institute of American Indian Arts, 1983. **Awards:** Grants from Southwestern

Association on Indian Affairs, Santa Fe, New Mexico, 1986, and Creative Glass Center of America, Wheaton Villages, New Jersey, 1988.

Individual Exhibitions

1979   Indian Pueblo Cultural Center, Albuquerque, New Mexico
1988   Southern Plains Indian Museum, Anadarko, Oklahoma
1990   Indian Pueblo Cultural Center, Albuquerque, New Mexico
1997   *Tony Jojola: Lasia-Glass,* Soumen Lasimuseuo, Helsinki, Finland

Selected Group Exhibitions

1981   Heard Museum, Phoenix, Arizona
1982   Isleta Arts and Crafts Exhibit, Isleta Pueblo, New Mexico
1983   *Institute of American Indian Arts Alumni Show,* Santa Fe, New Mexico
1984   *Red Cloud Indian Art Show,* Browning, Montana
1986   Fuller Lodge Art Center, Los Alamos, New Mexico
1987   Red Cloud Indian Art Show, Browning, Montana
        United States Department of Interior, Indian Arts and Crafts Board, Southern Plains Indian Museum and Crafts Center, Anadarko, Oklahoma
1988   Eileen Kremen Gallery, Fullerton, California
        Southern Alleghenies Museum of Art, Loretto, Pennsyl-vania
        Creative Glass Center of America, Heller Gallery, Soho, New York
1989   Isleta Arts and Crafts Exhibit, Isleta Pueblo, New Mexico
1990   *Crafts from the American Southwest,* Society for Art and Crafts, Pittsburgh, Pennsylvania
1992   Heard Museum, Phoenix, Arizona
        From the Earth VII, American Indian Contemporary Arts, San Francisco, California
        Native America: Reflecting Contemporary Realities, Craft and Folk Art Museum, Los Angeles, California
1993   Millicent Rogers Foundation Museum, Taos, New Mexico
1994   *Artists Who Are Indian,* Denver Art Museum, Denver, Colorado
        Native American Contemporary Realities, Warm Springs, California (traveling)
1995   Poeh Museum, Pojaque, New Mexico
1996   *Native Streams: Contemporary Native American Art,* Jan Cicero Gallery, Chicago, Illinois, and Turman Art Gal-lery, Indiana State University, Terre Haute, Indiana (traveling through 1997)

Collections

Institute of American Indian Arts Museum, Santa Fe, New Mexico; Museum of Indian Arts and Culture, Santa Fe, New Mexico; South-ern Plains Indian Museum, Anadarko, Oklahoma.

Publications

On JOJOLA: Books—*Native Streams: Contemporary Native American Art,* Chicago, Jan Cicero Gallery, and Terre Haute, Turman Art Gallery, 1996. **Articles**—"Anthony Jojola," by Gail Bird, *In-dian Market Magazine,* August 1988; "When Glass was King," by

Tony Jojola: Water jar. Courtesy of the artist.

Mark Cesarano, *Gloucester County Times* (Woodbury, New Jersey), 13 September 1988; "Will Success Spoil Art Society?," by Robert Silberman, *American Craft,* August/September 1990; "Glass Soldier Vies for Spot in Art Battle," by John Villani, *The Santa Fe New Mexican,* 15 August 1991. **Film**—*Indian Market: A Winter Event,* Southwestern Association on Indian Affairs, Inc., 1989.

*

Tony Jojola comments (1996):
  I rely on my Native American culture to create our old traditional and ceremonial forms such as seed jars, basket forms, ollas (water containers) in glass. To me, that seems like giving my culture an even longer existence. Pueblo people have always created in clay. I feel that glass relates to clay very strongly. To me, glass is like clay you can't touch. I have found that the best way to get from the idea to paper to reality is the team method. I will continue using the team method approach to achieve my ideas. My Native American culture gives me endless inspiration, so much so that I know I will never be able to create all that I have in mind. This is why each piece is very different. A few may be similar in form, but each varies in color and design, making each a unique piece of art. The work shown portrays a variety of the old forms that my culture has respected throughout time. (From the *Native Streams* catalog)

*   *   *

His vessels take the shape of pots from his native Isleta Pueblo, but they are formed in glass with breath and heat, not in clay by human hands. Anthony Jojola's choice of blown glass as a medium makes him unique among Native American artists, historic and contemporary. But if his medium is new, his inspirations are classic—the utilitarian forms of seed jars, baskets, and ollas, the symbol-laden images of rain and desert creatures.

Jojola was born in Albuquerque in 1958 and raised in the nearby Pueblo of Isleta. He still lives in Isleta, in a small house that belonged to his grandfather. Art runs in the family, and when Jojola was very young he watched his grandfather make jewelry. Other family members made pottery, and he would dabble in clay when he wasn't stretching silver for his grandfather. But it wasn't until he saw blown glass at the Institute of American Indian Arts that he found his true medium.

When Jojola move to Santa Fe to attend the IAIA in 1975, glass was a much-neglected medium. In 1971, renowned glass artist Dale

Chihuly built a small studio at the school in return for the Institute's exhibit of his native-inspired glasswork. The studio foundered, however, for lack of instructors and students. In 1975, a sculptor took over the studio and taught Jojola the basic skills of glass blowing. Another teacher noticed Jojola's enthusiasm and talent for the medium and suggested he apply to Chihuly's Pilchuck Glass School in Seattle, Washington. Jojola accepted the challenge, and in 1978 he became one of the first Native American students at the school. Jojola became Chihuly's apprentice in 1980. A year later, he started working on his own, using designs inspired by Isleta pottery.

At first, peers and patrons didn't know what to make of Jojola's glass vessels. "For the first few years, I received mixed reactions," Jojola said. "A lot of people thought it was really cool, but some asked, 'why aren't you doing pottery?'" Gradually Jojola received recognition as a glass blower and as a contemporary Native American artist. In 1991, he was selected to participate in the Heard Museum's Fifth Biennial Native American Fine Arts Invitational, where he exhibited *Night Keeper*, a radiant blue olla graced at the mouth by a blue glass serpent.

Jojola manages his own career and handles packing, shipping, client relations and promotion from his home in Isleta. Since there is no longer a studio at IAIA, Jojola makes annual pilgrimages from Isleta to Seattle, where he works with a hired crew to create a body of work based on previously-completed drawings. His techniques for decorating the glass includes sandblasting, electroforming, Graal overlay, and casting. The process is demanding, and Jojola relies on a team of experts to follow his directions. The finished products are elegant, brilliantly-colored vessels. Some of his forms adhere to conservative potted shapes, while others are swollen and distended, suggesting a cultural overflow or modern fullness not feasible with clay.

When he is not in Seattle or traveling to art shows, he applies pencil to paper to develop new designs. Like clay, glass is a medium with nearly infinite possibilities. Recently, Jojola has experimented with alternate shapes and processes, including lizard and bear fetishes made of solid glass. A ten-foot tall sculpture he fashioned from steel and glass graces the east yard of Santa Fe's Museum of Indian Arts and Culture.

Since the mid-1980s, Jojola has shown his wares at Santa Fe's annual Indian Market, where he requests customers to refer to his works as "pieces, not "pots," in recognition of their unique medium. His work is so distinctive, in fact, that he is forced to enter it as "Miscellaneous" in the annual Market competition. Because there is so little competition in this category, and because of the amazing quality, of course, Jojola routinely takes a top prize. Winning feels good, Jojola says, but at this point he would like some competition, and he takes every opportunity to encourage young Native artists to pursue the medium of hot glass.

—Margaret Dubin

JONES, Ruthe Blalock

Variant names: Chu-Lun-Dit
Tribal affiliations: Delaware; Shawnee; Peoria
Painter

Born: Claremore, Oklahoma, 8 June 1939. **Education:** Bacone College, AA, 1970; BFA in Painting, University of Tulsa, 1972;

University of Oklahoma, Museum Studies, 1985; Northeastern State University, MS, Humanities/Fine Arts, 1989. **Career:** Director of Art Department, Bacone College, Muskogee, Oklahoma, 1979-present; Associate Professor of Art, 1989-present; Juror, Red Earth Indian Arts Festival, 1989, Southwest Association of Indian Arts, Santa Fe, New Mexico, 1990; panelist, Forum on Indian Arts & Craft Act of 1990, Oklahoma City, Oklahoma, 1990, (moderator) "Traditional Culture in Native American Art," Oklahoma Historical Society, 1991,"Woodland Focus," Institute of American Indian Arts, 1995; Guest Artist, International Symposium on Polyaesthetic Culture, Salzburg, Austria, 1990; Co-Curator, "Native American Invitational & Oklahoma Masters," Gilcrease Museum, Tulsa, Oklahoma, 1995; Guest Artist, American Indian Cultural Awareness, University of Tulsa, Oklahoma; advisor, National Museum of Natural History, Smithsonian Institute, Washington, D.C.; Official Logo Design, Bacone College, 1992. **Awards:** Governor's Art Award, State of Oklahoma, Oklahoma City, Oklahoma, 1993; Oklahoma Women's Hall of Fame, State of Oklahoma, 1995; Woman of the Year, Oklahoma Federation of Indian Women, 1995; honors at juried shows, including Red Earth Indian Arts Festival, Oklahoma City, Oklahoma, 1987, Southwest Association of Indian Arts (SWAIA), Santa Fe, New Mexico, 1989-91, Tulsa Indian Summer Fest, "Best of Show," 1991, Philbrook Museum, "Best of Show," Tulsa, Oklahoma, 1993, Crumbo Memorial Award, SWAIA, Santa Fe, New Mexico, 1994; *Contemporary North American Indian Art* exhibit poster ("Shawl Women"), 1982.

Selected Group Exhibitions

1964	*International Indian Art Show and Handicraft Trade Fair*, sponsored by the Foundation of North American Indian Culture, Bismark, North Dakota
1964-65	*First Annual Invitational Exhibition of American Indian Paintings*, sponsored by the American Indian College Foundation, Charlotte, North Carolina
1967	*Biennial Exhibition of American Indian Arts and Crafts*, U.S. Department of the Interior, Washington, D.C.
1975	*Contemporary Indian Art Invitational*, Oregon State University, Corvallis, Oregon (traveling)
1980	*Centenial Touring Exhibit*, Bacone College, Bacone, Oklahoma (traveling)
1982	*Night of the First Americans*, Kennedy Center, Washington, D.C.
1985	*Daughters of the Earth: Works by Eight Native American Artists* (traveling)
1987	*Red Earth Indian Festival*, Myriad Plaza, Oklahoma City, Oklahoma
1992	*Pow-Wow Pride*, Wheelwright Museum, Santa Fe, New Mexico
	Benefit Exhibit for the Museum of the American Indian of Washington, D.C., Aspen, Colorado
1993	*Moving the Fire*, State Arts Council of Oklahoma, Official State Event for the Presidential Inauguration, Washington, D.C.
	The Women Students of Dick West, The University of Kansas, Lawrence, Kansas
1993-96	*Oklahoma Indian Art*, American Indian Heritage Center and the Philbrook Museum, Tulsa, Oklahoma
1994	*Tucson Indian Days*, Tucson, Arizona
	Watchful Eyes, Heard Museum, Phoenix, Arizona

Ruthe Blalock Jones: *Round Dance,* 1992. Courtesy of the artist.

Earth Works X, American Indian Contemporary Arts Gallery, San Francisco, California

Moving Murals of Oklahoma: Contemporary Native American Painting, Jacobson Foundation, Norman, Oklahoma (traveling)

1995   *Generations Exhibit*, Oscar Jacobson House, Norman, Oklahoma

Oklahoma Indian Painting, Thomas Gilcrease Institute of American History and Art, Tulsa, Oklahoma

Collections

Amerindian Circle, Washington, D.C.; Bacone College, Bacone, Oklahoma; The Five Civilized Tribes Museum, Muskogee, Oklahoma; Heard Museum, Phoenix, Arizona; Minnetrista Cultural Center, Muncie, Indiana; Museum of the American Indian, New York, New York; Northeastern State University, Tahlequah, Oklahoma; Okmulgee Independent School District, Okmulgee, Oklahoma; Philbrook Museum of Art, Tulsa, Oklahoma; Southwest Plains Indian Museum, U.S. Department of Interior, Anadarko, Oklahoma; The John H. Williams Center for the Performing Arts, Tulsa, Oklahoma.

Publications

By JONES: Essay—"Like Being Home," *Oklahoma Indian Painting,* Gilcrease Journal, Gilcrease Museum, Tulsa, Oklahoma, 1995.

Around 1994 Blalock Jones participated in an oral history project organized by Joan Frederick. Backed by a National Endowment for the Humanities fellowship funded by the Council for Basic Education (CBE), Frederick garnered a group of oral histories and remembrances from six traditionalist painters (and one descendant of the Kiowa Five). Apart from Jones, the participants were Dick West, Rance Hood, Leonard Black Moon Riddles, Doc Tate Nevaquaya, and Dennis Belindo (plus Vanessa Morgan Jennings, granddaughter of Stephen Mopope). Each one of these individuals contributed an extensive record of his or her experiences, memories, family histories, and so on. These oral histories are now ensconced as archives in the Western History Collections at the University of Oklahoma in Norman.

On JONES: Books—*Indian Painters and White Patrons,* by J. J. Brody, Albuquerque, 1971; *Minimyths and Legends of Oklahoma Indians*, by Lucelia Wise, Oklahoma City, 1978; *Bacone Indian University: A History*, by John Williams and Howard Meredith, Muskogee, 1980; *Keepers of Culture, Thoughts of a Southeastern Indian Artist,* Museum of Natural History, Anniston, Alabama, 1990; *Kiowa Art*, Muskogee Public Library, Muskogee, Oklahoma, 1992; *The Native Americans*, Turner Publishing, Atlanta, Georgia, 1993; *Watchful Eyes: Native American Women Artists,* Heard Museum, Phoenix, 1994. **Articles**—"Ruthe Blalock Jones," *Chronicles of Oklahoma*, Spring, 1980; "Traditional Painting in Oklahoma," by Joan Frederick, *Natives Peoples Magazine*, Summer, 1995.

*   *   *

An active painter and a prominent educator, Ruthe Blalock Jones is a major force in the Indian art world of Oklahoma. Jones, who sees herself as an artist who records the joys and experiences of a lifetime of attending and participating in traditional Indian social gatherings, is a contemporary exponent of the traditionalist approach in Oklahoma Indian painting. Jones has come full circle in her life insofar as she obtained her Associate in Arts degree at Bacone College (1970) and is now back there as Associate Professor of Art and Director of the institution's art program.

Jones was a student of the late W. Richard (Dick) West, Sr., who guided the learning process of countless numbers of young student proteges at Bacone and Haskell Institute in Lawrence, Kansas. West taught his students to be open to new approaches in art but also to have a concern for historical accuracy, fidelity to tribal customs, and precision in the execution of any work of art. Jones was not only taught by her mentor but chose, also, to prefer his traditionalist approach to Indian painting. Bacone College tradition is very important in the history of Oklahoma Indian painting, and now Jones is the trustee of that tradition. Indeed, Margaret Archuleta and Rennard Strickland, in their volume, *Shared Visions: Native American Painters and Sculptors in the Twentieth Century* (1991), argue for "The Bacone Period, 1935-Present," a major subdivision in the development of Native American art. According to Archuleta and Strickland, "The Bacone Period can be defined stylistically as using complex design elements in a decorative manner to "romance" in the past. The mythology was presented with a sense of the theatrical and the mysterious." Jones' stewardship of this tradition is no small matter in the context of Indian painting in Oklahoma. Naturally, she is bringing her own views and distinctive contributions to this task.

Around 1994 Jones participated in an oral history project organized by Joan Frederick. Backed by a National Endowment for the Humanities fellowship funded by the Council for Basic Education (CBE), Frederick garnered a group of oral histories and remembrances from six traditionalist painters (and one descendant of the Kiowa Five). Apart from Jones, the participants were Dick West,

Rance Hood, Leonard Black Moon Riddles, Doc Tate Nevaquaya, and Dennis Belindo (plus Vanessa Morgan Jennings, granddaughter of Stephen Mopope). Each one of these individuals contributed an extensive record of his or her experiences, memories, and family histories. These oral histories are now ensconced as archives in the Western History Collections at the University of Oklahoma in Norman. It is hoped, Frederick has written, that this collection "will someday influence young Indian artists to take up painting in the traditional manner and keep the old ways, revere them, and perpetuate them for their descendants, keeping them alive in good relation to all things."

As an active artist and an educational leader, Jones has an extremely active career. She has contributed illustrations to several books and articles, curated Indian art exhibitions, served as panelist at symposia, and assisted as juror in art competitions. Jones' success serves to make the point, sociologically speaking, that women have come a long ways in the post-World War II era in Oklahoma Indian art. There was a time when the would-be Kiowa artist (potentially making the group known as the Kiowa Five, the Kiowa Six), Lois Smoky, was discouraged by her tribal elders from pursuing a professional art career. But sociocultural change has now made it possible for many women to become successful artists, and Jones is a symbol of that kind of Progressive change. As an indication of that success, she was named in 1995 as the "Oklahoma Indian Woman of the Year" by the Oklahoma Federation of Women.

—John Anson Warner

KABOTIE, Fred

Variant names: Naqavoy'ma; Tawawiiseoma
Tribal affiliations: Hopi
Painter and muralist

Born: Naqavoy'ma (Day after Day; also transliterated as Nakayoma) in Shungopovi, Second Mesa, Arizona, 20 February 1900; also called Tawawiiseoma (Trailing Sun). **Education:** Indian school in Santa Fe; Santa Fe High School. **Career:** Book binder and painter, School of American Research, Santa Fe; participated in archaeological digs; commissioned in 1927 by the Heye Foundation to record details of Hopi ceremonials for the Museum of American Indian Art, New York; managed the Fred Harvey Company's gift shop at Lookout Studio in the Grand Canyon National Park; shepherd; initiated into the Wuwtsimt men's society; commissioned by René D'Harnoncourt, director of the Museum of Modern Art in New York, to reproduce kiva murals from the village of Awatobi, late 1930s; completed redrawings of prehistoric Mimbres ceramic designs and interpretations for his publication, *Designs from the Ancient Mimbreños*; created several murals for the Grand Canyon National Park (at Desert View Inn in 1933, Painted Desert Inn in 1948, and at Bright Angel Lodge in 1958); taught art at the Hopi High School in Oraibi, 1937-59; United States Goodwill Ambassador to Indian, 1960; community-based projects, 1959-86, including Hopi Craft Guild and Cultural Center; commissioned for a mural by the Museum of New Mexico in 1976 to mark the U.S. bicentennial. **Awards:** Numerous, including InterTribal Indian Ceremonials Grand Award, Gallup, New Mexico; Philbrook Art Center Grand Award; Guggenheim Fellowship, 1945; Indian Achievement Medal, Indian Council Fire of Chicago, 1949; Palmes d'Academiques, France, 1954; Certificate of Appreciation, Indian Arts and Crafts Board, 1958. **Died:** 28 February 1986.

Selected Group Exhibitions

1925   *American Indian Painting and Applied Arts*, Arts Club of Chicago, Illinois
1928   Museum of the American Indian, Heye Foundation, New York (now National Museum of the American Indian, Smithsonian Institution, Washington, D.C.)
1931   *Exposition of Indian Tribal Arts*, sponsored by the College Art Association (traveled through 1933)
1941   *American Indian Art of the United States*, Museum of Modern Art, New York
1947   *American Indian Paintings from the Permanent Collection*, Philbrook Museum (traveled through 1965)
1955   European tour, organized by the University of Oklahoma, Norman
1958   European tour, organized by the University of Oklahoma, Norman
1976   *Destruction of San Bartolome Church at Shungopovi, Hopi*, Museum of New Mexico, Santa Fe
1978   *100 Years of Native American Painting*, Oklahoma Museum of Art, Oklahoma City
1981   *Native American Painting*, organized by the Amarillo Art Center, Texas (traveled through 1983)
1984   *Indianascher Kunstler*, organized by the Philbrook Museum, Tulsa, Oklahoma (traveled in Germany)
1985   *The Hunt and the Harvest*, Paintings from the Museum of the American Indian, New York, organized by the Gallery Association of New York State (traveling)
1986   *When the Rainbow Touches Down*, Heard Museum, Phoenix, Arizona (traveling)
1991   *Shared Visions: Native American Painters and Sculptors in the Twentieth Century*, Heard Museum, Phoenix (traveled through 1993)

Collections

Amerind Foundation, Dragoon, Arizona; Bureau of Indian Affairs, United States Department of the Interior, Washington, D.C.; Elkus Collection of American Indian Arts and Artifacts, California Academy of Sciences, San Francisco; Cincinnati Art Museum, Cincinnati, Ohio; Corcoran Gallery of Art, Washington, D.C.; Columbus Gallery of Fine Arts, Columbus, Ohio; Cleveland Museum of Art, Ohio; Colorado Springs Fine Art Center, Colorado; Denver Art Museum, Denver, Colorado; Dartmouth College Collection, Hanover, New Hampshire; Thomas Gilcrease Institute of American History and Art, Tulsa, Oklahoma; Heard Museum, Phoenix, Arizona; Museum of Modern Art, New York City; Museum of New Mexico, Santa Fe; Museum of Northern Arizona, Flagstaff; Peabody Museum, Harvard University, Cambridge, Massachusetts; Philbrook Art Center, Tulsa, Oklahoma; Millicent Rogers Foundation Museum, Taos, New Mexico; Tweed Museum of Art, Duluth, Minnesota; Univeristy of Oklahoma, Norman, Oklahoma; Smithsonian Institution, Washington, D.C.; Woolaroc Museum, Bartlesville, Oklahoma; Wheelright Museum of the American Indian, Santa Fe.

Publications

By KABOTIE: Books—*Designs from the Ancient Mimbreños*, Grabhorn Press, San Francisco, 1949; *Fred Kabotie: Hopi Indian Artist*, with Bill Belknap, Northland Press and the Museum of Northern Arizona, Flagstaff, 1977.

On KABOTIE: Books—*Introduction to American Indian Art* by John Sloan and Oliver La Farge, Exposition of Indian Tribal Arts, Inc., New York, 1931; *American Indian Painting of the Southwest*

Fred Kabotie: *Tashaf Kachina Dance.* Courtesy Philbrook Museum of Art.

and Plains Areas by Dorothy Dunn, University of New Mexico, Albuquerque, 1968; *Indian Painters and White Patrons* by J.J. Brody, University of New Mexico Press, Albuquerque, 1971; *100 Years of Native American Painting*, exhibition catalog by Arthur Silberman, Oklahoma Museum of Art, Oklahoma City, 1978; *Hopi Painting: The World of the Hopis* by Patricia J. Broder, E.P. Dutton, New York, 1978; *The Arts of the North American Indian: Native Traditions in Evolution*, edited by Edwin L. Wade, Hudson Hills Press, New York, in association with Philbrook Art Center, Tulsa, Oklahoma, 1986; *When the Rainbow Touches Down*, exhibition catalog by Tryntje Van Ness Seymour, Heard Museum, University of Washington Press, 1988; *Shared Visions: Native American Painters and Sculptors in the Twentieth Century* by Margaret Archuleta and Dr. Rennard Strickland, New Press, New York, 1991. **Articles—** "American Indian Water Colors" by C. Norris Millington, *American Magazine of Art* vol. 25, no. 2, August 1932; "America's First Painters" by Dorothy Dunn, *National Geographic Magazine*, vol. CVII, no. 3, March 1955; "Hopi Artist Fred Kabotie, 1900-1986" by Ronald McCoy, *American Indian Art Magazine* no. 42, Autumn 1990; "Fred Kabotie" by Jeanne Snodgrass King, *American Indian Art Magazine* no. 21, Winter 1995.

*   *   *

In the Hopi village of Shungopovi at Second Mesa in northeast Arizona, a young boy by the name of *Naqavoy'ma*, Day after Day, scratched kachina figures on rocks down in the cornfields or with charcoal on walls of abandoned houses. In 1915 this young boy was sent to the Santa Fe Indian Boarding School where he became known as Fred Kabotie and developed into one of the pivotal figures in the early development of the American Indian watercolor painting tradition.

Pueblo Indians of the American southwest have a long history of painting for the decoration of religious and utilitarian objects, such as kiva murals and pottery. Painted artforms belonged to an established practice of producing objects for specific social purposes and adorning them with socially sanctioned designs and images. The beginning of what is now termed "modern" Pueblo Indian easel painting originated in the Santa Fe area around 1910-30 with a small group of artists from the pueblos of San Ildefonso, Zia, and Hopi. These artists produced secular watercolor paintings depicting scenes of daily life, ceremonial dances and dancers, stylized landscapes, and animal compositions for a predominantly European-American market. Fred Kabotie is one of the better known artists from this period and an important figure in Hopi history.

Until 1918 he attended the government-run Indian School in Santa Fe where, despite federal school policies prohibiting formal arts training, Kabotie was encouraged to draw and paint by the super-intendents' wife, Elizabeth De Huff (eventually costing her husband his job). Having admired the way Kabotie used watercolors to paint a map of the United States in class, De Huff invited him and a few other students to her home, where she provided them with watercolors and paper. Moved by loneliness, Kabotie drew the things that reminded him of home and his Pueblo identity, like the kachinas he drew for fun as a young boy. In *Fred Kabotie: Hopi Indian Artist*, he stated: "When you're so remote from your own people you get lonesome. You don't paint what's around you, you paint what you have in mind. Loneliness moves you to express something of your home, your background. The first time Mrs. De Huff saw my kachinas, she asked, 'What are these?' She didn't know anything about them."

While in school, Kabotie attracted the attention of his anglo teachers and supporters of Indian arts and culture in the Santa Fe area. Some of his first kachina drawings were purchased by his wood shop teacher, Mr. Jensen, who bought a dozen for seventy-five cents, or sold through the school arts club in order to raise money for extracurricular student activities. Through De Huff, Kabotie met Dr. Edgar Hewett, director of the Museum of New Mexico, who employed him part-time binding books and painting at the School of American Research. During the summer he also worked at archeological sites. Later, Kabotie enrolled in the Santa Fe High School, from which he graduated in 1925. Kabotie's early paintings, like those of his contemporaries, Velino Herrera, Tonita Peña, and Alfonso Roybal, epitomize the Pueblo Indian painting style characterized by flat colors, little modeling or perspective, outlined forms, and a lack of environmental backgrounds and groundlines.

After more than eleven years in Santa Fe, Kabotie began to feel that his urban experiences were adversely affecting his life and artwork. Encouraged by his good friend Dr. Harry Mera, Kabotie returned to Arizona in 1930. At first he managed the Fred Harvey Company's gift shop at Lookout Studio in Grand Canyon National Park during the tourist season, then he went home to Shungopovi where he herded sheep, hauled wood, and listened to the older generation talk about the past. He was initiated into the *Wuwtsimt* men's society. At home again, Kabotie had time to re-evaluate the importance of his Hopi heritage and realized his bahana [white man] life in Santa Fe was less important.

Some of his most accomplished works of art were painted during this next phase of his artistic career. Kabotie was comissioned by René D'Harnoncourt, director of the Museum of Modern Art in New York, to reproduce recently excavated kiva murals from the village of Awatobi for the landmark exhibition, *American Indian Art of the United States*, held at the MOMA in 1941. Four years later, in 1945, he received a Guggenheim Memorial Fellowship and completed redrawings of prehistoric Mimbres ceramic designs and interpretations for his publication, *Designs from the Ancient Mimbreños*. He continued to paint watercolors and created several murals for the Grand Canyon National Park (at Desert View Inn in 1933, Painted Desert Inn in 1948, and at Bright Angel Lodge in 1958).

Perhaps just as significant as Kabotie's artwork was his determination to preserve and foster greater appreciation for Hopi cultural traditions, both within and outside his pueblo community. His paintings from the 1940s to the 1950s show more developed perspective, detailed modeling, and specific backgrounds, and include nuances of his own artistic vision and personality. Certainly, as an artist Kabotie inspired future generations of Hopi artists, including his son, Michael.

Kabotie taught art at the Hopi High School in Oraibi from 1937 until it closed twenty-two years later. Afterward, Kabotie devoted his energies to painting and community-based projects. For example, during the 1950s he created designs used to develop a distinct Hopi jewelry style, and in the 1970s he became involved with the Hopi Craft Guild and Cultural Center. Although he rarely painted after 1950, his last significant painting, *Destruction of San Bartolome Church at Shungopovi, Hopi*, was commissioned by the Museum of New Mexico in 1976. This painting was commissioned to mark the U.S. bicentennial and dealt with the 1680 Pueblo revolt. Ten years later Kabotie died in Shungopovi. He left a substantial body of work—an appropriate testimony to the vitality and dedication he demonstrated throughout his life.

—Lisa Roberts

KABOTIE, Michael

Variant names: Lomawywesa
Tribal affiliations: Hopi
Painter

Born: Keams Canyon, Arizona, 3 September 1942; member of the Hopi Snow/Water Clan; initiated into the Wuwuchim, Hopi Men's Society, 1967, and given the adult name Lomawywesa, which means "Walking in Harmony." **Education:** Southwest Indian Art Project, University of Arizona, 1960; Haskell Institute, Lawrence, Kansas, 1961; University of Arizona, 1964-65, studio arts. **Career:** Artist, writer, lecturer; president, board of directors, Hopi Arts & Crafts Co-Op Guild, Second Mesa, Arizona, 1970-74, and manager, 1976-78; co-founder of Artist Hopid, 1973-1980s, a subsidiary of Hopi Arts & Crafts Co-Op Guild, promoting Hopi art through exhibits, lectures; muralist (with members of Artist Hopid, Hopi Cultural Center Museum, 1975; consultant, Hopi Cultural Center Museum, 1977, California Academy of Sciences, 1979-80; board of directors, Indian Arts & Crafts Association, Albuquerque, 1975-80; editorial advisory board, *American Indian Art Magazine*, 1975—; chairman, Hopi Cultural Center Museum Task Team, 1978—. **Awards:** Inter Tribal Indian Ceremonials (1968-70, 1978), fairs at the Museum of Northern Arizona (1970), Heard Museum (1969-70), and the Philbrook Museum of Art (1969-70).

Individual Exhibitions

1966   Heard Museum, Phoenix, Arizona

Selected Group Exhibitions

Kabotie's works have been exhibited continuously since the 1970s at Hopi Cultural Center Museum, Second Mesa, Arizona.

1975-80 *Pintura Amerindia Contemporanea/E.U.A.*, sponsored by
         the United States Department of State and Interna-
         tional Communications Agency, Washington, D.C.
1976   Katonah Gallery, New York
         Native American Center for the Living Arts, Niagara Falls,
         New York
1978   Wheelwright Museum of the American Indian, Santa Fe,
         New Mexico
         Indian Pueblo Cultural Center, Albuquerque, New Mexico
1980   Heard Museum, Phoenix, Arizona
         Museum of Northern Arizona, Flagstaff
1984-85 *Indianascher Kunstler* (traveling, Germany), organized
         by the Philbrook Museum, Tulsa, Oklahoma
1986   *When the Rainbow Touches Down*, Heard Museum, Phoe-
         nix, Arizona (traveling)
1988-89 *Four Sacred Mountains: Color, Form and Abstraction*,
         Arizona Commission on the Arts, Phoenix (traveling)
1989   *Paint, Bronze, and Sculpture*, Mitchell Indian Museum,
         Kendall College, Evanston, Illinois
1990-91 *One With the Earth*, organized by the Institute of Ameri-
         can Indian Arts and Alaska Culture and Arts Develop-
         ment, Santa Fe, New Mexico (traveling)
1991-92 *Shared Visions: Native American Painters and Sculptors
         in the Twentieth Century*, The Heard Museum, Phoenix,
         Arizona

Collections

Center for Great Plains Studies, University of Nebraska, Lincoln;
Colorado Springs Fine Arts Center, Colorado; Denver Art Museum, Denver, Colorado; Heard Museum, Phoenix, Arizona; Heritage Center, Inc., Collection, Pine Ridge, South Dakota; Hopi Cultural Center Museum, Second Mesa, Arizona; Institute of American Indian Arts Museum, Santa Fe, New Mexico; Museum of the
American Indian, Smithsonian Institution, Washington, D.C.; Museum of Northern Arizona, Flagstaff; Millicent Rogers Foundation
Museum, Taos, New Mexico; Roswell Museum and Art Center,
Roswell, New Mexico; Wheelwright Museum of the American Indian, Santa Fe, New Mexico.

Publications

By KABOTIE: Books written or edited—*Two Hopi Song Poets
of Shungopavi*, Hopi Arts and Crafts Co-Op Guild, Second Mesa,
Arizona, 1978; *Hopi Voices and Visions*, Intrepid Press, Buffalo,
1982; *Migration Tears*, Los Angeles, 1987. **Articles and anthologies**—*Many Fires: Inter Tribal Ceremonial Association Magazine*,
Gallup, 10 March 1975; *Arizona Living Magazine*, Phoenix, December 1975; *Intrepid: A Decade and Then Some: Contemporary
Literature*, Buffalo, 1976; *Church and Society*, New York, 1982.

On KABOTIE: Books—*Indian Painters and White Patrons*, by
J.J. Brody, Albuquerque, 1971; *Southwest Indian Art: A Changing
Tradition*, by Clara Lee Tanner, Tucson, 1973; *Hopi Painting: The
World of the Hopis*, by Patricia Janis Broder, New York, 1978; *The
Sweet Grass Lives On*, by Jamake Highwater, New York, 1980;
Indianascher Kunstler, by Gerhard Hoffmann, Munich, 1984; *The
Arts of the North American Indian: Native Traditions in Evolution*,
edited by Edwin L. Wade, New York, 1986; *When the Rainbow
Touches Down*, exhibition catalog by Tryntje Van Ness Seymour,
Heard Museum, University of Washington Press, 1988; *Beyond

Tradition: Native American Art and Its Evolution, by Jerry and
Lois Jacka, Flagstaff, 1988; *Shared Visions: Native American Painters and Sculptors in the Twentieth Century*, by Margaret Archuleta
and Dr. Rennard Strickland, The New Press, New York, 1991; *I
Stand in the Center of Good*, by Lawrence Abbott, Lincoln, Nebraska, 1994. **Articles**—"Artist Hopid: In Their Own Words," by
Max Benavidez, *Equal Opportunity Magazine*, June 1978.

*

Michael Kabotie comments:

The arts have always been an integral part of my life. It is through
the arts that I capture and share the values of people's spirituality,
agonies, contradictions, happiness, and through the arts that I clarify
my fears, passions, joy; my birth and my death.

*   *   *

Michael Kabotie, son of renowned Hopi artist Fred Kabotie, has
long since built a reputation of his own, and his work may be
regarded as a milestone in the development of modern Hopi painting. Unlike his father, he was exposed to and came under the influence of modern Western painting styles early on: Kabotie admired
the work of Picasso, Braque, Leger, as well as the French Impressionists and, in the late 1960s and 1970s, experimented with modern form elements mainly of Surrealism and Cubism. Characteristically, however, he used these techniques to portray the many aspects and levels of Hopi secular and spiritual life, as is suggested by
titles like *Kachina Lovers, Hopi Elements, Deer Dancer, Water
Serpent My Father*, and *Hopi Priest*. He had realized that modern
Western art, with its tendency towards stylization, corresponded
with the essential nature of Indian art and thus was easily adaptable
to its particular concerns.

The person that was instrumental in opening up young Kabotie's
eyes to the dignity of his people's art and its adaptability to modern Western art styles, was Cochiti painter Joe Herrera, himself a
mediator between Native American and European art. It was through
him that Kabotie became acquainted with the Awatovi kiva murals
excavated in the 1930s in a prehistoric Hopi village. The religious
paintings were to him living proof of his people's long history in
the arts, which had begun long before the white men set foot on the
American continent. Apart from establishing his pride in his people's
achievement, the Awatovi murals—as well as the pottery and basket designs—became a lasting influence on his own style and his
artistic development. Henceforth, two-dimensional images of
Kachinas, of holy plants and animals executed in the "four direction
colors" of black, white, red and green, the areas defined by heavy
contour lines, became his hallmark and can still be found in recent
paintings by Kabotie, like the *Kachina Still-Life Series* from 1990.

The spiritual element, so characteristic of Hopi Indian life and
art, is the basis of Kabotie's painting. It can be found in his use of
traditional fertility symbols of Hopi mythology, such as rainbows,
clouds, lightning bolts, and snow flakes. Migration spirals conjure
up the mythological Hopi wanderings through various worlds, and
Kachina figures are associated with Kabotie's prevalent themes of
blessing and purification.

These themes can be traced back to the stories of Hopi mythology, which gives Kabotie's paintings a narrative dimension, and
they are part of his personal credo. Accordingly, his initiation in
1967 into the Wuwuchim, the Hopi men's society of his pueblo,
meant a turning point in his life and in the development of his

artwork: "It was the beginning of my spiritual journey, seeking myself through art" (*Hopi Painting*, 1978).

As a consequence of this quest he lived through a time of disorientation when he abstained from painting. After he had clarified his ideas about art in general and the relationship of modern European and traditional pueblo art, he pursued his aims with renewed energy. Kabotie sought the community of fellow artists who shared his ideas and founded with them, in 1973, a painters' group they called the Artist Hopid.

The reconciliation of tradition and innovation, past and present, became the hallmark of the Hopi painters who became members of the group: Delbridge Honanie, Milland Lomakema, Mike Kabotie, Neil David, and Terrance Talaswaima. For several years they worked together, sharing a studio and their experiences, and participated as a group in the South American travelling expedition *Contemporary Amerindian Paintings/USA* in 1979.

The 1980s was a time when Kabotie was much concerned about the destructive influence of modern Western technology and mass media on Hopi life. He expressed this concern most explicitly in his poems of the time, which reflect his frustration about the disastrous changes that made the Hopis aliens to their own land. In an interview he spoke of a cultural clash and of the artists as "portraying the cultural clash symbolically in painting" (*I Stand in the Center of Good*, 1994). Some of his images, like *Hopi Babysitting*, became satirical comments on the changes of traditional tribal life and took on cartoon qualities

A decade later, his "cartoon era" was over and he made a fresh start. He now said: "I'm coming to a point where I want to go past the cultural and ethnic aesthetic barriers, when everything is merged into oneness." And a little later, "I think that every artist reflects his or her culture and values at a certain point. Now I"m going into a different plane or sphere or consciousness... It might be a point of my artistic maturity" (*I Stand in the Center of Good*, 1994).

—Gerhard and Gisela Hoffmann

KAI SA

Variant names: Percy Sandy
Tribal affiliations: Zuñi
Painter

Born: Percy Tsisete Sandy, Zuñi Pueblo, New Mexico, 1918: Kai Sa means "Red Moon." **Education:** Santa Fe Indian School, New Mexico. **Family:** Married Peggy Mirabal, Taos, 1940; one daughter and three sons. **Career:** Farmer; illustrator, *Sun Journey*, by Ann Nolan Clark, 1945; muralist, including schools at Zuni and Black Rock; gallery assistant; and painter. **Awards:** Inter-Tribal Indian Ceremonials and New Mexico State Fair. **Died:** 15 May 1974.

Selected Group Exhibitions

Exhibited at fairs, juried competitions and commercial galleries (particularly the Blue Door Gallery in Taos, New Mexico) throughout the southwest during the 1950s and 1960s.

1948	Philbrook Museum of Art, Tulsa, Oklahoma
1955	*An Exposition of American Indian Painters*, James Graham and Sons, New York
1963	*Contemporary American Indian Art*, United States Department of State, Washington, D.C.
1971	Laguna Gloria Art Museum, Austin, Texas
1972	Museum of New Mexico, Santa Fe
1978	Heritage Center Inc. Collection, Pine Ridge, South Dakota
1979-80	*Native American Paintings*, organized by the Mid-American Art Alliance and the Joslyn Art Museum, Omaha, Nebraska (traveling)
1981	*Native American Painting*, Amarillo Art Center, Texas
1981	Arizona State Museum, University of Arizona, Tucson
1983	Hampton University, Virginia
1985	*The Hunt and the Harvest*, Gallery Association of New York State
1987	Center for Great Plains Studies, University of Nebraska, Lincoln
1991	Heard Museum, Phoenix, Arizona
1996	*Vision and Voices: Native American Painting from the Philbrook Museum of Art*, Philbrook Museum of Art, Tulsa, Oklahoma

Collections

Amerind Foundation, Dragoon, Arizona; Center for Great Plains Studies, University of Nebraska, Lincoln, Nebraska; Thomas Gilcrease Institute of American History and Art, Tulsa, Oklahoma; Heritage Center Inc. Collection, Red Cloud Indian School, Pine Ridge, South Dakota; Heard Museum, Phoenix, Arizona; Indian Arts & Crafts Board, United States Department of the Interior, Washington, D.C.; Kiva Museum of the Koshare Indian, Boy Scouts of America, La Junta, Colorado; Museum of New Mexico, Santa Fe; Museum of Northern Arizona, Flagstaff, Arizona; National Museum of the American Indian, Washington, D.C.; Philbrook Museum of Art, Tulsa, Oklahoma; Riverside Museum, Riverside, California; Millicent Rogers Foundation Museum, Taos, New Mexico; Southeast Museum of the North American Indian, Marathon, Florida; United Pueblo Agency, Albuquerque, New Mexico; Woolaroc Museum, Bartlesville, Oklahoma.

Publications

By KAI SA: Books illustrated—*Sun Journey*, by Ann Nolan Clark, Washington, D.C., 1945.

On KAI SA: Books—*Indian Painters and White Patrons*, by J. J. Brody, Albuquerque, 1971; *Southwest Indian Painting: A Changing Art*, by Clara Lee Tanner, Tucson, 1973; *Native American Painting*, by Patrick Houlihan and Frederick Schmid, Omaha, 1979; *American Indian Painting and Sculpture*, by Patricia Janis Broder, New York, 1981; *Native American Painting*, by Jeanne Snodgrass King, Amarillo, 1981; *The Hunt and the Harvest*, by Nina Golder, Hamilton, New York, 1985; *Vision and Voices: Native American Painting from the Philbrook Museum of Art*, by Lydia Wyckoff, Tulsa, 1996.

* * *

Kai Sa, also known as Percy Sandy, was a versatile painter who adapted various techniques and styles to create original views of native themes involving Kachinas, ceremonial dances, and nature. This diversity is perhaps reflective of his background, having been

Kai Sa: *Deer Family,* c. 1970. Courtesy Challis and Arch Thiessen collection.

raised at Zuñi, studying briefly at the Santa Fe and Albuquerque Indian Schools during the 1930s artistic flowering, and living his adult life at Taos Pueblo, where he settled after having met and married a Taos woman. The Pueblo had also experienced an artistic flowering, and Kai Sa was well-acquainted with the Taos painter, Pop Chalee. This movement away from Zuñi may have been a series of personal choices, but some reports have suggested that his renderings of sacred dances and kiva gods led to his ostracism from that Pueblo.

From Zuñi, through the Indian Schools, to Taos, Kai Sa was immersed in a variety of Native American styles and also developed skill with perspective as practiced by European artists. His paintings of Kachinas are most often based on Zuñi ceremonies but are closer to the Hopi style of Fred Kabotie and Otis Polelonema than the less refined look typical of Zuñi painters. Kai Sa's renderings of plants and animals are vigorous in the manner of Navajo painting. These experimentations with varying trends continued throughout his career, which included early recognition while still in his twenties, including a strong showing at the initial annual exhibitions at the Philbrook Museum of Art in Tulsa during the late 1940s, to his most acclaimed work of the 1960s.

Along the way, Kai Sa's paintings reflect the flat style, though his line modeling could vary from thin to heavy to complete absence, and from slight to full coloring. Most of his work shows a concern for balance, presenting few figures and little background. Individual details, however, are rich: figures are individualized in physical appearance, costumes are minutely detailed, animals are robust, and figurative elements, such as the vibrant rainbow spilling into *Corn Dancer and Mudhead Meet Rainbow God,* are lively and arresting, given free space from other figures in his paintings.

Most of Kai Sa's paintings focused on dancers performing in Zuñi ceremonies and costumes. The dancers are often bulky, perform individually or in small groups, with no background, little ground line, and no audiences viewing their performances. Within this general subject concern he painted with great variety, drawing from developments in Pueblo in a seemingly cosmopolitan manner.

In 1940, Kai Sa described his purpose: "As an Indian artist, I hope to be instrumental in artistically and authentically depicting the customs of my people. This, I hope, will be my small contribution to a great race."

—Gregory Schaaf

KAKEGAMIC, Goyce

Tribal affiliations: Cree
Painter and printmaker

Born: Sandy Lake Reserve, Ontario, 1948. **Education:** Essentially a self-taught artist; classes at Confederation College, Thunder Bay, Ontario, and University of Western Ontario, London, Ontario. **Career:** Miner; high school counselor, Sioux Lookout, Ontario; Ontario Ministry of Culture and Recreation, Economic Development Program; Triple K Co-operative, Red Lake, Ontario, a silk screen print shop and the first native run operation of its kind.

Selected Group Exhibitions

1974   Aggregation Gallery, Toronto, Ontario
        Contemporary Native Arts of Canada, Oakville Centennial Gallery, Oakville, Ontario
1976   *Contemporary Native Art: The Woodland Indians,* Royal Ontario Museum, Toronto, Ontario
1977   *Contemporary Native Art of Canada—Triple K Co-operative,* Royal Ontario Museum, Toronto, Ontario
1978   *Art of the Woodland Indian,* McMichael Canadian Collection, Kleinburg, Ontario
1983   *Last Camp, First Song: Indian Art from the Royal Ontario Museum,* organized by the Thunder Bay National Exhibition Centre and Centre for Indian Art, Thunder Bay, Ontario
1984   *Norval Morrisseau and the Emergence of the Image Makers,* Art Gallery of Ontario, Toronto
1989   *Woodlands: Contemporary Art of the Anishnabe,* Thunder Bay Art Gallery, Thunder Bay, Ontario
1994   Thunder Bay Art Gallery, Thunder Bay, Ontario

Collections

Canadian Museum of Civilization, Hull, Quebec; Department of Indian and Northern Affairs, Canada, Ottawa, Ontario; McMichael Canadian Collection, Kleinburg, Ontario; Thunder Bay Art Gallery, Thunder Bay, Ontario.

Publications

On KAKEGAMIC: Book—*Contemporary Native Art of Canada: Silk Screens from the Triple K Co-operative,* exhibition catalog by Elizabeth McLuhan, Royal Ontario Museum, 1977. **Article**— "An Interview with Goyce Kakegamic: Painting for the Joy of It," by Bunny Sicard, *The Native Perspective,* vol. 3, no. 2, 1978.

*   *   *

Like most of his fellow Woodland School artists, Goyce Kakegamic was raised on the remote Sandy Lake Reserve in northwestern Ontario, and was a self-taught artist. His paintings exemplifies the style and motivation of the Woodland School artists of Ontario in several ways: his earliest work consisted of scenes, mostly landscapes, in oils, and painting was as much a hobby as a serious endeavor. In the late 1960s, Norval Morrisseau married Kakegamic's sister and moved to Sandy Lake. Morrisseau was the founder of the Woodland School, just beginning to gain momentum and widespread acclaim at this time. Under the influence of Morrisseau and others in the movement, including Kakegamic's younger brother, Joshim, Goyce Kakegamic abandoned his earlier, more traditional approach to the medium and began to paint in a distinct pictographic style of the Woodland School. The importance of family connections and communal efforts apparent in Kakegamic's development as an artist is characteristic of the movement and an important factor in the development of style and content in Woodland School painting.

In 1973 his brothers, Joshim and Henry, established the Triple K Cooperative, a silk screen print shop, in Red Lake, Ontario. Unlimited editions of the work of Goyce and Joshim were the primary products of the cooperative in its first years. Soon, however, they turned to the production of fine limited edition prints of their own work as well as many of the best known artists in the Woodland School. Kakegamic's style developed quickly in the fertile milieu of the cooperative, exhibiting clear relationships to the works of both Morrisseau and Carl Ray, another early teacher in the movement and also a resident of Sandy Lake Reserve. Kakegamic's style remains distinctively individual, nonetheless.

His early interest in traditional landscape painting is evidenced in his use of color and setting. Open areas tend to represent negative space in clearer terms than is often common in the style of most Woodland School painters. On the other hand, clearly defined positive form in Kakegamic's work is almost always filled with color, often vibrant but also subtle and subdued. There is a tendency to develop the segmented forms within the formline structure in concentric rings of related color, reminiscent of beadwork from Ontario. This use of color gives his style its distinctive quality, especially as applied to the relatively small design units within each figure, also characteristic of his style. His use of specific colors or color combinations is less consistent than others in the school, especially brother Joshim, but it is always an important factor in his compositions.

Kakegamic utilizes the typical black formline characteristic of all Woodland School painters, but it plays a much less significant role in the overall structure and definition of form than it does for most of his contemporaries. Formal elements tend to be more complex, far more so than those of his brother's, for example. That impression is due to the multiplication of smaller elements within the design and the use of color, breaking up the forms into a multiplicity of tiny elements, linked by the form line, but somehow not controlled by it. Long, curving lines of power—wavy lines radiating outward from the primary forms in his paintings—are a trademark as well. Never tense enough to be called serpentine, these lines form tenuous but crucial links between forms or run off the ends of them, like elongated drips of honey.

The impression of busy-ness that results from the multiplicity of segmented, highly colorful form in Kakegamic's work enhances its narrative quality, linking it formally to its mythological content. Unlike the work of some others in the school, whose emphasis upon design often begs an almost purely aesthetic reading, most of Kakegamic's paintings and graphics look like a story, told with a plethora of specific, if esoteric, information. His formal approach pushes the viewer to explore the narrative possibilities and details. An unusually strong emphasis upon the eyes of his subjects contributes to this impression as well. Eyes are enlarged and given equal status within compositions as much larger anatomical elements described by concentric bands of color.

Inconsistencies in Kakegamic's oeuvre, especially in his use of color, point to another aspect of style and motivation typical of many in the school. In addition to consciously appealing to the non-native art market in urban Canada and beyond, there is a decidedly didactic cast to the art of the Woodland School. The style was developed consciously as a distinctly indigenous medium for the exploration and elucidation of northern Algonkian culture and myth. Artists viewed the style as a means for strengthening Native identity in their communities, as well as promoting familiarity with traditional culture, especially among the young.

This insistence upon significant content and its relationship to the community at large is crucial. It means that many of the artists, like Kakegamic, are as deeply involved in practical approaches to the problems and needs of their communities as they are interested in aesthetics and the production of art. Kakegamic, for example, is not a full time artist: he also works as a counselor for the Red Lake Board of Education. The duality of purpose, of course, should not be read as somehow denigrating the relative seriousness of Kakegamic and the other Woodland School artists or the quality and significance of their creative work. On the contrary, it is the tension that arises from the need to respond to equally insistent and important, but very divergent, demands that gives much of this art its remarkable strength and appeal. Rising to the challenges presented by these professional and personal dichotomies renders the art distinctly native, on the one hand, and universally significant on the other. The resolution of similar tensions is basic to the production of all fine art, regardless of its origins.

In Kakegamic's art and that of the Woodland School, in general, the cultural and historical factors that have given rise to it are vital. The strong emphasis upon and dedication to the needs of the community proceeds from those realities and determines the general characteristics of the art produced, just as the historical and cultural milieu in which it develops has determined the nature of every major art movement.

—Amelia Trevelyan

KAKEGAMIC, Joshim

Tribal affiliations: Cree
Painter and printmaker

Born: Sandy Lake Reserve, Ontario, 1952. **Education:** Studied with Norval Morrisseau (his brother-in-law) and Carl Ray. **Career:** Founded, with older brother, Henry, Triple K Co-operative, Red Lake, Ontario, 1973, a silk screen print shop and the first native run operation of its kind.

Individual Exhibitions

1975	Aggregation Gallery, Toronto, Ontario
1976	Shayne Gallery, Montreal, Quebec
1977	Alice Peck Gallery, Toronto, Ontario
1977-79	Aggregation Gallery, Toronto, Ontario

Selected Group Exhibitions

1974	Aggregation Gallery, Toronto, Ontario
	Contemporary Native Arts of Canada, Oakville Centennial Gallery, Ontario

1975	*Indian Art '75*, Woodland Indian Cultural Education Centre, Brantford, Ontario
1976	*Contemporary Native Art: The Woodland Indians*, Royal Ontario Museum, Toronto
1977	*Contemporary Native Art of Canada—Triple K Co-operative*, Royal Ontario Museum, Toronto
1978	*Art of the Woodland Indian*, McMichael Canadian Collection, Kleinburg, Ontario
	Indian Art '78, Woodland Indian Cultural Education Centre, Brantford, Ontario
1980	New College, University of Toronto, Ontario
1981	*Indian Art '81*, Woodland Indian Cultural Education Centre, Brantford, Ontario
1983	*Last Camp, First Song: Indian Art from the Royal Ontario Museum*, organized by the Thunder Bay National Exhibition Centre and Centre for Indian Art, Ontario
1984	*Norval Morrisseau and the Emergence of the Image Makers*, Art Gallery of Ontario, Toronto
1989	*Woodlands: Contemporary Art of the Anishnabe*, Thunder Bay Art Gallery, Ontario

Collections

Cambrian College, North Bay, Ontario; Canadian Museum of Civilization, Hull, Quebec; Centre d'Exposition de la Gare, L'Annonciation, Quebec; Confederation College, Kenora, Ontario; McMichael Canadian Art Collection, Kleinburg, Ontario; Royal Ontario Museum, Toronto; Thunder Bay Art Gallery, Thunder Bay, Ontario; Woodland Indian Cultural Education Center, Brantford, Ontario.

Publications

On KAKEGAMIC: Books—*Contemporary Native Art of Canada: Silk Screens from the Triple K Co-operative*, exhibition catalog by Elizabeth McLuan, Royal Ontario Museum, 1977; *Norval Morrisseau and the Emergence of the Image Makers*, exhibition catalog by Elizabeth McLuan and Tom Hill, Art Gallery of Ontario, Toronto, 1984.

*   *   *

Joshim Kakegamic was one of the most important in the so-called second wave of artists in the Woodland School of eastern Canada. The style was developed during the late 1960s as way to express, explore and disseminate the traditional culture of the Algonkian peoples in the area. Kakegamic and his artist brothers were born on the Sandy Lake Reserve in northwestern Ontario. Sandy Lake was also home to Norval Morrisseau, founder of the Woodland School and Kakegamic's brother-in-law, as well as one of his first teachers. Kakegamic was an important innovator in the graphic arts, a central figure in the development of these media within the Woodland School. In 1973, he and his older brother, Henry, founded the Triple K Co-operative in Red Lake, Ontario, a silk screen print shop and the first native run operation of its kind.

Kakegamic worked in the essentially pictographic style of the school. Morrisseau initiated this distinctively Native formal expression and, with several others, passed it on to a new generation of young native artists in the early 1970s. They offered a series of summer workshops on Manitoulin Island and other native reserves in Ontario, sponsored by the Manitoulin Arts Foundation. Kakegamic was an enthusiastic participant.

Unlike those of Morrisseau and other founders of the tradition, Kakegamic's relatives were not important spiritual leaders. He had not experienced the deep immersion in traditional ritual and lore of the elder Woodland School artists. The result is a less spiritually intense expression, relying upon formal rigor more than personal angst to convey content and meaning.

From the outset, Kakegamic's approach to the style was more graphic than painterly. Early on, there is a tendency toward compacted forms defined by tightly controlled and extraordinarily heavy formline structure. The strength of his formline all but overpowers other elements of style in some of this early work. The tendency of the formline to absolutely control the composition increases over time, although it does so in increasingly subtler ways. In late works the formline thins out. It is still central to structure but wields that control with a less heavy hand.

In contrast, interior lines and even the typical feathering of the form line itself tend to be very delicate throughout Kakegamic's oeuvre, essentially calligraphic in quality as well as regularity. Variation of these linear elements almost always determines the overall feel and relative intensity of each composition. The results range from electrifying energy in some of his early work to an almost static, albeit sophisticated, beauty later on.

Color in Kakegamic's work, whether painting or silk screen, tends to be flat and subdued. He utilizes earth tones primarily, often quite elegantly combined with a lovely shade of blue, and laid down in relatively large interior areas with only minimal development of texture. The calligraphic delicacy of interior lines inevitably shows through. The results are often monumental in impression, much less narrative in overall feeling than the work of others in the school. His paintings almost always read more as compact and dynamic designs than illustrations. Even at his most narrative (e.g., *Boy in the Moon*, 1980), rough bilateral symmetry and measured control of each enclosed area of color gives the work the sophisticated graphic quality of an abstract design more than the illustration of a traditional story. One always has the impression that the formal elements of the design are as much the primary content as the details of the legend or tradition under consideration.

The same is true of the individual characters within these narrative works. In many examples, each figure appears as a more or less self-contained motif within the whole. Kakegamic's tendency to limit his palette to a few colors, closely related in value and intensity, contributes to this feeling. *Three Brothers*, featured in the *Image Makers* exhibition at the Art Gallery of Ontario in 1984, represents an important exception to this general rule in Kakegamic's style. Here, all three of the main figures are linked in a tight asymmetrical composition that opens only to the upper right in a more characteristic compartmentalization of form.

This approach to design is ideally suited to silk screen. Not surprisingly, Kakegamic became interested in graphic processes early on and began to experiment with silk screen in 1970s. However, he found the loss of artistic control in the translation of painting to screen and ink problematic. Given the subtle relationship between color and form in his work, these concerns are hardly surprising. Kakegamic responded to the difficulty by establishing his own graphic workshop in cooperation with his two brothers, after spending most of a year considering and coping with the logistical problems involved.

It was a unique concept, an entirely Native and artist run enterprise, deep in the forests of western Ontario, hundreds of miles from any urban center. The idea was to create images specifically designed for graphic processes and, thus, aesthetically different than those created after painted originals. In addition, each step of the process was controlled by the artist. Initially, they produced unlimited editions of their own work (Joshim and brother Goyce). They soon shifted from screening their own creations exclusively to the production of high quality limited editions by other members of the Woodland School, as well. The success of the enterprise was reflected in an exhibit of Triple K products at the Royal Ontario Museum, Toronto, in 1977. For seven years the Kakegamic brothers and the Triple K Cooperative were a central influence in the creation and production of graphic editions for the artists of the Woodland School.

—Amelia Trevelyan

KALVAK, Helen

Tribal affiliations: Inuit
Graphic artist

Born: Tahiryuak Lake, Victoria Island, Northwest Territories, Canada, 1901; last name also variously cited as Kalvakadlak, Kralvak. **Career:** Migratory hunter, graphic artist. **Awards:** Elected a member of the Royal Canadian Academy of Arts, 1975; Order of Canada, 1978. **Died:** 7 May 1984.

Individual Exhibitions

1968   *Helen Kalvak: Print Retrospective*, Canadian Guild of Crafts Quebec, Montreal
1969   *Kalvak Retrospective*, Canadian Guild of Crafts Quebec, Montreal
1970   *Helen Kalvak Drawings*, Canadian Guild of Crafts Quebec, Montreal
1992   *The Graphic Art of Helen Kalvak, R.C.A., 1965-1984*, Albers Gallery of Inuit Art, San Francisco, California

Selected Group Exhibitions

1965   *Arctic Values '65*, New Brunswick Museum, St. John
1970   *Graphic Art by Eskimos of Canada: First Collection*, Cultural Affairs Division, Department of External Affairs, Canada, Ottawa (traveling)
1972   *Kalvak - Nanogak Drawings*, Canadian Guild of Crafts Quebec, Montreal
1976-82 *Shamans and Spirits: Myths and Medical Symbolism in Eskimo Art*, Canadian Arctic Producers and the National Museum of Man, Ottawa (traveling)
1978   *The Coming and Going of the Shaman: Eskimo Shamanism and Art*, Winnipeg Art Gallery, Manitoba
1981   *Festival of Birds*, The Arctic Circle, Los Angeles, California
        Eskimo Games: Graphics and Sculpture/Giuochi Eschimesi: grafiche e sculture, National Gallery of Modern Art, Rome
1983   *The Arctic/L'Artique*, UNESCO, Paris
1985   *Uumajut: Animal Imagery in Inuit Art*, Winnipeg Art Gallery, Manitoba

1986   *Die Kunst aux der Arktis,* presented by Inuit Galerie, Mannheim, Germany (traveling)

1987   *The Matriarchs: Jessie Oonark, Helen Kalvak, Pitseolak Ashoona,* Snow Goose Associates, Seattle, Washington

1988   *Inuit Images in Transition,* Augusta Savage Gallery, University of Massachusetts, Amherst

1988-89 *Im Schatten der Sonne: Zeitgenossische Kunst der Indianer und Eskimos in Kanada/In the Shadow of the Sun: Contemporary Indian and Inuit Art in Canada,* Canadian Museum of Civilization, Ottawa (traveling)

1993   *The Prints Never Seen: Holman, 1977-1987,* Albers Gallery of Inuit Art, San Francisco, California

1994   *Arctic Spirit, 35 Years of Canadian Inuit Art,* Frye Art Museum, Seattle, Washington

Collections

Amon Carter Museum of Western Art, Fort Worth, Texas; Anchorage Museum of History and Art, Alaska; Beaverbrook Art Gallery, Fredericton, New Brunswick; Canada Council Art Bank, Ottawa; Canadian Guild of Crafts Quebec, Montreal; Canadian Museum of Civilization, Hull, Quebec; Clifford E. Lee Collection, University of Alberta, Edmonton, Alberta; Dennos Museum Center, Northwestern Michigan College, Traverse City; Department of External Affairs, Ottawa; Edmonton Art Gallery, Edmonton, Alberta; Glenbow Museum, Calgary, Alberta; Haffenreffer Museum of Anthropology, Brown University, Bristol, Rhode Island; Inuit Cultural Institute, Rankin Inlet, Northwest Territories; Inuit Cultural Institute, Rankin Inlet, Northwest Territories; Laurentian University Museum and Arts Centre, Sudbury, Ontario; McMaster University Art Gallery, Hamilton, Ontario; McMichael Canadian Art Collection, Kleinburg, Ontario; Musee des beaux-arts de Montreal, Montreal; Museum of Anthropology, University of British Columbia, Vancouver; National Gallery of Canada, Ottawa; Prince of Wales Northern Heritage Centre, Yellowknife, Northwest Territories; Smith College Museum of Art, Northampton, Massachusetts; University of Alberta, Edmonton, Alberta; Winnipeg Art Gallery, Winnipeg, Manitoba.

Publications

On KALVAK: Books—*Inuit: The Art of the Canadian Eskimo,* by W.T. Larmour, Indian Affairs and Northern Development, Ottawa, 1967; *The Coming and the Going of the Shaman: Eskimo Shamanism and Art*, exhibition catalog by Jean Blodgett, Winnipeg Art Gallery, Manitoba, 1978; *Kalvak/Emerak: Memorial Catalog,* by Bernadette Driscoll, Holman Eskimo Co-Op, Northwest Territories, 1987; *Contemporary Inuit Drawings* exhibition catalog by Marion E. Jackson and David Pelly, McDonald Stewart Art Centre, Guelph, Ontario, 1987; *In the Shadow of the Sun,* by Gerald McMaster, et al, Canadian Museum of Civilization, Hull, Quebec, 1993. **Articles**—"Eskimo Art from Holman," by Helen Burgess, *North,* vol. 13, no. 3, May/June 1966; "Kalvak," by Randy Sweetman, *Arctic in Colour,* vol. 6, no. 2, 1978; "Inuit Art: A Fantastic Arctic Success Story," by Sandra Souchotte, *Northwest Explorer* vol. 4, no. 4, Autumn, 1985; "Kalvak (1901-1984)," by Leo Bushman *Arctic: Journal of the Arctic Institute of North America* vol, 41, no. 1, March 1988; "More than Meets the Eye: The Clothing Motif in Inuit Legends and Art," by Robin McGrath, *Inuit Art Quarterly,* vol. 8, no. 4, Winter 1993.

*   *   *

In the western arctic, the only community to build a print-making program has been the hamlet of Holman (sometimes called Holman Island in the older literature), a community of about 300 Inuit on the west coast of Victoria Island. This program grew from the excitement and vision of an Oblate missionary from France, Father Henri Tardy, a resident of Holman for several decades starting in 1948. He knew of the great strides in the graphic arts being made in Cape Dorset in the early 1960s. This knowledge, combined with his despair at local prospects for subsistence led him to begin a small venture in his own community. The first exhibit and sale of Holman art in New Brunswick in 1965 included 37 prints by five artists, one of whom, Helen Kalvak, would become the luminary of Holman's graphic arts program.

Born on Victoria Island in the Western Canadian arctic in 1901, Kalvak spent her formative years as a migratory hunter in the company of her parents, Aluksit and Ingataomik. Like her mother, she was talented in the arts of skin sewing and parka making; indeed it was through this medium that the first glimmer of her talents as a graphic artist emerged. She moved into the settlement of Holman in 1960. In an interview, Father Tardy reminisced about his discovery of her creative powers in 1962:

> "I asked her to make me a parka. Usually they just look at you to size you up but this time she said she wanted to take some measurements. She took a pencil and drew the shape of a parka. I was really struck. You could feel the power of the lines. I asked her if she had ever drawn; she said not really, perhaps a little when she was young. So I said, 'let's try something.' She did a drawing, a shamanic seal. I was interested in using the story of the seal as a way of communicating with her and to allow me to practice the language. She became interested and started to produce quite a bit. We started very soon to use her drawings. She was very bright, didn't have much to do and so worked every day."

To encourage her work, Father Tardy paid her $1 per drawing and tape recorded the stories she told to accompany hundreds of the pieces. Many of the several thousand drawings that Kalvak made (most still housed in the archive at the Holman Eskimo Cooperative) reflect her own background and interests in shamanism, hunting, and women's needle arts.

Most of the Holman drawings (and the prints made from them during the 1960s and '70s) were the work of relatively unacculturated Inuit who had lived lives as migratory hunters for much of the 20th century. The imagery that fascinated them is older still—much of it reflected the lives of the Copper Eskimo recorded by explorers early in the 20th century; hunting caribou with bows and arrows, dancing the drum dance, and shamanic transformation are among the most frequent images.

In the annual corpus of prints produced at Holman, more were made from Kalvak's drawings than of any other artist's. Of the 677 prints issued by 1994, 155 were based on Kalvak's drawings. The process of making a stonecut print at Holman in the 1960s and 70s usually involved cutting away the stone that corresponded to the background space in the drawing and inking large surfaces, so that massive, blocky figures in one or two colors fill the space. The prints made in this way from Kalvak's drawings are bold and expressive, but they mask the delicacy and sureness of her line. In the 1960s, she drew primarily with pencil but came to prefer the felt-tipped pens that were made available in the 1970s. She was never interested in watercolor or any kind of brushwork, and never cut her own stone blocks for inking.

Leo Bushman has described the way in which Kalvak composed her drawings:

> Kalvak used her hands for placement of animals and figures in her compositions. She was composing with her hands and fingers in various positions to get a feeling of what the composition could be. All the while she hummed or sang and moved slowly and gently as if she were warming up for a dance instead of a drawing session. No drawing or marks were made on paper before going through these rituals of placing her hands on the paper and humming or singing. In several cases I watched her put her left hand, palm down, on the paper as if to trace it before drawing the complete figure or animal. This gesture was for compositional purposes.

The prints made from her drawings ranged from simple compositions done with great economy of line, to confident complex groupings that still retain great clarity and simplicity.

Kalvak's first print retrospective was held at the Canadian Guild of Crafts in Montreal (1968), followed by an exhibiting of her drawings there in 1970. Kalvak was elected to membership in the Royal Academy of Art in 1975, and in 1979 she was appointed a member of the Order of Canada, the highest official recognition of achievement of a Canadian citizen.

—Janet Catherine Berlo

KAROO Ashevak

Tribal affiliations: Inuit
Sculptor

Born: Near Spence Bay, Northwest Territories, 1940; also known as Mungnelli. **Career:** Traditional nomadic hunting existence until the 1960s, when he moved to Spence Bay and turned to carving. **Died:** October 1974.

Individual Exhibitions

1973   *Karoo Ashevak, Sculpture,* The Inuit Gallery of Eskimo Art, Toronto, Ontario
        Karoo Ashevak: Spirits, American Indian Arts Centre, New York, New York
1977   Winnipeg Art Gallery, Manitoba
        Karoo Ashevak, 1940-1974 Sculpture, The Upstairs Gallery, Winnipeg, Manitoba
1994-95 *Karoo in Ottawa,* National Gallery of Canada, Ottawa, Ontario

Selected Group Exhibitions

1970   *Sculpture,* Canadian Eskimo Arts Council, Yellowknife, Northwest Territories
1973   *Cultures of the Sun and the Snow: Indian and Eskimo Art of the Americas,* Musee des beaux-arts de Montreal, Quebec

1974   Lippel Gallery, Montreal, Quebec
1975-77 *Inuit Games/Inuit Pinguangit/Jeux des Inuit, 1975-77,* Department of Indian Affairs and Northern Development, Ottawa, Ontario (traveling)
1977   *White Sculpture of the Inuit,* Simon Fraser Gallery, Burnaby, British Columbia
1978   *The Coming and Going of the Shaman: Eskimo Shamanism and Art,* Winnipeg Art Gallery, Manitoba
1979-80 *Inuit Art in the 1970s,* Agnes Etherington Art Centre, Kingston, Ontario (traveling)
1980   *Whalebone Carvings and Inuit Prints Art Gallery,* Memorial University of Newfoundland, St. John's
1981   *Inuit Masks,* Inuit Gallery of Vancouver, British Columbia
1981-82 *Inuit Art: A Selection of Inuit Art from the Collection of the Canadian Museum of Civilization and the Rothman Permanent Collection of Inuit Sculpture,* (international tour)
1982   *Sculpture Inuit, Stone/Bone, c. 1960-79,* Canadian Galleries, Edmonton, Alberta
1983   *Inuit Masterworks: Selections from the Collection of Indian and Northern Affairs Canada,* McMichael Canadian Collection, Kleinburg, Ontario
1983-85 *Grasp Tight the Old Ways: Selections from the Klammer Family Collection of Inuit Art,* Art Gallery of Ontario, Toronto
1984-85 *Stones, Bones, Cloth, and Paper: Inuit Art in Edmonton Collections,* Edmonton Art Gallery, Alberta
1986   *The Spirit of the Land,* The Koffler Gallery, Toronto, Ontario
        Contemporary Inuit Art, National Gallery of Canada, Ottawa, Ontario
1988-89 *In the Shadow of the Sun: Contemporary Indian and Inuit Art in Canada/Im Schatten der Sonne: Zeitgenossische Kunst der Indianer und Eskimos in Kanada,* Canadian Museum of Civilization, Ottawa, Ontario (traveling)
1989   *Kitikmeot, Inuit Gallery of Vancouver,* British Columbia
        Masters of the Arctic: An Exhibition of Contemporary Inuit Masterworks, United Nations General Assembly, New York, New York (traveling)
1993-94 *The Inuit Imagination,* Winnipeg Art Gallery, Manitoba
1995   *Immaginario Inuit, Arte e cultura degli esquimesi canadesi,* Galleria d'Arte Moderna e Contemporanea, Verona, Italy

Collections

Art Gallery of Ontario, Toronto, Ontario; Canadian Museum of Civilization, Hull, Quebec; Amon Carter Museum of Western Art, Fort Worth, Texas; Glenbow Museum, Calgary, Alberta; Inuit Cultural Institute, Rankin Inlet, Northwest Territories; McMichael Canadian Art Collection, Kleinburg, Ontario; Musee des beaux-arts de Montreal, Montreal, Quebec; Museum of Anthropology, University of British Columbia, Vancouver, British Columbia; National Gallery of Canada, Ottawa, Ontario; Prince of Wales Northern Heritage Centre, Yellowknife, Northwest Territories; University of Alberta, Edmonton, Alberta; Winnipeg Art Gallery, Winnipeg, Manitoba.

Publications

On KAROO: Books—*Sculpture,* Canadian Eskimo Arts Council, Yellowknife/Ottawa, 1970; *Eskimo Fantastic Art,* by George

George Swinton, Winnipeg, 1972; *Karoo Ashevak: Spirits,* American Indian Arts Center, New York, 1973; *The Inuit Imagination: Arctic Myth and Sculpture,* by Harold Seidelman and James Turner, Vancouver/Toronto, 1993. **Articles**—"Operation Whalebone," by Abjon Bromfield, *North/Nord,* November/December, 1969; "Karoo Ashevak," by Judy McGrath, *artscanada,* December 1974; "The Spirit World of Karoo Ashevak," Robin McNeill, *North/Nord,* November/December 1975; "Karoo in Ottawa: Transcending the Specifics of Inuit Heritage," by Cynthia Cook, *Inuit Art Quarterly,* Summer 1995.

*   *   *

Karoo Ashevak lived a short life of 34 years, the last decade or so in the community of Spence Bay, where he had settled and concentrated on sculpture after having lived a nomadic existence. He quickly established himself as a creative force with a variety of animated sculptures, from dramatically-charged pieces to humorous images. Working primarily in whalebone, and often using ivory, antler, soapstone and baleen for embellishments, Karoo displayed excellent craftsmanship and a sense of playfulness in his work. Carefully selecting material to match the idea for a subject of his sculpture, working with natural colors, shapes, and contours of the material, and adding distinct features, Karoo sculptures have a refined, finished look and abstract expressiveness. His work was influential within his community and drew immediate acclaim outside of the Arctic in 1970 when first exhibited. He was beginning a celebrated career that was tragically cut short in 1974, when he died in a fire.

Karoo was raised in a traditional nomadic Inuit lifestyle, facing an ongoing struggle for subsistence through hunting and fishing. Many of the human figures he sculpted had small particles in their open mouths, suggesting that Karoo meant for them never to be without food. Such cleverness infuses his work in aspect and form, with some sculptures featuring removable parts, turning heads, several eyes, and mismatched feet, reflecting a sense of playfulness that Karoo brought to his art work. Most importantly, the original shape of whalebone pieces and stones he used inform the finished image, striking a balance between the natural world and how it is shaped into artwork, resulting in vivid and compelling sculptures.

The subjects of Karoo's works are human figures and such animals as birds, bears, and walruses, ranging from simple to otherworldly and shamanistic representations, often with spiritual undertones. Limbs or wings, edges of clothing, and similar features are incised in the whalebone and other materials, with eyes set in and often formed by rings of different materials, making them especially striking. The expressiveness of faces and Karoo's close adherence to the natural shape of his materials lends them a sense of exoticness and variety. A face can be rounded, squared, or take the shape of an inverted drop of water, as in *Head* (c. 1972), a whalebone sculpture with ringed eyes near the top, deep nostrils and an oval mouth; the piece is rounded at the top and tapers quickly to the base. *Two-Headed Figure* from 1971 is a delightful abstraction and a powerful example of Karoo's artistry. One head juts out from a solid piece of whalebone, bearing a serene expression with close, holed-out eyes, slightly protruding lips and a straightlined mouth. The other head is incised and rounded, wide-eyed with mouth agape, a figure perhaps pained or caught in a moment of surprise. Two arms are incised on either side of the squared-off torso, which is perched on a fish-shaped piece that fans out, curves back inward, then curves out again slightly where it meets a stone, parallelogram base that feeds into the curves. Karoo's cleverness in using natural

shapes is evident in manipulating the slightly curved-outward end to form the feet of the figure, and a holed-out center between the curving lines forms a graceful space between the legs.

Working natural shapes of material to wield expressive power, Karoo created works of increasing complexity, as facial features and appearances became more abstract: he set eyes in different locations, looking to the side or behind, and his poses became more dramatic and daring. His death cut short those developments, while frequent exhibitions of his work continue to show his accomplished artistry.

—Perry Bear

KASKALLA, Rod

Tribal affiliations: Zuñi
Jewelry designer

Born: Roderick Kaskalla at Zuñi Pueblo, New Mexico, 27 April 1955. **Education:** Fort Lewis College in Colorado. **Family:** Married Lela, governor of Nambe Pueblo; three children, Roland, Kayla, and Taya. **Career:** Jeweler, exhibiting regularly at fairs and markets.

Selected Group Exhibitions

1988   Smithsonian Institution, Washington, D.C.
1990   *Santa Fe Indian Market Collection,* Museum of Man in San Diego, California
1992   *The American Indian Tradition and Transition Exhibit,* Corpus Christi, Texas
1994   Smithsonian Institution, Washington, D.C.

Collections

Albuquerque International Airport, Albuquerque, New Mexico; Museum of Man, San Diego, California.

Publications

On KASKALLA: Books: *Southwest Indian Art Collectibles,* Carefree, Arizona, 1982; *Lost and Found Traditions: Native American Art 1965-1985,* by Ralph T. Coe, The American Federation of Arts, New York, 1986; *Southwestern Indian Jewelry,* by Dexter Cirillo, New York, 1992. **Articles**—"Southwest American Indian Art: A Contemporary View of Six Young Artists," by Leona M. Zastrow, *Arts & Activities Magazine,* 1981; "Roderick and Lela Kaskalla/ Jewelry Makers," by Suzanne Deats, *Indian Market Magazine* Santa Fe, 1989; "Zuni Jewelry Featured at Smithsonian," by Douglas Conwell, *The New Mexican,* Santa Fe, 21 July 1988; "Rod Kaskalla," by Sheila Tryk, *Santa Fe Indian Market,* Tierra Publications, 1993.

*

Rod Kaskalla coments:
I am fortunate to have grown up with grandparents, aunts and uncles whose livelihood was dependent on jewelry. Basically, I learned from watching the process. At the age of 13, I started to make channel inlay under the guidance of my grandparents. In the late 60s and 70s, the demand for jewelry became so great that my grandparents could not

keep up with their orders. They encouraged me to work on my own. The feeling of accomplishment that I experienced by doing a piece of jewelry from start to finish gave me the encouragement I needed, and I began to collect my own set of tools.

I continued this work throughout my high school years. In 1973, I graduated from Zuni High School and chose to go to Fort Lewis College in Durango, Colorado. While attending school, I met my lovely wife, Lela, who is from Nambe Pueblo. I taught her how to do inlay work. Lela has been a great inspiration to me. She was aware of the various art shows and encouraged me to enter the shows as well as juried competitions. We have now been working together for almost 23 years and in that time we have won numerous awards in a variety of categories. Lela and I have worked hard to establish a reputation of producing top quality pieces.

*   *   *

Rod Kaskalla is a noted Zuñi jeweler, who was taught as a young boy in the traditional Zuñi inlay style of stone work by his grandmother. He was raised in Zuñi Pueblo which is located in western New Mexico. After developing his craft during his high school years, Kaskalla attended Fort Lewis College in Colorado, where he expanded his study and practice of jewelry, the traditional art form of his people. Kaskalla particularly focused on working with silver, as well as stones and shells, and began developing his own style.

Kaskalla blends traditional Zuñi Inlay techniques of his ancestors with his own sense of design, which features simple patterns that complement inlays, and the personal dimension he infuses is valued by collectors. His jewelry designs, especially bracelets, feature patterns in stone and metal, and his work with stone and shell are meticulously designed and usually framed in either silver or gold, with color choices of stones, shells and metal providing a harmonious setting. The contemporary aspect of his channel inlay occurs through his use of different stones and shells to achieve desired designs, many of which are common in Zuñi but contemporized by Kaskalla's overall design. Among the mixture of indigenous and non-indigenous stones and shells he has used are turquoise, coral, abalone, green snail, and black jet.

Kaskalla has been recognized for his designs in both silver and gold as well as his craftsmanship. He has won numerous awards at the Santa Fe Indian Market, the Eight Northern Pueblos Indian Art Market, Eight Northern Indian Pueblo Art Show, and the Tulsa Indian Art Show. He has traveled extensively to participate in various art shows and to demonstrate his art. Kaskalla is represented by several major galleries in Arizona, Colorado, California, and New Mexico. In 1994, he was selected as part of New Mexico Artists delegation to the Smithsonian Museum, among the many sites where he has demonstrated the traditional inlay techniques of his people.

—Leona M. Zastrow

KAVIK, John

Tribal affiliations: Inuit
Carver, painter, and ceramist

Born: Gjoa Haven, King William Island, Rankin Inlet, Northwest Territories, 1897; member of the Utkusiksalingmiut tribe of Inuit, King William Island. **Family:** Married; five children; son Thomas

Udjuk (born 1921) is also a carver. **Career:** Hunter and fisherman; moved to the Keewatin community of Baker Lake in 1958 and then Rankin Inlet, 1959, where he worked in the newly opened nickel mine; began carving in 1960. **Died:** 28 March 1993.

Individual Exhibitions

1986   *Sculpture by John Kavik,* Guild Shop, Toronto, Ontario
       Johnny Kavik of Rankin Inlet, Inuit Gallery of Eskimo
       Art, Toronto, Ontario
1990   *John Kavik,* Inuit Gallery of Vancouver, British Columbia

Selected Group Exhibitions

1965   *Arctic Values '65,* New Brunswick Museum, St. John
1968   *Eskimo Ceramics,* Stewart Hall Cultural Centre, Pointe
       Claire, Quebec
1971   *Sculpture/Inuit: Masterworks of the Canadian Arctic,*
       Canadian Eskimo Arts Council, Ottawa (traveled
       through 1973)
1978   *The Zazelenchuk Collection of Eskimo Art,* Winnipeg Art
       Gallery, Manitoba
1979   *Inuit Art in the 1970s,* Department of Indian Affairs and
       Northern Development, and the Agnes Etherington Art
       Centre, Kingston, Ontario (traveled through 1980)
1981   *Rankin Inlet/Kangirlliniq,* Winnipeg Art Gallery, Manitoba
       *John Kavik: Rankin Inlet Sculpture/Mark Emerak:
       Holman Drawings,* Winnipeg Art Gallery, Manitoba
1983   *The Face of the Inuit,* Inuit Gallery of Eskimo Art, Toronto,
       Ontario
1985   *Masterwork Sculpture 1985,* Inuit Gallery of Vancouver
1986   *Pure Vision: The Keewatin Spirit,* Norman McKenzie Art
       Gallery, Regina, Saskatchewan (traveling)
1988   *The World around Me,* University of Lethbridge Art Gallery, Alberta
       *Im Schatten der Sonne: Zeitgenossische Kunst der Indianer
       und Eskimos in Kanada/In the Shadow of the Sun:
       Contemporary Indian and Inuit Art in Canada,* Canadian Museum of Civilization, Ottawa (traveling)
1989   *Mother and Child: Selections from the Inuit Collection of
       the Art Gallery of Ontario,* Art Gallery of Ontario,
       Toronto
1990   *Espaces Inuit,* Maison Hamel-Bruneau, Ste-Foy, Quebec
       (traveling)
1993   *Contemporary Inuit Drawings,* Muscarelle Museum of
       Art, College of William and Mary, Williamsburg, Virginia

Collections

Art Gallery of Greater Victoria, Victoria, British Columbia, Art Gallery of Ontario, Toronto; Canada Council Art Bank, Ottawa; Canadian Museum of Civilization, Hull, Quebec; Dennos Museum Center, Northwestern Michigan College, Traverse City; Eskimo Museum, Churchill, Manitoba; Inuit Cultural Institute, Rankin Inlet, Northwest Territories; Klamer Family Collection, Art Gallery of Ontario, Toronto; McMichael Canadian Art Collection, Kleinburg, Ontario; Mendel Art Gallery, Saskatoon, Saskatchewan; Musée des Beaux Arts de Montreal; Museum of Anthropology, University of British Columbia, Vancouver; National Gallery of Canada, Ottawa; Sarick Collection, Art Gallery of Ontario, Toronto; University of Lethbridge Art Gallery, Lethbridge, Alberta; Vancouver Art Gallery; Williamson Collection, Art Gallery of Ontario, Toronto; Winnipeg Art Gallery, Winnipeg, Manitoba.

Publications

On KAVIK: Books—*Rankin Inlet/Kangirlliniq,* Winnipeg Gallery, Winnipeg, 1981; *Pure Vision: The Keewatin Spirit* by Norman Zepp, Norman Mackenzie Art Gallery, Regina, 1986; *John Kavik,* Inuit Gallery of Vancouver, Vancouver, 1990; *The Inuit Imagination: Arctic Myth and Sculpture* by Harold Seidelman and James Turner, Douglas & McIntyre, Vancouver/Toronto, 1993. **Articles**—"The Spirit of Keewatin" by Robert G. Williamson, *The Beaver,* Summer 1965; "Kavik: The Man and the Artist" by Stanley Zazelenchuk, *Arts & Culture of the North,* vol. 4, no. 2, Spring, 1980; "Kavik: The Man and the Artist" by Stanley Zazelenchuk, *Arts & Culture of the North* vol. 4, no. 2, Spring 1980; "Some Wonderful, Creative Years in Rankin Inlet/ Les Annees Folles des Artistes de Rankin Inlet" by Claude Genier, *About Arts and Crafts/L'art et l'artisanat,* vol. 5, no. 1, 1982; "John Kavik's Son, Thomas Ugjuk, Speaks about His Father and Himself" by Simeonie Kunnuk, *Inuit Art Quarterly,* vol. 8, no. 4, Winter 1993; "Memories of John Kavik 1897-1993" by Norman Zepp, *Inuit Art Quarterly,* vol. 8, no. 3, Fall 1993.

*   *   *

John Kavik, a self-taught stone sculptor who lived and worked in the small Arctic community of Rankin Inlet, is considered one of Canada's foremost Inuit sculptors. Already elderly when he began producing art, Kavik quickly gained a reputation as an original and energetic talent. In fact, any discussion of Rankin Inlet art is dominated by the sculpture of Kavik and John Tiktak (1916-1981).

Kavik, a member of the Utkusiksalingmiut tribe of Inuit, was born in Gjoa Haven on King William Island in Canada's Northwest Territories in 1897. He moved south to the mainland where he maintained a traditional hunting existence for most of his life. Starvation forced him to move to the Keewatin community of Baker Lake in 1958. In 1959, at age 62, he was told to move to Rankin Inlet, and worked in the newly opened nickel mine, but was unable to continue for long. He stayed in the community, taking up carving in 1960. Known primarily as a stone carver, Kavik also experimented with pottery at the Rankin Inlet ceramics studio, which operated from 1965 until 1973, and produced several fine drawings as well. He carved only sporadically in the last five years of his life.

The human figure is a popular subject in the Keewatin. In the the art of Kavik, it dominates as well. Kavik generally portrayed single figures or depictions of mothers and children and other pairings. His figures are very often captured in motion or in some emotional state that energizes them. Joy, suffering, the maternal bond are clear for all to see and feel. When not preoccupied with the human figure, Kavik portrayed muskoxen in stone sculptures, in bas relief on ceramic pots, or in drawings.

Kavik's approach to carving is direct, uncalculated and unpolished. Tool marks—saw cuts, bored holes, file scratches—are everywhere in evidence, especially in his later works. The stone is slashed, gouged and drilled in a manner that probably has more to do with Kavik's advancing age than with violence against the material. In a sense, Kavik's sculpture is both impressionistic and expressionistic. Impressionistic because it is so immediate that it has

the effect almost of quick sketches in stone, devoid of unnecessary detail, almost blurred, giving us a sensory experience rather than a taste of objective reality. Expressionistic because of its powerful directness, almost raw in its emotional intensity. Stanley Zazelenchuk in his *Arts & Culture of the North* article (1980) stated: "Kavik's work is not pretty....Kavik's work is crude—yet his work is sensitively carved, his people have a soul and a power to evoke intense human feeling." Kavik's ceramics and drawings are as "crude" as his carvings. That is to say, they demonstrate the same direct, almost brutal physical presence and primal raw energy.

Kavik's sculptures have been included in fifty exhibitions in Canada and abroad, including *Sculpture/Inuit: Masterworks of the Canadian Arctic,* an international touring exhibition of 1971-73; *Rankin Inlet/Kangirlliniq* at the Winnipeg Art Gallery, 1981, and *Pure Vision: The Keewatin Spirit,* a touring exhibition of 1986-87. Of three solo exhibitions, *John Kavik* at the Inuit Gallery of Vancouver (1990) included an illustrated catalog. Major works by Kavik can be found in the collections of the National Gallery of Canada, the Canadian Museum of Civilization, the Art Gallery of Ontario, the Winnipeg Art Gallery and many other art galleries and museums.

—Ingo Hessel

KENOJUAK Ashevak
Tribal affiliations: Inuit
Carver and printmaker

Born: Ikerrasak, South Baffin Island, Northwest Territories, October 1927; name also variously spelled Kenoyuak, Kinoajuak, Kenoajuak. **Family:** Married 1) Johnniebo Ashevak, and 2) Joannasie Igiu; both were artists. **Career:** Artist, 1950-. **Awards:** The Order of Canada in 1967; election to the Royal Academy of Arts in 1974; appointment as Companion to the Order of Canada in 1982; Honorary Doctorate from Queens University in 1991; and an Honorary Doctor of Laws from the University of Toronto in 1992.

Individual Exhibitions

1967   *Kenojuak Prints,* National Library, Ottawa
1979   *Kenojuak Lithographs,* Waddington Galleries, Toronto, Ontario
1982   *Kenojuak: The Renowned Dorset Artist,* Canadiana Galleries, Edmonton, Alberta
1986   *Recent Drawings by Kenojuak,* The Innuit Gallery of Eskimo Art, Toronto, Ontario
1990   *Kenojuak Drawings,* Houston North Gallery, Lunenburg, Nova Scotia
1994   *Kenojuak Ashevak—Recent Drawings,* Feheley Fine Arts, Toronto, Ontario
1995   *Kenojuak: Original Drawings,* Albers Gallery, San Francisco, California

Selected Group Exhibitions

1965   *Contemporary Inuit Art at the National Gallery of Canada,* National Gallery of Canada, Ottawa

1967	*Inoonoot Eskima: Grafik och Skulptur fran Cape Dorset och Povungnituk,* Konstframjandet, Stockholm
1968	*Eskimo Sculpture, Eskimo Prints and Paintings of Norval Morrisseau,* Art Association of Newport, Newport, Rhode Island
1969	*Eskimo Sculpture '69,* Robertson Galleries, Ottawa
1970	*Graphic Art by Eskimos of Canada: First Collection,* Cultural Affairs Division, Department of External Affairs, Canada, Ottawa (traveling)
1984	*Demons and Spirits and those who wrestled with them,* The Arctic Circle, Los Angeles, California
1987	*The Swinton Collection of Inuit Art,* Winnipeg Art Gallery, Winnipeg, Manitoba
1987-89	*Contemporary Inuit Drawings,* Macdonald Stewart Art Centre, Guelph, Ontario (traveling)
1988	*The Sculpture of Kenojuak Ashevak & Joanassie Igiu,* Feheley Fine Arts, Toronto, Ontario
	Inuit Women and their Art. Graphics and Wallhangings, Gallery 210, University of Missouri, St. Louis
1989	*Spoken in Stone: An Exhibition of Inuit Art,* Whyte Museum of the Canadian Rockies, Banff, Alberta (traveling)
	A New Day Dawning: Early Cape Dorset Prints, University of Michigan, Ann Arbor
1991	*Sojourns to Nunavut: Contemporary Inuit Art from Canada,* at Bunkamura Art Gallery, Tokyo (traveling)
1995	*Immaginario Inuit, Arte e cultura degli esquimesi canadesi,* Galleria d'Arte Modernae Contemporanea, Verona, Italy

Collections

Anchorage Museum of History and Art, Alaska; Art Gallery of Greater Victoria, Victoria, British Columbia; Art Gallery of Hamilton, Ontario; Art Gallery of Nova Scotia, Halifax, Art Gallery of Ontario, Toronto; Art Gallery of Windsor, Ontario; Art Gallery of York University, Downsview, Ontario; Beaverbrook Art Gallery, Fredericton, New Brunswick; Canadian Museum of Civilization, Hull, Quebec; Dennos Museum Center, Northwestern Michigan College, Traverse City; Department of External Affairs, Ottawa, Ontario; Edmonton Art Gallery, Edmonton, Alberta; Agnes Etherington Art Centre, Queen's University, Kingston, Ontario; Glenbow Museum, Calgary, Alberta; Haffenreffer Museum of Anthropology, Brown University, Bristol, Rhode Island; Inuit Cultural Institute, Rankin Inlet, Northwest Territories; Macdonald Stewart Art Centre, Guelph, Ontario; McMichael Canadian Art Collection, Kleinburg, Ontario; Mendel Art Gallery, Saskatoon, Saskatchewan; Musee des beaux-arts de Montreal, Quebec; Museum of Anthropology, University of British Columbia, Vancouver; National Gallery of Canada, Ottawa, Ontario; New Brunswick Museum, Saint John, New Brunswick; Prince of Wales Northern Heritage Centre, Yellowknife, Northwest Territories; Red Deer College, Red Deer, Alberta; Royal Ontario Museum, Toronto; Tate Gallery, London; University of Alberta, Edmonton; University of Guelph, Ontario; University of Lethbridge Art Gallery, Lethbridge, Alberta; University of Michigan Museum of Art, Ann Arbor; Vancouver Art Gallery, British Columbia; Winnipeg Art Gallery, Manitoba; Woodstock Public Art Gallery, Woodstock, Ontario; World Wildlife Fund Collection, Switzerland.

Kenojuak Ashevak. Photograph by Marion Jackson.

Publications

On KENOJUAK: Books—*Cape Dorset: A Decade of Eskimo Prints and Recent Sculptures,* by James Houston, National Gallery of Canada, Ottawa, 1967; *Inuit: The Art of the Canadian Eskimo,* by W.T. Larmour, Indian Affairs and Northern Development, Ottawa, 1967; *Inuit Art in the 1970s,* catalog by Marie Routledge, Agnes Etherington Art Centre, Kingston, Ontario, 1979; *In the Shadow of the Sun,* by Gerald McMaster, et al, Canadian Museum of Civilization, Hull, Quebec, 1993; *The Inuit Imagination: Arctic Myth and Sculpture,* by Harold Seidelman and James Turner, Douglas & McIntyre, Vancouver/Toronto, 1993; *Inuit Women Artists: Voices from Cape Dorset,* edited by Odette Leroux, Marion E. Jackson, and Minnie Adola Freedman, Douglas & McIntyre, Vancouver, 1994. **Articles**—"Kenojuak," by Roy MacSkimming, *Inuit Art Quarterly,* vol. 1, no. 1, 1986; "The Power of the Pencil: Inuit Women in the Graphic Arts," by Janet Catherine Berlo, *Inuit Art Quarterly,* vol. 5, no. 1, Winter 1990.

*   *   *

Perhaps the best-known of all contemporary Inuit artists, Kenojuak Ashevak was one of the first Inuit women to involve herself in the new arts projects introduced at Cape Dorset by artist and South Baffin Area Administrator, James Houston. Kenojuak and her husband, Johnniebo, were still living on the land not far from Cape Dorset when James and Alma Houston settled in Cape Dorset in the 1950s and began encouraging Inuit of the area to make soapstone carvings and, later, prints and drawings to be sold in the cities of southern Canada and abroad.

In her twenties at the time and a young mother, Kenojuak welcomed the opportunity to augment her family's limited access to cash income by making objects of art. She discovered that she loved carving images (primarily birds and women) in white marble and in the soft green soapstone quarried in the nearby area. When she later tried her hand at drawing and at incising copper plates for engravings, she embraced these activities with equal enthusiasm.

Kenojuak has been an active contributor to the Cape Dorset annual print collections since their inception in 1959, and she displayed a natural talent and a distinctive lyrical style from the outset. Her early approach to graphic arts was informed by her experience in the traditions of her culture, particularly by her experience in sewing and piecing elegant designs with the furs she used to make traditional clothing and other objects of use. One of her first print images, *Rabbit Eating Seaweed* (1959), duplicated a sinuous silhouetted pattern she had created earlier as an appliqué on a leather pouch. This pattern was translated into a stencil print and included in the first catalogd print collection issued from Cape Dorset in 1959. Kenojuak's 1960 print image, *The Enchanted Owl*, remains emblematic of her work. This image of a young strutting owl—its head encircled with a fan of sinuous feathers suggesting rays of the sun and its long, curving tail feathers arching upward—is one of the most familiar images in contemporary Inuit art. *Enchanted Owl* was reproduced on the Canadian six-cent postage stamp in 1970.

Kenojuak has contributed nearly 200 images to the Cape Dorset collections. Primarily these are drawn images on paper, relying on the printmakers of the West Baffin Eskimo Cooperative at Cape Dorset to translate her images into stonecut, stencil or lithographic prints. However, during the 1960s Kenojuak incised a large number of drawings directly on copperplate for intaglio printing, and she has done some experimenting with the etching process and with working directly on the lithographic stone as well.

Bold, confident lines and closed, sinuous forms characterize Kenojuak's drawings, and many of her images have a strongly symmetrical organization. Her favored subjects are owls, birds, fish and women (particularly women's faces), and she is known for her lyrical use of decorative flat patterning and for appending ornamental floral forms to her figures to balance the composition and create visual interest. While her choice of subject matter clearly relates to her cultural experience, her images are more decorative than narrative in nature. The high degree of organization and flat patterning in her graphic work suggest an iconic quality, giving the impression that her images concentrate the very essence of Inuit tradition.

Works of art by Kenojuak Ashevak have appeared in almost every major group exhibition of Inuit art since 1960, and she has more than 100 exhibitions to her credit, including such landmark exhibitions as *Sculpture/Inuit: Masterworks of the Canadian Arctic* (1971-73), *The Inuit Print/L'estampe inuit* (1977-82), and *Isumavut: Inuit Women Artists—Voices from Cape Dorset* (1994-95). Kenojuak and her first husband, Johnniebo, were featured in a film, *The Living Stone* (1962), produced by the National Film Board, and she is the only Inuit artist to be featured in a book-length historical and interpretive monograph, Jean Blodgett's *Kenojuak* (1985).

Through the years, Kenojuak Ashevak has received a number of honors recognizing her outstanding artistic achievements. These tributes include the Order of Canada in 1967, election to the Royal Academy of Arts in 1974, appointment as Companion to the Order of Canada in 1982, and Honorary Doctorate from Queens University in 1991 and an Honorary Doctor of Laws from the University of Toronto in 1992. She has also executed many important commissions, including a 96 foot plaster mural that she created in collaboration with Johnniebo for the Canadian Pavilion at Expo '70 in

Osaka, Japan, and, more recently, a large hand-colored lithograph entitled *Nunavut (Our Land*, 1992) commemorating the signing of the agreement that will create the new Inuit territory, Nunavut, in 1999.

—Marion E. Jackson

KEYSER, Louisa

Variant names: Dat So La Lee
Tribal affiliations: Washoe
Basketweaver

Born: c. 1855. **Career:** Basketweaver and domestic helper; worked exclusively for patron Abe Cohn from 1895 to 1925. **Died:** 1925.

Individual Exhibitions

1995   Nevada State Museum, Carson City, Nevada

Selected Group Exhibitions

1977   Nelson Gallery of Art, Atkins Museum of Fine Arts, Kansas City, Missouri
1979   The Fine Arts Gallery, University of British Columbia, Vancouver
1994   *Passionate Hobby: Rudolf Frederick Haffenreffer and the King Philip Museum*, Haffenreffer Museum of Anthropology, Brown University, Bristol, Connecticut
1995-96 Marion Steinbach Indian Basket Museum at the Gatekeeper's Museum, Tahoe City, California
1996   *Weavers of Tradition and Beauty: Basketmakers of the Great Basin*, Nevada Historical Society, Reno, Nevada (on-going, permanent)

Collections

Brooklyn Museum, New York; Children's Museum of Indianapolis; Haffenreffer Museum of Anthropology; Phoebe A. Hearst Museum of Anthropology, University of California, Berkeley; Marion Steinbach Indian Basket Museum at the Gatekeeper's Museum, Tahoe, California; Natural History Museum of Los Angeles County, Los Angeles; Nevada Historical Society, Reno; Nevada State Museum, Carson City; Palm Springs Desert Museum, Palm Springs, California; Peabody Museum of Natural History, Yale University, New Haven, Connecticut; Philbrook Art Center, Tulsa, Oklahoma; Southwest Museum, Los Angeles, California; University of Pennsylvania Museum of Archaeology and Anthropology.

Publications

On KEYSER: Books—*Ledger of Datsolali Baskets,* by Abe Cohn, Archives of Nevada State Museum and Nevada Historical Society, Carson City and Reno, Nevada, n.d.; *The Queen of Basketry: Louisa Keyser,* by Emporium Company, Francis-Valentine Co., San Francisco, 1900; *Indian Basketry,* by James Wharton James, A.L. Hettrich and Co., San Francisco, n.d.; *Aboriginal American Bas-*

Louisa Keyser with two of her degikup baskets, dated 1916 (left) and 1907 (right). Courtesy Nevada State Museum.

ketry: Studies in a Textile Art Without Machinery, by Otis T. Mason, the U.S. National Museum, Washington, D.C., 1902; *How the L. K. Baskets Are Made: Dat So La Lee, Her Life and Work,* by Emporium Company, LeBerthon Publishing Co., Los Angeles, 1905; *Degikup: Washoe Fancy Basketry 1895-1935,* by Marvin Cohodas, The Fine Arts Gallery of the University of British Columbia, Vancouver, 1979; "Washoe Innovators and Their Patrons," by Marvin Cahodas, *Native Traditions in Evolution,* edited by Edwin L. Wade, Hudson Hills Press, New York, 1986; "Louisa Keyser and the Cohns: Mythmaking and Basket Making in the American West," by Marvin Cohodas, in *The Early Years of Native American Art History: The Politics of Scholarship and Collecting,* edited by Janet C. Berlo, University of Washington Press, Seattle, 1992; *Native American Art,* by David W. Penney and George C. Longfish, Hugh Lauter Levin Associates, Southport, 1994. **Articles**—"Dat so la lee," by Clara MacNaughton, *General Federation of Women's Clubs Magazine,* vol. 14, no. 2, 1915; "Dat-So-La-Lee, World-renowned Washoe Indian Basket Weaver," by Effie M. Mack, *Nevada Magazine,* February/March 1946; "Dat So La Lee, Queen of the Washo Basketmakers," by Jane Green Gigli, *Nevada State Museum Popular Series,* no. 3, 1967, republished in "Collected Papers on Aboriginal Basketry," *Nevada State Museum Anthropological Papers,* no. 6, 1974; "Dat So La Lee's Basketry Design," by Marvin Cohodas, *American Indian Art Magazine,* vol. 1, no. 4, 1976; "Dat So La Lee and the degikup," by Marvin Cohodas, *Halycon,* no. 4, 1982; "Abram Cohn of Carson City, Nevada, Patron of Dat-So-La-Lee," by Norton B. Stern, *Western States Jewish Historical Quarterly,* vol. 15, no. 4, 1983; "The Breitholle collection of Washoe basketry," by Marvin Cohodas, *American Indian Art Magazine,* vol. 9, no. 4, 1984; "Dat So La Lee: Washoe Basketmaker," by Donald R. Tuohy, *Nevada State Museum Newsletter,* no. 23, May/June 1995; "Two More Dat So La Lee's 'Modal' Baskets," by Donald R. Tuohy, *Nevada State Museum Newsletter,* no. 24, January/February 1996.

*   *   *

Louisa Keyser, better known as Dat So La Lee during her lifetime, is regarded by many as the finest Washoe Basket weaver of the 20th Century. Keyser was one of the first Indian craftspeople to be sponsored by a patron and thus able to devote all her time to her chosen craft. Her technical skills exceeded those of most, if not all, her contemporaries and prices paid for her work exceeded $1,000 even during her lifetime.

Keyser's technical and artistic skills cannot be disputed, but her notoriety was also due to considerable propaganda promulgated by her patrons, Abe and Amy Cohn of Carson City, Nevada. The Cohns began buying and selling Indian curios in the 1890s, and between 1895 and 1935, their store was the major retail outlet for Washoe baskets. Keyser was promoted as the premier representative of Washoe traditionalism, but in reality, her major basketry forms and designs were completely foreign to Washoe traditions. Indeed, much of the information the Cohns released about Keyser has since been proven to be partially, if not wholly, fabricated for marketing purposes. At the time, however, it went unquestioned by collectors, museum curators, and the media alike.

Keyser was born c. 1855 and was undoubtedly already an accomplished basket weaver when she and the Cohns first became acquainted, c. 1890s. Shortly thereafter the Cohns and Keyser entered into an agreement that lasted some 30 years, whereby the Cohns provided Keyser and her husband food, clothing, shelter, and medical care in exchange for all the baskets Keyser produced. Keyser was also expected to demonstrate her craft at fairs and other locations to increase public interest in her work and in Indian baskets, in general.

Keyser is best known for large spherical baskets, known as *degikup,* the best of which she produced during her years under the Cohn's patronage. The *degikup* was promoted as a traditional Washoe basket form that only Keyser was allowed to make. In truth, it blended the shape and designs of several California tribes, especially the Pomo and Maidu. Keyser began weaving this type of basket early in her career and preferred it over other shapes. Eventually, Amy Cohn recorded each of Keyser's major pieces in an ongoing ledger and completed an official registration certificate to accompany the baskets. These included Cohn's own fanciful interpretations of a basket's symbolism, as well as the starting and ending dates of its manufacture. Some baskets were given formal titles, much as a painting, and all major pieces were numbered sequentially, preceded by the weaver's initial's "LK".

Louisa Keyser's career can be divided into 3 periods, the first one extending from her birth until c. 1899. In these years she wove a variety of basket shapes, including the *degikup* for which she would later become famous. Baskets of this period were generally small and the heavy designs arranged in groups of three in vertical and diagonal bands. By the end of this period, Keyser had begun to use two colors and to experiment with different design layouts.

During the second phase, c. 1899-1914, Keyser's baskets dramatically increased in overall size and grew proportionately more vertical. An earlier design motif, based on a triangle with small attenuations, was further refined and made lighter in appearance. An infinite number of variations of this motif appear on many baskets from this period, with special attention always given to spatial arrangement, to insure that design elements lined up horizontally and vertically. In so doing, Keyser gave greater emphasis to design rather than form, her solution to the problem of placing designs on the two-dimensional surface of a three-dimensional form. The resulting designs seem to float in space. Keyser achieved her greatest technical proficiency during this period, averaging 28 stitches per inch on major pieces.

In the final period of Keyser's career, c. 1914-1925, overall size and vertical proportions increased even further and the contours became more even. Technical proficiency diminished slightly, and Keyser returned to designs and layouts used during her early years. She consciously made this change to make the designs a more integral part of the basket. Form now took precedence over design. Designs on her later baskets follow a basket's contours, making them appear more dynamic.

Louisa Keyser changed for all time the history of Washoe Basket making. Although she traded some of her personal freedom for the security offered by the patronage system, she remained an independent and innovative artist first and foremost. Indeed, her major works were marketed as works of art, albeit with a distorted link to age-old traditions. The *degikup* form and designs Keyser preferred were copied by many other weavers, both during and after her lifetime, and contemporary Washoe basketweavers still dream "of being the next Dat So La Lee."

—Russell P. Hartman

KI-KE-IN

Variant names: Ron Hamilton
Tribal affiliations: Nuu-Chah-Nulth
Graphic artist, carver, painter, illustrator, printmaker, and jewelry designer

Born: Aswinis, Barkley Sound, British Columbia, 1948. **Education:** Apprenticed to Henry Hunt, British Columbia Provincial Museum, Victoria, 1971; B.A. in Anthropology, University of British Columbia, 1992. **Career:** Fisherman, graphic artist, carver, painter, illustrator, speaker, writer, poet, draughtsman, printmaker, dancer, composer, drummer, and jewelry-maker; teacher, Northwest Coast Art, Malaspina College, 1995—.

Individual Exhibitions

1971	Port Alberni Museum, British Columbia
1974	British Columbia Archives, Victoria
	National Museum of Ethnology, Osaka, Japan
1995	British Museum, London
1996	Museum of Anthropology, University of British Columbia

Selected Group Exhibitions

1971-80	*The Legacy*, Royal British Columbia Museum, Vancouver (traveling)
1996	*Topographies: Aspects of Recent B.C. Art*, Vancouver Art Gallery

Publications

By KI-KE-IN: Book—*We Sing to the Universe: Poems by Ron Hamilton*, Vancouver, 1994. **Articles**—"I Invite Honest Criticism: An Introduction," "A Biography of Sorts," and "Poems," *B.C Studies* no. 89, 1991.

On KI-KE-IN: Books— *Northwest Coast Indian Graphics: An Introduction to Silk Screen Prints*, by Edwin S. Hall, Margaret B. Blackman, Vincent Rickard, Vancouver, 1981; *The Legacy: Tradition and Innovation in Northwest Coast Indian Art*, by Peter L. Macnair, Alan L. Hoover, Kevin Neary, Vancouver, 1984; *Topographies: Aspects of Recent B.C. Art*, by Grant Arnold, Monika Kin Gagnon, Doreen Jensen, Vancouver, 1996; *Ki-ke-in: The Drawings*, edited by Marjorie Halpin, University of British Columbia Press, Vancouver, 1997.

*

Ki-ke-in comments:

The drawings are somewhat like visual poems. They offer metaphoric kinds of representations that are full of complexity and welcome multiple interpretations. So, as with poems, I suppose they come from a very personal part of my being and I think that people should take them in whatever way they want, although they are sometimes rather loaded with information.

*   *   *

Ki-ke-in avoids the term "artist," for which there is no comparable concept in his own language. He prefers the ideas underlying the English word, "creator." In developing his creative skills as speaker, writer, poet, draughtsman, print-maker, dancer, composer, carver, drummer, and jewellery-maker, Ki-ke-in has also become a repository of knowledge about his people's culture, their history and expressive forms, at a time when they needed, if not salvaging, then careful research and recording. Marjorie Halpin, anthropologist and authority on the Northwest Coast, refers to Hamilton as "the most knowledgeable person of his generation on the history and culture of the entire Northwest Coast" (1996).

Ki-ke-in first began to draw seriously in 1965 when he went to Terrace, in the British Columbia interior, and was encouraged by being able to sell some of his works. He was apprenticed to the Kwakwaka'wakw carver Henry Hunt in Victoria for two years, before returning to his home on the west coast of Vancouver Island to play an active role in the political and ceremonial life of his people. He lived for some years in his late mother's house at Aswinis, but now makes his home on Sproat Lake near Port Alberni, from where he is able to combine his work among and for local communities with a growing international career. As an example of the former, Ki-ke-in worked for the Nuu-chah-nulth Tribal Council, interviewing over one hundred of his people who had suffered abuse in residential schools. This became the basis of a report that led to a successful court action against one of the offenders.

In the traditional way of a Nuu-chah-nulth creator, Ki-ke-in is adept in being able to turn his hand to a number of skills that are both time-sanctioned and contemporary: carving masks and other objects; print-making; making silver and gold jewellery, etched with his own re-working of the two-dimensional idiom of the region; painting ceremonial curtains, alive with the beings of a living cosmology; writing poetry; story-telling, passing on the old oral traditions as well as teaching all of the above. He is a rivetting storyteller, even, perhaps especially, for non-native audiences, having done a great deal to break down ignorance and build up an appreciation for the ways in which oral cultures communicate. He is also making an important contemporary contribution to knowledge of the Huupachesath. Halpin reports that his journals, kept over thirty years, "constitute perhaps the richest source of information about a Northwest Coast people and their culture that ever has been or, I daresay, ever will be, compiled." As such they are a rich source for others to tap into and should become widely known: "he scrupulously reports and records—verbatim—community and family events, political meetings, potlatches, including potlatch speeches, the amounts and sources of money donations, the songs, dances, masks and headdresses danced, the screen, the persons in attendance, family relationships of participants—and his thoughts, dreams, stories, poems."

Ki-ke-in became widely known for his innovative contribution to the genre of Northwest Coast silk-screen prints as it was developing in the 1970s. For example, *Lightning Snake, Thunderbird and Wolf* (1973) and *Whaler's Dream* (1977), which have been widely reproduced, can be seen to be amongst the most original of the genre. Having learned some of the lessons of modernism, Ki-ke-in took the flatness of the support into account rather than simply reproducing a design intended for three dimensions, and made original use of the rectangular field to make a new kind of abstract context for Nuu-chah-nulth cosmological dramas. This quality of the serigraphs, that they are partly illustrations of myths, partly liberations of myth into a new element, is also found in the drawings.

Ki-ke-in: *Ceremonial Screen,* 1996. Photograph by Trevor Mills; collection of the artist.

Most of Ki-ke-in's work is characterised by this ambivalence between the need to maintain a culture's historical integrity and the need, for the sake of that culture, to connect with other audiences, other aesthetics. Thus, in spite of his demonstrable ability to make saleable commodities, part of the western definition of art, Ki-ke-in now devotes most of his time to making objects and working as a creator/teacher in native communities. On the other hand a recent highly successful exhibition and forthcoming book of his casual drawings show that he has been drawing all his life, for all sorts of reasons and all sorts of people, in what is essentially an act of translation. What he aims to get across is the idea of *chihachitl*, which he translates as "being spooked"—the spiritual impact in songs, dances, masks, rituals and ceremonies.

Fundamental to his graphic skills is Ki-ke-in's knowledge of the graphic conventions involved in designing and painting the huge ceremonial curtains—*thliitsapilthim*—that are an essential element of Nuu-chah-nulth socio-religious events associated with the life-cycle and potlatching. He has devoted much time to enjoying, investigating, tracing the history of these screens. "This passionate interest and pursuit has coloured everything that I do, *everything* that I do," he says. He combines his rights to represent the beings of Nuu-chah-nulth cosmology and their stories with his rights to represent them in whatever manner he wishes.

Ki-ke-in combines the roles of a teacher of his culture and a highly individual creator in the pluralist, contemporary milieu. Contrary to simplistic, but widespread distinctions between the anonymous, collective nature of tribal representations and the individualism of the modern artist, Ki-ke-in's attitude and career suggest a synthesis much richer and more inspiring and with more to contribute in the contemporary world.

—Charlotte Townsend-Gault

KIMBALL, Yeffe

Variant names: Mikaka Upawixe
Tribal affiliations: Osage
Painter, illustrator, and textile artist

Born: Mountain Park, Oklahoma, 30 March 1914; Mikaka Upawixe means "Wandering Star." **Education:** East Central State College, Ada, Oklahoma; University of Oklahoma, Norman; Art Students League, New York, 1935-39; private instruction in France and Italy, summers 1936-39; studied intermittently with Fernand Léger, 1936-41. **Family:** Married Harvey Slatin, 1948. **Career:** Illustrator, textile designer, consultant on native arts, and painter; Art Students League, Vice-President and Board of Control Vice-President; consultant, American Indian art, Portland Art Museum, Oregon, and Chrysler Art Museum, Provincetown, Massachusetts; advisor, Americana Foundation. **Died:** Santa Fe, New Mexico, 10 April 1978.

Individual Exhibitions

1946   Rehn Gallery, New York
1947   Philbrook Museum, Tulsa, Oklahoma
        Denver Art Museum, Colorado
        Crocker Art Gallery, Sacramento, California
        Joslyn Memorial Gallery, Omaha, Nebraska
1948   University of New Mexico, Albuquerque
        Galerie Giroux, Brussels, Belgium
        Portland Art Museum, Oregon
1950   Fine Arts Gallery, San Diego, California
        Des Moines Art Center, Iowa
1951   Rochester Art Gallery, Minnesota
1952   Rehn Gallery, New York
1957   *Golden Jubilee Exhibition*, Municipal Building, Oklahoma
            City, Oklahoma

Art Museum, Santa Fe, New Mexico
University of New Mexico, Albuquerque
1958   Dayton Art Institute, Ohio
1959-65   Tirca Karlis Gallery, New York
1963   University of Virginia Museum, Charlottesville
          Norfolk Museum, Virginia
1966-67   *30 Year Retrospective*, Philbrook Museum of Art (travel-
          ing)

Selected Group Exhibitions

1942   National Academy, New York
1945   Whitney Museum of Fine Art, New York
          Carnegie Institute of Fine Arts, Pittsburgh, Pennsylvania
1946   Virginia Museum, Richmond
          University of Georgia, Athens
          Wesleyan Conservatory and School of Fine Art, Macon,
          Georgia
1947   William Rockhill Nelson Gallery, Kansas City, Missouri
1948   Toledo Museum, Ohio
          Mattatuck Historical Society, Waterbury, Connecticut
1949   La Jolla Art Association, California
1950   Birmingham Art Museum, Alabama
1951   Toledo Art Museum, Ohio
1952   Montclair Museum, New Jersey
1953   Pennsylvania Academy, Philadelphia
1954   De Young Memorial Gallery, San Francisco, California
1955   James Graham Gallery, New York
1958   Chrysler Art Museum, Provincetown, Massachusetts
1959   Philbrook Museum, Tulsa, Oklahoma
1960   Martha Jackson Gallery, New York
1961   Addison Gallery, Andover, Massachusetts
1961-64   *American Indian Paintings*, Philbrook Museum of Art,
          Tulsa, Oklahoma (traveling)
1962   Nova Gallery, Boston, Massachusetts
1964   *First Annual American Indian Art Exposition*, Charlotte,
          North Carolina
          Nelson-Atkins Museum of Art, Kansas City, Missouri
1965   Museum of Fine Arts, Boston, Massachusetts
          *Second Annual Invitational Exhibition of American In-
          dian Paintings*, United States Department of the Inte-
          rior, Washington, D.C.
1968   Santa Barbara Museum, California
1969   Trinity College, Hartford, Connecticut
1975-80   *Pintura Amerindia Contemporanea, E.U.A.*, United States
          Department of State and International Communica-
          tions Agency, Washington, D.C. (tour of South
          America)

Collections

Baltimore Art Museum, Maryland; Bureau of Indian Affairs, United States Department of the Interior, Washington, D.C.; Cincinnati Art Museum, Cincinnati, Ohio; Chrysler Art Museum, Provincetown, Massachusetts; Dayton Art Institute, Ohio; Indian Arts & Crafts Board, Department of the Interior, Washington, D.C.; Museum of Fine Arts, Boston, Massachusetts; Mattatuck Museum, Mattatuck Historical Society, Waterbury, Connecticut; Oklahoma State Art Commission, Oklahoma City, Oklahoma; Philbrook Museum, Tulsa, Oklahoma; Portland Art Museum, Portland, Oregon; Southern Plains Indian Museum and Craft Center, Indian

Arts and Crafts Board, United States Department of the Interior, Anadarko, Oklahoma.

Publications

By KIMBALL: Books illustrated—*Pagans Praying*, by Roy Keech, Clarendon, Texas, 1940; *The World of Manabozho. Tales of the Chippewa Indians*, by Thomas Leekley, New York, 1965; *The Art of American Indian Cooking*, by Yeffe Kimball and Jean Anderson, New York, 1965. **Article**—*Art Digest*, vol. 21, no. 19, 1947.

On KIMBALL: Books—*Songs from the Earth: American Indian Painting*, by Jamake Highwater, Boston, 1976; *Pintura Amerindia Contemporanea, E.U.A.*, by Lloyd Kiva New, Museo del Instituto de Artes Amerindos, 1979.

*   *   *

Yeffie Kimball was born to Martha Clementine and Other Good-Man Smith and given the name Mikaka Upawixe, or Wandering Star. The name aptly describes her art career for a few reasons, most notably because Kimball would travel extensively, took an interest in the subatomic world, which she recreated on the canvas with vibrant images and metaphors, and in later works painted scenes from outer space—fiery comets, otherworldly settings and radiant distant atmospheres. Kimball's works reflect a restless creativity and easy absorption into new subjects—from "primitive" African art to space travel—and she moved freely and rapidly between styles to express her visions and interests.

Kimball attended East Central State College, Ada, Oklahoma, and went on to the art department at the University of Oklahoma. Kimball's "star" first appeared over New York City in 1935 when she joined the Art Students League, then she wandered to Europe each summer from 1936 to 1939, receiving private instruction in France and Italy. She studied intermittently with the famous French modern master, Fernand Léger, from 1936 to 1941. At about this time she became fascinated with African art, which in turn inspired her to explore Native American history and art. Kimball settled in New York City during World War II and from her studio on West 55th Street launched her career as a painter, illustrator, textile designer and consultant on Native arts.

Kimball's early work generally features more open space and muted colors, with concentration on a particular image in a landscape. She enjoyed an excellent response to her first exhibition in 1942 and showed regularly in New York, establishing a strong reputation. Critic Henry McBride, in a review of her work in *The Sun*, 1946, said of Kimball: "Georgia O'Keeffe had better watch out. Her rival now appears on the desert horizon." In addition to capturing scenes and landscapes from her southern plains background, Kimball delved deeper into Native American art and began experimenting with such forms as the flat style and hide paintings.

During the late 1940s, Kimball became deeply interested in science and the subatomic world. She married Dr. Harvey Slatin, an atomic scientist, in 1948, and was influenced by his work at about the same time her paintings became less grounded in surface realism. Some critics have referred to this part of her career as her "fused earth" period, based on her comment that she had been captivated by a sample of earth, given to her by her husband, that had been fused as the result of an atomic explosion. Planets, stars and comets, fiery suns, and wildly shooting gases became frequent images in her work, accompanied by dynamic experimentation with color and texture on large, busy canvases. These works, which she continued painting into the 1960s, are generally grouped as Kimball's "space concept" paintings.

Kimball produced a formidable body of work, ranging from primitivist, to contemporary, to futuristic. The career of Wandering Star passed through many areas of interest, with early paintings suggesting wide open spaces, much like her native southern plains, to dense and almost clotted action scenes in later work. In a 1962 feature article in *The Christian Science Monitor,* Dorothy Adlow summed up her varied output: "Yeffe Kimball is a distinguished American painter who, while she works in what would be labeled a 'modern manner,' devises means which are appropriate to her ideas. These paintings bear titles relating to astronomical phenomena such as *Solar Aurora.* Her interest in nature manifested itself early in life, for her childhood was spent on the plains of Oklahoma. She operates with a great deal of imagination and much that she has to say is generated through the use of a new medium... Is it expressionism? Is it realism? Is it fantasy? One might say that Miss Kimball acquits herself in all or each of these styles."

Later in her career, the comets and spheres and the reaches of outer space gave way to blocks and ovals of hot-colored shapes in deeper abstraction. Because her work reflects ever-widening interests, she passed in and out of various phases and approaches, making Kimball a difficult artist to neatly classify. Kimball's constants were her dedication to art and her Native American heritage. She served as a consultant on American Indian art, literally from coast to coast, working with the Portland Art Museum in Oregon and the Chrysler Art Museum, in Provincetown, Massachusetts, was an advisor to the Americana Foundation, Vice-President of the Art Students League, and contributed illustrations for several books.

—Perry Bear

KUKA, King

Variant names: See Kooks Ee Nan
Tribal affiliations: Blackfeet
Painter and sculptor

Born: Browning, Montana, 1946; also known as Black Wolf. **Education:** Institute of American Indian Arts, Santa Fe, New Mexico, 1965-1966; University of Montana, BFA, 1973; Montana State University; studied watercolor painting with Milford Zornes in South Carolina. **Military Service:** U.S. Army, served in Vietnam. **Career:** Educator, gallery owner; personnel director, writer, poet, and artist; commissions include sculptures for Browning High School, Montana, and National Tekakwitha Conference and stained-glass windows, Little Flower Church, Browning. **Awards:** Numerous, including Heard Museum Guild Indian Fair and Market, Phoenix, Arizona, 1969, 1971-72; Red Cloud Indian Art Show, The Heritage Center, Pine Ridge, South Dakota, 1978-79, 1981-86, 1989-90, 1993; All American Indian Days, Sheridan, Wyoming, 1973; Great Falls Native American Art Show, 1987, 1989; Scottsdale Native American Indian Cultural Foundation Arts and Crafts Competition, 1988; Northern Plains Tribal Arts, 1988-89, 1991-92; Santa Monica Indian Ceremonial, 1990; Northern Plains Tribal Arts, poster artist, 1989.

Individual Exhibitions

1973   Museum of the Plains Indian, Browning, Montana
1984   *Great Falls Native American Art Show,* Great Falls, Montana
1991   Southwest Trading Company, St. Charles, Illinois

Selected Group Exhibitions

Exhibits widely at art fairs throughout the western half of the United States and the Canadian prairie provinces.

1965-66 *Young American Indian Artists,* Riverside Museum, New York
1966   Institute of American Indian Arts Museum, Santa Fe, New Mexico
1974   Hampton University, Virginia
1977   Philbrook Museum of Art, Tulsa, Oklahoma
1979   Cherokee National Museum, Tahlequah, Oklahoma
1981   Amon Carter Museum of Art, Fort Worth, Texas
        Night of the First Americans, John F. Kennedy Center for the Performing Arts, Washington, D.C.
1982   *Native American Painting: Selections from the Museum of the American Indian,* New York (traveling)
1985   Mathes Cultural Center Gallery, San Francisco, California
1986   Santa Fe Festival of the Arts, New Mexico
1987   American Indian Contemporary Arts, San Francisco, California
        Red Earth Festival, Myriad Plaza, Oklahoma City, Oklahoma
1989   International Festival of Native Arts, Calgary, Alberta
1989-92 *Willow Tree Festival,* Old Cowboy Museum, Gorden, Nebraska
1992   American Fair, Kumamoto, Japan
1993   *Let the Spirits Speak!,* Paul VI Institute for the Arts, Washington, D.C.
1993-94 *Native American Visual Arts and Montana,* Custer County Art Center, Montana (traveling)

Collections

American Indian Service, Sioux Falls, South Dakota; AmerIndian Circle, Washington, D.C.; Canadian Museum of Civilization, Ottawa, Ontario; Cleveland Museum of Natural History, Cleveland, Ohio; Deutsches Museum, Munich, West Germany; Thomas Gilcrease Institute of American History and Art, Tulsa, Oklahoma; Heard Museum, Phoenix, Arizona; Institute of American Indian Arts Museum, Santa Fe, New Mexico; Montana State Historical Society, Helena, Montana; Museum of the American Indian, New York; Museum of the Plains Indian, Browning, Montana; Native American Center for the Living Arts, Niagara Falls, New York; Vatican Permanent Collection, Vatican City, Italy; Whetung Art Gallery, Curse Lake, Ontario.

Publications

By KUKA: Poetry in anthologies—*The Whispering Wind,* edited by Terry Allen, Garden City, New York, 1972; *The Remembered Earth,* edited by Geary Hobson, Albuquerque, 1981; *Dancing on the Rim of the World,* edited by Andrea Lerner, Tucson,

1990; *Voices of the Rainbow*, edited by Kenneth Rosen, New York, 1993.

On KUKA: Books—*The Sweet Grass Lives On,* by Jamake Highwater, New York, 1980; *Native American Painting: Selections from the Museum of the American Indian,* by David M. Fawcett and Lee A. Callander, New York, 1982.

*

King Kuka comments:

I like to be free. I want my paintings to be the same. Realism and detail are fine for those who do it, but my temperament is not tolerant of that. People say "you have so much patience." I don't have any patience. If I did, I wouldn't be much of an artist. (From *Art Voices,* September/October 1981)

*   *   *

King Kuka, the Blackfeet artist also known as "Black Wolf," is most at home in nature, especially his homeland in the mountains of Montana, where he was born and raised and where he settled after schooling in Santa Fe, New Mexico, at the Institute of American Indian Arts, and after a tour of military duty that included Vietnam. His artwork developed from an early emphasis on realism to more abstract and mystical works, reflecting his frequent experimentation with media and materials. Studies of nature, animals, objects, and figures have become increasingly impressionistic. A sense of spirituality drawn from his Blackfeet and Christian backgrounds permeates his work, most often in a suggestive manner but also in motifs that employ the insignia of the Blackfeet tribe.

Kuka's early work featured realistic scenes of the wild west in the style of Charlie Russell. Through these pieces he quickly gained recognition, not only for their popular and nostalgic value but also as historically accurate depictions and finely-rendered natural scenes. Kuka, however, began drawing more on his spiritual heritage, creating a mystical style derived more from working in an impressionistic manner than through the subject matter. That is, ordinary scenes, including berry picking, take on mystical resonance. The influence of the abstract works of Jackson Pollock helped spur Kuka to blur realistic details with interpenetration of colors, which reflects the interpenetration of the human and natural worlds and the underlying interconnectedness that informs his spiritual vision. *Berry People* (1991), for example, is a misty forest scene, with shapes suggesting pines and bushes in which a man and woman robed in blankets with traditional Blackfeet designs are ensconced. White dots throughout the scene and the lightness in an open patch of sky suggest a snowfall and contribute to the mystical aura. Such dots, however, recur in Kuka's works: the artist has stated that the dots symbolize the spirit of Native Americans. Often taking the form of an element of nature, the dots, appearing in all parts of paintings, connect the constituents of a particular work. They also contribute to the sense of abstractness, but their importance must be considered vital in representing a reality that is spiritual at all times. The mystical scenes are often serene, but not static: symbols on garments or objects, the effects of wind, and other slight flourishes make Kuka's paintings active and suggest a glimpsed or passing moment, rather than a suspended, posed, or still life depiction.

King Kuka: *Deer Doctor.* Photograph by Seth Roffman; courtesy Dr. Gregory Schaaf collection.

An exhibition catalog for a show at the C.M. Russell Museum in Great Falls, Montana, noted that Kuka's art "is best described as ethereal American art. He paints with great spiritualism and love of the people and the country. Whether he is painting a traditional realistic watercolor or a pure landscape or one of his better known impressionistic Native American watercolors, a powerful feeling of the spiritual radiates from the finished work."

Being equally adept in oil paintings as in watercolors, Kuka works in pastels, mixed media, serigraphs and photo prints and produces bronze and stone sculpture. Kuka's sculptures tend to be grounded more in conventional realism than his paintings and often focus on traditions of the Northern Plains Indians. Integrating textures into the design of his watercolors and oils and mixing watercolor and wax resistance are among the numerous and varied techniques Kuka has employed to attain his dreamy scenes.

—Perry Bear

KUNUK, Zacharias

Tribal affiliations: Inuit
Filmmaker, video artist, and sculptor

Born: Near Igloolik, Northwest Territories, 1957. **Career:** Carving, 1969—; mining and carpentry, 1970s; video artist, 1981—; positions as assistant, station manager and senior producer, Inuit Broadcasting Corporation, 1980s-91; independent video producer, 1985—; founded, along with Norman Cohn, Paul Aapak and Paul Qulitaliq, Igloolik Isuma Production, a non-profit, Inuit-owned film-making company, 1991; films local events, televised daily on Igloolik community cable network. **Awards:** Canada Council Grant; Bell Canada Award for Video Art in 1994.

Films

1985   *From Inuk Point of View*, independent video
1989   *Qaggiq (Gathering Place)*, with Norman Cohn, independent video
1991   *Nunaqpa (Going Inland)*, independent video
1993   *Saputi (Fish Traps)*, independent video
1995   *Nunavut*, 13-episode television series, IBC

Selected Exhibitions

1989-93   Video Premiers, throughout Canada, and Tokyo, Japan, Copenhagen, Denmark, Washington, D.C., Alaska, Madrid, Spain, Geneva, Switzerland, Paris, France, New York
1991   *Land, Spirit, Power*, National Gallery of Canada, Ottawa, Ontario
1993   *Saputi*, Museum of Modern Art, New York (video premier)
1994   *From Icebergs to Ice Tea*, Thunder Bay Art Gallery, Ontario (traveling)

Collections

Avataq Cultural Institute, Montreal, Quebec; Canadian Museum of Civilization, Hull, Quebec; Museum of Anthropology, University of British Columbia, Vancouver; Museum of Northern Peoples, Hokkaido, Japan; National Gallery of Canada, Ottawa; New York University, New York; and the Winnipeg Art Gallery, Winnipeg, Manitoba.

Publications

On KUNUK: Catalogs—"Zacharias Kunuk," by Diana Nemiroff, Land, Spirit, Power, National Gallery of Canada, 1991; *From Ice-*

Zacharias Kunuk: Production still from *Qaggiq*, 1989. Collection of the National Gallery of Canada; courtesy of Igloolik Isuma Productions, Northwest Territories.

Zacharias Kunuk: Production still from *Nunaqpa*, 1991. Collection of the National Gallery of Canada; courtesy of Igloolik Isuma Productions, Northwest Territories.

bergs to Ice Tea, by Victoria Henry and Shelley Niro, Thunder Bay Art Gallery and Carleton University Art Gallery, 1994. **Articles**— "Zacharias Kunuk: Video maker and Inuit historian," *Inuit Art Quarterly*, Summer, 1991; "Local Channels: Zach Kunuk remodels TV / Chaînes locales: Zach Kunuk refaçonne la TV," by Kass Banning, *Parallelogramme*, vol. 17, no. 1, 1991; "Videographer racing against time," by Todd Phillips, *Nunatsiaq News* (Iqaluit), 15 March 1996; "Igloolik Video: An Organic Response from a Culturally Sound Community," by Kathleen Fleming, *Inuit Art Quarterly*, Spring 1996; "Time Travellers," by Sally Berger, *Inuit Art Quarterly*, Summer, 1996; "Inuit-made TV docudramas as popular as soaps in North," by Jane George, *Ottawa Citizen*, 26 February 1997.

*

Zacharias Kunuk comments (1991):
Up here, we point a camera at somebody and they know they have to tell the truth. We are trying to do everything from our own knowledge, and we expect the South to do the same. From television, we have a false idea of how people live in the South, but, of course, it works the other way around too. The South still thinks that we live in igloos. (From "Zacharias Kunuk: Video maker and Inuit historian," *Inuit Art Quarterly*)

*   *   *

From an isolated beginning in the Canadian Arctic, Zacharias Kunuk is now known internationally for his videos of Inuit life and culture and moves easily between his home community of Igloolik and contemporary art circles. As a filmmaker and visual historian, Kunuk is a pioneer. Through his experimentation with video he stands out as an artist exploring the potential of media other than the carvings, prints, and textiles synonymous with Inuit art.

Kunuk was born at a time when Inuit society was undergoing a vast transition, due largely to the involvement of the Canadian government in the North. As such, he belongs to a generation whose life experiences seem to straddle two cultures, a traditional, past way of existing in the arctic environment and a newer, settlement lifestyle permeated by outside influences. Although Kunuk was born on the land and remembers living in a sod house, at an early age he was separated from his parents to attend school in Igloolik. After a few years of high school in Iqaluit, Kunuk returned to his community, where he supported himself with jobs in mining and carpentry. He began to carve in 1969 and gained some recognition in this area before moving into video. Indeed, it was through the sale of his carvings that Kunuk bought his first video camera in 1981.

Igloolik was one of a few communities to refuse television broadcasts after the Anik-A satellite made this possible in 1972. They reversed their decision only after the creation of Inuit Broadcasting Corporation, in 1981, which ensured that programming would include shows in Inuktitut and on topics relating to the interests of Inuit. It was through IBC that Kunuk received his initial training, working his way up to station manager and then senior producer, until 1991. He produced his first independent video, *From Inuk Point of View* (1985) with funding from the Canada Council.

In 1988, Kunuk began to film *Qaggiq* (*Gathering Place,* 1989) with Norman Cohn, followed by *Nunaqpa (Going Inland,* 1991) and *Saputi* (*Fish Traps,* 1993. The three videos have come to form a loose trilogy based on the seasonal activities of Inuit. All are set in the past and attempt to recapture elements of Inuit life: from practical knowledge, such as how to build a fish wier, to the social interaction of camp life and family dynamics. Intimate details, including the sharing of a pipe between husband and wife, are given as much attention as the unapologetic depiction of the butchering of caribou after a successful hunt. There is no elaborate musical score to accompany the scenes. Instead, real sounds—running water, heavy breathing of Travellers carrying packs, and sounds of laughter, muted in the vast outdoor setting—create a sense of atmosphere. None of the scenes are staged. While Kunuk directs in terms of the idea for the overall film, the scenes are shaped through the collaboration of his partners as well as the actors. From Inuit elders to children, the actors come from Igloolik and may even represent generations of the same family. A script is not provided, but together with the producers, the "action" is discussed beforehand, relying especially on the input and knowledge of the elders. The scene, then, is allowed to unfold—partly spontaneous, partly re-

enacted. Kunuk's videos are unique through this process he calls "remembering by doing, using the technology ... to dramatically and artistically re-envision rather than journalistically document and record" (*Inuit Art Quarterly*, Summer, 1996). This combination of "lived and recreated experience" signifies a distinct approach to film that has roots in the traditional philosophy of Inuit, where skills and knowledge were passed on through observation and practice.

Before the completion of his second film, Kunuk, along with Norman Cohn, Paul Aapak and Paul Qulitaliq, founded Igloolik Isuma Production, a non-profit, Inuit-owned company. The main principle informing their videos is the need to preserve Inuit heritage in a way that incorporates self-representation. Kunuk noted: "We are recording history because it has never been recorded. It's been recorded by southern film makers...but we want our input, to show history from our point of view. We know it best because we lived it" (*Inuit Art Quarterly*, Summer, 1991).

In addition to major productions, Kunuk films local events that are televised daily on his community cable program. Winning the Bell Canada Award for Video Art in 1994 provided the finances to produce a 13 episode television series called *Nunavut*. Set in the mid-40s, each episode, like the videos, re-enacts aspects of life at that time. According to Kunuk, the programs are a reaction to television as a distortion of truth: "From television, we have a false idea of how people live in the South, but, of course, it works the other way around too. The South still thinks that we live in igloos" (*Inuit Art Quarterly*, Summer, 1991).

Since 1988, Kunuk has reached a broad audience through the screening of his videos in Canada as well as in cities around the world, including Tokyo, Copenhagen, Washington, Alaska, Madrid, Geneva, Paris and New York. In 1993, *Saputi* premiered at the Museum of Modern Art in New York. His work can be found in the collections of major institutions such as Avataq Cultural Institute, Montreal, Canadian Museum of Civilization, Hull, Museum of Anthropology, University of British Columbia, Vancouver, Museum of Northern Peoples, Hokkaido, Japan, National Gallery of Canada, Ottawa, New York University, New York, and the Winnipeg Art Gallery.

—Christine Lalonde

L

LA FONTAINE, Glen

Tribal affiliations: Chippewa; Cree
Sculptor

Born: Seattle, Washington 1949. **Education:** Institute of American Indian Arts, Santa Fe, New Mexico, 1968-70; Rhode Island School of Design, Providence, 1970-73.

Individual Exhibitions

1976   Amon Carter Museum of Western Art, Fort Worth, Texas

Selected Group Exhibitions

1973-74   *Heard Museum Guild Indian Fair and Market,* The Heard Museum, Phoenix, Arizona (annual)
1974   *Sculpture II,* The Heard Museum, Phoenix, Arizona
1978   Westwood Galleries, Portland, Oregon
        El Taller Gallery, Austin, Texas
1979   Turtle Museum, Native American Center for the Living Arts, Niagara Falls, New York
1985   *Native American Group Exhibition,* Santa Fe, New Mexico

Collections

Amon Carter Museum of Western Art, Fort Worth, Texas; Daybreak Star Arts Center, Fort Lawton, Washington; Heard Museum, Phoenix, Arizona.

Publications

On LA FONTAINE: Book—*Art in Seattle's Public Places,* by James M. Rupp, University of Washington Press, Seattle, 1992. **Articles**—"Cast Paper Sculpture," by Helen Littlepage, Mershom, *Southwest Art,* February 1982.

*   *   *

Sculpture often brings to mind symbols of strength, associated with materials like stone, bronze, wood, steel, plaster, and clay, but Glen La Fontaine pushed away from the traditional idea of strength and into the craft of delicacy. His cast paper sculptures portray images of commanding strength through a medium of delicate impermanence.

La Fontaine's unusual approach to three dimensional form involved taking paper, breaking it down and recreating images of the plains people from the past. The process involves making a clay tablet of the figure and creating a mold of polyester resin. His designs are cut into the original clay to an approximate depth of one half inch. Once the resin is set, he cleans the clay off the mold and packs the form with prepared rag paper pulp. He then subjected the entire piece to over twenty tons of pressure in a heat controlled, ventilated drying box for twenty four hours. In the process of drying, the paper sculpture shrinks away from the mold, taking a degree of control away from the artist.

In the process of creating many of the pieces, La Fontaine merges as many as five layers of coloured paper in his pulp mixture. These colours were all meticulously arranged within the mold to produce his desired effect. His use of brown, earth red, bright blue, and white created a carefully detailed collection of images with a startling degree of depth. Many of his other pieces were cast in solid colours and some were touched up with acrylic highlights.

In 1978, La Fontaine turned from these smaller scale pieces to what is considered by some his most monumental piece—the mural of ceramic tiles representing the vibrancy of the plains cultures at the Daybreak Arts Center near Seattle, Washington. More than 90 hand-painted and hand-carved tiles, filling a surface over eight feet by ten feet in dimension, became one of his most acclaimed pieces of work, *The Red Race.* The ceramic mural depicts a wild and vivid image of life for the people on the plains.

Although La Fontaine was originally known for his intricately detailed clay figures of plains Indians, his equally intricate use of paper in his sculptures has added an unusual dimension to his work. The method itself of creating these pieces, that of breaking down one fabric to reshape into another, has metaphoric significance far beyond the creation of art—suggesting a symbolic reversal of encroaching white influences in North America that broke down the fabric of native society. Although La Fontaine is believed to have stopped producing art in the 1980s, the products of his innovative methods stand as significant contributions to the artistic process.

—Vesta Giles

LaMARR, Jean

Tribal affiliations: Pit River; Paiute
Painter, printmaker, and mixed media artist

Born: Susanville, California, 24 July 1945. **Education:** San Jose City College, 1969-73; University of California, Berkeley, 1973-76; Kala Institute, Berkeley, 1976-86; color etching workshop, University of Oregon, 1991; Japanese paper/native fiber, NaoPaper, Oguni, Japan, 1991. **Career:** Educator, including San Francisco Art Institute, University of Oregon, and California Correctional Center, 1986-94; professor of printmaking, Institute of American Indian Arts, 1987-92; art instructor, College of Marin, San Francisco State University, California College of Arts and Crafts, Lassen

Community College, 1986-90; guest artist, Brandywine Workshop, Philadelphia, Pennsylvania, 1988, 1995; Los Angeles Festival Portfolio Project, 1990; international guest printmaker, Page 90 and Discovery Center, Wellington, and Poly-Technical Institute, Whanganui, New Zealand, 1993; artistic director and instructor, Native American Graphic Workshop, Susanville, California, 1986-94; project director and curator, *Weaving Contemporary Ceremony I, II, III*, Portfolio Project, 1993-98; Printmaking Workshops for Yakuts, Indigenous artists of Siberia, in screenpainting, etching, monoprinting, 1994; commissions, including *Commemoration of the Ohlone Way of Life*, public art project, San Jose, California, 1994-95, and Ohlone Mural Project, Ohlone Park, Berkeley, California, 1995. **Awards:** Scholarships and Fellowships, including Maple Creek Willies Scholarship, 1973-76, Brandywine Workshop fellowship, 1988; honors at juried competitions, including California Indian Days, Heard Museum Guild Indian Fair and Market, Cal Expo, Sacramento, and American Indian Festival of Arts, La Grande, Oregon.

Individual Exhibitions:

1975   C.N. Gorman Museum, University of California, Davis
1976   Marin Civic Center Gallery, San Rafael, California
1977   Trading Post Gallery, Berkeley, California
1981   Great Plains Indian Museum, Browning, Montana
1995   *Violently Viotaile, Selected Mixed Media Works, 1974-1995*, C. N. Gorman Museum, University of California, Davis

Selected Group Exhibitions:

1975   *Governor's Show*, State Capitol Building, Sacramento, California
        International Women's Exhibit, Artist Embassy, San Francisco, California
        Knowledge Through Vision and Tradition, Marin County Civic Center, San Rafael, California
1976   Humboldt Cultural Center, Eureka, California
        New Horizons in American Indian Art Southwest Museum, Los Angeles, California
1978   California State University, Hayward
        Circle of Tradition and Vision, Artist Embassy, San Francisco, California
1979   California State University Gallery, Sacramento
1980   *Das Andere Amerika*, touring Germany, France, and Italy
1981-86 *Art and Culture of the American Labor Movement*, touring Staadliche Kunsthalle, Berlin; Stadtische Galerie Schloss, Oberhausen, Germany; Stockhom Museum, Sweden; Frankfurt Museum, Germany; Kassel Museum, Germany; Chicago Historical Society Museum, Chichago, Illinois; D.Q. University, The International Indian Arts Festival, Davis, California; Gallery of the American Indian Community House, New York City
1982   Works Gallery, San Jose, California
        Vida Gallery, San Francisco, California
        Confluences of Tradition and Change, R.L. Nelson Gallery, University of California, Davis
        Native American Museum, Santa Rosa Junior College, California
1983   *Cultural Resistance Artist of the Bay Area*, La Pena Cultural Center, Berkeley, California

1984   *Six Native American Artists*, Jerome Evans Gallery, Sacramento, California
        Mother's Gift to her Children, Berkeley Art Center, Berkeley, California
        Bay Area Women Artists, LePena Cultural Center, Berkeley, California
        Faces, Helen Euphrat Gallery, DeAnza College, Cupertino, California
        Intergrafika 84, Berlin, Germany
        Bear Dance, Helen Euphrat Gallery, Cupertino, California
1985-86 *Extension of Tradition, Contemporary Northern California Native American Art in Cultural Perspective*, Crocker Art Museum, Sacramento, California, and Palm Springs Desert Museum, California
        Portfolio II: Eleven American Indian Artists, American Indian Contemporary Arts, San Francisco, California
1988-90 *Committed to Print*, Museum of Modern Art, New York, New York (traveling)
1990   *Intergrafik 90*, Berlin, Germany (traveling)
        Our Land/Our Selves: American Indian Contemporary Artists, University Art Gallery, State University of New York, Albany
1990-94 *Submuloc, In Response to the Columbus Wohs*, Evergreen University, Olympia, Washington, University of Oregon, Eugene, Oregon
1991   *Encentro: Invasion of the America and the Making of the Mestizo*, SPARC, Venice, California
1991-92 *Hosting Our Ancestors*, Richmond Art Center, Richmond, California
        Adeest'ii-Signs of Contradictions, Center of Contemporary Art, Santa Fe, New Mexico
        Counter Colon-ialismo, Centro Cultural de la Raza, San Diego, California; Mas Artspace, Phoenix, Arizona; Dinnerware Artist Cooperative, Tucson, Arizona; Diverse Works, Houston, Texas
1991-94 *Our Land/OurSelves: American Indian Contemporary Artists*, University Art Gallery, SUNY at Albany, New York (traveling)
1991-96 *Shared Visions: Native American Painters and Sculptors in the Twentieth Century*, Heard Museum, Phoenix, Arizona (traveling)
1992   *Centered Margins: Contemporary Art of the Americas*, Bowling Green University, Ohio
        With the Breath of Our Ancestors, Los Angeles Municipal Art Gallery, California
        Beyond 1992, Berkeley Art Center, California
        Alcove Show, New Mexico Museum of Fine Art, Santa Fe
        500 Years of Resistance Through Women's Eyes, Mission Cultural Center, San Francisco, California
        Four Directions: Women Honor Native Land, ProArts Gallery, Oakland, California
1992-95 *Ancestral Memories A Tribute for Native American Survival*, Falkirk Cultural Center, San Raphael, California
1993   *Generations: Her Story*, Berkeley Art Center, California
        Bridging Two Worlds, Pelham Art Center, New York
        Toi Te Ao: Aotearoa, Te Taumata Art Gallery, Auckland, New Zealand
1994   *Native People, Sacred Lands*, San Francisco Art Institute, California

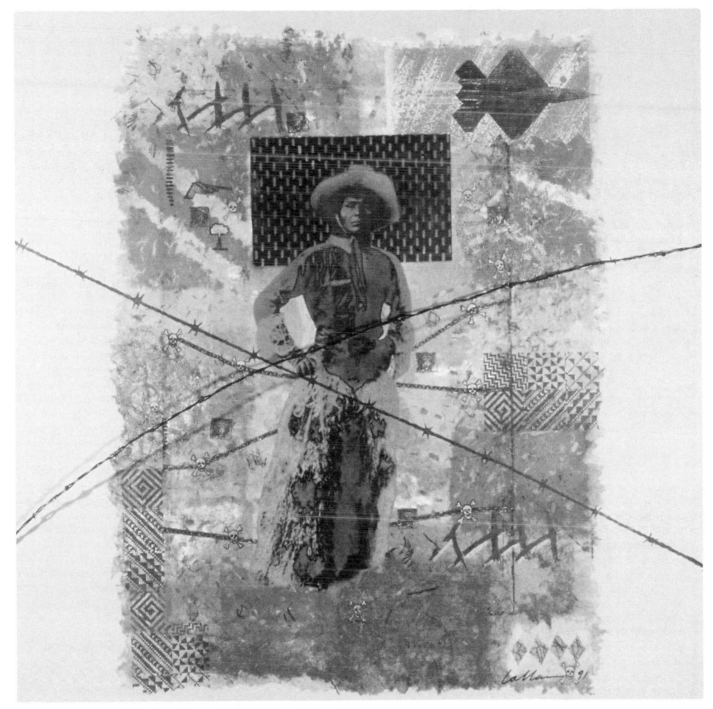

Jean LaMarr: *Some Kind of Buckaroo,* 1992. Courtesy of the artist.

Mirror, Mirror, San Jose Institute of Contemporary Art, California

Native American Voices, Sun Gallery, Hayward, California

Visions of Our Elders, Ancient Traditions Gallery, Minneapolis, Minnesota

Three Stories, University Art Gallery, Chico State University

1994-95 *Watchful Eyes,* Heard Museum, Phoenix, Arizona

Montana Project, Spiderwomen Theater, Bozeman, Montana

1994-97 *Indian Humor,* Center for the Arts, Yerba Buena Gardens, San Francisco, California

1994-98 *Spirit of Native America, South and Central America,* American Indian Contemporary Arts, San Francisco, California (also touring Mexico, Chile, Argentina, Colombia, Brazil, Venezuela, Dominican Republic)

1995   *Legacies: Contemporary Art by Native American Women,*
        Castle Gallery, New Rochelle, New York
        Weaving Contemporary Ceremony I and II, American
        Indian Contemporary Arts, San Francisco, California

Collections

Heard Museum, Phoenix, Arizona; Institute of American Indian
Arts, Santa Fe, New Mexico.

Publications

On LaMARR: Books—*Confluences of Tradition and Change,* edited by L. Price Amerson, Davis, California, 1981; *Committed to
Print,* by Deborah Wye, MOMA, New York, 1988; *Myths of Primitivism, Perspectives on Art,* Hiller, New York, 1989; *Intergrafik,* by
Verband Bildender, Kunstler der Deutschen Demokratischen
Republik, 1990; *Mixed Blessings,* by Lucy Lippard, New York,
1990; *Shared Visions: Native American Painters and Sculptors in
the Twentieth Century,* by Margaret Archuleta and Rennard
Strickland, Phoenix, 1991; *Creativity Is Our Tradition,* by Rick
Hill, Santa Fe, 1992; *The Submuloc Show/Columbus Wohs,* edited
by Carla Roberts, Phoenix, 1992; *Watchful Eyes: Native American
Women Artists,* edited by Anne Gully, Phoenix, 1994; *Feminist Art,*
by M. Roth & Y. Lopez, New York, 1995; *Native American Art,*
Penney/Longfish, Seattle, 1995; *Contemporary Art and Multi cul-
tural Education,* New Museum, New York, and SUNYPress, New
York, 1995. **Articles**—"Jean LaMarr," by Mark Miller, *Cultural
Survival,* Summer 1992; interview/cover, *Atlatl,* Summer 1994;
"Bolivian Sacred Textiles," *Native Peoples,* Winter 1994.

*   *   *

As a grassroots political activist and a teacher of other Native American
artists, Jean LaMarr use the genre of visual art as a vehicle for communication more than a medium to be manipulated according to a specific
aesthetic vision. Nevertheless, LaMarr's works are striking in their
graphic tension, appealing especially with their preponderance of dark
purple hues. Best known for prints on paper, LaMarr draws on her
personal experiences as a native California woman to create unique
images with strong commentary.

LaMarr was born in 1945 in Susanville, a reservation community
in central California. She was raised there and attended Lassen High
School before moving to Santa Clara, where she went to the Philco
Ford Technical Institute for one year. LaMarr continued her education at San Jose City College and University of California, Berkeley, where she majored in art. She has also taken specialized workshops in printmaking and papermaking at the Kala Institute in
Berkeley.

While she works in a wide range of media, including painting,
beadwork, and video installation, LaMarr is primarily known for
her graphic work on political issues, including women's status,
environmental protection and tribal sovereignty. Themes that might
turn maudlin in the hands of other artists, however, stay grounded
and sharp in LaMarr's work, which speaks in a distinctive language
of color and line. As one reviewer wrote, LaMarr "is too skilled an
artist ... to slip into romanticism or nostalgia, and her sense of
humor and knack for understatement enable her to be political without being ... polemical."

Humor becomes an educational tool in LaMarr's works, tempering her thoughtful commentary and political satire. In many pieces

she deconstructs negative sterotypes of Native women, as in *Land
O'Plenty* (1994), a mixed-media wall-hanging created for *Indian
Humor,* the touring exhibit organized by American Indian Contemporary Arts. In this piece LaMarr juxtaposes icons of Western
civilization—airplanes, Hollywood films—with a cartoon that
shows demeaning representations of Native American women.
Women are also featured in her *Cover Girl* series of prints, which
appropriate a patronizing female image from a historic photograph.
LaMarr takes this Native women, naked from the waist up, and
reinstates her as a dignified person, an individual of tribal heritage.

Positive images of women also appear, as in *Lena, 1922* and *Now,*
selected for the Heard Museum's *Second Biennial Native American
Arts Invitational.* This etching is a portrait of the aging process of a
beautiful Native woman, tender and yet telling of the changes
wrought by time and cultural change.

Other works confront environmental destruction and the technological world. In the catalog for *Forms of Address,* a 1994 show at
the San Francisco Art Institute, LaMarr is quoted as saying, "Christian thought has denied the existence of sacred lands in parts of the
world other than Jerusalem." While the U. S. Bombed the Middle
East in the Persian Gulf War, she continued, "[President] George
Bush remarked that efforts would be made not to destroy sacred
sites ... [but] the Supreme Court, however, continues to allow the
destruction of sacred lands in the United States."

Her concern derives also from her personal experience as a Native woman in California, where "sacred places are being destroyed,"
as she has written, "by industry, recreational needs, and by the
government." Nuclear waste sites planned for reservation lands are
protested in *Sacred Places Where We Pray* (1990), a mixed-media
on canvas in which bodies of Native Americans are surrounded by
missiles. In other works, contemporary people are shown wearing
mirrored sunglasses that reflect toxic dumpsites.

Community service is an important part of LaMarr's work. She
has taught classes in ethnic studies and Native American art at
various Bay area colleges, including San Francisco State University
and University of California, Berkeley. She has also designed posters and logos for local Native groups, creating greater public awareness of urban Indians. In her hometown of Susanville, LaMarr is
Director of the Native American Graphic Workshop, and she has
served as a consultant and educator in printmaking, papermaking,
videotape production, and curriculum development for Indian education. In 1991, she was asked to be a consultant for the Smithsonian
Institution's new National Museum of the American Indian.

—Margaret Dubin

LaPEÑA, Frank

Tribal affiliations: Wintu; Nomtipom
Painter, photographer, and mixed media artist

Born: San Francisco, California, 1937. **Education:** Maidu and
Northern California Native traditions from elders, including artists
Frank Day and Mabel McKay; California State University, Chico,
B.A., 1965; San Francisco State University, 1968; California State
University, Sacramento, MA, Anthropology, 1978. **Career:** Per-
forms traditional dance and ceremonies with the Maidu Dancers
and Traditionalists; writer and artist; contributing editor, *News from
Native California;* airplane construction, Port of Oakland, Califor-

nia; art instructor, Redding, California; Professor of Art and Ethnic Studies and Director of Native American Studies, California State University, Sacramento, California; consultant to the National Museum of the American Indian, Smithsonian Institution. **Awards:** Kingsley Show, Sacramento, California, 1961; Northern California Art Show, Chico, 1961, 1969; North Valley Art Show, Redding, 1969,1979; St. John's Religious Art Festival, Sacramento, 1969, 1976.

Individual Exhibitions

1960   Arts and Crafts Gallery, Chico, California
1964   New Image Gallery, San Francisco, California
1969   Raychem Gallery, Palo Alto, California
        Redding Museum and Art Center, California
1971   Redding Museum and Art Center, California
1973   Pacific Western Traders, Folsom, California
1974   Carl Gorman Gallery, University of California, Davis
        Southern Plains Indian Museum, Anadarko, Oklahoma
1980   Carl Gorman Gallery, University of California, Davis
1981   Graduate Fine Arts Center, Long Beach, California
1982   Clarence E. Smith Gallery, Hayward, California
1985   Candy Store Gallery, Folsom, California
1988   Sierra Nevada Museum, Reno
1994   *Art & Books*, California State Indian Museum, Sacramento, California
1995   *Shadows, Stones, and Still Water*, Grayhouse Gallery, Scottsdale, Arizona
1998   Natsoulas Gallery, Davis, California (in preparation)

Selected Group Exhibitions

1981   *Magic Images: Contemporary Native American Art*, Philbrook Art Center, Tulsa, Oklahoma
1982   *Walk in Beauty*, Fine Arts Museum, Santa Fe, New Mexico
1983   *First Biennial Invitational Exhibition*, Heard Museum, Phoenix, Arizona
1984   *Six Native American Artists*, Jerome Evans Gallery, Sacramento, California
        Ancient Visions in Contemporary Indian Art, Williamette University, Salem, Oregon
        Art of the Bear Dance, Euphrat Gallery, Cupertino, California
        No Beads, No Trinkets, American Indian Art Exchange, Seattle, Washington, and Palais des Nations, Geneva, Switzerland
        Native American Artists: California and the West Coast, American Contemporary Art, San Francisco, California
1985   *Eye of the Mind*, San Diego Museum of Man, California
        We Are the Seventh Generation, Atlanta, Georgia
1987   *The Artist and the Myth*, Monterey Peninsula Museum of Art, California
        Recent Generations: Native American Art 1950-1987, Heard Museum, Phoenix, Arizona
        Traditions in Progress, Berkeley Art Center Association, Berkeley, California
1988   *CSUS 40 Year Alumni Show*, Sacramento, California
        Bookart/Visual Literature, Matrix Gallery, Sacramento, California

1988-91 *Four Sacred Mountains*, Arizona Arts Council, a traveling exhibit
1990   *California Indian Shamanism*, C.E. Smith Museum, California State University, Hayward
1991-93 *Our Land, Ourselves*, University Art Gallery, State University of New York, Albany and New England and national tour
        Light on the Subject: The Environment, American Indian Contemporary Arts, San Francisco, California
        From the Source, Ink People Gallery, Eureka, California
        Robert Leach and Frank LaPeña, Artists Contemporary Gallery, Sacramento, California
1991-95 *Shared Visions*: Native American Painters and Sculptors of the Twentieth Century, Heard Museum, Phoenix, Arizona and national and international tour
1992   *Ancestral Memories*, Falkirk Cultural Center, San Rafael, California
1992-93 *Encounters*, Lincoln Plaza Gallery, Sacramento, California and tour to Vancouver, Canada and Mexico City
1993   *Visions and Voices*, U.C. Museum of Art, Science, and Culture, Danville, California
1994-95 *This Path We Travel: Celebrations of Native American Creativity*, Smithsonian Institution, National Museum of the American Indian at the Heye Center, Customs House, New York
        The Spirit of Native America, American Indian Contemporary Arts, San Francisco, California and travel to Mexico and South America
1995   *Native American Art*, Encina Art Gallery, California
        The Artist and A Flower, 37th Annual Invitation, Artists Contemporary Gallery, Sacramento, California
1996   *I Stand in the Center of Good*, American Indian Community House, New York
        Ancestral Memories: A Tribute to Native Survival, Ink People Center for the Arts, Eureka, California
        First People: Animals in Native Californian Art, Santa Barbara Museum of Natural History, California

Collections

California State University, Sacramento, California; Crocker Museum, Sacramento, California; Heard Museum, Phoenix, Arizona; Indian Arts and Crafts Board, Department of the Interior, Washington, D.C.; Mendocino Art Center, Mendocino, California; Mills College Rare Books Library, Oakland, California; Redding Museum and Arts Center, Redding, California; Turtle Foundation, Center for Living Arts, Buffalo, New York; University of Utah, Salt Lake City, Utah.

Publications

By LaPEÑA: Books—*Commemoration*, Okeanos Press, Berkeley, n.d.; *The World is a Gift*, San Francisco, 1987.

On LaPEÑA: Books—*Pintura Amerindia Contemporanea, E.U.A.*, by Lloyd Kiva New, Museo del Instituto de Artes Amerindos, 1979; *The Sweetgrass Lives On*, by Jamake Highwater, New York, 1980; *Confluences of Tradition and Change*, edited by L. Price Amerson, Jr., University of California, Davis, 1981; *Magic Images*, by Edwin L. Wade and Rennard Strickland, University of Oklahoma Press and Philbrook Museum, 1982; *The Arts of the North*

Frank LaPeña: *Horned Spirit,* **1979. Photograph by Rick Hill.**

American Indian: Native Traditions in Evolution, edited by Edwin L. Wade and Rennard Strickland, Hudson Hills Press, New York, 1986; *Portfolio II: Eleven American Indian Artists,* American Indian Contemporary Arts, San Francisci, 1988; *Shared Visions: Native American Painters and Sculptors of the Twentieth Century,* by Margaret Archuleta and Rennard Strickland, Heard Museum, Phoenix, 1991; *I Stand in the Center of Good,* by Lawrence Abbott, University of Nebraska Press, 1994. **Articles**—"Talking: Painter Frank LaPeña," by Jeanine Gendar, *Indian Artist,* Spring 1997. **Film**—*Frank LaPeña: Wintu Artist and Traditionalist,* Theo-Blount Media Productions, Fair Oaks, California, 1988; *Sacred Spaces, Spirit Places,* Department of Parks and Community Services, Sacramento, in cooperation with the California Department of Parks and Recreation, Office of Interpretive Services, Interpretive Programs Section, 1992; *The Heard Museum Presents Frank LaPeña, Artist and Lecturer,* Heard Museum, Phoenix, Arizona in conjunction with the exhibition, *Objects of Myth and Memory,* 1993.

*

Frank LaPeña comments (1987):

To understand the meaning of contemporary Indian art, it is necessary to consider the bond between the traditional arts and contemporary art as well as several other factors, such as the symbiotic relationship between human beings and nature, the function of traditional ceremony and storytelling, and the relationship of vision and dreams to imagery. In Northern California, as in other Indian areas and regions, certain themes flow through the conscious-

ness of the tribal society and its members. The themes are related through creation myths, stories, and songs. These, in turn, relate to understanding and controlling the philosophical and ethical foundation that helps one make a good and meaningful life. (From *The World Is a Gift*)

*   *   *

Frank LaPeña was born in San Francisco in 1937, to an Asian father and Wintu mother. When LaPeña was five years old, his father was killed and his mother was unable to care for him; consequently he spent much of his childhood in federal Indian boarding schools and in a foster home. It was not until after he graduated from public high school in Shasta County, California, that he reestablished relations with his Wintu relatives. As a young adult, LaPeña began seeking out elders from whom to learn traditional ways. In the process of becoming reconnected to his cultural heritage, LaPeña began painting and writing poetry. He first exhibited his work in 1960 in Chico, California, where he was working toward a B.A. in Art at the California State University.

LaPeña's art is deeply informed by his personal experience, the education he has received from those he considers his elders, and his own practice of traditional dance and ceremony. LaPeña has identified a trio of themes in his art: ceremony and dance, teaching and oral traditions, and traditional religion and symbolism. These themes appear in his work in both representational and abstract forms, departing from earlier Native American painting that reified these themes in literal, formulaic styles. The strength of LaPeña's art is its ability to freshly reinvent such images as the ubiquitous deer dancer, as in his *Deer Dance Spirit,* which conveys the spirituality and transformative power of the dance through symbolic use of color as well as visual referents to deer dance regalia.

Much of LaPeña's art makes reference to specific ceremonies and traditional motifs, but in ways that convey broad meaning, particularly of the unity of spirit and earth. Several of his works, among them *Big Head Design II* (1975), *Flower Dance Spirit* (1981), and *Spring Spirit* (1987), relate to the Hesi ceremony of his Wintun people, a ceremony that addresses the continuation of life, the maintenance of harmony and balance, and respect for life and living beings. Through color and impressionistic renderings of the Hesi ceremonial regalia, these paintings evoke such meanings without resorting to visual cliches.

Though LaPeña has been fundamentally concerned with tradition, both in his art and in his life, he understands tradition to be living and vibrant and continually in the process of recreating itself. This vitality informs the wide range of his work, which extends to a variety of media including acrylic, oil, woodblock engraving, lithographs, and photography. LaPeña, in discussing Native American artists and the interpretation of tradition, has said: "That's what we see in every generation, coming after every generation. They all [ask] the same thing, you know: 'Where are you? Who are you? Where are you going? What has happened to you?' How does [this process of questioning] happen? Well, art lets you see it. That's how it happens" (interview with essayist, 1994). In his continuing experimentation with addressing these questions, LaPeña visualizes what inspires him from California Indian traditions and thus holds out his answers for our consideration.

—Rebecca Dobkins

LARVIE, Calvin

Variant names: Umpan Hanska
Tribal affiliations: Lakota Sioux
Painter

Born: Wood, South Dakota, 6 July 1920; Lakota Sioux names means "Tall Elk." **Education:** Bacone College, 1938-40; University of Wichita, 1965. **Military Service:** U.S. Army, WWII; bronze star recipient. **Awards:** Statement of Recognition, *Bismark National Indian Art Show*, Bismark, North Dakota, 1963; commissioned for the U.S. Federal Pavilion, Golden Gate International Exposition, 1939. **Died:** 1969.

Individual Exhibitions

1942   Philbrook Museum of Art, Tulsa, Oklahoma
1964   Rosebud Arts and Crafts Museum, Rosebud, South Dakota
1969   Rosebud Arts and Crafts Museum, Rosebud, South Dakota

Selected Group Exhibitions

1939   San Francisco World's Fair, San Francisco, California
        U.S. Federal Pavilion, Golden Gate International Exposition, San Francisco, California
1955-56 European tour sponsored by the University of Oklahoma, Norman
1958-61 European tour sponsored by the University of Oklahoma, Norman
1964   *International Indian Art Show and Handicraft Trade Fair*, Foundation of North American Indian Culture, Bismark, North Dakota
        First Annual Invitational Exhibition of American Indian Paintings, United States Department of the Interior, Washington, D.C.
1970   *Contemporary Sioux Painting*, Sioux Indian Museum and Craft Center, Indian Arts and Crafts Board, United States Department of the Interior, Rapid City, South Dakota
1979-80 *Native American Paintings*, Joslyn Art Museum, Omaha, Nebraska (traveling)
1981-83 *Native American Painting*, Amarillo Art Center, Texas (traveling)
1996   *Visions and Voices: Native American Painting from the Philbrook Museum of Art*, Philbrook Museum of Art, Tulsa, Oklahoma

Collections

Denver Art Museum, Denver, Colorado; Thomas Gilcrease Institute of American History and Art, Tulsa, Oklahoma; Indian Arts & Crafts Board, United States Department of the Interior, Washington, D.C.; Museum of Art, University of Oklahoma, Norman, Oklahoma; Philbrook Museum of Art, Tulsa, Oklahoma; Sioux Indian Museum and Craft Center, Rapid City, South Dakota.

Publications

On LARVIE: Books—*American Indian Painters*, by Oscar B. Jacobson and Jeanne d'Ucel, Nice, France, 1950; *American Indian Painting of the Southwest and Plains Areas*, by Dorothy Dunn, Albuquerque, 1968; *Contemporary Sioux Painting*, by Miles Libhart, Rapid City, 1970; *Indian Painters and White Patrons*, by J. J. Brody, Albuquerque, 1971; *Native American Painting*, by Frederick Schmid and Patrick Houlihan, Mid-America Alliance Project, Kansas City, 1980; *Native American Painting*, by Jeanne Snodgrass King, Amarillo, Texas, 1981; *Visions and Voices: Native American Painting from the Philbrook Museum of Art*, edited by Lydia L. Wyckoff, Tulsa, Oklahoma, 1996. **Articles**—*The Rapid City Journal*, 3 December 1987.

*

Calvin Larvie comments (1961):
    I haven't made any paintings for 13 years but I am ready to start again. If you ever came to my reservation you could understand why I lost interest, but in the final analysis I must paint again and keep on painting to find those finer qualities my people must possess. (Larvie, in a letter to his friend, Raymond Piper)

*   *   *

    Calvin Larvie, who grew up on the Rosebud Reservation in South Dakota, became engrossed at an early age with his Lakota Sioux heritage, which included a grandfather, White Yellow Fox, who was a medicine man. Painting was Larvie's other passion. These two pursuits became intertwined in his life. His promising career as a painter was disrupted following a disabling wound in World War II, and he didn't paint again until the early 1960s. After painting scenes of the spirituality and heroism of his people, for which he received recognition by the time he was twenty, Larvie despaired at their plight on the reservation. As he began to overcome this view, as well as his own physical hardships, his art became a reflection of perseverance and promise.

    Larvie began developing his painting skills and wedding them to his interest in his heritage as early as grade school. One of his early works, *Sky People*, illustrated a Lakota legend in its depiction of warriors on horseback floating above rain clouds and lightning. In the autumn of 1938, Larvie entered Bacone College, the Oklahoma Indian school, where the noted Potawatomi artist, Woody Crumbo, was head of the art department. Larvie was penniless, but Crumbo encouraged his continuing education after recognizing his sense of color and composition as well as his rapid development in drawing. Larvie's early success came in 1939, when he received a commission to participate in developing the U.S. Federal Pavilion at the Golden Gate International Exposition, and that same year some of his works were displayed at San Francisco World's Fair.

    After these showings, Larvie painted a series of watercolors, several of which were purchased by the Philbrook Museum in Tulsa, Oklahoma. The list of titles documents Larvie's focus on Plains Indian culture, especially spiritual and ceremonial themes: *Prayers to the Elements, Supernatural Character, Sun Vow, Spiritual Vision, Sioux Dancer, Sioux War Dancer, Grass Dance, Peace Offering*, and *The Burial*. Larvie's spiritual visions portrayed supernatural figures floating in space or positioned atop a bold ground line. His horses are rendered in fantastic, vigorous action, often with tails and manes flying. The animated imagery carried over to Larvie's more secular paintings, including, *The Buffalo Hunt, Sioux Scout, Sentinels, Breaking Camp, The Duel*, and *Warrior on Horseback*. Here Larvie reveals the influence of nineteenth-century Plains ledger drawings. His horses are depicted in profile, drawn with a confident hand in graceful and muscular outlines. The Appaloosa and Painted Pony patterning complements the adornment of warriors wearing feathered bonnets and carrying shields and lances.

Larvie enlisted in the U.S. Army, took part in the D-Day invasion, and was wounded. His heroic service earned him the Bronze Star. The wounds left him permanently disabled, and he spent most of the rest of his life in government hospitals. From 1948 to 1961, Larvie stopped painting completely. His own physical hardships and a growing sense of hopelessness about the prospects of his people on the reservation led to a sense of despair. But in 1961, Larvie wrote a letter to a friend, Raymond Piper, in which he expressed determination to paint again. He returned to spiritual themes and Lakota legend, much like when he began painting nearly thirty years previously. Art evaluator Norman Meier viewed his work and encouraged him to continue. Larvie wrote to Meier in December 1962, thanking him: "You have no idea what a boost you [gave] me in recognizing my painting, *People of the Sky* because I worked very hard at it." In 1963, Larvie entered one of his new paintings in the *Bismark National Indian Art Show*, and the following year he participated in the *International Indian Art Show and Handicraft Trade Fair*, in Bismark. Larvie's work was selected for inclusion in *the First Annual Invitational Exhibition of American Indian Paintings*, sponsored by the United States Department of the Interior, in Washington, D.C., and his "comeback" was complete. Respected Indian art instructor Dorothy Dunn praised Larvie in 1968 as an "imaginative and promising artist," and while the same was said of Larvie thirty years earlier, he had, indeed, come a long way to return to a point of promise, and triumph.

In his secular and spiritual works, Larvie took great care to be authentic, and the fantastic and supernatural scenes reflect their basis in legend and spiritualism while embracing a vibrant worldview. The paintings can be admired and studied as well for telling details. Larvie devoted much research in preparation for his paintings. With respect for his spiritual and historical subject matter, great care was taken to be authentic. Larvie explained: "When I have an idea for a picture I spend a lot of time doing research for it—I can't explain it in the right terms but I have to be alone and make dozens of sketches before it proves satisfactory to me ... But the people I wish to paint appear to me as clear as day."

—Gregory Schaaf

LAVADOUR, James
Tribal affiliations: Walla Walla
Painter and printmaker

Born: Pendleton, Oregon, 18 July 1951. **Education:** High School. **Career:** Professional artist; founder, The Crow's Shadow Institute, dedicated to using art to advance social and economic development for the Umatilla Indian Reservation, 1992. **Awards:** Artist in Residence, Confederated Tribes of the Umatilla Indian Reservation, 1980; Artist in Schools Program, Eastern Oregon Regional Arts Council, La Grande, 1981; Art in Public Places, Washington State Arts Commission, 1983, 1985, 1987; Art in Public Places, Seattle Arts Commission, Seattle, Washington, 1984; Artist Advocate Program, Pendleton Arts Council, Pendleton, Oregon, 1985; Oregon Arts Fellowship, Oregon Arts Commission, Salem, 1986; Northwest Major Works Projects, Seattle Arts Commission, Se-

attle, 1989; National Print Making Fellowship to the Center for Innovative Print Making, Rutgers, University of New Jersey, New Brunswick, 1990; Betty Bowen Memorial Recognition Award, Seattle Art Museum, Seattle, Washington, 1991; Recognition Award, Seattle Art Museum, Seattle, Washington, 1994; Oregon Governor's Arts Award, Oregon Arts Commission, 1994.

Individual Exhibitions

1982	Oregon State Governors Office, Salem
1983	Sacred Circle Gallery, Seattle, Washington
1984	Museum of Art, University of Oregon, Eugene
	Sacred Circle Gallery, Seattle, Washington
1986	C.N. Gorman Museum, University of California, Davis
	Carnegie Center for the Arts, Walla Walla, Washington
1988	Elizabeth Leach Gallery, Portland, Oregon
1990	Cliff Michel Gallery, Seattle, Washington
	Portland Art Museum, Oregon
	Elizabeth Leach Gallery, Portland, Oregon
	Boise Art Museum, Idaho
1991	Elizabeth Leach Gallery, Portland, Oregon
	Elaine Horwitch Gallery, Scottsdale, Arizona
1992	Elizabeth Leach Gallery, Portland, Oregon
	Wentz Gallery, Pacific Northwest College of Art, Portland, Oregon
1993	Greg Kucera Gallery, Portland, Oregon
1995	Elizabeth Leach Gallery, Portland, Oregon
1997	Grover/Thurston Gallery, Seattle, Washington
	PDX Gallery, Portland, Oregon
	Gail Sevren Gallery, Ketchum, Idaho

Selected Group Exhibitions

1983	*Oregon Biennial*, Portland Art Museum, Oregon
	Indian Artists of the 1980s, Sacred Circle Gallery, Seattle, Washington
1984	*Seattle Urban League: Minority Artist Show*, Seattle Centre House, Seattle, Washington
	No Beads, No Trinkets: An Exhibition of Contemporary American Indian Artists, Elizabeth Leach Gallery, Portland, Oregon
	Contemporary Native American Art, Touchstone Gallery, Spokane, Washington
	Innovations: New Expression in Native American Painting, The Heard Museum, Phoenix, Arizona
1986	*The Artist Interprets the Landscape*, Blackfish Gallery, Portland, Oregon
	Oregon Artist Exhibition, Oregon Pavilion, EXPO 86, Vancouver, British Columbia
	Artists of Eastern Oregon on Tour, Eastern Oregon State College, La Grande, Oregon
	Northwest Now, Tacoma Art Museum, Washington
	Oregon Artists Show, Sacred Circle Gallery, Seattle, Washington
	Expo '86, Vancouver, British Columbia
1987	*Northwest '87*, Seattle Art Museum, Washington
	Recent Generations: Native American Art 1910-1987, The Heard Museum, Phoenix, Arizona
	New Directions Northwest: Contemporary Native Art, Portland Art Museum, Oregon

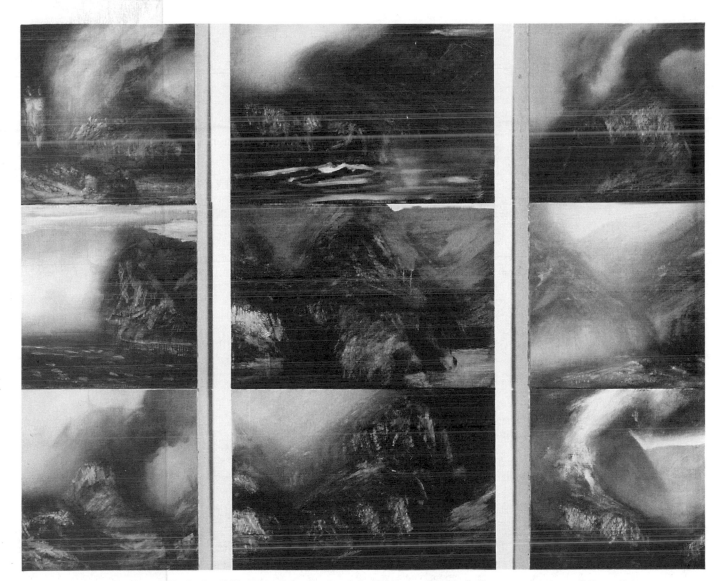

James Lavadour: *Bodies of My Body*. Collection of the Portland Art Museum, Portland, Oregon; courtesy of the artist.

Beyond Blue Mountains: A Travelling Collection of Contemporary Native American Artworks, Washington State Arts Commission, Olympia

Contemporary Visions: Fifteen Native American Artists, Read/Stremmel Gallery, San Antonio, Texas

Native American Art: Our Contemporary Visions, Stremmel Galleries, Reno, Nevada

1988   *Artists of the Blue Mountains: 1910-1988*, Sheehan Gallery, Whitman College, Walla Walla, Washington

Non-Objective Landscape, Marylhurst College, Oregon

1989   *Crossed Cultures: Five Contemporary Native Northwest Artists*, Seattle Art Museum, Washington

Roll on Columbia: Historic and Contemporary Landscapes of the Columbia River Gorge, Maryhill Museum, Goldendale, Washington

Figurative Show, Elizabeth Leach Gallery, Portland, Oregon

1990   *The Undiminished Landscape*, Security Pacific Corp Gallery, San Francisco, California

Northwest X Southwest: Painted Fictions, Museum of the Desert, Palm Springs, California (travelling show)

Celebrated Selections, The Heard Museum, Phoenix, Arizona

Tradition and Spirit: Contemporary Native American Art, Maryhill Museum of Art, Goldendale, Washington

Windhorse Gallery, Seattle, Washington

Printed in America, Walters Hall Gallery, Rutgers State University of New Jersey, New Brunswick

1991   *Shared Visions: Native American Painters and Sculptors in the Twentieth Century*, The Heard Museum, Phoenix, Arizona

1992   *Land, Spirit, Power: First Nations at the National Gallery of Canada*, National Gallery of Canada, Ottawa, Ontario (travelling)

Crossing Over/Changing Places: Artists and Collaborators, The Print Club, Philadelphia, Pennsylvania (travelling)

Decolonizing of the Mind, Center on Contemporary Art (COCA), Seattle, Washington

The Betty Bowen Legacy: Fourteen Years of Award Winning Art, Security Pacific Gallery, Seattle, Washington

MASTER PRINTS from the Rutgers Center for Innovative Printmaking: The First Five Years, The Gallery at Bristol-Myers Squibb, Princeton, New Jersey

1993 *The Sacred and the Profane*, Jan Baum Gallery, Los Angeles, California

1994 *From the Earth X,* American Indian Contemporary Arts, San Francisco, California

1995 Grove/Thurston Gallery, Seattle, Washington

1996 *Shared Visions: Native American Painters and Sculptors in the Twentieth Century,* The Heard Museum, Phoenix, Arizona (travelling, New Zealand)

Rediscovering the Landscape of the Americas, Gerald Peters Gallery, Santa Fe, New Mexico (travelling)

Romance of the Land: Native Northwest Visions, The Bellevue Art Museum, Washington

Twenty five American Print Artists: La Jeune Gravure, Mairie du Sixieme Arrondissement de Paris, Paris, France

Native Papers: Joe Fedderson, James Lavadour, Kay Walkingstick, Phil Young, Gallery 210, University of Missouri, St. Louis, Missouri

Gail Sevren Gallery, Ketchum, Idaho

Recent Northwest Acquisitions, Seattle Art Museum, Washington

Print and Paper Projects from the Rutgers Center for Innovative Print Paper, The Print Making Council of New Jersey, North Branch Station

Recent Acquisitions from the Rutgers Center for Innovative Print and Paper, The Jane Voorhees Zimmerli Art Museum, New Brunswick, New Jersey

1997 *Rising From Tradition*, The High Desert Museum, Bend, Oregon

Collections

Confederated Tribes of the Umatilla Indian Reservation, Pendleton, Oregon; Heathman Management Corporation, Portland, Oregon; The Heard Museum, Phoenix, Arizona; Hilton Corporation, Portland, Oregon; MicroSoft Corporation, Redmond, Washington; Oregon Health Sciences University, Portland, Oregon; Pacific Northwest Bell Corporation, Seattle, Washington; Perkins Coie, Seattle, Washington; Portland Art Museum, Portland, Oregon; Frank Russell & Company, Tacoma, Washington; Seattle Arts Commission, Seattle, Washington; Seattle Art Museum, Seattle, Washington; Washington State Arts Commission, Olympia, Washington; Western Heritage Savings and Loan, Pendleton, Oregon; West One Bank Corporation, Portland, Oregon; University of Washington Medical Center, Seattle, Washington; U.S. Department of the Interior, Indian Arts and Crafts Board, Washington, D.C.; Jane Voorhees Zimmerli Museum, New Brunswick, New Jersey.

Publications

On LAVADOUR: Books—*The Undiminished Landscape*, by Linda E. Evens, Security Pacific Gallery, San Francisco, 1990; *Shared Visions: Native American Painters and Sculptors in the 20th Century*, by Margaret Archuleta and Dr. Rennard Strickland, Heard Museum, Phoenix, Arizona 1991; *Master Prints from the Rutgers*

Center for Innovative Printmaking: The First 5 Years, by Judith Brodsky, Gallery at Bristol-Myers Squibb, Princeton, New Jersey, 1992; *Crossing Over/Changing Places: An Exhibition of Collaborative Print Projects and Paperworks,* by Jane Farmer, Print Club, Philadelphia, 1992; *Land, Spirit, Power: First Nations at the National Gallery of Canada*, by Diane Nemeiroff, National Gallery of Canada, Ottawa, Ontario 1992; *Land, Spirit, Power: First Nations at the National Gallery of Canada*, by Charlotte Townsend-Gault, National Gallery of Canada, Ottawa, Ontario 1992; *Native American Art*, by David Penney, and George Longfish, Hugh Lauter Levin Associates, Inc., Seattle, 1994; *A World of Art*, by Henry M. Sayre, Prentice-Hall Inc., New York, 1994. **Articles**—"Looking at Land," by Lois Allen, *Artweek*, 12 August 1990; "Visual Arts: James Lavadour at Elizabeth Leach," by Renardo Barden, *Reflex*, vol. 4, no. 5, September 1990; "Presence as Absence: James Lavadour at the Oregon Art Institute," by Randy Gragg, *Artweek,* San Francisco, September 1990; "Review of Exhibitions: James Lavadour at Cliff Michel, Seattle," by Ron Glowen, *Art in America*, vol. 78, no. 6, December 1990; "Reviews: James Lavadour at Cliff Michel, Seattle," by Lyn Smallwood, *ARTnews*, vol. 90, no. 1, January 1991; "Sex, Landscape, and Videotapes: The Pacific Northwest," by Patricia Failing, *ARTnews,* vol. 90, no. 10, December 1991; "Shared Visions-Part III," by Rennard Strickland, *Native Peoples Magazine*, vol. 5, no. 2, Winter, 1992; "Grounded in Oregon: Nature and Culture as the Local Ethnology in Portland," by Lois Allen, *Visions*, vol. 6, no. 2, Spring 1992; "Crow's Shadow, a Foundation for Art at the Umatilla," by Lois Allen, *Reservation Artweek*, vol. 23, no. 22, 20 August 1992; "Contemporary Landscape Painting," by Bruce Nixon, *Artweek*, vol. 23, no. 23, 3 September 1992; "Recent Native American Art," by W. Jackson Rushing, *Art Journal*, vol. 51, no. 3, Fall 1992; "Spirit Negatives: James Lavadour at Wentz Gallery, PNCA/Elizabeth Leach Gallery," by Nadine Fiedler, *Reflex*, vol. 7, no. 1, January/February 1993; "Contingent Histories, Aesthetic Politics," by W. Jackson Rushing, *New Art Examiner,* vol. 20, no. 7, March 1993; "Whose Nation?," by Scott Watson, *Canadian Art*, vol. 10, no. 1, Spring 1993; "New American Paintings: A Quarterly Exhibition Opens," by Steven T. Zevitas, *Studios Press*, vol. 1, no. VI, Spring 1996.

*

James Lavadour comments (1992):

For many years now, my main preoccupation in art has been the investigation of a phenomenon in the process of painting that I call the "extraordinary event of nature." Rather than the depiction or representation of a specific landscape scene, my object has been to display the occurrence of landscape inherent in the act of painting.

In paint there is hydrology, erosion, mass, gravity, mineral deposits, etc.; in me there is fire, energy, force, movement, dimension, and reflective awareness. For me landscape is not a picture, but a structure for a great experience. I use this structure to give form and identity to the vast and dynamic events that occur in the process of painting that are merely microcosms of the forces that shape the earth and mountains. To paint is to engage with nature, and this engagement produces knowledge and the love of being.

Whatever is in the earth is in me and whatever is in me is what I make art out of. I view making art as an expressive event of nature and a transfiguration of the experience of living. (*Land Spirit Power*)

*   *   *

"I am not concerned about what a painting means. I care only about what it does and how it does it." This statement by James Lavadour reflects his view that the act of creating and the act of walking on the earth are sacred, organic forces. As an active participant in the tribal affairs on the Confederated Tribes of the Umatilla Indian Reservation in Oregon, Lavadour believes that living and working on the reservation is a fundamental source of his art and creative process.

Lavadour is a self-taught artist. Growing up he watched his mother draw, and he absorbed from his father and uncle a passion for nature. Together these influences have weighed heavily on the style and development of Lavadour as a painter. While his work has been compared to landscape painters of the nineteenth century, with their thickly layered, sublime scenes, Lavadour prefers to liken his works to elements of nature, vessels for the human experience, and art as a spirit and light that can help bring illumination to the community.

Lavadour disputes the theories of various writers and critics who both look for and find social, psychological, and political themes in his work. Some have even gone so far as to discover "apocalyptic landscapes" within his pieces, which he finds most appalling. He is not a Christian and considers any kind of apocalypse, with its accompanying doom and damnation connotations, a concept outside of his experience and heritage. Lavadour holds a more hopeful viewpoint on the future of humanity and the earth, based on connections between human communities and nature.

Lavadour taps into elemental forces and an organic approach through the energy of inspiration, never feeling his work is completely in his control, and thus, he cannot purposefully inflict meaning on it in any form. Rather, he believes that just as nature is endowed with life and energy, the same is true in what we call "art"—regardless of the form. Lavadour's grand paintings bring to life emotions and sensations that hang in the breath of the viewer, while evoking few thoughts or arguments of remoter issues. Like the natural scenes he captures on canvas, painting, for Lavadour, is a catalyst for loving nature and life: it brings him healing and fills him with knowledge—reflecting his hopeful viewpoint. Lavadour cites his readings in the Baha Faith as motivation that has provided him with the courage and ongoing self-confidence to become and remain a professional artist.

—Vesta Giles

LEE, Charlie

Variant names: Hush Ka Yel Ha Yah
Tribal affiliations: Navajo
Painter

Born: Near Red Rock, Navajo Reservation, Arizona, 14 April 1926; Navajo name means "Warrior Who Came Out." **Education:** Santa Fe Indian School, 1945-46; Central Bible Institute, Springfield, Missouri. **Career:** Christian minister, silversmith, and painter. **Awards:** New Mexico State Fair, Albuquerque, 1947; Scottsdale National Indian Art Exhibition, Scottsdale, Arizona, 1963; Inter-Tribal Indian Ceremonial, Gallup, New Mexico, 1968-69, 1976.

Selected Group Exhibitions

Exhibited regularly at fairs and juried competitions in the Southwest during the 1960s and 1970s.

1947   New Mexico State Fair, Albuquerque, New Mexico
1962   Philbrook Museum of Art, Tulsa, Oklahoma
1968   Arizona State Museum, University of Arizona, Tucson
1975   Heard Museum, Phoenix, Arizona
1977   Laguna Gloria Art Museum, Austin, Texas
1978   Museum of New Mexico, Santa Fe
1996   *Vision and Voices: Native American Painting from the Philbrook Museum of Art*, Tulsa, Oklahoma

Collections

Amerind Foundation, Dragoon, Arizona; Thomas Gilcrease Institute of American History and Art, Tulsa, Oklahoma; Museum of New Mexico, Santa Fe; Museum of Northern Arizona, Flagstaff, Arizona; National Museum of the American Indian, Washington, D.C.; Peabody Museum of Salem, Massachusetts; Philbrook Museum of Art, Tulsa, Oklahoma; Millicent Rogers Foundation Museum, Taos, New Mexico; Smithsonian Institution, Washington, D.C.; Southwest Museum, Los Angeles, California; United Pueblo Agency, Albuquerque, New Mexico.

Publications

By LEE: Article—"Charlie Lee's Testimony," *The Pentecostal Evangel,* 17 April 1952.

On LEE: Books—*Indian Painters and White Patrons*, by J.J. Brody, Albuquerque, 1971; *Southwest Indian Painting: A Changing Art,* by Clara Lee Tanner, Tucson, 1973; *The Charlie Lee Story*, by David Mainse, Springfield, Missouri, 1976; *American Indian Painting and Sculpture,* by Patricia Janis Broder, New York, 1981; *Fine American Indian Art Auction*, by Will Channing, Santa Fe, 1992; *Vision and Voices: Native American Painting from the Philbrook Museum of Art*, edited by Lydia Wyckoff, Tulsa, 1996.

*   *   *

The paintings of Charlie Lee feature the terrain and animals, particularly horses, of the Navajo Reservation, where he was born, raised for much of his childhood, and returned as a missionary for the Pentecostal faith. His parents gave him a traditional Dene name, Hush Ka Yel Ha Yah, meaning "Warrior Who Came Out," and as a youngster he herded sheep and tended horses, experiencing life out on the land. While not deeply rooted in Navajo traditions, Lee paints in a style similar to other Navajo artists, including Harrison Begay, with whom he was friends, and those of the Santa Fe Indian School, where he studied art under Geronima Cruz Montoya during the mid-1940s. Like Begay, who painted ordinary life scenes rather than mythological themes, Lee recreated the Navajo landscape—red rocks and mountains, open spaces with hardy trees, cacti, and shrubs. His paintings usually focus on a lone human or animal figure, passing through or pausing; sometimes humans and animals encounter one another, or the subject is a group of sheep or horses. The figures are acutely stylized and are usually in motion. Earth tones predominate in his paintings, enlivened by his use of white that appears on his animals and on clothing. During the 1960s, he began painting more genre scenes of everyday Navajo life.

By the time he reached his early teens, Lee had been producing designs for silversmiths. This work was noticed and he was admitted to the Santa Fe Indian school in 1945. He became friends with Begay in Santa Fe and studied with Montoya at the Indian School; in addition to art studies, Lee was a soloist in the school choir and practiced piano. During this time he began receiving recognition for his art work, including winning first prize at the New Mexico State Fair in 1947. Paintings of a running deer and horses, particularly the blue horse featured in several of his works, became his most noted works. The musculature of his animals is finely outlined, with hairs, ears, and tails delicately rendered; landscapes are large and dominated by rocky terrain, with colors of vegetation and whites—as in the underside of deer, or spotted on horses—providing rich contrasts. Lee's painting, *White Indian Pony* (c. 1950), reflects influences from Harrison Begay and Beatien Yazz, another Navajo painter. Rendered with Lee's familiar curvilinear outlines, the horse

stands in profile, with a wispy mane and tail and a speckled texture on the horse's legs and rump, on a minimalist ground line; a few small rocks are scattered in the foreground and Shiprock Pinnacle, seen between the horse's legs, rises in the distance.

During his time in Santa Fe, Lee listened to preachers and became deeply interested in Christianity. After returning to the Navajo Reservation and feeling out of place, he turned to the Pentecostal Faith and attended the Central Bible Institute in Springfield, Missouri. In 1952 Lee wrote his personal "Testimony" in the *Pentecostal Evangel*: "During my high school days I became aware of the seriousness of life; the responsibilities that presented themselves, the opportunities for gain, prosperity, and a life of ease through my art work. But at the same time I became increasingly aware of the physical conditions among my own people, the Navajos." He returned as a missionary and eventually became a Christian minister on the Navajo reservation. Lee continued to paint in his spare time, focusing on horses and other animals and expanding into genre scenes during the 1960s. He exhibited regularly at southwestern

Charlie Lee: *Sunday Outing,* **c. 1970. Courtesy Challis and Arch Thiessen collection.**

Charlie Lee: *Appaloosa Horses*, 1976. Courtesy Challis and Arch Thiessen collection.

fairs, including the Scottsdale National Indian Art Exhibition, where he won honors in 1963, and the Inter-Tribal Indian Ceremonial, where he won honors in 1968, 1969 and 1976. Lee's work continues to be recognized in exhibitions and collections, particularly as representative of mid-century southwestern painting and for animated images of horses.

—Gregory Schaaf

LEWIS, Lucy

Tribal affiliations: Acoma Pueblo
Potter

Born: Lucy Martin, Sky City, Acoma Pueblo, New Mexico, c. 1898. **Family:** Married Toribio Luis (also known as Haskaya; died 1966). **Career:** Potter since adolescence; taught at Idyllwild School of Music and the Arts, Idyllwild, California. **Awards:** Numerous, including Maria Martinez Special Award, Santa Fe Fiesta, 1956; Indian Art Fund Award, 1958; first award, 7th Annual Amer-Indian Art Exhibition, Los Angeles, 1958; first prize Santa Fe Indian Market, 1960-61; Research Prize ("for overall excellence"), Indian Art Fund of the School of American Research, Santa Fe; six first prizes, five second prizes, two third prizes at the Inter-Tribal Indian Ceremonial; and First award, Scottsdale National Indian Arts Council, 1972; Governor of New Mexico Award for Outstanding Personal Contribution to the Art of the State, Santa Fe, 1983; Woman of Achievement Award, Northwood Institute, Houston, 1983; The Women's Caucus for the Arts (for her artistic accomplishments), 1992. **Died:** 1992.

Individual Exhibitions

1975   *A Tribute to Lucy M. Lewis, Acoma Potter,* Museum of North Orange County, Fullerton, California

1977   The White House, Washington, D.C.
1983   Northwood Institute, Houston, Texas
1987   Honolulu Academy, Hawaii
1988   Montclair Museum, New Jersey

Selected Group Exhibitions

1974   *Seven Families in Pueblo Pottery,* Maxwell Museum of
        Anthropology, Albuquerque, New Mexico
1980   *Master Pueblo Potters,* ACA Gallery, New York
1982   *Salute to Acoma Potters: Lucy Lewis and Marie Chino,*
        Wheelwright Museum of the American Indian, Santa
        Fe, New Mexico
1983   Driscoll Gallery, Denver Colorado; also organized exhibi-
        tion that toured the Peoples' Republic of China
        Museum of New Mexico, Santa Fe

Collections

Driscoll Gallery, Denver Colorado; Idyllwild School of Music and
the Arts, Idyllwild, California; Maxwell Museum of Anthropology, Albuquerque, New Mexico Montclair Museum, Trenton, New
Jersey; Museum of New Mexico, Santa Fe, New Mexico; Museum
of North Orange County, Fullerton, California; Northwood Institute, Houston, Texas; Wheelwright Museum of the American Indian, Santa Fe, New Mexico.

Publications

On LEWIS: Books—*Southwest Indian Craft Arts,* by Clara Lee
Tanner, University of Arizona Press, Tucson, 1968, reprinted 1975;
Seven Families in Pueblo Pottery, Maxwell Museum of Anthropol-
ogy, University of New Mexico Press, Albuquerque, 1974; *A Trib-
ute to Lucy M. Lewis, Acoma Potter,* by John E. Collins, Museum of
North Orange County, Fullerton, California, 1975; *Southwestern
Indian Arts and Crafts,* by Ray Manley, Ray Manley Photogra-
phy, Tucson, 1975; *Pottery Treasures: The Splendor of Southwest
Indian Art,* by Jerry Jacka with text by Spencer Gill, Graphic Arts
Center, Portland, 1976; "Acoma Pueblo," by Velma Garcia-Mason,
Handbook of North American Indians, edited by Alfonso Ortiz,
Smithsonian Institution, Washington, D.C., 1979; *Generations in
Clay: Pueblo Pottery of the American Southwest,* by Alfred E. Dittert
and Fred Plog, Northland Press, Flagstaff, 1980; *Master Pueblo
Potters,* by Susan Peterson, ACA Gallery catalog, New York, 1980;
Hewett and Friends, by Beatrice Chauvenet, Museum of New Mexico
Press, Santa Fe, 1983; *Lucy M. Lewis: American Indian Potter,* by
Susan Peterson, Kodansha International, Ltd., Tokyo, 1984; *Acoma
and Laguna Pottery,* by Rick Dillingham with Melinda Elliott, School
of American Research, Santa Fe, New Mexico, 1992; *Fourteen
Families in Pueblo Pottery,* by Rick Dillingham, University of New
Mexico Press, Albuquerque, 1994. **Articles**—"Lucy Lewis:
Acoma's Versatile Potter," by Minnie Oleman, *El Palacio,* vol. 75,
no. 2, 1968; "Nine Southwestern Indian Potters," by Rick
Dillingham, *Studio Potter,* vol. 6, no. 1, 1976; "Matriarchs of Pueblo
Pottery," by Susan Peterson, *Portfolio,* November/December, 1980;
"Pueblo Pottery: 2000 Years of Artistry," by David L. Arnold,
National Geographic, vol. 162, no. 5, November, 1982; "The Pot-
tery of Acoma Pueblo," by Rick Dillingham, *American Indian Art,*
vol. 2, no. 4, 1983; "Pueblo Pottery: Continuity and Change: Lucy
Lewis," by Melanie Herzog, *School Arts Magazine,* vol. 90, no. 5,
January 1991; "American Craft Council Gold Medalists," *Ameri-*

can Craft, August/September 1993; "Remembering Two Great
American Potters: Lucy Lewis and Maria Martinez," by Susan
Peterson, *Studio Potter,* December 1994.

*   *   *

Lucy Lewis learned to make pottery by watching other Acoma
women, through observation and experimentation, rather than formal art training. Her work was first influenced by the sacred pots
she saw in the kivas, which had traditional Acoma designs—parrots, flowers, and rainbows. Early in her career, Lewis, like many
other Acoma women, frequently sold works to tourists along the
highway.

The clay of Acoma differs from that of some of the eastern
pueblos, exhibiting a cream or buff color as opposed to the red clay
used in Santa Clara, San Ildefonso, and other pottery-making centers, and ground potshards are used to temper Acoma clay for
stability, rather than volcanic ash. Frequently, Acoma potters use
shards from their own pots that have been destroyed during firing.
Lewis, in contrast, used shards that she found on the ground, most
likely Anasazi in origin.

Lewis began to save the most interesting Anasazi shards, ultimately using them as inspiration for her work. She began to move
away from traditional Acoma designs and to develop her own black
on white fine-line hatch designs. A comparison of her black on
white patterns with Anasazi pottery reveals the strong influence
Anasazi styles had on her work. She ultimately became known for
her "star-burst" pattern, which consisted of fine black lines on a
white background. It wasn't until the late 1950s, when she visited
the New Mexico Museum of Anthropology, that she had an opportunity to see examples of fully intact ancient pottery (and was
surprised to find collections of her own work). Consequently, she
developed her hallmark style with only small fragments of ancient
pottery as inspiration. It is here that the skills of observation and
experimentation she developed as a child facilitated the development of her unique style.

Lewis produced her pottery in the traditional manner, digging
and preparing the clay herself. Using large coils of clay, she built her
vessels row by row, smoothing the coils as she progressed. After
scraping and smoothing a vessel, she covered it with white slip
made from watered down clay. Lewis painted her designs on the
pot with a yucca brush. In applying the design, she placed the
largest forms at the widest part of the vessel. She creates balance
and rhythm in her patterns by the manipulation of design elements
in relationship to the form. Her style is quite unique, employing all-
over, fine-line linear designs. Although the patterns seem to be
made of straight lines, they actually swell and contract to accommodate the contours of the pot.

Lewis represents one of a handful of women from her generation
that brought recognition to southwestern pottery through innovation and dedication to artistic traditions. Like Nampeyo, Maria
Martinez and Margaret Tafoya, Lucy Lewis built upon ancient
pottery styles in developing her own unique expression. Her influence on subsequent generations is still being realized, and it reaches
beyond the boundaries of Acoma Pueblo. For seventeen summers
she taught and demonstrated traditional Acoma pottery and firing
at the Idyllwild School of Music and the Arts, California. She
accumulated many awards and honors during her career. The
Women's Caucus for the Arts honored Lewis for her artistic accomplishments by presenting her with an award in 1992. Lewis, who
was ill at the time, was not present to accept the award. She re-

ceived the medal at her home at Acoma, and she died a few weeks later.

—Jennifer C. Vigil

LITTLECHILD, George

Tribal affiliations: Plains Cree
Painter

Born: George James Littlechild, Edmonton, Alberta, 16 August 1958. **Education:** Red Deer College, Diploma, Art and Design, 1984; Nova Scotia College of Art and Design, BFA, 1988; The Banff Centre, Independent Studies, 1988. **Awards:** First place scholarship award, Alberta Indian Arts and Crafts Society: ASUM MENA, 1988; British Columbia Cultural Services Award, 1996.

Individual Exhibitions

1988   *In Memory of the Late Rachel Littlechild,* Anne Leonowens Gallery II, Nova Scotia College of Art and Design, Halifax

How the Mouse Got Brown Teeth and *How the Birch Tree Got Its Stripes*, The Front Gallery, Edmonton, Alberta (book launch and illustrations sale)

1989   *Horse/Spirit Helper/Guide,* The Whyte Museum of the Canadian Rockies, Banff, Alberta
Painted Beads, The Front Gallery, Edmonton, Alberta

1990   *Regenerated Images,* Dunlop Art Gallery, Regina, Saskatchewan
Ancestral Passages, Gallery of Tribal Art, Vancouver, British Columbia
Red Horse, Red Indian, Thunder Bay Art Gallery, Ontario

1991   *George Littlechild,* Otto Van De Loo Gallery, Munich, Germany
Chief Noah Muddy Bull and the Warriors, Front Gallery, Edmonton, Alberta

1993   *Spirit of the Plains Cree,* Abokke Gallery, Kasama, Japan
Littlechild Paintings 1989-93, Sacred Circle Gallery, Day Break Star Indian Center, Seattle, Washington
Night Sky Visions, Gallery of Tribal Art, Vancouver, British Columbia

1994   *Dreamtime: The Other Side,* Gallery of Tribal Art, Vancouver, British Columbia

1995   *Heart Beat/Mother Earth,* Gallery of Tribal Art, Vancouver, British Columbia

George Littlechild: *Afro-Native Love,* 1992. Courtesy of the artist.

1996   *George Littlechild: Past & Recent Work,* Surrey Art Gallery, British Columbia

Selected Group Exhibitions

1981   *A Birthday Celebration,* Eagle Down Gallery, Edmonton, Alberta

1982   *Emerging Native Artists from Southern Alberta,* Bowman Arts Centre, Lethbridge, Alberta

1985   *Art Works Grand Opening,* Art Works Gallery, Saskatoon, Saskatchewan
        A Festival of Emerging Native Alberta Artists, Robert Vanderleelie Gallery, Edmonton, Alberta

1986   *Things from the Heart: A Festival of Native Art,* Legislative Pedway Main Concourse, Edmonton, Alberta

1987   *Alberta Inspirations: Five Man Exhibition of Contemporary Alberta Native Art,* Nova Gallery, Calgary, Alberta
        Innovation: Subject and Technique, The Gallery, University of Toronto, Scarborough
        London Life Young Contemporaries '87, London Regional Art Gallery, London, Ontario (traveling throughout the province)

1988   *Ritual Imagery,* Maltwood Art Museum and Gallery, University of Victoria, British Columbia
        Modern Echoes of Ancient Dreams, Art Court, Ottawa, Canada
        ASUM MENA: 5th Annual Native Art Festival, The Front Gallery, Edmonton, Alberta

1989   *Revelation of Inner Strengths,* Beaver House Gallery, Edmonton, Alberta
        Diversities, New Alberta, The Glenbow Museum, Calgary, Alberta
        Alberta Indian Artists, Dartmouth College, New Hampshire

1990   *Fear of Others: Art Against Racism,* The New Gallery, Calgary, Alberta
        Made in Canada, Virginia Christopher Galleries, Ltd., Calgary, Alberta

1991   *Bridging the Gap: Our Worlds Are One,* Triangle Art Gallery, Calgary, Alberta
        Cedar and Sweetgrass, Thunder Bay Art Gallery, Ontario
        Public, Private Gatherings: Recent Acquisitions, Indian and Inuit Art Gallery, Canadian Museum of Civilization, Hull, Quebec

1992   *Conrad House, George Littlechild, Jane Ash Poitras: Paintings,* Sacred Circle Gallery of American Indian Art, Daybreak Star Arts Centre, Seattle, Washington
        Unending Journey, Visual Arts Museum, School of Visual Arts, New York
        New Territories: 350/500 Years after Vision Planetaire, Maison de la Petite Patrie, Culture Rosemont, Montreal, Quebec

1993   *Canadian Artists to the Benefit of the Olga Havel Foundation,* Brezna Palace Gallery, Prague, Czechoslovakia
        Canada's First People: Syncrude Canada Limited Traveling Exhibition, Calgary, Winnipeg, Ottawa, Montreal, Toronto, Halifax, Vancouver, Fort McMurray, Tokyo, Japan, Czechoslovakia

1994   *Two Nations, One Voice: George Littlechild, Linda Frimer,* Gertrude Zack Gallery, Jewish Community Center, Vancouver, British Columbia
        First Nations Contemporary Art, Commonwealth Games 1994, Art Gallery of Greater Victoria, British Columbia

1995   *Voices of Vision...Resurgence,* Art Gallery of the South Okanagan, Penticton, British Columbia
        Abstracted on the Line, Grunt Gallery, Vancouver, British Columbia
        Voices of Vision ... Resurgence, Art Gallery of the South Okanagan, Penticton, British Columbia
        Who Speaks for the Rivers?, Gallery of Tribal Art, Vancouver
        We Are All Related, Surrey Art Gallery and Surrey Public Library, Vancouver Public Library, British Columbia (travelling)

1996   *Mother Earth: Important to All,* The Banff Centre Gallery, Calgary, Alberta
        Unity and Diversity in Arts & Culture, Prince George Art Gallery, British Columbia

Collections

Alberta Arts Foundation, Calgary; Banff Centre, Banff, Alberta; Canadian Museum of Civilization, Hull, Quebec; Dunlop Art Gallery, Regina, Saskatchewan; Edmonton Art Gallery, Edmonton, Alberta; Thunder Bay Art Gallery, Thunder Bay, Ontario; Trent University, Peterborough, Ontario.

Publications

By LITTLECHILD: Books Illustrated—*This Land is Your Land,* Children's Books Press, San Francisco, 1993.

On LITTLECHILD: Books—*The Trickster Shift: A New Paradigm in Contemporary Canadian Native,* by Allan J. Ryan, Unpublished PhD thesis, University of British Columbia, Vancouver, 1995; *George Littlechild: Past & Recent Work,* by Amir Alibhai, Surrey, British Columbia, 1996. **Articles**—"Recalling indignities with humor, not rage," by Ann Rosenberg, *The Vancouver Sun,* 27 October 1990; "A story of pain behind the paintings," by Marke Andrews, *The Vancouver Sun,* 31 December 1993; "Lost Heritage: George Littlechild's show tells a story of rediscovered roots," by Janice Foster, *The Peace Arch News,* 5 October 1996; "The Art of Self-Discovery," by Michael Scott, *The Vancouver Sun,* 21 September 1996.

*   *   *

In the late 1980s George Littlechild emerged from art college and the Canadian prairies as a hot young "Indian art star." His color-saturated acrylic paintings of maidens and warriors and mystical horses found an immediate audience. They stood in stark contrast to the darker and more politically-tinged works of fellow Albertans, Jane Ash Poitras and Joane Cardinal-Schubert, with whom he had occasionally exhibited. Within a short time his vibrant paintings were selling out gallery shows and appearing on posters, notecards, book covers and even a splashy wall calendar.

Littlechild revelled in the recognition. In hindsight, he now believes the aggressive marketing of his artwork damaged his credibility as a serious artist. There were also those who thought his paintings were merely decorative, lacking in substance and social relevance at a time when such things were expected, even demanded of a "serious" Native artist. Behind his back he was called "poster

George Littlechild with photographs of his great grandparents (Chief Francis Bull, wearing headdress, and Peggy Bull, woman on far right), 1995. Photograph by Chris Grabowski; courtesy of the artist.

boy" and a "sellout" to commercialism (even by other Native artists who a few years later would allow their own work to be marketed in similar fashion). Ironically, Littlechild says that his work has always had substantial social content but that viewers often didn't see it, or didn't want to see it. With increasing maturity and experience, he feels that his artistic voice has grown stronger and clearer, and his social critique more visible. In recent years, Littlechild has earned the respect and admiration of many critics, collectors and artistic contemporaries for his ongoing aesthetic investigations into his Plains Cree heritage. As a former foster child raised apart from his ancestral Cree community, Littlechild today creates art that documents his personal journey of cultural reclamation and reconnection. It is an unfolding visual narrative of self-discovery and identity reconstruction that clearly has universal resonance.

Littlechild is first and foremost a gifted colorist. His images on paper and canvas positively shimmer with chromatic energy. Few artists can combine hot pinks and peacock blues with deep greens and soft mauves in as sumptuous and seductive a fashion. His colors seem to glow with an inner life and light reflecting the inner life and light of Native cultures. This is no random correlation but an important part of the aesthetic. For Littlechild, colors are also imbued with spiritual properties; they have the power to cleanse and purify. In his best works regal (and sometimes wary) human figures are set against richly patterned backdrops of broad bars and sweeping arcs that rise and fall like powwow fringe or prayer ribbons fluttering in the wind. Not infrequently, playful five-pointed stars—always symbols of hope—dance across his skies. The artist's admiration for Marc Chagall is obvious.

Littlechild's themes are well-chosen and diverse: honoring the beauty and dignity of a powwow participant (*Ladies Traditional*, 1995), commemorating the traditional role of individuals born with both male and female qualities (*The Spirit of 2*, 1994), recognizing the reality of inter-racial romance (*Afro-Native Love*, 1992), wryly critiquing historical inter-cultural relations (*Mountie and Indian Chief*, 1991), or adopting a whimsical equine persona—much like Harry Fonseca's urban Coyote alter-ego—to affirm a contemporary Native presence (*Horse Plus Ancestor*, 1989).

Early on in his career Littlechild began appending assorted objects to his paintings—mirrors, brooches, shells, buttons, colored foils and ermine fur—to increase their tactile appeal. It was, however, the incorporation into his work of carefully collected, often haunting photographs of his Plains Cree ancestors that has had the most profound affect on his art—a means for Littlechild to raise up and honor the lives and memories of near-forgotten individuals, such as the aristocratic headman Louis Natuasis, or chiefs Bobtail and Francis Bull, and a way for him to affirm an all-important familial connection to these people, to get to know them a little better despite their grainy countenance. It is no less than a way of coming home to reclaim one's personal and cultural birthright.

Since the early 1990s, Littlechild has lived in Vancouver, British Columbia. During this time he has experimented with a variety of new techniques and media to satisfy both his need for aesthetic challenge and a desire to document his family history in a continually creative fashion.

George Littlechild: Past & Recent Work (1996), his recent solo show at the Surrey Art Gallery in Surrey, British Columbia, offers tangible proof of his willingness to explore new ground. Along with a mid-career retrospective of some of his better-known paintings, and a 1996 intaglio print honoring the famed Mohawk poet, Pauline Johnson, the exhibition includes a series of large hand-colored cibachrome photographs that interrogates, among other things, the mainstream beauty myth (*Aboriginal and Beautiful, Too,* 1995), his late mother Rachel's painful childhood experience at residential school (*An Indian Girl's First Communion,* 1996), a happier time when she later married her first husband, a white man (*Mixed Racial Marriage,* 1996), and Littlechild's own awkward childhood in foster care (*Indian Foster Boy,* 1996). The exhibition also includes *Displaced Indians: The Sixties Scoop,* Littlechild's first multi-media installation. Intentionally devoid of life-affirming color, it is reminiscent of many a solemn holocaust memorial. Through several poignant personal narratives the piece starkly documents the physical and psychological trauma inflicted upon Native children who, like Littlechild, were torn from their families during the infamous Canadian social services "scoop" of the nineteen-sixties.

Having discovered in his late teens that his now-deceased biological father was white, Littlechild is currently researching this side of his bi-racial and bi-cultural heritage. He has already acquired several intriguing photographs that will inevitably find their way into upcoming artworks. Without question, both he and his ever-expanding audience will be the richer for his ongoing explorations of aboriginal identity.

—Allan J. Ryan

LITTLE TURTLE, Carm

Tribal affiliations: Apache; Tarahumara
Photographer

Born: Carmelita Little Turtle in Santa Maria, California, 4 June 1952. **Education:** Navajo Community College, R.N., 1978; also studied photography at The University of New Mexico, Albuquerque, and the College of the Redwoods, Eureka, California. **Career:** Operating room nurse, 1978—; producer/photographer, Shenandoah

Films, Arcata, California, 1980-83; artist living in Flagstaff, Arizona. **Awards:** Western States Arts Federation Fellowship, 1993. **Agent:** Old Town Gallery, Flagstaff, Arizona.

Individual Exhibitions

1982   Harwood Foundation, Taos, New Mexico
1983   Southwest Museum, Los Angeles, California
1991   *Reflections in Time,* American Indian Contemporary Arts, San Francisco, California
1992   Center for Creative Photography, The University of Arizona, Tucson

Selected Group Exhibitions

1982   *Native Americans Now,* American Indian Museum, Santa Rosa, California
1983   *Indian Artists of the 80's,* Sacred Circle Gallery, Seattle, Washington
1984   *The New Native American Aesthetic,* Marilyn Butler Fine Arts, Santa Fe, New Mexico
        Contemporary Native American Photographers, Southern Plains Indian Museum, Anadarko, Oklahoma
        24 Native American Photographers, Gallery of the American Indian Community House, New York
1985   *The Photograph and the American Indian,* Library of Western Arts Americana, Princeton University, New Jersey
        Women of Sweetgrass, Cedar and Sage, American Indian Community House Gallery, New York
1986   *The Way of Life of the Real People,* C.E.P.A. Gallery, Buffalo, New York
1989   *As In Her Vision,* American Indian Contemporary Arts, San Francisco, California
1990   *Personal Preferences: First Generation Native Photographers,* American Indian Contemporary Arts, San Francisco, California
        Compensating Imbalances: Native American Photography, C.N. Gorman Museum, University of California, Davis
        Ed Singer and Carm Little Turtle: Contemporary Art, Old Town Gallery, Flagstaff, Arizona
        Ancestors Known and Unknown, Art in General Gallery, New York
        We Are Part of This Earth: Contemporary Native American Works on Paper, Centro Cultural de la Raza, San Diego, California
        Language of the Lens, The Heard Museum, Phoenix
1991   *Counter Colon-Ialismo,* Centro Cultural de la Raza, San Diego, California
        Our Land/Ourselves, University Art Gallery, State University of New York, Albany
        America, The Center for Contemporary Art, Sacramento, California
1992   *Message Carriers,* Photographic Resource Center, Boston University, Massachusetts
        Six Yeux: Three Women Photographers, La Cigale, Taos, New Mexico
        We, the Human Beings, College of Wooster Art Museum, Wooster, Ohio

Carm Little Turtle. Photograph by the artist.

Representatives: Women Photographers from the Permanent Collection, Center for Creative Photography, University of Arizona, Tucson
1993   *Silver Into Gold*, Ansel Adams Center for Photography, San Francisco, California
     Defining Our Realities: Native American Women Photographers, Sacred Circle Gallery, Seattle, Washington
1994   *Watchful Eyes*, The Heard Museum, Phoenix
     Traditions of Looking, The Institute of American Indian Arts Museum, Santa Fe, New Mexico
     Praising the Spirit, Local 803 Gallery/Group for Photographic Intentions, Tucson, Arizona
     Negatives and Positives, Street Level Gallery, Glasgow, Scotland
1995   *After the Ceremony*, Old Town Gallery, Flagstaff, Arizona
     Image and Self in Contemporary Native Photoart, Hood Museum of Art, Dartmouth College, Hanover, New Hampshire

1996   *Strong Hearts: Native American Visions and Voices*, Smithsonian Institution, Washington, D.C.
     I Stand in the Center of the Good, American Indian Community House Gallery, New York

Collections

The Center for Creative Photography, University of Arizona, Tucson; The Heard Museum, Phoenix; Southwest Museum, Los Angeles; Southern Plains Indian Museum, Anadarko; Western Arts Americana Library, Princeton University, Princeton, New Jersey.

Publications

By LITTLE TURTLE: Book—*I Stand in the Center of the Good*, edited by Lawrence Abbott, The University of Nebraska Press, Lincoln, Nebraska, 1994. **Articles**—Artist's Statement in *Watchful Eyes* (catalog), The Heard Museum, Phoenix, Arizona, 1994; Artist's Statement in *Image and Self in Contemporary Native Photoart* (cata-

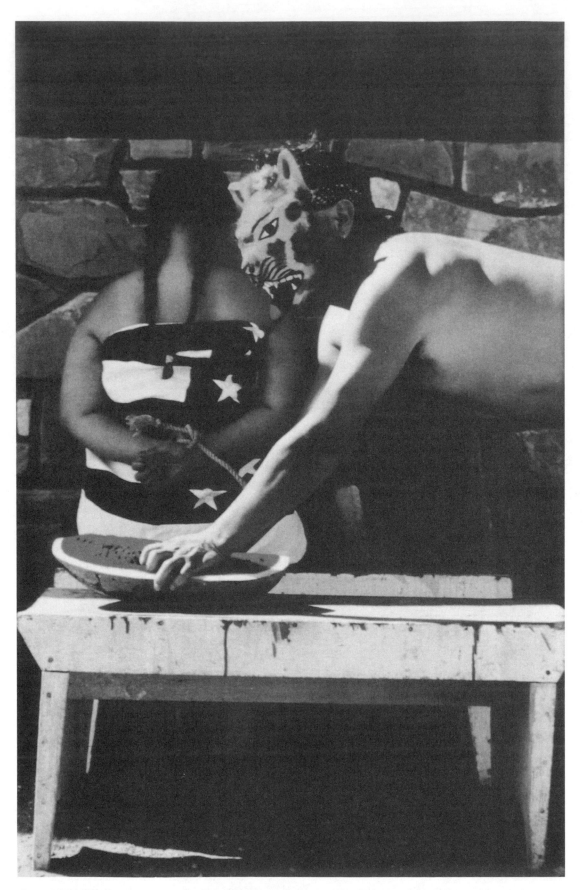

Carm Little Turtle: *El Diablo y Sandia with Woman Done Wrong,* **1992. Courtesy of the artist.**

log), Hood Museum of Art, Dartmouth College, Hanover, New Hampshire, 1995; "Strong Hearts," *Aperture*, no. 139, 1995; "Image and Self in Contemporary Native Photoart," in *American Indian Art Magazine* vol. 21, no. 2, 1996.

*

Carm Little Turtle comments:

The motivation behind my work as an artist is the same universal impulse that has always driven artists—the need to communicate based on knowledge and truth. The iconography in my work, by that I mean the props and costumes, is a private symbolism rather than one imposed by the dominant culture. The symbolism and mythology that dominant society attaches to indigenous people is nothing more than a salve for a troubled collective conscience. I have no need for that kind of mythology and symbolism. I attempt to imply a timelessness in my work which stimulates feelings that represent the past, present, and future. Photographs are typified by posed models either against a simple background, or, at times, against a background of actual nature. The rugged terrain of Northern Arizona or the mountains and clouds of New Mexico may serve as a backdrop to the politics played out symbolically between men and women. Models' faces are not seen in several of the staged images in order to suggest movement or solitary journeys that are dreamy visual poems.

*   *   *

Carm Little Turtle's selectively arranged photographs bring to life impossible moments, giving reality to her imagination. Laws of time and motion give way to the unexpected image, where the viewer's visual processing uncovers layers of meaning. Behind the ordinary and mundane lies an ethereal world. Little Turtle creates these multiple worlds in a Southwestern landscape that acts as a backdrop to the dynamics of interpersonal relationships. In her images there is a tension between stillness and action, between environment and the peopled world. There is a surrealistic effect, not only from her use of color but also from the juxtaposition of her props and her models. Although her props are derived from Native cultures her intent is to transcend a strict reference to experience. Likewise, her models' faces are often veiled or undisclosed. Her belief is that a specific face would draw the viewer away from the totality of the image and foreclose the viewer's participation in the making of meaning. For example, in *Day Dreamer* (1985), a male figure sits against what looks to be the wall of an old building in the desert. Hovering above him, with just her lower legs visible, is a woman. In *Parasol* (1983) three receding veiled faces create a sense of depth and represent the thoughts of the primary figure.

At the same time, there is another personal dimension to her work involving family history, and which further suggests the broader interaction between the Indian and the white man. The 1990 *Iron Horse* is based on a story she was told by her mother about her grandparents. This photograph superimposes an image of her grandparents and two petroglyph-like handprints over the image of a locomotive (the "iron horse"). According to the family story the artist's grandparents hopped trains and rode the rails and survived a TB epidemic through their daily doses of medicinal whiskey. Beyond this, though, the photograph raises questions about the exploitation of the West and the impact that expansionism had the way of life of indigenous peoples. There is a small-scale image of a buffalo under her grandfather's arm, which connotes both the im-

portance of the buffalo to Native people and the destruction of the buffalo for the laying of the railroad track.

However, the humor in Little Turtle's work should not be overlooked. Themes of harmony, fertility, and the regeneration of life emerge in such pieces as *She Was Used to Abiding by Her Own Decisions* (1989), *El Diablo con Sandia with Woman Done Wrong* (1991), and *Earthman Won't Dance, Except with Other Women* (1992). The relationships implied between men and women in these photographs are more playful. Humor becomes a way to communicate and heal.

Some of Little Turtle's other work utilizes brighter colors and edges into abstraction. The central image of *Mystery Figure in Time Warp* (1992) is a petroglyph on a rock face surrounded by other literal and abstract images. *Parajito's Terminated Dream Message* (1992) is a denser arrangement of colored swirls and forms. These two pieces, along with *Horse Reflections in Time* (1989), move Little Turtle's work away from the use of models and props, instead focusing exclusively on elements of nature.

Little Turtle's images, in both the actual photographing and the hand-painting, are highly-structured and intentional, often sketched out ahead of time. She was more influenced by Manuel Alvarez Bravo than by, for example, Ansel Adams and Edward Weston. She prefers to use photography as a means of creating an almost surrealistic world, rather than documenting the "real world."

—Larry Abbott

LOGAN, Jim
Tribal affiliations: Métis
Painter and mixed media artist

Born: New Westminster, British Columbia, 1955, of Cree, Sioux, and Scottish descent. **Education:** Learned to draw and paint from his mother (an amateur landscape and wildlife artist); travelled to Europe to study the work of Vincent van Gogh and Edvard Munch, 1975; studied graphic design, David Thompson University, Fort Nelson, British Columbia, 1982-83, Certificate in Graphic Design, 1983. **Career:** Graphic artist on the *Yukon Indian News*, Ne-Sa-To (Yukon Native Communications Society), Whitehorse, Yukon, 1983-88; part-time lay missionary; co-chair, Society of Canadian Artists of Native Ancestry (SCANA), 1993-94; member of the Second Circle Advisory Council of Atlatl, 1992—; founding member and captain of the executive committee of the Metis Art Council, 1993; curated *The Art of the Shuswap, A Legacy of Survival* and *Contemporary Native Art* at the Kamloops Art Gallery, 1993; printmaker (serigraphy) and painter. **Awards:** British Columbia Ministry of Culture, Aboriginal Arts Award, 1993; Canada Council award, 1993, 1995.

Individual Exhibitions

1985	*Images of a People*, Yukon Gallery, Whitehorse
1986	*Tutchone Images*, Town Square Gallery, Anchorage, Alaska
1987	*The Weight*, Territorial Gallery, Whitehorse
1988	*Recent Works of Jim Logan*, Bearclaw Gallery, Edmonton, Alberta

Sunny Side of Life, Yukon Gallery, Whitehorse
1989   *After the Gold Rush*, Bearclaw Gallery, Edmonton, Alberta
1990   *Recent Works of Jim Logan*, Leona Lattimer Gallery, Vancouver, British Columbia
        The Quiet Condition, Northern Passage Gallery, Victoria, British Columbia
        A Northern Mosaic, Yukon Gallery, Whitehorse
        A Requiem for Our Children, Territorial Gallery, Whitehorse, Yukon (travelled to Vancouver; Calgary, Alberta; and Camrose, Alberta)
1991   *Coming in from the Cold*, Bearclaw Gallery, Edmonton, Alberta
        Various Views, Canada House Gallery, Banff, Alberta
        Recent Works of Jim Logan, Leona Lattimer Gallery, Vancouver, British Columbia
        Heart Beats and Drum Beats, Northern Passage Gallery, Vancouver, British Columbia
        Recent Works of Jim Logan, Peters Gallery, Kamloops, British Columbia
1992   *Recent Works of Jim Logan*, Bearclaw Gallery, Edmonton, Alberta
        Recent Works of Jim Logan, Yukon Gallery, Whitehorse
        Recent Works of Jim Logan, Leona Lattimer Gallery, Vancouver, British Columbia
        Classical Aboriginal Series, Burnaby Art Gallery, British Columbia (travelled to Kamloops Art Gallery, British Columbia, 1992; Thunder Bay Art Gallery, Ontario, 1993; and the Yukon Arts Center, Whitehorse, 1994)
1993   *Recent Works of Jim Logan*, Peters Gallery, Kamloops, British Columbia
        Recent Works of Jim Logan, Youngfox Gallery, Toronto, Ontario
        Good Times, Canada House Gallery, Banff, Alberta
        Recent Works of Jim Logan, Yukon Gallery, Whitehorse
1995   *Nostalgic Resistance*, Bearclaw Gallery, Edmonton, Alberta
        Recent Works of Jim Logan, Yukon Gallery, Whitehorse
        Images in Collage, K'san National Exhibition Center, K'san, British Columbia

Selected Group Exhibitions

1981   *Caribou Regional Juried Exposition*, Studio 2880, Prince George, British Columbia
1983   *West Kootenay Regional Juried Exposition*, Nelson, British Columbia
        The Graphics Show, Views Gallery, Nelson, British Columbia
1984   *Points of View*, Yukon Territorial Government Building, Whitehorse
1985   South East Alaska State Fair, Haines
        Impressions and Expressions: The Work of Ray Ladue and Jim Logan, Territorial Gallery, Whitehorse, Yukon
1986   *Yukon Light*, St. John Public Library, New Brunswick
        Yukon Pavilion, *EXPO '86*, Vancouver, British Columbia
1987   *Yukon Indian Art Show*, Territorial Art Gallery, Whitehorse, Yukon
1988   *Peace Hill Trust Art Collection Show*, Edmonton, Alberta
        Spirit of the Lubicon, Bearclaw Gallery, Edmonton, Alberta
1990   *Explorations*, St. Jerome, Quebec and Kamloops, British Columbia

1992   *Indigena: Perspectives of Native People on Five Hundred Years*, Canadian Museum of Civilization, Hull, Quebec (travelled to Winnipeg, Manitoba; Halifax, Nova Scotia; Windsor, Ontario; Phoenix, Arizona; Calgary, Alberta; and Norman, Oklahoma)
        New Territories 150/500 Years After: An Exhibition of Contemporary Aboriginal Art in Canada, Cote de Neige Gallery, Montreal, Quebec
        Canada's First People: A Celebration of Contemporary Native Art, cross-Canada tour and Tokyo, Japan
1993   *Contemporary Native Art of the West Coast*, Western Gallery, Western Washington University, Bellingham
1994   *Challenging the Status Quo*, Art Gallery of Southern Alberta, Edmonton Public Art Gallery, tour of Alberta (to 1996), and Kelowna Art Gallery, British Columbia
1995   *Re-emergence*, Southern Okanagan Art Gallery, Penticton, British Columbia
        Basket, Bead and Quill, Thunder Bay Art Gallery, Ontario
1996   *New Aboriginal Works*, Gallery Gevik, Toronto
        Works from the Permanent Collection, Thunder Bay Art Gallery, Ontario

Collections

Alberta Government Tel, Edmonton, Alberta; Kamloops Art Gallery, Kamloops, British Columbia; National Heritage Collection of Native Art, Indian Art Centre, Department of Indian and Northern Affairs, Ottawa; Norwest Tel Art Collection, Whitehorse; Sohio Oil, Anchorage, Alaska; Thunder Bay Art Gallery, Thunder Bay, Ontario; Yukon Arts Centre, Whitehorse; Yukon Indian Development Corporation, Whitehorse; Yukon Permanent Collection, Yukon Territorial Government, Yellowknife.

Publications

On LOGAN: Books—*Indigena: Contemporary Native Perspectives*, exhibition catalog by Gerald McMaster and Lee-Ann Martin, Ottawa, 1992; *Jim Logan: A Question of Ideals*, exhibition catalog with an essay by Anna-Marie Larsen, Kamloops, 1992; *Jim Logan: Classical Aboriginal Series*, exhibition catalog with an essay by Allan J. Ryan, Whitehorse, 1994; *Thunder Bay Art Gallery Permanent Collection*, exhibition catalog by Janet Clark, Rick Hill, and Lee-Ann Martin, Thunder Bay, 1996. **Articles**—"Painting the Quiet Condition," *Up Here*, October/November 1985; "*The Weight*: Art and the Community," by Conrad Boyce, *Yukon News*, Whitehorse, 29 July 1987; "Logan Show Celebrates the Last Warriors" by Dave White, *Yukon News*, Whitehorse, 24 October 1990; "Lower Than the Angels: The Weight of Jim Logan's Art," *Canadian Journal of Native Studies*, vol. 10, no. 1, 1990; "School Horrors Recalled in Logan Art Show" by Dave White, *Yukon News*, Whitehorse, 14 September 1990; "Schools of Suffering and Shame" by Douglas Todd, *Vancouver Sun*, 3 November 1990; "Living with the Legacy of Abuse" by Terry O'Neill, *British Columbia Report*, 8 July 1991; "Jim Logan—The Painter Prophet," *Canadian Lutheran*, December 1991; "Aboriginal Art Series Interprets Work Done by Some 'Old Masters,'" by Annie Boulanger, *Burnaby Now*, Burnaby, 1992; "The Practice of Conflicting Art" by Alison Gillmor, *Border Crossings*, Winnipeg, 1992; "Dark Reflections: Native Artists Map the Legacy of Columbus" by Glen Allen, *Maclean's*, 4 May 1992; "Whose Nation?" by Scott Watson, *Canadian Art*, Spring 1993; "Jim Logan: Classical Aboriginal Series," *Imprint*, vol. 8, no. 3, Thunder Bay Art Gallery, September/October/November 1993; "Clever

Jim Logan: *The Diner's Club: No Reservations Required*, 1992. Photograph by Judy Flett; courtesy Thunder Bay Art Collection.

Logan Keeps the Issues on Canvas," *Yukon News*, Whitehorse, 1 June 1994; "Artist Takes Shrewd Look at Great Masters," *Yukon News*, 1 June 1994; "The Pun in Painting: Jim Logan's Comic Vision" by Allan J. Ryan, *Aboriginal Voices*, vol. 1, no. 4, Fall 1994; "Native Artists Maintain Ties to their Past," *Kelowna Courier*, 12 January 1995. **Film/Video**—*A Requiem for the Children*, for *Focus North*, Canadian Broadcasting Corporation Television, Whitehorse, 1990; *Drums*, CBC Television, 1991; *The Dispossessed: The War Against the Indians*, produced by Harry Rasky, National Film Board of Canada/Canadian Broadcasting Corporation, 1992; *Jim Logan*, interview for Rogers Cable, Ottawa 1994.

*

Jim Logan comments (1992):

It is vitally important to me that people out there in the art world audience don't say to themselves, "See, they may be a little poorer than us, but hell, they're happy and content," and put native society into the "quaint and rustic" file of their conscience. It is equally important to me that those same people don't say, "Hey, just like we've always known, Indians are drunks and neglect their kids!" So there is this dividing line in my work just like there is in the reality of living, there is a time to laugh and a time to weep. (From *Indigena*, Canadian Museum of Civilization)

*   *   *

Since the mid-1980s, Jim Logan has been producing paintings and mixed-media works that offer a sustained inquiry into the social realities faced by Native people in contemporary North America and an ongoing interrogation of the histories that have contributed to and masked those realities. Having grown up in a predominantly white, middle-class neighborhood of Port Coquitlam, British Columbia, Logan first began to wrestle with the issue of the place assigned to First Nations peoples within—or, more accurately, outside—the Canadian mainstream when he moved to Whitehorse in 1983 to work as a graphic artist. It was there, when he began to visit the nearby Indian village of Kwanlin Dun, that he had his first direct encounter with the extreme poverty of many northern Native communities.

His response to the conditions in the village took two forms: he began to work as a part-time lay missionary and, as he came to know the community and the stories of the individuals within it, he began to paint narrative scenes revealing the effects of poverty and cultural dislocation—the poor health and inadequate medical care, the alcoholism, violence, and despair. But, although always unsparing and unsentimental, his paintings from this period also depict the persistent strengths of the people of Kwanlin Dun, the effort to maintain community and family ties, the tenderness shown—especially between grandparents and grandchildren—and the humor.

Setting aside the landscape and wildlife subjects he had painted previously, Logan continued through the 1980s and early '90s to attempt to reveal the day-to-day truths of Native life. His most damning treatment of the forces that have undermined Native communities took the form of a series of fourteen paintings (three of them on blankets), *Requiem for Our Children* (1990). These works expose the emotional, physical, and sexual abuse endured in residential schools run by several religious denominations with the sanction of the federal government. Based on the recollections of people at Kwanlin Dun and several of his own relatives, the paintings vividly convey the isolation, shame, and helplessness experienced by hundreds of Native children forced to attend the schools for nine months of every year. To consider just one example, in *The Pee Parade* young girls who have wet their beds are shown forced to parade, draped in their wet sheets, in front of the other children. Each of the scenes is painted in a deceptively naive style that first attracts the viewer and then delivers its emotional content in an unavoidably direct manner.

Logan used this strategy again in *National Pastimes* (1991), a group of seven paintings that can be seen as the culmination of the themes he had been pursuing since 1983. In the title painting, young boys play hockey on a rink in the center of a village. This familiar scene, painted in a "folk-art" style and cheerful, poster-bright colors, seems to promise a nostalgic retreat to the innocence of childhood and the comfort of small-town values. A closer look, however, reveals a more complex reality: homes with boarded up windows; derelict cars; a couple brawling in the snow; a man slumped against the side of a house, drinking; another who has committed suicide; and, everywhere, the ambiguous presence of the church and the police. Six smaller paintings provide closer, more revealing, and often ironic views from different perspectives within the larger scene. In many of them, hockey, the national pastime, becomes both a means and a metaphor of escape. However, one of these close-ups, *Defensive Pair*, points toward a different possibility. Two defensive players wear hockey shirts with the names "Riel" and "Dumont"—the leaders of the Metis resistance of 1885—and two men watching the game from the sidelines wear kerchiefs over their faces and carry rifles—a reference to the stance taken at Oka, Quebec in 1990.

Other works from this period, such as the *Last Warrior* series of paintings of Native leaders (1990), also contain more overt political references and begin to explore issues of the representation of Native American history. Also from this period, the *Classical Aboriginal Series* (1991-92) examines the ways in which Western art history has marginalized Native American culture. The series of 36 works grew into a complex, many-barbed response to the Eurocentrism of art history as presented in standard texts; in particular, the persistent use of the term "primitive" to dismiss the artistic production of whole cultures, and the misrepresentation of Native American cultures as static, isolationist, and lacking a sense of history.

Using such strategies as parody, race and gender reversal, and other transgressions of canonical Western images, Logan repositioned Native values, issues, and images to be at the center of a new history, one told from a Native perspective. In *Wenapawawisk*, for example, Mona Lisa is displaced by a portrait of the artist's great-grandmother—a radically different image of beauty and worth. *A Rethinking on the Western Front* reworks Michelangelo's *Creation of Adam*, juxtaposing native creation myths with that of Christianity and challenging the representation of God and "man" as white Europeans. The work also exposes the racism in supposedly objective scientific representations in which homosapiens always appear to be a white.

Finally, to cite just one more example, in *Diners' Club (No Reservations Required)*, Manet's picnicking Parisians are replaced by Native Americans. However, to emphasize the importance of women in a matriarchal society, the men are nude while the women are clothed. Other details such as the bowl of Saskatoon berries, the Diet Coke can (no alcohol), and the scars on the mens' chests from participation in the Sundance ceremony subtly transform the scene into a statement of cultural survival.

The *Classical Aboriginal Series* deals with many other issues arising from the clash between Euro-American and Native values. But whatever problems he chooses to engage, Logan claims his right to express all the complexities and contradictions of contemporary Native life without being confined by histories and systems of representation imposed by others. In retrospect, this claim has been implicit in his work all along. Looking forward, Logan continues to explore new themes and new media in his ongoing effort to speak from the centre of First Nations culture at the end of the twentieth century.

—Deborah Burrett

LOLOMA, Charles

Tribal affiliations: Hopi
Painter, jewelry designer, and potter

Born: Hotevilla, Arizona, 7 January 1921. **Education:** Phoenix Indian School (with instruction by Hopi painter, Fred Kabotie); Fort Sill Indian School, Lawton, Oklahoma (mural instruction); following World War II, studied ceramics at the School for American Craftsmen, Alfred University, New York. **Military Service:** U.S. Army, World War II, stationed in the Aleutian Islands. **Family:** Married Otellie Pasiyava (divorced 1965). **Career:** Assisted in painting murals at San Francisco's Golden Gate International Exposition, 1939; assisted Kabotie in reproducing murals from the ancient Hopi village, Awatovi, at the Museum of Modern Art in New York, 1940; performed research of ceramics on the Hopi Reservation, 1949-54; owned and operated pottery shop with Otellie Loloma, 1954-60, and introduced Lolomaware pottery; jewery maker, 1955—; taught ceramics at the University of Arizona and the Arizona State University, late 1950s and early 1960s; taught summer sessions in the Southwest Indian Art Project at the University of Arizona, 1959-1962; was instrumental in establishing the Institute of American Indian Arts in Santa Fe in 1962 and served as the first head of its Department of Plastic Arts; established a studio and gallery near Hotevilla on the Hopi Reservation, 1966; National Education Administration artist-in-residence, Japan, 1974. **Awards:** Whitney Foundation Fellowship (to research Hopi ceramics), 1949; Arizona Governor's Art Award, 1990; Lifetime Achievement Award, Southwestern Association for Indian Affairs (SWAIA), Santa Fe, 1996; Appointed to various boards, including: First Convocation of American Indian Scholars, American Indian Historical Society, Princeton University, American Indian Center for Living Arts, New York, Arizona Commision on the Arts and Humanities, 1972-75, 1985-88; elected Fellow of the American Crafts Council; served on the Editorial Advisory Board of *American Indian Art Magazine*. **Died:** 1991.

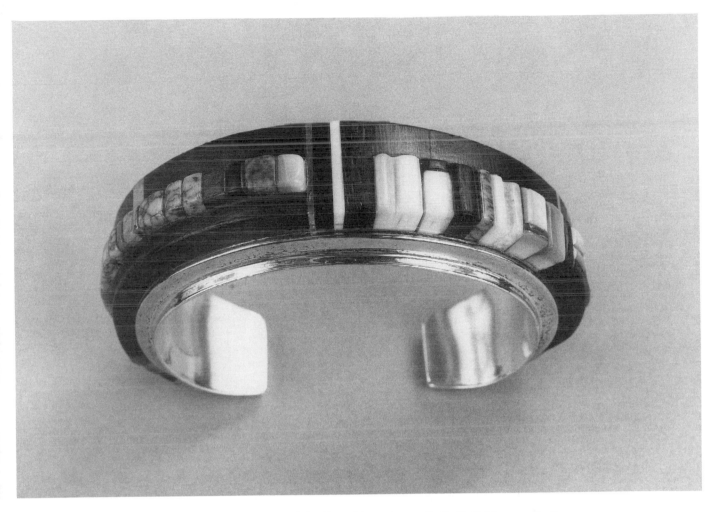

Charles Loloma: Silver bracelet, c. 1980. Photograph by Dong Lin; courtesy Ruth K. Belikove collection.

Individual Exhibitions

Exhibited regularly at his pottery shop in Scottsdale, 1954-1960, and his studio and gallery near Hotevilla on the Hopi Reservation, 1966-1990.

1963   Paris, France
1971   Heard Museum, Phoenix, Arizona

Selected Group Exhibitions

Exhibited regularly at the Scottsdale National Indian Arts Exhibition, the Arizona and New Mexico State Fairs, the Institute for American Indian Arts Museum, and the Santa Fe Indian Market

1970   *Objects USA*, American Craft Museum, New York (traveling)
1974   Museum of Contemporary Art, New York
1978   Museum of Contemporary Crafts, New York
1980   California Academy of Sciences, San Francisco, California
1981   Native American Center for the Living Arts, Niagara Falls, New York
        Native American Arts '81, Philbrook Art Center, Tulsa, Oklahoma

1982   Grand Palais, Salon d'Automne, Paris
1984   San Diego Museum of Man, California
1986   *When the Rainbow Touches Down*, Heard Museum, Phoenix, Arizona (traveling)
        American Craft Museum, New York
1996   Museum of Anthropology, Wake Forest University
1996-97 San Diego Museum of Man, California

Collections

Arizona State Museum, University of Arizona, Tucson; California Academy of Sciences, Elkus Collection, San Francisco; Children's Museum of Indianapolis; Heard Museum, Phoenix; Indian Arts and Crafts Board, U.S. Department of the Interior, Washington, D.C.; Millicent Rogers Museum, Taos, New Mexico; Museum of Anthropology, Wake Forest University; Museum of Northern Arizona, Flagstaff; San Diego Museum of Man; Wheelwright Museum of the American Indian, Santa Fe.

Publications

On LOLOMA: Books—*Objects: USA,* by Lee Nordness, Viking Press, New York, 1970; *Southwest Indian Art, A Changing Art,* by Clara Lee Tanner, University of Arizona Press, Tucson,

1973; *Art and Indian Individualists,* by Guy and Doris Monthan, Northland Press, Flagstaff, Arizona, 1975; *American Indian Art in the 1980's,* exhibition catalog by Lloyd Kiva New, Native American Center for the Living Arts, Niagara Falls, 1981; *Magic Images; Contemporary Native American Art,* by Edwin L. Wade and Rennard Strickland, University of Oklahoma Press, Norman, 1981; *The Elkus Collection, Southwestern Indian Art,* edited by Dorothy K. Washburn, California Academy of Sciences, San Francisco, 1984; *When the Rainbow Touches Down,* exhibition catalog by Tryntje Van Ness Seymour, Heard Museum, Phoenix, 1988; *Beyond Tradition: Contemporary Indian Art and Its Evolution,* by Lois Essary Jacka, Northland Publishing Co., Flagstaff, 1988; *Native America: Arts, Traditions and Celebrations,* by Christine Mather, Clarkson Potter, New York, 1990; *Southwestern Indian Jewelry,* by Dexter Cirillo, Abbeville Press, New York, 1992. **Articles**—"What You See Here Is a Lot of Soul," by Wesley Holden, *Arizona Highways,* vol. 50, no. 8, 1974; "American Indian Artist: Charles Loloma," by Marjel De Lauer, *Arizona Highways,* vol. 52, no. 8, 1976; "Beads, Boots and Jaguars: The Artists As They See Themselves," by Pam Hait, *Arizona Highways,* vol. 55, no. 4, 1979; "Innovations in Southwestern Indian Jewelry, Fine Art in the 1980s," by Jerry D. Jacka, *American Indian Art,* vol. 9, no. 2, 1984; "Charles Loloma," by Lois Essary Jacka, *American Indian Art,* vol. 21, no. 1, 1995. **Films**—*Three Indians,* produced by NET, 1972; *Loloma,* produced by the Public Broadcasting System, 1974, narrated by Rod McKuen.

*

Charles Loloma comments (1976):

Any creative act should bring joy or pleasure or satisfaction to both the creator and his audience.

*   *   *

An accomplished artist in many media, Loloma is best known for his trend-setting, innovative Hopi Jewelry. Throughout a long and illustrious career, he sought to create beauty for its own sake and to help others see the inner beauty in all things, animate and inanimate. He moved effortlessly between his traditional Hopi world and that of commercial galleries and famous people in the world's most cosmopolitan cities.

As a high school student in the 1930s, Loloma studied under Hopi painter, Fred Kabotie, and became an accomplished muralist. While still in his mid-teens, he assisted in painting murals at San Francisco's Golden Gate International Exposition, and in 1940, he assisted Kabotie in reproducing murals from the ancient Hopi village, Awatovi, at the Museum of Modern Art in New York.

During World War II, Loloma served in the U.S. Army and was stationed in the Aleutians. Upon his return, he enrolled under the GI Bill to study ceramics at the School for American Craftsmen, Alfred University, in Alfred, NY. While there, he was awarded a Whitney Foundation fellowship to research ceramics on the Hopi Reservation, a project that occupied him for five years. In 1954, he and his first wife, Otellie Pasivaya Loloma, established their own pottery shop in Scottsdale, which they operated for six years, producing innovative, wheel-thrown ceramic pieces marketed as Lolomaware.

Around 1955, Loloma first began to explore jewelry making, and over the next few years his interest was increasingly drawn in that direction. Through trial and error, he developed distinctive styles in sand casting, soldering, and lost wax casting. Like any artist working in a new medium, some of his early pieces now appear almost crude. Still, Loloma persevered and in 1963 he had a very successful show in Paris.

During Loloma's formative years of the late 1950s and early 1960s, he devoted much of his time to teaching ceramics, both at the University of Arizona and the Arizona State University. When the Rockefeller Foundation funded its Southwest Indian Art Project at the University of Arizona in 1959, Loloma was among the first participants and taught summer sessions for the project for the next three years. He was instrumental in establishing the Institute of American Indian Arts in Santa Fe in 1962 and served as the first head of its Department of Plastic Arts.

In 1966, Loloma returned to his birth place and established a studio and gallery near Hotevilla on the Hopi Reservation. There he continued to create internationally- acclaimed jewelry designs, incorporating ideas and materials from every part of the world and from many cultures. His designs combined many different settings in a single piece and can rightfully be considered sculpture as much as jewelry. As his designs became ever more innovative, his international following grew to include the world's best designers, and his clients included celebrities, monarchs, and presidents.

Loloma broke the barriers that separated traditionalism and modern art. From the beginning, his designs marked a major departure from what was regarded as traditional. His work being rejected at an early Gallup Inter-Tribal Indian Ceremonial, but his participation in other competitions often resulted in entry categories being redefined to match his innovations. At the Scottsdale National Indian Arts Exhibition, Loloma won First Prize awards for seven consecutive years during the 1970s. He was among the first Native American jeweler to use gold instead of silver and diamonds and other precious and semi-precious gems and minerals in addition to coral, turquoise, and shell. He was the first to place settings on the inside of a bracelet or ring, a reflection of his own strong belief in inner beauty, both in people and in natural materials and objects.

Loloma's influence on jewelry-making was international in scope, but nowhere is it more evident than in the works of many contemporary southwestern Native American silver and goldsmiths who have followed him. Many of these artists speak of Loloma's influence in terms of the confidence he instilled in them to follow their own intuitions and to continually challenge themselves.

Loloma's expertise and contributions to Native American art were often recognized and called upon in the form of speaking engagements, appointments to various boards, and other honors. In 1986, a terrible accident robbed Loloma of much of his energy and mobility. His nieces, Verma Nequatewa and Sherian Honhongva, who had worked under and along side him for many years, continued operating his studio for several years, with Loloma occasionally working at the bench or painting. After several years, however, the family made the painful decision to close the studio and to retire the Loloma hallmark. This Renaissance man died in 1991, but the honors continue. In 1996, Charles Loloma was selected for a Lifetime Achievement Award by the Southwestern Association for Indian Affairs in Santa Fe.

—Russell Hartman

LOLOMA, Otellie

Variant names: Sequafnehma
Tribal affiliations: Hopi
Ceramist, painter, jewelry designer, and painter

Born: Otellie Pasivaya in Sipaulovi Village, Second Mesa, Arizona, 1922; Sequafnehma means "The place in the valley where the squash blossoms bloom." **Education:** Oraibi High School, Arizona, with special classes in ceramics; School of American Craftsmen, Alfred University, 1947-49; University of Arizona, 1958-59; University of Northern Arizona, 1960-1961; College of Santa Fe, 1962. **Family:** Married Charles Loloma, 1942 (divorced, 1965). **Career:** Instructor, day schools in the Second Mesa area, 1940-45, and clay working, Shongopovy Day School, Second Mesa, Hopi Reservation, 1952-56; San Francisco State College, 1959; University of Arizona, Sedona, 1959-60; Southwestern Indian Art Project, University of Arizona, 1961-62; Institute of American Indian Arts (sculpture, painting, basic design, and traditional Indian dance), 1962-88; San Juan Pueblo (workshop), 1965; Indian Circle Project (workshop), Chippewa Ranch, Minnesota, 1966; Ramah Navajo School, New Mexico (workshop), 1968; School of Fine Arts, Miami University and Ceramics Department, Temple University, 1981; owned and operated pottery shop with Charles Loloma, 1954-60, and introduced Lolomaware pottery. **Awards:** Alfred University, New York, scholarship, 1947; National Women's Caucus for Art, Honor Award, 1991; danced in traditional groups at the 1968 Mexican Olympics and in a special invitational program at the White House; numerous awards for ceramics, including Arizona State Fair, Phoenix, Arizona, Philbrook Art Center, Tulsa, Oklahoma, Southwestern Association for Indian Arts, Indian Market, Santa Fe, Scottsdale National Indian Arts Exhibition, Arizona. **Died:** 30 January 1993.

Selected Group Exhibitions

1958	Tom Bahti Gallery, Tucson, Arizona
1959-62	Fifth Avenue Crafts Center, Scottsdale, Arizona
1963	Heard Museum, Phoenix, Arizona
1965	Blair House, Washington, D.C.
1966	Edinburgh Art Festival, Scotland
	Berlin Festival, Germany
1967	Museo de Belles Artes, Buenos Aires, Argentina
	Bibleotecha Nacionale, Santiago, Chile
1967-68	Center for Arts of Indian America, Washington, D.C.
1968	Philbrook Art Center, Tulsa, Oklahoma
1969	*Alaskan Centennial*, Anchorage, Alaska
1970	Marjorie Weiss Gallery, Bellevue, Washington
	Princeton University, New Jersey
1973	Museum of Fine Arts, Santa Fe, New Mexico
1977	Judith Stern Gallery, Minneapolis, Minnesota
1984	Turtle Museum of the Living Arts, Niagara Falls, New York
1985	American Indian Community House Gallery, New York City
	University of Michigan Art Museum, Ann Arbor
	Haffenreffer Museum, Brown University, Bristol, Rhode Island
	Brazos Gallery, Richland College, Dallas, Texas
	C.N. Gorman Museum, University of California, Davis
	American Indian Art Center Gallery, Minneapolis, Minnesota

Otellie Loloma: Ceramic pot, c. 1970. Courtesy Challis and Arch Thiessen collection.

1985-88	*Women of Sweetgrass, Cedar & Sage* (traveling)
1986	Oregon Institute of Art, Portland
	Wheelwright Museum, Santa Fe, New Mexico
	Evergreen Galleries, Evergreen College, Olympia, Washington
	Gardiner Art Gallery, Oklahoma State University, Stillwater
	North Museum, Lancaster, Pennsylvania
	Southwest Museum, Los Angeles, California
1988	Wheelwright Museum, Santa Fe, New Mexico

Collections

Heard Museum, Phoenix, Arizona; Indian Arts & Crafts Board, United States Department of the Interior, Washington, D.C.; Institute of American Indian Arts Museum, Santa Fe; National Museum of the American Indian, Washington, D.C.; Philbrook Art Center, Tulsa, Oklahoma.

Publications

On LOLOMA: Books—*Objects: USA,* by Lee Nordess, New York, 1970; *Indian Painters and White Patrons,* by J.J. Brody, University of New Mexico Press, Albuquerque, 1971; *Art and Indian Individuals: The Art of Seventeen Contemporary Southwestern Artists and Craftsmen,* by Doris and Gus Monthan, Northland Press, Flagstaff, Arizona, 1975; "Double Vision," by Lucy Lippard, and "My Mother's Daughter: A History of Native American Women in Art," interview with Ern Younger, *Women of Sweetgrass, Cedar & Sage,* edited by Harmony Hammond and Jaune Quick-to-See Smith, American Indian Community House Gallery, New York, 1985.

*

Otellie Loloma comments (1985):

Most of my ideas come from the stories told to me at home by uncles and my father and neighbors when I was growing up at Hopi. Winter at Hopi is cold and we stay inside a lot, and this is storytelling time. These are the stories of Soyoko, the Dachinas and Yaha times; these stories are of Hopi men and women, animals and birds and Spider Woman. Many of my paintings, clay figures and portraits on my pots are real characters at Hopi. Some of them are from my imagination and feelings about how I think they might look. Many are dressed in traditional Hopi fashion and are memories of early days. I want to show the young people the way things were before. When I work with figures in clay, I think of them as part of my life and visualize them as I work. When I make a bowl, I think of how it will be used, what will go in it like food or water, and I know it must be beautiful to hold such precious things like food or water.

*   *   *

Otellie Loloma made significant contributions as an artist, particularly as a ceramist, and as an instructor, drawing in both cases on her Hopi heritage. Her abilities as an instructor were, in fact, so inspirational that she nearly turned down a scholarship to the prestigious School of American Craftsmen, at Alfred University, to focus on her work as a teacher in the Second Mesa area of Arizona. She eventually forged legacies as an artist, instructor, and gallery owner. In addition to returning to teach Hopi children after graduating from Alfred University and instructing at such institutions as San Francisco State College, the College of Santa Fe, and the University of Arizona, Loloma was among the faculty at the Institute of American Indian Arts; numerous artists from that program cite her as a mentor. With her husband, famed jeweler Charles Loloma, to whom she was married from 1942 to 1965, Otellie Loloma participated in important Native American historical projects and operated a pottery shop, where the couple introduced the popular Lolomaware pottery, which modernized treatment of traditional clay pottery making of the Hopis but retained distinctive Hopi designs. Otellie assisted Charles in his Whitney Foundation research grant at Hopi, investigating local clays and earth stains for coloring.

The modern pottery and ceramic techniques Loloma learned at Alfred, including wheel-throwing and constructing, were combined with Hopi traditional hand-building methods. In the late 1950s, Otellie painted and potted with clay while Charles created his innovative jewelry. They showed and sold their wares at a shop they opened and operated, exhibited in 1958 at Tom Bahti Gallery in Tucson, and joined Cherokee textile-fashion designer, Lloyd Kiva New, who opened the Fifth Avenue Crafts Center in Scottsdale. They set up a studio and worked in the Phoenix area until fall of 1962, when all three artist moved to Santa Fe, New Mexico, to begin teaching at the Institute of American Indian Arts. Otellie taught ceramic sculpture, painting, basic design and traditional Indian dance at I.A.I.A. until her retirement in 1988. Otellie expressed her philosophy of teaching: "When I teach, which is so important to me and my own clay work, I try to instill belief in my students, whether Indian or non-Indian. When that belief is alive, their work is alive. This belief and aliveness gives the student strength in what they do in any art form or life work."

Loloma began each artwork with an idea drawn from Hopi legends or her experiences in the community. Though the initial idea might become subordinated as the final piece took shape, they remained an integral part of the finished product. Loloma's designs included male and female forms with recognizable Hopi traits deriving from masks, faces, and traditional hairstyles. Turquoise beading and leather were among the materials she used to enhance her ceramic works, lending them a uniqueness and beauty that were her contributions to Hopi traditional earthenware.

—Gregory Schaaf

LOMAHAFTEWA, Dan V.

Tribal affiliations: Hopi; Choctaw
Painter

Born: Dan Viets Lomahaftewa, Phoenix, Arizona, 3 April 1951. **Education:** Arizona State University, B.F.A., 1981. **Career:** Full-time artist, 1990—; singer and participant in ceremonials; lumberjack, mail clerk, road laborer; commissioned for a group of three paintings, Utah Opera Company; honorary U.S. delegate, United Nations' Earth Summit, Manchester, England, 1994. **Awards:** First Place, Santa Fe Indian Market, 1989 (painting: nontraditional), 1990 (oil painting: nontraditional), 1992 (Woody Crumbo Memorial Award, Excellence in Painting and Graphics), and 1994 (two awards: acrylic painting and graphics); First Place, Pueblo Grande Indian Market, Phoenix, Arizona, 1991 (poster design); Best of Division, Graphics, and Best of Classification, Painting, Drawing & Graphics, Heard Museum Guild Indian Fair & Market, Phoenix 1991; Visual Artist Fellowship, Utah Arts Council, 1989-90; Poster Artist, Pueblo Grande Indian Market, 1990, American Indian Art Festival, Dallas, Texas, 1993, and Santa Fe Indian Market, 1993.

Individual Exhibitions

1994   *New Spring Rain*, First Peoples Gallery, New York, New York

Green Art, Rainmaker Gallery, Manchester England

1995   Amer-Indian Gallery East, West Reading, Pennsylvania

Sundance Film Festival, Old Town Gallery Fine Art, Park City, Utah

Copeland-Rutherford Fine Arts, Santa Fe, New Mexico

Rainmaker Gallery, Manchester England

1996   Robins-Hyder Gallery, Santa Fe, New Mexico

Selected Group Exhibitions

1990   *Direction of the Sun*, brother & sister show (with Linda Lomahaftewa), American Indian Community House Gallery/Museum, New York

1991   *Living Room Pow Wow: Contemporary Native American Art*, Helio Galleries, SoHo, New York

1991-92 Heard Museum, Phoenix, Arizona

View of Six, Utah Arts Council Past Visual Arts Fellows (traveling)

1991-93 *Our Land/Ourselves: Contemporary Native American Indian Art*, premiered at University Art Gallery, State University of New York, Albany (traveling)

1992   *Recovery from Discovery: Native American Response to the Quincentenary*, Parents Association Gallery, University of Maryland, College Park

Dan V. Lomahaftewa: *Colors of Summer.* Courtesy of the artist.

From the Earth VIII, American Indian Contemporary Arts, San Francisco, California

1993   *For the Love of It*, Fenderson collection exhibit, Heard Museum, Phoenix, Arizona

Spirit of Native America, organized by American Indian Contemporary Arts, San Francisco, California, (traveling, South America and Paris, France)

1994   *East Meets West: Native American and Japanese Contemporary Art*, Copeland Rutherford Fine Art, Santa Fe, New Mexico

Art from New Mexico: The Governor's Show, Office of the Governor, Guadalajara, Mexico

New Art of the West, Eiteljorg Museum of American Indians and Western Art, Indianapolis, Indiana

1995   *Quintana*, Quintana Galleries, Portland, Oregon

One Moment In Time, First Peoples Gallery, New York, New York

Frog Pond Gallery, Sedona, Arizona

Southwest Gallery, Dallas, Texas

Evergreen Art Company, Colorado

1996-97   *Native Streams: Contemporary Native American Art,* Jan Cicero Gallery, Chicago, Illinois, and Turman Art Gallery, Indiana State University, Terre Haute (traveling)

Collections

Heard Museum, Phoenix, Arizona.

Publications

On LOMAHAFTEWA: Books—*Native Streams: Contemporary Native American Art,* Jan Cicero Gallery, Chicago, Illinois, and Turman Art Gallery, Indiana State University, Terre Haute, 1996.

*

Dan Lomahaftewa comments:

From when I was very young, it seems as though I was surrounded by expressions of beauty. As far back as I can remember, there were colorful and intricately designed baskets, pottery, rattles, bows and arrows, and katsina doll carvings, accenting all the households of my family. In addition, there were both ceremonial and social dancing and singing going on around me with an abundance of colorful regalia in which my family and I participate still....

The search for my own expression brought me to look at what had always influenced me and many other Native Americans, that being the inseparable interweaving of the lifeway of Indian people and their spirituality. This component of Native American expression was, and to some extent, still is, incorporated into all the different mediums of expression represented by form and symbol.

What I'm trying to create are images of my own interpretation of these symbolic representations of Native Americans.

*   *   *

Personal memories blend seamlessly into tribal references in the large, abstract oil paintings of Dan Lomahaftewa. Known for his modernist use of pictographic icons, Lomahaftewa is the logical successor to Michael Kabotie and the Artist Hopid, a group of contemporary Hopi artists co-founded by Kabotie in 1973. Lomahaftewa departs from these artists primarily in his preference for bright colors and his minimalization of design elements.

Lomahaftewa was born in Phoenix, Arizona in 1951, son of a Hopi man and a Choctaw woman. He was raised in Phoenix, where his family participated in the urban, intertribal community as well as the local Hispanic community. He spent summers on the Hopi reservation, where his father's family lived. During these visits he learned Hopi traditions and ceremonies and lived with his relatives, experiencing daily life on the reservation. During the school year, his mother introduced him to the pow-wow circuit, which provided a different Indian experience, less tribally-specific but just as socially satisfying. Lomahaftewa is still an active pow-wow singer.

Lomahaftewa was introduced to Western studio art by his older sister, Linda Lomahaftewa, who attended the San Francisco Art Institute in the late 1960s. Lomahaftewa was still in high school when he visited his sister at the Institute and was inspired to become a painter. But he remembers being advised against this, being told that the life of a real artist is very difficult. Lomahaftewa took this advice to heart, and sampled a number of other vocations—lumberjack, mail clerk, ditch digger—before finally enrolling at Arizona State University, where he earned his bachelor's degree in fine art. He continued for one year as a graduate student in the art department, but left to raise his family in Fort Duchesne, Utah, where his wife's relatives lived.

Lomahaftewa emphasizes the peaceful and beatific in his art. His vibrant acrylic images flow from a nostalgic sense of memory, of time spent herding sheep on the mesa tops, watching swollen rain clouds move high over the desert, listening to the whir of the grinding machine as his uncle cut turquoise for jewelry. On his canvases, pictograph-style images float over swirling fields of color, combining the warmth of childhood memories with more abstract tribal ideas, such as the attention paid to prayer, and respect for elders and for the natural world.

While traditional-style Hopi pictorial art tends to be flat and linear, Lomahaftewa applies his paint thickly, using wide, visible brush strokes and curvilinear forms. He builds texture by covering large canvases with a sea of pastel and jewel-toned colors before adding his minimalistic symbols. In comparing his approach to that of a friend who painted in a more traditional style, Lomahaftewa said, "My work is less direct, not like painting a man burning cedar. My painting is what's going on in his mind, this guy who's burning cedar."

In 1989, Lomahaftewa was awarded a Utah Arts Council Visual Artist Fellowship, which enabled him to spend time researching rock art in the Fort Duchesne area. Rock art appears throughout the Southwest, but Lomahaftewa was drawn to the Utah figures because they reminded him of Hopi kachinas. He

interprets these forms in his *Primordial Spirits* series, executed in a variety of media, including oil and acrylic paintings, collographs, monotypes, and etchings. Three of these works (*Moisture Bringers I*, monotype; *Singing Spirits*, acrylic on canvas; *Ancestor Myth*, acrylic on canvas) were included in the group show, *The Spirit of Native America*, curated by American Indian Contemporary Arts in San Francisco.

Building a career in the wake of his older sister has been a challenge. The siblings are close friends, living in the same city and occasionally working together, but Lomahaftewa has succeeded in finding his own path, developing his own network of galleries and collectors. One of his most recent projects was a group of three commissioned paintings for the Utah Opera Company productions of *La Boheme*, *The Barber of Seville*, and *Dreamkeepers*, a world premiere. Among Lomahaftewa's other major achievements are his selection for the Heard Museum's *Fifth Biennial Native American Fine Arts Invitational* in 1991, and his 1994 solo exhibit at Rainmaker Gallery in Manchester, England, scheduled to coincide with the United Nations' Earth Summit, at which Lomahaftewa was an honorary U.S. delegate.

—Margaret Dubin

LOMAHAFTEWA, Linda

Tribal affiliations: Hopi; Choctaw
Painter

Born: Phoenix, Arizona, 3 July 1947. **Education:** Institute of American Indian Arts; San Francisco Art Institute, B.F.A., 1970, M.F.A., 1971. **Career:** Teaching assistant, Santa Fe Art Institute in Santa Fe, New Mexico, 1970; assistant professor, Native American Art, California State College at Sonoma in Rohnert Park, 1971-73; professor of painting and drawing, Native American Studies, University of California, Berkeley, California, 1974-76, and Institute of American Indian Arts, Santa Fe, New Mexico, 1976—; board member, City of Santa Fe Arts Council, 1983-84, Wheelwright Museum of the American Indian, 1989-92, Southwestern Association for Indian Arts (SWAIA), 1993-96; visiting artist, Brandywine Workshop, Philadelphia, Pennsylvania, 1988, Heard Museum, Phoenix, 1993, Yavapai Art Institute, Prescott, Arizona, 1994, Rotorua Aotearoa, New Zealand, 1995, SWAIA Youth Camp, Santa Fe, 1996, McDougal Art Gallery, Christchurch, New Zealand, 1996; lecturer, University of South Dakota, Vermillion, 1996, Museum of Indian Arts and Culture, Santa Fe, 1997; juror, Eight Northern Pueblos Art and Craftsman Show and Northern Plains Tribal Arts, Sioux Falls, South Dakota. **Awards:** Center for the Arts of Indian America, 1967; Scottsdale National Indian Arts Exhibition, 1970-71; Indian Festival of Arts, 1st Place, Painting, La Grande, Oregon; Santa Fe Indian Market, 1974, 1982, 1987-90, and Helen Hardin Award, 1988; poster artist, Heard Museum Guild Indian Fair and Market, 1994 and 1997.

Individual Exhibitions

1989   *Lomahaftewa*, Verde Valley Art Association, Jerome, Arizona

Selected Group Exhibitions

1967   *Biennial Exhibition of American Indian Arts and Crafts*,
        United States Department of the Interior, Washington,
        D.C.

1974   *Institute of American Indian Arts Alumni Exhibition*,
        Amon Carter Museum of Western Art, Fort Worth,
        Texas

1976   *One With the Earth*, Institute of American Indian Arts
        Museum, Santa Fe, New Mexico

1980   *Pintura Amerinda Contemporanea*, Museo del Instituto
        Artes, Amerindos, Chile (touring Latin America)

1981-92 *Spirit of the Earth: An Exhibition of Contemporary Native
        American Art*, Confluences of Tradition and Change,
        organized by the R.L. Nelson Gallery and C. N.
        Gorman Museum, Davis, California (traveling)

1982   Native American Center for the Living Arts, Niagara Falls,
        New York

1985   *Women of Sweetgrass, Cedar and Sage*, American Indian
        Community House Gallery, New York (traveling)

1987   *Four Sacred Mountains' Contemporary Indian Arts Fes-
        tival*, Tuba City, Arizona

1988   College of Santa Fe Fine Arts Gallery, New Mexico
        Merging and Emergence, Wheelwright Museum of the
        American Indian, Santa Fe, New Mexico
        Portfolio II, American Indian Contemporary Arts, San
        Francisco, California
        Progressions of Impressions, Heard Museum, Phoenix,
        Arizona
        First Annual Hopi Foundation Arts Benefit Show, Lindavida
        Fine Arts, Ruidiso, New Mexico
        Artists from the Institute of American Indian Arts, Mount
        Scenario Coolege Fine Art Center, Ladysmith, Wisconsin

1989   *Monothon*, College of Santa Fe, New Mexico
        Changing Woman, Matrix Gallery, San Francisco, Cali-
        fornia
        As in Her Vision, American Indian Contemporary Arts,
        San Francisco, California
        American Indian Community House, San Francisco, Cali-
        fornia
        Native Proof, American Indian Contemporary Arts, San
        Francisco, California

1990   *We Are Part of the Earth*, Centro Cultural de la Raza, San
        Diego, California
        Direction of the Sun, American Indian Community House
        Gallery, New York
        *Contemporary Printmaking in New Mexico: A Native
        American Perspective*, Governor's Gallery and Stables
        Art Center, Taos, New Mexico
        Points of View: Mixed Media Show, Bridge Street Gallery,
        Big Fork, Montana
        American Indian Gallery, Steamboat Springs, Colorado

1990-91 *One With the Earth*, organized by the Institute of Ameri-
        can Indian Arts, Santa Fe, New Mexico (traveling)

1991   *Our Land/Ourselves*, University Art Gallery, Albany,
        New York (traveling)

1991-92 *Shared Visions: Native American Painters and Sculptors
        in the Twentieth Century*, Heard Museum, Phoenix,
        Arizona

1992   *Transformed Traditions*, Santa Rosa Junior College, Santa
        Rosa, California

**Linda Lomahaftewa. Courtesy of the artist and The Portrait
Studio, Santa Fe, New Mexico.**

        Lomahaftewa: Looking for Beauty in the Future, with
        brother, Dan V. Lomahaftewa, Galleria Posada, Sacra-
        mento, California

1993   *The Spirit of Native America*, American Indian Contem-
        porary Art, San Francisco, California
        Bridges and Boundaries, Pelper-Regraf Gallery, Frank-
        furt, Germany

1994   The Spirit of Native America, American Indian Contem-
        porary Arts, (touring six venues in Latin America and
        Lille, France)

1995   *Legacies: Contemporary Art by Native American Women*,
        Castle Gallery, College of New Rochelle, New York
        Spirit of the Pueblo People, East West Center, Honolulu,
        Hawaii
        *Native American and Native Artists of the South Pacific
        Islands*, Hei Tiki Gallery, Rotorua, New Zealand

1995-98 *Indian Humor*, American Indian Contemporary Arts, San
        Francisco, California

1996   *I Stand in the Center of Good*, American Indian Commu-
        nity House, New York

1996-98 *River Deep, Mountain High*, international traveling exhi-
        bition produced by Highland Council Culture and Lei-
        sure Services and Scottish Arts Council, Inverness,
        Scotland

1997   *New Art from Native America*, Center Gallery, Bucknell
        University, Lewisburg, Pennsylvania
        We are Many, We are One, University Art Center, Uni-
        versity of Wisconsin, La Crosse

Linda Lomahaftewa: *Parrot Migration I,* 1992. Courtesy of the artist.

Collections

American Indian Historical Society, San Francisco, California; Center for the Arts of Indian America, Washington, D.C.; Heard Museum, Phoenix, Arizona; Institute of American Indian Arts Museum, Santa Fe, New Mexico; Native American Center for the Living Arts, Inc., Niagara Falls, New York; Millicent Rogers Foundation Museum, Taos, New Mexico; Southern Plains Indian Museum, Anadarko, Oklahoma; University of Lethbridge, Native American Studies Department, Alberta, Canada; Wheelwright Museum of American Indian, Santa Fe, New Mexico.

Publications

On LOMAHAFTEWA: Books—*Alcatraz Is Not an Island,* edited by Peter Blue Cloud, Berkeley, 1972; *Spirit of the Earth,* edited by Ray Gonyea, 1980; *The Sweet Grass Lives On,* by Jamake Highwater, New York, 1980; *Magic Images: Contemporary Native American Art,* Norman, 1981; *Confluences of Tradition and Change,* edited by L. Price Amerson, Jr., Davis, California, 1982; *American Indian Women Artists,* by Charlotte Rubenstein, New York, 1982; *The American West: The Modern Vision,* by Patricia Janis Broder, Boston, 1984; *Women of Sweetgrass, Cedar and Sage,* New York, 1985; *Our Land/Ourselves,* edited by Deborah Ward, Albany, 1990; *Shared Visions: Native American Painting and Sculpture of the Twentieth Century,* by Margaret Archuleta and Rennard Strickland, Phoenix, 1991; *The Spirit of Native America,* American Indian Contemporary Art, San Francisco, 1993; *I Stand in the Center of Good,* by Larry Abbott, Lincoln, Nebraska, 1994; *Indian Humor,* exhibition catalog, American Indian Contemporary Arts, San Francisco, 1995.

*

Linda Lomahaftewa comments (1993):
Images that tend to recur in my work are animal spirits, petroglyphs, and Hopi symbols such as lightning, clouds, and rainbows. These images arise from a source deep within me that I can tap in an intuitive way. (From the catalog for *The Spirit of Native America*)

*   *   *

Like other contemporary Native American artists who work in abstractions, Linda Lomahaftewa relies on symbols to convey her memory of tribal landscape. But unlike the stark, hostile icons of Jaune Quick-to-See Smith, or Harry Fonseca's thickly textured *Stone Poems*, Lomahaftewa's symbols are gentle, prominent on the paper but translucent. If they were sounds, they would be windchimes. This is how the Hopi/Choctaw artist addresses her subjects, with patience and respect, like her father advised: "Whatever you do, always pray and sing a song because that's what makes your work good. You should always pray to the spirits to help you do your work."

Lomahaftewa was born in Phoenix in 1947. She spent part of her childhood in the Los Angeles area before moving back to Arizona. As a child she was encouraged to pursue her interest in art. Her father, who is Hopi, carved kachina dolls. Her mother, who is Choctaw, enjoyed crafts, especially quilts and ribbonwork applique. Her younger brother, Dan Lomahaftewa, studied art at Arizona State University and is now a successful painter. From this creative environment, Lomahaftewa moved to Santa Fe in 1962 to attend the Institute of American Indian Arts. At the time, the Institute was a high school, and under the directorship of Lloyd Kiva New it attracted enthusiastic and open-minded youths from tribes across the country. As a member of the cohort that included Earl Biss, T.C. Cannon, and Alfred Young Man, Lomahaftewa was part of a new generation of Native American artists that would set the standards for years to come.

After graduating from the Institute, Lomahaftewa joined several of her classmates in the journey west to the San Francisco Art Institute. There she received further formal training in painting, including the Western techniques of perspective, which she quickly rejected in her own work. She compares her favored technique to the painting on a piece of pottery, which is flat by Western standards, but assumes the fullness of the vessel in the Hopi aesthetic.

Lomahaftewa especially liked working with colors, and she soon gravitated to more abstract work. After several years of painting in the studio, she began to notice Hopi imagery in her pictures: "I started adding my own thing ... like corn would start popping up!" At first, her use of Hopi icons was generalized and vague, recalling "more of the totality of ... Hopi" than specific ceremonies or landmarks. Over the years her work has become more focused, especially in series such as *Cloud Maiden*.

Although trained as a painter, Lomahaftewa has leaned more towards printing techniques, which allow her to produce work efficiently while retaining her focus on design and color. Her monotypes are particularly strong, with their bold floating icons and softly textured backgrounds. A 1994 monotype, *Red Man's Path*, which was included in the exhibit *Legacies: Contemporary Art by Native American Women* (1995, Castle Gallery, College of New Rochelle, New York), is exemplary. In it, three striking figures dance in the light, partially within and partially outside a dark, textured frame. Inspired by petroglyphs near her home in Santa Fe, the figures appear caught in a passage between two worlds.

Unlike some of her peers, who have rejected the ethnic label, Lomahaftewa identifies as an Indian artist. As she told interviewer Lawrence Abbott in 1991, "because I'm an Indian whatever I paint is Indian ... [My] paintings contain the history of my people." For example, the 1987 monotype, *Awatovi Parrots,* refers to the prehistoric trade in parrot feathers between Hopi and Mexican tribes. The parrot design also pays homage to Hopi kiva murals, which often feature the colorful birds.

Lomahaftewa lives and works in Santa Fe, where she teaches at the Institute of American Indian Arts. Her work was featured in the Heard Museum's *Second Biennial Native American Fine Arts Invi-tational*, as well as Portfolio II (American Indian Contemporary Arts, San Francisco, 1988). Currently she exhibits her work in galleries throughout the United States, Canada, and Europe.

—Margaret Dubin

LOMAKEMA, Milland Dawa

Variant names: Dawakema
Tribal affiliations: Hopi
Painter

Born: Shungopovi, Second Mesa, Arizona, August 1941; member, One Horn Society and Corn/Water Clan; Hopi name means "House of the Sun." **Education:** Academy of Harding College, Searcy, Arkansas, 1957-59; Academy of Magic Valley Christian College, Delco, Idaho, 1960. **Career:** Detective, Phoenix, Arizona, mid-1960s; contributor, Hopi Project, 1965; Hopi police, 1968—; member, Hopi Arts & Crafts Co-Op Guild, Second Mesa, Arizona; co-founder, director, manager, Artist Hopid, 1973-80s, a subsidiary of Hopi Arts & Crafts Co-Op Guild, promoting Hopi art through exhibits, lectures; muralist, with members of Artist Hopid, Hopi Cultural Center Museum, 1975; commissioned for decal designs, Hopi Police Department and City of Winslow, Arizona. **Awards:** Numerous from fairs, including Inter-Tribal Indian Ceremonials, 1968, 1971, Arizona State Fair, 1969, Heard Museum Guild Indian Fair and Market, 1969, 1975, Navajo Tribal Fair and Rodeo, 1969, and Philbrook Museum of Art, 1971, 1975.

Selected Group Exhibitions

Lomakema's works have been exhibited continuously since the 1970s at Hopi Cultural Center Museum, Second Mesa, Arizona.

1970   *Hopi Life in Hopi Painting,* Museum of the American Indian, New York
1975-80 *Pintura Amerindia Contemporanea/E.U.A.*, sponsored by the United States Department of State and International Communications Agency, Washington, D.C.
1976   Native American Center for the Living Arts, Niagara Falls, New York
1978   Wheelwright Museum of the American Indian, Santa Fe, New Mexico
         100 Years of Native American Painting, Oklahoma Museum of Art, Oklahoma City, Oklahoma
1980   Heard Museum, Phoenix, Arizona
1984-85 *Indianascher Kunstler* (traveling, Germany), organized by the Philbrook Museum, Tulsa, Oklahoma
1988   Hopi-tu Tsootsvolla, Sedona, Arizona

Collections

Center for Great Plains Studies, University of Nebraska, Lincoln; Eiteljorg Museum of American Indians and Wester Art, Indianapolis, Indiana; Heard Museum, Phoenix, Arizona; Heritage Center, Inc., Collection, Pine Ridge, South Dakota; Hopi Cultural Center Museum, Second Mesa, Arizona; Museum of the American Indian, Smithsonian Institution, Washington, D.C.; Museum of Northern

Metropolitan State University
Library Services
St. Paul, MN 55106

Arizona, Flagstaff; Millicent Rogers Foundation Museum, Taos, New Mexico; Roswell Museum and Art Center, Roswell, New Mexico; Southwest Museum, Los Angeles, California; Wheelwright Museum of the American Indian, Santa Fe, New Mexico.

Publications

On LOMAKEMA: Books—*Southwest Indian Art: A Changing Tradition,* by Clara Lee Tanner, Tucson, 1973; *Hopi Painting: The World of the Hopis,* by Patricia Janis Broder, New York, 1978; *100 Years of Native American Painting*, exhibition catalog by Arthur Silberman, Oklahoma Museum of Art, Oklahoma City, 1978; *The Sweet Grass Lives On,* by Jamake Highwater, New York, 1980; *Indianascher Kunstler*, by Gerhard Hoffman, Munich, 1984; *The Arts of the North American Indian: Native Traditions in Evolution,* edited by Edwin L. Wade, New York, 1986.

*   *   *

Milland Dawa Lomakema is one of the main representatives of the second generation of Hopi painters who succeeded artists like Fred Kabotie, Otis Polelonema, and Waldo Mootzka. One of the Hopi elements in Lomakema's work is the spiritual subject matter of his paintings and his adherence to traditional designs. He shares the Hopi painters' love and reverence for the sacred Kachinas, the most frequent motifs of his images. And he looks to the kiva murals of ancient Awatovi for inspiration. He is modern insofar as his art is not so much representational as abstract and his goal is not to document the Hopi ceremonies, done so admirably by Fred Kabotie, but to conjure up the Hopi universe through ancient symbols and designs. Another modern trait is his experimentation with abstract forms and contemporary painting styles, like Cubism and Surrealism, though not to the same extent as other Hopi painters of his time.

Lomakema, who comes from Shungopovi, Second Mesa, on the Hopi reservation, is the same age as Mike Kabotie, also from Second Mesa, and has much in common with him. Both men have deep roots in the spiritual life of the Hopi, which are reflected in their work. They are also very active in the promotion of Hopi arts and crafts and have both been managers and directors of the Hopi Arts and Crafts Co-operative. In the 1970s they both were founding members of the Artist Hopid. The basic goal of these men was to experiment and test new ideas and techniques in art, using traditional Hopi designs and concepts. With this goal in mind, they worked so closely together, influencing each other, that, as Kabotie remembers, "in third year you couldn't tell which was Mike Kabotie, which was Milland (Lomakema) because a lot of our paintings began to look the same" (*Hopi Painting*, 1978).

Committed to the same artistic goal as Mike Kabotie, Lomekema's range of themes and expressive forms is not quite as broad. His artistic inspiration comes to a large degree from the rites of the One-Horn Society, in which he is an initiate. In several of his pictures he includes One Horn figures, as in *One Horn Priest*, an abstract painting organized around a stylized head with one horn, standing for the priest. This work conjures up the Hopi universe through abstract designs, like cloud terrasses, raindrops, migration-spirals and deer-tracks. Stylized little Hopi men with staffs represent the human world.

Lomakema has created his own Spirit World, which centers in the Spirit of Corn, the principal food of the Hopi. The Hopi believe that there is spiritual essence in each matter, which is the idea

behind Lomakema works such as *Cornmaidens* and *Cornspirits*. In one of many versions of "Corn Maidens," Lomakema portrays two spirits. He describes them as "corn plants with two ears of corn with heads on them. Their spirits meet at night and help the corn grow into healthy big corn, as corn is our principal food" (*Hopi Painting*, 1978). In another version, three maidens are rendered as the embodiment of corn—their bowed heads are the predominant expressive gesture. They bespeak humility and shyness, humility at the miracle of the ripening of the corn that takes place in them, shyness at the realization that the price they must pay is their virginity. No longer is a narrative painting style in the manner of the earlier Hopi painters used for the purpose of documentation; instead, abstraction becomes the idiom of a spiritual substance. *Corn Field* is in another respect remarkable. With strictly geometric forms, the impression of a cornfield is produced, bordered by mesas and surrounded by clouds and a rainbow. Beams of sunlight from a Sun Forehead symbol give the work surrealist effects.

Lomakema frequently paints the traditional leaders of his people as they go about their work for the well-being of the pueblo. In *The Old One: the Village Chief*, he depicts a "Mongwi" planting a prayer stick in the corn field. In *Hopi Chief in His Field*, the Chief carries sacred water to the field and sprinkles sacred corn on the ground, while a number of fertility symbols point to a good harvest.

The work of Lomakoma is abundant in Kachina paintings, as indicated by titles like *Cloud Kachina Symbol, Kachina Clan, Long Hair Kachina, Awatovi Motifs of the Kachina Clan*, and *Kachina Kivas on San Francisco Peaks*. These pictures are documents of Hopi culture, and to that extent traditional; but they can also be modern and comment on present day Hopi life. An example is *Symbols of the Home Dance*, in which the forms of the Hemis Kachinas are used to contrast the ancient rituals with modern industrial life. "By transforming the Kachinas into an industrial complex," notes Broder notes, Lomakema "emphasizes the ability of the Hopi culture to survive and flourish in the modern world" (*Hopi Painting*, 1978). This unshaken belief in the perseverance of the Hopis through the times is a distinctive feature of Lomakema's painting.

—Gerhard and Gisela Hoffmann

LONEWOLF, Joseph
Tribal affiliations: Santa Clara Pueblo
Potter

Born: Joseph Lonewolf Tafoya, Santa Clara Pueblo, New Mexico, 26 January 1932. **Family:** Member of the famed Tafoya family of Santa Clara Pueblo. **Career:** Mechanic, mining industry; full-time potter, 1971—.

Selected Group Exhibitions

Works have been consistently exhibited since the 1960s at Santa Clara Pueblo, through commercial galleries, and major art fairs in the southwest.

1977   Wheelwright Museum of the American Indian, Santa Fe, New Mexico

1981   *American Indian Art in the 1980s,* Native American Center for Living Arts, Niagara Falls, New York
Heard Museum, Phoenix, Arizona
Eiteljorg Museum of American Indians and Western Art, Indianapolis, Indiana

Publications

On LONEWOLF: Books—*The Pottery Jewels of Joseph Lonewolf,* Dandrick Publications, Scottsdale, Arizona, 1974; "Tafoya," *Seven Families in Pueblo Pottery,* by Rick Dillingham, Albuquerque, 1974; *Artistry in Clay,* by Don Dedera, Flagstaff, 1985; *Talking with the Clay: The Art of Pueblo Pottery,* by Stephen Trimble, Santa Fe, 1987; *Beyond Tradition: Contemporary American Indian Art and Its Evolution,* by Jerry and Lois Jacka, Flagstaff, 1988; *Fourteen Families in Pueblo Pottery,* by Rick Dillingham, Santa Fe, 1994; *Art of Clay: Timeless Pottery of the Southwest,* edited by Lee M. Cohen, Santa Fe, 1995. **Articles**—"American Indian Artists: Joseph Lonewolf, Grace Medicine Flower," by Marjel De Lauer, *Arizona Highways,* vol. 52, August 1976.

Collections

Eiteljorg Museum of American Indians and Western Art, Indianapolis, Indiana; Heard Museum, Phoenix, Arizona; Wheelwright Museum of the American Indian, Santa Fe, New Mexico.

*   *   *

The Pueblo Indians of the American Southwest have a long tradition in pottery-making. There are usually one or two families in a pueblo who have distinguished themselves and have handed down their knowledge and their skills from mother to daughter, and recently also from father to son. In Santa Clara, in the Rio Grande area, the Tafoya family, with their numerous descendants of the potter, Sarafina, are best known for their carved and incised blackware and redware, their miniatures and sgraffitos. Their most prominent member is Joseph Lonewolf (Tafoya), born in 1932. He has brought national, as well as international, fame to his pueblo. Strangely enough, his career did not start before he was thirty-nine years of age and had been forced by a back injury to give up his work as a journeyman mechanic in the mining industry in Colorado.

Having, as a child, helped his parents, Camilio Sunflower and Agapita, with their pots and having made and incised tiny pots over the years to give to family and friends, Lonewolf was prepared for the work ahead of him. Furthermore, he was and still is inspired by the prehistoric Mimbres vessels that he had studied in museums and private collections. The ancestors of the New Mexico puebloans, who lived in the region from the tenth to the fourteenth centuries, decorated their ware with a great variety of figurative designs representing birds, insects, mammals, the mythical water serpent, and fish. Lonewolf has taken up these stylized designs, refined them, and added his own more realistic wildlife motifs. He sees himself as a link in the long chain that has bonded Indian artists-in-clay together for untold years, feeling the influence of the ancient Mimbrenos: they show him, in visions and dreams, finished designs before he begins to form a pot.

Like many pueblo potters, Lonewolf feels a close relationship to the Earth, whose blessing he asks before he starts working. He also talks to the clay, which is a living being to him, and says he must be careful not to hurt a pot's feelings or it will take revenge and crack in the firing process. This relationship between the potter and his work is deeply rooted in Pueblo legends and mythology and unparalleled in the Western world.

Lonewolf is completely traditional in his pottery-making methods. He uses neither wheel nor kiln, and his only modern tool is a pocket-knife for incising the designs. He works on a pot for a very long time, up to two or three years in some cases, for "the clay requires feeling and patience." The clay comes mainly from the area near his studio in Santa Clara Pueblo, but he also seeks and gathers various clays that will serve later as slips and produce different colors. Working on a pot starts with cleaning and soaking the clay in water, making rolls and laying coil upon coil. Forming the pot can take up to three weeks, and then it is set aside for about three months to harden. Then comes the scraping stage, followed by water-smoothing the vessel with a soft cloth. Meanwhile, the pot is set aside for days, or even weeks. When the slip is prepared, it is applied on the entire surface and after another drying period the polishing begins. Polishing is an important phase that must be finished in one sitting or the potter has to start all over again at the scraping stage. Carving or incising the design is, in a way, the most creative and time-consuming part of the whole procedure, requiring a steady hand and a focused mind. Firing is the final and most exciting act, for it can lead to the fulfillment of the potter's dream or end in total disaster. If the pot has the slightest imperfection—a hairline crack, a tiny burn mark—Lonewolf will destroy it.

Lonewolf's pots range from 3/8 of an inch to 12-inches in height and bear a serial number and his signature. His versatility is such that no two vessels are alike. Their decors go by names like *Mimbres Past* (stylized Mimbres animals), *Possession of the Herd* (the battle of stags), *Flight of Fancy* (a Butterfly), or *Storm Maker* (the feathered serpent that brings the summer storm). Because of their excellence in craftsmanship and their high artistic value, Lonewolf's pots are much sought after and have become museum pieces and collectors' items. In spite of prices at several thousand dollars apiece, the waiting list is long, for he produces only about 60 pots a year. In recent years, in addition to making pots, Lonewolf has cast metal wolves in gold, silver, and bronze, and has also created a series of miniature pots in precious metals.

Lonewolf's artistry in clay has become an inspiration to the younger members of his family, like his daughters Susan Snowflake and Rosemary Appleblossom; they have become potters in their own right and pass on the gift of Old Clay Woman and the ancient Mimbrenos.

—Gerhard and Gisela Hoffmann

LONGFISH, George
Tribal affiliations: Seneca; Tuscarora
Painter

Born: Oshweken, Ontario, 22 August 1942. **Education:** Thomas Indian School near Gowanda, New York, 1945-56, and Tuley High School, Chicago, 1956-60; studied painting, sculpture, printmaking, and filmmaking at the School of the Art Institute of Chicago, B.F.A., 1970, M.F.A., 1972. **Career:** Teaching assistant in photography and filmmaking, School of the Art Institute of Chicago, 1971; taught art at Little Big Horn High School in Chicago, 1971-72; project director, Graduate Program in American Indian Art, University of Montana, Missoula, 1972-73; currently teaches historical and contemporary Native arts, Native American Studies program, University of California at Davis (assistant professor, 1973, associate professor, 1980, professor, 1985); director, C.N. Gorman Museum, University of California, 1974-96; active in ATLATL during the 1980s. **Awards:** Juror's Grand Award, Third Annual Contemporary Indian Art Exhibit, Ellensburg, Washington, 1974; First in sculpture and graphics, California Indian Days, Cal Expo, Sacramento, 1980; First in sculpture, October ArtFest, Davis, California, 1981.

Individual Exhibitions

1971   Hunt-Henry Studio, Chicago, Illinois
        Second Unitarian Church, Chicago, Illinois
1972   Gallery of Fine Arts, University of Montana, Missoula
1978   Walter Kelly Gallery, Chicago, Illinois
1979   Walter Kelly Gallery, Chicago, Illinois
1981   *George Longfish—Paintings*, South Alberta Art Gallery, Lethbridge, Alberta
1982   *G.C. Longfish: Work on Paper and Canvas*, Pence Gallery and Coleman Fine Arts, Davis, California
        George Longfish: Masks and Spirits, Fondo del Sol Visual Art and Media Center, Washington, D.C.
1983   College of the Redwoods Gallery, Eureka, California
1984   *Work of George Longfish*, Bernice Steinbaum Gallery, New York
        George Longfish: Recent Paintings and Masks, Crocker Art Museum, Sacramento, California
        Paintings by George Longfish, Museum of the Plains Indian and Crafts Center, Browning, Montana
1985   *George Longfish: Portraits*, Yuba College, Woodland Center, California
        George Longfish: Masks and Recent Paintings, American Indian Contemporary Arts Gallery, San Francisco, California
1986   *George Longfish*, Enthios Gallery, Santa Fe, New Mexico
        Common Ground: New Works by George Longfish, Bernice Steinbaum Gallery, New York
        Masks—George Longfish, Robert Else Gallery, California State University, Sacramento
1987   *George Longfish, New Works*, Heartwood Gallery, Davis, California
1988   *Circle in Transition: Works by George Longfish*, American Indian Contemporary Arts, San Francisco, California
1989   *George Longfish*, Jennifer Pauls Gallery, Sacramento, California
        George Longfish Paintings, LRC Gallery, College of the Siskiyous, Weed, California
1993   *Selected Paintings*, Dean Moniz Gallery, Sacramento, California
        Paintings and Masks: 1967 to the Present, Memorial Union Art Gallery, University of California, Davis

Selected Group Exhibitions

1973   *Native American Legacy*, Henry Gallery, University of Washington, Seattle

        Contemporary Indian Art Exhibition, Alaska State Council on the Arts (travelling show)
        Heard Museum Guild Indian Arts and Crafts Exhibit, Phoenix, Arizona
1974   *Scottsdale National Indian Arts Exhibition*, Scottsdale, Arizona
        Sacred Circle of Life, Oakland Museum, Oakland, California
        Heard Museum Guild Indian Arts and Crafts Exhibit, Phoenix, Arizona
1975   *Scottsdale National Indian Arts Exhibition*, Scottsdale, Arizona
        Knowledge through Vision & Tradition, Marin Museum Association, Marin Civic Center, San Rafael, California
        Heard Museum Guild Indian Arts and Crafts Exhibit, Phoenix, Arizona
1976   *American Indian Artists Exhibition*, Philbrook Art Center, Tulsa, Oklahoma
        New Horizons in American Indian Art, Southwest Museum, Los Angeles, California
        Indian Images, University Art Gallery, University of North Dakota, Grand Forks
1977   *Contemporary Native American Artists*, Center for International Arts, New York
        The Native American Heritage, Art Institute of Chicago, Illinois
        Circle of Tradition and Vision: Nine Native American Artists, Artists Embassy Gallery, San Francisco, California
1978   *Paintings, Fetishes, and Masks by George Longfish and Frank LaPena*, Art Space Gallery, Sacramento, California
        Messenger of the Earth, Main Gallery, California State University, Sacramento
1979   *Longfish/Lomahaftewa*, The Art Gallery, University of Lethbridge, Alberta
        Works on Canvas, Longfish/O'Neal, San Francisco Museum of Modern Art, California
        Contemporary Masks from Northern California, Palo Alto Cultural Center, California
        The Real People/El Autentico Pueblo, Galeria Latino-American, Cuba
1979-80 *Contemporary North American Indian Painting*, travelling exhibition in South America
1980   *Contemporary Iroquois Artists*, American Indian Community House Gallery, New York
        Spirit of the Earth, Buscaglia-Castellani Art Gallery, Niagara University, Niagara Falls, New York
        Respect for Traditions, Robert Else Gallery, California State University, Sacramento
1981   *Confluences of Tradition and Change*, Richard Nelson Gallery and C.N. Gorman Museum, University of California, Davis (traveled to Midland, Texas and New York)
        Return to the Central Fire, Oswego Art Center Gallery, New York
        American Indian Art in the 1980s, Native American Center for the Living Arts, Niagara Falls, New York
        Changing Myths, the Evolution of Tradition, Sacred Circle Gallery, Seattle

Native American Arts 81, Philbrook Art Center, Tulsa, Oklahoma

1982 *Institute of American Indian Art Museum 20th Anniversary*, Institute of American Indian Art, Santa Fe, New Mexico

American Indians Today, Works Gallery, San Jose, California

New Work by a New Generation, Mackenzie Art Gallery, University of Regina, Saskatchewan

Art of the Contemporary Iroquois People, The Gallery of the American Indian Community House, New York

1983 *Contemporary Native American Art*, Gardiner Art Gallery, Oklahoma State University, Stillwater

1984 *Six Native American Artists*, Jerome Evans Gallery, Sacramento, California

Emerging Voices I—Six Nations Artist, Fondo del Sol Visual Art and Media Center, Washington, D.C.

The New Native American Aesthetic, Marilyn Butler Fine Art Gallery, Santa Fe, New Mexico

The New West, John Edwards Hughes Gallery, Dallas, Texas

America 1984, Smith Anderson Gallery, Palo Alto, California

Signs and Messengers of the Earth, University Union Exhibit Lounge, California State University, Sacramento

1984-86 *Signale Indianisher Kunstler*, Akmak, Berlin (travelled through Germany, Austria, and Switzerland)

1985 *Cowboys and Indians: Common Ground*, Lock Haven Art Center, Orlando, Florida

Four Native American Painters, The College of Wooster Art Museum, Ohio

Post-1984 Show, Davis Art Center, California

1985-86 *Second Biennial Native American Fine Arts Invitational*, Heard Museum, Phoenix, Arizona

1986 *George Longfish/Jaune Quick-to-see Smith*, University of Northern Iowa, Cedar Falls

1986-87 *Other Gods: Containers of Belief*, Everson Museum of Art, Syracuse, New York (travelled to Washington, D.C., New Orleans, and Los Angeles)

1987 *Contemporary Visions: Fifteen Native American Artists*, Read Stremmel Gallery, San Antonio, Texas

The Soaring Spirit: Contemporary Native American Arts, Morris Museum, Morristown, New Jersey

1988 *Eight Native American Artists*, Fort Wayne Museum of Art, Indiana

Cultural Diversity: Seven Americans, University Art Gallery, California State University, Stanislaus

1989 *Continuity and Change: Trends in Contemporary Native American Art*, Ohio Historical Society, Columbus

1990 *The Power of Process*, American Indian Contemporary Arts, San Francisco, California

The Decade Show, New Museum of Contemporary Art, New York

New Art of the West, Eiteljory Museum of American Indian and Western Art, Indianapolis, Indiana

Artifacts for Seventh Generation, American Indian Contemporary Art Gallery, San Francisco, California

Endangered: Visual Art by Men of Color, Intermeda Art Gallery, Minneapolis, Minnesota

1991 *Submuloc*, Evergreen Galleries, Evergreen State College, Washington

Our Land/Ourselves, University Art Gallery, State University of New York, Albany (traveled to Burlington, Vermont; Stony Brook, New Paltz, and Syracuse, New York)

Shared Visions: Native American Painters and Sculptors in the Twentieth Century, Heard Museum, Phoenix, Arizona

America, Center for Contemporary Art, Sacramento, California

1992 *Acknowledging Our Host, Communal Sources*, Richmond Art Center, Richmond, California

500 Years Since Columbus, Triton Museum of Art, Santa Clara, California

Haudenosaunee Artist: A Common Heritage, Tower Fine Art Gallery, SUNY College, Brockport

Indigena: Perspectives of Indigenous Peoples on Five Hundred Years, Canadian Museum of Civilization, Hull, Quebec (travelled to Winnipeg, Manitoba; Halifax, Nova Scotia; Windsor, Ontario; Phoenix, Arizona; Calgary, Alberta; and Norman, Oklahoma)

Six Directions, Galerie Calumet, Heidelberg, Germany

We The Human Beings: 27 Contemporary Native American Artists, College of Wooster Art Museum, Ohio (travelling exhibit)

Decolonizing the Mind: End of 500 Year Era, Center of Contemporary Art, Seattle, Washington

Ancestral Memories: A Tribute to Native Survival, Falkirk Cultural Center, San Rafael, California

1993 *A Kindred Spirit: Contemporary Painting, Prints and Sculpture by Eight Native American Artists*, Bedford Gallery/Regional Center for the Arts, Walnut Creek, California

Publications

By LONGFISH: Books—"Artist's statement," Jamake Highwater, *The Sweetgrass Lives On: Fifty Contemporary American Indian Artists*, New York 1980; "New Ways of Old Visions: The Evolution of Contemporary Native American Art," with Joan Randall, *Artspace* no. 6, Summer 1982; "Contradictions in Indian Territory," with Joan Randall, *Contemporary Native American Art* catalog, Stillwater 1983; "Made by Choice," with Joan Randall, *The Extension of Tradition: Contemporary Northern California Native American Art in Cultural Perspective*, catalog edited by Frank LaPena and Janice Driesback, Sacramento 1985; "Runners Between the Tribes," with Joan Randall, *New Directions Northwest: Contemporary Native American Art* catalog, Portland, Oregon and Olympia, Washington 1987; artist's statement, *Indigena: Contemporary Native Perspectives*, catalog edited by Gerald McMaster and Lee-Ann Martin, Hull, Quebec 1992; artist's statement in *The Sublumoc Show/Columbus Wohs* catalog, Phoenix 1992; "George Longfish" interview in *I Stand in the Center of the Good*, edited by Lawrence Abbott, Lincoln, Nebraska 1994; *Native American Art*, with David W. Penney, Seattle, 1994.

On LONGFISH: Books—*Magic Images: Contemporary Native American Art*, Edwin Wade and Rennard Strickland, Norman, Oklahoma 1981; *The Arts of the North American Indian: Native Traditions in Evolution*, by Edwin Wade, New York 1986; *Mixed Blessings: New Art in a Multicultural America*, by Lucy Lippard, New York 1990. **Articles**—"Stating a Cross-cultural Identity: George

George Longfish: *The End of Innocence* triptych, 1991-92. Collection of the Museum of Man, Ottawa, Ontario; courtesy of the artist.

Longfish," by C. French, *Artweek*, no. 15, 14 July 1984; "The Second Biennial Native American Fine Arts Invitational," by Erin Younger and Robert Breunig, *American Indian Art Magazine*, no. 11, Spring 1986; "George C. Longfish at American Indian Contemporary Arts," by Jerome Tarshis, *Art in America*, no. 76, October 1988; "Like a Longfish out of Water," by Kay WalkingStick, *Northeast Indian Quarterly*, no. 7, Fall 1989; "George Longfish," by Jimmie Durham, *Kunstforum international*, May-June 1991; "Native American Art: Pride and Prejudice," by Robin Cembalest, *Art News*, no. 91, February 1992; "Indigena: Perspectives of Indigenous Peoples on Five Hundred Years" in *American Indian Art Magazine*, no. 17, Autumn 1992; "No Easy Solutions" by R. Davis in *Artweek*, no. 24, January 1993.

*

George Longfish comments (1992):

The more we are able to own our religious, spiritual, and survival information, and even language, the less we can be controlled... The greatest lesson we can learn is that we can bring our spirituality and warrior information from the past and use it in the present and see that *it still works*. (From *Indigena*, catalog)

*   *   *

Over the past three decades, George Longfish has emerged as a leading figure in contemporary North American Native art. As well as participating in close to 200 solo and group exhibitions in the United States, Canada, and Europe, he also has played an influential role as an educator, curator, and writer. As a professor of Native studies at the University of California, Davis, since 1973, and as director, from 1974 to 1996, of the C.N. Gorman Museum a gallery (associated with the Native studies program), Longfish has worked to further knowledge of traditional Native arts as a vital legacy and to promote recognition of contemporary Native arts as the independent and vigorous expression of an ongoing, transforming culture. In public lectures and published essays he has argued against narrow definitions of Native art, claiming all of contemporary life as the Native artist's wide-open turf. And in his own works, Longfish has staked the same claim.

As a student at the School of the Art Institute of Chicago in the 1960s and early 70s, Longfish was exposed to a barrage of compet-

ing art movements and styles—abstract expressionism, hard-edge, op art, pop art, minimalism, and realism. His early work was largely taken up with solving various "academic" problems posed by these influences. It was not until he moved to the University of Montana in 1972, to direct a program in American Indian arts, that he began to seek ways of incorporating in his work aspects of his Native heritage and his growing awareness of issues affecting Native people. Since then, although his range of styles and imagery has continued to evolve, his work has constantly centered on an exploration of the intersection of the personal and the cultural within the contradictions, dislocations, and open possibilities of life as a tribal person in the post-modern world. His vibrant, richly colorful paintings bring together elements of abstract painting styles, traditional symbols, historical references, pop culture fragments, and personal history to forge a language capable of expressing the complexity of his experience.

One of the central concerns in Longfish's art is the need for Native Americans to understand and gain control of what he refers to as their "cultural information"—the need to displace negative stereotypes and pop-culture cliches with knowledge and spiritual strength. In numerous paintings Longfish attempts to recover cultural information by looking back "to when art was called artifact," to find symbolic forms that he feels are "more honest to the feelings of the Indians who produced them" (Highwater, *The Sweetgrass Lives On*, 1977). In paintings such as *You Can't Roller-skate in a Buffalo Herd Even If You Have All the Medicine* (1979), *Spirit Guide/ Spirit Healer* (1983), and *Mother Earth Comes to the Rescue of the Two Brothers* (1983), for example, he uses expressionistic abstract shapes and animated brushwork and color relationships to create highly charged fields in which these symbolic forms are released to create new meaning. In *You Can't Roller-skate in a Buffalo Herd*, for example, the circle, groupings of sacred fours, zigzag mountain forms, and horse's hoofprints convey a sense of the need for spiritual growth in order to find one's way among large and contending forces.

In a series of paintings based on war shirts, Longfish again combines traditional elements with abstract expressionism, but on canvases in the shape of war-shirt silhouettes. These works again look to the cultural past, drawing it into the present in order to reflect on, among other things, the place of the warrior in contemporary life and the spiritual transformation and assumption of responsibility that accompanied the traditional warrior role.

Longfish takes up the theme of the warrior again, but in a humorous vein, in *Bless My Harley*, one of a number of assemblage masks he has created. This work brings into play multiple associations with the idea of the warrior in urban society and points at the dominant culture's ongoing fascination with those it designates as outsiders, whether biker gangs or Indians.

The need to regain control of the representation of Native subjectivity—to resist, in other words, the distorting power of the dominant culture's gaze—is also suggested in the 1989 painting *Goodbye Norma Jean, the Chief is Dead*, another work that examines stereotypes and mythmaking.

Many of Longfish's works explore such personal issues as relationships between men and women and his connection with his children; others deal with historical issues and more overtly political content. One example of this is *The End of Innocence* (1992), a large triptych that responds to the 1990 crisis at Oka, Quebec. The left and right panels of this complex work convey a sense of the economic and political forces against which Native people have had to fight in the past. And in the right panel, the Teenage Mutant Ninja Turtles, Michelangelo et al.—a tongue-in-cheek reference both to the Iroquois Turtle clan and to the leadership role that artists can play—take up fighting stances on a game board as the future threatens more of the same. In the central panel, the idea of the warrior is again invoked, this time by a leaping horse, based on Plains Indian horse dance sticks, surrounded by the words "spiritual," "warrior," and "information"—the keys, in Longfish's view, to cultural survival.

And in many ways, Longfish's work—as an artist, teacher, curator, and writer—can be understood as an ongoing effort to claim and communicate information, to show its continuing force in the contemporary world, and by so doing to resist all those who would impose limits on contemporary Native American art.

—Deborah Burrett

LONGMAN, Mary

Tribal affiliations: Saulteau
Mixed media artist

Born: Fort Qu'Appelle, Saskatchewan, 10 July 1964. **Education:** Emily Carr College of Art and Design, Vancouver, Fine Art Diploma, 1985-89; Concordia University, Montreal, Quebec, M.F.A. qualifying year, 1990-91; Nova Scotia College of Art and Design, M.F.A., 1991-93. **Career:** Archeologist, Museum Reserve, British Columbia, 1988; visual art and cultural enrichment instructor, Vancouver, 1988-90; artist and display technician, Vancouver Aquarium, 1989-1990; visual art instructor, Native Education Centre, Vancouver, 1989-90; illustrator, Alternatives to Racism, University of British Columbia, Vancouver, 1990; visual art and cultural enrichment instructor, Karionninoha School, Kanawake, Quebec, 1991; exhibitions technician, New Territories Exhibition, Montreal and Quebec City, Quebec, 1992; teaching assistant, Halifax, Nova Scotia, 1991-93; instructor in fine arts, Nicola Valley Institute of Technology, Merritt, British Columbia, 1993-96. **Awards:** Emily Carr College Award (First Citizens Fund), 1986; Mungo Martin Award (First Citizens Fund), 1988; Catholic Services Award, 1989; Canada Council, Canadian Native Arts Foundation (First Citizens Fund), 1992.

Individual Exhibitions

1988   *Wolves in Sheep's Clothing*, Emily Carr College of Art and Design, Vancouver, British Columbia
1993   *MFA Graduation Exhibition*, Anna Leonowens Gallery, Halifax, Nova Scotia
1995   *Coming Home*, Neutral Ground, Regina, Saskatchewan
1996   *Traces*, Kamloops Art Gallery, Kamloops, British Columbia

Selected Group Exhibitions

1990   *Four Days, Four New Directions*, 56 Gallery, Vancouver, British Columbia
        Artropolis, Co-operative Gallery, Vancouver, British Columbia
        Our Home and Native Land, Concordia University, Montreal, Quebec
        Depoteque, Co-operative Gallery, Montreal, Quebec
1991   *Strengthening the Spirit*, National Gallery of Canada, Ottawa, Ontario
1992-93 *Excursions*, Anna Leonowens Gallery, Halifax, Nova Scotia
        Contemporary Art in Nova Scotia, Art Gallery, Mount St. Vincent University, Halifax, Nova Scotia
        New Territories, Cultural Centres, Montreal, Quebec
        First Ladies, Pitt Gallery, Vancouver and A-Space, Toronto, Ontario
1993   *New Contemporaries*, London Regional Gallery, London, Ontario
        Contemporary Canadian Native Art, Kamloops Art Gallery, British Columbia
        Courants Rouges, La Gare Gallery, L'Annonciation, Quebec
        Canada's First Peoples, Founders Square, Halifax, Nova Scotia
1995   *Native Love*, Montreal and Manitoba
1996   *Topographies*, Vancouver Art Gallery, British Columbia

Collections

Indian Art Centre, Hull, Quebec; Kamloops Art Gallery, British Columbia; Native Law Society, Vancouver, British Columbia; United Native Nations, Vancouver.

Publications

By LONGMAN: Article—"First Ladies: Review," *Front*, November/December, 1992.

On LONGMAN: Book—*Mary Longman: Traces*, Kamloops Art Gallery (catalog), 1996. **Article**—"Old myths made new," *Vancouver Sun: Saturday Review*, 21 July 1990.

*

Mary Longman comments:

My work is mixed-media in either two or three dimensional form depending on the subject matter. Ultimately I try to achieve a poetic balance between aesthetics and content in order to arrive at a combination of subtle, enticing formal qualities with a strong, provocative message. The content of my work largely deals with First

Mary Longman in her studio with *Blue Thunderbird* (back, left) and *Co-Dependants* (right). Courtesy of Photography by Sharon.

Nations' current issues, concerns, struggles, and daily life within the dominant society. Topics that my work touches on may include Eurocentric systems and hierarchies, cultural dislocation and its ramifications, appropriation and stereotypes. In other cases I might focus on my daily life experiences, which always includes my cultural perspective and philosophy.

*   *   *

Longman is a passionate artist who tackles recurring themes—hope, loss, love and anger—and pushes them out into the world through blunt images and strong opinions. Yet, underneath these statements that demand the viewer's attention lie subtle textures of feeling. Longman's head-on approach pushes her to reach deep into her own personal life and experiences, into places where many people would give up and look away.

Longman chooses the subject matter for her pieces from volatile topics like the AIDS epidemic, suicide, adoption, land appropriation, and spiritual transformation. She uses traditional icons and

elements, mixing them with current issues facing herself and First Nations people. At times her images are shocking to viewers of any culture, yet each is absolutely appropriate.

For many of Longman's more abrasive pieces, such as the very personal *Goodbye to Romance*, she takes two or more strong images and places them in an unexpected situation together. In this case she presents a noose supporting the combination of an arrow piercing an anatomical heart, and places them in active relationship to each other. *Goodbye to Romance* is a tribute to a brother who committed suicide.

Longman's work often inspires and sustains a high level of energy that appears to cycle or pulsate, with no resolution in sight. Another recent larger-scale piece, *Co-dependants*, uses cottonwood and leather to create a vivid metaphor for human relationships, regardless of gender or type. Two large wishbones are arranged vertically in opposition, the first assuming a traditional wishbone position, representing love and hope, while the second is inverted and becomes a slingshot, a symbol for hate and anger. A strip of leather, which precariously holds together the images, forms a fine line between the two. The use of leather adds further symbolism since it is a manifestation of flesh—the human factor. As Longman indicates, most co-dependence stems from family dysfunctions and insecurity. Neither of these elements in the piece are secure in any manner without the other.

One reviewer referred to Mary Longman as an 'excellent propagandist,' which she clearly is. But rather than pushing a literal message on her audience, Longman chooses to display a metaphor for a captured moment in time, like looking in a window of someone's home, and viewers are left to decide for themselves exactly what is happening in the relationship and how they feel about it.

Much like *Co-dependants*, Longman's pieces metaphorically feature the many versions of relationships as they exist on macro and micro levels in all societies. In one stroke, she shows us all of the ways we as humans connect—within families, between cultures and communities, between similar and dissimilar people. She also manages to remind us that a person looking for their own spiritual truth is also in a private relationship.

—Vesta Giles

LOOKING ELK, Albert

Variant names: Albert Martínez
Tribal affiliations: Taos Pueblo
Painter

Born: Taos Pueblo, New Mexico, 1888. **Education:** Santa Fe Indian School; no formal art training. **Career:** Model and painter for Oscar E. Berninghaus, founding member of the Taos Society of Artists, c. 1900; exhibited regularly at the Santa Fe Indian Market and at Taos Pueblo. **Awards:** Southwestern American Indian Arts Indian Market, First Place, 1923; Governor of Taos Pueblo, 1938. **Died:** 30 November 1940.

Selected Group Exhibitions

ca 1928   School of American Research, Santa Fe, New Mexico

Collections

Museum of New Mexico, Santa Fe; Museum of Northern Arizona, Flagstaff; National Museum of the American Indian, New York; Philbrook Museum of Art, Tulsa, Oklahoma; School of American Research, Santa Fe, New Mexico; Southwest Museum, Los Angeles, California.

Publications

On LOOKING ELK: Books—*The Arts of the North American Indian: Native Traditions in Evolution*, by Edwin L. Wade, Hudson Hills Press, New York, in association with Philbrook Art Center, Tulsa, Oklahoma, 1986. **Articles**—"A Survey of Current Pueblo Indian Painting," by Anne Forbes, *El Palacio*, vol. 57, no. 8, August 1950; "Stylistic Plurality in the Paintings of Albert Looking Elk: An Examination of Patronage," by Samuel E. Watson, III, *American Indian Art Magazine*, Winter 1994.

*   *   *

Albert Looking Elk was an active artist throughout the early years of the Southwest Painting Movement. Nonetheless, it is difficult to place him within the context of that movement. Unlike his Santa Fe contemporaries Fred Kabotie and Velino Herrera, Looking Elk did not depict traditional Indian subject matter, such as ceremonial dancers, genre scenes, or stylized animal compositions, nor did he use the same medium or aesthetics sensibility. Looking Elk's adoption and mastery of European-American art styles is exemplified in the numerous impressionistic landscape images made of his surroundings and home-pueblo. In his paintings Looking Elk demonstrates a proficiency and skilled handling of illusionistic details, especially shading, light, and color. Because of his deviation from conventional Southwest Indian painting standards, Looking Elk was excluded from most of the early twentieth century Pueblo Indian painting exhibitions and much of the criticism and history from that period as well.

Looking Elk began modeling for Oscar E. Berninghaus, founding member of the Taos Society of Artists, around 1900. Eventually he quit to become a painter himself. He worked primarily in oils, utilizing European-American painting techniques and manners, including 3-point perspective, spatial depth, shading and modeling, explicit environmental settings, and atmospheric use of light and color. Looking Elk's naturalistic landscapes presumably reflect the influence of his friend and employer, the German born Berninghaus. At the same time, his refusal to conform to a standard of Indian painting, even at the sacrifice of art patronage, suggest a level of artistic agency on the part of this Taos artist. He was, however, not entirely alone. There were a few other artists in Taos, notably Albert Lujan and John Concha, who also did not entirely embrace the Pueblo Indian style of painting.

Unlike the Santa Fe area Pueblo Indian watercolorists, whose paintings centered on the social and cultural life of their people, Looking Elk depicted Taos Pueblo, the place or space itself often times epitomized by the adobe architecture. He portrayed the mood of the surroundings reflected by the effects of light and color rendered during specific times of the day. His atmospheric landscapes stress the land, architecture, and environment over the inhabitants and their daily customs or ceremonial practices.

Stylistically, his paintings fit into the genre of European-American landscape painting. Despite his proficiency and mastery of western art conventions and manners of representation, such as perspective and chiaroscuro, he is not included in discussions of the European-American artist colony at Taos either. Looking Elk, as an important figure historically, is ironically an anomaly to both the Southwest Indian painting movements and the American artist colony at Taos.

Looking Elk is known to have painted in the manner of the Southwest painting style (i.e. paint applied in blocks of color, outlined forms, emphasis on clothing details, little modeling, and a lack of groundlines, backgrounds or developed perspective). In 1927 Mary Cabot Wheelwright commissioned Looking Elk to create a series of watercolor paintings depicting creation myths. The resulting 14 paintings, collectively entitled *The Story of the Indian Creation* (accompanied with Looking Elk's own written explanations on the back) are now in the collection of the School of American Research in Santa Fe.

Despite the increased recognition and promotion of American Indian easel painting by Anglo-American patrons and supporters during the 1920s and 30s, Looking Elk remained to a certain extent obscure and excluded from an already small art market. Certainly the early promoters of American Indian easel painting were not

Albert Looking Elk: *Burros at Taos Pueblo.* Collection of Philbrook Museum of Art.

ready to acknowledge a painter working in otherwise 'untraditional' modes of representation. Promoters like American artist John Sloan denounced paintings that showed signs of European art influences. Even today, little is know of Looking Elk's life and work. Nonetheless, Looking Elk continued to paint, selling his small oil paintings (many of which are less than 12 inches) to tourists visiting Taos.

—Lisa Roberts

LOVATO, C. F.

Tribal affiliations: Santo Domingo Pueblo
Painter, potter, and textile artist

Born: Charles Frederick Lovato, Santo Domingo Pueblo, New Mexico, 23 May 1937. **Education:** Santa Fe Indian School; studied with Jose Rey Toledo. **Military Service:** U.S. Navy. **Awards:** Many between 1967, when he focused on painting full-time, through the 1970s, including Heard Museum Guild Indian Fair and Market, Phoenix, Arizona, 1968, Bialac Purchase Award, 1969 and 1971,

Avery Award, 1977; Inter-Tribal Indian Ceremonial, 1969, Keney Award, 1971-72, Elkus Award; Philbrook Museum Annual, 1970-71 and 1979; Red Cloud Indian Art, Show, 1971; Scottsdale National Indian Art Exhibition, 1970. **Died:** 1987.

Selected Group Exhibitions

Exhibited regularly from late 1960s through early 1980s at art fairs and commercial galleries in the southwest.

1969	Heard Museum, Phoenix, Arizona
1971	Heard Museum, Phoenix, Arizona
1978	Hastings College Art Center, Hastings, Nebraska
	Center for Great Plains Studies, University of Nebraska, Lincoln
1991	Wheelwright Museum of the American Indian, Santa Fe, New Mexico

Collections

Center for Great Plains Studies, University of Nebraska, Lincoln; The Heritage Center, Inc., Collection, Pine Ridge, South Dakota;

Heard Museum, Phoenix, Arizona; Indian Pueblo Cultural Center, Albuquerque, New Mexico; National Museum of the American Indian, Washington, D.C.; Museum of Northern Arizona, Flagstaff; Philbrook Museum of Art, Tulsa, Oklahoma; Millicent Rogers Foundation Museum, Taos, New Mexico.

Publications

By LOVATO: Books—*Life Under the Sun,* Santa Fe, 1982.

On LOVATO: Books—*American Indian Painting of the Southwest and Plains Areas*, by Dorothy Dunn, Albuquerque, 1968; *Southwest Indian Painting: A Changing Art,* by Clara Lee Tanner, Tucson, 1973; *Art and American Individualists,* by Guy and Doris Monthan, Flagstaff, 1975; *American Indian Painting and Sculpture,* by Patricia J. Broder, New York, 1981.

*   *   *

C. F. Lovato was born and raised at Santa Domingo Pueblo in a community of Keres-speaking families who maintain their traditional ceremonial cycles. Two art forms predominate in the Pueblo,

pottery and jewelry. The Lovato family artisans are known mostly for their fine sand cast jewelry and heishi bead making; Lovato worked within these traditions and he expanded from there to become the pueblo's most celebrated painter.

Artists are everywhere in Santa Domingo, but the community was not part of the flowering of modern Pueblo watercolor painting that took shape during the first third of the twentieth century. The Pueblo is known for its pottery, featuring bold designs often accentuated on black-on-cream wares, with symbols commonly relating to clouds, flowers and vines. A textile weaving tradition continues with such distinguishing articles as wool belts in vertical tapestry weaves, as well as embroidered kilts, breech cloths and other articles of ceremonial clothing. Over a hundred dancers participate in feast days at the Pueblo, offering strong images of spirituality and cultural continuity. The pueblo is quite conservative and insular, but the public is welcome to about half a dozen ceremonies per year, and their arts and crafts festival after the Santa Fe Indian Market is one of the largest events in the Pueblo world.

In this environment Lovato displayed restless creativity, learning to make jewelry, pottery, and textiles. Since Santo Domingo, unlike most of the other Pueblos, had not developed a tradition of modern painting, it is likely that Lovato first became exposed to

C. F. Lovato: *Bird and Deer Tracks.* **Photograph by Seth Roffman; courtesy Dick Howard collection.**

painting during his teenage years at the Santa Fe Indian School. Among the teachers there was the famed Pueblo painter Jose Rey Toledo (Zia/Jemez), an accomplished artist who had been mentored by an earlier great Pueblo painter, Velino Shije Herrera.

Lovato began developing his talents as a painter, continued practicing jewelry and pottery making, was also one of the most gifted of the artisans creating the heishi necklaces for which Santo Domingo Pueblo is well known, and became interested in poetry. After a stint in the Navy he continued pursuing these sundry art forms until the mid-1960s, when he began to focus most intensely on painting and poetry, and ways for blending the two.

Lovato enjoyed a quick run of acclaim from the late 1960s through the 1970s on the art fair circuit in the southwest, winning numerous awards. His abstract paintings were unique; unlike most Pueblo painters, who simultaneously mastered a style and began to incorporate individual flourishes, Lovato's work did not evolve from a painting tradition. Lovato used primary colors, with blacks, whites, and earth reds predominating. The power of his works resides in contrasting hues and juxtapositions of color that contribute to abstract images. The abstractions were often clarified by poetic titles (*He Is Pouring Out Stars, Upon the Earth Another Night*) and by poems occasionally accompanying them, which were placed adjacent to the paintings.

Lovato's timing for abstraction and mixed media was fortuitous, for several Native American artists were experimenting with some success with abstract expressionism and pop art in the Santa Fe area, including Fritz Scholder, T. C. Cannon, and R. C. Gorman. Gorman encouraged Lovato to pursue the style and helped introduce him to the art fair circuit and the artistic community around Santa Fe. Though Lovato did not receive the attention of these other artists, his presence at art fairs was an important "grass roots" complement to the efforts of the more showcased artists to make inroads into galleries and museums, to address the issue of what it means to be an Indian artist, and to make statements about Native American concerns. Lovato's work was contemporary but subtly incorporated Pueblo motifs from throughout the history of pictography and pottery, and Lovato developed a symbolism related to the southwest that also took on personal references, which could often be discerned and interpreted with accompanying poems. His works display a balance between the conservatism of his Keres culture, particularly because they often reflected a personal and sometimes Christian symbolism, and the more fantastic elements of Tewa culture as it is maintained through ceremonies, and he translated to the canvas the abstractions of Santo Domingo potters. In addition, his painting addressed scientific and social concerns. This weighty menu rendered in abstract forms was a strength, giving his works rich depth at a time when new forms of expression were flourishing; he developed his own expression individually, and brought it most directly to the people.

Lovato's multiple talents are reflected as well as in his bead making; even as he became Santo Domingo's best known painter, he was innovative as a bead maker and was honored with a posthumous exhibit at the Wheelwright Museum of the American Indian in Santa Fe in 1991. Lovato's important contribution to beadmaking is his introduction of shading, using very subtle gradations in color to animate a play of sparkle and shade. By stringing together tiny beads that became elegantly thin strands, and mixing a rich variety of colors to create dynamic and balanced jewelry, Lovato created a uniquely beautiful innovation.

—Gregory Schaaf

LOWE, Truman
Variant names: Ho-Chunk
Tribal affiliations: Winnebago
Sculptor and mixed media artist

Born: Black River Falls, Wisconsin, 1944. **Education:** University of Wisconsin-LaCrosse, B.S., 1969, University of Wisconsin, Madison, M.F.A., 1973. **Career:** Visiting lecturer in Art, Emporia State University, Emporia, Kansas, 1973-74; assistant dean and coordinator of Multicultural Programs, University of Wisconsin, 1974-75; coordinator, Native American Studies Program, 1975-88, assistant professor, 1975-84, associate professor, 1984-89, professor, 1989—, and chairman, Department of Art, 1993-present, University of Wisconsin; numerous lectures and panels, served on arts juries, and has led and participated in many workshops; consultant for art programs at universities and for cities and states; wide variety of services for the University of Wisconsin. **Awards:** Numerous grants and fellowships; art work selected for cover, Wisconsin telephone directory, 1983; Governor's Heritage Award, State of Wisconsin, 1984; artist-in residence, Rhinelander School of the Arts, 1990; member, Madison Committee for the Arts, Festival of the Lakes, 1990.

Individual Exhibitions

1977	College of St. Scholastica, Duluth, Minnesota
	Mt. Scenario College, Ladysmith, Wisconsin
1979	Mt. Scenario College, Ladysmith, Wisconsin
1983	American Intercultural Center Gallery, University of Wisconsin, Green Bay
1984	Field Museum, Chicago, Illinois
	Embassy Exhibition, Yaounde, Cameroon
1985	Embassy Exhibition, Lotonou, Benin
	Embassy Exhibition, La Paz, Bolivia
1986	University of Wisconsin, Madison Hospital and Clinics
1987	American Indian Center, Minneapolis, Minnesota
1988	Signature Gallery, Stoughton, Wisconsin
	Emporia State University, Kansas
1989	American Indian Community House Gallery, New York
1990	School of the Art, Rhinelander, Wisconsin
1991	Kathryn Sermas Gallery, New York
	Tula Foundation Gallery, Atlanta, Georgia
1992	Hopkins Gallery, Ohio State University, Columbus
1993	Cardinal Stritch College, Milwaukee, Wisconsin
1994	*Haga,* Eiteljorg Museum of American Indian and Western Art, Indianapolis, Indiana
1995	Jan Cicero Gallery Exhibition, Chicago, Illinois
1996	Eagle Gallery, Price Doyle Fine Arts Center, Murray State University, Kentucky

Selected Group Exhibitions

1980	*Woodland Structures,* Main Gallery, Memorial Union, University of Wisconsin, Madison
1981	*Trail Marker,* Indian Center Museum, Wichita, Kansas
	Sacred Circle Gallery of American Indian Art, Seattle, Washington
1982	*Night of the First Americans,* John F. Kennedy Center for the Performing Arts, Washington, D.C.

1983   *Northern Exposure,* Memorial Union, University of Wis-
        consin, Madison
        Mother Earth/Father Sun, Appleton Gallery, Appleton,
        Wisconsin
1984   Palais de Nations, United Nations, Geneva, Switzerland
        American Indian Community House, New York
        University of Oklahoma, Stillwater (traveling)
        No Beads, No Trinkets, Seattle, Washington
1985   Milwaukee Art Museum, Wisconsin
1986   *Visage Transcended: Contemporary Native American
        Masks,* American Indian Contemporary Arts Gallery,
        San Francisco, California (traveling)
        What is Native American Art, Philbrook Museum of Art,
        Tulsa, Oklahoma
1986-87 *Other Gods: Containers of Belief,* traveling, New Or-
        leans, Louisiana, Washington, D.C., Syracuse, New
        York, Los Angeles, California
1987   *Contemporary Visions, Fifteen Native American Artists,*
        San Antonio, Texas
1987-88 *Native American Artists,* Fort Wayne Museum of Art,
        Indiana
1988   *Native American Art of the Woodlands,* Museum of Art,
        University of Michigan, Ann Arbor
        Gallery Ten, Rockford, Illinois
1989   Lewellen/Butler Gallery, Santa Fe, New Mexico
1990   Sermas Gallery, New York, New York
        American Indian Contemporary Arts, San Francisco,
        California
        Maryhill Museum of Art, Washington, D.C.
1991   Sacred Circle Gallery of American Indian Art, Seattle,
        Washington
        Heard Museum, Phoenix, Arizona
1992   *Land, Spirit, Power,* National Gallery of Art, Ottawa,
        Ontario
        We the People, Wooster College Art Museum, Ohio (trav-
        eling)
        Without Boundaries, Jan Cicero Gallery, Chicago, Illinois
1992-96 *Shared Visions: Twentieth Century Native American Art-
        ists and Sculptors,* Heard Museum, Phoenix, Arizona
        (traveling)
1993   *Sticks!,* Leigh Yawkey Woodson Art Museum, Wausau,
        Wisconsin (traveling)
        We the Human Beings, The Riffe Gallery, Columbus, Ohio
        A Kindred Spirit, Bedford Gallery, Walnut Creek, Cali-
        fornia
        Golden West Galleries, Telluride, Colorado
1994   *Indian Humor,* American Indian Contemporary Art, San
        Francisco, California
        Artists Who Are Indian, Denver Art Museum, Colorado
1995   Jan Cicero Gallery, Group Exhibition, Chicago, Illinois
1996   *Watershed,* Minneapolis Museum of Art, Minnesota
1996-97 *Native Streams: Contemporary Native American Art,* or-
        ganized by Jan Cicero Gallery, Chicago, Illinois, and
        Turman Art Gallery, Indiana State University, Terre
        Haute, Indiana

Collections

Denver Art Museum, Colorado; Eiteljorg Museum, Indianapolis, Indiana; Ohio Arts Council, Columbus; Tucson Museum of
Art, Arizona.

Publications

On LOWE: Books—*The Arts of the North American Indian: Na-
tive Traditions in Evolution,* edited by Edwin L. Wade, Hudson Hill
Press, New York, New York, 1986; *Shared Visions: Native Ameri-
can Painters and Sculptors in the Twentieth Century,* by Margaret
Archuleta and Rennard Strickland, Heard Museum, Phoenix, Ari-
zona, 1991; *We the Human Beings,* edited by Kathleen McManus
Zurko, College of Wooster Art Museum, Wooster, Ohio, 1992;
Native Streams: Contemporary Native American Art, Jan Cicero
Gallery/Turman Art Gallery, Indiana State University, Terre Haute,
Indiana, and Chicago, Illinois, 1996. **Articles**—"Truman Lowe:
The Red Ochre Series," *The Atlanta Journal,* Atlanta, Georgia, 14
June 1991; "Truman Lowe at the Tula Foundation," *Art In America,*
December 1991; "Critical Issues in Recent Native American Art,"
by W. Jackson Rushing, *Art Journal,* vol. 51, no. 3, Fall 1992;
"Indigena and Land, Spirit, Power," *C,* Winter, 1993; "Truman
Lowe, Emerging Sculptor," by Robertson and McDaniel, *Sculpture
Magazine,* September 1996. **Film:** *Gottschalt Site,* State Historical
Society, Madison, interview, 1996; *From the Shadows of the River,*
Kentucky Educational Television, interview, 1996.

*

Truman Lowe comments (1996):
    This is what I am trying to do.
    To capture that image
    formed from that obscure place
    where past, present, and future are one.
    To know the universe for a moment
    on paper; with pigment or with sawdust.
(From *Native Streams: Contemporary Native American Art*)

*   *   *

    Truman Lowe (Ho-Chunk) occupies an important place in the
world of Native American contemporary fine art. His status is
comparable to Alan Houser (Chiracahua Apache) and George
Morrison (Ojibway/Chippewa). Houser was one of the forerunners of the Native American fine arts movement, and Morrison was
the first Native American to make an impact on the New York art
community. Lowe, like Houser, has achieved wide respect for his
sculpture within the context of the contemporary Native American
fine arts movement, and he is one of the most widely exhibited
contemporary Native American fine artists working today. And
like Morrison, Lowe enjoys as much respect from mainstream venues as he does from venues that focus primarily on Native American historic and contemporary culture and art. Lowe, Houser and
Morrison have all made significant contributions to the arts through
their influence in institutions of higher learning. Houser through his
work at the Institute of American Indian Arts in Santa Fe, New
Mexico; Morrison as a Professor of Art and the first American
Indian on faculty at the Rhode Island School of Design; and Lowe has
served as the Chairman of the Department of Art, University of Wisconsin, Madison, for three years and has been a member of the faculty
for nearly twenty-five years. They are, and have been, mentors for
many emerging American Indian and non-native artists alike.
    Reflected in all of Lowe's work is his love of nature and the
elements. This love is in part a product of his childhood. Lowe grew
up in Black River Falls, Wisconsin, and envelopes into his work
stories and images he experienced in the Winnebago community.

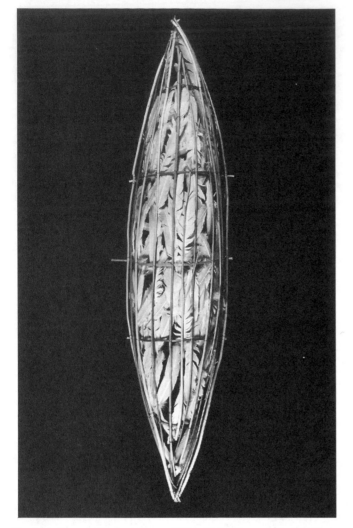

Truman Lowe: *Feather Canoe*, 1993. Collection of the Eiteljorg Musuem of American Indians and Western Art.

Lowe favors a minimalist approach that begs conceptual interpretation. His wood sculptures distill his subjects to the most elemental of forms. *Feather Canoe* is an excellent example of Lowe's facility with his materials and love of nature. In this work he has created a see-through wooden grid in the form of a canoe with a layer of feathers laid meticulously across the interior. This reference to air and water imbue the work with animated qualities despite the quiet and slow cadence of the piece. In Lowe's discussion of *Feather Canoe,* he describes the act of canoeing as "being on the earth while being suspended above it." This piece and description are classic examples of the poetic and metaphoric qualities of his sculpture.

Lowe's work from the 1990s is especially airy. At an exhibition at the Eagle Gallery, Murray State University, Kentucky, Lowe suspended Canoe forms from the ceiling and elevated wooden grids approximately 3 feet off the floor. These images that almost appear to levitate encourage the viewer to muse about the spiritual power of the work. Although this profoundly powerful vision appears in many aspects of Lowe's work, he never makes overt references to a works' particular power. His neglect to discuss this aspect of the work only adds to the mysterious qualities he has borrowed from

nature to create a serene and dignified presentation—a presentation that quite easily could be a metaphor for Lowe himself.

Another trademark of Lowe's work is his installation pieces. These works of art can be found in- and out-of-doors. They are responses to a particular geography or history of the landscape. Lowe's work in this context exemplifies his unique language. The installations appear to be a particular short-hand he uses for describing the historic and contemporary aspects of nature and its relationship to humankind.

Imbedded in Truman Lowe's work is the history of a people and the clarity of one person's vision. He knows two cultures, two ways of speaking, two ways of seeing, and is able to bring two universes together to give his viewer an object that can be interpreted on multiple levels.

—Jennifer Complo

LUNA, James

Tribal affiliations: Luiseño
Mixed media artist, performance artist, photographer, installation artist, and video artist

Born: Orange, California, 9 February 1950. **Education:** San Diego State University, M.S., 1983; University of California, Irvine, B.F.A., 1976. **Career:** Counselor, Extended Opportunities Programs and Services, and instructor in counseling and in American Indian studies courses, Palomar College, 1982—; instructor in studio arts, University of California, Irvine, 1992; board member, National Coalition for the Freedom of Expression (selected in 1993). **Awards:** Numerous grants and fellowships; several for distinguished faculty (resident and visting); and Bessie Creator Award (New York Dance Theatre Workshop), 1991.

Individual Exhibitions (including premier performances)

1981   Rolando Castilleon Gallery, San Francisco, California
1982   San Jose State University, San Jose, California
1989   *Two Worlds,* International Arts Relations Gallery, New York
1990   *Cultural Diversity in American Theatre,* University of California, San Diego, La Jolla
1992   *Indian Tails*, Center for Contemporary Arts, Santa Fe, New Mexico
        The Red Album, Randolph Street Gallery, Chicago, Illinois
        Sometimes It's Not So Beautiful to be Indian, Intermedia Art Minnesota and Two River Gallery, Minneapolis
        Multi-media Installations, The Center for Contemporary Arts, Sante Fe, New Mexico
        Action and Reactions: An Eleven Year Survey of Installation and Performance Work, 1981-1992, University of California, Santa Cruz
        Performances I've Been Thinking About, Portland Art Museum, Oregon
        The Sacred Colors, Galleria Posada, Sacramento, California
        ... Places for People to Meet, ART AWARENESS, Lexington, Kentucky

1993 *The Shameman Meets El Mexi-can't at the Smithsonian Hotel and Country Club*, Smithsonian Institution, Washington, D.C.

The Shameman, ART AWARENESS, Lexington, Kentucky

The History of the Luiseño People: La Jolla Reservation—Christmas 1990, Rochester Art Museum, Rochester, New York

New Basket Designs: No Direction Known, Randolph Street Gallery, Chicago, Illinois

Relocation Stories, Capp Street Project, San Francisco, California

1994 *The Shame Man Meets El Mexi-can't and the Cyber Vato in Chicago in Search of Their Lost Identities*, with Guillermo Gomez Pena, The Mexican Fine Arts Center Museum, Chicago, Illinois

Old Designs/New Messages, Montgomery Gallery, Pomona, California

James Luna: Works, Terrain Gallery, San Francisco, California

1996 *The Dream Hat Ritual*, Santa Monica Museum of Art, California

Tribal Identity, Scneider Art Museum, Ashland, Oregon

In My Dreams, Native Arts Network: 1996, University of Tulsa, Oklahoma

Selected Group Exhibitions

1975 Native American Art Exhibit for Governor Edmund G. Brown, Capitol Building, Sacramento, California

Native American Art, San Diego State University, California

1981 Carl Gorman Gallery, University of California, Davis

1986 *Made in Atzlan*, Centro Cultural de La Raza, San Diego, California

Hippodrone Gallery, Long Beach, California

1987 *Street Sets Show*, Sushi Gallery, San Diego, California

1988 *Mission Daze*, Installation Gallery, San Diego, California

Up Tiempo! Museo Del Barrio/Creative Tune, New York

1990 Washington Project for the Arts, Washington, D.C.

Disputed Identities, San Francisco Camerawork, California

Art History/AA Meeting, Atlanta College of Art, Georgia

Two Worlds, American Indian Community House Gallery, New York

1991 *Indigenous America: Honoring Our Heritage*, University of California, San Diego, La Jolla

Shared Vision, The Heard Museum, Phoenix, Arizona

SIT'Eseeing, Whitney Museum, New York

Facing the Finish, San Francisco Museum of Modern Art, California

1992 *Sites of Recollection*, Williams College Museum of Art, Williamstown, Massachusetts

Land, Spirit, Power, National Gallery of Canada, Ottawa

The People Themselves, Los Angeles Photography Center, California

1993 *Shared Experience/Personal Interpretations*, Sonoma State University, Rohnert Park, California

This is Not a Multicultural Show, St. Lawrence University, Canton, New York

1994 *Take a Picture with a Real Indian*, Creative Time, New York

1996 *Re: Public: Indian Having Coffee with Kerouac, Ginsberg and Hemingway*, Museum of Photographic Arts, San Diego, California

Collections

Denver Museum of Art, Colorado; Laguna Beach Museum of Art, California; New School of Social Research, New York, New York; San Diego Museum of Modern Art, La Jolla, California.

Publications

By LUNA: Articles—"Allow Me to Introduce Myself: The Performance Art of James Luna," *Canadian Theatre Review*, Fall 1991; "I've Always Wanted to Be an American Indian," *Art Journal* no. 51, Fall 1992.

On LUNA: Books—*James Luna: Two Worlds*, exhibition catalog by Judith McWillie, INTAR Latin American Gallery, New York, 1989; *The Decade Show: Frameworks of Identity in the 80s*, exhibition catalog by Museum of Contemporary Hispanic Art, The New Museum of Contemporary Art, The Studio Museum in Harlem, 1990; *Shared Visions: Native American Painters and Sculptors in the Twentieth Century*, by Margaret Archuleta and Dr. Rennard Strickland, The New Press, New York, 1991; *Land, Spirit, Power: First Nations at the National Gallery of Canada*, exhibition catalog by Charlotte Townsend-Gault, et al, National Gallery of Canada, Ottawa, 1992; *The Sacred Colors*, exhibition catalog by Rick Hill, LA RAZA/ Galeria Posada, Sacramento, California, 1992; *Sites of Recollection: Four Altars and a Rap Opera*, exhibition catalog by Julia Barnes Mandle, Deborah Menaker Rothschild, et al, Williams College Museum of Art, Williamstown, Massachusetts, 1992; *1993 Biennial Exhibition*, Whitney Museum of American Art, New York, in association with Harry Abrams, Inc., Publishers, 1993. **Articles**—"Call Me in '93: An Interview with James Luna," with Steve Durland, *High Performance*, no. 14, Winter 1991; "Multi-Site Exhibitions: Inside/Outside," by Calvin Reid, *Art in America*, no. 79, January 1991; "James Luna," by Jimmie Durham, *Kunstforum International*, no. 113, May/June 1991; "Art of the People," by Steve Chapman, et al, *Art Papers*, no. 12, November 1992; "Message Carriers: Native Photographic Messages," by Lisa G. Corrin, *Art Papers*, no. 18, July/August 1994; "Installing History," by Theresa Harlan, *Views*, no. 13-14, Winter 1993.

* * *

James Luna, counselor and artist, lives on the La Jolla Reservation, Valley Center, California, where he was born. Using his culture and experience as a base for his work, Luna's performance art, mixed-media installations, photography, and video works combine fiction with autobiography in an effort to express the narratives of his personal life and a collective existence of contemporary Native American people. His artwork is grounded by lived experiences and memories of life on the reservation.

Luna studied fine arts at the University of California at Irvine, graduating with a bachelors degree in 1976. He originally began as a painter but turned to the medium of performance because it did not have any real definitions or limiting boundaries. Luna found that he was able to vocalize and dramatize the concepts and ideas that otherwise could not be articulated in painting. Wanting something more tangible, more real than pictures and words, he began incorpo-

James Luna: *The Shameman* **performance piece. Photograph by Francisco Dominguez; courtesy of the artist.**

rating everyday objects from real life and transforming them into contextualized object-statements that educate, satirize, and highlight issues particular to the contemporary realities of American Indian identity.

Through his art Luna confronts serious yet sensitive issues like alcoholism and Indian stereotypes. Criticized at times for making fun or light of such serious matters, Luna insists that the only way to solve problems is by talking about them and includes his audience into each performance. Although he may push people at times to the point of anger, confusion, or make them uncomfortable, it is necessary to get people to think about things.

During the 1980s Luna did several mixed-media installations and photographic works that critiqued museum display techniques and modes of representation. *The Artifact Piece*, performed in 1987 and 1990, presented Luna lying in a museum display case full of sand and wearing a breechcloth. Surrounding labels identified the man in the case, even going so far as to document bodily scars. Additional display cases contained personal artifacts—his college diploma, divorce papers, clothing articles, family photographs, and samples from his music and literature collection, including a Sex Pistols album and a book by Allen Ginsberg. The presence of a real, or undead Indian displayed as artifact questioned the underlying premise of museums' authoritative role in defining perceptions of cultural authenticity and identity.

In Luna's thought-provoking performance *Shame-Man: My Way*, he confronted social attitudes, perceptions and behaviors towards Native American people in a parodic exercise of lifting the shame from non-Indians. Like other contemporary Native artists, one of Luna's strengths lies in his insightful ability to employ humor, irony, and parody as a tool to critique historically- and socially-rooted misconceptions about the realities of American Indian existence and identity.

Shame-Man: My Way opened with a barrage of photographs documenting the people of the La Jolla Reservation, historic photographs of the American Indian, landscapes of the interior and coastal land of southern California, and images of the cosmos set to background music of Frank Sinatra singing "My Way." The central personae, the Shame-man—part healer, preacher and satirical-judge—led the audience through a phantasmagoric ride, chastising mainstream cultures' treatment of marginalized peoples but also criticizing native people who have "sold out." Luna introduced modernized replicas of artifacts found in museums or marketed and sold by galleries: instead of the infamous dream catcher, Luna presented a new model, the wet-dream catcher. He challenged the romanticized, mythical perception of Native American identity as portrayed by such historically revered images as Farney's "End of the Trail" motif, a turn of the century image of an American Indian slumped over on a horse with his spear falling loosely to the ground. Luna contemporized the motif by replacing the horse with an old carpenters sawhorse and the spear with liquor bottle.

In a 1992 exposition and photo-montage, *I've Always Wanted To Be An American Indian*, Luna confronted similar stereotypes about Native American identity and endeavored to convey the reality of life on the La Jolla reservation with candor and explicitness. He combined photographs of children with images of dwellings and incorporated them with text that presented a barrage of statistics, including unemployment figures, education levels, and birth and death rates. The text concluded with the statement:

> There is much pain and happiness, there is success and there is failure, there is despair and there is hope for the future. Still I would live no place else because this is my home, this is where my people have come... [this] is the reality that we Indians live; this is it. This isn't the feathers, the beads of many colors, or the mystical spiritual glory that people who are culturally hungry want.Hey, do you still want to be an Indian?

Luna received a Masters in Counseling at the San Diego State University in 1983. He is active within his community and is a counselor at Palomar Community College. In recent years Luna has garnered a great deal of national recognition among the mainstream art market. He was included in the *1993 Whitney Biennial* and *The Decade Show: Frameworks of Identity in the 1980s*. He has performed throughout the United States at museums and galleries and received the New York Dance Theater Workshop's Bessie Award in 1991 for *The Artifact Piece* and *Take Your Picture with an Indian*.

—Lisa Roberts

MacDONALD, Mike

Tribal affiliations: Micmac; Beothuk
Video artist and photographer

Born: Sydney, Nova Scotia, 1941. **Career:** Taxicab driver, Toronto, 1970s; assistant to video producer and cameraman, Metromedia, British Columbia; independent photographer and filmmaker, working with travel councils, creating documentaries, and assisting in educational video conception and production; documented and gathered commission evidence for the Gitk'san Wet'suwet'en court case, 1980s. **Address:** c/o grunt gallery, 362 East 6th Ave., Vancouver, British Columbia, V5T 1K3.

Individual Exhibitions

1979   Cabana Room, Spadina Hotel, Toronto, Ontario
        Centre for Art Tapes, Halifax, Nova Scotia
        The New Era Social Club, Victoria, British Columbia
1980   *Punk, Rock, Culture, Revolution & Love*, Open Space, Victoria, British Columbia; Pumps, Vancouver, British Columbia
1981   *Amax and the Nishga*, Environment Conference, Ottawa
1982   Acid Rain Conference, Washington, D.C.
1983   *Walk For Peace: End the Arms Race*, Vancouver
1984   *Electronic Totem*, Newcomb Auditorium, Victoria, British Columbia; Video In, Vancouver, British Columbia
1987   *Electronic Totem*, Vancouver Art Gallery, British Columbia
1988   *Electronic Totem*, Ksan Exhibition Centre, Hazelton, British Columbia
1989   *Plants & Totems*, Terrace Art Gallery, Terrace, British Columbia
1990   *Photo Collages*, grunt gallery, Vancouver, British Columbia
1991   *Seven Sisters*, Mercer Union, Toronto, Ontario
1992   *Electronic Totem*, Art Gallery of Greater Victoria, British Columbia
        Recent Works, Video In, Vancouver, British Columbia
        Seeing Red, Seeing Green, Videographe, Montreal, Quebec; Pitt Gallery, Vancouver, British Columbia
1993   *Secret Flowers & Selected Works*, Confederation Art Gallery, Charlottetown, Prince Edward Island
        Secret Flowers, Presentation House, North Vancouver, British Columbia; Oboro Gallery, Montreal, Quebec
1994   *Secret Flowers & Seven Sisters*, Sacred Circle Gallery, Seattle, Washington
1996   *Seven Sisters*, Yukon Art Gallery, Whitehorse
        Touched By the Tears of a Butterfly, grunt gallery, Vancouver, British Columbia

Selected Group Exhibitions

1980   Nuclear Free Pacific Conference, Honolulu, Hawaii
1984   *Fish Story*, October Show, Vancouver, British Columbia
1987   *Photo Collages*, Kermodei Gallery, Hazelton, British Columbia
1988   *Revisions*, Walter J. Phillips Gallery, Banff, Alberta
1989   *Seven Sisters*, Grierson Festival, Toronto, Ontario
        Beyond History, Vancouver Art Gallery, British Columbia
1990   *A Training in the Arts*, Fine Art Gallery, University of British Columbia, Vancouver
1991   *Rat Art*, A.V.E. Festival, Arnheim, Netherlands (traveling)
        Okanata, A Space, Toronto, Ontario
        Visions of Power, Leo Kamen, Toronto, Ontario
        Spirit in the Land, Heritage Hall, Vancouver, British Columbia
1992   *Sacred ?*, Red Head, Toronto, Ontario
        New Territories, Montreal, Quebec
        Indigena, Canadian Museum of Civilization, Hull, Quebec
        Okanata, Woodlands Centre, Brantford, Ontario
1993   *Pe'l A'tukwey*, Art Gallery of Nova Scotia, Halifax, Nova Scotia
        Indigena, Dalhousie Art Gallery, Halifax, Nova Scotia; Winnipeg Art Gallery, Manitoba
        Community Hall, Walter Phillips Gallery, Banff, Alberta
        Contemporary Canadian Native Art, Kamloops Art Gallery, British Columbia
        Nomadis, Randolph St., Chicago, Illinois
        Contemporary Northwest Coast Art, Western Washington University Gallery, Bellingham
        Eh-toh simop, Muttart Gallery, Calgary, Alberta
1994   *These Are Your Instructions*, Mendel Art Gallery, Saskatoon, Saskatchewan
        Green the City, Halifax, Nova Scotia
        Pe'l A'tukwey, New Brunswick Museum, St. John, New Brunswick (traveling)
        Bath Fringe Festival, Bath, England
        Images Festival, Toronto, Ontario
        Indigena, Windsor Art Gallery, Ontario (traveling)
        Viva Awards Show, Charles Scott Gallery, Vancouver, British Columbia
1995   *Call of the Wild*, Walter J. Phillips Gallery, Banff, Alberta
        It's Time to Wear Our Blankets, Open Space, Victoria, British Columbia
        Annapolis Garden Project, Annapolis Art Gallery, Annapolis Royal, Nova Scotia
        Tea Party (Garden Project), Presentation House, North Vancouver, British Columbia
        Light Fantastic (Fringe Project), London

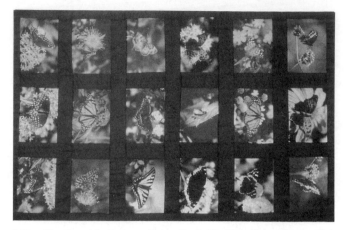

Mike MacDonald: *Eastern Butterfly Quilt.* Courtesy of the artist.

1996   *Romance of the Land*, Bellevue Art Museum, Seattle,
          Washington
        Metissages, Optica, Montreal, Quebec
        Beyond, A.K.A., Saskatoon, Saskatchewan
        All That Has Value Garden Project, Presentation House,
          North Vancouver, British Columbia

Collections

Kamloops Art Gallery, British Columbia; Vancouver Art Gallery,
British Columbia.

Publications

On MacDONALD: Books—*Indigena: Contemporary Native Per-spectives,* Douglas & McIntyre, Vancouver, 1992; *Indigena and Land, Spirit and Power* by Carol Podedworny, *C Magazine,* Winter, 1993. **Articles**—"In Absentia Video," by Karen Knights, *Video Guide,* August 1988; "'Beyond History' is powerful show by Indian artists," by Regina Hackett, *Seattle Post-Intelligencer,* 31 May 1989; "Indian Art bares both meanings of spirit world," by Elizabeth.Godley, *Vancouver Sun,* 7 June 1989; "Show of Native Art not Limited by Traditional Images," Laura Busheikin, *The Georgia Straight,* 16-23 June 1989; "Sniffy the Rat parody raises new thoughts about conceptual art," *Vancouver Sun,* 29 September 1990; "The Generic City and Its Dis-contents," by Scott Watson, *ART Magazine*, February 1991; "Inter-view," with Tom Sherman, *Mercer Union Interviews with Artists Se-ries*, March 1991; "Earth Spirit cultures celebrate similar visions," *Toronto Star,* 28 June 1991; "Electronic totem pole airs Gitksan cul-ture," by Adrian Chamberlain, *Times Colonist*, Victoria, British Colum-bia, 1 August 1992; "Aboriginal Artists open new territory," by Ann Duncan, *Montreal Gazette*, 8 August 1992; "Man of Flowers," by Donald Goodes, *hour,* 4-10 March 1993; "Whose Nation?," by Scott Watson, *Canadian Art*, Spring 1993; "Unendurable Boredom Not Part of This Video Show," by Robin Laurence, *Georgia Straight*, 14-21 May 1993; "Mike MacDonald: Secret Flowers," by Scott Watson, *Canadian Art,* Summer 1993; "VIVA award will help Mike MacDonald's video work bloom," by Peter Wilson, *The Vancouver Sun,* 27 May 1994; "Video Installations at Sacred Circle Gallery," Steve Garrow, *Reflex Magazine*, December 1994/January 1995.

*

Mike MacDonald comments:

One of the things I'm trying to do is to suggest that if we don't change our methods of resource extraction then the only place our grandchildren are going to see wildlife is stuffed in museums or on laserdiscs. The present resource extraction methods have got to change. We go into hemlock forests and clear cut them. The wood is not that great for building houses. It warps and twists and most of the hemlock in fact goes to pulp.

These forests take hundreds of years to grow. They provide an environment for hundreds of species of plants, many of which were exploited by the Native peoples for foods and medicines, many of which are still exploitable ... I'm suggesting that there's an incredible promise and potential in the area if we deal with it in the right way.

*   *   *

Since leaving Toronto for what began as a brief visit to the West Coast in 1977, Mike MacDonald has been a quiet and unassuming loaded gun in the slowly surging acceptability of video as an art form in Canada. Soon after arriving to the area, he began working on environmental and anti-nuclear videos that have acted as his version of a protester's sign at a rally—only his placard is the very screen many of us spend so many hours blankly staring at. His message is portrayed through images that are difficult to turn off.

More recently, this focus has expanded to First Nations people in Canada. He documents, through visual metaphor, their constant struggle to stop white society from needlessly destroying natural resources. In Northern British Columbia he documented the testi-mony of elders for Gitk'skan Wet'suwet'en Tribal Council's land claim process and, with his strong passion for ethnobotany, is creating a video on ethnobotany in the Maritimes and the tribal use of plants. Using technology as a tool for healing is one of MacDonald's prime intentions throughout his work. In this pro-cess, technology acts both as the medium for his message and as an integral component of the message itself.

It was in 1987 that MacDonald first became known in the con-temporary art world. His piece, *Electronic Totem,* features five vertically stacked monitors depicting contemporary images of the Gitk'skan Wet'suwet'en people, their environment and their active culture, totem images and the animals they represent, and elders singing the songs that make up the soundtrack of the piece. It was one of the first expressions of MacDonald's recurring theme, that dissecting the cadaver of an extinct race instead of preventing the extinction itself is not a viable option.

One of MacDonald's most acclaimed pieces, *Seven Sisters*, is named after a mountain range in Northern British Columbia and reflects his view that technology in the near future may contain the only remaining evidence of the natural environment we, as a soci-ety, claim to be so proud of.

As an example of the medium becoming part of MacDonald's message, the monitors, all of different sizes, are arranged not at eye level but on the floor, where they are dominated by the viewer. They are placed in relative position of the mountains to each other, each screen depicting, at one time, one of the mountains in the range. In this manner they appear vulnerable, almost cowering be-low us, as if they realize that our decisions determine their future. *Seven Sisters* carries a soundtrack of healing song cycles sung by Mary Johnson, a Kispiox Indian Chief and elder who was 82 when the pieces were recorded.

Another environmental piece, *Secret Flowers*, tells, in seven min-utes, a simple and sad story of blindly choosing one form of life at the expense of another. Recently purchased by the Vancouver Art Gallery, *Secret Flowers* features 16 video screens stacked four across by four high, that act as a canvas, with MacDonald's carefully placed images as a palette. Individually, each screen first features the flower of an endangered or rare plant from British Columbia. Combined, the colours of the single images are arranged in the tradition of a medicine wheel. As the images on each screen prepare to change every 30 seconds, there is a slight build up of activity and excitement—much like the anticipation of a stage of metamorphosis. Soon, the flowers attract bees and then butterflies, which increase the energy of the images even more. Suddenly, the simple and engaging colours of the flowers, bees and butterflies turns into the grey of the city skies as a plane flies overhead—a parallel to war with the Asian Gypsy Moth, as the plane drops a controversial insecticide over the City of Vancouver in the early 1990's. There is very little difference among these sixteen images. Next the screens feature scenes of stillness and death—a palette of butterflies pinned in boxes, neatly categorized, and most definitely dead. In this piece, Mike MacDonald uses the butterflies and endangered plants as a metaphor for the endangered cultural ways of indigenous peoples.

MacDonald has referred to himself as a First Nations artist of tradition using contemporary tools and media. His manner of using technology as part of the overall message is remarkable in itself and his own active participation in the process is also unusual. While creating *Seven Sisters*, MacDonald took a helicopter ride into the remote areas of northern British Columbia and walked his way out, shooting priceless footage all the way. As a result of this type of artistic field research, he has an intimate knowledge of his subject matter that goes beyond the collection and portrayal of pictures. As his knees prove less and less reliable, he is looking at further pursuing still photography, which boasts much lighter equipment than a camcorder, tripod, and camping gear.

MacDonald's technical style shuns current commercial video techniques and special effects in favour of straightforward images that tell their own story. He uses locked camera positions, precision framing, and allows the image to occur on it's own within the frame. The result is that the slightest movement within the frame completely captures the viewer's attention, proving that the subject itself is more than compelling enough. The outcome to the viewer is often a sense of dread mixed with longing, dread for what seems overwhelming and inevitable, and longing for ways that are rapidly disappearing—soon to be seen in static museum displays.

The video, television, and other tools of technology can be viewed as part of the problem itself. But, as becomes obvious with MacDonald's work, the tool is just a tool until we choose how to use it.

—Vesta Giles

MALOTTE, Jack

Tribal affiliations: Shoshone; Washoe
Painter, illustrator, and printmaker

Born: Jack Richard Malotte, Walker River Indian Reserve, Nevada, 5 December 1953. **Education:** California College of Arts and Crafts, 1971-74. **Career:** Firefighter and Wilderness Patrolman, United States Forest Service, Arizona and California, 1972-78; Paste-up and editorial artist, *Nevada State Journal*, 1979-80; Art Director, *Keepin' Track Magazine* and *Nevada State Journal*, 1980-81; self-employed graphic designer and illustrator since 1981. **Awards:** Intertribal Indian Ceremonial, Gallup, New Mexico, first place, 1976; Nevada State Council on the Arts Grant, 1982; Tanners All Indian Invitational Art Show, Scottsdale, Arizona, first place, 1982; Brandywine Fellowship, 1988.

Individual Exhibitions

1983   Charleston Heights Art Center, Las Vegas, Nevada
1985   Clark-Price Gallery, Incline Village, Nevada
1988   Sierra Nevada Museum of Art, Reno, Nevada

Selected Group Exhibitions

1982   *Night of the First Americans*, National Indian Art Show, Kennedy Centre, Washington, D.C.
1983   Staatliche Kunsthalle, Berlin, Germany
1984   Sierra Nevada Museum of Art, Reno, Nevada
        Charleston Heights Art Center, Las Vegas, Nevada
        Mission Cultural Center Gallery, San Francisco, California
1985   *Visage Transcended: Contemporary Native American Masks*, American Indian Contemporary Arts, San Francisco, California
1986   *Our Contemporary Visions*, Sierra Nevada Museum, Reno, Nevada
1987   *Traditions in a New Age*, Museum of the Rockies, Bozeman, Montana
        Third Biennial Invitational, The Heard Museum, Phoenix, Arizona
1989   *Native Proof: Contemporary American Indian Printmakers*, American Indian Contemporary Arts, San Francisco, California
1991   *Our Land / Ourselves*, State University of a New York, Albany, New York (traveling)
1993-94 Northeastern Nevada Museum, Elko
1994   *Indian Humor*, American Indian Contemporary Arts, San Francisco, California
1995   *Two Man Exhibition: Two Indian Guys at Cowboy Joe's*, Cowboy Joe's, Elko, Nevada

Collections

Heard Museum, Phoenix, Arizona; Sierra Art Museum, Reno, Nevada.

Publications

On MALOTTE: Books—*Portfolio: Eleven American Indian Artists*, by Kenneth Banks, San Francisco, American Indian Contemporary Arts, 1986; *Our Land/Ourselves*, American Indian Contemporary Artists, Albany, 1990. **Articles**—"Artist Profile: Jack Malotte," *Native Vision*, vol. 2, no. 3, May/June 1985; "Malotte Exhibit: Earthy but Electric," *Mountain Express*, 25 March 1982.

*   *   *

The paintings and drawings of Jack Malotte carry strong evidence of his extensive background in graphic design and illustration.

Jack Malotte. Photograph by Ruth Mills.

His style is a direct reflection of his continuing work in art direction for magazines and other publications, poster illustrations, and newspaper graphics. Using a clear cut style and vibrant, bold colors, Malotte successfully manages to create visually alluring pieces that draw the viewer into pleasing designs. Once captivated, Malotte's deep sense of irony and even anger at issues affecting Native Americans politically, environmentally and spiritually take over. He entices people to take a closer look at pretty colors while presenting an image of an atomic bomb or a representation of the militarization of Nevada.

Malotte wants his drawings and paintings to wake people up to see what's going on around them. He believes that society has been lulled into pacifism and away from activism by modern media. Often, particularly in his pieces that present a more political sentiment, Malotte's cunning sense of irony and humor is the thread that connects seemingly unrelated visual elements within his paintings. One particularly angry piece uses this irony in a manner that is both uncomfortable and compelling to witness. The painting displays a car accident scene where one native man is lying dead on a highway in the desert and two more are pinned in a wrecked car. A six pack of beer is spread around the scene and a billboard featuring the slogan "Pow Wow Beer" glares in triumph from above.

In each of his pieces, Malotte makes the communication of the idea the most important part of the structure and design. The state-ments are made even more powerful because he seldom presents his subjects in reaction to what is happening, allowing the viewers to react on their own, unable to defer pain or anger to a character on a canvas.

While one part of Malotte's repertoire is based on activism and strong political statements, another part, his work in landscapes, is peaceful and inspiring. Perhaps as a result of years of working deep in the woods as both a firefighter and a wilderness patrolman for the U.S. Forest Reserve, has instilled in Malotte forces of nature that drive many of the images in his work. Malotte's drawings and paintings reflect his deep personal feelings about native people and their spiritual and physical connection with the earth and sky. While presenting his images in a manner that fuses deep ancestral respect and reverence for the Earth and all of nature, his style is, however, undeniably modern.

In these pieces, Malotte seems particularly attracted to the manner in which elements in nature, such as the trees, or the mountains or sky, are connected. There is seldom a clear line of separation between them, rather, they blend and merge from one to the next. Likewise, in his paintings, Malotte strives to express that sense of connection between the images within his pieces. There may be the face of a woman in the clouds, or an old man blended into the branches of an ancient tree, connecting the human element to the tree or sky in a gentle yet pervasive way. Often, there is a lone native man standing off to the side, watching, perhaps a stand-in for the painter.

Featuring details of landscapes and Indian figures, Malotte portrays modern natives with modern dilemmas and concerns. In *It Is Hard to be Traditional When You Are Plugged In,* we see a very cool modern native man standing in the middle of his high tech living room. In one corner we see the technological clutter of the twentieth century in a TV, tuner, receiver, tape deck and VCR. On the other side traditional symbols of a more spiritual life float gently above the floor—a native person in a sweat lodge, a sacred fire, an eagle, and a moon, another example of juxtaposition that makes Malotte's work compelling. Malotte cites the neon and bright lights of Reno as a great influence on his early works, producing what he calls the 'electric Indian' effect, his trademark use of bright contrasted colors, clean lines and sharp images. He says his early art books were album covers, which he would buy for the cover and often not even listen to the music.

The exploding flashes of color in Malotte's pieces are accomplished in a variety of mediums which he moves between regularly to avoid getting bored with one set of tools. His work can be found in acrylics, pen and ink, watercolors, chalk, pastels, washes, and even colored pencils—the classic tools of the working graphic designer. Malotte's pieces convey a strong sense of meaning and symbolism and he prefers to let them speak for themselves. He likes his viewers to have the right to interpret his pieces on their own and, to that effect, often leaves his pieces untitled. He just presents what he sees in his mind, and tries to make his drawings "glow without electricity."

—Vesta Giles

MAMNGUKSUALUK, Victoria

Tribal affiliations: Inuit
Printmaker, sculptor, and weaver

Born: Near Garry Lake and Black River Area, Northwest Territories, 1930; daughter of famed artist Jesse Oonark; surname also tansliterated as Mamnguqsualuq, Mamnaguqsualuk. **Career:** Migratory existence until early 1963, when family settled at Baker Lake; drawer and printmaker at the Sanavik Co-operative, Baker Lake.

Individual Exhibitions

1983   *The Long Night: Mamnguqsualuq of Baker Lake,* The Innuit Gallery of Eskimo Art, Toronto
1984   *Victoria Mamnaguqsualuk Baker Lake Artist,* Northern Images, Whitehorse, Yukon
1986   *Keeveeok Awake! Mamnguqsualuk and the Rebirth of Legend at Baker Lake,* Ring House Gallery, University of Alberta, Edmonton

Selected Group Exhibitions

1970   Baker Lake Print Collection, annual collection
1971-73 *Sculpture/Inuit: Masterworks of the Canadian Arctic,* Canadian Eskimo Arts Council, Ottawa (traveling)

1972   Baker Lake Drawings, Winnipeg Art Gallery, Manitoba
        Eskimo Fantastic Art, Gallery 111, School of Art, University of Manitoba, Winnipeg (traveling)
1974   *Crafts from Arctic Canada/Artisanat de l'arctique canadien,* Canadian Eskimo Arts Council, Ottawa (traveling)
1976-82 *Shamans and Spirits: Myths and Medical Symbolism in Eskimo Art,* Canadian Arctic Producers and the National Museum of man, Ottawa (traveling)
1977   *The Inuit Print,* National Museum of Man, Ottawa
1978   *Polar Vision. Canadian Eskimo Graphics,* Jerusalem Artists' House Museum, Israel
1979   *Spirits and Dreams: Arts of the Inuit of Baker Lake,* Department of Indian Affairs and Northern Development, Ottawa (traveling)
        Baker Lake Wallhangings, Vancouver Art Gallery, British Columbia
1979-84 *Shamans and Spirits: Myths and Medical Symbolism in Eskimo Art,* Arts and learning Services Foundation, Minneapolis (traveling)
1980   *The Inuit Amautik: I Like My Hood To Be Full,* Winnipeg Art Gallery, Manibota
1981   *The Inuit Sea Goddess,* Surrey Art Gallery, organized to complement the Musee des beaux-arts de Montreal exhibit, Vancouver
1982   *Inuit Myths, Legends, and Songs,* Winnipeg Art Gallery, Manitoba
1983   *Mamnguqsualuk and Tookome of Baker Lake: Drawings on Black Paper,* The Upstairs Gallery, Winnipeg
1984-86 *Arctic Vision: Art of the Canadian Inuit,* Department of Indian Affairs and Northern Development and Canadian Arctic Producers, Ottawa (traveling)
1985-86 *Die Kunst aus der Arktis,* Department of Indian and Northern Affairs Canada, Ottawa, presented by Commerzbank, Frankfurt, Germany (traveling)
1991   *Qamanittuaq: The Art of Baker Lake,* National Gallery of Canada, Ottawa
1993   *Northern Lights: Inuit Textile Art from the Canadian Arctic,* Baltimore Museum of Art, Maryland (traveling)
1995   *Immaginario Inuit, Arte e cultura degli esquimesi canadesi,* Galleria d'Arte Moderna e Contemporanea, Verona, Italy
        Keeping Our Stories Alive: An Exhibition of the Art and Crafts from Dene and Inuit of Canada, Institute of American Indian Arts Museum, Santa Fe
1996   *Daughters of Oonark: Kigusiuq and Mamnguqsualuk,* Albers Gallery, San Francisco

Collections

Amway Environmental Foundation Collection, Ada, Michigan; Anchorage Museum of History and Art, Alaska; Art Gallery of Windsor, Ontario; British Columbia Ferries Corporation, Vancouver; Canada Council Art Bank, Ottawa; Canadian Guild of Crafts Quebec, Montreal; Canadian Museum of Civilization, Hull, Quebec; Dennos Museum Center, Northwestern Michigan College, Traverse City; Edmonton Art Gallery, Alberta; Glenbow Museum, Calgary, Alberta; Inuit Cultural Institute, Rankin Inlet, Northwest Territories; Kitchener-Waterloo Art Gallery, Kitchener, Ontario; Macdonald Stewart Art Centre, Guelph, Ontario; McMaster University Art Gallery, Hamilton, Ontario; McMichael Canadian Art Collection,

Kleinburg, Ontario; Mendel Art Gallery, Saskatoon, Saskatchewan; Musee des beaux-arts de Montreal, Quebec; Museum of Anthropology, University of British Columbia, Vancouver; National Gallery of Canada, Ottawa; Prince of Wales Northern Heritage Centre, Yellowknife, Northwest Territories; University of Alberta, Edmonton; University of Lethbridge Art Gallery, Lethbridge, Alberta; Winnipeg Art Gallery, Winnipeg, Manitoba.

Publications

On MAMNGUKSUALUK: Books—*Eskimo Narrative* by Jean Blodgett, Winnipeg Art Gallery, 1979; *Inuit Myths, Legends, and Songs* by Bernadette Driscoll, Winnipeg Art Gallery, 1982; *Keeveeok, Awake! Mamnguksualuk and the Rebirth of Legend at Baker Lake*, edited by Charles Moore, Boreal Institute of Northern Studies, University of Alberta, Edmonton, 1986. **Articles**—"Observations on Baker Lake Graphic Art and Artists," by Joanne Elizabeth Bryers, *Arts & Culture of the North,* vol. 3, no. 2, February, 1979; "Keeveeok, Awake!: Mamnguqsualuk and the Rebirth of Legend at Baker Lake," by Bente Roed Cochran, *Inuit Art Quarterly,* vol. 2, no. 2, Spring 1987; "Revealing the Truth of the Artist's Hand: Contemporary Inuit Drawings," by Judith Nasby, *Inuit Art Quarterly,* vol. 9, no. 3, Fall 1994.

* * *

Born near Garry Lake, in Canada's Northwest Territories, Mamnguksualuk lived a migratory existence on the land until she was in her early thirties. Because of the wide-spread disease and famine in the hunting camps of the Barren Lands region, many Inuit moved to the village of Baker Lake in the 1950s and 1960s. Mamnguksualuk's family settled there in 1963. The artist's mother was Jessie Oonark, one of the best-known of all Canadian Inuit artists. Mother and daughter both became active in the drawing and print-making program at the Sanavik Co-operative at Baker Lake, as have several Oonark's children, including Janet Kigusiuq.

While Mamnguksualuk is best known for her silk-screen and stencil prints, she has also done many drawings (upon which the prints are based), as well as sculpture and cloth wall-hangings. Eight Mamnguksualuk prints were part of the first edition of prints issued at Baker Lake in 1970; since then her work has been included in print editions almost every year that such editions have been issued. As a second generation Inuit artist to live in the settlements, Mamnguksualuk has been influenced by her exposure to pictorial images from the outside world. More than the artists of the previous generation, such as her mother, Mark Emerak, or Helen Kalvak, she employs the conventions of European art in her depictions of three-dimensional space and sequential action. Mamnguksualuk often draws violent, confrontive scenes of people, spirits, and animals in which multiple events and numerous protagonists fill the paper. Particularly interested in the visual depictions of Inuit myth, Mamnguksualuk credits her grandmother for telling her as a child many stories that enliven her drawings and prints. She also recalls that in the old days the elders cautioned children not to make sketches on the wall or ice windows of the igloo, because such images could come to life. In her many prints and drawings, Mamnguksualuk has brought to life a vivid picture of a traditional northern mode of existence and a shamanic way of thinking about the spiritual bonds between humans, animals and spirits. She is known for her illustrations of episodes in the myth of Keeveeok, an adventurer who has many escapades involving animals and the spirit world.

Her work has appeared in numerous group shows of Inuit art including *Sculpture/Inuit: Masterworks of the Canadian Arctic* (Canadian Eskimo Arts Council, Ottawa, 1971-73), *Baker Lake Drawings* (Winnipeg Art Gallery, 1972), *The Inuit Print* (National Museum of Man, Ottawa, 1977), and *Baker Lake Wallhangings* (Vancouver Art Gallery, 1979). Mamnguksualuk is represented in numerous museum collections including the Winnipeg Art Gallery, the Canadian Museum of Civilization, the Macdonald Stewart Art Center in Guelph, Ontario, the Prince of Wales Heritage Center in Yellowknife, the McMichael Canadian Collection in Kleinburg, Ontario, and the Glenbow Museum in Calgary.

—Janet Catherine Berlo

MARSHALL, Teresa

Tribal affiliations: Micmac
Installation artist and mixed media artist

Born: Truro, Nova Scotia, 1962; grew up on the Millbrook reserve near Truro and numerous Canadian Army Bases. **Education:** Nova Scotia College of Art and Design in Halifax, Nova Scotia, BFA in Art Education, in 1990, and studies with John Greer; administrative and curatorial internships; twice served as an artist-in-residence (Est Nord Est, Centre de Sculpture, Saint-Jean-Port-Joli, Quebec, and The Banff Centre for the Arts, Banff, Alberta); Dalhousie University, Theatre Studies, Halifax, Nova Scotia, 1996. **Career:** Active as a visting artist, guest speaker, panelist, instructor, and juror in the greater Canadian arts community since the early 1990s; participates in a wide range of art-related activites that focus on issues faced by Native peoples, with a specific concern for the cultural well-being of the Mi'kmaq; vocalist and poet. **Awards:** Peace Hill Trust; Nova Scotia Tourism and Culture Exhibition Grant; Confederacy of Mainland Micmacs Exhibition Grant; Micmac Association of Cultural Studies Exhibit Grant; Nova Scotia College of Art and Design Endowment Scholarship; Confederacy of Mainland Micmacs, Outstanding Scholastic Achievement Award; Assembly of First Nations, Outstanding Scholastic Achievement Award; Royal Trust Scholarship Competition Award; Canadian Native Arts Foundation Award; Native Arts Foundation Exhibition Grant; Canada Council Travel Award; Canada Council Project Grant; George Watchorn Memorial Scholarship, Banff Center; Theatre Center Research and Development Award; Canada Council B Grant; British Columbia Cultural Alliance Grant; City of Vancouver Cultural Sector, Residency Award of Artistic Excellence. **Address:** The Marshall Art Studio, 272 E. 4th Avenue, Vancouver, British Columbia, Canada V5T 1G5.

Individual Exhibitions

1990   *How the West Was Won*, Other Art Gallery, Halifax, Nova Scotia
1991   *Mother May I*, Art Gallery Mount Saint Vincent, Halifax, Nova Scotia
        Elitekey, Anna Leonowens Gallery, Halifax, Nova Scotia
1992   *Monopoly*, Gallery 101, Ottawa, Ontario
1994   *Re Search*, Connection Gallery, Fredericton, New Brunswick

Teresa Marshall: *Reservation*, 1993. Courtesy of the artist.

1994-95   *The Deportment Of Indian Affairs*, (traveling): Eye Level
          Gallery, Halifax, Nova Scotia; A Space Gallery, Toronto;
          Woodland Centre, Brantford, Ontario; Confederation
          Centre Art Gallery and Museum, Charlottetown, Prince
          Edward Island; Pitt Gallery, Vancouver; Latitude 53
          Gallery, Edmonton, Alberta; Galerie San Noms,
          Moncton, New Brunswick; Neutral Ground Gallery,
          Regina, Saskatchewan
1997   *Bandstands*, Thunder Bay Art Gallery, Thunder Bay,
          Ontario (traveling)

Selected Group Exhibitions

1990   *Four Days Four New Directions*, Pitt International Gal-
          lery, Vancouver, British Columbia
          STREETSMart, Gottingen Street Location, Halifax, Nova
          Scotia
          International Women's Day, Other Art Gallery, Halifax,
          Nova Scotia
1991   *Neo-Nativists*, Pitt International Gallery, Vancouver, Brit-
          ish Columbia
          First Nations 1991, Woodland Cultural Center, Brantford,
          Ontario
          Art Against Violence Against Women, Eye Level Gallery,
          Halifax, Nova Scotia
1992   *Land, Spirit, Power*, National Gallery of Canada, Ottawa
          (traveling)
          New Territories, Vision Planetaire, Montreal, Quebec
          First Ladies, Pitt International Gallery, Vancouver, (trav-
          eled to A Space Gallery, Toronto)
          Life in the Maritimes, Eye Level Gallery, Halifax, Nova Scotia
          Canada's First People, (traveling) Japan and Canada
          First Nations 1992, Woodland Cultural Center, Brantford,
          Ontario
          Subject/Matter, Art Gallery of Nova Scotia, Halifax, Nova
          Scotia
1993   *London Life Young Contemporaries*, London Art Gal-
          lery, Ontario (traveling)
          Pe'La'Tukwey, Art Gallery of Nova Scotia, Halifax, Nova
          Scotia
          Drawing the Future Close, Workscene Gallery, Toronto
1994   *I Put a Spell on You*, McGill Club, Toronto, Ontario
          Skijin Ao Waja: Indian Time, Brandts Klaederfabrik,
          Odense, Denmark (traveled to Roeniemi Art Museum,
          Roeniemi, Finland)
          First Nations Art 1994, Woodland Cultural Center,
          Brantford, Ontario
          Survivals, The New Gallery, Calgary, Alberta
          Internal Recall, Brock University Gallery, St. Catherines,
          Ontario, Woodland Cultural Center, Brantford, Ontario
          Naked State, The Power Plant, Toronto
1995   *Ceremonial Landscape*, Gallery 101, Ottawa
          Half Bred, The Grunt Gallery, Vancouver
          Painted Visions, Front Gallery, Edmonton, Alberta
          The Women's Monument Project, Vancouver Art Gallery,
          Vancouver (traveling)
          Invincible Spirit, Open Space Gallery, Victoria, British
          Columbia
1996   *Gifts of the Spirits: Masterworks by 19th and Contempo-
          rary Native American Artists*, Peabody Essex Museum,
          Salem, Massachusetts (traveling)

          First Nations Art 1996, Woodland Cultural Center,
          Brantford, Ontario
          Metissage, Optical Gallery, Montreal
          Topographies: Aspects of British Columbia Art, Vancouver
          Art Gallery
1997   *External Recall*, The Burnaby Art Gallery, Burnaby, Brit-
          ish Columbia

Collections

The Canadian Native Arts Foundation, Ottawa; The Confederacy
of Mainland Micmacs, Nova Scotia; Eskasoni Band Council, Nova
Scotia; Native Council of Nova Scotia; The Nova Scotia Museum
of Fine Arts and Artifacts, Halifax; The Royal Ontario Museum,
Toronto; The Vancouver Art Gallery, Vancouver, British Columbia;
Woodland Cultural Centre, Brantford, Ontario.

Publications

By MARSHALL: Books (poetry anthologies)—*Gatherings:
The En'Owkin Journal of First North American Peoples, Volume
IV*, Theytus Books, Penticton, British Columbia, 1993;
Kelusultiek: Original Women's Voices of Atlantic Canada, Insti-
tute for the Study of Women, Mount St. Vincent University
Press, Halifax, Nova Scotia, 1994; *Steal My Rage: New Native
Voices*, Douglas and McIntyre Vancouver, British Columbia,
1995; *Native Women in the Arts, In a Vast Dreaming*, Native
Women in the Arts, Toronto, Ontario, 1995. **Poetry in jour-
nals**—*Fireweed Feminist Quarterly*, no. 48, Toronto, Ontario,
Summer 1995; "SISTAHSPEAK," in *Absinthe Literary Journal:
Writings by Women of Color and Aboriginal Women*, vol. 8, no.
1, Calgary, Alberta, 1995.

On MARSHALL: Books—*Mother May I*, Mt. St. Vincent Univer-
sity, 1991; *Canada's First Peoples: A Celebration of Contemporary
Native Visual Arts*, Syncrude Canada, Fort McMurray, Alberta,
1992; *Subject Matter: Contemporary Paintings and Sculpture in
Nova Scotia*, Art Gallery of Nova Scotia, 1992; *LAND SPIRIT
POWER: First Nations At the National Gallery of Canada*, National
Gallery of Canada, 1992; *New Territories, 350/500 Years After: An
Exhibition of Contemporary Aboriginal Art of Canada 1992*, Ate-
liers Vision Planetaire, 1992; *London Life Young Contemporaries*,
London Regional Art and Historical Museums, 1993;
*Pe'La'Tukwey: Let Me ... Tell a Story. Recent Work by Mi'Kmaq
and Maliseet Artists*, Art Gallery of Nova Scotia, 1993; *Naked
State*, Power Plant Contemporary Art Gallery at Harbour Front
Centre, 1994; *The Deportment of Indian Affairs*, Eye Level Gallery/
A Space and Confederation Centre Art Gallery, 1995; *Internal Re-
call*, Woodland Cultural Center, 1995; *Skijin Ao Waja: Indian Time,
Contemporary Indian Art*, Kunsthallen Brandts Klaedefabrik, 1995;
Metissages, Le Centre de sculpture Est Nord Est, 1996. **Articles**—
"'Mother May I,'" review by Denis Gill, *Arts Atlantic Magazine*,
1991; "Concrete Statements," by Lee Parpart, *Artscraft Magazine*,
Winter 1991; *Matriart: Canadian Feminist Art Journal*, vol. 3, no.
2, 1992; "Teresa Marshall," by E. Paul, *Healthsharing, Canadian
Women's Health Quarterly*, Fall/Winter, 1992; "Land Spirit Power,"
review by Anne Whitelaw, *Parachute Magazine*, no. 70, 1992; "Subject Matter, Contemporary Sculpture and Painting in Nova Scotia,"
by J. Murchie, *Arts Atlantic Magazine*, no. 44, Fall 1992; "Land,
Spirit, Power," review by Mary Ann Barkhouse, *Matriart Magazine*, vol. 3, no. 2, 1992; "Y a t'il Encore Un Art Autochtone?," by

Teresa Marshall: Detail of *Reservation*, 1993. Courtesy of the artist.

John K. Grande, *Vie Des Arts,* no. 150, 1992; "Indigena and Land Spirit Power," by Carol Podedworney, *C Magazine,* Winter 1993; "Canada's 'Indigena' and 'Land, Spirit, Power': Contingent Histories, Aesthetic Politics," by W. Jackson Rushing, *The New Art Examiner,* March 1993; "Whose Nation," by Scott Watson, *Canadian Art Magazine,* vol. 1, no. 10, Spring 1993; "Spirit Landing," by Joseph Christianson, *Border Crossings Magazine,* December 1993; "It's a Cultural Thing," by Cheryl L'Hirondelle, *Parallelogramme Magazine of Contemporary Art,* vol. 19, no. 3, 1993-94; "Mora's Armour," by Lance Belanger, *Parrallelogramme Magazine of Contemporary Art,* vol. 19, no. 4, 1994; "'Re Search,'" by Brigid Toole Grant, *ArtsAtlantic Magazine,* no. 50, Fall 1994; *Matriart. Canadian Feminist Art Journal,* vol. 4, no. 4, 1994; "Fast Forward," by Oliver Girling, *Canadian Art Magazine,* Fall 1994; "'The Deportment of Indian Affairs,'" by R. Rosenfield, *ArtsAtlantic Magazine* no. 51, Winter 1995; "MONOPOLY Artist Project," *Fuse Magazine,* vol. 18, no. 4, Summer 1995; "Indian Acts," by Micheal Huppe, *Aboriginal Voices Magazine,* vol. 2, no. 2, July 1995; "Land Spirit Power: First Nations Cultural Production and Canadian Nationhood," by Anne Whitelaw, *Aboriginal Peoples and Canada. International Journal of Canadian Studies,* no. 12 Fall 1995; "Undressing Victim Art" by Jane Ash Poitras and Clint Beuhler, *Mix Magazine,* Fall 1995; "Confrontation and Redemption," by Debbie O'Rourke, *Espace Magazine,* Fall 1995.

*   *   *

Teresa Marshall defines herself as a "Mi'Kmaq artist living within the boundaries of occupied Canada." For those who have accepted the sanitized version of native/white relations in Canada (long propounded in academia and popular culture) Marshall's strident proclamation of identity is suggestive of a radical, if not slightly deluded, political stance. Yet by challenging conventional knowledge and uncovering the lesser known histories of genocide and treachery, Marshall's art pinpoints where the delusions really exist.

While Marshall's artistic aims are political, the means by which she presents her thoughts and findings are conceptual. Like other idea-based artists, Marshall utilizes a wide range of media, including the exhibition space itself, to explore issues of representation and to question the notion of *art as object.* Yet Marshall consistently expands on this mode of aesthetic inquiry; her installation, *Deportment of Indian Affairs* (1994), identifies the objectification and commodification of native peoples as a physically, sexually, and visually consumptive act.

Highly confrontational art is potentially self-defeating, for it can easily retrench old biases and provoke anger rather than critical thought or dialogue. Aware of this caveat, Marshall's sardonic sense of humor is key because it provides the initial allure that becomes the basis for more thoughtful reflections. For example, in a poem, "Shamon," that is included in *Deportment,* Marshall cleverly subverts and distorts the English language in fragmented and terse commentary:

. . .
Shamon you, at a table for two
feeding on the exotic,
something rare, under glass
with a vintage reserve; a Beothuk
a Natchez, a Mohican, a Yamasee,
or tobacco perhaps.
Shamon. You, with the silver spoon
stained with greed
lifting centuries of denial into your belly,
spitting out the indigestible morsels of reality
banging on the table for your just desserts.
We have some reservations.
Bone appetite.

While her cadence is quick and her analogies shrewd (Shamon being a word play with Shaman), Marshall ultimately seeks to elicit the nervous chuckle that accompanies more profound realizations.

Analogous to her verbal strategies is Marshall's frequent manipulation of scale. The physical counterpart to "Shamon" is *Reservation*, which consists of an anthropomorphic wire table surrounded by four matching chairs. Both the seats of the chairs and the tabletop contain naked, dark-skinned dolls pressed under glass. This display mocks both the containment of and voyeuristic fascination with Native Canadians, who are symbolically shrunk down to a palatable size to fit with the decor of a domestic dining space. The human body being a primary site of reception wherein meaning is both negotiated and internalized, the dolls also serve to transform Marshall's viewers into gigantic Epicureans partaking in this cannibalistic feast.

The spatial relationship between art and audience is inverted in *Monopoly* (1992). The main element in this installation is an oversized (12 by 12 feet) monopoly game board that is adapted to address the ongoing violence of colonization: instead of imaginary properties, the text consists of real events, including the confrontation at Wounded Knee, that are priced in temporal terms. The colossal scale of the board miniaturizes the audience, who are physically cast as pawns and lead to contemplate their own complicity within this grand game of "real-estate."

In addition to addressing historical and present-day injustices, Marshall recognizes the necessity of exposing her audience to the rich cultural legacy of First Nations art. Having researched the history of the Beothuk (an extinct neighbor of the Mi'Kmaq) and their last known survivor, Mary March, Marshall created *Receptionists* (1993). This piece consists of five oversized concrete reproductions of bone pendants associated with Beothuk adornment; they encircle a smaller grouping of the same reproductions strewn on the ground. Again, spatial exaggeration is key, for the size of the pendants physically defy the process of academic fetishization by which small-scale objects are collected, identified according to ambiguous categories such as "material culture" or "artifact," and indefinitely shelved for future study. Moreover, far from corroborating the nostaliga and romanticism surrounding the demise of the Beothuk, Marshall accepts the more difficult task of studying and adapting indigenous artistic traditions to function within a broader and more timely social context.

While Marshall speaks of the *Receptionists* as being "mediators between historical fiction, contemporary fact, and physical reality," she too can be considered in such terms. As a cultural researcher, Marshall is commited to uncovering "historical fictions." As an artist concerned with past and present day injustices, Marshall

acts with a sense of both urgency and commitment. While some of her more political works reflect an us *vs.* them mentality that is overly reductive (particularly for an artist who is part Scottish), Marshall's ambivalent spatial and linguistic puns and wide ranging (anti-)aesthetic sustain an ongoing art in which the confrontational and contemplative are poignantly integrated.

—Kristin Potter

MARTIN, Bobby C.
Tribal affiliations: Creek
Painter and printmaker

Born: Tahlequah, Oklahoma, 10 May 1957. **Education:** Northeast State University, Tahlequah, Oklahoma, B.A., 1989-92; University of Arkansas, Fayetteville, M.F.A., 1992-95. **Awards:** American Indian Graduate Center Fellowship, Albuquerque, New Mexico; College Art Association Professional Development Fellowship, New York City.

Individual Exhibitions

1994   *Drawing Closer, Looking Back: Recent Graphic Works of Bobby C. Martin*, Southern Plains Indian Museum, Anadarko, Oklahoma
1995   *Dwight I.T.S.: The Pursuit of Civilization*, Master of Fine Arts Thesis Exhibition, Fine Arts Center Gallery, University of Arkansas, Fayetteville

Selected Group Exhibitions

1992-95 *Five Civilized Tribes Annual Competitive Art Show*, The Five Civilized Tribes Museum, Muskogee, Oklahoma
1993   *Oklahoma Indian Artists: A Continuing Tradition*, Ziegler's Indian Art Gallery, Tulsa, Oklahoma
        Counterpoint: Drawing, Photography and Printmaking Exhibition, Hill Country Arts Foundation, Ingram, Texas
        Oklahoma Art Workshops Annual National Juried Competition, Tulsa, Oklahoma
        Trail of Tears Art Show, Cherokee Heritage Center, Tahlequah, Oklahoma
1994   *Dispelling the Myths: Controlling the Image*, American Indian Community House Gallery/Museum, New York
        CAJE '94: America's Cultural Diversity, The Center of Contemporary Arts, St. Louis, Missouri
        Continuity and Change: The Effects of Removal and Relocation on the Culture and Art of the Southeastern Tribes of Oklahoma, Philbrook Museum of Art, Tulsa, Oklahoma
        Lawrence Annual Indian Arts Show: A Juried Competition, University of Kansas Museum of Anthropology, Lawrence
1995   *Gilcrease Museum Native American Invitational & Masters Exhibition*, Gilcrease Museum, Tulsa, Oklahoma
        National Works on Paper Exhibition, University of Tennessee, Knoxville

Bobby C. Martin: *Dwight I.T.S. #8*, 1995. Photograph by Kevin W. Smith.

2nd Annual Student International Biennial, Skopje, Republic of Macedonia

Red Cloud Indian Art Show, Heritage Center, Pine Ridge, South Dakota

1996   *Oklahoma Indian Art Annual Competition*, sponsored by American Indian Heritage Center and Philbrook Museum of Art, Tulsa, Oklahoma, Philbrook Museum Native American Painting Gallery

Collections

Cherokee Nation of Oklahoma, Tahlequah; The Heritage Center Permanent Collection, Red Cloud Indian School, Pine Ridge, South Dakota; Philbrook Museum of Art, Tulsa, Oklahoma; Southern Plains Indian Museum, Anadarko, Oklahoma.

*   *   *

Bobby C. Martin's subject matter derives almost entirely from his beliefs regarding his family heritage and his role as an artist. Feeling affinity with neither the horse culture of the Plains Indians nor any other popular subjects of Native American art, Martin initially worked outside Native American art circles while earning both bachelor's and masters' degrees in painting and printmaking. He consciously resisted any pan-Indian themes in his work. Using his family as subject matter for class assignments led him to an alternative view of Native American heritage and art. Martin worked from the inside out, focusing first on an exploration his family history and second on expressing his discoveries through a personal artistic style. This process was more acceptable to him than imposing Native American art trends upon his own "Indianess." Martin's interest in his Muscogee (Creek) ancestry focused primarily on family history in the twentieth century. His research revealed a family history rooted in the Christian mission experience in Indian Territory. He poured over mission postcards, memorabilia, and family photos. Many of his works feature images from Dwight Mission in Indian Territory and, later, Indian Baptist campgrounds in Oklahoma.

Martin recreates life size images of figures from family photos and portraits using acrylic paint on unstretched canvas. This universal and nostalgic type of image, seen on a large scale, focuses the viewer's attention as if walking through an album of old photos. Martin also repeats these images in smaller lithographs, photo-transfers, paintings and etchings. His use of sepia color and hand-pulled printmaking produce photo realism without sacrificing the warmth or intimacy of portraiture in a familial context.

The content of the work centers on the forced assimilation of Native Americans into mainstream American society in the early twentieth century. Martin's characterization of that subject is one in which transition for Native American people was dramatic, troubled, and awkward. Martin expresses his characterization by depicting Native American people in non-Indian in settings rarely seen in Native American art and taken directly from the photo documentation mentioned above. There is poignancy in these paintings. This is visible, for instance, in the reworked images of fullbloods wearing tennis outfits. One painting features a snapshot image of Native Americans posing on the hood of a 1942 Plymouth. Like similar images of many American families of the period, this one seems to symbolize the anticipation of post-war prosperity. Yet the general public's unfamiliarity of this image of Native Americans reveals the history of social inequality that jeopardized equal prosperity for Native American families.

Paintings and prints often contain allusions to the historical events that were a part of the assimilation process. Blended in collage style with the photographic portrait images are fragments of the infamous Dawes commission lists and other government documents. The effect is like walking into a family photo album and experiencing a personal past haunted by fearful images of political ghosts. Cherished portraits of ancestors are juxtaposed against the threatening and impersonal instruments of assimilation. Within such imagery is an inquiry into the dynamics between personal experience and the impersonal political environment in which it exists. More specifically, it is an inquiry into both the fragility and the resiliency of Native American families during a specific time of acute social change and political stress. Martin's work is significant precisely because he successfully explores this vital part of Native American history overlooked by other artists.

—Kevin Smith

MARTIN, Mungo

Variant names: Nakapenkum
Tribal affiliations: Kwakiutl
Carver

Born: Fort Rupert, British Columbia, April, early 1880s (birth unrecorded, estimates range from 1879 to 1884); Nakapenkum means as "Ten Times a Chief"; also known as Hanagalesu ("invulnerable to ridicule"), Kasalas ("proficient on the shore"), Yayakalas ("always have a house full of wealth"), Gwoyimsi ("big whale"), Tlathbai ("leader of a school of whales"), Siekwalas ("proficient on the sea"), and Kisuyakulis ("great ceremony"). **Education:** Briefly attended Residential School in Alert Bay, British Columbia at the age of 10; apprenticed as carver with his stepfather, Charlie James. **Family:** Married Sarah Constance Abayah Hunt; children Tommy, Grace, and Agnes. **Career:** Commercial fisherman most of his adult life; restored several original Kwakwaka'wakw totem poles and houseposts, University of British Columbia's Museum of Anthropology, Vancouver, 1947-51; restored original totem poles, Provincial Museum of British Columbia, 1951; became Chief Carver of Totem Preservation Program, Provincial Museum, 1952-62; recorded, through the Provincial Museum, many of the 400 songs (Kwakwaka'wakw, Tsimshian and Navajo) that he knew, as well as his knowledge of customs, stories and traditions; served as mentor to many carvers, including David Martin, Henry Hunt and Tony Hunt. **Awards:** Canada Council Medal, posthumously, 1964. **Died:** Victoria, British Columbia, 16 August 1962.

Collections/Commissions

1902   *Raven-of-the-Sea* totem pole, University of British Columbia Museum of Anthropology, Vancouver
1952   *Wa'waditla* ("he orders them to come inside"; traditional big house built in Thunderbird Park; numerous poles, feast bowl, masks), Royal British Columbia Museum, Vancouver
1956   Kwakwaka'wakw totem pole, Beacon Hill Park, Victoria, British Columbia
1958   Royal Pole, copy, Vancouver, British Columbia
        Royal Pole, Windsor Great Park, London, England
1960   Memorial Pole, Courtenay, British Columbia

Publications

On MARTIN: Books—*Mungo Martin: Man of Two Cultures*, British Columbia Indian Arts Society, Vancouver, 1975.

*   *   *

Chief Mungo Martin is widely acknowledged for leading the resurgence of Northwest coast art and preserving the cultural traditions of the Kwakwaka'wakw nation in British Columbia in the twentieth century. From the time that Mungo Martin was a child, he was destined to become a great carver and artist. As a baby, his mother Nagayki, took him to a prominent Kwakwaka'wakw carver, Yakutglasomi, who performed a ritual in which he plucked four eyelashes from Mungo's eyelids and mixed them with porcupine bristles to make a paint brush. Yakutglasomi used the brush when painting so that Mungo Martin would become a great carver and artist. When his mother was widowed, she remarried a master carver, Charlie James, whom Mungo Martin apprenticed with as an artist.

Many traditional aboriginal ceremonies, including the potlatch, were banned by the Canadian Government between 1884 and 1951. It was unlawful for aboriginal people to create regalia and carve masks and poles that were associated with the dances, songs, gift giving and dedications associated with the potlatch ceremony. Although westcoast artists continued to carve and paint for the commercial market, the role of the master artist was reduced considerably in villages on the west coast. Many artists turned to fishing and logging to support their families. Mungo spent much of his adult life as a commercial fisherman.

In 1947, Mungo was visiting his niece, carver Ellen Neal, in Vancouver. The University of British Columbia Museum of Anthropology had invited her to repair some totem poles that had been purchased by Dr. Marius Barbeau at Fort Rupert and Alert Bay. Mungo discovered, among the poles, *Raven-of-the-sea*, which he had carved in 1902. Mungo took over the job of restoring the poles from Ellen.

In 1951, the Provincial Museum invited Mungo to Victoria and offered him studio space in Thunderbird Park, a small park adjacent to the museum (now called the Royal British Columbia Museum) where many original totem poles from various westcoast villages had been installed. Working in the open-sided carving shed, Mungo became a well-known and much-loved artist in Victoria, and he often carved with an audience of local residents and tourists. In 1952, Mungo was hired as the Chief Carver of the Totem Preservation Program in Thunderbird Park, with the task of replicating many of the original totem poles in the park that were becoming damaged through age and the elements. That year, he built a half scale replica in Thunderbird Park of the big house in which he was born in Fort Rupert. He named the house *Wa'waditla* ("he orders them to come inside"). In December 1953, to dedicate the house, Mungo held a three-day potlatch. It was the first time a potlatch was held in public since the ban had been lifted by the Canadian government in 1951.

In the final decade of his life, Mungo, who was in his 70s, worked tirelessly to capture many of the songs, stories and artistic traditions of his nation. He replicated as well as created new totem poles, feast dishes, masks, dance screens, and other ceremonial and utilitarian objects for the museum. He worked closely with anthropologists, primarily Wilson Duff, recording many of the 400 songs that he knew. His taped conversations with anthropologists reveal many of the oral histories and traditions of the Kwakwaka'wakw people.

Mungo Martin was fiercely determined to preserve the traditions of his people. He recognized that his knowledge was made more valuable and timeless if he passed it on to others. He served as a mentor to several artists who went on to become significant Canadian artists, including Henry Hunt and Tony Hunt. In turn, these artists became mentors to the next generation of prominent westcoast artists, including Richard Hunt, Tim Paul, Ron Hamilton and Art Thompson.

In 1956, the Victoria Times newspaper sponsored the carving of the "world's largest totem pole". Three thousand people attended the ceremony to dedicate the pole that Mungo had carved with a team of artists. The 127-foot, six-inch pole represented the crests and stories of his own family. Through a fundraising drive, 10,000 people had donated money to create the pole.

In 1958, Mungo was commissioned to create a totem pole commemorating the 100th Anniversary of the founding of the colony of British Columbia. The Royal Pole, which depicts crests of ten representative Kwakwaka'wakw clans, was presented to Her Majesty Queen Elizabeth II as a gift from the people of British Columbia. Mungo attended the dedication ceremony in England, at Windsor Great Park, at which the Queen Mother accepted the gift on behalf of her daughter (who was unable to attend the ceremony due to illness). A replica of the pole stands near the Maritime Museum in Vancouver, B.C.

In September 1959, Mungo's only son, David was lost at sea while out fishing. Two months later, at a ceremony in Wa'waditla, the grieving Mungo donated all of David's inheritance to the province, through the Ministry of Education. The collection included Mungo's own inherited masks, ceremonial items, and his Killer Whale Copper. In 1960, he carved a pole in memory of his son; it was erected in Centennial Park in Courtenay, British Columbia.

On August 16, 1962, Mungo Martin died at the height of his artistic career. He was 83 years old. An editorial by Brian Tobin in the Victoria Times on 17 August read, in part: "...In his hands the simple tools fashioned the inhabitants of the land and the ocean, the dreams of the young men and the memories of the old, the legends of his people and the story of man. Now the eyes are closed, the ears are deaf, the hands are stilled. But the genius of Mungo Martin lives on in the treasures he left us..."

Mungo's body laid in state in Wa'waditla, the house that he built. Hundreds of local residents, government officials, friends and family visited the house to pay their last respects. Following a private family ceremony, Mungo's casket was taken by the Royal Canadian Navy to the H.M.C.S. Ottawa, which was to carry him home to his village on northern Vancouver Island. The casket was placed reverently on the quarter-deck, where it was covered with flowers

and guarded by four sentries with fixed bayonets. A final memorial service was held in his village.

Mungo Martin's legacy continues to live on in the songs, stories and artistic traditions that he shared during his life as a result of his unrelenting passion and conviction that Kwakwaka'wakw heritage must be preserved for future generations.

—Barbara Hager

MARTÍNEZ, Crescencio

Variant names: Te E
Tribal affiliations: San Ildefonso Pueblo
Painter

Born: New Mexico, c. 1880; Te E means "Home of the Elk." **Family:** Married to Maximilliana Montoya, sister of potter Maria Martinez. **Career:** Maintenance, San Ildefonso Day School; Pajarito excavations, c. 1914-15; Rocky Mountain Camp Company, Santa Fe, tending horses; commissioned for paintings, Museum of New Mexico and School of American Research, Santa Fe, 1917-18. **Died:** 20 June 1918.

Selected Group Exhibitions

1917-19 Museum of New Mexico, Santa Fe
1918-19 Society of Independent Artists, New York
1920   American Museum of Natural History, New York
1927-36 CoronaMundi International Art Center, New York
1931-33 *Exposition of Indian Tribal Arts,* organized by the College Art Association (traveling)
1978   *100 Years of Native American Painting,* Oklahoma Museum of Art, Oklahoma City
1981   *Pueblo Dance: Perspectives from Paintings,* Millicent Rogers Foundation Museum, Taos, New Mexico (traveling)
1984-85 *Indianascher Kunstler* (traveling, Germany), organized by the Philbrook Museum, Tulsa, Oklahoma
1988   *When the Rainbow Touches Down,* Heard Museum, Phoenix, Arizona
1991-96 *Shared Visions: Native American Painters and Sculptors in the Twentieth Century,* The Heard Museum, Phoenix, Arizona (traveling)
1992   *A Bridge Across Cultures: Pueblo Painters in Santa Fe, 1910-1932,* Wheelwright Museum of the American Indian, Santa Fe, New Mexico

Collections

Thomas Gilcrease Institute of American History and Art, Tulsa, Oklahoma; Museum of New Mexico, Santa Fe; Millicent Rogers Foundation Museum, Taos, New Mexico; School of American Research, Santa Fe, New Mexico; Wheelwright Museum of the American Indian, Santa Fe, New Mexico.

Publications

On MARTÍNEZ: Books—*American Indian Painting of the Southwest and Plains Areas,* by Dorothy Dunn, University of New

Crescencio Martínez: *Four Figures of the Animal Dancers*, c. 1915. Courtesy Museum of Indian Arts and Culture, Santa Fe.

Mexico, Albuquerque, 1968; *Indian Painters and White Patrons,* by J.J. Brody, University of New Mexico Press, Albuquerque, 1971; *Song from the Earth: American Indian Painting,* by Jamake Highwater, Boston, 1976; *Great North American Indians: Profiles in Life and Leadership,* New York, 1977; *100 Years of Native American Painting,* exhibition catalog by Arthur Silberman, Oklahoma Museum of Art, Oklahoma City, 1978; *Indianascher Kunstler,* by Gerhard Hoffman, Munich, 1984; *The Arts of the North American Indian: Native Traditions in Evolution,* edited by Edwin L. Wade, Hudson Hills Press, New York, in association with Philbrook Art Center, Tulsa, Oklahoma, 1986; *When the Rainbow Touches Down,* exhibition catalog by Tryntje Van Ness Seymour, Heard Museum, University of Washington Press, 1988; *Shared Visions: Native American Painters and Sculptors in the Twentieth Century,* by Margaret Archuleta and Dr. Rennard Strickland, New Press, New York, 1991; *Exploring Human Worlds: A History of the School of American Research,* by Melinda Elliott, Santa Fe, 1991. **Articles**—"Crescencio Martínez—Artist," by Edgar L. Hewett, *El Palacio,* August 1918.

* * *

Martínez was one of a group of three extraordinary men from the Pueblo of San Ildefonso who began the modern American Indian watercolor painting movement and forever transformed a small, poor village to one of internationally artistic renown. He was probably born in about 1880 and died in Santa Fe on 20 June 1918 of influenza. The first Director of the Museum of New Mexico, Dr. Edgar Lee Hewett, wrote at his friend's death:

Crescencio Martínez was no ordinary man. He was one of a group whose names awake a deep sense of gratitude—the men on whom I have depended in my excavations in the Pajarito-Jemez region for the past twenty years.... During the year 1917 he turned his attention seriously to painting the figures of the performers in the two great cycles of Pueblo ceremonies (summer and winter) and found appreciation and sale for his work. In January 1918.... I commissioned him to paint a complete series of his designs [dancers]. The first twelve he finished and delivered late in the winter. These he signed. The last ten were finished in the spring. He lacked only one (the second eagle), of finishing the commission. He completed the first eagle just a few days before his death. It was his last work.

Crescencio first worked for Hewett during the summer of 1909 during archaeological investigations on the Pajarito Plateau (now Bandelier National Monument), ancestral homeland to San Ildefonso people. Also working on the excavations were Julian Martínez and Alfredo Montoya. All three men painted on paper to sell to a commercial market as a result of their association with Hewett. Alfredo Montoya, who died in 1913 at age twenty, seems to have been the first modern adult San Ildefonso painter. In 1909, he sold paintings from the Pajarito Plateau field camp that are now in the collections of the Museum of New Mexico.

It is reported that Crescencio Martínez, as early as 1910, was known to be painting single dance figures on the ends of cardboard boxes. Martínez had been a pottery decorator for several years prior to his association with Hewett and friends. He was married to Maximilliana Montoya, sister to the potter Maria Martínez, and served as pottery decorator for Maximilliana, Maria Martínez, and his sister Tonita.

It is probable that Crescencio Martínez started painting sometime between 1910-14, more than likely after he moved to Santa Fe in 1914, given that no extant documented work has yet been found which pre-dates that year. He and his wife groomed and fed horses at a Santa Fe hotel, and it was during this period that he found time to paint.

As a result of his working with the Museum of New Mexico, Crescencio associated with Santa Fe's artist community. His painting style was apparently uninfluenced by these other artists, although he learned early to consistently sign his works. Generally, Crescencio used no background, no foreground, no ground line; a dance figure or group of figures appears on a perfectly blank sheet of paper, which served as the ceremonial plaza of the village. Very often his figures are depicted at side view, moving across the page. In addition, the paintings gain vitality through his depiction of the minutest detail of dance costuming, his loose drawing, and his extraordinary use of subdued color.

Martínez was the first Pueblo artist to paint extensively; because of this and his contact with some the next generation of artists (Tonita Peña and Alfonso Roybal) he became influential. His name was also among the first to be known outside of Santa Fe, being included in a New York show in 1920. Although he was influenced by Alfredo Montoya to begin making watercolor paintings, Crescencio carried Pueblo painting many strides ahead and because of the greater influence and extent of his art, he has been considered the "father" of modern traditional Pueblo Indian painting.

—Bruce Bernstein

MARTÍNEZ, Julian and Maria

Variant names: Pocano (Julian); Poveka (Maria)
Tribal affiliations: San Ildefonso Pueblo
Painter (Julian) and potters

JULIAN. Born: 1897, San Ildefonso Pueblo; native name means "Coming of the Spirits." **Family:** Married Maria Montoya, 1904; four sons. **Career:** Assisted Museum of New Mexico Director Edgar Hewett's archaeological excavations on the Pajarito Plateau (now Bandelier National Monument); maintenance, Museum of New Mexico, c. 1909-15; farmer, pottery designer, painter; Governor, San Ildefonso Pueblo; commissioned for murals, including Santa Fe Indian School, Mesa Verde National Park, Colorado, School of American Research, Santa Fe; ceremonial dancer; demonstrator of pottery design. **Died:** 6 March 1943.

MARIA. Born: Maria Montoya, San Ildefonso, c. 1887; native name means "Pond Lily." **Career:** Potter; potterymaking demonstrations; ceremonial dancer. **Awards:** Special Recognition award and Bronze medal for "Indian Achievement," Chicago World's Fair, 1934; The Craftsmanship Medal, American Institute of Architects, 1954; Jane Adams Award for Distinguished Service, Rockford College, Santa Fe, 1959; Presidential Citation, American Ceramic Society, 1968; Symbol of Man award, Minnesota Museum of Art, 1969; Honorary Doctorate of Fine Arts, New Mexico State University, 1971; Catlin Peace Pipe award, American Indian Lore Association, 1974; Governor's award, New Mexico Arts Commission, 1974; Honorary Member of the Council, National Council on Education for the Ceramic Arts, 1976; Honorary Doctorate, Columbia College, 1977; Presbyterian Hospital Foundation Award for Excellence, 1977. **Died:** 10 June 1980.

Selected Group Exhibitions

Pottery of the Martínez's and those of many other San Ildefonso artists were exhibited from 1948 through the 1970s at Popovi Da Studio, Pueblo of San Ildefonso.

1904	*Louisiana Purchase Exhibition*, St. Louis World's Fair, Missouri
1914	*Panama-California Exposition*, San Diego World's Fair, California
1919-20	Museum of New Mexico, Santa Fe
1927	Corona Mundi International Art Center, New York
1928	Fair Park Gallery, Dallas, Texas
1931-33	*Exposition of Tribal Arts,* organized by the College Art Association (traveling)
1934	*Century of Progress,* Chicago World's Fair, Illinois
1937	*American Indian Exposition and Congress*, Tulsa, Oklahoma
1939	San Francisco World's Fair, Golden Gate International Exhibition, California
1953	University of Colorado, Boulder
1955-56	European tour sponsored by the University of Oklahoma, Norman
1958-61	European tour sponsored by the University of Oklahoma, Norman
1967	*Three Generations Show* (Maria, Popovi Da, and Tony Da), United States Department of Interior, Washington, D.C. and Institute of American Indian Arts, Santa Fe, New Mexico
1978	Renwick Gallery, National Collection of Fine Arts, Washington, D.C.
	100 Years of Native American Painting, Oklahoma Museum of Art, Oklahoma City
1979-80	*Native American Paintings*, organized by the Joslyn Art Museum, Omaha, Nebraska (traveling)
1982	*Native American Painting: Selections from the Museum of the American Indian*, Heard Museum, Phoenix, Arizona (traveling)

Julian Martínez: *Two Buffalo and Symbolic Figures*, c. 1925. Courtesy Museum of Indian Arts and Culture, Santa Fe.

Collections

American Museum of Natural History, New York; Amerind Foundation, Dragoon, Arizona; Arizona State Museum, University of Arizona, Tucson; Amon Carter Museum of Art, Fort Worth, Texas; Cincinnati Art Museum, Ohio; Cleveland Museum of Art, Ohio; Columbus Gallery of Fine Arts, Ohio; Denver Art Museum, Colorado; Dartmouth College Collection, Hanover, New Hampshire; Thomas Gilcrease Institute of American History and Art, Tulsa, Oklahoma; Joslyn Art Museum, Omaha, Nebraska; Koogler McNay Art Museum, San Antonio, Texas; Museum of the American Indian, New York; Museum of Art, University of Oklahoma, Norman; Museum of New Mexico, Santa Fe; Museum of Northern Arizona, Flagstaff; Millicent Rogers Foundation Museum, Taos, New Mexico; School of American Research, Santa Fe, New Mexico; Smithsonian Institution, Washington, D.C.; Southwest Museum, Los Angeles, California; University of Pennsylvania Museum, Philadelphia; Wheelwright Museum of the American Indian, Santa Fe, New Mexico.

Publications

On Julian and Maria MARTÍNEZ: Books—*Pueblo Indian Painting,* by Hartley Burr Alexander, Szewedzicki, Nice, France, 1932; *American Indian Painters,* by Oscar B. Jacobson and Jeanne D'Ucel, Nice, France, 1950; *Maria: The Potter of San Ildefonso,* by Alice Marriott, University of Oklahoma Press, Norman, 1948; *American Indian Painting of the Southwest and*

Plains Areas, by Dorothy Dunn, University of New Mexico, Albuquerque, 1968; *Indian Painters and White Patrons*, by J.J. Brody, University of New Mexico Press, Albuquerque, 1971; *Maria Martinez*, by Mary Carrol Nelson, Dillon Press, Minneapolis, 1972; "Martínez," by Rick Dillingham, *Seven Families in Pueblo Pottery*, University of New Mexico Press, Albuquerque, 1974; *Art and Indian Individualists*, by Guy and Doris Monthan, Northland Press, Flagstaff, 1975; *Song from the Earth: American Indian Painting*, by Jamake Highwater, Boston, 1976; *Great North American Indians. Profiles in Life and Leadership*, New York, 1977; *The Living Tradition of Maria Martinez*, by Susan Peterson, Kodansha, Tokyo and New York, 1977; *Maria Martinez: Five Generations of Potters*, by Susan Peterson, Smithsonian Institution Press, Washington, D.C., 1978; *100 Years of Native American Painting*, exhibition catalog by Arthur Silberman, Oklahoma Museum of Art, Oklahoma City, 1978; *Maria*, by Richard L. Spivey, Northland Press, Flagstaff, 1979; "Maria," *Exploration 1979*, School of American Research, Santa Fe, 1979; *American Indian Painting and Sculpture*, Patricia Broder, New York, 1981; *Maria: The Legend, the Legacy*, by Susan B. McGreevy, Sunstone Press, Santa Fe, 1982; *Indianascher Kunstler*, by Gerhard Hoffman, Munich, 1984; *The Arts of the North American Indian: Native Traditions in Evolution*, edited by Edwin L. Wade, Hudson Hills Press, New York, in association with Philbrook Art Center, Tulsa, Oklahoma, 1986; *Talking With the Clay: The Art of Pueblo Pottery*, by Stephen Trimble, Santa Fe, New Mexico, 1987; *When the Rainbow Touches Down*, exhibition catalog by Tryntje Van Ness Seymour, Heard Museum, University of Washington Press, 1988; *Beyond Tradition: Native American Art and Its Evolution*, by Jerry and Lois Jacka, Flagstaff, 1988; *American Indian Artists in the Avery Collection and the McNay Permanent Collection*, edited by Jean Sherrod Williams, San Antonio, 1990; *Shared Visions: Native American Painters and Sculptors in the Twentieth Century*, by Margaret Archuleta and Dr. Rennard Strickland, The New Press, New York, 1991; *Art of Clay: Timeless Pottery of the Southwest*, edited by Lee M. Cohen, Santa Fe, New Mexico, 1995. **Articles**—"Maria Martínez: Indian Master Potter," by Zahrah Preble Hodge, *Southern Workman*, vol. 62, no. 5, 1933; "Maria of San Ildefonso," by Ray Manley, *Arizona Highways*, May 1974; "The Legacy of Maria Martínez," by Roberta Ross Fine, *Santa Fean Magazine*, October 1980; "Maria: The Right Woman at the Right Time," by Betty Toulouse, *El Palacio*, Winter 1980-81.

*   *   *

Julian and Maria Martínez are the singularly most influential Southwestern artists and, arguably, Indian artists of the twentieth century. Their work is in public and private collections worldwide, and their work the subject of numerous individual and group shows internationally. There are three published biographies and hundreds of articles of which they are the subject. They did more than any other individuals in helping the world recognize Indian art as art, and not craft or scientific artifact. Maria was the most important Pueblo potter because of her unsurpassed artistic and technical skills and achievements, and also because her influence was the most widespread and far reaching. Her marriage to Julian Martínez created a team that revolutionized pottery.

Maria was probably born in 1887 and died on 10 June 1980. Julian was born in 1885 and died in 1943. They had four sons, two of whom (Popovi Da and Adam Martínez) became artists, inheriting and passing on the family's artistic legacy. Maria and Julian were married in 1904, spending their honeymoon in St. Louis demonstrating pottery and dancing for the visitors to the World's Fair. Maria learned to pot from her maternal aunt, Nicolosa Peña Montoya. Julian came from a family of farmers and basket makers. From 1907 to 1909, Julian worked as a laborer on Museum of New Mexico Director Edgar Hewett's archaeological excavations on the Pajarito Plateau, now Bandelier National Monument. Julian was the janitor at the Museum beginning in 1909, the year of the Museum's founding, and probably continued working at the Museum until 1914, when he and Maria went to San Diego to demonstrate at the Panama California Exposition. Julian filled notebooks with design ideas from archaeological as well as contemporary pottery (Hopi and Acoma wares in particular), which he later incorporated into his ingenious and innovative pottery decoration.

Maria was already recognized as one of best potters of her village in 1909, while Julian had been decorating her pottery since 1904. Julian was also an accomplished watercolorist, being one of the founders of the Pueblo Painting style with Crescencio Martínez and Alfredo Montoya. Maria was asked to make pottery similar to what was being found on the Pajarito Plateau. While she did not duplicate the soft and porous clay used in the fifteenth and sixteenth centuries, she did make a similar shaped bowl, and Julian recreated some of the designs of the ancestral Tewa pottery. Kenneth Chapman, a curator at the Museum of New Mexico, wanted to use pottery as a means to provide economic stability to the Pueblos. He desired to make pottery more art than curio, returning some dignity to Indian peoples' lives, and fortunately he found a willing and extraordinary accomplice in Maria Martínez. Although he probably kept asking Maria to "improve" her pottery, he most likely did not have a clear notion of what that pottery might look like, other than being duplicates of ancient styles.

Maria and Julian Martínez: Vessel, 1922. Courtesy Museum of Indian Arts and Culture, Santa Fe.

Herein lies part of the genius of Maria and Julian. In 1917 they brought to Chapman an exquisitely lustrous blackware water jar. They discovered that by lowering the firing temperature, Kapo black ceramics (dating from approximately 1550) would retain a highly polished finish. Subsequently, in the winter of 1919-20, Maria and Julian brought a decorated black pot to the Museum, called at first "two-blacks," and today internationally known as black-on-black. For their newly invented style of pottery, they developed an entirely new design repertoire, borrowing from rock art and ancestral pottery styles. By 1925, Maria and Julian reconstituted the pottery traditions of San Ildefonso. Not only did Maria share the secret of her new style of pottery with potters from her village, but she taught pottery to other pueblos as well. By the early 1930s, highly polished blackwares also dominated at Santa Clara Pueblo, and today this style of pottery is the most famous and widely associated with the Pueblos. In addition, by 1923, Maria and Julian were signing all of their work, another innovation practiced almost universally by Pueblo potters today.

Physically, pots were reformulated for the non-Indian market. Although situated in the traditions of Southwestern pottery, the designs and high polished surfaces were not derived from specific Tewa potting traditions. The design systems were largely taken from prehistoric contexts, probably found by or shown to Julian Martínez in books and museum collections. Maria Martínez possessed superb ceramic skills: no one could build pots faster or better, nor has anyone since been equal to her polishing skills. Together they created Pueblo-art pottery.

Julian died in 1943. Maria continued potting with her daughter-in-law, Santana Roybal Martínez. Indeed, Maria had begun potting with Santana from the moment of her entry into the Martínez household in 1939, and, in addition, Santana came from an illustrious potting heritage as well. Beginning in the early 1950s, Maria began a very fertile period of collaboration with her son, Popovi Da. Together they revitalized polychrome pottery and discovered new styles, such as gun metal finish, the sienna finish, and duotone, or the two firing process of black and sienna. Da also ensured that his mother's legacy would be remembered and understood from her perspective. Popovi died in 1971 and Maria stopped potting in 1972.

Maria Martínez was a superb ceramic technician, gathering and mixing her clay and shaping, smoothing and polishing to absolute perfection. With her husband, and later in life with her son, she was able to precisely control the outdoor firing of pottery to create brilliant surfaces and new finish colors. She was instrumental in the re-formulation of Pueblo pottery for the non-Pueblo world.

Maria lived her entire life in her village of San Ildefonso. She dismissed fame, reminding all that she was a Pueblo woman, nothing more, nothing less—a wife, mother, and member of her community. Although she was the first to consistently sign her pottery, individual achievement remained a foreign concept to her throughout her life. Nonetheless, with pottery she was able to allow a selective entry of the outside world to her Pueblo while using the money from pottery-making to support the ceremonial and social life of San Ildefonso. She gave the Pueblo world the gift of continued vigor in pottery and provided the non-Pueblo world with the beauty of her artistic vision as well as a glimpse into the Pueblo cosmos.

—Bruce Bernstein

MARTÍNEZ, Mario

Tribal affiliations: Yaqui
Painter

Born: Phoenix, Arizona, 1953. **Education**: School of Art, Arizona State University, B.F.A., 1979; San Francisco Art Institute, M.F.A., 1985. **Career:** Artist; educator, University of Tucson, San Francisco Art Institute, University of New Mexico; artist in residence, Vermont Art Center, 1994.

Individual Exhibitions

1990   Gorman Museum, University of California, Davis
1992   Ohio Wesleyan University, Delaware
1993   *Yaqui into Abstraction*, LaRaza/Galeria Posada, Sacramento, California
1995   *Visual Interpretations of Yaqui Myths and Legends*, American Indian Contemporary Arts, San Francisco, California
1996   *From Another World: Yaqui Visions*, Jan Cicero Gallery, Chicago, Illinois
        Yaqui Interpretations, Graythorne Gallery, Scottsdale, Arizona

Selected Group Exhibitions

1981   *3 Painters*, Moons Gallery & Cafe, Tempe, Arizona
1984   Diego Rivera Gallery, San Francisco Art Institute, California
1986   *Introductions '86*, Gallery Paule Anglim, San Francisco, California
1987   Walter and Atholl McBean Galleries, San Francisco Art Institute, California
1988   *Four Sacred Mountains: Color, Form, and Abstraction*, sponsored by the Arizona Commission of the Arts, Phoenix (traveling through 1989)
1990   *Six Directions: Sacred Places/Visual Messages*, American Indian Contemporary Arts, San Francisco, California
1991   *Without Boundaries: Contemporary Native American Art*, Jan Cicero Gallery, Chicago, Illinois
        Portfolio III, American Indian Contemporary Arts Gallery, San Francisco, California
        Our Land/Ourselves, originating at the University Art Gallery, State University of New York, Albany (traveling through 1995)
1992   *Hot Native Art*, American Indian Community House Gallery, New York
1992   *We the Human Beings: 27 Contemporary Native Artists*, College of Wooster Museum, Ohio
        The Submuloc Show/Columbus Wohs, Atlatl and Evergreen State College, Olympia, Washington
1993   *New Work by Four Gallery Artists: Mario Martínez, Duane Slick, Annette Turow, & Fern Valfer*, Jan Cicero Gallery, Chicago, Illinois
1995   *Living Tapestry: Contemporary Native American Artists*, Laney College Art Gallery, Oakland, California
1996   *Stand in the Center of the Good*, American Indian Community House Gallery/Museum, New York

New Art of the West V, Eiteljorg Museum of American Indians and Western Art, Indianapolis, Indiana
Native Streams, organized by Jan Cicero Gallery, Chicago, Illinois and Turman Art Gallery, Indiana State University, Terre Haute (traveling through 1997)

Collections

John D. and Catherine T. MacArthur Foundation, Chicago, Illinois; Tucson Museum of Art, Arizona; University of Arizona, Tucson.

Publications

By MARTÍNEZ: Article—"Visions," *Art Quarterly,* Fall 1989.

On MARTÍNEZ: Books—*Portfolio III: Native American Artists,* exhibition catalog by Janeen Antoine and Sara Bates, San Francisco, 1991; *The Submuloc Show/Columbus Wohs,* exhibition catalog by Carla Roberts, Phoenix, 1992; *Native American Art,* by David W. Penney and George C. Longfish, Seattle, 1994; *I Stand in the Center of the Good: Interviews with Contemporary Native American Artists,* edited by Lawrence Abbot, University of Nebraska Press, 1994; *Worlds in Collision: Dialogues on Multicultural Issues on Art,* San Francisco, 1995.

*

Mario Martínez comments (1996):

My work is a visual revelation of a dual cultural identity. I believe my work is abstract because abstract reasoning is primary to the mythic, enchanted qualities of Yaqui songs, dances, ceremonial rituals, and religions, as well as being the essence of Western European Modernist traditions.

My latest works include not only concepts and images for my specific cultural background, but also materials used by Yaquis in ceremonial traditions and ceremonial regalia. (From the *Native Streams* catalog.)

*   *   *

Martínez's thoughtful work reflects the persistence and continuity of a vision that does not remake itself in light of social or cultural trends. As a contemporary formalist with strong ties to his tribe and a great affinity for Abstract Expressionist use of color and form, Martínez has earned the respect of art critics as well as his peers in the Native American Fine Art Movement. For nearly 20 years, Martínez has represented the natural and supernatural worlds of his tribe, the Yaqui, with brightly colored paint thickly and laboriously applied. The paintings are abstractions, making reference to the artist's Western modernist art education while simultaneously paying respect to the sensitive nature of tribal traditions, ceremonial rituals and religion. Martínez has devised a unique visual language to recall and communicate the ceremonial tribal world of his childhood. On his canvases, biomorphic forms suggesting serpents, tree branches, and the petals of flowers float over large blocks of atmospheric color that fill every inch of canvas. The jewel tones and spare titles of the images leave association up the viewer. *Flowerland,* the large acrylic painting that anchored his 1995 solo show at Jan Cicero Gallery in Chicago, could be a window into another

Mario Martínez: *Yellow Flower Landscape.* **Photograph by Jerry Kobylecky; courtesy of the artist.**

world, where tall, spindly flowers dominate an eerie, sun-dappled landscape; or it could be a view through the lens of a microscope, where tiny life forms move in viscous fluids under glass. In any case, each canvas is a world unto itself. Representational forms only occasionally emerge, such as the deer with its heart visible in *Supernatural Fawn* (1995).

"For the Yaqui, the natural world consists not only of the actual or the real, but of a magical, supernatural counterpart as well. Our original poetry, songs, and dances vividly describe that double-world called the *Huya Ania* (Wilderness World) and the enchanted domains within the *Huya Ania,* the *Sea Ania* (Flower World) and the *Yo Ania* (the Ancient Realm of Respected Powers)," Martínez explains. In the artist's memory and his paintings, these worlds are connected to each other and to personal experiences, merging the natural and the supernatural, the personal and the tribal.

Martínez was born in 1953 in Phoenix, Arizona, and was raised there in a tricultural community—Yaqui, Mexican, and Anglo-American. He knew he wanted to be a painter from a very young age, and fondly recalls experimenting with colors in a kindergarten fingerpainting session. One of the few outspokenly gay contemporary Native American visual artists, Martínez is a minority within his own community. He addressed this position in an unusual acrylic and mixed media painting, *To My Lavender Siblings,* exhibited in *Portfolio III* (1991) at American Indian Contemporary Arts in San Francisco. This work combines an icon of homosexuality, the pink triangle, with a photographic image of a Yaqui deer dance. Gaudy texture is added by the incorporation of materials used in Yaqui ceremonial regalia, such as decorative fabric ribbons and glitter.

—Margaret Dubin

MATOUSH, Glenna
Tribal affiliations: Ojibway
Painter and sculptor

Born: Rama Reserve, Ontario, September 1946. **Education:** Quetico Park Centre, Quetico, Ontario, 1964; School of Fine Arts, Elliot Lake, Quebec, 1965; Museum of Fine Arts and Design, Montreal, Quebec, 1966-68; University of Alberta, Edmonton, Alberta; Guilde graphique de Montreal, Montreal, Quebec, 1976-80. **Awards:** Quebec Cultural Affairs honor. **Address:** c/o Monique Meunier, 53 rue McKenna, Montreal, Quebec H3T 1V2, Canada; phone 514-735-7726.

Individual Exhibitions

1988   Salle Augustin Chenier, Ville-Marie, Quebec
        Centre Socio-Culturel d'Amos, Quebec
1989   Centre d'Art Rotary, La Sarre, Quebec
1990   *Benvenuti,* Art Galery Moderna Venice, Italy
        Amerindian Museum, Pointe Bleue, Quebec
1995   *Matoush Retrospective*, Côte-des-Neiges-Cultural Centre, Quebec

Selected Group Exhibitions

1982   Department of Indian Affairs, National Arts Centre, Ottawa, Ontario
        Musée minier de Malartic, Malartic, Quebec
        Celebration of Survival, in conjunction with the international Assembly of First Nations, Assiniboia Gallery, Regina, Saskatchewan
1983   *Prints and Drawings,* Hazelton, British Columbia
        Galerie d'art et d'artisanat du Quebec, Quebec
1984   Meudon, Paris, France
1985   Centre Cultural de Val'Or, Val'Or, Quebec
1986   Gala des Grands Prix du Tourisme Quebecois, Val d'Or, Quebec
1987   International Symposium of the Northern Quebec Centre Socio-culturel d'Amos, Quebec
        Minstere des affaires culturelles du Quebec, Tolosane, France
        Cultural Centre, Val d'Or, Quebec
1988   National Indian Arts and Crafts Corporation, Ottawa, Ontario
        Salle d'exposition de Val d'Or, Quebec, with sculptor Steven Sheshamush, NIACC, Ottawa, Ontario
1989   Padova, Italy
        Changers: A Spiritual Renaissace, York Quay Gallery
        Changers: A Spiritual Renaissance, National Touring Exhibition, sponsored by NIACC
1990   *Hydro Quebec Exhibition,* Val d'Or-Amos-Rouyn-Noranda, Ville-Marie et la Sarre
1991   *Au de la tradition,* Rouyn-Noranda Exhibition Centre, Rouyn Noranda, Quebec
        Toronto Convention Centre, Ontario
        Palais de congres, Paris, France
1992   *New Territories: 350/500 Years After*, Montreal, Quebec City, Mexico City
        Bishop's University, Lennoxville, Quebec

1993   *Paperworks,* Trinity College, Toronto, Ontario
        Art Exploration Multimedia, from Whapmnagoostui Project 1991, Rouyn-Noranda, Quebec; Maison de Culture Mont-Royal, Montreal, Quebec
        Canadian Embassy at Guatemala, Guatemala
1994   *Nation to Nation Presents: Vision to Vision*, Metro Square Victoria, Montreal, Quebec
        Ramscale Art Associates Gallery, West Greenwich, New York
        Great Whale Ten, Exhibition of Native, French, and English Artists, Amsterdam; Burlington, Vermont; Montreal, Quebec
1995   *Foreign Affairs Collection of Native Art*, Ottawa, Moscow
        Peel Street, Montreal, Quebec
        Toronto Historical Board, Stone Powder Fort York
        Waterworks, De Pianofabriek Museum, Brussels, Belgium

Collections

Basilica del Santo, Padova, Italy; Canadian Cultural Centre, Rome, Italy; Canadian High Commission, London, England; Grand Council of the Crees (of Quebec), Val'Or; Guatemala School of Plastic Arts, Guatemala City, Guatemala; Indian and Northern Affairs Canada, Ottawa, Ontario; Woodlands Cultural Centre, Six Nations Reserve, Ontario.

Publications

On MATOUSH: Book—*Balance: Art and Nature*, by John K. Grande, Black Rose Books, Montreal, 1995.

*

Glenna Matoush comments:
    At present I am researching subject matter that holds particular relevance for native peoples. As a result of this exploration my new works show definite signs of being grounded in a realist's attitude while remaining far from pictorial in actuality. My epistomology is developing aesthetically. I am constantly balancing the delicate dialectic truth among the subjective and the objective. This process is slowly becoming the Golden mean of my artistic life.

*   *   *

    As an artist, Glenna Matoush's process is continually evolving, as she absorbs nature and the environment around her. In a style that has at times been loosley compared to American painter Jackson Pollock, her work is carefully planned while still spontaneous and alive.
    The most striking characteristic of Glenna Matoush's prints, paintings and mixed media works is her organic use of bright colours and her underlying sense of order that originates from within each piece. Her abstract pieces combine a sense of order and design, although far from being based in realism, with an exciting sense of surprise and unpredictability.
    While her work could be seen as abstract in nature, Matoush addresses specific and powerful themes with careful thought and technique. *Girl Paddling,* for example, is an etching that takes on a political tone, paying homage to the fragile native culture threatened by government and industry. In this case, the threat seems to come from the much debated James Bay hydro-electric project. These themes are simultaneously approached from both a personal and global perspective.

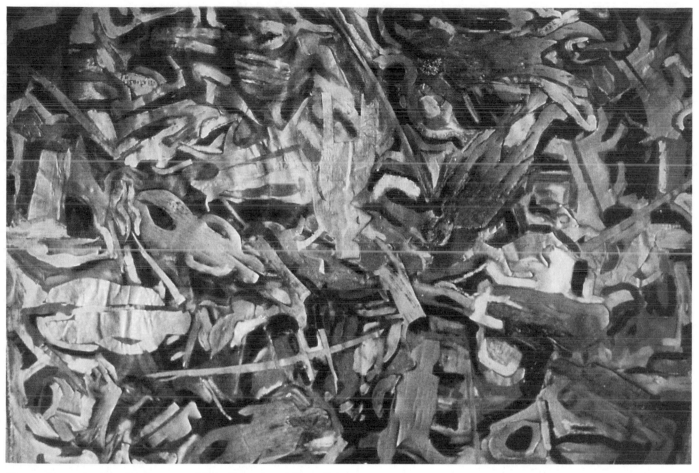

Glenna Matoush: *Dam Disharmony,* 1991. Courtesy of the artist.

Another piece by Matoush, *Ain't our mother earth no more* (1992), is a seventeen-foot totem pole encased in brightly painted canvas sections. This piece is both physically and emotionally imposing, as is much of her work. For the viewer, her work provides a sensation of racing or careening toward the unknown. During experiences such as these, the senses are overloaded and only pieces and fragments of what is passing can be grasped as a larger and more abstract truth is approached.

The art of Glenna Matoush draws deeply on a sense of order that reaches beyond logic and conscious understanding. The pieces access more primal sensibilities in the viewer and possibly the artist herself. Her work is immediate and tangible, embedded in a unique, entwined relationship with nature. It almost appears as though her artistic process and individual materials are all part of the nature of the work of art.

—Vesta Giles

MAYO, Sarah Jim

Tribal affiliations: Washoe
Basketweaver

Born: 1860. **Family:** Daughter of Captain James ("Captain" was a name of those recognized with authority for representing the com-

munity in dealings with whites); married Captain Pete Mayo, who died in 1918. **Career:** Self-supporting basketweaver. **Awards:** Made a presentation basket for President Woodrow Wilson, 1913. **Died:** 1945.

Selected Group Exhibitions

1990　　Philbrook Art Center, Tulsa, Oklahoma
1995-96　Marion Steinbach Indian Basket Museum at the Gatekeeper's Museum, Tahoe City, California
1996　　*Weavers of Tradition and Beauty: Basketmakers of the Great Basin*, Nevada Historical Society, Reno (on-going, permanent)

Collections

Philbrook Art Center, Tulsa, Oklahoma; Margaretta ('Maggie') Dressler Collection, Dresslerville, Nevada; Historical Society, Reno, Nevada.

Publications

On MAYO: Books—"Washoe Innovators and Their Patrons," by Marvin Cohodas, *The Arts of the North American Indians*, edited by by Edwin L. Wade, Hudson Hills Press, New York, and Philbrook Art Center, Tulsa, Oklahoma, 1986.

*   *   *

Around the turn of the century, Sarah Jim Mayo joined other Washoe women in selling baskets to tourists during the spring and summer around Lake Tahoe. The baskets she wove became most sought after, as she was among the first to introduce pictorial designs in beautiful coiled basketry. Her designs became progressively more complex, emphasizing dramatic colors, images, and large-scale motifs. The sense of boldness is reflected as well in her assertive and determined personal behavior—from her expectation of fair and equal treatment by white consumers, to her dealings with fellow Washoe, many of whom began to shun her, to taking on the name of her father after her husband's death because it commanded more respect, to the inscription on a basket she wove for presentation to President Woodrow Wilson, Mayo displayed a formidable talent and personality.

Sarah Jim Mayo was the daughter of Captain Jim, whose name denotes the authority for Washoe who represented their people in dealings with whites. As the daughter of a community leader, Mayo prided in a form of elevated status, and it was matched in the verve and daring of her basketmaking. Around 1905, pictorial designs began appearing in Washoe basketry, and none matched the complex and innovative designs of Mayo, who is sometimes credited for introducing the innovation. Regardless of whether or not she was the first to weave pictorial designs into her baskets, none exceeded her in execution of increasingly complex designs that became illusionistic and narrative, with fields of vibrant color. Far from the refined and precise excellence of the baskets of her contemporary, Louisa Keyser (Dat So La Lee), Mayo's baskets are daring and dramatic.

In 1914, her husband, Captain Pete Mayo, headed a delegation of Washoe that traveled to Washington D.C. to defend land claims for the tribe. Sarah created a basket for the occasion to be presented to President Woodrow Wilson. She wove an inscription into the spiraling design, with corresponding images of herself and her father as well as a likeness of eagles clutching arrows —similar to the design on the Presidential Seal; the matter-of-fact inscription emphasizes her father, herself, her region, and her tribe: "Nevada and California / Sarah, I am his daughter / Captain James, First Chief of Washoe Tribe / This basket is a special curio, 1913." It is interesting that Mayo mentions her father, whom she recognized as having a higher status than her husband, who was representing the Washoe at the time, and when Captain Pete Mayo died in 1918, Sarah assumed the name of her father.

Mayo gained an important patron in Margaretta Dressler, wife of William Dressler, owner of one of the largest ranch in Carson Valley, Nevada. While she continued to be independent, Mayo benefitted, historically, from Margaretta's record keeping; Mrs. Dressler also collected baskets from Sarah's contemporaries, Maggie James and Tillie Snooks. Sarah's style became the most popular among consumers, and though few could match her execution and results, many benefited from imitating her bold designs, rich color fields, and illusionism—the creation of optical effects that enhance and add depth to the design.

—Gregory Schaaf

McCOMBS, Solomon
Tribal affiliations: Creek
Painter

Born: Near Eufaula, Oklahoma, 17 May 1913. **Education:** Bacone College, studying with Acee Blue Eagle; Tulsa Downtown College. **Career:** Designer, illustrator, cartographer, and draftsman for the U.S. Government; Goodwill Ambassador, U.S. Department of State, traveling to Asia and Africa, 1954; founder and president, American Indian and Eskimo Cultural Foundation, Washington, D.C.; treasurer, Society of Federal Artists and Designers, 1956-57; commissioned for murals, including U.S. Post Office, Marietta, Oklahoma, and U.S. Army, painting for Congressional Medal of Honor ceremonies, 1980. **Awards:** Five Civilized Tribes Museum seal (selected), 1956; Waite Phillips Trophy, Outstanding Contributions to Indian Art, Philbrook Museum of Art, 1965; Shield Award, American Indian and Eskimo Cultural Foundation, 1968; designated as Master Artist, Five Civilized Tribes Museum, 1975. **Died:** 18 November 1980.

Selected Group Exhibitions

1936	*First American Indian Exposition*, Tulsa, Oklahoma
1937	*American Indian Exposition and Congress*, Tulsa, Oklahoma
1947-65	*American Indian Paintings From the Permanent Collection,* Philbrook Museum of Art, Tulsa, Oklahoma (traveling)
1955	*An Exhibition of American Indian Painters*, James Graham and Sons, New York
1955-56	European tour sponsored by the University of Oklahoma, Norman
1958-61	European tour sponsored by the University of Oklahoma, Norman
1963	Bismark National Indian Art Show, sponsored by the Chamber of Commerce and Bismark Art Association, North Dakota
1963	*Contemporary American Indian Art*, United States Department of State, Washington, D.C.
1964	*First Annual National American Indian Art Exposition*, Charlotte, North Carolina
1965	*Second Annual Invitational Exhibition of American Indian Paintings*, United States Department of the Interior, Washington, D.C.
1972	Cherokee National Museum, Tahlequah, Oklahoma
1975	*Contemporary Indian Art Invitational*, Oregon State University, Corvallis
1978	*100 Years of Native American Painting*, Oklahoma Museum of Art, Oklahoma City
1979-80	*Native American Paintings*, Mid-America Arts Alliance Project, organized by the Joslyn Art Museum, Omaha, Nebraska (traveling)
1980	*Midwest Professional Artistis Benefit Art Show*, Tulsa Garden Center, Oklahoma
1981	*Memorial Exhibition*, Thomas Gilcrease Museum Institute of American History and Art, Tulsa, Oklahoma
1991	*Mayfest International Festival*, Winston-Salem, North Carolina

1990   *American Indian Artists in the Avery Collection and the McNay Permanent Collection*, Marion Koogler McNay Art Museum, San Antonio, Texas

1993   Red Earth Indian Center, Kirkpatrick Center Museum Complex, Oklahoma City, Oklahoma

Collections

Bureau of Indian Affairs, United States Department of the Interior, Washington, D.C.; Creek Indian Council House and Museum, Okmulgee, Oklahoma; Denver Art Museum, Colorado; Thomas Gilcrease Institute of American History and Art, Tulsa, Oklahoma; Heard Museum, Phoenix, Arizona; Indian Arts and Crafts Board, United States Department of the Interior, Washington, D.C.; Joslyn Art Museum, Omaha, Nebraska; Museum of New Mexico, Santa Fe; Oklahoma State Art Collection, Oklahoma City; Philbrook Museum of Art, Tulsa, Oklahoma; University of Oklahoma, Fred Jones Jr. Museum of Art, Norman, Oklahoma; Wheelwright Museum of the American Indian, Santa Fe, New Mexico.

Publications

On McCOMBS: Books—*American Indian Painters,* by Oscar B. Jacobson and Jeanne D'Ucel, Nice, France, 1950; *Indian Artists from Oklahoma*, by Oscar B. Jacobson, Norman, 1964; *American Indian Painting of the Southwest and Plains Areas,* by Dorothy Dunn, Albuquerque, 1968; *Indian Painters and White Patrons,* by J.J. Brody, Albuquerque, 1971; *Art and Indian Individualists*, by Guy and Doris Monthan, Flagstaff, 1975; *100 Years of Native American Painting*, by Arthur Silberman, Oklahoma City, 1978; *Native American Art at the Philbrook*, by John Mahey, et. al., Tulsa, 1980; *Native American Painting*, by Fredrick Schmid and Patrick T. Houlihan, Kansas City, 1980; *American Indian Painting and Sculpture*, by Patricia Janis Broder, New York 1981; *American Indian Artists in the Avery Collection and the McNay Permanent Collection*, edited by Jean Sherrod Williams, San Antonio, 1990.

*   *   *

"Certainly, no artist has portrayed the Creek as extensively and in such depth as Solomon McCombs." These words appear in a short essay by Arthur Silberman, a collector and scholar of Native American art, prepared for the exhibit catalog, *100 Years of Native American Painting* (1978). *Fasting* (1975), one of McComb's pieces selected for the exhibition, illustrates Silberman's statement. The subject matter is Creek, and the authentically-rendered figures are dressed appropriately for Creek men, preparing for a ritual on Creek ceremonial grounds. The painting is rendered simply in the Woodland flatstyle, without any of the pan-Indian tribal motifs commonly found in flatstyle paintings of the period. At this point late in McCombs' career, he focused almost exclusively on Creek life and ceremonies, but the impetus for that decision came much earlier.

McCombs first studied Native American art under his cousin, Acee Blue Eagle, who became the first director of the art school at Bacone College in 1935. McCombs was impressed by Blue Eagle's advice to his students to preserve Native American traditions that were in danger of being lost. Like fellow student Dick West, McCombs would personalize this advice and give attention to preserving the heritage of his own tribe. West would later teach his students to paint only what they knew and to avoid painting traditions other than their own. McCombs was among the Bacone artists who took this ethic to heart. It should be noted, however, that he did occasionally paint other subjects. For instance, in 1942 he was commissioned to paint a Chickasaw subject for a mural (*Chickasaw Indian Family Making Sofkey*) in the United States Post Office in Marietta, Oklahoma.

A comparison of McCombs' works to those of two other noted artists who often painted Creek subjects, Fred Beaver and Jerome Tiger, illuminates the artists' major concerns. *Creek Women's Ribbon Dance* (1949) is very similar in subject and composition to many works by Beaver, who painted several ceremonial scenes featuring lines of dancers. The figures are somewhat stiff and virtually without expression in paintings by both artists, and the viewer focuses on the ceremonial itself. People become individual components of a whole, nearly types within a "blueprint" of the ceremony. Detail is on accurate clothing and placement, rather than on showing personality or emotion.

These characteristics are in contrast to Jerome Tiger's paintings of Creek and Seminole ceremonials. Tiger's figures have engaging facial expressions and dynamic movement. In creating his successfully dramatic paintings, Tiger sacrificed some of the authenticity that McCombs retained. Tiger also moved away from flatstyle painting and used European modeling and foreshortening to add visual impact. For McCombs, flatstyle was more than adequate for his purpose of preserving Creek customs. His choice of flatstyle was deliberate and significant to him. He defended it against those who called it "Bambi art," calling it a "true American art form." His *Creek Indian Social Ball Game* (1957) is an example of a mature flatstyle piece that delivers a great deal of information about the subject matter. It does not attempt to elicit emotional response as much as to provide a clear description of a communal activity. McCombs consistently painted many such straightforward depictions of Creek life, and in the process provided a rich history of Creek life.

—Kevin Smith

McHORSE, Christine

Tribal affiliations: Navajo
Potter

Born: Christine Nofchissey in Morenci, Arizona, 21 December 1948. **Education:** Institute of American Indian Art, Santa Fe 1963-67, post-graduate work in 1968. **Career:** Arts and crafts demonstrating, 1968-; potter and jeweler, 1970s-; Santa Fe Indian Market 1983-. **Awards:** Santa Fe Indian Market, 1985-96, annual awards in contemporary pottery, including first place, 1985, 1990, 1995; second place, 1992, 1994, 1996; third place, 1991; Annual Pottery Show, Denver Colorado, first prize, 1985; Inter-Tribal Indian Ceremonial, Gallup, New Mexico, first place, 1987, 1989, 1994.

Individual Exhibitions

1993   Andrea Fisher Fine Pottery, Santa Fe, New Mexico

Selected Group Exhibitions

1972   Taos Pueblo Arts and Crafts Shop, New Mexico (through 1977)

Christine McHorse: Navajo pitch-coated jar, 1990. Photograph by Dong Lin; courtesy Ruth K. Belikove collection.

1983	Brigham Young University, Provo, Utah
1985	Eileen Kremen Gallery, Fullerton, California
	Eight Northern Artist and Craft Show, San Ildefonso Pueblo, New Mexico
1987	Kornbluth Gallery, Fair Lawn, New York
1988	*anii ánáádaalyaa'íí: Continuity and Innovation in Recent Navajo Art*, Wheelwright Museum of the American Indian, Santa Fe, New Mexico
1989	*Navajo Pottery*, Southwest Museum, Los Angeles, California
	Scripps 45th Ceramics Annual, Lang Art Gallery, Scripps College, Claremont, California
	From this Earth: Pottery of the Southwest, Museum of Indian Arts and Culture, Museum of New Mexico, Santa Fe
1990	*The Cutting Edge*, traveling exhibit organized by the Museum of American Folk Art, New York; Venues: New Britain Museum of American Art, New Britain, Connecticut; Laguna Art Museum, Laguna Beach, California; Telfair Museum, Savannah, Georgia; Tampa Museum of Art, Tampa, Florida; Whatcom Museum, Bellingham, Washington
1994	*Honoring the Legacy*, Museum of Northern Arizona, Flagstaff
	Diversity of Expression: New Mexico Folk Art, New Mexico State Capitol/Governor's Gallery, Santa Fe
	Contemporary Art of the Navajo Nation, traveling exhibit

organized by Cedar Rapids (Iowa) Museum of Art; Venues: Albuquerque Museum, Albuquerque, New Mexico; University Art Museum, State University of New York, Albany, New York; Museum of the Southwest, Midland, Texas

1996 *Contemporary Women Artists of the West, 1946-1996*, Karan Ruhlen Gallery, Santa Fe, New Mexico

Collections

Denver Museum of Natural History, Colorado; Museum of Indian Arts & Culture, Museum of New Mexico, Santa Fe; Navajo Nation Museum, Window Rock, Arizona; School of American Research, New Mexico.

Publications

On McHORSE: Books—*Navajo Pottery: Traditions and Innovations*, by Russell P. Hartman, Northland Press, Flagstaff, 1987; *Beyond Tradition, Contemporary Indian Art and Its Evolution* by Lois Essary Jacka, Northland Publishing Co., Flagstaff, 1988; *anii ánáádaalyaa'íí: Continuity and Innovation in Recent Navajo Art*, exhibition catalog by Bruce Bernstein and Susan McGreevy, Wheelwright Museum, Santa Fe, 1988; *Museum of American Folk Art Encyclopedia of Twentieth-Century American Folk Art and Artists* by Chuck and Jan Rosenak, New York, 1990; *The People Speak: Navajo Folk Art* by Chuck and Jan Rosenak, Northland Publishing Co., Flagstaff, 1994; *Enduring Traditions, Art of the Navajo* by Lois Essary Jacka, Northland Publishing Co., Flagstaff, 1994; *Contemporary American Folk Art: A Collector's Guide*, by Chuck and Jan Rosenak, New York, 1996. **Articles**—*New York Times,* 17 March 1985; interview with Rebecca Friedman, *THE Magazine,* November 1994; "The 'Gold Pots' Stand Out in Elegant Beauty," by Dottie Indyke, *Santa Fe New Mexican's Pasatiempo,* 2 June 1995; "Meet the Masters," by Michael Hice, *Indian Artist Magazine,* Spring 1996; "Mother Earth's Shining Gift," by Melinda Elliott, *New Mexico Magazine* vol. 74, no. 7, August 1996.

*

Christine McHorse comments:

Beauty in simplicity is the basis for my work in clay and silver. The shiny earth and metal provide personal means of expression through the oldest crafts.

The micaceous clays I use are from the northern New Mexico mountains. Mica and sand are natural tempers within the clay that exclude the need for added ingredients, such as volcanic ash. After digging, hauling, soaking and cleaning the clay, it is set to a workable consistency. I begin each pot with a flat round clay disk that forms its base. The coil method is then employed with extreme care and concentration to shape while building thin even walls of a modified traditional form. After the dry pot has been sanded, a coat of fine clay slip might be applied. My burnishing tools are a worn round file that produces a light texture and a polishing stone for a smooth finish. Firing techniques vary, dependent on desired effects. I use cedarwood and cottonwood bark to fuel a traditional firing and to catch the dark random fire clouds, otherwise I may use a kiln. On fired pottery with incised design, an application of boiled pinon pitch is used much in the *Dine* manner of waterproofing, although I use it more for contrast than for tradition. Yesterday, today, and tomorrow ... pottery made of these uniquely beautiful and durable micaceous clays...was, and still is and will still be used for cooking.

*   *   *

Christine McHorse is among the leading Native American contemporary potters, recognized for her micaceous wares and her contemporary Navajo pieces. McHorse has forged new boundaries in both fields, and like several other Native American potters of her generation, her work is a blend of traditions from several cultures.

Although McHorse was born and raised outside the boundaries of the Navajo Reservation, she was taught to respect Navajo cultural traditions. Among the Navajo, pottery making skills are usually passed from mother to daughter, but in McHorse's family there were no known pottery traditions. While attending the Institute of American Indian Arts, McHorse met and later married Joel McHorse of Taos Pueblo, and it was from his grandmother, Lena Archuleta, herself a well-known Taos potter, that McHorse learned to make pottery, around 1970.

From those beginnings, McHorse has continually blended her own Navajo traditions with those of her husband's family from Taos Pueblo, with an occasional influence from other potters. Today, she uses several types of micaceous clay gathered in the mountains of northern New Mexico. Form has long been of primary interest to McHorse. Although her vessels are usually burnished smooth and mostly reflect traditional puebloan and Navajo shapes, her body of work also includes numerous asymmetrical shapes.

McHorse prefers firing her wares outdoors in the traditional manner, but occasionally uses an electric kiln, especially for pre-firing very large pieces, thereby reducing the chance of breakage. Pottery fired outdoors often shows black marks or fire clouds on its surfaces, the result of contact between the vessel and the burning fuel. Although these marks are a desired feature of Navajo pottery, pueblo potters have traditionally avoided them, especially in response to collectors. Use of a kiln completely eliminates the chance of fireclouding, but experience has taught McHorse how to control this during outdoor firing. Many of her Navajo-style pots are given a traditional coating of piñon pine pitch after they are fired.

From the very beginning, McHorse has produced pots intended as art pieces and has consistently worked to perfect her technique. Her large pieces, some measuring 25 inches, have the sound of glass when tapped. McHorse is ever aware of her cultural background but greatly treasures her artistic freedom as well. Although she works in a medium with traditions reaching back more than 1000 years in the Southwest, she does not let those traditions completely define or restrain her own creativity.

The work of Christine McHorse clearly stands out from the work of other southwestern Indian potters on the basis of its overall design and surface decoration. Many works emphasize only the natural beauty of the clay. Jars shaped like long-necked gourds or graceful double-spouted wedding vases are studies in line and form. Other examples are carefully sculpted with three-dimensional animals, some rendered in a stylized fashion of the ancient Mimbres culture of southwestern New Mexico, or in a more realistic style. Lizards are among McHorse's more popular motifs. From her Navajo culture, she sculpts and incises a whole different set of motifs, including more lizards, or wolves, or a young boy and his horse. Navajo pots traditionally have a decorative band around the neck, and McHorse has rendered some astonishing variations of this feature. Sometimes, she sculpts it in the style of the woven and intricately patterned sash belts worn by women on ceremonial occa-

sions or at dances. On other examples, this clay band is transformed into a bolt of lighting whose ends terminate as arrows. McHorse shows again and again that age-old stories and designs can still be given fresh interpretations.

Like many Native American artists who are very much part of the modern world around them, McHorse willingly shares her knowledge and skills, to ensure that the pottery tradition will continue. Her sister, Alberta Mason, is one of her most accomplished students. In 1994, McHorse participated at a week-long workshop for micaceous clay potters, hosted by the School of American Research in Santa Fe, where participants both learned from and taught each other. McHorse has also taught classes at the Poeh Cultural Center at Pojoaque Pueblo.

McHorse's pottery has caught the eyes of judges and collectors alike at leading competitions in the Southwest. Since 1984 she has won major awards at the annual Santa Fe Indian Market. She has also won several major awards at the Museum of Northern Arizona's Navajo Craftsmen Exhibition, including the coveted "Best of Show" award in 1990.

—Russell P. Hartman

McKAY, Mabel

Tribal affiliations: Pomo; Wintu; Patwin
Basketweaver

Born: Nice, Lake County, California, 12 January 1907; last representative of the Long Valley Cache Creek Pomo. **Family:** McKay's mother, grandmother and aunts were accomplished weavers and helped teach her the process of weaving. **Career:** Began basketweaving at age seven; taught basketry and lectured for fifty years; Medicine Woman, beginning 1925; interviewee and contributor to linguistic, anthropological, and folklore studies; worked for many years in an apple cannery. **Died:** June 1993.

Selected Group Exhibitions

1930	California State Indian Museum, Sacramento, California
1979	Pacific Western Traders, Folsom, California
1996	*The Fine Art of California Indian Basketry*, Crocker Art Museum, Sacramento, California

Collections

California State Indian Museum, Sacramento; Collection of Marchal McKay; Heard Museum, Phoenix, Arizona; Pacific Western Traders, Folsom, California; Smithsonian Institute, Washington, D.C.; State of California, Department of Parks and Recreation.

Publications

On McKAY: Books—*Mabel McKay: Weaving the Dream*, by Greg Sarris, University of California Press, Berkeley, 1995; *The Fine Art of California Indian Basketry*, by Brian Bibby, Crocker Art Museum, Sacramento, 1996. **Articles**—"On the Road to Lolsel: Conversations with Mabel McKay," by Greg Sarris, *News from Native California,* September/October 1988; "Big Times/Little Times,"

Mabel McKay: Feather basket. Photograph by Seth Roffman; courtesy Dick Howard collection.

by Vera Mae Fredrickson, *News from Native California,* July/August 1989; "Mabel McKay," by Bruce Bernstein, *American Indian Art Magazine,* Winter 1995. **Film**—*Mabel McKay and Bertha (Wright) Mitchell,* by Dorothy Hill, California State University, Chico, 1974.

* * *

Mabel McKay was born north of San Francisco on a ranch near Nice, California. Her Patwin maternal Grandmother, Sarah Taylor, raised her. Taylor's brother, Richard, was a Dream Dancer—a doctor and prophet—who revived the practice of spiritual healing among the Pomo. He prophesied one day that people would fly in the sky all the way to the moon. McKay was influenced by Sarah and Richard Taylor and was also close to Essie Parish, the great Kashaya Pomo prophet; upon her death McKay was buried next to Parish. By the time she was five, Mabel, who had been a sickly child, already experienced a number of powerful dreams that eventually would direct her to a life of traditional healing. She also linked her talent for basketweaving to her dreams. The spirit she experienced provided direction for her life and inspiration for her basketweaving. She was the last to practice the Bole Maru (Dream Dance) healing arts and the last representative of the Long Valley Cache Creek

Pomo, but she spread the wealth of culture, art, and medicine throughout her life in countless lectures and interviews, as well as through healing practices.

Medicine and healing were interwoven in her continuation of the 5,000 year old Pomo basketry tradition. She stated: "my basket-making goes with my healing. When I am asked to make a basket for a person, I put that person's name down in my book and I pray on it. I cannot finish the basket until that prayer is answered."

McKay was famous for her beautiful beaded and feather baskets in which a feather is woven-in on every other stitch, creating soft designs. Many of her "feathered jewels" were decorated with clam shell beads; in some pieces she added European trade beads and abalone shell pendants. Dorothy Hill made a videotape of McKay in 1974 in which the weaver explained, "I get most of my enjoyment working with the feathers. The bird is very sacred to us. Also, the traditional weavers, when they weave their baskets, when they kill their own birds, they eat the birds. They do not let it spoil. [When] Feather-basket weaving, we do not eat. We work hours first thing in the morning. And as you get hungry, you push it to side. And when you eat, you don't touch it no more till next day."

The process of weaving held special spiritual significance, beginning with the gathering of roots and other basketry materials. McKay was a master botanist. She prayed and often sang to the plants before selecting certain roots. Her tan material was sedge root from a grass that grows along creek banks. One of her favorite gathering spots was close to her grandmother's old village, called Wild Tobacco. Her baskets are prized examples of traditional weaving as well as the unique designs she created with materials she gathered.

Through McKay, a better knowledge of Pomo culture emerged as she shared her experiences, those of her area, and how they are applied not only to arts and medicine but to more mundane practices, including clothe swashing, fruit and nut picking and canning. Even as Pomo society became splintered by missionization and the dissipation of traditional villages, the dynamic spiritual life, which came through the medium of dreams, was sustained by McKay during her lifetime and through records of her talks and lectures, and perhaps best symbolized in her artwork, which contributed an important functionality as well as adornment from materials collected and woven with a sense of reverence.

—Gregory Schaaf

McMASTER, Gerald

Tribal affiliations: Plains Cree
Painter, mixed media artist, installation artist, and photographer

Born: Red Pheasant, Saskatchewan, 9 March 1953. **Education:** Institute of American Indian Arts, AFA, 1973-75; Minneapolis College of Art and Design, B.F.A., 1975-77; Banff School of Fine Arts, 1986; Carleton University, M.A., Anthropology, 1994; Ph.D. candidate, Amsterdam School of Cultural Analysis, Amsterdam, Holland, 1997. **Career:** Head, Indian Art programme, Saskatchewan Indian Federated College, University of Regina, 1977-81; curator of Contemporary Indian Art, Canadian Museum of Civilization, Hull, Quebec, 1981—; adjunct research professor, Carleton University, 1992—; sang with the Red Earth Singers on *Songs from Bismarck,* Indian Records, Taos, New Mexico, 1976; conference coordinator,

Second National Native Artists Conference, University of Regina, 1979; numerous commissions, including *Songs from the Battlefords*, record jacket, Canyon Records, Children's Book Illustrations, Saskatchewan Public Libraries, Regina, 1975, *Byron and his Balloon*, La Loche Learning Centre, La Loche, Saskatchewan, 12 watercolours, 1981, *Indian Hunting Traditions*, National Film Board, Montreal, 48 watercolours, 1982, record jacket for *Big, Big World*, The Parachute Club, Toronto, 1988, and murals for City of Ottawa/OC Transpo, Riverside Station, 1991, and Metro-Hall, Toronto, 1992; Juror, including *Art Amerindien '81*, Ottawa, Sculpture for the Olympic Oval, University of Calgary, Alberta, 1986, Canadian Mint, 1989 gold coin, St. Marie among the Hurons. **Awards:** Scottsdale Annual Indian Art Competition, 1976; First prize, *Byron and his Balloon* (illustrations), La Loche, Saskatchewan, 1981; several Canada Council Travel Grants. **Member:** Board, Inuit Art Foundation, 1991-93, Canadian Museums Association, 1991-93, Ontario Arts Council, 1991-94, ICOM-Canada, 1992-95, National Museum of the American Indian, Smithsonian Institute, Washington, D.C., 1995-98; Native Art Studies Association of Canada, vice-president, 1987, president, 1988-89, general editor, NASAC Newsletter, 1988-92. **Address:** c/o Canadian Museum of Civilization, 100 Laurier St., P.O. Box 3100, Station "B", Hull, Quebec J8X 4H2, Canada; phone 819-776-8443, fax 819-776-8300.

Individual Exhibitions

1981   *Sun Series*, Gallery 101, Ottawa, Ontario

1985   *Riel Remembered*, traveling exhibition organized by the Thunder Bay Art Gallery, Ontario

1988   *Ancients Singing*, Ufundi Gallery, Ottawa, Ontario
       T.P. Series, traveling exhibition organized by the Organization of Saskatchewan Arts Councils

1989   *Eclectic Baseball*, Ufundi Gallery, Ottawa, Ontario

1990-91 *The cowboy/Indian Show*, Ufundi Gallery, Ottawa, Ontario; McMichael Canadian Gallery, Kleinburg, Ontario

1992   *Savage Graces: "afterimages" by Gerald McMaster*, UBC-Museum of Anthropology, Vancouver, British Columbia

1993   *Crossfires of Identity*, Agnes Etherington Art Centre, Kingston & Carleton University Art Gallery, Ottawa, Ontario

1994-95 *Savage Graces: "afterimages" by Gerald McMaster*, Ottawa Art Gallery, Ontario; Southern Alberta Art Gallery, Lethbridge; Windsor Art Gallery, Ontario; Winnipeg Art Gallery, Manitoba; Memorial Art Gallery, St. John's, Newfoundland; Edmonton Art Gallery, Alberta

Selected Group Exhibitions

1974   *Indian Art '74*, Royal Ontario Museum, Toronto, Ontario
       Sculpture II, Heard Museum, Phoenix, Arizona

1975   *American Indian Artists Students' Exhibition*, Institute of American Indian Arts, Santa Fe, New Mexico

1977   *Graduating Show*, Minneapolis College of Art and Design, Minnesota

1979   *Indian Art Faculty Show*, Norman Mackenzie Art Gallery, Regina, Saskatchewan
       Three Prairie Artists, Kesik Gallery, Regina, Saskatchewan

1980   *Contemporary Art by Saskatchewan Indians*, Shoestring Gallery, Saskatoon, Saskatchewan

1981   *Tradition and Change*, University of Regina, Saskatchewan

1982   *Renewal*, Thunder Bay National Exhibition Centre and Center for Indian Art, Ontario

1983   *Indian Art '83*, Woodland Indian Cultural Educational Centre, Brantford, Ontario
       Directions: An Exhibition of Masterworks, Northwestern National Exhibition, Hazelton, British Columbia
       Contemporary Native American Art, Southern Plains Indian Museum, Anadarko, Oklahoma

1984   *Indian Art '84*, Woodland Indian Cultural Educational Centre, Brantford, Ontario
       Contemporary Native American Photography, Southern Plains Indian Museum, Anadarko, Oklahoma

1985   *Two Worlds: Contemporary Canadian Indian Art from the Collection of Indian & Northern Affairs, Canada*, Indian Art Centre, Hull, Quebec
       Indian Art '85, Woodland Indian Cultural Educational Centre, Brantford, Ontario

1988   *Indian Art '88*, Woodland Indian Cultural Educational Centre, Brantford, Ontario

1988-89 *T.P. Series*, Saskatchewan Arts Council (traveling)

1989   *Why Do You Call Us Indians?*, Ufundi Gallery, Ottawa, Ontario
       Indian Art '89 Woodland Indian Cultural Educational Centre, Brantford, Ontario

1990   *Why Do You Call Us Indians?*, Gettysburg College Art Gallery, Pennsylvania
       Last Chance, Saw Gallery, Ottawa, Ontario
       First Nations Art '90, Woodland Indian Cultural Educational Centre, Brantford, Ontario

1991   *Solidarity: Art After Oka*, Saw Gallery, Ottawa, Ontario

1992   *Eco-Art*, Rio de Frances, Brazil
       Contemporary First Nations Art, Ufundi Gallery, Ottawa, Ontario
       Enduring Strength, Intermedia Arts Minnesota/Two Rivers Gallery, Minneapolis

1994   *10 Contemporary Indian Artists from Canada and the United States*, Kunsthallen Brandts Klaedefabrik, Odense, Denmark
       Savage Graces "After Images," The Ottawa Art Gallery, Ontario
       Niya Nehiyaw: Crossfires of Identity, Carleton University Art Gallery, Ottawa, Ontario

1995   *Longing and Belonging: From the Faraway Nearby*, SITE Santa Fe, New Mexico

Collections

Canada Council Art Bank, Ottawa, Ontario; Canadian Museum of Civilization, Ottawa, Ontario; Carleton University, Ottawa; City of Ottawa, Ontario; City of Regina, Saskatchewan; Gettysburg College, Gettysburg, Pennsylvania; Guilford Native American Art Gallery, Greensboro, North Carolina; Indian Art Centre, Dept. of Indian Affairs, Ottawa; Institute of American Indian Arts, Santa Fe, New Mexico; Nickle Art Gallery, Calgary, Alberta; Norman MacKenzie Art Gallery, Regina, Saskatchewan; McMichael Canadian Collection, Kleinburg, Ontario; Museum fur Volkerkunde, Vienna, Austria; Peking Chinese Opera, Peking, People's Republic

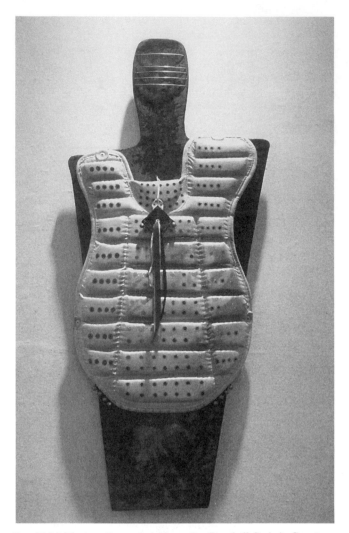

Gerald McMaster: *Protection* (from the *Baseball Series*). **Courtesy of the artist.**

of China; Walter Phillips Gallery, Banff Centre, Banff, Alberta; Saskatchewan Indian Cultural College, Saskatoon; Thunder Bay Art Gallery, Thunder Bay, Ontario; University of Regina, Saskatchewan; University of Saskatchewan, Saskatoon.

Publications

By McMASTER: Books and Catalogs—*Byron and his Balloon*, written by David May with direction from Lynn (Atkins) McMaster and illustrations by Gerald McMaster, Tree Frog Press, Edmonton, 1984; *CHALLENGES*, de Meervaart Cultural Centre, Amsterdam, 1985; *INDIGENA: Contemporary Native Perspectives*, edited by Gerald McMaster and Lee-Ann Martin, Douglas & McIntyre, Vancouver, 1992; *Edward Poitras Canada XLVI Biennale di Venezia*, Canadian Museum of Civilization, Hull, Quebec, 1995; *Jeffery Thomas: Portraits from the Dancing Grounds*, Ottawa Art Gallery, Ontario, 1996; *Mary Longman: Traces*, Kamloops Art Gallery, British Columbia, 1996. **Essays**—"A Wearable At Form: 19th Century Robe Paintings," *Canadian Home Economics Journal*, Edmonton, Summer 1983; "Tenuous Lines of Descent: Indian Arts and Crafts of the Reservation Period," *Im Schatten der Sonne*,

Stuttgart, Cantz, 1988, also published in *The Canadian Journal of Native Studies*, vol. 9, no. 2, 1989; "The Contemporary Indian Art Collection at the Canadian Museum of Civilization," with Lee-Ann Martin, *American Indian Art Magazine*, Autumn 1990; "How the West was Lost: An Artist's Perspective," *European Review of Native American Studies*, vol. 5, no. 2, 1991, also published in *Gatherings: The En'owkin Journal of First North American Peoples*, vol. 2, 1991; "INDIGENA: A Native Curator's Perspective," *Art Journal*, College Art Association, Fall 1992; "Paint, Sculpt, Draw!," in *ArtSource: Resource Guide to the Arts, Visual Arts in Canada: Painting, Drawing and Sculpture*, Secretary of State/Multiculturalism and Citizenship, Ottawa, 1992; "Colonial Alchemy: Reading the Boarding School Experience," *Partial Recall: Photographs of Native North Americans,* edited by Lucy Lippard, The New Press, New York, 1992; "Border Zones: The 'Injun-uity' of Aesthetic Tricks." *Cultural Studies*, vol. 9, no 1, 1994; "I Feel at Home With My Ancestors: A Canadian Perspective," in *American Visions: Artistic and Cultural Identity in the Western Hemisphere*, edited by Noreen Tomassi, Mary Jane Jacob and Ivo Mesquita, American Council for the Arts and Allworth Press, New York, 1994; "Gerald McMaster: Discovering the levels of Meaning," in *All Roads Are Good: Native Voices on Life and Culture*, National Museum of the American Indian and Smithsonian Press, Washington, D.C., 1994; "The Politics in Canadian Native Art," in *Mandate Study 1990-93: An Investigation of Issues Surrounding the Exhibition, Collection and Interpretation of Contemporary Art by First Nations Artists*, Thunder Bay Art Gallery, Ontario, 1994; "Bering Strait Jacket," in *Teresa Marshall: The Deportment of Indian Affairs*, exhibition catalog, A Space Gallery, Toronto, 1995; "Object (to) Sanctity: The Politics of the Object," *International Journal of Canadian Studies*, Fall 1995; "Creating Spaces," in *Thinking About Exhibitions*, edited by Reesa Greenberg, Bruce W. Ferguson, and Sandy Nairne, Routledge, New York, 1996; "The Subject of Displacement: A Response to the Judicial Decision Regarding What Constitutes a Work of Art that is Neither Canadian nor Indian Enough to be part of the said Collection," *FUSE* Magazine, Spring 1997; "Towards an Aboriginal Art History," in *20th Century Native American Art: Essays on History and Criticism*, edited by W. Jackson Rushing, Routledge, London, 1997. **Interviews**—"Crossfires of Identity: An Interview with Gerald McMaster," in *Talking Stick: First Nations Arts Magazine*, Winter 1994; "An Interview with Gerald McMaster," in *Akwe:kon Journal*, Spring 1994.

On McMASTER: Books—*The Second Generation: Fourteen Saskatchewan Painters*, by Norman Zepp and Michael Parke-Taylor, Norman MacKenzie Art Gallery, University of Regina, Saskatchewan, 1985; *Why Do You Call Us Indians?*, by Amelia M. Trevelyan, Gettysburg College Art Gallery, Pennsylvania, 1990; *The cowboy/Indian Show*, by Allan Ryan, *McMichael Canadian Art Collection*, Kleinburg, Ontario, 1990; *In the Shadow of the Sun*, Canadian Ethnology Service Mercury Series Paper 124, Canadian Museum of Civilization, 1993. **Articles**—"Exhibits Shouldn't Be Missed," by Lorna Burke, *Regina Leader Post*, 3 November 1979; "Indian Art Throws Off Limitations," by Jean Richards, *Edmonton Journal*, 4 April 1980; "Native art illuminated by sun's presence," by Nancy Baele, *Ottawa Citizen*, 17 October 1981; "Teacher-artist's commitment extends beyond work as curator," by Bill White, *Echo*, National Museums of Canada, October/November 1984; "Beside and Beyond the Mainstream," *Artweek*, 2 November 1985; "Token & Taboo," Alfred Young Man, *FUSE* Magazine, July 1988; "Baseball as a mystical art form," by Nancy Baele, *Ottawa Citizen*, 21

September 1989; "Review of Ancients Singing," by Jacqueline Fry, *PARACHUTE*, December-February 1990; "Native painter's criticism packs strong punchline," by Christopher Hume, *Toronto Star*, 8 February 1991; "Peeping across ignorance barriers," by Michael Valpy, *Toronto Globe and Mail*, 26 March 1991; "Stereotypes Under De (Construction)," by Charlotte Townsend-Gault, *Border Crossings*, vol. 11, no. 4, 1992; "Review," by Robin Laurence, *Canadian Art*, Winter 1992.

*   *   *

As writer, scholar and curator, as well as fine artist, Gerald McMaster is a central figure in the contemporary art world. In many ways, a look at the progress of his career is as revealing a look at his practice of art, as the objects themselves. He has moved from the examination and often ironic reinterpretation of historic photographs on a grand scale, to years of creating spectacularly beautiful and profound paintings. From there, he moved into a relatively brief period devoted to ironic constructions, then to a combination of all three of his earliest interests in the *cowboy/Indian* series. Most recently he has devoted himself to installations that re-present many of the ideas explored earlier but with a fresh twist and, often, in wholly new media.

Throughout, his work has been characterized by a strong aesthetic interest in surface. Regardless of medium and content, the creation of wonderfully rich surfaces has been a hallmark of his style, beginning with the monumental graphite works of the early 1980s. The haunting paintings of the mid- to late-1980s are characterized by McMaster's virtuoso application of paint on richly colored canvases. The wonderfully ironic works of the *Baseball* and *cowboy/Indian* series that followed include similarly spectacular treatment of surface, whether on painted baseballs or large canvases. Even his most recent work, although developed from new media and, in one case at least, constructed of objects created by others, proceeds clearly from McMaster's distinctly rich appreciation for the aesthetics of surface. The spectacular installation of beaded and quilled moccasins created for the opening of the National Museum of the American Indian in the Customs House in lower Manhattan (1994) is no exception to this general rule. McMaster's selection of the moccasins to use in this monumental spiraling construction serves once again to highlight his ongoing interest in rich surface texture, as well as a magnificent color sense.

In his paintings this aesthetic is manifested in many ways. First, there is a sense of almost total freedom in his wielding of the brush. Chronologically speaking, that comes as a bit of a surprise after the exacting precision of his early works in graphite. Despite that freedom, the brush is only rarely laden with paint—textures are almost never gooey—and passages of quickly applied paint often fade into raw canvas as the brush becomes increasingly dry. Where it is thick, the paint is applied in layers of rich and vibrant color. His use of pinks, reds and turquoises is especially striking and often punctuated by the addition of text or other linear elements, scratched and rubbed into the wet color.

Except for the quite literal and descriptive precision of the early graphite works, forms are rarely representational. Almost all of the paintings involve figure studies to some degree, but features are indistinct or left out entirely. If they exist at all, facial features are usually limited to the eyes. The figures themselves are little more than torsos with heads. This approach to the human/spirit form is common in the sacred arts of many Plains and Woodlands tribes. McMaster has examined and explored the nature and significance of

this form over many years and it is the basis for many of his most haunting and powerful works. The motif clearly has personal as well as aesthetic significance for him, since, when the head is presented in profile, it bears an unmistakable relationship to the artist's own features. The continual reappearance of this motif in McMaster's work, regardless of context—from the deeply spiritual paintings of the mid- to late-1980s to wryly comic works in the *cowboy/Indian* series—suggests that it may act as an important vehicle for self-examination. Small nucleated circles represent another recurring motif in McMaster's work, also drawn from traditional native art, especially that of Plains peoples.

Combined with the armless, legless and often horned torso form, they give his paintings a deeply spiritual quality, a sense of indistinct, but palpable sacredness. The profound character of some of these paintings eventually became problematic for McMaster. Comments by the artist in Allan Ryan's catalog of the *cowboy/Indian* exhibition suggest this, as well as McMaster's rather abrupt return to themes of ironic, if frequently biting, cultural and political humor that characterized his earlier work after deep immersion into this more somber mode.

These same haunting motifs continue to appear in later works, but their power is turned to different ends. The elements of humor and irony in paintings from the *cowboy/Indian* show and constructions like *Protection*, from the *Baseball* series, tend to redirect the heavier sacred content of the images. At the same time, the power of those forms lends a depth of significance and feeling to the lighter message of the paintings, providing each with an underlying profundity that belies the deceptively light-hearted content that moves across their surfaces.

Like other major figures in the world of mainstream contemporary native art, McMaster has become less active in the creation of new art work in the last few years. His time is increasingly taken up by writing on the subject, the curation of large exhibits and activity on the governing and advisory boards of major arts publications and institutions. This is a phenomenon of the multiple realities of life as a native person in a leadership role in North American society. The rich and often ironic content of contemporary native art is born, in part, of the dualities faced by all indigenous peoples in the postcolonial world. The need to process and express the complexities of that position, as well as the need to deal with the problems and conflicts faced by every citizen of the world today, regardless of ethnicity, is fundamental to the profound power of the best artwork created by artists like Gerald McMaster. It should not be surprising that the creative energy of such artists might be as readily applied to the concrete realities of life in the Americas as it is to their creative expression in artistic media.

—Amelia M. Trevelyan

McNEIL, Larry
Tribal affiliations: Tlingit; Nishga
Photographer

Born: Juneau, Alaska, 12 May 1955. **Education:** Brooks Institute School of Photographic Art and Science, Santa Barbara, California. **Career:** Commissions include Alaska Native Foundation, 1983, to illustrate Yupik Eskimo women weaving distinctive grass baskets, Kootznoowoo Corporation, 1986, seventeen portraits of tribal clan leaders, Northwest Arctic School District, 1986; vice-president, Native Indian Inuit Photographers Association; instructor, Institute of American Indian Arts; commercial photographer. **Awards:** Award of Excellence, Public Relations Society of America, 1983; Merit Award, Advertising Federation of America, 1983-86; Outstanding Photographic Technical Quality and Outstanding Outdoor Photography, Native Inuit Photography Association, 1992. **Address:** c/o American Indian Contemporary Arts, San Francisco, California.

Individual Exhibitions

1986   *Larry McNeil: NorthLight,* Western States Museum of Photography, Santa Barbara, California

Selected Group Exhibitions

1982   Anchorage Fine Arts Museum, Anchorage, Alaska
1983   Angoon Heritage Center, Alaska
1984   *Rarefied Light,* Artique Gallery, Anchorage, Alaska
        American Society of Magazine Photographers Exhibit, Stonington Gallery, Anchorage, Alaska
1985   *Photographing Ourselves,* Heard Museum, Phoenix, Arizona
        The Photograph and the American Indian, Princeton University, New Jersey
        Rarefied Light II, Cone Arts Gallery, Juneau, Alaska
1987   *New Directions Northwest,* Portland Art Museum, Oregon
1989   *Personal Preferences,* American Indian Contemporary Arts, San Francisco, California
        Northern Visions, American Indian Contemporary Arts, San Francisco, California
        Native American Expressions of Surrealism, Sacred Circle Gallery, Seattle, Washington
1990   *Compensating Imbalances,* Galeria Posada, Sacramento, California
        Contemporary Expressions, Southwest Museum, Los Angeles, California
1990-91 *Language of the Lens,* Heard Museum, Phoenix, Arizona
1991   *The Haida Project,* University of California, Davis
1992   *Ancestral Memories,* Falkirk Cultural Center, San Rafael, California
        Message Carriers, Photographic Resource Center, Boston University
        We the Human Beings, College of Wooster Art Museum, Wooster College, Ohio
1993   *Native American Connections Revisited,* Gallery 53 Artworks, Cooperstown, New York
1994-95 American Indian Contemporary Arts, San Francisco, California
1995   Institute of American Indian Arts Museum, Santa Fe, New Mexico
1996   *Native Arts Network,* University of Tulsa, Oklahoma, sponsored by Atlatl, Phoenix

Collections

Angoon Heritage Center, Alaska; Princeton University; Heard Museum, Phoenix, Arizona; Sealaska Heritage Foundation, Juneau, Alaska; University of Alaska, Fairbanks.

Publications

By McNEIL: Books—*Handbooks on North American Indians* (illustrations), Smithsonian Institution, Washington, D.C., 1981.

On McNEIL: Book—*New Directions Northwest: Contemporary Native American Art,* Portland Art Museum, 1986; *Stronghearts: Native American Visions and Voices,* Aperture, New York, 1995.

*   *   *

In the genre of photography, Larry McNeil's work stands out because it encompasses a wide range of subjects and formats, from formal realist portraits of tribal elders, to whimsical abstract cityscapes, to surreal electronic manipulations of tribal environments. McNeil's eye constantly roams the landscape, seeing physical beauty as well as political irony in a variety of people and places. As a result, he produces images that are personally meaningful, often eclectic and sometimes iconoclastic, but nevertheless representative of tribal realities and sensitive to the politics of representation.

McNeil was born in 1955 in Juneau, Alaska, to Tlingit and Nishga parents. He attended the Brooks Institute School of Photographic Art and Science, in Santa Barbara, California, where he majored in illustration. He recalls being asked by a teacher why he was interested in photography, and his original reply still holds true. "It always goes back to the same thing, even now. I still feel like Native Americans are not represented accurately in the media. And I thought, well, if I feel that way, what am I going to do about it?"

McNeil started out taking documentary-style photographs of his own people. In time his subject matter expanded, and he started experimenting with different photographic technologies. *Bananascape* (1986, published in *New Directions Northwest: Contemporary Native American Art*) is a trio of cibachrome prints that illustrate the trajectory of a banana flying through the air. The skyscraper background creates a juxtaposition that is both totemic, in a modern sense, and surreal. In his current work, McNeil returns to his native territory, but transfers photographic images of landscapes to the computer, where there is a greater possibility for manipulation.

A great honor bestowed on McNeil was a commission in 1983 from the Kootznoowoo Tribal Corporation, in the village of Angoon, Alaska. The corporation was building a tribal house that would serve as a museum and storehouse for regalia, and the tribal tradition was to commission artwork for the building. Someone in the village had seen McNeil's earlier documentary photography, and suggested commissioning formal portraits of village elders. McNeil was flattered by their request and surprised that elders wanted artwork in a contemporary medium for their tribal museum. The resulting silver gelatin photographs of clan leaders in their traditional regalia have been shown in several exhibits, including *Portfolio II* (1988). The images are powerful, especially when the viewer understands the cultural connection between the photographer and his subjects.

McNeil's recent work leans more toward the abstract and the metaphorical. In his black-and-white *Feather* series (1992), McNeil manipulates the image of a single object, the feather, to tell a story about indigenous peoples and fate. The first image of the series depicts a single, vertical feather held against a turbulent sky. Its title, *1491,* refers to the state of Native America before "interference," as McNeil calls it. The second image shows the same feather, horizontal, lying above a human skull. Wisps of smoke circle around the skull and feather, both objects stark white against the black background. This image is titled *1492*.

Another image in the series offers a ray of hope. In *Circle of Rebirth*, a tiny feather lies next to a larger feather, an "homage to fellow Native Americans who struggle, often against incredible odds, to maintain their identity, to continue the circle of life." Five images from the *Feathers* series are published in *Stronghearts: Native American Visions and Voices* (1995), a seminal collection of contemporary Native American photography.

—Margaret Dubin

MEDICINE FLOWER, Grace

Variant names: Wopovi Poviwah
Tribal affiliations: Santa Clara Pueblo
Potter

Born: Grace Tafoya, Santa Clara Pueblo, 13 December 1938. **Family:** Member of the renowned Tafoya family of potters that includes Camilio and Agapita Silva (her father and mother), Margaret (her aunt), and Joseph Lonewolf (her brother) from Santa Clara Pueblo. **Education:** Espanola high school, Brownings Commercial School; trained in potterymaking by her parents. **Career:** Temporary work, including secretarial, 1959-62; full-time potter beginning 1962; instructor, Santa Clara Pueblo. **Awards:** Numerous, from the annual Santa Fe Indian Market, Heard Museum Guild Arts and Crafts Exhibit, Scottsdale National Indian Art Show, Gallup Inter-Tribal Indian Ceremonial, American Indian Arts Show in Denver, and eight Northern Indian Pueblo Art Shows.

Selected Group Exhibitions

Works have been consistently exhibited since the 1960s at Santa Clara Pueblo and major art fairs in the southwest.

1974   *Pueblo Pottery*, Washington, D.C., venues include The White House, Smithsonian Institution, and National Gallery
1976   *Seven Families in Pueblo Pottery*, Maxwell Museum of Anthropology, University of New Mexico, Albuquerque
1977   Wheelwright Museum of the American Indian, Santa Fe, New Mexico
1979   *One Space, Three Visions*, Albuquerque Museum, New Mexico
1981   *American Indian Art in the 1980s*, The Native American Center for the Living Arts, Niagara Falls, New York
        Heard Museum, Phoenix, Arizona
        Eiteljorg Museum of American Indians and Western Art, Indianapolis, Indiana

Publications

On MEDICINE FLOWER: Books—*Seven Families in Pueblo Pottery* (1974) and *Fourteen Families in Pueblo Pottery* (1994), by Rick Dillingham, University of New Mexico Press, Albuquerque; *Southwestern Indian Arts and Crafts*, by Ray Manley, Ray Manley Photography, Tucson, 1975; *Art and Indian Individualists,* by Guy and Doris Monthan, Northland Press, Flagstaff, 1975; *Santa Clara Pottery Today*, by Betty LeFree, Albuquerque, 1975; "Interview," with Jane Katz, *This Song Remembers: Self Portraits of North Americans in the Arts*, by Mario Klimiades, Houghton Mifflin, Boston, 1980; *Artistry in Clay*, by Don Dedera, Northland Publishing, Flagstaff, 1985; *Talking with the Clay. The Art of Pueblo Pottery*, by Stephen Trimble, School of American Research Press, Santa Fe, 1987; *Beyond Tradition: Contemporary American Indian Art and Its Evolution*, by Jerry and Lois Jacka, Northland Publishing, Flagstaff, 1988. **Articles**—"Southwestern Pottery Today," by Patrick T. Houlihan, *Arizona Highways,* May 1974; "American Indian Artists: Joseph Lonewolf, Grace Medicine Flower," by Marjel De Lauer, *Arizona Highways,* August 1976; "Pueblo Pottery—2000 Years of Artistry," *National Geographic Magazine,* by David Arnold, November 1982; "Homage to the Clay Lady," by Ronald McCoy, *Southwest Profile*, March 1990. **Film**—*American Indian Artists*, PBS-TV, documentary series, produced at KAET-TV, Tempe, Arizona, 1976.

*   *   *

An innovator within the world of traditional Native American pottery, Grace Medicine Flower is best known for her carved, sgraffito miniature pieces. She applies red or black slip (liquid clay) to her miniature pieces of pottery that usually range in size from 3/8ths of an inch to about 2 inches. When the slip is dry, she carves intricate designs into the clay; many of the designs are based on those of the prehistoric Mimbres people. After firing the clay, the finished pieces are delicate, two colored designed vessels.

Medicine Flower was born into the famous Tafoya pottery family. She learned traditional pottery making from her mother and father, Agapita and Camilio Tafoya. She continues to employ traditional methods, gathering clay from the hills surrounding Santa Clara, drying it in the sun for several days, soaking the clay, and sifting it for impurities. She employs the coiling technique to build the pot and uses gourds to smooth the surface. After smoothing the piece, she applies a red earth clay and then polishes the piece with stones. Firing is done in the open, on metal grates over woodchips.

Medicine Flower began creating pottery seriously for art shows in 1964. She signed her pieces as Grace Hoover (her married name) or Grace with a flower symbol, and more recently as Grace Medicine Flower, with a flower symbol. Sometimes her pieces were signed with her name and that of her father, Camilio, who mentored her when she became a serious, full-time potter in the early 1960s. Her brother, Joseph Lonewolf, also collaborates with her on some pieces. Both siblings sign their names to the finished piece. Medicine Flower and Lonewolf are renowned for perfecting the sgraffito technique; the designs, incised after the slip is applied and before polish and firing, make the pottery a unique form of fine art. Medicine Flower has also introduced pastel-colored pottery, especially appropriate for the floral motifs she favors. Medicine Flower's designs, which are harmonious with the shape of each individual pot, include such traditional motifs as bear claws, serpents, feathers, and kiva steps as well as butterflies, hummingbirds, flowers, and deer.

Medicine Flower's pottery has won numerous awards over the years, and just as she has helped extend and expand the tradition of Santa Clara pottery, she is now teaching the techniques within her community.

—Leona Zastrow

MEDINA, Rafael

Variant names: Teeyacheena
Tribal affiliations: Zia Pueblo
Painter

Born: Zia Pueblo, New Mexico, 19 September 1929. **Education:** Santa Fe Indian School, where his teachers included Velino Shije Herrera, Jose Rey Toledo, and Geronima Cruz Montoya. **Awards:** Numerous at fairs and juried competitions during the 1960s and 1970s, including American Indian Art Exhibition, Detroit, Heard Museum Guild Indian Fair and Market, Phoenix, Inter-Tribal Indian Ceremonial, Gallup, 1970, Philbrook Museum of Art Annual Indian Art Exhibition, Tulsa, and Scottsdale National Indian Art Exhibition, Scottsdale.

Selected Group Exhibitions

Exhibited regularly at fairs in the southwest, southern Plains, and midwest during the 1960s and 1970s.

1955   *An Exhibition of American Indian Painting,* James Graham and Sons, New York
1968   *The James T. Bialac Collection of Southwest Indian Paintings,* Arizona State Museum, Tucson (traveling)
1978   *100 Years of Native American Painting,* Oklahoma Museum of Art, Oklahoma City
1979-80 *Native American Paintings,* organized by the Joslyn Art Museum, Omaha, Nebraska (traveling)
1980   *Native American Art at the Philbrook,* Philbrook Museum of Art, Tulsa, Oklahoma
1982   *Native American Painting: Selections from the Museum of the American Indian,* Heard Museum, Phoenix, Arizona
1984-85 *Indianascher Kunstler* (traveling, Germany), organized by the Philbrook Museum, Tulsa, Oklahoma
1990   *American Indian Artists in the Avery Collection and the McNay Permanent Collection,* Koogler McNay Art Museum, San Antonio, Texas
1996   *Drawn from Memory: James T. Bialac Collection of Native American Art,* Heard Museum, Phoenix, Arizona

Collections

Arizona State Museum, University of Arizona, Tucson; Museum of New Mexico, Santa Fe; Museum of Northern Arizona, Flagstaff; National Museum of the American Indian, Washington, D.C.; Philbrook Museum of Art, Tulsa, Oklahoma; Millicent Rogers Foundation Museum, Taos, New Mexico; Roswell Museum and Art Center, Roswell, New Mexico.

Publications

On MEDINA: Books—*Southwest Indian Painting: A Changing Art,* Tucson, 1973; *Song from the Earth: American Indian Painting,* by Jamake Highwater, Boston, 1976; *100 Years of Native American Painting,* exhibition catalog by Arthur Silberman, Oklahoma Museum of Art, Oklahoma City, 1978; *Native American Painting,* by Frederick Schmid and Patrick T. Houlihan, American Indian Painting and Sculpture, Kansas City, 1980; *Native American Art at the Philbrook,* by John Mahey, et. al, Tulsa, 1980, by Patricia Broder,

New York, 1981; *Indianascher Kunstler,* by Gerhard Hoffman, Munich, 1984; *American Indian Artists in the Avery Collection and the McNay Permanent Collection,* edited by Jean Sherrod Williams, San Antonio, 1990.

*   *   *

Rafael Medina's paintings are rendered in the traditional descriptive manner of Pueblo painting of the twentieth century, beginning with his early, conventional works most important for their authentic depiction of Pueblo ceremonies. He developed increasingly greater concern for telling details, modeling and movement of figures, and color patterning, most in evidence in his works from the 1960s onward. These individual flourishes coupled with his mastery of the style make him a major Pueblo painter of the second half of the twentieth century.

That Medina paints in the traditional Pueblo manner developed in the twentieth century is not surprising, considering two of his mentors at the Santa Fe Indian School he attended during the 1940s were early masters of the style—Jose Rey Toledo and Velino Shije Herrera. Herrera was among the first generation of modern Pueblo painters who began working previous to 1920, and Toledo, his nephew, was one of the major artists carrying the tradition into and beyond the middle of the century. Medina's early works were extremely faithful to his subjects, usually dancers, carefully recreating colors and controlled movement in a monotone setting, with no background or foreground. He later began adding symbols and design elements related to the ceremonies being performed by dancers and Koshares in blank spaces on the canvas. By the 1960s he became more adventurous: symbols are a larger and more important part of the presentation, details are even more intricate and capture the subtlest minutiae, figures are more active, and colors more vibrant. These elements can be viewed in *Answered Prayer* (1966) and *Desert Antelope Dance* (1969), both of which won awards at major southwestern art fairs. In both paintings designs symbolizing ritual activities and simple, decorative overtones contribute to the balance of the overall scene. Figures are more acutely rendered, with musculature and emotions more evident, revealing their individual personalities.

Koshares were of special interest to Medina and paintings featuring them are among his finest works. Especially in these paintings his technique for dispensing with background and foreground becomes most effective. Divorced from community settings, the Koshares dominate the paintings, stressing the necessity for the artist to capture them in acute detail in dynamic moments. His placement of symbols and design elements balanced with these animated figures. All of this Medina accomplishes, sometimes with great ingenuity. The dancer in *Koshare* (1968), for example, is captured in rhythmic movement, poised on one foot, with one arm crossing diagonally across the center of the painting, the other arm raised in open space and holding a rattle, and the other leg bent at the knee—a graceful image, tense with concentrated effort; this balance is further emphasized in the Koshare's body, where black stripes ring bodypaint half in yellow and half white. A piece of two-toned, ceramic pottery, finely detailed with images of a sinuous animal and Kachina masks, sits to the left of the dancer on one of three blocks, with the dancer on the middle block and needled vegetation to his right. The tiny mask motif on the pot is repeated in outline in the upper right corner of the painting, and a line that runs up from the vegetation, hovers over the dancer and comes down to the pot, unites the various elements and frames the dancer.

Medina's penchant for strong lines and geometric shapes are evident in this work, playing off the rounded muscles and animation of the dancer.

—Perry Bear

MEDINA, Trinidad
Tribal affiliations: Zia Pueblo
Potter

Born: Zia Pueblo, New Mexico, c. 1910. **Career:** Demonstrated potterymaking throughout the United States, 1930-46; instructed Zia potters, including her grandson, Raphael, and his wife, Sofia (neé Pino). **Awards:** Several, including first prize, Zia pottery, Santa Fe Indian Market, 1939. **Died:** Mid-1960s.

Selected Group Exhibitions

Medina's pottery was frequently exhibited at the Santa Fe Indian Market from 1936 through the 1950s as well as through traders, department stores, and at venues throughout the United States where she demonstrated potterymaking.

1933   Century of Progress Exhibition, Chicago, Illinois
1939   Golden Gate International Exposition, San Francisco, California

Collections

Museum of Indian Arts and Culture, Santa Fe, New Mexico; Museum of New Mexico, Santa Fe.

Publications

On MEDINA: Books—*Fourteen Families in Pueblo Pottery,* by Rick Dillingham, Santa Fe, 1994; *Art of Clay: Timeless Pottery of the Southwest,* edited by Lee M. Cohen, Santa Fe, 1995; *Southwestern Pottery: Anasazi to Zuni,* Flagstaff, 1996.

*   *   *

Trinidad Medina of Zia Pueblo was one of the best known potters of her village from the 1930s through her death in the mid-

Trinidad Medina: Storage olla, c. 1940. Courtesy Museum of Indian Arts and Culture, Santa Fe.

Trinidad Medina with her grandchildren at Zia Pueblo, c. 1960. Courtesy of the artist's family.

1960s. Medina toured the United States demonstrating Zia pottery-making from 1930-46 under the sponsorship of Wick Miller, a trader in the Southwest. She visited over a hundred cities throughout the country, demonstrating and selling her pottery mostly through the department store venues set up by Miller, who resided in San Isidro, New Mexico.

As one of the few potters of her generation from the conservative and insular Zia Pueblo willing to travel, Medina visited the Laboratory of Anthropology, Museum of New Mexico, in Santa Fe several times to study the Zia pottery collection. In 1939, she reportedly traveled to San Francisco to become part of the Indian Arts and Crafts Board exhibition at the 1939 International Exposition. This was the fist time an exhibition of American Indian arts and crafts was selected on the basis of aesthetic merit and not from the ethnological or anthropological viewpoint. She was a frequent exhibitor at Santa Fe's Indian Market (1936-50s), winning first prize in the Zia pottery category in 1939 for a magnificent olla that measures 22" in height and 78 ½" inches in circumference; this piece is in the collections of the Museum of Indian Arts and Culture, Santa Fe. She also made a number of larger ollas. Her pottery painting was always flawless. Although unsigned, her works are found in several museum and private collections.

Medina established a legacy of potters, which includes her granddaughter-in-law Sofia, and Sofia's children, daughter-in-law, and grandchildren: Marcellus, Elizabeth, Edan, Lois, Kimberly, and Marcella. As recorded by Rick Dillingham, Sofia Medina recalled Trinidad's view of Zia pottery: "She always told me instead of sitting around after the children went to school to work on pottery. Pottery making was important. Financially she could depend on that. She said she'd teach me—but first (she said), 'tell me and promise whatever I teach you, pass it on to my grandchildren so in the future they will profit from it and in the future my work would continue.'"

—Bruce Bernstein

MILLER, Kay
Tribal affiliations: Comanche; Métis
Painter

Born: Houston, Texas, 1946. **Education:** University of Houston, B.S., 1970; University of Texas, B.F.A., 1975; Naropa Institute, 1978; University of Texas, M.F.A., 1979. **Career:** Educator, Ohio State University, University of Nebraska, University of Iowa, University of Colorado; artist in residence, National Institute for Contemporary Art, New York.

Individual Exhibitions

1984   *Kay Miller/Paintings*, Formal Gallery, West Texas University, Canyon
1985   *Current Connector*, University of Iowa Museum of Art, Iowa City
1987   *Scouting*, Foxley/Leach Gallery, Washington, D.C.
1988   *Open Range*, University of Colorado Art Gallery, Boulder
        Light Gears, Arvada Center for the Arts, Colorado
1991   *Laughing Matters*, Artemisia Gallery, Chicago, Illinois
1993   *World Whirled*, Boulder Public Library, Colorado

Selected Group Exhibitions

1979   *Woman-In-Sight*, Doughtery Cultural Arts Center, Austin, Texas
1980   *Invitational*, Syracuse University, New York, and Massachusetts College of Art, Boston
1981   *Contemporary Native American Art*, Gardiner Gallery, Oklahoma State University (traveling)
1981   *Plain Primitive*, Gallery 71, Omaha, Nebraska
1982   *Delta Annual*, Little Rock Arts Center, Arkansas
1983   *Contemporary Native American Art* (travelled to Oklahoma, California, Montana, Iowa, New York)
        Discovery, Minnesota Museum of Art, St. Paul
1985   *Women of Sweetgrass, Cedar, and Sage*, American Indian Community House Gallery, New York (traveling)
        Corcoran Biennial of American Contemporary Painting, Corcoran Gallery of Art, Washington, D.C. (traveling)
        Kay Miller/Kay WalkingStick, Gorman Museum, University of California, Davis
        New Work: New York/Outside New York, New Museum of Contemporary Art, New York (traveling)
1986   Quintana Gallery, Portland, Oregon
        Seventh Heaven, New Museum of Contemporary Art, New York
1987   *Washington D.C. Artist Benefit for AIDS Research*
1988   *Colorado Women Artists*, National Museum of Women in the Arts, Washington, D.C. (traveling)
        Acts of Faith: Politics and the Spirit, Cleveland State University Art Gallery, Ohio (traveling)
1989   *Small, Curious Objects*, Carega/Leach Gallery, Washington, D.C.
        Sacred Objects, Boulder Art Center, Colorado
1990   *The Price of Power*, Cleveland Contemporary Art Center, Ohio
        True West, Cydney Payton Gallery, Denver, Colorado
        Away from the Center, Joslyn Art Museum, Omaha, Nebraska
1991   *Resident's Exhibit*, P.S. 1, National Institute for Contemporary Art, New York
        Show of Strength (Benefit for MADRE), Anne Plumb Gallery, New York
1992   *De-Colonizing the Mind*, Center for Contemporary Art, Seattle, Washington
        China Show, University of Southwest China Art Gallery, Chong Qing, China
        Remerika/Amerika! 1492-1992, Bertha and Karl Leubsdorf Art Gallery, Hunter College, New York
        Submuloc Society: Since 1492, (traveled through 1994)

1993   *The Seventh Generation*, New York (traveling)
1994   *Cultural Signs*, Herbert Johnson Museum of Art, Cornell University, Ithaca, New York
        Art from Detritus: Recycling with Imagination, Metro Center, Portland, Oregon
1995   *Maori and Overseas Artists*, Hei Tiki Gallery, Rotorua, New Zealand
        From Me to You, Higigashi, Hiroshima, and Fukuya Art Gallery, Tokyo, Japan
        On-Line Women Artists around the World, United Nations 4th World Conference on Women, Beijing, China
1996   *Tree of Life*, Boulder Public Library, Colorado

Collections

Apumoana Marae, Rotoruna, New Zealand; Denver Museum of Art, Colorado; Djerassi Foundation, Woodside, California; New Museum of Contemporary Art, New York; University of Arizona, Tucson; University of Houston, Texas; University of Iowa, Hospitals and Clinics, Iowa City; University of Iowa Museum of Fine Arts, Iowa City; University of South Dakota, Vermillion.

Publications

On MILLER:Books—*New Work: New York/Outside New York*, by Lynn Gumpert and Ned Rifkin, New Museum of Contemporary Art, New York, 1984; *The Corcoran Biennial of American Contemporary Painting*, by Lisa Lyons, Washington, D.C., 1985; *Women of Sweetgrass, Cedar and Sage*, exhibition catalog, American Indian Community House Gallery, Atlatl, Phoenix, 1985; *Scouting*, by Robert Hobbs, Leach Gallery, Washington, D.C., 1987; *Open Range*, by Lucy Lippard, Boulder, Colorado, 1988; *Revelations: The Transformative Impulse in Recent Art*, by John Perreault, Aspen Art Museum, Colorado, 1989; *Mixed Blessings*, by Lucy Lippard, Pantheon Books, New York, 1990; *The Price of Power*, by Don Desmett, Cleveland Contemporary Art Center, 1990; *Laughing Matters*, Artemisia Gallery, Chicago, 1991. **Articles**—"The Reality of Illusions," by Robert Hobbs, *No Bluebonnet, No Yellow Roses*, edited by Sylvia Moore, Midmarch Art Press, New York, 1988.

*

Kay Miller comments:

The imagery in my painting seems to be about opposites held in suspension which I hopefully unite: urban and tribal views, ghetto and ecological attitudes, White and Indian cultures, orthodox religion and personally intuited insights.

*   *   *

The juxtaposition of opposites forms the core of Kay Miller's work, at once lamenting the ultimate disparity of human existence and suggesting a path toward unity. A highly formal painter, Miller draws on themes and symbols from a variety of philosophies, applicable to but not centered in contemporary American Indian experience. As a consequence, she is frequently exhibited as a contemporary American artist, with little or no reference to her Comanche and Métis heritage.

Miller was raised in a poor Hispanic neighborhood, well acquainted with poverty but disenfranchised from her own or any other tribal community. The Indian aspects of her identity were

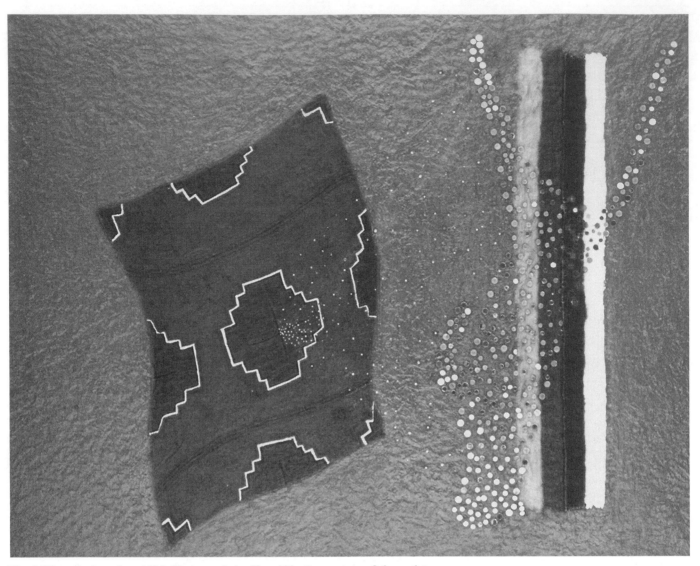

Kay Miller: *Reclamation,* **1994. Photograph by Ken Abbott; courtesy of the artist.**

realized as she grew older and came into contact with other indigenous people. These aspects are crystallized in Miller's sense of being a part of the universe, of the earth, of belonging. In her painting Miller expresses this feeling through ideas, rather than through formal references or styles.

Miller credits her parents for introducing her to the essential elements of art. Her father, a house painter, was a master at color-mixing. Her mother inspired her love of nature: "she taught me about light through gazing at water and the sun, through watching birds and animals, and through looking into the center of flowers." Miller's mother also told her stories about the hardships her Native American ancestors faced, stories that taught her the importance of perseverance.

After high school, Miller attended the University of Houston, where she majored in art education. She was always interested in being an artist, but survival took the highest priority, as she had to work full-time and occasionally lived out of her car. It was her own dedication and the support of friends and mentors that enabled her to graduate from college and continue her education at the Univer-

sity of Texas, where she received bachelors and masters degrees in fine art. Miller has also attended the Naropa Institute, in Boulder, Colorado, where she studied Tibetan calligraphy and tai chi.

An unenrolled Comanche, Miller has exhibited primarily in contemporary, non-Indian venues, such as the National Institute for Contemporary Art in New York City, where she was awarded a one-year residency in 1991, Artemisia Gallery in Chicago (1991), Cleveland Contemporary Art Center (1990), and various college and university art galleries throughout the country. Miller occasionally shows with other Indian artists in exhibits with a political theme. "I am a Taoist in terms of my spiritual practice, and I have never lived in an Indian community," Miller explained. "There is a core in my work that is American Indian, but I have many other identities."

Miller works in series, producing work on a cyclical but irregular basis. Each series addresses a particular intellectual or philosophical theme, always grounded in her overarching premise that any attempt to understand and merge opposites is healing. Working primarily in oil on large, horizontally oriented canvases, Miller applies paint thickly and carefully, creating rich fields of fully saturated color. Two icons of contrasting color and meaning are situated on these fields, suggesting at once connection and distance. The images are flat but not abstract, clearly developed for the two-dimensional environment of the canvas. As such, the objects become symbols. In *Stone Seed* (1983-86) a rock becomes a "meditative icon" in which the entire cosmos unfolds. In *Holy Orders* (1983-86) Miller juxtaposes a multicolor mudra (a hand meditation position) with an artists' paintbrush to speak about the spiritual nature of painting. Both paintings were exhibited in 1987 in *Scouting*, Miller's solo show at Foxley/Leach Gallery in Washington, D.C. According to Miller, the painted icons are "allusions rather than illusions or pictures of a particular object, place, or situation."

Symbols are useful to Miller because they allow her to focus on issues rather than objects. Often the visual juxtapositions will address political or social problems, as in her *Laughing Matters* series (1991). The title is ironic, for her subjects are human and earthly disasters such as nuclear waste, corruption, overpopulation, war and environmental destruction. In her treatment of these problems, Miller suggests a path toward healing, always grounded in human connectedness, recognition of the natural world, and spiritual enlightenment. Miller admits she is not an impartial observer of the universe: "I try to communicate the necessity for spiritual revolution."

—Margaret Dubin

MINTHORN, P. Y.

Tribal affiliations: Cayuse; Nez Percé
Mixed media artist and painter

Born: Pendleton, Oregon, Confederated Tribes of Umatilla, 1960.
Education: University of Colorado, Boulder, 1979; Institute of American Indian Arts, Santa Fe, New Mexico, A.F.A., 1981; Pacific Northwest College of Art, Portland, Oregon, 1983-84; American University, Washington, D.C., 1997. **Career:** Artist and poet; Socio-Cultural Technician, Confederated Tribes of Umatilla, 1987; Cultural Resource Technician, USFS, Wallowa-Whitman National Forest, 1988; Cultural Research Coordinator, Confederated Tribes of Umatilla, 1989; Archaeological Technician, Battelle Pacific Northwest Laboratories, 1989-91; Research Assistant, Tamustalik Cultural Institute, 1991; National Museum of Natural History, Smithsonian Institution, Contract Archaeologist, 1992-93, Museum Technician, 1993-96, and Museum Specialist, 1996-97; Committee Appointee, American Indian Council, Smithsonian Institution, 1994-97. **Awards:** Research grant, Crow Shadow Institute, 1996.

Selected Group Exhibitions

1980   *Contemporary Native American Art*, University of Colorado, Boulder
1983   Westwood Gallery, Portland, Oregon
1984   *Ancient Visions Through Contemporary Indian Art*, Hallie Ford Brown Gallery, Williamette University, Salem, Oregon; Lewis and Clark State College, Lewiston, Idaho
1985   *Northwest Art*, American Indian Contemporary Arts, San Francisco, California; Elizabeth Gallery, Portland, Oregon; Empire Gallery, Pendleton, Oregon

1986   *Contemporary Native American Art*, Read Stremmel Galleries, Reno, Nevada
        Artists of Eastern Oregon, NightingGale Gallery, La Grand, Oregon
        Beyond Blue Mountains, Public Art Space, Seattle, Washington
        Oregon Artists, Sacred Circle Gallery, Seattle, Washington
1987   *Contemporary Visions*, Read Stremmel Galleries, San Antonio, Texas; Sunbird Gallery, Bend, Oregon
        New Directions Northwest: Contemporary Native American Art, Portland Art Museum, Oregon
        Northwest 87, Seattle Art Museum, Washington
1989   *Ink, Stones, Blocks, and Plates: Contemporary Prints from the Institute of American Indian Arts*, traveling exhibit, Institute of American Indian Arts, Santa Fe, New Mexico
1990   *Tradition and Spirit*, Maryhill Museum of Art, Maryhill, Washington; Windhorse Gallery, Seattle, Washington
        P. Y. Minthorn, James Lavadour, and Holly Roberts, Elizabeth Leach Gallery, Portland, Oregon
1991   *Our Land/Ourselves: American Indian Contemporary Artists*, University Art Gallery, State University of New York at Albany, New York
        Underestimated Artists, American Indian Community House Gallery, New York
        Sapatq'ayn: Twentieth Century Nez Perce Artists, Nez Perce National Historic Park, Spaulding, Idaho
1992   *Monoprint Project*, Tamarind Institute, Albuquerque, New Mexico
        Decolonizing the Mind, Center on Contemporary Art, Seattle, Washington
1994   *The 1994 Reflex Print Portfolio*, Reflex MagArizonaine, Seattle, Oregon
        Artists Who Are Indian, Denver Art Museum, Colorado

Collections

Washington State Arts Commission, Olympia.

Publications

By MINTHORN: Books—*The Clouds Through This Light* (anthology, including poems by Minthorn), Institute of American Indian Arts Press, Santa Fe, 1980; *Ceremonious Blue*, Institute of American Indian Arts Press, Santa Fe, 1981; *Songs From This Earth and On Turtle's Back* (anthology, including poems by Minthorn), Greenfield Center, Greenfield Review Press, New York, 1983; *Sapatq'ayn: Twentieth Century Nez Perce Art* (introduction by Minthorn), Northwest Interpretive Association and Confluence Press, Lewiston, 1991.

On MINTHORN: Books—*Portfolio II: 11 American Indian Arts*, "P. Y. Minthorn," by Abby Wasserman, American Indian Contemporary Arts Gallery, San Francisco, 1986; *Our Land/Ourselves: American Indian Contemporary Artists*, by Jaune Quick-to-See Smith, University Art Gallery, Albany, New York, 1990. **Articles**— "P. Y. Minthorn," by Abby Wasserman, *Native Vision*, vol. 3, no. 3, July/August, 1986; "P.Y. Minthorn, James Lavadour, Holly Roberts at Elizabeth Leach," by Elizabeth Bryant, *Visions,* Winter 1990; "Exhibit Shows Off Minthorn's Magic," by Randy Gragg, *The*

Oregonian, 27 July 1990; "On Long Island, Photos, Portraits, Pollock and Stereotyping," by Roberta Smith, New York Times, 9 August 1990; "P.Y. Minthorn at Elizabeth Leach Gallery," *Reflex Magazine,* September/October 1990.

*   *   *

P. Y. Minthorn formally began his career as an artist in 1976 and two years later he decided to attend the Institute of American Indian Arts in Santa Fe. Like many other graduates of IAIA, Minthorn found the experience valuable and has commented that he "learned as much from [his] classmates as from the teachers." Additionally, the diversity of students (representing tribes from all of North America) opened up a whole new world for him, and he found it stimulating and enriching.

After graduating, Minthorn left Santa Fe for Portland, Oregon, where he spent a year and a half at the Pacific Northwest College of Art. He remained in Portland for three years after leaving Pacific Northwest College, supporting himself as a writer and artist. During this time, he was surrounded by art, poetry and jazz.

Rauschenberg was an important influence early in his career, especially "in terms of liberating [his] artistic expression." He was particularly inspired by a Rauschenberg collage on display at a local exhibition. Minthorn's resulting *Little-Big Culture Series* incorporated ordinary materials from the street into a collage. Minthorn describes these piece as an abstract collage with some traditional Native American design elements. Later he was impressed and inspired by the work of Antonio Tapies, Anselm Kiefer and other major neo-expressionists of the 1980s. According to Minthorn, "The visual symbolism, empty spaces, and intense gesture of Tapies had a spiritual sensibility that I longed for in my own work."

Experimentation is an important aspect of Minthorn's work. He uses various techniques to achieve rough textures on his canvases, combining ashes with acrylic paint in one work, for example, while using his whole hand in another. The combination of these various surface techniques and the strong single gestures that often dominate his canvases create intense contemplative works.

Minthorn's work references a way of life—his upbringing in a traditional home. His elders have told him, "Our people are considered dreamers." Consequently, Minthorn has been intrigued with "how to re-experience a dream visually through some artwork related to it," and his work has fragmented materials and arresting images. In an Untitled piece from 1989, a wing-shaped image dominates a painting referencing his participation in Crow Sundance ceremonies (Minthorn Sundanced with the Crow at Lodge Grass, Montana, for four years). A ball of white light with tracks leading into it appears as the central element of the composition. A bird wing protrudes from the light, symbolizing the sacred, and as a piece the painting captures the intense physical sensations of the Sundance.

Minthorn's work seems to be guided by the same forces that have directed his personal life. Working as a Museum Specialist at the National Museum of Natural History during the early-90s has exposed him to visionary-based material produced by Native Americans. He sees his own work as an extension of these traditions, in part because of his instruction about dreams by his elders. His participation in religious ceremonies has led to his involvement in repatriation—in particular the repatriation of the human remains of the Plateau region peoples. He has been trained by the elders of his tribe on how to handle human remains. This commitment and experience with repatriating is reflected in some of his recent prints appearing in Seattle and Denver: abstracted images of bones appear frequently in these works.

Despite his inclusion in many group exhibitions and strong reviews, Phil Minthorn has commented that no one has taken a serious look at his work. He came to this conclusion after sending his work to a gallery owner in Reno. Although she expressed interest and enthusiasm about his work, she rejected it, saying her clients were not sophisticated enough—that it was way ahead of her audience. Her clients were not ready for anything that broke from their preconceived notion of Native American art—the monolithic concept of a "Southwestern style" that has come to represent Native American art. Consequently, Minthorn attempts to create an authentic expression of who he is in his work. He draws on his traditional upbringing but refuses to fall prey to generic representations of "Indianness." Unfortunately his Native background at times hinders the reception of his work.

Minthorn's experience is not uncommon. Native American artists frequently fail to receive serious attention. This may be the result of several factors: the general lack of critical commentary on contemporary Native American artists by scholars and critics; the absence and at times segregation of Native artists by the mainstream art market; and the stereotyping of Native art and artists.

Currently he has been conducting research on pictographs and petroglyphs of the Plateau for a chapter he is writing for a book on Plateau Rock art. Pictographs and petroglyphs have provided a source of inspiration for Minthorn. As he describes it, "My interest in rock art is really based on an interest in their visual portrayal of ancient human experience and other-worldly phenomena. I sense a unique form of knowledge and history embedded in these images." There is a thread that weaves itself through all of Minthorn's work—as an artist, writer, anthropologist, Native rights activist—a deep commitment to his community and advocacy for Native rights and issues.

—Jennifer Vigil

MIRABAL, Vicente

Variant names: Chiu-tah
Tribal affiliations: Taos Pueblo
Painter

Born: Taos Pueblo, New Mexico, 1918; Chiu Tah translates as "Dancing Boy." **Education:** Santa Fe Indian School. **Military Service:** U.S. Army, World War II; fought in the Battle of the Bulge; killed in Germany. **Career:** Instructor, Santa Fe Indian School. **Award:** Poster Contest winner, San Francisco World's Fair, 1939. **Died:** 1944.

Selected Group Exhibitions

1934	Museum of New Mexico, Santa Fe
1935	Addison Gallery of American Art, Phillips Academy, Andover, Massachusetts
1939	San Francisco World's Fair, California
1978	Center for Great Plains Studies, University of Nebraska, Omaha (traveling)
1986	*When the Rainbow Touches Down,* Heard Museum, Phoenix, Arizona (traveling)

Vicente Mirabel: *Horsetail Dance,* c. 1940. Photograph by Seth Roffman; courtesy Dick Howard collection.

1995   Museum of Indian Arts & Cultures, Santa Fe, New
         Mexico
1996   *Vision and Voices: Native American Painting from the
         Philbrook Museum of Art,* Philbrook Museum of Art,
         Tulsa, Oklahoma

Collections

City Art Museum, St. Louis, Missouri; Center for Great Plains
Studies, University of Nebraska, Lincoln; Indian Arts & Craft Board,
Washington, D.C.; Museum of New Mexico, Santa Fe; Museum of
Northern Arizona, Flagstaff; National Museum of the American
Indian, Washington, D.C.; Owensboro Museum of Fine Arts, Ken-
tucky; Philbrook Museum of Art, Tulsa, Oklahoma; University of
Oklahoma, Norman; Woolaroc Museum, Bartlesville, Oklahoma.

Publications

On MIRABEL: Books—*American Indian Painters,* by Oscar B.
Jacobson and Jeanne d'Ucel, Nice, France, 1950; *American Indian
Painting of the Southwest and Plains Areas,* by Dorothy Dunn,
Albuquerque, 1968; *Modern By Tradition: American Indian Paint-
ing in the Studio Style,* by W. Jackson Rushing, Santa Fe, 1995;
Vision and Voices: Native American Painting from the Philbrook

Museum of Art, edited by Lydia Wyckoff, Tulsa, 1996. **Articles—**
"Remarkable Paintings by Indians at Art Museum," by Olive Rush,
Santa Fe New Mexican, 7 May 1934.

*   *   *

Vicente Mirabal was among the most promising of the great watercolorists who attended the Santa Fe Indian School during the
1930s. He received recognition as early as his mid-teens for his use
of color in capturing scenes from his native Taos Pueblo and later
won a contest for poster design for San Francisco's World Fair of
1939. By that time as well he had turned from student to instructor
at the school, where his contemporaries included Jose Rey Toledo,
Joe H. Herrera, and Pablita Velarde, among others, tutored by Dorothy Dunn. Tragically, Mirabel was killed fighting in World War II
at the age of twenty-six.

Mirabel left an impressive body of work that was respected but
increasingly fell into the background as his southwest contemporaries further developed and expanded their skills and formed a
tradition with important impact. Since the late 1970s, however,
interest in Mirabel's work has renewed through traveling exhibitions, reminding viewers about his remarkable strength with colors
and presentation. Rich earth tones of Taos Pueblo surround viv-
idly-realized characters in such works as *Taos Clowns, Taos Dancer,*

and *Woman Plastering Oven*, all painted by the time he was seventeen. In his ceremonial scenes, groups of people—rendered with lively flesh tones and mixed colors for their vibrant costumes and dyed or plain clothing—act and observe amid a balanced interplay of background elements patterned on the canvas, a blending that captures the mood of festivity or the commonplace. Play of light and shade and careful placement of figures and objects enhance the overall composition and coloring. *Turtle Dance on New Year's Eve* (1938) has fifty human figures, most of whom are clad in classic striped Pueblo wearing blankets. Eight dancers, in motion and with rattles shaking overhead, are adorned with parrot and eagle feathers on their heads, and fringed garters sway below their dance kilts, among details as colors grow more intense where action resides and fan off to more muted tones at the very edges of the painting—an accomplishment of form and patterning. Every element of the painting contributes to the effect. For example, as Professor W. Jackson Rushing has noted of this work, painted when the artist was twenty, "the mission church at Taos functions mostly as a space-generating formal device that sets off the indigenous ceremony being performed in the foreground."

In 1939, while teaching in Santa Fe, Mirabal's painting, *Taos Turtle Dance*, won the highly competitive poster contest for the World's Fair in San Francisco, California. Like his other works, this painting provides a perspective on life in the Pueblo, authentic in detail and vivid in overall impression. Mirabal's sister, Rose Cordova, recalled his painting technique: "I used to love to watch him painting. How he mixed his colors and the lines. . . Like if he drew a picture of a man singing, it was like [he] was actually singing because his mouth would be open a certain way. . . It was almost like he had in his mind just what he was going to draw. And he just did it freehand."

—Gregory Schaaf

MOMADAY, Al

Variant names: Haun Toa
Tribal affiliations: Kiowa
Painter

Born: Alfred Morris Momaday, Mountain View, Oklahoma, 2 July 1913. **Education:** Bacone College, 1931-34; University of New Mexico, 1936-37; University of California, Los Angeles, 1956. **Military Service:** U.S. Corps of Engineers, World War II. **Family:** Married noted artist and writer, Natachee; and son, N. Scott Momaday also noted writer and artist. **Career:** Principal and art instructor, Jemez Day School, 1947-67; assistant director, arts and crafts, New Mexico State Fair, 1946-60s; initiated art programs, including Jemez Pueblo Indian Arts Exposition and Pow Wow; director, All-American Indian Days, 1955-57, and American Indian Exposition, 1956-57; chairman, New Mexico Arts Commission; commissioned for altar plaques, St. Luke's Lutheran Church, Albuquerque, 1958. **Awards:** Honorary Doctorate, Lawrence University, Appleton, Wisconsin; Outstanding Southwestern Indian Artist, Dallas Exchange Club, Tribe of Teal Wing, 1956; Outstanding Indian Artist Award, Ho-ennywe Society, Western New York Art Association, 1965; Certificate of Appreciation, Indian Arts and Crafts Board, 1967; Waite Phillips Special Trophy, Philbrook Museum of Art, 1975; numerous awards at fairs, including All-American Indian Days, American Indian Exposition, Denver Art Museum,

Hollywood Festival of Arts, Inter-Tribal Indian Ceremonials, Museum of New Mexico; Philbrook Museum of Art, and Scottsdale National Indian Arts Exhibition. **Died:** November 1981.

Selected Group Exhibitions

1947	University of Oklahoma, Norman
	Bloomington Art Association, Illinois
	Syracuse Museum of Fine Art, New York
1948	Dallas Museum of Fine Arts, Dallas, Texas
	Detroit Institute of Arts, Michigan
	Joslyn Memorial Art Museum, Omaha, Nebraska
	Maryhill Museum of Art, Washington
	Isaac Delgado Museum, New Orleans, Louisiana
1949	Northeastern Oklahoma A&M College, Miami, Oklahoma
1950	Smithsonian Institution, Washington, D.C.
1951	Wichita Art Museum, Kansas
	Colorado Springs Fine Art Center, Colorado
1953	Texas Technology Museum, Lubbock
1954	George Thomas Hunter Gallery of Art, Chattanooga, Tennessee
	Rosicrucian Egyptian, Oriental Museum, Rosicrucian Park, San Jose, California
	Sioux Indian Exhibition & Crafts Center, Halley Park, Rapid City, South Dakota
	Chicago Art Institute, Illinois
1955	Sanford Museum, Cherokee, Iowa
	Albany Institute of History & Art, New York
	Currier Gallery of Art, Manchester, New Hampshire
1956	Norfolk Museum of Arts and Sciences, Virginia
1957	Drexel Institute of Technology, Philadelphia, Pennsylvania
1958	*We Shake Hands Conference,* Pierre, South Dakota
1959	Des Moines Art Center, Iowa
	Chappel House, Denver, Colorado
	Ponca City Art Association, Oklahoma
1960	Museum of American Indian, New York, New York
	Museum of the Plains Indian, Browning, Montana
1961	New Jersey State Museum, Trenton
1962	Heard Museum, Phoenix, Arizona
1964-65	*First Annual Invitational Exhibition of American Indian Paintings,* United States Department of the Interior, Washington, D.C.
1965	*Second Annual Invitational Exhibition of American Indian Paintings,* United States Department of the Interior, Washington, D.C.
1972	*Contemporary Southern Plains Indian Painting,* Southern Plains Indian Museum, Anadarko, Oklahoma (traveling)
1972-73	*Al Momaday* (with Natachee and N. Scott Momaday), Heard Museum, Phoenix, Arizona
1978	*100 Years of Native American Painting,* Oklahoma Museum of Art, Oklahoma City
1979-80	*Native American Paintings,* organized by the Joslyn Art Museum, Omaha, Nebraska (traveling)
1980	*Native American Art at the Philbrook,* Philbrook Museum, Tulsa, Oklahoma
1982	*Native American Painting: Selections from the Museum of the American Indian,* Heard Museum, Phoenix, Arizona
1984-85	*Indianascher Kunstler* (traveling, Germany), organized by the Philbrook Museum, Tulsa, Oklahoma

1988   *When the Rainbow Touches Down,* Heard Museum, Phoenix, Arizona (traveling)
1989   *Paint, Bronze and Stone,* Mitchell Indian Museum, Kendall College, Evanston, Illinois
1990   *American Indian Artists in the Avery Collection and the McNay Permanent Collection,* Koogler McNay Art Museum, San Antonio, Texas

Collections

Thomas Gilcrease Institute of American History and Art, Tulsa, Oklahoma; Kiva Museum of the Koshare Indian, La Junta, Colorado; Koogler McNay Art Museum, San Antonio, Texas; Museum of the American Indian, New York; Museum of New Mexico, Santa Fe; Museum of Northern Arizona, Flagstaff; Philbrook Museum of Art, Tulsa, Oklahoma; Millicent Rogers Foundation Museum, Taos, New Mexico; Roswell Museum and Art Center, New Mexico; Southwest Museum, Los Angeles, California.

Publications

On MOMADAY: Books—*A Pictorial History of the American Indian,* by Oliver LaFarge, New York, 1956; *American Indian Painting of the Southwest and Plains Areas*, by Dorothy Dunn, University of New Mexico, Albuquerque, 1968; *Indian Painters and White Patrons*, by J.J. Brody, University of New Mexico Press, Albuquerque, 1971; *Southwest Indian Painting: A Changing Art,* by Clara Lee Tanner, Tucson, 1973; *100 Years of Native American Painting*, exhibition catalog by Arthur Silberman, Oklahoma Museum of Art, Oklahoma City, 1978; *Native American Painting,* by Frederick Schmidt and Patrick T. Houlihan, Kansas City, 1980; *Kiowa Voices: Ceremonial Dance, Ritual and Song,* by Maurice Boyd, Fort Worth, 1981; *American Indian Painting and Sculpture,* Patricia Broder, New York, 1981; *When the Rainbow Touches Down*, exhibition catalog by Tryntje Van Ness Seymour, Heard Museum, University of Washington Press, 1988; *American Indian Artists in the Avery Collection and the McNay Permanent Collection,* edited by Jean Sherrod Williams, San Antonio, 1990.

*   *   *

Al Momaday may be counted among the pioneers of American Indian painting. His Kiowa predecessors repeatedly played an important role in the history of Indian painting: Paul Zotom (1856-1913) and Etadleuh Doanmoe (1856-88) were among the prisoner-artists of Fort Marion whose "ledger-drawings" of war and peace on the Southern Prairies mark the (visual and intellectual) transition to modern American Indian painting. In the 1920s and 1930s the Kiowa Five became the first group of Oklahoma artists to paint within the notions and developments of Western art. The decade of the 1930s also saw the founding of the famous art department at Bacone College in Muskogee, with which great names in American Indian painting (like Acee Blue Eagle and Woody Crumbo) are associated. Oklahoma thus can be said to have been a cradle of Indian painting and the Kiowa to have contributed remarkably to its emergence.

Momaday is both personally and artistically a representative of Kiowa-Oklahoma art. He was born into a family of strong and revered personalities, including his father, Mammedaty, mother, Aho, and grandfathers, who were tribal dignitaries (a judge and a medicine man). Thus, he knew the intricacies of tribal ceremonies, legends, and history and proudly identified with the Kiowa way.

Momaday's family background was conducive to his painting of Kiowa themes. Most of his images are inspired by ceremonies: the Kiowa Sun Dance, the Mountain Spirits Dance, and Buffalo Medicine, as well as the later Peyote movement. Mythical beings (spirit horses and water beasts) and Kiowa warriors and hunters are further sources of his imagery. Momaday's paintings are documents of Plains culture. The evocation of times past is sometimes extended to the material side of the painting. Momaday has, for instance, used buffalo and moose hide as his canvas, appropriate backdrops for Sun Dance Lodges rendered in a technique reminiscent of prehistoric Indian painting.

Momaday's paintings in general remind one of basic styles and forms introduced in the early days of modern Kiowa painting, although with variations and inventions. His images very often have an abstract quality and evoke an idea rather than depicting naturalistic scenes. Thus, the notion of a sun dance ceremonial lodge is established through a buffalo skull, a circle made of feathers, and the hand prints of a medicine man. Likewise, he adopts a kind of assemblage technique, displaying, for instance, the head of an Indian with a stylized buffalo headdress, a hand clutching a feather, and a drumstick with the sun as the background in order to give the impression of a traditional Prairie Indian amidst his world. The scale sometimes changes for emphasis on a symbol or idea, as in *Sun Worshipper*, where a head, magnified in scale, epitomizes the picture's theme by almost becoming one with the sun against which it is drawn. Another characteristic Momaday shares with his Kiowa forerunners is his primarily lineal composition and outlined color spaces.

Momaday's penchant for the decorative comes to the fore in the vigorous illustrations for N. Scott Momaday's book, *The Way to Rainy Mountain* (1969) as well as in four lithographs which he did a year before his death in 1981. This amalgamation of styles in the lithographs reflects Momaday's experience: from the late 1930s onward he lived in the Southwest and thus came in contact with the Pueblo cultures. The buffalo skulls, shields, mythic animals, hunters in the clouds are elements of style not unlike traditional decorations on Pueblo pottery.

For decades Momaday was principal as well as director of arts and crafts in Jemez Pueblo Day School in New Mexico and devoted himself to the furthering of young Native American artists and art, regardless of tribal affiliations. He initiated a number of Indian Art programs, including the annual Jemez Pueblo Indian Arts Exposition and Pow Wow, which attracted each year thousands of visitors from all over the country. His tremendous activity as an artist, with exhibitions inside and outside the United States, and as a leader in extending the art traditions of his and other tribal groups gained him many honors and awards. Nevertheless, he remained a Kiowa at heart. His pilgrimage every year to the Taipe Society Gourd Dance brought him back to his native Oklahoma, where elders still called him by his Kiowa name.

—Gerhard and Gisela Hoffmann

MONONGYE, Preston

Variant names: Snow Chief
Tribal affiliations: Hopi
Jewelry designer and painter

Born: Los Angeles, California, 6 September 1927. **Education:** Apprentice silversmith to his uncle, Gene Pooyouma, at Hopi,

Preston Monongye: *Corn Spirit,* c. 1980. Courtesy Challis and Arch Thiessen collection.

beginning in 1936; Haskell Indian Junior College; law courses, Occidental College, Los Angeles, mid-1950s. **Military Service:** U.S. Army, World War II, paramedic with paratroopers, South Pacific; also served in Korea, beginning in 1953. **Career:** Kachina painter and commercial painter, 1945-53; law enforcement with the Bureau of Indian Affairs, mid-1950s to early-1960s; full-time artist beginning in the mid-1960s; elected to Board of Directors, Inter-Tribal Indian Ceremonial, 1970; lecturer at civic clubs and schools; teacher, including Manuelito Hall, Gallup, University of Cincinnati, California Institute of the Arts, and Phoenix Indian Center. **Awards:** Numerous at fairs and juried competitions, including Inter-Tribal Indian Ceremonial, Gallup, New Mexico, 1966, 1970-77; Museum of Northern Arizona Annual Hopi Show, Flagstaff, Arizona; New Mexico and Arizona State Fairs; Santa Monica All Indian Ceremonial Show, Santa Monica, California; and Heard Museum Guild Indian Fair and Market.

Individual Exhibitions

1973   Heard Museum, Phoenix, Arizona
        Gila River Arts and Crafts Center, Sacaton, Arizona
1980-90 Margaret Kilgore Gallery, Scottsdale, Arizona

Selected Group Exhibitions

Exhibited regularly at fairs and commercial galleries throughout the southwest.

1973   European Tour of Hopi, Zuni, Pima, and Papago artists

Collections

Denver Art Museum, Colorado; Heard Museum, Phoenix, Arizona; Margaret Kilgore Gallery, Scottsdale, Arizona; Museum of Northern Arizona, Flagstaff; Smithsonian Institution, Washington, D.C.

Publications

By **MONONGYE: Articles**—"The New Indian Jewelry," *Arizona Highways,* June 1972; "Inter-Tribal Indian Ceremonial," *Arizona Highways,* July 1972.

On **MONONGYE: Books**—*Southwest Indian Art, A Changing Art,* by Clara Lee Tanner, Tucson, 1973; *Art and Indian Individualists,* by Guy and Doris Monthan, Flagstaff, 1975; *Beyond Tradition: Contemporary Indian Art and Its Evolution*, by Jerry and Lois Jacka, Flagstaff, 1988; *Hopi Silver,* by Margaret N. Wright, Flagstaff, 1989.

*

Preston Monongye comments (c. 1972):

When I am lecturing or touring, people always want to know where I get my designs or what silver techniques I use. I was taught by my uncle, Gene Pooyouma, one of the finest men I have ever known. He taught me to love my work, and to make the best of everything I do, whether it be painting, silversmithing, or whatever. He taught me how to live the "Hopi way."

To me, most Indians who have been exposed to their cultural heritage have an inner understanding of life. Therefore, if they go into the arts, something unique emerges.

Our art, as in non-Indian art, takes form from what we see today. We may use old techniques, along with old designs taken from potsherds or pictographs, but then we re-design them or add innovations of our own and we have "the new Indian art." The old Indian jewelry was great when it was made years ago, but so are the things we make today.

*   *   *

Preston Monongye was born in 1927 in Los Angeles to a Hopi father and a mother from a California Indian Mission nation. They moved to Hopi in 1934, where Monongye was raised in Hopi traditions by his extended family and began an apprenticeship when he was only nine with his uncle, Gene Pooyouma, in the art of silversmithing. His introduction to silversmithing came from pumping bellows to melt down Mexican silver pesos or American silver coins and hammering the metal into small bracelets, a process that often took days and retained a rough look. After numerous twists and turns in his career, he concentrated on art full time beginning in the 1960s and by the 1970s he was a leading designer of "New Indian Jewelry"—a term he coined to describe "highly refined items, beautifully decorated with polished turquoise and other precious stones" ("The New Indian Jewelry," *Arizona Highways,* June 1972).

Monongye's rise to prominence complemented that of another great Hopi artist, Charles Loloma. In a way, Loloma's international, critical, and academic acclaim was mirrored by Monogye on a more local, grass-roots level, though he, too, enjoyed recognition on a broader scale. Monongye's work generated overwhelming enthusiasm at the Inter-Tribal Indian Ceremonial in Gallup, New Mexico, beginning in 1966, and he was elected to the Ceremonial's Board of Directors in 1970. His efforts as an artist and teacher contributed greatly to the rise of the new Indian jewelry. However, though his works are distinct from more traditional Hopi jewelry, Monogye considered them more of an expansion of Hopi culture. He was a member of ancient Hopi clans, engraved his jewelry with a Peyote Prayer Bird (a messenger that requests blessings of rain and good health), and stated, "I feel that if my work were put into a time capsule, the beauty of the Hopi culture would shine through the art."

Monongye's early work in silversmithing was interrupted by his service in World War II. After the war, he concentrated on Kachina painting, including commercial projects, and continued to work with jewelry before undertaking another military stint, serving in Korea, after which he worked as a law enforcement officer with the Bureau of Indian Affairs from the mid-1950s to the early 1960s. He finally began focusing on jewelry-making full-time in the mid-1960s, producing his first examples of new Indian jewelry and winning instant recognition: he swept several prizes at the Inter-Tribal Indian Ceremonial, followed by more major awards in 1970, including Grand Prize for a silver, all-cast box, Best of Show, and 53 ribbons. His ceremonial painting and sculpture was also honored at the Museum of Northern Arizona Annual Hopi Show and at the state fairs of Arizona and New Mexico.

He once wrote to fellow artist Barbara Bovee: "When I began producing artwork, before World War II, there was no commercial outlet. What was produced was for the Indian and perhaps the occasional visitor under the portal at the railroad station. It is important to me that Indian Art be preserved as such. We make up an era much as the Ming Artists of China comprised. . . I'm just interested in survival for my art, my family and myself. When I do leave this life it will be as I entered, with nothing."

Monongye's work has been purchased or commissioned by the Prince of the Philippines and other noted dignitaries. Under the auspices of the State Department, he toured European countries displaying his jewelry. His artwork also included sculptures in silver and wood, and in later years his interest returned to painting, etching and lithography. One of his last lithographs, *Spirit of the Flute Player,* is deeply symbolic. The artist explained: "The figure depicted is a Flute Playing Kachina—the Kachina is our key to the Creator. We pray though the Kachina, not to the Kachina, and our prayers are carried to the Creator through the Kachina's spirit. The flute dance ceremonial alternates with the famous Hopi Snake Dance and is part of a harvest ritual and blessing."

There was often some young artist taking a lesson in Monongye's studio, for he was an accomplished teacher. He stated, "I feel the only way to perpetuate art is through teaching it. There are too many times when Indian artists are totally assimilated into the art world, not giving any tribal identity to their art. I feel this is a great injustice to the American Indian. In my feeling, true Americana is American Indian art. Indian art is just now finding its niche in the art world. This has come about through the efforts of Charles Loloma, Otellie Loloma, the Institute of American Indian Arts at Santa Fe, and through many fine Indian Teachers."

Though he created new Indian jewelry, Monongye employed some traditional methods, including carving a negative mold in tufa stone. Silver or gold is poured into the mold, then the design—for which he showed acute skill and elegance—is carved in a negative form. The designs related to Hopi culture, and embellishments,

usually in turquoise but often using other stones or shells as well, complemented the design to achieve balanced and timeless jewelry.

—Gregory Schaaf

MONTOYA, Geronima Cruz
Variant names: Potsunu
Tribal affiliations: San Juan Pueblo
Painter

Born: Born Geronima Cruz, San Juan Pueblo, New Mexico, 22 September 1915; Native name also transliterated as: P'otsunu, Po-Su-Nu, and Po-Tsunu. Daughter of Crucita Trujillo, potter, and Pablo Cruz. **Family:** Married Juan Montoya, 1939; three sons: Robert, Paul, and Eugene. **Education:** St. Joseph's Indian School, Santa Fe, 1935; University of New Mexico, 1935-1936; University of Albuquerque, BS, 1958; instructors included Dorothy Dunn and Kenneth Chapman. **Career:** Educator and art department director, Santa Fe Indian School, 1935-62; lecturer and artist. **Awards:** Henry Dendahl Award for Outstanding Student, Santa Fe Indian School; honorarium, when her student, Ben Quintana, won the National Youth Forum's art contest; Art and Cultural Achievement Award, National Museum of the American Indian, Washington, D.C., 1994; numerous from fairs and exhibitions, such as All American Indian Days, Inter-Tribal Indian Ceremonial, New Mexico State Fair; Scottsdale National Indian Art Exhibition; and those sponsored by Museum of New Mexico; Philbrook Museum of Art Center; School of American Research; and D.H. Young Museum, Fine Arts Museums of San Francisco.

Individual Exhibitions

1959	Museum of New Mexico, Santa Fe
1961	Museum of New Mexico, Santa Fe
	Amerika Haus, Nuremburg, Germany
1962	Philbrook Art Museum, Tulsa, Oklahoma

Selected Group Exhibitions

1934	Museum of New Mexico, Santa Fe
1948	Scripps College Art Gallery, Claremont, California
1955	*An Exposition of American Indian Painters*, James Graham And Sons, New York
1961	Museum of New Mexico, Santa Fe
1963	*Contemporary American Indian Art*, United States Department of State, Washington, D.C.
	Bismark National Indian Art Show, organized by the Chamber of Commerce and Bismark Art Association, North Dakota
1964	M.H. DeYoung Memorial Museum, Fine Arts Museums of San Francisco, California
1965	Arizona State Museum, University of Arizona, Tucson
1967	Millicent Rogers Foundation Museum, Taos, New Mexico
1982	*Native American Painting: Selections from the Museum of the American Indian,* (traveling)
1988	*When the Rainbow Touches Down*, Heard Museum, Phoenix, Arizona (traveling)

Geronima Cruz Montoya: *In Pursuit*, 1987. Photograph by Seth Roffman; courtesy Dick Howard collection.

1994   National Museum of the American Indian, Washington, D.C.
        Watchful Eyes: Native American Women Artists, Heard Museum, Phoenix, Arizona

Collections

M.H. DeYoung Memorial Museum, Fine Arts Museums of San Francisco, California; Heard Museum, Phoenix, Arizona; Indian Arts & Crafts Board, Washington, D.C.; Museum of New Mexico, Santa Fe; National Museum of the American Indian, Washington, D.C.; Philbrook Museum of Art, Tulsa, Oklahoma; Millicent Rogers Foundation Museum, Taos, New Mexico.

Publications

On MONTOYA: Books—*American Indian Painters*, by Oscar B. Jacobson and Jeanne d'Ucel, Nice, France, 1950; *American Indian Painting of the Southwest and Plains Areas*, by Dorothy Dunn, Albuquerque, 1968; *Indian Painters and White Patrons*, by J.J. Brody, Albuquerque, 1971; *Southwest Indian Painting: A Changing Art,* by Clara Lee Tanner, Tucson, 1973; *Native American Painting: Selections from the Museum of the American Indian,* by David. M. Fawcett and Lee A. Callander, New York, 1982; *When the Rainbow Touches Down*, by Tryntj Van Ness Seymour, Phoenix, 1988; *Santa*

Fe Indian Market, by Sheila Tryk, Santa Fe, 1993; *Watchful Eyes: Native American Women Artists,* edited by Anne Gully, Phoenix, 1994. **Articles**—"Remarkable Paintings by Indians at Art Museum," by Olive Rush, *Santa Fe New Mexican*, 7 May 1934; "Santa Fe Art," by Dorothy Morang, *El Palacio*, May 1940; *Native Peoples,* January/February/March 1995.

*

Geronima Cruz Montoya comments (1979):
My style of painting is very simple. My subjects are mainly traditional dances, home scenes, and designs. My inspiration also comes from Mimbres figures, pictographs, and petroglyphs. I continually experiment with new forms and styles.

*   *   *

Geronima Cruz Montoya was an important part of the burgeoning of Pueblo painting that began early in the twentieth century. As a student at the Santa Fe Indian School during the early 1930s, she displayed her early skill at painting and showed talent for teaching, and went on to pursue these professions simultaneously, making significant contributions in both areas. Montoya taught and administered the arts program at the Santa Fe Indian School from the mid-1930s to 1962, mentoring many students who became respected artists, like Ben Quintana, who won an art contest sponsored by the National Youth Forum. Her early works were done as a student at the Santa Fe Indian School in the mid-1930s and she continued painting in her spare time before becoming more prolific during the 1960s, winning several awards along the way and having her works regularly exhibited. For her excellence as a teacher and painter, Montoya was honored with the Art and Cultural Achievement Award by the National Museum of the American Indian, Washington, D.C., in 1994.

Montoya, who signed her paintings with her native name, Potsunu (also variously recorded as P'otsunu, Po-Su-Nu, and Po-Tsunu), was accomplished as an artist while still in her teens and participated in a 1934 exhibition at the Museum of New Mexico Olive Rush, a reviewer for the *Santa Fe New Mexican*, wrote "Remarkable Paintings by Indians at Art Museum," in which she discussed Montoya's work: "A San Juan girl, Po-Su-Nu, has a basket dance done in earth color on native ground. The design is a fine achievement through simple means, one great sweep of line for the shoulders of her women, and a clever use of triangles, circles, and straight lines for developing her theme." Montoya would build upon this reputation through her career and can be grouped as a major figure in any number of categories, including artist/educator, artist, Pueblo artist, and Pueblo woman artist. In the latter category she is linked with Santa Clara painter Pablita Velarde, a classmate at the Santa Fe Indian School; Lorencita Atencio, a fellow San Juan Pueblo artist who won early recognition as a watercolor painter but concentrated a greater part of her career on clothing design; Tonita Peña, a watercolor painter from San Ildefonso who preceded and encouraged both Montoya and Velarde; and on through Helen Hardin, Pablita Velarde's daughter, whose career began in the 1960s.

During the 1935-36 school semesters, Montoya assisted Dorothy Dunn in teaching the students at The Studio, Santa Fe Indian School, while taking classes at the University of New Mexico. Younger artists sought her advice freely and she contributed to the success of the program. She remained at the school for a major portion of her career, offsetting Dunn's strict emphasis on flatstyle painting by allowing students to more freely express themselves, offering guidance and principles for more rounded development. For the next 25 years, through various school administrations, periods of waning interest in preparing traveling exhibits and low funding cycles, Montoya maintained the original teaching objectives.

In her own work, Montoya favored a straightforward style, with detailed patterns providing depth and liveliness. The patterns resemble embroidered and woven designs typical of San Juan pueblo textile art, rendered in flat forms but with broader brush strokes and less emphasis on fine detail than Pueblo painting in general. She enjoyed a major solo exhibition at the Museum of New Mexico in 1959, and in 1961 the Museum awarded its highest purchase prize for *Rain God*, a placid, meditative painting with recognizable San Juan patterns and themes. Within her focused style and themes, Montoya displayed versatility in her approach to her subject matter and always showed painterly skill. The astonishing 1959 exhibition, from which every picture was sold, occurred more than twenty years after her most concentrated efforts as a studio artist, showing that she had matured privately as an artist during spare time from family and school.

In works after 1962 Montoya expanded her range. She worked in tempera, gouache, and dry brush, and moved from strict representational figures to expressionistic, abstract compositions that incorporate historic symbols from the southwest, which she imagina-

tively adapted to modern mediums. Her palette broadened as well in her later work, with brighter tones often blending with and off-setting more muted, earth tones, displaying the freedom and vibrancy of an artist with more time to play.

—Gregory Schaaf

MOOTZKA, Waldo
Tribal affiliations: Hopi
Painter and illustrator

Born: New Oraibi, Arizona, 1910; name also transliterated as Mootska. **Education:** Oraibi Day School, where he observed painter Red Kabotie at work; Albuquerque Indian School; The Studio, Santa Fe Indian School, New Mexico, studying under Dorothy Dunn **Career:** Painter, silversmith, and illustrator for John Louw Nelson's *Rhythm for Rain*, an ethnographic novel about the Hopi, 1937. **Died:** 1940.

Selected Group Exhibitions

1937   *American Indian Exposition and Congress,* Tulsa, Oklahoma
1947   New Jersey State Museum, Trenton
        University of Oklahoma, Norman
        Bloomington Art Association, Illinois
        Syracuse Museum of Fine Art, New York
1948   Dallas Museum of Fine Arts, Texas
        Detroit Institute of Arts, Michigan
        Joslyn Memorial Art Museum, Omaha, Nebraska
        Maryhill Museum of Art, Washington
        Isaac Delgado Museum, New Orleans, Louisiana
1949   Northeastern Oklahoma A&M College, Miami, Oklahoma
1950   Smithsonian Institution, Washington, D.C.
1954   George Thomas Hunter Gallery of Art, Chattanooga, Tennessee
        Rosicrucian Egyptian, Oriental Museum, Rosicrucian Park, San Jose, California
        Sioux Indian Exhibition & Crafts Center, Halley Park, Rapid City, South Dakota
        Chicago Art Institute, Illinois
1955   Sanford Museum, Cherokee, Iowa
        Albany Institute of History & Art, New York
        Currier Gallery of Art, Manchester, New Hampshire
1959   Chappel House, Denver, Colorado
        Ponca City Art Association, Oklahoma
1960   Museum of American Indian, New York, New York
        Museum of the Plains Indian, Browning, Montana
1978   *100 Years of Native American Painting,* Oklahoma Museum of Art, Oklahoma City
1979-80 *Native American Paintings*, organized by the Joslyn Art Museum, Omaha, Nebraska (traveling)
1982   *Native American Painting: Selections from the Museum of the American Indian*, Heard Museum, Phoenix, Arizona
1984-85 *Indianascher Kunstler* (traveling, Germany), organized by the Philbrook Museum, Tulsa, Oklahoma

Waldo Mootzka: *Mong Kachinas: Aholi, Eototo, and Crow Mother.* Photograph by Seth Roffman; courtesy Dick Howard collection.

1988   *When the Raibow Touches Down,* Heard Museum, Phoenix, Arizona (traveling)

1991-92 *Shared Visions: Native American Painters and Sculptors in the Twentieth Century,* The Heard Museum, Phoenix, Arizona

1996   *Drawn from Memory: James T. Bialac Collection of Native American Art,* Heard Museum, Phoenix, Arizona

Collections

Amerind Foundation, Dragoon, Arizona; Brooklyn Museum of Art, New York; Thomas Gilcrease Institute of American History and Art, Tulsa, Oklahoma; Koogler McNay Art Museum, San Antonio, Texas; Museum of the American Indian, New York; Museum of Northern Arizona, Flagstaff, Arizona; Philbrook Museum of Art, Tulsa, Oklahoma; Millicent Rogers Foundation Museum, Taos, New Mexico; Southwest Museum, Los Angeles, California; University of Oklahoma, Norman, Oklahoma; Woolaroc Museum,

Bartlesville, Oklahoma; Wheelwright Museum of the American Indian, Santa Fe, New Mexico.

Publications

On MOOTZKA: Books—*American Indian Painting of the Southwest and Plains Areas,* by Dorothy Dunn, University of New Mexico, Albuquerque, 1968; *Indian Painters and White Patrons,* by J.J. Brody, University of New Mexico Press, Albuquerque, 1971; *Southwest Indian Painting: A Changing Art,* by Clara Lee Tanner, Tucson, 1973; *100 Years of Native American Painting,* exhibition catalog by Arthur Silberman, Oklahoma Museum of Art, Oklahoma City, 1978; *American Indian Painting and Sculpture,* by Patricia Broder, New York, 1981; *Selections from the Museum of the American Indian,* by David M. Fawcett and Lee A. Callander, Museum of the American Indian, New York, 1982; *Indianascher Kunstler,* by Gerhard Hoffmann, Munich, 1984; *The Arts of the North American Indian: Native Traditions in Evolution,* edited by Edwin L. Wade, Hudson Hills Press, New York, in association with Philbrook Art Center, Tulsa, Oklahoma,

1986; *When the Rainbow Touches Down*, exhibition catalog by Tryntje Van Ness Seymour, Heard Museum, University of Washington Press, 1988; *Shared Visions: Native American Painters and Sculptors in the Twentieth Century,* by Margaret Archuleta and Dr. Rennard Strickland, The New Press, New York, 1991. **Articles**—"Mootzka, the Hopi Artist, Painter of Indian Tribal Ceremonies," by Pedro J. Lemos, *School Arts,* March 1935.

* * *

Among the first generation of Hopi painters, Frank Kabotie, Otis Polelonema, and Waldo Mootzka are the most important. Mootzka, the youngest of them, has a great deal in common with Fred Kabotie. Having been sent to school in Albuquerque before the establishment of art classes there, he had received no formal art training, but had observed Kabotie painting at Oraibi Day School and may have learned from him the technique of watercolor painting. During the 1930s, he was in Santa Fe, New Mexico, where he became associated with Dorothy Dunn's "Studio," an art center founded in 1932 for the furthering of young Natives in the arts. He also painted, together with other Hopi artists, scenes from everyday life for John Louw Nelson's *Rhythm for Rain*, an ethnographic novel about the Hopi. Toward the end of his life, Mootzka came under the influence of Frank Patania, who taught him silversmithing, a craft in which he was active until his death in 1940.

Mootzka's subject matter is quite varied. When he started painting in the 1920s, he focused on typical Hopi subjects—tribal ceremonies, kachinas, mythological scenes—and also painted scenes from everyday life and the animal world. Though his animals are stiff-legged creatures and quite conventional, they are beautifully colored, with pink and lavender often predominating. Mootzka also developed an interesting method for perspective in landscape backgrounds, by placing minute human figures in the distance, or in his arrangement of a pueblo village by drawing room above room.

Though influenced by Kabotie and traditional Hopi painting, Mootzka liked to experiment with other styles and modes, including three-dimensional quality in his portrayals as well as modeling in color. Mesas, for instance, are rendered in pastel shades, losing some dramatic impact for more subtle views. The stylized forms of leaves, flowers, and cloud formations suggest art deco, with a harmonizing and symbolic combination of decorative elements.

As a painter of Hopi subject matter, like kachinas, ceremonies, and mythology, Mootzka is an interesting transitional figure. On the one hand, he stands in the tradition of the kiva murals of Awatovi, a prehistoric settlement that also influenced Fred Kabotie. But in the rendering of fertility rites he broke new ground. His concept of the theme is modern, and he prefigures in his treatment of the background new possibilities that were pursued by Gilbert Atencio and Tony Da. For example, in *Pollination of the Corn* (1940), one of the most frequently reproduced milestones in the development of traditional Indian painting, Mootzka uses a rhythmical flow of forms for the symbolic rendering of the fertility rite. The figures celebrate the insemination of the corn in an overflowing sea of colors and shapes, mirroring the fertility theme, while sun, clouds, rain, and rainbow lend the ceremony significance. This painting was completed shortly before his death in an automobile accident in Phoenix in 1940. By then Mootzka's reputation had been solidly established, and his work was featured in numerous exhibitions during the following decades.

—Gerhard and Gisela Hoffmann

MOPOPE, Stephen
Variant names: Qued Koi
Tribal affiliations: Kiowa
Painter

Born: Kiowa Reservation, Oklahoma, 27 August 1898; Kiowa name means "Painted Robe." **Education:** Instruction in ceremonial dances and art by granduncles Charles White Buffalo Oheltoint (Ohet Toint) and Haungooah; St. Patrick's Mission School, Anadarko, Oklahoma, graduated in 1916; student at Susan Ryan Peters' special art education classes, 1918, art education at the University of Oklahoma, Norman, 1926 to 1929; Fort Sill Indian School, mural, secco and fresco painting instruction with Olle Nordmark, 1938. **Career:** Dancer and musician (Southern Plains Indian flute); an original member of O-HO-MAH Lodge, a ceremonial society of the Kiowa; commissioned for murals, including eight panels in memory of Father Isidore Ricklin, St. Patrick's Mission School, 1929, Fort Sill Indian School, 1938, U.S. Department of the Interior Building in Washington, D. C., Oklahoma Historical Society Museum, Federal Building in Muskogee, and U.S. Navy Hospital, Carville, Louisiana, 1940s, and for paintings, including sixteen on the walls of the Anadarko Post Office, 1936-37 (with James Auchiah); lecturer, including National Folk Festival, Chicago, Illinois, 1957. **Awards:** Certificate of Appreciation, Indian Arts and Crafts Board, Anadarko, Oklahoma, 1966. **Died:** 3 February 1974.

Individual Exhibitions

1975   *The Art of Stephen Mopope,* Southern Plains Indian Museum, Anadarko, Oklahoma

Selected Group Exhibitions

1928   *Five Kiowas*, traveling exhibition arranged by Oscar Brousse Jacobson
        Five Kiowas, First International Art Exposition, Prague, Czechoslovakia
1930   *Southwest States Indian Art Show*, Santa Fe, New Mexico
1931-33 *Exposition of Indian Tribal Arts,* Grand Central Galleries, New York
1937   *American Indian Exposition and Congress*, Tulsa, Oklahoma
1947-65 *American Indian Paintings from the Permanent Collection,* Philbrook Museum of Art (traveling)
1955-56 European tour sponsored by the University of Oklahoma, Norman
1958-61 European tour sponsored by the University of Oklahoma, Norman
1965   Kermac Mural Design Exhibit (traveling)
1967   Oklahoma Art Center Gallery, Oklahoma City
1972   *Contemporary Southern Plains Indian Painting*, tour organized by the Southern Plains Indian Museum and Oklahoma Indian Arts and Crafts Cooperative, Anadarko
1978   *100 Years of Native American Painting,* Oklahoma Museum of Art, Oklahoma City
1979   *Sharing Our Wealth*, Oklahoma Historical Society, Oklahoma City

Stephen Mopope: Detail of *Family on the Move* mural, U.S. Post Office, Anadarko, Oklahoma. Courtesy of J. A. Warner.

1980   *Midwest Professional Artists Benefit Show,* Tulsa Garden Center, Oklahoma

Plains Indian Paintings, organized by the University of Oklahoma Museum of Art (traveling)

1981   *Visions and Views: Symbolic Imagery of the Native American Church,* Southern Plains Indian Museum, Anadarko, Oklahoma

1981-83 *Native American Painting,* Amarillo Art Center, Texas (traveling)

1984-85 *Indianascher Kunstler* (traveling, Germany), organized by the Philbrook Museum, Tulsa, Oklahoma

1985   *Native American Fine Arts,* Heard Museum, Phoenix, Arizona

1990   *American Indian Artists: The Avery Collection and the McNay Permanent Collection,* Marion Koogler McNay Art Museum, San Antonio, Texas

1991   *Kiowa Murals,* The Southern Plains Indian Museum and Crafts Center, Anadarko, Oklahoma

1991-96 *Shared Visions: Native American Painters and Sculptors in the Twentieth Century,* Heard Museum, Phoenix, Arizona

Collections

Anadarko City Museum, Oklahoma; Cleveland Museum of Art, Ohio; Dartmouth College Collection, Hanover, New Hampshire; Thomas Gilcrease Institute of American History and Art, Tulsa, Oklahoma; Heard Museum, Phoenix, Arizona; Indian Arts and Crafts Board, Department of the Interior, Washington, D.C.; Fred Jones, Jr., Museum of Art, University of Oklahoma, Norman; Marion Koogler McNay Art Museum, San Antonio Texas; Museum of New Mexico, Santa Fe; Museum of Northern Arizona, Flagstaff; Museum of the American Indian, New York; Oklahoma Art Center Gallery, Oklahoma City; Oklahoma Historical Society Museum, Oklahoma City; Oklahoma Museum of Natural History, University of Oklahoma, Norman; Peabody Museum of Salem, Massachusetts; Philbrook Art Museum, Tulsa, Oklahoma; Millicent Rogers Foundation Museum, Taos, New Mexico; Southern Plains Indian Museum, Anadarko, Oklahoma; Southwest Museum, Los Angeles, California; Wheelwright Museum of the American Indian, Santa Fe, New Mexico; Woolaroc Museum, Bartlesville, Oklahoma.

Publications

On MOPOPE: Books—*Kiowa Indian Art,* by O.B. Jacobson, Nice, France, 1929; *Indian Painters and White Patrons,* by J.J. Brody, University of New Mexico Press, Albuquerque, 1971; *Song from the Earth, American Indian Painting,* by Jamake Highwater, New York Graphic Society, Boston, 1976; *100 Years of Native American Painting,* by Arthur Silberman, Oklahoma Museum of Art, Oklahoma City, 1978; *Kiowa Voices: Ceremonial Dance Ritual and Song* (1981) and *Kiowa Voices: Myths, Legends, and Folktales* (1983), by Maurice Boyd, Texas Christian University Press, Fort Worth; *Native American Painting: Selections from the Museum of the American Indian,* by David

M. Fawcett and Lee A. Callander, Museum of the American Indian, New York, 1982; *American Indian Artists: The Avery Collection and the McNay Permanent Collection,* by Jean Sherrod Williams, Marion Koogler McNay Art Museum, San Antonio, 1990; *Kiowa Murals,* Southern Plains Indian Museum & Crafts Center, Anardarko, Oklahoma, 1991; *Shared Visions: Native American Painters and Sculptors in the Twentieth Century,* by Margaret Archuleta and Dr. Rennard Strickland, Heard Museum, Phoenix, 1991; *Artists and Craftspeople,* by Arlene Hershfelder, Facts on File, Inc., New York, 1994. **Articles**—"American Inter-Tribal Indian Art," by Rose V.S. Berry, *Art and Archeology XXXII,* November-December 1931; "Indian Arts Fund Collection of Paintings," by Clara Lee Tanner and Anne Forbes, *El Palacio,* December 1948; "The Development of Modern American Indian Painting in the Southwest and Plains Areas," by Dorothy Dunn, *El Palacio,* November 1951; "Kiowa Indian Art, A Pochoir Portfolio," by Maybelle Mann, *American Art & Antiques,* January/February 1979; "The Kiowa Five," by W.K. Stratton, *Oklahoma Today,* November/December 1990; "Mopope," *American Indian Art,* Spring 1995.

* * *

Stephen Mopope was one of the best known members of the famous Kiowa Five group of artists who originated the classic flat style of painting on the Southern Plains. During his lifetime, Mopope established a strong personal and professional identity that enabled him to make enduring contributions to art in Oklahoma. Perhaps more than any other individual of the Kiowa Five, Mopope is remembered and admired by many contemporary painters who feel that he was an important influence or inspiration for their work. Mopope was a prolific artist who not only painted many pictures utilizing the casein media, but was also a muralist and a virtuoso with line and color. His paintings of dancers show elegance and motion, while his portraiture was almost always admirable. Like most of the other Kiowa Five artists, Mopope preferred to focus upon small groups and single figures in his art, as opposed to large ceremonial compositions that one might find in Southwestern art, and many pictures by Mopope and the Kiowa Five feature seated and rear-view figures, in addition to portraiture. Mopope was a master of all of the varieties of Oklahoma flat style painting.

Mopope is also very important because his personal history is a part of the continuities and changes in Southern Plains Indian painting. In particular, Mopope is organically related to the rich historic past of Kiowa male illustrative arts, which includes symbolic and pictographic designs on war shields, shield covers, and tipis as well as ledger art and the unforgettable memories of the Fort Marion imprisonment, when several Kiowas painted pictures to pass the time and earn extra money. One of Mopope's granduncles was Charles White Buffalo Oheltoint (Ohet Toint), who became an active artist and dance participant while a prisoner at Fort Marion, and Haungooah (James Silverhorn), one of the most talented and celebrated artists in Kiowa history, was another granduncle. According to Mopope, Oheltoint played an important role in teaching the young boy how to paint. Upon his return to Oklahoma from Fort Marion, Oheltoint continued to produce art for his people and ethnologists, like James Mooney of the Smithsonian Institution; Oheltoint took an interest in his young grandnephew's burgeoning interest in art. During one project when Oheltoint painted a reproduction of the famous

DO-GIAGYA-GUAT lodge (or Tipi of Battle Pictures), he allowed the young Mopope to paint the black and yellow stripes—distinctive feature of the tipi. Both Oheltoint and Haungooah worked on several commissions for Mooney, where they recreated painted miniature shields and tipis for the ethnologist's collection. Certainly these teachers and mentors were powerful influences in the artistic development of Mopope and his other relations—Jack Hokeah, Spencer Asah, George Silverhorn, and George Geionety. Moreover, this gave Mopope (and other members of the Kiowa Five) a direct connection to the historic past of Kiowa male painting.

Mopope's non-tribal educational experience is much like those of the other Kiowa Five artists: formal education at the St. Patrick's Mission School, Anadarko, from where he graduated in 1916; a student at Susan (Susie) Ryan Peters' special art education classes in 1918; and special art education at the University of Oklahoma in Norman from 1926-29. Like the other Kiowa Five artists, several of Mopope's paintings were included in 1928 in a traveling exhibit that went to Prague, Czechoslovakia, where they were featured in the First International Art Exposition. In 1929, some of Mopope's original paintings in the exhibition were reproduced in silkscreen print form (along with those of the other Kiowa Five painters) in the folio, *Kiowa Indian Art* (Nice, France).

Along with being a gifted painter, Mopope was a talented muralist. In 1929, he and three other Kiowa Five artists executed eight panels in memory of Father Isidore Ricklin at the St. Patrick's Mission School in Anadarko. Even more importantly, Mopope and Auchiah were commissioned in 1936 to do sixteen paintings on the walls of the new Post Office building in Anadarko. These treasures, depicting vignettes from traditional Kiowa life along with several works of portraiture, are still on view today. Each mural painting is marvelously appropriate for the particular space allotted. In 1938, Mopope enrolled in a course taught by the notable Swedish muralist, Olle Nordmark, on the techniques of secco and fresco painting. Afterwards, Mopope and Auchiah had the opportunity to work on murals for the U.S. Department of the Interior Building in Washington, D. C.

Mopope was also a very talented dancer and musician, remembered particularly for war dances and playing the traditional Southern Plains Indian flute. He was one of the original members of the Kiowa O-HO-MAH Lodge, a ceremonial society of the Kiowa, founded by culture bearers and leaders among the Kiowa and including many of the returned captives from the Fort Marion experience. Their ceremonial ritual derived from the Siouan Grass Dance that had spread throughout the Plains in the early reservation days. Many of Mopope's paintings featured dance scenes from the O-HO-MAH ceremony. Quite clearly, Mopope saw himself as a cultural traditionalist who devoted his life to recording the customs of his people for posterity.

Perhaps the best assessment of Mopope has been written by Rosemary Ellison, who offered these words in a 1975 exhibition brochure posthumously celebrating the life and career of Mopope. "The success of his endeavors is witnessed not only by the vast oeuvre which he produced in his lifetime but by his tremendous influence upon aspiring Native American artists. Stephen Mopope's artistic achievements will continue to provide inspiration to scores of future artists. His role is firmly established in the annals of American art."

—John Anson Warner

MORRISON, George

Tribal affiliations: Chippewa
Painter and sculptor

Born: Grand Marais, Minnesota, 30 September 1919. **Education:** Studied at Minneapolis College of Art and Design, 1938-43 (honorary M.F.A. 1969); Art Students League, 1943-46; University of Aix-Marseille, Aix-en-Provence, 1952-53. **Career:** Visiting artist, State College of Iowa, Cedar Falls, Iowa, 1961; visiting artist, Cornell University, Ithaca, New York, 1962; visiting artist, Pennsylvania State University, University Park, Pennsylvania; associate professor, Rhode Island School of Design, 1963-70; visiting professor of American Indian Studies and Studio Arts, University of Minnesota, 1970-73; Professor of Studio Arts, University of Minnesota, 1973-83, retired 1983. Received commissions for American Indian Center, Minneapolis, Minnesota, 1974; First Bank, Minneapolis, Minnesota, 1975; Daybreak Star American Indian Center, Seattle, Washington, 1978; Federal Forestry Building, Sandpoint, Idaho, 1979; Prudential Insurance Company, Plymouth, Minnesota, 1980. **Awards:** Vanderlip Traveling Scholarship, Minneapolis School of Art, 1943-44; Fulbright Scholarship, 1952-53; John Hay Whitney

Fellowship, 1953-54; first prize, Rhode Island Arts Festival, Providence, Rhode Island, 1965; Honorary Master of Fine Arts, Minneapolis College of Art and Design, Minneapolis, Minnesota, 1969; Merit Award, Ojibwe Art Expo Annual, Bemidji, Minnesota, 1978; Honorary Doctorate of Fine Arts, Rhode Island School of Design, Providence, Rhode Island, 1991.

Individual Exhibitions

1973	Walker Art Center, Minneapolis, Minnesota
	Bethel College, St. Paul, Minnesota
1976	Touchstone Gallery, New York
1977	Bemidji State University, Minnesota
1978	Macalester College, St. Paul, Minnesota
1981	*George Morrison: Entries in an Artist's Journal*, University of Minnesota, Minneapolis
1983	University Art Museum, University of Minnesota, Minneapolis
1984	University of North Dakota, Grand Forks
1987	*HORIZON: Small Painting Series, 1980-1987*, Tweed Museum of Art, University of Minnesota, Duluth
	Minnesota Museum of Art, St. Paul
1990	*Standing in the Northern Lights*, Minnesota Museum of Art, St. Paul
1992	*Drawings and Small Sculpture*, Bockley Gallery, Minneapolis, Minnesota
1993	Johnson Heritage Post Art Gallery, Grand Marais, Minnesota
	Horizon Series, Dolly Fiterman Fine Arts, Minneapolis, Minnesota
1995	*George Morrison: Recent Acquisitions*, The Minnesota Museum of Art, St. Paul

Selected Group Exhibitions

1971	*Images 1971*, Anoka-Ramsey State Junior College, Coon Rapids, Minnesota
	12th Red River Annual Exhibition, Fargo-Moorhead Art Association, Moorhead, Minnesota
1979	*New Works by Twin City Artists*, Landmark Center, St. Paul, Minnesota
	Vanderlip Award Winners Exhibition, Minneapolis College of Art and Design, Minnesota
1981	*Masterworks of American Indian Art*, Philbrook Art Center, Tulsa, Oklahoma
1987	*Traditions and Innovations: Seven American Artists*, Plains Art Museum, Moorhead, Minnesota
1990	*Our Land/Ourselves*, University Art Gallery, State University of New York, Albany
1991	*Shared Visions*, The Heard Museum, Phoenix
1992	*We, the Human Beings*, The College of Wooster Art Museum, Ohio
1996	*Gifts of the Spirit*, Peabody Essex Museum, Salem, Massachusetts

George Morrison. Courtesy of the artist.

Collections

Bezalel National Museum of Art, Jerusalem; Amon Carter Museum of Western Art, Fort Worth, Texas; Chrysler Museum of Norfolk, Norfolk, Virginia; Carl N. Gorman Museum, University of California, Davis; The Heard Museum, Phoenix; Joslyn Art Museum, Omaha, Nebraska; Kuopio Museum, Kuopio, Finland; Minnesota Museum of Art, St. Paul; Munson-Williams-Proctor Institute, Utica, New York; Philadelphia Museum of Art, Pennsylvania; Rose Art Museum, Brandeis University, Waltham, Massachusetts; Tweed Museum of Art, Duluth, Minnesota; Walker Art Center, Minneapolis; Whitney Museum of American Art, New York.

Publications

On MORRISON: Books—*George Morrison: The Story of an American Indian*, by Dragos Kostich, Dillon Press, Minneapolis, Minnesota, 1977; "George Morrison," in *This Song Remembers*, edited by Jane Katz, Houghton Miflin, Boston, 1980; "Artist's Statement" in *The Sweetgrass Lives On*, edited by Jamake Highwater, Lippincott and Crowell, New York, 1980; *Magic Images*, by Edwin Wade and Rennard Strickland, Philbrook Art Center, Tulsa, Oklahoma, and the University of Oklahoma Press, Norman, 1981; *The Arts of the North American Indian: Native Traditions in Evolution*, edited by Edwin Wade, Hudson Hills Press, New York, 1986; "Standing in the Northern Lights," in *Standing in the Northern Lights* by Katherine Van Tassell, Minnesota Museum of Art, St. Paul, 1990; "George Morrison," in *Many Voices, Many Visions*, edited by Lawrence Abbott, 1997. **Articles**—"An Interview with George Morrison," by Elizabeth Erickson, *Artpaper*, Summer 1987; "George Morrison," in *The Canadian Journal of Native Studies 15*, no. 1, 1995. **Transcript**—Transcription of recorded remarks in *Shared Visions: Native American Painters and Sculptors in the Twentieth Century: Conference, May 8-11, 1991, Phoenix, Arizona: Proceedings*, The Heard Museum, Phoenix, Arizona, 1992. **Film**—*George Morrison: Indian Artist*, KTCA-TV, Minneapolis, Minnesota, 1978; *Standing in the Northern Lights*, produced by Linda Kuusisto and Daniel Gumnit, Grace Productions, Minneapolis, Minnesota, 1991.

*

George Morrison comments:

There is a spirituality in the landscape at my studio in Grand Portage: the water and the air and the atmosphere. All those elements are coming into me from what I see. I'm not looking at it like I'm painting it. But all of these things are in my mind even though I'm not looking at the lake when I'm painting. I'm looking at the lake at other times, just for the sake of looking at it because it's there. I'm always very conscious and aware of this large body of water, which is like a presence in itself. It is alive and it changes by the hour. Perhaps that very thing has been transplanted into my head, and then I'm transforming that onto the canvas. I think that's the kind of transformation that an artist does—taking what's in his head and putting it on canvas to create his interpretation of what is there.

I think that all art from every source has a certain element of magic. I like to feel that every work has that kind of special quality by virtue of the artist doing it in some reverential manner. When I say that, more and more of the word "magic" is coming into my own head. It's not like I'm saying that I want to do a magic piece today, but by and large, in the back of my mind, I like to think that way. Even in the *Horizon Series* there was a certain spirituality coming from the subject matter that somehow enters into the work from my head and through my hands, and then the images come and

they give forth their own kind of power through the essence of what the subject is.

* * *

For over fifty years George Morrison has followed his unique individual vision, from Minnesota to New York to Europe to Rhode Island and back to Minnesota. In that sense he has come full circle, and he admits to having had to leave his Northern Minnesota roots in order to hone his talents and then return to the shores of Lake Superior. In another way, certain forms and images have persisted and recurred in Morrison's work throughout his career, regardless of the materials used or the nature of the project. Morrison uses wood, tempera, pencil, ink, acrylics, crayon, and watercolor, and his work can be both small (like the 4 1/2 x 7 1/2 inch *Red Rock: Imaginative North Shore Landscape*, 1981) or monumental (the 18 x 98 foot exterior mural for the American Indian Center in Minneapolis).

One constant in most of his later work is the horizon line, which appears not only in his paintings but also in his sculptures. One recurrent theme in Morrison's work is the presence and livingness of nature and organic forces, which can be seen in his early pieces focusing on elements of nature, such as *Starfish* (1945) and *Sun and the River* (1949). This focus on nature is reflected in one of the names his cousin Walter Caribou received for him in a dream, "Standing in the Northern Lights."

Morrison graduated from the Minneapolis School of Art in 1943, where he was exposed to the Bauhaus as well as Matisse, and Picasso. He went on to the Art Students League in New York City, graduating in 1946, and later to study in France and travel in Italy and Spain. Because of his exposure to Cubism, Surrealism, and Abstract Expressionism, Morrison has integrated elements of these styles into his work, although certainly in the case of the former not in "orthodox" ways. His is a Surrealism of personal uses of color to

George Morrison: *Cube,* 1987. Courtesy of the artist.

NATIVE NORTH AMERICAN ARTISTS

create images transformed in the process of moving from observation to reflection. *Surrealist Landscape: Leaping Figure* (1984) and the similar *Red Rock Variation* (1986) are still very much based on Morrison's familiar Lake Superior environment with his signature horizon line. One does not find melting watches in Morrison's work. Beyond this, though, Morrison's interests branched out into many other areas, to the arts of Central America, to the Aztecs and Mayans, and to indigenous art from all over the world.

More to the point is the influence of Abstract Expressionism in his drawings and paintings. *The Antagonist* (1956) and *Reunion* (1962) use blocks of contrasting colors; *Pennsylvania Landscape* (1963) is a swirl of color. However, even some of the abstractions are transformations of observed reality. *Untitled Drawing* (1977) echoes a number of works detailing another of Morrison's recurring subjects, the Witch Tree on the shore of Lake Superior near his studio. *Witch Tree* (1981), *Witch Tree: Direct Observation* (1982), and *Witch Tree Variation* (1988) interpret the subject in varying degrees of literalness. It might not even be too extreme to say that the aforementioned *Surrealist Landscape: Leaping Figure* depicts the Witch Tree broken into its essential forms and unloosed from its earthbound moorings.

Two series that have occupied Morrison's energies over the past fifteen years have been the *Horizon* series and the *Red Rock Variations*. The *Horizon* paintings, small-scale in a variety of styles, are Morrison's interpretations of the sky, land, and water he sees from his studio window in Grand Portage. Seeking variation, he uses different techniques to delineate the organic structural elements of each painting. For example, in some works the paint is thin, in others thick; in still others there may be four layers of paint, with the underlayer showing through, and in others up to twenty layers. Each of these techniques creates the variation in texture that Morrison sought. Further, some of the paintings have a sense of flatness because shapes go against one another, while in others the colors blend because they are more pastel in tone and lower in value.

The *Red Rock Variations* are inspired by the location of Morrison's studio. These works have some resonances with the *Horizon* series, in terms of the palette and the horizon line, but more characteristically use blocks of color to create shapes. Paintings like *Memory of the Shore. Red Rock Variation: Lake Superior Landscape* (1993), *Red Rock Variation: Sentinels* (1993), and *Red Rock Variation: Procession* (1993) use reds predominantly in interlocking shapes to interpret the physical environment.

Morrison also uses wood, steel, and brass to create collages, totems, lingas and chiringas, and even coffee table tops, and he experiments with the shapes of found objects. Morrison's collages further reflect his concerns with natural elements. Using found and prepared wood, these pieces are analogs of his paintings of Lake Superior. His first redwood and red cedar totems derive from numerous sources, including the Northwest Coast, but Morrison's do not represent animal and human heads but are more constructivist mosaics of carved shapes placed on a plywood core to give the appearance of incisions. These were stained dark red to relate them indirectly to the Northwest Coast totem poles. Poles done with exotic woods like padouk and bubinga and other materials become more abstract forms, some with smaller vertical columns within the larger column, like *Vertical Wood Column* (1988).

Morrison's interpretations of large and small linga and chiringa forms include his horizon line as his "mark." These forms become sculptures in themselves. *Red Totem* (1980) and the lithograph *Red Cube* (1983) could be seen as foreshadowing Morrison's later constructions of coffee table tops, cubes, and boxes. The table tops are

also reminiscent of his wood collages, but he uses exotic woods and less geometrical shapes.

Morrison continuously experiments with forms and materials and is open to new sources. For example, the design of *Solar Form* (1991), made from padouk wood, was based on an old wooden gear Morrison found in a friend's studio, and reminded him of a calendar form of the Mayans. The search for new forms and a sense of transformation is the hallmark of George Morrison's art.

—Larry Abbott

MORRISSEAU, Norval
Variant names: Copper Thunderbird
Tribal affiliations: Ojibway
Painter, printmaker, and illustrator

Born: Beardmore, Sandy Point Reserve, Ontario, 14 March 1931. **Family:** Married Harriet Kakegamic, 1957; six children. **Education:** Self-taught. **Awards:** Commissions, including Indians of Canada Pavilion Expo '67, Montreal, Quebec, and McMichael Canadian Collection, Kleinburg, Ontario; Appointed as member of the Royal Canadian Academy of Art (RCAA), 1970. **Awards:** Order of Canada, 1978; Honorary Doctorate of Laws Degree, McMaster University, Montreal, Quebec, 1980; honorary doctorate, McMaster University, 1980; honoured by the Assembly of First Nations, 1995.

Individual Exhibitions

1962-63	Pollock Gallery, Toronto, Ontario
1964	Red Door Gallery, Winnipeg, Manitoba
1965	Galerie Agnes Lefort, Montreal, Quebec
	Hart House Gallery, University of Toronto, Ontario
1966	St. Paul de Vence, France
1967	Musee du Quebec, Quebec City
	La Galerie Cartier, Montreal, Quebec
1969	Gallerie Saint-Paul, Saint-Paul-de-Vence, France
1972	*Retrospective*, Pollock Gallery, Toronto, Ontario
1974	Bau-xi Gallery, Toronto, Ontario
	Pollock Gallery, Toronto, Ontario
1975	Shayne Gallery, Montreal, Quebec
1978	First Canadian Place, Toronto, Ontario
1979	Pollock Gallery, Toronto, Ontario
	The Gallery Stratford, Stratford, Ontario
	Cardigan-Milne Gallery, Winnipeg, Manitoba
1980	Canadian Galleries, Edmonton, Alberta
	Bayard Gallery, New York, New York
1981	Anthony's Gallery, Toronto, Ontario; Vancouver, British Columbia
	Thunder Bay National Exhibition Centre, Ontario
1982	The NewMan Gallery, London, Ontario
	Nexus Art Gallery, Toronto, Ontario
1983	Art Imperial Gallery, Toronto, Ontario
	Native American Centre for the Living Arts, Niagara Falls, New York
1984	Ontario North Now, Ontario Place, Toronto
1988	Sinclair Centre, Vancouver, British Columbia

1989	The Art Emporium, Vancouver, British Columbia
1990-91	Kinsman Robinson Galleries, Toronto, Ontario
1992	*The Spirit Within,* Kinsman Robinson Galleries, Toronto, Ontario
	Jenkins/Showler Galleries, Whiterock, British Columbia
1994	Kinsman Robinson Galleries, Toronto, Ontario

Selected Group Exhibitions

1963	Kitchener-Waterloo Gallery, Kitchener, Ontario
	Canadian Contemporary Art, Canadian National Exhibition, Toronto, Ontario
1965	University of Waterloo Art Gallery, Ontario
1967	Expo '67, Montreal, Quebec
1971	*Festival of Canada,* Robertson Art Centre, Binghamton, New York
1973	*Canadian Contemporary Painting,* University of Waterloo Art Gallery, Ontario
	Canadian Indian Painting, Royal Ontario Museum, Toronto
1974	McMichael Canadian Collection, Kleinburg, Ontario
	Contemporary Native Arts of Ontario, Oakville Centennial Gallery, Ontario
1975	Dominion Gallery, Montreal, Quebec
	Professional Native Indian Artists Incorporated, The Art Emporium, Vancouver, British Columbia
1976	Bergens Kunsfoeing, Bergen, Norway
	Contemporary Native Art of Canada: The Woodland Indians, Royal Ontario Museum for travel to Canada House Gallery, London, England, Aula Luisen Schule, Lahr, Germany
1977	*Painting Now,* Agnes Etherington Art Centre, Queens University, Kingston, Ontario
	Contemporary Indian Art: The Trail from the Past to the Future, Mackenzie Gallery and Native Studies Programme, Trent University, Peterborough, Ontario
	Links to a Tradition, Department of Indian Affairs and Northern Development, for travel to centres in Brazil
1978	*Morrisseau/Thomas/Odjug,* Pollock Gallery, Toronto, Ontario
	Art of the Woodland Indian, McMichael Canadian Collection, Kleinburg, Ontario, for travel to Surrey, British Columbia, Thomas, Ontario, and North Bay, Ontario
	Images of Man in Canadian Painting, 1878-1978, McIntosh Gallery, London, Ontario
	Thunder Bay National Exhibition Centre, Ontario
1979	*Kinder des Nanabush,* Interversa Gallerie, Hamburg, West Germany
1980	Bearclaw Gallery, Edmonton, Alberta
1982	Moore Gallery, Hamilton, Ontario
	Renewal, Masterworks of Contemporary Indian Art from the National Museum of Man, Thunder Bay, Ontario
1983	*New Growth from Ancestral Roots,* The Koffler Gallery, Willowdale, Ontario
	Contemporary Indian Art at Rideau Hall, from the permanent collection of the Department of Indian Affairs and Northern Development, Ottawa, Ontario
1983-85	*Contemporary Indian and Inuit Art of Canada,* organized by the Department of Indian and Northern Affairs for travel in the United States and Canada

1984	*Norval Morrisseau and the Emergence of the Image Makers,* organized by the Art Gallery of Ontario, Toronto
1985	*Two Worlds,* Norman MacKenzie Art Gallery, Regina, Saskatchewan
1986	*New Beginnings,* Native Business Summit, Toronto, Ontario
	The Shaman Art of Morrisseau and Marion, First Canadian Place, The Gallery, Toronto, Ontario
	The Birch Bark Sings, Ontario North Now, Ontario Place, Toronto, Ontario
1987	*A Celebration of Contemporary Native Art,* Southwest Museum, Los Angeles, California
1989	*Woodlands: Contemporary Art of the Anishnabe,* Thunder Bay Art Gallery, Ontario
1993	*Art of the Anishnabe: Works from the Permanent Collection,* Thunder Bay Art Gallery, Ontario
1994	Thunder Bay Art Gallery, Ontario

Collections

Art Gallery of Hamilton, Hamilton, Ontario; The Art Gallery of Ontario, Toronto, Ontario; Art Gallery of Windsor, Toronto; Canada Council ArtBank, Ottawa, Ontario; The Canadian Museum of Civilization, Ottawa, Ontario; City of Toronto Collection, Toronto, Ontario; Confederation Centre Art Gallery and Museum, Charlottetown, Prince Edward Island; Department of Indian Affairs and Northern Development, Ottawa, Ontario; Dodd's Coal Mines, South Edmonton, Alberta; Glenbow Museum, Calgary, Alberta; Guardian Capital Group, Toronto, Ontario; Hart House Art Gallery, University of Toronto; Humber College Collection, Toronto, Ontario; McMichael Canadian Collection, Kleinburg, Ontario; The Montreal Museum of Fine Art, Montreal, Quebec; Musée du Quebec, Quebec City, Quebec; Robertson Art Centre, Binghamton, New York; Ross Memorial Hospital, Lindway, Ontario; Royal Ontario Museum, Toronto, Ontario; Seneca College, Toronto, Ontario; Thunder Bay Exhibition Centre and Centre for Indian Art, Thunder Bay, Ontario; Winnipeg Art Gallery, Winnipeg, Manitoba.

Publications

By MORRISSEAU: Books—*Legends of My People: The Great Ojibway* (Morrisseau researched and transcribed the legends), edited by Selwyn Dewdney, Ryerson Press, Toronto, 1965; *Windigo and Other Tales of the Ojibway,* Herbert T. Schwarts, McCelland and Stewart, Toronto, 1969.

On MORRISSEAU: Books—*Indian Arts in Canada,* by Olive Patricia Dickason, Department of Indian Affairs and Northern Development, Ottawa, Ontario, 1972; *The Art of Norval Morrisseau,* by Lister Sinclair, Methuen, Toronto, 1979; *Norval Morrisseau and the Emergence of the Image Makers,* by Elizabeth McLuhan, Toronto, 1984; *The Sound of the Drum: The Sacred Art of the Anishnabec,* Boston Mills Press, Erin, Ontario, 1984; *Im Shatten der Sonne: Zeitgenossische Kunst der Indianer und Eskimos in Kanada,* Edition Cantz and Canadian Museum of Civilization, Ottawa, 1987; "Messages from the Past: Oral Traditions and Contemporary Woodlands Art," by Ruth B. Phillips, *In the Shadow of the Sun: Perspectives on Contemporary Native Art,* Canadian Museum of Civilization, Ottawa, 1993; **Articles**—"Cooper Thunderbird: An Ojibway Paints His People's Past," by Bill Brown,

Weekend Magazine, Toronto Daily Star, 12 June 1962; "Self-Taught Ojibway Artist Find Fame Overnight," by Lenore Crawford, *London Free Press,* 29 September 1962; "Myths and Symbols," *Time,* September 28, 1962; "Norval Morrisseau," by Selwyn Dewdney, *Canadian Art,* January/February 1963; "Canadian Indian Artists Death and Rebirth," by Tom Hill, *Art Magazine,* Summer 1974; "Interview with Norval Morrisseau," by James Stephens, *Art Magazine,* Summer 1974; "New Morrisseau Works Show He's Settled Inner Conflict," by James Purdie, *The Globe and Mail,* 19 August; "Fierce Clarity and Sophistication," *Time,* 25 August 1975; "Shaking Tents and Medicine Snakes: Traditional Elements in Contemporary Woodland Art," by Nancy-Lou Patterson, *Art Magazine,* Summer 1976; "North American Indian Art A Special Way Of Seeing," by Jamake Highwater, *Artwest,* vol. 8, no. 5, May 1983; "Salute To A Vibrant Revolutionary," by Gilliam MacKay, *MacLean's,* 5 March 1984; "Meeting Morrisseau (excerpt from Jack Pollock's memoir *Dear M*)," *Canada Forum,* vol. 4, 1989. **Films**—*The Colours of Pride,* National Film Board Of Canada, 1973; *The Paradox of Norval Morrisseau,* National Film Board of Canada, 1974; *Spirits Speaking Through: Canadian Woodland Artists,* CBC Spectrum Series, 1982; *The Originals: Norval Morrisseau,* by Moses Znaimer and Jim Hanley, City TV, Toronto, 1990.

*

Norval Morrisseau comments:

All my painting and drawing is really a continuation of the shaman's scrolls.

*   *   *

Norval Morrisseau is generally regarded as the founder of a new art movement, sometimes called the Woodlands School, or (less accurately) the Legend Painting movement. In this art, traditional Anishnaabe sacred iconography that had historically been expressed in rock art and incised birchbark Midewiwin scrolls was reinscribed in the Western media of easel painting and printmaking.

When Morrisseau burst on the attention of the Toronto public after his sell-out first show at the Pollock Gallery in 1962, his work was received as a direct survival of ancient Ojibway art reemerging after a century of repressive assimilationist policies. In fact, he is better characterized as a brilliant innovator who created a new kind of art out of inherited traditions and a modernist-primitivist painterly vocabulary, both informed by the artist's highly individual aesthetic sensibilty and his need to resolve his dual religious heritage. The power of his inventions, in terms both of form and content, together with his immediate commercial success in the cosmopolitan Toronto art market inspired a whole generation of young Anishnabek painters to take up the brush and the pen.

Morrisseau was, from his youth, intensely drawn both to the making of art and to ritual and mystical practices. From his early years two systems of belief competed for his allegiance: the Catholic faith of his grandmother that was sanctioned by government-sponsored institutions, and the ancient shamanstic practices taught to him by his grandfather, Moses Nanakonagos, that had been systematically repressed by government and church and that had been forced to go underground. Both because Midewiwin knowledge is not intended for disclosure outside of the society and because of government policies of supression secretized it even further, Morrisseau was greatly criticized within the Native community when he first began to paint scenes of traditional spirituality. But the artist's sense of his own mission to conserve and to assert the greatness of Native traditions was even stronger than this community disapproval, as indicated by his early decision to sign his works in syllabics with the name his grandfather gave him at the age of nineteen, Copper Thunderbird. In 1976, when Morrisseau joined the Eckankar sect, a further layer of mystical belief and practice began to influence his art.

Morrisseau's art is figurative, and his canvases are usually organized around large central images of animals or human beings connected by power lines and divided circles, the latter an image he invented to symbolize the principle of cosmic duality. Heavy black formlines surround his figures, and they are internally articulated by ex-ray motifs. The formlines are infilled with a mosaic of bright, saturated colours. The style of his maturity developed between about 1958 and 1965 in response to, but not always in agreement with, the advice given him by two important early patrons, Dr. Joseph Weinstein and Selwyn Dewdney. Morrisseau met Dr. Weinstein during the mid 1950s while he was working at a mine for which Weinstein was the regional doctor. Weinstein was an amateur painter of abstract works who had studied in Paris before World War II. He lent Morrisseau books from his extensive library on modern and world arts and introduced the young artist to his own art collection. Most importantly, he encouraged Morrisseau to paint images from Aboriginal oral tradition. The important collection of Morrisseau's work assembled by Dr. Weinstein in the late 1950s and now in the Canadian Museum of Civilization includes paintings of ancestors in nineteenth-century dress, of the divination ritual of the shaking tent, and of the transformation of man into thunderbird. Selwyn Dewdney, an artist and amateur archaeologist who was carrying out an important study of Anishnaabe rock art in Northern Ontario in the late 1950s, was introduced to Morrisseau about 1960 by a police officer who knew of their common interest in rock art and Ojibway traditions. Dewdney used Morrisseau as a consultant in his research and offered him instruction in Western art media and techniques. He encouraged a high standard of craftsmanship and an "authentic" Native style, as free as possible of white influence. Perhaps most importantly, through their mutual researches into rock art Morrisseau refined his graphic style through the assimilation of the bold, simplified forms found in rock painting. The colourful palette that the artist eventually adopted, however, went against his mentor's advice, for Dewdney thought that earth colours were more authentically Native.

After his initial success in Toronto, and the further mentoring of his dealer, Jack Pollock, Morrisseau's range of subjects expanded. He began painting powerful syncretistic images showing subjects such as as Christ as a shaman, and self portraits in which he depicted himself wrestling with serpents that probably represent sexual temptation and his terrible struggles with alcoholism. He has also accepted commissions for large dyptychs and tryptychs, as well as murals for such sites as the Indians of Canada Pavillion at Expo '67. Morrisseau's subsequent involvement with the Eckanckar sect led to canvases exploring concepts of spiritual aura and visionary experiences. During the 1980s and 1990s Morrisseau has continued to paint, although his productivity has been much affected by his continuing struggles with addiction. He currently lives in British Columbia and has exhibited periodically since 1990 with the Kinsman Robinson Gallery in Toronto.

—Ruth B. Phillips

NAHA, Raymond

Tribal affiliations: Hopi
Painter

Born: Polacca, First Mesa, Arizona, 5 December 1933. **Education:** Phoenix Indian School and Inter-Mountain Indian School; studied under Fred Kabotie, probably at the Hopi High School in Oraibi. **Military Service:** U.S. Army. **Career:** Painter and sculptor. **Awards:** Numerous from early-1960s through early-1970s at fairs and juried competitions, including Indian Arts Fund Award, 1962; American Indian Art Exposition, 1964; Inter-Tribal Indian Ceremonial, 1968, 1970, 1972; Scottsdale National Indian Art Exhibition, 1967 and 1970.

Selected Group Exhibitions

1963   *Contemporary American Indian Art*, United States Department of State, Washington, D.C.
1964   *First Annual Invitational Exhibition of American Indian Paintings*, United States Department of the Interior, Washington, D.C.
1965   *Second Annual Invitational Exhibition of American Indian Paintings*, United States Department of the Interior, Washington, D.C.
1978   *100 Years of Native American Painting*, Oklahoma Museum of Art, Oklahoma City
1984-85 *Indianascher Kunstler* (traveling, Germany), organized by the Philbrook Museum, Tulsa, Oklahoma
1988   *When the Rainbow Touches Down*, Heard Museum, Phoenix, Arizona (traveling)
1990   *American Indian Artists in the Avery Collection and the McNay Permanent Collection*, Koogler McNay Art Museum, San Antonio, Texas
1996   *Vision and Voices: Native American Painting from the Philbrook Museum of Art*, Tulsa, Oklahoma

Collections

Amerind Foundation, Dragoon, Arizona; Arizona State Museum, University of Arizona, Tucson, Arizona; Bureau of Indian Affairs, United States Department of the Interior, Washington, D.C.; Eiteljorg Museum, Indianapolis, Indiana; Hastings College Art Center, Hastings, Nebraska; Heritage Center Inc. Collection, Pine Ridge, South Dakota; Heard Museum, Phoenix, Arizona; Indian Arts & Crafts Board, United States Department of the Interior, Washington, D.C.; Marion Koogler McNay Art Museum, San Antonio, Texas; Museum of Northern Arizona, Flagstaff, Arizona; National Museum of the American Indian, Washington, D.C.; Oklahoma Museum of Art, Oklahoma City, Oklahoma; Millicent Rogers Foundation Museum, Taos, New Mexico; Southwest Museum, Los Angeles, California; Woolaroc Museum, Bartlesville, Oklahoma.

Publications

On NAHA: Books—*American Indian Painting of the Southwest and Plains Areas*, by Dorothy Dunn, Albuquerque, 1968; *Indian Painters and White Patrons*, by J.J. Brody, Albuquerque, 1971; *Southwest Indian Painting: A Changing Art*, by Clara Lee Tanner, Tucson, 1973; *Song from the Earth: American Indian Painting*, by Jamake Highwater, Boston, 1976; *100 Years of Native American Painting*, exhibition catalog by Arthur Silberman, Oklahoma Museum of Art, Oklahoma City, 1978; *Indianascher Kunstler*, by Gerhard Hoffman, Munich, 1984; *When the Rainbow Touches Down*, exhibition catalog by Tryntje Van Ness Seymour, Heard Museum, University of Washington Press, 1988; *American Indian Artists in the Avery Collection and the McNay Permanent Collection*, edited by Jean Sherrod Williams, San Antonio, 1990; *Vision and Voices: Native American Painting from the Philbrook Museum of Art*, edited by Lydia Wyckoff, Tulsa, 1996.

*   *   *

Raymond Naha was raised in the rich cultural environment of Hopi of the mid-twentieth-century, after such painters as Fred Kabotie and Otis Polelonema had won recognition to complement the revitalized potterymaking tradition inspired by Nampeyo. Naha contributed paintings that record Hopi life, using acrylic, casein, watercolor, pen and ink. His most noted works depict ceremonies, many of which involved Kachinas, in a rich and striking style that found enthusiastic viewers and jurors at fairs in the 1960s and early-1970s, until his early death at 42 in 1975. Since then his work has been included in several important exhibitions featuring the most noted Native American artists of the southwest.

Naha was born at Polacca, First Mesa, Arizona, which was named after Tom Polacca, brother of the famous Tewa potter Nampeyo. Naha was related to the Nampeyo family. Hopi pottery designs and Kachinas were among his earliest introductions to the ancient symbols of his cultural heritage. During his high school years Naha studied under Fred Kabotie, one of the most famous Hopi painters. Kabotie was among a group of artists from the pueblos of San Ildefonso, Zia, and Hopi who initiated what is now termed "modern" Pueblo Indian easel painting during the first three decades of the twentieth century. Perhaps just as significant as Kabotie's artwork was his determination to preserve and foster greater appreciation for Hopi cultural traditions, both within and outside his pueblo community, which included teaching art at the Hopi High School in Oraibi.

Naha developed the general characteristics associated with the Pueblo style, taking Pueblo life and ceremonies as subject matter and essentially painting in a flat style enhanced with modeling and

Raymond Naha: *Redtail Hawk Kachina,* c. 1950. Photograph by Murrae Haines; courtesy Dr. Gregory Schaaf collection.

perspective. Naha's particular talent rests with his use of color and his play of light and shade, including night scenes where illumination from fires and lamps catches dramatic effects of color, costume, and action. Naha's striking effects were often daring, evoking a sense of vigorous and intense activity, telling details within larger images, and bold touches of coloring; ceremonial dancers, for example, are stylized and vibrant images within the larger scene of the ceremony being performed, with colors in minute details blending to achieve an overall dramatic effect. Naha's most impressive work focuses on Kachinas, individually and in groups, and ceremonies with large groups of dancers and other participants. He also painted indoor scenes and portraits, sketched designs, and occasionally sculpted.

Naha's strength with telling character details is exhibited in various ways—from the comical merriment of Koshares to intense expressions of concentration and movement in dancers, as in *Snake Dance* (1969). Always the play of light and shade is important, particularly in night settings, as in *Mixed Kachina Dance* (1969), with bustling activity and captivating details of Kachinas in the glow of lamps. In each instance, Naha provided a fresh perspective, inventive rendering, and an uncanny ability to capture the sense of purpose in the performers, through expressions, body motion, and color of costume or dress. *Redtail Hawk Kachina Dancer* has a dancer in classic stance, one leg up, before a kiva, holding a bow embellished with eagle feathers in one hand and a ceremonial dance rattle in the other. His regalia is authentic: a headdress composed of finely painted hawk feathers positioned straight up on either side, with a plumed cluster atop; face paint with a rainbow of colors on the chin; red wool belt and brocaded Kachina sash, deerskin kilt, moccasins adorned with quilled anklets, and turquoise nuggets on the dancer's necklace. Naha's special achievement lies in drawing the viewer in to notice and appreciate such particulars.

—Gregory Schaaf

NAILOR, Gerald

Variant names: Toh Yah; Walking by the River
Tribal affiliations: Navajo
Painter, illustrator, and designer

Born: Pinedale, New Mexico, 21 January 1917. **Education:** Attended Albuquerque Indian School; entered fine arts program at the Santa Fe Indian School, where he studied under Dorothy Dunn; attended University of Oklahoma, where he and classmate Allan Houser studied under muralist Olaf Nordmark. **Military Service:** U.S. Army, World War II. **Career:** Established studio with Allan Houser in 1938; painted murals in the gift shop of the Indian Arts and Crafts Board at the Department of the Interior Building in Washington, D.C., 1938, and painted murals in the penthouse in 1940; later painted murals at the Mesa Verde National Park post office and at the Navajo Tribal Council Chamber in Window Rock, Arizona; rancher; illustrator; designer. **Died:** 13 August 1952.

Selected Group Exhibitions

1937   American Indian Exposition and Congress, Tulsa, Oklahoma
1941   *Exhibit of Indian Art*, Museum of Modern Art, New York

1947-65 *American Indian Paintings from the Permanent Collection*, Philbrook Art Center, Tulsa, Oklahoma (traveling)
1953   *Contemporary American Indian Painting*, National Gallery of Art, Washington, D.C.
1955-56 International traveling exhibit organized by University of Oklahoma on behalf of U. S. Information Service in Rome
1968   *The James T. Bialac Collection of Southwest Indian Paintings*, Arizona State Museum, University of Arizona, Tucson
1973   *American Indian Art, 1920-1972*, Peabody Museum of Archaeology and Ethnology, Harvard University, Cambridge, Massachusetts
1978   *100 Years of Native American Painting*, Oklahoma Museum of Art, Oklahoma City
1979-80 *Native American Paintings*, Mid-Amercian Arts Alliance Project, Joslyn Art Museum, Omaha, Nebraska (traveling)
1981-83 *Native American Painting,* Amarillo Art Center, Texas (traveling)
1984-85 *Indianscher Kunstler*, exhibit tour of West Germany organized by the Philbrook Museum of Art, Tulsa, Oklahoma
1986-90 *When the Rainbow Touches Down*, Heard Museum, Phoenix (traveling)
1995-96 *With a View to the Southwest: Dorothy Dunn*, Museum of Indian Arts & Culture, Museum of New Mexico, Santa Fe
1996   *The Studio: The Santa Fe Indian School*, Fred Jones Jr. Museum of Art, University of Oklahoma, Norman

Collections

Arizona State Museum, University of Arizona, Tucson; California Academy of Sciences, Elkus Collection, San Francisco; Thomas Gilcrease Institute of American History and Art, Tulsa, Oklahoma; Heard Museum, Phoenix, Arizona; Indian Arts and Crafts Board, U.S. Dept. of the Interior, Washington, D.C.; Fred Jones Jr. Museum of Art, University of Oklahoma, Norman; Museum of Indian Arts and Culture, Museum of New Mexico, Santa Fe; Museum of Northern Arizona, Flagstaff; National Museum of the American Indian, Smithsonian Institution, Washington, D.C; Philbrook Art Center, Tulsa, Oklahoma; Milicent Rogers Museum, Taos, new Mexico; School of American Research, Santa Fe; Southwest Museum, Los Angeles; Woolaroc Museum, Bartlesville, Oklahoma.

Publications

On NAILOR: Books—*American Indian Painting of the Southwest and Plains Areas,* by Dorothy Dunn, University of New Mexico Press, Albuquerque, 1968; *The James T. Bialac Collection of Southwest Indian Paintings*, exhibition catalog by Clara Lee Tanner, University of Arizona Press, Tucson, 1968; *Southwest Indian Painting: A Changing Art* by Clara Lee Tanner, University of Arizona Press, Tucson, 1973; *100 Years of Native American Painting* by Arthur Silberman, Oklahoma Museum of Art, Oklahoma City, 1978; *American Indian Painting & Sculpture*, by Patricia Janis Broder, Abbeville Press, New York, 1981; *Navajo Painting*, by Katherine Chase, Museum of Northern Arizona Press, Flagstaff, 1983; *The Elkus Collection, Southwestern Indian Art*, edited by Dorothy K.

Gerald Nailor: *Deers and Hunters,* 1937. Photograph by Dong Lin; courtesy California Academy of Sciences, Elkus Collection.

Washburn, California Academy of Sciences, San Francisco, 1984; *When the Rainbow Touches Down,* exhibition catalog by Tryntje Van Ness Seymour, The Heard Museum, Phoenix, 1988; *Modern by Tradition: American Indian Painting in the Studio Style,* by Bruce

Bernstein and W. Jackson Rushing, Museum of New Mexico Press, Santa Fe, 1995. **Articles**—"Modern Navajo Water Color Painting," by Linzee King Davis, *Arizona Highways*, vol. 32, no. 7, July 1956; "Indian Art in Washington: Native American Murals in the

Department of the Interior Building," by Christine Nelson, *American Indian Art Magazine,* Spring 1985 and Spring 1995.

*   *   *

Gerald Nailor numbers among a small group of Navajo painters trained in the Santa Fe Studio Style by Dorothy Dunn at what would become known as the Santa Fe Studio, an experimental fine arts program at the Santa Fe Indian School and forerunner of the Institute of American Indian Arts. Dunn sought to instill in her students a natural style of painting, whereby the students would draw upon their own tribal cultural experiences for inspiration.

Nailor was already a graduate of the Albuquerque Indian School when he entered the Studio around 1936. As evidenced by some of his first works produced there, he probably enrolled expecting to receive basic instruction in non-Indian, American painting techniques, but soon adopted and excelled in the flat, two-dimensional style of painting espoused by Dunn. Dunn, herself, remembered him as a "suave stylist-decorator".

At the Studio, Nailor established a close friendship with a classmate, Apache artist Allan Houser. In 1938, the two established their own studio in an apartment they shared. The venture earned them very little money, but later that same year they were among several former Studio students commissioned to paint murals in the gift shop of the Indian Arts and Crafts Board at the Department of the Interior Building in Washington, D.C. They received further mural commissions for the penthouse of the same building in 1940. Nailor and Houser both subsequently studied mural painting at the University of Oklahoma, under Olle Nordmark of Sweden. Nailor later completed murals at the post office at Mesa Verde National Park and at the Navajo Tribal Council Chamber in Window Rock, Arizona. This latter work comprises eight large panels, each measuring approximately 150 to 200 square feet, that wrap around the interior walls of the building and trace Navajo history up to the signing of the Treaty of 1868 between the Navajo Tribe and the United States Government. It is, without doubt, Nailor's most monumental work.

Like others trained at the Studio under Dunn, Nailor produced highly stylized paintings whose subject matter is both conventionalized and limited. Neverthless, his work is easily distinguished from that of his contemporaries on the basis of his delicate brushwork and palette. Nailor was far more sophisticated in his sense of design and layout than most other students his age. In the typical Studio-style, his figures are flat and two-dimensional, but they are posed in a way that suggests movement even though no foreground is rendered. Plants are particularly stylized, and decorative elements often fill the overhead space, such as a deity figure arching over an otherwise mundane scene from daily life. Nailor accomplished shading by applying bands of paint in varying hues, starting from dark to light. He often experimented with color and design as an integral part of a painting.

In 1952, at the very young age of 35, Nailor was tragically killed when he intervened in a domestic dispute. During his short life, he produced an amazing body of work, now included in numerous museum and private collections. The number of Native American painters, both Navajo and non-Navajo, who emulated Nailor's style is a testimony to his contributions.

—Russell P. Hartman

NAMINGHA, Dan
Tribal affiliations: Hopi
Painter

Born: Polacca, Arizona, 1 May 1950. **Education:** University of Kansas, Lawrence, Kansas; Institute of American Indian Arts, Santa Fe, New Mexico; American Academy of Art, Chicago, Illinois. **Military Service:** U.S. Marine Corps, 1970-72. **Career:** Professional artist; owner, Niman Fine Art, Santa Fe, New Mexico. **Awards:** The Harvard Foundation, 1994; Distinguished Artist of the Year, Santa Fe Rotary Foundation, 1995; Governor's Award for Excellence and Achievement in the Arts, 1995.

Individual Exhibitions

1977   Museum of Northern Arizona, Flagstaff, Arizona
        Orange Coast College, Costa Mesa, California
1978   *Namingha: Imagery of a Hopi Indian,* Sonoma County Library, Santa Rosa, California
1978-79 *Extensions of the Nampeyo Creative Spirit,* California Academy of Sciences, Golden Gate Park, San Francisco, California
1980   *Dan Namingha Retrospective,* The Arizona Bank Galleria, Phoenix, Arizona
1983-86 International European Exhibit, United States Information Agency Cultural Affairs Department (traveling)
1986   The Gallery Wall, Scottsdale, Arizona and Santa Fe, New Mexico
1987   *Dan Namingha: Tewa-Hopi Reflections,* Heard Museum, Phoenix, Arizona
1988   *Images of the Southwest,* National Academy of Sciences, Washington, D.C.
        Gerald Peters Gallery, Dallas, Texas
1989   Governor's Gallery, State Capitol Building, Santa Fe, New Mexico
        Gerald Peters Gallery, Santa Fe, New Mexico
1990   Niman Fine Art, Santa Fe, New Mexico
1991   *Timeless Land and Enduring Images,* Palm Springs Desert Museum, California
1992   *Dan Namingha: Pueblo Reflections of Land and Symbolism,* Southwest Museum, Los Angeles, California
        Susan Duval Gallery, Aspen, Colorado
        The Art Guild, Farmington, Connecticut
        Dan Namingha: Extending Pueblo Imagery, Nevada State Museum, Las Vegas
1994   *Fragments of Symbolism and Landscape,* The Fogg Museum, Harvard University, Cambridge, Massachusetts
        Dreamscapes, Susan Duval Gallery, Aspen, Colorado
1995   Bently Gallery, Scottsdale, Arizona
1996   *Metaphors of Culture and Place: The Paintings and Sculpture of Dan Namingha,* Museum of Fine Arts, Santa Fe, New Mexico
1997   *Structural Dualities,* Wheelwright Museum of the American Indian, Santa Fe, New Mexico
1998-99 Montclair Art Museum, New Jersey

Selected Group Exhibitions

1972   Philbrook Museum of Art, Tulsa, Oklahoma
        The Jamison Galleries, Santa Fe, New Mexico

1973   Mary Livingston Gallery, Santa Ana, California
1974   *Nampeyo Family Exhibition*, Muckenthaler Cultural Center, Fullerton, California
1977   *Alumni Exhibition*, Institute of American Indian Arts Museum, Santa Fe, New Mexico
        Invitational Sculpture III Exhibition, The Heard Museum, Phoenix, Arizona
1978   *Graphics Invitational*, New Britain Museum of American Arts, New Britain, Connecticut
        Messengers of the Earth, California State University, Sacramento, California
1980-81 *Hopi Kachina Spirit of Life*, California Academy of Sciences, Golden Gate Park, San Francisco, California
1981   Salon d'Automne, Grand Palais, Paris, France
1982   University of Nebraska, Sheldon Memorial Art Gallery, Lincoln, Nebraska
        Inaugural Art Exhibit, Armand Hammer United World College, Montezuma, New Mexico
1983   *FIAC International Exhibit*, Grand Palais, Paris, France
        Flagstaff Festival of Native American Arts, Flagstaff, Arizona
1986   *Contemporary Visions of New Mexico*, Sangre de Cristo Arts and Conference Center, Pueblo, Colorado
1988   Western Heritage Center, Oklahoma City, Oklahoma
        Visions of Flight, Kennedy Space Center, Cape Canaveral, Florida

1989   *Glyphs of New Mexico: New Interpretations*, Governor's Gallery, State Capitol Building, Santa Fe, New Mexico
        Sights and Sounds, Kennedy Space Center Art Gallery, Cape Canaveral, Florida
1992   *Creativity is Our Tradition*, Institute of American Indian Art Museum, Santa Fe, New Mexico
1993   Middlebury College Museum of Art, Middlebury, Vermont
1994   *The Artist as Native: Reinventing Regionalism*, Albany Institute of History and Art, Albany, New York
        Westmoreland Museum of Art, Greensburg, Pennsylvania
        Maryland Institute and College of Art, Baltimore, Maryland

Collections

British Royal Collection, London, England; City of Phoenix Collection, Sky Harbor International Airport, Phoenix, Arizona; City of Scottsdale Fine Arts Collection, Scottsdale, Arizona; Dahlem Museum, Berlin, Germany; Fogg Art Museum, Harvard University, Cambridge, Massachusetts; The Gallery of East Slovakia, Kosice, Czech Republic; Heard Museum, Phoenix, Arizona; Intrawest Financial Corporation, Denver, Colorado; Montclair Art Museum, Montclair, New Jersey; Mountain Bell Collection, Albuquerque, New Mexico; Museum of Fine Arts, Santa Fe, New Mexico; Museum of Northern Arizona, Flagstaff, Arizona; NASA Art Collection, Washington, D.C.; The Naprstkovo Museum, Prague, Czech

Dan Namingha: *Pueblo Fragments,* 1996. Courtesy of the artist and NIMAN Fine Art, Santa Fe, New Mexico.

Dan Namingha. Courtesy of the artist and NIMAN Fine Art, Santa Fe, New Mexico.

Republic; Opto 22 Corporation, Huntington Beach, California; Palm Springs Desert Museum, Palm Springs, California; Millicent Rogers Museum, Taos, New Mexico; United States Department of the Interior, Indian Arts Collection, Washington, D.C.; United States' Embassies, Brazil, Denmark, Senegal, Bolivia.

Publications

On NAMINGHA: Books—*Dan Namingha: Extensions of the Nampeyo Creative Spirit,* California Academy of Sciences, San Francisco, 1978; *The Sweet Grass Lives On,* by Jamake Highwater, Lippincott and Crowell, New York, 1980; *American Indian Art in the 1980's,* by Lloyd Kiva New, Native American Center for the Living Arts, Niagara Falls, New York, 1981; *Magic Images: Contemporary Native American Indian Art,* by Edwin Wade and Rennard Strickland, University of Oklahoma Press, Norman, 1981; *Hopi,* by Jake Page and Susanne Page, Harry N. Abrams, New York, 1982; *Art of the Native American: The Southwest from the Late 19th Century to the Present,* Lloyd Kiva New, et. al., Owensboro Museum of Fine Art, Kentucky, 1985; "Frames of Reference: Native American Art in the Context of Modern and Postmodern Art," by Gerhard Hoffman, *The Arts of the North American Indian: Native Traditions in Evolution,* edited by Edwin Wade, Philbrook Art Center, Tulsa, 1986; *Beyond Tradition,* by Jerry and Lois Jacka, Northland Pub-

lishing Company, Flagstaff, Arizona, 1988; *Dreamscapes,* Susan Duval Gallery, Aspen, Colorado, 1994; "Dan Namingha," *This Path We Travel: Celebrations of Contemporary Native American Creativity,* Smithsonian Institution, Washington, D.C., 1994. **Articles**—"Dan Namingha," *Arizona Highways,* vol. 59, no. 2, February 1983; "Reaching Out, Reaching In," by Pam Hait, *Air & Space,* June-July 1986; "Blazing Colors," by Rebecca Clay, *New Mexico Magazine,* vol. 66, no. 5, May 1988; "Namingha," by M. Hal Sussmann, *Southwest Art,* January 1989; "Dan Namingha: American Indian Artist on the World Stage," *The Christian Science Monitor,* 4 March 1991; "American Indian Artist Brings Southwest Images, Myths to the Fogg," by Lisa Amand, *Cambridge Chronicle,* vol. 148, no. 33, 18 August 1994; "Dan Namingha," by Joanne Silver, *ARTnews,* vol. 93, no. 10, November 1994; "Namingha Paintings Carry Spirit of All Human Kind," by Gussie Fauntleroy, *New Mexican,* Santa Fe, 27 October 1995; "Dan Namingha," by Candelora Versace, *El Palacio,* vol. 101, no. 2, Summer/Fall 1996; "Metaphors of Culture & Place," by Daniel Vaillancourt, *Pasatiempo,* Santa Fe, 16-22 August 1996. **Films**—*American Indian Artists: Part II,* produced by the Native American Public Broadcasting Consortium, Lincoln, Nebraska, 1984; *Two Worlds of Dan Namingha,* produced by Matthew Smeddon, Colores Series, KNME-TV, Albuquerque, 1992.

*　　*　　*

Dan Namingha's artistic roots run deeply. He is the great-great-grandson of Nampeyo, the famed revivalist of Hopi pottery. His mother and great-grandmother also followed in the tradition of pottery-making, and his father carved kachinas. His uncle, Raymond Naha, was also a carver and painter. Namingha's work is decidedly different from those of his ancestors, but the same spirit of creativity and personal vision infuses his art. Growing up in this tradition was one aspect of his education. He also credits his art lessons at the Polacca Day School for exposing him to watercolors and techniques of design. More formally, after a summer program at the University of Kansas, Namingha entered the Institute of American Indian Art in Santa Fe, at age 16, completing two years of study. At IAIA Namingha was influenced by instructor and artist Otellie Loloma. He then moved to Chicago and enrolled at the American Academy of Art. While at the AAA, Namingha was inspired by the work of such artists as De Kooning, Hofmann, Kline, Pollack, and Rothko, using the vocabulary of these artists to express a range of images, most of which center on aspects of Hopi life and experience. He captures the ceremonial rhythm of chants, songs, and dances, often using such fragmented images as kachina faces, the sun, corn stalks, rainbows, parrot feathers, and black-and-white strips connoting the Koshare to create complete compositions. Not so oddly, one of Namingha's subjects has been the 1985 lift-off of the space shuttle *Discovery* and its return in 1988. In his painting *Emergence* (1985), Namingha places an astronaut bursting from the bounds of the earth and inhabiting the same space as Kokopelli, signifying warmth and beauty, and the Twin War Gods, watchers over the land and the water. These interconnections appear in different ways in the three areas that Namingha has explored in his nearly thirty-year career: architecture, landscape, and spiritual imagery. While Namingha's images may appear to be discrete fragments, but are rather metonyms that represent the wholeness of Hopi experience.

Architectural structures are one of the recurrent themes in Namingha's work. Some of these works representationally depict scenes of Hopi and the Arizona of Namingha's memory. *Autumn Light* (1988), for example, is a straightforward scene of a mesa-top structure. Namingha transforms the familiar images of his upbringing into a painting notable for its compositional balance and use of color. *Hopi Dwelling* (1990) takes a different approach in both color and form. Although the buildings are recognizable, especially with the upraised kiva ladders, the bottom section of the work coalesces into a wash of reds. In this work Namingha takes a long view of the pueblo, accentuating the surrounding space. These aspects of the land, the immensity of space and the colors of earth and sky emerge in such pieces as *Desert Arroyo* (1994), *Jemez* (1992) and *West of Kykotsmovi* (1996).

In an early piece, *View from Walpi* (1979), a 27-foot-long painting shown at the Sky Harbor International Airport in Phoenix, Namingha uses blocks of color to take us to the mesa top and experience the desert floor below. In *West of Oraibi* (1991) Namingha views a red mesa from a distance. The canvas, some 96 inches by 80 inches, is split horizontally. In the top half, the mesa is dwarfed by a huge expanse of light blue sky. The lower portion of the work is comprised of blocks of abstract and symbolic elements, such as a series of spirals, which could refer to the evolution or migration of Hopi people. The same motif is revisited in the 1996 *Hekytwi Sunrise*. The mesa becomes a raised black line dividing the canvas between a brilliant sunrise of gold and splashes of red above and two panels below, separated vertically by a thin black-and-white band suggesting the Koshare, or Koyaala—the Hano sacred clown

seen only at First Mesa. The lower left panel also includes the black-and-white bands, along with three spirals and a series of crosses representing stars, and the right panel also includes spirals and other symbolic figures. These pieces reflect Namingha's interest in the expanses of the Southwest, but beyond simply illustrating space and scale in the landscape Namingha invests these pieces with elements connected to Hopi beliefs. The landscape is not simply land, but also homeland and sacred land, the spiritual center of Hopi life. Through his use of symbols in work ostensibly about the land and architecture Namingha gives them an added dimension. Namingha may be best known for the work that focuses on ceremonial figures, such as kachinas, primary figures in Hopi spirituality. Clearly, Namingha's images of dancers have evolved as he has continued to explore ways of recreating in a static medium the total experience of a ceremony. The softer figures in *Kiva Dancers* (1990) give way to the vibrant and shimmering *Pueblo Kachina Images* (1991) and *Hopi Kachinum* (1991), where the acrylic is applied by knife blade to create elongated dagger-shaped forms. The 1993 *Dream State Series, #14* replicates this style and uses elements of abstraction to suggest a dancer. In *Kwahu Dance* (1994), Namingha unreins his palette to create a piece where the movement of the dancer is a swirl of reds, oranges, blues, greens, and whites. In the 1995 *Dance Series, #9* and the *1996 Ceremonial Dance Series I and II*, Namingha creates more of a collage effect with patterns of abstract imagery and the simple suggestion of a dancer's mask.

Namingha also develops his themes in wood and bronze sculpture. *Cloud Image* (1996) uses acrylic and collage on two upright wood panels and on the base; the panels are set off from each other but connected by a small strip of blue wood. On the front side of this piece is a spiral and the dagger-like dancer and what could be an elongated mask. On the back side, on the base, is a spiral and blocks of color. The black-and-white strip of the Koshare runs partially across the top, while a thin bar of red and a curved bar of white, in addition to the blue strip connecting the two panels and the yellow along the edge of the panel, may refer to cardinal directions.

Namingha's bronzes are of two styles: those like *Katchina Symbolism I and II* (1995) are similar to the paintings, using fragments of images in a single plane and negative space to create the final form; others, like *Pueblo Eagle Dancer* (1995) and *Tewa Maidens* (1995), are more representational, emphasizing the forms of the figures, and reminiscent of some of Allan Houser's smaller work.

In the same way that his great-great-grandmother Nampeyo extended pottery imagery by utilizing fragments from the past to create new designs, Namingha uses fragments of ritual and memory to construct windows into the Hopi experience.

—Larry Abbott

NAMPEYO

Tribal affiliations: Hopi
Potter

Born: Hano, First Mesa, Arizona, in 1859. **Family:** Married 1) Kwivoya, 1879; 2) Lesso (also spelled Lesou), 1881; five children, Annie Healing Nampeyo, William Lesso (1893-1935), Nellie Nampeyo Douma (1896-1978), Wesley Lesso (1899-1985), and Fannie Polacca Nampeyo (1900-1987). **Died:** 20 July 1942.

Selected Group Exhibitions

Some sources list the 1898 *Santa Fe Railway Exposition*, Coliseum, Chicago, Illinois, as the first showcase for Nampeyo's work outside of Hopi lands, but no conclusive documentation or records of the show exist; the following selected exhibits outside of Hopi, where her work was accessible beginning in the latter part of the nineteenth century.

1905-10   Hopi House, Grand Canyon, Arizona
1910   United States Land and Irrigation Exposition, Chicago, Illinois
          National Museum, Washington, D.C.
1911   Milwaukee Public Museum, Milwaukee, Wisconsin
1973   Museum of Northern Arizona, Flagstaff, Arizona
1974   Muckenthaler Cultural Center, Fullerton, California
          American Indian and Western Relic Show, Los Angeles
1989   *Nampeyo: A Gift Remembered*, Mitchell Indian Museum, Evanston, Illinois
1996   *The Nampeyo Legacy Continues: The Art of Five Generations of a Renowned Tewa / Hopi Family*, Santa Fe Indian Market, Santa Fe, New Mexico

Nampeyo: Sikyatki revival/Hano polychrome pottery by Nampeyo and her family. Photograph by Seth Roffman; courtesy Dr. Gregory Schaaf collection.

Collections

Thomas Burke Memorial Washington State Museum, Seattle; Field Museum of Natural History, Chicago, Illinois; Heard Museum, Phoenix, Arizona; Logan Museum of Anthropology, College of Beloit, Wisconsin; Milwaukee Public Museum, Milwaukee, Wisconsin, Museum of Indian Arts and Culture, Santa Fe, New Mexico, National Museum, Washington, D.C.; Southwest Museum; Los Angeles, California; University of Colorado Museum, Boulder, Colorado.

Publications

On NAMPEYO: Books—*The Hopi Indians*, by Walter Hough, Cedar Rapids, Iowa, 1915; "Designs on Prehistoric Hopi Pottery," by Jesse Walter Fewkes, *Bureau of American Ethnology 33rd Annual Report 1911-1912*, Washington, D.C., 1919; *Hopi Journal of Alexander M. Stephen*, by Alexander Stephen, New York, 1936; "The Influence of J. Walter Fewkes on Nampeyo: Fact or Fancy," by Theodore R. Frisbie, *The Changing Ways of Southwestern Indians: A Historic Perspective*, edited by Albert H. Schroeder, Glorieta, New Mexico, 1973; *Nampeyo, Hopi Potter: Her Artistry and Her Legacy*, by John Collins, Fullerton, California, 1974; "Nampeyo," by Rick Dillingham, *Seven Families in Pueblo Pottery*, Albuquerque, 1974; *Seven Families in Pueblo Pottery*, by Rick Dillingham, et. al., Albuquerque, 1978; "Nampeyo: Giving the Indian Artist a Name," by Ronald McCoy, *Indian Lives: Essays on Nineteenth- and Twentieth-Century Leaders*, edited by L.G. Moses and Raymond Wilson, Albuquerque, 1985; *Beyond Tradition: Contemporary Indian Art and Its Evolution*, by Jerry and Lois Jacka, Flagstaff, 1988; *Nampeyo: A Gift Remembered*, by Martha Lanman Cusick, Evanston, Illinois, 1989; *Fourteen Families in Pueblo Pottery*, by Rick Dillingham, Albuquerque, 1994; *Creation's Journey: Native American Identity and Belief Washington*, edited by Tom Hill and Richard W. Hill, Sr., Washington, D.C., 1995; *Nampeyo and Her Pottery*, by Barbara Kramer, Albuquerque, 1996. **Articles**—"Land Show is On," *Chicago Sunday Tribune*, 20 November 1910; "A Revival of the Ancient Hopi Pottery," by Walter Hough, *American Anthropologist*, vol. 19, no. 2, 1917; "Death of Nampeyo," by Fredrick W. Hodge, *Masterkey*, 1942; "Nampeyo, Famous Hopi Potter," by Edmund Nequatewa, *Plateau*, January 1943; "An Appreciation of the Art of Nampeyo and Her Influence on Hopi Pottery," by Mary Russell F. and Harold S. Colton, *Plateau*, January 1944; "Nampeyo and Lesou," by Robert Ashton, Jr., *American Indian Art Magazine*, Summer 1976; "Pueblo Pottery: 2000 Years of Artistry," by David L. Arnold, *National Geographic Magazine*, November 1982; "Nampeyo, Hopi House, and the Chicago Land Show," by Barbara Kramer, *American Indian Art Magazine*, Winter 1988.

*   *   *

Nampeyo and her descendants are best known for reviving and expanding a beautiful ancient style of pottery called Sikyatki. Her inspiration for drawing on and recreating the style probably began in the 1880s, and she certainly mastered the style by the mid-1890s, when she had already established a reputation as an excellent potter and her work began being promoted by the Santa Fe Railroad and the Fred Harvey Company. Her husband, Lesso, was working with Dr. Jesse Walter Fewkes on his excavation of the village of Sikyatki in the mid-1890s, and either he or Dr. Fewkes showed Nampeyo shards of Sikyatki pottery, which inspired her to recreate the style. However, just when and how she was first inspired to introduce a modern version that would win worldwide acclaim is a matter of conjecture, and her personal discoveries and invention should certainly be considered.

Nampeyo's Corn Clan ancestors were Tewa-speaking people from New Mexico who moved to Hopi in Arizona after the 1680 Pueblo Revolt. They settled atop First Mesa in the village of Hano. At the time of Nampeyo's birth, around 1860, Hopi pottery in the style of Polacca Polychrome was experiencing a decline in quality. Nampeyo had learned to make pottery after having watched her grandmother make ollas—vessels for everyday use. She began introducing subtle variations on traditional designs, and her works began to draw good prices from white traders. Because Nampeyo was of Tewa ancestry, however, she was discouraged from using designs claimed by Hopi potters. Her dilemma was solved by switching to symbols found on old pottery shards of types known as Kayenta Anasazi and Sikyatki Polychrome.

By the early 1890s, Nampeyo had entertained ideas of reviving older designs. It is believed that she found inspiration from shards at Kikyatki and ruins at Awatovi, Tsukuvi, and Payupki. A controversy still rages over the influences on Nampeyo's pottery revival. Biographer Barbara Kramer recently challenged Dr. Jesse Walter Fewkes inference over his role in showing Nampeyo pottery shards from his excavation of the village of Sikyatki. Fewkes was influential in artistic developments in the southwest, and his classic study, *Designs on Prehistoric Hopi Pottery,* is still avidly studied by First Mesa potters. Kramer contends that Nampeyo and Lesso were drawing from designs on old pottery shards long before the arrival of Fewkes. The classic pottery unearthed at Sikyatki at least provided further inspiration and the 1895 date begins a larger flourishing of Nampeyo's art and reputation.

Sikyatki symbols of parrots, butterflies, eagles and other designs appear on pottery of Nampeyo and her descendants. Sikyatki style potters worked with artistic tenets comparable to Cubism, as championed by Picasso and Braque. Design elements were compressed, reduced to basic forms and abstracted. For example, a parrot design sometimes would be divided into four quadrants. The curling beak, the flowing wings and sharp-tipped tail feathers were rotated in space and then fit back together like a mosaic. The effect is sophisticated and ingenious, like a great Cubist painting. Nampeyo was responsible as well for other design and form innovations and revivals. Her use of background space is essential to the overall design, and she revived such forms as the low, wide-shouldered jars of Kikyatki.

Nampeyo was first and foremost an innovator, drawing on forms and designs of the past to refresh the present. At the beginning of the twentieth century, Nampeyo was the first Pueblo potter to gain fame beyond the American Southwest. During the first decade of the twentieth century her fame grew rapidly from exhibits at the Grand Canyon and in Chicago and Washington, D.C. Her photograph was often used in promotional brochures for southwest travel, and she demonstrated potterymaking at the Grand Canyon for two periods between 1905 and 1910. But amid the hoopla of promotion, Nampeyo focused on her artistry, and her legacy rests with revolutionizing Hopi pottery, drawing great attention to the art form, and sharing her knowledge and skill with her family and community.

Nampeyo and Lesso's three daughters were potters. The eldest, Annie Healing, who accompanied her mother to demonstrations in the Hopi House at the Grand Canyon, was noted for Redware pots, bowls and compressed seed jars with black, and occasionally white,

Sikyatki-inspired designs. Nellie Douma, the middle daughter, accompanied Nampeyo to the 1910 Chicago Exposition. As Nampeyo's eyesight began to fail, her youngest daughter, Fannie Polacca Nampeyo, helped her mother by painting on the designs. Fannie's favorite design was the fine line migration pattern featuring curling waves with parrot tail tips. Among Nampeyo's grandchildren from Annie, Nellie and Fannie, thirteen became potters, and twenty-five great-grandchildren are acclaimed potters.

—Gregory Schaaf

NARANJO-MORSE, Nora

Tribal affiliations: Santa Clara Pueblo
Potter and ceramist

Born: Espanola, New Mexico, 1953. **Education:** College of Santa Fe, B.A., 1980; Institute of American Indian Arts, Santa Fe, Silversmithing Program, 1991. **Career:** Artist in residence Santa Fe Indian School, Santa Fe, New Mexico, 1982; toured Denmark and Germany teaching basic techniques in Santa Clara Pueblo Pottery, 1984; panel participant on Indian Awareness, sponsored by the Department of Social Services, Houston Community College, Houston, Texa, 1985; various poetry readings 1986-95. **Awards:** Third place, single figure clay sculpture, SWAIA Indian Market, Santa Fe, 1979; second place single figure clay sculpture, SWAIA Indian Market, Santa Fe,1980; first place in contemporary clay forms, Annual Pottery Show, Denver, Colorado, 1981; second place in clay sculpture, SWAIA Indian Market, Santa Fe, 1982; first place in contemporary clay forms Annual Pottery Show, Denver,1982; first place clay scenes, SWAIA Indian Market, Santa Fe, 1983.

Individual Exhibitions

1987   *One Woman Exhibition,* Many Goats Gallery, Tucson, Arizona
1992   *One Woman Exhibition*, Maxwell Museum, Albuquerque, New Mexico
1993   *One Woman Exhibition,* American Indian Contemporary Arts, San Francisco, California
1994   *What Was Taken ... What We Sell*, Institute of American Indian Arts, Santa Fe

Selected Group Exhibitions

1980   *Rising Stars*, Gallery 10, Scottsdale, Arizona
1983   *Two Person Show,* Many Goats Gallery, Tucson, Arizona
1984   Squash Blossom Gallery, Denver, Colorado
        Adobe Wall Gallery, Houston, Texas
1985-86 *Two Person Show,* Squash Blossom, Vail, Colorado
1988   *Earth, Hands and Life*, Heard Museum, Phoenix, Arizona
        Two Woman Show, The Four Winds Gallery, Pittsburgh, Pennsylvania

Publications

By NARANJO-MORSE: Books—*Sun Tracks*, vol. 3, no. 2, Spring 1979; *Ceremony of Brotherhood*, University of New Mexico Press,

Albuquerque, 1981; *Gathering of Spirits*, Sinister Wisdom Press, Canada, 1982; *Fireweed*, Ontario Arts Council, 1986; *Mud Woman: Poems from the Clay,* The University of Arizona Press, Phoenix, 1992.

On NARANJO-MORSE: Books—*Seven Families in Pueblo Pottery*, Maxwell Museum of Anthropology, University of New Mexico Press, Albuquerque, 1974; *Talking With Clay: the Art of Pueblo Pottery* by Stephen Trimble, School of American Research Press, Santa Fe, 1987; *American Encounters: A Companion to the Exhibition at the National Museum of American History,* by Howard Morrison, et al, Smithsonian Institution Press, Washington, D.C., 1992. **Articles**—"Nora Naranjo-Morse: Working With Enchantment," by Ashley Peterson, *Artists of the Sun: Official Indian Market Program*, 20 August 1981; "Brown Earth and Laughter: The Clay People of Nora Naranjo-Morse," by Stephen Trimble, *American Indian Art*, vol. 21, no. 4, Autumn 1987; "Nora Naranjo-Morse: Pearlene Plays Poker at the Pueblo," by Susan Bryan, *Phoenix Home and Garden,* April 1988; "Making Ceramic Figures Remains a Living Art Form," by Lynn Pyne, *Phoenix Gazette*, 13 April 1988; "Earth Symbols," by Diana Pardue and Kathryn Coe, *Native Peoples*, vol. 2, no. 2, Winter 1989; "The Only One Who Knows: A Separate Vision," by Linda Eaton, *American Indian Art*, vol. 14, no. 3, Summer 1989; "The Evolution of a Craft Tradition," by Grace Lichtenstein, *Ms*, April 1983; "Tracks to Culture," by Jocelyn Lieu, *Indian Market Magazine*, Summer 1992; "Nora Naranjo-Morse," by Jackson Rushing, *The New Art Examiner,* vol 21, no. 5, January 1994; "Molding Identity: The Ceramic Sculpture of Nora Naranjo-Morse and Pablita Abeyta," by Jennifer Vigil MA Thesis The University of Iowa, Iowa City, 1994. **Film**—*A Separate Vision*, Museum of Northern Arizona, 1989.

*

Nora Naranjo-Morse comments (1991):

All of my art asks, "Where do I fit in? How do I make a place for myself in these two worlds?" Where I come from, you're always going back [to] basic natural things, but I couldn't move forward as a human being, mother, wife, Towa without a strong cultural base. Who would think of dancing for water or corn, but that was their [the ancient people's] life. In the transition, I needed to go back to that water and that corn.

*   *   *

Nora Naranjo-Morse, a Santa Clara ceramicist who lives in Espanola, New Mexico, is keenly aware of the issues that confront contemporary Native Americans, attempting to find a balance between the sometimes very contradictory worlds that she lives in (Santa Clara and American). She achieves this balance through her art and poetry. Her work helps to bridge the cultural gap—bringing both sides a little closer.

Understanding tradition and her place in it is central to Nora Naranjo-Morse's art and poetry, as she attempts to balance her identity through her work. Coming from a Santa Clara family of master potters, she had to find her own niche—her own sense of self within the community of her family. Throughout her career she has continued to reinvent herself through her work. Naranjo-Morse's work is constantly evolving, not only a result of her interest in experimentation, but also a result of her effort not to be labeled.

Women's themes are pervasive; her female figures are constantly evolving as she confronts different issues. One of her earlier works,

Mud Woman's First Encounter With the World of Money and Business (1987), was produced at a time when she was struggling with her twins. On a personal level, the two *Kosa* (ceremonial clowns) that Mud Woman holds represent Naranjo-Morse's children, while on another level, as the title suggests, they represent Mud Woman's first attempts to market her work. She is presenting her work for display as well as for sale, whether to the gallery owner or curious tourist. Ironically the *Kosa*, while representing the sale of her cultural heritage, also defies the "non-Indian" consumption of her culture, and Mud Woman becomes like the *kosa*—poking fun at the tourists' attempt to purchase her culture. There is also an element of disillusionment, as the first encounter with the world of money and business is a defeat as well. It is disillusioning to find that tribal values do not necessarily carry over to the mainstream American world, where traditions are valued as a commodity with a corresponding price tag and an artist's importance is tied to success and marketability, often over creativity and originality. As a result the *kosa* are popular because of their aesthetic appeal, not because of their meaning.

The image of Mud Woman is contrasted with *Pearlene's Roots*, created two years later. Here the roles are reversed. Pearlene is a consumer with her American Express card in hand. She determines the value—she has the purchasing power. Pearlene is a Pueblo woman living in two worlds. She is in control. This is quite a change from Mud Woman, who was disillusioned by money and business.

A Towa Woman's Clothesline, an installation in her 1993 San Francisco show, attempted to educate the viewer about the complexity of a Pueblo woman's world and identity. On the floor lay a thick layer of dirt, over which was suspended a clothesline: on it were all the clothes that a Pueblo woman today might wear: a sexy blue bra, traditional dance outfit, a free Leonard Peltier T-shirt, jeans, etc. The clothes represented Nora Naranjo-Morse and the complexity of her life, which cannot be labeled or described easily. A Native American writer's workshop T-shirt, listing her as one of the participants, reveals her strong commitment to her writing, and all of the objects reveal the connectedness of her art, political struggle, cultural adaptation, domesticity, and erotic expression. As Nora Naranjo-Morse's work has become more issue oriented, she has expanded into mixed media. Clay now acts as a metaphor in her work—still there connecting her but no longer the dominant factor.

In addition to her art work, Nora Naranjo-Morse is also known for her poetry. Many of the same themes that dominate her ceramic work are also present in her writing. These two creative acts—writing and sculpting clay—are linked for Nora Naranjo-Morse. Each offers her a vehicle to address issues—sometimes with coyote-like humor, sometimes with irony and often through unavoidable confrontation with the realities of life.

—Jennifer Vigil

NEEL, David

Tribal affiliations: Kwakiutl
Photographer, mixed media artist, and carver

Born: Vancouver, 1960. **Education:** Studied fine arts and anthropology, Mount Royal College, Calgary, 1978-80; University of Kansas, Lawrence, 1980-82. **Career:** Photographer, Texas and Mexico, 1982-86; multimedia artist, lecturer, and art activist, British Columbia, 1986—.

David Neel with Chief Charlie Swanson Nisga'a. Courtesy of the artist.

Individual Exhibitions

1991   *To Speak for Ourselves: Portraits of Chiefs and Elders by David Neel*, National Archives of Canada, Ottawa, Ontario (touring through 1995)

1993   *Photographs of Native Leaders and Related Works*, Canadian Museum of Contemporary Photography, Ottawa, Ontario (touring through 1995)

        Spirit of the Earth, Vancouver Museum, Vancouver, British Columbia (touring through 1996))

Selected Group Exhibitions

1992   *Canadian Inuit: Northwest Coast Indian Art*, Seoul Arts Centre, Korea

        Native America: Reflecting Contemporary Realities (toured United States)

        New Territories: 350/500 Years After, Maison de la Culture, Montreal, Quebec

1993   *Guatemalan/Canadian Indigenous art Exhibition*, Guatemala City, Guatemala

1994   *First Nations Contemporary Art*, Art Gallery of Greater Victoria, British Columbia

1995   *First Nations Art*, Canadian Embassy, Moscow

1996   *Partial Recall: Photographs of Native North America*, National Museum of the American Indian, New York

Collections

Art Gallery of Greater Victoria, British Columbia; Burke Museum, Seattle; Canada Council Art Bank, Ottawa; Canadian Embassy, Guatemala City, Guatemala; Canadian Museum of Civilization, Hull, Quebec; Canadian Museum of Contemporary Photography, Ottawa; Glenbow Museum, Calgary, Alberta; Indian Art Centre, Ottawa; Kwagiulth Museum, Cape Mudge, British Columbia; National Museum of the American Indian, New York; Royal B.C. Museum, Victoria, British Columbia; Thunder Bay Art Gallery, Ontario; UBC Museum of Anthropology, Vancouver; Vancouver Museum.

Publications

By NEEL: Books—*Our Chiefs and Elders: Words and Photographs of Native Leaders*, Vancouver and Seattle, 1992; *The Great Canoes: Reviving a Northwest Coast Tradition*, Vancouver and Seattle, 1995. **Article:** "Artist's Statement," *B.C. Studies, Special Issue in Celebration of Our Survival*, no. 89, 1991.

*   *   *

David Neel is the grandson of Ellen Neel, the first woman carver on the Northwest Coast. Both his father, David Neel, and his great-grandfather, Charlie James, were carvers, and his uncle was the renowned Mungo Martin. After a number of years living and working as a photographer in Mexico and Dallas, Neel returned in 1986 to the Pacific Northwest and began to identify himself with his father's people.

Neel is a versatile artist working in a number of media, some of which are traditional, like wood carving. Jewellery is a more recent tradition, having developed since the introduction of precious metals and the techniques for working them. Others, like photography would not be called traditional. However, Neel is not the first to point out that innovation is part of his tradition and that it is a curious contradiction, in the name of cultural purity, to deny native artists access to whatever materials or techniques enable them to make expressions of their culture.

In this belief Neel's collection of masks, exhibited under the title *Spirit of the Earth*, combined a modified version of traditional Kwagiulth form with contemporary subjects. They were made to be danced as well as displayed. Among the twenty masks was *Racism*, a representation of Rodney King, the black man whose beating by the police sparked the Los Angeles riots, *Greed*, which is decorated with five-dollar bills, and *Pollution*. His representations of these modern evil spirits continue the tradition of the smallpox masks that were one of the ways in which his people dealt with that nineteenth-century scourge. Although Neel's masks make a strong impact, it is to some extent dependent on their novelty. Neel's carving skills do not show the imaginative confidence of a Robert Davidson nor the exquisite inventiveness of Dempsey Bob, but the conviction that he shares with them that this time-honoured form of cultural expression is still valid is fully justified by the vitality he gives it.

As a photographer, Neel's greatest influences have been the strong documentary images of Donald McCullin, W. Eugene Smith, and Henri Cartier-Bresson. Photography and First Nations have had an uneasy history. In too many cases photography has been used to record and pry in ways that are demeaning, invasive and often sacrilegious. Neel has encountered some opposition in Native communities from those for whom innovation in representation means an erosion of the culture as they define it. But the contribution that he has made by giving First Nations people contemporary images of themselves, while replacing stereotypes with understanding, has convinced most people. Outside of specialist literature these cultures are little known. Neel uses photography for a dual purpose: to record the remarkable people and remarkable technologies of the Northwest Coast cultures, but also to make the point that these things are not disappearing, but are rather moving to new positions of strength.

The photographs for which Neel is best known have been widely exhibited and are collected in his two successful books, *Our Chiefs and Elders* and *The Great Canoes: Reviving a Northwest Coast Tradition*. The latter documents the resurgence of making and using the ancient dug out canoes of the Pacific Northwest, and the dramatic effects it has had on people who are working to retain their culture in a modern world. The former pairs images of men and women in everyday and ceremonial regalia, revealing the transformative powers of the latter. Neel's ability to establish a rapport with his subjects so that the sense of a living breathing individual comes over strongly is complemented by the remarks made by these men and women, which add greatly to the book's value as a record. Their own voices tell of the great range of ideas and opinion about land claims, Native languages, education, about their own youth and the youth of today. They provide a necessary antidote to the tendency to essentialise or romanticise Native people, both of which perpetuate misunderstanding.

In 1995 Neel completed his own 25-foot ocean-going canoe, *Wulas Kwisgila (Travels Great Distances)*, from a 500 year old cedar log. Neel has lectured widely on his work and contributes frequently to debates on First Nations issues in the national and provincial press. Every aspect of his work is inseparable from his sense of responsibility to his community. It is shared by many other artists of the Northwest Coast, for whom the unspoken requirement to "give something back" is one of the defining traditions of their cultures.

—Charlotte Townsend-Gault

NEW, Lloyd Kiva

Variant names: Lloyd Kiva
Tribal affiliations: Cherokee
Textile artist

Born: Fairland, Oklahoma, 18 February 1916. **Education:** Undergraduate studies, Oklahoma State University, University of New Mexico, and University of Chicago; Art Institute of Chicago, B.A.E; Laboratory of Anthropology, Santa Fe, New Mexico; Arts Management Institute, Harvard University; apprenticeships to Olle Nordmark, muralist, and D.D. and Leslie Tillet, designers. **Military Service:** World War II, battalion artist, Fifth Special CB Battalion, Aleutian Islands, Alaska, and beginning in 1943, U.S. Navy, Boat Wave Commander, lieutenant. **Career:** Arts supervisor and instructor, Phoenix Indian School, 1938-42; founder, Lloyd Kiva Art Studios, 1946-50, Lloyd Kiva Craft Center, featuring 45 studios and shops, and developer of Fifth Avenue, a premier resort arts and crafts center, Scottsdale, Arizona, 1950-1961; trainer, Indian art teachers, Bureau of Indian Affairs; supervisor, interior color decoration and execution of mural projects, B.I.A. schools and hospitals; co-director and conceptual leader, Southwest Indian Arts Project, a research and development program in Arts education for young Indian adults, University of Arizona, 1958-61; Arts Education Consultant on the formation of the Institute of American Indian Arts, 1962, Arts Director and instructor in Fabric design, 1962-67, President, 1967-78; consultant, curator, fabric and fashion designer, entrepreneur; poet (including "Forever Indian," commissioned by the Arizona State Fair), lyricist (including "The Gods Will Hear," for a choral work by Louis Ballard), writer, and dramatist (including "Catch the Eagle, Feather the Shrine" acts for an Indian dance drama); Vice President, IAIA Development Foundation; Commissioner and Chairman, Indian Arts and Crafts Board, Washington, D.C.; trustee, Heard Museum, Plains Indian Museum, Buffalo Bill Historical Center, and National Council of the Museum of the American Indian; curator, including *Pintura Amerindia Contemporanea/E.U.A* and *Indian Art in the 1980s;* adjudicator, National Foundation for Talents in the Arts, Educational Testing Service, and Dade County University; advisor to the Director, National Museum of the American Indian, Smithsonian Institution, Washington, DC.; board member, International Council of Indian Arts, American Crafts Council, and World Crafts Council; chairman, Inter-cultural committee, American Council for Arts in Education. **Awards:** Cultural Services Medal, University of Arizona, 1960; honorary membership, American Institute of Interior Designers; lifetime honorary fellowship, American Crafts Council; The Lloyd New Room is dedicated in his honor at the Institute of American Indian Arts; named "The Honored One," an annual award to a "Native American who has a distinguished record of service on behalf of promoting and contributing to Native American Art," Red Earth Indian Arts Festival, 1994. **Member:** TACT (Technology and Cultural Transformation), UNESCO.

Individual Exhibitions

1946-50 Lloyd Kiva Studio, Scottsdale, Arizona
1950-61 Kiva Craft Center, Scottsdale, Arizona
1996   *Lloyd Kiva New: Traditional Pathways, Innovative Journeys,* Taliesin West, Scottsdale, Arizona

Selected Group Exhibitions

1946-50 Lloyd Kiva Studio, Scottsdale, Arizona
1950-61 Kiva Craft Center, Scottsdale, Arizona
1957   University of Arizona, Tucson
1961   *Textiles U.S.A.*, Museum of Modern Art, New York
1965   Edinborough Festival, Scotland
1968   Cultural Olympics, Mexico City, Mexico
1981   *Indian Art of the 1980s*, Native American Center for the Living Arts, Niagara Falls, New York
1988   *World Crafts Country Exhibit,* Lima, Peru
1992   *Creativity Is Our Tradition*, Institute of American Indian Arts Museum, Santa Fe, New Mexico
1994   *Selections from the Permanent Collection: Past and Present Faculty*, Institute of American Indian Arts Museum, Santa Fe, New Mexico

Collections

Casa de las Americas, Havana, Cuba; Institute of American Indian Arts, Santa Fe, New Mexico; Museum of Modern Art, New York.

Publications

By NEW: Books—*The Institute of American Indian Arts Alumni Exhibition,* Fort Worth, 1974; *American Indian Art in the 1980s,* Niagara Falls, New York, 1981; *Art of the Native American: The Southwest, from the late 19th Century to the Present,* Owensboro, Kentucky, 1985; *Selections from the Permanent Collection: Past and Present Faculty,* Institute of American Indian Arts Museum, Santa Fe, 1994. **Articles**— "A New Vitality: Contemporary Influences of Native American Arts Traditions," *House Beautiful* magazine, June 1971; "The Role of Art in the Education of the American Indian," *Arts in Society,* vol. 9, no. 3, 1973; "Contemporary Indian Arts in the U.S.A.," in *Handbook on the American Indian,* Smithsonian Institution, Washington, D.C., 1987; "Lloyd Kiva New," in *Creativity Is Our Tradition,* edited by Richard Hill, Santa Fe, 1992.

On NEW: Books—*Indian Painters and White Patrons,* by J.J. Brody, Albuquerque, 1971; *Song from the Earth,* by Jamake Highwater, Boston, 1975; *American Indians Today,* Tucson, 1979. **Articles**—"New, 'Honored One,' at Red Earth," *Cherokee Observer,* August 1994; "Honoring Lloyd Kiva New," by Marilyn LaFountain, *Indian Artist,* Winter 1997.

*

Lloyd Kiva New comments:

It is for the Indian Artists of the future to realize that within their artistic traditions lies the spirit and soul of the nation, reaching back into the very primordial beginnings of this continent. It will be they who will be able to answer the question far into the future of "who are we Americans, really?" Through careful nurturing of the everlasting and fundamental human truths—that lie both at the base of the civilizing process and the core of Indian culture—and their careful analysis and synthesis with the new wisdoms of the world, Native Americans through their cultural and arts expressions will maintain the thread of cultural continuity that will truly distinguish the American throughout the world. (From "Credo for Indian Artist: 'As Long as the Rivers Flow.'"

*   *   *

Lloyd Kiva New, 1997. Photograph by Seth Roffman; courtesy Southwest Learning Centers collection.

As an artist, entrepreneur, educator and administrator, Lloyd Kiva New stands tall in the twentieth century arts scene. He has successfully created and promoted artwork that expands on traditional Native American artistic expression in contemporary forms, as reflected in his own fabric and fashion designs and those marketed through the internationally respected studios and shops he played a major role in developing in Scottsdale, Arizona. Among his many accomplishments as an educator and administrator is having helped lead the establishment of the Institute of American Indian Arts, where he served as an instructor from 1962 through 1967 and as Director through 1978. With its emphasis on individual expression, where the issue of what constitutes Native American art is defined by artists themselves, and sharing of Native American traditions, the Institute has greatly impacted art since its doors opened in 1962. Similarly, New has been a major force for contemporary Native American art and education through his memberships with academic and government institutions, his curatorial activities, instruction, and his own example as artist and entrepreneur.

New's artwork and the time he has available to practice art have been overshadowed by his other endeavors and accomplishments. As an artist he has been primarily known for creating wearable art, in which contemporary designs on clothing and accessories preserve Native American traditions. This reflects his philosophy as an art educator—of evolving traditions through original approaches to expand and sustain them. New acknowledges that any art done by a Native American is Native American art, whether or not it directly ties with tradition. His own work most consistently shows an extension of tradition through more contemporary styles and designs. For example, his works in leather include a handbag with a form adapted from pouches used by medicine men of the Plains, adorned with conches that give it an original look.

New grew up in Oklahoma. Hopping a freight train to Chicago to attend the World's Fair while in his teens, New discovered the Art Institute of Chicago, where he later enrolled and became the first American Indian to obtain an Arts Education degree from its school of arts. His studies in ancient Native American architecture awakened in him a sense of pride and inspiration. He pursued postgraduate studies in Southwest Indian Art at the Laboratory of Anthropology in Santa Fe, New Mexico. During these early years, New apprenticed with Olle Nordmark, the noted Swedish muralist technician in fresco and secco mural painting. New then moved to New York City, accepting an apprenticeship in Fabric design and printing in the studios of D. D. and Leslie Tillet, a noted design team.

New's teaching experience began in 1938 as an art instructor in the Phoenix Indian School, (K-12). His teaching career neatly coincides with the end of Dorothy Dunn's association with The Studio at Santa Fe Indian School. New's emphasis on working with an artist's original approaches contrasts with Dunn's strict emphasis on teaching and promoting flatstyle painting and emphasizing strict adherence to traditional styles. During the following four years, he supervised special students in illustrating a series of bi-lingual text books, his curricula was sensitive to the needs of his Indian students, and he also silk screened and lithographed posters for bilingual adult education, used on the Navajo Reservation. Soon New was promoted to master teacher, training incoming Indian art teachers under the Bureau of Indian Affairs, and he supervised interior color decoration and execution of large scaled mural projects in various B.I.A. schools and hospitals.

During World War II, New served as one of two official Battalion Artists in the Fifth Special CB Battalion in the Aleutian Islands, Alaska. In 1943, he transferred to the Navy and served as a Boat Wave Commander. After his honorable discharge in 1946, he opened a design/crafts fashion studio named "Lloyd Kiva" in Scottsdale, Arizona. His center featured haute couture works in leathers, Cherokee hand-woven tweeds and hand dyed fabrics. He worked from basic American Indian design and color motifs. As New's vision grew, he developed the "Fifth Avenue and Craftsman Court." From sections of raw land in Scottsdale, New designed and constructed "Kiva Craft Center," featuring 45 studios and shops. This original arts and crafts theme helped propel spectacular growth of the small village of Scottsdale into a nationally known resort shopping community.

New served as co-Director and conceptual leader of the Southwest Indian Arts Project, sponsored from 1958 to 1961 at the University of Arizona by the Rockefeller Foundation, a research and development program in arts education for young Indians. A prototype philosophy was developed that resulted in a theory of education that emphasized complete creative freedom for Indian artists, which was subsequently institutionalized with the founding of the Institute of American Indian Arts (IAIA) by the U. S. Government in 1962, in Santa Fe, New Mexico. New served as an instructor and later as President of the IAIA.

During his tenure at IAIA, New wrote and produced, in 1964, two American Indian dance-drama theater productions in Washington, D. C., *Sipapu* and *Feather the Shrine*. After a decade of service as commissioner of the Indian Arts and Crafts Board by the Secretary of the Interior, New was selected Chairman in 1971. He supported the chartering of a non-profit sister institution, the National Foundation for American Indian Art, an organization devoted to the promotion of contemporary Indian expressions in all major media. While working on the federal level as a advocate for Indian arts, New simultaneously promoted art education on the local level in support of museums and schools. He was appointed to the charter group of trustees for the Heard Museum in Phoenix, Arizona, and served as a member of its National Advisory Council. For years New worked on the National Council of the Museum of the American Indian, Heye Foundation, in New York City, and remains active as informal transitional advisor in the subsequent transfer of National Museum of the American Indian to Washington, D.C., by the Smithsonian Institution. New continued to teach and lecture during this period.

In 1988, New completed a four year appointment as Adjudicator of Fine Arts, the National Foundation for Talents in the Arts, Educational Testing Service, Princeton, New Jersey, and Dade County University, Miami, Florida. It is from the list of winners of this annual competition that the Presidential Scholars in the Arts are selected. During the 1980s, New curated and lectured at the *Pintura Amerindia Contemporanea/E.U.A*, an exhibition of American Indian painting which toured the capital cities of Colombia, Ecuador, Peru, Bolivia, and Chile.

Recognition for his work in support of the arts continues. In 1992, the "Lloyd New Room" was named and dedicated at the IAIA Museum. He was honored as part of a Committee of Elders, who serve as advisors to the architects for the design of the National Museum of the American Indian to be built on the Mall, Washington, D.C. In 1994, New was selected by the Oklahoma-based Red Earth Indian Arts Festival to the position of "The Honored One," an annual award to a "Native American who has a distinguished record of service on behalf of promoting and contributing to Native American Art."

—Gregory Schaaf and Perry Bear

NIRO, Shelly

Tribal affiliations: Mohawk
Photographer, painter, and filmmaker

Born: Niagara Falls, New York, 1954. **Education:** Durham College, Oshawa, Ontario, Graphics Program, 1978; Ontario College of Art, HFA, 1990; Banff School of Fine Arts, summer classes. **Career:** Teaches part-time at the University of Western Ontario. **Awards:** Walking in Beauty Award, for *It Starts with a Whisper*, 1992; Two Rivers Film and Video Festival, Minneapolis, Minnesota; First Projects Grant and Photographer's Exhibition Assistant Grant, Ontario Arts Council.

Individual Exhibitions

1992   *Mohawks in Beehives and Other Works*, Mercer Union, Toronto, Ontario
1992   *This Land Is Mime Land*, Ufundi Gallery, Ottawa, Ontario
1994   *Sense of Self*, London Regional Art and Historical Museums, London, Ontario

Selected Group Exhibitions

1993   *Defining Our Realities: Native American Women Photographers*, Sacred Circle Gallery, Seattle, Washington
1993   *Cultural Contrasts*, Stamford Museum and Nature Center, Stamford, Connecticut
1994   *From Icebergs to Ice Tea*, Thunder Bay Art Center, Ontario
         Watchful Eyes, Heard Museum, Phoenix, Arizona
1995   *The Female Imaginary*, Agnes Etherington Art Centre, Kingston, Ontario
1995   *Image and Self: In Contemporary Native American Photoart*, Hood Museum of Art, Dartmouth College, Hanover, New Hampshire
1995   *Alter*Native: *Contemporary Photo Compositions*, McMichael Canadian Art Collection, Kleinburg, Ontario

Collections

Laurentian Art Centre, Sudbury; Indian and Northern Affairs, Indian Art Bank; Canada Council Art Bank, Ottawa; Canadian Museum of Civilization, Hull, Quebec; Woodland Cultural Centre, Brantford, Ontario; and the City of North Bay.

Publications

By NIRO: Film—*It Starts With a Whisper*, with Anna Gronau, 1992.

On NIRO: Books—*Watchful Eyes: Native American Women Artists*, by Theresa Harlan, The Heard Museum, Phoenix, 1994; *AlterNative: Contemporary Photo Compositions*, by Lynn A. Hill, McMichael Canadian Art Collection, Kleinburg, Ontario, 1995. **Articles—**"I Enjoy Being a Mohawk Girl: The Cool and Comic Character of Shelly Niro's Photography," by Allan Ryan, *American Indian Art Magazine*, vol. 20, no. 1, Winter 1994; "Image and Self: In Contemporary Native American Photoart," by Jennifer Skoda, *American Indian Art Magazine*, vol. 21, no. 2, Spring 1996.

*   *   *

As a photographer, painter and filmmaker, Shelly Niro is most well known for her whimsical photos of women. She uses herself, her family and friends as subjects in her works. Themes of self-determination, sisterhood and the commodification of Native women, cultures and histories appear frequently in Niro's work. Through the inclusion of text in her photos and the use of diptychs and triptychs, Niro expands the narrative potential of photography. Niro's photographic works frequently address the complexity of female identity.

Niro hand-tints and sepia-tones her black-and-white photographs. Additionally, she mounts her diptychs and triptychs on mat board. The photographs are united on the mat background through the pinhole designs, which are reminiscent of Mohawk beadwork designs. Niro references Mohawk women's art traditions with these designs—connecting her work and message to the continuing importance of women in Native communities. This theme of sisterhood is strong. The texts written on the photographs create layers of meaning that aid the viewer in exploring the complexity of Niro's themes.

Through the use of humor and trickster-like satire, Niro's earlier works challenge and deconstruct stereotypical images of Native women, as illustrated in *The Rebel* (1987), which shows her mother, June Chiquita Doxtater, lounging across an AMC Rebel automobile. She is not the stereotypical young, thin (frequently blond), sexy model often used to sell cars. This work challenges notions of ideal feminine beauty and the commodification of Native women, whose images are used to sell everything from butter to beer.

In a defiant act of sisterhood, Niro's sisters sport beehive hairdos and irreverently kick up their heels in front of a statue of a Mohawk chief in *Red Heels Hard*. One wonders for whom is this a memorial: was it to honor a great Mohawk leader who fought to defend his people and culture or is it a monument to the colonizer—a reminder that "the only good Indian is a dead Indian." Either way, the defiant act of sisterhood attests to the resistance of cultural annihilation. Here images of earth mothers and Indian princesses fade away, as her sisters become contemporary tricksters subverting the history of the colonizer. So, on another level Niro's work urges both non-native and Native viewers to give up their nostalgia—to recognize that there is no going back—that what is left is history and who controls and shapes it.

In her more recent work the female form takes a secondary role in the overall composition. In the series *Flying Human Being*, for example, Niro probes her psyche, which is embodied in *Flying Woman*. For Niro, *Flying Woman* is the archetype of freedom and abandonment, representing the "subconscious as it passes through time and space, past and present." In *Flying Woman #8*, the figure has been pushed to the border, no longer dominating the composition. In this piece the emphasis is on the beaded details of the legging, which has opened up, creating a kaleidoscopic image. In this series the reference to beadwork has moved from a decorative matting element to a fundamental element in the composition. The connection of Flying Woman to the beaded legging represents Niro's tie to her culture.

Niro represents a growing number of Native photographers who are turning their cameras on themselves and their communities in an attempt to subvert the history of voyeurism and to create new photographic histories that speak of Native cultural survival, not cultural decline.

—Jennifer Vigil

NOGANOSH, Ron

Tribal affiliations: Ojibway
Graphic artist, photographer, and installation artist

Born: Magnetewan Reserve, 3 May 1949. **Education:** Shawnaga Indian Day School; public and secondary schools in Nobel, Garson, Parry Sound, and Toronto, Ontario; studied welding at George Brown College, Toronto, 1967-68, diploma; studied graphic design at George Brown College, Toronto, 1968-70, diploma; studied visual arts at the University of Ottawa, taking courses in sculpture, painting, drawing, and lithography, beginning 1980, B.A. **Career:** Wide range of jobs, including welding, tree pruning, underground mining, truck driving, carpentry, and construction; graphic designer, silkscreen artist, and photographer, and display and installation work; served as Band Administrator, Ojibways of Magnetawan Band Council, Byng Inlet, Ontario, 1972-79; served on the Board of Directors,

Ontario Trappers Association, North Bay, Ontario, 1977-80; involved as actor and artist in a production of *The Loon's Necklace* at the Great Canadian Theatre Company, Ottawa, Ontario, 1981; conducted workshop in sculpture at SAW Gallery, Ottawa, 1982 and the Contemporary Indian and Inuit Art and Sculpture Workshop at the McMichael Art Gallery, Kleinburg, Ontario, 1985; during the 1980s, taught art at the College d'Enseignement General et Professionel de l'Outaouais, Hull, Quebec. **Awards:** Regional Municipality of Ottawa-Carleton, 1992; Scholarship and artist's residency (Nomad Program) at the Banff Centre for the Arts, Banff, Alberta, 1993; Ontario Arts Council, 1993; Canada Council, 1994.

Individual Exhibitions:

1992   *Ron Noganosh: Recent Work,* Ufundi Gallery, Ottawa, Ontario

Selected Group Exhibitions

1981   *Viewpoints,* Gallery 101, Ottawa, Ontario
1982   *Sculpture,* SAW Gallery, Ottawa, Ontario
1984   *Points of View: Works by Five Native American Artists,* The Community Gallery, New York
1985   *Contemporary Indian Art at Rideau Hall,* Congress Centre, Ottawa, Ontario
        Installation, Ottawa School of Art, Ontario
        Indian Art '85, Woodland Cultural Centre, Brantford, Ontario
1986   *Indian Art '86,* Woodland Cultural Centre, Brantford, Ontario
        Winterlude Festival: Artist in Residence, Ottawa Congress Centre, Ontario
        Contemporary Indian and Inuit Art, United Nations, New York
1987   *Artists Choose Artists,* Jamaica Arts Center, New York
1988   *Doux amer,* Axe Neo 7, Hull, Quebec
        Snakes in the Garden, Arts Court, Ottawa, Ontario
        Solstice d'Ete: La Fraise, Galerie l'Imagier, Aylmer, Quebec
        Zeitgenossische Kunst der Indiane und Eskimos, Museum am Ostwal, Dortmund, Germany
1989   *Beyond History,* Art Gallery of Vancouver, British Columbia
        Decelebration, SAW Gallery, Ottawa, Ontario
        In the Shadow of the Sun: Contemporary Indian and Inuit Art, Canadian Museum of Civilization, Hull, Quebec; Stuttgart Museum, Stuttgart, Germany
        Solstice d'Ete: La Grand-Mere, Galerie l'Imagier, Aylmer, Quebec
1990   *Cardinal Points: Amerindian Art Today,* La Macaza, Quebec
        Hard and Soft, University of Sherbrooke Cultural Centre, Sherbrooke, Quebec
1991   *En Hommage a un Cadeau d'Eva Hesse, a Sol LeWitt,* Axe-Neo 7, Hull, Quebec
        L'Amerindienne: Regards sur l'Animal, Museum of Civilization, Quebec
        Strengthening the Spirit, National Gallery of Canada, Ottawa, Ontario
        Visions of Power, Earth Spirit Festival, Toronto, Ontario

1992   *Summer Solstice*, Galerie l'Imagier, Aylmer, Quebec
        Canada's First People, travelled across Canada and Japan
        Autobiography: First Nations Art, Ufundi Gallery, Ottawa, Ontario
        Extra-Muros: Five Artists at Jeanne d'Arc, organized by Artscourt, Ottawa, Ontario
        New Territories—350/500 Years After, Les Maisons de la Culture, Montreal, Quebec
        Contemporary First Nations Art, Ufundi Gallery, Ottawa, Ontario
1993   *Nomads: Artists in Residence*, Banff Centre for the Arts, Banff, Alberta

Collections

Canadian Museum of Civilization, Hull, Quebec; Indian Art Centre, Department of Indian and Northern Affairs, Ottawa.

Publications

On NOGANOSH: Books—*Snakes in the Garden*, exhibition catalog, Ottawa, 1988; *Beyond History*, exhibition catalog by Tom Hill and Karen Duffek, Vancouver, 1989; *Decelebration*, exhibition catalog, Ottawa, 1989; *Hard and Soft*, exhibition catalog by Jaqueline Fry, Sherbrooke, 1990; "Ron Noganosh," *Mixed Blessings: Contemporary Art in a Multicultural America*, by Lucy Lippard, New York, 1990; *Visions of Power—Contemporary Art by First Nations, Inuit and Japanese Canadians*, exhibition catalog, Toronto, 1991; *En Hommage a un Cadeau d'Eva Hesse a Sol LeWitt*, exhibition catalog, Hull, 1991; *New Territories—350/500 Years After*, exhibition catalog, Montreal, 1992; "Postmodern Culture and Indian Art," *In the Shadow of the Sun: Perspectives on Contemporary Native Art* by Gerhard Hoffman, Hull, 1993. **Articles**—"Noganosh's Roadside Collection," by Alexis Mantel, *Low Down to Hull and Back News,* Wakefield, Quebec, August 1982; "Decking the Halls in Lower Midtown," by Diana Freedman, *Art Speak*, New York, vol. 6, no. 8, December 1984; "Artist Conveys Political View in Visual Satire," by Nancy Baele, the *Ottawa Citizen*, 2 February 1985; "Le Dur et le Flexible, Viviane Gray and Ron Noganosh," *Tribune*, Sherbrooke, December 1989; "Art and Issues," by Olive Robertson, *FUSE*, August 1989; "Issues and Trends in Contemporary Native Art," by Alfred Young Man, *Artscraft*, Ottawa, Winter 1989; "Decelebration," by Lee-Ann Martin and Gerald McMaster, *Artscraft*, Ottawa, 1990; "Decelebration" by Jacqueline Fry and Brian Maracle, *Runge Press*, Ottawa, 1990; "Indian Sculptor Practises Art of the Cosmic Giggle," by Nancy Baele, the *Ottawa Citizen*, 8 May 1990; "Hard and Soft: Collaborative Works by Ottawa Artists Viviane Gray and Ron Noganosh," by Mike Anderson, *Artscraft*, Ottawa, Spring 1990; "Will the Canoe Ever Look the Same?," interview with the artist by Gerald McMaster, *Artscraft*, Ottawa, Winter 1990; "Earth Spirit," *Artscraft*, Spring/Summer 1991; "Extra Muros: Arts Court's Haunting New Exhibit," by Mike Anderson, *Metro*, Ottawa, August/September 1992; "Aboriginal Artists Open New Territory," by Anne Duncan, *Gazette*, Montreal, August 1992; "Post Modern Parody: A Political Strategy in Contemporary Canadian Native Art," by Allan J. Ryan, *Art Journal*, Fall 1992. **Broadcasts**—"Lubicon Art Exhibit," an interview with the artist on *As It Happens*, CBC Radio, 1 June 1989; "Aboriginal Voices," with Doug MacKenzie, CHRO TV, Ottawa, 1993.

*

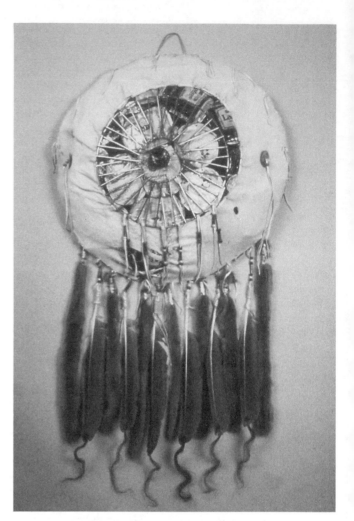

Ron Noganosh: *Shield for a Modern Warrior: No Concessions to Beads and Feathers in Indian Art,* 1985. Collection of the Indian Art Centre, Department of Indian and Northern Affairs, Ottawa, Canada; courtesy of the artist.

Ron Noganosh comments:

I am according to the Government of Canada, a real INDIAN. The number that has been assigned to me is BO47957 and my band number is 99. This has helped me to find my place in society, for without this information, I would, in all probability not know that I was an Indian, says the government.

I spent my youth on the Shawnaga Indian Reservation, attending various and sundry schools, after which I was pronounced CIVILIZED. Upon completing a Graphic Design course in Toronto in 1980, I was officially declared an ARTIST, and let loose upon an unsuspecting world. Thereafter I obtained gainful employment in diverse occupations ranging from car washer to screen washer and discovered that jobs for CIVILIZED INDIAN ARTISTS are not profuse.

During this time, caught up in the mystique of being a CIVILIZED INDIAN ARTIST, I began making prints of a realistic nature and this approach continues to this day.

I entered the Fine Arts Program at the University of Ottawa and began teaching art at the CEGEP de l'Outaouais in Hull, Quebec. At the university I began to explore the political, economic, ecological and social issues which confront people in their everyday lives, through the medium of sculpture, using found objects. Perhaps I am becoming a MYSTICAL CIVILIZED INDIAN ARTIST...say the reviewers. Their pronouncements have led to exhibitions in Ottawa, Hull, Toronto, Brantford, New York, Tokyo and Munich. My work has been acquired by the Department of Indian and Northern Affairs, the Canadian Museum of Civilization and several private collectors.

Someday I may even be a RICH MYSTICAL CIVILIZED INDIAN ARTIST. (From Artist's File, Indian Art Centre, Department of Indian Affairs)

(1993) As an "ignoble savage," I seek to shock and dismay audiences out of their comfortable realities — realities that exchange life for death, nature for contamination, peace for genocide. I seek to speak out against institutions that would categorize, stereotype, trivialize and colonize. I do this, knowing full well that there are more comfortable ways to earn a living. I do this for my children and for the world. (From *Nomads*, Banff Centre for the Arts)

*   *   *

Mixing discarded auto parts, tin cans, empty liquor bottles, plastic toys, and other detritus of contemporary society, Ron Noganosh constructs assemblages and installation works that convey humorous but always incisively critical comments on social, cultural, and environmental issues. He belongs to the generation of Native artists who emerged in Canada in the early 1980s—artists whose art-school training has given them access to all the techniques and formal strategies of modernist and post-modernist art. They have freely drawn on those options to create the means through which to explore their experiences within the dual contexts of traditional Native values and those of a post-industrial, media-saturated, consumerist society.

Indeed, Noganosh's choice of medium in itself can be seen as a response to the conflict between those two sets of values. Although the use of found objects and the creation of "junk sculpture" have been part of Western art since early in this century, it is not aesthetic debates or art-historical precedents that concern Noganosh; his use of discarded objects is motivated instead by a desire to put into practice his belief that nothing should be wasted, while at the same time confronting society with the evidence of its excesses.

As well as informing his choice of medium, the belief that one should use only what is necessary and leave the land the way one found it for the sake of future generations has inspired a number of works that deal overtly with the destruction of the environment. In *Canoe 92* (1989), for example, a camouflage shirt draped on a coat rack, a Girl Guides' scarf, and a gas mask make up the head and torso of a seated figure paddling a canoe across a styrofoam base carved and painted to suggest rippling water, the surface of which is littered with trash. Already a vivid and blunt statement of the inability of nature to absorb any more of society's waste, the work gains an ironic edge when gallery goers take their cue from the trash already present and add their own litter to the piece.

The loss of Native lands—and all that follows from that loss as a result of relentless resource exploitation is the subject of a number of Noganosh's works. *Massey-Harris* (1985), named after the manufacturer of the ploughs and combines that transformed the Canadian prairies into wheat farms, includes miniature plastic buffalo stampeding over the edge of a tractor seat from which hangs a mobile of hide thongs, bones and money. All of this is gracefully suspended in mid-air from a bow-shaped metal form and counter-balanced by the large metal spring and engine part to which the bow is affixed. The work is at once a playful balancing of weights and forces (reminiscent of Calder perhaps) and a not-so-playful reminder of the destruction of a way of life.

Lubicon (1988), a major installation work, presents a more stark condemnation of the forces that continue to destroy Native lands and communities. The work addresses the long struggle of the Lubicon Cree of northern Alberta to regain lands taken over by oil companies. Against the backdrop of a Canadian flag rising from (or sinking into) the ground, "Lubicon" is spelled out in empty whiskey bottles connected by a plastic intravenous tube. Liquid runs continuously through this tube into the mouth of a plastic skull set at the head of a traditional Woodland beaded costume, which is laid out on a pole burial platform. There appears to be no hope for a people kept alive on this most meagre and pernicious of life supports. On a taped soundtrack, laughter and crying alternate endlessly.

Other works such as *Dominus Vobiscum* (1985), with its rosary of bullets, and *Darryl Strawberry* (1987), with its juxtaposition of the image of a priest giving the sacrament to a kneeling Indian with a traditional story of the choice to remain among the dead, deal with the role of the church and the residential schools in undermining Native value-systems.

At first glance, *If You Find Any Culture Send It Home* (1986) also appears to focus on the loss of traditional culture. However, far more than a simple lament, this work is a sly and knowing critique of the presumption of non-Native experts who take it upon themselves to determine what is and is not "authentic." The work consists of a rough-hewn wooden mask accompanied by a letter from a father to his son who is studying art at university. The father recounts how a man "from the museum" gave him "800 bucks" for the mask—the one his grandfather used before he died—because it was "a fine exampel [sic] of the culture." He didn't tell this "authority" that he almost burned the mask once when he needed firewood. He writes that he spent the money on a VCR, and ends the note with "PS. If you find any culture send it home." Adding to the irony that the no-longer-meaningful mask has been exchanged for access to the mainstream culture, and that the expert is uninterested in the present, living culture of the Natives with whom he deals, is the appearance of the mask itself. It does not resemble any specific traditional style; however, it does look suspiciously like the "primitivism" favoured by modernism and its champions—a visual comment on the twists and turns of art-world fashions in relation to Native arts.

Shield for a Modern Warrior: No Concessions to Beads and Feathers in Indian Art (1985) is another work that targets those who would limit Native culture to preconceived notions of the traditional. The shield, constructed from a hub cap and crushed beer cans, as well as more customary materials such as hide and feathers, insists, among other things, on the right of Indian artists to make works that draw on and are relevant to the world in which they now live.

Ron Noganosh has been called a "junk-yard satirist" (Mike Anderson, 1990)—a fitting title for this resourceful, irreverent artist. Whether parodying the experts, challenging narrow definitions of tradition, accusing the ongoing forces of colonialiasm, or just shaking his head over human folly, Noganosh transforms the cast-off and overlooked into works that speak with intelligence, humor, and power to the needs of the present.

—Deborah Burrett

NO TWO HORNS, Joseph

Variant names: He Nupa Wanica; White Butterfly
Tribal affiliations: Hunkpapa Lakota
Carver and painter

Born: 1852. **Career:** Warrior who fought in approximately forty battles, including Little Big Horn; served with Sitting Bull. Keeper of Winter Count (pictograph records); craftsman of weaponry; painter and carver. **Died:** 1942.

Group Exhibition

1992-93   *Visions of the People*, Minneapolis Institute of Arts, Minnesota

Collections

Denver Art Museum, Colorado; State Historical Society of North Dakota, Bismark; Science Museum of Minnesota, St. Paul.

Publications

On NO TWO HORNS: Books—*The History of Joseph No Two Horns*, by Henry Murphy, State Historical Society of North Dakota, Bismark, 1927; *Visions of the People: A Pictorial History of Plains Life*, by Evan Maurer, The Minneapolis Institute of Arts, Minneapolis, and University of Washington Press, Seattle, 1992; *Plains Indian Drawings 1865-1935: Pages from a Visual History* edited by Janet Catherine Berlo, Harry Abrams, Inc., New York, 1996. **Articles**—"Joseph No Two Horns, He Nupa Wanica," by David Wooley and Joseph D. Horse Capture, *American Indian Art Magazine* vol. 18, no. 3, 1993.

*   *   *

One of a large group of Hunkpapa artists active at the Standing Rock Agency at the turn of the century, No Two Horns worked in several medias, including wood, hide, cloth and paper. He was most active as an artist between 1890 and 1920. The Reverend Aaron

No Two Horns: *No Two Horns, in a battle with the Assiniboine, rescues a member of the Strong Heart Society.* **Courtesy State Historical Society of North Dakota.**

McGaffey Beede, who was an Episcopal minister and director of Indian mission work in North Dakota, collected more than forty drawings on paper from No Two Horns and gave them to the Historical Society of North Dakota. They depict events from No Two Horn's early years as a warrior as well as incidents in the life of his father, Red Hail, and other Hunkpapa warriors.

Despite the fact that his right hand was crippled on a hunting expedition in his youth, No Two Horns was a skilled carver of dance sticks memorializing the blue roan horse he rode as a young warrior. Ten such carvings have been attributed to him.

Two painted canvas tipis and two other drawings on muslin are known to have been crafted by No Two Horns. In the tipi drawings and some of the pictographic drawings on paper, No Two Horns used stencils ingeniously (perhaps because of his hand injury) to create repeating images of horses. Like the drawings on paper, the painted tipis illustrate the war-making and horse-capture activities of traditional Lakota men, including the artist himself, Red Hail, Sitting Bull, Red Bow, and others. No Two Horns depicted the historical traditions of the Lakota people in at least two winter counts—pictographic records of key historical events of many years. One of these survives in the collection of the State Historical Society of North Dakota.

No Two Horns' painted shield is one of the most familiar images of late nineteenth century Plains iconography. It depicts a frontal thunderbird with extended claws and wavy lines of power extending from its outstretched wings. Several variants of this shield exist in museum collections, and depictions of it appear in No Two Horns' drawings as an element that identifies him as the protagonist.

Like many Lakota artists of his generation, including Standing Bear, Moses Old Bull, and White Bull, No Two Horns has one foot in the nineteenth-century warriors' way of life and one foot in the early twentieth-century settled life on the reservation. In his art, he continued the traditions of the nineteenth century warrior-artists who memorialized their deeds in narrative drawings and their visions on painted war shields. He did so at a time when many outsiders commissioned such works from elderly Lakota men in order to have a record of a vanishing way of life. All of these artists helped preserve Lakota traditions for successive generations, who have revived the Sun Dance and other ceremonial activities, ensuring the vitality of Lakota life into the twenty-first century.

—Janet Catherine Berlo

ODJIG, Daphne
Tribal affiliations: Ojibway
Painter

Born: Wikwemikong Indian Reserve, Manitoulin Island, Ontario, 1919; surname means "Kingfisher," and sometimes spelled Adjudge. **Career:** Numerous important commissions, including Expo '70, the Manitoba Museum of Man & Nature, and the National Museum of Man, Ottawa, among others; founder and member of several cultural organizations, including Indian Prints of Canada Ltd., 1970, co-founders of Professional Native Indian Artists Inc., (the "Indian Group of Seven"), 1973, opened the Warehouse Gallery in Winnipeg, Manitoba, 1974; taught at the Manitou Arts Foundation, Schrieber Island, early 1970s; resource person, Society of Canadian Artists of Native Ancestry (SCANA), 1985. **Awards:** Presented Eagle Feather by Chief Wakageshigon on behalf of the Wikwemikong Reserve, in recognition of artistic accomplishments, an honour previously reserved for men to acknowledge prowess in hunting or war, 1978; elected to the Board of the Canadian Native Arts Foundation, 1986, Royal Canadian Academy of Art, 1989; honourary degrees from Laurentian University, Sudbury, the University of Toronto, and Nipissing University, North Bay; The Order of Canada, 1986.

Individual Exhibitions

1967 The Lakehead Art Centre, Port Arthur, Ontario
1969 *Viscount Gorte*, sponsored by the Manitoba Indian Brotherhood, Winnipeg, Manitoba
1970 Canadian Guild of Crafts, Place Bonaventure, Montreal, Quebec
Canadian Pavilion, Osaka, Japan
Minot State University, North Dakota
1971 *Smotra Folklore Festival*, Yugoslavia
The Agence de Cooperation Culturelle et Technique, toured France, Belgium, Canada
1972 Winnipeg Art Gallery, Manitoba
1974 Warehouse Gallery of Native Art, Winnipeg, Manitoba
1976 Jerusalem Series, Bashford and Schwartz Gallery, Calgary, Alberta
1977 Wah-sa Gallery, Winnipeg, Manitoba
Lefebvre Gallery, Edmonton, Alberta
Images for a Canadian Heritage, Vancouver, British Columbia
The Bashford's and Schwarts Gallery, Calgary Inn, Bow Vallery Square, Calgary Alberta
1980 *Parallels of Nature*, Assiniboia Gallery, Regina, Saskatchewan
Children of the Raven Gallery, Vancouver, British Columbia
Behind the Mask, Robertson Gallery, Ottawa, Ontario

1981 Gold Design Fine Arts, Calgary, Alberta
Children of the Raven Gallery: Childhood Memories, Vancouver, British Columbia
1982 Robertson Gallery, Ottawa, Ontario
Assiniboia Gallery, Regina, Saskatchewan
Gold Design Fine Arts, Calgary, Alberta
1983 Shayne Gallery, Montreal, Quebec
1984 Gallery Phillip, Toronto, Ontario
1985 *A Retrospective 1946-1985*, Thunder Bay Exhibition Centre and Centre for Indian Art, toured Laurentian University Museum and Arts Centre, Sudbury, Ontario; McMichael Canadian Collection, Kleinburg, Ontario; Woodland Indian Cultural Educational Centre, Brantford, Ontario
Robertson Gallery, Ottawa, Ontario
Shayne Gallery, Montreal, Quebec
1986 Gallery Phillip, Toronto, Ontario
1987 Gallery Phillip, Toronto, Ontario
1988 Shayne Gallery, Montreal, Quebec
1989 Phillip Gallery, Toronto, Ontario
Robertson Gallery, Ottawa, Ontario
Woodlands: Contemporary Art of the Anishnabe, Thunder Bay Art Gallery, Gallery Phillip, Toronto, Ontario
1990 Hamilton Galleries, British Columbia
Gallery Shayne, Montreal, Quebec
1991 Hamilton Galleries, Kellowan, British Columbia
1993 Gallery Indigena, Stratford, Ontario
1995 Hambleton Galleries, Kellowan, British Columbia

Selected Group Exhibitions

1970 Canadian Guild of Crafts, Montreal, Quebec
Expo '70, Indians of Canada Pavilion, Japan
Minot State University, South Dakota
1971 L'Agence de Co-operation Culturelle et Technique, Canada, France, Belgium
1972 *Treaty Numbers 23, 287, 1171: Three Indian Painters of the Prairies*, (with Alex Janvier & Jackson Beardy) Winnipeg Art Gallery, Manitoba
1973 P.N.I.A. Group Exhibition, Gallery Anthropos, London, England
1974 *Oakville Exhibition of Native Art*, Centennial Gallery, Oakville, Ontario
The New Warehouse Gallery, Winnipeg, Manitoba
Canadian Indian Art '74, Royal Ontario Museum, Toronto, Ontario
1975 Winnipeg Art Gallery, Manitoba
Professional Native Indian Artists Incorporated, P.N.I.A. Group Exhibition, Dominion Gallery, Montreal, Quebec
1976 Laurentian University, Sudbury, Ontario

From Women's Eyes: Women Painters in Canada, Agnes Etherington Art Centre, Queen University, Kingston, Ontario

Etobicoke Civic Centre, Ontario

Janet Ian Cameron Gallery, University of Manitoba, Winnipeg

Indian Art '76, Woodland Cultural Educational Centre, Brantford, Ontario

The Woodland Indians, Royal Ontario Museum, Toronto, touring: Canada House Art Gallery, London, England, and Aula Luisen Schule, Lahr, West Germany

1977 *Links to Tradition*, touring exhibition sponsored by Indian and Northern Affairs Canada for travel to centres in Brazil

Contemporary Indian Arts : The Trail from the Past to the Future, MacKenzie Gallery Trent University, Peterborough, Ontario

1978 *One Hundred Years of Native American Painting*, Oklahoma Museum of Art Oklahoma City

Eagle Down Gallery, Edmonton, Alberta

1979 Glenhyrst Gallery, Brantford, Ontario

Woodland Cultural Educational Centre, Brantford, Ontario

1981 SUB Theatre, Edmonton Centre, Alberta

Traditions and Change, Rothman's Gallery, Sudbury, Ontario, touring

1982 *Wandering Spirits: Contemporary Native Artists and Their Art*, Windsong Galleries Mississauga, Ontario

Renewal, Masterworks of Contemporary Indian Art, Thunder Bay National Exhibition Centre for Indian Art from the Canadian Museum of Civilization, Ontario

The Indian Individualist Show, joint project of the Assiniboia Gallery, The World Assembly of First Nations and Saskatchewan Indian Federated College, Regina, Saskatchewan

1983 *Contemporary Indian and Inuit Art of Canada,* General Assembly Building, United Nations, New York

Touring: Organization of American States; Duke University, Durham, North Carolina; The Hall of State, Fair Park, Dallas, Texas; The South West Museum, Los Angeles, California

Contemporary Indian Art, from the collection of Indian and Northern Affairs Canada, Rideau Hall Ottawa, Ontario

1984 *Norval Morrisseau and the Emergence of the Image Makers*, Art Gallery of Ontario

The Best of Our Collections, In the Spirit of Sharing, Woodlands Indian Cultural Educational Centre, Brantford, Ontario

1985 *Challenges*, Meervaart Cultural Centre, Holland Festival, Amsterdam, Holland.

Holland Festival, Amsterdam, Holland, sponsored by the Canadian Museum of Civilization, Ottawa, Ontario

Two Worlds, Norman MacKenzie Art Gallery Regina, Saskatchewan

1986 *Ascending Culture*, Les Terrasses de la ChaudiereHull, Quebec

New Beginnings, Native Business Summit, Toronto, Ontario

Keepers of Our Culture, Woodland Indian Cultural Educational Centre Brantford, Ontario

1987 *A Celebration of Contemporary Canadian Native Art*, Southwest Museum, Los Angeles, California

Manitoulin Island: The Third Layer, Thunder Bay Art Gallery, Ontario

1988 *An Exhibition of Contemporary Indian Art*, Joseph D. Carrier Art Gallery, Columbus Centre, Toronto, Ontario

1989 *Woodlands: Contemporary Art of the Anishnabe*, Thunder Bay Art Gallery, Ontario

1996 *20th Anniversary Highlights,* Thunder Bay Art Gallery, Ontario

Collections

Ameco Canadian Petroleum Ltd., Calgary, Alberta; Helen E. Band Collection, Toronto, Ontario; Brandon University, Brandon, Manitoba; Canada Council Art Bank, Ottawa, Ontario; Canadian Museum of Civilization, Ottawa, Ontario; Glenview Corporation, Ottawa, Ontario; Government of Israel, Jerusalem, Israel; Government of Newfoundland, St. John's, Newfoundland; Government of Ontario, Toronto, Ontario; Government of Manitoba, Winnipeg, Manitoba; Laurentian University Museum and Art Centre, Sudbury, Ontario; Manitoba Indian Brotherhood, Winnipeg, Manitoba; Manitoba Museum of Man and Nature, Winnipeg, Manitoba; McMichael Canadian Art Collection, Kleinberg, Ontario; New College, University of Toronto, Toronto, Ontario; Ojibwe Cultural Foundation, West Bay, Ontario; Prince Edward Island Museum and Heritage Foundation, Charlottetown, Prince Edward Island; Royal Ontario Museum, Toronto, Ontario; Sir Wilfred Laurier University, Waterloo, Ontario; Thunder Bay National Exhibition Centre and Centre for Indian Art, Thunder Bay, Ontario; Winnipeg Art Gallery, Winnipeg, Manitoba; Woodland Indian Cultural and Education Centre, Brantford, Ontario.

Publications

By ODJIG: Books—*Tales of the Nanabush: Books of Indian Legends for Children,* 10 vols., Toronto, 1971; *A Paintbrush in My Hand*, with R.M. Vanderburgh and M.E. Southcott, Toronto, 1992.

On ODJIG: Books—*Indian Arts in Canada,* by Olive Dickason, Ottawa, 1972; *The Sound of the Drum: The Sacred Art of the Anishnabec,* by Mary E. Southcott, Erin, Ontario, 1984; *Daphne Odjig: A Retrospective, 1946-1985,* by Elizabeth McLuhan and R.M. Vanderburgh, Thunder Bay, Ontario, 1985; *Woodlands: Contemporary Art of the Anishnabe,* edited by Marcy Menitove and Joanne Danford, Thunder Bay, Ontario, 1989; *Time for Dialogue,* by Joanne Cardinal-Schubert, Calgary, 1992; *In the Shadow of the Sun,* by Gerald McMaster, et. al., Hull, Quebec, 1993. **Films**—*Three Artists Three Styles*, Henning Jacobsen Productions, 1973; *The Colours of Pride*, National Film Board of Canada, 1973; "Spirits Speaking Through," *Spectrum*, Canadian Broadcasting Company, 1981; *Window On Canada: Daphne Adjudge/Painter,* Tokyo Television, Japan, 1989.

*   *   *

Daphne Odjig was born in 1919 on the Wikwemikong Indian Reserve, Manitoulin Island, Ontario. As an originating member of the New Woodland School of painting, Odjig is a forerunner and example to the generations of First Nations artists who have participated with and challenged the Canadian mainstream art world since 1960.

Daphne Odjig: *Meares Island,* 1985. Photograph by Theodore Johns; collection of the artist; courtesy Thunder Bay Art Gallery.

Daphne Odjig has been the recipient of numerous important commissions and has been exhibiting in important group and solo exhibitions since 1967, among them the following groundbreaking exhibitions: *Treaty Numbers 23, 287, 1171*, Winnipeg Art Gallery (1972); *Indian Art '74*, Royal Ontario Museum (1974); *Contemporary Indian Art at Rideau Hall*, Indian Affairs & Northern Development, Ottawa, (1983); *Norval Morrisseau & the Emergence of the Image Makers*, Art Gallery of Ontario, Toronto, (1984); *Two Worlds*, Mackenzie Art Gallery, (1985); *Challenges*, de Meervaart Cultural Centre, Amsterdam, Holland, (1985); and *Canadian Contemporary Native Art*, Southwest Museum, Los Angeles, California, (1987).

Odjig was the founder and member of several cultural organizations whose efforts have been pivotal in terms of the development of a history of First Nations artistic production in Canada. For instance, in 1970 the artist created Indian Prints of Canada Ltd. In 1973, Odjig was one of the co-founders of Professional Native Indian Artists Inc., (the "Indian Group of Seven"). In 1974 she opened the Warehouse Gallery in Winnipeg, Manitoba. The artist taught at the Manitou Arts Foundation, Schrieber Island in the early 1970s and acted as a resource person for the Society of Canadian Artists of Native Ancestry (SCANA) in 1985. The following year, Odjig was elected to the Board of the newly formed Canadian Native Arts Foundation.

Odjig's work is important on the one hand for its acumen in defining the contemporary Indian experience in Canada, and on the other hand because it distinguishes itself from the work of other artists of the New Woodland School, particularly from that of its patriarch, Norval Morrisseau. Odjig's visual vocabulary was predicated on the New Woodland School's tendency to a distinctive black formline, a palette of high intensity colours, and a blank background. Volume is left to the formline to define, and this is achieved through the line's flow from thick to thin and back again, rather than through any attempted illusion of three-dimensional space. Yet, there are a variety of decorative aspects to Odjig's work that has made it unique among that produced by adherents of the school's formal style. While the formline in New Woodland School work often merely serves to contain—and specifically, to contain colour—Odjig's formline seems intent rather on expression. There is a lyricism present in Odjig's canvases that signals an innovative liberation of the formline.

While Odjig's earliest works depicted scenes of Ojibway culture as well as the essence of its worldview, by the late 1970s a change began to take place. In beginning to address issues of contemporary cultural relevance, Odjig's thematic focus became overtly political. Recalling the injustices of the past and the moment in her work, the artist began to gain a reputation as a cultural spokesperson. "Odjig found the means to express an Indian reality, with all its tragedy and contradiction, on a scale equal to the monumental injustice and irrationality of the experience." (McLuhan & Hill, 1984). Themes of spiritual renewal and social activism became the focus of much of Odjig's work well into the 1980s.

From the late 1980s to the present, Odjig's formline has shifted in significance, its importance to the overall composition has lessened while colour has become the predominant focus in terms of area, purity, and variety. Concomitantly, the artist's themes have shifted as well, becoming more reflective and personal. What was once complex and agitated has become lyrical and serene, not only in theme but in form. Recounting the events of a career of great breadth and power, Odjig's most recent work seems to reside peacefully in recognition of a significant contribution made, in terms of both aesthetic and socio-political change.

Much has happened during the span of Odjig's professional career; the old anthro/art debates regarding Native art have been laid to rest; the art of the First Nations is recognized and applauded in mainstream art institutions in Canada; Native artists have dealers and independent control of their careers and art; and the social injustices against Native peoples in Canada are no longer ignored or hidden but are at the forefront of media attention and political agendas. Issues of self-determination and land claims remain outstanding, yet the period of Canadian history from which we are currently emerging, a period in which Daphne Odjig made significant cultural and political contributions, has changed much and a path has clearly been made toward a more just future.

Daphne Odjig is an important figure in the history of contemporary Canadian art. Her contribution to the cultural life of Canada has been acknowledged in her election to the Royal Canadian Academy of Art in 1989, and in the honourary degrees which have been bestowed upon her by Laurentian University, Sudbury; the University of Toronto; and Nipissing University, North Bay. In 1986, Daphne Odjig was awarded The Order of Canada.

—Carol Podedworny

OLANNA, Melvin
Tribal affiliations: Inupiaq
Sculptor and jewelry designer

Born: Born Melvin Azittauna Olanna, Ikpik, Alaska, 5 May 1941. **Education:** Chemawa Indian School, Salem, Oregon; Institute of American Indian Arts, Santa Fe; Native Arts and Crafts Extension Program, University of Alaska, Fairbanks. **Family:** Married Karen Jenkins in 1976; three children. **Career:** Instructor, Village Art Upgrade Program, University of Alaska, Fairbanks, 1969-71; Artist in Residence, Fairbanks schools, 1975-76, Shishmaref Elementary School, 1983, Nome Community College Workshop, Shishmaref, Alaska, 1984; founded the Shishmaref Carving Center (now the Melvin Olanna Carving Center), Shishmaref, Alaska, 1988. **Awards:** First prize, silver jewelry, Festival of Native Arts, Anchorage, Alaska 1969; first prize, sculpture, Exxon USA Salon for Alaskan Artists 1973; Rassmussen Award, sculpture, All-Alaska Juried Show 1976; first prize, sculpture, Festival of Native Arts, Anchorage, Alaska 1976; Fellowship, American Center, Cite International des Arts, Paris, 1985; Public Art Commissions in Alaska—University of Alaska, Fairbanks, Northwest Community College, Nome, Egan Convention Center, Anchorage, North Star Borough School District, Fairbanks, Anchorage School District, Bering Straits School District, Fairbanks Correctional Center. **Died:** Seattle, Washington, 31 August 1991.

Individual Exhibitions

1969	Alaska Festival of Native Arts, Tundra Times Exhibit, Anchorage Historical and Fine Arts Museum, Alaska
1974	Alaska Native Arts and Crafts, Anchorage, Alaska
1976	Artworks Gallery, Fairbanks, Alaska
1979	The Snow Goose Gallery, Seattle, Washington
1981	*Whalebone, Ivory and Wood,* Alaska Native Arts and Crafts, Anchorage, Alaska
	The Legacy Ltd., Seattle
1989-90	Anchorage Museum of History and Art, Alaska
1990	Glenn Green Galleries, Scottsdale, Arizona

Selected Group Exhibitions

1971   *Contemporary Alaska Native Arts*, University of Alaska, Fairbanks

1973   *Alumni Exhibition*, Institute of American Indian Arts, Santa Fe, New Mexico

1977   *Survival: Art of the Alaskan Eskimo*, Newark Museum, New Jersey

1978   *Contemporary Arts from Alaska*, Smithsonian Institution, Washington, D.C.

1982   *Inua: Spirit of the Bering Sea Eskimo*, Smithsonian Institution, Washington, D.C.

Contemporary Eskimo and Northwest Coast Indian Arts, Field Museum of Natural History, Chicago, Illinois

The Craft Show, Washington State Museum, Olympia

1983   *Remains To Be Seen:*, John Kohler Arts Center, Sheboygan, Wisconsin

Contemporary Alaskan Artists, The Senate, Washington, D.C.

1985   *Alvin and Melvin*, Stonington Gallery, Anchorage, Alaska

1992   *Friends, a Special Tribute to Melvin Olanna*, Stonington Gallery, Anchorage, Alaska

Collections

Anchorage Museum of History and Art; Bell Telephone Company, Rainier Bank, Seattle-First National Bank, Old National Bank, Skinner Corporation, Seattle, Washington; Amon Carter Museum, Fort Worth, Texas; Indian Arts and Crafts Board, US Department, of the Interior, Washington, D.C.; Marshal Field, Chicago, Illinois; University of Alaska, Fairbanks; Whatcom County Museum, Bellingham, Washington.

Publications

On OLANNA: Articles—"Melvin Olanna," *Alaska Journal*, vol. 1, no. 4, 1971; "From Souvenirs to Contemporary Sculpture," *Alaska Fish Tales & Game Trails*, Winter 1981; "Melvin Olanna, Alaskan Artist, a Solo Exhibition Series, 1989-90," *Anchorage Museum of History and Art*, Fall 1989; "After the Art Boom, What? Alaskan and Inuit Art: a Resurgence" in *Inuit Art*, vol. 7, no. 1, 1992; "Melvin Olanna," *American Indian Art Magazine*, vol. 12, no. 1, 1995.

*   *   *

One of the best known of the Alaskan carvers, Melvin Olanna began wedding older Alaskan Eskimo sculptural design with modernist forms. Olanna was brought up in Shishmaref in a traditional Eskimo life of subsistence hunting. As a child he learned ivory carving, and later, graphic techniques, from local artists, including George Ahgupuk and Wilbur Walluk. At about age fourteen he found he could support himself by carving souvenir ivory billikens to sell to tourists, and thus began his career as a sculptor. That he and others were able to make a living from their art remained an abiding concern throughout his life.

After attending the Chemawa Indian School in Oregon, Olanna spent two years in the mid 1960s at the Institute of American Indian Arts in Santa Fe, where he studied sculpture under Alan Houser, then went on to the Native Arts Center, University of Alaska, Fairbanks, to work with Ronald Senungetuk in silversmithing. In the 1970s he established a permanent studio in Shishmaref and later a second one in Suquamish, Washington. He and his family divided their time between the two.

Olanna produced some prints and jewelry but preferred sculpture. Although he worked part of the time outside the state, his subjects always referenced Alaska, which he spoke of as "my backbone," and many were rooted in his specialized knowledge as a skilled, traditional hunter. "When I am hunting, my heart is full of joy, and I never get tired," he stated, and a sustained exploration of the form and movement of the walrus, seal and bear he had come to understand dominated his art, bonding large, sleek sculptures with much smaller work in ivory, the material of centuries of Eskimo hunter-carvers before him. Like theirs, his work translates the essential sensitivity of a hunter to the meaning of a subtle shift in an animal's profile or gesture against the flat arctic light.

The broad planes, simple surfaces, and flowing contours of Olanna's work reflect a personal, sometimes whimsical sensibility lensed through traditional Eskimo sculptural practices and also reflect his admiration for the sculpture of Henry Moore and Alan Houser. Olanna described the process through which he created his sleek, abstracted forms, as coming out of the Eskimo sense of form and approach to narrative: "The old storytellers tell you 'When you tell a story, you change it around to make it sound right.' So I do that with art, taking the idea and turning it around."

Olanna worked in wood, ivory, and whalebone, as well as bronze, especially for works to be sited outdoors. In later years alabaster and marble were his favorite materials. Upon return from a fellowship period at the American Center of the Cite International des Arts in Paris in 1985, he shipped tons of Cararra marble to his

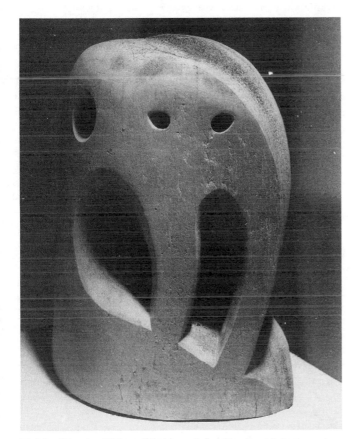

Melvin Olanna: *Walrus.* Photograph by Jim Benedetto; courtesy Anchorage Museum of History and Art.

studio at Suquamish. "Marble slows me down, allowing me to think about my next piece before I'm even finished with the one I'm working on."

Over his career, Olanna enjoyed critical acclaim, commercial success, and the respect of his fellow Native Alaskans. He was especially successful at garnering corporate and public commissions. Occasionally his work was characterised as slick and clever, but more often has been appreciated for its sedate, compact forms, serenity, graceful modulations, and visual rhythm. The later works in marble capture a cool strength and vitality. At the time of his death he had just completed several large bronze sculptures, and a series of small "studies" for others were cast in bronze posthumously.

Throughout his career Olanna was committed to encouraging younger artists and helping them find both purpose and income through carving. He was deeply aware of the problems and despair among young Alaskan Natives and the challenges they faced in balancing a subsistence lifestyle with the needs of a cash economy in communities with few jobs. For years he was active in Native Arts programs, especially the Artists in the Schools Program and Village Artists Upgrade Program, instructing design and production workshops in villages across Alaska. In the late 1980s, building on what he had learned through those experiences, he and his wife initiated a grant to fund tools, equipment, and workshop space, and established the Rural Alaska Native Arts Workshop in Shismaref. Now named the Melvin Olanna Carving Center, its program has been instrumental to a burst of innovative whalebone sculpture coming out of Shishmaref in the 1990s.

—Kate C. Duncan

OLNEY, Nathan Hale, Jr.

Tribal affiliations: Yakima; Hupa
Painter

Born: Wapato, Washington, 21 January 1936. **Education:** University of Washington; University of Wurzburg (Germany); San Francisco Art Institute. **Military Service:** 1960-62, U.S. Army, battle group artist. **Career:** Worked with Central Washington State College collecting legends of the tribes of Washington State; co-founder, Washington State Indian Arts Association; Printer and artist for the *Yakima Nation Review.* **Awards:** All-American Indian Days, Sheridan Wyoming, 1970 and 1973, first place; Heard Museum Guild Indian Fair and Market, 1971, and Scottsdale National Indian Art Exhibition, first place, 1967. **Death:** Yakima, Washington, 6 January 1980.

Individual Exhibitions

1976   *Paintings and Drawings by Nathan Olney, Jr.,* Muscum of the Plains Indian and Crafts Center, Browning, Montana

Selected Group Exhibitions

Exhibited regularly during the 1960s and 1970s at All-American Indian Days, Sheridan, Wyoming, Heard Museum Guild Fair and Market, Phoenix, Arizona; Scottsdale National Indian Art Exhibi-

tion, Arizona; Inter-Tribal Indian Ceremonies, Gallup, New Mexico; and arts and crafts fairs in Washington and Oregon.

1961   Southern Command Art Show, Schweinfurt, Germany
1964   *International Indian Art Show and Handicraft Trade Fair,* Bismark, North Dakota

Collections

Collection of Estate of Senator Robert F. Kennedy, The Smithsonian Institution, Washington, D.C.

Publications

On OLNEY: Book—*Indian Painters and White Patrons*, by J.J. Brody, Albuquerque, 1971. **Article**—"Nathan H. Olney, Jr. passes away," *Yakima Nation Review,* 15 January 1980.

*   *   *

In hatched lines and haunting images, Nathan Hale Olney, Jr., created portraits of the people and world of his Yakima ancestors. These simple sketches become textured landscapes worn with time, trial and triumph. All of Olney's pieces, from those that depict home and family life to proud warriors and hunters on horseback, carry a sense of topography and contour. The deep lines that meander across the faces of his subjects are a constant reminder of the intricate relationship between land and people.

Other pieces by Olney show movement and force from both within and around the central image. An image of a horse and rider carries a sweeping sense of tension; the horse appears to be desperately trying to stop as the elaborately dressed rider fights the reversal of momentum in vain. The layout adds to the sense of depth and texture, from which a central image of strength or power emerges. What makes the piece as a whole most interesting is the way in which Olney accentuated the commanding strength of the image by portraying it with a complex illustration style, while leaving the depiction of the surrounding environment vast and simple.

Perhaps the most unusual quality of Olney's work is his use of a fairly traditional portrait style to captured multiple images: within the expression on a human face are more complex issues surrounding his community and history. His simple sketch work also blended human figures within landscapes, uniting the spirit of an individual human being and the rich land that is so essential for physical and spiritual survival.

—Vesta Giles

OONARK, Jessie

Variant names: Taviniq; S. Toolooklook
Tribal affiliations: Inuit
Weaver and printmaker

Born: Back River area, Northwest Territories, Canada, 1906; last name also transliterated as Una, Unaaq. **Family:** Married Qabluunaq; seven of Oonark's thirteen children became artists—Janet Kigusiuq, Victoria Mamnguqsualuk, Miriam Qiyuk, Mary Yuusipik, Peggy Qabluunaq, Nancy Pukirngnak, and William Noah. **Career:** Child care; preparing skins and making the tailored fur clothing; custodial worker; artist.

Jessie Oonark. Photograph by Marion Jackson.

Awards: Elected a member of the Royal Canadian Academy of Arts, 1975; named an Officer in the Order of Canada, her country's highest civilian honor, 1984; commemorated by having the Jessie Oonark Arts and Crafts Centre in Baker Lake named in her honor. **Died:** 1985.

Individual Exhibitions

1970   *Oonark Drawings,* The Innuit Gallery of Eskimo Art, Toronto

1971   *Oonark Wallhangings,* National Arts Centre, Ottawa
1973   *Oonark Drawings,* Canadian Guild of Crafts—Quebec, Montreal
1977   *Jessie Oonark, R.C.A.: Prints and Drawings 1970 through 1976,* The Upstairs Gallery, Winnipeg, Manitoba
1984   *Jessie Oonark—A Retrospective,* Raven Gallery, Minneapolis
1986-88 *Jessie Oonark—A Retrospective,* Winnipeg Art Gallery, Manitoba (traveling)
1993   *Jessie Oonark: Selected Works from the Permanent Collection,* National Gallery of Canada, Ottawa

Selected Group Exhibitions

1960   Cape Dorset Graphics (annual collection)

1967   *Cape Dorset - A Decade of Eskimo Prints & Recent Sculpture,* National Gallery of Canada, in cooperation with the Canadian Eskimo Art Committee, Ottawa (traveling)

1970   *Oonark/Pangnark,* National Arts Centre, curated by the National Museum of Man, Ottawa (traveling)

1972   *Baker Lake Drawings,* Winnipeg Art Gallery, Manitoba (traveling)

1973   *Three Artists from Baker Lake,* Mazelow Gallery, Toronto

1975   *The Art of Eskimo Women: in Sculpture, Prints, Wallhangings,* The Arctic Circle, Los Angeles, California

1976   *The People Within - Art from Baker Lake,* Art Gallery of Ontario, Toronto (traveling)

1976-82 *Shamans and Spirits: Myths and Medical Symbolism in Eskimo Art,* Canadian Arctic Producers and the National Museum of Man, Ottawa (traveling)

1977   *Kenojuak/Oonark: Prints, Wallhangings, Sculpture,* Inukshuk Galleries, Waterloo, Ontario

1978   *Looking South,* Winnipeg Art Gallery Manitoba (traveling)
         Polar Vision: Canadian Eskimo Graphics, Jerusalem Artists' House Museum, Israel

1979-81 *Keewatin Wallhangings 1979-1981,* Canadian Arctic Producers LTd., Ottawa (traveling)

1980   *La deesse inuite de la mer/The Inuit Sea Goddess,* Musee des beaux-arts de Montreal, Quebec (traveling)

1981   *Eskimo Games: Graphics and Sculpture/Giuochi Eschimesi: grafiche e sculture,* National Gallery of Modern Art, Rome

1984   *Drawings from Baker Lake,* The Innuit Gallery of Eskimo Art, Toronto
         Die Kunst aus der Arktis, Iniut Galerie, Mannheim held at Humanities and Social Sciences Research Institute, University of Siegen at Villa Waldrich, Wiegen, Germany

1986   *The Spirit of the Land,* The Koffler Gallery, Toronto

1987   *The Matriarchs: Jessie Oonark, Helen Kalvak, Pitseolak Ashoona,* Snow Goose Associates, Seattle

1988-89 *Im Schatten der Sonne: Zeitgenossische Kunst der Indianer und Eskimos in Kanada/In the Shadow of the Sun: Contemporary Indian and Inuit Art in Canada,* Canadian Museum of Civilizaion, Ottawa (traveling)

1991   *Soujourns to Nunavut: Contemporary Inuit Art from Canada,* Bunkamura Art Gallery, Tokyo (traveling)

1992   *Each Depends on the Other,* Houston North Gallery, Lunenburg, Nova Scotia

1994   *Kunst aus der Arktis,* Volkerkundmuseum der Universitat Zurich, Switzerland

Collections

Agnes Etherington Art Centre, Queen's University, Kingston, Ontario; Amon Carter Museum of Western Art, Fort Worth, Texas; Art Gallery of Greater Victoria, Victoria, British Columbia; Art Gallery of Nova Scotia, Halifax; Art Gallery of Ontario, Toronto; Art Gallery of Windsor, Ontario; Canada Council Art Bank, Ottawa; Art Gallery of York University, Downsview, Ontario; Beaverbrook Art Gallery, Fredericton, New Brunswick; Canada Council Art Bank, Ottawa; Canadian Catholic Conference Art Collection, Ottawa; Canadian Guild of Crafts Quebec, Montreal; Canadian Museum of Civilization, Hull, Quebec; Churchill Community Centre, Churchill, Manitoba; Clifford E. Lee Collection, University of Alberta, Edmonton; Collection of His Holiness John Paul II, Vatican City, Rome; Collection of the Supreme Patriarch of All Armenia, His Holiness, Catholicos Vazken I; Dennos Museum Center, Northwestern Michigan College, Traverse City; Edmonton Art Gallery, Alberta; Glenbow Museum, Calgary, Alberta; Art Gallery of Ontario, Toronto; Eskimo Museum, Churchill, Manitoba; Glenbow Museum, Calgary, Alberta; Inuit Cultural Institute, Rankin Inlet, Northwest Territories; Macmillan-Bloedel Limited, Vancouver; McMichael Canadian Art Collection, Kleinburg, Ontario; Museum of Anthropology, University of British Columbia, Vancouver; National Gallery of Canada, Ottawa; Prince of Wales Northern Heritage Centre, Yellowknife, Northwest Territories; Sarick Collection, Art Gallery of Ontario, Toronto; University of Lethbridge Art Gallery, Lethbridge, Alberta; Winnipeg Art Gallery, Manitoba.

Publications

On OONARK: Articles—"Tattoos, Hairsticks and Ulus: The Graphic Art of Jessie Oonark," by Bernadette Driscoll, *Arts Manitoba,* vol. 3, no. 4, Fall 1984; "Jessie Oonark: Giver of Life," by Sandra Souchotte, *Up Here: Life in Canada's North,* June/July 1985; "The Power of the Pencil: Inuit Women in the Graphic Arts," by Janet Catherine Berlo, *Inuit Art Quarterly,* vol. 5, no. 1, Winter 1990.

*   *   *

One of the best known and most respected Inuit artists of her generation, Jessie Oonark has been widely acclaimed throughout North America and abroad for her appliquéd wool duffel wall hangings, her stonecut and stencil prints, and her bold drawings. There was little in her early experience, however, that would prepare Oonark for the international attention she was to receive during her lifetime.

Born near the turn of the century in the Back River area, approximately 150 miles north of Baker Lake, when the area was still extremely isolated from the outside world, Oonark grew to maturity immersed in traditional Inuit culture and had almost no contact with the world beyond her immediate camp. As a young girl, Oonark became acquainted with the traditional beliefs and stories of her elders, and she learned the essential Inuit women's skills, such as caring for children, preparing skins and making the tailored fur clothing necessary to survival on the Barren Lands. As a young woman Oonark married a strong hunter, Qabluunaq, and together they had 13 children.

Oonark's life, however, was to take a direction very different from that of her elders and from what she herself could have imagined. Widowed in her 40s when her family was still young, Oonark and her children became vulnerable and dependent upon other hunters of their camp for the meat and furs necessary for survival. Life became a difficult struggle for Oonark and her children. When she was in her early 50s, starvation and epidemic disease hit the Back River area and she and others in weakened condition were eventually air-lifted by government rescue teams to the small but growing settlement of Baker Lake. Regaining her strength, Oonark sought employment as custodial worker for the church and school in Baker Lake and involved herself in the community's new sewing project in a proud effort to provide for herself and her children.

Oonark's sewn garments of fur and of wool duffel were admired in the community. Her bold patterning and extraordinary sense of design distinguished her boots and parkas from those of others associated with the fledgling sewing project. Sensing Oonark's artistic talent, wildlife biologist Andrew MacPherson provided her with pencils and paper and encouraged her to try her hand at drawing. Some of Oonark's early drawings were sent to Cape Dorset, where three of her images were translated into prints issued in the 1960 and 1961 annual Cape Dorset print collections. Despite experimental efforts with printmaking in Baker Lake during the 1960s, it was not until 1970 that Baker Lake developed its own successful printmaking program.

Jessie Oonark became one of the influential mainstays in this program, creating hundreds of drawings to support printmaking at the new Sanavik Cooperative. More than 100 of Oonark's drawings were translated into prints in the Baker Lake print collections between 1970 and 1985, and her energy and discipline set an example for others in the community. Seven of her own children became active artists at the Baker Lake Sanavik Cooperative as did several other relatives from the Back River area. During this same period, Oonark continued to make sewn garments for her family and also produced numerous large scale wool and felt wall hangings, including major commissions for public sites in Canada.

Oonark's drawings, prints, and wallhangings are all informed by a strong sense of graphic design and are frequently organized around a figure or figures emblematic of the traditional Inuit culture. Her favored subjects include traditional women's implements (primarily the crescent-bladed knife, the "ulu"), traditional clothing styles, women's facial tattoos, shamanic themes, and isolated episodes from traditional Inuit legends. Images relating to the coming and the teachings of Christian missionaries in the Arctic and references to personal biographical experiences occasionally occur in her work as well. She typically works in large flat areas of color, and her figures are usually isolated on a contrasting ground.

Works by Jessie Oonark have been widely exhibited and are included in many important public and private collections, and she was the recipient of numerous prestigious awards during her lifetime. In 1975 Oonark was elected to the Royal Canadian Academy of Arts, and in 1984 she was named an Officer in the Order of Canada, thus receiving her country's highest civilian honor. Oonark's legacy continues in Baker Lake through her offspring who continue as active artists today and through the naming of the Jessie Oonark Arts and Crafts Centre.

—Marion E. Jackson

OQWA PI
Variant names: Abel Sanchez
Tribal affiliations: San Ildefonso Pueblo
Painter

Born: San Ildefonso Pueblo, 1 August 1899; Oqwa Pi means "Red Cloud." **Education:** Santa Fe Indian School; self-taught artist. **Career:** Painter, beginning in 1919; elected governor of San Ildefonso six times, and served in other secular and spiritual roles. **Awards:** Honors at fairs, including Inter-Tribal Indian Ceremonials and Museum of New Mexico; recognition of accomplishments by All Indian Pueblo Council, signed by the 19 governors, 1971. **Died:** 21 March 1971.

Selected Group Exhibitions

1931-33 *Exposition of Indian Tribal Arts*, sponsored by the College Art Association (traveling)
1937   *American Indian Exposition and Congress*, Tulsa, Oklahoma
1959-60 *Contemporary American Indian Paintings*, New Jersey State Museum, Trenton
1979-80 *Native American Paintings*, Mid-American Arts Alliance Project, organized by the Joslyn Museum, Omaha, Nebraska (traveling)
1982   Museum of the American Indian, New York (traveling)
1985   *The Hunt and the Harvest: Paintings from the Museum of the American Indian*, organized by the Gallery Association of New York State (traveling)
1987   *Contemporary Pueblo Indian Art*, Philadelphia Art Alliance, Pennsylvania
1988   *When the Rainbow Touches Down*, Heard Museum, Phoenix, Arizona
1990   *American Indian Artists in the Avery Collection and the McNay Permanent Collection*, Koogler McNay Art Museum, San Antonio, Texas
1992   *A Bridge Across Cultures: Pueblo Painters in Santa Fe, 1910-1932*, Wheelwright Museum of the American Indian, Santa Fe, New Mexico
1993-94 *Contemporary Native American Works*, Montclair Art Museum, Montclair, New Jersey

Collections

American Museum of Natural History, New York; Amerind Foundation, Dragoon, Arizona; Brooklyn Museum of Art, New York; Columbus Gallery of Fine Arts, Columbus, Ohio; Cranbrook Institute of Science, Bloomfield Hills, Michigan; Cleveland Museum of Art, Ohio; Denver Art Museum, Denver, Colorado; Joslyn Museum, Omaha, Nebraska; Marion Koogler McNay Art Museum, San Antonio, Texas; Museum of the American Indian, Washington, D.C.; Museum of New Mexico, Santa Fe; Museum of Northern Arizona, Flagstaff, Arizona; Philbrook Museum of Art, Tulsa, Oklahoma; Millicent Rogers Foundation Museum, Taos, New Mexico; School of American Research, Santa Fe, New Mexico; Southwest Museum, Los Angeles, California; Wheelwright Museum of the American Indian, Santa Fe, New Mexico; Wilmington Society of Fine Arts, Delaware Art Center, Wilmington, Delaware.

Publications

On OQWA PI: Books—*Introduction to American Indian Art*, by John Sloan and Oliver La Farge, Exposition of Indian Tribal Arts, New York, Inc., 1931; *Pueblo Indian Painting*, by Harley Burr Alexander, Nice, France, 1932; *American Indian Painters*, by Oscar B. Jacobson and Jeanne D'Ucel, Nice, France, 1950; *American Indian Painting of the Southwest and Plains Areas*, by Dorothy Dunn, University of New Mexico, Albuquerque, 1968; *Indian Painters and White Patrons*, by J.J. Brody, University of New Mexico Press, Albuquerque, 1971; *Southwest Indian Painting: A Changing Art*, by Clara Lee Tanner, Tucson, 1973; *The Life and Art of the North American Indian*, by John Anson Warner, New York, 1975; *Native American Painting*, by Frederick Schmid and Patrick Houlihan, Kansas City, 1980; *American Indian Painting and Sculpture*, by Patricia Broder, New York, 1981; *Native American Paint-*

Oqwa Pi: *Buffalo,* c. 1930. Courtesy Museum of Indian Arts and Culture, Santa Fe, Dorothy Dunn Kramer Collection.

ing: Selections from the Museum of the American Indian, New York, 1982; *When the Rainbow Touches Down,* exhibition catalog by Tryntje Van Ness Seymour, Heard Museum, University of Washington Press, 1988; *American Indian Artists in the Avery Collection and the McNay Permanent Collection,* edited by Jean Sherrod Williams, San Antonio, 1990.

*   *   *

During the first two decades of the twentieth century, modern Indian painting came alive in the Santa Fe area among artists usually referred to as part of the "San Ildefonso school." Like the first important San Ildefonso painter, Crescencio Martinez, most started as pottery decorators and simply translated their designs into another medium, while others depicted ceremonial dances and scenes of everyday life. Thus, two distinct styles evolved, one decorative and abstract, the other realistic and descriptive. Both styles merged in the work of Romando Vigil and Oqwa Pi.

Crescencio Martinez died suddenly in 1918, but his work, the paintings by Julian Martinez, and the pottery of Maria Martinez, drew great attention outside of San Ildefonso and further encouraged arts and crafts within the Pueblo. Oqwa Pi was raised in a

traditional lifestyle and actively participated in ceremonial and secular activities. He attended the Santa Fe Indian School, but only started painting late in his teens, probably having been inspired by the bustling artistic activity in the Pueblo, for in addition to more traditional Native art forms, such as pottery, painting with watercolors had become a popular activity. And just as Oqwa Pi was influenced by this flowering of modern painting, he played a major role in the formative years of water color painting in the Southwest, by quickly developing a distinctive style that captured communal activities and sights and expressed a personal vision that featured bright colors and strong, harmonious decorative elements.

Oqwa Pi was somewhat of an overnight sensation. He started painting around 1919 to 1921 and immediately attracted patrons. He was fond of noting that painting brought in good income that helped him raise a large family. He coupled this personal success with deep involvement in secular and spiritual matters of San Ildefonso, being elected governor of the pueblo on six occasions and regularly participating in ceremonies. This example of commitment to personal vision and community activism no doubt helped feed the continued excellence of twentieth-century arts in San Ildefonso; from the Martinez's, through the generation that included Oqwa Pi, Romando Vigil, Rose Gonzales, and Encarnacion Pena, through mid-century artists like Gilbert Atencio, Popovi Da, and Jose D. Roybal, and on to flourishing artists of the final quarter of the century, including Tony Da and Jody Folwell. Twentieth-century artists of San Ildefonso have made great and lasting cultural contributions.

Oqwa Pi's untrained hand and bright palette combined for a kind of art that can be compared with Cubism and Fauvism. Oqwa Pi painted in a flat style with little concern for spatial depth. His style remained consistent and personal: realistic, descriptive, and flat, decorative through solid color blocks, and bordering on the abstract, which was likely due to the fact that he remained free to pursue his original manner without being unduly influenced by training or styles. The combination of realism and abstractness, then, is a source of vitality in his work. Figures and objects are simply rendered, and vast, outlined blocks of color lend the paintings a great sense of decorativeness, but since the colors are not overtly stylized they impress with their bold simplicity. *Koshares*, from the collection at the Museum of New Mexico, has four dancing Koshares spaced in a diamond configuration on the canvas, each engaged in a particular part of a ceremony—one clowning, one dancing, one bent to a knee, one poised with a rattle—in a solid block of color as a captured, impressionistic moment. Important details in dress, ceremonial objects, and ritual are present within a colorful, individualized expression, a work that can be admired for telling detail and as an imaginative flourish. Similarly, the early *Chorus—Corn Dance* (c. 1925) has a stiff group of chanters and a standard bearer, with one dancer contrasting the rigidness of the other figures. The dress of the chorus members, all of whom have their backs to the viewer, are rendered as variously colorful blocks; the half-raised standard sweeps across diagonally over the center of the painting, with subtle details of feathers on the standard; set against a solid background, the images are stark in essence, with splashes of color providing dramatic and pleasing impact—a recognizable communal activity represented as colored geometric shapes, balanced as a whole with telling details.

—Perry Bear

OSBURN-BIGFEATHER, Joanna

Tribal affiliations: Cherokee
Mixed media artist, ceramist, and sculptor

Born: Felixstone, England, 1952. **Education:** Institute of American Indian Art, A.A., 1987; University of California, Santa Cruz, B.A., 1990; State University of New York, Albany, M.F.A., 1993. **Career:** Marketing Director, Austin-Hansen Architects, 1978-81; curator, American Indian Community House Gallery/Museum, 1993-present; teacher, Diversity Committee, University of California, Santa Cruz, 1989; Diversity Committee, Arts and Humanities College, State University of New York, Albany, 1990-92; Artist Board of Advisors, New York Foundation for the Arts, 1995-present; Advisor at Large, Rice University Art Gallery, 1995-present; juror, College Art Association Fellowships Program, 1994, Hillwood Art Museum, Project Residencies in Painting, 1993, HarperCollins Publishing, Center for Multicultural Children's Literature, poster selection, National Literacy Campaign, 1995; speaker and panelist at various conferences, lecture series, and seminars, 1993-present. **Awards:** First prize monoprint and ceramic sculp-

ture, Native American Art Exhibition, Heard Museum, Phoenix, Arizona, 1987; nine awards, Santa Fe Indian Market, 1988-92; Merit Award, University of Kansas and Haskell Junior College, 1993. **Address:** c/o American Indian Community House Gallery/ Museum, New York City, New York.

Individual Exhibitions

1995 *One Woman Exhibition,* University of Massachusetts, Augusta Savage Gallery, Amherst, Massachusetts

Selected Group Exhibitions

1990 *Bronze from UCSC Foundry,* Dancing Man Gallery, Santa Cruz, California
   Six Directions, American Indian Contemporary Arts, San Francisco
1992 *Portfolio III Show,* American Indian Contemporary Arts, San Francisco
   We're Still Here, American Indian Community House Gallery/Museum, New York
   Women's Sculpture Group Show, Kingsboro Community College Art Gallery, New York
   Native America: Reflecting Contemporary Realities, American Indian Contemporary Arts
   Rediscoveries: The Myth Makers, Jamaica Arts Center, Jamaica, New York
   From the Earth VIII, American Indian Contemporary Arts, San Francisco, California
   Bridging Two Worlds, Pelham Art Center, Pelham, New York
   For the Seventh Generation: Native American Arts Counter the Quincentenary, New York
1992-96 *Expanded Visions: Contemporary American Crafts,* California Crafts Museum, San Francisco, national traveling exhibition
1993 *Artists of the Mohawk-Hudson Regional,* juried, Albany Institute of History and Art, Albany, New York
   The Atmosphere: Art, Native Wiscom and Science, University at Albany, State University of New York, Albany, New York
   Indian Arts Exhibition, Haskell Junior College and University of Kansas Museum of Anthroplogy, Lawrence Kansas
1993-94 *Artist As Native: Reinventing Regionalism,* (traveling)
1994 *The Long and the Short of It,* Smithtown Township Arts Council, St. James, New York
   From Mother Earth, Works in Clay, American Indian Community House Gallery/Museum, New York
   Contemporary Native American Artists, Reflections on Their Past, Susquehanna Art Museum, Harrisburg, Pennsylvania
   Cultural Signs in Contemporary Native American Art, Cornell University, Herbert F. Johnson Museum of Art, Ithaca, New York
1994-96 *Indian Humor,* American Indian Contemporary Art, San Francisco, California (traveling)
1995 *Volume I: Book Arts by Native American Artists,* American Indian Community House Gallery/Museum, New York, New York (traveling)

Legacies: Contemporary Art by Native American Women, College of New Rochelle, Castle Gallery, New Rochelle, New York

From the Earth XI, American Indian Contemporary Art, San Francisco, California

Collections

Brooklyn Museum, Brooklyn, New York; A.P. Fenderson, Modesto, California; Haskell, Jr. College, Lawrence, Kansas; Heard Museum, Phoenix, Arizona; Institute of American Indian Arts, Santa Fe, New Mexico; Smithsonian Institute, Washington, D.C.

Publications

On OSBURN-BIGFEATHER: Catalogs—*Portfolio III Show,* American Indian Contemporary Arts, San Francisco, 1991; *For the Seventh Generation: Native American Arts Counter the Quincentenary,* New York, 1992; *Bridging Two Worlds,* Pelham Art Center, New York, 1993; *Contemporary Native American Artists, Reflections on Their Past,* Susquehanna Art Museum, Harrisburg, Pennsylvania, 1994; *Cultural Signs in Contemporary Native American Art,* Cornell University, Ithaca, New York, 1994; *Indian Humor,* American Indian Contemporary Art, San Francisco, California, 1995; *Legacies: Contemporary Art by Native American Women,* College of New Rochelle, New Rochelle, New York, 1995. **Articles**—"Brave Hearted Native American Women Artists," by Charleen Touchett, *Signals,* Santa Fe, July 1993; "Light and Heat From American Indian Women," by William Zimmermer, *The New York Times,* 24 September 1995; "AIDS: The Latest Epidemic Native Art Explores Denial Fear," by Carol Kalafatic, *The Circle,* Minneapolis, November 1995; "AIDS/HIV Focus of Art Exhibition," by Mark Fogarty, *Indian Country Today,* Rapid City, South Dakota, 2 November 1995; "Osburn-Bigfeather: Challenging Perception with Art," by Margaret Dubin, *Indian Country Today,* Rapid City, South Dakota, 5 October 1995.

* * *

Ideas supersede images in Joanna Osburn-Bigfeather's multimedia ceramic sculptures, and as her ideas have grown increasingly political over the years, this thoughtful artist has found herself on the front line of contemporary American Indian political art. One of the few women in this artistic subgenre, Osburn-Bigfeather tempers confrontational statements with bouts of playfulness, humor and nostalgia.

Osburn-Bigfeather's busy schedule as curator, teacher and artist requires her to take advantage of weekends and holidays to use her studio. She always works in series, each year producing a new body of work that addresses a particular theme. Over the years, as her themes have grown more complex and more political, her clay has acquired new textures from the incorporation of found materials, such as chicken wire, X-rays, and nails. Her work has also expanded physically into large-scale installations, such as *The White Man's Boarding School* (1993). The clay, however, remains central, an homage to her Cherokee ancestors who created functional pottery.

Osburn-Bigfeather was born in 1952 and raised primarily in New Mexico. Her career began at the Institute of American Indian Arts in Santa Fe, New Mexico, where she studied printmaking and ceramic sculpture. After graduating with the highest academic and artistic honors, Osburn-Bigfeather continued her education at the University of California-Santa Cruz. It was here that she encountered radical political ideologies for the first time in her life. Taking courses in the American Studies department, particularly with the prolific American Indian author, Gerald Vizenor, provided new, critical ways of looking at American Indian history and current events. As she later recalled, "those courses helped frame my thinking."

New thoughts fomented a new kind of art. While a graduate student at the State University of New York-Albany, where she earned her M.F.A. in 1993, Osburn-Bigfeather started exhibiting sculptural ceramic works that spoke about her identity as a modern native woman, and about the political and social positions of native people in the United States. In *Portfolio III* (1991), a group show curated by American Indian Contemporary Arts in San Francisco, Osburn-Bigfeather's drawings, monoprints and clay sculptures constituted what she called a "visual rewriting of our [tribal] history." Two series were represented in this exhibit: her *Turtle Series,* in which turtle bodies serve as metaphors for the cultures and belief systems of indigenous America, and her *Collectors Series,* in which historic art forms, such as ledger books and parfleche bags, are recreated in clay then ossified in the firing process to simulate the spiritually-gutted possessions of non-Indian collectors of Native American artifacts.

In 1992 Osburn-Bigfeather participated in several group exhibits that confronted the legacy of Christopher Columbus' "discovery" of America. In *For the Seventh Generation: Native American Artists Counter the Quincentenary,* she contributed a piece about the impact of western expansion on her native Cherokee people. The rectangular slab of clay in *I am Cherokee: Do You Know Who You Are?* serves as a canvas to portray travelers on the newly completed railroad. Incised around this scene, in the form of a frame, are characters from the Cherokee syllabary.

Mass media images frequently garnish Osburn-Bigfeather's work, adding an element of humor while simultaneously providing a familiar visual reference. Unabashedly fond of the icons of popular culture, the artist incorporated plastic toys and miniature slip-cast ceramic busts of Indian chiefs in *May I Serve You?—Cultural Artifacts,* exhibited in the group show, *Indian Humor* (1994). The headdress of the Statue of Liberty (e.g. *Liberty Series: Just Another Headdress,* 1992) is another favorite icon, used not as a symbol of freedom, but as a reminder of colonization.

Since 1993, Osburn-Bigfeather has been director and curator of the American Indian Community House Gallery/Museum in New York City, a position she has used effectively to gain wider exposure for the great variety of art, especially conceptual and political art, being created by native people.

—Margaret Dubin

OSUITOK Ipeelee

Tribal affiliations: Inuit
Sculptor, printmaker, and carver

Born: Cape Dorset, Northwest Territories, 23 October 1923; native name also transliterated as Oshoweetook, Oshaweetuk, Osoetuk, and Oshewetok. **Career:** Traditional nomadic Inuk lifestyle; learned to carve by watching his father. **Awards:** Elected a member of the Royal Canadian Academy of Arts, 1978.

Individual Exhibitions

1973   *Sculptures by Oshoweetook "B" of Cape Dorset,* Canadian Guild of Crafts Quebec, Montreal, Quebec
1978   *Exhibition of Eskimo Carvings by Cape Dorset Artist, Oshewetok,* Waddington Galleries, Toronto, Ontario
        Oshoweetok, Pucker/Safrai Gallery, Boston, Massachusetts
1979   *Oshewetok,* Waddington Galleries, Montreal, Quebec
1980   *Osuitok Aipellie, Cape Dorset,* Theo Waddington & Company, New York, New York
1983   *Ipillie Oshoweetok,* Inuit Galerie, Mannheim, Germany
1987   *Osuitok Ipeelee: One Man's Sculpture,* Feheley Fine Arts, Toronto, Ontario
        Oshaweetok Ipeelee, Eskimo Art Gallery, Toronto, Ontario
1993   *Osuitok Ipeelee R.C.A.,* Inuit Gallery of Vancouver, Vancouver, British Columbia

Selected Group Exhibitions

1951   *Eskimo Art,* National Gallery of Canada, Ottawa, Ontario
1953   *Eskimo Carvings: Coronation Exhibition,* Gimpel Fils, London, England
1967   *Cape Dorset - A Decade of Eskimo Prints & Recent Sculpture,* National Gallery of Canada, in cooperation with the Canadian Eskimo Art Committee, Ottawa, Ontario (traveling)
1969   *The Eskimo,* Museum of Fine Arts, Houston, Texas
1970   *Graphic Art by Eskimos of Canada: First Collection,* Cultural Affairs Division, Department of External Affairs, Canada, Ottawa, Ontario (traveling)
1972   *Eskimo Fantastic Art,* University of Manitoba, Winnipeg, Manitoba (traveling)
1973   *Inuit Art Exhibition,* Canadian Trade Centre, Sydney, Australia (traveling)
1974   *Ten Masterworks Exhibition Artists,* Gallery of the Arctic, Victoria, British Columbia
1975-79 *We Lived by Animals/Nous Vivions des Animaux,* Department of Indian Affairs and Northern Development in cooperation with the Department of External Affairs, Ottawa, Ontario (traveling)
1981-83 *The Murray and Marguerite Vaughan Inuit Print Collection,* Beaverbrook Art Gallery, Fredericton, New Brunswick (traveling)
1986   *Contemporary Inuit Art,* National Gallery of Canada, Ottawa, Ontario
1989   *Spoken in Stone: an exhibition of Inuit Art,* Whyte Museum of the Canadian Rockies, Banff, Alberta (traveling)
1995   *Immaginario Inuit, Arte e cultura degli esquimesi canadesi,* Galleria d'Arte Moderna e Contemporanea, Verona, Italy

Collections

Art Gallery of Greater Victoria, Victoria, British Columbia; Art Gallery of Nova Scotia, Halifax, Nova Scotia; Art Gallery of Ontario, Toronto, Ontario; Canada Council Art Bank, Ottawa, Ontario; Canadian Guild of Crafts Quebec, Montreal, Quebec; Canadian Museum of Civilization, Hull, Quebec; Amon Carter Museum of Western Art, Fort Worth, Texas; Dennos Museum Center, Northwestern Michigan College, Traverse City, Michigan; Department of External Affairs, Ottawa, Ontario; GE Canada Inuit Art Collection, Mississauga, Ontario; Glenbow Museum, Calgary, Alberta; Inuit Cultural Institute, Rankin Inlet, Northwest Territories; Macdonald Stewart Art Centre, Guelph, Ontario; Macmillan-Bloedel Limited, Vancouver, British Columbia; McMaster University Art Gallery, Hamilton, Ontario; McMichael Canadian Art Collection, Kleinburg, Ontario; Museum of Fine Arts, Houston, Texas; National Gallery of Canada, Ottawa, Ontario; Nunatta Sunaqutangit Museum, Iqaluit, Northwest Territories; Rothmans Permanent Collection of Eskimo Sculpture, Toronto, Ontario; Sarick Collection, Art Gallery of Ontario, Toronto, Ontario; Tom Thomson Memorial Gallery and Museum of Fine Art, Owen Sound, Ontario; University of Alberta, Edmonton, Alberta; University of Lethbridge Art Gallery, Lethbridge, Alberta; University of Michigan Museum of Art, Ann Arbor, Michigan; Whyte Museum of the Canadian Rockies, Banff, Alberta; Winnipeg Art Gallery, Winnipeg, Manitoba.

Publications

By OSUITOK: Books—*Oshoweetok,* Pucker/Safrai Gallery, Boston, 1978.

Osuitok Ipeelee: *The Young Drum Dancer.* **Courtesy Inuit Gallery of Vancouver.**

On OSUITOK: Books—"Osuitok Ipeelee," *Inuit Art: An Anthology,* by Jean Blodgett, Watson and Dyer, Winnipeg, 1988; *The Inuit Imagination: Arctic Myth and Sculpture,* by Harold Seidelman and James Turner, Douglas & McIntyre, Vancouver/Toronto, 1993. **Articles**—"The Creation of Anoutoaloak," by James A. Houston, *The Beaver,* Winter 1955; "Anoutoaloak: The Mace of the Northwest Territories," by Irene Baird, *Canadian Geographical Journal,* vol. 55, no. 3, September 1957; "Janus in Baffinland," by John Noel Chandler, *artscanada,* vol. 27, no. 6, December/January 1972.

                    *   *   *

Osuitok Ipeelee was born into a traditional Inuk lifestyle where survival was harsh and the line between the physical and the spirit world was faint. He learned to carve by watching his father and has continued ever since. Strength, pride and confidence are the hallmarks of his style, as is a resistance to producing pieces that are overly dramatic or exaggerated.

Although he worked on prints early in his career, sculpture has been the primary focus for Ipeelee. He most frequently uses the animals and legends of the north for the subjects of his carvings: caribou, musk-oxen, and birds that grace the arctic landscape are represented in the majority of his pieces, while others feature characters from arctic myth, or strong and beautiful Inuit women.

Osuitok is inspired by Inuit transformation myths and shamans, who can be seen as both animal and human at the same time. The concept of transformation appears in several of his pieces. He also experiments occasionally with non-representative forms and shapes, producing sculptures that carry a powerful appearance of energy rather than exact likeness. In more recent years, Osuitok has ventured into representing more complex and interactive scenes in his sculptures over singular isolated figures.

His exploration of arctic myth appears many times in his pieces, including *Sea Goddess, Taleelayo* (1983), which is carved from green stone and offers examples of many of Osuitok's thematic and structural considerations. This elegant green creature, half woman, half sea creature, is delicate and quiet in mood, which nearly belies her physical strength. She is swimming, her body diving at an easy angle further down into the water, and her arms are long, thin, and graceful with fins for hands that she has positioned behind her in a manner of one who is moving quickly and efficiently. Her head is thrust forward and flowing behind are two long and delicate braids. The figure is balanced on her breasts at an angle that seems to defy gravity, yet the weight throughout the entire piece is carefully distributed to give her an illusion of movement—an excellent accomplishment of a piece of stone lying on a flat surface.

As with many of his other pieces, *Sea Goddess* consists of a strong sense of volume, incorporating thoughtful use of negative and positive space. The braids, flowing behind the woman's head, meet up with her elbows in only one place, resting on the air below and creating the effect of a smooth, flowing current. Likewise, there is negative space pushing around her arms, back and fins, as if she needs to use her considerable physical strength to keep them in their streamlined position.

This ability to ingeniously balance the weight of his figures on fine, delicate points is almost unique to Ipeelee. He must carefully consider the weight of a piece, the centre of gravity, and the visual effect the balance will produce. Through all these considerations, the movement and goals of the central figure remain the highest priority. Overall, this creates an effect similar to a gesture drawing, with a dynamic sense of tension, as a subject is captured in the process of moving.

Working primarily in soapstone and occasional with ivory, Osuitok also experiments with other materials, like tusk, antler, and copper, but prefers to work in stone. In these stone sculptures, the artist's interest in fine details within the finished work is apparent. The smallest elements in his pieces, like the scales of a tiny fish or hatched markings on the face of a shaman, make the figures within the sculptures look more real and alive.

Osuitok Ipeelee is one of the original artists to bring high quality, originality, and thought provoking Inuit art to the southern world. He has inspired generations of carvers with his high standards and his interest in the art world as a business. Artistically, his pieces are of priceless value to all nations while at the same time, they are essential historical and cultural documentaries of the world in which Osuitok Ipeelee has spent his life.

—Vesta Giles

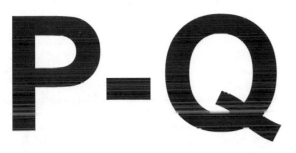

P-Q

PALADIN, David Chethlahe
Variant names: Chethlahe
Tribal affiliations: Navajo
Painter and jewelry designer

Born: Canyon de Chelly, Arizona, 1926; Chethlahe means "Little Turtle Who Cries in the Night." **Education:** Santa Fe Indian School; City College, San Mateo, California; California School of Fine Arts, Oakland; Art Institute of Chicago, Illinois. **Military Service:** U.S. Army, World War II; prisoner of war for 2 ½ years. **Career:** Variety of odd jobs, including sailor, window designer, broadcaster, teacher, and writer; Unitarian minister, volunteer chaplain, Albuquerque Police Department; sculptor, jeweler, and painter; lecturer; guest professor, Iliff School of Theology, University of Denver, Colorado; commissioned for numerous commercial murals, posters, including the Scottsdale National Indian Arts Exhibition, 1975, Christmas card designs, including UNICEF, 1970, Foundation for Blind Children, 1975, and New Mexico Easter Seals, 1978, fabric designs for City of Phoenix, Arizona, four tapestries, 1972, and Cannon River Mills, 1977. **Awards:** Carnegie Medal for Achievement in the Arts, 1968; Distinguished Service to the Arts and Education Commendation, Cambridge University, 1970; Italian Academy of Art, Gold Medal, 1981; *Santa Fean* magazine, Artist of the Year, 1981; several at fairs and juried competitions, including Scottsdale National Indian Art Exhibition, Arizona, 1967-68, 1970-71, and American Indian and Cowboy Artists National Western Art Exposition, San Dimas, California, 1978. **Died:** 19 December 1984.

Individual Exhibitions

1967	Heard Museum, Phoenix, Arizona
1968	Pittsburgh Educational Institute, Pittsburgh
	Vagabond House, Sedona, Arizona
1969	William Penn Memorial Museum, Harrisburg, Pennsylvania
	Austin Gallery, Santa Barbara, California
1970	Vagabond House, Sedona, Arizona
1971	Turquoise Kiva, Cave Creek, Arizona
1971-74	Martin Gallery, Scottsdale, Arizona
1973	Cassidy Gallery, Albuquerque, New Mexico
1974	Squash Blossom Gallery, Cincinnati, Ohio
	Plymouth House Gallery, Plymouth, Michigan
1975	Museum of Texas Technological University, Lubbock, Texas
	Museum of American Indian Arts, New York
	Heard Museum, Phoenix, Arizona
1975-76	Hayloft Gallery, Sedona, Arizona
1976	Thomson Gallery, Phoenix, Arizona

1977-82	Martin Gallery, Scottsdale, Arizona
1978	Los Llanos Gallery, Santa Fe, New Mexico
	Turtle Mountain Gallery, Pittsburgh, Pennsylvania
1980	Eastern New Mexico University, Portales, New Mexico
	Iowa State University, Ames, Iowa
1981-83	Christof's, Santa Fe, New Mexico
1985	Illuminarium Gallery, Larkspur, California

Selected Group Exhibitions

1966	Amon Carter Museum, Fort Worth, Texas
1967	*Washington Biennial Exhibition Of American Indian Arts and Crafts*, Washington, D. C.
1968	Northern Arizona University, Flagstaff
1972	Charles Bowers memorial Museum, Santa Ana, California
	Yevapi College, Prescott, Arizona
1973	Mathes Cultural Center Gallery, San Francisco, California
1973-74	Mary Livingstone's Gallery 2, Santa Ana, California
1975	*Contemporary Indian Prints,* Museum of Albuquerque, New Mexico
1976	Pueblo Indian Cultural Center, Albuquerque, New Mexico
1979-80	*Native American Paintings*, organized by the Joslyn Art Museum, Omaha, Nebraska (traveling)
1980	*Native American Art at the Philbrook*, Philbrook Museum of Art, Tulsa, Oklahoma
1983	Museum of Northern Arizona, Flagstaff
1985	Albuquerque Museum, Albuquerque, New Mexico
	Museum of Man, San Diego, California
1986	Wheelwright Museum of the American Indian, Santa Fe, New Mexico
1996	*Drawn from Memory: James T. Bialac Collection of Native American Art,* Heard Museum, Phoenix, Arizona

Collections

Albuquerque Museum, Albuquerque, New Mexico; Boston Museum of Fine Art, Boston, Massachusetts; Bowers Museum of Cultural Art, Santa Ana, California; Carnegie Museum of Art, Pittsburgh, Pennsylvania; Detroit Institute of Arts, Michigan; Heritage Center Inc. Collection, Pine Ridge, South Dakota; Heard Museum, Phoenix, Arizona; Institute of American Indian Arts, Santa Fe, New Mexico; Minnesota Museum of Art, Minneapolis, Minnesota; Museum of Fine Arts, Boston, Massachusetts; Museum of New Mexico, Santa Fe; Navajo Tribal Museum, Window Rock, Arizona; William Penn Memorial Museum, Harrisburg, Pennsylvania; Phoenix Civic Center Concert Hall, Arizona; Portland Art Museum, Portland, Oregon; Millicent Rogers Foundation Museum, Taos, New Mexico; San Francisco Palace of the Legion of Honor, San Francisco, California; Stanford University, Palo Alto, California; United Nations Building, New York; West Texas Museum, Lubbock, TX; Wheelright Museum of the American Indian, Santa Fe, New Mexico; The White House, Washington, D. C.

Publications

On PALADIN: Books—*Indian Painters and White Patrons*, by J.J. Brody, Albuquerque, 1971; *One With the Earth,* by Lloyd Kiva New and David C. Young, Santa Fe, 1976; *Native American Painting*, by Patrick Houlihan and Fredrick Schmid, Kansas City, 1979; *Painting the Dream: The Visionary Art of Navajo Painter David Chethlahe Paladin,* by Lynda Paladin, Rochester, Vermont, 1992. **Articles**—"Grains of Sand," *Newsweek,* 14 April 1975; "Paladin's Modern Vision," by Alan Weisman, *American Indian Art,* Spring 1977; "Contemporary Navajo Artists," by John Anson Warner, *Southwest Art,* April 1977; "David Chethlahe Paladin," by Mary Carroll Nelson, *Art Voices/South,* September/October 1980; "David Chethlahe Paladin, Artist," by Don Jones, *The Santa Fean,* July 1981; "Navajo Painting," by Katherin Chase, *Plateau,* vol. 54, no. 1, 1982; "David Chethlahe Paladin: Shaman with a Palette and a Pulpit," by Kathryn Gabriel, *Albuquerque Journal,* 18 October 1983. **Films**—*Discover '70,* UNICEF and ABC TV, 1970; *American Indian Arts,* KAET-TV, Public Broadcasting System, Tempe, Arizona, 1971; *Three Indian Artists,* KAET-TV, Public Broadcasting System, Tempe, Arizona, 1972.

*

David Chethlahe Paladin comments:

Indian artists are contemporaries of their time. In the truest sense, there isn't a traditional Navajo ... So many variables enter in and influence the individual—including, his relation with the tribe, his interactions with others, and the individual's overview of his culture

... Art is individual and must be freed from limited boundaries.

*   *   *

The lively, abstract works of David Chethlahe Paladin reflect a variety of influences and his own sense of independence and daring. In addition to drawing on his Navajo heritage and experiences in the wide open spaces of northern Arizona—where the natural rock formations and colors as well as designs in sandpainting and wall drawings are recreated in his work—Paladin derived symbols from diverse cultures in a free form manner where images may or may not be related, and swirls and rounded shapes flow amid solid blocks of color. *Phantasies*, one of a series of exhibitions of his work held in Santa Fe in the early 1980s, aptly describes his canvasses. Moving between sandpainting, acrylics, oils, and watercolors and frequently mixing media, Paladin's work became an increasingly playful blend of overlapping colors, images, symbols, and shapes, vivid and yet mystical as reveries.

Whether painting subjects like Southwestern landscapes, mythological themes, animals or more non-representational images, Paladin brought the same boldness to painting with which he approached life—from living out on the land as a youngster, to stowing away on ship while in his teens, to working with a special unit behind enemy lines in World War II, to restlessly seeking new forms of creative expression. He created a body of work that was at times fiercely unconstrained, at other times played for humor, and at other times instructional, reflecting his interest in education.

Just as Paladin drifted among styles, his life was not particularly rooted in traditions. His father was Anglo—once a Roman Catholic priest, and his mother was Navajo. During his childhood, Paladin often moved physically between these two worlds, the Arizona homeland of his mother and the California towns where his father's relatives resided. On Navajo lands he herded sheep, and his nomadic experiences, where he discovered petroglyphs, cave paintings, and shrines as well as learning the stories and worldview of his uncle, a medicine man, inform his work. During trips to California and in his classes at the Santa Fe Indian School, however, Paladin's life was much less free: he resisted his relatives' attempts to Christianize him (but would later become a Unitarian minister and theologian of his own volition) and found painting classes at the famed Studio too restrictive. "I was told I should paint Indian when I was at the Indian school," he told Don Jones of the *Santa Fean*, "and at that time in my life there was only one thing that existed on this earth that was beautiful and that was wildflowers. I was damned if I was going to sit and paint blue horses. It may have been someone's idea of what Indian's should paint, but it sure wasn't my idea of what I felt or what I was experiencing."

When he was fourteen, Paladin stowed away with a cousin on a ship that embarked from San Francisco and the two spent two years traveling the Pacific. Soon after his return he enlisted in the U.S. Army in 1941, and eventually landed assignments as a cartographer working behind enemy lines. He was captured by Nazis during a clandestine mission in which he wore a German uniform. Paladin spent two and a half years in a prisoner of war camp. Upon his release, Paladin drifted in the United States until meeting a Navajo medicine man who helped him reclaim and appreciate part of his heritage. He attended classes at the Chicago Art Institute, where he met famed artist Marc Chagall, whose surrealistic paintings employed deep symbolism and probed the unconscious. When Paladin returned to Santa Fe and later moved to Sedona in the late 1950s, he worked a series of odd jobs while painting and making jewelry. His early work was highly stylized, much like that associated with The Studio and recalled traditional Indian painting. Gradually, however, Paladin became more experimental and abstract, infusing his paintings with dreamlike images, with symbols and references to his Navajo heritage and his memories of life on the land. A study of traditional Navajo sand painting techniques found their way onto his canvasses. From the mid-1960s through his death in 1984, Paladin painted prolifically, using symbols and unconscious designs and patterns to form lively works that were regularly exhibited in the Southwest. He also pursued his interests in education, metaphysics, and spirituality He was involved with UNICEF, for example, and with a think-tank—the Meninger Clinic's Counsel Growth Conferences, and served as a Unitarian minister.

Paladin's most noted work is generally of two kinds—free form mixtures of symbols, images, and flowing lines amid color blocks, and paintings that have a clear setting and subject. The former is reflected in works like *Wind Spirits Altar,* a sandpainting with a square-within-a-square composition and dual circular images which rest among swirling lines of color, with Navajo symbols for mountains and suggestions of a mesa and pueblo. The latter style can be seen in *Acoma Shrine* (1981), which shows his great talent for textures. The painting depicts huge boulders with rock art paintings of horned deities; spiritual symbols of spiral migration and the Zia sun blend with images of tadpole and big horn sheep. An individual hand print rests on the edge of a stone, a gesture, perhaps, of his expression for personal freedom.

—Perry Bear

PANGNARK, John

Tribal affiliations: Inuit
Sculptor

Born: Windy Lake, Northwest Territories (Keewatin region, just north of the Manitoba border), 1920. **Career:** Traditional semi-nomadic existence, trapper and hunter, professional carver, artist-in-residence at Expo '70 in Osaka, Japan. **Died:** 1980.

Individual Exhibitions

1972   *Pangnark,* The Arctic Circle, Los Angeles

Selected Group Exhibitions

1970   *Oonark/Pangnark,* National Arts Centre, curated by the National Museum of Man, Ottawa (traveling)
1971-73 *Sculpture/Inuit: Masterworks of the Canadian Arctic,* Canadian Eskimo Arts Council, Ottawa (traveling)
1978   *The Coming and Going of the Shaman: Eskimo Shamanism and Art,* Winnipeg Art Gallery, Winnipeg, Manitoba
1979   *Sculpture of the Inuit: Lorne Balshine Collection/Lou Osipov Collection/Dr. Harry Winrob Collection,* Surrey Art Gallery, Surrey, British Columbia
1981-82 *Inuit Art: A Selection of Inuit Art from the Collection of the National Museum of Man, Ottawa, and the Rothmans Permanent Collection of Inuit Sculpture,* Canada National Museum of Man, Ottawa and Rothmans of Pall Mall Canada Ltd., Toronto (traveling)
1984-85 *Stones, Bones, cloth, and paper: Inuit Art in Edmonton Collections,* Edmonton Art Gallery, Alberta
1985   *Uumajut: Animal Imagery in Inuit Art,* Winnipeg Art Gallery, Manitoba
       Masterwork Sculpture 1985, Inuit Gallery of Vancouver, British Columbia
1986-87 *Pure Vision: The Keewatin Spirit,* Norman McKenzie Art Gallery, Regina, Saskatchewan (traveling)
1987   *The Williamson Collection of Inuit Sculpture,* Norman Mackenzie Art Gallery, University of Regina, Regina, Saskatchewan (traveling)
       Rugged and Profound—Sculpture from Eskimo Point, The Innuit Gallery of Eskimo Art, Toronto
1988-89 *Im Schatten der Sonne: Zeitgenossische Kunst der Indianer und Eskimos in Kanada/In the Shadow of the Sun: Contemporary Indian and Inuit Art in Canada,* Canadian Museum of Civilizaion, Ottawa (traveling)
1990-91 *Espaces Inuit,* Maison Hamel-Bruneau, Ste-Foy, Quebec
1993   *The Art of Keewatin,* Arctic Artistry, Hastings-on-Hudson, New York
1994   *Share the Vision, Philadelphians Collect Inuit Art,* Art Space Gallery, Philadelphia
1995   *Immaginario Inuit,* Arte e cultura degli esquimesi canadesi, Galleria d'Arte Moderna e Contemporanea, Verona, Italy

Collections

Art Gallery of Ontario, Toronto; Canadian Museum of Civilization, Hull, Quebec; Amon Carter Museum of Western Art, Fort Worth, Texas; Dennos Museum Center, Northwestern Michigan College, Traverse City; Edmonton Art Gallery, Alberta; Agnes Etherington Art Centre, Queen's University, Kingston, Ontario; Inuit Cultural Institute, Rankin Inlet, Northwest Territories; Klamer Family Collection, Art Gallery of Ontario, Toronto; Musee des beaux-arts de Monteal, Quebec; Museum of Anthropology, University of British Columbia, Vancouver; British National Gallery of Canada, Ottawa; Surick Collection, Art Gallery of Ontario, Toronto; Williamson Collection, Art Gallery of Ontario, Toronto; Winnipeg Art Gallery, Manitoba.

Publications

On PANGNARK: Books—*Oonark-Pangnark: An exhibition selected from the collections of the National Museum of Man,* National Museum of Man, Ottawa, 1970; *Eskimo Point/Arviat,* Winnipeg Art Gallery, Winnipeg, 1982; "Pangnark," by Norman Zepp, *The Canadian Encyclopedia,* edited by James H. Marsh, Hurtig Publishers, Edmonton, 1985; *Pure Vision: The Keewatin Spirit,* by Norman Zepp, Norman Mackenzie Art Gallery, Regina, 1986. **Articles**—"Eskimo Art Reconsidered," by George Swinton, *Artscanada,* vol. 27, no. 6, December/January 1971-72; "Arviat Stone Sculpture: Born of the Struggle with an Uncompromising Medium," by Ingo Hessel, *Inuit Art Quarterly,* vol. 5, no. 1, Winter 1980.

*   *   *

John Pangnark, a self-taught stone sculptor who lived and worked in the small Arctic community of Arviat, is generally considered the foremost proponent of the "minimalist" style of sculpture that developed in that community in the 1960s. Though not a conscious movement, the Arviat style is considered to be unique in Inuit Art. In it the human form is greatly simplified or abstracted, and the raw or barely worked stone often takes precedence over details of clothing or anatomy.

Pangnark was born in 1920 at Windy Lake, about 200 miles west of Arviat, in the Keewatin region of the Northwest Territories just north of the Manitoba border. Like many of the Caribou Inuit (specifically Ahiamiut) who were decimated by starvation and disease in the late 1950s, he was relocated to one of the communities on the west coast of Hudson Bay. Until then Pangnark and his family had led a traditional semi-nomadic existence. Pangnark settled in Arviat (then known as Eskimo Point) and remained there for his entire life. He trapped and hunted as long as he was able and supported himself through carving and odd jobs. Pangnark married Joy Kitterselerk (born 1898) in 1958. Pangnark died in the nearby community of Rankin Inlet in 1980.

Like most Arviat artists, Pangnark concentrated on the human form in his sculpture, working with small hand tools in the grey to black stone of the region and very occasionally in antler and bone. However, rather than depicting mothers and children or families as is typical of Arviat sculpture, he depicted small-scale solitary figures almost exclusively. Pangnark's art is the epitome of the so-called "minimalist" style of Arviat community sculpture. He began in the mid-1960s with fairly angular, simplified and abstracted yet clearly recognizable human shapes. There is evidence of an interest in a subtle kind of geometry in his compositions of this period. By the late-60s Pangnark seemed to be more interested in working with gentle undulating curves and planes of stone than he was in representing the human figure. By the early 1970s Pangnark had stripped down the human form to its barest essentials: faint slits delineating facial features were incised on smoothly filed but often irregular chunks of stone. The sex of his subjects was no longer apparent, and gestures were so subtle as to be obscure.

It could be said that Pangnark expressed the human form in terms of volumes, planes and curves rather than heads, torsos and limbs. Quite apart from their visual appeal, his sculptures have a sensuous tactile quality. His work quickly invited comparisons with modern European sculptors, such as Brancusi. Among Inuit artists, his work can be compared with the sculpture of Andy Miki (1918-83), of Arviat, and Lucy Tasseor Tutsweetok (1934—), also Arviat, who said of Pangnark's work: "It's the imagination of the shape that I like. It does not look just like a real thing. If it looked like a real person, you would simply see a copy of what is alive."

Pangnark was one of four Inuit artists invited to spend six months as artist-in-residence at Expo '70 in Osaka, Japan, in March 1970, but found the pace too hectic and returned home after six weeks. Although he achieved some critical acclaim in Inuit Art curatorial circles, his work was generally unappreciated during his lifetime; it now fetches relatively high prices on the auction block. Pangnark's sculptures have been included in more than forty exhibitions in Canada and abroad. The most notable of these are *Oonark-Pangnark*, a touring exhibition of 1970; *Sculpture/Inuit: Masterworks of the Canadian Arctic*, an international touring exhibition of 1971-73; and *Pure Vision: The Keewatin Spirit*, a touring exhibition of 1986-87. Major works can be found in the collections of the National Gallery of Canada, the Canadian Museum of Civilization, the Art Gallery of Ontario, the Amon Carter Museum of Western Art in Fort Worth, and other art galleries and museums.

—Ingo Hessel

PAPIALOOK, Josie

Variant names: Pamiutu; Puppy
Tribal affiliations: Inuit
Carver

Born: Josie Pamiutu Papialook near Povungnituk, Northwest Territories, Canada, in 1918; last name also spelled Papialuk. **Family:** Married Martha (died 1978) and one son, Peter; brother, Isah Papialuk is also an artist. **Career:** Hunter, trapper, artist.

Individual Exhibitions

1980   *Josie Papialuk: Print Retrospective with Carvings,* Inuit Gallery of Vancouver, British Columbia
1983   Marion Scott Gallery, Vancouver
1984   *Josie Papialook: Drawings and Carvings,* Houston North Gallery, Lunenburg, Nova Scotia
1985   *Original Drawings by Josie Papialuk,* The Guild Shop, Toronto

Selected Group Exhibitions

1962   Povungnituk Print Collection (annual collection)
1971   *Eskimo Carvings and Prints from the Collection of York University,* Art Gallery of York University, Downsview, Ontario

1980-81   *Things Made by Inuit,* La Federation des Cooperatives du Nouveau-Quebec, Montreal (traveling)
1983-85   *Contemporary Indian and Inuit Art of Canada,* Department of Indian Affairs and Northern Development, Ottawa, presented at the General Assembly Building, United Nations, New York (traveling)
1985-87   *Chisel and Brush/Le ciseau et la brosse,* Department of Indian Affairs and Northern Development, Ottawa (traveling)
1987   *The Williamson Collection of Inuit Sculpture,* Norman Mackenzie Art Gallery, University of Regina, Regina, Saskatchewan (traveling)
1988-89   *Im Schatten der Sonne: Zeitgenossische Kunst der Indianer und Eskimos in Kanada/In the Shadow of the Sun: Contemporary Indian and Inuit Art in Canada,* Canadian Museum of Civilizaion, Ottawa (traveling)
1989   *Art Inuit, la Sculpture des Esquimaux du Canada,* presented by l'Iglou Art Esquimau, Douai at Chapelle de la Visitation, Thonon, France
1990   *Arctic Mirror,* Canadian Museum of Civilization, Hull, Quebec
        Art Inuit: Autour de la Collection de Cape Dorset 1990, presented by l'Iglou Art Esquimau, Douai at Centre Culturel Canadien, Paris
1991   *Aux frontieres de l'imaginaire inuit,* Galerie du Trait-Carre, Charlesbourg, Quebec
1992   *Prints from Povungnituk 1962-1988,* Albers Gallery of Inuit Art, San Francisco
1994   *Arctic Spirit, 35 Years of Canadian Inuit Art,* Frye Art Museum, Seattle
        Kunst van de Inuit Eskimo's, Gemeentelijk Kunstcentrum, Huis Hellemans, Edegem, Belgium

Collections

Art Gallery of Nova Scotia, Halifax, Nova Scotia; Art Gallery of York University, Downsview, Ontario; Avataq Cultural Institute, Montreal; Canadian Guild of Crafts Quebec, Montreal; Canadian Museum of Civilization, Hull, Quebec; Confederation des caisses populaires et d'economie Desjardins, Levis, Quebec; Dennos Museum Center, Northwestern Michigan College, Traverse City, Michigan; Eskimo Museum, Churchill, Manitoba; Glenbow Museum, Calgary, Alberta; Macdonald Stewart Art Centre, Guelph, Ontario; McMichael Canadian Art Collection, Kleinburg, Ontario; Ministere des affaires culturelles du Quebec, Quebec City; Musee de la civilisation, Quebec City, Quebec; Musee des beaux-arts de Montreal, Quebec; Musee du Quebec, Quebec City; Museum of Anthropology, University of British Columbia, Vancouver; National Gallery of Canada, Ottawa; Red Deer College, Red Deer, Alberta; Saputik Museum, Povungnituk, Quebec; University of Lethbridge Art Gallery, Lethbridge, Alberta; Winnipeg Art Gallery, Manitoba; York University, Toronto.

Publications

On PAPIALOOK: Article—"Josie Papialook," by Marybelle Mitchell, *The Beaver,* Summer 1982.

*

Josie Papialook comments (1982):
There are all different kinds of wind. Yes, all different kinds.

Josie Papialook: *This is the Wind.* Courtesy Macdonald Stewart Art Center, Guelph, Ontario.

Some very strong and some not strong enough. Sometimes it makes clouds and rain. It is also all different colors... I see it almost every day. I feel it strongly. That's how I see it. Not with my eyes but with my hands and face. The wind is different all the time. It never stays the same.

*   *   *

Like many Inuit artists of his generation, Papialook spent the early decades of his life immersed in a traditional hunting lifestyle approximating that of his Inuit ancestors, living "on the land" in traditional camps and traveling occasionally to the Hudson Bay Company post at Povungnituk to trade white fox furs for supplies. Art as a concept was not a part of Papialook's early life experience, nor did a word for "art" exist in his native Inuktitut language.

It was not until Papialook was in his 40s that, as a result of a tuberculosis epidemic, large numbers of Inuit from the camps surrounding Povungnituk (the *Povungnitungmiut)* abandoned traditional camp life and settled close to the trading post, where supplies and support were more readily available. Within a few years, a school and nursing station were built and a government welfare

program established. By 1960, Povungnituk had became a small, permanent settlement.

The new Oblate missionary in the community, Father André Steinmann, encouraged relocated Inuit to produce soapstone carvings for sale in the South as a means to stabilize their fragile economic circumstances. Living in the settlement, they could no longer survive solely as hunters and trappers and were becoming increasingly dependent on government welfare. Papialook was among those who responded positively to the encouragement to take up stone-carving as a regular supplement to, or even a substitute for, welfare payments. He also became one of the first to involve himself in the experimental printmaking projects introduced by Father Steinmann in the early-1960s. However, not liking what he considered the messiness and repetitiveness of the stone block printing process, Papialook gravitated away from executing full editions of prints from the stone blocks he had prepared. He preferred to make drawings on paper with felt markers, crayons and colored pencils.

From his earliest involvement in the art activities, Josie Papialook exhibited a distinctive personal style. His work is easily identifiable by his sense of play and his whimsical handling of a favored and limited repertoire of subjects—birds, faces, hunters, igloos and the occasional frame house, and various implements and paraphernalia of the traditional Inuit hunter. Papialook's drawings and prints are particularly distinctive because of their vivid and varied colors and because of his convention of presenting both the seen and unseen elements of nature. In his drawings, for example, Papialook typically includes colorful notations depicting the singing or chirping of birds in the form of lines of slanting "V's" emanating from the birds' open beaks.

Papialook also pictures the sounds and sensations of the wind and other natural forces in his graphic works. Papialook's life experience in the traditional culture has made him particularly sensitive to qualities of wind and its directions and intensities. An understanding for wind was critical to the Inuit hunter's ability to predict weather, determine appropriate times for hunting particular animals, and even for ascertaining one's location in times of bad weather and limited visibility. Papialook's drawing, *This Is the Wind* (1980), typifies this interest. In the drawing, Papialook features a standing man (perhaps a self-portrait) surrounded by vibrating shapes and icy droplets in various colors representing the ever-present and ever-shifting arctic winds. Papialook once explained his sensitivity to the wind to sociologist, Marybelle Mitchell, with the following statement:

> There are all different kinds of wind. Yes, all different kinds. Some very strong and some not strong enough. Sometimes it makes clouds and rain. It is also all different colors...I see it almost every day. I feel it strongly. That's how I see it. Not with my eyes but with my hands and face. The wind is different all the time. It never stays the same.

Papialook often inscribes titles on his drawings with the syllabic characters of his native Inuktitut language, and he frequently signs his works in Roman characters. *This is the Wind* is signed "JOSIE (P) PAPIALOOK" with a circle carefully-drawn around the middle "P," attesting to Papialook's pride of authorship. The circle is derived from his awareness of the typographical convention of using an encircled "c" as a symbol to designate copyright.

While Papialook's drawings rarely illustrate traditional stories, as do many of the graphic images and sculptures by other Povungnituk artists, his art provides access to what artist George Swinton, has termed "decorative reality." Papialook provides straight-forward access to his personal experience. His bright color sense and his playful handling of form and subject resonate with qualities of his own personality, but suggest as well the empowering optimism characteristic of the traditional Inuit culture.

—Marion E. Jackson

PARKER, Julia

Tribal affiliations: Kashia Pomo; Coast Miwok
Basketweaver

Born: Julia Domingues, Graton, California, 8 March 1929. **Education:** Graduated from Stewart Indian School, Stewart, Nevada, 1948. **Family:** Married Ralph Parker (Mono Lake Paiute/Miwok) 1948; four children. **Career:** Maid and housekeeper in Yosemite; cultural demonstrator for National Park Service, Yosemite National Park, 1960—; Manager of Pohono Indian Shop, 1970-1972.

Individual Exhibitions

The artist has never kept a listing of the many exhibitions in which her baskets have appeared. The following is a partial listing:

1966	Norwegian Ski Association Headquarters, Oslo, Norway
1973	Yosemite Museum, Yosemite National Park, California
1990	*Festival At The Lake*, Oakland, California
1990	Museum of the American Indian, Heye Foundation, New York
1991	Sacramento County Fair, California
1991	Native American Craft Days, Bridgeport, California
1992	Native American Craft Days, Bridgeport, California
1993	Native American Craft Days, Bridgeport, California
1994	Native American Craft Days, Bridgeport, California
1994	*Tallac Festival*, Lake Tahoe, California
1995	Native American Craft Days, Bridgeport, California
1995	Chawse State Park, Jackson, California
1996	Native American Craft Days, Bridgeport, California

Collections

Yosemite Museum, National Park Service, Yosemite National Park, California.

Publications

On PARKER: Books—*Tradition and Innovation: A Basket History of the Indians of the Yosemite-Mono Lake Area*, by Craig D. Bates and Martha J. Lee, Yosemite, 1990; *It Will Live Forever: Traditional Yosemite Acorn Preparation*, by Beverly R. Ortiz, Berkeley, 1991/1996. **Articles**—"Miwok-Paiute Basketry 1920-1928: Genesis of an Art Form," by Craig Bates, *American Indian Art Magazine*, vol. 4, no. 4, 1979; "Made For Sale: Baskets from the Yosemite-Mono Lake Region of California," by Craig Bates, *Moccasin Tracks*, vol. 7, no. 4, 1981; "Ethnographic Collections at Yosemite National Park," by Craig Bates, *American Indian Art Magazine*, vol. 7, no. 32, 1982; "Yosemite Miwok-Paiute Basketry: A Study in Cultural Change," by Craig Bates *American Indian Basketry Magazine*, vol 2, no. 4, 1982; "Yosemite: A Melting Pot for Indian People and Their Baskets," by Craig Bates and Martha J. Lee, *Strands of Time: Yokuts, Mono and Miwok Basketmakers*, Fresno, 1988.

*   *   *

Julia Parker's place in the history of Yosemite-Mono Lake basketry is unique; by the 1990s she was the only practicing weaver who had been taught by women who wove baskets during the 1900-1920 era. In addition, she blended their teachings with her own creativity to produce basket styles that are uniquely her own, as well as baskets that emulate older Pomo, Miwok and Mono Lake Paiute pieces.

Parker, of Pomo and Coast Miwok ancestry, met her future husband while attending Stewart Indian School near Carson City, Nevada. Ralph Parker was the grandson of famed Yosemite weaver Lucy Telles. After their marriage, the couple settled in Yosemite in 1948, and Julia Parker began to learn the traditional skills of her husband's family.

In 1960 Park Naturalist Douglas Hubbard revived demonstrations of Indian basket weaving at the Yosemite Museum, and he

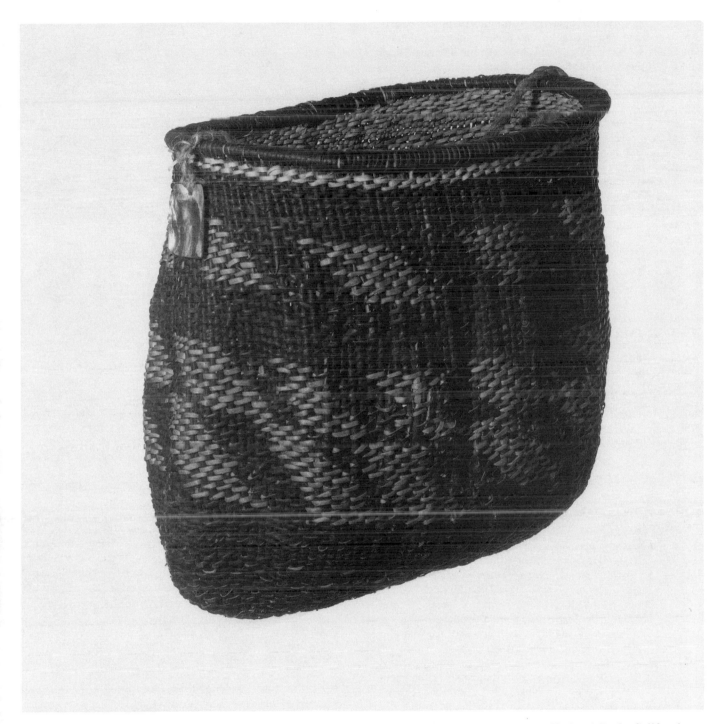

Julia Parker: Twined basket, c. 1980. Courtesy National Park Service, Yosemite Museum, Yosemite National Park, California.

asked Parker if she would be interested in the job. That weekend the Parkers went to Coleville to visit Ralph's great-aunt, Tina Charlie, who gave Julia basic instructions for weaving a coiled, single-rod basket and provided her with materials. Parker immediately began giving demonstrations at the Yosemite Museum, a job which she has held for over thirty years.

Parker's knowledge about weaving was further augmented through the next several years by visits with well-known weaver Carrie Bethel and Bethel's sister, Minnie Mike, both of whom lived near Lee Vining, California. The baskets that Parker wove in the 1960s were primarily coiled with single-rod, three-rod or grass-bundle foundations in a variety of shapes and sizes; their patterns were based on Miwok and Paiute designs, or occasionally, were invented by Parker. She also made beaded baskets in Paiute style.

By the 1970s Parker was well known throughout California as a basketweaver, and she traveled to a number of Native American cultural events to demonstrate her skills. She also taught basketry classes for Yosemite and Mariposa-area Indian women through the American Indian Council of Mariposa County, and attended classes at the newly formed Sierra Mono Museum in North Fork to improve her skills in twined basketry. By the mid-1970s she began to experiment with Pomo weaving and patterns, studying museum collections and learning from Pomo weavers Elsie Allen and Mabel McKay. During this time, the Indian Cultural Program in Yosemite was enlarged at the Yosemite Museum, and Parker began to train new employees in basketry skills as part of their work as cultural demonstrators.

Parker was making many styles of baskets by the 1980s. They ranged from coarse baskets of whole, unpeeled willow and dogwood shoots in Pomo style, to finely stitched miniature beaded baskets in the style of her teacher Carrie Bethel. Parker also began to teach classes in beadwork and basketry throughout California in the 1980s. She continued teaching and demonstrating into the 1990s. She is perhaps the last direct link with the weavers who were the creators of the fancy basket style of the Yosemite-Mono Lake region.

—Craig Bates

PARSONS, Neil

Variant names: O'mahk-pitawa
Tribal affiliations: Blackfeet
Painter

Born: Browning, Montana, 2 March 1938; O'mahk-pitawa means "Tall Eagle"; also known as Little Dog. **Education:** Montana State University, B.A., 1961, M.A., 1964.

Selected Group Exhibitions

1964   *Own Your Own Invitational*, Denver Art Museum, Denver, Colorado
        Intermountain Painting and Sculpture Exhibition, Salt Lake Art Center, Salt Lake City, Utah
1965   *Second Annual Invitational Exhibition of American Indian Paintings*, United States Department of the Interior, Washington, D.C.
1966   *Edinburgh Art Festival*, Edinburgh, Scotland
1971   *Contemporary Indian Artists,* Museum of the Plains Indian, Browning, Montana (traveling)
1975   *Pintura Amerinda Contemporanea,* sponsored by United States Deartment of State and International Communication Agency, Washington, D.C. (traveling in South America through 1980)
1981   *Confluences of Tradition and Change: 24 Native American Artists,* Richard L. Nelson Gallery, University of California, Davis (traveling)
        Buffalo Bill Historical Center, Cody, Wyoming
1984   *Indianascher Kunstler,* organized by the Philbrook Museum, Tulsa, Oklahoma (traveling in Germany through 1985)
1986   *New Directions Northwest*, Evergreen State College, Olympia, Washington
        Coyote Indian Art Exhibit, Montana Indian Artist Project, Missoula, Montana
1990   *Our Land/Ourselves: American Indian Contemporary Artists,* State University of New York, Albany

Neil Parsons: *Sweetgrass Series #49.* **Photograph by Rick Hill.**

1991   *One with the Earth*, organized by the Institute of American Indian Arts and Alaska Culture and Development, Santa Fe (traveling through 1992)
1992   *Submuloc Show/Columbus Wohs*, organized by Atlatl, Phoenix, Arizona (traveling)

Collections

Bureau of Indian Affairs, U.S. Department of the Interior, Washington, D.C.; Heard Museum, Phoenix, Arizona; Institute of American Indian Arts Museum, Santa Fe, New Mexico; Maryhill Museum of Art, Goldendale, Washington; North Dakota Museum of Art, University of North Dakota, Grand Forks; Salt Lake Art Center, Salt Lake City, Utah.

Publications

On PARSONS: Books—*The Sweet Grass Lives On,* by Jamake Highwater, New York, 1980; *Indianascher Kunstler*, edited by Gerhard Hoffman, Munich, 1984; *Confluences of Tradition and Change: 24 American Indian Artists,* C. N. Gorman Museum, University of California, Davis; *American Indian Art in the 1980s,* by Lloyd Kiva New, Niagara Falls, New York, 1984; *New Directions Northwest*, Olympia, Washington, 1987; *Our Land/Ourselves: American Indian Contemporary Artists,* Albany, New York, 1990; *The Submuloc Show/Columbus Wohs*, Phoenix, 1992; *Native American Painters of the Twentieth Century: The Work of 61 Artists*, by Robert Henkes, Jefferson, North Carolina, and London, 1995. **Articles**—"The Second Biennial Native American Fine Arts Invitational," by Erin Younger and Robert Breunig, *American Indian Art* magazine, Spring 1986; "Whirling, Dreaming, Feeling," by Erin Snow, *Reflex,* May/June/July 1994.

*   *   *

Neil Parsons, a modernist painter throughout much of his long and productive career, has aimed for a synthesis of traditional Native American creativity and spirituality with contemporary Western painting styles. Distinct periods are evident in Parsons's oeuvre. His earliest paintings were dark and self-contained, while in his middle period during the late 1960s, 1970s and early 1980s his works have delicacy and formal beauty. At this time he was influenced by color field painting. His latest works, from the second half of the 1980s and 1990s, are less handsome but quite strong, with gestural qualities and disjunctive collage elements predominating. Quite prolific, Parsons has worked with oil, acrylic, graphite, charcoal, pastel, mixed media, and monoprints.

Parsons's M.F.A. thesis was a large mural created for the Museum of the Plains Indian in Browning, Montana, in 1966. An oil painting on masonite, it is abstract yet inspired by themes drawn from his Blackfeet heritage. Wishing to allude to the timeless components of native life and physical environment, he succeeded in evoking the color and texture of deer hide and buckskins, the precipitous structure of the Rocky Mountains and the bleak horizon line of the Badlands.

Exploring formal relationships, Parsons's work from his middle period tended to begin with an idea, usually a Native American reference (for example, *Osage, Arapaho, Two Medicine Series #27* and *Crow Child Series #7),* which the artist condensed into non-objective works. Since color field painters such as Barnett Newman and Mark Rothko were often inspired by the spiritual underpinnings of Native American art, it was logical for Parsons to ally his paintings with his Plains Indian sacred heritage. Thus, the artistic movement offered an important way to connect his inherent native beliefs with a desire to do abstract painting.

These diamond-shaped canvases, like his earliest works, also made reference to nature. Parsons's preference for diagonal compositions during the 1970s imply the Rocky Mountains and other structural aspects of nature, whereas his delicate washes of color evoke water or sky. In *Crow Child #18* (acrylic on canvas) subtle washes of color enliven a diamond-shaped flat canvas having as its principal formal characteristic a dark/light opposition on both the top and bottom of the composition. This contrasts with the lighter middle section, which has ethereal washes of darker colors streaked though, creating a very fluid overall appearance. *Bannock* (1972) repeats the diamond shape and dark hues pressing in from the top and bottom of the composition. It also has borders of warm red glowing mysteriously beside/behind the earth-colored center panel.

During a transition to his latest period of work, of the late 1980s and 1990s, Parsons began to include collage elements that have a relationship with his childhood and his memories of family heirlooms and clothing. For example, his *Napumi* series (1990, monoprint/collage) has an agitated linearity with strokes that record his gestures and then often wipe them partially away. Floral patterns from cutout textiles are collaged onto the support. These added elements are somewhat disjunctive and work better conceptually than formally. Conceptually they could refer to the turmoil of the conquest, when alien values and decorative impulses interfered with the native aesthetic heritage.

Parsons's willingness to change his style and engage with his deepest personal struggles and triumphs reveal his integrity. *Night of the Star Dance* (1992, charcoal and graphite on paper), is full of explosive energy and gestural eloquence. The artist's lyrical titles seem to belie darker meanings in these works. Layers of modulated values give subtlety to volatile drawings. They are natural forms, however, since some of the dark patterns suggest leaping frogs, a

whimsical element in an otherwise aggressively executed piece. The drawings and monoprints that characterize Parsons's latest work from the 1990s are dissonant and harsh and have a deliberately unfinished aspect—paint rarely touches the edge of the paper—yet these works are strong and alive.

Catalysts of personal change and engagement, his latest works oscillate between conscious control and the unconscious power of creativity. There are, nevertheless, threads of continuity with the earlier parts of his oeuvre. Parsons continues to grapple with the formal aspects of the language of vision and an attempt to unite the spiritual and decorative traditions of his ancestors with abstract styles of painting, printmaking and drawing.

—Ann Storey

PAUL, Leonard
Tribal affiliations: Micmac
Painter and printmaker

Born: Halifax, Nova Scotia, 4 September 1953. **Education:** B.F.A., Nova Scotia College; B.A. (Art History and Political Science), Acadia University; Masters in Philosophy and Religion, Acadia University; travelled to Europe, India, Hawaii, New York and Florida to study works of the great masters, particularly the Dutch Masters on a trip to Amsterdam and Paris. **Career:** Taught art education to adults and children for one year on the Eskasoni Indian Reserve; professional artist since 1970s. **Awards:** Tom Longboat award, 1974; Governor General's medal, 1993; nominated for National Aboriginal Achievement Award, 1993; inducted into Canadian Who's Who, 1996. **Address:** c/o Fox Trail Editions, Inc., P.O. Box 848, Wolfville, Nova Scotia, B0P 1X0, Canada.

Individual Exhibitions

1978	*Portrait of a People*, Mount Saint Vincent Art Gallery, Halifax, Nova Scotia
1979	*Portrait of a People* (Provincial Art Tour), Art Gallery of Nova Scotia, Halifax
1980	Landmark Art Gallery Exhibition, Fredericton, New Brunswick
1985	Manuge Art Gallery, Halifax
1987	Private Art Exhibition, Wolfville, Nova Scotia
1988	Private Art Exhibition, Wolfville
	Hollis Galleries Art Exhibition, Halifax
1991	*Still Moments*, Acadia University Art Gallery, Wolfville
1992	*Nova Scotia Salmon River Series*, Chateau Halifax, Halifax

Selected Group Exhibitions

1976	Graphics Atlantic Art Exhibition, Halifax
1979	Landmark Gallery Exhibition, Fredericton
	Art Survival, Atlantic Style, Halifax
1980	Zwicker's Gallery Exhibition, Moncton, New Brunswick
	Carriage House Gallery, Wolfville
1981	*Art Amerindian Contemporary Tradition*, Ottawa
1982	Dalhousie Medical Research Foundation, Halifax
	Regional Realism, Halifax

Leonard Paul: Untitled. Courtesy of the artist.

New Works by a New Generation, Regina, Saskatchewan
1983   Manuge Galleries Atlantic Symphony Art Auction, Halifax
1984   *Indian Art, 1984*, Brantford, Ontario
1986   Federal Department of Indian and Northern Affairs Art
        Exhibition, Halifax
1987   Bowater - Mersey Paper Company, Ltd., Brooklyn, Nova
        Scotia
1989   33rd Annual Art Charity Auction, Montreal
1991   Ducks Unlimited Art Auction, Wolfville
        Micmac Heritage Gallery, Halifax
1992   Ducks Unlimited Art Auction, Kentville, Nova Scotia
1993   *Pe 'l A 'tukwey*, Art Gallery of Nova Scotia, Halifax

Collections

Indian Arts Centre of the Federal Department of Indian and Northern Affairs, Halifax; Nova Scotia Art Bank, Halifax.

Publications

On PAUL: Articles—"Major crowd gathers for opening of show by Leonard Paul," *The Chronical-Herald*, Halifax, Nova Scotia, 23 April 1991; "Jam Packed Opening: Still Moments: A Tribute to Leonard Paul's Father," *Micmac-Maliseet Nations News*, May 1991. **Film**—*Kwa 'nu 'te'*, National Film Board documentary, 1991.

*   *   *

Paul turns to the techniques of the great European masters, and a deep spiritual well of experience, to bring to visual life the Nova Scotia rivers and landscape he has known since childhood. Like the American Hudson River School of the 1850s, Paul's artwork is greatly influenced by the painting styles of the Renaissance and the European Watercolorists of the 1800s.

For sources of inspiration, Paul relies not only on rives and lakes, which frequently become the subject matter of his paintings, but reaches out to the varied experiences he has absorbed from his native culture, from an artistically and spiritually profound journey to southern India in 1992, and several trips to the United States and Europe. As a painter, Paul visualizes his own process of painting as a union between his native background and the natural world around him.

Paul concentrates on capturing feelings in order to preserve them on canvas through his paintings. He has commented that nature is his greatest teacher, and it is during his long walks and mountain bike rides that his senses are most heightened. As a painter Paul attempts to recreate the vividness of these experiences. His task is to freeze pieces of motion in order to create a "super-real" image that exists outside of time or era—prehistoric, today, or a long way into the future. Paul's attempt at environmental education aims not at blaring, abrasive, message driven pieces, but at images of real and tangible beauty. Thus, the viewer is left with memories of these waterways and landscapes on which to base their own activism.

Although Paul was formally trained in art and started with a solid background in draftsmanship, he considers himself self-taught in watercolours and painting. In the 1970s he showed several times with works in graphite pencil. More recently, though, he has been drawing in soft pastels, which offer a more expressive, impressionistic range of effects that directly contrast these earlier, more rigid, pencil pieces. His latest efforts have taken him in the direction of watercolors.

Paul takes his studies in technique and style very seriously. In 1993 he travelled to Amsterdam and Paris, undergoing extensive research into the techniques of the Dutch Masters, particularly Vermeer, with special emphasis on their specific techniques for glazing. Choosing his subjects with great care, Paul looks for spots along the water with turbulence for his desired effect, often seeking them out after a storm. His work has qualities of a photograph and the realism is haunting.

—Vesta Giles

PEÑA, Tonita

Variant names: Quah Ah
Tribal affiliations: San Ildefonso Pueblo
Painter

Born: Maria Antonia Peña at San Ildefonso, New Mexico, 10 May 1893; also known as Quah Ah (White Coral Beads) and Tonita Vigil Peña (her mother was Ascencion Peña, and after her mother's death in 1905, Tonita was raised by her aunt, Martina Vigil, of Cochiti). **Education:** Trained in pottery making by Martina Vigil; San Ildefonso Public Day School; St. Catherine's Indian School, Santa Fe. **Career:** Painter, art instructor; copied Parajito murals during the restoration process on the Parajito Plateau; muralist, Chicago World's Fair, 1939, and Santa Fe Indian School. **Died:** 1 May 1949.

Selected Group Exhibitions

1931-33 *Exposition of Indian Tribal Arts*, sponsored by The College Art Association (traveling)
1937 *American Indian Exposition and Congress*, Tulsa, Oklahoma
1955-56 European Tour, University of Oklahoma, Norman
1958-61 European Tour, University of Oklahoma, Norman
1980 *Native American Painting*, sponsored by the Mid-American Arts Alliance, (traveling)
1984-85 *Indianascher Kunstler*, organized by the Philbrook Museum, Tulsa, Oklahoma (toured Germany)
1988 *When the Rainbow Touches Down*, Heard Museum, Phoenix (traveling)
1991-92 *Shared Visions: Native American Painters and Sculptors in the Twentieth Century*, Heard Museum, (traveling)
1994 *Watchful Eyes: Native American Women Artists*, Heard Museum, Phoenix

Collections

American Museum of Natural History, New York; Amerind Foundation, Dragoon, Arizona; Center for Great Plains Studies, University of Nebraska, Lincoln; Cincinnati Art Museum, Ohio; City Art Museum, S. Louis, Missouri; Cleveland Museum of Art, Ohio; Columbus Gallery of Fine Arts, Ohio; Corcoran Gallery of Art, Washington, D.C.; Cranbrook Institute of Science, Bloomfield, Michigan; Dartmouth College Collection, Hanover, New Hampshire; Denver Art Museum, Colorado; Thomas Gilcrease Institute of American History and Art, Tulsa, Oklahoma; Heard Museum, Phoenix, Arizona; Phoebe Hearst Museum, University of Califor-

Tonita Peña: *Women Weaving and Supervising Kiln.* **Gift of Miss Amelia White, courtesy Detroit Institute of Arts.**

nia, Berkley; Museum of New Mexico, Santa Fe; Museum of Northern Arizona, Katheryn Harvey Collection, Flagstaff; Philbrook Art Center, Tulsa, Oklahoma; Milliccnt Rogers Foundation Museum, Taos, New Mexico; Roswell Museum and Art Center, Roswell, New Mexico; Univeristy of Oklahoma, Norman; Smithsonian Institution, Washington, D.C.

Publications

On PEÑA: Books—*Introduction to American Indian Art*, by John Sloan and Oliver La Farge, The Exposition of Indian Tribal Arts, Inc., New York, 1931; *American Indian Painting of the Southwest and Plains Areas*, by Dorothy Dunn, University of New Mexico, Albuquerque, 1968; *Indian Painters and White Patrons* by J.J. Brody, University of New Mexico Press, Albuquerque, 1971; *100 Years of Native American Painting*, exhibition catalog by Arthur Silberman, Oklahoma Museum of Art, Oklahoma City, 1978; *When the Rainbow Touches Down*, Heard Museum exhibition catalog by Tryntje Van Ness Seymour, University of Washington Press, Seattle & London, 1988; *Tonita Peña,* by Samuel L. Gray, Avanyu Publishing, Albuquerque, 1990; *Shared Visions: Native American Painters and Sculptors in the Twentieth Century*, by Margaret Archuleta and Dr. Rennard Strickland, The New Press, New York, 1991. **Articles**—"American Indian Water Colors," by C. Norris Millington, *The American Magazine of Art*, vol. 25, no. 2, August 1932; "America's First Painters," by Dorothy Dunn, *National Geographic Magazine*, vol. CVII, no. 3, March 1955; "Tonita Peña

(Quah Ah), Pueblo Painter: Asserting Identity Through Continuity and Change," by Marilee Jantzer-White, *The American Indian Quarterly* vol. 18, no. 3, Summer 1994.

*   *   *

A pioneer in the Southwest Easel Painting Tradition, Tonita Peña was the first and only female painter among the early San Ildefonso watercolorists (1910-30). Throughout her career as a painter Peña depicted ceremonial dances, dancers and genre scenes of women producing pottery. In her paintings she frequently focused attention on womens' roles and activities. She can be credited with breaking down gender barriers that traditionally confined women's artistic roles to pottery production.

Born in San Ildefonso, she began painting as a young girl while attending the Day School there (1899-1905). The teacher, Esther B. Hoyt, encouraged Peña and a few others to use watercolors, but she is generally considered a self-taught painter. Following the death of her mother and sister, Peña was sent to Cochiti in 1905 to live with her aunt and uncle, well known potters Martina Vigil and Florentino Montoya. In Cochiti, Peña helped produce her aunt's pottery and even made some of her own. Although she attended St. Catherine's Indian School in Santa Fe on and off from about 1912-15, it was in Cochiti that Peña raised a family and painted her entire life. During the early period Dr. Edgar Lee Hewett, of the Museum of New Mexico and School of American Research, encouraged Peña and became one of her first patrons.

Peña faced many challenges during her life. Having lost her first two husbands to accident and disease she was for a time the sole supporter of her family. Peña's paintings provided her with a much needed income and personal creative satisfaction. At a time when Pueblo social, religious, and artistic traditions were being threatened and denounced by federal policies and government organizations, Peña recorded what she deemed culturally significant. According to her son, Sam Aquero, Peña produced paintings as permanent records for future generations: "she had a strong feeling for preserving our traditional things. . . she was concerned, and that was one way of preserving those things."

As if that wasn't enough, she faced further opposition from tribal members who did not agree with the recording of religious or sacred practices, not to mention that it was being done by a woman. When Cochiti elders tried to prevent Peña from painting images of pueblo ceremonies and dancers, her third husband, Epitacio Arquero, helped convince them that if others were permitted to produce works of art decorated with sacred tribal designs, such as pottery, then Peña should be allowed to paint ceremonial dances. Eventually, Peña received permission from the governor of Cochiti, excusing her from agricultural duties so that she could pursue painting full-time. Peña, in turn, hired others to help fulfill her communal obligations.

Peña's use of varying poses, her attention to detail, and use of color to model forms are examples of the illusionistic intentions that have resulted in her realistic style. Peña's work has always been praised for the way in which she portrayed her dancers as real people, as opposed to conventionalized renderings of the human form. Her paintings were exhibited regularly at museums and galleries throughout the United States. During the 1930s she also worked under the WPA painting a series of murals for the Santa Fe Indian School.

As an established artist, Peña occasionally worked as an art instructor at the Santa Fe and Albuquerque Indian Schools. Like most of her contemporaries, Peña had a tremendous effect upon following generations of Pueblo painters. Her son, Joe H. Herrera, painted under his mother's guidance as a child and become a famous painter, while Pablita Velarde, the esteemed female painter from Santa Clara, cited Peña as one of her early influences. Both graduated from the Santa Fe Indian School art program, better known as the Studio.

—Lisa Roberts

PEPION, Victor

Variant names: Double Shields
Tribal affiliations: Blackfeet
Painter

Born: Birch Creek, Blackfeet Indian Reservation, Montana, 10 March 1907. **Military Service:** U.S. Marines, Asian Theatre, 1941-42; U.S. Army Air Corps, 1942-45, photographer, European Theatre. **Education:** Private instruction with Winold Reiss, including summer classes in portraiture, 1937, and muralist Olaf Nordmark, 1940; Los Angeles County Art Institute, 1939-1940; Army Art School, Shrivenham, England, 1945; University of Oklahoma, 1945; University of New Mexico, 1946-1947; University of South Dakota, B.F.A., 1948; New Mexico Highlands University, M.A., 1949.

Career: Muralist, Museum of the Plains Indian, Browning, Montana, 1941, and at Oglala Boarding School, Pine Ridge Indian Agency, Fort Sill Indian School, and New Mexico Highlands University (MA thesis, *Dances of All Nations*); painted diorama, Museum of the Plains Indian; art instructor, Chilocco Indian School, 1950-51, Phoenix Indian School, 1951-52. **Awards:** Philbrook Museum of Art, 1956. **Died:** Cut Bank, Montana, 4 March 1956.

Individual Exhibitions

1991   *Paintings by Victor Pepion,* Museum of the Plains Indian, Browning, Montana

Selected Group Exhibitions

1941   Museum of the Plains Indian, Browning, Montana
1956   Philbrook Museum of Art, Tulsa, Oklahoma
1960   Philbrook Museum of Art, Tulsa, Oklahoma
1961   Historical Society of Montana, Helena
1971-72 *Contemporary Indian Artists: Montana/Wyoming/Idaho,* Museum of the Plains Indian, Browning, Montana (traveling)

Collections

Historical Society of Montana, Helena; Museum of Art, University of Oklahoma, Norman; Museum of the Plain Indian, United States Department of the Interior, Indian Arts & Crafts Board, Browning, Montana; Philbrook Museum of Art, Tulsa, Oklahoma.

Publications

On PEPION: Books—*American Indian Painters*, by Oscar B. Jacobson and Jeanne d'Ucel, Nice, France, 1950; *Indian Painters and White Patrons*, by J.J. Brody, Albuquerque, 1971; *Contemporary Indian Artists: Montana/Wyoming/Idaho*, by Dorothy Jean Ray, Rapid City, 1972; *American Indian Painting and Sculpture*, by Patricia Janis Broder, New York, 1981; *Paintings by Victor Pepion,* catalog by John Ewers, Browning, 1991.

*   *   *

Visitors to the Museum of the Plains Indian in Browning, Montana, encounter colorful murals painted in secco dry fresco on the four walls of the entrance lobby. These murals were the finest artistic achievement of Victor Pepion, who had only started painting seriously a few years earlier, during the 1930s, before completing the murals in 1941. Pepion had several other important paintings and murals during a career of many starts and stops: he was active in the arts and music at the Holy Family Boarding School through the early 1920s and painted intermittently until his talent was recognized during the mid-1930s by Winold Reiss, a German portraiture artist whose Indian paintings were frequently featured in calendars. Reiss invited Pepion and several other Blackfeet artists for summer classes near Glacier National Park in 1937. Pepion continued to work with Reiss and also composed sketches for murals for the lobby of the Museum of the Plains Indian, scheduled for opening in 1941 by the Department of the Interior in Browning, Montana. The mural sketches were accepted and Pepion was commissioned to paint them, with advising by the museum's first director, John Ewers, who would enjoy a long career in administration of museums with Native American art collections.

Soon after Pepion completed the murals, he enlisted in the Marines and was stationed first in Asia, then in Europe as a member of the Army Air Corps. After the war, Pepion studied art at several schools, attained a BFA and an MA, was commissioned for several more murals, and taught art at Chilocco Indian School and Phoenix Indian School. At about the time Pepion was beginning to concentrate on art full-time for an extended period, he died in an accidental explosion and fire in 1956. At his brother's home, Pepion had turned on a small heater; gas accumulated without igniting, and then exploded, killing Pepion instantly. At the time Pepion was considered the most distinguished painter of the Blackfeet tribe.

Pepion's works were showcased for the fiftieth anniversary of the Museum of the Plains Indian, 1991, and John Ewers, then Curator Emeritus of the Smithsonian Institution, returned to the Museum to discuss Pepion's art, the founding of the Museum, and to be honored at anniversary festivities.

In addition to the murals, Pepion painted watercolors of current and historical events associated with his tribe, from hunting scenes, to ceremonies, to games, to portraits, including *Night Rider* (pastel and tempera on illustration board, c. 1937), which was executed under the direction of Reiss and painted directly from life. *Happy Hunting Ground,* an unfinished work, reflects his skills as a graphic artist. One half of this work is devoted to a hunter clad in furs and standing by his tipi, upon which are drawings concerning the hunt, while beyond in the other half is a vast plain where buffaloes feed. The fact that this work was unfinished proved important for displaying Pepion's graphic skills before he applied the paint. The painting won an award later that year, after his death, at the Philbrook annual fair.

Pepion's mural at the Plains Indian Museum depicts four stages in a buffalo hunt. Pepion conferred with his great uncle, Mountain Chief, who was the oldest Indian living in the area and had participated in buffalo chases on horseback near the site of the museum. The first mural depicts a small party of buffalo hunters approaching a herd in the distance. The second presents the action of the chase and the hunters bringing down a buffalo. The third portrays a woman helping a man to butcher one of the fallen buffalo, while another woman leads a heavily loaded pack horse toward camp bearing the meat and hide of the butchered animal. The last mural shows a scene in camp and many of the ways Blackfeet Indians made use of materials taken from buffalo.

—Perry Bear

PIQTOUKUN, David Ruben

Tribal affiliations: Inuit
Carver

Born: Paulatuk, Northwest Territories, 10 May 1950. **Career:** Hunter, artist, instructor and cultural ambassador; visiting artist-in-residence in the Dominican Republic, Mexico, Ivory Coast. **Awards:** Grants from Canadian Eskimo Arts Council, Canada Council, and UNESCO Committee for the World Decade of Cultural Development.

Individual Exhibitions

1973   Arctic Arts Ltd., Edmonton, Alberta
1974   Gallery of British Columbia Arts, Vancouver

1983   Family Hall, Inuvik, Northwest Territories
1986   Expo 1986, Northwest Territories Pavilion, Vancouver

Selected Group Exhibitions

1974   *British Columbia Nephrite Jade Show,* Dallas Trade Show, Texas (traveling)
1979-80   *Inuit Art in the 1970s,* Department of Indian Affairs and Northern Development, and the Agnes Etherington Art Centre, Kingston, Ontario (traveling)
1979   *Sculpture of the Inuit: Masterwork Exhibitors of the Canadian Arctic,* Inuit Gallery of Vancouver, British Columbia
1984-86   *Arctic Vision: Art of the Canadian Inuit,* Department of Indian Affairs and Northern Development and Canadian Arctic Producers, Ottawa (traveling)
1985-86   *Sanaugasi Takujaksat: A Travelling Celebration of Inuit Sculpture,* presented by Canadian Arctic Producers Ltd., with the assistance of Indian and Northern Affairs Canada, Ottawa (traveling)
1986   *Die Kunst aus der Arktis,* presented by Inuit Galerie, Mannheim, Germany (traveling)
1989   *Out of Tradition: Abraham Anghik/David Ruben Piqtoukun,* Winnipeg Art Gallery, Winnipeg, Manitoba
               Masters of the Arctic: An Exhibition of Contemporary Inuit Masterworks, Presented by the Amway Corporation at the United Nations General Assembly, New York (traveling)
1992   *Nouveau Territories...350/500 Ans Apres,* presented at Les Maisons de la Culture Cote-des-Neiges, Notre-Dame-de-Grace, and Rosemont-Petite Patrie, Montreal Recreation and Community Development Service and les Ateliers Visions Planetaire, Montreal (traveling)
1993   *Multiple Realities: Inuit Images of Shamanic Transformation,* Winnipeg Art Gallery, Winnipeg, Manitoba
1995   *Immaginario Inuit, Arte e cultura degli esquimesi canadesi,* Galleria d'Arte, Modernae Contemporanea, Verona, Italy
               Keeping Our Stories Alive: An Exhibition of the Art and Crafts from Dene and Inuit of Canada, Institute of American Indian Arts Museum, Santa Fe

Collections

Amway Environmental Foundation Collection, Ada, Michigan; Art Gallery of Ontario, Toronto; Canadian Museum of Civilization, Hull, Quebec; Confederation Centre of the Arts, Charlottetown, Prince Edward Island; Inuit Cultural Institute, Rankin Inlet, Northwest Territories; Klamer Family Collection, Art Gallery of Ontario, Toronto; McMichael Canadian Art Collection, Kleinburg, Ontario; Museum of Anthropology, University of British Columbia, Vancouver; Prince of Wales Northern Heritage Centre, Yellowknife, Northwest Territories; Sarick Collection, Art Gallery of Ontario, Toronto; University of Alberta, Edmonton; Winnipeg Art Gallery, Winnipeg.

Publications

By PIQTOUKUN: Articles—"Trip to Abidjan, Ivory Coast, Africa," *Inuktitut,* January, 1983, pp. 19-32; "A Journey to the Ivory Coast," *About Arts and Crafts,* vol. 5, no. 3, 1982, pp. 1-8.

On PIQTOUKUN: Books—*Arctic Vision: Art of the Canadian Inuit*, by Barbara Lipton, Ottawa: Canadian Arctic Producers, 1984; *Out of Tradition: Abraham Anghik/David Ruben Piqtoukun*, by Darlene Wight, Winnipeg, MB: Winnipeg Art Gallery, 1989. **Articles**—*Arts & Culture of the North*, vol. 5, no. 4, Fall, 1981, pp. 375-77; "Paulatuk Exhibition Shows Spirit, Power," by Martha Devine, *Native Press*, July 24, 1987; "David Ruben Piqtoukun: Sculpting a Magic Past," by Nancy McLeod, *Up Here*, vol. 3, no. 6, October/November, 1987, p. 34; "David Ruben Piqtoukun-Inuit Artist: Releasing the Figure in the Stone," by Sheila Noble, *Intercom*, December, 1988, pp. 1-2; "David Ruben Piqtoukun," by Ronnie Seagren, *Edges: New Planetary Patterns*, vol. 1, no. 4, 1989, pp. 23-25; "David Ruben Piqtoukun," by John Ayre, *Inuit Art Quarterly*, 9, 3 (Fall 1994), 17-22; "Six Sculptors, Abraham Anghik," *Inuit Art Quarterly*, 10, 3 (Fall 1995), 40-41.

*

David Ruben Piqtoukun comments:

With the introduction of modern religion, the shaman has slowly disappeared, but they live through the artist in this day and age. Myself and my brother—we are the extensions of that. We are just a tool for somebody else. Some of the sculptures that I create are so powerful—it's as if they are emitting a life force.

*　　*　　*

David Ruben Piqtoukun's ancestry combines Bering Sea Inupiaq from Alaska and Mackenzie Delta Inuit from Canada. In his early childhood he learned to hunt on the land, but then experienced cultural isolation in the residential schooling system. Inuit as well as "southern" themes and styles are synthesized in his work.

Piqtoukun credits his younger brother, Abraham Anghik, with being his main artistic influence:

"I ended up in Vancouver with my brother Abraham Anghik in May of 1972. He had studied art at the University of Alaska for a few years and I was fascinated by what he was doing. I decided to try my hand at carving. I took his stone scraps and he gave me instructions about how to use the tools. I left a few months later and kept carving. I was determined to make the material work. The first carvings I did were small stone pendants into which I carved animals in relief. Edith Clark of the Gallery of British Columbia Arts bought my first stone carvings for $56 and I suddenly realized I could make a living out of this."

By the 1980s, Piqtoukun, like his brother, was achieving notable success with his work. One of Piqtoukun's strongest pieces is *Shaman Chanting* (1984), carved from Brazilian soapstone. Slightly smaller than human size, it depicts the head and shoulders of a shaman whose upraised hands grasp rattles. On one face of the work, the shaman chants, his brow furrowed and his eyes closed in contemplation. On the reverse, we see the result—he has achieved transformation: his mouth sprouts fierce tusks, which were made from bear claws.

Shamanistic iconography has potent meaning for Piqtoukun, as it does for his brother. Both revere the stories of the powerful practitioners in their ancestry. It is hard to resist the interpretation that shamanistic transformation, and the doubling of images in *Shaman Chanting* and other works by this artist, also represents the doubling of identity for a young man who is both northern and southern, both rural Inuk and cosmopolitan city-dweller, both spokesman for an emergent Inuit identity and an individual artist forging his own identity.

Piqtoukun is interested in cross-cultural communication through art. At the invitation of the Canadian government he traveled to the Ivory Coast, Africa, in 1984, where he demonstrated stone carving techniques and interacted with local sculptors. Since then he has also led carving workshops in Mexico and the Dominican Republic.

In addition to many corporate and private collections, Piqtoukun's work is found in major Canadian museums, including the Art Gallery of Ontario, the Canadian Museum of Civilization, the McMichael Canadian Collection, and the Winnipeg Art Gallery, as well as the Staatliche Museum für Volkerkunde in Munich, Germany.

—Janet Catherine Berlo

PITSEOLAK

Variant names: Pitseolak Ashoona; Sea Pigeon
Tribal affiliations: Inuit
Printmaker

Born: Nottingham Island, Northwest Territories, c. 1904. **Family:** Married Ashoona, and together they had twelve children—four of whom became well-known artists (Koomwartok, Kaka, and Kiawak Ashoona, and Napatchie Pootoogook), two died in infancy, and four were adopted by other families. **Career:** Hunting, fishing, sewing, artist. Portrait was featured on a Canadian postage stamp that was part of a series honoring Canadian women, issued on International Women's Day, 1993. **Awards:** Elected to the Royal Canadian Academy of Arts in 1974; won a Canada Council Senior Arts Grant in 1975; received the Order of Canada in 1977. **Died:** 1983.

Individual Exhibitions

1971　　*Print Retrospective, 1962-1970,* Canadian Guild of Crafts Quebec, Montreal
　　　　The Inuit Gallery of Eskimo Art, Toronto
1975-77　*Pitseolak,* Department of Indian and Northern Affairs in cooperation with the West-Baffin Eskimo Cooperative, Cape Dorset, Ottawa (traveling)
1982　　*Pitseolak Ashoona (1904-1983): An Unusual Life,* Ring House Gallery, University of Alberta, Edmonton

Selected Group Exhibitions

1960　　Cape Dorset Graphics (annual collection)
1967　　*Inoonoot Eskima: Grafik och Skulptur fran Cape Dorset och Povungnituk,* Konstframjandet, Stockholm, Sweden
1970　　*Graphic Art by Eskimos of Canada: First Collection,* Cultural Affairs Division, Department of External Affairs, Canada, Ottawa (traveling)
1973-74　*Lies Eskimos/De Eskimo's,* Studio 44 - Passage 44, Brussels, Belgium

1975-79 *We Lived by Animals/Nous Vivions des Animaux,* Department of Indian Affairs and Northern Development in cooperation with the Department of External Affairs, Ottawa (traveling)

1975-77 *Inuit Games/Inuit Pinguangit/Jeux des inuit,* Department of Indian Affairs and Northern Development, Ottawa (traveling)

1976-82 *Shamans and Spirits: Myths and Medical Symbolism in Eskimo Art,* Canadian Arctic Producers and the National Museum of Man, Ottawa (traveling)

1978 *Polar Vision: Canadian Eskimo Graphics,* Jerusalem Artists' House Museum, Israel

1980 *The Dorset Group of Four: Drawings and Prints by Kenojuak, Lucy, Parr and Pitseolak,* Canadiana Galleries, Edmonton, Alberta

La deesse inuite de la mer/The Inuit Sea Goddess, Musee des beaux-arts de Montreal, Montreal (traveling)

1981 *Eskimo Games: Graphics and Sculpture/Giuochi Eschimesi: grafiche e sculture,* National Gallery of Modern Art, Rome

1981-83 *Cape Dorset Engravings,* Department of Indian Affairs and Northern Development, circulated by the Art Gallery of Ontario, Toronto (traveling)

1983-85 *Contemporary Indian and Inuit Art of Canada,* Department of Indian Affairs and Northern Development, Ottawa, presented at the General Assembly Building, United Nations, New York (traveling)

1987 *The Matriarchs: Jessie Oonark, Helen Kalvak, Pitseolak Ashoona,* Snow Goose Associates, Seattle

1988-89 *Im Schatten der Sonne: Zeitgenossische Kunst der Indianer und Eskimos in Kanada/In the Shadow of the Sun: Contemporary Indian and Inuit Art in Canada,* Canadian Museum of Civilization, Ottawa, (traveling)

1989 *Spoken in Stone: an exhibition of Inuit Art,* Whyte Museum of the Canadian Rockies, Banff, Alberta (traveling)

1991 *Soujourns to Nunavut: Contemporary Inuit Art from Canada,* Bunkamura Art Gallery, Tokyo (traveling)

1994 *Kunst aus der Arktis,* Volkerkundmuseum der Universitat Zurich, Switzerland

1995 *Immaginario Inuit,* Arte e cultura degli esquimesi canadesi, Galleria d'Arte Moderna e Contemporanea, Verona, Italy

Collections

Agnes Etherington Art Centre, Queen's University, Kingston, Ontario; Amon Carter Museum of Western Art, Fort Worth, Texas; Anchorage Museum of History and Art, Alaska; Art Gallery of Greater Victoria, British Columbia; Art Gallery of Windsor, Ontario; Art Gallery of York University, Downsview, Ontario; Beaverbrook Art Gallery, Fredericton, New Brunswick; Canada Council Art Bank, Ottawa; CIBC Collection, Toronto; Canadian Guild of Crafts Quebec, Montreal; Canadian Museum of Civilization, Hull, Quebec; Clifford E. Lee Collection, University of Alberta, Edmonton; Cultural Affairs Division, Department of External Affairs Canada, Ottawa; Dennos Museum Center, Northwestern Michigan College, Traverse City; Edmonton Art Gallery, Alberta; Fitzgerald Collection, Whyte Museum of the Canadian Rockies, Banff, Alberta; Glenbow Museum, Calgary, Alberta; Haffenreffer Museum of Anthropology, Brown University, Bristol, Rhode Island; Kitchener-

Waterloo Art Gallery, Kitchener, Ontario; Klamer Family Collection, Art Gallery of Ontario, Toronto; Laurentian University Museum and Arts Centre, Sudbury, Ontario; London Regional Art Gallery, Ontario; MacDonald Stewart Art Centre, Guelph, Ontario; McMichael Canadian Art Collection, Kleinburg, Ontario; Mendel Art Gallery, Saskatoon, Saskatchewan; Musee des beaux-arts de Montreal, Quebec; Museum of Anthropology, University of British Columbia, Vancouver; Museum of Modern Art, New York; National Gallery of Canada, Ottawa; Prince of Wales Northern Heritage Centre, Yellowknife, Northwest Territories; Royal Ontario Museum, Toronto; Simon Fraser Gallery, Simon Fraser University, Burnaby, British Columbia; Smith College Museum of Art, Northampton, Massachusetts; Tom Thomson Memorial Gallery and Museum of Fine Art, Owen Sound, Ontario; University of Alberta, Edmonton; University of Lethbridge Art Gallery, Alberta; University of New Brunswick, Fredericton; Vancouver Art Gallery, British Columbia; Whyte Museum of the Canadian Rockies, Banff, Alberta; Winnipeg Art Gallery, Manitoba; Woodstock Public Art Gallery, Woodstock, Ontario.

Publications

On PITSEOLAK: Book—*Pitseolak: Pictures Out of My Life,* with Dorothy Eber, Montreal, Design Collaborative Books, in association with Oxford University Press, Toronto, 1971. **Articles**—"The Ashoonas of Cape Dorset: In Touch with Tradition," by Marion E. Jackson, *North/Nord,* vol. 29, no. 3, Fall, 1982; "Pitseolak Ashoona: An Unusual Life," by Bente Roed Cochran, *Inuit Art Quarterly,* vol. 2, no. 2, Spring, 1987; "The Power of the Pencil: Inuit Women in the Graphic Arts," by Janet Catherine Berlo, *Inuit Art Quarterly,* vol. 5, no. 1, Winter, 1990; "The Ashoona Family of Cape Dorset," by Alison Gillmore, *Inuit Art Quarterly,* vol. 10, no. 2, Summer, 1995. **Film**—*The Way We Live Today* and *Spirits and Monsters,* produced by the International Cinemedia Centre Ltd, 1971.

*

Pitseolak comments (1971):

"I am happy doing the (drawings). After my husband died I felt very alone and unwanted; making (drawings) is what has made me happiest since he died. I am going to keep on doing them until they tell me to stop. If no one tells me to stop, I shall make them as long as I am well. If I can, I'll make them even after I am dead."

*   *   *

Born in the first decade of the twentieth century, Pitseolak belongs to the last generation of Inuit to grow to maturity in the old traditions of the Inuit culture. She was born on Nottingham Island in Hudson Bay where her family spent the winter after their migration by skin boat from Arctic Quebec to Baffin Island. As a child, Pitseolak (which means "sea pigeon" in the Inuktitut language) learned to prepare skins, to sew skin garments and to manage the traditional women's roles of the Inuit culture. Her childhood was one of traditional life on the land, of hunting and fishing, of absorbing the legends and wisdom of the elders, and of experiencing shamans performing.

As a very young woman, Pitseolak was married to a young and self-reliant hunter, Ashoona, and they made their life together along the coast and inland on the Foxe Peninsula of Baffin Island. Pitseolak and Ashoona had twelve children, two of whom died in infancy and

Pitseolak. Photograph by Marion Jackson.

four of whom were adopted by other families. Then suddenly, when Pitseolak was in her forties, Ashoona died of illness, leaving her with young dependent children. Pitseolak moved with her children to Cape Dorset and settled in the small but growing community where government health and social services were becoming available and where efforts were already under way to establish arts projects to bring income into the settlement.

Eager to provide for herself and her children, Pitseolak used her traditional skills to make parkas, boots and other items for the local sewing project. Later, encouraged by the artist and local Govern-

ment Administrator, James Houston, and inspired by her cousin Kiakshuk, Pitseolak hesitantly tried her hand at drawing. Four of Pitseolak's images were selected to be translated into stonecut prints in Cape Dorset's second annual print collection in 1960, and she remained an active contributor to Cape Dorset's yearly collections until her death in 1983.

Though Pitseolak engraved a few copper plates during the 1960s, she disliked the process (and the frequent cuts she suffered when the tools slipped) and concentrated primarily on drawing. In the last two decades of her life, Pitseolak Ashoona made more than

7,000 images, 233 of which were translated into prints in the annual Cape Dorset collections. Her lively images are often playful and characterized by a sense of humor and *joie de vivre*. Subject matter is most often taken from her memories of her years on the land. Scenes of camping, families traveling, children playing, and fanciful vignettes of animals and birds adopting patterns of human behavior are among her favored subjects. Her drawings sometimes make references to traditional legends and include representations of Taleelayu, or fantasy figures. Regardless of their content, however, Pitseolak's images are consistently expressive of her own resilience and optimism, qualities essential to survival in the traditional Inuit culture. Her lively line, her joyful color combinations and her attention to small but amusing details make her drawings a source of enjoyment and viewing pleasure.

Prolific and consistently active as an artist, Pitseolak Ashoona became a model and inspiration for others in Cape Dorset. Four of her own children became well-known artists. Her daughter, Napachie Pootoogook, became a famous graphic artist, and three of her sons—Kiawak, Kaka and Koomwartok—became well-known sculptors. Others artists in the community, such as her daughter-in-law, Sorosilutu, also looked to Pitseolak for encouragement and guidance. Through her success as an artist, Pitseolak rose from a position of poverty to a position of independence in her community, and she became a respected matriarch, frequently representing the artists' cooperative and meeting dignitaries visiting Cape Dorset.

During her lifetime, Pitseolak Ashoona received considerable recognition outside the community of Cape Dorset as well. Almost every major group exhibition of Inuit art after 1960 has included work by Pitseolak Ashoona, and she received several special commissions for commemorative folios of print images. In 1971, Pitseolak collaborated with Montreal writer, Dorothy Eber, to produce a bilingual book of drawings and reminiscences in English and Inuktitut, *Pitseolak: Pictures Out of My Life*. A film by the same name was produced later that same year by the National Film Board of Canada. In addition, Pitseolak Ashoona was accorded various honors, including election to the Royal Canadian Academy of Arts in 1974, a Canada Council Senior Arts Grant in 1975, and the Order of Canada in 1977. In 1993, Pitseolak's portrait was featured on a Canadian postage stamp as part of a series of stamps honoring Canadian women issued on International Women's Day. Although Pitseolak Ashoona initially turned to art for pragmatic reasons, a way to earn an income to support herself and her family, she began to find great enjoyment in drawing, and it eventually became central to her life.

—Marion E. Jackson

PITT, Lillian

Variant names: Wakamu
Tribal affiliations: Warm Springs Yakima; Wasco
Ceramist and sculptor

Born: Warm Springs, Oregon, 10 October 1943. **Education:** Mt. Hood Community College, Gresham, Oregon, 1981; study papermaking with a Japanese Master and techniques in willow and bronze in Wisconsin. **Career:** Hairstylist for 15 years; while studying Human Services, she took a ceramics class as an elective and has

Lillian Pitt. Courtesy of the artist.

been a self-employed artist since 1981. **Awards:** 1990 Governor's Award for the Arts, Oregon; 1986 Purchase Award, Metropolitan Arts Commission, Portland, Oregon.

Individual Exhibitions

1991   Galleria Posada, Sacramento, California
        Spirit Square Art Center, Charlotte, North Carolina
1992   *Out of the Earth*, Salishan Lodge, Gleneden Beach, Oregon
1993   Governor Barbara Roberts Office, Salem, Oregon
        Art of the People, Sunbird Gallery, Bend, Oregon
1994   *Honoring our Ancestors*, Quintana Gallery, Portland, Oregon
        Plateau Spirits: Works by Lillian Pitt, Institute of American Indian Studies, Washington, Connecticut
1995   *Plateau Spirits*, Quintana Gallery, Portland, Oregon
        Carolyn Ruf Gallery, Minneapolis, Minnesota
        Memorial Union Gallery, U.C. Davis (During conference "Rewriting the Pacific: Cultures, Frontiers and Migration of Metaphors")
1996   Sunbird Gallery, Bend, Oregon
        Detroit Art Gallery, Detroit, Michigan
        Forest Spirits, Quintana Gallery, Portland, Oregon
        Native American Tradition/ Contemporary Responses, Society for Contemporary Crafts, Pittsburgh, Pennsylvania

Selected Group Exhibitions

1984   *No Beads No Trinkets*, Palais de Nations, Geneva, Switzerland

1986   *Women of Sweetgrass, Cedar & Sage*, American Indian Community House, New York (traveling, U.S. and Canada)

1987   *New Directions Northwest: Contemporary Native American Art*, travelling show (catalog)

1990   *Contemporary Native American Art*, Montana State University, Bozeman

1991   *Ancient Images from the Columbia River Gorge*, Maryhill Museum, Goldendale, Washington

Wood Spirits, Galleria Mesa, Mesa, Arizona

1992   Ceramic Invitational, Renshaw Gallery, Linfield College, McMinville, Oregon

1993   *Dear Sister*, (Show with Amy Cordova), Carolyn Ruff Gallery, Minneapolis, Minnesota

Crosscut, Portland Art Museum, Portland, Oregon

Tribal Member's Show, Museum at Warm Springs, Warm Springs, Oregon

Contemporary Art Work, Te Taumata, Aukland, New Zealand

Buyer's Market, Rosen Art and Crafts Exposition, Philadelphia, Pennsylvania

Spirits Keep Whistling Us Home, Sacred Circle Gallery, Seattle, Washington

Northwest Native American and First Nations Peoples Art, Western Washington University, Bellingham, Washington

Art of the People, Sunbird Gallery, Bend, Oregon

1994   *Feats of Clay*, Lincoln Arts Center (Juried Show), Lincoln, California

Works of Three Native American Women, Adobe East Gallery, Summit, New Jersey

Watchful Eyes: Native American Women Artists, Heard Museum, Phoenix, Arizona

Artists Who are Indian, Denver Art Museum, Denver, Colorado

1995   *Indian Humor*, American Indian Contemporary Arts, San Francisco, California

Setting the Stage: A Contemporary View of the West, Eiteljorg Museum, Indianapolis, Indiana

Te Atinga, International Exhibit, Rotorua, New Zealand

Contemporary Totems, Bush Barn Gallery, Salem, Oregon

Sisters of the Earth, Holter Museum, Helena, Montana

Tacoma Art Museum, (Juried Show), Tacoma, Washington

Sculpture '95, Sacred Circle Gallery, Seattle, Washington

Oregon Biennial, Portland Art Museum, Portland, Oregon

1996   *Art of the People*, Sunbird Gallery, Bend, Oregon

Collections

City of Hillsboro, Justice Center, Hillsboro, Oregon; City of Oguni, Japan; R.C. Gorman Gallery, Taos, New Mexico; Heard Museum, Phoenix, Arizona; Indian Arts & Crafts Board, Washington, D.C.; Indianhead Gaming Center, Warm Springs, Oregon; Native Arts Council of the Portland Art Museum, Portland, Oregon; Oregon

State Bar Association, Portland, Oregon; Sapporo City Hall, Sapporo, Japan; Washington State Historical Museum, Tacoma, Washington; Yakima Cultural Heritage Museum, Yakima, Washington.

Publications

On Pitt—*Women in American Indian Society*, by Rayna Green, New York: Chelsea House Publishers; *The Craft Person Speaks: Artists in Varied Media Discuss Their Crafts*, Joan Jeffri (Ed.), Westwood, Connecticut: Greenwood Press, *American Women Sculptors*, by Charlotte Streifer Rubenstein, Boston: G.K. Hall & Co.; *A Time of Gathering: Masterworks of Washington Native Art*, Robin K. Wright (Ed.), Seattle: University of Washington Press; *Columbia River Basketry: Gifts of the Ancestors, Gifts of the Earth*, by Mary Schlick, Seattle: University of Washington Press.

*

Lillian Pitt comments:

The focus of my current sculptural work has been to combine diverse materials to create a rich visual context for the stoneware forms I hand build and fire. I combine beads, feathers, shells, strands of copper wire, stones, tread, and peeled or weathered wood—materials which allow for startling juxtapositions of texture and color that move the eye. With these materials, sometimes I adorn the work; at other times I mend or reassemble things that have been torn asunder. My aim is to heal the things of this wounded planet by creating a consciousness of the need for healing and a sense of the transformative magic in ordinary things and beings. I orient my work in relation to the four directions, the seven directions, and at times celebrate the ancient stories of my Warm Springs, Wasco, and Wishxam ancestors in the imagery I create. There are also times when new characters are born in response to the contradictions caused by remembering the traditions that reveal the madness of current culture, which destroys so much that has sustained life in our world. These characters tell their own stories and new myths are born as I reflect on their meaning. In this work, I aim to create a visual language that will translate the stress on things in the natural world into a voice that will make everyone aware of the responsibility we all have to work inside the circle of things that supports life on earth.

*   *   *

Lillian Pitt has been pursuing her art for a relatively short time, yet, her work reaches across time and geography. Her pieces are creations of characters and reminders. Primarily acclaimed as a maker of ceramic masks in the ancient methods of Raku, from 17th century Japan, and Anagama, from 8th century Korea, Pitt continually pushes to expand her basic forms through new media such as sculpture and installations.

For inspiration, Pitt looks to pictographs of the Columbia River Gorge area of the Northwestern United States—the lands of her ancestors. Many of her masks are born from legends and the characters portrayed in them. One of her most easily recognizable pieces, *She-Who-Watches*, comes from these pictographic images and recounts the legend of the last of the woman chiefs who, after teaching her people to live in the manner that was right, was turned into a rock to watch over them. Her well known "stick people," or Steah-hah in Chinook jargon, easily distinguished by their pursed

Lillian Pitt: *Wannapambhe Who Watches*, **1993. Courtesy of the artist.**

lips, are known for leading good people who are lost to safety and bad people who are lost to a painful demise. Pitt is the first person to create a visual image for these mythical forest dwellers.

Pitt has drawn from a variety of ancient and contemporary sources to fuel the development of other series of works. One series depicts women from her ancestry. Another consists of animal masks created as a reaction to the 1988 fire in Yellowstone National Park where loss of animal life was devastating. With these mask creations, the animals, through the clay, were not destroyed by the fire (kiln) but rather born from it, thus completing the circle and leaving a permanent visual reminder.

The masks Pitt creates are not intended to convey a hidden meaning, rather they are made with the simple desire to make people feel better about their circumstances and the world around them, and with luck, this will lead to a domino effect where one person feels good and passes it on to the next. She makes no spiritual claims regarding her pieces, yet, she has also indicated that she aims to "heal the things of this wounded planet by creating a consciousness of the need for healing and a sense of the transformative magic in ordinary things and beings." The strongest reactions to Pitt's work, therefore, may not be intentional manipulations on her part. These masks may instead act simply as doors for the viewer, enabling him or her to explore their own personal journey.

After 15 years as a hairdresser, back problems forced Pitt to explore other career options. While attending college in the field of social services she enrolled in a ceramics course as an elective. Unable to sit at a potter's wheel for long periods of time, her instructor encouraged her to try the Raku method instead.

Initially, she studied the traditional mask forms of many of the Northwest Coast peoples, including the Tlingit, Haida, and even Inuit. Her investigations led her further away from home to other cultures around the world, developing a special interest in Maori people and styles of New Zealand. It is interesting that, although many of her basic images come from her own ancestral lands, the methods she chooses to establish these images come from a net she has cast around the globe. The primary methods she chooses to develop her masks stem from ancient traditions in Japan and Korea. Both the Japanese Raku and the Korean Anagama methods indicate Pitt's lack of a need to control both the reactions of the viewers and her own process of creation. Through both of these processes, Pitt controls the choice of clay, the sculpted shape, and the placement within the kiln. She has no control over how the unpredictable forces of heat, fire, and smoke will affect the mask. Anagama, in particular, is a creative act of faith, since this process of using an uphill kiln embedded in the earth, requiring a fire to be meticulously stoked by a team of volunteers for 56 hours, actually destroys half of the pieces in the process.

After the firing, Pitt's masks undergo a process that brings them home, back to her Northwest roots. Each mask, to a greater or lesser extent, is embellished with objects that come mostly from the area of her ancestry and her current home in Portland. Adornments include prominent feathers, shells, beads, sticks, wire and other pieces of metal, buckskin, peeled or weathered wood, bones and clay—all representing the natural world.

Conscious of the potential to limit her scope as an artist, Lillian Pitt seeks opportunities to expand her works into new forms and media. She has recently started working in freestanding sculpture and installation pieces while still using the mask work as a seed for the new creations. Further, she looks for new skills, textures and materials to influence her main body of work. Her exploration has led to her being invited to study papermaking with a Japanese Master and travelling to Wisconsin to learn techniques in willow and bronze.

Pitt indicates that she is not involved in rituals, although people read many ritualistic meanings into her masks. Whether lavishly adorned or starkly simple, Pitt's masks have an energy all of their own, and each have long ties to many societies. Given the traditional role of masks in many societies, it may be that her involvement in rituals comes from the act of creating, which is a form of ritual in itself. She has stated: "My tradition, my heritage, my love for the land and the people are spoken through my work. My masks reveal my feelings about our land, trees, animals; ancient ones . . . ancient ways. Other feelings may occur along with this love—such as concern, hope, respect and sometimes, anger and angst."

—Vesta Giles

POINT, Susan

Tribal affiliations: Coast Salish
Painter, jewelry designer, carver, and sculptor

Born: Alert Bay, British Columbia, 5 April 1952. **Education:** Academic artistic training in Interior Design (Primary School of Design,

Burnaby, British Columbia), engraving, metallurgy, metal deformation (Vancouver Community College), printmaking Behnson Graphics and Prism Graphics (Vancouver), Woodblock printing and stone litho at New Leaf Press, acrylic painting at Cannell Agencies, bas relief at Image Concrete, pattern making and asting at Seattle Metro Transit Design and Urban Accessories (Seattle, Washington), handmade paper making with Sharon Yuen (Vancouver, British Columbia), wood carving with master carver John Livingstone (Victoria, British Columbia), glass carving with David Montpetit (North Vancouver, British Columbia). **Career:** Professional artist; various commissions, including Vancouver International Airport, Vancouver, Parliament Buildings, Victoria, British Columbia, and U.B.C. First Nations House of Learning, Vancouver, British Columbia. **Family:** Married Jeff Cannell, 1980; four children: Brent Sparrow, Rhea Sparrow, Thomas Cannell, Kelly Cannell. **Career:** Professional Artist, Council Member for Musqueam Indian Band, Board Member for Emily Carr Institute of Art and Design. **Agent:** c/o Coast Salish Arts, 3917 West 51st Ave., Vancouver, British Columbia, V6N 3V9; phone: (604)266-7374, fax (604)261-5683.

Individual Exhibitions

1983 *Native Indian Exhibition*, Delta Museum and Archives, Ladner, British Columbia

1985-86 *Procope - Coast Salish Limited Edition Seriographs by Susan A. Point*, Vancouver, British Columbia

1986 *New Visions - Seriographs by Susan A. Point, Coast Salish Artist*, U.B.C. Museum of Anthropology, Vancouver, British Columbia (traveling)

1987 *Coast Salish Impressions*, Gateway Theatre, Richmond Art Gallery Exhibition, Richmond, British Columbia
 Eskimo Art Gallery, Edmonton, Alberta

1988 *New Visions - Seriographs by Susan A. Point, Coast Salish Artist*, Stellacoom Tribal Museum, Stellacoom, Washington (traveling)

1989 *Susan A. Point*, SANDIA, Galerie fur Indianerkunst Nordamerikas, Basel, Switzerland

1990 *Salish Point*, Canadian Museum of Civilization, Ottawa, Ontario
 The Art Space Gallery, Philadelphia, Pennsylvania

1992 Ronin Gallery, Victoria, British Columbia
 Northwest Coast Prints, Sacred Circle Gallery of American Indian Art, Daybreak Star Arts Center, Discovery Park, Seattle, Washington

1994 Ancestral Journey Gallery, Victoria, British Columbia

1994-96 *Point on Granville Island*, New Leaf Editions, Vancouver, British Columbia

1996 Emily Carr House, Victoria, British Columbia

Selected Group Exhibitions

1982 *Art of the Northwest Coast*, London Regional Art Gallery, London, Ontario.

1985 *The Northwest Coast Native Print*, Art Gallery of Greater Victoria, Victoria, British Columbia
 Images of Coast Salish Culture, Fraser Valley College, Abbotsford, British Columbia
 Northwest Coast Indian Prints, Richmond Art Gallery, Richmond, British Columbia
 Coast Salish Art, East Lake Gallery, Belleview, Washington

Susan Point in her studio. Courtesy of the artist.

1986   *Northwest Coast Native Art Show*, Sacred Circle Gallery
         of American Indian Art, Seattle, Washington, USA
         *Salish Images: Northwest Coast Artists Tribute to Salish
         Art*, U.B.C. Museum of Anthropology, Vancouver,
         British Columbia
         Cultural Treasures, U.B.C. Museum of Anthropology,
         Vancouver, British Columbia
         Western Pacific Engravers, Vancouver, British Colum-
         bia
         All Native Indian Womens' Show, Images of Canadian
         Heritage, Vancouver, British Columbia
         Northwest Coast Indian Art, Robson Media Centre,
         Vancouver, British Columbia
         Pacific Northwest Art Expo, Seattle Trade Centre, Seattle,
         Washington
         Sacred Circle Gallery of American Indian Art, Seattle,
         Washington
1987   *Quintana's Northwest Coast Indian Art Show*, Gallery of
         Indian Art, Portland, Oregon
1988   Centre Culturel de Pointe Claire, Montreal, Quebec

In the Shadow of the Sun, (traveling exhibition in Ger-
many, Canada, USA, France, England, and Japan), Ca-
nadian Museum of Civilization, Ottawa, Ontario
Gallerie: Womens Art, 45 Women Artists from Across
Canada and USA, Book Launching and Art Show,
Women in Focus, Vancouver, British Columbia
Gateway to Art :The $100,000 Art Auction, Richmond
Art Gallery, Richmond, British Columbia
1989   *Art Salish*, Guilde Canadienne des Metlers d'art Quebec,
         Canadian Guild of Crafts Quebec, Montreal, Quebec
         Susan A. Point, Joe David, Lawrence Paul, Indianische
         Kunstler der Westkuste Kanadas Volkerkundemuseum
         der Universitat Zurich, Zurich, Switzerland
         Beyond Revival, Emily Carr College of Art, Charles Scott
         Gallery, Vancouver, British Columbia
         *Fear-Of-Others, International Art Exhibit Against Rac-
         ism*, Vancouver, British Columbia (traveling)
1990   Thunder Bay Art Gallery, Thunder Bay National Exhibi-
         tion Centre & Centre for Indian Art, Thunder Bay,
         Ontario

Susan Point: *Images.* **Courtesy of the artist.**

Contemporary Coast Salish, Thomas Burke Memorial, Washington State Museum, University of Washington, Seattle

Changing Forms, Enduring Spirit, Anne Gould Hauberg Gallery, Pacific Arts Centre at the Seattle Centre, Seattle, Washington

Salish Design: Drums, Paintings and Prints by Susan A. Point, Coast Salish Artist, The Legacy Ltd., Seattle, Washington

In the Shadow of the Sun, Art Gallery of Nova Scotia, Halifax, Nova Scotia (travelling)

Dance, The Legacy Ltd., Seattle, Washington

The Legacy 1500: Small Treasures from the Northwest Coast, The Legacy Ltd., Seattle, Washington

1992 The Art Space Gallery, Philadelphia, Pennsylvania

Here Today, Open Space Gallery, Victoria, British Columbia

Museu Da Gravura Cidade De Curitiba, Parana, Brasil

First Northwest Native Women's Art Exhibit, Granville Native Art, Vancouver, British Columbia

1993 The Western Gallery, Western Washington University, Seattle, Washington

Mythological Creatures of the Northwest, Stonington Gallery, Seattle, Washington

Wear It!—Northwest Coast Designs in Contemporary Clothing and Jewelry, The Legacy Ltd., Seattle, Washington

1994 *Frogs: Leaps of Imagination*, Stonington Gallery, Seattle, Washington

Bit Im Presseclub, Zeitgenossische Kunst der Indianer der Nordwestkuste Kanada, Bonn, Germany

Exhibition of Northwest Coast Indian Art, Nordamerican Indian Museum, Zurich, Switzerland

First Nations Print Exhibition, Art Gallery of Greater Victoria, Victoria, British Columbia

Life of the Copper: A Common Wealth of Tribal Nations, Alcheringa Gallery, Victoria, British Columbia

1995 *The 6th Native American Fine Arts Invitational*, Phoenix, Arizona

Agents of Change: New Views by Northwest Women, Seafirst Gallery, Washington State Convention & Trade Centre, Seattle, Washington

Women Across the Arts, Friesen Gallery, Seattle, Washington

Expressions of Spirit: Contemporary American Indian Art, Wheelwright Museum of the American Indian, Santa Fe, New Mexico

Creatures of the Deep, Stonington Gallery, Seattle, Washington

1996 *Remember the Way - Art of the Native Northwest*, American Indian Contemporary Arts, San Francisco

New Directions Northwest, Royal British Columbia Museum, Victoria, British Columbia

Metamorphosis: Recent Work by Artists, Richmond Art Gallery, Richmond, British Columbia

1996-97 *Topographies: Aspects of Recent British Columbia Art*, Vancouver Art Gallery, Vancouver, British Columbia

Collections

King County Arts Commission, Seattle, Washington; Natural Resource Building (Washington State Arts Commission), Olympia,

Washington; Volkerkundemuseum der Universitat Zurich, Zurich, Switzerland; U.B.C. Museum of Anthropology, Vancouver, British Columbia.

Publications

On POINT: Books—*Indianische Kunstler der Westkuste Kanadas Volkerkundemuseum der Universitat Zurich. Susan A. Point, Joe David, Lawrence Paul*, Zurich, Switzerland, 1989; *From Periphery to Centre: The Art of Susan and Krista Point*, by Joanne Danford, Thunder Bay Art Gallery, Thunder Bay, Ontario, 1989. **Articles**—"Preserving the Traditions of the Coast Salish," *The Georgia Straight*, July 25-August 1, 1996; "Galleries," *Where Vancouver*, July 1996; "Northwest Coast Carving: An Evolving Tradition," by Barbara Hager, *Indian Artist*, Fall 1996.

*

Susan Point comments:

Coast Salish art is relatively unknown to most people today as it was an almost lost art form after European contact; the reason being is that Salish lands were the first to be settled by the Europeans, which adversely affected my people's traditional life-style.

Today, much of the native art associated with the Pacific northwest coast is from principle tribes of northern British Columbia. Because of this, over the years, I spend a great deal of my time, as a Coast Salish artist, trying to revive traditional Coast Salish art in an attempt to educate the public to the fact that there was, and still is, another art form indigenous to the central Pacific northwest coast.

Although most of my earlier work is very traditional, today I am experimenting with contemporary mediums and themes. However, I still incorporate my ancestral design elements into my work to keep it uniquely Salish. Sometimes I address issues of gender conditioning as well as social and economic conditions.

In creating my art, I feel a need to continually express my cultural background and beliefs yet, at the same time, my work continues to evolve with changes within and outside of my community.

*　*　*

When people think of the great traditions of Northwest Coast art, it is usually the Haida and various Vancouver Island styles of totem poles that come to mind. Thanks to Susan Point, the distinct and luxurious Coast Salish style is gaining the attention it deserves. Point has spent years studying museum artifacts to learn the unique secrets of Coast Salish pieces. She is now leading the way by example as this form takes its place as one of the major styles of the coastal peoples. With over 15 major monumental public art pieces around the world and over 60 commissioned pieces in the past six years alone, her reputation as a prominent artist is well established.

Circles often recur in Point's work, reflecting her use of the spindle whorl, a hand held traditional wooden disk-shaped tool used in the process of spinning wool, as a basis for structuring prints, carvings and even large monumental sculptures. Pieces made with this tool were some of the first she was able to study in museum collections. Their form and elaborately carved surfaces have become a favorite starting point for Point in her work because of their inherent sense of movement and flow.

The circles that make up the framework for the whorls are classic and reach into nearly every civilization in the world. The spindle whorl itself is a traditional woman's tool, and circles have been associated with feminine spiritual symbolism to indicate the circle of life, change, transformation, birth, death and rebirth, evolution and even time. The whorls are in constant motion. Point allows, but does not force, feminine themes to drive the direction of many of her pieces, and has used the whorl form to express modern ideas of flight, gender issues and even violence against women. Choosing elemental materials, such as glass, cedar, metal and stone, she pushes the boundaries of her work into deep tradition and feminine spirituality.

In her work, Susan Point uses her detailed craftsmanship to bring the singular Coast Salish art forms into the public's awareness, extending the perception of Northwest Coast art beyond more familiar styles of the Haida and Vancouver Island communities. Yet, at the same time, she has indicated that she is against classification and distinctions between culture and environment, art and craft, traditional and contemporary.

Point has explored a wide variety of mediums and scales to further her explorations of the modern potential for the Salish style. She has turned to precious metals, serigraphs, acrylic paints, glass etchings, wood carving, as well as large scale monumental art in wood, stainless steel, glass and concrete. Through these modes Point takes advantage of identifiable Salish design elements such as the U forms, crescents and wedges in a style that is looser and less constricted than the more familiar northwest forms. Images portrayed are the traditional figures of birds, animals, and humans, all with a distinct sense of realism and movement that is uniquely Salish.

Another distinctive Salish carving trait is the frequent creation of multi-level engraved surfaces, producing a unique, three-dimensional series of figures that often overlap. This has been described as a blend of block engraving and low relief sculpture in the same piece. Point's personal style has evolved with clean lines her own way of blending forms in two dimensional pieces.

In each medium she works in, explores all possible aspects of the relationship between positive and negative space and the individual secrets of each. As a result, the viewer never sees a flat or static image. Even in her serigraphs and paintings, the viewer is required to continually dissect, reassemble and even reconsider the images and their relationships to the rest of the piece, as the weight of the images seems to move and change before the eyes.

Point is now taking another step in absorbing and defining the Coast Salish style. In 1995 she was commissioned by the U.B.C. Museum of Anthropology to reconstruct a group of Coast Salish artifacts using only badly charred prehistoric fragments of bone, wood, and antler, all dated in the last century B.C.E., as a frame of reference. She is recreating these images as pen and ink illustrations, colored renderings, and actual carvings in antler and bone for an upcoming exhibition, *Written in the Earth: Coast Salish Prehistoric Art.*

Point has been quite successful in educating the public about her ancestral artistic forms. Some of her recent public displays include several large pieces at the new terminal for the Vancouver International Airport. There a 17 foot "female" house post, a 16 foot red cedar spindle whorl with a flight theme, carved cedar panels, and 37" by 47" glass panels greet visitors arriving in Vancouver and the traditional lands of the Coast Salish people.

—Vesta Giles

POITRAS, Edward
Tribal affiliations: Métis
Sculptor and installation artist

Born: Regina, Saskatchewan, 1953. **Education:** Saskatchewan Indian Cultural College, Saskatoon, 1974; Manitou College, La Macaza, Quebec, student and teaching assistant, 1975-76. **Career:** Instructor, Indian Art, Saskatchewan Indian Cultural College, Saskatoon, 1976-78; graphic artist, *New Breed* magazine, Association of Métis and Non-Status Indians of Saskatchewan, Regina; Lecturer, Indian Art Department, Saskatchewan Indian Federated College, University of Regina, Saskatchewan, 1981-84, 1989-90, and University of Manitoba, Winnipeg in 1978.

Individual Exhibitions

1983   *Day Break Sentinel,* A.K.A., Saskatoon, Saskatchewan
1985   *Artist-in-Residence Exhibition,* Department of Indian Affairs, Hull, Quebec
        Edward Poitras, Department of Indian Affairs, Ottawa, Ontario
1987   *Warm Gun: Works on the Wall,* Cultural Exchange Society, Regina, Saskatchewan
1988   *Edward Poitras: Indian Territory,* Mendel Art Gallery, Saskatoon, Saskatchewan
        Big Iron Sky, Thunder Bay Art Gallery, Thunder Bay, Ontario
1989   *Nation Sauvage,* Galerie Le lieu, Quebec
        Et in America Ego ..., Art Speak, Vancouver
1991   *Marginal Recession,* Dunlop Art Gallery, Regina, Saskatchewan
        Edward Poitras: Installation, Articule, Montreal
1993   *Three Lemons and a Dead Coyote,* Ottawa School of Art
1996   Canadian Museum of Civilization, Hull, Quebec

Selected Group Exhibitions

1975   *Contemporary Native Art,* Native North American Institute, Montreal
1976   Heard Museum, Phoenix, Arizona
1980   Rosemont Art Gallery, Regina, Saskatchewan
        Traditions and Change, touring
1982   *New Work by a New Generation,* Norman Mackenzie Art Gallery, Regina, Saskatchewan
1983   *The 2nd Annual Wild West Show,* Alberta College of Art, Calgary, Alberta
        Twp Way Risk, A.K.A. Gallery, Saskatoon, Saskatchewan
1984   *Horses Fly Too: Bob Boyer/Edward Poitras,* Norman Mackenzie Art Gallery, Regina, Saskatchewan
        Susan Whitney Gallery, Regina, Saskatchewan
1985   *Small Matters, Neutral Ground,* Regina, Saskatchewan
1986   *Stardusters,* Thunder Bay Art Gallery, Thunder Bay, Ontario
        Another Prairie, The Art Gallery at Harbourfront, Toronto, Ontario
        Cross Cultural Views, National Gallery of Canada, Ottawa
1987   *Drawing Out the Form: Sculpture Touched by Drawing,* The Nickel Art Museum, Calgary, Alberta

1988   *In the Shadow of the Sun,* Canadian Museum of Civilization, Hull, Quebec
        Revisions, Walter Phillips Gallery, Banff, Alberta
1989   *Canadian Biennial of Contemporary Art,* National Gallery of Canada, Ottawa
1990   *Toward a History of the Found Object,* Mendel Art Gallery, Saskatoon, Saskatchewan
        Seeing Red, Agnes Etherington Art Centre, Kingston, Ontario
        Savoire-Vivre, Savoir-Faire, Savoir-Etre, Centre International d'Art Contemporain de Montreal, Quebec
1991   *Humans and the Environment,* Museum of Modern Art, Tampere, Finland
        L'oeil amerindien. Regards sur l'animal, Musee de la civilisation, Hull, Quebec
1992   *New Territories,* city-wide exhibition organized by Vision Planetarie, Montreal, Quebec
1993   *Rethinking History,* Mercer Union: A Centre for Contemporary Visual Art, Toronto
        As Snow before the Summer Sun (outdoor installation), Woodland Cultural Centre, Brantford, Ontario
        A Billboard Exhibition, Mendel Art Gallery, Saskatoon, Saskatchewan
        Indigenia, Canadian Museum of Civilization, Hull, Quebec
1995   *Le Canada a la XLVI biennale de Venise des Arts Visuels,* Venice, Italy

Collections

Canadian Broadcasting Corporation, Regina, Saskatchewan; Canadian Museum of Civilization, Hull, Quebec; City of Regina, Saskatchewan; Department of Indian and Northern Affairs, Hull, Quebec; Agnes Etherington Art Centre, Kingston, Ontario; Norman Mackenzie Art Gallery, Regina, Saskatchewan; Mendel Art Gallery, Saskatoon, Saskatchewan; Saskatchewan Arts Board, Regina, Saskatchewan; SakTel Corporation, Regina, Saskatchewan; Thunder Bay Art Gallery, Thunder Bay, Ontario.

Publications

On POITRAS: Books—"Moderne-Postmoderne: Edward Poitras," by Gerald McMaster and Deidre Tedds, Zeilgenoosische Kunst der Indianer und Eskimos in Kanada, Ottawa, 1988; *In Eye of Nature,* Dana Augaitas, editor, Banff, Alberta, 1991. **Articles**—"Art Amerindian Contemporary Tradition," by Kay Woods, *Art West* 6, no. 10, 1981; "Horses Fly, Too," *Indian Art Sketch Book,* Spring 1985; "Edward Poitras," by Jacqueline Fry, *Parachute,* 41, September, 1986;"The Story Began Long Ago," by Gail Bourgeois, *Harbour Magazine of Art and Everyday Life,* Vol. 1, No. 3, 1991; "Reclaiming History: Robert Houle, Carl Beam and Edward Poitras," by Michael Bell, *Currents,* Vol. 7, No. 4, 1991; "Interview with Edward Poitras: Black Horse Offerings," *ArtsCraft,* Vol. 2, No. 4, 1991; "A Review of the Edward Poitras Installation at Articule," *Espace,* Vol. 7, No. 5, 1991; "Métis Artist's Coyotes are Hit of Venice Biennale," *The Montreal Gazette,* 17 June, 1995.

*   *   *

Throughout his career, Edward Poitras has been particularly distinguished by his installations, though the artist has produced some

sculptural work as well. From the outset, Poitras' production has
included the juxtaposition of found objects from nature and those
that are man-made. Often the latter are those that reflect the technological make-up of the contemporary world. The sometimes incongruous combination of the natural with the fabricated lends a
Duchampian air to the artist's work. Too, Poitras' work reveals the
influence of two of his teachers: Sarain Stump and Domingo
Cisneros. Poitras' work reflects their teachings in its concern with
traditional indigenous values regarding the land; with the ritualizing
of the art process; and with a self-imposed intention to be culturally responsible. Poitras has chosen to achieve the latter by producing works of art that rethink issues of representation and place.

The themes of many of Poitras works in the early years of his
career often dealt with the gap existing between the world views of
"traditional" Native communities and those that exist in the contemporary urban milieu. Often the work detailed a brutal exchange;
for example, in works such as *Internal Recall* and *Mythical Balance*
(both 1986), taut steel cables and twisted hemp ropes intimate the
tension accompanying the physical and psychological movement
"between two worlds," as well as the consequences of colonial
expansion.

Poitras' more recent work, such as *Offensive/Defensive* and *Rock
Hearts* (1988), have revealed the artist's exploration of issues of
identity and place, while works such as *Small Matters*, also 1988,
have found Poitras re-writing history from an aboriginal perspective. All of these activities—history-writing, identity politics, and
border crossing—are intimately connected with the artist's intention to construct aboriginal sites of location and self.

Poitras began exhibiting professionally in 1975. Subsequently,
he has been included in numerous important Canadian-produced
group exhibitions of the art of the First Nations, among them *Cross-
Cultural Views* (1986)—the first Native exhibition at the National
Gallery of Canada in Ottawa since 1927, and *In the Shadow of the
Sun* (1988), the inaugural exhibition for the Indian and Inuit Galler-
ies at the newly constructed Canadian Museum of Civilization,
Hull, the among many other prestigious and groundbreaking ef-
forts. As well, Poitras' work has been the focus of several solo
exhibitions, such as *Indian Territory* (1988) at the Mendel Art
Gallery, Saskatoon, and *Marginal Recession* (1991) at the Dunlop
Art Gallery, Regina.

Having built a body of work that is recognized as among the
most innovative in the country, Poitras is considered one of the
principal installation artists in Canada. Poitras was one of three
artists chosen to represent Canada at the XLVI Biennale di Venezia
in 1995.

—Carol Podedworny

POITRAS, Jane Ash

Tribal affiliations: Cree
Mixed media artist and printmaker

Born: Fort Chipewyan, Alberta, 11 October, 1951. **Education:**
University of Alberta, Edmonton, BS in microbiology, 1977, BFA
in printmaking, 1983; Columbia University, New York, MFA,
Printmaking, 1985; also studied at Yale University, New Haven,
Connecticut, 1982. **Career:** Industrial microbiologist, instructor,
artist. **Awards:** Several scholarships.

Individual Exhibitions

1985   Robert Vanderleelie Gallery, Edmonton, Alberta
1986   *Print and Collages,* Brignall Gallery, Toronto, Ontario
1987   *Sweat Lodge Etchings,* Museum of Anthropology, Uni-
        versity of British Columbia, Vancouver
1988   *Fort Chip Breakfast Club,* Fort Chipewyan, Alberta
1989   *Indigenous Blackboards,* Woltjen/Udell, New York
1990   *Power Shields,* New York; West End Gallery, Edmonton,
        Alberta
1991   *Peyote Visions,* Woltjen/Udell, New York; Vancouver,
        British Columbia
        Dream Vision, Elaine Horwitch Galleries, Phoenix, Ari-
        zona, Scottsdale, Arizona, Santa Fe, New Mexico
1992   *Americas,* Andalusian Pavilion at Expo '92, Seville, Spain
        Recycled Blackboards, Leo Kamen Gallery, Toronto,
        Ontario
1993   Thunder Bay Art Gallery, Thunder Bay, Ontario
1993-94 Leo Kamen Gallery, Toronto, Ontario
1994   Robertson Gallery, Ottawa, Ontario
1995   Hamburg Art Academy, Hamburg, Germany
        NewZones Gallery of Contemporary Art, Calgary,
        Alberta

Selected Group Exhibitions

1981   Canadian Galleries, Edmonton, Alberta
1982   Shadows Gallery Group, Edmonton, Alberta
        UCLA Third National Print Exhibition, Los Angeles, Cali-
        fornia
        Universiade '83, Kaleidoscope Native Art Exhibit,
        Edmonton, Alberta
1984   *Izbagranfic '84,* Museo de Art Contemporeano, Ibiza,
        Spain
        International Independent Exhibition of Prints, Prefec-
        tural Gallery, Kanagawa, Japan
        Cabo Frio International Print Biennial, Cabo Frio, Brazil
1985   *Keepers of Our Culture,* Woodland Indian Cultural Cen-
        tre, Brantford, Ontario
1986   *New Beginnings,* Native Small Business Summit, Toronto,
        Ontario
        Cross Cultural Views, National Gallery of Canada, Ot-
        tawa, Ontario
1986-87 *Stardusters,* Thunder Bay Art Gallery, Thunder Bay,
        Ontario (traveling)
1987   *Los Angeles Celebration of Canadian Contemporary
        Native Art,* Southwest Museum of Los Angeles, Cali-
        fornia
1988   *Modern Echoes of Ancient Dreams,* Arts Court, Ottawa,
        Ontario
        *Zeitgenossische Kunst der Indianer und Eskimos in
        Kanata,* Canadian Museum of Civilization, Hull, Que-
        bec; opened in Dortumd, Germany, toured Canada
1989   *Revelation of Inner Strengths,* Beaver House Gallery,
        Edmonton, Alberta
        The Mainstream Move, Nova Gallery, Calgary, Alberta
        In The Shadow of the Sun, Canadian Museum of Civiliza-
        tion, Hull, Quebec
1990   *Eleven Stories: Mixed Media Work by Eleven Native
        American Artists,* Sacred Circle Gallery of American
        Indian Art, Seattle, Washington (traveling)

Seeing Red, Agnes Etherington Art Centre, Queen's University, Kingston, Ontario

Ritual and Magic, Winnipeg Art Gallery, Winnipeg, Manitoba

Carriers of the Fire, American Indian Community House, New York

1991-92   *Changes: A Spiritual Renaissance* (traveling)

1992   *Indigena*, Museum of Civilization, Hull, Quebec

Americas, Monasterio de Santa Clara, Moguer (Huelva), Spain

New Territories... 350/500 Years After, Antelier Vision Planetaire, Montreal, Quebec

1993   Kamloops Art Gallery, Kamloops, British Columbia

1994   *Together—Alone*, NewZones Gallery of Contemporary Art, Calgary, Alberta

1994-95   *Women and Paint*, Mendell Art Gallery, Saskatoon, Saskatchewan

1995   *Basket, Bead and Quill Forum*, Thunder Bay Art Gallery, Thunder Bay, Ontario

1997   *Transitions: Contemporary Canadian Indian and Inuit Art*, Indian and Northern Affairs Canada, Department of Foreign Affairs and International Trade, Paris, France

Collections

Alberta Indian Arts & Crafts Society Collection, Edmonton; Alberta Art Foundation, Edmonton; Art Gallery of Ontario, Toronto; Brooklyn Museum, New York; Canada Council Art Bank, Ottawa, Ontario; Canadian Museum of Civilization, Hull, Quebec; City of Edmonton, Alberta; Columbia University, New York City; Edmonton Art Gallery, Alberta; Department of Indian and Northern Affairs Canada, Ottawa, Ontario; McMichael Art Gallery, Kleinburg, Ontario; Peace Hills Trust, Edmonton, Alberta; Peguis Indian Band, Winnipeg, Manitoba; Thunder Bay Art Gallery Collection, Thunder Bay, Ontario; University of Alberta; Winnipeg Art Gallery, Winnipeg, Manitoba; Woodland Indian Cultural Centre, Brantford, Ontario; Yale University, New Haven, Connecticut.

Publications

On POITRAS: Books—*Stardusters*, by Gary Mainprize, Thunder Bay Art Gallery, 1986; *Beyond History*, by Karen Duffek and Tom Hill, Vancouver Art Gallery, 1989; *The 4th Biennial Native American Fine Arts Invitational*, by Margaret Archuleta, Phoenix, Heard Museum, 1989. **Articles**—"The Travels of Jane Ash Poitras," *Visual Arts Newsletter-Alberta Culture*, August 1984; "Cree Orphan Reached Out to Achieve," by Phyllis Matousek, *Edmonton Journal*, September 1, 1985; "Jane Ash Poitras," by Diedre Hanna, *Now Magazine*, August 1989; "The Synchronic Spirit: An Interview with Jane Ash Poitras,"*Border Crossings*, September 1992; "Indigena: Perspectives of Indigenous Peoples on Five Hundred Years," by Gerald McMaster and Lee-Ann Martin, *American Indian Art Magazine*, Autumn 1992; "Lady Oracle," by Gillian Mackay, *Canadian Art*, Fall 1994; "Jane Ash Poitras," by Laura Mark, *Artforum*, Vol. 33, January 1995; "Mummy Dearest—Gallery Goers," *Toronto Globe and Mail*, 13 May, 1995; "Reflections on Nationhood," by Victor Dwyer, *Mcleans*, 1 July, 1995. **Film**—*Hands of History*, by Loretta Todd, 1994.

*   *   *

Jane Ash Poitras was born in Fort Chipewyan and raised in Edmonton, Alberta, after being orphaned at age six by her mother's death from tuberculosis. It was not until after receiving her bachelor's degree in microbiology from the University of Alberta that Poitras began to search for her roots. After finding her mother's death certificate, she returned to Fort Chipewyan to find her family. This reconnection with her roots was a turning point in her life that ultimately led to her completing a Master of Fine Arts degree in printmaking from Columbia University, New York City, in 1985.

Despite her success as a printmaker, Poitras abandoned the practice because of an allergy to the chemicals in ink. Turning to painting and mixed media collages, Poitras focused on themes relating to heritage, genealogy, identity and history both personal, communal and national. Poitras prefers to exploit an idea or image completely, frequently working in series. In her early series, she incorporated traditional Cree iconography. In *Family Background* (1989), for example, Poitras positions a family photo in the center surrounded by examples of writing as symbols of civilization: Egyptian hieroglyphs, Chinese characters, pages of invalid credit card numbers, and a Canadian one-dollar bill with Queen Elizabeth wearing a headband with a feather. Also included is a page from a Cree dictionary with the Cree word for orphan—an obvious reference to Poitras. A blackboard dominates the upper third of the composition with three rows of writing: the first two are of upper and lower case, cursive style letter "a," the third row is filled with characters from the Cree syllabary. This piece, from her *Indian Blackboard* series, examines the effects of acculturation and assimilation of Native people through education. Poitras challenges the viewer to examine their assumptions of what determines "civilized," as she reflects writing traditions from diverse cultures and periods in history. Ultimately, this piece critically examines the "education of Indians" as the last frontier of colonialism—the colonization of the mind.

In her 1994 series, Poitras incorporates images of important figures in Native and non-Native history to draw a connection between genealogies and histories—to tie us all to the ideas and individuals who had an impact on history. In ironic twists, Poitras takes historical figures who generally claim more attention and puts them in secondary positions. For example, in *Generations Late*, Black Elk and his descendants share the composition with Christopher Columbus in a multi-image collage. The picture of Black Elk from 1930 was taken in Germany, when he toured with the "Wild West" show. Although the photo of Black Elk and his sons reflects the colonial influences on their lives, the image attests to Native cultural survival over five hundred years of colonization and genocide that would follow Columbus' landing in North America. Consequently, this juxtaposing of Columbus and Black Elk challenges the current historical constructions of European colonization of the Americas. The indigenous people who inhabited the Americas, then, have not been eliminated or assimilated. They are still here.

Where her earlier collages were more chaotic in the arrangement of images, resulting in an intense visual experience, her 1994 collages embrace a new type of order. Images are isolated on the page, no longer layered and competing for attention or challenging each other. Photographs seem to dominate, as she creates new narratives, new histories, in her arrangement of images. These works are embellished with Navajo rug designs, such as crosses, diamond shapes and ziggurats.

Poitras search for her own family—her own identity—has expanded. The intense search for herself has turned into an exploration of Native identity and history. This journey is manifested in her work, as she addresses issues of forced education of Native people, acculturation and assimilation, and the larger ramifications of colonization. She exploits painting and mixed media collages to poignantly address these ideas.

—Jennifer Vigil

POLELONEMA, Otis

Variant names: Lomadamociva
Tribal affiliations: Hopi
Painter

Born: Shungopovi, Second Mesa, Arizona, 2 February 1902; Lomadamociva means "Springtime." **Education:** Santa Fe Indian School, including Elizabeth De Huff's watercolor classes. **Career:** Illustrations for *TayTay's Tales,* by Elizabeth De Huff, published in 1922; farmer; poet and composer. **Awards:** Numerous, including Heard Museum Guild Indian Fair and Market (1969, 1976), Inter-Tribal Indian Ceremonials (1970), Scottsdale National Indian Arts Exhibition (1970), Santa Fe Indian Market, and fairs sponsored by the Museum of New Mexico, the Museum of Northern Arizona, and the Philbrook Museum of Art. **Died:** 1981.

Selected Group Exhibitions

1925	*American Indian Painting and Applied Arts,* Arts Club of Chicago
1939	San Francisco Exposition, California
1954	Denver Art Museum, Denver, Colorado
1955	De Young Museum, San Francisco, California
1955-56	European tour sponsored by the University of Oklahoma, Norman
1968	Heard Museum, Phoenix, Arizona
1978	*100 Years of Native American Painting,* Oklahoma Museum of Art, Oklahoma City, Oklahoma
1979-80	*Native American Paintings,* organized by the Joslyn Ary Museum, Omaha, Nebraska (traveling)
1981	Colorado Springs Fine Arts Center, Colorado Springs, Colorado
1982	*Native American Painting: Selections from the Museum of the American Indian,* Heard Museum, Phoenix, Arizona
1984-85	*Indianascher Kunstler* (traveling, Germany), organized by the Philbrook Museum, Tulsa, Oklahoma
1987	Fulton-Hayden Memorial Art Gallery, Dragoon, Arizona
1988	*When the Rainbow Touches Down,* Heard Museum, Phoenix, Arizona
1990	*American Indian Artists in the Avery Collection and the McNay Permanent Collection,* Marion Koogler McNay Art Museum, San Antonio, Texas
	James T. Bialac Collection of 20th Century Native American Art, Nelson Fine Arts Center, Arizona State University Art Museum, Tempe
1991-92	*Shared Visions: Native American Painters and Sculptors of the Twentieth Century,* Heard Museum, Phoenix, Arizona (traveling)
1992	*A Bridge Across Cultures: Pueblo Painters in Santa Fe, 1910-1932,* Wheelwright Museum of the American Indian, Santa Fe, New Mexico

1994	*Sharing the Heritage: American Indian Art from Oklahoma Private Collections,* Fred Jones, Jr. Museum of Art, University of Oklahoma, Norman
1996	*Drawn from Memory: James T. Bialac Collection of Native American Art,* Heard Museum, Phoenix, Arizona

Collections

Amerind Foundation, Dragoon, Arizona; Columbus Gallery of Fine Arts, Columbus, Ohio; Denver Art Museum, Denver, Colorado; Thomas Gilcrease Institute of American History and Art, Tulsa, Oklahoma; Heard Museum, Phoenix, Arizona; Museum of New Mexico, Santa Fe; Museum of Northern Arizona, Flagstaff, Arizona; Philbrook Museum of Art, Tulsa, Oklahoma; Millicent Rogers Foundation Museum, Taos, New Mexico; Southeast Museum of the North American Indian, Marathon, Florida; University of Oklahoma, Norman, Oklahoma; Smithsonian Institution, Washington, D.C.; Wheelwright Museum of the American Indian, Santa Fe, New Mexico.

Publications

On POLELONEMA: Books—*Introduction to American Indian Art,* by John Sloan and Oliver La Farge, New York: The Exposition of Indian Tribal Arts, Inc., 1931; *American Indian Painting of the Southwest and Plains Areas,* by Dorothy Dunn, Albuquerque: University of New Mexico, 1968; *Indian Painters and White Patrons,* by J. J. Brody, Albuquerque: University of New Mexico Press, 1971; *100 Years of Native American Painting,* exhibition catalog by Arthur Silberman, Oklahoma Museum of Art, Oklahoma City, 1978; *Hopi Painting: The World of the Hopis,* by Patricia J. Broder, New York: E.P. Dutton, 1978; *The Arts of the North American Indian: Native Traditions in Evolution,* Edwin L. Wade, ed., New York: Hudson Hills Press in association with Philbrook Art Center, Tulsa, Oklahoma, 1986; *When the Rainbow Touches Down,* exhibition catalog by Tryntje Van Ness Seymour, Heard Museum, University of Washington Press, 1988; *Shared Visions: Native American Painters and Sculptors in the Twentieth Century,* by Margaret Archuleta and Dr. Rennard Strickland, New York: The New Press, 1991. **Articles**—"Pueblo Tribe Aesthetic Giants, Indian Art Reveals," *El Palacio,* 24 March, 1928; "American Inter-Tribal Indian Art," by Rose Berry, *Art and Archaeology,* November-December, 1931; "Contemporary Indian Art," by Clara Lee Tanner, *Arizona Highways,* February 1950; "America's First Painters," by Dorothy Dunn, *National Geographic Magazine,* March 1955.

*   *   *

Otis Polelonema seems to steadily gain more respect posthumously, even beyond earlier periods of recognition, including the 1920s and 1930s and again when he returned to full-time painting in the 1960s and 1970s. His work is pictorial and detailed, with little background or sense of environment, and his figures and objects are not as finely detailed as those of other Hopi painters, artists of The Studio, or flatstyle painters of the Plains. But his more crudely-rendered scenes and his technique for presenting subjects up close and statically posed generate a dynamic intensity not always as evident in some of his more acclaimed contemporaries, including Fred Kabotie, Velino Shije Herrera, and Waldo Mootzka, who painted similar scenes with more acute detail. In fact, Polelonema's less-polished skills as a draftsman may have resulted in paintings with greater resonance. Since Polelonema's return to full time painting in the 1960s and winning numerous awards in the 1970s before his death in 1981, his work has been included consistently in major exhibitions and his stature as an individual artist is growing.

Polelonema started painting at the government run Indian School in Santa Fe, where despite federal school policies prohibiting formal arts training, talented students like Kabotie and Herrera were encouraged to draw and paint by the superintendents' wife, Elizabeth De Huff (eventually costing her husband his job). De Huff invited these students to her home, where she provided them with watercolors and paper. Polelonema was a close friend of Kabotie and began tagging along to the sessions, soon becoming a regular. Of this situation, Kabotie once said, "Polelonema paints because I paint." De Huff recognized Polelonema's talents and asked him to compose a series of illustrations that she used for *TayTay's Tales,* a book of stories based on Hopi legends De Huff published in 1922.

Preparing for the Buffalo Dance (watercolor on paper, 1918) shows traits that distinguish Polelonema's work throughout his career: the dancers laying out costumes and feathers, the baskets and wall-hangings in the room they inhabit, all are rendered crudely, but the images splash on the canvas, and they are projected close to the viewer, giving a sense of immediacy, power and expressiveness. Kabotie painted a similar scene at about the same time, with figures more finely rendered and placed at a more relaxed distance. Where Kabotie's painting evokes a sense of ease in the scene and viewing, Polelonema's work impresses as more urgent and energetic.

The artists encouraged by De Huff won recognition for secular watercolor paintings depicting scenes of daily life, ceremonial dances and dancers, stylized landscapes, and animal compositions. Both Kabotie and Polelonema painted a series of Kachina paintings that are well-regarded and can be studied for better understanding of the roles and symbolism of this aspect of Hopi culture. Polelonema focused more specifically on everyday reality and details of costumes and people. He developed techniques for presenting a real world environment with shadows and robust people, as opposed to flatstyle figures, though a sparseness of environmental details remains throughout his work. His people seem especially strong, serene, active, meditative. During the early 1930s, a period in which Polelonema was prolific, this expressive intensity is wrought through tiny, meticulously rendered and repeated brush strokes, and static figures gain a sense of vibrancy though their heavy forms and a bulkiness in clothing, blankets, and shawls.

Polelonema remained at Hopi all of his life, painting less and less while participating regularly in tribal affairs and ceremonies, particularly those related to the Snow Clan, of which he was a member, and raising a family of six. When he began painting consistently again in the 1960s, his works were much like those from his first period, particularly the watercolors of Kachinas he produced during the 1920s. Other small and telling details appeared as well; for example a close look at *Hopi Rainbow Dance* from late 1960s rewards with such minute details as a tiny, abstract expression of a bean on a Kachina mask, appropriate for a ceremonial for rain to feed the crops. The seemingly stilled procession in *Women's Society Dance* (casein on paper, 1967) would be entirely static except the dancers are so up front, as if the viewer is watching them pass from a seated position just over an arm's length from the procession.

Polelonema's return to painting was highly successful, as he won major awards at the major Indian fairs and juried competitions from 1969 through the mid-1970s, followed by showings in over a dozen major group exhibitions since then.

—Perry Bear

POOLAW, Tom

Tribal affiliations: Kiowa; Delaware
Painter

Born: Thomas Lee Poolaw, Fort Sill, Oklahoma, 24 February 1959. **Education:** University of Oklahoma, BA, painting, 1992, and MFA, 1997. **Career:** Artist; Curator of Exhibitions, Jacobson Foundation, Norman, Oklahoma. **Awards:** Award of Merit, Oklahoma Painting Biennial III, 1994.

Individual Exhibitions

1981   *Paintings by Thomas Poolaw,* Southern Plains Indian Museum and Crafts Center, Anadarko, Oklahoma
1996   *Thomas Poolaw,* MFA Midway Exhibition, Lightwell Gallery, University of Oklahoma, Norman

Selected Group Exhibitions

1979   *Cultures and Arts of Native Americans, Inc., Invitational,* Fred Jones Art Center Museum, Norman, Oklahoma
1992   *Native Peoples ... Our Ways Shall Continue,* Denver Art Museum, Denver, Colorado
1993   *Pahdopony, Poolaw, Connywerdy, Mahetsky,* Jacobson Foundation, Norman, Oklahoma
1994   *Sixth Annual Indian Arts Show,* Museum of Anthropology, University of Kansas, Lawrence
            Moving Murals Collection Traveling Exhibition, Jacobson Foundation, Norman, Oklahoma (traveling)
            Volume One: Book Arts by Native Americans, American Indian Community House, New York, and American Indian Contemporary Arts, San Francisco
1995   *Revolving Wall: Mixed Media Works by Wendy Mahetsky and Tom Poolaw,* Living Arts Exhibition and Performance Space, Tulsa, Oklahoma
            Oklahoma Painting Biennial III, Oklahoma Visual Arts Coalition/City Arts Center, Oklahoma City, Oklahoma
            Native American Invitational and Masters Exhibition, Thomas Gilcrease Museum of American History and Art, Tulsa, Oklahoma
1996   *Infinite Choices: Mixed Media Works by Wendy Mahetsky and Tom Poolaw,* Kirkpatrick Gallery of Oklahoma Artists, Oklahoma City, Oklahoma
            Eighth Annual Indian Arts Show, Museum of Anthropology, University of Kansas, Lawrence
1997   *We Are Many, We Are One: National Exhibition of Contemporary Native American Art,* University Art Gallery, University of Wisconsin-LaCrosse
            Days of Invention: Emerging Artists of the South Plains, Institute of American Indian Arts Museum, Santa Fe, New Mexico

Collections

Fred Jones Art Center Museum, University of Oklahoma, Norman, Oklahoma; Southern Plains Indian Museum and Crafts Center, Anadarko, Oklahoma.

*

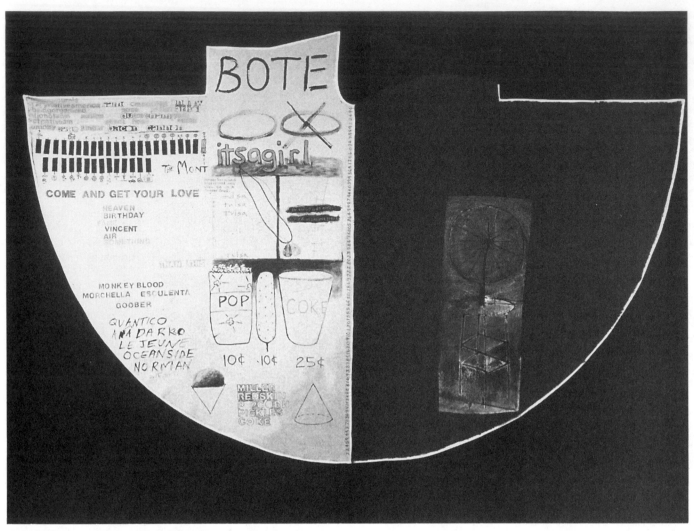

Tom Poolaw: *Autoblograffitipi,* 1992. Courtesy of the artist.

Tom Poolaw comments:

Since 1980 my work has gone through several transitional periods. My recent paintings reflect an interest in process and use of various media. I am currently moving towards a non-objective approach to painting. I am doing this in order to rely less on cultural appropriation. I want to look toward current issues and situations presented daily. It is out of respect for past generations of people, their lives and cultures, that I omit any comment on my part. This also ensures avoidance of exploitation, intentional or unintentional.

For me, the Indian culture is alive in songs, ceremonies, memories and voices of the people. Interaction with fellow Native American people is a gift. My role as an artist carries with it a responsibility to produce work based on integrity and honesty.

*   *   *

Tom Poolaw is one of the most promising members of a new generation of Native American painters just making the transition from the insularity of art school to the larger art community. Educated at a mainstream art school in the wake of stereotype-shattering painting careers of T. C. Cannon and Fritz Scholder, Poolaw has been influenced by such diverse artists as the Kiowa Five, Blackbear

Bosin, Francis Bacon, Bryce Marden, and professors Gene Bavinger and Hachivi Edgar Heap of Birds. An avid researcher of art history and fully aware of contemporary art issues, Poolaw has nevertheless developed his own distinct style, which, like that of many of his peers, presents Native identity from an intensely personal perspective.

Poolaw is deeply tied to his tribal and family home in Anadarko, Oklahoma, and the creative legacy of his family emerges in his art. Poolaw has drawn on the imagery found in the extraordinary photography collection, touring the country in the mid-1990s in an exhibition organized by Stanford University, that was left by his grandfather, documentary photographer Horace Poolaw. But recalling that during his childhood these photos represented the history of everyday family and tribal life rather than art for public consumption, Poolaw has also created his own series of snapshots, which he often integrates into mixed media works. *Oklahoma Photo Album* juxtaposes photographic images of his own family and the region surrounding the family home with old record album jackets, resulting in a witty homage to his grandfather.

The conventions and imagery of the Kiowa calendar counts kept by Poolaw's great-grandfather also emerge in the younger artist's work. *Autobiograffitipi,* a painting created on a tipi hide-shaped canvas, serves as a personal calendar. Like scribbled notes for a documentary of the artist's life, rudimentary marks count off his age at the time of its creation, the names of towns where he lived as the son of a U.S. Marine are listed, and images of indeterminate meaning emerge from the black and white minimalist palette. Perhaps in a concerted effort to counteract this barrage of personal symbolism, however, Poolaw has chosen to provide a painterly rendition of Ducahmp's *Bicycle Wheel* as the central image on the right side of the bisected canvas. The painting, which was created for the Jacobson Foundation's traveling exhibit of Native American art, is easily read as a metaphor for the Native artist's struggle to negotiate two distinct art worlds—Native and non-Native. However, Poolaw rejects the prevailing dualistic truism that Native artists have "one foot in each world." "I'm a Native person and I'm an artist," he states. "My Kiowa and Delaware heritage is my birthright. Being an artist is a career choice. I don't want these two elements of my life to be seen as mutually dependent. But, of course, they aren't mutually exclusive either."

Most recently, Poolaw has been developing two series that rely on more abstract imagery. Traditional Kiowa traveling songs are the inspiration for the *Journey Series,* in which the canvas serves as a map upon which a change of place and time is documented in paint. These journeys may recall the historically nomadic way of the Kiowa, but they also evoke modern wanderlust, metaphorical spiritual pilgrimages of self-discovery, the power of fate in our lives, and even the expeditionary process of creating a painting.

The *Door Series,* in which a planer, abstract passageway is centered on a four-foot square canvas, also serves as a vessel for Poolaw's masterful manipulation of paint and for the viewer's own personal interpretation. The artist describes the imagery in terms of the spiritual transformations of birth and death, and indeed there is the sense of glimpsing in another dimension. But the aperture, which typically throws light and its own color scheme into the lower portion of the painting, can also be read as the threshold we stand upon at the dawn of any life transition—with all the uncertainty of imminent evolution. It is Poolaw's attitude toward this accessible, open-ended imagery that led Hachivi Edgar Heap of Birds, curator of *Days of Invention: Emerging Artists of the South Plains* at the Institute of American Indian Arts Museum, to declare: "The artist exhibits a great deal of promise in the broad latitude by which he is willing to have his symbols diversely interpreted by the viewer."

—Lisa Cooley

POP CHALEE

Tribal affiliations: Taos Pueblo
Painter

Born: Merina Lujan (later Merina Lujan Hopkins) in Castle Gate, Utah, 20 March 1906; Pop Chalee means "Blue Flower." **Family:** Married Otis Hopkins; two children, Jack and Betty. **Education:** Santa Fe Indian School through the mid-1920s; The Studio, Santa Fe Indian School, mid-1930s. **Career:** Professional artist beginning mid-1930s; painted murals for the Albuquerque International Airport, 1940s, airports in Roswell and Santa Fe, New Mexico, Santa Fe Railroad (now in the Wheelwright Museum collection); numerous other private and public mural commissions, including New Mexico State Capitol Building, Santa Fe, Grand Hotel, Mackinac

Island, Michigan, and the General Holmes House, La Cienega, California; entertainer, including radio singer; art instructor and lecturer. **Awards:** Governor's Award for Excellence and Achievement in the Arts, State of New Mexico, 1990; Woman of Distinction Award, New Mexico Democratic Party, 1992; Grand Award, Inter-Tribal Indian Ceremonials, Gallup, New Mexico. **Died:** 11 December 1993.

Selected Group Exhibitions

1937   *American Indian Exposition and Congress,* Tulsa, Oklahoma
1964   Read Mullan Gallery of Western Art, Phoenix, Arizona
1965   *Second Annual Invitational Exhibition of American Indian Paintings,* United States Department of the Interior, Washington, D.C.
1978   *100 Years of Native American Painting,* Oklahoma Museum of Art, Oklahoma City, Oklahoma
1981   *Walk in Beauty,* Santa Fe Festival of the Arts, New Mexico
1982   *Night of the First Americans,* Kennedy Center for the Performing Arts, Washington, D.C.
1984-85 *Indianascher Kunstler* (traveling, Germany), organized by the Philbrook Museum, Tulsa, Oklahoma
1988   *When the Rainbow Touches Down,* Heard Museum, Phoenix, Arizona
1991-92 *Shared Visions: Native American Painters and Sculptors in the Twentieth Century,* The Heard Museum, Phoenix, Arizona
1992   Museum of Natural History, Albuquerque, New Mexico
1994   Museum of New Mexico, Santa Fe
        Watchful Eyes: Native American Women Artists, Heard Museum, Phoenix, Arizona

Collections

Amerind Foundation, Dragoon, Arizona; Arizona State Museum, University of Arizona, Tucson; Denver Art Museum, Denver, Colorado; Eiteljorg Museum of American Indians and Western Art, Indianapolis, Indiana; Thomas Gilcrease Institute of American History and Art, Tulsa, Oklahoma; Heard Museum, Phoenix, Arizona; Heritage Center, Inc., Collection, Red Cloud Indian School, Pine Ridge, South Dakota; Joslyn Art Museum, Omaha, Nebraska; Koogler McNay Art Museum, San Antonio, Texas; Montclair Art Museum, Montclair, New Jersey; Museum of New Mexico, Santa Fe; Museum of Northern Arizona; Philbrook Museum of Art, Tulsa, Oklahoma; Millicent Rogers Foundation Museum, Taos, New Mexico; School of American Research, Santa Fe, New Mexico; Smithsonian Institution, Washington, D.C.; Southeast Museum of the North American Indian, Marathon, Florida; Southwest Museum, Los Angeles, California; Stanford Fine Arts Museum, Stanford, California; University of Oklahoma, Norman, Oklahoma; Wheelwright Museum of the American Indian, Santa Fe, New Mexico; Woolaroc Museum, Bartlesville, Oklahoma.

Publications

On POP CHALEE: Books—*American Indian Painters,* by Oscar B. Jacobson and Jeanne D'Ucel, Nice, France, 1950; *American Indian Painting of the Southwest and Plains Areas,* by Dorothy Dunn, Albuquerque: University of New Mexico, 1968; *Indian Painters and White Patrons,* by J. J. Brody, Albuquerque: University of

Pop Chalee: *Water Serpent and Dancers*, c. 1950. Photograph by Seth Roffman; courtesy Dick Howard collection.

New Mexico Press, 1971; *100 Years of Native American Painting*, exhibition catalog by Arthur Silberman, Oklahoma Museum of Art, Oklahoma City, 1978; *American Indian Painting and Sculpture,* Patricia Broder, New York, 1981; *Indianascher Kunstler*, by Gerhard Hoffmann, Munich, 1984; *When the Rainbow Touches Down*, exhibition catalog by Tryntje Van Ness Seymour, Heard Museum, University of Washington Press, 1988; *Shared Visions: Native American Painters and Sculptors in the Twentieth Century,* by Margaret Archuleta and Dr. Rennard Strickland, New York: The New Press, 1991; *Watchful Eyes: Native American Women Artists,* Anne Gully (editor),Phoenix, 1994.

*

Pop Chalee comments (1988):

When I am painting you can hardly stop me. I get into that and there is something ... peaceful. I think people should get into color, into paint, even if they just dabble and do pretty little things, because there is something in that mellows you. You are just out of this world. When I am painting, I don't know anything that is going on around me. I don't hear anything, I don't see anything. I am just in with my painting. And it is so relaxing. I just love to paint. (From the catalog, *When the Rainbow Touches Down*.)

*   *   *

Merina Lujan, who was born in Utah in 1906 to an East Indian mother and a Taos father, grew up in Taos Pueblo, New Mexico. It was here that she received the lasting influences on her life and had her first exposure to easel painting. Her grandfather, who gave her the name Pop Chalee (Blue Flower), also instilled in her a love of nature and told her the Native legends that would later be the motifs of her paintings. Her aunt, art patron Mabel Dodge (Lujan), intro-

duced her to the Anglo art colony established in a nearby settlement, and Pop Chalee would go to the artists' studios.

It was after several years in Salt Lake City, Utah, where she married and had two children, that she returned to Taos determined to be an art instructor for her people. For an education in the arts she went to Santa Fe and attended the recently founded "Studio" of Dorothy Dunn, where she became a classmate of Harrison Begay and Gerald Nailor. Upon graduation, Dunn presented her with a certificate on which she wrote, "Pop Chalee, it would be better for you to go out and be an artist, and not a teacher, because you will encourage others to go out."

She did, and she immediately established a strong reputation, showing at the *American Indian Exposition and Congress* in Tulsa, Oklahoma, and soon gaining commissions that would keep her busy and financially secure for the next few decades. Chalee's paintings and murals are valued for their rich colors and scenes of ceremonies, dances, and everyday community activities, presenting Native American life in a lively, animated manner.

Pop Chalee is best known today as a painter of fantastic forest wonderlands. In paintings like *The Black Forest* and *Enchanted Forest* her decorative trees with tiny leaves or filmy needles stand out in bright colors on a dark ground. Dainty flowers and shrubs are strewn over the earth. Elegant birds flit about the trees, squirrels nibble on their nuts, rabbits run, and, in the center of the picture, a group of blue or brown deer with decorative antlers chase in long leaps across the picture plane.

Pop Chalee's "fairy-tale paintings," like the pastoral scenes of Navajo painter Harrison Begay, were for a time very popular with Anglo buyers. After the Walt Disney films of the 1940s, however, they became highly controversial. Modern art critics dismissed them as "Bambi art," and kitsch, maintaining they lacked originality, profundity, and truth. Recently voices have been raised from various quarters protesting this dismissal of Chalee's work. Patricia

Janice Broder and others have pointed out that her first "Bambi paintings" were painted as early as 1936, thus making the question of Disney's influence an impossibility. Disney visited Santa Fe and Taos to recruit Indian artists from The Studio for work at Disney Studios; Disney felt the artists' practiced attention to detail, crisp lines, and flat style of painting translated well to animation. While in Taos, Disney met Chalee and bought a forest scene painting from her; it believed that Disney's famous animal character, Bambi, was stylized from deer in Chalee's painting.

Apart from the question of authenticity, a re-evaluation of Pop Chalee's "Bambi-pictures" has taken place in recent years, according to changes in aesthetics and taste in postmodern times. Her paintings are now widely understood as "design" pictures that do not intend to compete with reality or beautify it. Their charm is the result not of sentimentalization, but of stylization committed to decorative patterns, and as such they possess a quality that is at the very foundation of Indian art.

Chalee was skilled as well at more realistic depictions of ceremonial dances and Native American community life, which retain the rich palette and vigor of her forest scenes. *Masks and Mexican Horses,* in mixed media, offers a glimpse of her technique and subject concerns: over a series of heavy- to light- colored arcs that form a background, dynamic masked figures arrest the viewer with their otherworldly appearance, counterpointed by the arced, muscularly-necked horses they ride, who wear happy expressions.

Pop Chalee received numerous commissions that kept her extremely active as a professional artist. Just before her death in 1993 she recalled that she painted every day of her life beginning in 1936.

—Gerhard and Gisela Hoffmann

POV, Abraham

Variant names: Abraham Talirunnilik
Tribal affiliations: Inuit
Sculptor

Born: Abraham Talirunnilik at Sarollie's Camp, north of Inukjuak, Quebec, 1927; surname Pov comes from the region of his birth, Puvirntuq (formerly Povungnituk, or P.O.V.), and he was also known as Samson Abraham, P.O.V., Peow, Piuvi Aipara, Talirunaalik, and Talirunili. **Family:** Third child and first son of artist Joe Talirunnilik; married to Alicie Arngajuk Uppatitsiaq, with whom he had three sons, one daughter and five adopted children. **Career:** House construction in Inukjuak, hunter, and carver; carving of five Inuit building an igloo was reproduced on a postage stamp, 1979. **Died:** July 1994.

Selected Group Exhibitions

1955   *Eskimo Sculpture,* arranged by the Department of Northern Affairs and National Resources, and the National Gallery of Canada, Ottawa, Ontario
1959   *Contemporary Eskimo Sculpture,* St. James Church, New York
1965   *Arctic Values 65,* New Brunswick Museum, St. John, New Brunswick
1967   *Eskimo Sculpture,* Winnipeg Art Gallery, Winnipeg, Manitoba

1971   *Eskimo Carvings and Prints from the Collection of York University,* Art Gallery of York University, Downsview, Ontario
1971-73 *Sculpture/Inuit: Masterworks of the Canadian Arctic,* Canadian Eskimo Arts Council, Ottawa, Ontario (traveling)
1979   *Sculpture of the Inuit: Masterwork Exhibitors of the Canadian Arctic,* Inuit Gallery of Vancouver, British Columbia
1980   *A Taste of Arctic Quebec,* Marion Scott Gallery, Vancouver, British Columbia
1981   *Inuit Masks,* Inuit Gallery of Vancouver, British Columbia
1982   *Les Inuit du Nouveau-Quebec,* Musée du Quebec, Quebec City
1983   *An Enduring Tradition: Inuit Carving from Arctic Quebec,* Inuit Gallery of Vancouver, British Columbia
         Artists of Arctic Quebec, Inuit Gallery of Vancouver, British Columbia
1984   *Sculptures Inuit du Nouveau-Quebec,* Quebec 84, Quebec City
         Heritage of the Inuit: Masterpieces of the Eskimo, Colorado Galleries of the Arts, Littleton, Colorado
         Treasures from Canada's Arctic, Heritage Place, Uxbridge, Ontario
         Takamit—Canadian Eskimo Art: Selections from Private Collections and the Government of Canada, Rutgers University, New Brunswick, New Jersey
1985   *Masterwork Sculpture 1985,* Inuit Gallery of Vancouver, British Columbia
1986   *Inuit: Eskimo Art of Arctic Canada,* Miharudo Gallery, Mejiro, Japan
         The Spirit of the Land, The Koffler Gallery, Toronto, Ontario
         The Art of the Eskimo, Newman Galleries, Bryn Mawr, Pennsylvania
1987-88 *Inuitkonst från Kanada - skulptur och grafik,* Millesgarden, Lidingo, Sweden
1988   *Nouveau-Quebec/Arctic Quebec,* Galerie le Chariot, Montreal, Quebec
1989   *Art Inuit, Sculpture des Esquimaux du Canada,* presented by l'Iglou Art Esquimau, Douai at Galerie La Poutre, Marseille, France
1990   *Arctic Mirror,* Canadian Museum of Civilization, Hull Quebec
         Beeldhouwkunst van de Inuit (Canada), by l'Iglou Art Esquimau, Douai, France at Amphora Finippon pvba, Sint Andries, Brugge, Belgium
         Art Inuit, Galerie Saint Merri, Paris
         Small Sculptures from Across the Canadian Arctic, Feheley Fine Arts, Toronto, Ontario
         Art inuit Autour de la Collection de Cape Dorset 1990, L'iglou Art Esquimau-Douai, Centre Culturel Canadien, Paris, France
1990-92 *The First Passionate Collector: The Ian Lindsay Collection of Inuit Art,* Winnipeg Art Gallery, Winnipeg, Manitoba (traveling)
1992   *Hudsons Bay Company's Collection of Inuit Art,* Winnipeg Art Gallery, Winnipeg, Manitoba
1993   *Kunstwerke der Inuit,* Hotel am Badersee, Grainau, Germany

1994   *Kanuipit? Kunst un Kulturen der Eskimo*, Eine Auswahl
        aus den Museumssammlungen Staatliches Museum
        fur Volkerkunde Munchen, Munich, Germany
        Share the Vision: Philadelphians Collect Inuit Art, Art
        Space Gallery, Philadelphia, Pennsylvania
        Kunst van de Inuit Eskimo's, Gemeentelijk
        Kunstcentrum, Huis Hellemans, Edegem, Belgium

Collections

Art Gallery of Ontario, Toronto, Ontario; Canadian Museum of
Civilization, Hull, Quebec; Dennos Museum Center, Northwest-
ern Michigan College, Traverse City, Michigan; Eskimo Museum,
Churchill, Manitoba; Glenbow Museum, Calgary, Alberta; Inuit
Cultural Institute, Rankin Inlet, Northwest Territories; McMichael
Canadian Art Collection, Kleinburg, Ontario; Museum of Anthro-
pology, University of British Columbia, Vancouver, British Co-
lumbia; National Gallery of Canada, Ottawa, Ontario; Prince of
Wales Northern Heritage Centre, Yellowknife, Northwest Territo-
ries; University of Lethbridge Art Gallery, Lethbridge, Alberta;
Winnipeg Art Gallery, Winnipeg, Manitoba.

Publications

On POV: Books—*Eskimo Sculpture/Sculpture esquimaude*, by
George Swinton, Toronto, Canada, 1965; *Sculpture of the Eskimo*, by George Swinton, Toronto, 1972; *The Inuit Artists of
Inoucdjouac, P.Q.: Historical and Biographical Information for
the Viewers and Collectors of Eskimo Art,* by Barry A. Roberts,
Montreal, 1978; *Sculpture of the Inuit: Masterwork Exhibitors
of the Canadian Arctic*, Inuit Gallery of Vancouver, Vancouver,
1979; *Canadian Guild of Crafts Quebec: The Permanent Collection: Inuit Arts and Crafts c. 1900-1980*, Canadian Guild of Crafts
Quebec, Montreal, 1980; *Singing Songs to the Spirit/The His-
tory and Culture of the Inuit: A Heritage Stamp Collection/Un
chant au grand esprit: L'histoire et la culture des Inuit: Une
collection de timbres consacre au patrimoine text,* by Michael
Mitchell, Ottawa, 1980; *Inuit Masks*, Inuit Gallery of Vancouver,
Vancouver, 1981; *An Enduring Tradition: Inuit Carving from
Arctic Quebec,* Inuit Gallery of Vancouver, Vancouver, 1983;
Winnipeg Collects: Inuit Art from Private Collections, by Darlene
Wight, Winnipeg Art Gallery, 1987; *Inuit Sculpture: In the Col-
lection of the Art Gallery of York University*, by Cynthia Waye
Cook, North York, Ontario, 1988; *The First Passionate Collec-
tor: The Ian Lindsay Collection of Inuit Art/Le premier
collectionneur passionne: La Collection d'art inuit Ian Lindsay*,
by Darlene C. Wight, Winnipeg Art Gallery, 1990; *Nunavimiut:
Art inuit,* by Michel Noel, Pointe-Claire, Quebec, 1992.

*   *   *

Abraham Pov was born in an encampment situated 50 miles
south of Puvirntuq (formerly Povungnituk, or P.O.V.). His surname, Pov, is in reality a nickname based on the region of his
birth. He followed a nomadic life until marrying Alicie Arngajuk
Uppatitsiaq, when he settled in Inukjuak and still pursued the
traditional activities of hunting and fishing while occasionally
taking odd jobs in the settlement.

He became one of the most prolific and admired Inuit artists
of his generation, practicing the art of sculpture regularly beginning in the 1950s. However, in spite of an impressive career, he
never had a solo exhibition nor was he ever the subject of a monograph—surprising because his works are widely known in Canada
and the United States and have been displayed in over forty
group exhibitions, including some in Europe and Asia.

In general, Pov's works have a monolithic bearing, ample in
volume and forming compact masses. His figures lack naturalism, which does not lessen their effect, for the forms sculpted
by Pov suggest elements represented more than they define them.
Moreover, the pieces are massive and dominated by a roundness
of angles creating harmonious whole forms pleasant to the touch.

The sculptures of Pov have very little elaboration, even of
standard details. The surfaces are rarely pierced and never engraved. His sculptures possess a simple geometry, resembling
conic and cylindrical forms. One also observes a distinct preference for whole compositions of trapezoids, manifested by a
progressive diminution from the base toward the top. Indeed,
this particular structure strengthens the effect of stability in his
work and contributes to the expression of monumentality. The
subjects of Pov's work are always figures on a slim base that
juts out slightly. If this sculptural element subsumes the Inuit
landscape, by the contrast of dimension it confers even more the
giganticism of the personages of Pov, reaffirming their placing at
a conventional distance of the socle.

A comparative examination of the works of Pov during the 1950s
and those made during the course of the last year of his life reveals
that he came to simplify the shape of the bulk and geometry of his
images. In preserving little relief, faces gained depth through the
dramatic intensity of their introspective glances, remaining nevertheless somewhat wild-eyed and haggard.

Most particularly, one notices that the heads of his characters are
habitually disproportionate, often more than bulky. They polarize
attention on what remains most striking in his sculptures—the
expression of astonishment on the faces of his characters. In fact,
with large foreheads covered by straight hair, eyes opened wide and
mouth gaping on the whole amplitude of the chin, the bearing of his
characters combines a sentiment of surprise and gravity, a symmetry that gives them a rigid look—with effects emphasized by the
recurrent presence of a perimeter in relief to evoke the thick ornamental border of a parka hood. In spite of the profound difference
of the effects, similarities exist between the enlarged eyes in his
work and those of his father, Joe Talirunnilik, the celebrated Inuit
sculptor.

Pov's meticulousness as a sculptor is evident in several ways,
from the dark green and marbled stones he collected, to his precise
sculpting, to the smooth and polished surfaces that shine to maxi-
mum effect. Yet, at the end of his career, Pov created a few works in
which he sought the effects of thin, rough texture. He generally
signed his sculptures in syllabic characters and at times simply as
Abraham, in roman letters.

Pov mostly represented subjects inspired by daily life of the
past. Even though he rarely illustrated legends or stories, one
can identify few works in which he evoked shamanic expression.
Pov principally devoted himself to representing solitary subjects, above all Inuit women in traditional activities and often
carrying a child in their amauti (women's parkas), or Inuit hunters in typical postures. One also finds magnificent animal scenes,
which by the accuracy of execution confirm the classicism of
Pov sculptures.

—Louis Gagnon

POWLESS, Bill

Tribal affiliations: Mohawk
Painter

Born: Six Nations Reserve, Ohsweken, Ontario, 21 January 1952. **Education:** Studied commercial art at Mohawk College, Brantford, Ontario. **Career:** Painted bridges and industrial steel, early 1970s; graphic designer, Woodland Cultural Centre, Brantford, Ontario, beginning in 1976; Museum Design Preparator, Woodland Cultural Centre; illustrator of children's books, including a four-part series on sexual abuse; satirical cartoons published in *Tekawennake*, an Ontario newspaper; numerous commissions

Selected Group Exhibitions

1975-96   *First Nations Art Show* (annual), Woodland Cultural Centre, Brantford, Ontario
1986   *Art of the Seventh Generation: Iroquois Symbols on Canvas and Paper*, Roberson Center for the Arts and Sciences, Binghamton, New York
1995   *Smoke and Mirrors: Art by Ann Pineault and Bill Powless*, Brock Centre for the Arts Gallery, Brock University, St. Catharines, Ontario
1996   *Smoke and Mirrors: Art by Ann Pineault and Bill Powless*, Woodland Cultural Centre, Brantford, Ontario
       Be It So, It Remains In Our Minds, The Art Gallery of Ontario, Toronto

Collections

Joseph Brant Museum, Burlington, Ontario; Schoharie Museum of the Iroquois Indian, Schoharie, New York; Woodland Cultural Centre Museum, Brantford, Ontario.

Publications

By POWLESS: Books (illustrated)—"Bandaids," *From Nose to Toes*, Toronto, Institute for Studies in Education, 1984; "All Kinds of Weather," in *Skipping Over Rainbows*, Toronto, Institute for Studies in Education, 1984; "Oh Norman!," in *The Yummy Book*, Toronto, Institute for Studies in Education, 1984; "The Surprise Package," in *Lots to Do*, Toronto, Institute for Studies in Education, 1984; "Monster Party," Toronto, Institute for Studies in Education, 1984; "A Seneca Indian Legend," in *Time Spinners*, Toronto, Nelson Canada, 1984; "Illustrations for The Iroquois," Grollier Ltd. of Canada, 1984; "The First Day, Bingo," *Thin Ice*, Toronto, Institute for Studies in Education, 1986; *Illustrations for Teacher's Helpers*, Toronto, Institute for Studies in Education, 1987

On POWLESS: Articles—"Legends Come Alive in Colourful Indian Art," by Trish Wilson, *Kitchener-Waterloo Record*, 20 October 1979; "Poetry, Photographs Unusual Combination of Artistic Mediums," by Grace Inglis, *Hamilton Spectator*, 19 January 1985; "Six Nations Artist Profile On TV Ontario," by Dave Harrison, *Brant News*, 23 January 1985; "Artist Keeps Heritage Alive," by Kim Novak, *Brant News*, 6 October 1990; "Postmodern Parody: A Political Strategy in Contemporary Canadian Native Art," by Allan J. Ryan, *Art Journal*, Fall, Vol. 51(3), 1992; "Thayendanegea Revisited By Powless,"

Bill Powless. Drawing by and courtesy of the artist.

Waurihwa: Quarterly Newsletter of the Woodland Cultural Centre, April 1993; "Exhibit Timely Commentary On Natives' Plight," by Sean Condon, *The Standard*, 23 September 1995.

*   *   *

Bill Powless is largely unknown outside "Iroquois country"—southern Ontario and upstate New York. This is unfortunate since he is an artist of considerable ability. His relative anonymity on the national and international scene is for the most part the result of a deliberate choice. Forsaking a full-time career as a fine artist, Powless chooses to devote his talents to improving the public profile of Native peoples at the Woodland Cultural Centre in his home community of Six Nations, near Brantford, Ontario. As Museum Design Preparator at the Centre he works with a team of people dedicated to preserving First Nations history.

Powless has still managed to maintain a modest personal profile as a painter, sketch artist and cartoonist. For the last twenty years he has contributed work to the annual First Nations Art Show at the Woodland Cultural Centre and designed many of the show's catalogs as well. This show has been the principal public venue for Powless's acrylic paintings.

Over the same two decades he has produced a yearly calendar of pencil, pen and ink drawings that has found an ever-widening audience. Since the late 1980s he has also been a regular contributor of wry and insightful editorial cartoons to the local community newspaper, *Tekawennake*.

Certainly, Powless has created many memorable images, with humor providing distinctive flavor to much of his acrylic painting. It is a Trickster's humor that delights in the interplay between image and title, revelling in clever (and sometimes outrageous) puns and surprising juxtapositions. His work is informed by the same

Bill Powless: *Indians' Summer,* 1984. Courtesy of the artist.

comic spirit that inspires some of his better known contemporaries, artists like Harry Fonseca, T.C. Cannon, Richard Glazer-Danay, Bob Haozous, David Bradley, Gerald McMaster, Ron Noganosh, Shelley Niro and Nora Naranjo-Morse.

Powless often portrays single human figures that assume archetypal significance by virtue of their singularity. Rendered in a naturalistic manner, they symbolize the persistence of Native culture in a constantly changing world. Inevitably, they challenge non-Native stereotypes and attitudes. One of Powless's best known images is *Indians' Summer* (1984), a picture of self-satisfied contemporary reality that wickedly inverts the classic Indian warrior portraits of yesteryear. Sporting bikini briefs, yuppie sweatband and "Indianized" umbrella beanie, this "warrior" seems more interested in "communing with nature" than performing vigorous acts of bravery. When first exhibited, this painting caused a minor furor on the Six Nations Reserve among those who felt it promoted a slothful Indian stereotype; Powless says they preferred the romantic stereotype.

Runs With Roosters (1991) is another painting of present-day reality. It depicts a mature Native woman jogging in a zebra-patterned spandex outfit. Clearly, an "Earth Mother with attitude" possessed of a healthy zest for life, she puts the lie to lingering Hollywood fictions of cowering squaws and vacuous Indian princesses.

Powless is well aware of Hollywood stereotypes, and is not above using them to his own ends. In *Home of the Brave* (1986), for instance, he surrounds the image of a seated warrior with selected symbols of popular culture to once again affirm a contemporary indigenous presence. In this case, a pink plastic flamingo vies with

the warrior for viewer attention. (Do Indians have plastic flamingos on their front lawns? Powless does.) Paintings such as *Beer Garden* (1984) reflect the artist's penchant for punning and verbal/visual mischief. Interpreting the title literally rather than metaphorically, he portrays two men at work in the garden: one scattering beer caps on the ground in the manner of Johnny Appleseed while the other tills the soil with a hoe. Above them, a sequence of time-lapse images illustrates how the bottle caps take root and grow into mature bottles of beer ready for harvest.

As accomplished a painter as Powless is, he demonstrates even greater proficiency with pen and ink and pencil. Preliminary sketches for paintings often exhibit fluid lines and subtle nuances that sometimes get lost when the images are transferred to canvas. The drawings that Powless creates for his annual calendars range from quick pen and ink studies to detailed pencil portraits. The sketches depict people in both traditional and modern dress enjoying a variety of tribal activities, from planting crops to playing lacrosse, sharing a pipe to sampling soup, cavorting in the snow to courting in the moonlight. Powless is not above including an occasional fearless warrior or comely maiden as well. After all, this is a calendar. More importantly, it is an opportunity to share his uplifting vision of Iroquoian life and culture with his home community and beyond.

The Six Nations community is also the primary inspiration for (and consumer of) Powless's immensely appealing editorial cartoons. Like fellow cartoonists, Vincent Craig (Navajo) and Robert Freeman (Dakota/Luiseno), Powless has developed a personal style of comic commentary well suited to visualizing the many ironies and issues that dominate Native life today. These issues invariably concern band politics, control of Native education, federal government relations and the impact of global events on the local community.

Inspired by the work of Ojibway artist, Ron Noganosh, Powless occasionally constructs whimsical three dimensional sculptures from found objects. *Wowie Zowie: A Tribute to the Maestro*, for instance, is a recent "portrait head" of the late rock music innovator, Frank Zappa, constructed of coiled metal shavings and stereo speaker components.

Powless' versatility is reflected in his numerous commissions: *The Battle of Beaver Dam*, mural, Woodland Cultural Centre Museum, Brantford, Ontario; A Dream of Unity, mural group project, *"Spirit of Sharing" Festival*, West Bay, Ontario, 1984; Poster, Buffy Sainte-Marie Benefit Concert, Chiefswood Restoration Committee, Six Nations Reserve, Ontario, 1986; Fundraising design, James Bay Cree Band Council, in support of their challenge to Phase II of the James Bay Hydro Electric Project, 1991; various projects for the new Oliver Smith Elementary School, Six Nations.

—Allan J. Ryan

PRATT, Charles

Tribal affiliations: Arapaho; Sioux; Cheyenne
Sculptor

Born: Concho, Oklahoma, 8 November 1937. **Education:** El Reno High School, Oklahoma; self-taught artist; learned to mold clay from his grandfather. **Career:** Watercolor painter, 1950s; traditional dancer and flutemaker; painter and then welder, auto body repair, 1950s; began welding sculptures, 1960s; built and operated a foundry in Oklahoma, mid-1970s; commissions, including Murray Federal Building, Oklahoma City, Oklahoma; lecturer and craft demonstrator. **Awards:** More than 250 from fine art shows and invitationals, including Inter-Tribal Indian Ceremonials (1972, 1975, 1977), Santa Fe Indian Market (1973-74), Heard Museum Guild Indian Fair and Market (1975), Scottsdale National Indian Art Exhibition (1975), Philbrook Museum of Art Annual Indian Art Exhibition (1975), American Indian and Cowboy Association (1979), Kirkpatrick Center (1979-80), Cherokee National Museum, 1980, and Indian Arts and Crafts Association, (artist of the year, 1986, and 1993).

Individual Exhibitions

1981   Southern Plains Indian Museum, Anadarko, Oklahoma

Selected Group Exhibitions

Exhibits regularly at art fairs, powwows, and invitationals and at galleries in Oklahoma, New Mexico, and California

1972   Red Ridge Art Museum, Oklahoma City, Oklahoma
1975   Heard Museum, Phoenix, Arizona
        Door County Museum, Sturgeon Bay, Wisconsin
1976   Philbrook Museum of Art, Tulsa, Oklahoma
1977   Bowlus Fine Arts Museum Iola, Kansas
1978   Heritage Center, Inc., Pine Ridge, South Dakota
1980   Casa de las Americas, Havana, Cuba
        Oklahoma Fine Arts Foundation, Oklahoma City
1981   Native American Center for the Living Arts, Niagara Falls, New York
1982   Nassau County Museum, Glen Cove, New York
1983   Cherokee National Museum, Tahlequah, Oklahoma
1986   American Indian Contemporary Arts, Albuquerque, New Mexico
1989-90 *Excellence* (annual), Christof's, Santa Fe, New Mexico
1992   Franco American Institute, Rennes, France
1996   Kiva Fine Arts, Santa Fe, New Mexico

Collections

American Indian Contemporary Arts, Albuquerque, New Mexico; Heard Museum, Phoenix, Arizona; Heritage Center, Inc., Pine Ridge, South Dakota; Philbrook Museum of Art, Tulsa, Oklahoma; Red Ridge Museum, Oklahoma City, Oklahoma; Red River Museum, Idabell, Oklahoma; St. Gregory's College, Shawnee, Oklahoma; Southern Plains Indians Museum, Anadarko, Oklahoma.

Publications

On PRATT: Articles—"Excellence Old and New at Christof's," *Art Talk*, June-July 1987; "Charlie Pratt," by Julie Pearson, *Southwest Art*, May 1989.

                    *   *   *

Like his grandfather, who molded animals, people, and buildings from clay as a way to entertain the three boys in his care, Pratt has creatively used resources available to him to reflect on and express a unique vision of his heritage. His successful career as an artist—having won over 250 prizes on the art fair circuit, enjoying regular commissions, and having work displayed and sold consistently in galleries—is a reflection of his determination, resourcefulness, and the spark of creativity that shapes ordinary and discarded material into works of art, in Pratt's case as wide-ranging works of metal sculpture.

Pratt was raised in southwestern Oklahoma with three siblings by his grandfather, who kept the boys entertained through storytelling, by creating toys he molded from clay, and by instructing the boys on how to mold their own objects. The combination of practiced technique and developing personal creativity made a lasting impression. Pratt became a self-trained artist while in his teens. Painting materials were the most readily available art supplies, and Pratt began creating watercolor works that he was able to sell on occasion in Oklahoma City. To make ends meet, he took a job at an automotive shop, first as a painter, then filling in when a body repairman failed to show for work, becoming involved in welding and collision repair. In off-work hours, he remained in the shop, using tools and scrap metal to form pieces he hand-welded into such objects as war shields and dancers. Encouraged by interested observers, informal sales, and visitors to his residence to view his pieces, Pratt left his job, completed a collection of works, and hit the art fair and powwow circuit, where he quickly made sales and attracted representation from galleries from the Plains to the far west.

In addition to larger sculptures, like the war shields, which have representative Plains Indians designs and are adorned with likenesses of feathers, Pratt also created smaller-sized metal figures, much like the clay pieces he fashioned as a boy. Among these were several series, including a set of miniature bronzes, *Ten Little Indians*, that proved immensely popular. The playfulness and skill of Pratt's work is evident in these pieces, from the title of the series to the figures represented, including Indian dancers and warriors, people praying or hunting, and all rendered with serious attention to telling, authentic detail. This early 1970s series was a breakthrough, but being restlessly creative Pratt became prolific in a wide variety of sculptures, from miniatures, to masks, to full-sized pieces, including dancers over six feet tall with ceremonial regalia and paraphernalia. Through research and discussions with people from many tribes, whom he met at fairs or sought for consultation, Pratt was able to make his figures more authentic—using his imagination to represent the real and avoiding fanciful stereotypes or distorted warrior and ceremonial elements.

Pratt's sculptures can be basically divided into two kinds: those meant as a rough, representational art and more polished pieces that reflect skill of craftsmanship. The more polished pieces are seamless and can include paint, inlays, engravings, and a such materials as semiprecious stones and leather, all designed to achieve a harmonious balance and accurate representation. Other works remain rough, with fused sheet metal, rods, tubes, nuts and bolts, evoking more abstract forms. Pratt's subjects have ranged broadly: examples from his vast inventory include bronze buffalo skulls, shields, feathers, masks, small animals, plumage, monumental outdoor sculpture, kachinas, and chess sets. A ceremonial dancer since he was a boy, Pratt is careful to attend to the dignity of his subject matter while also remaining playful, as exemplified in a metal sculpture of a Kachina at rest eating a candy bar and enjoying a soft drink.

                                                —Perry Bear

PROKOPIOF, Bill

Tribal affiliations: Aleut
Sculptor and mixed media artist

Born: Juneau, Alaska, 20 May 1944. **Education:** Institute of American Indian Arts, AA, 1966; San Francisco Art Institute, 1967-68; additional courses in sculpting and casting at University of Kansas and through the Southwestern Association for Indian Artists (SWAIA). **Career:** Assistant, Oceanic/Atmospheric Administration, St. George's Island, Alaska; bronze casting, Santa Fe, Tesuque, New Mexico, and Loveland, Colorado; designer, technical advisor, and traveling curator, *One With the Earth* bicentennial exhibition sponsored by the Institute of American Indian Arts, 1976-80; sculpting full time since 1980. **Awards:** Grand Award winner, Red Earth, Oklahoma City, Oklahoma, 1989-90; Best of Show, American Indian Contemporary Arts, San Dennis, California, 1992; Best of Show, Eiteljorg Museum, Indianapolis, 1995.

Individual Exhibitions

1985	Southern Plains Indian Museum, Anadarko, Oklahoma
1990	Carlin Gallery, New York, New York
	Minnesota Skyway, Minneapolis, Minnesota

Selected Group Exhibitions

1966	Edinburgh Festival, Scotland
	Alaska Centennial Exhibition, Anchorage, Alaska
	Berlin Festival, Berlin, West Germany
	Philbrook Museum of Art, Tulsa, Oklahoma
1972	*Night of First Americans*, Kennedy Center for the Performing Arts, Washington, D.C.
	Heard Museum, Phoenix, Arizona
1976-80	*One With the Earth Bicentennial*, Institute of American Indian Arts, Santa Fe, New Mexico (traveling)
1987	Riverside Museum, New York City, New York
1989-94	*Red Earth Festival*, Anadarko, Oklahoma
1992-96	Santa Fe Indian Market
1995	Eiteljorg Museum, Indianapolis, Indiana

Collections

Anchorage Museum of Natural History, Anchorage, Alaska; Eiteljorg Museum, Indianapolis, Indiana; Institute of American Indian Arts Museum, Santa Fe, New Mexico; Southern Plains Museum, Anadarko, Oklahoma; Southwest Museum, Los Angeles, California.

Publications

On PROKOPIOF: Articles—"From Alaska to Santa Fe with Love," by Katherine Anthony, *Focus Santa Fe*, August/September 1987; "Bill Prokopiof," by Julie Pearson, *Southwest Art*, April, 1992; "Sculptor Bill Prokopiof Returns Full Circle to his Alaskan Roots," by Julie Weinberg, *Pasatiempo*, 20-26 August 1993; "Monumental Sculpture Enthralls a Growing Audience," by Ann Lawrence Ryan, *Santa Fe Reporter: Indian Market Special Insert*, August 1996; "A Career of Random Events," by Michael Koster, *Pasatiempo*, 16-22 August 1996.

* * *

Bill Prokopiof: *Dances with Walrus.* **Courtesy of the artist.**

Bill Prokopiof makes no romantic or spiritual claims about his sculptures. They are pieces filled with humor and whimsy and, most importantly, even though they are made primarily of welded steel, they are to be taken very lightly. Although he originally produced works that favored the more visible Southwestern styles where he settled, Prokopiof now produces pieces that rely heavily on his Aleut upbringing in Alaska. His recent characters are almost exclusively based on fish, walrus, seals, fishermen, and mythical creatures from the very North of North America.

Throughout his career, Prokopiof has experimented extensively with unusual media and techniques. Stone, steel, bronze, cast paper and wood are among the variety of materials that have appeared in his pieces. Prokopiof has been known to combine these in startling ways, producing an effect based on the contrasting relationships between the materials and the subjects they represent within the sculptures.

Prokopiof seems to find most of his professional satisfaction, though, through working with welded steel. For him, the appeal of building layers seems preferable to the techniques of working primarily in stone, as many other sculptors do. With steel, the artist is not limited by the grain of the stone or the size of the original piece. Most recently, Prokopiof has been using metal and stone together in direct and startling interactions.

In all of his pieces, a strong sense of character laced with his trademark ironic whimsy is one of the prominent forces in Prokopiof's work. *Bird Woman with Egg* (welded steel and alabaster) features a woman made of steel, her spindly features bringing Disney characters to mind, yet there is something moving about the tenderness and gentleness in which she cradles the white alabaster egg in her lap.

Prokopiof's sculptures also carry a strong sense of balance and design. In *Walking Wally* (welded steel and marble), the sculptor presents us with a steel human figure topped by the head of a walrus carved in marble. Wally's arms are raised in the tradition of a politician on a soap box, and he stands with one leg raised in mid-step. It makes one wonder whether Wally is preaching or protesting—or both.

Like *Walking Wally*, a number of Prokopiof's characters are captured in mid-stride, or mid-waddle. Some, like *Dances With Walrus*, appear to be dancing or even skipping down the street. Each of them, though, is definitely going somewhere.

Prokopiof also creates more abstract pieces, such as *Village Gossip (Can We Talk?)*. Carved out of Utah alabaster, this piece has the sideways whispering expression of the gossip, yet only the face and hand are representational. The rest of the piece projects the image of a woman leaning over to talk to her neighbor, only the face and hand are clearly defined.

Wherever whimsy takes him, Prokopiof seems to be skipping down a road that few other artists are traveling. Yet, the irony of his pieces keep them from floating off without substance.

—Vesta Giles

PUDLO

Variant names: Pudlo Pudlat
Tribal affiliations: Inuit
Carver and printmaker

Born: In a camp near Kamadjuak, in the vicinity of Cape Dorset, Northwest Territories, 1916; name also transliterated as Padluq, Padlo, Padloo, Pudloo. **Career:** Hunter, fisherman, artist. **Awards:** Design chosen for UNICEF greeting card, 1972; one of four Cape Dorset artists commissioned by United Nations Habitat Conference to produce a collection of prints, 1976; *Aeroplane* (1976) reproduced on Canadian postage stamp, 1978; commissioned by Department of Indian Affairs and Northern Development, 1978, Canadian Guild of Crafts Quebec, 1979, Queen Elizabeth Hotel, Montreal, 1979, Canadian Guild of Craftsman, 1980. **Died:** 28 December 1992.

Individual Exhibitions

1976   *Pudlo Prints*, Department of Indian Affairs and Northern Development, Ottawa (traveling through 1977)
1978   *Pudlo: Acrylic Paintings*, Inuit Gallery of Eskimo Art, Toronto
        Pudlo Pudlat: Acrylic Paintings, Canadian Guild of Crafts Quebec, Montreal
1980   *Pudlo Pudlat: Ten Oversize Works on Paper*, Theo Waddington, New York
1981   *Arctic Landscapes*, Theo Waddington, New York
1982   Department of Indian Affairs and Northern Development, Ottawa (traveling through 1984)
1983   Confederation Centre Art Gallery and Museum, Charlottetown, Prince Edward Island
1987   Inuit Gallery of Eskimo Art, Toronto
1989   Inuit Galerie, Mannheim, Germany

Gallery Indigena, Stratford and Waterloo, Ontario
1990   *Pudlo Pudlat: New Drawings*, Inuit Gallery of Eskimo Art, Toronto
        Uffundi Gallery, Ottawa
        Pudlo: Thirty Years of Drawing, National Gallery of Canada, Ottawa (traveling through 1991)
1993   *Pudlo Pudlat: A Meeting of Cultures*, McMichael Canadian Art Collection, Kleinburg, Ontario
1994   *Pudlo Pudlat aus Cape Dorset*, Inuit Galerie, Mannheim, Germany
1995   *Pudlo: Original Drawings*, Albers Gallery, San Francisco

Selected Group Exhibitions

1961   Cape Dorset Graphics (annual through 1993)
1967   *Cape Dorset: A Decade of Eskimo Prints & Recent Sculpture*, National Gallery of Canada in cooperation with the Canadian Eskimo Art Committee, Ottawa (traveling)
        Inoonoot Eskima: Grafik och Skulptur fran Cape Dorset och Povungnituk, Konstframjandet, Stockholm, Sweden
1968   *Eskimo Sculpture, Eskimo Prints, and Paintings of Norval Morriseau*, Art Association of Newport, Newport, Rhode Island
1969   *Arctic Art*, Lippel Gallery, presented at Place Bonaventure, Montreal
1970   *Graphic Art by Eskimos of Canada*, Cultural Affairs Division, Department of External Affairs, Ottawa (traveling)
1971   *Sculpture/Inuit: Masterworks of the Canadian Arctic*, Canada Eskimo Arts Council, Ottawa (traveling through 1973)
1972   *Eskimo Fantastic Art*, Gallery 111, School of Art, University of Manitoba, Winnipeg
1973   *Les Eskimos/De Eskimos*, Studio 44 - Passage 44, Brussels, Belgium
1975   *We Lived by Animals/Nous Visions des Animaux*, Department of Indian Affairs and Northern Development in cooperation with the Department of External Affairs, Ottawa (traveling through 1979)
1976   *Shamans and Spirits: Myths and Medical Symbolism in Eskimo Art*, Canadian Arctic Producers and the National Museum of Man, Ottawa (traveling through 1982)
1977   *Contemporary Eskimo Prints and Sculpture*, Amon Carter Museum of Western Art, Fort Worth, Texas
1978   *The Coming and Going of the Shaman: Eskimo Shamanism and Art*, Winnipeg Art Gallery, Manitoba
        Polar Visions: Canadian Eskimo Graphics, Jerusalem Artists' House Museum, Israel
1979   *Creative Flight*, Surrey Art Gallery, Surrey, British Columbia
1980   *The Inuit Amautik: I Like My Hood to Be Full*, Winnipeg Art Gallery, Manitoba
1981   *Eskimo Games: Graphics and Sculpture/Giuochi Eschimesi: grafiche e sculture*, National Gallery of Modern Art, Rome
        Inuit Art: A Selection of Inuit Art from the Collection of the National Museum of Man, Ottawa, and the Rothman's Permanent Collection of Inuit Sculpture, Canada (traveling through 1982)
1982   *Noel au Chateau: Art Inuit de la collection Macdonald Stewart Art Centre*, Chateau Dufresne, Montreal

473

1983   *The Arctic/L'Artique*, UNESCO, Paris
        *Hunter of the Sacred Game: Traditional Life on the Land,
        Arts and Services Foundation*, Minneapolis, Minne-
        sota (traveling)
1985   *Alaska Eskimo Dolls/Inuit Prints*, Provincial Museum of
        Alberta, Edmonton, Alberta (traveling)
1986   *From Drawing to Print: Perceptions and Process in Cape
        Dorset Art*, Glenbow Museum, Calgary, Alberta
1988   *Im Schatten der Sonne: Zeitgenossische Kunst der Indianer
        und Eskimos in Kanada/In the Shadow of the Sun:
        Contemporary Indian and Inuit Art in Canada*, Cana-
        dian Museum of Civilization, Ottawa, (traveling
        through 1989)
1991   *Soujourns to Nunavut: Contemporary Inuit Art from
        Canada*, Bunkamura Art Gallery, Tokyo (traveling)
1992   *Oonark, Pudlo, Kananginak*, Winnipeg Art Gallery,
        Manitoba (traveling through 1993)
1995   *Keeping Out Stories Alive: An Exhibition of the Art and
        Crafts from Dene and Inuit of Canada*, Institute of
        American Indian Arts Museum, Santa Fe

Collections

Anchorage Museum of History and Art, Anchorage, Alaska; Art Gallery of Greater Victoria, Victoria, British Columbia; Art Gallery of Nova Scotia, Halifax, Nova Scotia; Art Gallery of Windsor, Windsor, Ontario; Beaverbrook Art Gallery, Fredericton, New Brunswick; Canada Council Art Bank, Ottawa; Canadian Guild of Crafts Quebec, Montreal, Quebec; Canadian Museum of Civiliza-tion, Hull, Quebec; Amon Carter Museum of Western Art, Fort Worth, Texas; CIBC Collection, Toronto; Confederation Centre of the Arts, Charlottetown, Prince Edward Island; Dennos Museum Center, Northwestern Michigan College, Traverse City, Michigan; Agnes Etherington Art Centre, Queen's University, Kingston, Ontario; Glenbow Museum, Calgary, Alberta; Klamer Family Col-lection, Art Gallery of Ontario, Toronto; Laurentian University Museum and Arts Centre, Sudbury, Ontario; Clifford E. Lee Col-lection, University of Alberta, Edmonton; London Regional Art Gallery, London, Ontario; Macdonald Stewart Art Centre, Guelph, Ontario; Macmillan-Bloedel Limited, Vancouver; McMaster Uni-versity Art Gallery, Hamilton, Ontario; McMichael Canadian Art Collection, Kleinburg, Ontario; Mendel Art Gallery, Saskatoon, Saskatchewan; Musée des Beaux Arts de Montreal; Museum of Anthropology, University of British Columbia, Vancouver; Mu-seum of Modern Art, New York; National Gallery of Canada, Ot-tawa; Owens Art Gallery, Mount Allison University, Sackville, New Brunswick; Prince of Wales Northern Heritage Centre, Yellowknife, Northwest Territories; Province of British Columbia, Victoria; Royal Ontario Museum, Toronto; Simon Fraser Gallery, Simon Fraser University, Burnaby, British Columbia; Surrey Art Gallery, Surrey, British Columbia; Teleglobe Canada, Montreal; University of Alberta, Edmonton; University of Lethbridge Art Gallery, Lethbridge, Alberta; University of Michigan Museum of Art, Ann Arbor; University of New Brunswick, Fredericton; Vancouver Art Gallery; Winnipeg Art Gallery, Manitoba; York University, Toronto.

Publications

On PUDLO: Books—*Sculpture of the Eskimo* by George Swinton, Toronto, 1972; *Art of the Eskimo: Prints* edited by Ernst Roch with text by Patrick Furneaux and Leo Rosshandler, Toronto, 1974; *The Eskimo and His Art* by Carson I. A. Ritchie, Toronto, 1974; *Umajut: Animal Imagery in Inuit Art* by Bernadette Driscoll, Winnipeg Art Gallery, 1985; *From Drawing to Print: Perception and Process in Cape Dorset Art* by Dorothy LaBarge, Calgary: Glenbow Museum, 1986; *Kunst aus der Artiks* by Gitta Hassler, Zurich, 1994; *Keep-ing Our Stories Alive: An Exhibition of Art and Crafts from Dene and Inuit of Canada,* Santa Fe: Institute of American Indian Art Museum, 1995. **Articles**—"Pudlo Hangings for Indian and North-ern Affairs Lobby," *About Arts and Crafts,* Winter 1978; "Inuit Painter Best with Airplanes as He Dares to Do What Others Shun" by Gary Michael Daunt, *Toronto Star,* 17 February 1978; "No Hunting, Just Art for Pudlo" by Evelyn Brakeman, *Edmonton Jour-nal,* 31 October 1978; "Personal vs. Cultural Expression in Inuit Prints" by Marion E. Jackson, *Print Voice: A Publication on Printmaking and Print Artists,* Edmonton, 1984; "Christianity and Inuit Art" by Jean Blodgett, *The Beaver,* Autumn 1984; "Northern Exposure: Inuit Images of Travel," *Inuit Art Quarterly,* vol. 1, no. 2, 1986; "From Drawing to Print: Perception and Process in Cape Dorset Art" by Monique Westra, *Inuit Art Quarterly,* vol. 1, no. 3, 1986; "Inuit Drawings: 'Prompted' Art-Making" by Robert Chris-topher, *Inuit Art Quarterly,* Summer 1987; "Pudlo Pudlat's Force-ful Legacy: Who Will Follow the Master?" by Terrence Ryan, *Arc-tic Circle,* Spring 1993. **Film**—*Interview with Pudlo Pudlat,* Canadian Eskimo Arts Council in collaboration with the Inuit Art Section, Inuit Art Centre, and the National Film Board of Canada, 1985.

*   *   *

Well known in the history of contemporary Inuit art is the story of James Houston, the Canadian artist who ventured into the Arctic in 1948 and encouraged the Inuit to carve soapstone sculptures to sell in southern Canada. Today contemporary Inuit art (including sculpture, prints, drawings, textiles and jewelry) has gained inter-national recognition from scholars, patrons and institutions. While Houston initially solicited anyone, the increasing focus on aes-thetic quality that accompanied the growing popularity of Inuit art aided in distinguishing the gifted artists from those simply trying to make a living. Among the first generation of artists encountered by Houston was Pudlo Pudlat.

Pudlat's career as an artist was initially born of misfortune. In the spring of 1957, at the age of forty-one, he had a hunting acci-dent. Having dismissed the incident as minor, within a month he was in need of emergency medical care and was flown south for surgery. A few days after returning north Pudlat was diagnosed with tuberculosis and was again sent south to recover. In part due to these complications, Pudlat and his wife, Innukjuakju, eventu-ally gave up their traditional semi-nomadic hunting lifestyle and settled at a camp near Cape Dorset in the spring of 1958.

The late 1950s were a pivotal and productive time at Cape Dorset, the best-known artistic community in the Canadian Arctic. Suc-cessful experimentation with hand printing in 1957-58 lead to the creation of the West Baffin Eskimo Co-operative, a printshop that began marketing an annual collection in 1959. Here Pudlat came into regular contact with Houston, other Inuit artists such as Kenojuak, as well as the photographer and Inuit historian Peter Pitseolak. Pudlat was initially encouraged to carve but later started to draw. His early works consist of bold and relatively uncomplicated black-and-white images that float unimpeded in the center of the page. This stylistic emphasis on form favored by many Inuit artists has been associated with indigenous artistic traditions and is also easily translatable into prints. Consequently, ten of Pudlat's early images were chosen for the 1961 print collection.

While his talent as a graphic artist was immediately apparent, Pudlat's reputation was formed later, in the mid-1970s. Pudlat became known for his depiction of modern, non-Inuit subject matter, with controversy surrounding his image, *Aeroplane*, which was included in the 1976 print collection. Although he was not the first Inuit to depict modern technology, he was the first to treat it as an integral aspect of everyday life rather than a passing anomaly, and reaction was mixed. While many saw the denigration of tradition in *Aeroplane*, others applauded Pudlat's candid representation of Western subject matter.

In addition to his documentary style, Pudlat is also known for his more imaginative works in which he experiments with fantasy and visual punning. For example, *New Parts for an Inuk* (1981) is a self-portrait of a standing human figure with horns, antlers, hooves and a wrist watch—the design of which is enlarged and repeated over the figure's heart cavity. Having just recovered from an operation in which he received a pacemaker, Pudlat's image is a clever and sophisticated interpretation of this event.

Due to the suggestive iconography in works such as *New Parts*, some of Pudlat's drawings have been misconstrued as expressions of Inuit Shamanism. Because non-Western art with religious subject matter has historically been valued over that with secular themes, such misunderstandings are common and often remain undisputed. Fortunately, the artist himself has addressed the discrepancy between his intentions and his audiences' interpretations. When asked by art historian Marion Jackson in a 1978 interview if one of his drawings is representative of a shaman, Pudlat replied, "No. I don't think of her as a shaman, maybe only you do." In fact, Pudlat has been an Anglican for most of his life, and many of his images incorporate symbols of this adopted faith.

With increasing interest in his work, Pudlat attended several openings in his later years, including his own retrospective, *Pudlo: Thirty Years of Drawing* (1990). Pudlat is remembered with reverence within his community while his work continues to attract critical art historical attention. Consisting of over 4,500 drawings, Pudlat's *oeuvre* is the product of a prolific and visionary mind as well as an extensive visual record that documents changes in Canadian Inuit society.

—Kristin Potter

PUSHETONEQUA, Charles

Variant names: Charlie Push; Wawabano Sata
Tribal affiliations: Sauk and Fox
Painter

Born: Tama, Iowa, 1915; Wawabano Sata means Dawn Walker. **Education:** Haskell and Santa Fe Indian Schools. **Military Service:** U.S. Air Force, World War II. **Awards:** America Discovers Indian Art, 1967, regional award. **Died:** 25 August 1987.

Selected Group Exhibitions

1946-59   *America Discovers Indian Art*, Smithsonian Institution touring exhibition
1963   Association on American Indian Affairs, Inc., New York
1969   Philbrook Museum of Art, Tulsa, Oklahoma

1996   Museum of Indian Arts and Cultures, Santa Fe, New Mexico
          Vision and Voices: Native American Painting from the Philbrook Museum of Art, Philbrook Museum of Art, Tulsa, Oklahoma

Collections

Denver Art Museum, Denver, Colorado; Mexico; Historical Society of Marshall County, Marshalltown, Iowa; Museum of Indian Arts and Cultures, Santa Fe, New Mexico; Philbrook Museum of Art Center, Tulsa, Oklahoma; Tama Indian Crafts Organization, Tama, Iowa.

Publications

On PUSHETONEQUA—*Indian Painters and White Patrons*, by J. J. Brody, Albuquerque, University of New Mexico Press, 1971; *American Indian Painting and Sculpture*, by Patricia Janis Broder, New York, Abbeville Press, 1981; *Vision and Voices: Native American Painting from the Philbrook Museum of Art*, Lydia Wyckoff, editor, Tulsa, Philbrook Museum of Art, 1996.

*   *   *

Charles Pushetonequa was one of few painters among the Sauk and Fox Woodlands people and his art is considered especially important as one of the few illustrated documentations from within the Sauk and Fox nation on the customs, dress, and ceremonies of Woodlands Indians of the Mississippi River area. An Algonquian speaking people, the Sauk and Fox are a Woodlands group who originally lived east of the Mississippi. While most of the Sauk (People of the Yellow Earth) live today in northeast Oklahoma, near Stroud, most of the Fox live in Tama, Iowa. Pushetonequa was from Tama, Iowa, indicating that most of his ancestors probably were Fox, a people who call themselves Mesquakie (People of the Red Earth). The two tribes were long united as one nation, but split in the nineteenth century over the issue of removing to Indian Territory in Oklahoma. Pushetonequa's ancestors were the group that held onto part of their homeland in Iowa. They also preserved traditional culture.

Pushetonequa's first love was baseball, and his pursuit of becoming a pitcher led, inadvertently, to instruction in the arts through which he eventually became a painter. Pushetonequa came from the same nation as Olympic champion and professional baseball and football player Jim Thorpe. Wayne Pushetonequa, the artist's son, recalled his father saying, "first thing I wanted to do was to be a ball player." Pushetonequa was sent to boarding school and started playing baseball, developing into a strong pitcher. He was recruited by the Haskell Indian School in Oklahoma, but was stricken with tuberculosis. Pushetonequa moved on to the Santa Fe Indian School, where the drier climate helped improve his health; it was there that he was exposed to painting, was influenced by fellow artists who rendered ceremonial and secular depictions of their communities, and found an audience for his work.

One of Pushetonequa's early patrons was Margretta S. Dietrich, a social activist who provided both financial and emotional support for many Indian artists. Her circle included Museum of New Mexico founding director Edgar L. Hewett, poet Alice Corbin Henderson and Santa Fe artist Olive Rush. These collectors and promoters favored decorative paintings that provided ethnographic information, particularly colorful and detailed renderings of the secular and spiritual life of Indian communities. Dietrich bought a painting from Pushetonequa that was donated as part of a group of Dorothy Dunn Studio-style works to the Museum of Indian Arts and Cultures in Santa Fe. The painting, *Woodland Buffalo Dance*, exhibited with a selection of 85 paintings at the Museum in 1996, was one of few in the exhibit by Woodlands artists.

Woodland Buffalo Dance was painted in tempera on board in 1942. At first glance, the painting shows influences of the Southwest and Plains, and only closer inspection reveals unique cultural symbolism. For example, the blue sky is represented with rain clouds painted in the Pueblo style, above a stepped terrace. Lightning bolts zig-zag toward the center, framing a buffalo shield with horns emerging from a Pueblo sun symbol. In the foreground, five buffalo dancers are escorted by three dancing women. They move across the field in profile, a composition familiar to most Pueblo artists. The lead buffalo dancer is blowing a flute topped with a carved buffalo effigy. It is here that the artist reverts to his own Woodland traditions. The dancers have beaded arm bands, while Pueblo arm bands are generally made of painted leather. The bodies of the dancers are blue and their moccasins are yellow, atypical in Pueblo scenes. Their garters are black and without tassels, while Pueblo garters are generally red or a mix of bright colored yarns. The moccasins have long cuffs, unlike Puebloan fringed anklets. Breech cloths are blue with green ribbon edges and tassels, while Pueblo ones are generally white with red, green and black embroidery, or dark indigo blue. The details that unmistakably identify the work as Woodlands are in the women's dress. Their skirts are long blue stroud with colorful ribbon applique in strips down the front and around the bottom border. Close examination also reveal the bottoms of their leggings are blue stroud with ribbonwork applique. No Pueblo and other Southwestern woman dress in this woodlands style, which spread from the Great Lakes region and Prairie tribes. The technique was carried by dispossessed Eastern tribes to Indian Territory in Oklahoma in the nineteenth century and is still popular today.

Pushetonequa served in World War II and returned to the Tama Indian Settlement. He continued painting intermittently while raising a family, and his works were reproduced and widely distributed by the Tama Indian Crafts organization. Pushetonequa focused on the traditional activities of the Mesquakie tribe, including gathering and preparing maple syrup, weaving, drying squash, and some early dances of the tribe. He probably was the first person to bring the concept of modern painting forward to his people, and notice he received through reproductions and purchases of originals brought some recognition to the settlement as well here. His son, Wayne, notes that Pushetonequa's paintings "were more or less all over the place in the businesses downtown and banks. So his artwork was out there. And I think that inspired other people to start on their own." He added: "we have ended up a tribe with quite a few artists ... The official tribal logo of our tribe was his design. So there's evidence that he is still here."

—Gregory Schaaf

QOYAWAYMA, Polingaysi

Variant names: Elizabeth White
Tribal affiliations: Hopi
Painter

Born: Oraibi, Arizona, c. 1892. **Education:** First Hopi child taught in the Anglo public school system; Sherman Institute in Riverside;

California, 1906; Bethel Academy (Kansas), 1910; Bible Institute in Los Angeles, undergraduate work. **Family:** Married Lloyd White, 1931. **Career:** Taught on Hopi and Navajo reservations, early 1930s to 1954; established Hopi Scholarship Fund, 1959; operated a guest house on the Hopi Reservation, where she entertained anthropologists, scholars, writers (including Ernest Hemingway), and statespersons (including Theodore Roosevelt); potter, in the latter part of her life. **Awards:** Department of the Interior's Distinguished Service Award, 1954; Museum of Northern Arizona honors, 1976 (bronze sculpture of Polingaysi by Una Hanbury); Arizona Indian Living Treasure tribute (Heard Museum's Gold Medal), 1978; Bethel College honors, Outstanding Alumna, 1979; Arizona Author Award, Arizona State Library Association and the Libraries Limited Group, 1989; Arizona Women's Hall of Fame, 1991.

Individual Exhibitions

1978   Heard Museum, Phoenix, Arizona

Selected Group Exhibitions

1974   *Indian Arts and Crafts Exhibit,* Heard Museum, Phoenix, Arizona
1977   Heard Museum Indian Fair and Market, Phoenix, Arizona

Collections

Heard Museum, Phoenix, Arizona

Publications

By QOYAWAYMA: Books—*The Sun Girl*, Phoenix, 1941; *No Turning Back: A Hopi Indian Woman's Struggle to Live in Two Worlds* (with Vada F. Carlson), Albuquerque, 1964.

On QOYAWAYMA: Books—*When I Met Polingaysi Underneath the Cottonwood Tree,* edited by Jo Linder, privately published, 1983; *Talking with the Clay,* by Stephen A. Trimble, Santa Fe, 1987; *Polingaysi Qoyawayma (Elizabeth Q. White)*, Arizona Women's Hall of Fame, Phoenix, 1991. **Article**—"Polingaysi Qoyawayma," *American Indian Art*, Winter 1995.

*   *   *

Polingaysi Qoyawayma was a rebel and a pioneer of thought and education, gracefully blazing a pathway between the Hopi and Anglo worlds and fulfilling the prophecy of her grandmother, who once told her that she would form a bond between the Hopi and the Anglo people. Qoyawayma was the first Anglo-educated Hopi woman, choosing to attend Mennonite schools, and she eventually became an innovative teacher in native education and an award-winning writer. In the second phase of her life, following her retirement from teaching in 1954, Qoyawayma created breathtakingly beautiful pottery—and once again, she was a pioneer.

Qoyawayma's pottery is easily distinguished for its simple style and balance. Her pieces, whether vases, corn maiden wind bells, or other unusual shapes, were all made with an eye for clean lines and balance. Her distinctive style of using the images of an ear of corn,

Dextra Quotskuyva: Sikyatki-style pottery, c. 1990. Photograph by Seth Roffman; courtesy Dick Howard collection.

or a Kokopelli, created through the use of high relief techniques on the surface of the pots, has yet to be matched.

Singlehandedly, Qoyawayma created this unique style by producing unpainted, off-white colored pottery with the large and clear figure of the ear of corn pushing or bursting from the surface as a tribute to the Hopi "Mother Corn" and a return to her ancestral ways. She was also one of the first potters to progress to new forms of Hopi pottery while still using Native materials and styles. Here, Qoyawayma continued her grandmother's prophesy again, blending traditional Hopi materials with a new style to fashion a variety of colors, from off-white to buff pink and red.

In between worlds defined by race and religion she moved easily and thoughtfully. In the Hopi language, her name roughly translates to "butterfly sitting among flowers in the breeze." As a woman who was able to find spiritual beauty wherever she was, Polingaysi Qoyawayma's name seems deeply appropriate. Her sentiments are stated beautifully in words from her corn grinding song:

> Oh for a heart as pure as pollen on corn blossoms,
> And for a life as sweet as honey gathered from the flowers,
> And beautiful as butterflies in sunshine.

—Vesta Giles

QUOTSKUYVA, Dextra
Tribal affiliations: Hopi
Potter

Born: Polacca, Arizona, 7 September 1928. **Family:** Fourth generation descendant of Nampeyo, the Tewa potter who revived Sityatki-style pottery on First Mesa at Hopi; granddaughter of Annie and Willie Healing, daughter of Rachel and Emerson Namingha, wife of Edwin Quotskuyva, mother of Hisi (Camille) Nampeyo and Dan Namingha, grandmother of Lowel Chereposy, Erica Quotskuyva, and Reid Ami. **Education:** Phoenix Indian School, Oraibi High School. **Career:** Full-time potter since 1967. **Awards:** Many, including First Place, American Indian and Western Relic Show, Los Angeles, 1974, and proclaimed an "Arizona Living Treasure," 1995.

Selected Group Exhibitions

The artist has exhibited frequently at fairs throughout the Southwest.

1973   Museum of Northern Arizona, Flagstaff, Arizona
1974   Muckenthaler Cultural Center, Fullerton, California

477

1989 American Indian and Western Relic Show, Los Angeles
Mitchell Indian Museum, Evanston, Illinois
1994 Museum of Indian Arts and Culture, Santa Fe, New Mexico
1996 *The Nampeyo Legacy Continues: The Art of Five Generations of a Renowned Tewa/Hopi Family,* Santa Fe Indian Market, Santa Fe, New Mexico

Collections

Museum of Indian Arts and Culture, Santa Fe, New Mexico.

Publications

On **QUOTSKUYVA: Books**—*Seven Families in Pueblo Pottery,* Maxwell Museum of Anthropology, Albuquerque: University of New Mexico Press, 1974; *Nampeyo: A Gift Remembered,* by Martha Lanman Cusick, Evanston, Illinois, 1989; *Fourteen Families in Pueblo Pottery,* by Rick Dillingham, Albuquerque, 1994; *Creation's Journey: Native American Identity and Belief,* Tom Hill and Richard W. Hill, Sr., editors, Washington, D.C., 1995; *The Nampeyo Legacy Continues,* Martha Hopkins Struever, Santa Fe, 1996. **Articles**— "Dextra Quotskuyva Nampeyo," *American Indian Art Magazine,* by Guy and Doris Monthan, Autumn 1977; "Pueblo Pottery: 2000 Years of Artistry," by David L. Arnold, *National Geographic,* November 1982; "Potter Dextra Quotskuyva," by Martha Hopkins Struever, *Indian Artist,* Summer 1996.

*

Dextra Quotskuyva comments:

I started my pottery work around 1967 and have been working on it constantly ever since. My mother, Rachel, watched and supervised me. I would help my mother with the firing but began to fire on my own. I have experimented with the use of shells and turquoise on my pottery like some of the potters at San Ildefonso. My mother isn't happy about the break from tradition. I am always working on new experiments. I want to keep my pottery unique.

*   *   *

Dextra Quotskuyva is recognized as one of the most eminent contemporary Pueblo Indian potters. Following in the heritage of Nampeyo, her Tewa great-grandmother, Quotskuyva honors her ancestors while going beyond tradition, with work that features thin walled coiling, perfect symmetry, a range of traditional and contemporary forms, and intricate painting that patterns traditional symbols and motifs in a rich complexity of designs that create a contemporary look.

While Quotskuyva had tremendous opportunities for education in pottery surrounding her in the Hopi community, she displayed natural talents as well as hard-earned success through practice. During her childhood she asked her mother one day to let her paint pots and was given a cracked one to start with, but her painting came so effortlessly that it was the last imperfect vessel her mother gave her for practice. Her pottery making began similarly, under the tutelage of her mother, Rachel, beginning with filling up solid places on pots, followed by molding, making tiny pots, making bigger ones, and then making round pots, which she found easier and discovered as well that it is easier to design larger pots than smaller ones. "But before all of that happened," she told Martha Hopkins Struever (*Indian Artist,* Summer 1996), "I had a dream . . . of being at Sand Hills where all the trees were in the midst of the sand dunes. It was so beautiful. . . . We used to play there all the time, rolling down those big hills. In this dream I was sitting on the hill by myself. I kept smoothing the sand and then I felt something round. I went, 'What is this?' I kept digging on the right hand side, and finally I saw a pot. I dug it out, and it was really pretty with beautiful designs on it. I kept picking up pots, all with those beautiful designs. There were so many of them! After that, I thought the dream was wiped away, but when I was firing, it came back. Then it dawned on me that some of those designs were on one of the pots that I had designed."

Making an original contribution to the history of pottery in the Southwest, Quotskuyva enjoys great demand for her work, which is among the most difficult to obtain and most pieces are sold as quickly as they become available. Even as she creates new pieces, Quotskuyva helps sustain traditional culture, teaching and encouraging young people at Hopi in the art while giving young artists the freedom to be creative: "You need to almost surrender yourself to what you're doing. You're talking to clay all the time. It's just like talking to another person. Once clay gets hold of you, you drop everything. The clay has a lot of energy . . . the clay wants you home. It's got that energy to pull you back . . . I'm just in my own world. Once you start feeling that way, the clay wants to work along with you, and let you make this beautiful pot. These are things that you feel, but I never really felt I was an artist."

—Gregory Schaaf

RAY, Carl
Variant names: Tall Straight Poplar
Tribal affiliations: Cree
Painter and printmaker

Born: Sandy Lake Reserve, Ontario, 18 July 1943. **Education:** Essentially a self-taught artist; apprentice to Norval Morrisseau, mural for Expo '67. **Career:** Worked as a trapper, logger, and miner; writer, editor, printmaker; taught summer workshops sponsored by the Manitoulin Arts Foundation, early 1970s; numerous mural commissions, including Expo '67, Indian Pavilion (1967), Sandy Lake Primary School (1971), Sioux Lookout Fellowship and Communication Centre, Sioux Lookout, Ontario (1973). **Awards:** Grants from Canada Council, Indian and Northern Affairs Canada, and Department of National Health and Welfare. **Died:** September 1978.

Individual Exhibitions

1969	Brandon University, Brandon, Manitoba
	Indian-Metis Friendship Centre, Winnipeg, Manitoba
1969-70	Confederation College, Thunder Bay, Ontario
1972	Fort Francis Public Library, Fort Francis, Ontario
	Gallerie Fore, Winnipeg, Manitoba
1972-77	Aggregation Gallery, Toronto, Ontario
1973	Terryberry Library, Hamilton, Ontario
1979	Wah-sa Gallery, Winnipeg, Manitoba
1984	Ethel Flavelle Gallery, Willowdale, Ontario

Selected Group Exhibitions

1968-69	Brandon University, Brandon, Manitoba
1970	Confederation College, Thunder Bay, Ontario
1971	Minnesota State College, International Falls, Minnesota
1972	University of Minnesota, Duluth
	Gallerie Fore, Winnipeg, Manitoba
	Northern Ontario Art Show, sponsored by Indian and Northern Affairs, Canada, Ottawa, Ontario (traveling)
1974	*Canadian Indian Art '74,* Royal Ontario Museum, Toronto, Ontario
	Contemporary Native Art of Ontario, Oakville Centennial Gallery, Oakville, Ontario
1975	*Indian Art by the Seven Members of the Professional Native Artists, Inc.,* Wallack Galleries, Ottawa, Ontario
1976	*Contemporary Native Art of Canada: The Woodland Indians,* Royal Ontario Museum, Toronto, Ontario, and touring London, England, and Lahr, West Germany
1977	*Contemporary Indian Art: The Trail from the Past to the Future,* Mackenzie Gallery and Native Studies Programme, Trent University, Peterborough, Ontario
	Contemporary Native Art of Canada: Silk Screens from the Triple K Co-operative, Royal Ontario Museum, Toronto, Ontario
1978	*The Art of the Woodland Indian,* McMichael Collection, Kleinburg, Ontario
1979	*Kinder des Nanabush,* organized by McMichael Collection, Kleinburg, Ontario, touring West Germany
1980	*Contemporary Woodland Indian Paintings,* New College, University of Toronto, Ontario
1983	*Contemporary Indian Art,* Rideau Hall, Ottawa, Ontario
1984	*Norval Morrisseau and the Emergence of the Image Makers,* Art Gallery of Ontario, Toronto
1993	*The Art of the Anishnabe: Works from the Permanent Collection,* Thunder Bay Art Gallery, Thunder Bay, Ontario
	In the Shadow of the Sun, organized by the Canadian Museum of Civilization, Ottawa, Ontario (traveling)
1994	*Moose Season,* Thunder Bay Art Gallery, Thunder Bay, Ontario
1997	*Water, Earth, and Air,* Thunder Bay Art Gallery, Thunder Bay, Ontario

Collections

Canadian Museum of Civilization, Hull, Quebec; Department of Indian and Northern Affairs, Canada, Ottawa, Ontario; Fort Francis Public Library, Fort Francis, Ontario; Manitoba Centennial Corporation, Winnipeg, Manitoba; McMichael Collection, Kleinburg, Ontario; New College, University of Toronto, Ontario; Queens's Park, Toronto, Ontario; Red Lake Fellowship Centre, Red Lake, Ontario; Royal Ontario Museum, Toronto, Ontario; Sioux Lookout Public Library, Sioux Lookout, Ontario; Thunder Bay Art Gallery, Thunder Bay, Ontario; Winnipeg Art Gallery, Winnipeg, Manitoba.

Publications

By RAY: Books—*Legends of the Sandy Lake Cree,* by Carl Ray and James Stevens, McCelland and Stewart, Toronto, 1971.

On RAY: Books—*Canadian Native Art,* by Nancy-Lou Patterson, Collier-Macmillan Canada, Ltd., 1973; *Contemporary Native Art of Canada: Silk Screens from the Triple K Co-operative,* exhibition catalog by Elizabeth McLuan, Royal Ontario Museum, 1977; *Norval Morrisseau and the Emergence of the Image Makers,* exhibition catalog by Elizabeth McLuan and Tom Hill, Art Gallery of Ontario, Toronto, 1984.

*　　*　　*

Carl Ray was a central figure in the Woodland School of painting and graphics that developed and flourished in the 1960s and 1970s on the native reserves of Ontario. Ray and others developed a distinctive pictographic style designed to present traditional myth and legend to a native audience as well as the Euro-American art world. Younger and more approachable as a teacher, Ray provided an essential link between the acknowledged founder of the Woodland School, Norval Morrisseau, and the dozens of young people they both taught to paint in summer workshops sponsored by the Manitoulin Arts Foundation. The workshops were held on Manitoulin Island and other native reserves throughout Ontario during several consecutive summers in the early 1970s.

Like Morrisseau, Ray was essentially self taught, developing a narrative style that grew ultimately from the pictographic and mnemonic motifs used to record and illustrate sacred ceremonies among the Ojibwa and Cree. The older artist introduced him to the style and provided important formal influence when Ray worked as his apprentice on a large mural project for *Expo '67* in Montreal. Both lived on the remote Sandy Lake Reserve in northwestern Ontario, where Ray grew up, and both had intimate knowledge of ancient ritual.

Since his grandfather and brother were practicing medicine men in the Cree tradition, Ray had ample exposure to native ceremony and related art. The richness of his traditional background undoubtedly accounts, in part, for the deep spirituality that characterizes many of his works. However, there is no direct relationship in style or medium between Ray's creative work and Cree traditional arts. The art of the Woodland School was a fine art tradition from the outset, a conscious affirmation and explication of ancient tradition but fully grounded in the modes and media of western art history.

Ray's early paintings and graphics concentrated on illustrating myth and legend adapted from his own Cree heritage and the special knowledge of his relatives. This kind of narrative approach is typical of much of the work created by Woodland School artists, especially in the first years of the development of the style. That focus was determined, in part, by the dual interests of most of the artists involved, including Ray. It was an art that targeted at least two very different audiences: its combination of exotic, essentially pictographic form and traditional native subject matter consciously appealed to the non-native, art-buying public and achieved considerable success in catering to the tastes of that audience; for artists like Ray, however, the native audience was at least as important, as well as occasionally problematic. Among Cree traditionalists within his community, works that incorporated sacred knowledge and legend were greeted with considerable suspicion. Nevertheless, the Woodland School and related developments, especially in its early and central focus on native education, were part of a self-conscious revival of native culture, a way to explore, define, and, in some cases, reformulate native identity.

Both style and content reflect this mildly didactic purpose as well as important aesthetic ones. One of Ray's most important commissions, the illustrations for James Stevens' book, *Legends of the Sandy Lake Cree*, is a prime example of this focus. The heavy black and brown form lines characteristic of this series and basic to Ray's later style are an important hallmark of the Woodland School painters, a descriptive technique developed first by Morrisseau and strongly related to beadwork styles in the region, often worked on dark fabric or leather foundations. Its function in establishing basic structure, dynamic, and descriptive qualities is central to the appeal of the paintings and graphics for both of the audiences targeted. Ray's approach to the style was far more dynamic than that of his mentor. His form lines tend to be thinner and less regular.

Both the descriptive form line and the interior spaces defined by it are full of agitated, even violent, movement. There is always a visceral quality in the feathering of the form lines in Ray's work, an approach that is distinctly his own.

The rounded and segmented interior spaces defined by those lines are energetically charged as well. Delicate lines like tiny maps of arteries and veins fill many of the spaces, especially in the spiritually and physically potent areas of his human and animal subjects. Even when done in blue or brown, the linear delicacy is reminiscent of tree branches against a winter sky, which effectively links the figures' interior with the surrounding landscape in many of Ray's works, whether implied or actually described within the painting. In fact, the aesthetics of the formline style itself seem intimately related to the visual milieu of the woodlands, where throughout the long winter months, as well as in early spring and late fall, the landscape is defined almost exclusively by the deep black and swelling linearism of leafless trees.

Still, early on Ray thought of himself as a colorist and his work from the late 1960s and early 1970s includes examples in which the descriptive form line gives way to a less stylized rendering of subject matter set against a rich painterly background (e.g., *Thunderbirds,* 1972-73). A narrative- and legend-based approach remains consistent throughout, though, and the visceral character of linear elements is distinctly his, even in these more painterly works.

When his segmentation of the subject matter is filled with less linear design, the overall effect in much of Ray's work is still more distinctly a matter of drawing than heavy application of paint. Many of the interior areas are left open, defined by a single, often delicate wavy line. The overall result is less solid, less slick and sophisticated than some others—more full of tense agitation, less settled. This quality in Ray's artwork increases as time goes on, almost certainly related to his personal struggles with violent alcoholism that ultimately resulted in his death at 35 in 1978.

As that moment grew nearer, Ray's work took on an increasingly personal content. The shift from a recounting of legend and tradition to the exploration of personal identity, apparent in Ray's final years, paralleled developments throughout the Woodland School. Building on the confidence gained through the explication of traditional culture, Ray and the other Woodland artists pushed style and content into the more complex realms of personal and native identity in a post-colonial world.

—Amelia Trevelyan

RED ELK, Herman
Variant names: Hegaka Wambdi
Tribal affiliations: Yanktonai Lakota
Painter

Born: Poplar, Montana, on the Fort Peck Indian Reservation, 27 March 1918. **Education:** Chemawa Indian School, Salem Oregon, 1935-39; studied drawing in workshops in South Dakota; studied under Dr. Oscar Howe at the University of South Dakota, 1964-65. **Military Service:** U.S. Army, World War II. **Career:** U.S. Army Corps of Engineers, after World War II; electrician and general contractor; museum aide; researched techniques and materials of traditional Plains painting on hide, 1963-64; teacher, Sioux Indian Museum, 1969-85; commercial artist and painter. **Died:** 1986.

Individual Exhibitions

1970   *Paintings by Herman Red Elk,* Sioux Indian Museum and
        Crafts Center, Rapid City, South Dakota

Selected Group Exhibitions

1965   Sioux Indian Museum and Craft Center, Indian Arts and
        Crafts Board, U.S. Department of the Interior, Rapid
        City, South Dakota
        Second Annual Invitational Exhibition of American In-
        dian Paintings, U.S. Department of the Interior, Wash-
        ington, D.C.
1967   *Black Hills Indian Art Exposition,* Rapid City, South Dakota
1970   *Contemporary Sioux Painting,* Sioux Indian Museum and
        Craft Center, Rapid City, South Dakota
1972   Philbrook Museum of Art, Tulsa, Oklahoma
1973   Southern Plains Indian Museum and Craft Center, Indian
        Arts and Crafts Board, U.S. Department of the Inte-
        rior, Anadarko, Oklahoma
1975   Heritage Center Inc. Collection, Red Cloud Indian School,
        Pine Ridge, South Dakota
1979-81 *Native American Paintings,* Joslyn Art Museum, Omaha,
        Nebraska (traveling)
1992-93 *Visions of the People,* Minneapolis Institute of Arts, Min-
        neapolis, Minnesota

Collections

Heritage Center, Inc., Red Cloud Indian School, Pine Ridge, South
Dakota; Indian Arts & Crafts Board, United States Department of
the Interior, Washington, D.C.; Sioux Indian Museum and Crafts
Center, U.S. Department of Interior, Indian Arts & Crafts Board,
Rapid City, South Dakota.

Publications

On RED ELK: Books—*Paintings by Herman Red Elk,* Rapid City,
1970; *Contemporary Sioux Painting,* by Myles Libhart, Rapid City,
1970; *Indian Painters and White Patrons,* by J. J. Brody, Albuquerque,
1971; *Painted Tipis by Contemporary Plains Indian Artists,* by Cecil
Blackboy, et. al., Anadarko, Oklahoma, 1973; *Native American Paintings,* by Frederick Schmid and Patrick Houlihan, Kansas City, 1979;
Visions of the People, by Evan Maurer, Minneapolis, 1992. **Articles**—
"Hide Painting," *Smithsonian,* November 1992.

*

Herman Red Elk comments (1970):

"I enjoy painting; trying to recapture and preserve the very early
traditions and life of our Sioux of the plains — their religion, their
ceremonies, and their many ways of expressing themselves in their
various art media." (From *Contemporary Sioux Painting*)

*   *   *

In 1960 Herman Red Elk moved his family from Montana to
Rapid City, South Dakota, to recuperate from tuberculosis at the
Sioux Sanitarium. Participating in an art therapy program introduced him in his early forties to serious painting. He furthered his
artistic interests in 1963 through summer workshops at Black Hills

State College, where he was influenced by Diane Tollefson, a Rapid
City artist and educator. From 1963 to 1964, Red Elk worked on a
project sponsored by the Indian Arts and Crafts Board of the Sioux
Indian Museum and Crafts Center in Rapid City. He conducted
historical and technical research and became preoccupied with Plains
painting traditions. He began painting on buffalo hides, applying
powdered pigments with bone tubes and brushes and working in
the traditional narrative style of winter counts, pictographic histories or biographies of a warrior's or medicine person's life experiences. Along with images on full-sized buffalo robes, he produced
smaller hide paintings and designed wall hangings for modern home
decor.

Red Elk's ledger drawing style based on winter counts is illustrated in his 1965 piece *Roping Wild Horses,* rendered in colored
marking pens on commercial skin (now in the Sioux Indian Museum
and Crafts Center collection). The work is similar in appearance to
Sitting Bull's early ledger books, featuring two-dimensional Indian
figures with shirts, breech cloths and leggings throwing their lariats
toward galloping horses. The horses' front and rear legs are extended, and the active images, grouped in twos and threes, appear
to be floating in space.

From 1964 to 1965, Red Elk studied under Dr. Oscar Howe, an
internationally renowned Lakota artist and educator who had introduced startlingly modern, vital, and innovative techniques to flatstyle
Native American painting that developed during the twentieth century. Red Elk benefited both stylistically and technically: Howe's
dynamic stylistic influence can be seen in Red Elk's 1969 acrylic on
illustration board, *Eagle Dancer.* The painting portrays a fancy
dancer in whirling, circular motion. The dancer's eagle feathers are
abstracted into flat parallelograms, angular patterns appear in the
background, and even moccasin ties and dance bells have the appearance of being on planes. The painting is signed with Red Elk's
antler-like logo and dated "69."

Red Elk was responsible for the marked revival of hide painting
among the Sioux, starting in the 1960s. Through his participation in
the early-1960s research project, Red Elk learned to prepare bone
brushes and earth pigments in the old ways. In addition to creating
original works based on biographies and histories, Red Elk recreated hide paintings by earlier artists. For example, *Robe with biography of a Lakota warrior* is based on the hide-painting autobiography of George Saves Life. A Sioux warrior, Saves Life made a hide
painting that roughly spanned the years 1880 to 1920 and is part of
the Sioux Indian Museum and Crafts Center collection, where Red
Elk studied the work and later became a guide and teacher. *Robe
with biography of a Lakota warrior* depicts scenes of war and horse
roundups as well as images of courting and the Elk Dreamers'
Dance. Horses in action and at rest and details of clothing are especially well-rendered in this visually rich narrative that appears as a
large (69" by 80") panorama filled with various stories.

—Gregory Schaaf

RED STAR, Kevin
Tribal affiliations: Crow
Painter

Born: Crow Reservation, Montana, 9 October 1943. **Education:**
Institute of American Indian Arts, 1962-65; San Francisco Art

Institute, 1965-66; Montana State University, 1968-69; Eastern Montana College, 1971-72. **Career:** Instructor and consultant, Crow Tribal Art and Lodge Grass High School, 1973-74; helped found Crow-Cheyenne Fine Arts Alliance to promote art and organize exhibitions and lectures; artist-in-residence, Institute of American Indian Arts, 1976; Copenhaver Scholar-in-Residence, Roanoke College, 1996. **Awards:** Numerous, including Heard Museum Guild Indian Fair and Market, 1964 and 1971, Scottsdale National Indian Art Exhibition, 1965 and 1969, Museum of New Mexico, 1967, All American Indian Days, 1968; Artist of the Year, *Santa Fean* magazine, 1976-77; Honorary Doctorate, Rocky Mountain College, Billings, Montana, 1996. **Address:** c/o Kevin Red Star Gallery, 15 S. Broadway, P.O. Box 1377, Red Lodge, Montana, 59068.

Individual Exhibitions

1971   Museum of the Plains Indian, Browning, Montana
1975-79   Squash Blossom Gallery, Chicago
1976-77   Nadler's Fine Arts, Scottsdale, Arizona
1977   Jamison Gallery, Santa Fe, New Mexico
1978   Hukashee Fine Arts Gallery, Scottsdale, Arizona
1979   Carol Thornton Gallery, Santa Fe, New Mexico
1980   Good Company Gallery, New York

Kevin Red Star. Courtesy of the artist.

1980-82   Via Gambaro Gallery, Washington, D.C.
1983   *Crow Indianer Acrybilder,* Galerie Amak, Berlin
1984   *Eye of My Mind,* San Diego Museum of Man, California
          Galeria Capistrano, San Juan Capistrano, California
1985   Segal Gallery, New York
1988-90   El Taller Gallery, Santa Fe, New Mexico
1988-96   Merida Gallery, Red Lodge, Montana
1995   Museum of the Rockies, Bozeman, Montana
1996   Kevin Red Star Gallery, Red Lodge, Montana
1997   Autry Museum of Western Heritage, Los Angeles

Selected Group Exhibitions

1964-65   *First Annual Invitational Exhibition of American Indian Paintings,* U.S. Department of the Interior, Washington, D.C.
1965   Institute of American Indian Arts, Santa Fe, New Mexico
1965-66   *Young American Indian Artists,* Riverside Museum, New York
1966   Edinburgh Art Festival, Edinburgh, Scotland
1968   U.S. Dept. Of Interior, Washington, D.C.
1971-72   *Contemporary Indian Artists—Montana/Wyoming/Idaho,* Museum of the Plains Indian, Browning, Montana
1973   *Painted Tipis,* Southern Plains Indian Museum, Anadarko, Oklahoma
1977   *'77 West Coast Experience,* Asahi Gallery, Tokyo
1977-78   Institute of American Indian Arts, Santa Fe, New Mexico
1978   *100 Years of Native American Painting,* Oklahoma Museum of Art, Oklahoma City
1979   *The Real People, International Native American Council of Arts,* Casa de las Americas, Havana, Cuba
          Espace Pierre Cardin, Paris
          Kevin Red Star and Earl Biss, Mackler-Kleban Gallery, Kansas City, Missouri
1980   *Kevin Red Star and Doug Hyde,* Galleria Capistrano, San Juan Capistrano, California
          Kevin Red Star and Earl Biss, Whitney Gallery, Taos, New Mexico
1981   Native American Center for the Living Arts, Niagara Falls, New York
          Peking Art Exhibit, organized by the Driscoll Gallery, Denver, Colorado (touring China)
1982   *Night of the First Americans,* Kennedy Center for the Performing Arts, Washington, D.C.
1984-85   *Indianascher Kunstler* (traveling, Germany), organized by the Philbrook Museum, Tulsa, Oklahoma
1989   *Paint, Bronze and Sculpture,* Mitchell Indian Museum, Kendall College, Evanston, Illinois
          Willow Tree Festival, Old Cowboy Museum, Gordon, Nebraska
1990   Creighton Preparatory School, Omaha, Nebraska
1991   *One With the Earth,* organized by the Institute of American Indian Arts and Alaska Culture and Arts Development, Santa Fe, New Mexico
1992   *Creativity Is Our Tradition,* Institute of American Indian Arts Museum, Santa Fe, New Mexico
1996   Russian Academy of Art, Moscow

Collections

Pierre Cardin Collection, Paris; Denver Art Museum, Denver, Colorado; Eiteljorg Museum, Indianapolis, Indiana; Heard Museum,

Kevin Red Star: *White Hawk.* Courtesy of the artist.

Phoenix, Arizona; Heritage Center, Inc., Pine Ridge, South Dakota; Institute of American Indian Arts Museum, Santa Fe, New Mexico; Museum of the American Indian, New York; Museum of the Plains Indian, Browning, Montana; Millicent Rogers Foundation Museum, Taos, New Mexico; San Diego Museum of Man, San Diego, California; Southwest Museum, Los Angeles, California; Wheelwright Museum of the American Indian, Santa Fe, New Mexico.

Publications

On RED STAR: Books—*Kevin Red Star,* catalog, Museum of the Plains Indian, Browning, Montana, 1971; *Contemporary Indian Artists—Montana/Wyoming/Idaho*, by Dorothy Jean Ray, Rapid City, South Dakota, 1972; *Painted Tipis by Contemporary Plains Indian Artists,* Cecil Blackboy, et. al., Anadarko, Oklahoma; *100 Years of Native American Art,* by Arthur Silberman, Oklahoma City, 1978; *The Sweet Grass Lives On,* by Jamake Highwater, New York, 1980; *Indianascher Kunstler*, by Gerhard Hoffman, Munich, 1984; *The Arts of the North American Indian: Native Traditions in Evolution*, Edwin L. Wade, ed., New York: Hudson Hills Press in association with Philbrook Art Center, Tulsa, Oklahoma, 1986; *Lost and Found Traditions,* by Ralph T. Coe, Seattle, 1986; *Creativity Is Our Tradition,* by Rick Hill, Santa Fe, 1992. **Articles**—"Kevin Red Star," by Jo-Ann Swanson, *Southwest Art,* July 1990; "Where Are They Now?," *Art Talk,* April/May 1995.

*

Kevin Red Star comments (1971):

Indian culture has in the past been ignored to a great extent. It is for me, as well as for many other Indian artists, a rich source of artistic expression... An intertwining of my Indian culture with contemporary art expression has given me an enlightenment and greater insight concerning my art. I hope to accomplish something for the American Indian and at the same time achieve personal satisfaction in creative statement through my art. (From *Kevin Red Star,* catalog, Museum of the Plains Indian, Browning, Montana)

*   *   *

Among the early students at the Institute of American Indian Arts in Santa Fe, New Mexico, which opened its gates in 1962, was Kevin Red Star, a Crow Indian from Montana. The Institute strives for a synthesis of tradition and innovation in Indian art, in accord with the innermost feeling of the artist. Red Star is inspired by the traditions of the nineteenth-century Northern Plains Indians, but reviews them through twentieth-century perspectives.

Inspiration for the subject matter of his paintings and lithographs are the feasts and celebrations, the vision quests and dream states of his forebears, together with the people themselves and the land, preferably under the moon at night. Red Star bases many of his paintings on fading Crow photographs of life on the Crow Reservation; he tapes old tales told by the elders, has a fine collection of ancient beadwork, and has read most books on Crow history and culture. All this lends his paintings authenticity in imaginative flourishes.

Red Star's main interest is portraiture. He paints half-length figures, as in *Side Stepper*, and figures in full-length, as in *Rainbow Woman*. No matter who the "real" people are, his portraits bear the stamp of his own personal and unique style. Like R. C. Gorman's graceful Navajo woman, Red Star created a type—the male face of the wise Crow, determined and strong. *Side Stepper* is an example. It shows a Crow Indian in full headdress, with buffalo horns, buffalo hide, ornamental feathers, and a necklace of bear claws. The face has a nocturnal, alien expression, a mien that bespeaks knowledge of the depth of life; a hint of stoicism and contrariness resides in the eyes, which gaze proudly past the viewer, as if in a trance.

Occasionally, Red Star, like T. C. Cannon, adds an ironic touch to his portraits. In *Rainbow Woman*, for example, he paints an Indian woman on horseback resembling an eighteenth-century English noblewoman. Her clothing, however, is ornamented with elk teeth, shells, and beadwork. It is the portrait of a noble woman cognizant of her power and authority, and who can represent it ceremonially.

Red Star's paintings also bespeak his love of the land. Even though he has spent a great part of his life in Santa Fe, he returns to his native Montana whenever he feels the need to be "revitalized." In 1990 (*Southwest* magazine) he stated, "I get nostalgic for the Pryor Mountain area and Arrow Creek Valley where I was raised." He loves the vast expanses of unspoiled land, the limitless horizons and the big sky. His landscapes are often night scenes, with figures lit by an eerie unknown light source and accompanied by an orange-yellow moon. Moon and sun, typically rendered perfectly round, are celestial bodies and also sacred Crow symbols. His most recent art is moving away now, in landscapes and in portraiture, from the realism of his earlier years. Meanwhile, Red Star returned to Montana in the mid-1990s to stay.

The Santa Fe years had been fruitful. During his time in the mid-1970s as the first artist in residence at the Institute of American Indian Arts, a friend, painter Earl Biss, suggested to him to try graphics—stone lithography, serigraphy, and etching—and another friend offered to teach him. Thus, he was introduced to a new medium in the Southwest, and its artists and galleries have also been conducive to the development of his style in general. His delicate use of colors has become one of his hallmarks. His paintings are characterized by a compelling balance of muted, dark colors, which may be attributed to the old photographs he uses, and bright accents. Faces are usually dark and blend in with the likewise dark, often yellowish-brown tones of the background. Costumes, especially details, are often exaggerated in bright colors, which make his works more vibrant.

Red Star's reputation has increased ever since he started exhibiting in 1965. He is nationally and internationally known, with shows in Paris, London, Munich, and Berlin as well as Tokyo, Peking, and Latin America. The secret of his success is not talent alone, but also discipline and hard work. He likes to stress this: "The more you practice, the luckier you get."

—Gerhard and Gisela Hoffmann

REID, Bill
Tribal affiliations: Haida
Carver, sculptor, illustrator, and filmmaker

Born: Victoria, British Columbia, 1920. **Education:** Ryerson Technical Institute of Jewelry, Toronto, 1948; apprenticed with his grandfather, Charles Gladstone, and studied Haida art. **Career:** Radio announcer, Canadian Broadcasting Corporation and privately-owned stations; commissions for totem pole, Shell Oil Centre, London, England, wood screen, New Provincial Museum, Victoria, British Columbia, and carvings for Museum of Anthropology, University of British Columbia and Vancouver Airport Authority, British Columbia. **Awards:** Honorary degrees, University of British Columbia and Trent University, 1976, York University, 1978, University of Victoria and Canadian Conference of the Arts, 1979; Molson Award, 1977; Lifetime National Aboriginal Achievement Award, 1994.

Individual Exhibitions

1974   *A Quarter-Century of Bill Reid Work*, Vancouver Art Gallery, British Columbia
1980   *Bill Reid Retrospective*, Children of the Raven Gallery, Vancouver, British Columbia
1993   Miriam Shell Fine Art, Toronto, Ontario

Selected Group Exhibitions

1966   *Arts of the Raven*, Vancouver Art Gallery, British Columbia
1967   Canadian Pavilion at EXPO '67, Montreal, Quebec
1980   *The Legacy*, British Columbia Provincial Museum, Victoria
1986   EXPO '86, Montreal, Quebec
        Museum of Anthropology, University of British Columbia, Vancouver
1989   Musee de l'Homme, Paris
1992   *Time for Dialogue*, organized by the Aboriginal Awareness Society, Calgary, Alberta (traveling)
1993   *In the Shadow of the Sun*, Canadian Museum of Civilization, Ottawa, Ontario (traveling)
1994   Museum of Anthropology, University of British Columbia, Vancouver (permanent display of jewelry and small sculptures)
        The Spirit of Haida Gwaii, Vancouver Museum, British Columbia

Collections

Canadian Embassy, Washington, D.C.; Department of Indian and Northern Affairs, Ottawa, Ontario; Museum of Anthropology, University of British Columbia, Vancouver; Vancouver Airport Authority, Vancouver, British Columbia.

Publications

By REID: Books—*The Raven's Cry*, by Christie Harris (illustrations by Reid), Vancouver, 1965; *Out of the Silence*, by Adelaide de Menil (with text by Reid), Toronto, 1970; *Indian Art of the Northwest Coast*, by Bill Holm and Bill Reid, Houston, 1975; *Islands at the Edge*, Toronto, 1984; *The Raven Steals the Light*, by Reid with Robert Bringhurst, Vancouver, 1988. **Films**—*The Salvage of the Last of the Totem Poles from the Queen Charlotte Islands*, Canadian Broadcasting Corporation, 1958; *People of the Potlach*, Canadian Broadcasting Corporation, 1958.

On REID: Books—*The Legacy: Continuing Traditions of Canadian Northwest Coast Art*, by Peter Macnair, et. al., Victoria, British Columbia, 1980; *The Bill Reid Retrospective*, by Hilary Stewart, Vancouver, 1980; *Northwest Coast Indian Graphics*, by Edwin S. Hall, Jr., et. al., Seattle, 1981; *Cedar*, by Hilary Stewart, Vancouver, 1984; *Bill Reid: Beyond the Essential Form*, Vancouver, 1986; *Bill*

Reid, by Doris Shadbolt, Vancouver, 1987; *Time for Dialogue*, by Joanne Cardinal-Schubert, Calgary, 1992; *In the Shadow of the Sun*, by Gerald McMaster, Hull, Quebec, 1993; *The Black Canoe: Bill Reid and the Spirit of Haida Gwaii*, text by Robert Bringhurst, illustrations by Ulli Steltzer, Vancouver, 1995. **Articles**—"Bill Reid and the Native Renaissance," by Joan M. Vastokas, *ArtsCanada*, June 1974; "Haida Art Alive Again," by Susan Mertens, *The Vancouver Sun*, July 31, 1974; "Bill Reid: A Retrospective," by Deidre Spencer, *Dimensions*, February-March 1975; "The Haida Arts of Robert Davidson and Bill Reid," *Artswest*, Vol. 3, no. 2, 1978; "Bill Reid: Master Sculptor of Contemporary Haida Art," by Arthur Perry, *Art Magazine*, June 1978; "Artist Bill Reid Maintains Classic Haida Heritage," by David General, *The Native Perspective*, Vol. 3, no. 32, 1979; "The Myth Maker," *Saturday Night*, February 1982; "Child of the Raven Bill Reid," by Joan Loundes, *Vanguard*, February 1982; "Bill Reid and the Washington Embassy Project," by Stephen Godfry, *Canadian Art*, Spring 1992; "The Big Money in West Coast Native Art," by Alan Bayless, *Financial Times of Canada*, August 28, 1993.

*   *   *

A sculptor in the classic Haida style of the Northwest Coast, Canada, Bill Reid has long been recognized as occupying the first rank of international artists. His importance has been attested to time and time again in public exhibitions mounted and commentary published over the course of the last several decades.

His early training was in European jewelry-making methods. He avers that his interest in Haida carving began comparatively late. His early career was as an announcer in private sector radio and with the Canadian Broadcasting Corporation. Yet, by his early twenties he was examining at close quarters the work of two formidable artists, Charles Gladstone (1877-1954), his Haida grandfather, and Charles Edenshaw (1840-1920), his grandfather's uncle and teacher. Reid learned that his grandfather was the last in a direct line of Haida silversmiths and was also a noted argillite carver. Reid's apprenticeship continued through long hours spent in his grandfather's company and in studying Haida art in various museum collections. He said that he became wholly conversant with the underlying dynamics of Haida art through an exhaustive analysis of the work of Charles Edenshaw.

Reid's use of new techniques and materials in his art has been widely acknowledged. He demonstrates a talent for innovation while remaining true to the essential principles of the formline style of Haida art. This is as true of his sculpture as his jewelry, beginning in the late 1950s. He applied European techniques to fabricating jewelry based on the old Haida designs. In his bracelets, for instance, he was able to achieve real three-dimensional volume for the first time. His lifelong fidelity to traditional Haida designs paradoxically gave him the freedom to be unusually innovative.

In his sculpture, Reid demonstrates at once a rather awesome fidelity to the old Haida tradition and a rare ability to revivify it. If Reid breathes new life into the existing Haida aesthetic, he does so not only through technical innovation but through exploring and giving tactile form to the primordial mythos that underlies it. The remarkable ethos of his own work stems from the living mythos that infuses each and every articulation of form in his sculpture with salient atavisms. Every *line* in his sculpture seems somehow alive. The hand that carves here speaks in the most eloquent of voices. The barest nuance, the loveliest contour, the overall expressiveness of the design—these seem as necessary as breathing in his

Bill Reid and his sculpture *The Raven and the First Men*. Photograph by William McLennan; courtesy UBC Museum of Anthropology.

compositions. Archaic images are resurrected and made powerfully new. But only an artist with an uncanny familiarity and understanding of his materials could make them so.

Certainly, this is true of many of the piles of the Haida Village in Totem Park, such as the monumental raven and beaver memorial pole, with their capacity to induce a simple awe in the observer. The treatment of the origin myth in his well-known yellow cedar carving, *Raven Discovering Mankind in a Clamshell,* haunts us long after we have left the actual carving behind. The resplendent 10,800 pound cast-bronze shaped canoe, *The Spirit of Haida Gwaii,* in the courtyard of the Canadian Embassy in Washington, D.C., has a hauntingly mythic grandeur and formal integrity. Replete with its 13 beasts, *The Spirit of Haida Gwaii* is a Northwest Coast version of Noah's Ark, rife with mythological entities and tribal memories. Reid once said that "Western art starts with the figure. West Coast Art starts with the canoe." We can see the truth of this statement in this magnificent work of public art.

Wilson Duff, a professor of anthropology at the University of British Columbia, once wrote that Reid "has been using his eye and intuition to jump the seeming chasm between Picasso and Edenshaw, his voice to urge the building of a bridge, and his hand to trace out its very foundations." And this testament is still as topical concerning Bill Reid's work as it is intuitively true.

—James D. Campbell

RENWICK, Arthur

Tribal affiliations: Haisla
Photographer and installation artist

Born: Kitimaat, British Columbia, 9 February, 1965. **Education:** Vancouver Community College, Langara Campus, fine arts program, Vancouver, British Columbia, 1984-86; Emily Carr College of Art and Design, fine arts diploma, photography, Vancouver, British Columbia, 1986-89; Concordia University, MFA graduate program, photography, Montreal, Quebec, 1991-93. **Career:** Assistant photo technician, Emily Carr College of Art and Design, Vancouver, British Columbia, 1988-89; research assistant, Indian Art Centre, Department of Indian Affairs, Hull, Quebec, and photographer, *Indigena* (exhibition catalog), Canadian Museum of Civilization, Hull, Quebec, 1991; teaching assistant, Concordia University, Montreal, Quebec, 1991-92; advisory board member, *New Territories: 350/500 Years After,* Maison de la Culture, Montreal, Quebec, 1992; photography workshop facilitator, Concordia University, Montreal, Quebec 1992-93; orientation program, National Gallery of Canada, Ottawa, Ontario, elected board member of Toronto Photographer's Workshop, 1993; curatorial intern, The Power Plant, Toronto, Ontario, 1993-95; assistant curator to Gerald McMaster, Canadian Museum of Civilization, Hull, Quebec, 1995-97. **Awards:** Scholarship Grant, Cultural Services Branch, Province of British Columbia, 1985; Canadian Native Arts Foundation Grant, 1991; Canada Council, Short Term Grant, Photography, 1992; Canadian Native Arts Foundation Grant, 1994; Canada Council, Short Term Grant, Photography, 1995.

Selected Group Exhibitions

1988   *Photophelia*, Concourse Gallery, Emily Carr College of Art and Design, Vancouver, British Columbia

1989   *Souvenir / Les Souvenirs*, 23 West Cordova Street, Vancouver, British Columbia

       Photonoesis, Concourse Gallery, Emily Carr College of Art and Design, Vancouver, British Columbia

1990   *Our Home and Native Land*, VAV Gallery, Concordia University, Montreal, Quebec

1991   *Contemporary Indian and Inuit Photography*, La Maison de la Culture Notre-Dame-de -Grace, Montreal, Quebec

       Strengthening the Spirit, The National Gallery of Canada, Ottawa, Ontario

       OKANATA, A Space, Toronto, Ontario

       Solidarity: Art After Oka, SAW Gallery, Ottawa, Ontario

1992   *Tracing Locations*, Bourget Gallery, Concordia University, Montreal, Quebec

       Experimental Photographic Artworks, NIIPA Gallery, Hamilton, Ontario

       New Territories: 350l500 Years After, La Maison de la Culture Cote-des-Neiges, Montreal, Quebec

1993   *Social Studies / Still Lives*, Les Mois de la Photo, Maison de la Culture, Cote-des-Neiges, Montreal, Quebec

       Contemporary Camera, Red Head Gallery, Toronto, Ontario / The Pitt Gallery, Vancouver, British Columbia

       First Nations Art '93, Woodland Cultural Centre, Brantford, Ontario

1993-94   *Multiplicity: A New Cultural Strategy*, U.B.C. Museum of Anthropology, Vancouver, British Columbia

1994   *Art Bingo*, Art Exhibition and Performance, Montreal, Quebec

       Nation to Nation, Art Exhibition and Performance, Montreal, Quebec

1995   *AlterNative*, McMichael Canadian Art Collection, Kleinburg, Ontario / Canadian Museum of Contemporary Photography, Ottawa, Ontario

       Native Love, DAS Communication, Montreal, Quebec / Art Space, Peterborough, Ontario / A.K.A., Saskatoon, Saskatchewan

       HERMIT, The Monastery, Plasy, Czech Republic

1996   *Dis/Location Markers*, Toronto Photographer's Workshop, Toronto, Ontario

Collections

Canada Council Art Bank, Ottawa, Ontario; Canadian Museum of Civilization, Hull, Quebec; Indian Art Centre, The Department of Indian and Northern Affairs, Hull, Quebec; National Gallery of Canada, Ottawa, Ontario; Vancouver Community College Langara Campus, Vancouver, British Columbia; Winnipeg Art Gallery, Winnipeg, Manitoba; Woodland Cultural Centre, Brantford, Ontario.

Publications

On RENWICK: Books—*Solidarity: Art After Oka*, Lee-Ann Martin, SAW Gallery: Ottawa, 1991; *New Territories: 350/500 Years After*, Ateliers Vision Planetaire: Montreal, 1991; *Social Studies / Still Lives*, by Cheryl Simon and Joanne Sloan, Les Mois de la Photo, Montreal: Vox Populi, 1993; *AlterNative*, by Lynn Hill, Kleinburg: McMichael Canadian Art Collection, 1995. **Articles**—"Our Home and Native Land," *Thursday Report*, October 25, 1990; "Recovering and Discovering," *The Link*, October 30, 1990; "Eagle-

Arthur Renwick: *Conductor* **(installation view). Photograph by Gary Hall.**

Eyed," *Montreal Mirror*, December 5-12, 1991; "Native art exhibits should not all be treated the same," *The Vancouver Courier*, December 12, 1993; "Native Traditions spoken in the language of post-modernism," *The Weekend Sun*, Vancouver, British Columbia, December 23, 1993; "Looking at reality through alterNative eyes," by Nancy Baele, *The Ottawa Citizen*, April 21, 1996.

*   *   *

Arthur Renwick is a photographer and installation artist who describes himself as a "displaced totem pole maker who has lost his tools to carve and uses the next best thing at hand." His photo essays document the dangerous and unjust effects of encroaching industry and uneducated decisions regarding extraction of natural resources on First Nations communities. They also touch more personal issues of the search for identity and community.

Assembling the subject matter in his photographs, Renwick metaphorically depicts his own stories and experiences using traditional elements mixed with contemporary methods. His themes include references to land claims and ownership, natural resource manage-

ment, historical markers and futuristic predictions—all within one photo or a series of connected images. His work derives from the traditional Northwest Coast art forms and is portrayed through the use of unconventional materials.

One of his pieces, *The Great One*, is a mixed media installation that features the image of a child and an image of water. In between the two is an aluminum sheet, harkening to the presence of Alcan Aluminum intrusion on Renwick's ancestral Haisla territory. Lying on the floor, propped against a wall in a position reminiscent of a fallen totem pole, the child and the water are low in status, without power, and it is the observer's point of view, from well above the image, that theoretically prioritizes the demands of the piece. It's graphic content asks the question of whether the child, as a symbol for future generations, would ever see the clean water again or maintain the right to relate to the water in the manner that is the Haisla ancestral heritage.

Another of Renwick's more well known pieces, *A Prophetical Transformation of the Kitwancool Natural Museum 1995*, is a tryptic featuring three poles. The first is an old totem pole, covered with white paint, a possible symbol of envelopment by European society. Next to it is a fence pole, and the third image is a light pole. Each pole is a symbol of one or more forms of power. The totem pole indicates traditional or ancestral power, with the white paint a reminder of the coating of non-native power infringing on the reality of lives for the aboriginal people under the guise of protection. The fencepost carries the sign Private Property, no hunting or trespassing; this metaphorically matches the first totem pole, which was a marker of family and resource ownership in the village, but here the power becomes threatening with barbed wire at the top. The power in this instance is that of ownership and law with hints at retaliation. The phrase "Trespassers will be shot" comes to mind immediately. The third image, the light post, metaphorically relates to the totem at the entrance to a traditional house, similar to the regional "hole in the sky" totem pole. Here the power is obviously electric. But with the electric power come the tools for natural destruction—dammed rivers, irresponsible resource extraction, and a world progressively more and more out of balance.

Renwick pursues traditional artistic forms of the Northwest Coast people in an art form that is a further sign of times to come and a symbol for how technology can be used responsibly to further mankind. His photography "brings to light" reminders of ancestral traditions, historical turning points and contemporary issues within the one medium that is entirely based on "carving with light." His meticulously chosen elements and subjects are a passionate cry to address the internal and external issues affecting all people, and especially those of the First Nations.

—Vesta Giles

RIDDLES, Leonard
Variant names: Black Moon
Tribal affiliations: Comanche
Painter

Born: Walters, Oklahoma, 28 June 1919; also called Black Moon.
Education: Fort Sills Indian School (Valedictorian, 1941); mural

instruction with Olaf Nordmark. **Military Service:** U.S. Army, World War II. **Career:** Rancher and carpenter, artist, involved with Indian affairs and farm programs. **Awards:** Fair and exhibitions, including American Indian Exhibition, Anadarko, Oklahoma (Grand Award, 1961 and 1964), Bismark National Indian Art Show (1963), Inter-Tribal Indian Ceremonies (1963), Philbrook Art Center (first place, 1962, 1969, 1972), Waurika Arts Festival (first place, 1988-90); Indian Arts and Crafts Board, special award for contributions to art, 1976; commissioned for several murals, including Fort Sills Indian School and Oklahoma Indian Arts and Crafts Cooperative, Anadarko.

Individual Exhibitions

1994   Southern Plains Indian Museum, Anadarko, Oklahoma

Selected Group Exhibitions

Riddles' works have most often been exhibited at Native American art fairs in Oklahoma.

1963   *Contemporary American Indian Art,* U.S. Department of State, Washington, D.C.
1964-65   *First Annual Invitational Exhibition of American Indian Paintings,* U.S. Department of the Interior, Washington, D.C.
1972   Contemporary Southern Plains Indian Painting, organized by Southern Plains Indian Museum Indian Arts and Crafts Co operative, Anadarko, Oklahoma (traveling)
1973   *Painted Tipis by Contemporary Plains Indian Artists,* Southern Plains Indian Museum, Anadarko, Oklahoma
1978   *100 Years of Native American Painting,* Oklahoma Museum of Art, Oklahoma City, Oklahoma
1979-85   *Oklahomans for Indian Opportunities,* Galleria, Norman (annual)
1980   *Plains Indian Paintings,* organized by the Museum of Art, University of Oklahoma, Norman
1981   *American Indian Art in the 1980s,* Native American Center for the Living Arts, Niagara Falls, New York

Collections

Bureau of Indian Affairs, Department of the Interior, Washington, D.C.; Heritage Center, Inc., Collection, Red Cloud Indian School, Pine Ridge, South Dakota; Indian Arts and Crafts Board, Department of the Interior, Anadarko, Oklahoma; Philbrook Art Center, Tulsa, Oklahoma; Southern Plains Indian Museum, Anadarko, Oklahoma; University of Oklahoma.

Publications

On RIDDLES: Books—*American Indian Painters,* by Oscar B. Jacobson and Jeanne d'Ucel, Nice, France, 1950; *Indian Painters and White Patrons,* by J. J. Brody, Albuquerque, New Mexico, 1971; *100 Years of Native American Art* (exhibition catalog), by Arthur Silberman, Oklahoma City, 1978; *American Indian Art in the 1980s,* New York, 1981.

*

Leonard Riddles comments (1978):

Preserving the Comanche's cultural life is very important to me. All my art work is based on the Comanche people and I try to get it as accurate as possible. I never dress up the subject; I mean, put extra beadwork just for color or paint a buffalo hunter with a war bonnet. You don't paint just what comes to your mind, you paint Comanche. When I was trying to find myself at the Fort Sill Indian School, I would sketch a fire dancer but after that I began to paint and study only Comanche. I was looking at some of my older paintings done when I was about eleven or twelve years old and most of them were in the Indian flat type painting. I don't know how I got started doing that type of work. Later, in high school, I studied with Spencer Asah who was the instructor at the Fort Sill School. He'd help me with my figures and I would help him with his horses. We did some mural painting. After graduation, Cecil Murdock and I went to Riverside [Indian School] for the summer and painted murals....It's always been a deep concern of mine to keep what the Comanches had. I would like to be remembered as the artist of historical values. (From an interview with Arthur Silberman)

*   *   *

Leonard Black Moon Riddles is one of the Southern Plains' leading artist-historians. Riddles and his wife, Eva, have spent many years collecting information from the elders of the Comanche tribe so that the artist can use this data in his numerous paintings. During his high school years, Riddles studied art under the tutelage of Spencer Asah, one of the members of the "Kiowa Five" group who established the "classical" or "traditional" flat style in Oklahoma Indian painting. Thus, Riddles has been a traditionalist Indian painter whose central purpose it has been to depict cultural elements of the Comanche past.

According to the artist, Riddles began his process of learning Comanche lore at the foot of his grandfather in an evening ritual of telling stories of battles, war dances, and religious ceremonies. True to the Comanche tradition that men should seek to become successful warriors, Riddles spent World War II in the United States Army, where he saw action in France and Germany. He was decorated with a Service Ribbon, two Bronze Stars, the 8 P Service Ribbon, and an American Defense Ribbon. Once the war was over, Riddles resumed his quest to learn more about the Comanche cultural heritage and history. Traveling throughout the Southern Plains region, he recorded stories and songs told to him in the Comanche language and he sketched images pertinent to the Comanche past. Riddles stays true to the traditionalist flat style of painting pioneered in easel art form by the Kiowa Five.

In 1968, Riddles was authorized by the Indian Arts & Crafts Board of the U.S. Department of the Interior to create a series of special hide paintings on rawhide shields and historical paintings on buckskin and elkhide. Among the most noted of these are a Comanche Rattlesnake Medicine Shield and paintings representative of his concerns—*Battle of Adobe Walls* and *Peyote Ceremony.* In 1973, Riddles was commissioned to do a full-scale reproduction of the Comanche Bear Paw Tipi for the Southern Plains Indian Museum's catalog and exhibition, "Painted Tipis by Contemporary Plains Indian Artists." In recognition for his services to Indian art, the Indian Arts & Crafts Board of the U.S. Department of the Interior presented him with a "Certificate of Appreciation" in 1976.

—John Anson Warner

RIVET, Rick

Tribal affiliations: Sahtu; Métis
Painter

Born: Richard James Rivet, Aklavik, Northwest Territories, 10 November 1949. **Education:** University of Alberta, Edmonton, BA, 1972; University of Victoria, BFA, painting, 1980; Banff Centre, School of Fine Arts, 1980-81; University of Saskatchewan, Saskatoon, MFA, painting, 1985, BE and Professional "A" Teaching Certificate, 1986. **Career:** Full-time artist since 1976; art instructor, Newfoundland and Manitoba, 1987-89; jurist for the selection of work for the Indian Art Centre for Indian and Northern Affairs Canada, 1983; board member, Society of Canadian Artists of Native Ancestry, Ottawa, Ontario; jurist, selection for the Canada Council Arts Awards (short term and travel grants), 1995. **Awards:** The Mungo Martin Student Award, British Columbia, 1978, 1983; The Victoria Arts Council Award, 1979; The Vancouver Foundation Bursary Award, 1980; The Banff Centre School of Fine Arts Scholarship, 1980; The First Citizen's Fund for Native Students, 1982; Northwest Territories Government Supplementary Grant, 1983, 1985-86; B.C. Cultural Fund Grant, 1983-84, 1984-85; Graduate Student Scholarship, Saskatchewan 1983-84, 1984, 1984-85;

Saskatchewan Arts Board Grant, 1986; Government of Newfoundland Arts and Letters Competition Award, 1988; Canadian Native Arts Foundation Grant, 1990; Canada Council Short Term Grant, 1992; Canada Council Travel Grant, 1994.

Individual Exhibitions

1985   *Graduate Show*, The Gordon Snelgrove Art Gallery, University of Saskatchewan, Saskatoon, Saskatchewan
1990   Houston North Gallery, Halifax, Nova Scotia
1991-92 *Directions*, The Thunder Bay Art Gallery, Thunder Bay, Ontario
1994   *Axis-North by Northwest*, The Virginia Christopher Gallery, Calgary, Alberta
        The Prince of Wales Northern Heritage Centre, Yellowknife, Northwest Territories
        Matter, Space and Time, Simon Patrich Gallery, Vancouver, British Columbia
1995   The Alcheringa Gallery, Victoria, British Columbia
1996   *Mask Series*, Virginia Christopher Gallery, Calgary, Alberta
        The Yukon Arts Centre, Whitehorse, Yukon.
1997   Simon Patrich Gallery, Vancouver British Columbia

Rick Rivet, 1995. Photograph by Donna Rivet.

Selected Group Exhibitions

1979   *Graduating Students Art Show*, The Maltwood Museum and Art Gallery, University of Victoria, Victoria, British Columbia

1980   *The Armouries Building Show*, Victoria, British Columbia

Graduating Students Art Show, The Maltwood Museum and Art Gallery, University of Victoria, Victoria, British Columbia

1981   *Visual Arts Participants Show*, The Walter Phillips Gallery, The Banff Centre, Banff, Alberta

1983   *Faculty Club Show*, University of Saskatchewan, Saskatoon, Saskatchewan

1984   *The Saskatchewan Open 84*, The Mendel Art Gallery, Saskatoon, Saskatchewan

University of Saskatchewan Art '84, Travelling Group Exhibition.

Graduate Students Group Show, The Gordon Snelgrove Art Gallery, University of Saskatchewan, Saskatoon, Saskatchewan

1986   *The Saskatchewan Open '86*, The Mendel Art Gallery, Saskatoon, Saskatchewan

Vinish Gallery, Saskatoon, Saskatchewan

1988   Memorial University of Newfoundland Art Gallery, Arts and Culture Centre, St. Johns Nfld.

1990   Other Art Gallery, Halifax, Nova Scotia

Great Northern Arts Festival, The Inuvialuit Corporate Centre, Inuvik, Northwest Territories

1991   *Public-Private Gatherings: Recent Acquisitions, Indian and Inuit Art Gallery*, The Canadian Museum of Civilization, Hull, Quebec

The Toronto Symphonys Annual Presidents Evening in support of the Canadian Native Arts Foundation, (Auction and Benefit Show), Roy Thompson Hall, Toronto, Ontario,

1992   The Marion Scott Gallery, Vancouver, British Columbia

New Territories, 350-500 Years After, Les Ateliers Vision Planetaire, Montreal/Quebec City, Quebec

The Great Northern Arts Festival, The Inuvialuit Corporate Centre, Inuvik, Northwest Territories

Recent Acquisitions, The Thunder Bay Art Gallery, Thunder Bay, Ontario

1992-93   *Canada's First People: A Celebration of Contemporary Native Visual Arts*, (touring exhibit, Canada/Japan), Alberta Part Art Publications Society (with Syncrude Canada, Ltd.), Edmonton, Alberta

The National Arts Centre and Indian Art Centre Gallery, Indian and Northern Affairs, Ottawa, Ontario

1992-94   *Indigena: Perspectives of Indigenous Peoples on Five Hundred Years*, (travelling exhibition - Canada/USA), The Indian and Inuit Gallery, the Canadian Museum of Civilization, Hull, Quebec

1993   *The Ethics of Gesture*, The Burnaby Art Gallery, Burnaby, British Columbia

Native American Art and First Nations Peoples Art, The Western Gallery, Western Washington University, Bellingham, Washington

Artropolis 93, The Woodwards Building, Vancouver, British Columbia

1993-95   *Arts From the Arctic*, (Russia, Canada, Alaska, Greenland, Scandanavian Lapland), The Vancouver Inuit Art Society

1994   *Discoveries '94*, Simon Patrich Gallery, Vancouver, British Columbia

Arts From the Arctic, The Maltwood Art Museum and Gallery, University of Victoria, Victoria, British Columbia

1995   *Recent Acquisitions*, Dept. of Foreign Affairs and International Trade, Ottawa, Ontario

The Great Northern Arts Festival, Inuvik, Northwest Territories

1996   Gallery Gevick, Toronto, Ontario

1996-97   *Topographies: Aspects of Recent British Columbia Art*, Vancouver Art Gallery, Vancouver, British Columbia

Collections

Alberta Energy Company, Calgary, Alberta; Canadian Museum of Civilization, Hull, Quebec; Chateau Champlain, Montreal, Quebec; Department of Foreign Affairs and International Trade Art Collection, Canadian Embassy, Moscow; Government of British Columbia Art Collection, Victoria, British Columbia; Indian Art Centre, Indian and Northern Affairs Canada, Ottawa, Ontario; Maltwood Museum and Art Gallery, University of Victoria, Victoria, British Columbia; Memorial University Art Gallery, Memorial University, St. Johns, Newfoundland;Gordon Snelgrove Art Gallery, University of Saskatchewan, Saskatoon, Saskatchewan; Thunder Bay Art Gallery, Thunder Bay, Ontario; Vancouver Inuit Art Society, Vancouver, British Columbia.

Publications

On RIVET: Books—*New Territories: 350/500 Years After*, Ateliers Vision Planetaire; Tétrault/Williams; Montreal, 1992; *Indigena: Contemporary Native Perspectives*, Gerald McMaster, editor, Vancouver/Toronto, 1992; *Artropolis '93*, Langford Kelly, editor, Vancouver, British Columbia, 1993; *Topographies*, Arnold, Gagnon, and Jensen, editors, Douglas & McIntyre; Vancouver, 1996.

*   *   *

The work of Rick Rivet revolves and evolves around the concept of dualities. His Métis-Canadian ancestry is anchored with dualities of culture and social status. His painting style blends abstract, earthy strokes and the formality and structure of traditionally European based art education.

It was in the mid-1980s, during his period researching his masters thesis at the University of Saskatchewan, that Rivet began his exploration of the ethnic textures of his own voice as an art and as a person. He has become a collector, interpreter and connoisseur of cultural symbols and imagery. Rivet continually takes an intellectual point of view in seeking out his sources of inspiration, which he draws from aboriginal peoples from around the world—North America, South America, and Asia, as well as ancient European cultures, such as the Norse. In the light of his dualistic explorations, Rivet is also inspired by more Western and contemporary influences. The German and French Impressionists, Abstract Impressionists, Primitivist Art, Art Povera and artists who themselves probed the secrets of Primitive Art, all to various degrees of influence, have played a part in molding the style that is uniquely Rivet's.

In much of his work, the spiritual influences of shamanism encounter and interact with contemporary social and economic issues. Rivet makes use of traditional icons, manipulating them into

Metropolitan State University
Library Services
St. Paul, MN 55106

Rick Rivet: *Smallpox Jack #1*, 1992. Courtesy of the artist.

catalysts for the transformation of the spirit. Thematically, he often traces the affect of European colonization on Native people. In this respect his focus is not only the well-rehearsed and repeated history of contact, but of the continuing and more subtle effects of Western Society on Native people. As a teacher, communicator, and healer, the shaman image in Rivet's work is compelling. The shaman as intervenor and guardian to the spirits also eases tensions in the variety of relationships involved, that of Aboriginal and Western people and philosophies, of art and viewers of any background, and perhaps of Rivet and the artwork itself.

Known for the strong graphic element that pervades his work, Rick Rivet's paintings are filled with subtle contrasts that require a great deal of work on the part of the viewer to piece together the elements of the work and to play with the layers and the relationships between the dualities expressed within them. The representations of spirit and flesh, mythic and contemporary, intimate and impersonal, realistic and surreal, are not readily apparent and are often difficult to absorb, especially without concentrated effort, but that effort is rewarding.

Rivet's examination and representation of history and all of its affects on today's aboriginal people comes from both his educational and personal experiences. They are at the same time both introspective and expansive studies. Continuing his balanced perspective, Rivet's themes move from the political to the spiritual, where shamanism of many native cultures promotes a true harmony of the earth and the creatures on it, while the Western beliefs lean much more toward domination and mastery of the earth by humanity. This simultaneous global and personal perspective weaves in and out of the images Rivet creates.

Tied by both blood and spirit to the Western and native worlds, Rivet manages to find a balance between the contradictions that bind his work through disciplined study and meticulous thought.

—Vesta Giles

ROMERO, Diego

Tribal affiliations: Cochití Pueblo
Potter and ceramist

Born: Berkeley, California, 1 June 1964. **Education:** Institute of American Indian Arts, AFA, 1986; Otis/Parsons Art Institute, BFA,

1990; University of California, Los Angeles, MFA, 1993. **Career:** Lab Technician, Otis/Parsons Art Institute, 1988-90; teaching associate, University of California, Los Angeles, 1991-93; guest lecturer, University of New Mexico Fine Arts Department, 1993; visiting artist and guest lecturer, Institute of American Indian Arts, 1993-94; ceramics Instructor, Institute of American Indian Arts, 1995-96. **Awards:** First Place, Best of Division and Best of Class, Contemporary Pottery, Southwestern Association on Indian Arts Annual Market, Santa Fe, New Mexico, 1995 and 1996. **Address:** c/o Robert F. Nichols Gallery, 419 Canyon Road, Santa Fe, New Mexico 87501.

Selected Group Exhibitions

1986   *Graduation Show*, Institute of American Indian Arts Museum, Santa Fe, New Mexico

1990   *Clay Ninety, Eighty-Nine, Eighty-Eight*, Otis/Parsons Art Institute North Gallery, Los Angeles

1992   *Creativity is Our Tradition*, Institute of American Indian Arts Museum, Santa Fe, New Mexico

1993   *MFA Exhibition*, Wright Art Gallery, University of California, Los Angeles

Into the Forefront: American Indian Art in the 20th Century, Denver Art Museum, Denver, Colorado

N.C.E.C.A. '93, National Council on Education for the Ceramic Arts, San Diego, California

1994   *American Highway Series*, Two Person Show, Robert F. Nichols Gallery, Santa Fe, New Mexico

Crow Canyon Archaeological Invitational, Chicago

Mimbres in the 20th Century, Museum of New Mexico, Museum of Indian Arts and Culture, Santa Fe, New Mexico

1995   *Chongo Brothers: Third Generation Cochití Artists*, Museum of New Mexico, Museum of Indian Arts and Culture, Santa Fe, New Mexico

1996   *Gifts of the Spirit: Works by Nineteenth-Century and Contemporary Native American Artists*, Peabody Essex Museum, Salem, Massachusetts

Native American Traditions/Contemporary Responses, The Society for Contemporary Craft, Pittsburgh, Pennsylvania

Innovations in Clay, Robert F. Nichols Gallery, Santa Fe, New Mexico

Southwest '96, Museum of New Mexico, Museum of Fine Arts, Santa Fe

To Touch the Past, Weisman Museum, Minneapolis, Minnesota

Gallery 10, Scottsdale, Arizona

A Labor of Love, The New Museum of Contemporary Art, New York

1997   Gallery 10, Carefree, Arizona

Collections

Denver Art Museum, Denver, Colorado; Institute of American Indian Arts Museum, Santa Fe, New Mexico; Museum of New Mexico, Museum of Indian Arts and Culture, Santa Fe, New Mexico; Peabody Essex Museum, Salem, Massachusetts; Poeh Museum, Pueblo of Pojoaque, New Mexico; Weisman Museum, Minneapolis, Minnesota.

Publications

On ROMERO: Books—*Creativity Is Our Tradition*, by Rick Hill, Santa Fe, Institute of American Indian Arts, 1992; *Gifts of the Spirit—Works by Nineteenth-Century and Contemporary Native American Artists*, Salem, Massachusetts, Peabody Essex Museum, 1996. **Articles**—"Chongo Brothers Meet Mimbres," by William Clark, *El Palacio*, Summer 1994; "A Cross-Cultural Mix, Modern Imagery Meets Traditional Shape in the Innovative and Expressive Pottery of Diego Romero," by Robert F. Nichols, *Focus/Santa Fe*, October 1994; "Coding the Universe, An Interview with Diego Romero, Cochití Potter," by Gerry Williams, *The Studio Potter*, December 1994; "1 Potter + 1 Painter = 2 Brothers," by Lis Bensley, *Pasatiempo, The Santa Fe New Mexican*, December 9, 1994; "Showcasing Works of Remarkable Cochití Family— A Marriage of Modern, Traditional," by Jason Silverman, *Pasatiempo, The Santa Fe New Mexican*, August Silverman, August 11, 1995; "Gallery Section," by MaLin Wilson, *Santa Fean*, September 1995; "Clay Lady's Children, Southwestern Pottery's Spirit of Invention," by Ron McCoy, *Indian Artist Magazine*, Summer 1996; "The Mimbres Tradition: Past and Present," by Robert Silberman, *American Craft*, August/September, 1996;

*

Diego Romero comments:

I'm developing my own language through symbolism. I'm dealing with a language of symbols and metaphors... My dialogue centers around industrialization of Indian land, cars, automobiles, broken hearts, bars, Indian gaming. And I've developed a whole new set of symbols and symbology for that. That's somewhat universal I think. That transcends language. I've always felt that a person from Japan or Germany can come and look at one of my pots and see exactly what's going on. There doesn't need to be a text. It's obvious. This guy's breaking up with his girlfriend.

*   *   *

Diego Romero's major contribution to the contemporary Indian art movement is his sophisticated use of traditional pottery forms and techniques, laden with modern social commentary. His execution of narratives, whether in Greek hero figures or Keresan styled comic book characters, places his work outside any established Indian art genre. Viewers who in all likelihood may choose to avoid the "heavy" or "angry" messages of overtly politicized native artists are innocently led to Romero's work through the innocuous medium of pottery, long considered a craft form. Pueblo Indian contact, oppression, resistance and revolt are poignantly traced along with playful renderings of space travel, broken hearts, and the industrialized landscape. A stylistic congruence with classic Mimbres design elements links Romero's work inescapably to those of his Cochití ancestors, whose own highly formalized symbolism conveyed the essential messages of their time, relating to such subjects as fertility and the elements. Diego Romero's *American Highway* series successfully stretches historic Southwestern polychromia conventions to accommodate the all-pervasive pop culture of our global society at the end of the 20th century.

While it has been noted by art critics that Romero's ceramics "mesh the intellectual component associated with contemporary works with the high craft of American Indian art" (Jason Silverman 1995), a simple cultural bridging does not account for the sophis-

Diego Romero: *The Martyrdom of Father Fray Jesus.* **Courtesy of the artist.**

tication of this artist's aim. The inherent assumption that American Indian art traditions (categorized as craft) contain no intellectual component is evidenced by some critics. Certainly, it takes an artist trained both in method and analysis to undertake the multiple layerings of interpretation that infuses Romero's work. Yet, the use of precise construction based on older technical forms does not mean that the content is any less meaningful. The seamless merging of these two categories (technical adeptness and intellectual observation) is the hallmark of Romero's career. An inability to see how indigenous technique and modern analysis can coexist is responsible for the way in which Indian art theory is lodged in a seemingly unaltered state of marginality.

Romero's skill in moving smoothly between the perceived disparate influences of modern art and traditional ceramics was forged by his experience growing up in Berkeley, California, and Cochití Pueblo. At age 19, Romero entered the Institute of American Indian Arts and was influenced by Hopi ceramics instructor Otellie Loloma, who taught hand-built ceramics using commercial materials. At IAIA, Romero began making and selling stylized ceramic coyotes. Realizing this vocation was almost "too easy," he returned to the West Coast to continue his education. At UCLA, his involvement with the American Indian Students Union led to a political awareness that began being reflected in his work.

Describing the reaction to his artwork at school, Romero notes: "All through grad school and undergrad school, I wanted to do Indian art. I just don't do traditional Indian art. But it's still very Indian, still very pop, too." While some saw his use of Cochití designs as a "crutch" or even as something other than art, Romero says this denial only "made me more determined to recontextualize that trend—art/craft." He observes, "It's interesting that when an Anglo gets plugged into Indian art and starts painting pictures of shamanism or Indian spirituality it's quote/ unquote 'high art.' But when an Indian does it, like in art school, you can use the argument it's a crutch." Romero's premise is that symbolism is a highly sophisticated "Universal" form of communication.

Romero's adept use of humor to convey complex social realities is fully in line with the great tradition of delivering a grim message in a palatable manner. That his use of satire is executed in a medium that most would consider apolitical is evidence of his ability to communicate adeptly using illustration that combines old and new symbols. All of this is nothing more extraordinary than simple cultural change and adaptation. As Romero observes, "It's not like we didn't do it before."

—Nancy Marie Mithlo

ROMERO, Mateo

Tribal affiliations: Cochití Pueblo
Painter

Born: Berkeley, California, 9 December 1966. **Family:** Son Vance Romero born in 1994 to Jody Archambault; daughter Jopovi Romero born in 1995 to Melissa Talachy. **Education:** San Francisco Academy of Art College, 1984; University of Oregon, Architectural Seminar, 1984; B.A. in Visual Studies, modified Art History, Dartmouth College, 1989; Institute of American Indian Arts, 1989-90; Dartmouth College Reynolds Scholar, Guanajuato Mexico, 1991-92; M.F.A. University of New Mexico, 1996. **Career:** Production assistant, Dartmouth College, Hopkins Center Design Studio, 1987; preparator, Oakland Museum of Art, 1988; painting instructor, Native American Preparatory School at Cushing Academy, 1989; Fading Sun Gallery, Santa Fe, New Mexico, 1989; board of directors, Southwestern Association for Indian Arts (SWAIA), 1994-96; drawing and printmaking instructor, graduate assistant, University of New Mexico, 1994-96; instructor, Southwestern Association for Indian Arts Summer Youth Camp, 1995; chairman of Artists Advisory Council, Southwestern Association for Indian Arts, 1995-96; Atlatl Second Circle Board of Directors, 1996; assistant director, Poeh Cultural Center and Museum, Pueblo of Pojoaque, 1996. **Awards:** Several at juried shows, including the Southwestern Association of Indian Arts Annual Market, Santa Fe, New Mexico, and the Indian Nations Rendezvous Trade Fair, Denver, Colorado; Language Study Abroad, Facultad de Transducir, Granada, Spain, 1987; Endowed Scholar, Native American Education Fund, 1988; Daniel S. Simon Award, Dartmouth College, 1989; Wolfendine Fine Arts Award, Dartmouth College, 1991-92; several fellowships and scholarships, 1991-96.

Individual Exhibitions

1991   Institute of American Indian Arts Museum, Santa Fe
        Trading Company, Aspen, Colorado
1993   Mural Project, Denver International Airport Western
        American Indian Chamber of Commerce
1994   Wheelwright Museum of the American Indian, Santa Fe
1996   *Tales of Ordinary Violence*, Gallery 10, Santa Fe
1997   Mural Project, Cities of Gold Casino, Pueblo of Pojoaque,
        New Mexico

Selected Group Exhibitions

1991   *The Nude in Native American Art (Cultural Reality or
        Sexual Fantasy?)*, Institute of American Indian Arts
        Museum, Santa Fe
        Southwest Connection, Hudson, New Hampshire

1992   American West, Chicago
        Crow Canyon Archaeological Invitational, Chicago
        Creativity is Our Tradition, Institute of American Indian
            Arts Museum, Santa Fe
1993   *Into the Forefront: American Indian Art in the 20th Cen-
            tury*, Denver Art Museum, Colorado
1994   American West, Chicago
        Graphics Show, Gallery 10, Scottsdale, Arizona
        Crow Canyon Archaeological Invitational, Chicago
        Tamarind Institute Collaborative Lithographic Workshop,
            Albuquerque
        University of New Mexico, University Art Museum,
            Albuquerque
        American Highway Series, Robert Nichols Gallery, Santa Fe
1995   Wheelwright Museum of the American Indian, Santa Fe
        Chongo Brothers: Third Generation Cochiti Artists,
            Museum of New Mexico, Museum of Indian Arts and
            Culture, Santa Fe
1995-96 *Building Blocks: Recent Additions to the American Indian
            Collection*, Denver Art Museum, Colorado
1996   *Southwestern Association for Indian Arts Masters Show*,
            Cast Iron Gallery, New York
        Gallery 10, Scottsdale, Arizona
        *Gifts of the Spirit: Works by Nineteenth-Century and Con-
            temporary Native American Artists*, Peabody Essex
            Museum, Salem, Massachusetts
1998   Group Installation Show, Canadian Museum of Civiliza-
            tion, Hull, Quebec

Collections

Denver Art Museum; Denver International Airport; Institute of
American Indian Arts Museum, Santa Fe; Museum of New Mexico,
Museum of Indian Arts and Culture, Santa Fe; Poeh Museum,
Pueblo of Pojoaque, New Mexico; Cities of Gold Casino, Pueblo of
Pojoaque, New Mexico.

Publications

By ROMERO: Article—"Tales of Ordinary Violence," MFA Catalog, University of New Mexico Fine Arts Department.

On ROMERO: Books—*Gifts of the Spirit: Works by Nineteenth-
Century and Contemporary Native American Artists*, Peabody Essex
Museum, Salem, Massachusetts, 1996. **Articles**—"Blooming: A
Look at Student Mateo Romero," *Institute of American Indian Arts
Newsletter*, 1989; "Artist Links Pueblo Roots, Urban Life," by
William Clark, *The Albuquerque Journal*, August 1992; "The Evo-
lution of American Indian Art," by Richard Johnson, *Denver Post
Magazine*, July 4, 1993; "Council at SWAIA Elects New Chair-
man," by Hollis Walker, *The Santa Fe New Mexican*, May 24, 1995;
"Showcasing Works of Remarkable Cochiti Family: A Marriage of
Modern, Traditional," by Jason Silverman, *Pasatiempo—The Santa
Fe New Mexican*, August 11, 1995; "Gallery Section," by Marlin
Wilson, *Santa Fean*, September, 1995; "On the Wind," *Indian Art-
ist Magazine*, Fall 1995; "Hybrid Vigor," by Daniel Vallincourt,
Pasatiempo: The Santa Fe New Mexican, May 10, 1996; "Don't
Miss Too-Short MFA Exhibit," by Marlin Wilson, *Albuquerque
Journal*, May 16, 1996.

*   *   *

The lithographs and paintings of Cochiti artist Mateo Romero are
deceptive in their starkness. While the viewer may experience nostalgia
over his renderings of pueblo dancers, humor at viewing the Coke Can
fetish work, or grief at contemplating his *Tales of Ordinary Violence*,
the artistic intent is constant—to communicate and humanize a uniquely
Indian point of view. Aside from this central approach to his work, it is
Romero's underlying intent, his self-described "pin prick of conscience"
that characterizes his placement as a major figure in the development of
contemporary Indian Art practice and theory.

Raised in the urban environment of the Greater California Bay
Area, Romero exercises a highly sophisticated use of images and
materials. Even the language in which he describes his art is difficult
for the average Indian Art enthusiast to follow. His ability to "work"
these processes to such an accelerated degree places Romero
squarely in a no-man's land of artistic development; beyond the
confines of the mainstream Indian art marketplace, yet too content-
laden to be fully acceptable to established Western fine art paradigms. This quandary, however, has not limited his ability to trans-
gress successfully in the world of higher education.

Romero's story could be described as a classical "two worlds"
scenario (Art Critic Marlin Wilson writes of Romero's ability to
"bridge the White man's world and the Native American world"),
but the formula isn't nearly as simple as this cliche suggests. His
extensive formal training in the arts combined with the influence of
family and community does lend itself to the expectation that a
discrepancy between these influences exists. Addressing this famil-

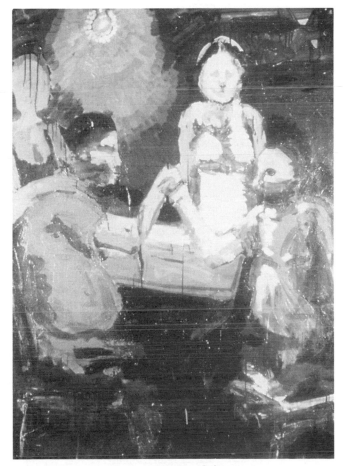

Mateo Romero: Untitled. Courtesy of the artist.

iar argument, Romero responds, "I just function, participate in the society; I do my art, and the two are related, but in ways that are divorced. No, I don't perceive this as a conflict." Perhaps it is precisely Romero's realism, fed by his worldly experiences, that sets him apart from other artists of his generation who lean towards a romantic depiction of the more traditional aspects of native culture. Of his art, he says "It has to do with what the Indian society is now," which of course includes Coke cans, alcoholism, gambling, and domestic violence.

Romero's body of work has developed over time from looming surreal landscapes to what he terms "social landscapes." His concern with expressing "the nuances of Indigenous thought" has recently led to what some might describe as a bleak portraiture of human existence. It is this documentation of the personal and domestic experience that Romero identifies as a prerequisite to a healing process and possible raising of conscience for both native and Non-native audiences. He states of his work, "Conspicuously absent are the images of historically accurate Indians dancing to an imaginary song, replaced by uncomfortable, sensual, sleek, dangerous images of present day urban Indians" (Romero, 1996). This is a far reach from his earlier concern with pop culture icons, expressed, for example, in his *Indian Marilyn Monroe Series* and the *Bonnie and Clyde Series*. These developments suggest a maturation process that seems sure to express the sincerity he strives for.

Commenting on the role of the artist in society, Romero states, "At the most sincere level, I think it (art) has to deal with communication. I think the artist ideally is ... someone who has responsibility for informing society ... and communicating ideas that are viable and that are important." Beyond even this function of art in society, Romero recognizes that it is the content of that communication that ultimately makes the work valuable to the audience. Of knowing just what to communicate, he concludes:

"You have to have a statement to make. You have to have a message to make ... underlying that, even, is just your own sense of motivational worth ... your own motivational sense of drive, regardless of whether you're an artist, a mechanic or anything. It has to do with your own sense of ability, your own goals, your own drive. Endurance is important. Training is important. It all goes back to motivation—just being able to function, not just as an artist, but as a human being, to make things happen."

It is this "cultural desire to express something" that makes his narratives so compelling. Issues of ethnicity, spirituality, and pluralism are laid bare for his audience to resolve. This reluctance to finish every story may frustrate a public spoon-fed with spiritual explanations, but they do not cease to entice those hungry for a more realistic rendering of contemporary Indigenous society.

—Nancy Marie Mithlo

ROYBAL, José D.
Variant names: Oquwa
Tribal affiliations: San Ildefonso Pueblo
Painter

Born: José Disiderio Roybal, San Ildefonso Pueblo, New Mexico, 7 November 1922; also known as Oquwa, which translates as Rain

God. **Family:** Mother and father (Tonita and Juan Cruz Roybal) were potters, and he was related to Awa Tsireh, a famous painter; married Julia Dasheno, 1951, two children. **Education:** San Ildefonso Day School; St. Catherine's Indian School, Santa Fe, graduating in 1942; Santa Fe Business College, 1959-60. **Military Service:** U.S. Army, World War II, disability discharge. **Career:** Potter and painter; council member, San Ildefonso Pueblo. **Awards:** Southwestern Association for Indian Arts Santa Fe Indian Market, 1942, 1962-63, 1972-74, 1976; Heard Museum Guild Indian Fair and Market, 1969; Inter-Tribal Indian Ceremonials, Elkus Award, 1972; Scottsdale National Indian Arts Exhibition, 1971. **Died:** 28 June 1978.

Selected Group Exhibitions

Exhibited regularly at Southwestern Association for Indian Arts Santa Fe Indian Market, the Eight Northern Pueblos Arts and Crafts Show, and New Mexico State Fair, 1940s through 1970s.

1968   *James T. Bialac Collection of Southwest Indian Paintings,* Arizona State Museum, University of Arizona, Tucson

1978   *100 Years of Native American Painting,* Oklahoma Museum of Art, Oklahoma City, Oklahoma

1979-80 *Native American Paintings,* organized by the Joslyn Art Museum, Omaha, Nebraska (traveling)

1982   *Native American Painting: Selections from the Museum of the American Indian,* Heard Museum, Phoenix, Arizona

1984-85 *Indianascher Kunstler* (traveling, Germany), organized by the Philbrook Museum, Tulsa, Oklahoma

1990   *Selections from the James T. Bialac Collection of 20th Century Native American Art,* Nelson Fine Arts Center, Arizona State University Art Museum, Tempe, Arizona

1996   *Drawn from Memory: James T. Bialac Collection of Native American Art,* Heard Museum, Phoenix, Arizona
        Vision and Voices: Native American Painting from the Philbrook Museum of Art, Philbrook Museum of Art, Tulsa, Oklahoma

Collections

Heritage Center, Inc., Collection, Red Cloud Indian School, Pine Ridge, South Dakota; Museum of the American Indian, Washington, D.C.; Museum of Northern Arizona, Flagstaff; Museum of New Mexico, Santa Fe; Millicent Rogers Foundation Museum, Taos, New Mexico; Southwest Museum, Los Angeles, California.

Publications

On ROYBAL: Books—*American Indian Painting of the Southwest and Plains Areas,* by Dorothy Dunn, Albuquerque: University of New Mexico, 1968; *Indian Painters and White Patrons,* by J. J. Brody, Albuquerque: University of New Mexico Press, 1971; *Song From the Earth: American Indian Painting,* by Jamake Highwater, Boston, 1976; *100 Years of Native American Painting,* exhibition catalog by Arthur Silberman, Oklahoma Museum of Art, Oklahoma City, 1978; *Native American Painting,* by Frederick Schmid and Patrick T. Houlihan, Kansas City, 1980; *American Indian Painting and Sculpture,* by Patricia Broder, New York, 1981; *Indianische Kunst im 20 Jahrhundert,* Munich, 1984; *Vision and*

José D. Roybal: *Kiva Dance.* Courtesy Ron and Doris Smithee collection.

Voices: Native American Painting from the Philbrook Museum of Art, Lydia Wyckoff, editor, Tulsa, 1996.

*   *   *

José D. Roybal carried on the tradition of his famous relative, Awa Tsireh, one of the original great Pueblo watercolorists noted for depicting genre scenes, ceremonial dances and dancers, and stylized compositions of animals and landscapes. Conservative with color, favoring warm, rich earth tones, and focusing on the same themes and subjects as his predecessors, Roybal created finely detailed paintings. Lively, animated characters and touches of humor make his work especially distinctive and pleasing.

Roybal was born in 1922 at San Ildefonso Pueblo, to Tonita and Juan Cruz Roybal, who gave him a traditional Tewa name, Oquwa, "Rain God." In the Tewa world, most ceremonies are directed at bringing gentle rains for bountiful harvests. Rain symbols and dancers appear frequently in Roybal's work, reflecting as well his penchant for blending realistic depictions—characterized by blocks of outlined color with little modeling, considerable detailing of costume, and little use of backgrounds or three-dimensional perspective—with symbolic images.

Roybal grew up under artistic influence of his uncle, Awa Tsireh; there has been debate over their actual relation, as some, including Santa Fe Indian Market judge and collector Dick Howard, claim that J. D. Roybal was not the nephew, but rather the cousin of Awa Tsireh. Regardless, Roybal grew up in a fertile artistic environment. In addition to learning from Awa Tsireh, Roybal attended San Ildefonso Day School from 1927 to 1934 and graduated from St.

Catherine's Indian School in 1942, from which many Indian artists emerged. Following military service in World War II, where he was wounded and received a disability discharge, Roybal began to paint more frequently and seriously. He attended Santa Fe Business College from 1959 to 1960, developing skills helpful to artists seeking to make a living through their art. During the 1950s he was also encouraged by Popovi Da, the son of renowned potters Julian and Maria Martinez. In 1948, Da and his wife, Anita, opened the Popovi Da Studio in the Pueblo of San Ildefonso. It was not until the early 1960s, however, that Roybal reached his stride and began winning competitions and having his work exhibited regularly. He remained a popular and respected artist through to his death in 1978.

Roybal is best known for his paintings of ceremonials, including the Corn Dances, usually focusing on the Winter, or Turquoise Dancers, where the men have painted bodies, wear kilts embroidered with rain symbols, and are adorned with evergreen boughs, a symbol of growth; women wear black sashes and turquoise-colored headdresses in the familiar terraced shape that represents clouds; Koshares are painted in black and white stripes, and musicians and singers have brightly colored clothes. *Corn Dance* (1968) depicts such a scene in a familiar Pueblo manner, as the group proceeds across the bottom portion of the painting. A kiva, with steps leading up in the center of the painting, is a unique background device in this work, as is Roybal's infusion of humor: while the procession passes, Koshare clown dancers atop the Kiva are taking breaks—eating watermelon and napping. In other works by Roybal, similar ceremonies are taking place while Koshares off to the sides or away from the action are relaxing, talking, smoking, and helping each other with their costumes.

Close inspection of Roybal's work usually rewards the viewer with such incidental touches; for example, his human figures often have animated facial expressions, and peripheral characters are often engaged in mundane matters. Roybal also used familiar Pueblo images, such as the rainbow, in novel ways, as in *Koshare and Rainbow,* where a rainbow spills into a scene with six Koshare clowns, three of whom ride the arc while three others wrestle with a snake at rainbow's end. A conventional symbol is, thus, playfully rendered, similar to the joviality and mischievousness exhibited by Koshares themselves in their actions amid more serious events.

The humor is made more poignant by the conventional, realistic manner and respect for ceremony reflected in the works; Roybal's humor has its place among the many facets of Pueblo life he depicts.

—Perry Bear

S

SAHMIE, Ida

Tribal affiliations: Navajo
Painter

Born: Ida Nobell, Pine Springs, Navajo Nation, Arizona, 27 May 1960. **Family:** Married Andrew Sahmie, 1986, one son, one daughter. **Awards:** Several at the Santa Fe Indian Market, the Museum of Northern Arizona's Navajo Craftsman Exhibition, and the Navajo Nation Fair.

Individual Exhibitions

1990   Museum of Northern Arizona, Flagstaff
1996   Second Mesa Cultural Center, Second Mesa, Arizona
        Arizona State Museum, University of Arizona, Tucson
        Mesa Verde National Park, Mesa Verde, Colorado
        Crow Canyon Archaeological Center, Cortez, Colorado

Ida Sahmie: Navajo polychrome bowl, c. 1989. Photograph by Dong Lin; courtesy Ruth K. Belikove collection.

Selected Group Exhibitions

1988   *anii ánáádaalyaa'íí: Continuity and Innovation in Recent Navajo Art*, Wheelwright Museum of the American Indian, Santa Fe

1989   Southwest Museum, Los Angeles

1993   *Leets'aa bi Diné Dáályé: It Is Called Navajo Pottery*, Phoebe A. Hearst Museum of Anthropology, University of California, Berkeley

1994   *Contemporary Art of the Navajo Nation*, traveling exhibit organized by Cedar Rapids Museum of Art, Iowa; Venues: Albuquerque Museum, Albuquerque, New Mexico; University Art Museum, State University of New York, Albany; Museum of the Southwest, Midland, Texas

Permanent Public Installations

Navajo Nation Museum, Window Rock, Arizona

Collections

Arizona State Museum, University of Arizona, Tucson; Carnegie Museum of Art, Pittsburgh; Navajo Nation Museum, Window Rock, Arizona; Peabody Museum, Harvard University, Cambridge, Massachusetts; School of American Research, Santa Fe.

Publications

On SAHMIE: Books—*Navajo Pottery: Traditions and Innovations* by Russell P. Hartman, Flagstaff: Northland Press, 1987; *anii ánáádaalyaa'íí: Continuity and Innovation in Recent Navajo Art*, exhibition catalog by Bruce Bernstein and Susan McGreevy, Santa Fe: Wheelwright Museum, 1988; *Museum of American Folk Art Encyclopedia of Twentieth-Century American Folk Art and Artists* by Chuck and Jan Rosenak, New York: Abbeville Press, 1990; *The People Speak; Navajo Folk Art* by Chuck and Jan Rosenak, Flagstaff: Northland Publishing Co., 1994; *Enduring Traditions: Art of the Navajo* by Lois Essary Jacka, Flagstaff: Northland Publishing Co., 1994; *Fourteen Families in Pueblo Pottery* by Rick Dillingham, Albuquerque: University of New Mexico Press, 1994; *Trading Post Guidebook* by Patrick Eddington and Susan Makov, Flagstaff: Northland Publishing Co., 1995; *Southwestern Pottery: Anasazi to Zuni* by Allan Hayes and John Blom, Flagstaff: Northland Publishing Co., 1996.

*   *   *

Ida Sahmie is among a handful of younger, Navajo Potters who have come to their craft indirectly. Traditionally, pottery making has been handed down from mother to daughter in Navajo society, but Sahmie learned from her mother-in-law, noted Hopi potter Priscilla Namingha. Thus, her pottery has a decidedly puebloan sense but clearly is Navajo in design.

Sahmie's painted wares contrast sharply with the plain brown wares made by most Navajos. Using only natural clay slips and a brush made from a yucca leaf, she executes designs that are both delicate and bold at the same time. These include rows of masked Navajo dancers, geometric rug patterns, and designs taken from Navajo wedding baskets and sandpaintings, especially those of Mother Earth and Father Sky. On a number of vessels, the background is painted black to depict a night sky, against which ceremo-

nial dancers are shown. On some vessels, Sahmie has shown both day time and night time aspects of Navajo healing ceremonies, which encompass nine days.

To date, Sahmie's body of work is still not large, partly because of the high standards she sets for herself and partly because her vessels are so thin-walled that many break during the firing process. Clay gathered from several locations on the Hopi Indian Reservation is used to build up each vessel, using the coiling method. After the clay has been shaped to the desired form and allowed to partially dry, it is polished with a smooth river stone. Many puebloan potters completely slip the exterior of their pottery to provide an even smoother surface on which to paint the design. Sahmie, however, polishes her work so highly that an underlying slip is unnecessary. Instead, she prefers to paint directly onto the natural clay surface, using only natural clay slips that yield a subtle palette of earth colors, including black, white, red, brown, yellow, and gray. She has won awards for her work at the Santa Fe Indian Market, the Museum of Northern Arizona's Navajo Craftsman Exhibition, and the Navajo Nation Fair. These events, as well as features in several publications and marketing by leading galleries, have all contributed to rapid success for Sahmie. Her work is eagerly sought by collectors of contemporary Native American pottery because of its uniqueness and quality.

—Russell P. Hartman

SAKIESTEWA, Ramona

Tribal affiliations: Hopi
Textile artist

Born: Albuquerque, New Mexico, 1948. **Education:** Self-taught in traditional Pueblo spinning and weaving techniques; attended the School of Visual Arts, New York City, 1966-67. **Career:** Weaver since 1966; worked at an Albuquerque Trading Post, 1960s; arts administrator, Museum of New Mexico; helped establish Atlatl, a national Native American arts and cultural services organization; founded Ramona Sakiestewa Ltd., 1982; commissions, including Bandelier National Monument, beginning in 1975, Smithsonian Institution, 1987-92, Frank Lloyd Wright Foundation, 1987-89, limited edition blankets for Santa Fe Pendleton, 1990—, Bernice Steinbaum Gallery, a weaving for painter Paul Brach, and Sundance, Provo, Utah; lecture tour of Japan, United States Information Service; Design Consultant, National Museum of the American Indian, Washington, D.C., 1993-2001; lay member, New Mexico State Bar Arbitration Committee; commissioner, New Mexico Arts Commission; trustee, International Folk Art Foundation, Santa Fe, New Mexico; board member, Southwest Association on Indian Affairs, Wheelwright Museum of the American Indian; panelist, National Endowment for the Arts. **Awards:** First Place, contemporary weaving, Santa Fe Indian Market, 1982-91; fellowships, including Southwest Association on Indian Affairs, 1984, National American Indian Arts Foundation, 1988, Smithsonian Research grant, 1988. **Address:** c/o Horwitch LewAllen Gallery, 129 West Palace Avenue, Santa Fe, New Mexico 87501.

Individual Exhibitions

1987-88   *Kokoma: Colors of the Southwest,* LTV Center Pavillion, Trammell Crow, Dallas, Texas

Ramona Sakiestewa: *Facets/5*, 1990. Courtesy of the artist.

1989   *Ramona Sakiestewa, Patterned Dreams*, Wheelwright
        Museum of the American Indian, Santa Fe, New Mexico
1991   *Ramona Sakiestewa/Frank Lloyd Wright, Themes and
        Variations*, Newark Museum, Newark, New Jersey
1993   *Between Four Sacred Mountains: Contemporary
        Weavings of Ramona Sakiestewa*, Southwest Museum,
        Los Angeles, California
1994-97 Horwitch LewAllen Gallery, Santa Fe, New Mexico
1995   *Patterns of the Southwest: Tapestries by Ramona
        Sakiestewa*, John Michael Kohler Arts Center,
        Sheboygan, Wisconsin

Selected Group Exhibitions

1984   *Five Directions*, Museum of Northern Arizona, Flagstaff
1985-86 *Women of Sweetgrass, Cedar and Sage: Contemporary
        American Art by Native American Women*, American
        Indian Community House, New York (traveling)
        Gail Bird, Yazzie Johnson, and Ramona Sakiestewa, Tay-
        lor Museum, Colorado Springs, Colorado
1986   *In the Spirit of Tradition*, Heard Museum, Phoenix, Ari-
        zona
        Contemporary Native American Artists, Governor's Gal-
        lery, State Capitol, Santa Fe, New Mexico
1989   *Six from Santa Fe*, Gibbes Art Museum, Charleston, South
        Carolina
1989-90 *The Alcove Show*, Museum of Fine Arts, Santa Fe, New
        Mexico
1990   *Southwest '90*, Museum of Fine Arts, Santa Fe, New
        Mexico
        Society for Arts and Crafts, Pittsburgh, Pennsylvania

Beyond Tradition, Cowboy Hall of Fame, Oklahoma City,
        Oklahoma
1991   *Contemporary Concepts*, Los Colores Museum, Albu-
        querque, New Mexico
1992   *American Encounters 1992*, Smithsonian National Mu-
        seum of History, Washington, D.C.
        Colorado University Art Gallery, Boulder, Colorado
1993   *Weaving*, Albuquerque Museum, Albuquerque, New
        Mexico
1994   *Homeland: Use and Desire*, Massachusetts College of
        Art, Boston, Massachusetts

Collections

Albuquerque Museum New Mexico; Cleveland Museum of Art,
Ohio; Denver Art Museum, Colorado; Heard Museum, Phoenix,
Arizona; Museum of Fine Arts, Santa Fe, New Mexico; Newark
Museum, New Jersey; St. Louis Museum, Missouri; Wheelwright
Museum of the American Indian, Santa Fe, New Mexico.

Publications

By SAKIESTEWA: Essays—"Ramona Sakiestewa," *The* magazine, December 1992; "Weaving for Dance," *Partial Recall*, edited
by Lucy Lippard, New York, 1993.

On SAKIESTEWA: Books—*Women of Sweetgrass, Cedar and
Sage*, exhibition catalog, Albuquerque, 1986; *Beyond Tradition:
Contemporary Indian Art and Its Evolution*, by Jerry and Lois
Jacka, Flagstaff, Arizona, 1988; *Six from Santa Fe*, exhibition cata-
log, Gibbes Museum of Art, Chareston, South Carolina, 1989;

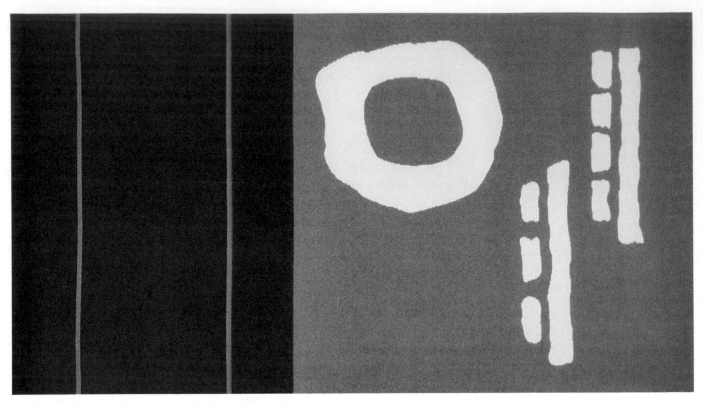

Ramona Sakiestewa: *Blue Corn,* 1993. Courtesy of the artist.

Ramona Sakiestewa, Patterned Dreams, by Suzanne Baizermann, Wheelwright Museum of the American Indian, Santa Fe, 1989; *Native American Arts: Traditions and Celebrations,* by Christine Mather and Jack Parsons, New York, 1990. **Articles**—"Southwest Reflections," by Mary Rawclift Colton, *The Weaver's Journal,* Summer 1986; "The Patterned Dreams of Ramona Sakiestewa," by Suzanne Baizcrman, *Artspace,* Fall 1988; "Patterned Dreams: Tapestries of Ramona Sakiestewa," by Patricia Harris and David Lyon, *Fiber Arts,* Spring 1990; "Blanket Statement," by Michael Haederle, *Los Angeles Times Magazine,* 1991; "Weaving Old into New," by M.S. Mason, *Christian Science Monitor,* January 13, 1992; "Ramona Sakiestewa," *Indian Artist* magazine, Spring 1995; "Dream Weaver," by Emily Drabanski, *New Mexico* magazine, August 1996.

*

Ramona Sakiestewa comments (December 1992):

I started weaving in 1966 when I was 17 years old. I'm self-taught. I learned on the vertical loom. The first weavings I did were wall hangings for my mom. I learned how to weave from looking at diagrams. I began by doing restoration and reclamation projects...

My work derives from indigenous icons, like Kachinas. I take a set group of colors. Basically, it's variations on a theme. Or, in a scrics called *Basket Dance,* I take the colors and designs of Hopi flat wicker basketry plaques and make them linear. I don't work representationally, only abstractly. (From *The* magazine)

*   *   *

Ramona Sakiestewa's hand-woven textiles allude to native themes, with colorful flat designs and suggestive titles like *Basket Dance*

and *Blue Corn.* But their resemblance to the wicker plaques and woven belts of her Hopi tradition is fleeting, rooted more in memory and research than experience. Sakiestewa, who taught herself how to weave because there were no weavers in her family, draws inspiration from abstract painters like Mark Rothko. For this reason, her tapestries stand apart from other Native American weavings, created as conscious abstractions of cultural icons.

Sakiestewa was born in 1948 and raised in Albuquerque. She was exposed to art at an early age, as her family collected Navajo and Pueblo textiles, as well as other cultural artifacts. She started weaving at the age of 17, learning techniques and designs from diagrams in books. According to Sakiestewa, the people who most influenced her career were Kate Peck Kent and Ruth Underhill, both anthropologists who wrote about Native American crafts of the Southwest.

After teaching herself traditional Pueblo spinning and weaving techniques, Sakiestewa sought formal training. From 1966 to 1967 she attended the School of Visual Arts in New York City, where she took classes in textile design, color, drawing, and commercial art. Upon her return to the Southwest, she visited the Hopi reservation, where she re-established ties with her extended family, thus augmenting learned culture with experience.

"By nature," Sakiestewa told *The* magazine in December 1992, "I am a very curious person. I read a lot, mostly science, art, and anthropology." The artist's inquisitive nature, combined with her active imagination and openness to experimentation, has enabled her to produce innovative and critically acclaimed bodies of work.

Sakiestewa's weavings are internationally known for their exquisite craftsmanship, particularly their tight construction, which recalls the tension of a stretched canvas. On more than one occasion, in fact, paintings have provided models for her tapestries.

The Bernice Steinbaum Gallery in New York City commissioned her to create a weaving for painter Paul Brach, and a series a tapestries were woven after the abstract paintings of Kenneth Noland.

Her most publicized commission was a series of 13 tapestries based on the architectural designs of Frank Lloyd Wright. This project was suggested in 1987 by Lee Cohen, the late owner of Gallery 10 in Scottsdale, Arizona. Although Sakiestewa usually only accepts commissions that allow her freedom of design, she took on the Wright project as a challenge as well as an homage to the late architect. Rather than duplicating entire drawings, Sakiestewa isolated and enlarged small segments, thus recasting the designs according to her own aesthetic sensibilities. The resulting series of weavings, including *Imperial Hotel/A*, a striking interpretation of a Tokyo hotel fireplace, and *Maybasket/2*, a recreation of Wright's stylized design for linoleum, were exhibited in 1991 at the Newark Museum, where reviewers marveled at Sakiestewa's "immaculate craftsmanship" as well as her creative interpretations.

Sakiestewa's own designs arise from her immediate experience of the Southwestern desert as well as other images that attract her eye. As art historian Suzanne Baizerman wrote in the catalog for Sakiestewa's 1989 solo exhibit at the Wheelwright Museum in Santa Fe, "Her works explore the patterns reflected in her surroundings, which return in her dreams. Her patterned dreams represent a synthesis of what she has actively sought out and integrated and what has more silently crossed her path and become fixed within her." Thus her aesthetic repertoire easily accommodates detailed work commissioned by private clients, as well as the more minimalist works that recall historic Pueblo and Navajo blankets. She has also experimented with hand-made paper and lithographic reproductions.

"Being an Indian artist is a wonderful springboard to have begun from, but my goal is not to have any label attached to my work, be it 'woman' or 'Indian' or 'Southwestern' or 'American.' I just want people to see my work and have some feeling about it," Sakiestewa told *Indian Artist* magazine in 1995. Since the mid-1980s, Sakiestewa's home base has been Santa Fe, where her new company, Sakiestewa Textiles Ltd., creates designs for blankets and other functional items. Among her other achievements, Sakiestewa is the first person of native descent to design a series of blankets for Pendleton Mills, the Oregon company that started selling native-inspired wool blankets more than 100 years ago.

—Margaret Dubin

SAPP, Allen

Tribal affiliations: Plains Cree
Painter

Born: Red Pheasant Reserve (near North Battleford, Saskatchewan) in 1929; direct descendant of Chief Red Pheasant, for whom the reserve is named; his paternal grandfather, Flying Eagle Saposkum, was a first cousin to the famous Cree leader, Poundmaker. **Education:** Traditional, but childhood illnesses prevented schooling; painting lessons in the 1960s with Saskatchewan artist Wynona Mulcaster. **Career:** Woodcutter, clerk in hobby shop, professional artist. **Awards:** Elected an Associate of the Royal Canadian Academy of Art in 1975, received the Order of Canada, 1987.

Individual Exhibitions

1968	St. Thomas Moore College, University of Saskatchewan, Saskatoon, Saskatchewan
1970	Alwin Gallery, London
1971	Downstairs Gallery, Edmonton, Alberta
1972	The Gainsborough Galleries, Calgary, Alberta
	Gallery of the Golden Key, Vancouver, British Columbia
1974	Zachary Walter Gallery, Los Angeles
1976	Rowe House Gallery, Washington, D.C.
1977	Continental Galleries, Montreal, Quebec
1978	Assiniboia Gallery, Regina Saskatchewan
1981	Robertson Galleries, Ottawa, Ontario
1985	Heffel Galleries, Vancouver, British Columbia
1989	La Galerie Continentale, Montreal, Quebec
1990	*Allen Sapp Gallery: The Gonor Collection*, North Battleford, Saskatchewan
	Wilfert's Hambleton Galleries, Kelowna, British Columbia
1991	West End Gallery, Edmonton, Alberta
1992	Clymer Art Museum & Gallery, Ellensburg, Washington, D.C.
	Lourie Gallery, Toronto, Ontario
1993	Hollander-York Gallery, Toronto, Ontario
	Masters Gallery, Calgary, Alberta
1994	Assiniboia Bessborough, Saskatoon, Saskatchewan
	Wilfert's Hambleton Galleries, Kelowna, British Columbia
1995-96	*Allen Sapp Retrospective*, McKenzie Art Gallery, Regina, Saskatchewan

Selected Group Exhibitions

1974	*Canadian Indian Art '74*, Royal Ontario Museum, Toronto, Ontario
1977	*Links to a Tradition*, Department of Indian Affairs and Northern Development (traveling in Brazil)
1982	*Tailfeathers/Sapp/Janvier: Selections from the Art Collection of the Glenbow Museum*, Thunder Bay Art Gallery, Ontario
	Renewal, Masterworks of Contemporary Indian Art from the National Museum of Man, Thunder Bay Art Gallery, Ontario
1983	*Contemporary Indian Art At Rideau Hall*, from the permanent collection of Department of Indian Affairs and Northern Development, Ottawa, Ontario
1983-85	*Contemporary Indian and Inuit Art of Canada*, organized by the Department of Indian Affairs and Northern Development (traveling)
1985	*Two Worlds*, MacKenzie Art Gallery, Regina, Saskatchewan
1986	*New Beginnings*, Native Business Summit, Toronto, Ontario
	A Celebration of Contemporary Canadian Native Art, Southwest Museum, Los Angeles
1987	*Eight from the Prairies*, Thunder Bay Art Gallery, Ontario

Publications

On SAPP: Books—"Allen Sapp: By Instinct a Painter," by J.W. Grant MacEwan, *Portraits from the Plains*, Toronto/New York:

McGraw-Hill Co. of Canada, 1971; *A Cree Life: The Art of Allen Sapp,* by John Anson Warner and Thecla Bradshaw, Vancouver: J.J. Douglas Ltd., 1977; *The Sweetgrass Lives On: Fifty Contemporary North American Indian Artists,* by Jamake Highwater, New York: Lippincott & Crowell Publishing, 1980; *Two Spirits Soar: The Art of Allen Sapp,* by W.P. Kinsella, Toronto: Stoddart Publishing Co., 1990. **Articles**—"Allen Sapp: Paintings," by Robert M. Percival, *artscanada,* nos. 148-149, October/November 1970; "The Cree Artist Allen Sapp," by John Anson Warner, *The Beaver,* Winter 1973; "Allen Sapp, Cree Indian Artist," by Janice Lovoos, *Southwest Art,* January 1975; "Allen Sapp: Paintings," by Robert M. Percival, *artscanada,* no. 148-149, October/November 1979; "Chronicler of the Cree: Allen Sapp Paints the Story of His People," by Max McDonald, *Canadian Geographic,* August-September 1990; "Retrospective Features Work of Talented Aboriginal Artist," by Shelia Stevens, *First Perspective,* February 1995. **Films**—"Allen Sapp: By Instinct a Painter," *The Nature of Things,* CBC Television, Bill Zborowsky producer, November 23, 1971; *Colours of Pride,* Henning Jacobsen Productions Limited for the Department of Indian Affairs and Northern Development, National Film Board of Canada, 1973; *Four Prairie Artists,* Donnalu Wigmore producer, CBC Television, 1983; "Allen Sapp," *For Art's Sake,* Bill Morrison producer STV Television Saskatoon, 1985.

*   *   *

Born in 1929 on the Red Pheasant Reserve, Allen Sapp is a direct descendant of Chief Red Pheasant, for whom the reserve is named, and his paternal grandfather, Flying Eagle Saposkum, was a first cousin to the famous Cree leader, Poundmaker. Sapp began painting professionally in the late 1960s, continuing a "tradition" of prairie realism initiated a decade and a half earlier by Gerald Tailfeathers in Alberta. The narrative style, which favours the representation of documentary and visionary genre scenes from Native cultural life, is carried on today in the work of a younger generation of artists, such as Sanford Fisher, among others. Passing on knowledge regarding artistic practice as well as cultural history to a younger generation of artists and viewers alike, Sapp has been concerned very much with both cultural relevance and persistence. In documenting the culture of the Northern Plains Cree, Sapp has revealed both the visionary qualities of a worldview as well as the historical directions that are informed by practical experience.

In the early 1960s, Sapp was befriended by a local Saskatchewan merchant, Eileen Berryman, who would supply him with materials to paint. In 1966, Sapp met and began a business association with Dr. A. Gonor, who initially purchased the artist's work and initiated a series of painting lessons from the recognized Saskatchewan painter, Wynona Mulcaster. Later, Gonor would take on the duties of an agent, organizing—through various connections and advertising programs—exhibitions for Sapp throughout Europe and Canada in both commercial and public venues. This relationship lasted until Gonor's death in 1985.

Sapp's earliest work is considered to be representative of a realist vision common to that found in magazine illustrations and on calendars, sources which the artist apparently drew from early on. Much of the literature on the artist maintains that this naive vision continues to dominate Sapp's output to this day. Yet, a recently published collection of essays written on the occasion of Sapp's retrospective exhibition at the McKenzie Art Gallery in Regina, assesses the artist's work anew. Native art historian, teacher, and artist Bob Boyer notes that Sapp's work is equally informed by a realist vision, and by that developed from dream imagery. Drawing upon the knowledge that Northern Plains Cree culture has traditionally used dreams and visions as providers of guidance and direction to individuals and the community, as well as on the knowledge that the Cree often illustrate dreams in the visual arts through story telling, music, dance, or visual art (i.e., beadwork, carving, paintings, or other media), Boyer relates Sapp's artistic practice to his Native roots.

According to Boyer and Alfred Young Man, the main body of Sapp's work—that is, the work produced by the artist from approximately 1968 through to 1985—concentrates on the life of the Cree after 1900 but "before the era of government houses." The cut-off date for these themes appears to coincide with Jamake Highwater's analysis in 1980. During this period, 1968 to 1985, Sapp created work that reveals a worldview through the documentation of day-to-day occurrences and occasions.

Since 1985, Sapp's palette has been considerably lightened, and his brushstroke has become more loose and animated. Too, the artist's themes have been enlivened with humour, expression, and an interest in the contemporary scene. Boyer notes that "the paintings of the nineties have shifted to a timeless quality that no longer represents just the past or the present. They have come to represent the Indian community in continuity as strong, vital, happy, and alive. Whereas Sapp's early work often represented a sombre past, his recent work is free of angst and portrays an eternal Plains Cree community."

As representative of the "first generation" of Native artists in Canada to join the mainstream Canadian art world in the development of histories and the creation of cultures specific to this country, Sapp's work is important and influential. As a cultural documentarian of the Northern Plains Cree, the artist has been responsible for both making history, and more recently, for revealing the continuity of Cree life.

—Carol Podedworny

SCHILDT, Gary

Variant names: Netostimi
Tribal affiliations: Blackfeet
Painter and sculptor

Born: Gary Joseph Schildt, Helena, Montana, 5 June 1938; variant name, Netostimi, means Lone Bull. **Education:** University of Montana; San Francisco City College, AA, 1962; San Francisco Academy of Fine Arts. **Career:** Painter and sculptor since the early 1960s; lecturer, C.N. Russell Museum; commissions, including sculpture of Senator Lee Matcalfe for Montana State Capitol Building, 1984, and Montana Historical Society Museum, Helena, three paintings, 1988; guest artist, Havre Art Show, Montana (1988), Florence Arts Festival, Arizona (1991), guest artist and juror, Great Falls Native American Art Show, 1983-87. **Awards:** San Francisco Academy of Fine Arts scholarship; prizes at fairs and juried competitions in Montana, Arizona, and Washington.

Individual Exhibitions

1966   C. M. Russell Museum, Great Falls, Montana
1971   C. M. Russell Museum, Great Falls, Montana

1973	Willoby-Taush Gallery, San Francisco, California
	Montana Historical Society, Helena, Montana
1980	Montana Historical Society, Helena, Montana
	C. M. Russell Museum, Great Falls, Montana
1981	Museum of the Plains Indian, Browning, Montana
1988	Holter Museum of Art, Helena, Montana
1990	C. M. Russell Museum, Great Falls, Montana
1991	Shellenberg Gallery, Livingston, Montana

Selected Group Exhibitions

1967	*America Discovers Indian Art*, Smithsonian Institution, Washington, D.C.
1969	Plein Air Painter's Art Show, Santa Catalina, California
1969-83	Museum of Native American Cultures, Spokane, Washington
1970-74	Museum of the Rockies, Bozeman, Montana
1972	*Western Art Exhibition*, Glacier National Park, Montana
1977	*First Annual Governor's Salute to the Arts*, Helena, Montana
1980	National Sculpture Society Exhibition, New York
	Glacier Gallery, Kalispell, Montana
	St. George Art Festival, St. George, Utah
1981	Annual Art Show and SIDS Benefit, Denver, Colorado
1983-87	Western Heritage Center, Billings, Montana
1990	*Art for the Parks: Top 100*, Jackson Hole, Wyoming (national tour)
1991	Pueblo de los Suenos, Coolidge, Arizona
1992	Museum of the Plains Indian, Browning, Montana
1993	Red Mesa Art Center, Gallup, New Mexico
1994	Robert Drummond Gallery, Coeur d'Alene, Idaho
1995	Hockaday Center for the Arts, Kalispell, Montana
1994-97	Fenn Gallery, Santa Fe, New Mexico

Collections

Montana Historical Society, Helena, Montana; C. M. Russell Museum, Great Falls, Montana; Smithsonian Institution, Washington, D.C.

Publications

On SCHILDT: Books—*Contemporary Indian Artists—Montana/ Wyoming/Idaho*, by Dorothy Ray, Rapid City, South Dakota, 1972; *American Indian Painting and Sculpture*, Patricia Broder, New York, 1981. **Articles**—"The Art of G. Schildt," *Flathead Valley Outdoor Journal*, Vol. 3, No. Winter, 1981; "Gary Schildt," *Southwest Art*, February 1988; "Arizona Impressionists," *Phoenix Magazine*, October 1992. **Film**—*Show of Hands*, 1983.

*   *   *

Often categorized as a Western artist in the mode of Charles Russell, Gary Schildt is known primarily for depicting scenes of life among the Blackfeet in Montana, frequently focusing on everyday activities in the open spaces of the countryside and towns. Schildt's paintings have ranged from documenting historical topics to capturing the flavor of contemporary life. The transitional post-World War II era of which he is witness involved the kind of change to urban culture that came more slowly to the wide open spaces of Montana, and subtle images of this transition are often evident in his paintings. His works with contemporary settings are especially noteworthy for documenting life among the Blackfeet of today, often portrayed in isolated, spontaneous moments of people at work and children at play, as well as portraits that bring forth their subjects in natural backgrounds that retain a sense of the open frontier. As a sculptor, Schildt models his subjects to feature telling character details in naturalistic forms, much like Russell.

Schildt was raised by his grandparents on a ranch west of Browning, Montana. By the time he reached age fourteen both of his grandparents had passed away and he was unable to live with his parents. Schildt moved from home to home, living for awhile with noted Montana educator, Vina Chattin. She and other teachers, along with local university professors, encouraged him to keep practicing art. Schildt painted wall murals while still a junior in high school, and at age nineteen, after taking some classes at the University of Montana, he enrolled in art school at the City College in San Francisco, where he earned an Associate of Arts degree in 1962 and a scholarship to attend the San Francisco Academy of Fine Arts. From there he began pursuing a full-time career as an artist.

Returning to northwestern Montana, Schildt attracted a regional following with his paintings of common activities. *Fixing Fence* (1966, in the collection of the Museum of the Plains Indian and Crafts Center), for example, shows three laboring men taking a break—one wiping his brow, another drinking from a canteen, with a horse feeding in the foreground and a wide vista sweeping out to the distance beyond. The painting is strongly grounded in realism and character study while blending in impressionistic natural details that enliven the presentation—a balance that gives the work a distinctly western appearance. This same counterpointing is seen as well in his portrait paintings, where human figures are acutely rendered while the natural setting is more suggested, has more varied colors, and approaches abstraction. The artist's talent is revealed in subtle character details and in imaginative renderings of the natural world.

This recurring technique became more prominent in Schildt's work as he moved from an early emphasis on historical subjects, like life on the frontier, to a focus on contemporary scenes, where he strives to capture the spontaneous moment in largely rural settings.

—Gregory Schaaf

SCHOLDER, Fritz
Tribal affiliations: Luiseño
Painter

Born: Fritz William Scholder in Breckenridge, Minnesota, 6 October 1937. **Education:** Studied in high school under Oscar Howe; Wisconsin State College, Superior, Wisconsin, 1957-58; Sacramento City College, 1958; Sacramento State College, BA, 1960; Southwest Indian Art Project, University of Arizona, summers, 1961-62; University of Arizona, MFA, 1964. **Family:** Married Peggy Stephenson, 1958, divorced, one child; married Romona Attenberger. **Career:** Arts and crafts instructor, Sacramento YMCA, 1958; participated in Southwest Indian Art Project, 1961-62 (the second summer as a faculty member), which led to the founding of the Institute of American Indian Arts; fellow, John Hay Whitney Foundation, 1962-63; graduate assistant instructor, University of Arizona, Tucson; instructor, Institute of American Indian Arts, 1964-69; full-time painter beginning in 1969; juror at art fairs, including Philbrook Museum of Art, 1968; lecturer, including First Convocation of American Indian Scholars, Princeton University, 1970; artist in residence, Dartmouth College, 1973; visiting artist, American University, Washington, D.C., Black Hills State College, Spearfish, South Dakota, Dakota Centennial Arts Congress, Aberdeen, South Dakota, Oklahoma Summer Arts Institute, Santa Fe Art Institute, University of Southern California, Idylwild, Vermont Studio School, Taos Institute of Art. **Awards:** Honorary degrees, College of Santa Fe, Concordia College, Ripon College, University of Arizona; American Academy of Arts and Letters Award in Painting, 1977; Governor's Award in the Visual Arts, State of New Mexico; Distinguished Achievement Award, Arizona State University; appointment, Societaire, Salon d'Automne, Paris, France; numerous awards at fairs and festivals, including 10th Southwestern Painters' Festival, Tucson (1960), California Spring Festival (1961), West Virginia Centennial (1963), All-American Indian Days (1968), Scottsdale National Indian Exhibition (1968-69), Intergrafiks, Berlin, Germany (international prize in lithography, 1980).

Individual Exhibitions

1958	Sacramento City College, Sacramento, California
1959	Artists' Cooperative Gallery, Sacramento, California
	E. B. Crocker Art Gallery, Sacramento, California
1963	Hali's, Tucson, Arizona
1964	M.F.A. Exhibition, Museum of Art, University of Arizona, Tucson
1967	*Fritz Scholder Paintings: Stripes, Butterflies, Indians,* Collectors Gallery, Bellevue, Washington
	College of Santa Fe, New Mexico
1968	Roswell Museum and Art Center, Roswell, New Mexico
1969	Fairmont Gallery, Dallas, Texas
1970	*Fritz Scholder: New Indian Oils,* Lee Nordness Galleries, New York
	Janus Gallery, Santa Fe, New Mexico
1971	Heard Museum, Phoenix, Arizona
	Esther Bear Gallery, Santa Barbara, California
	Indians and Women, Jamison Galleries, Santa Fe, New Mexico
	Tally Richards Gallery of Contemporary Art, Taos, New Mexico
1972	Michael Smith Gallery, Los Angeles
	Peter M. David Gallery, Inc., Minneapolis, Minnesota
	Marquiot Gallery, San Francisco, California
	St. John's College, Santa Fe, New Mexico
1972-73	Cedar Rapids Art Center, Cedar Rapids, Iowa (traveling)
1972-74	Cordier & Ekstrom, New York
1972-79	Elaine Horwitch Galleries, Santa Fe, New Mexico, and Scottsdale, Arizona
1973	*Fritz Scholder, Indians/Vampires,* Art Wagon Galleries, Scottsdale, Arizona
	Hayden Gallery, Massachusetts Institute of Technology, Cambridge, Massachusetts
	Hopkins Center, Dartmouth College
	Tally Richards Gallery of Contemporary Art, Taos, New Mexico
1974	Brooks Memorial Art Gallery, Memphis, Tennessee
	Gallery Moos, Ltd., Toronto, Ontario

	Fritz Scholder, Indians in Gallup, New Mexico, International Art Fair, Basel, Switzerland
1974-78	Jamison Galleries, Santa Fe, New Mexico
1975	Summit Art Center, Trenton, New Jersey
	De Saisset Art Gallery, University of Santa Clara, California
1976	Cordier & Ekstrom, New York
	University of Notre Dame, South Bend, Indiana
	University of New Mexico Art Museum, Albuquerque
1977	Oakland Art Museum, Oakland, California
	Gimpel and Weitzhoffer, New York
	Fritz Scholder: Major Indian Paintings, 1967-1977, Wheelwright Museum of the American Indian, Santa Fe, New Mexico
1978	Tally Richards Gallery of Contemporary Art, Taos, New Mexico
	Cordier & Ekstrom, New York
1979	*Indian Kitsch,* Heard Museum, Phoenix, Arizona
	Fritz Scholder: Paintings and Prints, 1966-1978, Boise Gallery of Art, Boise, Idaho (traveling)
1979-80	*Fritz Scholder Monotypes,* organized by the Western Association of Art Museums (traveling)
1980-81	Museum of the Plains Indian, Browning, Montana (traveling)
1981	*Retrospective: 1960-1981,* Tucson Museum of Art, Tucson, Arizona
	Fritz Scholder Monotypes, organized by the Art Museum Association of America (traveling)
	Fresno Art Museum, California
1982	El Paso Museum of Art, Texas
	North Dakota Heritage Center, Bismark
1983	Rizzoli Gallery, Chicago
1983-84	ACA Galleries, New York
	Gallery 10, Aspen, Colorado
1983-87	Marilyn Butler Fine Art, Scottsdale, Arizona, and Santa Fe, New Mexico
1984	University of Texas, Odessa
	Smith Anderson Gallery, Palo Alto, California
1985	Museum of Art, University of Arizona, Tucson
	Southwest Museum, Los Angeles, California
1986-88	Sena Galleries West, Santa Fe, New Mexico
1987	Rourke Gallery, Moorehead, Minnesota
	Louis Newman Galleries, Beverly Hills, California
1990	Schneider Museum of Art, Ashland, Oregon
1990-91	Charlotte Jackson Fine Art, Scottsdale, Arizona
1991	Temple Gallery of Art, Tucson, Arizona
1992-96	Riva Yares, Scottsdale, Arizona, and Santa Fe, New Mexico
1997	*Fritz Scholder: Millenium and Other Works,* Niman Fine Arts, Santa Fe, New Mexico
	Scottsdale Fine Arts Center, Scottsdale, Arizona

Selected Group Exhibitions

1956	Memorial Union Gallery, University of Wisconsin, Madison
1959	The Print Room, Sacramento, California
	E. B. Crocker Art Gallery, Sacramento, California
1960	Tucson Art Center, Tucson, Arizona
	Palacio de la Virreina, Barcelona, Spain
1961	E. B. Crocker Art Gallery, Sacramento, California

1962   Museum of Fine Arts, Houston, Texas

1963   *Centennial Exhibition of Painting and Sculpture,* Huntington Galleries, Huntington, West Virginia

1965   University of New Mexico, Santa Fe

1967   *Biennial Exhibition of American Indian Arts and Crafts,* Department of the Interior, Washington, D.C.

1972   *Two American Painters* (Fritz Scholder and T. C. Cannon), National Collection of Fine Art, Smithsonian Institution, Washington, D.C., and later toured Berlin, Germany, Belgrade, Yugoslavia, Istanbul, Turkey, Madrid, Spain and London, England

1973   Museum of Fine Arts, Santa Fe, New Mexico

1976-77 *America 1976,* bicentennial touring exhibit organized by the U.S. Department of the Interior

1977   Heard Museum, Phoenix, Arizona
         Tamarind: Suite Fifteen, University Art Museum, University of New Mexico, Albuquerque

1978   *100 Years of Native American Painting,* Philbrook Museum of Art, Tulsa

1979-80 *Native American Painting,* Mid-American Arts Alliance Project, organized by the Joslyn Museum, Omaha, Nebraska

1979-81 *Western States Biennial,* organized by the Western States Art Foundation (traveling)

1980   *Intergrafik '80,* Ausstellungszentrum am Fernshtrum, Berlin, Germany
         Prints in the Cliche-verre, 1839 to the Present, Detroit Institute of Art, Detroit, Michigan

1981   Scottsdale Center for the Arts, Scottsdale, Arizona
         Walk in Beauty, Santa Fe Festival of the Arts, Santa Fe, New Mexico

1982   Native American Center for the Living Arts, Niagara Falls, New York

1984-85 *Indianascher Kunstler* (traveling, Germany), organized by the Philbrook Museum, Tulsa, Oklahoma

1990   *American Indian Artists in the Avery Collection and the McNay Permanent Collection,* Koogler McNay Art Museum, San Antonio, Texas

1990-91 *One with the Earth,* organized by the Institute of American Indian Arts, Santa Fe, New Mexico (traveling)

1991-96 *Shared Visions: Native American Painters and Sculptors in the Twentieth Century,* The Heard Museum, Phoenix, Arizona

1996   *Drawn from Memory: James T. Bialac Collection of Native American Art,* Heard Museum, Phoenix, Arizona

1997   *Namingha, Houser and Scholder,* Niman Fine Art, Santa Fe, New Mexico

Collections

Alaska State Museum, Juneau; Albany Institute of History and Art, Albany, New York; Albright-Knox Art Gallery, Buffalo, New York; Arkansas Art Center, Little Rock, Arkansas; Art Gallery of Ontario, Toronto, Ontario, Canada; Art Museum, Princeton University, Princeton, New Jersey; Art Museum, University of New Mexico, Albuquerque, New Mexico; Baltimore Museum of Art, Baltimore, Maryland; Bibliotheque Nationale, Paris, France; Brigham Young University, Provo, Utah; Brooklyn Museum, Brooklyn, New York; Centre Culturel American, Paris, France; Charles M. Russell Museum, Great Falls, Montana; Chicago Art Institute, Chicago, Illinois; Cincinnati Art Museum, Cincinnati, Ohio; Civic Fine Arts

Fritz Scholder: *One Navajo.* Photograph by Larry McNeil; courtesy Institute of American Indian Arts Museum, Santa Fe, New Mexico.

Association, Sioux Falls, South Dakota; Cleveland Museum of Art, Cleveland, Ohio College of Santa Fe, Santa Fe, New Mexico; Colorado Springs Fine Arts Center, Colorado Springs, Colorado; Corcoran Gallery of Art, Washington, D.C.; E. B. Crocker Art Gallery, Sacramento, California; Currier Gallery of Art, Manchester, New Hampshire; Dallas Museum of Fine, Dallas, Texas; De Saisset Art Gallery, University of California, Santa Clara, California; Delaware Art Museum, Wilmington, Delaware; Denver Art Museum, Denver, Colorado; Detroit Institute of Art, Detroit, Michigan; El Paso Museum of Fine Arts, El Paso, Texas; Everson Museum of Art, Syracuse, New York; Fogg Art Museum, Cambridge, Massachusetts; Fogg Art Museum, Cambridge, Massachusetts; Heard Museum, Phoenix, Arizona; High Museum of Art, Atlanta, Georgia; Hirschhorn Museum and Sculpture Garden, Washington, D.C.; Honolulu Academy of Arts, Honolulu, Hawaii; Hopkins Center, Dartmouth College, Hanover, New Hampshire; Indianapolis Museum of Art, Indianapolis, Indiana; Joslyn Art Museum, Omaha, Nebraska; Marion Koogler McNay Art Institute, San Antonio, Texas; Memorial Art Gallery of the University of Rochester, Rochester, New York; Metropolitan Museum and Art Center, Miami, Florida; Milwaukee Art Center, Milwaukee, Wisconsin; Montgomery Museum of Fine Arts, Montgomery, Alabama; Museum of Art, Carnegie Institute, Pittsburgh, Pennsylvania; Museum of Contemporary Art, Chicago, Illinois; Museum of Fine Arts, Boston, Massachusetts; Museum of Modern Art, New York, New York; Museum of New Mexico, Santa Fe, New Mexico; National Museum of American Art, Smithsonian Institution, Washington, D.C.;

Newark Museum, Newark, New Jersey; Philadelphia Museum of Art, Philadelphia, Pennsylvania; Philbrook Museum of Art, Tulsa, Oklahoma; Portland Art Museum, Portland, Oregon; Roswell Museum and Art Center, Roswell, New Mexico; San Francisco Museum of Modern Art, San Francisco, California; Scottsdale Fine Arts Center, Scottsdale, Arizona; Seattle Art Museum, Seattle, Washington; State Historical Society of North Dakota, Bismarck, North Dakota; Tucson Museum of Art, Tucson, Arizona; University Art Museum, University of California, Berkeley, California; University of New Mexico Art Museum, Albuquerque, New Mexico; Vermont Museum, Montpelier, Vermont; Wichita Art Museum, Wichita, Kansas; Worcester Art Museum, Worcester, Massachusetts; Yale University Art Gallery, New Haven, Connecticut; Yellowstone Art Center, Billings, Montana.

Publications

On SCHOLDER: Books—Centennial Exhibition of Painting and Sculpture, Huntington Galleries, Huntington, West Virginia, 1963; *Two American Painters: Fritz Scholder and T. C. Cannon*, Smithsonian Institution, Washington, D.D., 1972; *Fritz Scholder: Lithographs*, by Clinton Adams, Boston, 1975; *Native Americans: Five Hundred Years After*, by Michael Dorris, New York, 1975; *America 1976*, U.S. Department of the Interior, Washington, D.C., 1976; *100 Years of Native American Painting*, exhibition catalog by Arthur Silberman, Oklahoma Museum of Art, Oklahoma City, 1978; *The Sweet Grass Lives On*, by Jamake Highwater, New York, 1980; *Fritz Scholder*, by Joshua C. Taylor, et. al., New York, 1982; *Indianascher Kunstler*, by Gerhard Hoffman, Munich, 1984; *The Arts of the North American Indian: Native Traditions in Evolution*, Edwin L. Wade, ed., New York: Hudson Hills Press in association with Philbrook Art Center, Tulsa, Oklahoma, 1986; *Shared Visions: Native American Painters and Sculptors in the Twentieth Century*, by Margaret Archuleta and Dr. Rennard Strickland, New York: The New Press, 1991. Articles—"Artists in the Art News," *Artnews*, September 1962; "Indian Affairs, New Style," by Robert M. Coates, *New Yorker*, June 17, 1969; "The Santa Fe Art Scene Today," by Robert A. Ewing, *Western Review: A Journal of the Humanities*, Spring 1972; "Scholder on Scholder: A Self-Interview," by Fritz Scholder, *American Indian Arts Magazine*, Spring 1976; "Prints and the Indian Artist at the Heard Museum," by Patrick T. Houlihan, *American Indian Arts Magazine*, Spring 1979; "Fritz Scholder: New Work, New Assessment," by Barbara Cortwright, *Artweek*, March 23, 1981; "Fritz Scholder," *The*, August 1994.

*

Fritz Scholder comments:

I've always been an individual and have done exactly what I wanted to do. I've painted only for myself and never for others. I think this is the only way one can approach what is a very strange role of being a painter.

*   *   *

Fritz Scholder will be remembered as the artist who revolutionized Native American painting, both in form and content, and gave it a new direction. Strangely enough, he had not intended to ever paint Indian subject matter when he started out, and being Indian had not mattered to him at all until the early 1960s.

Born in Minnesota in 1937 to a father who was one-half California Mission Indian and part German, part French, and a mother who was English and Irish, Fritz was not particularly interested in his Native heritage. He was, in fact, hardly aware of it. His interest in the arts, however, began already in high school, when Sioux artist Oscar Howe became his teacher. Howe, who had been in Paris during World War II and had been greatly influenced by the contemporary art of Europe, instilled his enthusiasm in the young student. When his family moved to Sacramento, California—his father worked for the Bureau of Indian Affairs—Scholder studied at Sacramento City College with Wayne Thibaud, who introduced him to the world of abstract expressionism and pop art. Scholder's interest in Indian art was aroused when, in 1961 and 1962, he participated in a Rockefeller Foundation-supported project at the University of Arizona, which inquired into the possibilities of combining Indian art traditions with contemporary non-Indian idioms and techniques and eventually led to the founding of the Institute of American Indian Art in Santa Fe, New Mexico. In 1964, Scholder, with an MA degree from the University of New Mexico, joined the faculty of the IAIA as an art instructor. In the following years, until 1969, he introduced his students to trends in contemporary painting: abstract expressionism, pop art and op art and started painting Indians.

As a painter of Indian subject matter, Scholder had an entirely new approach that has been called "Indian Pop" and was described by him as "a merger of traditional subject matter ... and my previous allegiance to Abstract Expressionism and Pop Art. Put this all together and you have Pop Indian Art!" (*The Navajo Times*, March 19, 1970). Indian art during the 1960s was in a crisis. The traditional Southwest painting style established by the "Studio" in the 1930s had exhausted itself and was in need of a transformation. Moreover, some Indian painting had become synonymous with "Bambi art" and the "Waters of the Minnetonka school" and needed to be freed from romanticized clichés of the noble Indian and the pastoral and/or heroic Indian world. Indian art was in the 1960s in search of its own identity.

Scholder made a fresh start by painting Indians from an entirely new perspective. He was one of the first "New Indian Artists," but interestingly enough, he uses the familiar motifs—Indians in traditional costumes, with feather bonnet and buffalo hide, on horseback and engaged in beadworking. His Indians, however, are not romanticized or glorified, rather he shows their human side, their strength as well as their weaknesses. He sees them critically in *Indian with Beer Can* and *Screaming Indian*, with a humorous note in *Indians with Umbrellas* or *Super Indian No. 2*, in which a buffalo dancer with a forbidding headdress is shown holding an ice cream cone in his hand. He paints Indians with understanding, with an awareness of their tragedy (*End of the Trail*), or at a mysterious and mystical distance, as in *Forest Shaman*.

Scholder"s paintings of demythicized Indians of the 1960s and 1970s were received with mixed reviews—delight and horror, and even hatred, due to the fact that his images smashed the familiar clichés and that his style is entirely "un-Indian." Scholder was stylistically inspired by Francis Bacon, Diebenkorn, Thibaud, and Oliveria: distorted figures, bold lines, strong colors, and daring color combinations are his hallmark. He maintains that color is of prime importance in a painting, that it is very personal, and that no color stands alone: surrounding colors, blending and contrasting are equally important.

Scholder paints in series about subjects that interest him at a given time and may fascinate him for a longer or a shorter period.

During the late 1970s, he began to move away from motifs that were generally considered to be Indian, and his painting, while retaining a mystic and mythical quality, became more abstract in nature. There followed series titled *Shaman, Portrait, Dream, Monster Love, Felix the Dog, Mystery Women*, and others, and recently he returned to Indian subjects again.

Scholder has said of himself and that he is a non-Indian Indian artist, or that he is artist first, Indian next. He has always stressed the individual aspect of his personality. This very individualistic Indian painter has, nevertheless, in his way and through his pictures, honored the American Indian.

—Gerhard and Gisella Hoffmann

SCHOPPERT, James

Tribal affiliations: Tlinget
Carver

Born: Robert James Schoppert, Juneau, Alaska, 28 May 1947.
Education: Anchorage Community College, AA, 1975; Instituto de Allende, San Miguel de Allende, Mexico (bronze casting and stone lithography), 1975; University of Alaska, BFA in sculpture and printmaking, 1978; University of Washington, MFA in sculpture, 1981. **Career:** Chairman, Traditional Native Arts Advisory Panel, Alaska State Council on the Arts, 1979-82; assistant professor of visual arts, University of Alaska, 1981; member, Spring Season Committee for the Festival Fairbanks, 1981-82, Native Cultural Steering Committee, State of Alaska, 1981-82, Art Selection Committee, Alaska State Council on the Arts, 1982; artist in residence at Sitka Fine Arts Camp, 1987; Dillingham Schools, 1986; trustee, Institute of Alaska Native Arts, 1985-88; commissioner, Washington State Arts Commission, 1986-89; visiting professor of visual art, University of Alaska, 1987; board of directors, Atlatl, 1987-88. **Awards:** First Prize-Ivory, Eleventh Festival of Alaska Native Arts and Juror's Choice, *Earth Fibre Fire VIII*, 1976; Juror's Award, Contemporary Maskmaking, *Alaskameut '80*; Outstanding Native American Poet, Native American Center for the Living Arts, 1985. **Died:** 2 September 1992.

Individual Exhibitions

1974   Alaska Native Arts and Crafts Gallery, Anchorage
1980   Snow Goose Gallery, Seattle, Washington
1981   The Gathering Gallery, Ketchikan, Alaska
1982   Sacred Circle Gallery, Seattle, Washington
1983   Alaska Native Arts and Crafts Gallery, Anchorage, Alaska
1984   Stonnington Gallery, Anchorage, Alaska
1985   Governor's Gallery, Alaska State Museum, Anchorage, Alaska
1987   American Indian Contemporary Arts, San Francisco
1997-98 *An Instrument of Change: Jim Schoppert Retrospective*, touring: Anchorage Museum of History and Art, University of Alaska, Fairbanks, Alaska State Museum, Juneau, and other venues

Selected Group Exhibitions

1977   *Two-person Show*, Art, Inc., Anchorage, Alaska
1980   *Native Arts*, The Gathering Gallery, Ketchikan, Alaska
1981   *Walk in Beauty*, Santa Fe Festival of Arts, Santa Fe, New Mexico
        Inaugural Exhibit, Sacred Circle Gallery, Seattle, Washington
1982   *Maritime Exhibit*, Field Museum, Chicago, Illinois
1983   *Regional Crafts: An Historical Perspective*, Bellevue Art Museum, Bellevue, Washington
        Northwest Coast: A Living Tradition, Stonnington Gallery, Anchorage, Alaska
1984   *Native American Artists of California and the West Coast*, American Indian Contemporary Arts, San Francisco, California
        Second Annual Santa Fe Invitational: The New Native American Aesthetic, Marilyn Butler Fine Art Gallery, Santa Fe, New Mexico
1985   *Second Biennial Invitational*, Heard Museum, Phoenix, Arizona
        New Ideas from Old Traditions, Yellowstone Arts Center, Wyoming
1986   *What is Native American Art?*, Philbrook Art Center, Tulsa, Oklahoma
        Journey into Spirit, Stonnington Gallery, Seattle, Washington
1987   *Group Exhibit: Masks*, Art With Texture Gallery, Seattle, Washington
        New Directions Northwest: Contemporary Native American Art, Portland Art Museum, Portland, Oregon
1989   *Native American Expressions of Surrealism*, Sacred Circle Gallery, Seattle, Washington
1990   *Eleven Stories*, Sacred Circle Gallery, Seattle, Washington
        Northern Lights, Sun Runner, Ojai, California
1991   *A Northern Perspective*, The Legacy Ltd., Seattle, Washington
        Raw Materials, Sacred Circle Gallery, Seattle, Washington
1992   *Visions of Alaska*, Denise Wallace Gallery, Santa Fe, New Mexico
        Salmon: Ritual and Resource, Stonington Gallery, Seattle, Washington

Collections

Alaska State Council on the Arts, Juneau; Alaska State Museum, Juneau; Anchorage Community College, Alaska; Anchorage Museum of History and Art, Alaska; Calista Corporation, Anchorage, Alaska; City of Seattle, Washington; The Heard Museum, Phoenix, Arizona; Microsoft Corporation, Seattle, Washington; Newark Museum, Newark, New Jersey; Seattle-Tacoma International Airport, Washington; University of Alaska, Fairbanks; Washington State Arts Commission Art Bank, Olympia, Washington; Washington State Portable Art Collection, Olympia, Washington; Yukon Baha'i Institute, Yellowknife, Yukon.

Publications

By SCHOPPERT: Books—"Between the Rock and the Walrus," exhibition catalog essay in *Wood, Bone, and Ivory*, Alaska State Council on the Arts, 1981; "Give It Eyes and Teeth and I'll Buy It," exhibition catalog essay in *Setting It Free: An Exhibition of Modern Eskimo Ivory Carving*, University of Alaska, Fairbanks, 1982; *New Traditions: An Exhibition of Alaska Native Sculpture*, Institute of

James Schoppert and his work. Photograph by Mary Randlett.

Alaska Native Arts (exhibition catalog), 1984; "Masks 1991," exhibition catalog essay in *Alaskameut '86,* Institute of Alaska Native Arts, 1986; *Sam Fox: The Life and Art of a Yup'ik Eskimo,* exhibition catalog, 1986; *Native Arts Network: A Special Report,* Phoenix, Atlatl, 1986. **Poems**—*Journal of Alaska Native Art,* November/December, 1985; *Turtle Quarterly* 5 no. 2, 1985; *The Greenfield Review* 14 no. 1-3, 1987.

On SCHOPPERT: Books—*Portfolio: Eleven American Indian Artists,* American Indian Contemporary Arts, 1986; *The Arts of the North American Indian,* Edwin L. Wade, Hudson Hill Press, 1986; *New Directions Northwest* (exhibition catalog), Portland Art Museum, 1987. **Articles**—*The Alaska Journal* 9, no. 2, 1979; Interview with David, R. Francis, *The Christian Science Monitor,* January 15, 1987; "Review," by Barry Johnson, *The Oregonian,* January 23, 1987.

*   *   *

Considering his prolific artistic career and keen understanding of the art market, it is hard to believe that the late Tlingit artist James

Schoppert only fortuitously stumbled into artmaking in 1973 at the age of twenty five. At the time Schoppert was working as a carpenter and was placed in a precarious economic position when one of his freelance jobs fell through in Anchorage. As the story goes, with the last of his money Schoppert purchased and carved a piece of soapstone into two small birds, one of which he sold at a local gift shop, and from that moment on he dedicated himself to the creation of art. Today Schoppert's oeuvre is widely known and appreciated, for it consists of work in which his skill as a carver, his respect for indigenous artistic traditions, and his personal vision as a contemporary artist are masterfully combined.

Because he saw a lack of understanding about Native American cultural expressions, Schoppert envisioned himself, in part, as an educator and used the written word (both poetry and prose) to challenge stereotypes and convey the importance of art in relation to cultural and individual identity. This is evident in a short poem/artist statement of 1985:

> I offer
> in my art, a view
> into our Alaskan Heritage.

A view that takes us
a step beyond the
gloved intimacy
of Anthropology; to where
latex ripped from flesh
explores
the hidden recess
of thigh.

In addition to his writing, Schoppert is known for his low relief carvings consisting of multiple panels in which Northwest Coast design units are enlarged, cropped, and placed next to each other. Like traditional art of the area there is a tension between figure and ground and an emphasis on the overall pattern. However, in contrast to Northwest Coast art, in which there is an adjustment of form to surface, Schoppert arranges the panels to create the formal and compositional tension. Also, rather than utilizing bright colors to emphasize and echo the design, Schoppert uses thin translucent layers of muted color to bring out the sculptural qualities of his work. While they consist of a complex interplay of light, color, texture and depth, these compositions are calm and contemplative. Titles such as "*Blueberries*" (1986) and "*Stillwater #2*" (1984) indicate that Schoppert draws on the natural world around him for inspiration. The 6 by 15 foot multipaneled "*Raven's Descent*" (1983) consists of shallow yet grand swoops that are suggestive of avian flight paths intersecting with atmospheric patterns. Splashes of paint, like the crashing of waves, hint at a journey between earthly realms—from wind to water—and are indicative of one of the many stories involving the raven, a key figure in Northwest Coast mythology.

Having been born and raised in Juneau, Alaska, Schoppert expressed a deep admiration for Eskimo art and culture, and found artistic inspiration in Eskimo masks. Although they are not meant to be worn in a ceremonial context, Schoppert's masks are similar in design and form to traditional Eskimo masks, which visually allude to the profound process of transformation. Schoppert also often constructs a "halo" of materials, often with feathers and wood splints, that surround the facade, which is known to be symbolic of the heavens and the interconnectedness of the macrocosm/microcosm.

The degree to which native artists deviate from tradition, and how to achieve and maintain artistic integrity in the late twentieth century, were main concerns of Schoppert. In his writing he often referred to "tradition" as both a burden and a blessing. As he has observed, the ethnic art market is often defined in accordance to narrow perceptions of "traditional," which can be stifling to present day artists. At the same time, however, he acknowledged that native artists must produce work that appeals to market demands if one hopes to survive economically, and he consistently sought to demystify the creative process by emphasizing the practical, "9 to 5" aspects of art making.

Fond of drawing analogies when addressing these issues, Schoppert has compared the Native artist of today with the hunter of the past. Just as the hunter knew the land and the nature of his prey, according to Schoppert, the Native artist must have a keen sense of the marketplace. Moreover, Native artists must learn about the complexities of cross-cultural interaction in order to succeed artistically and, more importantly, gain both personal and cultural empowerment. According to Schoppert: "Knowledge becomes the new harpoon, and the carver, the new hunter."

—Kristin Potter

SEAWEED, Willie

Variant names: Heyhlamas; Kwaghitola
Tribal affiliations: Kwakiutl
Carver, mask maker, and painter

Born: Blunden Harbour, British Columbia, 1873; Seaweed, his official Canadian name, is a Kwakiutl Chief's name (Paddling Recipient, or Many Travel by Canoe to Be at His Potlatches); Heyhlamas (Rights Maker, or The One Able to Set Things Right) was his name as chief of the Nakwaktokw, and Kwaghitola (Smoky-Top, like a volcano) is his informal name. **Education:** Apprenticed in carving with his older, half-brother, Johnny Davis. **Career:** Kwakiutl Chief; fisherman and artist; commissioned by people from neighboring Kwakiutl villages to make masks, totem poles and other ceremonial objects. **Died:** 1967.

Selected Group Exhibitions

1983-84 *Smoky-Top: The Life and Times of Willie Seaweed*, Pacific Science Center, Seattle

Collections

Thomas Burke Memorial Washington State Museum, University of Washington, Seattle; Campbell River Museum, Campbell River, British Columbia; Canadian Museum of Civilization, Hull, Quebec; Central Washington University, Ellensburg, Washington; Denver Art Museum, Colorado; Denver Museum of Natural History, Denver; Detroit Institute of Arts, Michigan; Glenbow Museum, Calgary, Alberta; McMichael Canadian Collection, Kleinburg, Ontario; Royal British Columbia Museum, Victoria, British Columbia; U'mista Cultural Centre, Alert Bay, British Columbia; University of British Columbia Museum of Anthropology, Vancouver; Vancouver City Museum, British Columbia.

Publications

On SEAWEED: Books—*Northwest Coast Indian Art: An Analysis of Form* by Bill Holm, Seattle/London: University of Washington Press, 1965; *The Crooked Beak of Heaven: Masks and Other Ceremonial Art of the Northwest Coast* by Bill Holm, Seattle/London: University of Washington Press, 1972; *Spirit and Ancestor: A Century of Northwest Coast Indian Art at the Burke Museum* by Bill Holm, Seattle/London: University of Washington Press, 1973; *The Struggle for Survival: Indian Cultures and the Protestant Ethic in British Columbia* by Forest La Violette, Toronto: University of Toronto Press, 1973; "The Art of Willie Seaweed, a Kwakiutl Master," by Bill Holm in *The Human Mirror, Material and Spatial Images of Man,* edited by Miles Richardson, Baton Rouge, Louisiana: Louisiana State University Press, 1974; *Sacred Circles*, by Ralph Coe, London: Arts Council of Great Britain, 1976; *Looking at Indian Art of the Northwest Coast*, by Hilary Stewart, Seattle/London: University of Washington Press, 1979; *Kwakiutl Art,* by Audrey Hawthorn, Seattle/London: University of Washington Press, 1979; *Innovations for a Changing Time: Willie Seaweed, A Master Kwakiutl Artist*, by Patricia Cosgrove-Smith, exhibition catalog, Seattle, Washington: Pacific Science Center, 1983; *The Box of Daylight: Northwest Coast Indian Art*, by Bill Holm, Seattle/London: University of Washington Press, 1983; *Smoky-Top: The Art and*

Willie Seaweed: *Wolf Mask*. **Photograph by William McLennan; courtesy UBC Museum of Anthropology.**

Times of Willie Seaweed, by Bill Holm, Seattle/London: University of Washington Press, 1983; *The Legacy: Tradition and Innovation in Northwest Coast Indian Art*, by Peter L. Macnair, Alan L. Hoover, and Kevin Neary, Vancouver/Seattle: Douglas & McIntyre/University of Washington Press, 1984; *Totem Poles of the Pacific Northwest Coast*, by Edward Malin, Portland, Oregon: Timber Press, 1986. **Films**—*Blunden Harbour*, Orbit Films, Seattle, 1951; *Dances of the Kwakiutl*, Orbit Films, Seattle, 1951.

*　　*　　*

A Kwakiutl (Kwakwaka'wakw) artist and chief from Blunden Harbour, British Columbia, Willie Seaweed was one of a handful of Kwakiutl artists who kept older traditions alive, including the production of artwork associated with potlatches and winter ceremonials, during a time when there was tremendous pressure from missionaries and Canadian governmental authorities to abandon time-honored customs to assimilate native inhabitants into mainstream Canadian society. Seaweed, along with many other Kwakiutl leaders and artists, resisted these forces and helped keep the old ways and art alive. As an artist he is considered to be something of an innovator, taking the relatively more austere style of nineteenth-century Kwakiutl art and developing it into a more fantastic and flamboyant mode of expression. Employing bright enamel paints and exercising a stupendous technique, Seaweed and his associates created a more expressive, extravagant, and theatrical kind of Kwakiutl art. While he was not alone in his efforts to retain the traditional culture and arts, he has become the most famous and celebrated symbol of this effort.

Sociologically speaking, it is important to situate Seaweed within the context of his times. From 1884 to 1951 the Canadian government outlawed the potlatch, the most vital of Kwakiutl institutions. Christian missionaries came to Indian communities to dispar-

age old beliefs and customs in the name of a new religion; children were sent to boarding schools for deculturization and resocialization with the norms and values of white culture. Nevertheless, many Kwakiutl leaders resisted these policies of social change by forms of passive resistance. Through secrecy and subterfuge, the potlatch continued to be practiced, especially in remote villages where governmental authorities found it more difficult to operate efficiently. In this connection, then, Blunden Harbour, where Seaweed was born and raised, was one of those out-of-the-way communities.

It is important to bear in mind, however, that Seaweed did not carry his cultural and artistic mandate alone. Two brothers, Chief George and Charley George, Sr., and George Walkus from nearby Smith Inlet, combined with Seaweed to create a new style in Kwakiutl art that was more colorful and flamboyant than the preceding works. They have since become grouped as the "Kwakiutl Four," but it should also not be forgotten that there were other artists of the Southern Kwakiutl nation who were active in the first half or so of the twentieth century: Dick Price, Arthur Shaughnessey, Henry Speck, Charlie James, Mungo Martin, and Ellen Neel. Although these individuals were born and worked at slightly differing times, together they constitute the vital connection or link between the past and the contemporary artists of today.

As a boy Seaweed was able to avoid the boarding school experience and it is said that he only spoke the Kwakwala language during his lifetime. Traditionally raised to take his place as a chief and artist, Seaweed became a leader of the "Kwakiutl Four" innovators. One of his alterations of the traditional approach occurred around 1920, when he began to substitute older matte paints with the newly imported enamel paints—a practice dramatically altering the appearance of his carvings. He usually painted a piece with a white enamel background and applied his decorations with bright and shiny hues of red, black, orange, yellow, blue, and green. This gave his work a more showy and bold appearance than was possessed by the late nineteenth century art. As well, Seaweed used new tools such as the straight-edge and compass. Patricia Cosgrove-Smith has noted that "the addition of the compass and straight edge really gave the art a strong sense of symmetry and composition. Seaweed carried this development even further by refining his carving technique so there were no unexpected bumps or bulges. What was meant to be straight was exactly straight, and his curves were precisely and gracefully arched. He used the compass to lay out the three concentric circles which formed the eye on his masks. His artwork can be identified by such stylistic characteristics and a row of three compass point holes on the eye can be seen as a kind of Seaweed signature."

Out of these changes came an art that Bill Holm has called the Blunden Harbour/Smith Inlet style. Holm is considered to be the leading authority on Seaweed, and his book, *Smoky-Top: The Art and Times of Willie Seaweed* (1983), is regarded as definitive. Holm has been able to identify anywhere from 120 to 130 Kwakiutl art works created by Seaweed and divides Seaweed's production into ten major categories: Totem poles (both full-sized and models); house-fronts and panels; coppers; drums; whistles and horns; rattles; singers' batons; painted screens; masks; and headdresses. The range and assortment of this creativity is nothing short of astonishing. Quite clearly, as Holm points out, Seaweed understood virtually every aspect of Kwakiutl culture.

Nearly two-thirds of Seaweed's output was in the category of masks. These items are crucial in the winter ceremonies, and Seaweed carved masks for and participated in these events. The variety of Kwakiutl masks is quite staggering; Seaweed carved various types of masks in the following ceremonial divisions: Hamatsa (Cannibal Raven), Atlakam (Spirits of the Forest), Wolf Dance, Tsonoqua (Cannibal Grandmother), and Tla'sa la. Most scholars are in agreement that Seaweed is best known for his production of the fabulous and impressive Hamatsa Cannibal Raven masks.

Over his lifetime, Seaweed carved many Hamatsa masks for different Kwakiutl clientele. The Hamatsa or Cannibal Spirit dances and accompanying ritual activities are perhaps the most highly regarded of all Kwakiutl winter ceremonies. Only the highest ranking persons in a village can join the society responsible for these rituals. In these ceremonies there is an initiate who is known as a man-eating spirit (called Baxwbakwalanuksiwe). He is accompanied by associates who take the appearance of bird-like beings and are identifiable (despite variations) because of their staring eyes, large articulated and nostriled beaks, and heavy manes of cedar bark (shredded and dyed red) hanging downwards. The long beaks of these Cannibal Raven birds are said to be strong enough to crack the skulls of their victims so their brains can be sucked out. These beings accompany the initiate in the complex dance ritual wherein he is pacified and tamed. These are spectacular creatures, and the masks, appearing in the flickering light and shadows of a cedar plankhouse on a winter's evening, can be startling and terrifying. The visual experience of these masks is augmented when the audience hears the loud snapping sound made when the beaks are cracked against each other. Upon such masks as these, Seaweed lavished his skill and imagination for several decades.

Seaweed and his colleagues in the Blunden Harbour and Smith Inlet area left behind a legacy that was taken up by their own offspring—Charley George, Jr., Charley G. Walkus, and Joe Seaweed. In a larger sense, however, they bequeathed a living tradition—and a connection between past and present—for the preservation of a heritage.

—John Anson Warner

SENUNGETUK, Joseph

Variant names: Inusuyauq Sinuyituq
Tribal affiliations: Inupiaq
Printmaker and carver

Born: Joseph Engasongwok Senungetuk, Wales, Alaska, 29 March 1940. **Education:** Nome High School; University of Alaska Fairbanks, 1959-61; San Francisco Art Institute, BFA, 1970. **Career:** Began art career in 1964; assisted in founding Indian Historian Press, San Francisco, 1968-71; ongoing involvement in arts programs throughout Alaska, including residencies and the Artists in the Schools Program; instructor, Village Art Upgrade Program, University of Alaska, Fairbanks (1971-72), Artists in Prisons Program, Alaska (1976-84), Alaska Native Arts Workshop, Visual Arts Center of Alaska, Anchorage (1985-86), Sheldon Jackson College, Sitka (1974-77), and Alaska Pacific University, Anchorage (1986); director, Alaskan Educational Program for Intercultural Communications, Center for Northern Educational Research, University of Alaska Fairbanks, 1973-74; cultural coordinator, Cook Inlet Native Association, Anchorage, 1980-84; consultant, Maritime Peoples Exhibit, Field Museum, Chicago, 1979-84; columnist, *Anchorage Daily News,* 1989-90, *Anchorage Gazette,* 1992-94; board member, Visual Arts Center of Alaska, Anchorage (1976-86), Institute of Alaska Native Arts, Fairbanks (1979-85), University of Alaska, Anchorage, Chancellor's Select Task Force on Alaska Native Higher Education (1992-93); Public Art Commissions, Anchorage Airport, Bethel, Chugiak, Nome. **Awards:** Second Place, Alaska Centennial Arts Exhibit, 1967; First Place, mixed media sculpture, National Graphic Exhibit, Indian Arts and Crafts Board, 1969; First Award, Earth, Fire and Fibre, Anchorage Museum of History and Art, 1977; First Prize, Alaska Native Woodcarving Competition, Institute of Alaska Native Arts, Fairbanks, 1980; National Endowment for the Arts Emerging Artist Fellowship, 1980; New Langdon Arts project grant, 1993.

Individual Exhibitions

1967-68	American Indian Historical Society, San Francisco
1979-84	Sindin Gallery, New York
1990	*New Works,* Visual Arts Center of Alaska, Anchorage
1995	*Ilitkusiq,* Acanthus Gallery, Portland, Oregon

Selected Group Exhibitions

1967	Indian Arts and Crafts Board, Washington, D.C.
1967-68	American Indian Historical Society, San Francisco, California
1976	*Survival: Life and Art of the Alaskan Eskimo,* Newark Museum, New Jersey
1978	*Contemporary Art from Alaska,* Smithsonian Institution, Washington, D.C.
1982	*Exhibition of Contemporary Pacific Rim Art,* Field Museum, Chicago
1984	*Bridges from the Past,* Stonington Gallery, Anchorage, Alaska
	New Traditions, Anchorage History and Fine Arts Museum, Alaska
1986	*Alaskameut '86,* Native Artists Mask Carving Workshop I, Fairbanks

Joseph Senungetuk: *Bering Straits: Soul on Ice.* Photograph by Joel Berger; courtesy Anchorage Museum of History and Art.

Stonington Gallery, Anchorage

1987   Alaskameut '87, Native Artists Mask Carving Workshop II, Fairbanks

1988   *Crossroads of Continents: Cultures of Siberia and Alaska,* Smithsonian Institution, Washington, D.C.
Die Eskimo, Rautenstrauch Joest Museum, Germany

1988-95 *Artists Respond, A People in Peril,* traveling exhibit sponsored by Visual Arts Center of Alaska, Anchorage

1989   Contemporary American Indian Art Gallery, San Francisco

1989-90 *Metamorphosen,* Staatliches Museum, Munich

1990   Institute of Alaska Native Arts, Fairbanks

1993   *Indianer und Eskimo,* Jagd und Fischereimuseum, Munich

1995   *Kunst der Eskimo und Indianer der Nordwestkoste Nordamerikas,* Kunst und Anitquittenmesse, Munich; Stand Museen, Munich

1996   *Les Olseaux,* Fondation Cartier pour l'art contemporain, Paris

Collections

Alaska State Museum, Juneau; Anchorage Museum of History and Art, Alaska; Centennial Building, Alaskaland, Fairbanks; Field Museum, Chicago; Governor's House Collection, Juneau, Alaska; Indian Arts and Crafts Board, Washington, D.C.; Metropolitan Museum of Art, New York; Seatac Airport, Seattle, Washington; Seattle City Light Collection, Washington; University of Alaska, Anchorage; University of Alaska, Fairbanks; Whatcom Museum, Bellingham, Washington.

Publications

By SENUNGETUK: Books—*Give or Take a Century: An Eskimo Chronicle,* San Francisco, 1972; illustrations, foreword, and glossary, *Favorite Eskimo Tales Retold,* by Ethel Ross Oliver, 1990.

On SENUNGETUK: Books—*Graphic Arts of the Alaskan Eskimo,* by D.J. Ray, Seattle, 1969; "Joseph E. Senungetuk," *Crossroads of Continents: Cultures of Siberia and Alaska,* Washington, D.C., 1988; *Artists Respond: A People in Peril,* Anchorage, 1988. **Articles**—"After the Art Boom, What? Alaskan and Inuit Art: A Resurgence," *Inuit Art Quarterly,* 7, no. 1, 1992.

*

Joseph Senungetuk comments (1995):

On the mask, *and the White Man Came . . . and He Hung Around . . . and He Hung Around:* This mask was begun during a Bent Wood Workshop, which my brother, Ron Senungetuk, coordinated when he still was an art professor at University of Alaska Fairbanks and Director of the Center for Alaska Native Art. He has since then retired.

At first all I had was the antler or bone maskett above the Philippine Mahogany primary mask and skinny little quarter inch dowels connecting the hands and feet to the primary mask body. And it didn't look all that interesting. But it did have that intriguing title. So, recently I began searching for ideas on how to get the white man more gesturally and interesting visually. Bleached caribou antler, which had lain on the tundra for a few years, did the trick.

A strange thing has recently happened with this mask. We hung the mask in our bedroom in order to temporarily store it before shipping. There is a plant, a fern, hanging next to the mask, which hangs on a hook attached to the ceiling. Since it is summer time in Anchorage, there are two new vines growing from the fern, which later on will mature into the furry and broad fern the main plant is composed of. During the first two days of the mask hanging there, one of the new vines entwined itself around the hoop between the left hand and the left leg of the appendages of the mask. Not tightly but definitely going around one and a half times. The next two days or so it unwound itself and started heading towards the mouth of the mask. Now it is definitely inside the mouth heading towards the light of the window behind the mask. And we thought this was a simple and non-gregarious plant. (From "Joe Senungetuk: Descriptions of Artwork," Acanthus Gallery, Portland, Oregon)

* * *

More than any other contemporary Alaskan Native artist, Joseph Senungetuk has throughout his career been committed to political activism—as an artist, writer, and teacher. Unlike most established contemporary Alaskan Native artists, he has chosen to live in Alaska permanently, rather than "outside" at least a part of the year, and to be involved ongoing in Alaskan civic affairs. His work and activities support his dedication to the revitalization of Alaskan Native art and the needs of Alaskan Native artists, a deep concern over the effects of politics and economic development on the fragile relationship between land and people in Alaska, and the importance and costs of maintaining artistic integrity.

As a child growing up in Nome, Senungetuk was taught to carve ivory by an uncle. After study at the University of Alaska, Fairbanks, and an Indian Arts and Crafts Board-sponsored artist residency in Sitka in the mid-1960s, he left Alaska for the San Francisco Art Institute. The politicized climate of the Bay area urban Indian community and the open atmosphere at the school freed him to break from the traditional framework of what he has called stereotypical Eskimo art, to explore new mediums, techniques, and forms, and to make strong emotional and political statements through his work.

While in San Francisco, Senungetuk assisted in setting up the Indian Historian Press, the first American Indian-controlled publishing house in the United States, and wrote *Give or Take a Century: An Eskimo Chronicle* (1971). An autobiographical/historical essay on cultural change, the book, like his art at the time, explores the struggle of an artist living in two cultures, moving between village and urban worlds. This theme pervades his later art and writing as well.

Prints (woodblocks and some etchings) dominate Senungetuk's work from the San Francisco years through the 1970s. In the block prints, sinuous forms often evocative of skeletal motifs common in precontact Eskimo art are layered in jarring colors, musings on personal and Eskimo identity, continuities and disconnections with the past. "My woodcuts sort of meander around the theme of

where I am from and how I go out into the universe with my artwork." His sculptures of this period and later often combine wood and metal, and frequently reference Eskimo mask forms.

Senungetuk speaks of the deep responsibility he feels as a Native artist and to the cultural and individual integrity of his own art. "It's my interest to disclose to other people what is most important about my culture . . . I represent native people in my work and I have to be truthful and honest about it." His art and writing are sometimes unsettling, sometimes whimsical, often both, and usually thought provoking. His refusal to create "Alaskana" curios and his use of disturbing visual forms has sometimes put him at odds with his own people as well as with art buyers who prefer more conservative images.

Senungetuk's interest in the revival of dying arts has been focused especially through mask making, drum making, and explorations with oral literature integrated into drama. The three were unequivocally united in Eskimo ceremonies no longer practiced, which honored and showed respect to animals and life forces, and their spirits.

Senungetuk has worked with mask forms through his career, exploring their transformational, spiritual, and storytelling powers. Like several other Alaskan artists of his generation (Ron Senungetuk, James Schoppert, Larry Beck, Melvin Olanna), he was deeply influenced in the 1970s through contact with old masks and prehistoric Eskimo objects brought to Alaska in *The Far North* and later exhibitions. "I am always interested in museum pieces done by Alaska native peoples hundreds of thousands of years ago. They themselves are my 'teachers,' as it were." Other teachers have been elders with whom he participated in Alaskan maskmaking workshops in 1978, 1980, and 1986, where artists of several generations shared a two-way flow of ideas and experimented with combinations of natural and industrialized world materials.

In a 1985 workshop on traditional drum making, which brought rural and urban artists together to explore the spiritual and art, Senungetuk learned to construct a tambourine drum in the old way. In 1993 he was awarded a New Langdon Arts Grant to begin experimentation with electronically altering the drum sound to create a new percussive instrument.

As an Anchorage newspaper columnist through the early 1990s, Senungetuk commented regularly on the impact of the oil industry on Alaska and on the insufficient support for Native art and culture in the state. He took up these themes in the sculptures and statements in a 1995 one-man exhibition, *Ilitkusiq*. "In my art and writings, I have asked the public to see what is happening . . . the automobile industry, the highway systems, the oil companies . . . eating up real estate, clean air and water, and asking for more permission to search and destroy." He also spoke with anger and sarcasm about Anchorage plans to build a "Native Heritage Park," with authentic-looking Native igloos and underground pre-contact houses and having "a few select Native innocents . . . sing a few songs, dance a few dances, carve a few billikens, in short, act like Natives for the tourist dollar. Meanwhile the (University and other schools of Anchorage have not) any sort of viable Native studies programs." Senungetuk's work in the *Ilitkusiq* show was primarily mixed media sculpture, often incorporating found objects. Frequently inscrutable and whimsical, sometimes raunchy, it combined visual puns in form with literary ones in titles. His work has been especially appreciated in Europe, where he has participated in four major group exhibitions during the early 1990s.

Like his older brother, artist Ronald Senungetuk, who taught for years at the Native Arts Center of the University if Alaska,

Fairbanks, Joseph Senungetuk has been an important influence in leading younger Alaskan Native artists into exploring modernist forms and non-traditional media.

—Kate C. Duncan

SHILLING, Arthur

Tribal affiliations: Ojibway
Painter

Born: Rama Reserve, near Orillia, Ontario, 1941. **Education:** Attended New School of Art and Ontario College of Art. **Career:** Draftsman and Painter. **Awards:** *Globe and Mail* Art Fund Award for Aspiring Young Artists, 1962; scholarship, Department of Indian and Northern Affairs, 1964; Centennial Medal, 1967, and first prize, Canadian Indian Christmas Card Design. **Died:** 1986.

Individual Exhibitions

1963	Orillia Public Library, Orillia, Ontario
1966	Blue Easel Studios Gallery, Toronto
	Kitchener/Waterloo Gallery, Kitchener, Ontario
1967	Wells Gallery, Ottawa, Ontario
	Tom Thompson Gallery, London, Ontario
1970	McIntosh Gallery, London, Ontario
1976	Nancy Poole Studio, Toronto
1977	Beckett Gallery, Ottawa, Ontario
1979	Beckett Gallery, Ottawa, Ontario
	Wells Gallery, Ottawa, Ontario
1980	Sundance Gallery, Calgary, Alberta
	Beckett Gallery, Ottawa, Ontario
1981	Keenlyside Gallery, Vancouver, British Columbia
	Sundance Gallery, Calgary, Alberta
	Beckett Gallery, Ottawa, Ontario
1989	Joseph D. Carrier Gallery, Toronto
1993	Gallery Indigena, Stratford, Ontario

Selected Group Exhibitions

1974	*Canadian Indian Art '74*, Royal Ontario Museum, Toronto
1976	*Contemporary Native Art of Canada, The Woodland Indians*, Royal Ontario Museum, Toronto (touring, Canada, England, and Germany)
	Links to a Tradition, organized by Department of Indian and Northern Affairs for the Canadian embassy in Brazil
1977	*Contemporary Indian Art: The Trail from the Past to the Future,* Mackenzie Gallery and Native Studies Programme, Trent University, Peterborough, Ontario
1977-82	*Canadian Indian Art,* Royal Ontario Museum, Toronto (annual)
1978	*Canadian Indian Art,* Royal Ontario Museum, Toronto
1979	*Kinder des Nanbush,* McMichael Canadian Collection, Hamburg, Germany
1982	*Renewal: Masterworks of Contemporary Indian Art from the National Museum of Man,* Thunder Bay, Ontario

1983	*Contemporary Indian Art at Rideau Hall,* Department of Indian Affairs and Northern Development, Ottawa, Ontario
1983-85	*Contemporary Indian and Inuit Art of Canada,* Department of Indian Affairs and Northern Development, Ottawa, Ontario (touring, Canada and the United States)
1992	*Two Natives Masters,* Beckett Gallery, Toronto
1996	*The Helen Band Collection,* Thunder Bay Art Gallery, Thunder Bay, Ontario

Collections

Canadian Museum of Civilization, Ottawa, Ontario; Indian and Northern Affairs Canada, Ottawa, Ontario; McMichael Canadian Collection, Kleinburg, Ontario; Royal Ontario Museum, Toronto, Ontario; Sundance Gallery, Calgary, Alberta; Woodlands Indian Art Gallery, Brantford, Ontario.

Publications

By SHILLING: Book—*The Ojibway Dream,* Tundra Books, Montreal, 1967.

On SHILLING: Book—*Indian Arts in Canada,* by Olive Dickason, Department of Indian Affairs and Northern Development, Ottawa, 1972. **Articles**—"Working in Solitude," *Atlantic Monthly,* May 1967; "An Interview with Arthur Shilling," *Tawow,* Vol. 7, no. 1, 1980; "Arthur Shilling," by Karen Mills, *Artwest,* Vol. 6, no. 9, 1981; "Seven Portrait Painters—A Personal Choice," by Deborah Goden, Vol. 7, no. 1, 1981-82.

*   *   *

Arthur Shilling began painting in the early 1960s, during a period when fledgling "schools" of artistic activity by artists of the First Nations in Canada were developing across the country. From the Northwest Coast graphic tradition on the West Coast, through the Plains Pictorial tradition on the prairies, to the Woodland School in the Great Lakes region, and the eastern craft movement across Ontario, Quebec, and the Maritimes, artists of the First Nations were creating work that extended Native artistic traditions while rivalling the art history of Euro-Canadians. What has distinguished the work of Arthur Shilling, however, is that he chose to work outside of any of these styles, creating an oeuvre that is innovative in its expression of an Ojibway worldview through a medium and style that are predominantly European influenced.

Shilling is recognized by a body of work that is comprised of paintings in oil on canvas or board and some works in graphite on paper. Shilling's oeuvre is representational, featuring some landscapes and a significant body of portraiture. Indeed it is in the latter genre that Shilling excelled, creating during his career a number of innovative portrait formats as well as a unique palette. For the artist, colour was the element that tied his paintings together, being responsible for both form and expression at once. Shilling once said, "Colour is form, space and reflection . . . colour is everything." The artist would eventually develop a vibrant palette that reflected the exuberance of spirit his expressionistic statements demanded.

From the early 1960s and throughout the 1970s, Shilling experimented with a diversity of portrait formats, a variety of palettes, and surfaces marked by thinly applied washes to thickly impastoed areas. But in 1980, the artist's work underwent a transformation that would herald a formal change and designate a shift in his conceptual approach to the subject. The effects of the transformation would remain evident in Shilling's work until his untimely death in 1986.

In 1980, following a decision to reside full time on the Rama Reserve (previously the artist had divided his time between the Reserve and Toronto), and following a close brush with death, Shilling's work would begin to reveal a commitment to imparting the relevance of an Ojibway worldview. Through images of "his people" —whom he stated were his inspiration—the artist found a genre within which he could effectively present an Ojibway symbology, reminiscent of, but visually very different than, that developed by such artists as Norval Morrisseau, Daphne Odjig, and others of the New Woodland School. In 1980, Shilling began to include indigenous semiotics in his portraits: the equal-armed cross, circles, power lines and spirit figures, all depicted according to Shilling's interpretation of the traditional teachings. The motifs appeared first in the background planes of the paintings, and later would be placed on shawls and other garments worn by the sitters. It was also at this time that Shilling would begin to associate himself with the raven, a symbol of friendship, freedom, keenness, and survival. In the self-portraits of the period the raven is often found placed in Shilling's hand where previously only the brush had been.

Shilling's iconographic "breakthrough" would be accompanied by formal developments that echoed and represented the thematic and ideological shifts his work had undergone. His palette was by this time increasingly subjective, characterized by vibrant hues and decisive placement of brushstrokes, a unique combination of impressionistic and expressionistic tendencies. Too, Shilling would create portrait formats that would transcend European traditions in this genre and would mark a particularly indigenous idiom—multiple figure and totemic formats, for example.

Shilling is recognized as an artist who in the early 1960s "took Indian art beyond the old images," and as such he can be credited with inspiring other artists of the First Nations to transcend the stereotypes of art and culture.

—Carol Podedworny

SILVERHORN, James

Variant names: Haungooah
Tribal affiliations: Kiowa
Painter

Born: Oklahoma, 1861. **Family:** Dohasan, his father, kept a pictographic calender, and his brother, Ohettoint, was among the prisoner-artists at Fort Marion; uncle of Stephen Mopope. **Career:** Warrior (participated in Kiowa resistance, 1874); medicine man; scout, Fort Sill, Oklahoma, 1890s; consultant on Native American culture and commissioned to reproduce power images, illustrations of ceremonies, and heraldry of the Kiowa nation. **Died:** c. 1941.

Selected Group Exhibitions

1978   *100 Years of Native American Painting,* Oklahoma Museum of Art, Oklahoma City, Oklahoma

1990   *American Indian Artists in the Avery Collection and the McNay Permanent Collection,* Koogler McNay Art Museum, San Antonio, Texas
1992-93 *Visions of the People,* Minneapolis Institute of Art, Minneapolis, Minnesota (traveling)
1994   Museum of Natural History, Washington, D.C.

Collections

American Museum of Natural History, New York; Claremont College, Claremont, California; Field Museum of Natural History, Chicago, Illinois; Fort Sill Museum, Fort Sill, Oklahoma; Marion Koogler McNay Art Museum, San Antonio, Texas; Museum of the Great Plains, Lawton, Oklahoma; Newbery Library, Chicago, Illinois; Philbrook Museum of Art, Tulsa, Oklahoma; Smithsonian Institution, Office of Anthropological Archives, Washington, D.C.

Publications

On SILVERHORN: Books—*Sioux Indian Painting,* by Hartley Burr Alexander, Nice, France, 1938; *The Kiowas,* by Mildred Mayhall, Norman, Oklahoma, 1962; *Song from the Earth,* by Jamake Highwater, Boston, 1976; *The Native American Heritage: A Survey of Native American Indian Art,* by Evan Maurer, Lincoln, Nebraska, 1977; *100 Years of Native American Painting,* exhibition catalog by Arthur Silberman, Oklahoma Museum of Art, Oklahoma City, 1978; *The Arts of the North American Indian: Native Traditions in Evolution,* Edwin L. Wade, editor, New York: Hudson Hills Press in association with Philbrook Art Center, Tulsa, Oklahoma, 1986; *American Indian Artists in the Avery Collection and the McNay Permanent Collection,* Jean Sherrod Williams, editor, San Antonio, 1990; *Visions of the People,* by Evan Maurer, Minneapolis, Minnesota, 1992.

*   *   *

James Silverhorn, a medicine man and descendant of Chief Tohausen, is an historic and cultural link between the warrior-artists of Fort Marion in the 1870s and the artists of the 1930s known as the "Kiowa Five." His family background was conducive to his drawing and painting: his father, Dohasan, was keeper of the winter count, a pictographic calender, and his brother, Ohettoint, among the prisoner-artists at Fort Marion, acquainted him with the "ledger painting style." Silverhorn, in turn, influenced his nephew, Stephen Mopope, who was among the five artists that brought international reputation to the Kiowa painting style.

The end of the nineteenth century was a time of great upheaval on the Plains, when Native cultures were threatened with extinction. Ethnologists like James Mooney of the Smithsonian Institution in Washington, D.C., endeavored to rescue documents of the Plains culture for posterity. Mooney commissioned Silverhorn, a prolific drawer and painter, to produce drawings and models of traditional shields and teepee designs that embodied the power images and heraldry of the Kiowa nation. Another student of Plains Indian culture, though an amateur, was Hugh L. Scott, commander of Fort Sill in the 1990s, when Silverhorn served there as a scout. Scott acquired from him illustrations of the Kiowa Sun Dance, the most important Kiowa ceremony. Silverhorn was also acquainted with the Peyote rituals and produced a number of drawings at about 1891; they are of great documentary value and are considered the first painted documents of Peyotism, an intertribal Indian religion that emerged in the 1890s on the Plains and was later recognized (institutionalized) as the Native American Church.

Silverhorn was both a versatile and a prolific painter. Hundreds of pictures have survived, covering a broad range of subjects, such as warfare, hunting, and religious ceremonies; they also depicted various aspects of life at the agency, including games, courting, and recreation activities. His materials were both of traditional use and of modern acquisition: he painted on hides as well as on muslin and paper and he used crayon, pencil, and watercolor.

Recollections of Historical Incidents, painted with crayon and pencil on muslin, reflects the traditional composition of hide paintings with their great number of persons and animals spread over the same surface. Various combat scenes are depicted, most of them encounters between soldiers and Indian braves. *Young Kiowa Brave,* painted in 1887, shows the influence of the Fort Marion style of ledger drawing. The rider and his horse are rendered with close attention to detail and fill the whole picture. The theme of a mounted warrior is taken from Plains Indian experience and tradition and is rendered in a way that shows the painter's pride in being a Kiowa. The Indian brave is clad in finery and wearing an impressive feather bonnet, trousers with rich ornamentation, and a decorative lance with a great number of paired feathers. His horse is elegantly drawn and likewise richly adorned. There is a nostalgic flair about the picture; it recalls the free and independent lifestyle of times past that is in sharp contrast to the misery and the hardships of reservation life.

Some of Silverhorn's later paintings, the Peyote pictures that Mooney collected in 1904, show an artistic development in his work. The figures in a Peyote ceremony are rendered more naturalistic, are shown in three-quarter poses and from the front, and are captured during a high point of a ritual event. Thus, these pictures are not only of documentary value in Indian ethnology but also a milestone in the development of Native North American painting.

—Gerhard and Gisela Hoffmann

SIMON, Luke

Tribal affiliations: Micmac
Painter and ceramist

Born: Big Cove Reserve, New Brunswick, 30 May 1953. **Education:** George Brown College of Applied Arts and Technology, Toronto, 1975-77 Graphic Design Technician Certificate; Institute of American Indian Arts, Santa Fe, New Mexico, 1980-83, AFA; College of Santa Fe, BFA, 1985. **Career:** Self-employed artist, elementary school language and art instructor, Big Cove Reserve. **Awards:** Institute of American Indian Arts, T. C. Cannon Award, 1983; Outstanding Student's Award, 1983; National Dean's List Award, 1982-83; First Place, Sculpture Division (Bronze), Santa Fe Indian Market, 1983; First Place, Sculpture, Red Earth Festival, Oklahoma City, Oklahoma, 1988.

Selected Group Exhibitions

1979   La Maison Des Artisans, Moncton, New Brunswick
1981   *American Indian Art in the 1980s,* The Native American Centre for the Living Arts, Niagara Falls, New York
1982   *Graduate Show,* Institute of the American Indian Arts, Santa Fe, New Mexico
1983   Institute of American Indian Arts, Santa Fe, New Mexico
        Ceramics by Southwest Native American Artists, Gallery Mack, New York
        American Indian Ceramic Art: Yesterday, Today and Tomorrow, Sacred Circle Gallery of the American Indian Arts, Seattle, Washington
1984   *Flash and Fire,* Santa Fe Festival of the Arts, Santa Fe, New Mexico
1985   Sheila Nussbaum Gallery, Millburn, New Jersey
        The Magic Mountain Gallery, Taos, New Mexico
1986   *El Parian de Santa Fe,* Plaza Mercado, Santa Fe, New Mexico
1987   *Fiesta del Tlaquepaque,* Fourth Native American Invitational Exhibition, Sedona, Arizona
        Secrets Shared, Whitehorse Gallery, Santa Fe, New Mexico
1988   Regent Gallery, Fredericton, New Brunswick
        Red Earth Festival, Oklahoma City, Oklahoma
1990   Kimball Art Centre, Park City, Utah
1992   *Indigena,* Canadian Museum of Civilization, Ottawa, Ontario
1993   *P'el A'tukwey,* Art Gallery of Nova Scotia, Halifax, Nova Scotia

Collections

Art Gallery of Nova Scotia, Halifax; Institute of American Indian Arts Museum, Santa Fe, New Mexico; National Indian Art Collection, Department of Northern and Indian Affairs, Ottawa, Ontario.

Publications

On SIMON: Books—*Indigena: Contemporary Native Perspectives,* by Gerald McMaster and Ed Martin, Vancouver/Toronto, 1992; *Pe'l A'tukwey: Let Me Tell A Story—Recent Work by Mi'kmaq and Maliseet Artists,* Art Gallery of Nova Scotia, 1993.

*

Luke Simon comments:

Life, like art, is a struggle for balance between forces that pull at us from many directions. In a world that doesn't stand still, my native history and culture act as beacons from which I align my sights, even as this heritage widens and changes. A culture that is alive adapts to changing conditions, yet I am concerned that the societies we are adapting to are out of control.

The present system is good at overdoing things and creating a lot of waste in the process, even as people go hungry. The poor, in turn, are being put to work by short-sighted leaders further to exploit lands and resources. Those who are in power are proving incapable of adapting to the earth's needs. While governments are pursuing economic growth policies for their voracious populations, no one is even sure whether the planet is now on an irreversible path to ecological disaster.

Natives can't rely on the non-native masses to practice restraint when harvesting natural resources, nor can they rely on bureaucrats and political opportunists to safeguard their rights or turn things around. Natives should also be on guard against racist manipulation of ecological issues to the detriment of native rights and land claims.

Luke Simon: *We Are All Connected,* 1993. Courtesy of the artist.

These are some of the things I think about as I struggle with my work. But after all is said and done, I get the feeling that it is the earth that will soon have the last word.

*   *   *

Luke Simon's paintings are beautiful in their simple and deceptively primal use of intense emotional images, and they are highly arresting. Simon paints complex, intricately evolved graffiti that

address issues at the forefront of Native Canadian politics, presenting them in raw fragments of basic rage. These works illustrate the "civilizing" of Native peoples by European conquerors through history, whom Simon declares formed a complex mythology between itself and "primitive" peoples and concluded that these peoples must "disappear."

There is little room for questions in the intent behind Simon's work. Everything is in plain view and there is no doubt as to his feelings on these highly charged subjects. His anger at white governments and their failure to live up to treaty agreements signed in good faith is obvious. His choice of images to convey these messages is compelling and thrilling to view.

In his *Columbus Decelebration Series*, Simon illustrates, in plain terms, the harsh effects of the arrival of Christopher Columbus to North America. *The Crucifixion* (1991, oil on masonite) from this series depicts a Christ figure in the form of an anguished skeleton on a white, tombstone-like cross, with a feather coming down its cheek like a tear. The image is flanked to either side and from above by painted representations of photo negatives filled with stark images of suicide, industrial waste, and the natural contrasts of a moose, a buffalo, and a fish in the negatives along the top. At the heart of the Christ figure are the scales of justice. The scales, supported by the Canadian parliament buildings and a Canadian flag, are severely out of balance. Above the head of the Christ figure, written as though on a headstone, are the letters D-I-A—presumably for the Department of Indian Affairs.

The series "decelebrates" the arrival of Columbus in North America and focuses on the horrors of the victims of repeated colonization. Simon uses a mockingly primitive style, featuring images reminiscent of the skeletons found in Mexican art, although not nearly as peaceful, and exposed jagged lines that appear sharp and dangerous to the touch. The repeated use of the skull images also brings to mind the standard symbol for poison.

In another piece from the same series, *Exploitation* (1991, oil on masonite), the field of view is divided into four corners, representing the many breeds of conquerors who came to civilize the native people, taking land and anything else they wanted as a reward. Along the sides of the painting are representations of the four elements, and in the centre is an image of native culture being ripped apart and sliced open from all sides.

The block-like divisions within Simon's paintings highlight a fragmented society legislatively dissected and disconnected. Yet, through all of this anger and disruption, there winds a faint thread of hope.

Simon has said that "art is creative expression through playful and serious imagination." His is a process of intuition, and he doesn't always begin his work with a precisely mapped-out plan. He keeps his relationship with his work intuitive and organic, leaving room for the back and forth process of analysis, synthesis, creation, and reanalysis. Collectively, his work becomes an active part of the process of change in society, which also involves analysis, synthesis, and creation.

—Vesta Giles

SINGLETARY, Preston

Tribal affiliations: Tlinget
Glassblower

Born: San Francisco, California, 1963. **Education:** Pilchuck Glass School, 1984, studied with Dan Dailey and Lino Tagliapietra, 1987, studied with Benjamin Moore, Lino Tagliapietra, and Dorit Brand, 1995, studied with Lino Tagliapietra and Cecco Ongaro. **Career:** Glassblower, The Glass Eye Studio, Seattle, Washington, 1982-85; Glassblower assistant to Benjamin Moore, Richard Royal, Dale Chihuly, Dan Dailey, Fritz Dreisbach, and Dante Marioni, 1985—; gaffers assistant, Pilchuck Glass School, Stanwood, Washington,

1988-90; co-founded Maggio Gallery, New Orleans, Louisiana, 1993 (closed in 1995 due to fire); demonstrations, Itala, Finland, Konstfak College, Sweden, Kosta Boda, Sweden, 1993; blew light fixtures for the St. Ignatius Chapel, Seattle University, Seattle, Washington, 1997; teaching assistant to Therman Statom and Susan Stinsmullen-Amend, Pilchuck Glass School, and instructor, Pratt Fine Arts Center, Seattle, Washington, 1986; instructor, Goblet Workshop, Fujugawa Glass Workshop, Minamikoma, Japan, 1990; teaching assistant for "Masterpiece Workshop," Pilchuck Glass School, 1992; guest instructor at the College of Arts and Crafts, Helsinki, Finland, and Konstfak University, Stockholm, Sweden, 1994; instructor, Pratt Fine Arts Center, Seattle, Washington, 1994—. **Awards:** The Glass House Goblet Competition Purchase Award, 1988-90; various grants, including work study grant, The Institute of Alaska Native Arts, 1985.

Individual Exhibitions

1991   The Glass Gallery, Bethesda, Maryland
1993   Maggio Gallery, New Orleans, Louisiana

Selected Group Exhibitions

1986   The Hundred Waters Gallery, Seattle, Washington
1987   *The Gift Is in the Giving*, Seattle, Washington
1988-92   *Annual Goblet Show*, Glass House, Seattle, Washington
1989   *11th Annual International Pilchuck Exhibition*, William
             Traver Gallery, Seattle, Washington
           International Glass Trade Show, Tokyo
           Pilchuck Staff Show, Stanwood, Washington
1990   *Goblet Show*, Maurine Littleton Gallery, Washington, D.C.
           Goblet Show, Kurland Summers Gallery, Washington, D.C.
1991   *The Americans: A Venetian Tradition*, West End Gallery,
             Corning, New York
1991-92   *Goblet Show*, Gallery Nakama, Tokyo
1992   *Twist Gallery*, Portland, Oregon
           New Visions, The Visual Arts Center of Alaska, Anchorage, Alaska
1993   Margo Jacobson Gallery, Portland, Oregon
           Susan Duvall Gallery, Aspen, Colorado
1994   *16th Annual International Pilchuck Exhibition*, William
             Traver Gallery, Seattle, Washington
           Six Glass Artists, Gallery Glass 1, Stockholm, Sweden
1995   *A Powerful Presence: Pilchuck 25 Years*, Bumpershoot
             Arts Festival, Seattle, Washington
           Leedy Volkus Gallery, Kansas City, Missouri
1996   *Echoes of Scandinavia*, Glass Gallery, Bethesda, Maryland
           A New Generation, William Traver Gallery, Seattle, Washington
1997   *4 in Glass*, Lubbock, Texas
           Kiva Fine Arts, Santa Fe, New Mexico
           Northwest Coast Images in Glass, Vetri International
             Glass, Seattle, Washington
           Margo Jacobson Gallery, Portland, Oregon
           5 Northwest Artists, GUMPS, San Francisco

Collections

Glass House, Seattle, Washington; Group Health Cooperative, Seattle, Washington; Handlesbank, Stockholm, Sweden; Museum of

Preston Singletary: *Frog,* **1997. Photograph by Roger Schreiber; courtesy of the artist.**

Natural History, Anchorage, Alaska; Pilchuck Glass School, Stanwood, Washington.

Publications

On SINGLETARY: Articles—"The Glassblowers of the Pacific Northwest," by Dick Weiss, *Glasswork Magazine,* Number 11, 1992; "A New Generation," by Geoff Wichert, *Glass Magazine,* Number 63, 1996; "Many Nurturing Artworks of Varied Media...," by Robin Updike, *The Seattle Times,* March 14, 1996; "A Place to Reflect," by Robin Updike, *The Seattle Times,* March 30, 1997; "Enlightened Spaces," by John Pastier, *Seattle Weekly,* April 16, 1997.

*　　*　　*

For most of his career as a glass artist, Preston Singletary has drawn inspiration from his environment. In keeping with the clean lines and abstracted forms of his peers and mentors at the Pilchuck Glass School, Singletary has produced elegant blown-glass vessels reminiscent of classic Venetian or modern Danish styles. In his newest works, Singletary uses the same precision techniques to render images from within, symbolic of his Tlingit heritage.

In a unique attempt to wed a Northwest Coast aesthetic to the hard-edged medium of glass, Singletary has etched and sandblasted familiar formlines into clear and translucent glass, infusing the usually dark, brooding images with light. In *Bear* (1997), a yellow-hued blown-glass cylinder is carefully sand-blasted to reveal a bear totem, with each feature glowing softly as if lit from within. Large, shallow feast bowls are emblazoned with animal crests, painstakingly blasted through a colored layer of glass. The most spectacular pieces are flat-bottomed vessels, up-ended versions of woven Tlingit clan hats, with the inner surface of the brim etched with eagle and wolf crests.

The Tlingit-inspired forms weren't nearly as challenging for Singletary as the two-dimensional techniques for rendering tribal moiety and crest symbols. Traditionally, the rule-governed vocabulary of formlines and ovoids is learned through a lengthy apprenticeship. Singletary recently sought the advice of Marvin Oliver, an accomplished painter and carver based in Seattle. But for the most part, Singletary taught himself, studying other artists' work and images published in books. "I had the idea about six years ago, and made prototypes," he noted. "Then I started to work on the graphics, and figure out how to apply two dimensional images to three-dimensional glass."

Singletary was born in 1963 in San Francisco, but was raised in Seattle. His maternal grandmother was Tlingit, from southeast Alaska. His mother, half Tlingit and half Filipino, is a musician and an artist, and throughout his childhood Singletary was interested in music. He plays piano and guitar and intended to be a musician before he discovered glass.

Due to its proximity to the internationally known Pilchuck Glass School, Seattle is home to an unusually large number of professional glass artists. In high school, Singletary met Dante Marioni, son of the renowned glassblower Paul Marioni and now a successful glassblower in his own right. Through the younger Marioni, Singletary discovered the art of glass and was immediately intrigued. After graduating from high school, he worked as a glassblower at the Glass Eye, a small local studio. From there he moved on to Pilchuck, where he studied with Lino Tagliapietra, Benjamin Moore, and Cecco Ongaro.

His first works reflected this exposure to international talents. In the *Scribble Vases* series (1991), Singletary adhered thin curlicues of colored glass to sleek glass vases. The *Prestonuzzis* pay homage to classical Italian form, transforming solid, brightly colored jugs into flower vases. *The Genies,* produced after a six-month sojourn in Finland and Sweden, recall the spare geometry of modern Scandinavian style.

Singletary is excited about incorporating tribal designs into his work. "Tlingit culture wasn't impressed on me as a child. We knew we were of Indian descent, but at the time the trend was more to assimilate," he explains. Through studying and practicing his tribal aesthetic, he has rediscovered this part of his heritage. "I feel like I am at the beginning of a long path with these pieces," he writes. "It is a process of discovery."

—Margaret Dubin

SLICK, Duane

Tribal affiliations: Sac Fox; Winnebago
Painter and performance artist

Born: Waterloo, Iowa, 1961. **Education:** State University of New York, Plattsburg, 1983; West Chester University, Pennsylvania, 1984; Skowhegan School of Painting and Sculpture, Maine, 1986; University of Northern Iowa, B.F.A., 1986; Vermont Studio School, 1989; University of California, Davis, M.F.A., 1990. **Career:** Studio assistant to Judy Pfaff (1977), Guy Goodwin (1980), and David Reed (1990); guest artist, Tamarind Institute, 1992-93; painting instructor at the Institute of American Indian Art, Santa Fe, University of Northern Iowa, and Rhode Island School of Design; Southwest Representative, Second Circle Board of Governors,

Duane Slick: *White Bouquet,* **1995. Courtesy Jan Cicero Gallery, Chicago.**

Atlatl. **Awards:** Fellowships, Skowhegan School of Painting and Sculpture, 1986, University of California, Davis, 1988-90, Vermont Studio School, 1989, Fine Arts Work Center, 1990-92.

Individual Exhibitions

1988	*Mayors Choice Exhibit*, City Hall, Cedar Falls, Iowa
1990	C. N. Gorman Museum, University of California, Davis
1991	Hudson D. Walker Gallery, Provincetown, Massachusetts
1992	Farnham Galleries, Simpson College, Indianola, Iowa
	UFO Gallery, Provincetown, Massachusetts
1993	*Looking for Orozco,* Lawrence Arts Center, Lawrence, Kansas
1996	UFO Gallery, Provincetown, Massachusetts

Selected Group Exhibitions

1987	*24th Annual McNeider Exhibit,* Charles H. McNeider Museum, Mason City, Iowa
1988	*Iowa Competitive,* Metropolitan Gallery, Cedar Falls, Iowa

1989	*Artist for Amnesty,* Natsoulas/Novelozo Gallery, Davis, California
1990	*MFA Thesis Exhibit,* C. N. Gorman Museum, University of California, Davis
1991	*Without Boundaries: Contemporary Native American Art,* Jan Cicero Gallery, Chicago
	Submoloc Show or Columbus Wohs, An Alternative View by Contemporary Native American Artists, Evergreen College, Washington (traveling through 1993)
	Our Land/Ourselves: Contemporary Native American Artists, State University of New York, Albany (traveling through 1994)
1992	*Four Directions: Contemporary Native American Art,* University of Massachusetts, Amherst
	We the People: Native American Autobiography, Wooster College, Wooster, Ohio
	Six Directions, Galeria Calumet, Heidelberg, Germany
	For the Seventh Generation: Native American Artists Counter the Quincentenary, Chenango Council of the Arts & Golden Artist Colors, Inc., Columbus, New York

1993   Hudson P. Walker Gallery, Fine Arts Work Center,
           Provincetown, Massachusetts
        Art and Techno Culture, Evergreen College, Olympia,
           Washington
        Come to the Raz, James Hearst Art Center, Cedar Falls,
           Iowa
        New Mexico Repertory Theatre, Santa Fe
        Gallery Artists Works on Paper, Jan Cicero Gallery, Chicago
1994   *Artists Who Are Indian,* Denver Art Museum, Denver
        Indian Humor, American Indian Contemporary Arts, San
           Francisco
        Heard Invitational, Heard Museum, Phoenix
1995   *Abstract Painting,* Jan Cicero Gallery, Chicago
1996   *Native Streams: Contemporary Native American Art,* or
           ganized by Jan Cicero Gallery, Chicago, and Turman
           Art Gallery, Indiana State University, Terre Haute (trav-
           eling through 1997)

Performances

1991   *Coyote Looks into His Mind,* Fine Arts Work Center,
           Provincetown, Massachusetts
1992   *Coyote Looks into His Mind,* University of Massachu-
           setts, Amherst, and Bernice Steinbaum Gallery, New
           York
1993   *Coyote Looks into His Mind,* Richard Levy Gallery, Albu-
           querque, and Golden West Gallery, Telluride, Colorado
1994   *Coyote Looks into His Mind,* C. N. Gorman Museum,
           University of California, Davis, and University of New
           Mexico, Albuquerque

Publications

On SLICK: Books—*Our Land/Ourselves: American Indian Contemporary Artists,* exhibition catalog, Albany: SUNY, 1991; *Submoloc
Show, or Columbus Wohs: An Alternative View by Contemporary Native American Artists,* exhibition catalog, Washington: Evergreen College, 1991; *For the Seventh Generation: Native American Artists Counter
the Quincentenary,* New York: Columbus, 1992; *Native Streams: Contemporary Native American Art,* exhibition catalog, Chicago, 1996.
Article—"Gorillas in the Dunes: A Field Report from Provincetown,"
by Ann Wilson Lloyd, *Provincetown Arts Magazine,* 1992.

Collections

Gallery of Art, University of Northern Iowa; C.N. Gorman Museum, University of California, Davis; Skowhegan School of Painting and Sculpture, Maine; State University of New York, Plattsburg.

*

Duane Slick comments (1992):
    I consider my work a blend of storytelling and abstraction. I treat
the canvas as a fictitious space where anything can happen. (From
*For the Seventh Generation: Native American Artists Counter the
Quincentenary*)

*   *   *

    Duane Slick's work has evolved on two distinct planes: abstract
painting and storytelling. In both areas, his formal training provides

him a wide repertoire of symbols, techniques, and media, while his
experience as an urban Native American offers endless raw material. This combination results in a fresh and thoroughly modern, if
not postmodern, interpretation of contemporary Native life.
    Slick is interested in political as well as formal aesthetic or philo-
sophical issues. *The History of North America,* a piece he contributed to *For the Seventh Generation: Native American Artists Counter
the Quincentenary,* for example, combines painterly techniques for
abstraction with his penchant for storytelling. A small oil and collage on linen, it effectively inserts narrative into abstracted forms,
incorporating symbols from rock art, ledger drawings, and industrial America on layered fields of white and gray.
    In another exclusively Native American exhibit, Slick takes a
more direct approach to narrative. *Family Tree* (1992), a larger
mixed-media drawing included in *The Submoloc Show/Columbus
Wohs,* also looks back in time but finds stories that are at once more
personal and more political. The vertically oriented canvas lists the
names of Native leaders and activists, including some of Slick's
relatives. Small chunks of narrative recall Wovoka, the Ghost Dance
Messiah, and others who provided inspiration for their people.
Names and narratives are connected by a maze of thick lines in
Slick's signature white paint. "I approach art making as an act of
asking questions," Slick explains. "How do you talk rationally about
genocide when it is a part of *your own history*? The works I am
presenting [are attempts] at remaking, remembering, and re-telling
that history."
    Tamarind Institute of the University of New Mexico has twice
invited Slick to be a guest artist. In 1993, he produced two lithographs there that incorporate images of Coyote, the legendary Indian character whom Slick calls his "alter-ego." Just as he builds
texture in paintings, Slick layers symbols and references in these
prints, rearranging and reconstructing images of Coyote, historical
figures, and other meaningful icons. Each mass of images is connected, as before, by a maze of lines. As the images are superimposed, iconic references fade into an abstract form, reminding the
viewer that Coyote is a visual trickster. Layered images of Coyote
appear again in *The Coyote Flower: Red Snapper* (1994), selected for
the Heard Museum's Sixth Native American Fine Arts Invitational.
    While Slick's prints are nervous, highly energetic composites of
images, his paintings are serene, contemplative studies of light and
form. His recent canvases have been small, sometimes no bigger
than a square foot. This forces him to use every inch carefully.
White Bouquet (1995), included in the Cicero Gallery's *Native
Streams: Contemporary Native American Art,* is simultaneously
exquisite and forlorn. Using a subtle palette of whites and browns,
Slick renders a bouquet of roses, but only the round petal lips are
visible. Leaves and stems are shrouded by "veils of white," as Slick
terms it, in some places so thin the canvas shows through. And
again, through the haze of pale washes, a maze of lines appears.

—Margaret Dubin

SMITH, Ernest
Variant names: Gaon Yah
Tribal affiliations: Seneca
Painter and mixed media artist

Born: Akron, Tonawanda Reservation, New York, 28 October 1907;
Gaon Yah translates as From the Middle of the Sky. **Education:**

Public schools in Akron and Buffalo. **Career:** Sculptor, painter, and illustrator; commissioned regularly by the Rochester Museum of Arts and Sciences, and contributed to workshops; consultant on Iroquois myths and legends to authors William N. Fenton, Arthur Parker, and Jeanette Collamer; worked at the U.S. Gypsum Mines in Oakfield, New York, mid-1940s to the mid-1950s, and the Akron Parks Department, Akron, New York, 1960s. **Awards:** Iroquois of the Year, 1972. **Died:** 26 February 1975.

Individual Exhibitions

1950	Rochester Museum of Arts and Sciences, Rochester, New York
1972	First Unitarian Society, Schenectady, New York
	Everson Museum, Syracuse, New York
1975	Sioux Indian Museum and Craft Center, Indian Arts and Crafts Board, Sioux City, Iowa

Selected Group Exhibitions

1945-60	Ongoing exhibits at the Rochester Museum of Arts and Sciences, Rochester, New York, including *Longhouse Paintings of Iroquois Life,* 1950
1970	First Unitarian Society, Schenectady, New York
	Albany Unitarian Church, Albany, New York
1973	Sienna College, Londonville, New York
1974	First Unitarian Society, Schenectady, New York
	Museum of the American Indian, New York
	James T. Bialac Collection of 20th Century Native American Art, Nelson Fine Arts Center, Arizona State University Art Museum, Tempe
1991-92	*Shared Visions: Native American Painters and Sculptors in the Twentieth Century,* The Heard Museum, Phoenix, Arizona (traveling)
1993	*In the Shadow of the Sun,* Canadian Museum of Civilization, Hull, Quebec (traveling)

Collections

Indian Arts and Crafts Board, United States Department of the Interior, Washington, D.C.; Rochester Museum of Arts and Sciences, Rochester, New York; Schoharie Museum of the Iroquois Indian, Schoharie, New York; Smithsonian Institution, Washington, D.C.

Publications

On SMITH: Books—*The American Indian,* by Oliver LaFarge, New York, 1960; *Red Man's Religion,* by Ruth M. Underhill, Chicago, 1965; *Native American Painting: Selections from the Museum of the American Indian,* by David M. Fawcett and Lee A. Callander, New York, 1982; *Shared Visions: Native American Painters and Sculptors of the Twentieth Century,* by Margaret Archuleta and Rennard Strickland, Phoenix, 1991; *In the Shadow of the Sun,* by Gerald McMaster, et. al., Hull, Quebec, 1993.

*   *   *

In 1907 on Tonawanda Seneca land in upstate New York, a baby boy was born and given a traditional name, Gaon Yah, meaning

"From the Middle of the Sky." In accordance with Iroquoian cosmology, the middle of the sky is the place of the North Star, and from around this center point the cosmos turns. Stargazers traditionally asked the deeper question as to what is behind the North Star? Here, some believe, is the source of creation.

Gaon Yah was destined to be a creative artist. He began painting at the age of ten in a Buffalo public school, where he was addressed by his other name, Ernest Smith. Although he grew up in a matrilineal society, by this time the custom of taking the father's last name was accepted. Gaon Yah was the son of Pete Smith and Rose Spring, both members of artistic families. Pete's brother was a traditional Seneca wood carver, fashioning masks, condolence canes, burl wood bowls, maple spoons, pipe stems, and many other items both spiritual and utilitarian. Rose Spring was a fine beadworker; Seneca beadworkers are noted for making beaded jackets, leggings, moccasins, shoulder bags, as well as many whimsical items for collectors. Their unique style is called "embossed beadwork," where the beads raise up off the surface in clusters. Gaon Yah was raised around arts and crafts and was essentially a self-taught artist who mastered illustrating and expanded from there to paintings in oils and watercolors. He rarely strayed from the Tonawanda Reservation area of New York, where he found ample subject matter and work to sustain a career in which he made important contributions to understanding the history of New York Native American tribes. He was honored as Iroquois of the Year in 1972—"for preservation of Iroquois culture through painting"—the first such honor bestowed by the Iroquois Conference representing six nations of the northeast.

Smith's works relate Iroquois myths and legends, most of which he learned through the storytelling of his great grandmother. He participated in Iroquois rituals as a young man and was known as a talented singer, dancer, and storyteller. These experiences gave him deep understanding of the customs and cultures of the six nations comprising the Iroquois, carefully recreated in his artwork. He knew, for example, that each of the six nations had unique arrangements for the feathers in their head dresses, among the differentiating cultural styles he was careful to represent in his work.

Like several American artists and writers, Smith benefited by participating in the Works Project Administration during the Depression, finding employment as an illustrator on the Tonowanda reservation from 1935 to 1939, which led to a position at the Rochester Museum of Arts and Sciences from 1939 to 1945 and regular commissions from the Museum. Anthropologist William N. Fenton recognized his talent and asked him to illustrate a series of books on Iroquoian oral traditions. Fenton recorded stories told by Iroquoian people, including tales of the dawn of creation, the seven sisters of the Pliades, the dark age of war, and the arrival of the Great Peacemaker. In 1936, Fenton published "An Outline of Seneca Ceremonies at Coldspring Longhouse," *Yale University Publications in Anthropology,* and in 1941 he compiled "Tonawanda Longhouse Ceremonies: Ninety Years After Lewis Henry Morgan," *Bureau of American Ethnology Bulletin.* Here we find recorded the roots of Smith's Seneca spirituality, the essence being that life is sacred, the Earth is alive and maternal, and the cosmos is filled with living spirits. The life force of this spiritual power is called Orenda. Smith was also consulted by Dr. Arthur Parker, a Seneca anthropologist, on Iroquois history and legends, and the experience benefited Smith as well, who focused his attention on authentic detail, which he recalled from his grandmother's stories and furthered through experience and research. Smith's illustrations for Parker's books, along with those by Ruth Underhill and Jeanette Collamer, were rendered with India ink and watercolor wash on heavy white board. They reveal deep understanding of cultural details and meticulous care in depicting faithfully each element of his compositions. He knew that his elders were going to see these pictures.

In the exhibition *Longhouse Paintings of Iroquois Life* at the Rochester Museum & Science Center, Smith had 128 paintings on display. *Longhouse Under Construction* (1939) portrays three bare-chested Iroquois men wearing leggings and breach cloths and building a birchbark house. Everything down to the beadwork in their moccasins is authentic. The spare background maintains focus on the activity and the men. Smith's understanding of anatomy is evident, and his brush strokes are confident.

Smith's artistic output tapered off sharply from the late 1940s through the 1960s. He continued painting occasionally and developed a preference for watercolor. In the later works through his death in 1975, Smith continued to recreate Iroquois myths and legends as well as more historical depictions of everyday life. *Curing the Sick* (oil on canvas, 1968), for example, is spare in background, focusing all attention on a medicine man applying traditional methods for healing. The clothing and medicinal herbs are authentic, the figures are sharply drawn, and the work achieves its purpose of providing an illustration of commonplace community events. In other works, like *Legend of the Seven Brothers (Story of the Little Dipper)*, Smith created a visual accompaniment for oral, mythic narratives that had been passed on for generations among the Iroquois, and which he learned, in turn, from his great grandmother. For these reasons and his heroic but not romanticized portrayals, Smith's work is an invaluable resource for the history of Native America life in New York state.

—Gregory Schaaf

SMITH, Jaune Quick-to-See

Variant names: Insightful Awareness
Tribal affiliations: Salish; Cree; Shoshone
Painter

Born: St. Ignatius, Indian Mission Flathead Reservation, Montana, 15 January 1940; also named Insightful Awareness. **Education:** Framingham State College, Massachusetts, B.A., 1976; University of New Mexico, M.A., 1980. **Career:** Public commissions, including Terazzo Floor, Denver Airport, Cultural Museum, Flathead Reservation, and Yerba Buena Park, Sculpture Garden, San Francisco, 1991, and National Museum of the American Indian, Smithsonian Institution, Washington, D.C. (artist on design team), 1993; curator, including *Contemporary Native American Art*, Ken Phillips Gallery, Denver, Colorado, 1980, *Women of Sweetgrass, Cedar and Sage* (co-curator, traveling, catalog), 1985, *The Submuloc Show/Columbus Wohs* (traveling), 1990, *Positives and Negatives: Native American Photographers*, (traveling Europe), 1995; juror, including New Mexico Women Artists Exhibition, 1983, National Endowments for the Arts, 1986, Millay County for the Arts, 1995-96; Trustee, including Atlatl, 1984-94, American Indian Community Arts, 1984-88, Institute of American Indian Arts, 1986-90, College Art Association, 1989-95, and Salish Kostenai College Foundation, board member, 1995; printmaking, including Tamarind Lithography Workshop, Albuquerque, New Mexico, 1978-82, 1988-89, 1995-96; numerous conferences and panels; lecturer; catalog contributor, editor, and producer; writer. **Awards:** Fellowships; honorary doctorate, Minneapolis College of Art and Design, 1992; master artist-in-residence, Santa Fe Institute of Fine Arts, 1994; Wallace Stegner Award, Center of the American West, University of Colorado, 1995; Joan Mitchell Foundation Award for Painting, 1996; Women's Caucus for Art Award for Outstanding Achievement in the Visual Arts, 1997. **Address:** c/o Steinbaum Krauss Gallery, 132 Greene Street, New York, New York, 10012.

Individual Exhibitions

1978	*Jaune Quick-to-See Smith*, Pastel and charcoal drawings, Clarke Benton Gallery, Santa Fe, New Mexico
1980	Galleria de Cavallino, Venice, Italy
1981	Clarke Benton Gallery, Santa Fe, New Mexico
1982	North Dakota Arts Council and NEA (traveling)
	Jaune Quick-to-See Smith: The Red Lake Series, paintings, works on paper, Marilyn Butler Gallery, Scottsdale, Arizona
1983	Montana Art Gallery Directors Association (traveling)
	Jaune Quick-to-See Smith: The Site Paintings, Marilyn Butler Gallery, Santa Fe, New Mexico
1984	*Flathead Wellspring: The Art of Jaune Quick-to-See Smith*, Washington State Arts Commission (traveling)
1985	*Jaune Quick-to-See Smith*, Bernice Steinbaum Gallery, New York
1986	*Jaune Quick-to-See Smith: Speaking Two Languages*, Yellowstone Art Center, Billings, Montana
1987-88	Marilyn Butler Gallery, Santa Fe, New Mexico
1989	*Centric 37: Jaune Quick-to-See Smith*, University Art Museum, California State University, Long Beach
1990	*Jaune Quick-to-See Smith, New Works: Chief Seattle Series*, LewAllen/Butler Gallery, Santa Fe, New Mexico
1992	*The Quincentenary Non-Celebration*, Steinbaum Krauss Gallery, New York
1993	*Jaune Quick-to-See Smith*, Chrysler Museum, Norfolk, Virginia, Parameters Series (traveling)
1994	Jan Cicero Gallery, Chicago
	LewAllen Gallery, Santa Fe, New Mexico
	Santa Fe Institute of Fine Arts, Santa Fe, New Mexico
1995	*Talking Pictures*, Steinbaum Krauss Gallery, New York
	University of Wyoming Museum, Laramie
	Jaune Quick-to-See Smith, Wabash College Art Museum, Crawfordsville, Indiana
1996	*Subversions/Affirmations: Jaune Quick-to-See Smith, A Survey*, Jersey City Museum, Jersey City, New Jersey (traveling)

Selected Group Exhibitions

1976	Whittemore Gallery, Framingham State College, Massachusetts
1977	*The Woman as Artist*, Galleria, Albuquerque, New Mexico
	Indian Art Now, Wheelwright Museum of the American Indian, Santa Fe, New Mexico
1978	*Grey Canyon*, Albuquerque Museum Plaza Gallery, New Mexico
1979	*Summer Show*, Droll/Kolbert Gallery, New York
	Grey Canyon Artists, Ken Phillips Gallery, Denver, Colorado

1980   *The Grey Canyon Artists*, Wheelwright Museum, Santa
        Fe, New Mexico (traveling)
        Work from the Tamarind Institute, Scottish Arts Council,
        Edinburgh, Scotland
        Cavillino Gallery, Venice, Italy
        Conceptual Art, Southern Plains Indian Museum,
        Anadarko, Oklahoma
1981   Philbrook Art Center, Tulsa, Oklahoma
        Richard L. Nelson Gallery, University of California, Davis
        Museum of the Southwest, Midland, Texas
        Fiber Arts, Banff Center for the Arts, Banff, Alberta
1982   Galleria D'arte L'Argentario, Trento, Italy
        Smithsonian Institution, Washington, D.C.
1983   *The Horse Show,* Robert Freidus Gallery, New York
        Common Ground, American Indian Community House,
        New York
        Contemporary Native American Art, Gardiner Art Gal-
        lery, Oklahoma State University, Stillwater, Oklahoma
        Grey Canyon, Portland Art Museum, Oregon
        The New Feminism, Ohio State University, Columbus
        Western States Biennial, traveling; venues include Corcoran
        Art Gallery, Washington, D.C., San Francisco Museum
        of Modern Art, Museum of Albuquerque, Long Beach
        Museum of Art, and Brooklyn Museum
1984   *Expanding Powers,* University of Tennessee, Knoxville,
        and California State College, Stanislaus
1985   *Women of Sweetgrass, Cedar and Sage: Contemporary
        American Art by Native American Women,* American
        Indian Community House, New York (traveling)
        New Ideas from Old Traditions, Yellowstone Art Center,
        Billings, Montana
1986   *AdoRnmenTs,* Bernice Steinbaum Gallery, New York (trav-
        eling)
        Personal Symbols, two person exhibition with George
        Longfish, Northern Iowa Gallery of Art, Ames
1987   *Motion and Arrested Motion: Contemporary Figurative
        Drawing,* Chrysler Museum, Norfolk, Virginia
1988   *Earth and Sky,* Anne Reed Gallery, Sun Valley, Idaho
        Alice, and Look Who Else, Through The Looking Glass,
        Bernice Steinbaum Gallery, New York (traveling)
1989   *Zeitgenossische Indianische Kunst II,* Dorothee Peiper-
        Riegraf Gallery, Frankfurt, Germany
1990   *Coast to Coast-The Box Show,* Art in General, New York
        (traveling)
        The Decade Show, New Museum of Contemporary Art,
        Studio Museum in Harlem, New York
1991   *Okanta,* A-Space, Toronto, Ontario
        Without Boundaries, Jan Cicero Gallery, Chicago
        *The Enabling Spirit, Michael Naranjo and Significant New
        Mexico Artist* Very Special Arts Gallery, Washington, D.C.
        Myth and Magic in the Americas, Museo de Arte
        Contemporaneo de Monterrey, Monterrey, Mexico
1992   *For the Seventh Generation: Native American Artists Counter
        the Quincentenary,* Chenango County Council of the Arts
        Gallery, Norwich, New York and Golden Artist Colors
        Gallery, Columbus, New York (traveling)
        Counter Colon-ialismo, Centro Cultural Tijuana, Mexico
        (traveling)
        *Shared Visions: Native American Sculptors and Painters
        in the Twentieth Century,* The Heard Museum, Phoenix,
        Arizona (traveling)

1993   *Spirits Keep Whistling Us Home,* Sacred Circle Gallery of
        American Indian Art, Seattle, Washington
        *Into the Forefront: American Indian Art in the 20th Cen-
        tury,* Denver Art Museum, Colorado
1993-96 *Current Identities: Recent Paintings in the United States,*
        traveling exhibition, including Panama, Honduras, Sal-
        vador, Costa Rica, Ecuador, Columbia, Uruguay, Ven-
        ezuela, Paraguay and the Dominican Republic
        The Spirit of Native America, organized by American In-
        dian Contemporary Arts, San Francisco, California
        (traveling)
1994   *Weltpremier: Remember the Earth Whose Skin You Are,*
        Kunsthalle, Bonn, Germany
1994-95 *Current Identities: IV Biennal International de Pintura
        94-95,* South America traveling exhibition
1995   *Bridges and Boundaries: Brucken und Abgrenzungen,*
        Peiper-Riegraf Gallery, Frankfurt, Germany
        Indian Humor, organized by the American Indian con-
        temporary Arts, San Francisco, California (traveling)
1996   *Objects of Personal Significance,* Exhibits USA and East-
        ern Illinois University, Charleston, Illinois (traveling
        through 1999)
        Native Streams: Contemporary Native American Art, Jan
        Cicero Gallery, Chicago
        I Stand in the Center of Good, American Indian Commu-
        nity House, New York
        *American Kaleidoscope: Themes and Perspectives in Re-
        cent Art,* National Museum of American Art,
        Smithsonian Institution, Washington, D.C
        Summer Group Exhibition, Steinbaum Krauss Gallery,
        New York
1996-99 *Objects of Personal Significance,* organized by Exhibits
        USA and Eastern Illinois University, Charleston (trav-
        eling)

Collections

Albuquerque Museum, Albuquerque, New Mexico; American Medi-
cal Association, Chicago; Art Museum Framingham State College,
Framingham, Massachusetts; AT&T Corporate Art Collection;
Birmingham Museum of Art, Birmingham, Alabama; Bruce Museum, Greenwich, Connecticut; Bureau of indian Affairs, Washing-
ton, D.C.; Cornell University, Ithaca, New York; Denver Art Museum, Denver, Colorado; Eastern New Mexico State University,
New Mexico; Fine Arts Museum, Santa Fe, New Mexico; Thomas
Gilcrease Museum, Tulsa, Oklahoma; Heard Museum, Phoenix,
Arizona; Home Box Office Productions, New York; Jersey City
Museum, Jersey City, New Jersey; Memorial Art Museum, Roch-
ester, New York; Minneapolis Art Institute, Minneapolis, Minne-
sota; Montclair Art Museum, Montclair, New Jersey; Mount
Holyoke Art Museum, Mount Holyoke, Massachusetts; Museum
of Mankind, Vienna, Austria; Museum of Modern Art, New York;
Muscum of New Mexico, New Mexico; National Museum of Ameri-
can Art, Washington, D.C.; National Museum of Women in the
Arts, Washington, D.C.; Nebraska 1% for Arts Program, Lincoln,
Nebraska; Newark Art Museum, Newark, New Jersey; Roswell
Museum and Art Center, Roswell, New Mexico; Smith College
Museum of Art, Northampton, Massachusetts; Southern Plains
Indian Museum, Anadarko, Oklahoma; Stamford Museum, Stam-
ford, Connecticut; Steinberg Museum, St. Louis, Missouri; Sweet
Briar College, Sweet Briar, Virginia; University of California, Davis

Jaune Quick-to-See Smith: *Tree of Life* diptych. Courtesy Steinbaum Krauss Gallery, New York, and Jan Cicero Gallery, Chicago.

Nelson Gallery, California; University of Colorado, Boulder, Colorado; University of North Dakota Museum, North Dakota; University of Oklahoma Museum of Art, Norman, Oklahoma; University of Regina, Saskatchewan

Publications

By SMITH: Books—*Women of Sweetgrass, Cedar, and Sage,"* (catalog with essay), New York, 1985; "Curator's Statement," *Our Land/Ourselves: American Indian Contemporary Artist*, Albany: University Art Gallery, State University of New York, 1990; "Artist's Statement," *Portfolio III*, San Francisco: American Indian Contemporary Arts, 1991; "Artist's Statement," *Counter Colonlalismo*, San Diego, California: Centro Cultural de la Raza, 1992; "Curator's Statement," *The Submuloc Show/Columbus Wohs*, Phoenix: Atlatl, 1992; "We, the Human Beings," *We, the Human Beings*, Wooster, Ohio: College of Wooster Art Museum, 1992; **Books illustrated**—*That's What She Said*, Rayna Green, editor, Bloomington, Indiana University Press, 1984; *I Become Part of It*, D.M. Dooley and Paul Jordan-Smith, editors, New York, 1989. **Articles**—"Women of Sweetgrass, Cedar and Sage." *Women's Studies Quarterly* 15, 1 and 2 (Spring- Summer 1987): 35-41.

On Smith: Books—*Magic Images: Contemporary Native American Art*, by Edwin Wade and Rennard Strickland, Norman: Philbrook Art Center and University of Oklahoma Press, 1981; *The American West: The Modern Vision*, by Patricia Janis Broder, New York Graphic Society and Little, Brown and Company, Boston, 1984; *The Arts of the North American Indian: Native Traditions in Evolu*

tion, Edwin Wade, editor, New York: Hudson Hill Press and The Philbrook Art Center, Tulsa, 1986; *The Decade Show: Frameworks of Identity in the 1980s*, Museum of Contemporary Hispanic Art, The New Museum of Contemporary Art, The Studio Museum in Harlem, 1990; *Mixed Blessings: New Art in a Multicultural America*, by Lucy Lippard, New York: Pantheon Books, 1990; *Shared Visions: Native American Painters and Sculptors in the Twentieth Century*, Margaret Archuleta and Rennard Strickland, New York: The New Press, 1991; *Land, Spirit, Power: First Nations at the National Gallery of Canada*, by Diana Nemiroff, Robert Houle, and Charlotte Townsend-Gault, Ottawa: National Gallery of Canada, 1992; *I Stand in the Center of the Good,* Lawrence Abbott, editor, Lincoln and London: University of Nebraska Press, 1994. **Articles**—"The Gray Canyon Artists," by Richard Hill, *The Turtle Quarterly*, Vol. 2, Spring-Summer, 1980; "Native American Art and Influence," by Peter Jemison, *Artspeak*, April 15, 1982; "Native Intelligence," by Lucy Lippard, *Village Voice*, December 1983; "In Stamford Art Exhibit, Life Imitates Art," by Vivien Raynor, May 21, 1989; "Sovereignty over Subjectivity," by Robert Houle, *C 30.* (Summer 1991); "Critical Issues in Recent Native American Art," by Jackson Rushing, *Art Journal*, Vol. 51, no. 3, Fall 1992; "Native American Art in the Postmodern Era," by Kay WalkingStick, *Art Journal*, Vol. 51, no. 3, Fall 1992; "Jaune Quick-to-See Smith: Steinbaum Krauss Gallery," by Jennifer P. Borum, *Artforum*, January, 1993; "Social Turf Gives a Multicultural Tour," by Jeffery Cullum, *Atlanta Journal*, May 12, 1995; Jeff Huebner, "Holding Pattern," *The New Art Examiner*, Summer, 1995, Vol. 22, No. 10; "X-Sightings," by Victor Mathieu, *ArtVoice*, June 21-July 4, 1995; "A Celebration of Tamarind Institute Artist," by Lynn Hunter

Cline, *Pasatiempo*, February 2, 1996. **Other Media**—*American Indian II: Juane Quick-To-See Smith*, Public Broadcasting System, 1980; *Indian Women (Wir, die undiamischen Frauen)*, Georg Eich, producer, ZDF TV, Germany; *American Journey: Women in America*, CD-ROM, Primary Source Media, Woodbridge, Connecticut, 1995.

*   *   *

Flathead, French-Cree, and Shoshone artist, Jaune Quick-to-See Smith takes her middle name, meaning insight and perception, from her grandmother. Born on the Confederated Salish and Kootenai Reservation in St. Ignatius, Montana, Smith was raised on several reservations by her father, an accomplished horseman and trader. Leading a nomadic childhood traveling the Pacific northwest and entertained herself artistically by working with rocks, ferns and dirt. These childhood experiences influenced her solemn attitude towards land and nature and her artistic sense of texture and color.

At the age of thirty and as a mother of two she returned to school in 1970, receiving a bachelors in art education from Framingham State College in 1976 and her masters at the University of New Mexico in 1980. Her abstract paintings and mixed-media collages reflect a range of modernist influences, including Robert Rauschenberg, Anselm Keifer, and Oscar Howe, as well as symbols, techniques, and media derived from her Native American heritage.

For the past twenty years land has been an ever-present theme in her work and life, especially such highly charged topics as the devastation of her homeland and destruction of the earth. Her commitment to the land, as it is expressed in her art, articulates a profound link between place and identity, and between the production of art and cultural survival.

Regardless of the manner or subject of representation, the rendering of the natural world by generations of American Indian artists signifies a profound conceptual difference between their relationship to the land and that of Western cultures. Rather than land as a commodity or landscape as a visual temporal record, it refers to a sense of one's connection to place, a spatial reality signified by a spiritual alliance. In addition to the religious and philosophical connections, there are historical and political components as well, involving underlying issues of land loss and cultural sovereignty. Therefore, the embodiment of the earth in art functions as the central metaphor used to critique mainstream society, while at the same time it is employed to reaffirm and redefine a sense of contemporary cultural identity.

Most of Smith's paintings, like *Buckskin*, 1989, begin with a multidimensional and compressed view of space and time. These are not empty or static landscapes depicting majestic mountains or romantic valleys, not images of unclaimed wilderness waiting to be settled and cultivated. According to Smith, her abstracted landscapes are inhabited, living entities within which move various elements from the natural world and a multitude of life-forms.

Smith's ideological and metaphysical conceptions of the natural world is made physically manifest in the application of paint. The layering of paint reveals large brushstrokes and drips that duplicate the tactile quality of an animated landscape: reflections of light on water, rain rivulets in the soil, the color of moss and foliage, or the qualities of sand and snow. At other times Smith utilizes blocks of color to render impressions of broad expanses of space, suggesting prairies, ranges, and valleys.

Superimposed over the land are symbols, including figures, animals, tools, trees, and vessel forms. The images are depicted in forms that make reference to ancient pictographic languages and historic peoples. Frequently, the forms are rendered as outlined shapes, suggesting they are part of or embedded within the land, as opposed to solid forms that might be interpreted as dominating or superimposed upon the land. The earth shows clearly through these lucid shapes, creating the impression of equal significance with the other natural elements. In fact, pictorially and metaphorically the elemental forms and background swatches of land provide each other with substance and sustenance.

Another recurring motif in Smith's work is the image of a horse. Smith has stated that the image is frequently a stand in for herself, a form through which she expresses the narrative of her personal life as well as the collective memory of her Native American ancestry. In a recent painting, *Indian Horse*, made in 1992 for the de-celebration of the Quincentenary of Columbus' arrival, Smith juxtaposes family photographs and an image of Chief Joseph on a beaded vest with newspaper clippings and advertisements. She merges these iconic elements within the contoured form of a horse, which stands entrenched in drips and swatches of red paint. Scattering these images, Smith explores contemporary Native American identity and instigates a questioning of existing historical narratives. Art, history, and popular culture are used to point out fictions and actualities of post-colonial life.

In order to convey her identity as both a modern painter and an artist of American Indian ancestry, Smith is mindful to communicate the realities of her contemporary existence along with the received, or inherited history of her Native American heritage. She borrows elements from historic Indian art that now seem particularly modern, like the juxtapositioning of organic and geometric motifs in weaving and the vibrant combination of colors in painted parfleches and beadwork. By incorporating materials, processes, and images related to pictographs, ledger book art, and the painted parfleche, Smith uses her art to reaffirm the continuity of Native American artistic traditions.

As an artist Smith journeys across borders that separate Indian from non-Indian worlds, using her paintings as her voice, her conduit to enlighten, and her artistic talents and education to network and trade information. Smith is active with tribal activities, boards, and conferences, lectures frequently, teaches, and works collaboratively with other artists. She has curated numerous exhibitions and has been the subject of three PBS documentaries. Smith has achieved international recognition and her artwork is represented in numerous museum collections throughout the United States and Europe.

—Lisa Roberts

SMOKY, Lois

Variant names: Bougetah
Tribal affiliations: Kiowa
Painter and basketweaver

Born: Near Anadarko, Oklahoma, 1907; native name means Of the Dawn. **Education:** Art classes at the University of Oklahoma, 1927. **Career:** Beadworker and painter; concentrated on raising a family by the late 1920s. **Awards:** Certificate of Appreciation, Indian Arts and Crafts Board, 1966.

Lois Smoky: *Kiowa Mother & Children*. Courtesy Thomas Gilcrease Museum of History and Art, Tulsa, Oklahoma.

Individual Exhibitions

1975   Southern Plains Indian Museum, Anadarko, Oklahoma

Selected Group Exhibitions

1936   *American Indian Exposition*, Tulsa, Oklahoma
1947-65 *American Indian Paintings from the Permanent Collection*,
         Philbrook Art Center, Tulsa, Oklahoma (traveling)
1972   *Contemporary Southern Plains Indian Painting*, tour or-
         ganized by the Southern Plains Indian Museum and
         Oklahoma Indian Arts and Crafts Cooperative,
         Anadarko, Oklahoma
1979   *Sharing Our Wealth*, Oklahoma Historical Society, Okla-
         homa City
1980   *Plains Indian Paintings*, Museum of Art, University of
         Oklahoma, Norman (traveling)
1981-83 *Native American Painting*, Amarillo Art Center, Ama-
         rillo, Texas (traveling)
1982   *Native American Painting: Selections from the Museum of
         the American Indian*, Heard Museum, Phoenix, Arizona
1990   *American Indian Artists: The Avery Collection and the
         McNay Permanent Collection*, Marion Koogler McNay
         Art Museum, San Antonio, Texas
1991-96 *Shared Visions: Native American Painters and Sculptors in
         the Twentieth Century*, Heard Museum, Phoenix, Arizona
1996   *Visions and Voices: Native American Painting from the
         Philbrook Museum of Art*, Tulsa, Oklahoma

Collections

Thomas Gilcrease Museum of American History and Art, Tulsa,
Oklahoma; Marion Koogler McNay Art Museum, San Antonio
Texas; Museum of the American Indian, New York; National Cow-
boy Hall of Fame and Western Heritage Center, Oklahoma City,
Oklahoma; Philbrook Museum of Art, Tulsa, Oklahoma; Millicent
Rogers Foundation Museum, Taos, New Mexico.

Publications

On SMOKY: Books—*Kiowa Indian Art*, by Oscar B. Jacobson,
Nice, France, 1929; *American Indian Painters*, by Oscar B. Jacobson
and Jeanne d'Ucel, Nice, France, 1950; *Oklahoma Indian Painting
and Poetry*, by Acee Blue Eagle, Tulsa, 1959; *American Indian
Painting of the Southwest and Plains Areas*, by Dorothy Dunn,
Albuquerque, New Mexico, 1968; *Song from the Earth: American
Indian Painting*, by Jamake Highwater, Boston, 1976; *American
Indian Painting and Sculpture*, Patricia J. Broder, New York, 1981;
Shared Visions, by Margaret Archuleta and Rennard Strickland,
Phoenix, 1991; *Vision and Voices: Native American Painting from
the Philbrook Museum of Art*, Lydia Wyckoff, editor, Tulsa, 1996.

*   *   *

Lois Smoky stands as the first Kiowa woman of note to break
into the male tradition of figure painting. An original Kiowa Five
artist, Smoky studied at the University of Oklahoma with Stephen
Mopope, Monroe Tsatoke, Spencer Asah, and Jack Hokeah in
1927. However, she has often been overshadowed, indeed almost
replaced, by James Auchiah, who later joined the artists and is more
commonly known as one of the Kiowa Five. Smoky used the gen-

eral aesthetic vocabulary developed by these early Kiowa easel
painters. This stylistic genre, later to be called traditional flat art,
employed opaque planes of flat color to develop elegantly postured
figures silhouetted against plain backgrounds with movement and spatial depth suggested by contour lines. Based on these principles of
design, Smoky originated her own distinctive expression of flat-style
painting, which emphasized geometric patterns of design.

Smoky's treatment of these decorative elements, a strength in her
work, reflects her ties to traditional women's art of Plains societies.
While figurative painting was reserved for men, womens' artistic
sphere included parfleche painting and beadwork. A highly developed sense of design, with a repetition of form and graphic interplay between color, is seen in the geometric and floral designs that
characterize Smoky's work. *Kiowa Mother and Children*, published
in Oscar Jacobson's 1929 portfolio on Kiowa art, is a good example. In this painting, Smoky centers on the upper bodice of the
women's buckskin, which is produced by bold applications of blue
and green. This floral design is set off by the white area of negative
space. Similar to ledger work, the rhythmic patterns of color in the
beadwork designs shift across the surface of the painting, producing a patchwork effect. Moreover, the carefully executed line
coupled with the vivid color contrasts activates the surface of the
painting—the designs nearly hover above the painting's surface.

In *Kiowa Mother and Children*, both the mother and son gaze
directly at the viewer while the small girl shyly peers around her
mother's skirt. This interaction between subject and viewer is a
device often used to bring the viewer into the work; however, these
solid and still figures stand their ground and invite you no further.
The familial relationship between the figures is underscored by this
repetition of design from one figure to another.

In a 1930 piece, *Kiowa Woman*, from the Silberman Collection of
the National Cowboy Hall of Fame, Smoky experiments with spatial depth and movement by adding contour lines. However, her
approach is inconsistent, shifting from flat geometric planes to
contoured areas within the same figure. The contour lines around
the blanket suggest the volume and shape of the figure's shoulder
and back, though there is no modeling. This volumetric blanket area
conflicts with the rectangular flat skirt area that suggest no movement or volume. Smoky introduces a simplicity and restraint in her
use of color: a simple patch of pale beadwork decorates the surface
of the leggings in contrast to her vivid colors in other works.

Raising a family became primary over Smoky's painting career,
leaving only rare examples in museum collections. The past decade has
seen a renewed interest in Smoky's work and a desire to recognize her
achievements in painting. Despite time constraints, Smoky continued
in bead work and exhibited her work at the Southern Plains Museum in
Anadarko, Oklahoma, in 1975. Smoky, daughter of Enoch Smoky,
belonged to a long familial tradition of esteemed Kiowa beadworkers
that included Gladys Parton and Lucy Jackson.

—Marla Redcorn

SOQWEEN

Variant names: Soukwawe; Jose Encarnacion Peña
Tribal affiliations: San Ildefonso Pueblo
Painter

Born: Jose Encarnacion Peña, San Ildefonso Pueblo, New Mexico,
25 March 1902; also signed his work as Soqueen; also named

Soqween: *Pumpkin Dance,* 1970. Photograph by Murrae Haines; courtesy Dr. Gregory Schaaf collection.

Soukwawe, which means Frost on the Mountain. **Education:** School of American Research, Santa Fe, New Mexico, and Santa Fe Indian School. **Awards:** Museum of New Mexico, Santa Fe, "Best example of original use of traditional material," 1957; Santa Fe Indian Market, 1978. **Died:** 19 October 1979.

Selected Group Exhibitions

1955	*An Exhibition of American Indian Painters,* James Graham and Sons, New York
1957	Museum of New Mexico, Santa Fe
1968	Arizona State Museum, University of Arizona, Tucson
1972	Denver Art Museum, Denver, Colorado
1979-80	*Native American Painting,* Joslyn Museum, Omaha, Nebraska (traveling)
1981	*Native American Painting,* Amarillo Art Center, Amarillo, Texas

1996	*Honoring the Weavers,* Poeh Museum, Pueblo of Pojoaque, New Mexico
	Museum of New Mexico, Santa Fe, New Mexico
	Heard Museum, Phoenix, Arizona

Collections

Bayou Bend Collection, Museum of Fine Arts, Houston, Texas; Cleveland Museum of Art, Ohio; Denver Art Museum, Colorado; Museum of New Mexico, Laboratory of Anthropology, Santa Fe; Museum of Northern Arizona, Flagstaff; National Museum of the American Indian, Washington, D.C.; Millicent Rogers Foundation Museum, Taos, New Mexico; Southwest Museum, Los Angeles.

Publications

On SOQWEEN: Books—*Pueblo Indian Painting,* by Hartley Burr Alexander, Nice, France, 1932; *Southwest Indian Painting,* by Clara

Lee Tanner, Tucson, 1957; *American Indian Painting of the Southwest and Plains Areas,* by Dorothy Dunn, Albuquerque, 1968; *Indian Painters and White Patrons,* by J. J. Brody, Albuquerque, 1971; *Southwest Indian Painting: A Changing Art,* by Clara Lee Tanner, Tucson, 1973; *Native American Painting,* by Frederick Schmid and Patrick Houlihan, Kansas City, 1979; *Native American Painting,* by Jeanne Snodgrass King, Amarillo, 1981. **Articles—** "Jose Encarnacion Peña," by Barbara Nelson, *Sunstone Review,* Vol. 5, no. 1, 1976; "Southwest Textile Traditions," by Gregory Schaaf, *Indian Artist,* Summer 1997.

*   *   *

Soqween is best known for his watercolors of Pueblo ceremonies, classic scenes with rows of dancers, sacred clowns and spectators. He was among the original San Ildefonso group of Pueblo painters that includes Crescencio Martinez, Julian Martinez, Alfonso Roybal (Awa Tsireh), Tonita Peña, Luis Gonzales, Abel Sanchez (Oqwa Pi), and Romando Vigil. Together with artists from other pueblos, they started a movement in watercolor painting that rendered colorful ceremonies and symbols of the southwest. Along with other promising Pueblo artists, Soqween attended art classes at the School of American Research in Santa Fe. One of the young artists, Hopi painter Fred Kabotie, who became one of the most significant of the pueblo painters, was praised by Soqween as the artist from whom he "learned the most."

Soqween's early work was described by Dorothy Dunn, who taught at The Studio in the Santa Fe Indian School, which Soqween attended, as "Decorative Naturalism." Similar to the work of other Pueblo painters, Soqween's paintings feature stylized figures performing in ceremonies without background details. His flatstyle approach is less precise and refined, not as smooth as those of most other Pueblo artists, as he emphasized emotional qualities that were often rendered through his technique of applying uneven textures. This manner of painting, the colors he selected, and his active approach to subject matter, from initial sketches to the applications of paint, all reflect his interest in relaying emotional and spiritual power. In addition to depicting ceremonial figures, such as Koshares, Soqween also painted wildlife of the area, often infused with mythological associations. *Avanyus of East and West Fighting* (c. 1920) is one of the best examples, with two Avanyus struggling in a dynamic pattern of curving horns and billowing clouds.

Soqween ceased painting during the 1930s while he worked on his farm to support his family. In the 1940s, he returned to his favorite themes: abstract Avanyus, semi-naturalistic dancers in classic Pueblo ceremonials, and the sacred clowns. Soqween was himself a Koshare, an initiated member of the clown society, and took part in fertility rituals and satirical performances. His work from the late 1960s through the mid-1970s, a period in which he was most prolific since the 1920s, brought together his experiences and memories of some of the rarer ceremonies, including the Yucca Dance and Pumpkin Flower Dance. A painting on the latter ceremony from this period is remarkably detailed: six dancers, rendered in bright watercolors, are composed in a slight diagonal composition; orange pumpkin flowers combined with eagle and red scarlet macaw parrot feathers make up their headdresses, fir boughs form their collars, spring from arm bands and are held in their left hands, black rattles shake in their right hands in rhythm with their right raised legs; each wears a white cotton rain sash and red and green embroidered kilt with red garters and fur cuffs. Before the dancers stand three elders wrapped in classic Pueblo striped wear-

ing blankets, so acutely and accurately rendered that the painting was used to illustrate part of a traveling exhibit of pueblo textiles, *Honoring the Weavers* (Poeh Museum, Pueblo of Pojoaque, 1996). In *Yucca Dance* (1975), three black and white striped Koshare clowns perform their antics in the foreground, while ten Yucca dancers are lined up in a strong, horizontal composition. A powerful visual statement is made through the rows of design elements. From top to bottom, the tips of scarlet macaw parrot feathers are flanked by eagle feathers, composing the dancers headdresses. Their painted eyes are framed by their hairstyle, and fir green collars and turquoise armbands create vibrant color bands. Careful examination reveals the more subtle rain and water symbols in the cotton sash and red embroidered kilts. The yucca wands held by the dancers evoke the deeper inner meanings of the ceremony.

—Gregory Schaaf

SOZA, Bill

Variant names: Bill War Soldier
Tribal affiliations: Cahuilla Apache
Painter

Born: Santa Ana, California, 1949. **Education:** Institute of American Indian Arts, Santa Fe, New Mexico, 1964-69. **Career:** Artist and activist.

Selected Group Exhibitions

1966	Institute of American Indian Arts, Santa Fe, New Mexico
1970	Tempe Art Center, Tempe, Arizona
	American Indian Community House, New York
1973-74	*New Directions,* Institute of American Indian Arts Museum, Santa Fe, New Mexico (traveling)
1974	*Institute of American Indian Arts Alumni Exhibition,* Amon Carter Museum of Western Art, Fort Worth, Texas
1975-80	*Pintura Amerindia Contemporanea/E.U.A.,* sponsored by the United States Department of State and International Communications Agency, Washington, D.C.
1981-92	*Confluences of Tradition and Change,* organized by the Richard L. Nelson Gallery and C.N. Gorman Museum, University of California, Davis (traveling)
1987	*Four Sacred Mountains Contemporary Indian Arts Festival,* Tuba City, Arizona
1988-89	*Four Sacred Mountains: Color, Form, and Abstraction,* Arizona Commission on the Arts, Phoenix, Arizona (traveling)
1990-91	*One with the Earth,* organized by the Institute of American Indian Arts and Alaska Culture and Arts Development (traveling)

Collections

Institute of American Indian Arts Museum.

Publications

On SOZA: Books—*Institute of American Indian Arts Alumni Exhibition,* by Lloyd Kiva New, Amon Carter Museum of Western Art, Fort Worth, Texas, 1974; *The Arts of the North American*

Bill Soza: *Self-Portrait.* Photograph by Larry Phillips; courtesy Institute of American Indian Arts Museum, Santa Fe, New Mexico.

Indian: Native Traditions in Evolution, Edwin L. Wade and Rennard Strickland, editors, New York: Hudson Hills Press, 1986; *Creativity Is Our Tradition: Three Decades of Contemporary Indian Art,* by Rick Hill, Santa Fe: Institute of American Indian and Alaska Native Culture and Arts Development, 1992.

*   *   *

Bill Soza was one angry young man. He came to the Institute of American Indian Arts in Santa Fe, New Mexico, on the tidal wave of rebellion that was sweeping the nation. In his mind, everything was corrupt and the treatment of Indians, then and now, was evidence of the depth of the social corruption that existed in American society. He first vented is anger through his work. Soza can be credited with creating the first angry Indian images on canvas in the modern era. He used color, shape, and emotion to present Indians as less than the idealized stereotype, but more than was commonly granted to Indians in the racist environment many Indians grew up in during Soza's youth.

At IAIA, Soza was part of a unique mixture of energetic and talented Indian students who met Indian artists at the right time. Soza, as a contemporary with T.C. Cannon and Alfred Young Man, turned the Indian art world on its head and delighted at it. His work at IAIA had the emerging elements that have become commonplace and his contributions to the field have often been overlooked because of his extreme personality and problems with the law. He firmly believes that it was the students who taught the faculty at IAIA and has stated that the student work influenced what Fritz Scholder (one of the IAIA instructors at the time) has become famous for in the Indian art field. Soza's student work at the IAIA collection seems to bear this out. In many of the student paintings we can see the origins of the tortured features, massive brushwork and intensity of imagery that emerged as the new style of art from Santa Fe. In fairness to all, it was the mixture of talents and the willingness to experiment, oftentimes beyond what even IAIA found

acceptable, that produced the Indian/Pop/Abstract movement. Soza was the spiritual heart of that movement.

Soza's *Ghost Dance* triptych shows the bold use of color, the juxtaposition of Indian symbols and written text on the art itself, and the intense emotional message that was the strength of Soza's early work. Soza, like many of the student artists at IAIA, focused on the warrior and past struggles for freedom. However, the past and present collided in Soza's life. He became very active in protest movements, leading him to the takeover of the Mayflower at Plymouth Rock on Thanksgiving Day, 1970, and later occupations of Alcatraz Island and the Bureau of Indian Affairs building in Washington D.C. Soza became a federal fugitive and spent years on the run. He served time in prison and turned back to his art to express himself. He found that he could say the same kind of things as he did during the protests, but that because it was art, he would not suffer legal reprisals. In 1991, he returned to Santa Fe to focus more directly on his career, but legal problems caught up to him again and he has returned to prison. Unfortunately, the brilliance that he once demonstrated in the arts has been weakened by his real-life travails. At the same time, we need to recognize that Soza opened the artistic doors through which many have walked. Without his work at IAIA, it is difficult to imagine where the careers of Scholder, Cannon, and many others might have led instead of the creative and challenging nature they realized—made possible, in part, by the volatile and feisty nature of Soza, the artistic war soldier.

—Rick Hill

SPANG, Bently

Tribal affiliations: Cheyenne
Sculptor and installation artist

Born: Crow Agency, Montana, 1960. **Education:** Eastern Montana College, B.S. in art (extended sculpture) and marketing, 1991; University of Wisconsin, M.F.A., 1996. **Career:** Pipe fitter; graduate assistant, 1993, teaching assistant, 1995, University of Wisconsin; co-curator, Toucan Gallery, 1991, and Northcutt-Steele Gallery, 1992, Billings, Montana; artist-in-residence, Fondo del Sol Visual Arts, Washington, D.C., 1992; guest curator, Denver Museum, 1993-95, Fort Lewis College, 1994-95, for *Artists Who Are Indian,* Custer County Art Center, Miles City, Montana, 1995, Fifth Eiteljorg Museum Invitational, Inidanapolis, Indiana, 1996; panelist, various symposia, conferences, and selection committees; site evaluator, National Endowment for the Arts Expansion Arts Program, Washington, D.C., 1994; executive director, Montana Indian Contemporary Arts. **Awards:** ARCO Academic Undergraduate Scholarship, 1987; Community Scholar Fellowship, Smithsonian Institution, National Museum of Natural History, American Indian Program, and National Museum of the American Indian, research project exploring geometric design and mythology of Plains Indians tribes, 1992; various other scholarships and fellowships. **Address:** c/o Montana Indian Contemporary Arts, Billings, and Jan Cicero Gallery, 221 W. Erie, Chicago, Illinois 60610.

Individual Exhibitions

1992   *The Healing* (mixed media installation), Western Heritage
        Center, Billings, Montana
1994   Dahl Fine Arts Center, Rapid City, South Dakota

Bently Spang: *Hoxouestaue (Journey Across Country)*, Arapahoe County, Aurora, Colorado. Courtesy of the artist.

1995   *Transitions,* Northern Plains Tribal Arts Gallery, Sioux Falls, South Dakota

Selected Group Exhibitions

1990   *Celebrate Montana,* Haynes Hall Gallery, Montana State University, Bozeman
        Montana Indian Contemporary Arts Symposium, Pablo, Montana
        The International Icon Show, Castle Gallery, Billings, Montana
        Electrum XIX, Holter Museum of Art, Helena, Montana
        Introductions, Montana Indian Contemporary Art (traveling through 1992)
1991   *Ten Views,* Invitational Group Show, Toucan Gallery, Billings, Montana
        Submuloc Show/Columbus Wohs, Atlatl, Phoenix (traveling through 1993)
1992   *Submuloc Show,* Montana Indian Contemporary Art (traveling)
        The Contemporary Room, permanent invitational group show, traveling, based at Plains Indian Museum, Buffalo Bill Historical Society, Cody, Wyoming
1993   *Native Peoples,* Denver Art Museum

Signals in Sculpture, Institute of American Indian Art Museum, Santa Fe
Bountiful Bowls, Sutton West Gallery, Missoula, Montana (annual homeless benefit)
The Spirit of Native America, American Indian Contemporary Arts, San Francisco (traveling through 1995)
1994   *Sixth Heard Native American Fine Art Invitational,* Heard Musem, Phoenix
        The Fourth Eiteljorg Museum Invitational: New Art of the West, Eiteljorg Museum, Indianapolis
        Native Expressions, Golden West Gallery, Telluride, Colorado
        Native Hotheads, Santa Fe Arts Center
1994   *Indian Humor,* American Indian Contemporary Art, San Francisco (traveling through 1997)
1995   *Native Streams,* Indian State University and Jan Cicero Gallery, Chicago (traveling)
        American Indian Community House Gallery, New York
        Recent Acquisitions, Institute of American Indian Arts Museum, Santa Fe (traveled to Bogota, Columbia)
        Phoenix Gallery, New York
        Spirit of Native America, Festival de Lille, France and Salt Lake Arts Center, Utah
1996   *Group Show,* University of North Carolina, Charlotte

Wisconsin Triennial, Madison Arts Center, Wisconsin

Gifts of the Spirit, Peabody Essex Museum, Salem, Massachusetts

Much Ado about Something, 23rd Avenue Gallery, Denver, Colorado

Mexican Cowboys and Indian Lowriders (performance), Holter Museum, Helena, Montana

Publications

On SPANG: Catalogs—*The Sixth Heard Native American Fine Art Invitational,* Heard Musem, Phoenix, 1994; *The Fourth Eiteljorg Museum Invitational: New Art of the West,* Eiteljorg Museum, Indianapolis, 1994; *Native Streams Contemporary American Indian Art,* Jan Cicero Gallery, Chicago, and Indianapolis State University, Terre Haute, 1996. **Articles**—"Rice Krispies to Mixed Media," *Indian Country Today* (Rapid City, South Dakota), 5 October 1994; "Art in Transition" by Richard Nilson, *Arizona Republic,* 5 October 1994; "Danny's Column" by Danny Madina, *ArtTalk* (Scottsdale, Arizona), November, 1994;"Sculptor Strives to Define Himself in Modern Times" by Lynn Taylor, *Rapid City Journal,* 24 October 1994; "Bently Spang's Sculptures Deserve Our Attention" by Darrel D. Nelson, *Rapid City Journal,* 6 November 1994; "Metastasis en la Cultura," *La Prensa* (Bogota, Colombia), 15 September 1994; "Art and Soul" by Susan Blocker, *Wisconsin State Journal* (Madison), 19 March 1995; "Land Put in Context" by Ann Gravugol, *Argus Leader,* Sioux Falls, South Dakota, 13 July 1995; "Indians' Tribute" by Alan Snel, *Denver Post,* 23 December 23; "Forward to the Past" by Mary Chandler, *Rocky Mountain News* (Denver) 26 March 1996. **Television**—Interview, Public Broadcasting System (PBS), station WYOU, 14 April 1995.

Collections

Eiteljorg Museum of American Indian and Western Art, Indianapolis; Heard Museum, Phoenix; Institute of American Indian Art Museum, Santa Fe; Montana State University, Billings; University of North Carolina, Charlotte.

*

Bently Spang comments:

My work explores the issues surrounding my identity as a contemporary Northern Cheyenne and the challenges inherent in that existence. Each of the mediums that I choose have personal significance and thus act as metaphor for various aspects of my existence. My use of natural materials juxtaposed with man-made speaks of my mixed blood heritage (Cheyenne, Ogala Lakota, Chippewa, Cree, Spanish, and French) and the complexity of my experience being raised Cheyenne in a contemporary world. I grew up both on and off the reservation and was influenced by both worlds—worlds that are often on a collision course with each other. I have always identified with my Cheyenne heritage and my work examines how that identity manifests itself in these contemporary times. In speaking of the nature of my existence today, I feel that I am continuing a tradition of making which my ancestors and my relatives passed on to me. It is a way of making that has always defined our existence as Native people from within the culture (too often we are defined from without), and, in so doing, provided strategies for our continued survival. (From *Native Streams: Contemporary Native American Art*)

*   *   *

Striking a sophisticated balance between the personal and the tribal, the aesthetic and the political, Bently Spang's sculptures have earned him a position in the forefront of the Native American Fine Arts Movement. As an occasional curator, panelist, and performance artist, Spang has helped define this movement verbally as well as visually, calling for a politically responsible and materially original body of work.

Spang identifies himself as a political artist, but says his messages are often quite subtle. Much of his work addresses the challenges he has faced as a man of mixed heritage (Cheyenne, Oglala Lakota, Chippewa Cree, Spanish, and French) growing up in a highly mobile, multicultural society. Born in 1960 at the Crow Agency hospital, on the Crow reservation in Montana, Spang was raised both on and off the reservation he calls home, Northern Cheyenne. His father worked for the Bureau of Indian Affairs, so the family was constantly moving, never spending more than a few years in one place. Consequently, Spang grew up in Alaska, Washington, Oregon, and Montana, but was always around Indian people.

Spang received his artistic training at the University of Wisconsin-Madison under the tutelage of Truman Lowe, an internationally acclaimed Winnebago sculptor and multi-media artist. But before committing himself to the life of an artist, Spang took business classes at Eastern Montana College, and worked in the construction industry for five years as a pipe fitter. This experience helps explain Spang's affinity for industrial materials and large-scale works, exemplified in a recent outdoor installation, *Hoxouestaue (Journey Across Country,* 1996), commissioned by Arapaho County, Colorado, which measures 22 feet tall, 50 feet long, and incorporates structural steel and lodgepole pine into the form of a travois.

His juxtaposition of natural and man-made materials is simultaneously intellectual and experimental. Materials such as the cast aluminum, cow bone, slate, cedar, steel, and sinew used in *The Healing Series: Metastasis* (1993) make literal and metaphoric references to the artist's bicultural existence, to the survival and persistence of Native peoples and values in the modern, industrialized world, and to the ability of all indigenous peoples to overcome adversity. The focus on healing is personal, reflecting Spang's search to find a balance between the native world and the non-native world.

"This self-healing really was a combination of understanding the power of the creative process and my place in the continuum of making that my people handed on to me," Spang explains. Hailing from a family of traditional bead artists, Spang appreciates the value of cultural adaptability. "The realization that I, as a contemporary Native person, am creating in much the same way that my ancestors created, combining indigenous materials with materials outside the culture to speak about life at that moment, was very powerful and very humbling."

The cocoon form found in Spang's work is related to the theme of healing, representing transition and change. Human beings enter cocoons during difficult parts of their lives in order to experience change or growth, and emerge renewed, the artist explained. This sensation of wholeness and renewal is directly at odds with the sense of "cultural dismemberment" Spang says he feels when faced with Anglo-American representations of Native American cultures and peoples.

As a relative newcomer to the Native American art world, Spang has achieved rapid success. He was chosen for the Sixth Heard Native American Fine Art Invitational in 1994, and was invited to curate the exhibit *Artists Who Are Indian* at the Denver Art Museum the same year.

—Margaret Dubin

SPYBUCK, Ernest

Tribal affiliations: Shawnee
Painter

Born: Potawatomi-Shawnee Reservation, Oklahoma, 1883. **Career:** Painter, historian, farmer. **Died:** 1949.

Selected Group Exhibitions

1937   American Indian Exposition and Congress, Tulsa, Oklahoma
1978   *100 Years of Native American Art,* Oklahoma Museum of Art, Oklahoma City (traveling)
1982-84 Museum of the American Indian, New York
1991-92 *Shared Visions: Native American Painters and Sculptors in the Twentieth Century,* Heard Museum, Phoenix, Arizona (traveling)

Collections

Gilcrease Museum, Tulsa, Oklahma; Heard Museum, Phoenix, Arizona; Oklahoma Historical Society Museum, Oklahoma City; Museum of the American Indian, Smithsonian Institution, Washington, D.C.

Publications

On SPYBUCK: Books—*Religion and Ceremonies of the Lenape,* by Mark Raymond Harrington, New York: Museum of the American Indian, 1921; *A Pictorial History of the American Indian,* by Oliver LaFarge, New York: Crown Publishers, 1956; *The American Indian,* by Oliver LaFarge, New York: Golden Press, 1960; *Memoirs of a Pioneer Teacher,* by Harriet Patrick Gilstrap, Oklahoma City: Oklahoma Historical Society, 1960; *Red Man's Religion: Beliefs and Practices of the Indians North of Mexico,* by Ruth M. Underhill, Chicago: University of Chicago Press, 1965; *Indian Painters and White Patrons,* by J. J. Brody, Albuquerque: University of New Mexico Press, 1971; *Great North American Indians: Profiles in Life and Leadership,* by Frederick J. Dockstader, New York: Van Nostrand Reinhold Company, 1977; *100 Years of Native American Art,* by Arthur Silberman, Oklahoma City: Oklahoma Museum of Art, 1978; *Many Smokes, Many Moons: An American Indian Chronology,* by Jamake Highwater, New York: J. B. Lippincott, 1978; *Native American Painting - Selections from the Museum of the American Indian,* by David M. Fawcett and Lee A. Callander, New York: Museum of the American Indian, 1982; *Home Life: The Paintings of Ernest Spybuck Shawnee,* by Lee A. Callander and Ruth Slivka, New York: Museum of the American Indian, 1984; *Shared Visions: Native American Painters and Sculptors of the Twentieth Century,* by Margaret Archuleta and Renard Strickland, Phoenix: The Heard Museum, 1991.

*   *   *

Ernest Spybuck's painting is unique among well-known Oklahoma Native American artists for not being affected by the same influences that defined the Kiowa or Studio styles. Spybuck's work developed and matured before either of those dominant Native American painting styles were codified. Spybuck's work is easily identifiable as having been created by an untrained artist. In fact, in Western European art history terms, it is naive art. Yet, it is different from most naive painting in two important ways. First, it shows the influence of ethnographic patronage and is consequently more inclusive of certain details than naive painting in general. Second, it is infused with a sense of humor and personality rarely seen in naive painting of similar style.

Spybuck shows a meticulous attention to detail in the depiction of the ceremonial life of the Shawnee and other Oklahoma tribes. This is partly due to the influence of his chief patron, the ethnologist M.R. Harrington. However, Spybuck was drawing images of Shawnee daily life long before his association with Harrington. He simply continued what he had been doing since childhood. As he grew, his drawing matured and developed concurrently with his participation in Shawnee ceremonies and gatherings. Spybuck also portrayed the ritual practices held in common by tribes who associated with his own, including depictions of peyote ceremonies of the Kickapoo or Delaware. For ethnologists, his paintings are documentation of those practices as well as daily life. Spybuck was himself a participant in peyote ceremonies and was especially attentive to details when depicting them, as evidenced by the addition of inserts to represent different phases of the ceremony.

Formal and informal community gatherings are the subjects of most of Spybuck's paintings. The composition usually provides an overall sense of the activity very clearly read as a dance, a prayer meeting, or a ball game. Within this overall view is a more intimate treatment of the individuals within the group. Spybuck subtly hints at attitudes and personalities of those individuals. A sideways glance, a stooped posture, a thoughtful bowing of the head, all show the vitality of the group through the sum of the individual personalities. These whimsical inclusions on the periphery often contrast the more serious central focus of the piece. A depiction of a war dance ceremony shows dignified men engaged in the somber event, yet a carefree dog trots through camp in the background. In *Sauk and Fox Buffalo Dance,* the center of attention is the group of alert dancers in ceremonial dress. Yet, to the side is contrasted a singular figure, plainly dressed, sleeping with a hat over his face. Such a contrast in action and rest, respect and unconcern, activity and leisure is the essence of Spybuck's humor that adds a level of interest. This is in contrast to the exclusively ethnographic interest that might have been expected from commissions by Harrington. Ethnographic information is viewed within the context of friends and family, and the subtle details of daily life. This makes the "charm" of Spybuck's work all the more important. It reveals an insider's intimate perspective. Ironically, this makes Spybuck's paintings even more valuable to ethnologists, as well as to more general audiences.

—Kevin Smith

STANDING BEAR

Variant names: Mato Najin
Tribal affiliations: Oglala Lakota
Painter

Born: 1868. **Career:** Warrior, participated in the Battle of Little Big Horn. Buffalo Bill's Wild West Show, 1887-91; historian and artist. **Died:** 1933.

Selected Group Exhibitions

1992   *Visions of the People*, Minneapolis Museum of Art (traveling through 1993)

Collections

Beuchel Memorial Museum, St. Francis Mission, St. Francis, South Dakota; Denver Art Museum, Colorado; Foundation for the Preservation of American Indian Art and Cultures, Inc., Chicago; Milwaukee Public Museum, Wisconsin; Philbrook Museum, Tulsa, Oklahoma; St. Joseph Museum, St. Joseph, Missouri; State Historical Society of South Dakota, Pierre.

Publications

On STANDING BEAR: Books—*The Sixth Grandfather: Black Elk's Teachings Given to John Neihardt*, edited by Raymond DeMallie, Lincoln: University of Nebraska Press, 1984; "Sacrifice Transformed Into Victory: Standing Bear Portrays Sitting Bull's Sun Dance and the Final Summer of Lakota Freedom" by Peter Powell, *Visions of the People*, edited by Evan Maurer, Minneapolis: The Minneapolis Institute of Arts, 1992.

*   *   *

Standing Bear was born into Crazy Horse's band of the Oglala division of the Lakota and spent his early years as a migratory hunter and warrior. At age seventeen he participated in the Battle of Little Big Horn, an event that he would depict in several paintings on muslin at the beginning of the twentieth century. In 1887 he joined Buffalo Bill's Wild West Show, traveling in Europe until 1891, when he returned to the Pine Ridge Reservation, where he lived until his death in 1933.

Standing Bear's most ambitious work is a six-feet-square muslin painted with vignettes of Lakota ceremonialism and scenes from the Battle of Little Big Horn. Like Amos Bad Heart Bull, he was among the first Lakota artists to experiment with ambitious visual narrative and detailed depictions of traditional life. His work comprises a visual ethnography of Lakota ceremony and history. Unlike most Lakota artists of his generation, he focused both on male and female experiences, not just male warrior iconography. His visual narratives include genre scenes of the camp circle, women moving household goods by travois, and scenes of courtship and food preparation.

Other painted muslins by Standing Bear are found in the Philbrook Museum in Tulsa and the State Historical Society of South Dakota in Pierre, both of which also focus on Lakota warfare and traditional life. A series of drawings on paper were commissioned as illustrations of the recollections of Standing Bear and his friend, Black Elk, published in *Black Elk Speaks*. These illustrate scenes of the Battle of Little Big Horn of 1876, the Wounded Knee Massacre of 1890, the Horse Dance, and scenes in the life of Black Elk, including his renowned visions. Another series of unpublished drawings on paper resides in the Beuchel Memorial Museum, St. Francis Mission, St. Francis, South Dakota. Depicting clothing and implements of Lakota ceremonial practitioners and military societies, these drawings were commissioned by Father Eugene Beuchel as part of his study of Lakota traditions and practices.

Standing Bear (not related to Luther Standing Bear, a well-known Sioux author of the same generation) was the great-grandfather of Arthur Amiotte; his image appears as an important iconic element in Amiotte's work. Standing Bear lived at a time when the old traditions were under siege and apparently disappearing. His impulse to record the historical and ceremonial traditions of the Lakota has served as inspiration for successive generations of Lakota artists, who find in his work validation of Lakota history and art history from a native perspective.

—Janet Catherine Berlo

STEVENS, Maxx
Tribal affiliations: Seminole
Mixed media artist and installation artist

Born: Charlene Maxine Stevens in Wewoka, Oklahoma, 6 May 1951. **Education:** Haskell Indian Junior College, Lawrence, Kansas, A.A., fine arts, 1972; Wichita State University, Wichita, Kansas, B.F.A., sculpture and ceramics, 1979; Indiana University, Bloomington, Indiana, M.F.A., sculpture, 1987; also studied at United Welding Institute, Wichita, Kansas. **Career:** Associate instructor, sculpture and foundation departments, Indiana University, Bloomington, Indiana, 1982-85; visiting artist, sculpture department, Wichita State University, Wichita, Kansas, 1985-86; theatre artisan, Music Theatre of Wichita, Wichita, Kansas, 1986-90 (summers); visiting artist, technical assistant, Iron Pour Class, The School at Ox-Bow, Saugatuck, Michigan, August, 1989; visiting artist, sculpture department, School of the Art Institute of Chicago, 1989-91; professor of foundation and three-dimensional arts and chair, foundation arts department, The Institute of American Indian Arts, Santa Fe, New Mexico, 1991-96; visiting professor, fine arts, University of Northern Iowa, Cedar Falls, Iowa, 1996 (summer). **Awards:** Indian Arts Studies, Fine Arts Award, Haskell Indian Junior College, Lawrence, Kansas, 1972; Minority Studies Scholarship, Wichita State University, Wichita, Kansas, 1978-79; American Indian Graduate Studies Scholarship, New York, 1982-85; New Forms Regional Grant, Alternative Arts Category, Randolph Street Gallery, Chicago, 1990; SITE Santa Fe, Regional and Local Artist Endorsement Award, Santa Fe, New Mexico, 1995.

Individual Exhibitions

1987   *Fans, Installation #1*, Lawrence, Kansas
1995   *Ghost Lights* (collaboration with Melanie Yazzie), Institution of American Indian Arts Museum, Santa Fe

Selected Group Exhibitions

1988   *1/2 Mile Art Show*, Century II Gallery, Wichita, Kansas
1989   *Bodies and Walls*, Wicker Park, Chicago
1990   *Re-collecting Memory*, Kalpulli Gallery, Chicago
        Graceland Art Rodeo II, Graceland Sculpture Yard, Calgary, Alberta, Canada
1991   *Gigantic Women-Miniature Art Show*, Gallery Two, School of the Art Institute of Chicago
        Symbolic Language, North Lakeshore Culture Center, Chicago
1992   *Graceland Art Rodeo IV*, Graceland Sculpture Yard, Calgary, Alberta, Canada

Maxx Stevens: *History: True or False*, 1993. Courtesy of the artist.

Like That There Show, C.A.G.E. Gallery, Cincinnati, Ohio

1993   *501 Blues/501 Years of Post Columbian Resistance in the Americas*, Core Gallery, Denver

Before There Were Borders/Beyond Imaginary Lines, The Gallery at the Rep, Santa Fe

Santa Fe Outdoor Sculpture Show, College of Santa Fe, New Mexico

1994   *Watchful Eyes: Native American Women Artists*, Heard Museum, Phoenix

Crows Carry the Story, Kansas University Student Union Gallery, Kansas University, Lawrence

Tres Caras/Three Faces, Dustin Gallery, Gallup, New Mexico

Artists Who Are Indian, Denver Art Museum, Colorado

Volume I: Book Arts by Native American Artists, American Indian Community House Gallery, New York

1995   *SITE Santa Fe Endorsement Show*, Warehouse, Santa Fe

CSF Sculpture Project, College of Santa Fe, New Mexico

Mapped Out: Reinventing the New Mexico Landscape, Fine Arts Gallery, School of the Arts, University of California, Irvine

Volume I: Book Arts by Native American Artists, American Indian Contemporary Arts, San Francisco

Artists Who Are Indian, Part II, Fine Arts Gallery, Fort Lewis College, Durango, Colorado

Something Borrowed, Santa Fe Fine Arts Museum, Santa Fe

1996   *The Shrine Show of 1996/A Night of 100 Drummers*, Institute of American Indian Arts Museum, Santa Fe

Up and Running, Center for Contemporary Arts, Santa Fe

Women of Color, Federal Bank Gallery, Boston

Publications

On STEVENS: Book—*Watchful Eyes: Native American Women Artists*, The Heard Museum, Phoenix, Arizona, 1994. **Article**—"Voices: Contemporary Artists Speaking About Their Lives," *Indian Artist 1*, No. 1, 1995.

*

Maxx Stevens comments:

Working from the Native point of view in my art work, I have drawn upon issues about history, archeology, and the stereotyping placed upon Native people. I have been developing my own language through the use of materials based upon my own personal reactions and looking for new directions to work out these important questions and concepts. Being an urban Indian has always been a source of dualism in my work, and that sometimes gives the viewer a sense of the conflict it generates. I find that I work dramatically, using space as my "canvas" in developing visual stories, placing various objects in that space to give the viewer hints as to what I am trying to say. My art work reflects me as a human being who is an artist, but most importantly draws upon my own culture, the Seminole Nation of Oklahoma.

*   *   *

Maxx Stevens' art tells stories of identity, family, culture, and history and explores the interrelationships among them. She uses the techniques she learned as a theater artisan, sculptor, and welder to create diverse multi-media installations, some of which literally strip away external environments to interrogate the meanings of history, while others present autobiographical details of the artist's experience and the impact of family and culture on that experience.

Space and lighting take on significance in Stevens' installations and reveal her training in theatre. She typically utilizes yellow, blue, red, and white lights to emphasize certain figures and to make an area dominant. She tries to create a sense of calm or agitation, for example, in the viewer by the use of light.

Fragments of Life (1994) centers on a small, battered, multiple-drawer filing cabinet that was cut in half with a blowtorch and suggested an open book. The drawers of the cabinet, representing pages in an autobiography, contained documents, statements, photos, and drawings that provide details of Stevens' life. The pages begin with the history of Native people, move to the history of the Seminole Nation, to Stevens' personal history of being Seminole and growing up in an urban environment, and finally to the present concerns of Native people. Titles of the multi-media pages included "Removal," "Where the Indians Lived Excavation," "Enrollment," "Urban Indians Fighting Surviving in Cities," "Mother," and "Future."

The image of the book also figures in *History: True or False* (1993), an outdoor installation that was on the grounds of the College of Santa Fe. Stevens placed four old school chairs on the inside edge of a circular excavation. Bolted onto each of these four chairs was a mold of a book that she made from a high school history text. Written on the cover of the first one was "History," followed by "True," "Or," and "False" on the successive books. The installation dealt with the stereotypical portrayal and damaging myths that surround Native people. In the central excavation were figures in different stages of completeness. One figure is fully formed with a cement head; the second figure has to do with breaking away from that solid form; while the third figure was very fragmented, made of barbed wire and a little concrete. This particular piece spoke about the creation of false histories, the schoolbook histories, which, she suggests, persist to this day.

Much of Stevens' work concerns the stripping away of facades to reveal the interiority of spaces. *FANS, Installation #1* (1987), was a piece that was built as a room in part of Stevens' loft. She constructed the room with no nails or screws, using wood, paper, sticks, and found objects. The audience walked directly up the stairs of her loft into the environment. The construction reflected her philosophy that, as a Native person, she is living in two worlds and must maintain a balance between the two.

A similar piece in the *Gigantic Women/Miniature Art* show (1991) revealed interior spaces. Stevens had a small room that used to be a vault for chemicals. The whole space was a metaphor for the human being, with the room being the center. There was a box in the middle of the space, which was the miniature installation, that had the same icons on the exterior of the room, but they had a distressed and aged feel; in the center of the box was another small box, and

inside of that one was a heart. Stevens sought to create a contrast between surface appearance and internal reality, not only in terms of the space itself but also as it relates to individual psychology.

In *Dreaming of Circles and Chairs* (1991) she used two rooms to stress the exterior and interior architecture of the site. In each room were ambiguous figures suggesting human form in psychological dilemma, perhaps asleep, perhaps dead. The piece reflected on her exploration of the disparity between her rural experience with her tribe and her residence in Wichita. The work posed a question: "If you're urban, are you Indian? If you're not, what are you?" The work was her response.

Where *Fragments of Life* and Stevens' larger installations focus on history and identity, an installation from 1994, *Aunt Nelly: My Story*, focuses on family, specifically her Aunt Nelly, and her aunt's impact on her life. Stevens built a small kitchen table with four small benches that were raised up on a porch-like element. On the table were familiar objects of domesticity, coffee cups, and plates, and on each bench was a book of images, depicting Stevens as a child, her aunt, her father, and his family. The images represent the inhabitants of the house and the unity of the family. On the porch she placed putty, which cracked like dried dirt, and scattered twigs and sticks to suggest her rural experience. Hanging over the installation was her aunt's apron, which was left to the artist after her aunt's death.

This work, like many others of hers, connects past with present, history with the individual, and makes a bridge between cultural and personal memory. It can be viewed as a visual analogue of the oral tradition, in this case conveying the teachings of her aunt. Stevens' work is a way of passing on personal, familial, and cultural information.

—Larry Abbott

STEWART, Kathryn

Variant names: Carries the Colors; Kathryn Livermore
Tribal affiliations: Crow; Blackfeet
Painter

Born: Kathryn Marie Stewart Livermore, California, 25 June 1951. **Education:** Mills College, Oakland, California, BA, painting, 1974; Montana State University, Bozeman, Masters in Education, 1984. **Career:** Coordinator, American Indian Research Project, Montana State University, 1984-88; Executive Director, American Indian Contemporary Arts, San Francisco, 1989; Coordinator, Native American Graduate Fellowship Program, Center for Native American Studies, Montana State University, 1989-93; founder (with her sister, Susan Stewart), Montana Indian Contemporary Arts (MICA), a nonprofit regional Native arts service organization; board member, American Indian Art Organization; curator; instructor and lecturer on Native American art. **Died:** 22 October 1993.

Selected Group Exhibitions

1969   Dallas Summer Arts Festival, Texas
1972   *Teacher's Choice,* University Gallery, University of Nevada, Reno

1975   *American Indian Contemporary Art,* Marin County Civic
        Center, San Rafael, California
1976   *In'Din Art'I Faks,* Humboldt Cultural Center, Humboldt,
        California
        Painted Desert National Park, Holbrook, Arizona
1977   *New Horizons in American Indian Art,* Southwest Mu-
        seum, Los Angeles
        Three Indians, Two Dimensions, C. N. Gorman Museum,
        University of California, Davis
1978   *Native American Contemporary Art,* International Art-
        ists Embassy Gallery, San Francisco, California
1979   Museum of the Plains Indian, Browning, Montana
1981   *Sweet Pea Festival,* Artifacts Gallery, Browning, Montana
1982   *Night of the First Americans,* Via Gambaro Art Gallery,
        Washington, D.C.
1983   Danforth Art Gallery, Livingston, Montana
1984   Touchstone Art Gallery, Spokane, Washington
        Sacred Circle Gallery, Seattle, Washington
1985   *Homecoming,* North Dakota Museum of Art, Grand
        Forks, North Dakota
1986   Black Orchid Gallery, Butte, Montana
1987   *Traditions in a New Age,* Museum of the Rockies, Mon-
        tana State University, Bozeman
1988   Marilyn Butler Fine Arts, Santa Fe, New Mexico
        About Survival, Multi cultural Arts Festival, Berkeley,
        California
1989   *Four Sacred Mountains: Color, Form & Abstraction,*
        Arizona Commission on the Arts, Phoenix
        WARM Gallery, Minneapolis, Minnesota
        *Women's Work, The Montana Women's Centennial Art
        Survey Exhibition, 1889-1989* (traveling)
1989-90 *Native Proof,* American Indian Contemporary Arts Gal-
        lery, San Francisco, California
1992   *Submuloc Show/Columbus Wohs,* Evergreen College,
        Olympia, Washington (traveling)

Collections

Museum of the Plains Indians, Browning, Montana.

Publications

On STEWART: Books—*New Horizons in American Indian Art,*
Southwest Museum, Los Angeles, 1976; *Sublumoc Show/Colum-
bus Wohs,* Atlatl, Phoenix, 1992. **Articles**—"Completing the Circle:
The Lifework of Kathryn Stewart," by Bently Spang, *Montana
Crossroads Magazine,* Vol.1, Issue 1, April 1997 (slightly revised
version reprinted below, with permission of the author).

*   *   *

The first time I met Kathryn Stewart was in 1989, across a table
cluttered with my litho prints at the Big Sky Indian Market in
Billings, Montana. I was an undergraduate art major at Eastern
Montana College and had volunteered for the market, so they gave
me some space to show my work. I reluctantly accepted, knowing
that people would see my abstract work and think, "that's not
Indian art! Where's the tipi's, where's the buffalo, how come there's
no hill with an Indian on it?" I had suffered the looks and unspoken
questions all day when Kathryn and her sister, Susan, approached
my table.

They saw my work, handed me a business card, and said, "Your
work doesn't belong here, it belongs in museum shows or galleries.
Give us a call, we can help." As they left a feeling of relief washed
over me. They had read my mind. The business card read, "Montana
Indian Contemporary Arts (MICA), Kathryn Stewart, Executive Director." I eventually made the call, and the rest, as they say, is history.

As I was to later learn, Kathy and MICA, the Native arts organization she co-founded, were synonymous, inseparable. As inseparable as her connection to her sister Susan, her daughter Maya, and
her artwork. One cannot speak of Kathy's life without, in large
part, speaking of these connections to family and to her organization. Over the next four years I came to know Kathryn as mentor,
colleague, and friend, until her much-too-soon death in 1993. She
was a gentle, passionate, brilliant person, gifted artist, and a patriot
within the Contemporary Native North American art movement.
Her example has greatly influenced my life.

Though they were born two years apart, the Stewart sisters
seemed more like twins, doing everything together. They were so
close people often mistook one for the other throughout their lives.
Those of us in the Indian arts movement who knew them often
referred to them as simply "The Stewart Sisters." One of the few
divergences in their life occurred when they chose colleges to attend. Kathy, the more demure, introspective of the two, chose
Mills College in Oakland, an all girls liberal arts college with an ivy
league reputation. Susan's more brash, outgoing personality lead
her to the California College of Arts and Crafts in San Francisco.
Both obviously pursued art degrees.

Stylistically speaking, the Stewart's art work seemed to match
their personalities near perfectly. Though their palettes were at
times similar, their approach to the work was quite different.
Kathryn's work is measured and deliberate, with a soft, ethereal
edge. Susan's is all about expressed energy, frenetic and intuitive.
Both expressed personal concepts specifically surrounding their
spiritual connection as Crow women with the earth. Kathryn's
signature, besides her gossamer-soft handling of the medium, was
her use of the crow as a central motif. For her the bird represented
the Crow people, herself included. The Crow believe themselves to
be the children of "The Big Beaked Bird." The bird, known to them
as Absaaloogke, was a Thunderbird-like being that created the Crow
people. Crow people say "bay' Absaalookge," "we are
Absaaloogke."

Throughout her artist's life Kathryn would return to the crow
again and again, placing one, two, perhaps three within surreal,
numinous landscapes. She, in fact, spoke of the influence of the
surrealists in her work who, ironically, were influenced by early
Native art. The art historian Rennard Strickland refers to this as,
"A mirror reflecting back on a mirror," implying that the Indian
artist accesses their culture only after it has been run through the
filter of Western culture. I disagree. Strickland's analogy implies a
separation of Indian people from the art and culture of our past. To
the Indian way of thinking, Kathryn's work really represents the
completion of the circle of existence. It is a handing on. Just as her
ancestors interpreted their experience in their time period with the
materials at hand, so too did Kathryn, and both have handed it on to
the next generation through the artwork. And, inherent in the artwork, in the handing on, is a wealth of cultural information thousands of years old.

After college, the sisters naturally gravitated toward other Indian
artists in the bay area. They joined forces with people like Jean
LaMarr, George Longfish, Frank LaPena, and Linda Lomaheftewa,
all household names within the Contemporary Native North Ameri-

Kathryn Stewart: *Night Spirits,* 1989. Collection of Maya Bronston; courtesy of Susan Stewart.

can arts movement today. At the time there weren't many opportunities for contemporary Native artists to show their work: the art world wasn't quite sure what to make of this "radical" shift in Indian art. The group strategized ways to get exposure, learned the ropes of the art business, and eventually started to get some exhibitions in the area as well as across the nation. They connected with other Native artists around the country and a network began to develop, like a national version of the Indian community, where artists dialogued and referred each other to exhibition opportunities. It would prove to be an invaluable experience for both Kathryn and Susan, one they would draw from often in the future.

In the late 70's the sisters made their way back to Montana. Kathryn moved to Hardin, Montana, and worked for the Crow tribe, Susan married and moved to Bozeman. They each birthed children, Kathryn had Maya and Susan had Vanessa and Noah. Kathryn eventually moved to Bozeman to pursue a masters degree in education, and graduated from Montana State University in 1981. The longer they were back in Montana the more they began to notice a wealth of talented Native artists in the state and the region. With their own work established in exhibitions nationally, Kathryn and Susan began pursuing regional and Montana venues for their work and the work of other Montana Indian artists. One thing became painfully clear in this process: as limited as the opportuni-

ties were for contemporary Indian artists nationally, they were even more limited in Montana and the region.

Instead of being discouraged, however, the sisters took the situation as a challenge. They re-started the network they had established in California and began a dialogue with other Native artists concerning how to get more exposure for Native artists in Montana and the region. What became obvious is that it would take an organized effort to make any kind of effective change. What was really needed was a Native arts service organization.

In 1986, as they were beginning to explore ways to create this organization, Kathryn received devastating news: she had a brain tumor. She endured a harrowing four hour surgery and the tumor was removed. Although the tumor was found to be cancerous, the doctors were confident they had gotten all of it. Kathryn recovered fully and resumed her work.

In lieu of a formal organization, the Stewart's took it upon themselves to become watchdogs for the contemporary Indian art movement in Montana. They challenged art institutions and art agencies throughout Montana to make a greater commitment to contemporary Indian artists in the state. Finally, in 1989, the sisters got the break they were looking for: they were asked to become board members of a fledgling organization called the Montana Indian Arts and Culture Association (MIACA).

Susan and Kathryn agreed to join and were elected as President and Secretary of the board respectively. With only $5,000 in the organization's bank account, they set about the task of recruiting Indian artists and friends to help structure the organization to better serve the needs of Montana Indian artists. They brought Montana Indian artists like Juane Quick-to-See Smith, Corwin Clairmont, and Dwight Billedeaux, from the Salish-Kootenai Nation and Neil Parsons and Ernie Pepion from the Blackfeet Nation onto the board and MICA was born. The mission of the organization became to provide Montana Indian artists with networking opportunities and to promote awareness of high quality contemporary Indian art in the region. While both the sisters dedicated themselves to the organization, it was Kathryn who most enjoyed the "nuts and bolts" administrative work that the organization required, so much so that she volunteered her time as Executive Director of MICA in order to ensure the fulfillment of the organization's mission. By day she worked as Coordinator of the Native American Graduate Fellowship Programs at Montana State University in Bozeman, but her heart was really in her work with MICA. Her personal dream was to quit the university and work for MICA full time. In the mean time, she worked tirelessly to secure grant monies for the organization, develop programming, and promote the mission of the organization.

With the combined efforts of the sisters and the support of MICA's board, the organization began to grow. Programming dreams for MICA—a performing arts series, art exhibitions, a reservation-based art symposium, and a permanent gallery—all began to take shape with National Endowment for the Arts and Montana Arts Council grant support. Several major traveling exhibitions of Native work organized by MICA toured Montana, two MICA symposiums (one on the Salish-Kootenai reservation and one on the Crow reservation) took place, and MICA artists began appearing in national exhibitions. It looked as though Kathryn's dream would be realized.

Then, in 1992 the unthinkable happened: Kathryn's cancer returned. Another brain tumor was discovered and she endured yet another operation. This time, however, the prognosis was not so positive. Still willing but unable to devote as much time to the organization, she turned much of her attention to her artwork. Within her surreal landscapes, situated among her beloved crows, began to appear stylized, mask-like human faces. They are reminiscent of the spirit figures seen on beaded pipe bags from earliest times and emanate a similar spiritual power. She eventually gave the faces full bodies and her groupings of the figures became like families; mother with children, sisters, and lone figures surrounded by the spirit faces.

Though she has passed, Kathryn's artwork and her dreams for MICA still live on. Her legacy has been taken up by her daughter Maya who, now 18, has been accepted to a prestigious art school in Washington state. A gifted young artist like her mother, she will no doubt be a force in the contemporary Indian arts movement as well.

Her sister Susan has also dedicated herself to the dream her and Kathryn conjured for MICA and the dream continues to be realized. MICA is now in its eighth year of existence in the Emerson Cultural Center in Bozeman with a new gallery space, studio space, and expanded programming firmly in place. The organization has been involved in networking and exchanges with groups as far away as New Zealand and France and as close as the Rocky Boy reservation in north central Montana. Built on the foundation of Kathryn's love and commitment to the Indian arts and the Indian community, "her" MICA continues to thrive and her art intrigues and enriches us. The circle completes itself again.

(Revised version of "Completing the Circle: The Lifework of Kathryn Stewart," *Montana Crossroads Magazine,* April 1997; reprinted with permission)

—Bently Spang

STEWART, Susan

Variant names: Esh-Ba'-E-Loua-It-Chay
Tribal affiliations: Crow; Blackfeet
Painter, printmaker, installation artist, performance artist, and video artist

Born: Livermore, California, 22 May 1953; Esh-Ba'-E-Loua-It-Chay translates as Her Colors are Good. **Education:** California College of Arts and Crafts, Oakland; Montana State University, BA, Fine Arts, 1981, working on M.F.A., mid-1990s. **Career:** Artist, arts administrator, curator, and community activist; co-founded (with her late sister, Kathryn Stewart) and Program Director, Montana Indian Contemporary Arts (MICA), a non-profit regional Native arts service organization; represented Partners of America, a private group that creates partnerships with South American communities and businesses; board member, Montana Indian Art and Cultural Association; National Performance Network Steering Committee, National Association of Artist's Organizations; Atlatl, Second Circle Regional Board. **Awards:** Grace Richardson Trust Grant, Montana Artist Fellowship, Partners of America Travel Grant. **Contact information:** Montana Indian Contemporary Arts (MICA), Bozeman, Montana; (406)587-2993.

Individual Exhibitions

1988 *Montana Dream Reflections: Absoolaka,* American Indian Contemporary Arts Gallery, San Francisco, California

Selected Group Exhibitions

1974 *Watercolor Exhibit,* California College of Arts and Crafts, Oakland
1976 *New Horizons in American Indian Art,* Southwest Museum, Los Angeles
1977 *Three Indians, Two Dimensions,* C. N. Gorman Museum, University of California, Davis
1979 Museum of the Plains Indian, Browning, Montana
1980 Artifacts Gallery, Browning Montana
1981 University of Montana, Missoula
1982 *Night of the First Americans,* Kennedy Center for the Performing Arts, Washington, D.C.
        Smithsonian Institution, Washington, D.C.
1983 Danforth Gallery, Livingston, Montana
1984 Sacred Circle Gallery, Seattle, Washington
1985 *Homecoming,* North Dakota Museum of Art, Grand Forks
1986 Beall Park Art Center, Bozeman, Montana
        Expressions of a Living Culture, Custer County Art Center, Miles City, Montana

Native American Visual Arts in Montana, Sierra Nevada Museum of Art, Reno (traveling)

Native American Art: Our Contemporary Visions, Thomas Segal Gallery, Boston, Massachusetts

1987 *The Mountain Indian Nation's Rendez-vous in Helena,* Governor's Mansion, Helena, Montana

1988 Marilyn Butler Fine Arts, Santa Fe, New Mexico

Equis, Beall Park Art Center, Bozeman, Montana

1989 *Four Sacred Mountains: Color, Form & Abstraction,* Arizona Commission on the Arts, Phoenix

WARM Gallery, Minneapolis, Minnesota

Women's Work, The Montana Women's Centennial Art Survey Exhibition, 1889-1989 (traveling)

1989-90 *Native Proof,* American Indian Contemporary Arts Gallery, San Francisco, California

1990 *Poetry: An Image in Mind,* Beall Park Art Center, Bozeman, Montana

We Are part of the Earth, Centro Cultural de la Raza, Balboa Park, San Diego, California

1991 *Submuloc Show/Columbus Wohs,* Evergreen College, Olympia, Washington (traveling)

Treaty Times, Missoula Museum of Art, Missoula, Montana

1992 *Translating Indian Memory,* American Indian Contemporary Arts Gallery, San Francisco, California

Discovering Ourself, Not Columbus, American Indian Community House, New York

Luna Luna, installation, Bozeman, Montana

Without Words, site-specific performance, Portland Art Museum, Portland, Oregon

Survival, installation, Institute of American Indian Arts Museum, Santa Fe, New Mexico

1993 Sutton West, Missoula, Montana

1994-95 *The Spirit of Native America,* American Indian Contemporary Arts Gallery, San Francisco, California (touring Central and South America and Europe)

Artists Who are Indian, Denver Art Museum, Denver, and Fort Lewis College, Boulder, Colorado

1995 *Native American Women Artists,* Castle Gallery, New Rochelle, New York

Indian Humor, American Indian Contemporary Arts Gallery, San Francisco, California (traveling)

1996 *Expressing the West,* Paris Gibson Square Museum, Great Falls, Montana

Mexican Cowboys Indian Lowriders, installation performance with Guillermo Gomez-Pena, and Roberto Sifuentes, Premier Holter Museum of Art, Helena, Montana

I Stand in the Center of Good, American Indian Community House Museum, New York

Collections

Museum of the Plains Indians, Browning Montana; North Dakota Museum of Art, Grand Forks, North Dakota; Washington State Arts Commission, Olympia, Washington.

Publications

On STEWART: Books—*New Horizons in American Indian Art,* Southwest Museum, Los Angeles, 1976; *Our Land/Our Selves,*

State University of New York, 1990; *Sublumoc Show/Columbus Wohs,* Atlatl, Phoenix, 1992; *The Spirit of Native America,* American Indian Contemporary Arts, San Francisco, 1994. **Articles**—"Art Review," by William Zimmer, *New York Times,* September 26, 1995.

*   *   *

As is often the case with artists situated in the mainstream of the contemporary Native North American art movement, Susan Stewart wears an array of different artistic hats. She is variously a painter, printmaker, installation artist, performance artist, video artist, arts administrator, curator, and self-avowed community activist. Her focus in all of these areas is the articulation of life as a contemporary Native North American.

This multiplicity of identities is not a unique phenomenon within the continuum of art making by Native people. A Native artist of the past often worked not only in visual forms (utilizing mediums from within the culture and without), but also ritual and performance, as well as the spoken word. Artistic content in all of these forms ran from social issues and political statements to personal expression and spiritual invocation. Art and life melded in such a way that they were unrecognizable as autonomous entities and, consequently, there often exists no word for art in most Native languages. This has been carried forward to today, as the words of Crow Sundance Chief Dan Old Elk, one of the elders from Stewart's tribe, so eloquently expressed to her: "Religiosity and art are integrated into Native existence to such an extent that they are inseparable from daily experience. Utilitarian items and artworks often are indistinguishable."

Stewart's multi-faceted ouevre grapples with all this and more, literally functioning as a contemporary manifestation of the complex role the Native artist has held historically. Her paintings provide the most tangible evidence of this complexity in their structure and handling. In the painting *Spirit Shield,* for example, Stewart's unrestrained handling of the paint creates a frenetic, charged atmosphere, within which hints of symbols, stylized landscape, and a monumental shield form interact freely, metamorphosing and merging with one another. It is as if she has stripped away the layer of conscious human experience to reveal an unseen layer of activity that occurs naturally all around us—an unseen life of symbols that is understood to exist by Native people. These forms emerge from her life experience as a member of the Crow tribe, growing up on and off the reservation, and she references concepts and forms specific to her tribe, including the Crazy Mountains, Crow beadwork colors, and geometric design.

Though schooled in Western European technique and visual structure, Stewart uses this knowledge as a tool to access a level that modernists like Klee and Pollock, who were influenced by early Native art, sought but could never completely enter, for it is an access that comes most effectively through Stewart's lived experience as a Native person. It is an experience that, to coin a phrase, is "often imitated but never duplicated." The artist's chosen palette is rich and vibrant, echoing traditional Crow beadwork colors.

Stewart's works on paper are no less vibrant, particularly her most recent mono-print series, *Biliiadaacha,* a Crow word meaning "almost like water." Though not as complex as her works on canvas, the prints convey much of the same mood in a smaller format. The most distinct difference between the paintings and the prints is Stewart's use of more overt imagery: stenciled forms such as buffalo skulls, howling-at-the-moon "rez" dogs (mocking the south-

Susan Stewart: *Spirit Shield,* 1990. Courtesy of the artist.

west coyote stereotype), and outlines of running horses float in front of a polychromatic, constantly shifting backdrop. The more telling nature of these works suggest a direct confrontation of the stereotypes and misconceptions that confront contemporary Native existence. It is as if the artist is saying these forms also inhabit that unseen layer expressed in the paintings.

Performance is also a distinct component of Stewart's oeuvre, but her focus in this area is decidedly more pragmatic, as she deals with specific issues confronting Native culture. Her most significant performance to date involved a cross-cultural collaboration with four other artists, Guillermo Gomez-Pena, Roberto Sifuentes, Tyler Medicine Horse, and Bently Spang, *Mexican Cowboys and Indian Lowriders*. The five hour performance/installation was presented at the Holter Museum in Helena, Montana, and involved recreating a roadside museum/curio shop, complete with the performers acting as living dioramas. The space was filled with stereotypical artworks—a wooden Indian, velvet paintings, and all manner of pop imagery offensive to every group of color imaginable. The performers assumed the following distinct personas: Gomez-Pena was "The Mexterminator," a schizophrenic hybrid of Mexican and cowboy stereotypes in a plexiglass case, who handled snakes, drank tequila, performed karate moves, while sitting in an antique wheelchair; Stewart was the "Hollywood Squaw / Undercover AIM Activist," replete in elk tooth dress and activist gear (a rifle, hand grenades, the classic bandanna, and mirrored shades) who, also in a plexi case, held a rifle overhead (classic AIM pose), fanned herself diva-like with a peyote fan, and gave birth; Sifuentes assumed the role of "El Lowrider Warrior," a tattooed gang member bent on self destruction and violence, who variously turned a gun on himself, "huffed" spray paint and whipped himself; Medicine Horse became a "New Age Shaman/Special Agent Assbury," a shaman for hire selling Indian names and love songs and busting audience members for offering him alcohol; and I, Bently Spang, became "El Undercover Indian Anthropologist Delbert Sellyersoul," a fence-riding Indian anthropologist who studied and documented the non-Indian audience.

The artists performed simultaneously and continuously throughout the five hour piece, as Mexican, cowboy, and Native American music blared and a video monitor flashed images of old cowboy and Indian and Mexican movies. The mood of the piece was at once chaotic and bizarre. Stewart's character silently performed a series of movements, each appearing to be purely maudlin and stereotypical at the outset. After closer examination, however, one could sense that her character possessed a hidden power. Her characterization, while humorous at the outset, eventually forced the viewer to painfully face his or her own personal misconceptions about Indian culture. The most hauntingly powerful movement in her repertoire was a standing pose where she held a ceramic "Indian maiden" mask in front of her face with one hand, and waved a classic princess wave to the audience with the other. Because the mask was slightly smaller than her own face it gave the pose a distorted, surreal quality, effectively transforming the stereotypical Indian princess into a grotesque, sideshow-like figure. Stewart's other performance work has been done in a collaborative format also, and the characters she portrays are most often done with a biting satirical edge designed to keep the viewer off balance.

Even more pointed than her performance work, however, is Stewart's work as a Native arts advocate and community activist. In 1989, together with her late sister Kathryn Stewart, a prolific artist in her own right, she co-founded Montana Indian Contemporary Arts (MICA), a non-profit regional Native arts service organi-

zation. The two co-directed the organization until Kathryn's death in 1993, at which time Susan took the helm. Since its founding, the organization has focused on cutting edge forms in Native art, providing Native artists from the state and region with opportunities to exhibit, perform, and participate in an on-going dialogue about Native art issues. It has been a labor of love for both the sisters, whose ultimate commitment was to provide opportunities for the Native voice to be heard. The organization is still in existence today, with Susan acting as programming director.

In 1990, a pivotal event took place in Stewart's life that affected her deeply and shaped much of her work. She had a dream in which she was taken to several sites sacred to indigenous people throughout the world. In the dream she questioned why she was being shown these sites. A person in the dream approached her and told her, "the world is out of balance," and that all her questions about the dream would be answered if she would travel "south." Intrigued and puzzled by the vivid dream, Susan sought an answer to its meaning. She was approached soon after by an organization called Partners of America, a private group that creates partnerships with South American communities and businesses. They needed a Native representative to accompany a delegation that was traveling to Argentina. She agreed to go and, though the funding fell through for the delegation, the organization felt that she should make the trip on her own. The only stipulations were that she would have to live for one month with a tribal people in Argentina called the Mapuche and, if their spiritual leaders deemed it appropriate, she would have to participate in one of their major ceremonies.

Ultimately, she went to Argentina and was invited to participate. During the four day ceremony she was continually struck by the similarity of the ceremony to the Crow-Shoshone Sundance of her own people. Several profound occurrences during the earth-centered ceremony, and during her month long stay, ensured both her and the Mapuche that she had been lead to this place. The experience also brought her to several significant realizations: that indigenous people throughout the world are interconnected on a powerful spiritual plane, that indigenous spiritual practitioners have the knowledge to restore the balance of our planet, that speaking about her existence as a contemporary Native person through her art work was an absolute necessity, and that she needed to commit herself to helping affect positive change in the perception of Native art and culture.

Stewart returned to Montana invigorated and decided to articulate her experience (in her words, "literally join together the Mapuche and the North") through a multi-media artwork combining painting, performance, and installation. Soon after beginning the project she was introduced to the Russian filmmaker, Arvo Iho. He recognized her immediately from a vivid dream he himself had experienced just prior to their meeting. In the dream Susan was lying on a large boulder in the middle of a body of water. It was an experience that Stewart admitted had actually happened during her visit with the Mapuche. Both agreed that their meeting was no coincidence and they decided to collaborate on a project. What resulted was a film directed by Iho documenting the multi-media piece Susan had planned, which she called *The Crow-Mapuche Connection*.

Stewart credits the experience with providing her a clearer perspective in her life as a Native person, and helping her work reach its current level of maturation. The impact of the experience is clearly evident in her personal commitment to Native arts issues and the community. However, the true essence of the experience seems to emanate most from her visual work. It exists in her ability to strip away the conscious world, to reveal to the viewer a realm that does truly exist in the Indian world and to remind us to honor that realm as she does in her work.

—Bently Spang

SWAZO HINDS, Patrick

Variant names: Grey Squirrel
Tribal affiliations: Tesuque
Painter

Born: Born Jose Patrico Sawazo, Tesuque Pueblo, New Mexico, 25 March 1929; adopted by Dr. Norman A. E. Hinds, an honorary member of the Tesuque Pueblo. **Education:** Hill and Canyon School of Art, Santa Fe, 1948; California College of Arts and Crafts, Oakland, B.A., 1952; Mexico City College, 1952; Chicago Art Institute, 1953-55. **Military Service:** U.S. Marine Corps; served in Korea. **Career:** Instructor at the University of California, Berkeley; active in several artist organizations, including the Oakland Art Association, the Okland Museum Association, Arts & Crafts Co-Op (Berkeley), California League for the American Indian, Berkeley Art Festival Guild, East Bay Artists Association, and the American Indian Historical Society; painted full time after 1968; served as judge in juried competitions. **Awards:** Many from fairs and juried competitions, including Scottsdale National Indian Art Exhibition (1966-68, 1970-71), Berkeley Art Festival (1966-68), Philbrook Annual Indian Art Exhibition (1967, 1969, 1971), All American Indian Days (1968), Center for Indian Art (1968), San Francisco Art Festival (1968-69), Heard Museum Guild Indian Fair and Market (1969-71), Inter Tribal Indian Ceremonial (1969), Southwestern Association for Indian Arts, Santa Fe Indian Market (1969-71, 1973). **Died:** 30 March 1974.

Individual Exhibitions

1964-65	Cork Wall, Berkeley, California
1964-68	Heard Museum, Phoenix, Arizona
1965	Student Union, University of California, Berkeley
	Pacific School of Religion, Berkeley, California
1966	Beaux Arts Gallery, Oakland, California
1967	E. Smalle and Associates, Novato, California
1967-68	Cincinnati Gallery, San Francisco, California
	American Indian Historical Society, San Francisco California
1969	Brick Wall Gallery, Berkeley, California
1970	Heard Museum, Phoenix, Arizona
1974	*Patrick Swazo Hinds Memorial,* Santa Fe Indian Market, New Mexico

Selected Group Exhibitions

1955	Art Institute of Chicago, Illinois
1966-68	National American Artists Exhibition, Kaiser Center, Oakland, California
1967	*California College of Arts & Crafts Alumni Show,* Oakland
1968	San Francisco Museum of Art, San Francisco, California
1968-69	Town & Country Gallery, Palo Alto, California
1970	Oregon State University, Corvallis
1971	Arizona State Museum, University of Arizona, Tucson
	University of Oregon, Eugene
1974	Museum of New Mexico, Santa Fe
1975	Wheelwright Museum of the American Indian, Santa Fe
1984-85	*Indianascher Kunstler* (traveling, Germany), organized by the Philbrook Museum, Tulsa, Oklahoma

Collections

American Indian Historical Society, San Francisco; Bureau of Indian Affairs, Department of the Interior, Washington, D.C.; California College of Arts and Crafts, Oakland; Heard Museum, Phoenix, Arizona; Oakland Museum, Oakland, California; Scottsdale National Indian Art Collection, Scottsdale, Arizona.

Publications

On SWAZO HINDS: Books—*Indian Painters and White Patrons,* by J .J. Brody, Albuquerque, 1971; *Southwest Indian Painting: A Changing Art,* by Clara Lee Tanner, Tucson, 1973; *Art and Indian Individualists,* Flagstaff, 1975; *Indianische Kunst im 20 Jahrhundert,* by Gerhard Hoffman, et al., Münich, Germany, 1984.

*   *   *

In his art, as in his life, Patrick Swazo Hinds blended his experiences in two cultural traditions, those of the Native American pueblo and Western academia. His Pueblo heritage is evident in the themes and subjects of his paintings, many of which focus on images from Pueblo secular and spiritual life, and his schooling in Western Art traditions is especially reflected in his abstract interest in color and background. Swazo Hinds adapted Western techniques to create impressionistic images of Pueblo subjects, thus extending and expanding on the tradition of Pueblo painting in the twentieth century. Swazo Hinds' interest in color, qualities of light and shade, and blending of central images and surroundings included other subjects, but his paintings on Pueblo themes were especially well-realized.

Swazo Hinds was born in Tesuque Pueblo and adopted at age nine by geologist Norman A. E. Hinds, who had often performed fieldwork in and around Tesuque and was recognized as an honorary member of the pueblo. Hinds taught at the University of California, Berkeley, where Patrick was raised during the academic year, and they usually spent summers at the pueblo. Swazo Hinds settled in Berkeley during the 1960s, maintained a studio there, was active in the northern California arts scene, and taught at the University.

Just as parts of each year of his childhood after age nine were divided between Berkeley and Tesuque, Swazo Hinds worked within two artistic traditions. He mastered authentic Tewa art forms and worked them with precision, skill, and confidence. He experimented more freely with various international styles, and his paintings were exhibited regularly in the San Francisco Bay area during the 1960s. Of his dual backgrounds, Swazo Hinds stated: "In my student days at the California College of Arts and Crafts and at the Chicago Art Institute, I thought of myself simply as a painter, not an Indian painter. Many of my fellow students were already professional painters and my survival in this intense competition was to be, first, a good painter. My only goal was to master techniques, to learn how to control the various media. I have worked hard to learn to paint and now I have chosen to paint the Indian, to paint

Patrick Swazo Hinds: *Forgotten Faces,* c. 1970. Courtesy Challis and Arch Thiessen collection.

the Indian and his religion and his culture as I understand it. I can paint an Indian as ugly as I want, because there is paint, there is sorrow, there is suffering. I can paint him beautiful, because that is there, too."

Mastering techniques and learning how to control media was what Swazo Hinds set out to do in education at Hill and Canyon School of Art, Santa Fe, the California College of Arts and Crafts, Oakland, Mexico City College, and the Chicago Art Institute. He returned, first to Berkeley, then to Santa Fe, with a wide range of skills to apply to his Native subject matter, not only recreating images from the Pueblo but doing so with imagination and freshness, perhaps best exemplified in the popularity of works at fairs. Using a palette knife, oils, drybrush, soft brush with spatter, acrylics, mixed-media and other tools to achieve background effects in paintings with Pueblo motifs, Swazo Hinds bathed his central images in muted colors for impressionistic effects: squared shapes of Pueblo buildings provide form within a haze of muted colors, dancers are sharply rendered in indistinct backgrounds that suggest different auras of light—from brilliant to diffused and coming into play upon the scene and around the figures. Impressionistic and abstract qualities through soft colors or shades brought into play visual and abstract qualities new or rare in the rich tradition of

Pueblo painters—far from the more realistic watercolor works that preceded Swazo Hinds, but his figures and scenes retain representative details to celebrate the subject matter.

In 1969, Swazo Hinds completed a circle in his decision to return to his native state, where he and his family settled in Santa Fe, just eight miles from Tesuque. It proved to be an auspicious new beginning, and an ending too soon. A rich new dimension was added to the broad spectrum of his art in 1972 when Swazo Hinds began working in lithograph stone, and his last major work was a suite of four lithographs executed at Tamarind in February 1974. Hinds died shortly threafter. The Southwestern Association on Indian Affairs, which sponsors the Santa Fe Indian Market, featured the lithographs at the 1974 Santa Fe Indian Market and set up a Patrick Swazo Hinds Memorial Award to be presented annually for excellence in painting.

It had been a long-time dream of Swazo's to build a home in Tesuque, and he was engaged in final plans for this in the months prior to his death. In the fall of 1974, his wife, Rita, and his two teen-aged children, Mark and Marita, moved into the completed home at the pueblo he had left 40 years before.

—Gregory Schaaf

SWEEZY, Carl

Variant names: Wattan
Tribal affiliations: Arapaho
Painter

Born: Oklahoma (near Darlington, on the former Cheyenne-Arapaho Reservation), c. 1879; Wattan means Black. **Education:** Federal Indian schools at Carlisle, Pennsylvania, and Chilocco, Oklahoma, and Mennonite Mission schools in Darlington, Oklahoma, and Halstead, Kansas; essentially a self-taught artist. **Career:** Drew regularly as a boy and worked with anthropologist James Mooney, restoring shield paintings and copying excavated designs; farmer; baseball player (local teams); civil service, Indian agent. **Died:** 28 May 1953.

Selected Group Exhibitions

1932   American Indian Exposition, Anadarko, Oklahoma
1947-65 *American Indian Paintings from the Permanent Collection,*
            Philbrook Art Center, Tulsa, Oklahoma (traveling)
1978   *100 Years of Native American Painting,* Oklahoma Museum of Art, Oklahoma City, Oklahoma
1981   *Native American Painting,* Amarillo Art Center, Amarillo, Texas
1984-85 *Indianascher Kunstler* (traveling, Germany), organized by the Philbrook Museum, Tulsa, Oklahoma
1990   *American Indian Artists in the Avery Collection and the McNay Permanent Collection,* Koogler McNay Art Museum, San Antonio, Texas
1991-92 *Shared Visions: Native American Painters and Sculptors in the Twentieth Century,* The Heard Museum, Phoenix, Arizona
1996   *Drawn from Memory: James T. Bialac Collection of Native American Art,* Heard Museum, Phoenix, Arizona

Collections

Field Museum of Natural History, Chicago, Illinois; Thomas Gilcrease Institute of American History and Art, Tulsa, Oklahoma; Heard Museum, Phoenix, Arizona; Indian Arts and Crafts Board, Department of the Interior, Washington, D.C.; Museum of the American Indian, New York; Museum of Art, University of Oklahoma, Norman; Oklahoma Historical Society Museum, Oklahoma City, Oklahoma; Oklahoma Museum of Natural History, Oklahoma City, Oklahoma; Philbrook Museum of Art, Tulsa, Oklahoma; Smithsonian Institution, Washington, D.C.; Southwest Museum, Los Angeles, California.

Publications

On SWEEZY: Books—*American Indian Painters,* by Oscar B. Jacobson and Jeanne d'Ucel, Nice, France, 1950; *Indian Painters and White Patrons,* by J. J. Brody, Albuquerque, 1971; *100 Years of Native American Painting,* by Arthur Silberman, Oklahoma City, 1978; *American Indian Painting and Sculpture,* by Patricia Janis Broder, New York, 1981; *Native American Painting,* by Jeanne Snodgrass King, Amarillo, Texas, 1981; *Indianascher Kunstler,* by Gerhard Hoffman, Munich, 1984; *The Arts of the North American Indian: Native Traditions in Evolution,* Edwin L. Wade, ed., New York: Hudson Hills Press in association with Philbrook Art Center, Tulsa, Oklahoma, 1986; *Shared Visions: Native American Painters and Sculptors in the Twentieth Century,* by Margaret Archuleta and Dr. Rennard Strickland, New York: The New Press, 1991.

*   *   *

Carl Sweezy ranks with Ernest Spybuck as one of the outstanding figures in the formative years of modern Native American painting. In federal Indian schools at Carlisle, Pennsylvania, and Chilocco, Oklahoma, he first tried painting under the tutelage of white teachers. At age 14 Sweezy returned to his reservation, where he unsuccessfully tried farming and played baseball for an Indian team. He painted what he saw around him—life at the agency as well as great chieftains, like Little Raven and Left Hand. Moreover, he painted scenes from the tales and stories of traditional life and customs the old men told him. A new phase in his life as a painter began late in the nineteenth century when he came under the influence of anthropologists, like James Mooney of the Smithsonian Institution and George A. Dorsey of the Field Museum in Chicago. They had come to study the Cheyenne and Arapaho way of life, which was changing dramatically, and employed Sweezy as an assistant to copy old shield designs and paint scenes from the daily life and religious ceremonies of his people. Before leaving near the end of World War I, Mooney gave him the advice that Sweezy was to follow for the rest of his life: "Keep on painting ... Paint Indian." Henceforth, Sweezy painted in what he called "the Mooney way."

Sweezy's work offers insight into the beginning of modern Indian painting. Most of his pictures have a documentary character and record both the old Plains Indian way and the new. For Mooney and Dorsey he painted scenes of warfare, the hunt, and traditional ceremonial life and customs. He also painted Peyote religious paraphernalia in pictures like *Peyote Road Man,* which deals with the Native American Church that emerged on the plains in the late nineteenth century. Pictures of historic events, like the battle of Little Big Horn, are interesting insofar as they are rendered from a Native perspective.

Sweezy's works, of which many are in the collections of the Smithsonian and the Field Museum, make clear that a kind of folk art beyond mere documentation was in the making. For the joy of artistic expression, he developed a self-confident stance and an independent position. Sweezy shows tribal brethren earnest and deliberate in their ceremonies, or paints them as stylized riders who hunt the buffalo before the backdrop of the endless prairie. Formally, his works rest on the development of contrasts in coloration and composition that manifests the pleasure of motion and the play of colors. With this, Sweezy stands at the head of a tradition that, in the 1920s, became formalized into a "school" in the works of the Kiowa Five and had decisive influence on all of Indian painting.

—Gerhard and Gisela Hoffmann

SWENTZELL, Roxanne

Tribal affiliations: Santa Clara Pueblo
Sculptor and potter

Born: Taos, New Mexico, 9 December 1962. **Education:** Portland Museum Art School, Portland, Oregon, 1980-81; The Institute of American Indian Arts, Santa Fe, New Mexico, 1978-80 Ralph

Pardington a highly respected ceramics teacher; printmaking instruction from Frank Flinn, Santa Fe, New Mexico, 1971; sculpting instruction from Michael Naranjo, Santa Clara Pueblo, New Mexico, 1976. **Career:** Instructor, private ceramics classes, Santa Fe, New Mexico, mid-1970s; self-employed artist since 1980; secretary/treasurer, Flowering Tree Permaculture Institute, since 1989; participates in conferences, workshops, and panels, including career education art workshop, Shiprock, New Mexico, 1982, and "Touch the Earth," at the University of California, Irvine, 1988; artist in residence, San Juan Elementary, San Juan Pueblo, New Mexico, 1979, Santa Fe Indian School, 1981-82, Santa Clara Elementary, Santa Clara Pueblo, and Tesuque Elementary, Tesuque Pueblo.

Individual Exhibitions

1990   Fort Mason, San Francisco, California

Selected Group Exhibitions

1991   *Shared Visions: Native American Painting and Sculpture of the Twentieth Century,* Heard Museum, Phoenix, Arizona
        Not by Bread Alone, Amarillo, Texas
1992   Four Winds Gallery, Pittsburgh, Pennsylvania
1993   Museum of the Blackhawk, Danville, California
        Allan Houser Art Park, Institute of American Indian Arts Museum, Santa Fe, New Mexico

Publications

On SWENTZELL: Books—*Shared Visions: Native American Painters and Sculptors in the Twentieth Century,* by Margaret Archuleta and Dr. Rennard Strickland, New York: The New Press, 1991. **Articles**—"Indian Market Supplement," by Nancy Gillespie, *The New Mexican,* August 18, 1988.

*

Roxanne Swentzell comments (1993):

I sculpt, to reach out to you. Hoping to go past the words and thoughts that rings us to a shallow world. Hoping to catch a moment of direct connection between your soul and mine. Then, for that second, we will remember what is important. In remembering there is hope. (From Catalog, Institute of American Indian Arts, 1993)

*   *   *

Part of a Santa Clara Pueblo family that spans five generations of potters, sculptors, architects and educators, Swentzell draws upon a great tradition of clay workers to create an innovative form of what has been called folk art, in which she embodies clay figures with human characteristics. Her most acclaimed work centers on *kosharis,* of whom she shows uncanny ability to recreate costumes, gestures, and expressions that animate her figures with a profound sense of liveliness. "I want them to look like they're emerging from the earth," says Swentzell of her *kosharis,* impish figures that symbolize her ties to Pueblo-Indian mythology. "The four *kosharis* symbolize the four directions," she adds. "They're the ones who came out of the earth first and brought the rest of the people to the surface. My message is, 'Remember where you came from.'" Fascinated by *kosharis,* the Pueblo-Indian clowns, Swentzell adds, "They imitate people, and so do I."

Like many Pueblo-Indian artists, Swentzell grew up with clay. She accompanied her mother, a potter, on clay-digging expeditions, learned how to find and use different colors, how to mix, and how to fire. Swentzell's particular gift for sculpture arose in childhood, not only because there were so many gifted potters around her but also as a means for expressing herself, since she had difficulty learning to talk. She made little people out of clay that expressed feelings she wasn't able to communicate through words. For example, she expressed sadness at school by fashioning a figure of a little girl with her head down on her desk, crying. Additional figures represented other feelings and observations—figures of men sitting in chairs reading, because her father read constantly, craftspeople making pottery—and through this practice Swentzell has created a unique mode of art through which she continues to express feelings and represent the daily lives and concerns of her community.

Her parents both recognized and supported her talent. In high school, Swentzell was offered an unusual opportunity to study at the Institute of American Indian Arts, an invitation rarely extended, since students have to apply and gain admittance to the school. By her junior year in high school, Swentzell was spending more than half of each day at the Institute and studying with Ralph Pardington, a highly respected ceramics teacher. Just as her talent had been recognized by her family, the pueblo community, and the Institute, so too came commercial potential. She has supported herself form her sculpture since she was 17 years old.

Swentzell's sculpture has grown progressively larger in size since the small figures she first created as a child and is limited only by the size of the kiln. Because Swentzell builds with coil construction, her sculpture, which can appear massive, is light and easily handled. Along with a desire to pursue more monumental forms, Swentzell is addressing problems of commercial success, where popularity and constant demand for her work challenge her concern for quality and craft. Dealers have proposed that she make editions in bronze, a prospect about which Swentzell has mixed feelings: "I see bronze as cold and hard, a material that can't crumble back into earth. I was reminded of that one day when the rain was pouring in on my sculpture through an open window. I found myself thinking how easy it would be for my figures to melt back into the earth. There's something pleasing and natural about that idea. So I'll hold off on bronze until I do a piece that could work in any material—and might translate into bronze. Maybe large pieces that you could sit on, or even hug."

—Gregory Schaaf

TAFOYA, Margaret

Tribal affiliations: Santa Clara
Potter

Born: Santa Clara Pueblo, New Mexico, 1904. **Education:** Taught pottery and material collection by her mother; Santa Fe Indian School, 1914-1918. **Family:** Daughter of well-known potters, Geronimo and Fina Guiterrez Tafoya; married Alcario Tafoya in 1924, thirteen children, including three adopted. **Career:** Potter; housekeeper and waitress, 1918-early 1920s; full time potter beginning 1924. **Awards:** Numerous (69 awards at various shows in 1977 alone), including consistent honors at Santa Fe Indian Fair beginning in the 1940s, at the Inter-Tribal Indian Ceremonials beginning in the 1950s; dominated awards at various fairs beginning in the 1970s, including Best of Show, Santa Fe Indian Market, 1977-78; Lifetime Achievement Award, Santa Fe Indian Market, 1996; National Heritage Fellowship Award, 1981, New Mexico Governor's Award for Excellence in the Arts, 1984, Master Artist Award, National Endowment for the Arts, 1984; Margaret Tafoya Heritage and Legacy Museum, Santa Clara Pueblo (planned). **Contact information:** Toni Roller Indian Pottery Studio and Gallery, Santa Clara Pueblo, New Mexico.

Individual Exhibitions

1983   Wheelwright Museum of the American Indian, Santa Fe, New Mexico
1984   Colorado Springs Fine Arts Center, Colorado Springs, Colorado
          Denver Museum of Natural History, Denver, Colorado

Selected Group Exhibitions

Has exhibited regularly at Santa Fe Indian Market since the 1930s.

1996   *Lifetime Achievement Awards* (Margaret Tafoya and Charles Loloma), Southwestern Association for Indian Arts, Santa Fe, New Mexico

Collections

Denver Art Museum, Colorado; Museum of Indian Arts and Culture, Santa Fe; Museum of New Mexico, Santa Fe; Toni Roller Indian Pottery Studio and Gallery, Santa Clara Pueblo, New Mexico; Wheelwright Museum of the American Indian, Santa Fe, New Mexico.

Publications

On TAFOYA: Books—*Margaret Tafoya: A Tewa Potter's Heritage and Legacy,* by Mary Ellen and Laurence Blair, Santa Fe,

Margaret Tafoya: Storage jar, 1930. Courtesy Museum of Indian Arts and Culture, Santa Fe.

1986; *Fourteen Families in Pueblo Pottery,* by Rick Dillingham, Santa Fe, 1994; *Art of Clay: Timeless Pottery of the Southwest,* Lee M. Cohen, editor, Santa Fe, 1995. **Articles**—"A Good Heart, A Good Life: The Legacy of Potter Margaret Tafoya," by Brandt Morgan, *Indian Artist* magazine, Spring 1997.

*

Margaret Tafoya comments:
    You have to have a good heart when you sit down to make this pottery; otherwise, it will show up in your work. You have to live a good life, because the clay knows. (From *Indian Artist* magazine, Spring 1997)

*   *   *

    Margaret Tafoya is one of most influential potters of the twentieth century and is matriarch to five generations and nearly 75 individual potters. Since the 1960s her work and that of her family has helped shift to her village the success and eminence of Pueblo pottery making. Born in 1904, she has worked consistently and quietly throughout her life, creating a legacy of superbly crafted and beautifully polished wares. Tafoya, too, is the inheritor of a great pottery tradition, both of her village and that of her mother, Sara Fina

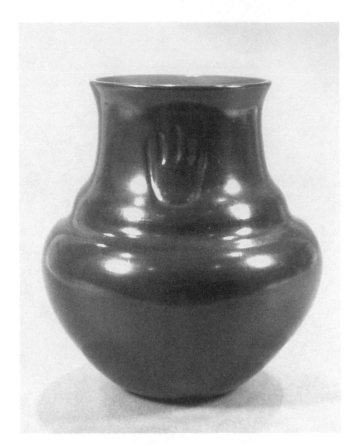

Margaret Tafoya: Water olla, c. 1960. Courtesy Museum of Indian Arts and Culture, Santa Fe.

Tafoya. Margaret learned to make pottery by watching her maternal aunts and through direct instruction by her mother.

She briefly attended Santa Fe Indian School (1914-18), leaving early to work at a variety of housekeeping, waitressing and cooking jobs in Dulce, Espanola and Santa Fe. After her marriage to Alcario Tafoya in 1924, the couple moved back to Santa Clara. Tafoya's name first appears in the records of the Santa Fe Indian Fair in 1930, when Kenneth Chapman paid the then enormous sum of $20.00 for a piece of her pottery. This indicates that she was already making her signature large ollas at this juncture, as is also documented by a pot purchased for $12.00 and a raccoon coat in 1930 and now in the collection of the Museum of Indian Arts and Culture, Santa Fe.

Tafoya began entering the revived Indian Market in 1936 and has received numerous awards beginning in the 1940s. During the 1950s she began entering the Gallup Inter-Tribal Ceremonial Fair, which was at that time the most important annual judged Indian art show, and she was a consistent winner there, as well. But it would not be until the 1970s and 1980s that she and her family dominated the awards and Margaret Tafoya would rise to a position of acknowledged prominence. In 1978 and again in 1979 she won best of show at the Santa Fe Indian Market.

Tafoya's pottery is best known for being highly-polished and often huge, with olla or water jars up to three feet tall. There are a series of remarkable skills needed to precisely build, shape, sand and smooth, polish, and outdoor fire her magnificent pottery. While her finished pieces are splendid to behold, knowing the technical

difficulty can only increase the finished pottery's aesthetic appreciation. The technique to which she and her family adhere to strictly involves clay digging and gathering, kneading the clay with hands and feet, gathering fuel for the firing process, and carefully designing, sanding and polishing the pieces. Only through these methods, Tafoya insists, can a piece be called traditional pottery. "My grandma would be very upset if we didn't dig our own clay and fire it in this way," notes Nancy Youngblood; "She always told us, 'if you kids don't carry this on, it's gonna be lost." Accordingly, she dismisses other processes, including using commercial kilns for firing.

During the 1930s and 1940s Tafoya experimented with polychrome painting and orange outlined designs, adopting Greek and Roman forms, and produced carved pottery. Once she stopped experimenting and concentrated on polished red or black sculpturally elegant vases, storage jars, ollas, and bowls, she began to receive recognition. In 1983, the Wheelwright Museum of the American Indian had the first major showing of Margaret's work, followed later by the Colorado Springs Fine Arts Center and Denver Museum of Natural History. In 1984 Tafoya was selected as a recipient of a prestigious National Endowment for the Arts, Master Artist award, and in 1985 she received the New Mexico Governor's Award for outstanding achievement in the arts.

—Bruce Bernstein

TAHOMA, Quincy

Tribal affiliations: Navajo
Painter

Born: Tuba City, Arizona, 1920; Tahoma means Water Edge. **Education:** The Studio, Santa Fe Indian School, 1936-40. **Military Service:** U.S. Army, World War II, Code Talker. **Career:** Shepherd and painter; worked briefly in Hollywood as a painter, 1940s; commissioned for murals and posters. **Awards:** Several from fairs, including Inter-Tribal Indian Ceremonials, New Mexico State Fair, and Philbrook Museum annual. **Died:** 1956.

Selected Group Exhibitions

1939   Art Gallery of the Museum of New Mexico, Santa Fe
1939-40   San Francisco World's Fair and Golden Gate International Exposition, San Francisco, California
1941   Foundation of Western Art, Los Angeles, California
1947-65   *American Indian Paintings from the Permanent Collection,* Philbrook Art Center, Tulsa, Oklahoma (traveling)
1949   *Man Becomes an Artist,* Museum of New Mexico, Santa Fe
1955   *An Exhibition of American Indian Paintings,* James Graham and Sons, New York
1978   *100 Years of Native American Painting,* Oklahoma Museum of Art, Oklahoma City, Oklahoma
1981-83   *Native American Painting,* Amarillo Art Center, Amarillo, Texas (traveling)
1982   *Native American Painting: Selections from the Museum of the American Indian,* Heard Museum, Phoenix, Arizona

1984-85 *Indianascher Kunstler* (traveling, Germany), organized by the Philbrook Museum, Tulsa, Oklahoma

1988 *When the Rainbow Touches Down,* Heard Museum, Phoenix, Arizona (traveling)

1990 *American Indian Artists in the Avery Collection and the McNay Permanent Collection,* Koogler McNay Art Museum, San Antonio, Texas

1991-92 *Shared Visions: Native American Painters and Sculptors in the Twentieth Century,* The Heard Museum, Phoenix, Arizona

1996 *Drawn from Memory: James T. Bialac Collection of Native American Art,* Heard Museum, Phoenix, Arizona

Collections

Amerind Foundation, Dragoon, Arizona; Thomas Gilcrease Institute of American History and Art, Tulsa, Oklahoma; Heard Museum, Phoenix, Arizona; Phoebe Appearson Hearst Museum of Anthropology, Berkeley, California; Kiva Museum of the Koshare Indian, La Junta, Colorado; Museum of the American Indian, New York; Museum of New Mexico, Santa Fe; Museum of Northern Arizona, Flagstaff, Arizona; Philbrook Museum of Art, Tulsa, Oklahoma; Millicent Rogers Foundation Museum, Taos, New Mexico; Southwest Museum, Los Angeles, California; United Pueblo Agency, Albuquerque, New Mexico; University of California, Berkeley; University of Oklahoma, Norman, Oklahoma; Wheelwright Museum of the American Indian, Santa Fe, New Mexico; Woolaroc Museum, Bartlesville, Oklahoma; Wheelwright Museum of the American Indian, Santa Fe, New Mexico.

Publications

On TAHOMA: Books—*American Indian Painters,* by Oscar B. Jacobson and Jeanne D'Ucel, Nice, France, 1950; *A Pictorial History of the American Indian,* by Oliver LaFarge, New York, 1956; *Indian Art in America: The Arts and Crafts of the North American Indian,* by Frederick J. Dockstader, Grenwich, Connecticut, 1962; *American Indian Painting of the Southwest and Plains Areas,* by Dorothy Dunn, Albuquerque: University of New Mexico, 1968; *Indian Painters and White Patrons,* by J. J. Brody, Albuquerque: University of New Mexico Press, 1971; *Song from the Earth: American Indian Painting,* by Jamake Highwater, Boston, 1976; *100 Years of Native American Painting,* exhibition catalog by Arthur Silberman, Oklahoma Museum of Art, Oklahoma City, 1978; *American Indian Painting and Sculpture,* Patricia Broder, New York, 1981; *Indianascher Kunstler,* by Gerhard Hoffmann, Munich, 1984; *The Arts of the North American Indian: Native Traditions in Evolution,* Edwin L. Wade, ed., New York: Hudson Hills Press in association with Philbrook Art Center, Tulsa, Oklahoma, 1986; *When the Rainbow Touches Down,* exhibition catalog by Tryntje Van Ness Seymour, Heard Museum, University of Washington Press, 1988; *Beyond Tradition: Native American Art and Its Evolution,* by Jerry and Lois Jacka, Flagstaff, 1988; *American Indian Artists in the Avery Collection and the McNay Permanent Collection,* Jean Sherrod Williams, editor, San Antonio, 1990; *Shared Visions: Native American Painters and Sculptors in the Twentieth Century,* by Margaret Archuleta and Dr. Rennard Strickland, New York: The New Press, 1991; *Enduring Traditions: The Art of the Navajo,* by Jerry and Lois Jacka, Flagstaff, 1994. **Articles**—"Modern Navajo Water Color Painting," by Linzie W. King Davis, *Arizona Highways,* July 1956; "Navajo Painting," by Katherin Chase, *Plateau,* Vol. 54, No. 1, 1982.

*   *   *

Tahoma had lived the life of a shepherd until he went to Santa Fe Indian School in 1936 and received his first formal art training in Dorothy Dunn's Studio. His early paintings reflect his pastoral background and show the influence of "Studio art": he painted mothers with children, shepherds with their flocks, and proud Navajos on horseback. It is the same kind of genre scenes for which Navajo artist Harrison Begay, who also attended Dunn's Studio in the late 1930s, would become famous. Tahoma's idealized landscape environments are rendered with Studio techniques, though with remarkably imaginative use of color, and there is the same attention to conventional detail: birds and butterflies hovering in the air, tufts of grass dotting the ground, and bizarre rock formations standing against the horizon, giving the scene local color and "Native flavor."

Tahoma distinguished himself from the beginning. As early as 1939, when he was 18 and participated in an exhibition at the Art Gallery of the Museum of New Mexico, he was hailed as a promising young artist. Some of Tahoma's early paintings of horses show yet another trait that would be his hallmark in later years: his depiction of action and vitality. He had, however, considerable difficulty with perspective and especially foreshortening, a technical aspect of painting that he had not learned to deal with at the Santa Fe Studio and which is absent from two-dimensional, traditional Indian painting. It was only after individual studies of foreshortening and anatomy that Tahoma was able to render pictures of dramatic movement.

In the mid-1940s, after his return from World War II, a new phase in Tahoma's work began. He had discovered pure action as subject matter and translated it into dynamic movement. Motifs and themes like the buffalo hunt or the driving of wild horses as well as battle scenes now came to the fore, and he turned to the early days of American Indian life, to the "days of the plentiful," when the buffalo herds still roamed the country and Indian braves fought for honor and glory. In a picture like *In the Days of the Plentiful* (1946), every detail is drawn in expressive distinctiveness: the wild, determined mien of the hunter, the strain and fright of the horse, the exhaustion and fear of the buffalo. In another picture of a struggle between man and beast, *Driving Wild Horses* (1947), Tahoma achieves a kind of spiritualization of the horses, expressed in wildly flying manes and the twists and contortions of bodies in full gallop.

Tahoma has been criticized for welcoming opportunities to depict blood and gore, yet his rendering of pure energy and strength gave his work a whole new expressive dimension that drew attention of the Native art world. Tahoma's wild images had a decisive influence on the further development of Indian painting, on other Navajos like Andy Tsinajinnie and Beatien Yazz and on artists like Allan Houser and Blackbear Bosin. He also set a new standard for the depiction of horses, which in his and Tsinajinnie's work often took on an inspired, and even "spiritual" character. The glorification of times past had yet another impact: the stereotyped image of the noble savage found valid expression in Indian painting and was accepted as one vision of the Indian"s own ideal form of existence.

Tahoma's later pictures are not all dramatic or even wild. He depicted proud people in quieter moments and on festive occasions: in *Going to the Navajo Chant,* a family on their horses are rendered almost static—the man and his wife in stiff, upright postures, the horses ambling with almost symmetrical movements. Man and beast give the impression of quiet beauty and dignity as befits the purpose of their journey. Quietude is also at the core of *Navajo Sing*, a large picture that shows Tahoma's mastership in dealing with masses of people and animals as well as perspective. Beyond the lines of people on horseback or afoot the land is spread out, stripe upon stripe, with towering rocks and decorative cloud formations above. Close attention to detail, including costumes and jewelry, saddle blankets and rugs, wagons and a car, hogans and other dwellings, makes Tahoma, here and in other pictures, a chronicler of Navajo life.

In some instances, the artist acts as a commentator on Indian\White relationships. *Tourist Season*, for instance, depicts an Indian family, ice-cream cones in hand, posing happily and shyly for a tourist couple, wearing such typical costumes as short pants and Navajo bracelets and armed with the inevitable camera. Tahoma's sense of humor, also evident in pictures such as one showing a bear fleeing before a swarm of bees, has in *Tourist Season* taken on a satiric touch, which anticipates American Indian painters of the 1970s and 1980s.

—Gerhard and Gisela Hoffmann

TAILFEATHERS, Gerald

Variant names: Omuka-nista-payh'pee; Eets-pahp-awag-uh'ka
Tribal affiliations: Blood, Blackfoot
Sculptor and painter

Born: Standoff Blood Reserve, Alberta, 14 February 1925; native names translate as Big Walking Away (Omuka-nista-payh'pee) and Walking on Top (Eets-pahp-awag-uh'ka). **Education:** Summer art school, St. Mary's Lake, Montana; Banff School of Fine Arts, under the direction of Charles Comfort, Walter Phillips, and H.G. Glyde; Provincial Institute of Technology and Art, Calgary, 1942-44. **Career:** Commercial artist, Hudson's Bay Company, draftsman, sculptor and painter; commissioned for painting for the Indian Pavilion at Expo '67, Christmas Card for the Calgary Indian Friendship Centre (1971), sketches of medicinal herbs and paintings of Plains life, Glenbow Museum, and Canada Post Office, Ottawa, 1972; Band Council member and activist. **Died:** 1975.

Individual Exhibitions

1967   Gainsborough Galleries, Lethbridge, Alberta
1970   *Gerald Tailfeathers Retrospective Exhibition,* Glenbow-Alberta Art Gallery, Calgary, Alberta
1973   Glenbow-Alberta Art Gallery, Calgary, Alberta
1975   Framecraft Gallery, Calgary, Alberta

Selected Group Exhibitions

1960   Indian Handicraft Exhibition, YMCA, Calgary, Alberta (sponsored by Calumet Indian Club of Calgary)
        Gainsborough Art Galleries, Lethbridge, Alberta
1961   *All Indian Show,* Chautauqua House, San Francisco, California

1966   *American Indian Artist Show,* Oakland California
1967   Indian Pavilion, Expo '67, Montreal, Quebec
1968   University of Calgary, Alberta
        Medicine Hat Museum, Medicine Hat, Alberta
1969   Art Gallery of the Whitehorse Public Library, Whitehorse, Yukon
1970   Glenbow-Alberta Art Gallery, Calgary, Alberta
1981   *Tradition and Change in Contemporary Indian Art,* Edmonton Centre and Student Union Building, Edmonton, Alberta
1983   *Contemporary Indian Art at Rideau Hall,* Ottawa, Ontario General Assembly Building, United Nations, New York
1992   *Time for Dialogue,* Calgary, Alberta

Collections

Centennial Museum, Vancouver, British Columbia; Department of Indian and Northern Affairs, Ottawa, Ontario; Galt Museum, Lethbridge, Alberta; Glenbow Museum, Calgary, Alberta; National Art Gallery, Ottawa, Ontario; Royal Ontario Museum, Toronto.

Publications

On TAILFEATHERS: Books—*Tailfeathers: Indian Artist,* by Hugh A. Dempsey, Glenbow-Alberta Institute, 1978; *Gerald Tailfeathers: Fifty Years,* by Joan Stebbins, Southern Alberta Art Gallery, 1981; *Time for Dialogue,* Joanne Cardinal-Schubert, Calgary, 1992; *In the Shadow of the Sun,* by Gerald McMaster, et. al., Hull, Quebec, 1992. **Articles**—"This Is Quite a Thrill," by Rickard D'arcy, *Lethbridge Herald,* April 15, 1971; " Indian Artists on the Move," *Edmonton Journal,* April 22, 1981.

*   *   *

Gerald Tailfeathers had a long formal art education and utilized its lessons in both the field of commercial art and in the fine art forum. Tailfeathers' careers, as artist, draughtsman, and Indian rights activist, kept him moving back and forth between his reserve and the city throughout his short life. In 1970, the Glenbow Museum produced a retrospective exhibition of the artist's work. Tailfeathers died suddenly in 1975.

Tailfeathers' oeuvre is distinguished by works in charcoal, pastel, watercolour, tempra, pen & ink, and oil, and his preferred subjects were those that documented Native life on the prairie—genre scenes of the moment. Tailfeathers was particularly interested in portraiture, amassing a significant body of work over his lifetime. For a time, Tailfeathers emulated the "cowboy" scenes of western American artists, like Charles M. Russell, Frederic Remington, and Will James.

Prior to his formal art education, Tailfeathers worked in charcoal and pastel, two media that he perfected while under the tutelage of Winold Reiss and Carl Linck, artists running a summer art school in St. Mary's Lake when Tailfeathers was a young man. In addition to the artistic education he learned during this time, Tailfeathers also developed a knowledge of the Blood people and their traditions. Rooming with a number of elders of the Blood, who had jobs posing for the participants in the summer school, Tailfeathers was privy to their evening stories around the campfire.

In 1941, Tailfeathers began studies at the Banff School of Fine Arts where under the direction of Charles Comfort, Walter Phillips, and H.G. Glyde, he was introduced to watercolours. Subsequently, again with Walter Phillips as instructor, Tailfeathers began a three

Gerald Tailfeathers: Untitled #2, 1969. Photograph by Lawrence Cook; courtesy Indian Art Centre, Department of Indian and Northern Affairs, Ottawa, Ontario.

year programme at the Provincial Institute of Technology and Art in Calgary in 1942. Here the artist learned the rudimentary skills of the commercial art and design trade, skills he would apply in his position as commercial artist for the Hudson's Bay Co. for many years to come.

While Tailfeathers continued to paint and draw after he graduated and pursued a professional, commercial career, his art had to take a backseat to his daily responsibilities. In 1957 Tailfeathers began to make a concerted effort to be accurate in terms of the historical significance of his work, depicting incidents and events in the history of the Blood Indians of Alberta. In 1959, after 18 years as a city dweller, Tailfeathers moved back to the Blood Reserve and began painting in earnest. He would continue to be prolific until his death.

Early on in Tailfeathers career as a visual artist, he was instructed to anglicize his name to avoid the racism in Canadian society. As early as 1941, Tailfeathers was signing his name Gerald T. Fethers. He would continue to alter the spelling of his name until 1963, when he finally began to sign his work as Tailfeathers.

As one of the first Native artists to be active within the mainstream Canadian visual arts community, exhibiting in commercial and public venues and gaining wide national acclaim as a visual artist, rather than an ethnographic curiosity, Tailfeathers stands out as an important precursor to the generations of First Nations artists who have followed in his footsteps. Melding a career marked by a commitment to his art, his community, and to social activism in respect to the position and rights of First Nations peoples in Canada, Tailfeathers emulated the characteristic roles in which Native artists have placed themselves ever since.

—Carol Podedworny

TALIRUNNILIK, Joe

Tribal affiliations: Inuit
Sculptor and printmaker

Born: Neahungnuk, in the land of Kooalik, South of Puvirnituq, c. 1899; last name also transliterated as Talirunili, Talirunilik. **Fam-**

ily: Married Lydia Arnasuk Panialuk Surusiq; 7 children. **Career:** Nomadic existence; began making carvings, prints and drawings during the last 15 years of his life; his sculpture, *Migration*, was reproduced on a 1978 Canadian postage stamp. **Died:** 13 September 1976.

Individual Exhibitions

1976   *Joe Talirunili from Povungnituk: Sculpture, Prints, Drawings*, The Innuit Gallery of Eskimo Art, Toronto, Ontario

1978   Canadiana Galleries, Edmonton, Alberta

Selected Group Exhibitions

1966   *Esquimaux, Peuple du Quebec*, Musée du Quebec, Quebec City, Quebec

1971-73   *Sculpture/Inuit: Masterworks of the Canadian Arctic*, Canadian Eskimo Arts Council, Ottawa, Ontario (traveling)

1973   *The Tactile Eskimo Art Collection/Collection de sculptures esquimaudes appreciables par le toucher*, Department of Indian Affairs and Northern Development, in cooperation with the Canadian National Institute for the Blind, Ottawa, Ontario (traveling)

1975-77   *Inuit Games/Inuit Pinguangit/Jeux des inuit*, Department of Indian Affairs and Northern Development, Ottawa, Ontario (traveling)

1979-81   *By the Light of the Qulliq: Eskimo Life in the Canadian Arctic*, Smithsonian Institution, a traveling exhibit of Inuit art from the Feheley Collection, Washington, D.C. (traveling)

1979   *Eskimo Narrative*, Winnipeg Art Gallery, Winnipeg, Manitoba (traveling)

Sculpture of the Inuit: Masterwork Exhibitors of the Canadian Arctic, Inuit Gallery of Vancouver, Vancouver, British Columbia

1982   *Les Inuit du Nouveau-Quebec*, Musée du Quebec, Quebec, Quebec

1983-85   *Grasp Tight the Old Ways: Selections from the Klamer Family Collection of Inuit Art*, Art Gallery of Ontario, Toronto, Ontario (traveling)

1985-86   *Sanaugasi Takujaksat: A Travelling Celebration of Inuit Sculpture*, presented by Canadian Arctic Producers Ltd., with the assistance of Indian and Northern Affairs Canada, Ottawa, Ontario (traveling)

1985-87   *Chisel and Brush/Le ciseau et la brosse*, Department of Indian Affairs and Northern Development, Ottawa, Ontario (traveling)

1988   *Mythmakers: Davidialuk and Talirunili*, Winnipeg Art Gallery, Winnipeg, Manitoba

1988-90   *Stories in Stone: Soapstone Sculptures From Northern Quebec and Kenya*, La Federation des Cooperatives du Nouveau-Quebec, Montreal, Quebec (traveling)

1988-89   *Im Schatten der Sonne: Zeitgenossische Kunst der Indianer und Eskimos in Kanada/In the Shadow of the Sun: Contemporary Indian and Inuit Art in Canada*, Canadian Museum of Civilization, Ottawa, Ontario (traveling)

1990   *Arctic Mirror*, Canadian Museum of Civilization, Hull, Quebec

1990-92   *The First Passionate Collector: The Ian Lindsay Collection of Inuit Art*, Winnipeg Art Gallery, Winnipeg, Manitoba (traveling)

1992   *Each Depends on the Other*, Houston North Gallery, Lunenburg, Nova Scotia

1992-93   *Inuit Art: Tradition and Regeneration*, Canadian Museum of Civilization, Hull, Quebec

1994   *On Collectors and Collecting: Selections from the Herb & Cece Schreiber Family Collection*, The Art Gallery of Hamilton, Hamilton, Ontario

Collections

Art Gallery of Ontario, Toronto, Ontario; Art Gallery of Windsor, Windsor, Ontario; Art Gallery of York University, Downsview, Ontario; Avataq Cultural Institute, Montreal, Quebec; Canada Council Art Bank, Ottawa, Ontario; Canadian Guild of Crafts Quebec, Montreal, Quebec; Canadian Museum of Civilization, Hull, Quebec; Confederation des caisses populaires et d'economie Desjardins, Levis, Quebec; Dennos Museum Center, Northwestern Michigan College, Traverse City, Michigan; Eskimo Museum, Churchill, Manitoba; Agnes Etherington Art Centre, Queen's University, Kingston, Ontario; Glenbow Museum, Calgary, Alberta; Laurentian University Museum and Arts Centre, Sudbury, Ontario; McMichael Canadian Art Collection, Kleinburg, Ontario; Musée d'Art Contemporain de Montreal, Montreal, Quebec, Canada; Musée de la civilisation, Quebec City, Quebec; Musée des beaux-arts de Montreal, Montreal, Quebec; Musée du Quebec, Quebec City, Quebec; Museum of Anthropology, University of British Columbia, Vancouver, British Columbia; National Gallery of Canada, Ottawa, Ontario; Saputik Museum, Povungnituk, Quebec; University of New Brunswick, Fredericton, New Brunswick; Winnipeg Art Gallery, Winnipeg, Manitoba; York University, Toronto, Ontario

Publications

By TALIRUNNILIK: Books—*A Grace Beyond the Reach of Art*, Joe Talirunili, memoirs edited by Marybelle Myers, Montreal: La Federation des Cooperatives du Nouveau-Quebec, 1977.

On TALIRUNNILIK: Articles—"Mythmakers: Davidialuk and Talirunili," by Robert Bilan, *Inuit Art Quarterly*, vol. 3, no. 3, Summer, 1988; "Joe Talirunili: le dernier temoin (A Witness to Terror)," by John D. Furneaux, *Musée des beaux-arts de Montreal*, vol. 6, no. 2, 1974; "Mythmakers: Davidialuk and Talirunili," by Darlene Wight, *Tableau*, vol. 1, no. 5, 1988.

*   *   *

A significant figure in Inuit art, Joe Talirunnilik worked in a manner uncommon among most contemporary Inuit artists by chronicling the lived experiences of the artist. Thus, in carvings, prints, and drawings, Talirunnilik has undertaken a narrative illustration of his life and most intimate memories. Despite a short career of about 15 years in which he was fairly active during the last five years of his life, his art rapidly impressed art specialists. His works have been shown in over 20 group and two solo exhibitions, most of which occurred after his death.

He is principally known for migration scenes in umiaks (large Inuit boats), of which he produced about 50 versions. Talirunnilik intensely recounts his childhood recollections of a voyage with dramatic vicissitudes. Around age five, he took part in a northern trek from Kuujjuarapik along the east coast of Hudson Bay. Along the way, four Inuit families were stopped by a sand bank and suffered famine as they attempted to find a way to reach a coastline full of game. They succeed by transforming their qamutiiks (dog sleds) and poles for drying skins into the framework of a sail, which they filled with okino they had available. After a risky embarkation and many misfortunes, the entire group reached the island of Ottawa, which faces Puvirnituq. This experience affected Talirunnilik deeply, and in efforts to authentically recall all of the details, he sometimes scribbled a list of about 40 people involved and includes the list with a finished piece of sculpture to commemorate these actual events. His failing memory in later years led to varying numbers of people on the list.

It is interesting to know that in spite of the slight amount of elaboration (along with schematic forms and rough textures) of people appearing in migration scenes, some of them are distinguishable and one of them often represents Talirunnilik himself. There is frequently a woman who appears dominant within the group of people; this is his grandmother, Audlayuk, who was chosen to be responsible for the lifesaving operation.

Talirunnilik has explored fewer themes than most other Inuit artists, but he was not less inventive in contriving to illustrate with descriptive details subjects like migration aboard the umiaks, where occupants travel with all of their personal belongings, sometimes with and sometimes without sails and waves. He also describes, with details, a tragic story of the wreck of a small boat made with 45 gallon barrels. Also praised are his depictions of caribou, owls, arctic hares, women, and poised hunters, standing or squatting, as well as hunting scenes of marine mammals.

There are never bases or lines representing the earth in his sculptures. His people and animals often have eyes popping out of their sockets and most often stand directly on their feet. When not coifed with a round hat, his males have a bowled hairstyle, while his females have hair braided on their backs or formed in a bun on their nape. His land mammals are represented with long bodies and short limbs.

Talirunnilik generally makes his sculptures more complex by representing such elements as a harpoon, rifle, bow, knife or a ulu (a woman's knife with the form of a half-moon) made of ivory, wood, and sometimes even plastic. One may occasionally find a bag chiseled in the stone for holding possessions or a sail. Many of his migration scenes include busts of nomadic people. A peculiar element and one exclusive to his work appears on many of the umiaks in his migration scenes, where a small piece of oblong paper with corners bent is glued to the prow. This slip of paper is used to place his signature. As in many of his pieces, the migration scenes are signed Joe, in roman letters, or with his whole name written in Inuit characters.

Without grand virtuosity, his jack-of-all-trades attitude is reflected in improvised repairs he makes on portions of broken sculpture utilizing diverse adhesive materials and even binding pieces with string. His artwork is not deeply sophisticated, but very expressive. Moreover, his multiple characters in migration scenes sustain a strong principle of accumulation, which is also evidenced in the majority of his prints and drawings, where the repetition of motifs take on an enumerative value.

Even as he has been a prolific sculptor, Talirunnilik developed a passionate interest in printmaking and drawing. Like his cousin, Davidialuk Alaasuaq Amittuq, Talirunnilik belongs to the first group associated with the Atelier de gravure of Puvirnituq. There are at least 68 prints attributed to Talirunnilik and more not catalogd. Sarah Joe Talirunnilik Qinuajuak, his oldest daughter, inspired him

with her singular manner of constructing images and themes, such as the reclusive egret, *The Grand Duke*, that one finds frequently in Talirunnilik's work.

For Talirunnilik, the prints and drawings become his privileged means to bear witness to traditional Inuit life, a nomadic existence he knew so well. In a single image, he usually adds a multitude of activities and animals. In others one observes a preponderance for scenes of hunting with dogs and scenes of transport in such traditional means as kayak, umiak (boat) and quamutik (dog sleds).

Without considering influences, one can identify in his pictorial works rules that regulate his drawing strips. In effect, the images are frequently devised, fully, or line-by-line, in horizontal registers or in quadrants that evoke either simultaneous or subsequent events. Those concentrations or groupings combine to form the overall image. The logical organization of these images results, apparently, from an organic impulse where the objective is to fill the blank spaces on the page (or of the matrices where one always feels the limits of his engravings, even when they are cut off) and, as in collage, without regard for other scenes that sometimes seem reversed to each other.

Moreover, the gradation of elements represents a fading into distance: that which is largest in a picture is apparently closest. But, this perspective effect does not produce a result in itself, rather it generally combines to a sensible play of expectation that could be called "spherical." This other manner allows the viewer to proceed from a central image around which diverse elements cluster. For example, a hunter in a kayak appears as the center of a scene that shows seals left and right, above and under the kayak. The animals seem small and remote as they would appear to the hunter. By this manner of centering the view, Talirunnilik successfully immerses the spectator within the figurative scene.

Some writers have described Talirunnilik's work as being folk art, without a doubt in reference to the "naive" execution and idiosyncratic content showing traditional values that have faded, but this artistic categorization is unfair because it reveals a Westernized conception of art often perceived through the theme of the struggle of classes. The concept of social class is in no way suitable in regards to traditional Inuit culture, whose ancient structure bears no equivalence with those of post-industrial Western cultures.

A clever storyteller in the sense of proverbial humor, Talirunnilik recounts his miraculous survival from numerous adventures. Whether in complete distress during a difficult migration or in badly planned hunting expeditions, and having been shot accidentally in the right arm when he was young, Talirunnilik witnessed real hardships. His stories tell of resourcefulness, practical sense, and determination, all of which saved his life many times. These stories take on mythic character (as reflected in the imprecise dating of his birth—at times 1893, 1896, 1899, and even 1906) of life and death, happy endings, and tragic drama.

—Louis Gagnon

TELLES, Lucy
Tribal affiliations: Mono Lake Paiute; Miwok
Basketweaver

Born: Lucy Tom in Mono Lake, California, 1885. **Family:** Married 1) Jack Parker, c. 1900 (died); 2) John Telles, 1914; three

Lucy Telles and her grandson David Telles with coiled basket, 1941. Courtesy National Park Service, Yosemite Research Library, Yosemite National Park, California.

children. **Career:** Housekeeper for Yosemite Valley residents; wove baskets for sale to non-Indians by 1911 and was a major innovator of new ideas and producer of baskets throughout her life; demonstrator at the Yosemite Museum, c. 1948-1950s. **Died:** Yosemite Valley, 24 February 1955.

Individual Exhibitions

The artist is not known to have kept records of exhibition data. The following is an incomplete list that has been re-constructed:

1912   Salter's Yosemite Store, Yosemite Valley, California
1916   Bishop Harvest Days, Bishop, California
1923   Indian Field Days, Yosemite Valley, California
1924   Indian Field Days, Yosemite Valley, California
1925   Indian Field Days, Yosemite Valley, California
1926   Indian Field Days, Yosemite Valley, California
1939   Golden Gate International Exposition, San Francisco
1953-66 Yosemite Museum, Yosemite National Park, California
1973   Yosemite Museum, Yosemite National Park, California
1986   Taylor Museum, Colorado Springs Fine Arts Center, Colorado
1990   *Yosemite 100*, California Academy of Sciences, San Francisco

Collections

Academy of Sciences, San Francisco; Field Museum of Natural History, Chicago; Laboratory of Anthropology, Museum of New Mexico, Santa Fe; National Museum of the American Indian, New York; Taylor Museum, Colorado Springs Fine Arts Center, Colorado; Yosemite Museum, National Park Service, Yosemite National Park, California.

Publications

On TELLES: Books—*Tradition and Innovation: A Basket History of the Indians of the Yosemite-Mono Lake Area* by Craig Bates and Martha J. Lee, Yosemite 1990. **Articles**—"Miwok-Paiute Basketry 1920-1928: Genesis of an Art Form," by Craig Bates, *American Indian Art Magazine* 4(4):54-59, 1979; "Lucy Telles: Outstanding Weaver of the Yosemite Miwok-Paiute," by Craig D. Bates, *Pacific Historian* 24(4):396-403, 1980; "Made For Sale: Baskets from the Yosemite-Mono Lake Region of California," by Craig Bates, *Moccasin Tracks* 7(4):4-9, 1981; "Ethnographic Collections at Yosemite National Park," by Craig Bates, *American Indian Art Magazine* 7(32):28-35, 1982; "Yosemite Miwok-Paiute Basketry: A Study in Cultural Change," by Craig Bates, *American Indian Basketry Magazine* II(4):23-29, 1982; "Lucy Telles: A Supreme Weaver of the Yosemite Miwok-Paiute" by Craig D. Bates in *American Indian Basketry Magazine* 11(4):23-29, 1979; "Yosemite: A Melting Pot for Indian People and Their Baskets" by Craig D. Bates and Martha J. Lee in *Strands of Time: Yokuts, Mono and Miwok Basketmakers*, Fresno 1988.

*   *   *

Lucy Telles was one of the most influential basket weavers of the Yosemite-Mono Lake region. Her weaving was consistently of high quality. She perfected such forms as lock-lidded baskets, and she refined new patterns for use on baskets, such as butterflies. Lucy Telles learned the art of basketry from her mother, and as a young girl she wove baskets for traditional use. By 1911 she had produced many single-rod and three-rod baskets for sale. Although these baskets were made in traditional forms, some made use of newly invented patterns.

By 1912, when Telles sold three baskets to Nelson Salter's Yosemite Store, her tightly stitched baskets showed a refinement of the two-color black and red patterns in vogue at the time. Woven with sedge root sewing strands for the buff-colored background, and with patterns in red-brown split redbud shoots and black-dyed bracken fern roots, the baskets had motifs that were new to Yosemite basketry. They included floral and flame designs, as well as patterns that were variations on those developed in the previous decade, such as beadwork-inspired eight-pointed stars. Two of the baskets that she sold to Salter's Store were based on an older, globular-type of Miwok gift basket, but Telles had added basketry lids that snapped into place, a feature that had apparently been introduced on much smaller baskets made for sale in the 1890s. By 1914, and perhaps as early as 1911, Telles was proficient at making beaded baskets, a new art form that developed sometime around 1908 near Mono Lake. Although she made many, few have survived that can be positively attributed to her. She also produced great numbers of beaded objects, including sashes, hatbands, belts, lapel pins, bracelets, beaded buckskin cradlebasket covers, and gloves, most of which she sold primarily to Yosemite visitors.

Telles' reputation as a master weaver was established by the 1920s. She was a regular competitor in the Yosemite Indian Field Days basketry contests, and was a frequent prizewinner. She won first prize for best basket in 1924. Some of her baskets sold for $100 to $200 each, an amazing price during the 1920s. She experimented with many design styles, and by the end of the decade had incorporated designs derived from crochet pattern books in some of her baskets. Telles developed a new serrated zigzag design that she used on at least four baskets. Based on what was probably an old Miwok design, it consisted of a connecting, serrated pattern encircling each basket.

By the 1930s, Telles began to make very large new-style baskets. Her first such basket, exhibited unfinished at the 1929 Indian Field Days, was completed and sold the following year. In 1930 she began what was to become her most famous basket, finishing it in 1933. The largest basket known to have been woven in the Yosemite region, it was 40 inches in diameter and 20 inches in height. It was exhibited at the Golden Gate International Exposition in San Francisco in 1939, where Telles was both a demonstrator and sold baskets at the Indian trading post there. The basket appeared on postcards sold in Yosemite and, after its purchase by collector James H. Schwabacher in 1953, was exhibited at the Yosemite Museum.

Like other weavers of her generation, Telles continued to weave all her life. Her later baskets were often more simply made, with larger coils and stitching. These she could sell for a quite reasonable price to park visitors. At the time of her death, however, she had in her possession the start to a basket that would have been even larger than her 1933 piece, had it been completed.

Telles' influence on other weavers, and her work in refining and introducing new design ideas into the basketry of the Yosemite-Mono Lake region was profound, matched only by the work of weaver Carrie Bethel.

—Craig Bates

TETERS, Charlene

Tribal affiliations: Spokane
Installation artist and performance artist

Born: Spokane, Washington, 25 April 1952. **Family:** Son George Raymond born in 1971; daughter Kristal Raymond born in 1976; married Don Messec in 1995. **Education:** M.F.A. University of Illinois at Urbana-Champaign, 1994; B.F.A. College of Santa Fe, New Mexico, 1988; A.F.A. Institute of American Indian Arts, New Mexico, 1986; New York Arts Internship Program, Great Lakes College Association, 1989; Fritz Scholder Workshop, Santa Fe Institute of Fine Arts, 1988. **Career:** Receiving Home Manager, Colville Confederated Tribes, Nespelem, Washington, 1976-1978; Illustrator, Colville Confederated Tribes, 1978-1979; Technical Advisor, "A Tradition Lives. Part One: Pow Wow Dance Outfits," Videomasters Production, 1980-1982; Interpretive Advisor and Liaison for Spokane Tribe, National Park Service, Coulee Dam, Washington, 1983; Johnson O'Malley Tutor and Counselor, Grand Coulee Dam Junior High, Grand Coulee, Washington, 1983-1984; Teaching Assistant, Printmaking Workshop Community Outreach Program, Louis Armstrong School of Fine Arts, New York, 1986; Printmaking Instructor, Bob Blackburn Workshop, New York Arts Internship Program, Great Lakes College Association, 1989; Co-Founder of American Indian Midwest Alliance, 1990; Co-Founder and President, Native American Students for Progress at the University of Illinois, 1989-1991; Teaching Assistant, University of Illinois Urbana-Champaign, 1989-1991; Board of Directors, Illinois, Iowa, Missouri American Indian Center, Quincy, Illinois, 1991; Racial Justice Coordinator, National Congress of American Indians, Washington, D.C., 1991-1992; Speakers Bureau, International Indian Treaty Council, 1992—; Guest Visiting Artist, Univeristy of Arizona at Tucson, 1992, University of Illinois at Urbana-Champaign, 1994; Professor and Director of Student Placement and Alumni Affairs, Institute of American Indian Arts, 1992-1995; National Board of Directors, National Coalition on Racism in Sports and the Media, 1992—; Juror, *Sculpture Project*, College of Santa Fe, 1995-1996; Visiting Lecturer, Ohio State University, 1995-1996; Juror, *Southwest 96*, Museum of New Mexico Museum of Fine Arts, 1996; Senior Editor, *Indian Artist Magazine* 1996; Guest Curator, *Beyond the Trails End*, Ohio State University, 1996. **Awards:** Several graduate fellowships; Young Women's Christian Association Racial Justice Award, 1991; W. Ellison Chalmers Memorial Award, American Civil Liberties Union Champaign County Chapter, 1991; Art Matters Fellowship, Art Matters Foundation, 1995; New Forms Regional Initiative Grant, DiverseWorks, Art Space, 1995.

Individual Exhibitions

1991   *What We Know About Indians*, Gallery 9, Urbana, Illinois
1993   *Into Indian Country*, Center for Contemporary Arts Museum, Santa Fe
1994   *It Was Only An Indian*, American Indian Community House, New York
            It Was Only An Indian, Institute of American Indian Arts Museum, Santa Fe
1996   *We the Invisible People*, Cheney Cowles Museum, Spokane, Washington
            The Good White Man, Spokane Falls Community College, Spokane, Washington

Selected Group Exhibitions

1990   Beacon Street Gallery, Chicago
1991   Krannert Art Museum, Champaign, Illinois
            Illinois State Museum, Bloomington, Illinois
1992   *Sculpture Project*, College of Santa Fe, New Mexico
1994   *Old Tracks, Old Land*, Institute of American Indian Arts Museum, Santa Fe
            Sculpture Project, College of Santa Fe, New Mexico
1995   *Native American Women Artists*, College of New Rochelle, New York
            Visiting Artists Exhibit, Ohio State University

Collections

Illinois State University, Normal; Institute of American Indian Arts, Santa Fe.

Publications

By TETERS: Articles—"Stop Degrading Indians With Worn Out Stereotypes," *Palm Beach Post*, November, 1991; "Challenging the Myth," *Indian Artist Magazine*, Fall 1995; "Meeting, Shan Goshorn," *Indian Artist Magazine,* Spring 1996; "Juror's Essay," *Southwest 96,* Museum of New Mexico, Museum of Fine Arts.

On TETERS: Book—*Personal Accounts by American Indians 1790 to the Present*, Arlene Hirschfelder, editor, New York, 1995. **Articles**—"Teters, Munoz, Open at CCA with Powerful Statements," by John Villani, *Santa Fe New Mexican, Pasatiempo,* 27 August, 1993; "Brave Hearted Native American Women Artists," by Charlene Touchette, *Signals Magazine,* July/August, Vol. 2, no. 2, 1993; "Artist Wants Others to Walk in Indians' Shoes," by Minerva Canto, *Albuquerque Journal,* February 11, 1994; "Images of Racism and Americana," by Tom Collins, *Santa Fe Reporter,* March 9, 1994; "Demonstrations of Culture, Charlene Teters: The Rosa Parks of Campus Racism," by Nancy Marie Mithlo, *Crosswinds*, March, Vol. 6, no. 4, 1994; "Indian Activists Attack Disney," by Wren Propp, *Albuquerque Journal,* February 11, 1996; "Charlene Teters: Art on the Line," by Ross Coates and Marilyn Lysohir, *High Ground,* 1996. **Videos**—*False Traditions, False Idols*, Marie Kate Mendosa (Producer), New Mexico: KNME, 1994; *In Whose Honor?,* Jay Rosenstein (Producer), Champaign, Illinois: Smoking Munchkin Video, 1996.

*   *   *

The artistic career of Spokane artist Charlene Teters is exemplary in its evolution. While many other native artists of her generation are still producing the same predictable Indian themes they established 20 years ago, Teters has taken a visible and vocal stand against the oppressive forces that seek to demean the integrity of native culture. In a manner uncharacteristic of what many consider the proper role of a "successful" Indian artist she has expanded her medium from saleable paintings to temporary installation works that no one can own. Like the ceremonies of her tribe, her art exists only through the internalized experience. In this way she challenges her audience and her colleagues to think about the ways in which Native Americans are portrayed: "It is my intention to bring a noise into the silence, to make visible the invisible," she states.

Teters' journey began in earnest in 1989 when she entered a graduate art program at the University of Illinois, Urbana, and discovered that the "U of I" was home to the "Chief Illiniwek" mascot. During halftime intermission at games, a non-Indian student dressed in traditional buckskin Sioux regalia (complete with an eagle-feathered headdress) would mockingly enact a war dance for the crowd's entertainment. Angered at how this image embarrassed her children, she realized she had to address the racism on campus—"because if I don't protect the integrity of my cultural identity, then how are (my children) going to know that it's something important to protect?" Her first "performance piece" was protesting alone in front of U of I games holding a sign that simply read "Indians are not mascots. We are human beings." Eventually, the National Coalition on Racism in Sports and the Media was formed with Teters serving on the Board of Directors. Although many of the blatant uses of the Indian mascot at the University of Illinois have been removed, Teters comments that "the attitude is still there ... the hostility and the feeling that you don't belong is still there."

In her first major installation, What *We Know About Indians* (Gallery 9; Urbana, Illinois, 1991), Teters establishes the tone of her subsequent works by drawing from her personal family experience to "make real" her statement. This strategy of relying on personal experience to demonstrate broader issues (such as stereotypes) is effective in conveying visually the political statements she feels strongly about.

Teters stated, "I think there's no such thing as apolitical work. Because you're either reinforcing the status quo or you're not. I think all work is political." That the personal is also political is reminiscent of the rallying cry of feminist ideology. This additional component of gender added to the interpretation of Teters' work is what gives her statements the reserved dignity of a firm, but contained objection while simultaneously infusing it with a potent punch of self-awareness. By owning her own implicit participation in systems of oppression (Bureau of Indian Affairs census numbers, anglicized names), Teters allows herself adequate room to name the wrongs of her own people. This internal criticism is a scarce commodity to find in the world of Indian arts and the grace with which Teters aims her focus is admirable, considering the possible negative consequences of censure or rebuff.

Her timing in response to critical issues is precise. The title of the installation *It Was Only an Indian* (Institute of American Indian Arts Museum, 1994) comes from a reported reaction by a U.S. Forest Service Official to the death of a Jemez Pueblo firefighter: "I don't understand what the big deal is; it was only an Indian." As this installation was nearing completion, New Mexico state Senate Republican leader Billy McKibben was quoted at a press conference likening a group of Democrats to "ugly little Indians." The statement was not lost on Teters, who immediately enshrined his quote on the walls of the museum exhibition. McKibben publicly apologized for his comment, calling it a mistake "I'll regret forever." It is likely that without the additional attention Teters focused on these issues, the public would never be aware of their existence.

The expansion of the role Native American artists now occupy is directly linked to the goals Teters has established for herself. This tradition of activism can be traced to earlier groups (certainly A.I.M. members have influenced her, and *vice versa*). However Teters has breathed new life into their actions. Her participation with Vernon Bellecourt against Walt Disney's *Pocahontas* film (the headlines

Charlene Teters: *It Was Only an Indian* (detail). Photograph by Don Messec; courtesy of the artist.

read "Indian Activists Attack Disney") is characteristic of this merging. "You don't compromise your principles," she stated; "Once you've done that you've abandoned your goal." Her example proves integrity can exist in Indian arts despite the pull of a commercial market.

—Nancy Marie Mithlo

THOMAS, Roy

Variant names: Gahgahgeh
Tribal affiliations: Ojibway
Painter

Born: Longlac, Ontario, 1949. **Education:** Self-taught artist; Arts Program of the Saskatchewan Indian Federated College at the University of Regina. **Career:** Various odd jobs, including truck driver, railroad worker, guide, and painter.

Individual Exhibitions

1966   The Delta, Ottawa
        Gallery 103, Toronto

Roy Thomas: *Turtle Island,* 1996. Courtesy of the artist.

1967	Confederation College, Thunder Bay, Ontario
1968	Mary J. Black Library, Thunder Bay, Ontario
1970	University of Toronto, Ontario
1974	Gallery 103, Toronto
	Kar Gallery, Toronto
1977	Pollock Gallery, Toronto
1978	Pollock Gallery, Toronto
	Wah-sa Gallery, Winnipeg, Manitoba
1979	Pollock Gallery, Toronto
	Shayne Gallery, Montreal
1980	Pollock Gallery, Toronto
	Shayne Gallery, Montreal
1982	Gallery Quan, Toronto
1983	The Delta, Ottawa
1994	Maslak-McLeod Canadian Art, Toronto

Selected Group Exhibitions

1974	*Contemporary Native Arts of Ontario*, Oakville Centennial Gallery, Oakville, Ontario
1975	McMichael Canadian Collection, Kleinburg, Ontario
1976	*Contemporary Native Art of Canada: The Woodlands Indians*, Royal Ontario Museum, Toronto (traveling)

1976	*Indian Aer '76,* Woodland Indian Cultural Educational Centre, Brantford, Ontario
	Wells Gallery, Ottawa
1977	*Contemporary Native Arts of Canada*, CMS, Ottawa
1978	*Morrisseau/Thomas/Odjig*, Pollock Gallery, Toronto
	Nicholas Gallery, Toronto
1978	*Art of the Woodland Indian,* McMichael Canadian Collection, Kleinburg, Ontario
1979	*Kinder des Nanabush,* Hamburg, West Germany
1980	New College, University of Toronto, Ontario
	Pollock Gallery, Toronto
1982	Turtle Art Gallery, Niagara Falls, Ontario
	Ermineskin Band, Hobbema, Alberta
	Gallery Quan, Toronto
1983	*Indian Art '83,* Woodland Cultural Educational Centre, Brantford, Ontario
	Last Camp, First Song: Indian Art from the Royal Ontario Museum, Thunder Bay Art Gallery, Thunder Bay, Ontario
1984	*Norval Morriseau and the Emergence of the Image Makers,* Art Gallery of Ontario, Toronto
1986	Native Business Summit, Toronto Convention Centre, Toronto
	Oil Sand Museum, Fort McMurray, Alberta

Manu-life Place, Edmonton, Alberta
The Birch Bark Sings, Ontario North Galleries, Ontario
Place, Toronto
1987   Calgary Stampede, Calgary, Alberta
Bearclaw Gallery, Edmonton, Alberta
Manu-life Place, Edmonton, Alberta
International Child Welfare Conference, Calgary, Alberta
Celebration of Contemporary Canadian Native American Art, Southwest Museum, Los Angeles
1989   *Woodlands: Contemporary Art of the Anishabe,* Thunder Bay Art Gallery, Thunder Bay, Ontario
1991   *Mizinatik The Painting Stick,* Thunder Bay Art Gallery, Thunder Bay, Ontario
1993   *Kunstler Aus 'Kanada,* Ausstellung, Universitstsbibliothek Osnabruck, Alte munse/Kamp
1996   *The Art of the Anishnawbek,* Three Perspectives, Gallery of Indigenous Peoples, Royal Ontario Museum, Toronto
1996   *Thunder Bay Art Gallery 20th Anniversary Celebration,* Thunder Bay Art Gallery, Thunder Bay, Ontario

Collections

Alexander Education Centre, Morinville, Alberta; Art Gallery of Ontario, Toronto; Business Assistance for Native Albertans, Edmonton, Alberta; Canadian Museum of Civilization, Ottawa; Citicorp Canada, Toronto; Crown Life Insurance Company, Toronto; Department of Indian and Northern Affairs, Hull, Quebec; Edmonton Art Gallery, Vancouver; Ermineskin Band, Hobbema, Alberta; Imperial Oil, Toronto; Inuit Gallery, Manheim, Germany; McMichael Canadian Collection, Kleinburg, Ontario; Ministry of Colleges and Universities Building, Thunder Bay, Ontario; Museum of Man and Nature, Thunder Bay, Ontario; Nakoda Institute, Morley, Alberta; National Gallery of Canada, Ottawa; National Museum of Ethnology, Osaka, Japan; Peace Hills Trust, Edmonton, Alberta; Primeau School, Morinville, Alberta; Royal Ontario Museum, Toronto; Sawridge Band, Slave Lake, Alberta; Thunder Bay Art Gallery, Thunder Bay, Ontario; Turtle Art Gallery, Niagara Falls, New York; University of British Columbia, Vancouver; University of Regina, Regina, Saskatchewan; Vancouver Art Gallery, British Columbia; Winnipeg Art Gallery, Manitoba.

Publications

On THOMAS: Articles—"Spotlight on Artists: Roy Thomas," *Artscraft,* 1976; "Shaking Tents and Medicine Snakes: Traditional Elements in Contemporary Woodland Indian Art," *Art Magazine,* Vol. 7, No. 28, 1977; "Contemporary Algonkian Legend Painting," by John Anson Warner, *American Indian Art,* Vol. 3, No. 3, 1978; "Contemporary Canadian Indian Art," by John Anson Warner, *The Masterkey,* Southwest Museum, Vol. 58, No. 4, 1984; "Artscene," by Sam Middleton, *The Edmonton Sun,* April 24, 1991; "Contemporary Canadian Native Art: Newly Emerging Art Styles," by John Anson Warner, *Journal of Inquiry and Research, Kansai Gaidai University,* Osaka, Japan, No. 63, February, 1996; "Profile: Roy Thomas, Artist," by John Copley, *Alberta Native News,* August, 1996; "Roy Thomas Rooted in Woodlands Tradition," by Gussie Fauntleroy, *Pasatiempo,* August 16-22, 1996.

*

Roy Thomas comments:

Once I used to try and paint for recognition and praise. That was the wrong way, and for me, the troubled way. I was popular but not happy. I made mistakes and became heavily involved with alcohol. The elders helped me to recover, to find myself. They told me to be careful what I was saying with my work. They told me stories. They told me of life. They told me of the importance of tradition and culture. They told me in ways that made me understand that you can not treat tradition and culture lightly. You must have respect for who you are and where you come from.

*   *   *

An Ojibway (Ahnishnabe) from the Northwestern Ontario community of Long Lac, Roy Thomas is an outstanding member of the so-called Ahnishnaebae Woodland School of art, situated in Northwestern Ontario and northeastern Manitoba. This approach to painting, pioneered by its founder, Norval Morrisseau (Ojibway), came to prominence in the 1970s and is one of the major paradigms of contemporary Native painting in North America. It features boldly painted and very colorful works whose subject matter encompasses the legends, stories, myths, and philosophy of these Woodlands Canadian peoples. Most of the canvases by these artists (and especially Thomas) are striking and unforgettable in their impact. While deference must be paid to the efforts of Morrisseau, in my judgement Thomas is today the most talented and prolific member of this group. His technical skills—wedded to a fecund imagination and a penchant for brilliant colors—has attracted much critical acclaim, and understandably so.

This group of painters engages in "Contemporary Algonkian Legend Painting." The mode of consciousness informing these works stems organically from the sort of imagination that originated in the original Ojibway/Cree legends and myths. Whatever newer themes are present in these works are sourced from the spiritual and mystical frame of mind present in their traditional culture. This contention is seen to good advantage by inspecting the four inter-related themes of their art: (1) Scenarios of traditional legends and stories; (2) Vignettes of Ojibway/Cree cultural history; (3) Spiritual ideas about the appropriate relationship between humans and nature; and (4) Personal beliefs, experiences, philosophies, and odysseys. However, most of my Canadian colleagues do not appear to have agreed with me since they seem to prefer the very generic name of 'Woodlands Art' for these works. Be that as it may, this painting school can be termed either as the 'Algonkian Legend Painting' or the 'Ahnishnaebae Woodlands Art' paradigm.

Another way of looking at this art is to interpret it as an example of 'innovative traditionalism' in Native American arts. This type of art occurs when a traditional concept (e.g., legends) receives a new and tangible artistic treatment that is organically associated with that tradition. An excellent example of this sort of art is found among the Ahnishnaebae painters like Thomas. The art usually requires its viewers to have some knowledge of and appreciation of the concepts being presented. It is not a "decorative" art, since messages and communication are central to its identity and sometimes have to be "read" by those viewing it. Hence, the subject matter of this art is a very important of its nature.

It was Morrisseau who created paradigmatic conventions, featuring formlines that outline each figure or subject clearly and the

Roy Thomas. Courtesy of the artist.

use of circles. Employing formlines, Thomas' images almost always include stylized fish, birds, land animals, and people; these elements usually share borders like puzzle pieces or are connected by lines representing the unity of all creatures and nature. Circles are an especially important part of Thomas' art because, as he says, "The circle has several meanings. First, it is the symbol of our Creator. It is the shape of the world, the shape of the sun, the shape of the moon, the shape of equality. The circle is the sun, the life giver, fire." Another characteristic of this art (most certainly including Thomas') is the X-ray technique, integrating both the exterior and the interior view of subjects, particularly fish, bird, and animals. The X-ray technique is often utilized by artists who come from hunting and fishing peoples and who consequently are as familiar with the insides of fish, animals, and birds as they are with their exterior appearance. Thus, the spinal column, major bones, and entrails are often incorporated in an artistic fashion into the overall rendition of various subjects.

It is possible that some of the images in this paradigm are drawn from ancient pictographs (created between 400 and 600 years ago) that were drawn on the granite rock of the Canadian Shield. Thomas has referred to these possible origins with the following observation: "I strongly believe that my great-great-great-great grandfather was responsible for some of this art. I know for a fact where the pictographs are and who put them there, but I have no idea of the

meaning. But the feeling of the art is there.... I like to bring out the same kind of feeling of that art."

In a more personal vein, Thomas recalls that his first efforts at art occurred when he was a small boy who used to draw pictures in the dirt, snow, or sand with a stick. In the evenings Thomas reports that he used to listen to his grandmother tell stories and legends, which had a profound effect upon him. When there was an opportunity, he would try to paint pictures of the subjects about which his grandmother had spoken. Naturally, such pictures were ephemeral, and when he complained to his grandmother that they were all gone, she would reply, "They're not gone. Some day they'll come back. They'll come back in full color." And so they have.

Thomas professes to have a deep and profound respect for his hard working and principled grandmother: "I am very fortunate. My grandmother and the teaching she bestowed upon me have never left me, have never let me down. And even though she is no longer with us in person, her spirit is very strong within me. Her teachings and her presence are vivid."

When he was around 14 years of age, Thomas' parents died in a car accident and he dropped out of school to travel around Ontario and the United States by hitchhiking and jumping trains. It was around this time, he says, that he began to paint in whatever locales he found himself. While he states that he is self-taught and that there were no outside influences on his art, this cannot be strictly true. No doubt he acquired his superlative technique on his own, although he was enrolled for a period of time in the Arts Program of the Saskatchewan Indian Federated College at the University of Regina where he studied under Bob Boyer. However, this experience came after he had already been painting for some years. More significantly, there is little question that Thomas had ample opportunities to see the art of not only Norval Morrisseau but others who were active in this school: Carl Ray (Cree), Jackson Beardy (Cree), Joshim Kakegamic (Cree), Goyce Kakegamic (Cree), Saul Williams (Ojibway), and many others. In a sense, he was immersed in the culture and milieu of this art.

Since, as already noted, this art characteristically contains messages and meanings derived from elements of traditional Ahnishnaebae (Algonkian) culture, it is exceedingly thoughtful of Thomas to append statements to his work that help the viewer to understand and interpret the images. Thomas' paintings are amenable to silkscreen and lithograph print editions. In those instances when many copies of a work will reach the public, he adds a statement about the iconography and meanings to be found thereupon. He frequently paints works about "Turtle Island" (Ojibway legend says that they live on the back of a giant turtle). Thomas offers this commentary:

> The Elders of our nation remind us that this land belongs to our Creator and this is Turtle Island. The purpose of Turtle Island is to provide for all living creatures. Our relationship with this land is to be the keepers of this earth, knowing the ways of Turtle Island. The life elements given to all life are the "fire", "air", "land", "water", and "time". These life givers care for us during our cycle of life on this Turtle Island....We bless Turtle Island by keeping our mind, body and spirit clean. We keep our families, our communities, our nation and the elements in this same condition. We bless Turtle Island by giving natural offerings before we take, taking only what we need. We treat the environment as we treat ourselves because they are our spirit relatives.

—John Anson Warner

THOMPSON, Art

Tribal affiliations: Nuu-chah-nulth
Carver and printmaker

Born: Whyac, Nitinaht Indian Reserve, Vancouver Island, British Columbia, 1948; of Coast Salish and Nuu-chah-nulth (also known as the Westcoast or Nootka) descent. **Education:** Commercial art program, Camosun College; studied under Joe David and Ron Hamilton. **Career:** Logger; carver, silversmith and painter; tribal band leader. **Awards:** Commissions, including Commonwealth Games, Victoria, British Columbia, and Aboriginal Affairs Ministry Office, Victoria, British Columbia, both 1994.

Selected Group Exhibitions

1980   *The Legacy*, British Columbia Provincial Museum, Victoria, British Columbia

1987   *A Celebration of Contemporary Canadian Native Art*, Woodland Indian Cultural Education Centre, Brantford, Ontario

1993   *Art of the Mask: Works from the Peacock Collection*, Thunder Bay Art Gallery, Thunder Bay, Ontario
        In the Shadow of the Sun, Canadian Museum of Civilization, Hull, Quebec

Collections

Department of Indian and Northern Affairs, Ottawa, Ontario; Heritage Center Inc., Collection, Red Cloud Indian School, Pine Ridge, South Dakota; Washington State Arts Commission, Olympia.

Publications

On THOMPSON: Books—*The Box of Daylight: Northwest Coast Indian Art*, by Bill Holm, University of Washington Press, 1983. **Articles**—"Spirits in the Gallery," by Pamela Young, *MacLean's Magazine*, November 13, 1989.

*

Art Thompson comments:
    Cultural activities have greatly enhanced my art-works, for it is my belief that they truly do go hand in hand. Many times I've seen artists of the Northwest who just do art-work, but have no idea of their cultural backgrounds. Many continue without anything culturally... that is their prerogative, I'm glad I have the opportunity.

*   *   *

Thompson is especially noted for his successful efforts to revive and recreate the classic arts of the Nuu-chah-nulth people. After careful investigation of museum and book resources, in addition to work with other similarly-minded tribal artists, Thompson is busy producing works directly inspired by the nineteenth century Nuu-chah-nulth tribal style. It might be said that he and his fellow artists are a special part of the Northwest Coast Indian art renewal, since they are rediscovering an art style that was thought by many to be virtually extinct. Thompson has distinguished himself especially in the field of serigraphy, but he is also renowned as a carver and silversmith. From his meticulous studies of the older tribal style of the Nuu-chah-nulth, he has emerged with a personal approach of his own that has made him one of the leaders in the field.

Thompson came from a father and grandfather who were both artists known for their carved totem poles and canoes, as well as ceremonial regalia. However, because of tuberculosis at an early age, Thompson was unable to spend much time with his family. He was hospitalized for his malady and then was sent to the Port Alberni Indian residential school, where he had a miserable experience with formal education. After running away from the boarding school several times, he finally got work in the logging industry. After that experience he drifted for a number of years, from Vancouver to Florida. Upon his return to British Columbia in 1967, he enrolled in the commercial art program at Camosun College in Victoria and majored in two-dimensional mediums. It was around this time period when Thompson became interested in his Nuu-chah-nulth artistic heritage. In the early 1970s he was fortunate to meet up with Joe David and Ron Hamilton, both Nuu-chah-nulth

Art Thompson: *Thunderbird Chief's Chest Supported by Slave Figures*, 1996. Photograph by Kenji Nagai; courtesy of the artist.

artists; their friendship and advice were to prove helpful to Thompson in terms of his own learning endeavors. Hamilton, in particular, had already studied nineteenth century tribal arts in museum collections, and Thompson still thinks of his mentor as "an encyclopedia of Westcoast art."

Thompson began to produce silkscreen prints (and some carvings) around 1974 or so. As was not untypical for a fledgling Northwest Coast Indian artist (even if he was a Nuu-chah-nulth), many of his earlier works were done in the 'Northern Style' of the Haida/Tsimshian/Gitksan/Nishga/Tlingit. After all, the market for works in this tradition was significant. Nevertheless, by 1978 Thompson was beginning to work more and more with two-dimensional designs from his own tribal tradition. The period from 1978 to 1981 was significant because he had an association with two leading non-Native Northwest Coast artists and pedagogues, Duane Pasco and Steve Brown. Thompson acknowledges that he learned a great deal from his experience with these teachers and was strengthened in his desire to develop a more personal style.

The wish of Thompson, David, and Hamilton to revive the essence of nineteenth century Nuu-chah-nulth art and to develop it in new ways was easier said than done, however. Apart from the fact that there was not much of this art around (except in a few museums), it has to be said that traditional Nuu-chah-nulth art was regarded by many analysts as a somewhat "inferior" art style when compared with the Kwakiutl, Haida, and so on. Thus, there were a lot of prejudices to overcome, not least of all in the art marketplace. With sincerity, talent, and enthusiasm, the artists addressed these challenges, and it must be said that they have definitely found a "niche" in the Northwest Coast art market for themselves and for Nuu-chah-nulth inspired art works.

Students of classical nineteenth century Nuu-chah-nulth art have concluded that it is a hybrid of the old Wakashan style (that goes back into antiquity) and the incoming influences from the northern two-dimensional (or graphic) style.

Characteristically, the figures most commonly featured in this art are the Wolf, Thunderbird, Whale, and Lightning Serpent. The Wolf Society (Tlu-Kwalla) is particularly important in tribal life, and it is notable that Thompson was inducted into it just before his twelfth birthday. Two very important historic screens (one in Fort Worth's Amon Carter Museum and the other in New York's American Museum of Natural History), for example, feature the classic dyad of "Thunderbird with Killer Whale".

Nuu-chah-nulth masks are identifiable at a glance due to their angularity and the distinctive appearance of the humanoid face. Bill Holm has described Nuu-chah-nulth masks as follows:

Deep from front to back, with the sides forming planes angled away from the median line, the mask achieves strong, sculptural form with minimal carving. The large, open eye rimmed with long eyelids, tapered to points, on the slightly modeled cheek plane is a typical feature of this style of carving. The area above the eye is wide and gently slanted up to the narrow arched eyebrow. Flaring nostrils and a wide, straight mouth above a short chin complete the form.

In "The Legacy" collection at the Royal British Columbia Museum in Victoria, there are three Thompson pieces: one is a humanoid, *Changing Mask*, and two are headdresses (male and female) featuring the "Lightning Snake" (or Haietlik) imagery. Evident in these and other works by Thompson is the great variety of colors preferred by Nuu-chah-nulth artists: black and red, of course, along with white and a vibrant blue, plus bright hues of green, yellow, orange, gold, and silver. The colorfulness of Nuu-chah-nulth art is one of its pronounced traits, especially noticeable in many of Thompson's silkscreen prints. Given the richness of the traditional art, Thompson has commented that there is enough material in the old Nuu-chah-nulth style to hold his interest for a lifetime. It would seem, too, that there are more and more discerning collectors for this art.

Thompson's reputation as an artist is especially strong in the area of serigraphy because he has produced a very great number of silkscreen prints. Many collectors are impressed with his bold style with its simple lines and brilliant colors. Since the late 1970s, he has been producing more woodcarvings, and these have attracted a considerable amount of critical acclaim. Thompson has also become increasingly involved with the culture of his people, as a tribal band leader and an active participant in the ceremonial dancing and singing.

—John Anson Warner

Art Thompson. Photograph by Kenji Nagai; courtesy of the artist.

TIGER, Dana

Tribal affiliations: Creek; Seminole; Cherokee
Painter

Born: Dana Irene Tiger, Tahlequah, Oklahoma, 9 December 1961. **Education:** Oklahoma State University; art instruction with her uncle, artist Johnny Tiger, Jr., brother of famous artist Jerome Tiger. **Career:** Lecturer and artist. **Awards:** Several from juried competitions as a student (Five Civilized Tribes Museum and Heard Museum) and as a professional artist, including Five Civilized Tribes Museum (1978, 1980, 1987), Tulsa Indian Art Festival and Pow Wow (1988-89), and Cherokee National Museum (1988-89).

Selected Group Exhibitions

1979   Five Civilized Tribes Museum, Muskogee, Oklahoma
1980   Five Civilized Tribes Museum, Muskogee, Oklahoma
1981   Five Civilized Tribes Museum, Muskogee, Oklahoma
1985   *Native American Rights Fund*, Boulder, Colorado

Dana Tiger: *Patrol of the Light Horse.* **Courtesy Gilcrease Museum, Tulsa, Oklahoma.**

1986	*New Harmony Indian Arts Festival,* South Dallas Cultural Center, Dallas, Texas
1989	Featured artist, Tulsa Indian Arts Fair, Tulsa Oklahoma
1990	Cherokee National Museum, Tahlequah, Oklahoma
1991	Inter-Tribal Arts Experience, Dayton, Ohio
1992	American Indian Art Festival, Houston, Texas
1993	Featured artist, Tallasi Winter Festival, Tulsa, Oklahoma
1995	Philbrook Museum of Art, Tulsa, Oklahoma
1996	Thomas Gilcrease Institute of American History and Art, Tulsa, Oklahoma

Collections

Gilcrease Museum, Tulsa, Oklahoma.

*   *   *

Dana Tiger's goal as an artist is to create new and positive images of women. That people recognize her work as feminist is particularly pleasing to her because painting is her chief means of expressing her views. Her art, then, is politically motivated: she embraces the term *feminist* and doesn't consider it negative in spite of what she feels are society's attempts to make it "another negative word to describe women."

There are certainly other factors that contribute to her popularity. Her style and her focus on Native American subjects make her works appealing, and Tiger's success is partly due to the way in which she presents her subject matter. The use of an already established style popularized by her own family increases the potential for Tiger's message to also receive wide acceptance. Jerome Tiger, Dana Tiger's father, successfully developed a unique style combining European draftsmanship with Native American flatstyle painting. Jerome Tiger died when Dana was five years old. When she dedicated herself to painting at age 24, she began to emulate her father. She also learned from the tutelage of her uncle Johnny Tiger, Jr., who encouraged all of Jerome's children to create art and to enter contests.

Dana Tiger's paintings incorporate pastel colors, graceful line and delicate composition like that of her father. Figures gradually fade into a wispy, light rendering, sometimes disappearing before the figure is complete. Works like *Freedom to Choose* and *Gathering Strength* compare to her father's pieces, like *A Walk through the Great Mysteries*, or *Observing the Enemy*. When modeling faces and figures that are more solid and complete, as in *Ritual Tradition of Human Woman*, she uses a gradual shading technique like her uncle, rather than the separate areas of differing value usually seen in her father's work.

Tiger's works gain further depth through her expression of feminist sentiments within the context of Native American culture. Drawing upon authentic traditions of Native American women adds a unique dimension to the feminist message. In some cases, Tiger does not have to look far for inspiration to support her cause. *Ritual Tradition of Human Woman* and *Sacred Power* were inspired by stories of a medicine woman from her own family. *Cherokee Women's Council* reflects the tribe's characteristic of honoring women, who share in positions of leadership. In addition to drawing upon specific traditions, Tiger composes works that portray anonymous women who serve as types representing all Native American women, and by extension, all women. These works usually have titles that bring attention to a specific issue, such as in *Freedom to Choose*. Tiger's practice of providing Native American context adds power and interest to her message, enhanced by her use of a popular "Indian" style of painting. Tiger draws upon her own heritage to give vitality to more universal messages.

—Kevin Smith

TIGER, Jerome

Variant names: Kocha
Tribal affiliations: Creek; Seminole
Painter

Born: Jerome Richard Tiger, Tahlequah, Oklahoma, 8 July 1941. **Education:** Cooper School of Art, Cleveland, 1962, and Cleveland Engineering Institute, 1963-64. **Military Service:** U.S. Marine Corps. **Career:** Sculptor and painter, laborer and prizefighter. **Awards:** Honors at major Native American fairs and juried competitions, including All-American Indian Days, Sheridan, Wyoming; inter-Tribal Indian Ceremonials, Gallup, New Mexico; Scottsdale National Indian Art Exhibition, Arizona; National Exhibition of

American Indian Art, Oakland, California; and fairs sponsored by the Philbrook Museum of Art, Tulsa, Oklahoma, and the Museum of New Mexico, Santa Fe. **Died:** 13 August 1967.

Individual Exhibitions

1965   Philbrook Museum of Art, Tulsa, Oklahoma
1967   Cherokee National Museum, Tahlequah, Oklahoma
1968   Five Civilized Tribes Museum, Muskogee, Oklahoma

Selected Group Exhibitions

1964-65 First Annual Invitational Exhibition of American Indian Paintings, United States Department of the Interior, Washington, D.C.
1967   Oklahoma Art Center Gallery, Oklahoma City
1978   *100 Years of Native American Painting*, Oklahoma Museum of Art, Oklahoma City, Oklahoma
1980   *Midwest Professional Artists Benefit Art Show*, Tulsa Garden Center, Tulsa, Oklahoma
       Native American Art at the Philbrook, Philbrook Museum, Tulsa (traveling)
1981   *Native American Painting*, Amarillo Art Center, Amarillo, Texas
1982   *Native American Painting: Selections from the Museum of the American Indian*, organized by the Museum of the American Indian, New York (traveling)
1984-85 *Indianascher Kunstler* (traveling, Germany), organized by the Philbrook Museum, Tulsa, Oklahoma
1990   *American Indian Artists in the Avery Collection and the McNay Permanent Collection*, Koogler McNay Art Museum, San Antonio, Texas (traveling)
1991-96 *Shared Visions: Native American Painters and Sculptors in the Twentieth Century*, The Heard Museum, Phoenix, Arizona (traveling)

Collections

Bureau of Indian Affairs, Department of the Interior, Washington, D.C.; Five Civilized Tribes Museum, Muskogee, Oklahoma; Thomas Gilcrease Institute of American History and Art, Tulsa, Oklahoma; Museum of New Mexico, Santa Fe; Philbrook Museum of Art, Tulsa, Oklahoma; Smithsonian Institution, Washington, D.C.; Woolaroc Museum, Bartlesville, Oklahoma.

*   *   *

Jerome Tiger's painting was influenced by both European and Native American artistic traditions. Some of his first "Indian" paintings occurred after he had already taught himself to work with European techniques. Even after success in the Indian art market, Tiger sought more training in European art techniques. Paintings done at the Cooper School of Art in Cleveland, such as *Futuristic City* (1962), show Tiger's mastery of those techniques. Tiger also sought direction from Native American painting traditions in the development of his own style. He tried flatstyle painting, the most accepted type of Native American painting at the time, viewed paintings collected by patrons such as Nettie Wheeler, and when he saw Oscar Howe's award-winning entry in the 1965 Philbrook Annual, he was inspired to experiment. Tiger's fully developed

Jerome Tiger: *The Four Moons.* **Courtesy Gilcrease Museum, Tulsa, Oklahoma.**

style exhibits the best of what he learned from these various influences. Flatstyle esthetics, sometimes flatstyle technique entirely, are combined with skilled European draftsmanship in works painted late in his career, such as *Seminole Fisherman* (1967).

Tiger's unique style is seen in works that are sometimes not as concerned with historical accuracy as with narrative action, dramatic impact, or even design, but is also evident in paintings that accurately portray aspects of tribal heritage. *Medicine Man's Help* (1964) shows a healing ceremony that was characteristicly common to many tribes but does not identify a specific tribe. This type of painting was created with more of a concern for dramatic design and narrative action, as are his many "Trail of Tears" paintings. On the other hand, Tiger often accurately portrayed such subjects as stickball games and stomp dances. *Stomp Dance* (1967), in fact, includes several traditional activities presented in vignettes. In paintings like *Waiting to Dance* (1967), Tiger shows the western type clothing actually worn by southeastern people at ceremonials. He did not add artificial or pan-Indian clothing as did many of his contemporaries. Deviations from authentic details were more often motivated by his own creative design, rather than by pan-Indian trends. As a result, his style developed in a recognizably unique direction.

Because of his successful manipulation of that style in dealing with subject matter, Tiger stood alone among his peers in his sensitive portrayal of intimate personal and family experience. His paintings were explorations of the personal human experiences occurring within Native American history and culture. He created, for instance, several pieces that illustrate the close relationship between mother and child. *Indian's Precious Cargo* (1964) shows an Indian woman carrying a child in a cradleboard, bearing the child in her arms rather than on her back, accentuating her attentiveness. *Protector* (1966) portrays a kneeling mother holding her sleeping children in her lap, one of many Tiger paintings that address family affection and concerns.

Tiger's consideration of the individual human experience is exhibited in many of the paintings done toward the end of his career. *Taking a Breather* (1966), *The Stomp Dance Looker* (1967), and *Into the Wind* (1966) all show individuals engaged in personal activities. This humanistic concern motivated Tiger to create art that contrasted with that of many of his contemporaries. Indian painting of the day generally focused on tribal community as a whole, with the individual being an anonymous component of that whole. Even portraits were concerned with either specific tribal representation or with pan-Indian types. In neither case was the personality of the individual of chief concern. Tiger asked viewers to see not only individual personalities, but also to consider the universal human experiences that they had. *Overplayed Stickballer* (1966) and *Agony* (1966) display Tiger's success in focusing the viewer's attention on a recognizable inner state of the individual.

—Kevin Smith

TIKTAK, John
Tribal affiliations: Inuit
Sculptor

Born: Karcak (a temporary Padlermiut camp situated between Arviat and Whale Cove), on the west coast of Hudson Bay, Keewatin Region, Northwest Territories, January, 1916. **Family:** Married Atunga; several children. **Career:** Nomadic hunter and fisherman; moved to Eskimo Point, mid-1950s, and Rankin Inlet, where Tiktak was a nickel miner; full-time carver, beginning 1963. **Awards:** Elected a member of the Royal Canadian Academy of Arts, 1974. **Died:** 1981.

Individual Exhibitions

1970   *Tiktak: Sculptor from Rankin Inlet, Northwest Territories,* Gallery 111, School of Art, University of Man, Winnipeg, Manitoba

Selected Group Exhibitions:

1967   *Eskimo Sculpture,* Winnipeg Art Gallery, presented at the Manitoba Legislative Building, Winnipeg, Manitoba
1969   *Eskimo Sculpture '69,* Robertson Galleries, Ottawa
1971-73 *Sculpture/Inuit: Masterworks of the Canadian Arctic,* Canadian Eskimo Arts Council, Ottawa (traveling)
1972   *Eskimo Sculpture: Selections from the Twomey Collection,* Winnipeg Art Gallery, Winnipeg, Manitoba
1978   *The Zazelenchuk Collection of Eskimo Art,* Winnipeg Art Gallery, Winnipeg, Manitoba
1979   *Canadian Eskimo Art: a representative exhibition from the collection of Professor and Mrs. Philip Gray,* Fine Arts Gallery, Montana State University, Bozeman, Montana
        Eskimo Narrative, Winnipeg Art Gallery, Winnipeg, Manitoba (traveling)
1980   *Collectors' Choice, An Exhibition of Important Inuit Sculpture,* Waddington Galleries, Toronto
        The Klamer Family Collection of Inuit Art from the Art Gallery of Ontario, University of Guelph, Guelph, Ontario
1981   *Rankin Inlet/Kangirlliniq,* Winnipeg Art Gallery, Winnipeg, Manitoba
1981-82 *Inuit Art: A Selection of Inuit Art from the Collection of the National Museum of Man, Ottawa, and the Rothmans Permanent Collection of Inuit Sculpture,* Canada National Museum of Man, Ottawa and Rothmans of Pall Mall Canada Ltd., Toronto (traveling)
        The Jacqui and Morris Shumiatcher Collection of Inuit Art, Norman Mackenzie Art Gallery, University of Regina, Regina, Saskatchewan
1982   *Sculpture Inuit: Stone/Bone circa 1960-1979,* Canadiana Galleries, Edmonton, Alberta
1983-85 *Grasp Tight the Old Ways: Selections from the Klamer Family Collection of Inuit Art,* Art Gallery of Ontario, Toronto (traveling)
1984   *Takamit, Canadian Eskimo Art: Selections from Private Collections and the Government of Canada,* organized by La Federation des Cooperatives du Nouveau-Quebec and the Jane Voorhees Zimmerli Art Museum, Rutgers University, New Brunswick, New Jersey
1984-86 *Arctic Vision: Art of the Canadian Inuit,* Department of Indian Affairs and Northern Development and Canadian Arctic Producers, Ottawa (traveling)
1986   *Pure Vision: The Keewatin Spirit,* Norman Mackenzie Art Gallery, Regina, Saskatchewan

John Tiktak: *Mother and Child.* Photograph by Kenji Nagai; courtesy Inuit Gallery of Vancouver.

1986-88 *Selections from the John and Mary Robertson Collection of Inuit Art,* Agnes Etherington Art Centre, Queen's University, Kingston, Ontario (traveling)

1988-89 *Im Schatten der Sonne: Zeitgenossische Kunst der Indianer und Eskimos in Kanada/In the Shadow of the Sun: Contemporary Indian and Inuit Art in Canada,* Canadian Museum of Civilizaion, Ottawa (traveling)

1990 *Inuit Masterworks,* Inuit Gallery of Vancouver, British Columbia

1991-92 *Moving Around the Form: Inuit Sculpture and Prints,* Agnes Etherington Art Centre, Queen's University, Kingston, Ontario

1995 *Immaginario Inuit, Arte e cultura degli esquimesi canadesi,* Galleria d'Arte Moderna e Contemporanea, Verona, Italy

Collections

Art Gallery of Ontario, Toronto; Canadian Muscum of Civilization, Hull, Quebec; Edmonton Art Gallery, Edmonton, Alberta; Eskimo Museum, Churchill, Manitoba; Agnes Etherington Art Centre, Queen's University, Kingston, Ontario; Inuit Cultural Institute, Rankin Inlet, Northwest Territories; Klamer Family Collection, Art Gallery of Ontario, Toronto; McMichael Canadian Art Collection, Kleinburg, Ontario; Mendel Art Gallery, Saskatoon, Saskatchewan; Musée des beaux-arts de Montreal, Montreal, Quebec; National Gallery of Canada, Ottawa; Prince of Wales Northern Heritage Centre, Yellowknife, Northwest Territories; Red Deer and District Museum and Archives, Red Deer, Alberta; Vancouver Art Gallery, British Columbia; Williamson Collection, Art Gallery of Ontario, Toronto; Winnipeg Art Gallery, Manitoba.

Publications

On TIKTAK: Books—*Tiktak: Sculptor from Rankin Inlet, N.W.T.,* with an essay by George Swinton, Gallery 111, Winnipeg: University of Manitoba School of Art, 1970; *Tiktak: Mother and Child, Landmarks of Canadian Art* by Peter Mellen, Toronto, McClelland and Stewart, 1978; *Rankin Inlet/Kangirlliniq* Winnipeg: Winnipeg Art Gallery, 1981; *Pure Vision: The Keewatin Spirit* by Norman Zepp, Regina: Norman Mackenzie Art Gallery, 1986. Articles—"The Spirit of Keewatin, Northwest Territories," by Robert G. Williamson, *The Beaver,* Summer, 1965; "Artists from the Keewatin," by George Swinton, *Canadian Art,* No. 101, April 1966; "Eskimo Art Reconsidered," by George Swinton, *Artscanada,* vol. 27, no. 6, December-January, 1971-72; "Some Wonderful, Creative Years in Rankin Inlet, Les Années folles des artistes de Rankin Inlet," by Claude Grenier, *About Arts and Crafts/L'art et l'artisanat,* vol. 5, no. 1, 1982.

*   *   *

John Tiktak, a self-taught stone sculptor who lived and worked in the small Arctic community of Rankin Inlet, is considered one of Canada's foremost Inuit artists. Any discussion of Rankin Inlet art is dominated by the sculpture of Tiktak and John Kavik (1897-1993). Recognition of his status as an important sculptor in his own right led to Tiktak being the first Inuit artist to be given a major retrospective exhibition and catalog: *Tiktak: Sculptor from Rankin Inlet, N.W.T.* was presented at the University of Manitoba School of Art in Winnipeg, 1970.

Tiktak was born at Kareak, a small temporary Padlermiut camp situated between Arviat (formerly Eskimo Point) and Whale Cove, on the west coast of Hudson Bay in the Keewatin Region of Canada's Northwest Territories in 1916. For much of his life he led a traditional Inuit hunting and camping life. By the 1950s many Keewatin Inuit were moving to the small permanent coastal communities because of famine and disease; Tiktak first moved to Eskimo Point, where he married Atunga and where their first two of several children were born. The family then moved to Rankin Inlet in 1958 so that Tiktak could work at the newly opened nickel mine. He began carving as early as 1961 to make extra cash. Tiktak was seriously injured in a mine accident; the mine then closed prematurely in 1962, so he turned to carving full-time in 1963. Tiktak gave up carving a few years before his death in Rankin Inlet in 1981.

Tiktak, like many Keewatin artists, was preoccupied with the human form and the human condition. Tiktak's sculptures usually represent mothers and children, single figures and heads, or clusters of heads or faces. Clearly recognizable as human images, they are nevertheless simplified and stripped of superfluous detail. Tiktak's sculptures are noted for their strong, often rounded shapes, and are perforated by round or oval holes, which can indicate the spaces between torso and arms, for example. His faces, too, are distinctive, with slit eyes and prominent cheeks; in later works, facial features are even more exaggerated, resembling crudely plowed furrows. Heads tend to dominate Tiktak's works, especially later ones; they can comprise as much as one-third of a figure. Tiktak's sculptures exude an air of static calm and timelessness, as well as monumentality. Thus they can be read as universal symbols of humanity, not merely visual images. In that sense they transcend the simple cultural content that informs much of Inuit Art.

In the opinion of George Swinton ("Artists from the Keewatin," *Canadian Art*, April 1966), Tiktak is "a primordial artist." Swinton adds, "He is primitive like Henry Moore, or Wotruba. That is to say, his sophistication of form is such that he arrives at primal shapes ... he communicates elemental matter through primal form." Tiktak's sculptural shapes, with their volumes and hollows, have often been compared to Moore's, and Moore was known to be an admirer of Tiktak's work. Tiktak's sculptures have been included in 50 exhibitions in Canada and abroad.

—Ingo Hessel

TIMECHE, Bruce
Tribal affiliations: Hopi
Painter

Born: Shungopovi, Second Mesa, Arizona, 9 November 1923. **Education:** Phoenix Indian School; Kachina School of Art, Phoenix, Arizona, 1955-1958; Phoenix College; Arizona State University, B.F.A., 1975. **Career:** Sales clerk, barber; Hopi House, Grand Canyon, 1940s; teacher, Phoenix Indian School and the Hopi Junior/Senior High School, mid-1970s to mid 1980s; katsina carver, commercial muralist, and painter. **Awards:** Whitney Scholarship, Katchina School of Art, 1955; various awards at juried competitions, including Inter-Tribal Indian Ceremonial, Heard Museum Guild Indian Fair and Market, Museum of New Mexico, Santa Fe, Philbrook Museum of Art, and Scottsdale National Indian Art Exhibition. **Died:** April 1987.

Selected Group Exhibitions

Exhibited regularly during the 1960s and 1970s at fairs and competitions, including Arizona State Fair, Phoenix; Heard Museum Guild Indian Fair and Market, Phoenix; Inter-Tribal Indian Ceremonial, Gallup, New Mexico; Maricopa County Fair, Mesa, Arizona; Museum of New Mexico, Santa Fe; Museum of Northern Arizona, Flagstaff; Philbrook Museum of Art, Tulsa; and Scottsdale National Indian Art Exhibition, Scottsdale, Arizona.

1956   *Waldorf-Astoria Scholarship Fund Exhibition*, New York
1962   Heard Museum, Phoenix, Arizona
1964   *First Annual Invitational Exhibition of American Indian Paintings,* United States Department of the Interior, Washington, D.C.
1988   *When the Rainbow Touches Down,* Heard Museum, Phoenix, Arizona (traveling)

Collections

Indian Arts & Crafts Board, United States Department of the Interior, Washington, D.C.; Logan Museum of Anthropology, Beloit, Wisconsin; Museum of Northern Arizona, Flagstaff; National Museum of the American Indian, Washington, D.C.; Southeast Museum of the North American Indian, Marathon, Florida;

Publications

On TIMECHE: Books—*American Indian Painting of the Southwest and Plains Areas*, by Dorothy Dunn, Albuquerque, University of New Mexico Press, 1968; *Indian Painters and White Patrons*, J. J. Brody, Albuquerque, University of New Mexico Press, 1971; *Southwest Indian Painting: A Changing Art*, by Clara Lee Tanner, Tucson, University of Arizona Press, 1973; *When the Rainbow Touches Down*, by Tryntje Van Ness Seymour, Phoenix, Heard Museum, 1988.

*   *   *

Bruce Timeche created art nearly his entire life but it was only when he reached his thirties that he came to regard himself as an artist. "I always thought only certain people could do art," Timeche explained humbly, but, in fact, his artistic talents had been recognized from a very early age. Timeche's first compositions were done with a stick on the ground while he was herding sheep. Traditional spiritual leaders of Hopi encouraged him to paint inside the kivas, and he carved and painted kachina dolls, given to the children to educate them about more than 300 Hopi spiritual "friends."

He grew up in Shungopavi, the mother village of Second Mesa, about a hundred miles from the Grand Canyon, where he was surrounded by scores of talented textile weavers, kachina doll carvers, jewelers, potters and painters. Most of the Hopi painters were devoted to ceremonial themes, and Hopiland in the mid-20th century was home of great masters, including Fred Kabotie and Waldo Mootzka. Timeche's education began in the kivas and the Shungopavi Day School. Like many other Hopi children, Timeche was sent away from his family to the U.S. government boarding school in Phoenix. He lived there through the end of the Great Depression. The focus of the industrial arts training there prepared students for blue collar jobs. Timeche learned to be a barber, and since the federal government seemed determined to have every Indian child's hair cropped as a symbol of "civilization," had steady work. Ironically, when Timeche went to work at the Hopi House at the Grand Canyon during the 1940s, the Fred Harvey Company wanted him to grow his hair long for a traditional Indian look expected by tourists. At the Hopi House Timeche met Catherine Poley; they married in 1948 and had one daughter, Christina.

With encouragement from his wife and friends, Timeche decided to go to art school rather late in life, enrolling at the Kachina School of Art in Phoenix shortly after he turned 32. Mrs. Cornelius Vanderbilt Whitney, one of America's wealthiest women and namesake of the Whitney Museum, admired Timeche's work and awarded him with a full scholarship. From 1955 through 1958, Timeche attended the school and began formal training in easel painting. After 30 months of art classes, a teacher told him, "I think I have taught you all I can. I'll let you graduate early because you have talent. Teach yourself as you go along."

Timeche began painting full time, initially with two-dimensional styles that had been established as a twentieth-century tradition at Hopi, and moving gradually to three-dimensional styles based on his study of European and American masters. Timeche executed beautiful portraits, landscapes and narrative themes. His paintings show affinities to Michelangelo's rendering of muscular models, Titian's rich coloration and Rembrandt's dramatic diagonal compositions while representing his own, unique style. Working in oils, Timeche specialized in portraits and painted with such confidence and speed that he could complete a full sized portrait in two weeks.

By the early 1960s, he had established himself as a respected artist and began winning awards regularly on the art fair circuit.

Timeche, who was initiated into the Hopi Kachina Society, followed the tradition of Pueblo artists by painting Kachina ceremonies in watercolors. Timeche had special feelings when he painted Kachina subjects: "I enjoy painting the katsinas— because I have taken part in the Katsina dances. . . I have seen the katsina and I know just what it is. . .I have painted the masks, I have performed in it." In his Katsina paintings, Timeche was careful only to depict those things shown in public ceremonies. What happens inside the kivas is considered sacred, and he was careful not to break taboos. Yet, excellent attention to detail is among the hallmarks of his work and combined with his infusion of Western techniques, Timeche helped expand on traditions of Hopi painting established by Kabotie and Mootzka. The social, cultural, and artistic experience he brought to his modern-styled renditions of Hopi traditions make his work particularly important, as historical illustrations and as fine art.

Traditional values were part of his curricula as well when he taught children to paint. After graduating from Arizona State University while in his forties, Timeche taught art at Phoenix Indian School and the Hopi Junior/Senior High School. He encouraged Indian students, "Think about your history of your tribe, and then try to portray it," as he had done.

—Gregory Schaaf

TOLEDO, José Rey

Variant names: Shoba Wonhon
Tribal affiliations: Jémez Pueblo; Zia Pueblo
Painter

Born: Jemez Pueblo, New Mexico, 28 June 1915; names include Shona Wonhon (Morning Star), Tia Na (Northeast Place), Aluh Hochi (Lightning), and Mus Truwi (A Little Mountain Creature with Great Power). **Education:** San Diego Mission School, Jemez Pueblo; Albuquerque Indian School; mentored in painting by his uncle, Velino Shije Herrera, with whom he lived in Santa Fe beginning in 1935; University of New Mexico, 1937-40 (studying painting with mentor and friend Dr. Florence M. Schroeder) and 1950-51, B.A.; M.A., Art Education, University of New Mexico, 1965; M.A. Comprehensive Health Planning, University of California, Berkeley, 1972. **Family:** Married Amelita Toya (Jemez; Pecos), 1938; eight children. **Career:** Decorated his mother's Zia pottery and designed the diploma for his high school graduating class before he turned twenty; professional painter beginning late 1930s; painter, Museum of Navajo Ceremonial Art (now known as the Wheelwright Museum of the American Indian); instructor, Santa Fe Indian School, mid-1930s; painter, Work Project Administration, 1939-1942; draftsman, Phoenix airplane factory, 1941-44; art instructor, Santa Fe Indian School (1949-1956) and Albuquerque Indian School (1956-1957); educator and Bureau of Indian Affairs health official, New Mexico, Colorado, and South Dakota, 1960s, New Mexico, 1970s; muralist, Indian Pueblo Cultural Center, Albuquerque, New Mexico; actor, including eleven feature films, numerous documentaries, and a television commercial for an Albuquerque-based pizza establishment. **Awards:** Numerous from fairs sponsored by the Philbrook Museum of Art, Tulsa, Oklahoma, Heard Museum, Phoenix, Arizona, Southwest Museum, Los Angeles, California, and the

José Rey Toledo, 1991. Photograph by Nura Stone; courtesy Museum of Indian Arts and Culture, Santa Fe.

Museum of New Mexico, Santa Fe, as well as the New Mexico State Fair and the Inter-Tribal Indian Ceremonials. **Died:** 1 April 1994.

Individual Exhibitions

1978   Indian Pueblo Cultural Center, Albuquerque, New Mexico
1994   Museum of Indian Arts and Culture, Santa Fe, New Mexico
        Dancing Spirits: José Rey Toledo, Tewa Artist, Museum of New Mexico, Santa Fe

Selected Group Exhibitions

1937   American Indian Exposition and Congress, Tulsa, Oklahoma
1939-40 Golden Gate International Exposition and San Francisco World's Fair, San Francisco
1947-65 *American Indian Paintings from the Permanent Collection,* Philbrook Art Center, Tulsa, Oklahoma (traveling)
1955-56 European tour sponsored by the University of Oklahoma, Norman

1958-61 European tour sponsored by the University of Oklahoma, Norman

1978 *100 Years of Native American Painting,* Oklahoma Museum of Art, Oklahoma City, Oklahoma

1979-80 *Native American Paintings,* organized by the Joslyn Art Museum, Omaha, Nebraska (traveling)

1980 *Native American Art at the Philbrook,* Philbrook Museum, Tulsa, Oklahoma (traveling)

1981 *Native American Painting,* Amarillo Art Center, Texas,

1984-85 *Indianascher Kunstler* (traveling, Germany), organized by the Philbrook Museum, Tulsa, Oklahoma

1985 *The Hunt and the Harvest: Pueblo Paintings from the Museum of the American Indian,* organized by the Gallery Association of New York State (traveling)

1988 *When the Rainbow Touches Down,* Heard Museum, Phoenix, Arizona (traveling)

1996 *Drawn from Memory: James T. Bialac Collection of Native American Art,* Heard Museum, Phoenix, Arizona

Collections

Center for Great Plains Studies, University of Nebraska, Lincoln; Thomas Gilcrease Institute of American History and Art, Tulsa, Oklahoma; Heard Museum, Phoenix, Arizona; Museum of the American Indian, New York; Museum of Indian Arts and Culture, Santa Fe, New Mexico Museum of New Mexico, Santa Fe; Museum of Northern Arizona, Flagstaff, Arizona; Muskogee Public Library, Muskogee, Oklahoma; Philbrook Museum of Art, Tulsa, Oklahoma; Millicent Rogers Foundation Museum, Taos, New Mexico; San Diego Museum of Man, California; School of American Research, Santa Fe, New Mexico; Smithsonian Institution, Washington, D.C., Southwest Muscum, Los Angeles, California; University of New Mexico, Albuquerque; University of Oklahoma, Norman, Oklahoma; Woolaroc Museum, Bartlesville, Oklahoma.

Publications

On TOLEDO: Books—*American Indian Painters,* by Oscar B. Jacobson and Jeanne D'Ucel, Nice, France, 1950; *American Indian Painting of the Southwest and Plains Areas,* by Dorothy Dunn, Albuquerque: University of New Mexico, 1968; *The American Indian Speaks,* John R. Milton (editor), Vermillion, South Dakota, 1969; *Indian Painters and White Patrons,* by J. J. Brody, Albuquerque: University of New Mexico Press, 1971; *Song from the Earth: American Indian Painting,* by Jamake Highwater, Boston, 1976; *100 Years of Native American Painting,* exhibition catalog by

José Rey Toledo: *Navajo Woman Rider,* 1942. Dr. Florence Shroeder Collection, Museum of Indian Arts and Culture, Santa Fe.

Arthur Silberman, Oklahoma Museum of Art, Oklahoma City, 1978; *Native American Art at the Philbrook,* by John Mahey, et. al., Tulsa, 1980; *American Indian Painting and Sculpture,* Patricia Broder, New York, 1981; *Native American Painting,* by Jeanne Snodgrass King, Amarillo, Texas, 1981; *Indianascher Kunstler,* by Gerhard Hoffmann, Munich, 1984; *The Hunt and the Harvest: Pueblo Paintings from the Museum of the American Indian,* by Nina Golder, Hamilton, New York, 1985; *The Arts of the North American Indian: When the Rainbow Touches Down,* exhibition catalog by Tryntje Van Ness Seymour, Heard Museum, University of Washington Press, 1988; *Dancing Spirits: José Rey Toledo, Tewa Artist,* by Susan Scarberry-Garcia, Santa Fe, 1994.

*   *   *

José Rey Toledo was born to Refugia Moquino from Zia Pueblo and José Ortiz (Jemez; Pecos). Toledo's mother's spoke Keres (the language of Zia Pueblo) as well as Towa the language of his father's village. As a child, José Rey spoke these native languages as well as Spanish and English, which he learned when he attended San Diego Mission school in the pueblo. His childhood was typical of its time, rather isolated from the non-Pueblo world except for schooling and a few goods available at the local trading post, filled with the self-reliance of a rich agricultural and ceremonial life.

He was artistically inclined from a very young age, Toledo recalled to biographer Susan Scarberry-Garcia: "I did a lot of drawing" (*Dancing Spirits,* 1994). He drew on paper sacks in pencil or crayola, or on the inside of labels from canned goods, and with his uncle he would sketch hunting scenes in charcoal on the kitchen walls. He helped his mother decorate her Zia pottery to sell. A series of realistic drawings captured in photographs taken in 1926 by a visitor to San Diego Mission School show him to be a talented young artist who demonstrated a gift for rendering visual images of the natural world. Following the death of his father and grandfather in 1928, Toledo suffered greatly and probably in an attempt to ease some of the pain he was sent to the Albuquerque Indian School, where he attended fifth through twelfth grades. In 1935 he designed the diploma for his graduating class.

Following high school he moved to Santa Fe to live with his uncle, Zia painter Velino Shije Herrera. His uncle had been a successful artist since the early 1920s and served as mentor for Dorothy Dunn's and Geronima Montoya's art classes at the Santa Fe Indian School. He would provide an excellent model for José Rey, and, as a result, during the next 15 years Toledo produced some of his very best paintings. Toledo would imitate his uncle's work, painting some of the same scenes, such as those rendered in *Matachine Dancer* and *Pine Tree Ceremonial.* He found work with the Museum of Navajo Ceremonial Art (now the Wheelwright Museum of the American Indian), taught the lower grades at the Santa Fe Indian School, and experimented with painting a series of studies of shields, medicine bowls, and Pueblo iconography, all of which are contained in the Alice Shively Collection, Museum of Indian Arts and Culture, Santa Fe.

From 1939-1942, José Rey painted for the WPA, producing some of his finest works, which were mostly sold or given to public collections. These paintings include *Dancing Spirits, Pecos Bull Dance,* and *Eastern Ceremonial.* The culmination of this period and his first major award was in 1947, when he won the grand prize at the Annual Indian Painting exhibition at the Philbrook Museum of Art in Tulsa, Oklahoma.

In 1937 Toledo took the bold step of enrolling at the University of New Mexico, financing his education through his painting. He also found a lifelong mentor and friend in faculty member Dr. Florence M. Schroeder. In 1938 he married Amelita Toya (Jemez; Pecos); together they raised a family of eight children. During World War II, Toledo moved to Phoenix to work as a draftsman in an airplane factory. After the war he returned to Santa Fe Indian School serving as an art instructor (1949-1956), and at the Albuquerque Indian School (1956-1957). He also completed his B.A. from University of New Mexico in 1951. In 1965, he received his M.A. in art education from the University of New Mexico, and in 1972 he earned a second M.A. in comprehensive health planning from the University of California at Berkeley. From the 1960s to the 1980s Toledo worked as an educator and Bureau of Indian Affairs health official in New Mexico, Colorado, and South Dakota. In 1972, he and his family were able to permanently return to Jemez Pueblo.

The combined loss of a child and a busy professional life significantly slowed José Rey's art production during the 1950s and 1960s. While he never stopped painting, he began to experiment with linoleum block prints, jewelry design, and silk screening, and he illustrated the book, *The Misadventures of Coyote: Indian Tales From the Pueblos* (1979). In addition, Toledo found other ways to express his artistic propensity, including a successful acting career. Beginning with a small part in the movie *Flap,* he eventually appeared in 11 films, including *The Man and the City, Bobby Joe and the Outlaws, The Legend of the Lone Ranger,* and *Nightwing.* Additionally, he appeared in numerous documentaries, as well as the well-loved locally produced television commercial for an Albuquerque based pizza establishment.

—Bruce Bernstein

TOM, Leanna

Tribal affiliations: Mono Lake Paiute; Miwok
Basketweaver

Born: Leanna Sam in Yosemite Valley, c. 1850. **Family:** Married Bridgeport "Mack" Tom, four children. **Career:** Trained in weaving Paiute-twined utilitarian baskets, c. 1860s; wove baskets in the new style as early as 1916; housekeeper and cook in Yosemite Valley. **Awards:** Received numerous awards at Indian Field Days exhibits, Yosemite Valley, California. **Died:** Mariposa, California, 4 May 1965.

Selected Group Exhibitions

The artist is not known to have kept any substantial records, therefore exhibition data is incomplete; the following is reconstructed from various historic documents.

1916	Bishop Harvest Days, Bishop, California
1923	Indian Field Days, Yosemite Valley, California
1924	Indian Field Days, Yosemite Valley, California
1925	Indian Field Days, Yosemite Valley, California
1926	Indian Field Days, Yosemite Valley, California
1928	June Lake Field Days, June Lake, California
1929	Indian Field Days, Yosemite Valley, California
1973	Yosemite Museum, Yosemite National Park, California

Leanna Tom: Coiled basket, c. 1926. Courtesy National Park Service, Yosemite Museum, Yosemite National Park, California.

Collections

Field Museum of Natural History, Chicago; P.A. Hearst Museum of Anthropology, University of California, Berkeley; Yosemite Museum, National Park Service, Yosemite National Park, California.

Publications

On TOM: Books—*Tradition and Innovation: A Basket History of the Indians of the Yosemite-Mono Lake Area* by Craig D. Bates and Martha J. Lee, Yosemite 1990. **Articles**—"Miwok-Paiute Basketry, 1920-1928: Genesis of an Art Form," by Craig Bates, *American Indian Art Magazine* 4(4):54-59, 1979; "Made For Sale: Baskets from the Yosemite-Mono Lake Region of California," by Craig Bates, *Moccasin Tracks* 7:4, 1981; "Ethnographic Collections at Yosemite National Park," by Craig Bates, *American Indian Art Magazine* 7(32):28-35, 1982; "Yosemite Miwok-Paiute Basketry: A Study in Cultural Change," by Craig Bates, *American Indian Basketry Magazine* ll(4):23-29, 1982; "Yosemite: A Melting Pot for Indian People and Their Baskets," by Craig D. Bates and Martha J. Lee, *Strands of Time: Yokuts, Mono and Miwok Basketmakers*, Fresno 1988.

* * *

Leanna Tom was a prolific and innovative weaver whose early works (c. 1915-1925) helped set a standard for the fancy basketry of the Yosemite-Mono Lake region. The major period of her basketry appears to be prior to 1940; during the last two decades of her life Leanna Tom is remembered for weaving utilitarian culinary baskets, which she had produced since childhood.

Tom mastered the art of weaving Paiute-twined utilitarian baskets during the 1860s, when she was a child. Baskets were then still necessary for the many food-preparation tasks of Mono Lake Paiute and Miwok peoples. Early in her life she specialized in making diagonally twined cooking baskets, which were used to stone-boil acorn mush, from willow shoots. Patterns were worked in either fern root or split redbud shoots. Leanna's sister, Louisa, who was also married to Leanna's husband, specialized in the making of diagonally twined acorn flour sifting baskets, also from willow. Each sister thus filled a special niche in the basketry needs of their family. The sisters' marriage at the same time to the same man, a not uncommon practice among the Mono Lake Paiute, must have contributed to their influencing each other's weaving.

As early as 1916 Tom wove baskets in the new style that had been refined and made popular by her niece (and husband's daughter) Lucy Telles. Tom's earliest documented new-style basket, entered in the 1916 Bishop Harvest Days Festival, displayed both old-style geometric patterns, and a new-style eight-pointed star design. Additionally, this basket has a high-shoulder and small base, a shape not formerly used in the basketry of Tom's people. The basket's form was probably based on a modification of the so-called bottleneck basket, long a part of the repertoire of the neighboring Yokuts and Western Mono.

Tom continued to produce fancy baskets, often with the highest stitch-per-inch count of any Yosemite-Mono Lake weaver, during the 1920s. Her baskets were frequent prize winners at the Yosemite Indian Field Days basket contests and she also entered her baskets in the June Lake Field Days contests. She continued to use a blending of old-style Miwok patterns and new patterns (such as realistic arrows, flames, and eight-pointed stars) in many of her baskets.

While producing baskets for sale to non-Indians was the major part of Tom's weaving, she also made baskets for use by local Indian people. She wove many utilitarian baskets, but also on occasion made baskets in the fancy style for family members. Tom returned to making primarily utilitarian baskets in the 1950s, although at the time of her death an unfinished fancy basket was in her possession. Worked in an extremely complex pattern using primarily black-dyed bracken fern root with redbud and sedge root highlights, it was about 16 inches in diameter and recalled the negative-patterned baskets of Tina Charlie.

—Craig Bates

TOPPAH, Herman

Variant names: Al Qua Kou
Tribal affiliations: Kiowa
Painter

Born: Carnegie, Oklahoma, 17 August 1923; Kiowa name means Yellow Hair. **Education:** St. Patrick's Mission School and Riverside Indian School, Anadarko, Oklahoma, and Chilocco Indian School, Chilocco, Oklahoma; mural instruction under Olaf Nordmark; personal instruction from noted Kiowa painters James Auchiah, Spencer Asah, Leonard Riddles, Archie Blackowl, and Cecil Murdock. **Career:** Member of the Native American Church, painter. **Awards:** Several from juried exhibitions, including American Indian Exposition (posthumous, 1982), Inter-Tribal Indian Ceremonial, Philbrook Museum of Art, and Regional Motorola Art Show. **Died:** 1980.

Selected Group Exhibitions

1963   Bismark National Indian Art Show, Bismark, North Dakota

       Philbrook Museum of Art, Tulsa, Oklahoma
1964   *First Annual National American Indian Art Exposition*, Charlotte, North Carolina
1972   *Contemporary Southern Plains Indian Painting*, Southern Plains Indian Museum and the Oklahoma Indian Arts and Crafts Co-operative, Anadarko, Oklahoma (traveling)
1981   *Native American Painting*, Amarillo Art Center, Amarillo, Texas
1982   *American Indian Exposition*, Anadarko, Oklahoma

1996   *Visions and Voices: Native American Painting from the Philbrook Museum of Art,* Philbrook Museum of Art, Tulsa, Oklahoma

Collections

Carnegie High School, Carnegie, Oklahoma; Philbrook Museum of Art, Tulsa, Oklahoma; Southern Plains Indian Museum and Craft Center, Indian Arts and Crafts Board, United States Department of the Interior, Anadarko, Oklahoma; United States Department of the Interior, Washington, D.C..

Publications

On TOPPAH: Books—*American Indian Painters*, by Oscar B. Jacobson and Jeanne d'Ucel, Nice, France, 1950; *Indian Painters and White Patrons*, by J. J. Brody, Albuquerque, University of New Mexico Press, 1971; *Native American Painting*, by Jeanne Snodgrass King, Amarillo, Texas, 1981; *Kiowa Voices*, by Maurice Boyd, Fort Worth, Texas Christian University Press, 1981; *Visions and Voices: Native American Painting from the Philbrook Museum of Art*, Lydia L. Wyckoff, editor, Tulsa, Philbrook Museum of Art, 1996. **Audio tapes**—*Kiowa Historical Notes*, by James Auchiah, Kiowa Tribal Museum, Carnegie, Oklahoma, January 23, 1974.

*   *   *

Herman Toppah is best known for paintings related to the Native American Church, of which he was a devoted follower respectful of its strictest tenets. The symbols and compositions painted by artists associated with the church and its peyote-based rituals were subject to scrutiny and critique from other members. Toppah created a legacy of work that can be appreciated for authenticity and historical detail as well as imaginative and visionary effects, rendered in a flatstyle manner. Peyote, a cactus with hallucinogenic properties, is a sacrament in the Native American Church, and Toppah's bursts of visionary imagery reflects spiritual traditions and symbolism popular among peyotists.

The religion stresses strong community values, family connections and the freedom of individuals to experience personal, spiritual visions. The Church was legalized with the aid of Smithsonian Institution ethnographer James Moody, who was sent to Oklahoma around the turn of the century to be among Toppah's Kiowa ancestors and gather information for pending legislation that threatened to make the "Peyote Way" illegal. Moody met many peyotists, attended their meetings and eventually became an advocate for their religious freedom.

Toppah maintained a humble existence and rarely left his native area. His son, Bryon, recalls that his painting routine consisted of finding a lamp and setting it up near the dining room table: "that's where he did most of his work. He had just what he absolutely needed, his brushes, and his paints." As a devoted insider of the Church, Toppah expresses an immediacy about his community through his art that few others have achieved. Recognizing his talent, several artists offered him training, including such noted painters as James Auchiah and Spencer Asah, both of whom also painted peyote rituals. Auchiah and Asah differ from Toppah for their much more practiced and skillful techniques as well as wider range of subject matter, but Toppah's less trained and refined manner and more exclusive focus are precisely the traits that make his work important. His careful detail and fanciful imagery offer historical illustrations of the particular ceremonies and beliefs of the Church.

Among Toppah's most noted works is the watercolor, *Peyote Ceremony* (1963). With smoke from a Peyote altar swirling upward, flanked by a Kiowa man and woman in deep meditation, a Peyote Road Man, or religious leader, sprinkles cedar onto the fire from his upraised hand. Above the smoke are stars in a darkening sky, where a Scissor Tail and a Water Bird soar. These are the two most important birds to Peyotists: from them come feathers used in Peyote fans, and they symbolize the freedom of spiritual visions. The painting balances between realism and fantasy, too finely detailed to be abstract but presenting layers of interpretation and meaning through symbolism and depth of images.

The history of the Kiowa and their visions of the future emerge through paintings and song. Toppah merged the two by singing while he painted. Native American Church songs mostly are high pitched and fast in tempo. Toppah's son recalled an image of his father hard at work: "He'd be painting and he'd be singing Indian songs while he was doing it or humming along." When Toppah received a vision, he would sit down and paint it.

—Gregory Schaaf

TRIPP, Brian

Tribal affiliations: Karok
Painter, sculptor, mixed media artist, basketweaver

Born: Eureka, California, 1945. **Education:** Humboldt State University, 1970-76. **Military Service:** U.S. Army, 1967-69, served in Vietnam. **Career:** Educator in art, Humboldt State University; cultural consultant; public information officer, Tricounty Indian Development Council, Eureka, California; member, board of directors, Clarke Memorial Museum, Eureka, and Native American advisory committee, California State Parks, Sacramento, California; graphic art consultant and artist; California Arts Council artist in residence, The Ink People, Eureka; traditional dancer and singer.

Selected Group Exhibitions

1975   Humbolt State University, Arcata, California
1976   *New Horizons,* Southwest Museum, Los Angeles
1977   Alternati Center for International Arts, New York
1981   *American Indian Art in the 1980s,* Native American Center for the Living Arts, Niagara Falls, New York
        Confluences of Tradition and Change, Richard L. Nelson Gallery, Davis, California
1983   *Innovations: New Expressions in Native American Painting,* Heard Museum, Phoenix, Arizona
1984   *Landscape, Landbase, and Environment,* American Indian Community House Gallery, New York
1986   *The Extension of Tradition: Contemporary Native American Art in Cultural Perspective,* Crocker Art Museum, Sacramento, California
1988   Chaw'se Cultural Center, Pinegrove, California
1989   *Works by Burns, LaMarr, Noble, and Tripp,* American Indian Contemporary Arts Gallery, San Francisco

1990   *Recent Works by Five Northern California Indian Artists,* Gallery Route One, Point Reyes, California
        Art Faculty Exhibition, Humboldt State University, Arcata, California
        Tradition and Change: Contemporary California Indian Art, University of California, Riverside
1991   *Keeping Indian Tradition Alive,* Tsurai, California
1992   Humboldt Cultural Center, Eureka, California
1993   Edinboro State College, Edinboro, Pennsylvania
1994   Carnice Cultural Arts Center, Oxnard, California
        Gardiner Art Gallery, Oklahoma State University, Stillwater, Oklahoma
1996   C.N. Gorman Museum, University of California, Davis
        Crocker Art Museum, Sacramento, California
1997   Hupa Tribal Museum, Hoopa, California

Collections

Crocker Art Museum, Sacramento, California; Washington State Art Commission, Olympia, Washington.

Publications

On TRIPP: Books—*New Horizons,* exhibition catalog, Southwest Museum, Los Angeles, 1976; *Confluences of Tradition and Change: 24 American Indian Artists,* edited by L. Price Amerson, Jr., Davis, California, 1981; *American Indian Art in the 1980s,* by Lloyd Kiva New, Niagara Falls, New York, 1981; *The Fine Art of California Indian Basketry,* by Brian Bibby, Sacramento, 1996. **Article**—"Brian Tripp," by Darryl Wilson, *News from Native California,* Spring 1992.

*

Brian Tripp comments:

Through my body flows the blood of singers and dancers, makers of the dance regalia, carvers, and basketmakers, hunters and fishermen, all believers in the traditional religion of the old ways. I know I am these people and I have done all those things before many, many years ago.

*   *   *

Brian Tripp uses art as a means for extending and expanding on the traditions of his Karok culture and clarifying, perhaps reclaiming, an identity threatened by Western culture. His very act of conceptualizing and creating becomes part of an ongoing ritual his people have been performing for thousands of years in northern California, and its results—reflected on an individual level in his art and on a community level in ceremonial and everyday use and appreciation of such works—represents the most significant, profound and clearest expression of cultural identity. These concerns are reflected in artworks in various media that draw from traditional symbols and beliefs of his culture, which Tripp reworks into contemporary forms, giving new expression and often addressing contemporary issues. *They Think They Own the Place* (1992), for example, presents the image of a traditional Karok housepit with streams of silver descending upon it, suggesting encroaching forms of modern urban life represented in silver to symbolize material values.

Tripp has always identified with artistic expression, as he told Darryl Wilson (*Notes from Native California,* Spring 1992): "I have always known that I was going to be an artist. Ever since I was a little kid. Somewhere along the line I discovered that an artist was an actual thing. I said, 'whoa, that is me. That is what I want to be.'" Tripp took part in Karok ceremonies, became immersed in understanding the historical artifacts of his people (symbols commonly found woven in basketry, a 10,000-year-old tradition, recur in his work), and began carving and painting. Being a member of the Karok Nation, the artist draws from a sophisticated coastal culture: excellent examples of wood carving range from canoes used for ocean salmon fishing to fluted elk horn spoons; shell necklaces and feathered headdresses are among the other forms of traditional craft, and the World Renewal ceremony features dancers who hold cylindrical basketry purses with designs of spiritual symbolism. Tripp grew up with these and many more ancient and symbolic objects to inspire his art and sense of cultural appreciation.

It was not until he was in his mid-twenties, after a tour of duty in Vietnam, that Tripp began to forge his personal expression; his career reflects a steady progression from modest and small-scale drawings, paintings, and carvings, to larger and more complex works. His studies at Humboldt State exposed him to a variety of practices and techniques, which helped him expand his approaches while he furthered his commitment to tribal values. He began exhibiting his work during the mid-1970s and was included in several important exhibitions of the 1980s, including *American Indian Art in the 1980s, Confluences of Tradition and Change, Innovations: New Expressions in Native American Painting, Landscape, Landbase, and Environment,* and *The Extension of Tradition: Contemporary Native American Art in Cultural Perspective.* Tripp had discovered modes of contemporary expression for representing and reflecting on the past and present concerns of his people: "Just as the people before me explained their world, I try to understand and bring purpose to mine. My art is a personal reflection of that time and that reality" (*The Extension of Tradition* catalog, 1985). Additionally, Tripp became active in promoting these concerns in a variety of activities in northern California.

Tripp continues to participate in ceremonies as a dancer and singer. His artwork, though often a distinctly contemporary extension of more traditional forms, is also, nevertheless, connected to ritual. In the solitude of the far northwestern wilderness of California, he gathers materials, muses, and finds ideas and inspiration for his work—collecting, exploring and conceptualizing in the manner of his forebears.

—Gregory Schaaf

TSABETSAYE, Roger J.

Tribal affiliations: Zuñi
Painter, jewelry designer, and ceramist

Born: Zuñi Pueblo, New Mexico, 29 October 1941. **Education:** Southwest Indian Art Project, University of Arizona, summers 1960-63; Institute of American Indian Arts, Santa Fe, New Mexico, 1962-63; School for American Craftsmen, Rochester Institute of Technology, 1963-65. **Career:** Instructor and administrator, Institute of American Indian Arts; representative in government conferences that helped launch programs associated with The War on Poverty during President Lyndon Johnson's administration; founder

and owner, Tsabetsaye Enterprises, Zuñi Pueblo; silversmith, ceramist, and painter; numerous commissions, by President Lyndon Johnson for a necklace to present to the wife of Costa Rican president Orlich, by the Inter-Tribal Indian Ceremonial, Gallup, New Mexico, for a commemorative poster, 1975, by the Zuñi Tribe for the Zuñi Veteran's Medal of Valor, presented to Zuñi veterans of foreign wars, and by the Turkey-Bear Clan, Inc., for commemorative posters, among others; member, Board of Directors, New Mexico Indian Business Association, 1979-82, All-Indian Pueblo Marketing, Indian Pueblo Cultural Center, 1982-86, and new Mexico State Commission on Indian Affairs, 1984-88 and 1988-90; Tribal Councilman (1979-86), Head Tribal Councilman and Tribal Treasurer (1982-86), Zuñi Tribal Council. **Awards:** Rochester School of Technology, New York, scholarship; Albuquerque Indian School, New Mexcio, Arts and Crafts Department Certificate of Merit and Student Service Certificate; Institute of American Indian Arts, Santa Fe, New Mexico, Outstanding Student, 1963; Outstanding Minority Retailer, State of New Mexico Office of Minority Business, 1975; numerous at juried competitions, including Inter-Tribal Indian Ceremonial, poster contest award, 1959, 1964-66, and Museum of New Mexico, Santa Fe, Philbrook Museum of Art, Tulsa, Oklahoma, and Scottsdale National Indian Art Exhibition, Scottsdale, Arizona, Santa Fe Indian Market, 1989-91, and Museum of Northern Arizona, 1995.

Selected Group Exhibitions

Exhibits regularly at art fairs and juried competitions throughout the southwest.

1965-66 *Young American Indian Artists*, Riverside Museum, New York
1967   Indian Arts & Crafts Board, United States Department of the Interior, Washington, D.C.
1968   Arizona State Museum, University of Arizona, Tucson
1981   Philbrook Museum of Art, Tulsa, Oklahoma
1982   Heard Museum, Phoenix, Arizona
1986   Museum of New Mexico, Santa Fe
1987   Tulsa Indian Art Festival and Pow Wow
1996   *Visions + Voices: Native American Painting from the Philbrook Museum of Art,* Tulsa, Oklahoma

Collections

Arizona State Museum, University of Arizona, Tucson; Indian Arts & Crafts Board, United States Department of the Interior, Washington, D.C.; Museum of New Mexico, Santa Fe; Museum of Northern Arizona, Flagstaff; Philbrook Museum of Art, Tulsa, Oklahoma.

Publications

On TSABETSAYE: Books—*Indian Painters and White Patrons*, by J. J. Brody, Albuquerque, 1971; *Southwest Indian Painting: A Changing Art*, by Clara Lee Tanner, Tucson, 1973; *Native Americans: 23 Indian Biographies,* by Dr. Roger W. Axford, Indianapolis, 1980; *Zuñi Jewelry*, by Theda and Michael Bassman, West Chester, Pennsylvania, 1992; *Visions + Voices: Native American Painting from the Philbrook Museum of Art,* Lydia Wyckoff, editor, Tulsa, 1996. **Articles**—"In the Name of Progress, Is History Being Repeated?," by Jeanne Snodgrass-King, *American Indian Art Magazine*, Spring 1985.

*

Roger J. Tsabetsaye comments (1993):

I think the ultimate depth of who you really are as a person or as an artist . . . can be found through the freedom of expression to understand universal art.

At the University of Arizona, where I studied (in the Southwest Indian Art Project, which led to the formation of the Institute of American Indian Arts), they stressed there are no limits and nothing is one-sided. So what you're doing is you're beginning to understand the depth of life or who you are. You were born at a certain time, year, and so on. All of a sudden you're like a soulless, nameless individual. Now you feel like you've been stripped of everything else and you begin to think for yourself. You're given the whole world. And I think once you begin to analyze all that contains life and understand the profession yourself, the true art world, there's no divisions.

I think you can do traditional art forms as well as contemporary abstract forms if you come through with what you intend to interpret and express. (From *Visions + Voices,* 1996)

*   *   *

A talented artist in several media and an activist who has worked through community, educational and governmental systems to address Native American issues and concerns, Roger J. Tsabetsaye has been a highly visible artist and spokesperson as well as a kind of "grass roots" organizer, working from within his Pueblo and actively engaging in the business and everyday life of Zuñi to help further the interests of the community. At various times in his life, Tsabetsaye has been an innovative painter, a talented student and educator, a spokesperson for Native American concerns in government conferences, a ceramist working within traditional forms and methods, an art promoter through a Zuñi-based business he founded, and a jeweler whose striking designs are stirring excitement during the 1990s. His sister, Edith Tsabetsaye, is a renowned jeweler as well.

Tsabetsaye has been involved in some of the major developments in Native American art and social issues, but neither as flamboyantly as abstract painter Fritz Scholder nor as defiantly as some other fellow artists. Tsabetsaye was an innovative artist during the 1960s period of change and new developments, working in abstract forms that incorporated elements of his culture in markedly contemporary manners. He was one of the first students of the Institute of American Indian Arts, after having participated in the "Southwest Indian Art Project" in 1961 that helped launch the school, and he taught at the Institute as well as helping develop its overall curricula. The purpose of the Southwestern Arts Project, held at the University of Arizona, as described by participants, was to provide "young potential artists a thorough knowledge of their own artistic heritage and tradition, of the great world art tradition, of design as it applies to their own art products, and of contemporary tools, materials and techniques." The curricular approach was "to instruct primarily by participation and demonstration." The instructors included Charles Loloma (jewelry), Professor Andreas Anderson and Joe Herrera (painting), and Lloyd Kiva New (fabrics).

Tsabetsaye can be counted among the initial Native American painters to practice contemporary abstract forms that developed after the mid-twentieth century. Many of his paintings depict activities and ceremonies at Zuñi, incorporating traditional motifs, designs, symbols and subjects while displaying an approach markedly different than Pueblo painters that preceded him. *Shalako Ceremonial* (1962), for example, features lively Kachinas and stilted figures with headdresses and masks, dancing in an animated rite; designs on kilts, robes, breech cloths, and other regalia are acutely rendered. Unlike the outdoor settings, flatstyle manner, and sparse background of his predecessors, Tsabetsaye sets the painting indoors with viewers, arranged flatly in the style of medieval paintings, peering on through a window. The freedom with which he mixes styles, adds telling details, and strives for an implied setting give the work a decidedly contemporary feel. Originality and incorporation of an array of techniques flourish throughout the piece, whereas traditional Pueblo painters often expressed originality by blending flourishes upon painstaking realistic detail. Authenticity and the dynamics of a lively ceremony are displayed in Tsabetsaye's work, despite its obvious break from "traditional Indian painting." The painting, in fact, extends the tradition, and the central ceremonial activity, with all other elements in the painting removed, could stand itself as a traditional painting. In many ways, then, this painting fulfills the stated purpose of the Southwestern Arts Project.

During the mid-1960s, after teaching at the Institute for American Indian Arts, Tsabetsaye represented Indian concerns at several governmental conferences and on panels that became part of President Lyndon Johnson's War on Poverty. Tsabetsaye then returned to his native Zuñi Pueblo to work on the community level, which included founding Tsabetsaye Enterprises to help promote Zuñi art.

In his paintings, Tsabetsaye has ranged from traditional styles to more abstract works. Many of his paintings depict ceremonies, with the abstract works generally considered superior. Tribal designs and cubist perspectives enrich the spiritual elements of these paintings, where a wild array of colors and unbridled motion evoke a sense of spiritualism and action. Tsabetsaye's early abstracts regularly won awards at art fairs during the 1960s.

Tsabetsaye's work in ceramics and jewelry is more traditional, aligned with the long history of practice of these arts at Zuñi. Four pieces he entered in the 1991 Gallup Inter-Tribal Indian Ceremonial represent his jewelry work: a raised inlay, 14 kt gold bracelet composed of a row of domed cabochons tapering gracefully toward the ends, with large oxblood coral and lapis lazuli inlays in highly polished gold settings; a ring matches nicely, also in coral and lapis, while another ring adds turquoise in an oval whirlwind design; a larger ring is a vertical rectangle with four inlays stacked in columns, evoking a monumental effect.

—Perry Bear

TSATOKE, Monroe

Tribal affiliations: Kiowa
Painter

Born: Near Saddle Mountain, Oklahoma, 29 September 1904. **Education:** Bacone College and informal painting classes at the University of Oklahoma. **Career:** Artist, singer and dancer, and farmer. **Awards:** Among several commissions, painted murals for the Oklahoma Historical Society Museum, Oklahoma City, and the U.S.

government the Federal Building in Anadarko, Oklahoma; University of Oklahoma colophon is adopted from one of his paintings. **Died:** 3 February 1937

Selected Group Exhibitions

1928   *Five Kiowas,* traveling exhibition arranged by Oscar Brousse Jacobson
        Five Kiowas, First International Art Exposition, Prague, Czechoslovakia
1930   Southwest States Indian Art Show, Santa Fe
1933   *American Indian Exposition,* Anadarko, Oklahoma
1936   *First American Indian Exposition,* Tulsa, Oklahoma
1945   United Nations Conference, San Francisco, California
1947-65 *American Indian Paintings from the Permanent Collection,* Philbrook Art Center, Tulsa, Oklahoma (traveling)
1955-56 European tour sponsored by the University of Oklahoma, Norman
1958-61 European tour sponsored by the University of Oklahoma, Norman
1972   *Contemporary Southern Plains Indian Painting,* tour organized by the Southern Plains Indian Museum and Oklahoma Indian Arts and Crafts Cooperative, Anadarko, Oklahoma
1978   *100 Years of Native American Painting,* Oklahoma Museum of Art, Oklahoma City, Oklahoma
1979   *Sharing Our Wealth,* Oklahoma Historical Society, Oklahoma City, Oklahoma
1980   *Plains Indian Paintings,* Museum of Art, University of Oklahoma, Norman (traveling)
1981-83 *Native American Painting,* Amarillo Art Center, Amarillo, Texas (traveling)
1982   *Native American Painting: Selections from the Museum of the American Indian,* The Heard Museum, Phoenix, Arizona
1984-85 *Indianascher Kunstler,* organized by the Philbrook Art Museum, Tulsa, Oklahoma (touring Germany)
1990   *American Indian Artists: The Avery Collection and the McNay Permanent Collection,* Marion Koogler McNay Art Museum, San Antonio, Texas
1991   *Kiowa Murals,* The Southern Plains Indian Museum and Crafts Center, Anadarko, Oklahoma
1991-92 *Shared Visions: Native American Painters and Sculptors in the Twentieth Century,* The Heard Museum, Phoneix, Arizona

Collections

Anadarko City Museum, Oklahoma; Cleveland Museum of Art, Ohio; Thomas Gilcrease Institute of American History and Art, Tulsa, Oklahoma; Heard Museum, Phoenix, Arizona; Indian Arts and Crafts Board, Department of the Interior, Washington, D.C.; Josylyn Art Museum, Omaha, Nebraska; Marion Koogler McNay Art Museum, San Antonio Texas; Museum of Art, University of Oklahoma, Norman; Museum of the Great Plains, Lawton, Oklahoma; Museum of Northern Arizona, Flagstaff; Oklahoma Historical Society Museum, Oklahoma City; Millicent Rogers Foundation Museum, Taos, New Mexico; Woolaroc Museum, Bartlesville, Oklahoma.

Publications

By TSATOKE: Book—*The Peyote Ritual: Visions and Descriptions,* San Francisco, 1957.

On TSATOKE: Books—*Kiowa Indian Art,* by Oscar B. Jacobson, Nice, France, 1929; *American Indian Painters,* by Oscar B. Jacobson and Jeanne d'Ucel, Nice, France, 1950; *American Indian Painting of the Southwest and Plains Areas,* by Dorothy Dunn, Albuquerque, New Mexico, 1968; *Indian Painters and White Patrons,* by J. J. Brody, Albuquerque, New Mexico, 1971; *Song from the Earth: American Indian Painting,* by Jamake Highwater, Boston, 1976; *100 Years of Native American Art* (exhibition catalog), by Arthur Silberman, Oklahoma City, 1978; *Kiowa Voices: Ceremonial Dance, Ritual and Song,* by Maurice Boyd, Fort Worth, Texas, 1981; *Native American Painting* (exhibition catalog), by Jeanne Snodgrass King, Amarillo, Texas, 1981; *Native American Painting: Selections from the Museum of the American Indian,* New York, 1982; *Shared Visions,* by Margaret Archuleta and Rennard Strickland, Phoenix, 1991. **Articles**—"The Development of Modern American Indian Painting in the Southwest and Plains Area," by Dorothy Dunn, *El Palacio* LVIII, November, 1951; " Kiowa Indian Art," by Maybelle Mann, *American Art and Antiques,* January-February, 1979.

*   *   *

Monroe Tsatoke died tragically young from tuberculosis but he did manage to leave behind a legacy of his creative work. He was a member of the famous group of "Kiowa Five" artists who were the founders of the "flat style" of two-dimensional painting on the Southern Plains of Oklahoma. Along with Spencer Asah, James Auchiah, Jack Hokeah, and Stephen Mopope, Tsatoke established the primary paradigm in the 1920s and early 1930s for Oklahoma Indian painting, which is still popular among many artists today. Unlike his colleagues, Tsatoke did not attend St. Patrick's Mission School in Anadarko. However, he did participate in the art classes organized in 1918 by Susan (Susie) Ryan Peters and the special art courses created for the Kiowa Five at the University of Oklahoma in Norman from 1926 to 1929. Since Tsatoke was already married by the time OU courses were set up, he lived in an apartment off campus with his wife (as did the similarly situated James Auchiah). In 1928, some of Tsatoke's work completed at OU went on a touring exhibition with the oeuvre of his colleagues. The collected works of these artists were sent to the First International Art Exposition in Prague, Czechoslovakia, and in 1929 a folio set of their art in silkscreen form, titled *Kiowa Indian Art,* was published in Nice, France.

In the early 1930s Tsatoke accompanied his friends to the Inter-Tribal Indian Ceremonials in Gallup, New Mexico. While his four friends performed as dancers, Tsatoke accompanied them with song. Unfortunately, his health was already beginning to fail and he was not strong enough to engage in the dances. Tsatoke's supreme talent as a painter was unable to reach its fullest development due to an early death in 1937 from tuberculosis. During his illness, Tsatoke became a strong believer in the Native American Church (peyote cult). While all of the Kiowa Five artists had some familiarity and appreciation for this belief, only Tsatoke and Auchiah became ardent members of the faith. It was natural, therefore, that many of Tsatoke's paintings featured symbols and paraphernalia, along with persons and scenarios, associated with peyote ceremonies. *Member of the Peyote Cult,* (1929; now in the collection of the Oklahoma

Historical Society in Oklahoma City) shows a single figure replete with peyote fan, gourd rattle, water drum, and beadwork accoutrements all pertinent to peyote religious activities. After his death, *The Peyote Ritual Visions and Descriptions of Monroe Tsatoke*, a book of his thoughts, prayers, and songs in connection with the peyote ritual, was published.

Despite the fact that he did not live long enough to produce as many works as some of the other Kiowa Five painters, Tsatoke won strong critical acclaim; indeed, some art historians, like Jamake Highwater, believed that he was the best of the five. Highwater stated:

> Tsatoke was unquestionably the master, standing apart in his highly sophisticated individuality. His paintings possess the kind of precision and depth which is seen in the primal imagery of Paul Gauguin: a curiously unreal realism, a pervasive sense of mystery arising out of the simplest detail, and an extraordinary sense of color, which, though the hues are familiar, blends to create an entirely unexpected and vivid harmony. Tsatoke was an Indian painter whose work would astonish us if we saw it without the least information about his race, training, tradition, or place in history.

—John Anson Warner

TSINAHJINNIE, Andy

Variant names: Yazzie Bahe
Tribal affiliations: Navajo
Painter

Born: Andrew Van Tsinahjinnie; birth dates vary, from as early as 1908 and 1909 to 16 February 1916, and military discharge papers list November 14, 1916; Yazzie Bahe translates as Little Grey. **Education:** Santa Fe Indian School, 1932-36. **Military Service:** U.S. Air Force, World War II, Pacific Theatre. **Career:** Translated Navajo for a medicine man, Chicago World's Fair, 1933; book illustrator, beginning late 1930s, most often for textbooks (Bureau of Indian Affairs, 1930s and 1940s; Navajo Curriculum Center, 1970s); full-time artist and muralist following World War II. **Awards:** Numerous, including Arizona Living Treasure Award; Paul Coze Award and Palmes d'Academiques, France; and honors from Heard Museum Guild Indian Fair and Market, Inter-Tribal Indian Ceremonials, Museum of New Mexico, Museum of Northern Arizona, Philbrook Musuem of Art, and Scottsdale National Indian Arts Exhibition.

Selected Group Exhibitions

1933	Chicago World's Fair, Chicago, Illinois
1937	*American Indian Exposition and Congress,* Tulsa, Oklahoma
1947-65	*American Indian Paintings from the Permanent Collection,* Philbrook Art Center, Tulsa, Oklahoma (traveling)
1955-56	European tour sponsored by the University of Oklahoma, Norman
1958-61	European tour sponsored by the University of Oklahoma, Norman
1964	Read Mullan Gallery of Western Art, Phoenix, Arizona
1964-65	First Annual Invitational Exhibition of American Indian Paintings, United States Department of the Interior, Washington, D.C.
1978	*100 Years of Native American Painting,* Oklahoma Museum of Art, Oklahoma City, Oklahoma
1980	*Native American Painting at the Philbrook,* Philbrook Museum of Art, Tulsa, Oklahoma (traveling)
1981-83	*Native American Painting,* Amarillo Art Center, Amarillo, Texas (traveling)
1982	*Native American Painting: Selections from the Museum of the American Indian,* Heard Museum, Phoenix, Arizona
1984-85	*Indianascher Kunstler* (traveling, Germany), organized by the Philbrook Museum, Tulsa, Oklahoma
1988	*When the Rainbow Touches Down,* Heard Museum, Phoenix, Arizona (traveling)
1990	*American Indian Artists in the Avery Collection and the McNay Permanent Collection,* Marion Koogler McNay Art Museum, San Antonio, Texas
1991-92	*Shared Visions: Native American Painters and Sculptors in the Twentieth Century,* The Heard Museum, Phoenix, Arizona
1996	*Drawn from Memory: James T. Bialac Collection of Native American Art,* Heard Museum, Phoenix, Arizona

Collections

American Museum of Natural History, New York; Amerind Foundation, Dragoon, Arizona; Center for Great Plains Studies, University of Nebraska, Lincoln; Columbus Gallery of Fine Arts, Columbus, Ohio; Denver Art Museum, Denver, Colorado; Denver Museum of Natural History, Denver, Colorado; Thomas Gilcrease Institute of American History and Art, Tulsa, Oklahoma; Heard Museum, Phoenix, Arizona; Heritage Center, Inc., Pine Ridge, South Dakota; Indian Arts and Crafts Board, Washington, D.C.; Logan Museum of Anthropology, Beloit, Wisconsin; Marion Koogler McNay Art Museum, San Antonio, Texas; Museum of Navajo Ceremonial Art, Santa Fe, New Mexico; Museum of New Mexico, Santa Fe; Museum of Northern Arizona, Flagstaff, Arizona; Philbrook Museum of Art, Tulsa, Oklahoma; Millicent Rogers Foundation Museum, Taos, New Mexico; Southeast Museum of the North American Indian, Marathon, Florida; University of Oklahoma, Norman, Oklahoma; Smithsonian Institution, Washington, D.C.; Wheelwright Museum of the American Indian, Santa Fe, New Mexico.

Publications

By TSINAHJINNIE: Books illustrated—*Who Wants to be a Prairie Dog?,* by Ann Nolan Clark, Phoenix, 1940; *Navajo Life Series,* by Hildegard Thompson, Phoenix, 1948; *The Pollen Path: A Collection of Navajo Myths Retold,* by Margaret Schevill, Stanford, California, 1956; *Peetie the Pack Rat, and Other Indian Stories,* by Ann Nolan Clark, Caldwell, Idaho, 1960; *Snake Skin and Hoops,* by Leland C. Wyman, Flagstaff, Arizona, 1966; *Black Mountain Boy,* by Vada Carlson and Gary Witherspoon, Washington, D.C., 1968; *Navajo Biographies,* Vol. 1, by Virginia Hoffmann, Phoenix, 1974; *A History of Navajo Clans,* by Regina Lynch, Cortez, Colorado, 1987.

On TSINAHJINNIE: Books—*American Indian Painters,* by Oscar B. Jacobson and Jeanne D'Ucel, Nice, France, 1950; *A Pictorial History of the American Indian,* by Oliver LaFarge, New York, 1956; *Southwestern Indian Arts and Crafts,* by Tom Bahti, Flagstaff, 1966; *American Indian Painting of the Southwest and Plains Areas,* by Dorothy Dunn, Albuquerque: University of New Mexico, 1968; *Indian Painters and White Patrons,* by J. J. Brody, Albuquerque: University of New Mexico Press, 1971; *Song from the Earth: American Indian Painting,* by Jamake Highwater, Boston, 1976; *100 Years of Native American Painting,* exhibition catalog by Arthur Silberman, Oklahoma Museum of Art, Oklahoma City, 1978; *American Indian Painting and Sculpture,* Patricia Broder, New York, 1981; *Indianascher Kunstler,* by Gerhard Hoffman, Munich, 1984; *The Arts of the North American Indian: Native Traditions in Evolution,* Edwin L. Wade, ed., New York: Hudson Hills Press in association with Philbrook Art Center, Tulsa, Oklahoma, 1986; *When the Rainbow Touches Down,* exhibition catalog by Tryntje Van Ness Seymour, Heard Museum, University of Washington Press, 1988; *Beyond Tradition: Native American Art and Its Evolution,* by Jerry and Lois Jacka, Flagstaff, 1988; *American Indian Artists in the Avery Collection and the McNay Permanent Collection,* Jean Sherrod Williams, editor, San Antonio, 1990; *Shared Visions: Native American Painters and Sculptors in the Twentieth Century,* by Margaret Archuleta and Dr. Rennard Strickland, New York: The New Press, 1991. **Articles**—"Modern Navajo Water Color Painting," by Linzie W. King Davis, *Arizona Highways,* July 1956; "Navajo Painting," by Katherin Chase, *Plateau,* Vol. 54, No. 1, 1982.

*   *   *

Andy Tsinahjinnie displayed a sense of vibrancy and playfulness as well as an ability to change styles, continually expanding his possibilities for artistic expression. From energetic action scenes to reflective moments, always presented in thoughtful perspectives and intriguing colors, Tsinahjinnie passed through several periods of experimentation and refinement, creating a rich body of diverse approaches to scenes from Navajo communities and landscapes.

Most reports indicate that Tsinahjinnie was born in 1916 on the Navajo Reservation and that by the age of 20 had displayed a strong will and resourcefulness. According to some sources, including Tsinahjinnie, he was sent to the Indian School at Fort Apache, on the Apache Reservation, but ran away and returned home, and in 1933 made his way to the Chicago World's Fair, where he worked as a translator for a Navajo Medicine Man and showed some of his early artwork. By the time he graduated from the Santa Fe Indian School in 1936, his artwork had been praised and already showed an individual approach to common scenes—using active poses and various colors to animate images of people at work. Tsinahjinnie was employed at the Indian Service at the Navajo Agency in Window Rock, Arizona, where he landed commissions as an illustrator, including contributions for *Who Wants to be a Prairie Dog,* a children's story by Ann Nolan Clark. In the years immediately prior to World War II, Tsinahjinnie traveled and worked odd jobs before entering the U.S. Air Force and serving in the Pacific in World War II; he is rumored to have painted creatively in Tokyo, including designing the decor of a bar.

Following the war, Tsinahjinnie established a studio in Scottsdale, Arizona, and was involved in the local arts scene, becoming friends with such noted Native artists as Lloyd Kiva New and Charles and Otellie Loloma, among others. Later, from the mid-1960s through the early 1970s, Tsinahjinnie taught at a school and community college on the Navajo Reservation.

From the earliest part of his career, Tsinahjinnie painted Navajo subjects familiar to him with a singularity of style that stressed activity and warm colors. In paintings of Navajo weavers (*Woman Spinning Yarn,* 1935, and *Navajo Weaver,* 1952), for example, the play of color—reds and browns enriched to maroon and mauve, and a sense of action through active poses or suggestions of a passing breeze are of primary importance in otherwise quotidian scenes. Tsinahjinnie showed great versatility throughout his career in his approach to secular and spiritual subject matter. Color sets the mood for representation of Navajo fire dancers—their painted white bodies accentuated against a black background from which they burst forth, an animated color contrast he also employed in showing wild horses at full gallop in the night. More sober moods are evoked in muted and blended colors in depictions of wedding, purification, and other ceremonies. In other works, color can be subordinated to small, telling, and authentic details in dress or landscape, as in crowded scenes of public gatherings for games or meetings. The more crowded the scene, the more various the activities individuals are found engaging in, from spirited gestures, to casual conversations, to perimeter figures taking naps.

The constant in Tsinahjinnie's art is his subject matter—usually based in Navaho themes and often featuring horses and landscapes, but rendered in varying colors and perspectives, which lend a distinct originality to his paintings, and occasional experimentation with style. *Enchanted Forest* (1965) displays some characteristics of Asian painting Tsinahjinnie may have observed during his tour of military duty, for example. *Council Meeting* (1961), with three men paused on horseback in the foreground and others approaching from a background of foothills and a butte, is an undramatic moment greatly enlivened by a reflecting pool of water and slight details that make the individuals and their horses unique and interesting, in many ways the hallmark of his work. Horses appear in paintings throughout Tsinahjinnie's career, in almost every color and with great attention to shapes and muscles.

Nearly every aspect of twentieth-century Navajo life was rendered by Tsinahjinnie, in varying tones and perspectives. If his output was uneven—with exhibitions, collections, and honors seeming to favor his work through the late 1940s and his later work of the 1960s and 1970s, his works reflect a wealth of perspectives on Navajo culture, captured with rich colors and thoughtful details. Arthur Silberman (*100 Years of Native American Painting*), noted that he fully explored every aspect of Navajo life: "Imaginative, creative, uninhibited, Tsinahjinnie has always innovated, developed and discarded—moving on to new challenges."

—Perry Bear

TSINHNAHJINNIE, Hulleah

Tribal affiliations: Seminole; Creek; Navajo
Photographer and installation artist

Born: Phoenix, Arizona, 1954. **Education:** Arcosanti, Cordes Junction, Arizona, 1975; Haystack Mountain School of Arts, Deer Isle, Maine, 1977; Institute of American Indian Arts, Santa Fe, New Mexico, 1975-1978; California College of Arts and Crafts, Oakland, B.F.A., 1981. **Career:** Visiting artist, Bug-Ga-Na-Ge-Shig

School, Cass Lake, Minnesota, 1992-present; instructor, Institute of American Indian Arts, Santa Fe, the San Francisco Art Institute, University of California, Davis, and the California College of Arts and Crafts, Oakland; served as board member for the Inter-Tribal Friendship House in Oakland, California, and American Indian Contemporary Arts, San Francisco; professional graphic designer and photographer since 1980.

Individual Exhibitions

1993   *Nobody's Pet Indian*, San Francisco Art Institute, California
1994   C.N. Gorman Museum, University of California, Davis, traveling
1994   *Photographic Memoirs of an Aboriginal Savant*, Multimedia Sacred Circle Gallery, Seattle, Washington
1997   *Women of Hope: Portraits of Indigenous Women*, 1199 Union Gallery, New York

Selected Group Exhibitions

1977   *Indian Art Today: Traditional and Contemporary*, Albuquerque Fine Arts Museum, Albuquerque, New Mexico
1986   *The Photograph and the American Indian*, Princeton University Library, Princeton, New Jersey
1990   *Language of the Lens: Contemporary Native Photographers*, traveling exhibition, Heard Museum, Phoenix, Arizona
        Native Photographers, Stewart Indian School Museum, Reno, Nevada
1991   *Counter Colon-ialismo*, Centro Cultural de la Raza, San Diego, California
        Shared Visions, Heard Museum, Phoenix, Arizona, traveling exhibition
1992   *Message Carriers*, traveling exhibition, Photographic Resource Center, Boston University, Massachusetts
        International Istanbul Biennial, Istanbul Municipality Nejat F. Eczacibasi Art Museum, Halic, Turkey
        Ancestral Memories: A Tribute to Native Survival, Falkirk Cultural Center, San Rafael, CA, traveling exhibition
        Partial Recall, traveling exhibition
1994   *Watchful Eyes*, Heard Museum, Phoenix, Arizona
        This Path We Travel, National Museum of American Indian, New York

Publications

By TSINHNAHJINNIE: Book—*This Path We Travel: Celebrations of Contemporary Native American Creativity*, Washington, D.C.: Smithsonian Institution Press, 1994. **Article**—"Compensating Imbalances," *Exposure*, Vol. 29, No. 1, Fall 1993.

On TSINHNAHJINNIE: Books—*Mixed Blessings: New Art in a Multicultural America*, by Lucy Lippard, New York: Pantheon Books, 1990; *Ancestral Memories: A Tribute to Native Survival*, by Theresa Harlan and Carrie Lederer, San Rafael, California: Falkirk Cultural Center, 1992; *Partial Recall*, by Lucy Lippard, editor, New York: The New Press, 1992; *Watchful Eyes: Native American Women Artists*, by Theresa Harlan, Phoenix, Arizona, The Heard Museum, 1994. **Articles**—"Cultural Confrontations," by Casey Fitzsimons, *Artweek*, Vol. 22, November 21, 1991; "A Conversa-

tion with Hulleah Tsinhnahjinnie," Steven Jenkins, *Artweek*, Vol. 24, May 6, 1993; "Sovereignties," by John Rapko, *Artweek*, Vol. 24, May 6, 1993; "A Curator's Perspective: Native Photographers Creating a Visual Native American History," by Theresa Harlan, *Exposure*, Vol. 29, No. 1, Fall 1993; "Sovereignty: A Line in the Sand," by Jolene Rickard, *Aperture*, No. 139, Summer 1995; "Image and Self: In Contemporary Native American Photoart," by Jennifer Skoda, *American Indian Art Magazine*, Vol. 21, No. 2, Spring 1996.

*   *   *

Hulleah Tsinhnahjinnie represents a growing number of Native American photographers who are using photomontage and collage as a way of layering meaning in their work as they address critical issues facing Native Americans in the twentieth century. Tsinhnahjinnie exploits the narrative potential of photography through the use of collage, photomontage, installations and mixed media constructions. This layering allows Tsinhnahjinnie to create complex and rich metaphorical images that challenge myths of colonial authority. Consequently, Tsinhnahjinnie has developed various strategies to force the viewer to examine stereotypes and their roles in perpetuating the myth of colonial authority.

One strategy she employs capitalizes on international human rights issues that Americans become passionate about as a way to focus their attention on similar issues within the United States. During the mid-1980s she created a series of photocollages centered around "Mattie," a young Native girl. In *Mattie Looks for Steve Biko*, the image of Mattie sitting in the back seat of an old car is seen on the screen of a TV. Mattie, wearing a wing dress and moccasins, sits on a Pendelton blanket. Through the window to her right there is an African-American family on their way to church, suggesting that Americans were outraged by apartheid in South Africa but were and are unable to see the same types of injustice in the U.S. Consequently, Tsinhnahjinnie chooses a young Native girl Mattie as the seeker of justice—as the one who will bring these issues forward, much like young children who often ask questions that people avoid or are afraid to discuss.

Tsinhnahjinnie also addresses the issue of "blood quantum" and construction of identity in her work. In an installation for the *Partial Recall* exhibition, she positioned photographs of artists on the wall with phrases written over them: *My Number?* and *Nobody's Pet Indian*. The images are united on the wall by large black dots. Her recent work is an extension of her interest in the myth of colonial authority. In *Grandma and Me* (1994), she uses a page from a 1950s travel magazine that showed pictures of Navajos with the title "Arizona's noble people" to address the history of voyeurism that such advertisements have perpetuated. Tsinhnahjinnie has inserted images of her grandmother and herself with their relationship written in Dine (grandmother on the father's side and granddaughter). Tsinhnahjinnie states, "These Dine captions recognize intimacy and responsibility, whereas an *Arizona Highways'* caption, 'Aged Navajo,' denies a whole range of her possible identities—a council woman, a medicine woman, a master rug weaver, a star gazer, a translator, a teacher, a writer, a singer, a traveler, an organizer, a woman of thought."

Where much of her early work was focused on revealing issues to non-Native audiences, Tsinhnahjinnie's later work is increasingly directed towards indigenous communities. There was a corresponding shift in themes from manipulation of American history to contemporary social issues facing Native people. In 1996, Tsinhnahjinnie was commissioned by Bread and Roses to do 12 portraits of Native women for an ongoing poster project (the two previous series focused on Latina women and African-American women respectively). The resulting series, *Women of Hope: Portraits of Indigenous Women*, opens at 1199 Union Gallery in 1997, but will ultimately be a public art project with the posters being displayed in schools, clinics, community centers and mass transit stops. In the portraits of 12 important and influential Native women, Tsinhnahjinnie visually connects the women to the land—*their* land. Each of the women has a strong tie and commitment to the issue of land: in fighting for it, preserving it and maintaining community connections to it. Consequently, the resulting images are not studio portraits. Rather, Tsinhnahjinnie has photographed them (except for Jaune Quick-to-See Smith, who is seen in her studio) on the land—within the context of their issues and struggles.

Tsinhnahjinnie continues to expand and exploit photography, photomontage and collage to relay her political commentary. Like other contemporary Native American photographers, she is pushing the limits of photography in an attempt to challenge the "truth" of photographs, ultimately creating new visual realities and truths.

—Jennifer Vigil

TSO, Faye

Tribal affiliations: Navajo
Painter and potter

Born: Faye Bilagody, Tuba City, Navajo Nation, Arizona, 1933; member of the *Naakaii Dine's* (Mexican clan). **Career:** Herbalist, potter, rug-weaver, teacher and demonstrator of pottery-making. **Family:** Married Emmett Tso, four sons, four daughters. **Awards:** Numerous from the Museum of Northern Arizona, Flagstaff.

Selected Group Exhibitions

1987 Permanent installation, Navajo Nation Museum, Window Rock, Arizona

1988 *anii ánáádaalyaa'íí: Continuity and Innovation in Recent Navajo Art,* Wheelwright Museum of the American Indian, Santa Fe

1990 *Navajo Junction: Where Navajo Potteries Meet*, Arizona State Museum, University of Arizona, Tucson
   The Cutting Edge, traveling exhibit organized by the Museum of American Folk Art, New York; Venues: New Britain Museum of American Art, New Britain, Connecticut; Laguna Art Museum, Laguna Beach, California; Telfair Museum, Savannah, Georgia; Tampa Museum of Art, Tampa, Florida; Whatcom Museum, Bellingham, Washington.

1993 *Leets'aa bi Diné Dáályé: It Is Called Navajo Pottery*, Phoebe A. Hearst Museum of Anthropology, University of California, Berkeley

1994 *Contemporary Art of the Navajo Nation*, traveling exhibit organized by Cedar Rapids Museum of Art; Venues: Albuquerque Museum, Albuquerque, New Mexico; University Art Museum, State University of New York, Albany; Museum of the Southwest, Midland, Texas.

1996 San Diego Museum of Man

Faye Tso: Navajo pitch-coated jar, c. 1988. Photograph by Dong Lin; courtesy Russell P. Hartman collection.

Collections

Arizona State Museum, University of Arizona, Tucson; Heard Museum, Phoenix, Arizona; Museum of Northern Arizona, Flagstaff; Logan Museum of Anthropology, Beloit College, Beloit, Wisconsin; Navajo Nation Museum, Window Rock, Arizona; P. A. Hearst Museum of Anthropology, University of California, Berkeley; San Diego Museum of Man.

Publications

On TSO: Books—*Navajo Pottery: Traditions and Innovations* by Russell P. Hartman, Flagstaff: Northland Press, 1987; *Folk Art of the People: Navajo Works*, exhibition catalog by Charles Rosenak, St. Louis: Craft Alliance Gallery, 1987; *anii ánáádaalyaa'íí: Continuity and Innovation in Recent Navajo Art,* exhibition catalog by Bruce Bernstein and Susan McGreevy, Santa Fe: Wheelwright Museum, 1988; *Museum of American Folk Art Encyclopedia of Twentieth-Century American Folk Art and Artists* by Chuck and Jan Rosenak, New York: Abbeville Press, 1990; *The People Speak; Navajo Folk Art* by Chuck and Jan Rosenak, Flagstaff: Northland Publishing Co., 1994; *Enduring Traditions: Art of the Navajo* by Lois Essary Jacka, Flagstaff: Northland Publishing Co., 1994; *Trad-*

ing Post Guidebook by Patrick Eddington and Susan Makov, Flagstaff: Northland Publishing Co., 1995. **Articles**—"Techniques in Navajo Pottery Making" by Jan Bell, and "Potters and Their Work" by H. Diane Wright and Jan Bell, *Plateau* 58, no. 2, 1987; "Navajo Pottery: Contemporary Trends in a Traditional Craft" by Diane Wright, *American Indian Art* 12, no. 2, 1987.

*

Faye Tso comments (1990):

If the clay doesn't like you, you will never be able to make a good pot

*　　　*　　　*

Faye Tso's work successfully and easily bridges the gap between traditional, utilitarian Navajo pottery and that made for sale to non-Indian collectors. She learned pottery-making approximately 40 years ago from Mabel Begay and Rose Williams, her husband's mother and aunt, respectively. As a practicing herbalist and a very traditional woman, Tso produced pottery during the 1960s and 1970s primarily for the common, ceremonial needs of her patients. This was a period when the number of practicing potters was very limited, primarily because demand for pottery was low. The current ongoing revival of Navajo pottery-making was just beginning, as the public increasingly responded to innovations introduced by several potters.

Despite her traditional viewpoint regarding most matters, Tso began to test age-old beliefs relating to pottery very early in her career. The fact that her husband is a traditional medicine man, as well as her own training in the healing arts, have perhaps eased her concerns about stretching the boundaries of Navajo pottery.

Tso was one of the first of today's Navajo potters to experiment with the use of clay slips of contrasting colors for decorating her work. Traditionally, Navajo pottery is coated only with piñon pitch, giving it a characteristic sheen. Tso nearly always applies a heavy coating of red slip to her work before firing. After firing, she applies the piñon pitch in the traditional manner.

One of the innovations introduced by Navajo potters during the 1950s was appliquéed designs. This too was an extension of a traditional design, namely an appliquéed band around the neck of a vessel, called a fillet, or in the Navajo language, *biyo'*. Whereas other potters have been content to appliqué various plant and animal motifs on their pots, Tso tackles more challenging subject matter, including rows of ceremonial dancers, Hopi corn maidens, large ears of corn, or individual deity figures that virtually cover an entire vessel. Most of these are modeled in low relief; others are further outlined and accentuated with incised and stamped designs. Finally, the motifs are selectively painted with clay slips with colors that contrast the red slip used as a background. Some pieces use two or more decorative slips, such as white and yellow, on a red field.

Tso has taught her craft to many other potters, including several of her children and other relatives. Such instruction always includes lessons about respecting the clay provided by Mother Earth. Decorating pottery with clay slips has been adopted by a number of Tso's students, including her daughter, Myra Tso, and her clan relative, Jimmy Wilson, each of whom has individualized the technique to suit their own senses of design. She has frequently demonstrated pottery-making at museums and regional craft shows, including the Museum of Northern Arizona, where she has often won awards.

During the 1980s, Tso produced a number of unusually large vessels, some measuring 36 inches or more. Vessels of such size required use of a different type of clay to support their own weight as the walls were built up. Once completed, they further required consummate skill to prevent breakage during firing. This large size provided Tso a much larger "canvas" for her appliquéed designs. However, it also limited their appeal to most collectors, and thus Tso turned increasingly to smaller pieces.

Also an accomplished rug weaver, Tso travels widely to market her pottery and herbal medicines. Her contributions toward preserving and promoting Navajo pottery has been recognized through numerous awards and inclusion in museum collections and exhibits throughout the country, particularly in the Southwest.

—Russell P. Hartman

TUNGILIK, Mark

Tribal affiliations: Inuit
Carver

Born: Netjilik Ilani, Boothia Peninsula region, Northwest Territories, 1913. **Family:** Married, first wife died early 1940s; married Louise Anguatsiark, carver and crafts artist, and settled with family in the community of Repulse Bay in 1948; his brother, Anthanese Ullikatar, was also a Repulse Bay artist. **Career:** Nomadic hunter and fisherman; trapper and trader, mid-1940s; professional carver, beginning in mid-1940s; worked at the Roman Catholic Mission, Our Lady of Snow, in Repulse Bay. **Died:** 22 September 1986.

Individual Exhibitions

1973　　*Mark Tungilik,* Canadian Guild of Crafts Quebec, Montreal, Quebec
　　　　Sculpture by Mark Tungilik of Repulse Bay, Snow Goose, Ottawa, Ontario
1982　　*Marc Tungilik: Recent Sculpture,* Images Art Gallery, Toronto, Ontario
　　　　Miniature Ivory Sculptures by Tungilik from Repulse Bay, Le Centre d'Art, Montreal, Quebec
　　　　Recent Sculpture, Ottawa, Canadian Arctic Producers Co-operative Limited

Selected Group Exhibitions

1949　　Canadian Handicraft Guild, Ottawa, Ontario
1951　　*Eskimo Art,* National Gallery of Canada, Ottawa, Ontario
1953　　*Eskimo Carvings: Coronation Exhibition,* Gimpel Fils, London, England
1967　　*Eskimo Sculpture,* Winnipeg Art Gallery, presented at the Manitoba Legislative Building, Winnipeg, Manitoba
1971-73　*Sculpture/Inuit: Masterworks of the Canadian Arctic,* Canadian Eskimo Arts Council, Ottawa, Ontario (traveling)
1973　　*The Bessie Bulman Collection,* Winnipeg Art Gallery, Winnipeg, Manitoba

Mark Tungilik: *Angel*, 1982. Collection of the National Gallery of Canada.

Sculpture Inuit 25 Years After, Canadian Guild of Crafts Quebec, Montreal, Quebec

1975-79 *We Lived by Animals/Nous Vivions de Animaux,* Department of Indian Affairs and Northern Development in cooperation with the Department of External Affairs, Ottawa, Ontario (traveling)

1976 *The Mulders' Collection of Eskimo Sculpture,* Winnipeg Art Gallery, Winnipeg, Manitoba

1977 *White Sculpture of the Inuit,* Simon Fraser Gallery, Simon Fraser University, Burnaby, British Columbia

1978 *Repulse Bay,* Winnipeg Art Gallery, Winnipeg, Manitoba

1979 *Inuit Sculpture from the Collection of Mr. and Mrs. Eugene B. Power,* University of Michigan Museum of Art, Ann Arbor, Michigan

1980 *The Abbott Collection of Inuit Art,* Winnipeg Art Gallery, Winnipeg, Manitoba

1981 *Ivory Sculpture,* Snow Goose, Ottawa, Ontario

1985 *Uumajut: Animal Imagery in Inuit Art*, Winnipeg Art Gallery, Winnipeg, Manitoba

Masterwork Sculpture 1985, Inuit Gallery of Vancouver, Vancouver, British Columbia

1985-86 *Sanaugasi Takujaksat: A Tavelling Celebration of Inuit Sculpture,* presented by Canadian Arctic Producers Ltd., with the assistance of Indian and Northern Affairs Canada, Ottawa, Ontario (traveling)

1986 *Contemporary Inuit Art,* National Gallery of Canada, Ottawa, Ontario

1986-88 *Selections from the John and Mary Robertson Collection of Inuit Art,* Agnes Ehterington Art Centre, Queen's University, Kingston, Ontario (traveling)

1987 *The Swinton Collection of Inuit Art,* Winnipeg Art Gallery, Winnipeg, Manitoba

1988-89 *Im Schatten der Sonne: Zeitgenossische Kunst der Indianer und Eskimos in Kanada/In the Shadow of the Sun: Contemporary Indian and Inuit Art in Canada*, Canadian Museum of Civilizaion, Ottawa, Ontario (traveling)

1990-92 *The First Passionate Collector: The Ian Lindsay Collection of Inuit Art,* Winnipeg Art Gallery, Winnipeg, Manitoba (traveling)

1992-93 *Inuit Ivories from the Collection,* Winnipeg Art Gallery, Winnipeg, Manitoba

Collections

Art Gallery of Ontario, Toronto, Ontario; Canadian Guild of Crafts Quebec, Montreal, Quebec; Eskimo Museum, Churchill, Manitoba; Canadian Museum of Civilization, Hull, Quebec; Klamer Family Collection, Art Gallery of Ontario, Toronto, Ontario; Metropolitan Museum of Art, New York; Museum of Anthropology, University of British Columbia, Vancouver, British Columbia; National Gallery of Canada, Ottawa, Ontario; Prince of Wales Northern Heritage Centre, Yellowknife, Northwest Territories; University of Lethbridge Art Gallery, Lethbridge, Alberta; Winnipeg Art Gallery, Winnipeg, Manitoba.

Publications

On TUNGILIK: Books—*Sculpture/Inuit: Sculpture of the Inuit: masterworks of the Canadian Arctic/La sculpture chez les Inuit: chefs-d'oeuvre de l'Arctique canadien,* Canadian Eskimo Arts Council, Toronto: University of Toronto Press, 1971; *Repulse Bay,* by Jean Blodgett, Winnipeg: Winnipeg Art Gallery, 1978; *Canadian Guild of Crafts Quebec/Guilde Canadienne des metiers d'art Quebec: The Permanent Collection: Inuit Arts and Crafts, c.1900-1980,* Canadian Guild of Crafts Quebec, Montreal: Canadian Guild of Crafts Quebec, 1980; *Marc Tungilik: Recent Sculpture,* by Darlene Wight, Ottawa: Canadian Arctic Producers Cooperative Limited, 1982. **Articles**—"Eskimo Sculpture in Stone," by Douglas Leechman,*Canadian Geographical Journal,* vol. 49, no. 3, September, 1954; "Christianity and Inuit Art," by Jean Blodgett, *The Beaver,* Autumn, 1984.

*   *   *

Born in the Boothia Peninsula region of the Northwest Territories, Mark Tungilik spent the first half of his life as a hunter in the nomadic tradition of Inuit. In an interview shortly before his death in 1986, Tungilik described this way of life without romanticism: "Life was not exciting, a matter of everyday survival, hunting caribou by walking inland, and seal from a little home-made boat, and catching fish when they came up the river." By the mid-40s, however, he had settled first at Pelly Bay and later at Wager Bay to be close to the Hudson Bay post. The trapping and trading of fur pelts soon became an important source of income, all but replacing traditional subsistence hunting. Tungilik was among the few families to remain at Wager Bay after the closing of the post in 1946. After the death of his first wife, he married Louise Anguatsiark and together they settled in the community of Repulse Bay in 1948 to raise their family and turn their skills to carving.

Although Tungilik had carved since he was a teenager, making miniatures of tools and other objects such as fox traps, it was not until the mid-40s that his carvings began to be noted as such. His first well-documented piece is a small ivory bust of Christ (now in the Eskimo Museum collection in Churchill), which was carved at the request of Father Franz van der Velde in 1945.

In 1949, the Canadian Handicraft Guild hosted the first show and sale of carvings collected from the Eastern arctic by James Houston. Within a few years of this event, distinctly regional and individual styles began to emerge. The difficulties in obtaining locally quarried stone may account for the small scale sculptures generally characteristic of Pelly Bay and Repulse Bay artists. While the continued use of ivory links these work to the miniature tradition of the Historic period (post-1949), no longer were artists exclusively making models of domestic or hunting items.

Tungilik is one of the finest artists within this genre of small scale work, his carvings often measuring no more than a few centimeters. In 1948, Pope Puis XII was presented with a carving made from a walrus tooth. Tungilik's working method would be to place the ivory in a vise and shape the piece with the use of files. Details, such as facial expressions, were added later while he held the miniature carving in his hand, often wearing two pairs of glasses to compensate for his poor eyesight. Despite their diminutive scale, Tungilik's carvings contain a heraldic quality, communicated through the frontal and static poses of his figures. Rather than physical gesture, Tungilik relies on the facial expressions of the figures to enliven his carvings. Regardless of size, each animal, spirit or human, has distinct facial features, with expressions that can range from humourous to disturbing grimaces. Often his ivory figures are so small, as in *Men and Foxes* (1982), that he places them on a base or ledge. Whether the base is of stone, bone or ivory, Tungilik allows the natural shape of the material to suggest landscape. While the figures do not appear to interact, they are encompassed within their own separate microcosm.

Tungilik is also well known for his depictions of Christian subject matter. In addition to the encouragement and commissions he received from the various missionaries, Tungilik worked at the Roman Catholic Mission, Our Lady of Snow, when he first arrived in Repulse Bay. Such contact may explain his sustained interest, even when not directly commissioned, in religious themes, of which *Angel* (1982) is an excellent example. Traditional Inuit beliefs are also prevalent, however, in his depictions of spirits and transforming humans and beasts. In *Bird Spirit* (1982), two small animals are perched on top of a figure with the face of a human but the body of a bird. Despite the complexity of parts, the creatures are integrated so closely and harmoniously that they do not appear as separate entities. The connection between animal helpers, particularly birds, and shamanistic ritual has been well documented in Inuit oral traditions.

In common with other artists of his generation, Tungilik's work is testament to the grace and ability of Inuit to adapt to the vast changes they have experienced during their lifetimes. Created during a period of transition, it is no surprise that Tungilik's works contain elements of the past and present, intermingled, in his carvings. The use of ivory and intimate scale of his sculptures links them to the period prior to 1949, when carvings were made for trade to whalers, scientists, and other travelers to the North. The references to both Christianity and shamanism in his work reflects, perhaps, the way in which these dual belief systems coexisted for many Inuit. Yet Tungilik's carvings are contemporary expressions, inspired by his own vision and aesthetic, and it is here that the power and fascination of his works resides.

—Christine Lalonde

TUNNILLIE, Ovilu

Tribal affiliations: Inuit
Sculptor and jewelry designer

Born: In a camp, Kangia, on Baffin Island, Northwest Territories, 20 December, 1949; first name also transliterated as Oviloo, surname as Toonoo. **Family:** Daughter of Toonoo Toonoo and Sheojuke Toonoo; brother, Kiperqualuk, and sister, Napatchie; married Iola Tunnillie, five children and one grandchild. **Career:** Artist (sculpting, drawing, jewelry making); leads workshops on soapstone carving.

Individual Exhibitions

1981	Canadian Guild of Crafts, Montreal, Quebec
1992	Inuit Galerie, Mannheim, Germany
1993	*An Inuit Woman Challenges Tradition: Sculpture by Oviloo Tunnillie,* Burdick Gallery, Washington D. C.
1994-95	Marion Scott Gallery, Vancouver, British Columbia

Selected Group Exhibitions

1976	*Baffin Island Sculpture Exhibition,* Baffin Regional School, Iqaluit, Northwest Territories
	Debut: Cape Dorset Jewellery, Canadian Guild of Crafts Quebec, Montreal, Quebec
1979	*Cape Dorset: Recent Sculpture,* Gallery of the Arctic, Victoria, British Columbia
	Sculpture of the Inuit: Lorne Balshine Collection/ Lou Osipov Collection/ Dr. Harry Winrob Collection, Surrey Art Gallery, Surrey, British Columbia
1983	*Fantasy and Stylization — Cape Dorset Sculpture,* Inuit Gallery of Vancouver, British Columbia
1984	*On the Land,* The Arctic Circle, Los Angeles, California
1984-86	*Arctic Vision: Art of the Canadian Inuit,* Department of Indian Affairs and Northern Development and Canadian Arctic Producers, Ottawa, Ontario (traveled)
1987	*Art Inuit,* Canadian Guild of Crafts Quebec, Montreal, Quebec
1987-88	*Inuitkonst fran Kanada, skulptor och grafik,* Millesgarden, Lidingo, Sweden
1988	*Building on Strengths: New Inuit Art from the Collection,* Winnipeg Art Gallery
	Opening Exhibition, Nunavut Fine Arts Limited, Toronto, Ontario

1989   *Hermitage '89: New Exhibits*, Hermitage Museum, Leningrad, Soviet Union

Birds: Sculpture from Cape Dorset and Rock Ptarmigan Limited Edition, Print by Kananginak, The Guild Shop, Toronto, Ontario

1990   *Small Sculptures from across the Canadian Arctic*, Feheley Fine Arts, Toronto, Ontario

1991   *Art Inuit: Autour de la Collection de Cape Dorset 1991*, l'Iglou Art Esquimau, Douai at Le Colombier, Ville D'Avray, France

The Hand: Images in Inuit Sculpture, The Isaacs/Inuit Gallery, Toronto, Ontario

Cape Dorset Stone Sculptures: Masters and the Next Generation, Inuit Gallery of Vancouver, British Columbia

Glaciopolis: Art Inuit, Presented by l'Iglou Art Esquimau, Douai at Maison de Pesey, Les Arcs, France

Art Inuit, l'Iglou Art Esquimau, Douai at Chapelle de la Visitation, Thonon, France

Cape Dorset Sculpture, McMaster Art Gallery, Hamilton, Ontario

1992   *Small Sculptures by Great Artists I*, Feheley Fine Arts, Toronto, Ontario

Inuit Sculpture: New Acquisitions, Pucker Gallery, Boston, Massachusetts

Arctic Ice: Sculptures in Marble by the Artists of Cape Dorset, Northwest Territories, Marion Scott Gallery, Vancouver, British Columbia

Women of the North: An Exhibition of Art by Inuit Women of the Canadian Arctic, Marion Scott Gallery, Vancouver, British Columbia

Images of Influence: Contemporary Inuit Art, Surrey Art Gallery, Surrey, British Columbia

1993   *Inuit Sculpture*, Canadian Guild of Crafts Quebec, Montreal, Quebec

Sculpture Inuit et Retrospective Pudlo Pudlat, Canadian Guild of Crafts Quebec, Montreal, Quebec

Sculpture and Graphics from Cape Dorset, Art Space Gallery, Philadelphia, Pennsylvania

1993-94   *The Inuit Imagination*, Winnipeg Art Gallery, Winnipeg, Manitoba

1994   *Small Sculptures by Great Artists III*, Feheley Fine Arts, Toronto, Ontario

Sculpture by Women, Feheley Fine Arts, Toronto, Ontario

Kunst van de Inuit Eskimo's Gemeentelijk Kunstcentrum, Huis Hellemans, Edegem, Belgium

The Tunnillie Family of Cape Dorset, Albers Gallery, San Francisco, California

Small Sculptures by Great Artists II, Geheley Fine Arts, Toronto, Ontario

1994-95   *Isumavut: The Artistic Expression of Nine Cape Dorset Women / Inuit Women Artists: Voices From Cape Dorset*, Canadian Museum of Civilization, Hull, Quebec

1995   *Sunakutagnuvalautut: Things from the Past*, Feheley Fine Arts, Toronto, Ontario

Keeping Our Stories Alive: An Exhibition of the Art and Crafts from Dene and Inuit of Canada, Institute of American Indian Arts Museum, Santa Fe, New Mexico

1995-96   *Inuit Art: From the Collection of Maurice Yacowar*, Collector's Gallery, Calgary, Alberta

1996   *Major/ Minor*, Marion Scott Gallery, Vancouver, British Columbia

Birds: Sculpture from Cape Dorset and Rock Ptarmigan Limited Edition, Print by Kananginak, The Guild Shop, Toronto, Ontario

Sedna: Spirit of the Sea, Feheley Fine Arts, Toroto, Ontario

Collections

Canada Council Art Bank, Ottawa, Ontario; Canadian Guild of Crafts Quebec, Montreal; Canadian Museum of Civilization, Hull, Quebec; GE Canada Inuit Art Collection, Mississauga, Ontario; Hermitage Museum, Leningrad, Soviet Union; McMaster University Art Gallery, University of British Columbia, Vancouver, British Columbia; National Gallery of Canada, Ottawa, Ontario; University of Lethbridge Art Gallery, Lethbridge, Alberta; Winnepeg Art Gallery, Winnipeg, Manitoba.

Publications

On TUNNILLIE: Books—*Cape Dorset: Recent Sculptures*, Ottawa: Canadian Arctic Producers Cooperative Limited, 1979; *Cape Dorset Sculpture: Fantasy and Stylization*, Inuit Gallery of Vancouver, 1983; *Arctic Vision: Art of the Canadian Inuit*, by Barbara Lipton, Canadian Arctic Producers, 1984; *Winnipeg Collects: Inuit Art from Private Collections*, by Darlene Wight, Winnipeg, Winnipeg Art Gallery, 1987; *Oviloo Tunillie*, Inuit Galerie, Mannheim, F. D. R., 1988; *Die Kunst Der Arktis*, Inuit Galerie, Mannheim, F. D. R. 1988; *Moments in Stone: Recent Sculpture from Cape Dorset*, Toronto, Innuit Gallery of Eskimo Art, 1988; *Cape Dorset Stone Sculpture: Masters and the Next Generation*, Inuit Gallery of Vancouver, 1991; *Arctic Ice: Sculptures in Marble by the Artists of Cape Dorset*, Northwest Territories, Vancouver, Marion Scott Gallery, 1992; *Sculpture of the Inuit*, George Swinton, Toronto: McClelland and Stewart, 1992; *Women of the North: An Exhibition of Art by Inuit Women of the Canadian Arctic*, Vancouver, Marion Scott Gallery, 1992; *Keeping Our Stories Alive: The Sculpture of Canada's Inuit*, Inuit Art Section, Indian and Northern Affairs Canada, 1993; *The Inuit Imagination: Arctic Myth and Sculpture*, Harold Seidelman and James Turner, Vancouver/Toronto: Douglas and McIntyre, 1993; *Inuit Women Artists: Voices From Cape Dorset, Catalog*, ed. by Odette Leroux, Marion E. Jackson and Minnie Aodla Freeman, Vancouver, Toronto, Hull, Quebec, University of Washington Press, 1994; *Sculpture by Celebrated Inuit Artist Oviloo Tunillie*, Vancouver, Marion Scott Gallery, 1994; *Keeping Our Stories Alive: An Exhibition of Arts and Crafts from Dene and Inuit of Canada*, Catalog, Institute of American Indian Arts, Santa Fe, New Mexico, 1995; *Inspiration: Four Decades of Sculpture by Canadian Inuit*, Vancouver, Marion Scott Gallery, 1996. **Articles**—"Christianity and Inuit Art," by Jean Blodgett, *The Beaver*, Autumn 1984; "Arctic Vision: Art of the Canadian Inuit," by Barbara Lipton, *Archaeology*, January/February 1985; "Building on Strengths: New Inuit Art From the Collection," by Darlene Wight, *Tableau* 1, no. 5, 1988; "Women of the North: An Exhibition of Art by Inuit Women of the Canadian Arctic," by Peter Millard, *Inuit Art Quarterly* 7, no. 3 Summer/Fall 1992; "The Artists Speak: About learning from each other; about pleasing buyers; about personal power," by Marybelle Mitchell, *Inuit Art Quarterly* 7, no. 4, Fall/Winter 1992; "Mediations on Womanhood: Oviloo Tunillie," by Peter Millard, *Inuit Art Quarterly* 9, no. 4 Winter, 1994; "An Exhibition, A Book, and an Exaggerated Reaction," a review by Janet Catherine Berlo, *Inuit Art Quarterly*, 10, vol. 1,

Spring 1995. **Film**—*Keeping Our Stories Alive: The Sculpture of Canada's Inuit*, Indian and Northern Affairs of Canada, 1993.

* * *

After almost five decades of growth and change, contemporary Inuit art can no longer be defined solely in terms of sculptures and prints suited to the ethnic art market. While the 1950s and 60s were dominated by James Houston's vision of a uniquely Canadian "primitive" art, during the 1970s and 80s Inuit artists experimented with a variety of media and subject matter. Currently, contemporary Inuit art is both a mature tradition and a loose term that encompasses an increasingly wide and sophisticated range of artistic production. One who is at the forefront of this, addressing the complexities of cultural and personal interaction in her art is Oviloo Tunnillie.

Tunnillie was born in 1949 on Baffin Island in the Northwest Territories. Due to illness, as a young girl she spent repeated and prolonged periods of time hospitalized in southern Canada. Having regained her health, at the age of 11 Tunnillie returned to the north. Upon her return Tunnillie was received by her family with a great degree of antipathy because, according to her mother, she had lost a great degree of her cultural identity. While experiences such as these are potentially devastating for a child, they undoubtedly contributed to Tunnillie's keen perspective, evident in her sculptures.

Although Tunnillie created her first soapstone sculpture in 1966, she did not begin steadily carving until 1972, after her second daughter was born. Like many other Inuit, Tunnillie initially began producing art for economic reasons, yet there is no question concerning her talent or vision. Rather than sate the demand for stereotypical images of Inuit life, Tunnillie's *oeuvre* consists of technically accomplished and conceptually challenging works of art.

While Tunnillie draws on her natural surroundings, childhood memories, and pop culture for inspiration, she also addresses more complex issues in her work. For example, *Woman Passed Out* (1987) depicts a man holding an unconscious woman in his arms. While the woman lies corpse-like with a distended neck and expressionless face, the man looks to the sky in mourning. The solemnity of this contemporary pieta is established in the simple poses that lead one to consider, in personal terms, the evils of alcoholism. More abstract works include *Thoughts Create Meaning* (1980), which consists, in part, of a giant hand that points to a person who is drinking. According to Tunnillie, the hand is symbolic of the grip of alcohol on Inuit people and also functions to identify the figure—a government official—as the source of the problem. Both of these works are characteristic of Tunnillie's carving style, which includes an emphasis on mass, the interlocking forms, and the surface texture of the stone itself.

Although Inuit artists today have a great degree of artistic freedom, there are difficulties in straying from standard expectations, as Tunnillie is well aware. In the catalog that accompanies the recent show, Voices *of Cape Dorset: Nine Inuit Women*, Tunnillie discusses her pieces individually. In relation to all of her sculptures that are about alcoholism, Tunnillie claims: "This is a work of aesthetic inspiration and not intended as a social commentary." While this statement does distance Tunnillie from the critical content of her work, it only does so in a highly problematic and superficial way. To emphasize the aesthetic aspect of her work to the exclusion of the historical context surrounding their creation or the social critiques embedded within them is a nostalgic and anachro-

nistic strategy associated with modernist-primitivism of mid-century. However, such disclaimers indicate that Tunnillie is keenly aware that "the white man," once the invaders of the Arctic, are now her best patrons. For Inuit artists today, odd compromises such as the blatant discrepancies between Tunnillie's statement and sculptures, provide a means (albeit an ironic one) by which one succeeds within the established market with historically important works of art.

Tunnillie is currently enjoying a great degree of attention due to the recent show, *Inuit Women Artists: Voices From Cape Dorset*. In contrast to her childhood experiences in the north, Tunnillie is now a well-respected member of the Cape Dorset community (she was elected to the board of the West Baffin Island Co-operative in 1992).

—Kristin Potter

TUTSWEETOK, Lucy Tasseor

Variant names: Tasseor
Tribal affiliations: Inuit
Carver

Born: Nunalla (Nunaalaaq, a trading post on the west coast of Hudson Bay), Manitoba, 1934 **Family:** Married Richard Tutsweetok in Rankin Inlet in 1960; the couple moved to Arviat (then known as Eskimo Point) soon after and have several children and grandchildren. **Career:** Nomadic hunter and carver. **Awards:** Commissioned by the Earth Spirit Festival to carve a piece for the *Visions of Power* exhibition in Toronto, 1991.

Selected Group Exhibitions

1970   *Sculpture*, Yellowknife, Northwest Territories
1971-73 *Sculpture/Inuit: Masterworks of the Canadian Arctic*, Canadian Eskimo Arts Council, Ottawa, Ontario
1972   *Eskimo Sculpture: Selections from the Twomey Collection*, Winnipeg Art Gallery, Winnipeg, Manitoba
1973   *Eskimo Sculpture*, Central Ontario Exhibition, Kitchener, Ontario
1973-74 *Les Eskimos/De Eskimo's*, Studio 44 - Passage 44, Brussels, Belgium
1975   *The Art of Eskimo Women: In Sculpture, Prints, Wallhangings*, The Arctic Circle, Los Angeles, California
1976   *The Mulders' Collection of Eskimo Sculpture*, Winnipeg Art Gallery, Winnipeg, Manitoba
1977   *Eskimo Point Sculpture: Stone & Bone*, The Inuit Gallery of Eskimo Art, Toronto, Ontario
1979   *Sculpture of the Inuit: Masterwork Exhibitors of the Canadian Arctic*, Inuit Gallery of Vancouver, Vancouver, British Columbia
1982   *Eskimo Point/Arviat*, Winnipeg Art Gallery, Winnipeg, Manitoba
        Inuit Sculpture 1982, The Raven Gallery, Minneapolis, Minnesota
1983-85 *Grasp Tight the Old Ways: Selections from the Klamer Family Collection of Inuit Art*, Art Gallery of Ontario, Toronto, Ontario

1985   *Our Hoods are Full*, Arctic Artistry, Hartsdale, New York

1986   *Keewatin Sculpture: Reflections of the Spirit*, Inuit Gallery of Vancouver, Vancouver, British Columbia

1986-87 *Pure Vision: The Keewatin Spirit*, Norman Mackenzie Art Gallery, Regina, Saskatchewan (traveling)

1987   *Rugged and Profound - Sculpture from Eskimo Point*, The Innuit Gallery of Eskimo Art, Toronto, Ontario

1987-88 *Inuk, Inuit: Art et tradition chez les esquimax d'hier et d'aujourd'hui*, Musée des Beaux-arts d'Arras, Arras, France

1988   *Tundra & Ice: Stone Images of Animals and Man*, Adventurers' Club, Chicago, Illinois

1988-89 *Im Schatten der Sonne: Zeitgenossische Kunst der Indianer und Eskimos in Kanada / In the Shadow of the Sun: Contemporary Indian and Inuit Art in Canada*, Canadian Museum of Civilization, Ottawa, Ontario

1989   *Iglou Art Esquimau*, Douai at St. Marcellin, France

1989-90 *The Stone Sculpture of Arviat*, McMichael Canadian Art Collection, Kleinburg, Ontario

1990   *Art Inuit, l'Art des Esquimaux du Canada*, Maison Falleur, Cambrai, France

1990-91 *Espaces Inuit*, Maison Hamel-Bruneau, Ste-Foy, Quebec

1991   *Art Inuit*, Le Theatre, La Ciotat, France

       Visions of Power, York Quay Gallery and Leo Kamen Gallery, Toronto, Ontario

1992   *Inuit Art: Drawings and Recent Sculpture*, National Gallery of Canada, Ottawa, Ontario

       Our Hoods are Full, Arctic Artistry, Hastings-on-Hudson, New York

       Nouveau Territories... 350/500 ans apres, Les Ateliers Visions Planetaire, Montreal, Quebec (traveling)

1993   *The Treasured Monument*, Marion Scott Gallery, Vancouver, British Columbia

1994   *Kanuitpit? Kunst und Kulturen der Eskimo: Eine Auswahl aus den Museumssammlungen*, Staatliches Museum fur Volkerkunde Munchen, Munich, Germany

       Inuit Art from the Canadian Arctic, Bayly Art Museum, University of Virginia, Charlottesville, Virginia

1995   *Inspiration, Four Decades of Sculpture*, Marion Scott Gallery, Vancouver, British Columbia

1995-96 *Inuit Art: from the collection of Maurice Yacowar*, Collector's Gallery, Calgary, Alberta

1996   *Emerging Spirit*, Banff Centre, Banff, Alberta

Collections

Art Gallery of Ontario, Toronto, Ontario; Canadian Museum of Civilization, Hull, Quebec; Dennos Museum Center, Northwestern Michigan College, Traverse City, Michigan; Inuit Cultural Institute, Rankin Inlet, Northwest Territories; Klamer Family Collection, Art Gallery of Ontario, Toronto, Ontario; McMichael Canadian Art Collection, Kleinburg, Ontario Museum of Anthropology, University of British Columbia, Vancouver, British Columbia; National Gallery of Canada, Ottawa, Ontario; Prince of Wales Northern Heritage Centre, Yellowknife, Northwest Territories; Sarick Collection, Art Gallery of Ontario, Toronto, Ontario; Winnipeg Art Gallery, Winnipeg, Manitoba.

Publications

On TUTSWEETOK: Books—*Sculpture of the Eskimo*, by George Swinton, Toronto, 1972; *Sculpture of the Inuit: Masterwork Exhibi-*

tors of the Canadian Arctic, Inuit Gallery of Vancouver, 1979; *Lords of the Stone: An Anthology of Eskimo Sculpture*, by Alistair Macduff, North Vancouver: Whitecap Books, 1982; *Grasp Tight the Old Ways: Selections from the Klamer Family Collection of Inuit Art*, by Jean Blodgett, Toronto: Art Gallery of Ontario, 1983; *Keewatin Sculpture; Reflections of the Spirit*, Inuit Gallery of Vancouver, 1986; *Pure Vision: The Keewatin Spirit*, Norman Zepp, Regina: Norman Mackenzie Art Gallery, 1986; *Espaces Inuit: Dessins et Sculpture*, by Louis Gagnon, Sainte-Foy, Quebec: Maison Hamel-Bruneau, 1990; "Contemporary Inuit Art," by Ingo Hessel, in *Visions of Power: Contemporary Art by First Nations, Inuit and Japanese Canadians,* Toronto: The Earth Spirit Festival, 1991; *Canadian Inuit Sculpture*, Department of Northern and Indian Affairs, Ottawa: Inuit Art Section, 1992; *Indigena: Contemporary Native Perspectives,* Gerald McMaster and Lee-Ann Martin, editors, Vancouver/Toronto, Canadian Museum of Civilization, 1992; *Nouveaux Territories: 350/500 Ans Apres: Une exposition d'art aborigene contemporain du Canada*, Vision Planetaire, Montreal, 1992; *Pelts to Stone: A History of Arts & Crafts Production in Arviat*, Mark Kalluak, editor, Ottawa: Indian and Northern Affairs Canada, 1993. **Articles**—"Arviat Stone Sculpture: Born of the Struggle with an Uncompromising Medium," by Ingo Hessel, *Inuit Art Quarterly*, vol. 5, no. 1, Winter, 1990.

*   *   *

Lucy Tasseor Tutsweetok (who is generally known in Inuit art circles by her own Inuktitut name, Tasseor) is a self-taught stone sculptor living and working in the small Arctic community of Arviat. She is one of the leading proponents of the "minimalist" style of sculpture developed in that community in the 1960s. Though not a conscious movement, the Arviat style is considered to be unique in Inuit Art. In it the human form is greatly simplified or abstracted, and the raw or barely worked stone often takes precedence over details of clothing or anatomy.

Tasseor was born at Nunalla (Nunaalaaq), a trading post on the west coast of Hudson Bay in northern Manitoba, just south of the border with the Northwest Territories. Her father was named Otsuvialik Katjuak, and her mother Ottuk (Christian name Rachael). After the death of her father, Tasseor went to live with her grandparents in and around Nunalla and Churchill, Manitoba. Her grandfather Ulibbaq Isumatarjuaq worked for the trading posts there, and Tasseor would often accompany him on his trips hauling supplies by dog team or canoe. She considers her grandfather to have been the greatest influence on her life. Tasseor married Richard Tutsweetok in Rankin Inlet in 1960. The couple moved to Arviat (then known as Eskimo Point) soon after and have lived there ever since. Tasseor and her husband travel and hunt on the land whenever they can. They have several children and grandchildren.

Tasseor began carving in the early 1960s. Her first few carvings of seals and polar bears were rejected by the local buyer, and Tasseor waited for some time before trying again. The next time she picked up a piece of stone she remembered something her grandfather had done on one of their hunting trips together. He had drawn a shape in the sand and placed stones along its edges, telling his granddaughter stories as he did so. Tasseor transformed that memory into a sculpture. The shape in the sand was the stone itself; her grandfather's stones became faces carved on the stone's surface and along its edges. Tasseor had invented a personal style that would make her famous.

Tasseor's sculptures are carved in a semi-abstract style that flows with the natural irregular shape of the stone. The stone is usually worked completely but very sparingly. The greater part of the stone forms a background, so to speak, for the faces, representing groups of people—usually mothers and their children—that are Tasseor's favourite subjects. The human figure is never defined in its entirety but rather suggested by a face, perhaps an arm or a leg, and sometimes the outline of a parka. These features seem to emerge from the solid mass of the stone, often only along the edges of the stone; the carving is essentially done in relief. Tasseor also occasionally incises drawings of tents, igloos or birds on large flat surfaces. Tasseor's faces are distinctive; although other Arviat carvers also employ the "multiple face" technique, Tasseor's faces are filed and cut into the stone in a trademark fashion. But for Tasseor, the surface of the stone, with its rasp and file marks, is as expressive as the faces emerging from it. She does not attempt to master the stone, but works in complete harmony with it.

A great part of the attraction of Tasseor's sculptures is their tactile quality, and even her small works have a sense of the monumental. Among Inuit artists, Tasseor's works can be compared with the multiple face style sculptures of Luke Anowtalik (born 1932) and his wife, Mary Ayaq (born 1938), also of Arviat. Tasseor herself feels a close affinity with the art of John Pangnark (1920-1980).

Tasseor works almost exclusively with the grey to black stone found near the community or imported from nearby, and has occasionally carved caribou antler. She begins work with a hacksaw and axe, then switches to files and rasps, and sandpaper. For years Tasseor was afraid to use electric tools, but now occasionally begins carving with a small electric grinder.

Tasseor's sculptures have been included in over 70 exhibitions in Canada and abroad. The most notable of these are *Sculpture/Inuit: Masterworks of the Canadian Arctic*, an international touring exhibition of 1971-73, and *Pure Vision: The Keewatin Spirit*, a touring exhibition of 1986-87. Major works by Tasseor can be found in the collections of the National Gallery of Canada, the Canadian Museum of Civilization, the Art Gallery of Ontario, the Winnipeg Art Gallery and other museums and art galleries. Tasseor has received several commissions and has been invited to "the South" on numerous occasions.

—Ingo Hessel

TUTTLE, Frank

Tribal affiliations: Yuki-Wailaki; Concow Maidu
Painter

Born: Oroville, California, 1957. **Education:** Humboldt State University, Arcata, California, B.A., 1981. **Career:** Lecturer in art and Native American Studies, Mendocino College, Ukiah, California.

Individual Exhibitions

1982	Mendocino County Museum, Willits, California
1990	Bear n' Coyote Gallery, Jamestown, California
1992	C.N. Gorman Museum, University of California, Davis, California
	The One Looking Back, Meridian Gallery, San Francisco
1993	*Frank Tuttle at the Galleria Posada*, La Galleria Posada, Sacramento, California

Selected Group Exhibitions

1981	*American Indian Art in the 1980's*, Center for Living Arts, Niagara Falls, New York
1982	*Native Americans Now: Contemporary Artforms*, Jesse Peters Museum, Santa Rosa Junior College, Santa Rosa, California
1983	*American Indian International Tribunal*, C.N. Gorman Museum, University of California, Davis, California
	Innovations: New Expressions in Native American Painting, The Heard Museum, Phoenix
1984	*Signs and Messengers of the Earth*, Union Gallery, California State University, Sacramento, California
1985	*The Extension of Tradition: Contemporary Northern California Native American Art in Cultural Perspective*, The Crocker Art Museum, Sacramento, California
1987	*Healing That Way*, Humboldt State University, Arcata, California
	American Dreams, Memorial Union Gallery, University of California, Davis, California
1990	*Recent Work by Five Northern California Indian Artists*, Gallery Route One, Point Reyes Station, California
1991	*From the Source*, Ink People Gallery, Eureka, California
	Acknowledging the Host, Richmond Art Center, Richmond, California
	Sacred Spaces, Spirit Places, Memorial Union Art Gallery, University of California, Davis, California
1992	*Transformed Traditions*, Santa Rosa Junior College, Santa Rosa, California
	Ancestral Memories: A Tribute to Native Survival, Falkirk Cultural Center, San Rafael, California
	From the Center of the World, Humboldt Cultural Center, Eureka, California
	From the Source II, Ink People Gallery, Eureka, California
1993	*Shared Experiences/Personal Interpretations: Seven Native American Artists*, University Art Gallery, Sonoma State University, Rohnert Park, California
1994	*Three Times Three*, Humboldt Cultural Center, Eureka, California
	From the Source III, Humboldt Cultural Center, Eureka, California
1995	*Vessels from the Land*, Meridian Gallery, San Francisco
	Walking Stones, Still Water, Artists Contemporary Gallery, Sacramento, California
	Facing Eden: 100 Years of Landscape Art in the Bay Area, M.H. DeYoung Museum, San Francisco
1996	*Weavers and Artists: The Sisters Series*, California State Indian Museum, Sacramento, California
	Paths of Familiar Patterns: The Influence of Basketry on Contemporary California Indian Art, La Raza/La Galleria Posada, Sacramento, California

Collections

Crocker Art Museum, Sacramento, California.

Publications

By TUTTLE: Books—"Artist's Statement," *Innovations: New Expressions in Native American Painting*, Phoenix, Arizona: The Heard Museum, 1983; "Artist's Statement," *Ancestral Memo-*

ries: A Tribute to Native Survival, San Rafael, California, Falkirk Cultural Center, 1992.

On TUTTLE: Books—"Franklin D. Tuttle, Jr.," *The Extension of Tradition: Contemporary Northern California Native American Art in Cultural Perspective*, Frank LaPena and Janice Driesbach, eds., Sacramento, California, The Crocker Art Museum, 1985; "Frank Tuttle," *Recent Work by Five Northern California Indian Artists*, Point Reyes Station, California, Gallery Route One, 1990; "Frank Tuttle," *I Stand in the Center of the Good*, ed. by Lawrence Abbott, Lincoln, Nebraska, The University of Nebraska Press, 1994. **Articles**—"Contemporary Northern California Native American Art," by Frank LaPena, *California History LXXI*, No. 3, 1992; "The Artist's Vocation," by Bruce Nixon, *Artweek*, June 17, 1993; "A Conversation with Frank Tuttle," by Mary Hull Webster, *Artweek 24*, No. 12, June 17, 1993; "Frank Tuttle's Re-imagining of Native America," by David Roth, *Artview*, August (2nd Saturday issue), 1993.

*

Frank Tuttle comments:

First, I am a California Indian, and second, I am an artist. My primary concerns at this moment focus on the imagery strongly derived from my ethnic background. This focus is a personal choice. I choose to work with this type of imagery not because I am a California Indian but because I make the decisions regarding my imagery. When my imagery is not immediately identifiable as a traditional California Indian image, it will still remain California Indian because I am the source and I choose to always work from that angle of vision. I am the artist and I am not giving up that claim.

*   *   *

The art of Frank Tuttle can be seen within the context of both an individual exploration of the meaning and continuity of certain Northern California indigenous traditions and within the dynamics of an evolving group of artists who, through their work, maintain and extend those traditions by searching for the essences and then revitalizing those traditions through contemporary imagery and technique. Artists like Jean LaMarr, Karen Tripp, Brian Tripp, Frank LaPena, Dal Castro, George Blake, and Frank Tuttle investigate the form, practice and meaning of tradition.

The diversity of Tuttle's imagery is grounded in such an exploration of tradition in a contemporary context. He combines Indian imagery and art traditions with modern techniques. He searches for the essences of the ceremonies and rituals of the indigenous peoples of Northern California. Works derived from ceremony can take two forms, the literal and the abstract. Paintings such as *Centerman* (1989), based on the jump dance, and *Thursday Night, Brush Dance* (1989), based on the brush dance, are straightforward depictions of moments in Yurok ceremonial occasions. In the latter, Tuttle does not focus on the beauty of the dance regalia but on the simpler activities of three figures in rolled-up blue jeans. Other paintings use abstract imagery to depict ceremony. *The Abundance of Things* (1983) and *When the Earth Rolls Up* (1984) use elements of ceremony but transform those elements into highly-structured compositions. However, even these abstract compositions are deceptive. In *Shaking All 'Round* (1983), Tuttle employs cloth and netting, which refer to the energy he discerns in the traditional dances of Northern and central California. His marks on the canvas, often in groups of threes, symbolize the rhythms and sounds

that characterize a particular dance. The abstract works become more of the artist's sensory response to the dance rather than a literal depiction.

This is not to say that Tuttle ignores the political dimensions of Native history. In such works as *Coloma* (1989), from his series of "devotional icons" from the late 1980s, Tuttle subtly contrasts the California Indian world view with the European world view, and raises questions about the process of missionization in the eighteenth century and the continuing process of social change and community fragmentation. There is often a juxtaposition between his specific imagery and his use of color that helps to bring out this contrast.

The colors, textures, and structures in Tuttle's paintings are metaphoric representations of the design and materials utilized in ceremonial dress and objects. Designs in the paintings often mirror the designs of such items as purses, baskets, headbands and headgear nets, dance feathers, and skirts. Certain colors recur in Tuttle's work that also have a metaphoric meaning: reds may suggest woodpecker feathers and their mythological associations; greens with elements of nature, growth and life; blues the sky. Lines define and create boundaries and also make vertical connections between earth and sky and form a sense of upward movement. In this way Tuttle invests the static image of the painting with the color and movement associated with ceremonial dances.

—Larry Abbott

TUU'LUUQ, Marion
Tribal affiliations: Inuit
Textile artist

Born: Back River delta of the Northwest Territories, 1910. **Family:** Married (widowed) with five children; married artist Luke Anguhadluq in 1955. **Career:** Traditional Inuit nomadic life; moved to Baker Lake and became a professional artist. **Awards:** Member of the Royal Canadian Academy of Arts since 1978; honorary doctorate, University of Alberta and in 1990.

Individual Exhibitions

1980   *Marion Tuu'luq Wallhangings,* The Upstairs Gallery, Winnipeg, Manitoba

Selected Group Exhibitions

1974   *Baker Lake Print Collection,* (annual collection)
1976   *Tuu'luq/Anguhadluq,* Winnipeg Art Gallery, Winnipeg, Manitoba
         Anguhadluq/Tuu'luq: Husband and Wife of Baker Lake, The Upstairs Gallery, Winnipeg, Manitoba
1977-82 *The Inuit/Print/L'estampe Inuit,* Department of Indian Affairs and Northern Development and the National Museum of Man, Ottawa, Ontario (traveling)
1980   *The Inuit Amautik: I Like My Hood To Be Full,* Winnipeg Art Gallery, Winnipeg, Manitoba
1983-85 *Grasp Tight the Old Ways: Selections from the Klamer Family Collection of Inuit Art,* Art Gallery of Ontario, Toronto, Ontario (traveling)

Marion Tuu'luuq: *Animals Disguised as People.* Photograph by Kenji Nagai; courtesy Inuit Gallery of Vancouver.

1987-89 *Contemporary Inuit Drawings,* Macdonald Stewart Art Centre, Guelph, Ontario (traveling)

1988-89 *Im Schatten der Sonne: Zeitgenossische Kunst der Indianer und Eskimos in Kanada/In the Shadow of the Sun: Contemporary Indian and Inuit Art in Canada,* Canadian Muscum of Civilizaion, Ottawa, Ontario (traveling)

Women of the North: An Exhibition of Art by Inuit Women of the Canadian Arctic, Marion Scott Gallery, Vancouver, British Columbia

1993 *Northern Lights: Inuit Textile Art from the Canadian Arctic,* Baltimore Museum of Art, Baltimore, Maryland (traveling)

1994-97 *Qamanittuaq: Where the River Widens. Drawings by Baker Lake Artists,* Macdonald Stewart Art Centre, Guelph, Ontario (traveling)

1995 *Immaginario Inuit,* Arte e cultura degli esquimesi canadesi, Galleria d'Arte Moderna e Contemporanea, Verona, Italy

1995 *Qamanittuaq, Drawings by Baker Lake Artists,* Macdonald Steward Art Centre, Guelph, Ontario (traveling)

Collections

Canada Council Art Bank, Ottawa, Ontario; Canadian Museum of Civilization, Hull, Quebec; Dennos Museum Center, North-western Michigan College, Traverse City, Michigan; Inuit Cultural Instituc, Rankin Inlet, Northwest Territories; Klamer Family Collection, Art Gallery of Ontario, Toronto, Ontario; Macdonald Stewart Art Centre, Guelph, Ontario; McMaster University Art Gallery, Hamilton, Ontario; McMichael Canadian Art Collection, Kleinburg, Ontario; Mendel Art Gallery, Saskatoon, Saskatchewan; Museum of Anthropology, University of British Columbia, Vancouver, British Columbia; National Gallery of Canada, Ottawa, Ontario; Prince of Wales Northern Heritage Centre, Yellowknife, Northwest Territories; Simon Fraser Gallery, Simon Fraser University, Burnaby, British Columbia; University of Alberta, Edmonton, Alberta; University of Lethbridge Art Gallery, Lethbridge, Alberta; Winnipeg Art Gallery, Winnipeg, Manitoba.

Publications

On TUU'LUQ: Books—*Tuu'luq/Anguhadluq,* by Jean Blodgett, Winnipeg: The Winnipeg Art Gallery, 1976; *Northern Lights: Inuit Textile Art from the Canadian Arctic,* by Katharine W. Fernstrom and Anita E. Jones, Baltimore Museum of Art, 1993; *Qamanittuaq, Where the River Widens: Drawings by Baker Lake Artists,* by Marion Jackson with Judith Nasby and William Noah, Guelph: Macdonald Stewart Art Centre, 1995. **Articles**—"Wall Hangings from Baker

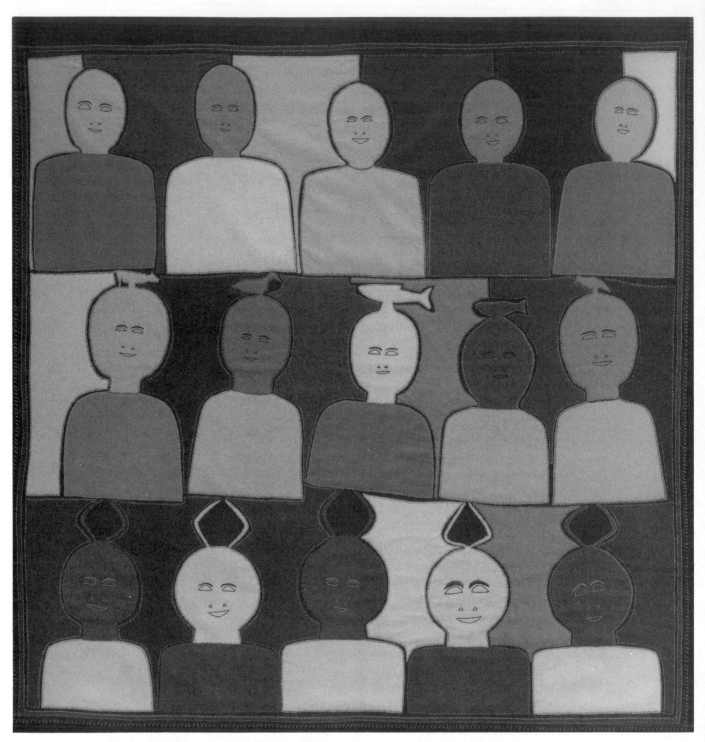

Marion Tuu'luuq: *People, Shamans, and Spirits,* 1978. Collection of the National Gallery of Canada.

Lake," by Sheila Butler, *The Beaver,* Autumn, 1972; "The Tapestries of Marion Tuu'luq," by Marilyn Baker, *Branching Out,* vol. 7, no. 2, 1980; "Marion Tuu'luq Wallhangings at Upstairs Gallery," by Eleanor Hannan, *Artmagazine,* 48/49, May/June, 1980; "Sewing Fine Seams: the Needlecraft of Baker Lake Women, by Alison Gillmore, *Arts Manitoba*, Vol.3, No.4, Fall 1984; "A Woman's Vision, A Woman's Voice: Inuit Textile Art from Arctic Canada," by

Bernadette Driscoll-Engelstad, *Inuit Art Quarterly*, Vol. 9, No. 2 Summer, 1994.

*   *   *

Born in 1910 on the Back River delta of the Northwest Territories, Marion Tuu'luuq has experienced first-hand the dramatic changes to Inuit society over the course of this century. She grew to maturity living the traditional way of Inuit on the land. Widowed with five children, she married Luke Anguhadluq in 1955. Together they continued to live self-sufficiently until the cyclical depletion of caribou caused a period of starvation, which forced many Inuit families to move gradually into settlements. After living in tents on the outskirts for a time, Tuu'luuq recalls that they finally moved into a house in the community of Baker Lake (Qamanittuaq) in 1967. She resides there still and is one of the community's most respected elders.

Tuu'luuq emerged from among the first generation of Inuit artists to become internationally renown. Handicrafts programs across the Canadian Arctic gave Inuit an alternative income and provided stability during the transition from camp to settlement life. The visual expressions of artists have strengthened Inuit cultural values and have become a way of passing on knowledge to future generations.

Tuu'luuq is best known for her vibrant and richly coloured wall-hangings. Traditionally, when living on the land, a mother passed on the skills of animal skin preparation and sewing to her daughter. Although the death of her mother when Tuu'luuq was an infant meant that she was self-taught, she acquired the technical knowledge and manual dexterity for which Inuit women are famous. The link between traditional clothing production and the making of modern images has often been noted. The sense of design, pattern and symmetry necessary for the making of clothing are fundamental to visual artists everywhere. In particular, Baker Lake women have distinguished themselves for their needlecraft through their textile arts.

In her new role as artist, Tuu'luuq was able to adapt these skills to the making of souvenir clothing and handicrafts, and later to the creation of drawings and appliqued wall-hangings.

Tuu'luuq's style is easily distinguished by her use of bold colours and strong visual design. Rather than creating narrative scenes, intricate and repetitive decorative motifs, which can range from Arctic animals to hearts and faces, cover the fabric surface. Over the years, she has developed a number of compositional devices, such as radiating patterns from a central motif, as in *One Man's Dream* (1988). The delicately embroidered tattooed face at the center serves as a focal point and visual anchor from which the complex of radiating circles and repeating motifs seem to ripple forth in layers.

Tuu'luuq's images are characteristically symmetrical, yet never stiff. The use of registers, as in *People, Shamans, and Spirits* (c.1978) affords a strong compositional structure into which Tuu'luuq introduces an offbeat visual rhythm through her controlled yet irregular placement of colours. The image is enlivened through the subtle variations between the repeating shapes and forms of the figures. In particular, it is the embroidery of the faces, for example, in the fine stitches used for the eyebrows that create visual interest without discord to the overall design. It is tempting to relate this well developed sense of design to the making of clothing for the human body, which, while balanced, is never perfectly symmetrical. The impact of these large anthropomorphic patterns, with their interplay between animals and humans, is a harmony that perhaps reflects the integrated relationship of Inuit with their physical environment and spiritual worlds.

Tuu'luuq also excels as a graphic artist. After several attempts, the print shop in Baker Lake published their first collection of prints in 1970 under the direction of Jack and Sheila Butler. Over 20 of Tuu'luuq's drawings have been translated into stonecut or stencil prints. As in *People and Graylings* (1974), her drawing style tends to flow over the paper with large composite creatures and transforming figures that evoke mystery and wonder. Without an obvious narrative, her drawings occasionally relate to legends or myths and likewise these tend toward the fantastic.

In 1976, the Winnipeg Art Gallery organized an exhibition which featured the work of Tuu'luuq and Anguhadluq. More recently, her wall-hangings were shown in *Northern Lights, Inuit Textile Art from the Canadian Arctic* (1993), while her drawings have been included in *Qamanittuaq, Drawings by Baker Lake Artists* (1995). She has been a member of the RCA since 1978, and in 1990 received an honorary doctorate from the University of Alberta. Her work is well represented in numerous Canadian institutions, such as the Winnipeg Art Gallery, Art Gallery of Ontario, Toronto, National Gallery of Canada, Ottawa, Canadian Museum of Civilization, Hull, Prince of Wales Heritage Center, Yellowknife, and Macdonald Stewart Art Center, Guelph.

—Christine Lalonde

ULLULAQ, Judas
Variant names: Judas Ooloolah
Tribal affiliations: Inuit
Carver

Born: Community of Taloyoak, Gjoa Haven, Kitikmeot region (meaning "in the centre"), Northwest Territories. **Family:** Brothers Nelson Takkiruq and Charlie Ugyuk and nephew Karoo Ashevak are noted artists.

Individual Exhibitions

1983   *Ooloolah of Spence Bay,* The Inuit Gallery of Eskimo Art, Toronto, Ontario

1983   Alaska Shop, Gallery of Eskimo Art, New York, New York

1985   *Whalebone Sculpture: Gjoa Haven Featuring Judas Ooloolah,* Northern Images, Edmonton, Alberta

1987   *Judas Ooloolah, Gjoa Haven,* The Upstairs Gallery, Winnipeg, Manitoba

1991   *Judas Ululaq,* Houston North Gallery, Lunenburg, Nova Scotia

Selected Group Exhibitions

1977   *Miniatures from Pelly Bay, Repulse Bay, Spence Bay,* The Innuit Gallery of Eskimo Art, Toronto, Ontario

1982   *Spence Bay Sculpture,* Inuit Gallery of Vancouver, Vancouver, British Columbia

1983   *Inuit Masterworks: Selections from the Collection of Indian and Northern Affairs Canada,* McMichael Canadian Collection, Kleinburg, Ontario

1983-85   *Contemporary Indian and Inuit Art of Canada* (traveling)

1984   *Spence Bay Artists,* Galerie Elca London, Montreal, Quebec

1984-86   *Arctic Vision: Art of the Canadian Inuit,* organized by the Department of Northern and Indian Affairs and Canadian Arctic Producers, Ottawa, Ontario (traveling)

1985   *Spence Bay Sculpture by Ooloolah and Ugjuk,* Gallery Indigena, Waterloo, Ontario

1985-86   *Sanaugasi Takujaksat: A Traveling Celebration of Inuit Sculpture,* organized by Canadian Arctic Producers with the Department of Northern and Indian Affairs and Ottawa, Ontario (traveling)
       Die Kunst aus der Arktis, Department of Northern and Indian Affairs (touring Germany)

1986   *Northern Exposure: Inuit Images of Travel,* Burnaby Art Gallery, Burnaby, British Columbia

1987   *Useful Bits of Bone,* Winnipeg Art Gallery, Winnipeg, Manitoba

Judas Ullulaq: **Shaman.** Courtesy Inuit Gallery of Vancouver.

1988   *Building on Strengths: New Inuit Art from the Collection,* Winnipeg Art Gallery, Winnipeg, Manitoba

1988-89   *Im Schatten der Sonne: Zeitgenossische Kunst der Indianer und Eskimos in Kanada/In the Shadow of the Sun: Contemporary Indian and Inuit Art in Canada,* Canadian Museum of Civilization, Ottawa, Ontario (traveling)

1989   *Brothers: Nelson Takkiruq, Judas Ullulaq, Charlie Ugyuk,* Gallery Indigena, Stratford, Ontario

1990   *Small Sculptures from across the Canadian Arctic,* Feheley Fine Arts, Toronto, Ontario

1990-91   *Espaces Inuit,* Maison Hamel-Bruneau, Ste-Foy, Quebec

1991   *Taste of the Wild,* Orca Art, Chicago, Illinois
       Art Inuit, Galerie Saint Merri, Paris, France
       Mother and Child: Sculpture and Prints, Albers Gallery, San Francisco, California

1992   *The Arctic Project: A Photographic Exchange,* Surrey Art Gallery, Surrey, British Columbia
       Salon International Europ'art '92, presented by Galerie Saint Merri, Geneva, Switzerland
       Nouveau Territories... 350/500 ans apres, Les Ateliers Visions Planetaire, Montreal, Quebec (traveling)

1993   *Umingmak-Muskox,* Houston North, Lunenburg, Nova Scotia
       The Bear: Sculpture, Albers Gallery, San Francisco, California

1994   *Mythic Image,* Ancestral Spirits Gallery, Port Townsend, Washington

1995   *Immaginario Inuit, Arte e cultura degli esquimesi canadesi,* Galleria d'Arte Moderna e Contemporaranea, Verona, Italy

        Tundra & Ice: Exceptional Sculpture from Canada, Orca Art Gallery, Chicago, Illinois

        Keeping Our Stories Alive: An Exhibition of the Art and Crafts from Dene and Inuit of Canada, Institute of American Indian Arts Museum, Santa Fe, New Mexico

        Inspiration, Four Decades of Sculpture, Marion Scott Gallery, Vancouver, British Columbia

1995-96 *Inuit Art: from the collection of Maurice Yacowar,* Collector's Gallery, Calgary, Alberta

1996   *Emerging Spirit,* Banff Centre, Banff, Alberta

Collections

Ackland Art Museum, Chapel Hill, North Carolina; Art Gallery of Ontario, Toronto, Ontario; Canadian Museum of Civilization, Hull, Quebec; Dennos Museum Center, Northwestern Michigan College, Traverse City, Michigan; Inuit Cultural Institute, Rankin Inlet, Northwest Territories; Macdonald Stewart Art Centre, Guelph, Ontario; McMichael Canadian Art Collection, Kleinburg, Ontario; Musée des beaux-arts de Montreal, Montreal, Quebec; Museum of Anthropology, University of British Columbia, Vancouver, British Columbia; National Gallery of Canada, Ottawa, Ontario; Peary-MacMillan Arctic Museum, Brunswick, Maine; Prince of Wales Northern Heritage Centre, Yellowknife, Northwest Territories; Sarick Collection, Art Gallery of Ontario, Toronto, Ontario; Winnipeg Art Gallery, Winnipeg, Manitoba.

Publications

On ULLULAQ: Books—*Images and Words from Spence Bay, N.W.T.,* by Pam Harris and Judy McGrath, Artscanada, 1972; *Judas Ooloolah,* Canadian Arctic Producers, Ottawa, 1983; *Arctic Vision: Art of the Canadian Inuit,* by Barbara Lipton, Ottawa, Canadian Arctic Producers, 1984; *Im Schatten der Sonne: Zeitgenoessische Kunst der Indianer und Eskimos in Kanada (In the Shadow of the Sun: Contemporary Art of the Indians and Eskimos in Canada),* Stuttgart: Edition Cantz, Ottawa: Canadian Museum of Civilization, 1988; *Brothers: Nelson Takkiruq, Judas Ullulaq, Charlie Ugyuk,* Gallery Indigena, Stratford, 1989; *Espaces Inuit: Dessins et Sculpture,* by Louis Gagnon, Sainte-Foy, Quebec, 1990; *Sculpture of the Inuit,* (revised and updated edition of *Sculpture of the Eskimo*), by George Swinton, Toronto, 1992; *The Inuit Imagination: Arctic Myth and Sculpture,* by Harold Seidelman and James Turner, Vancouver/Toronto, 1993; *Keeping our Stories Alive: An Exhibition of Art and Crafts from Dene and Inuit of Canada,* Institute of American Indian Arts Museum, Santa Fe, 1995. **Articles**—"Focus on Artists: The Central Arctic," by Darlene Wight, *Inuit Art and Crafts,* December 1984; "Spence Bay has Come a Long Way Against Formidable Odds," *Inuit Art Quarterly,* vol. 4, no. 1, Winter, 1989; "Storytellers in Stone," by Jeanne L. Pattison, *Up-Here,* October / November 1991; "Judas Ullulaq: An Interview by Simeonie Kunnuk, with Additional Questions by Janet McGrath," *Inuit Art Quarterly,* Summer 1995.

*   *   *

Judas Ullulaq is a member of one of the most talented families of Inuit artists in Canada. He and brothers Nelson Takkiruq and Charlie Ugyuk were featured in their own 1989 exhibition, *Brothers,* at Gallery Indigena, Stratford, Ontario. Together, they have made an outstanding contribution to the development of Inuit sculpture and can certainly be credited, in part, with the growing interest in Kitikmeot sculpture. The communities of Taloyoak and Gjoa Haven are in the Kitikmeot region (meaning *in the centre*) of the Northwest Territories.

Originally from Taloyoak, Ullulaq was one of the first in the community to begin carving in the late 1960s. It was in these early years that he admired and was inspired by the work of his nephew, Karoo Ashevak, whose innovative whalebone carvings of the spirit world had a dramatic impact on the future of Inuit art and artists. Karoo's influence is perhaps most apparent in the striking facial expressions and the boldness of his uncle's compositions. Much of the tremendous energy and imagination in Ullulaq's sculpture may have been motivated by Karoo's fearless creativity.

While spirit figures are commonly featured in much of the sculpture from the region, Ullulaq also tends to draw on his own experience and concentrates on the environment he knows best when choosing his subjects. There is, however, a spirit-like quality inherent in his carvings, a sense of mischief and whimsy that is most often reserved for creatures of the imagination. His human, animal and spirit figures exude personalities so animated in their appearance and interaction that it seems as if they are performing for an audience. The wonderful humour in Ullulaq's work comes, in part, from the wildly expressive faces—eyes wide with fear, joy or surprise, large, flaring nostrils and contorted mouths dotted with ivory teeth. These signature elements also demonstrate the artist's attention to detail and an obvious interest in materials. In the early 1980s Ullulaq moved to Gjoa Haven, where whalebone was the carving material of choice, yet he still prefers dark, greenish-black stone that will take a fairly high polish. He is particularly adept at introducing different materials, providing an effective contrast in colour and texture, in a single piece. It is not unusual to find various combinations of caribou antler, whalebone, sinew, ivory and stone in an Ullulaq composition. He is a master of mixed media amongst Inuit sculptors.

In his carvings, Ullulaq often illustrates the connection between humans and animals in the arctic, a relationship that the Inuit of his generation understand completely. The hunt, a very important aspect of Inuit life, is a key theme in Ullulaq's work. He presents the hunter and his prey not in a life and death struggle, but almost as if at play. The adversaries become equals in a carving that depicts a hunter with his spear being tossed into the air by an aggressive musk-ox, apparently taking them both by surprise. Such intriguing compositions also show off the artist's grasp of balance and unique sense of space. Ullulaq's uninhibited approach results in works that are consistently startling, exciting and amusing.

Ullulaq's work has been shown in over 60 exhibitions, including five solo shows, in Europe and North America. In 1988 he travelled to Germany to attend the opening of *In the Shadow of the Sun,* a touring exhibition of Inuit and Indian art in Canada. He also participated in the opening of the exhibition, *Contemporary Indian and Inuit Art of Canada,* which was held at the General Assembly Building of the United Nations, and the 1995 *Immaginario Inuit* exhibition in Verona, Italy. His work is prized by private collectors, and is well represented in such major permanent collections as the Winnipeg Art Gallery, Musée des beaux-arts de Montreal and the National Gallery of Canada. Ullulaq's carving, *Mother Carrying*

Pot (1988) was featured on the cover of the Summer 1995 issue of the *Inuit Art Quarterly* magazine.

—Lori Cutler

VELARDE, Pablita

Variant names. Tse Tsan
Tribal affiliations: Santa Clara Pueblo
Painter

Born: Santa Clara Pueblo, New Mexico, 19 September 1918; native name Tse Tsan means Golden Dawn. **Family:** Married Herbert Hardin in 1942, divorced early 1960s; two children, Herbert II and artist Helen Hardin. **Education:** St. Catherine's Indian School, Santa Fe; Santa Fe Indian School, 1932, where she studied with Dorothy Dunn, educator for the U.S. Civil Service, at the Studio; also encouraged by watercolorist Tonita Peña. **Career:** Artist, lecturer, teacher, illustrator, author; muralist, commissioned by the Museum of Fine Arts, Santa Fe, New Mexico, Bandalier National Monument (where she was artist-in-residence), and Santa Clara Day School. **Awards:** Numerous, including first place honors at All American Indian Days, Sheridan, Wyoming, Trail of Tears Show, Cherokee National Museum, Tahlequah, Oklahoma; Inter-Tribal Indian Ceremonies, Gallup, New Mexico, (4 times), and Indian Market, Santa Fe, (7 times, including the Helen Hardin Award); French Government, Palmes d'Academiques, 1954, and New Mexico Governor's Award for Outstanding Achievement in the Arts.

Individual Exhibitions

1966   Desert Museum, Palm Springs, California
1993   *Woman's Work: The Art of Pablita Velarde*, Wheelwright Museum of the American Indian, Santa Fe, New Mexico
1995   Museum of New Mexico, Santa Fe

Selected Group Exhibitions

1931-33 *Exposition of Indian Tribal Arts*, sponsored by The College Art Association, (traveling exhibit)
1934   Chicago Century of Progress, Chicago, Illinois
1947-65 *American Indian Paintings from the Permanent Collection*, Philbrook Art Museum, Tulsa, (traveling)
1955   *An Exhibition of American Indian Painters*, James Graham and Sons, New York
1955-56 University of Oklahoma European Tours, organized by University of Oklahoma, Norman
1958-61 University of Oklahoma European Tours, organized by University of Oklahoma, Norman
1963   *Contemporary American Indian Art*, United States Department of State, Washington, D.C., (traveling)
1978   *100 Years of Native American Art*, Oklahoma Museum of Art, Oklahoma
1979-80 *Native American Paintings*, Mid-America Arts Alliance Project, organized by the Joslyn Art Museum, Omaha, Nebraska, touring
1980   *American Indian Woman's Spring Art Festival*, Indian Pueblo Cultural Center, Albuquerque, New Mexico

Native American Art at the Philbrook, Tulsa, Oklahoma
1981   *Walk in Beauty, A National Invitational Native Art Show*, Santa Fe Festival of the Arts, New Mexico
1981-83 *Native American Painting*, organized by the Amarillo Art Center, Amarillo, Texas, (traveling)
1984-85 *Indianischer Kunstler*, organized by the Philbrook Museum, Tulsa, Oklahoma, traveling, West Germany
1986   *When the Rainbow Touches Down*, Heard Museum, Phoenix, Arizona, (traveling)
1987   Cherokee National Museum, Tahlequah, Oklahoma
1990   Koogler McNay Art Museum, San Antonio, Texas
1990-91 *One With the Earth*, organized by the Institute of American Indian Arts and Alaska Culture Arts and Development, (touring exhibit)
1991-92 *Shared Visions: Native American Painters and Sculptors of the Twentieth Century*, Heard Museum, Phoenix, Arizona, (traveling)

Collections

Amerind Foundation, Dragoon, Arizona; Denver Art Museum, Colorado; Thomas Gilcrease Institute of American History and Art, Tulsa, Oklahoma; Heard Museum, Phoenix, Arizona; Joslyn Art Museum, Omaha, Nebraska; Kiva Museum of the Koshare Indian, Boy Scouts of America, La Junta, Colorado; Logan Museum of Anthropology, Beloit, Wisconsin; Museum of New Mexico, Santa Fe; Museum of Norther Arizona, Flagstaff; National Museum of the American Indian, Smithsonian Institution, Washington, D.C.; Oklahoma University Fred Jones, Jr., Museum of Art, Oklahoma City; Philbrook Museum of Art, Tulsa, Oklahoma; Roswell Museum and Art Center, Roswell, New Mexico; San Diego Museum of Man, California; Southwest Museum, Los Angeles, California; University of California, Berkeley; United Pueblo Agency, Albuquerque, New Mexico; Wheelwright Museum of the American Indian, Santa Fe.

Publications

By VELARDE: Book—*Old Father, The Storyteller*, Globe, Arizona, 1960.

On VELARDE: Books—*American Indian Painting of the Southwest and Plains Areas*, by Dorothy Dunn, Albuquerque: University of New Mexico, 1968; *The Arts of the North American Indian: Native Traditions in Evolution*, Edwin L. Wade, editor, New York: Hudson Hills Press in association with Philbrook Art Center, Tulsa, Oklahoma, 1986; *When the Rainbow Touches Down*, by Tryntje Van Ness Seymour, Heard Museum exhibition catalog, Seattle & London: University of Washington Press, 1988; *Changing Woman: The Life and Art of Helen Hardin*, Jay Scott, Flagstaff, Northland Press, 1989; *Shared Visions: Native American Painters and Sculptors in the Twentieth Century*, by Margaret Archuleta and Dr. Rennard Strickland, New York: The New Press, 1991; *Woman's Work: The Art of Pablita Velarde*, by Sally Hyer, Santa Fe, Wheelwright Museum of the American Indian, 1993. **Articles**—"Helen Hardin: A Retrospective," by LouAnn Culley, *American Indian Art Magazine*, Summer 1977; "Pablita Velarde," Mary Carroll Nelson, *American Indian Art Magazine*, Spring 1978. **Film**—*Pablita Velarde: An Artist and Her People*, National Park Service, 1984.

*   *   *

In 1918 a baby girl by the Tewa name of Tse Tsan (Golden Dawn) was born at the Santa Clara Pueblo. Named by her grandmother, the child later became one of the most influential female painters in the modern Indian painting movement, Pablita Velarde. She is considered the pre-eminent female artist from the second generation of American Indian painters associated with the Santa Fe Indian Boarding School. Velarde shares the title with her predecessor, first generation painter Tonita Peña (1893-1949), of being the first Pueblo Indian women to pursue careers as easel painters. Velarde's paintings are derived from her experiences and memories as a Santa Clara woman. Her subjects illustrate the dance ceremonies she participated in, the stories heard as a child, and the more routine task of selling pottery and paintings—all from the female perspective.

As a young child Velarde was blinded by a serious eye infection, which lasted until she was six or seven years of age. Having already lost her mother and several siblings to disease, she was cared for by her father and grandmother. Perhaps it was this temporary loss of sight combined with her commitment to preserving Santa Clara cultural traditions that first kindled Velarde's desire to become an artistic observer and recorder of the world around her.

Velarde attended the St. Catherine's Indian School in Santa Fe as a young girl. Her formal artistic training began when she was transferred to the Santa Fe Indian School in 1932 where she studied with Dorothy Dunn. Dunn, an educator for the U.S. Civil Service, established the first fine arts program and painting department at SFIS, called the Studio. Velarde and her sister were the first female art students. Velarde credits Dunn with providing her first encouragement as an artist. At the school in Santa Fe she also met and was inspired by the watercolorist Tonita Peña. At the time, Peña was a well-established easel painter who visited the school periodically while working on mural projects during the 1930s.

Although Velarde rarely strayed from what she herself termed traditional subject matter, ceremonial dances and scenes of everyday pueblo life, her stylistic and technical approaches to painting were diverse. Like most early painters Velarde used tempera and watercolor paints on paper and even experimented with oils. Eventually she worked in a technique using natural earth pigments she produced herself. Velarde collected rocks and minerals near her home, ground them into a fine powder and mixed them with a binder of glue and water, a technique encouraged by Dunn at the Studio. During the 1950s and 1960s she experimented with style by using abstracted depictions of symbolic designs, drawing on motifs from pottery and ancient murals. Occasionally Velarde used stories and aesthetic elements from other American Indian cultures as sources for her own paintings.

By the time Velarde graduated from high school in 1936 her paintings had been exhibited in Chicago, Washington D.C., and

Pablita Velarde: *Koshares of Taos.* **Collection of the Philbrook Museum of Art.**

New Mexico. She went back to Santa Clara where she worked at the day school for two years. In 1939 Velarde and several of her contemporaries were commissioned to paint murals for the facade and entry of the Maisel Trading Post in Albuquerque, New Mexico. Not long after, at the age of 20, Velarde was hired as an artist-in-residence at Bandelier National Monument, where she produced a large collection of paintings portraying scenes from everyday, traditional Pueblo Indian life. She worked at Bandelier for two different appointments completing 84 paintings between 1939 and 1948 as part a Works Progress Administration project.

In spite of cultural attitudes and social pressures that discouraged women from becoming painters, Velarde persevered. In part, she maintained that her purpose as an artist was to record the old ways, the traditions and practices that were slowly disappearing. "As time went on I began to think, someday this is not all going to be the same. So I started recording. I think that is my main purpose of getting into this subject." Velarde had always disliked the tasks and roles that were considered typical women's work, like housework and cooking. She attempted to find satisfaction through various jobs but in the end painting was the only profession that provided her with pleasure and a sense of personal fulfillment.

Although Velarde enjoyed artistic success early on, she had to rely on additional means of economic support. She left her studio in Santa Clara to find work in Albuquerque. There she met and married Herbert Hardin in 1942. They settled in Albuquerque and raised two children, Herbert II and Helen Hardin. Velarde did not return to her Santa Clara home until the 1960s after her marriage ended. The homecoming was not easy however, and she struggled once again to define and defend her role as a pueblo woman artist. By this time she had received numerous awards and museum exhibitions. Fortunately, despite the criticism she continued to paint and is today one of the most celebrated modern painters from Santa Clara.

—Lisa Roberts

VIGIL, Romando

Variant names: Tse Ye Mu
Tribal affiliations: San Ildefonso Pueblo
Painter

Born: San Ildefonso Pueblo, New Mexico, 23 January 1902; Tse Ye Mu translates as Falling in Water. **Education:** Santa Fe Indian School. **Career:** Professional painter from around 1918 through the 1960s; commissioned muralist, including The Corcoran Gallery of Art, Washington, D.C. (with Oqwa Pi and Velino Shije Herrera and Santa Fe Indian School; studio employee and painter, Walt Disney Studios, 1960s and 1970s. **Died:** 1978

Selected Group Exhibitions

1925   *Exhibition of American Indian Paintings and Applied Arts,* Arts Club of Chicago, Illinois
1931-33 *Exposition of Indian Tribal Arts,* organized by the College Art Association (traveling)
1935-37 Mesa Verde National Park, Colorado
1937   *American Indian Exposition and Congress,* Tulsa, Oklahoma

1955-56 European tour sponsored by the University of Oklahoma, Norman
1958-61 European tour sponsored by the University of Oklahoma, Norman
1978   100 Years of Native American Painting, Oklahoma Museum of Art, Oklahoma City, Oklahoma
1979-80 *Native American Paintings,* organized by the Joslyn Art Museum, Omaha, Nebraska (traveling)
1982   *Native American Painting: Selections from the Museum of the American Indian,* Heard Museum, Phoenix, Arizona
1984-85 *Indianascher Kunstler* (traveling, Germany), organized by the Philbrook Museum, Tulsa, Oklahoma
1986   Denver Art Museum, Denver, Colorado
1988   *When the Rainbow Touches Down,* Heard Museum, Phoenix, Arizona (traveling)
1989   *2,000 Years of Southwest Indian Arts and Culture,* Museum of New Mexico, Santa Fe
1990   *American Indian Artists in the Avery Collection and the McNay Permanent Collection,* Koogler McNay Art Museum, San Antonio, Texas
1991-92 *Shared Visions: Native American Painters and Sculptors in the Twentieth Century,* The Heard Museum, Phoenix, Arizona
1996   *Drawn from Memory: James T. Bialac Collection of Native American Art,* Heard Museum, Phoenix, Arizona

Collections

Amerind Foundation, Dragoon, Arizona; Center for Great Plains Studies, University of Nebraska, Lincoln; Denver Art Museum, Denver, Colorado; Thomas Gilcrease Institute of American History and Art, Tulsa, Oklahoma; Heard Museum, Phoenix, Arizona; Joslyn Art Museum, Omaha, Nebraska; Koogler McNay Art Museum, San Antonio, Texas; Mesa Verde National Park Museum, Colorado; Mitchell Indian Museum, Kendall College, Evanston, Illinois; Museum of New Mexico, Santa Fe; Museum of Northern Arizona, Flagstaff, Arizona; Philbrook Museum of Art, Tulsa, Oklahoma; Millicent Rogers Foundation Museum, Taos, New Mexico; University of Oklahoma, Norman, Oklahoma; Woolaroc Museum, Bartlesville, Oklahoma.

Publications

On VIGIL: Books—*Pueblo Indian Painting,* by Hartley Burr Alexander, Nice, France, 1932; *American Indian Painting of the Southwest and Plains Areas,* by Dorothy Dunn, Albuquerque: University of New Mexico, 1968; *Indian Painters and White Patrons,* by J. J. Brody, Albuquerque: University of New Mexico Press, 1971; *100 Years of Native American Painting,* exhibition catalog by Arthur Silberman, Oklahoma Museum of Art, Oklahoma City, 1978; *Selections from the Museum of the American Indian,* by David M. Fawcett and Lee A. Callander, New York: Museum of the American Indian, 1982; *Indianascher Kunstler,* by Gerhard Hoffmann, Munich, 1984; *The Arts of the North American Indian: Native Traditions in Evolution,* Edwin L. Wade, ed., New York: Hudson Hills Press in association with Philbrook Art Center, Tulsa, Oklahoma, 1986; *When the Rainbow Touches Down,* exhibition catalog by Tryntje Van Ness Seymour, Heard Museum, University of Washington Press, 1988; *I am Here: 2,000 Years of Southwest Indian*

Romando Vigil: *Charging Warrior on Yellow Horse,* c. 1960. Photograph by Seth Roffman; courtesy Dr. Gregory Schaaf collection.

Arts and Culture, by Andrew Whiteford, Santa Fe, 1989; *American Indian Artists in the Avery Collection and the McNay Permanent Collection,* Jean Sherrod Williams, editor, San Antonio, 1990; *Shared Visions: Native American Painters and Sculptors in the Twentieth Century,* by Margaret Archuleta and Dr. Rennard Strickland, New York: The New Press, 1991.

*   *   *

Modern Indian painting began in the Santa Fe area in the early decades of the 20th century among artists usually referred to as part of the "San Ildefonso school." The first important San Ildefonso painter, Crescencio Martinez, had been encouraged to move from painting pottery to working on canvas by Dr. Edgar L. Hewett of the School of American Research, but Martinez died in 1918 in a flu epidemic. By 1920 almost every man of San Ildefonso, Romando Vigil among them, and some women had begun painting pictures.

Like Julian Martinez, some of these artists had started as pottery decorators and simply "translated" their designs—primarily birds and the mythical "Avanyu" (snake)—into another medium, while others depicted ceremonial dances and scenes of everyday life. Thus two distinct styles evolved, one decorative and abstract, the other realistic and descriptive.

The two modes were combined by Vigil, who began painting about 1918 and became a prolific artist. His main interest was the dances of his pueblo, but he also painted animals as well as men and women at work. His dance-pictures are good examples of the dif-

ferent tendencies. In his oil painting, *San Ildefonso Woman's Dance,* the dancers, seen from the side, are lined up in three rows with a drummer in front. They are all depicted in the same posture, looking straight ahead, with arms outstretched in front of them and both feet on the ground. The only variation, which avoids monotony, is in the coloration of the shawls and dresses. There is neither a ground line nor a background, and the overall impression is that of bareness and rigidity. Quite different is *San Ildefonso Scalp Dance,* which has figures distributed all over the picture plane; the dancers here are looking in various directions, holding different weapons, and are depicted in a number of positions, thus contributing to a dynamic, rhythmic impression.

Animals comprise the subject matter in *Legend of the Game,* which shows the dichotomy between the artist's decorative and realistic goals in a different way. There is no symmetry or "order" in the picture; miscellaneous animals, scattered over the picture plane, are moving towards a hunter at the far right. Even though not realistic in size—some of the birds are as big as the deer and the deer are the same size as the buffalo—the animals are well observed and represented in different postures and vivid movements. The "realistic" scene, however, is framed by an abstract, partly geometric pattern with a stylized, decorative sun.

Vigil has also painted scenes of every day life. *Ceremonial Corn Grinding,* from around 1920, with its strict formal structure and the static positions of four women grinding corn, has the charm of the unmediated and unreflected. The monotony of the arrangement of the women is interrupted by the variation in their poses: from left to right they bend over their work progressively, and the rigorous serialism is relieved by the figures in the foreground and the two brimming bowls. In the background, a rainbow repeating the harmonious colors of the image rounds off the composition, like a frame.

The different trends in Romando Vigil's work reflect the changes that took part in the development of the San Ildefonso school, whose members strongly influenced each other. Except for the pottery decorators, they started out with attempts at illusionistic, representational, and realistic pictures. In the early 1920s there was a shift toward abstract decoration, and that mode came to dominate. The contrasting visual goals are represented by Vigil's *Woman and Skunk* (c. 1920-25), in which the female figure is running fast, with one arm raised, her shawl, sash, and braid fluttering behind her, and *The Bird* of 1935, a highly abstract, decorative design merely suggesting an animal.

Romando Vigil seems to have made a living as an artist. He was, for instance, employed, together with other Pueblo painters, at producing the mural decorations for the 1933 Exposition of Indian Tribal Arts at the Corcoran Gallery in Washington, DC. In the 1950s he was obviously in California and employed as a painter at the Walt Disney Studios. While still in Los Angeles in the 1960s, he apparently did very little painting. He died in 1978.

—Gerhard and Gisela Hoffmann

VIGIL GREY, Darren

Tribal affiliations: Jicarilla Apache; Kiowa
Painter

Born: Dulce, New Mexico, 29 July 1959. **Family:** Married to actress and model Jill Momaday, daughter of Pulitzer Prize-winning author, N. Scott Momaday. **Education:** Institute of American Indian Arts, 1975-77; College of Santa Fe, 1978-79; University of New Mexico, Albuquerque, 1985-86. **Career:** Painter; musician (played and recorded with popular performers, including Rita Coolidge, and is a member of musical group, The Mud Ponies); commissions, including Southwest Ballet Company poster, 1975, *Saturday Night Live* (NBC-TV) backdrop, 1988. **Agent:** c/o Peyton-Wright Gallery, Santa Fe, New Mexico.

Individual Exhibitions

1981	Twenty First Century Fox Gallery, Santa Fe, New Mexico
1982	Twenty-Six Horses Gallery, New York, New York
1988	Lakota Gallery, Santa Monica, California
	The Santa Fe Gallery, London England
1989	The Common Ground, New York, New York
	Lakota Gallery, Santa Monica, California
1990-91	The Friesen Gallery, Sun Valley, Idaho

Selected Group Exhibitions

1979	Museum of the American Indian, New York, New York
1981	*American Indian Art in the 1980s*, Native American Center for the Living Arts, Niagara Falls, New York
	Santa Monica Indian Art Show, Santa Monica, California

	Turtle Museum Premier Art Show, Niagara Falls, New York
1982	Armand Hammer United College of the American West, Montezuma, New Mexico
	One with the Earth Exhibit, Trumbull Art Guild, Warren, Ohio
	Smithsonian Institution, Washington, D.C.
	Stanford University Faculty Club, Palo Alto, California
1983	The Institute of the American West, Sun Valley, Idaho
	Musée de l'homme, Paris, France
	Three Person Show, Twenty Six Horses Gallery, New York, New York
1983-84	Telluride Film Festival, Gallery of the Twenty First Century, Telluride, Colorado
1984	Lincoln Center for the Performing Arts, Avery Fisher Hall, New York, New York
	The Object is Graphic, Wheelwright Museum of the American Indian, Santa Fe, New Mexico
	Haffenreffer Museum of Anthropology, Brown University, Bristol, Rhode Island
	Walk in Beauty, The Festival of the Arts, Santa Fe, New Mexico
	U.S. Customs House Museum, New York, New York
	Mendocino County Museum of Art, Willits, California
	Seton Hall University, West Orange, New Jersey
	Quinnipiac College, New Haven, Connecticut
	Scribbs College, Lang Museum, Claremont, California
1985	*The Art of the Native American: The Southwest from the Late 19th Century to the Present*, Owensboro Museum of Fine Art, Owensboro, Kentucky
	Los Angeles Art Expo, Los Angeles, California
	Two-Man Show, Sacred Circle Gallery, Seattle, Washington
	Oklahoma City Ballet, Artists of Santa Fe, Inc., Oklahoma City, Oklahoma
1986	*New York Art Expo*, Westwood Galleries, New York, New York
	Taos Spring Arts Celebration: Sixty Contemporary Southwestern Artists, Taos, New Mexico
	Politics Now Exhibit, Reinventing Politics Symposium, Telluride, Colorado
1987	*Fifteen Contemporary Native American Artists*, Governor's Gallery, Santa Fe, New Mexico
1988	Enthios Gallery, Santa Fe, New Mexico
1989	*Five Contemporary Native American Artists*, The Gibbs Museum, Charleston, South Carolina
1990	*Printmaking in New Mexico: A Native American Perspective*, Stables Art Center, Taos, New Mexico
	The Art of the West Invitational, Eiteljorg Museum, Indianapolis, Indiana
	Art and Cuisine at the French Culinary Institute, New York, New York
1991	Peyton-Wright Gallery, Santa Fe, New Mexico
1992-93	The Friesen Gallery, Sun Valley, Idaho
1994	Lone Pine Gallery, Irvine, California
	The Friesen Gallery, Seattle, Washington
1995	Ramscale, New York, New York
1996	Peyton-Wright Gallery, Santa Fe, New Mexico

Collections

Bruce Museum, Greenwich, Connecticut; Denver Art Museum, Denver, Colorado; Thomas Gilcrease Institute of American His-

Darren Vigil Grey: *Ascencion #7,* 1988. Photograph by Seth Roffman; courtesy Southwest Learning Center collection.

tory and Art,Tulsa, Oklahoma; Heard Museum, Phoenix, Arizona; Indian Arts and Crafts Board, Washington D.C.; Institute of American Indian Arts Museum, Santa Fe, New Mexico; Institute of the American West, Sun Valley, Idaho; Norman Mackenzie Museum, University of Regina, Regina, Saskatchewan; Museum of Mankind, Vienna, Austria; Museum of the American Indian, Heye Foundation, New York, New York; National Museum of American Art, Smithsonian Institution, Washington D.C.; Philbrook Museum of Art, Tulsa, Oklahoma; Stamford Museum, Stamford, Connecticut; Wheelwright Museum of the American Indian, Santa Fe, New Mexico.

Publications

On VIGIL GREY: Books—*American Indian Art in the 1980s,* by Lloyd Kiva New, Niagara Falls, Native American Center for the Living Arts, 1981; *New Art of the West,* by Thomas Gentry, et. al., Indianapolis, Eiteljorg Museum, 1990; *Creativity is Our Tradition: Three Decades of Contemporary Indian Art,* by Rick Hill, Santa Fe, Institute of American Indian Arts, 1992. **Articles**—*American Indian Art,* Summer 1981; "Seventh Son gets the blues from all over," by Emily Van Cleve, *Masters of Indian Market Exhibition Guide,* supplement in the *New Mexican,* 22 May 1996.

*   *   *

Darren Vigil Grey is among the best-known artists on the contemporary Santa Fe art scene, for his paintings, which are exhibited locally and internationally, and for other activities, including his work as a musician with The Mud Ponies, a popular local band. He has been a session musician as well, playing drums on recordings by Rita Coolidge and others. Additionally, he has supported the Santa Fe Indian Market with concerts, is active in various causes, and works on occasion with the Institute of American Indian Arts. He studied at the Institute in his mid-teens, when he left the Jicarilla Apache Reservation to enroll in art classes. "When you're living on the reservation, you're living a very isolated existence," Vigil Grey recalled. "So, when I came to Santa Fe, it seemed like almost a different world. It didn't seem like any other place I ever dreamed about. It was so, kind of eclectic and bohemian. That . . . appealed to me."

At the IAIA, Vigil Grey experimented and expanded his penchant for using vibrant colors, symbols and images common to southwest cultures, and techniques for blending social commentary and vivid abstractions. In several ways Vigil Grey continued the spirit of modernistic painting among Native American artists that had become a hallmark at the Institute through the works of such artists as T.C. Cannon, Fritz Scholder, and Alfred Young Man. From the 1960s, these artists helped promote a movement toward abstraction, satire and social commentary. The works of Cannon, a Kiowa/Caddo painter who died in May 1978, after Vigil Grey had completed his studies at the Institute, influenced Vigil Grey's early painting, which shows a representational and pop style while making statements on contemporary Native American life. "I always wanted to say something," Vigil Grey reflected; "I thought there was a great need for Native Americans to say certain things, and it was maybe only through the arts that anybody was going to try and understand, or try to relate."

After graduating from IAIA in 1977, Vigil Grey continued his formal training at the College of Santa Fe through 1979, when his work began to receive wider recognition. His paintings were included in an exhibit at the Museum of the American Indian and another important group show, *American Indian Art in the 1980s*, at the Native American Center for the Living Arts, Niagara Falls, New York. A representative early work, *The Round Up* (acrylic on canvas), from these exhibits, depicts a cowboy with darkened eyes on horseback in front of a palisaded, frontier fort. In the foreground the powerful faces of five Indians stare directly at the viewer. Their outlines are dark and bold, the grass and sky are vibrant and flowing. Paint is applied thickly, with a balance of serpentine lines and small, solid blocks of color. Another early work, *Hopi*, demonstrates Vigil Grey's technical mastery of line and form, balancing of wavy lines and solid areas in its rendering of a traditional Hopi woman, her hair adorned in "Butterfly whorls."

Numerous important exhibitions soon followed: by 1982, Vigil Grey's work had been shown at the Smithsonian Institution and Stanford University, and the following year his paintings traveled from the Institute of the American West, in Sun Valley, Idaho, to the Musée de l'homme, in Paris, France. His work was popular at the Telluride Film Festival, and he was chosen to participate in an annual exhibit at the Lincoln Center for the Performing Arts in New York City. All this was accomplished before he was 25 years old. Meanwhile, Vigil Grey continued to expand his craft, taking classes at the University of New Mexico, studying serigraphy with Kate Karasin, and experimenting with intaglio etching, a process of printmaking made famous by Rembrandt.

During the 1990s, Vigil Grey has worked with these various methods and experimented with several styles, expanding from the mid-70s Pop Genre into what he terms "a larger arena" that can encompass abstraction, modern Western art developments, Native American symbolism, and other styles through original expression. He is concentrating on "just an age-old thing of how native peoples relate to the work, and how they're closely bonded to nature, and to the earth, and to the land, and to the people. Just real basic things that people just don't have a grasp on anymore." His latest paintings in the mid-1990s are imbued with the reddish landscapes of northern New Mexico. Indian figures appear with animals and birds, spiritual transformations emerge through half human/half bird figures, drawing from ancient traditions in modern contexts, reflecting the interplay of the natural world and "supernatural" realms.

—Gregory Schaaf

WAANO-GANO, Joseph

Tribal affiliations: Cherokee
Painter and textile artist

Born: Salt Lake City, Utah, 3 March 1906. **Education:** Los Angeles Metropolitan High School, CA, 1922; Von Schneidau School of Art, 1924-1928; University of California, Los Angeles, extension courses. **Military Service:** U.S. Air Force, WWII. **Career:** Decor designer, actor, dancer, director, outdoor display artist, commercial artist, textile designer, writer, lecturer, sculptor, potter, and painter; chairman, California International Flower Show Art Exhibition, 1958; mural commissions, Community Chest, Los Angeles General Hospital, and Los Angeles Public Library, Los Angeles, California; fundraising, including the painting, *Green Virgin of Mexico*, for education in Mexico, 1948; masthead design, *The Amerindian*. **Awards:** Over 100, including American Indian and Cowboy Artists National Western Art Exposition, Inter-Tribal Indian Ceremonial, Kern County Fair, Los Angeles County Fair, Los Angeles Indian Center, Laguna Beach Art Association Gallery, Philbrook Museum of Art, Scottsdale National Indian Art Exhibition. **Died:** 1982

Selected Group Exhibitions

Exhibited regularly at art fairs throughout the Southwest and in the Los Angeles area.

1934   Chicago Century of Progress, Chicago, Illinois
1964   *First Annual Invitational Exhibition of American Indian Paintings*, United States Department of the Interior, Washington, D.C.
1965   *Second Annual Invitational Exhibition of American Indian Paintings*, United States Department of the Interior, Washington, D.C.
1975   *Contemporary Indian Art Invitational*, Oregon State University, Corvallis, Oregon
1978   *American Indian and Cowboy Artists National Western Art Exposition*, San Dimas, California

Collections

Gardenia Public Schools, California.

Publications

On WAANO-GANO: Books—*Indian Painters and White Patrons*, by J. J. Brody, Albuquerque, University of New Mexico Press, 1971; *Indians of Today*, by Marion Gridley, Washington, D.C., I.C.F.P., Inc., 1971.

*   *   *

Joseph Waano-Gano is best known for his dramatic paintings of the Old West, rendered in the tradition of Frederick Remington and Charlie Russell. Like those artists, Waano-Gano frequently painted action scenes in the wilderness depicting the struggle for survival. Waano-Gano's human figures in action reflected a strong grounding in realism, based on his strength for accurately capturing details of anatomy, of tensed muscles that convey the toil of his figures, as well as visual harmony and discord, with landscape features representing harshness and beauty. As well, Waano-Gano developed an intense attention on nature, becoming especially focused on the interplay of light and darkness and evolving an almost surreal imagery within stark settings. On occasion, he also blended designs and symbols into otherwise ordinary scenes.

Waano-Gano began painting and drawing as a child and became interested in traditional Cherokee pottery, studying many different styles. The most spectacular traditional Cherokee pottery featured three-dimensional lizards, squirrels, bears and other animal effigies modeled on the surface and handles of globular pottery forms. Surface designs were either engraved or imprinted. In his painting, Waano-Gano established a practice of blending human figures and two dimensional design, as in cubism, but he filled spaces with design elements from Indian pottery, basketry and beadwork. The human figures became a world of mythical characters inhabiting a realm increasingly filled with surrealistic animals and spirit beings.

These otherworldly qualities derived from Waano-Gano's passion for reflecting the qualities of moonlight. He devoted over a decade of his artistic career on recreating the properties of moonlight, capturing ethereal glows with an uncanny sense of how they play on natural scenes. These often eerie, nocturnal effects were executed with the aid of his own personal set of homemade pastels. Like a scientist studying the elements of his craft, Waano-Gano experimented with colors that took the silvery qualities in reflected moonlight, and found iridescence through layers of pastels. His goal, in a thematically-linked series called "moonlight nocturnes," was to "produce the exact strange and unreal colors of a moonlit night."

Waano-Gano's work displayed a range of styles, from naturalistic renderings of three-dimensional scenes to two dimensional natural scenes that show a concern with geometric configurations. When Waano-Gano sought authenticity in his paintings, he consulted Indian elders and professional anthropologists, including Frederick W. Hodge and Mark. R. Harrington, scholars for the Bureau of American Ethnology. Hodge compiled the two volume *Handbook of American Indians North of Mexico*, and Harrington wrote ethnological essays as well as novels.

Along with his formal painting, Waano-Gano was involved in a host of other activities, including textiles design and special logos and insignias. For example, during his World War II service in the Air Force, Waano-Gano created more than two-dozen insignias for combat and transport aircraft. After the war, he was deeply involved in the arts in southern California, painting murals, attending and participating in cultural affairs, and becoming involved in acting and stage production. He directed a major production at the Hollywood Bowl of *The Song of Hiawatha*, coordinating roles of over 100 Indian actors and performers, and won many awards and mural commissions. After his hands were permanently injured in a car accident in 1961, Waano-Gano quickly rebounded and continued his active career, persevering to find new ways to paint.

—Gregory Schaaf

WADHAMS, Lloyd

Tribal affiliations: Kwakiutl
Jewelry designer, carver, and printmaker

Born: Lloyd James Wadhams, 3 September 1939, in Bones Bay (Alert Bay), British Columbia. **Education:** Residential School Grade 6; self-educated as an adult. **Family:** Married Virginia, 30 September 1965 (died 1980); five children, Lloyd, Jr., Kathleen, Beverly, Benita, Judith. **Career:** Carved from age 9 and maintained this as his profession with the exception of a brief stint as a gillnetter; taught carving in informal studio sessions. **Agent:** c/o Kwakwala Indian Art, #3, 1548 Lonsdale Ave., North Vancouver, British Columbia; ph 604-983-9389. **Died:** 10 October 1992

Selected Group Exhibitions

There are no official records of most of Wadham's exhibitions; he did participate at various times in shows at the Vancouver Art Gallery, the University of British Columbia Museum of Anthropology, the Hyatt

Lloyd Wadhams: *Thunderbird with Tsonoqua* silver bracelet. Photograph by W. McLennan; courtesy University of British Columbia Museum of Anthropology.

Regency in Vancouver, Hills Indian Crafts in Vancouver, and in 1987 at the Quintana Gallery in Portland, Oregon.

Collections

University of British Columbia Museum of Anthropology.

*   *   *

Wadhams developed a unique style of carving and engraving and, at the same time, taught and influenced many artists in informal gallery and workshop settings. Yet, very little is known about him as an individual artist. He was press-shy, but gallery owners, colleagues and private collectors all invariably praise his style of deep engraving and carving.

Wadhams used the same designs repeatedly, particularly the thunderbird, his family crest, yet was always interested in experimenting with new images or mediums. Wadhams also used whale, eagle, and loon, images. The characters in his pieces move through the work with a great deal of life and energy. Open air designs and strong deep lines, consistent and clean, are signatures of his style, from bracelets to totem poles, and this style continues to flourish among his students, particularly in jewelry design.

Among his more notable pieces was a chalice Wadhams was commissioned to carve for presentation to Pope John Paul III on a visit to Ottawa. Another acclaimed piece is a totem pole for the Centennial School of Coquitlam, British Columbia.

—Vesta Giles

WALKINGSTICK, Kay

Tribal affiliations: Cherokee
Painter

Born: Syracuse, New York, 1935. **Education:** Beaver College, Glensdale, Pennsylvania, B.F.A., 1959; Pratt Institute, Brooklyn, New York, M.F.A., 1975. **Career:** Painter; instructor in painting, Edward Williams College, Farleigh Dickinson University, 1970-73, Upsala College (also lecturer on twentieth-century art), 1975-79, Art Center of Northern New Jersey, 1978-85, Montclair Art Museum, 1986-88, Atlantic Center for the Arts, 1995, and Vermont Studio Center, 1995; assistant professor of art, Cornell University, 1988-90, and State University of New York, Stony Brook, 1990-92; associate professor of art, Cornell University, 1992- ; artist-in-residence, Fort Lewis College, 1984, Ohio State University, 1985, and Heard Museum, 1995; guest artist, Printmaking Workshop, New York, and Brandywine Workshop, Philadelphia, 1989; guest lecturer and panelist, numerous symposia, including "Women of Sweetgrass, Cedar & Sage," University of California at Davis, 1985, Contemporary American Arts conventions, 1989-90, 1994, and Heard Museum Symposium, "Shared Visions," 1991; member of advisory boards and juries, including Women's Caucus for Art, New York State Council on the Arts (visual arts panel), New Jersey State Council for the Arts (painting fellowship panel), William Carlos Williams Center for the Performing Arts (exhibitions coordinator), New York Foundation for the Arts (painting fellowship panel), and nominator for the Tiffany Awards, New York. **Awards:** Residencies, McDowell College, 1970-71, Yaddo Artists' Colony,

1976, William Flanagan Memorial Creative Person's Center, Montauk, New York, 1983, Rockefeller Conference & Study Center, Bellagio, Italy, 1992; Golden Disk Award for Distinguished Achievement, Beaver College; National Endowment for the Arts, Visual Artist Fellowship in Painting, 1983-84; Richard A. Florsheim Art Fund Award, 1991; New York Foundation for the Arts, NYCSA grant in painting, 1992.

Individual Exhibitions

1969	Cannabis Gallery, New York
1976	Soho Center for the Visual Arts, New York
1978	Bertha Urdang Gallery, New York
1979	Wegner Gallery, San Diego, California
1981	Bertha Urdang Gallery, New York
1984	Wegner Gallery, San Diego, California
	Bertha Urdang Gallery, New York
	Fine Arts Gallery, Fort Lewis College, Durango, Colorado
1985	Hopkins Hall Gallery, Ohio State University, Columbus
	Spruance Art Gallery, Beaver College, Glenside, Pennsylvania
1987	M-13 Gallery, New York
1988	Wegner Gallery, Los Angeles
1989	Union College, Cranford, New Jersey
1990	M-13 Gallery, New York
1991	Elaine Horwitch Gallery, Scottsdale, Arizona
	Hillwood Art Museum of Long Island (also traveled to Heard Museum, Phoenix, Arizona, and Hartwick College Gallery, Oneta, New York)
1992	Morris Museum, Morristown, New Jersey
1993	Hartell Gallery, Cornell University, Ithaca, New York
	Galerie Calumet, Heidelberg, Germany
1994	June Kelly Gallery, New York
1995	Atlantic Center for the Arts, New Smyrna Beach, Florida

Selected Group Exhibitions

1975	*Contemporary Reflections, 1974-75*, Aldrich Museum, Ridgefield, Connecticut
1976	*Viewpoint '76*, Morris Museum of Arts and Sciences, Morristown, New Jersey
1980	Southern Plains Indian Museum, Anadarko, Oklahoma
	Marking Black, Bronx Museum, New York
1981	*Dark Thoughts, Black Paintings*, Pratt Manhattan Center, New York
1983	*Contemporary Native American Art*, traveling exhibit, Gardner Art Gallery, Oklahoma State University, Stillwater
1984	*A Personal Choice*, Harm Bouckaert Gallery, New York
	Signals, Gallery Akmak, Berlin (traveled in Europe through 1986)
1985	*Women of Sweetgrass, Cedar & Sage*, American Indian Community House, New York (traveled U.S. and Canada)
	40 New York Artists, Modernism Gallery, San Francisco, California
	New Ideas from Old Traditions, Yellowstone Art Center, Billings, Montana
	AdoRnmenTs, Bernice Steinbaum Gallery, New York (traveled the United States through 1987)

1986	*Native Business Summit*, Foundation of Canada, Toronto
1987	*Native American Art: Our Contemporary Visions*, Sierra Nevada Museum, Reno, Nevada
	Traditions in a New Age, Montana State University, Bozeman
	We the People, Artists Space, New York
1988	*Autobiography: In Her Own Image*, Intar Gallery, Pindell, New York
1989	*100 Women Artists' Drawings*, United States Information Agency, traveling, South America; also organized by Hillwood Gallery, C.W. Post College, Long Island to tour the United States
1990	*The Decade Show: Framework of Identity in the 1980s*, The New Museum, The Studio Museum in Harlem, and Museum of Contemporary Hispanic Art, New York
1991	*The Submuloc Show, in Response to the Columbus Wohs*, Evergreen State College, Olympia, Washington (traveled the United States through 1993)
	Presswork: The Art of Women Printmakers, National Museum of Women in the Arts, Washington, D.C.
	Shared Visions: Native American Painters and Sculptors of the Twentieth Century, organized by the Heard Museum (traveled the United States 1991-94, New Zealand, 1995-96)
	Our Land/Ourselves, American Indian Contemporary Artists, University Art Gallery, State University of New York, Albany (traveled the United States through 1995)
1992	*Six Directions*, Calumet Galerie, Heidelberg, Germany
	Artifacts of Various Civilizations, Howard Yezerski Gallery, Boston
	Land, Spirit, Power, National Museum of Canada, Ottawa (traveled internationally)
	We the Human Beings, Wooster College Art Museum, Wooster, Ohio (traveled through 1995)
1993	*The Environmentalists*, Gallery North, Setauket, New York
	Multiplicity: A New Cultural Strategy, Museum of Anthropology, University of British Columbia, Vancouver
1994	*Strategies of Narration*, USA Exhibit, Cairo Biennial (traveled in Africa through 1997)
1995	*Phil Young and Kay WalkingStick*, Atrium Gallery, University of Connecticut, Storrs
1996	Rose Art Museum, Brandeis University, Boston
	Retreat and Renewal: Painting and Sculpture by MacDowell Art Colonists, Currier Gallery of Art, Manchester, New Hampshire (traveling)

Publications

By WALKINGSTICK: Articles—"Like a Longfish Out of Water," interview with George Longfish, *Northeast Indian Quarterly*, Fall 1989; "Democracy, Inc., Kay WalkingStick on Indian Law," *Artforum International*, 1991, reprinted in *Native American Expressive Culture*, New York: National Museum of the American Indian, 1991; "Bob Blackburn's Printmaking Workshop: Artists of Color," *College Art Association Journal*, Fall 1992; "Woodworker" (on Truman Lowe). **Book**—*HAGA (Third Son)*, exhibition catalog, Eiteljorg Museum of American Indian and Western Art, Indianapolis, 1994.

Kay WalkingStick: *The Four Directions/Vision* diptych. Courtesy of the artist.

On WALKINGSTICK: Books—*The Decade Show: Frameworks of Identity in the 1980s,* exhibition catalog, Museum of Contemporary Hispanic Art, New Museum of Contemporary Art, Studio Museum in Harlem, 1990; *Mixed Blessings* by Lucy R. Lippard, New York, 1991; *Kay WalkingStick, Paintings 1974-1990,* exhibition catalog by Holland Cotter, Brookville, New York: Hillwood Art Museum, 1991; *Shared Visions: Native American Painters and Sculptors of the Twentieth Century* by Margaret Archuleta and Rennard Strickland, Phoenix: Heard Museum, 1991; *I Stand in the Center of Good: Interviews with Contemporary Native American Artists* by Lawrence Abbott, University of Nebraska Press, 1994; *Understanding Art* by Lois Ficher-Rathus, Englewood Cliffs, New Jersey: Prentice Hall, 1995; *History of Art,* by H. R. Janson, Englewood Cliffs, New Jersey: Prentice Hall and Abrams, 1995. **Articles**—review by Laurel Bradley, *Arts Magazine,* Summer, 1978; review by Marjorie Welish, *Art in America,* September-October, 1978; review by Robert Yoskowitz, *Arts Magazine,* June 1980; review by Deborah C. Phillips, *Art News,* June 1981; review by Vivien Raynor, *New York Times,* 19 June 1981; review by Meg Perlman, *ARTnews,* December 1983; "The Meaning of 'Duality' in Art" by Pat Malacher, *New York Times,* 22 December 1985; review by Marlena Donohue, *Los Angeles Times,* 26 February 1989; "Kay WalkingStick" by Kellie Jones, *The Village Voice,* 16 May 1989; "A Special Regard for Nature's Forces" by Phyllis Braff, *New York Times,* 14 April 1990; "Painting the Native Soul: Mother Earth Talks through Artist's Work," *Arizona Republic,* 16 September 1991; "Artist Wants Her Work to Whisper" by Lyn Dyne, *Phoenix Gazette,* 23 September 1991; "Charcoal on Paper" by William Zimmer, *New York Times,* 21 June 1992; "Myths of the American Indian and Significant Photographs" by Phyllis Braff, *New York Times,* 21 June 1992; "Critical Issues in Recent Native American Art" by Jackson Rushing, *Art Journal* 51, no. 3, Fall 1992; "Native Tradition Spoken in Language of Post-Modernism" by Robin Lawrence, *The Weekend Sun, Saturday Review* (Vancouver), 31 December 1993; "Mistaken Identity: Between Death and Pleasure in the Art of Kay WalkingStick" by Erin Valentino, *Third Text,* Spring 1994; review by Richard Vine, *Art in America,* January 1995.

                         *

Kay WalkingStick comments:

   My present paintings are concerned with the balance between the concrete visual landscape and our archtypal memory of the earth, or one could say, between the physical and spiritual view of the earth. I see the landscape as a "stand-in" for ourselves—our body. We speak metaphorically of grandmother earth. The earth is life, so to use landscape as a stand-in for ourselves seems appropriate.

   I see balance also between the physical self and the spiritual self. Just as one side of the diptych is not the abstraction of the other but the extension of the other, so, too, is the spiritual not the opposite of the physical but its natural extension. The active layered paint surface and the division of the two sides of the painting is thus necessary to convey these ideas of the spiritual and the sacred. They are different, but one. As a bi-racial woman this unity is important to my psyche.

   It is content expressed through form, and a multiplicity of readings that I like in all painting, including my own.

                *   *   *

   WalkingStick's paintings are informed by Native American views about land and space, time and place. Of mixed parentage, WalkingStick was raised by her non-Indian mother, who continually emphasized her Cherokee ancestry. Much of her work and thought has involved re-identifying with her absent Cherokee father and exploring that heritage. She is best known for her two-paneled paintings that combine naturalistic and abstract representations of the earth.

   In her diptych paintings, a format she developed in the mid-1980s, two canvases joined side by side are meant to be viewed as complimentary parts of a whole. The panels are related extensions of one another, intuitively summarizing temporal and spatial kinds of knowing or relating to the natural world. In her 1991 charcoal drawing, *Spirit Center*, for example, WalkingStick visualizes two representations of the earth. The panel on the right displays a conception of land that is particular and immediate. The left panel articulates a spiritual, non-specific, inner view of the earth as interminable. The naturalistic rendering of trees embedded in boulders and cascading over rocks is made more comprehensive, more tangible and real when paired with the abstracted side.

WalkingStick compares the relationship between the panels to short and long term memory. The naturalistic rendering of land is considered short-term, or an immediate visual memory, like a "snap-shot." It becomes more concrete when paired with the abstracted side, the long-term or archetypal form of memory. The non-representational panel together with the illusionistic side of the painting treats the earth and life as it exists along a continuum that, as WalkingStick states, "reaches back into history to the beginning of time, but also stretches forward to the unknown future." Through this coupling of perceived opposites exists a complex interrelational set of balanced and complimentary dualities, like realistic/abstraction, empirical/spiritual, temporal/spatial, seen/sensed, and microcosm/macrocosm.

Embedded within the abstracted layers of scraped paint or smudged charcoal are symbols whose meanings are unclear. Possibly they are iconographic signs or visual references to the four cardinal directions and the whole of creation. Frequently this central image is geometrically centered in the non-objective panel or related to the canvas as a whole. Sometimes there is a center line creating a subtle visual distinction between panels. At other times the paint or charcoal from each panel merges into one another. In both instances the relationship between parts and whole constitutes a balance and identifies a mythic and physical relationship between the two portions of the painting and two manners of perception, which provides a deeper understanding of life on earth, in space, and in time.

WalkingStick's artwork also involves an investigation into what it means to be bi-racial, Cherokee and Anglo-American—raised away from the traditional community structures of reservation life and artistically trained in Western-based art institutions. Her paintings explore the dichotomy between European-based and Native American world views and seek to establish an equilibrium, a unification of two states of being found in nature and in our own lives. It only makes sense that much of WalkingStick's painting is about process, spiritual and ideological. In many of her paintings the surface is activated with marks and scratches, leftover signs and traces of the artist's hands and the creative process. For WalkingStick the significance of working with the hands to create an activated and tactile surface is linked not just to the artistic presence, but to the artist's own bodily presence as well. The physical activation of the painted surface along with the spiritual vibrancy of an animated, spatial earth-scape mirrors WalkingStick's transcendental view and very personal approach to her identity, artwork, and relationship with the earth.

—Lisa Roberts

WALLACE, Denise

Tribal affiliations: Sugpiaq
Jewelry designer

Born: Denise Hottinger, Seattle, Washington, 6 March 1957. **Education:** Institute of American Indian Arts, Santa Fe, A.A., Fine

Arts, 1977-81. **Career:** Owns and operates dw Studio, Inc., Santa Fe, with husband, Samuel; produces annual show, *Visions of Alaska*, during the Santa Fe Indian Market, held in August. **Awards:** Numerous awards from the Southwestern Association of Indian Artists, the Eight Northern Pueblos, and the Heard Museum, among others. **Address:** dw Studio, Inc., P.O. Box 5321, Santa Fe, New Mexico, 87502.

Individual Exhibitions

1989   Anchorage Museum of History and Art, Alaska
1990   *Secret of Transformation,* American Museum of Natural History, New York
        Gene Autry Museum, Los Angeles, California
1991   *Northern Images,* Southwest Museum, Los Angeles, California
1992   *Crossroads of Continents,* Canadian Museum of Civilization, Hull, Quebec
1996   *Denise & Samuel Wallace: Ten Year Retrospective Exhibition,* Graythorne Gallery, Santa Fe, New Mexico

Selected Group Exhibitions

1987-96 *Visions of Alaska,* dw Studio, Inc., Santa Fe, New Mexico
1988   *Sun, Moon, and Stone,* Southwest Museum, Los Angeles
1989   *Native Art to Wear,* Heard Museum, Phoenix, Arizona
1993   *Voices and Visions,* University of California Museums at Blackhawk, Danville, California
1994-95 *This Path We Travel,* National Museum of the American Indian, New York
1996-97 *Native American Traditions/Contemporary Responses,* Society for Contemporary Crafts, Pittsburgh, Pennsylvania
        Gifts of the Spirit, Peabody Essex Museum, Salem, Massachusetts

Collections

Anchorage Museum of History and Art, Alaska; Institute of American Indian Arts, Santa Fe, New Mexico; Wheelwright Museum of the American Indian, Santa Fe, New Mexico

Publications

On WALLACE: Books—*This Path We Travel,* National Museum of the American Indian, Smithsonian Institution, Washington, D.C., 1994; *Denise & Samuel Wallace: Ten Year Retrospective Exhibition,* Graythorne Gallery, Santa Fe, 1996. **Articles**—"Wearable Sculpture: Denise Wallace's Versatile Metalsmithing," by Robin J. Dunitz, *Southwest Art,* November 1988; "Spirits and Souls: Denise and Samuel Wallace," by Carolyn L. E. Benesh, *Ornament* 15, no. 2, 1991; "Layered with Significance," *Lapidary Journal,* September 1992.

*

Denise Wallace comments:
    Most of my designs are inspired by my cousins, the Yup'ik of the Bering Sea. My ancestors are the Pacific Eskimo known as the Sugpiaq. We are from the south central part of Alaska, the Prince William Sound, or Chugach region.

Denise Wallace: Pin pendant (two views). Courtesy of the artist.

I am grateful for the ingeniousness of my ancestors to survive and adapt to their environment. Survival was, and continues to be, highly dependent on a hunting subsistence lifestyle. [In the] process of this lifestyle, which involved an understanding and respect for the natural world, our ancestors created many wonderful and magical objects. These objects speak of the various interlinking connections between all living and spiritual entities. It is from this idea that I receive my inspiration.

Many of the designs are a combination of the ancient and the contemporary. Not only do I seek inspiration from those who have been here before me, but from my contemporaries as well. My husband, Samuel, a lover of stone and an exceptional lapidarist, continues to inspire and strengthen me.

*   *   *

Denise Wallace was born in Seattle to an Aleut mother who maintained ties to her extended family in Cordova on Prince William Sound in southern Alaska. Wallace credits her maternal grandmother for her interest in her Alaska Native heritage, which since 1984 Wallace has expressed through her award-winning jewelry with northern themes.

Wallace attended the Institute of American Indian Art in Santa Fe from 1977-1981, although her interest in silversmithing and the lapidary arts predates that formal schooling. She settled in Santa Fe after graduation from IAIA and maintains a busy jewelry studio with her husband and partner, Samuel Wallace. Most of their work is collaborative: he cuts and polishes the stones, she designs the works and, formerly, fabricated them. Today she has a large studio staff to work on fabricating the technologically complex pieces she designs.

Wallace's jewelry designs are mixed media. She uses gold, silver, carved and incised walrus ivory fossil, and semi-precious stones.

Some pieces have multiple uses: a portion of a bracelet or necklace can be removed for wearing as a separate pendant, and some figures have hinged faces or abdomens, revealing other figures beneath in a shamanistic fashion.

Wallace is profoundly influenced by the archeological and historical arts of her own Aleut heritage as well as other Alaskan Native people, including Eskimo and Tlingit. Native arts of many media, including basketry and other fiber arts, as well as wood and ivory carving, form the inspiration for her work. For example, Eskimo wooden mask forms are miniaturized and put on bracelets, Native dancers and dollmakers wearing traditional ornamented parkas are formed out of semi-precious stones, and fossilized walrus tusk is meticulously set in silver channels.

Wallace's superb techniques and unique Northern imagery were first revealed to an international audience at the 1984 Santa Fe Indian Market, where she won a First Award, a Best of Class (Jewelry) and a Best of Division Award. Numerous other honors and awards have followed.

Among her most ambitious works are the figural belts that she devised as a unique amalgam of the Native southwestern concha belt style and her Alaskan iconography. One of the most complex was made in response to the artist's viewing of the ambitious *Crossroads of Continents* exhibit sponsored by the Smithsonian Institution in the late 1980s, which traced the cultural relationships of numerous circum-polar people, including Siberian, Alaskan and Canadian. Wallace's concha belt features ten human figures of various northern ethnic groups, including the Chukchi, Koryak, Tlingit, and Aleut. Removable pieces include scrimshaw pails, which can be worn as earrings, and an Eskimo infant, which can be worn as a pendant. Other concha belts depict northern women and children, or seals and sea otters.

Like many Native artists of her generation, Denise Wallace forms connections between diverse genres, styles, and iconographies in her work. As the only internationally-known jeweler of Aleut heritage, she has helped to bring a stronger knowledge of Alaskan Native imagery to an audience used to thinking of Navajo and Pueblo jewelers as the dominant creators in this medium.

—Janet Catherine Berlo

WARRIOR, Antowine
Variant names: Takotokasi
Tribal affiliations: Sauk and Fox
Painter and sculptor

Born: Stroud, Oklahoma, 4 January 1941; Sauk and Fox name means Roaring Thunder. **Education:** Bacone College in Muskogee, Oklahoma; Penn Valley Junior College, Kansas City, Missouri; Haskell Institute, Lawrence, Kansas; Southwest Indian Art Project," University of Arizona. **Career:** Visual and performing artist. **Awards:** American Indian Exposition, Colorado Indian Market (Best of Show, 1986), Inter-Tribal Indian Ceremonies, Philbrook Museum (Wolf Robe Hunt Award, 1978, first place, 1979), Red Earth Festival (first place, 1993), Santa Fe Indian Market (1982-83).

Individual Exhibitions

1958   Philbrook Museum, Tulsa, Oklahoma

Selected Group Exhibitions

Participates regularly in fairs, expositions, and juried competitions, including American Indian Exposition, Anadarko, Oklahoma; American Indian Exposition, Chicago, Illinois; Inter-Tribal Indian Ceremonies, Gallup, New Mexico; Philbrook Museum Annual Indian Art Exhibition, Tulsa, Oklahoma; Red Earth Festival Indian Art Competition, Oklahoma City; and Santa Fe Indian Market.

1980   *Native American Art at the Philbrook,* Tulsa, Oklahoma
1992   *Franco American Institute Exhibit,* Rennes, France

Collections

Arizona State Museum, University of Arizona, Tucson; Bureau of Indian Affairs, Department of the Interior, Washington, D.C.; Thomas Gilcrease Institute of American History and Art, Tulsa, Oklahoma; Philbrook Museum, Tulsa, Oklahoma.

Publications

On WARRIOR: Books—*Indian Painters and White Patrons,* by J. J. Brody, Albuquerque, 1971; *Native American Art at the Philbrook,* catalog by John Mahey, et. al., Tulsa, 1980; *Arizona Galleries and Their Artists,* by Danny Medina, Phoenix, 1981.

*

Antowine Warrior comments:

I'm trying to go back with my paintings, to relive the days my Grandfather told me about. He had the Great Plains to roam on and

be free; I have the canvas. I am free when I paint—reliving my people's vision. If I used a painting style from another culture, I would also have to use the thought processes that go with it; and that's not the Indian way.

*   *   *

Antowine Warrior is a prominent painter and sculptor who is an exponent of the traditionalist (or neo-traditionalist) approach in Oklahoma Indian art. He is much admired for his technically sophisticated and dynamic paintings that adhere to the basic artistic contours of the flat style. Warrior's popularity rests primarily upon lithographic prints of some of his best work that have been widely distributed.

It is significant that Warrior received art education at both Bacone College in Muskogee, Oklahoma, and Haskell Institute in Lawrence, Kansas. Early influences towards traditionalism were both deepened and modified by his experience at Bacone, where Dick West, who personally used a narrative/illustrative style that emphasized careful and detailed drawing, taught in the art program. Equally important, he taught his students that their work should be historically and ethnographically accurate and serve as a cultural record. Although West himself experimented with various modernist approaches, both he and the bulk of his students (like Warrior) were basically traditionalist in orientation. As Margaret Archuleta and Rennard Strickland noted, "The Bacone Period can be defined stylistically as using complex design elements in a decorative manner to 'romance' the past. The mythology was presented with a sense of the theatrical and the mysterious" (*Shared Visions,* Archuleta and Strickland, 1991).

Consistent with the approach taught at Bacone by a series of talented instructors (Acee Blue Eagle, Woody Crumbo, Dick West, and Ruthe Blalock Jones), was the work of two non-Bacone educated artists—Quincy Tahoma and Blackbear Bosin. In the post-World War II period they took their fundamentally traditionalist painting and added to it an approach emphasizing greater degrees of motion, drama, tension, and theatricality. What emerged, in effect, was a new attitude in traditionalist painting that can be called neo-traditionalism, a category in which Antowine Warrior can be situated.

This categorization is illustrated in one of Warrior's most famous paintings (issued in lithographic print form), *Monarchs of the Plains,* a large work featuring a line of five charging Plains Indian warriors in full battle gear and dress. In fundamental ways, this painting adheres to the traits of the classic flat style (or two-dimensional) art codified by the Kiowa Five artists: nostalgic subject matter, harkening back to classical warrior activities on the Great Plains, handled in an idealized fashion, with figures clearly outlined, an emphasis on line to separate discrete color areas, sinuous curves, and only the simplest of ground line. The background is largely nonexistent (except for a few low-lying, shadowy hills) in order to focus attention upon the warriors, and there is a pervasive quality of symmetry and balance in the painting. This sense of due proportion, so evident in the work of the Kiowa Five, is immediately discernible: the center figure is a warbonneted leader whose horse directly faces the viewer; the two Indians flanking him on either side ride horses that are increasingly proportionately pointed to the sides of the picture. Moreover, the craftsmanship evident in execution of the painting is meticulous and impressive. And like the work of the Kiowa Five, subject matter is kept simple, focused, and uncomplicated.

However, it is also evident that this work exhibits considerably more drama, tension, and dynamism than was usual in the paintings of the Kiowa Five. Here is where we can discern the contributions of the post-war artists (especially Bosin) and the learning experienced by Warrior at Bacone (and Haskell). Thus, herein we encounter the evidence for the neo-traditionalist classification.

As might be expected of an artist with his reputation, Warrior has won many honors and prizes at various exhibitions/shows/competitions, not the least of which was the Wolf Robe Hunt Award in 1978 from the Philbrook Art Center in Tulsa, Oklahoma. The commercial release of some of Warrior's work in lithograph print form has done much to enhance his popularity throughout the United States. In addition to his painting and sculpture, Warrior is also an accomplished dancer, flute player, and craftsman who enjoys creating colorful beadwork, leathercrafts, and woodcarvings.

—John Anson Warner

WA WA CHAW

Variant names: Wawa Calac Chaw
Tribal affiliations: Luiseño
Painter

Born: Valley Center, Rincon Reservation, California, 25 December 1888, originally named Wawa Calac Chaw (Keep from the Water); also known as Princess Wa Wa Chaw, and later as Benita Nunez and Benita Wawa Calachaw Nunez. **Family:** Adopted by Dr. Cornelius Duggan, and raised by his sister, Mary; married Manuel Carmonia-Nunez, divorced. **Education:** Private schools in the eastern United States; Sherman Institute, Riverside, California; private instruction with Albert Pinkham Ryder. **Career:** Activist and lecturer, Indian and women's causes; entertainer, including dancing and vaudeville; illustrator for medical journals, and painter.

Selected Group Exhibitions

1980   Philbrook Museum of Art, Tulsa, Oklahoma
1996   *Vision and Voices: Native American Painting from the Philbrook Museum of Art*, Tulsa, Oklahoma

Collections

National Museum of the American Indian, Washington, D.C.; Philbrook Museum of Art Center, Tulsa, Oklahoma.

Publications

On WA WA CHAW: Books—*The New Indians,* by Stan Steiner, New York, 1968; *Spirit Woman: The Diaries and Paintings of Bonita Wa Wa Calachaw Nunez, An American Indian,* edited by Stan Steiner, San Francisco, 1980; *The Arts of the North American Indian: Native Traditions in Evolution,* Edwin L. Wade, ed., New York: Hudson Hills Press in association with Philbrook Art Center, Tulsa, Oklahoma, 1986; *Vision and Voices: Native American Painting from the Philbrook Museum of Art,* Lydia Wyckoff, editor, Tulsa, 1996.

*   *   *

Wa Wa Chaw was a free-spirited artist and activist involved with some of the major cultural and social issues of the twentieth century, including women's rights and matters pertaining to Native Americans, and she was among few American painters working in the Expressionist mode, a turn-of-the-century trend characterized by intense emotionalism and dark, haunting images. She had intermittent periods of public recognition, primarily as a lecturer and portrait painter as well as an entertainer, performing vaudeville and dancing, including a stint with famed dancer Isadora Duncan. She was also out of the public eye, searching for her mother and residing among the Luiseño Indians in southern California, and among Indians in major cities, ultimately living in poverty at the end of her life in New York City. It was there that she had been brought as an adopted child, raised in a wealthy household, tutored by a famous professional artist, and became an artist and activist. Her unique position as an American expressionist painter, as well as her activism, has led to renewed, posthumous, interest in her work since the late 1970s.

Wa Wa Chaw was born on the Rincon reservation at Valley Center, California. A sickly newborn, she was delivered by Dr. Cornelius Duggan, a doctor who had paused among the Mission Indians of southern California during a storm; his sister, Mary, "adopted" Wa Wa Chaw from her poverty-stricken mother. Some reports suggest the mother had died, others that she was too poor and ill to raise the infant. The Duggans were wealthy New Yorkers who provided Wa Wa Chaw with a comfortable upbringing and education in private schools. They dressed her as they thought a young Indian child might dress. Wa Wa Chaw was a child prodigy in art and received encouragement to pursue her talents, including instruction in studio art techniques and anatomy. During her teens she started painting portraits and showed great talent at sketching medical specimens. She subsequently received several commissions from medical journals to illustrate articles.

As she became more accomplished in painting, Wa Wa Chaw was accepted as a student by Albert Pinkham Ryder. A visionary artist who applied paint thickly on canvases and was noted primarily for moody landscapes and seascapes, Ryder was in the latter stage of his career, living as a recluse and frequently repainting his compositions. He encouraged her to blur images and mute her bright palette, and it has been suggested that the experience was significant in her development to a more intense personal expression.

After achieving a reputation as an illustrator and portrait painter, as well as an outspoken advocate of women's rights while in her teens, Wa Wa Chaw began painting increasingly dark and imaginative works and found an audience for them in Greenwich Village, mostly in informal settings; she was never associated with a gallery or a promoter, and her distinctly Expressionist artworks were only exhibited intermittently. She sold her first works on Greenwich Village street corners and found the environment conducive to her personal growth. Her paintings, with dense shadows, bold outlines and strong dark colors, were imaginative and often reflected an inner sense of anger that was coming to the forefront in her personal life.

She joined one of her friends, Dr. Carlos Montezuma, an early leader in the Indian rights movement, in social activism for Native Americans and championed women's rights as well, lecturing throughout the country. Her own people, the Luiseño, had suffered harsh treatment, including missionization and enslavement by Spaniards. This social activism, while it took time away from her career, spilled over into the arts, where she challenged all artists to depict real scenes from their experience and to express emotion in their work, much like the Expressionists of Europe, who challenged more intellectual and academic-based approaches to art. Wa Wa Chaw pointed out, for example, that California Mission Indians did not look like the typical Indian stereotypes: "Our Indian People are plain people. . . The Indians on the Reservations do not wear beads or feathers. Indians that live outside of Reservations wear them for Money. It is the White Man's way of keeping Indianism."

Wa Wa Chaw was married and divorced, bore a child who died at age three, searched for her mother among the Luiseño of southern California, and lived for periods among urban Indians in such cities as Chicago and Philadelphia, as well as New York, where she lived most of her life. Her activism for Native American causes and for women often took place at local levels.

Though she did not produce a large body of work and was never part of a major exhibit in her lifetime, Wa Wa Chaw's artwork is important; her portraits are skillfully rendered, and her Expressionist pieces are among the most powerful in that style by an American artist. The *Vision and Voices* exhibit at the Philbrook Museum of Art in 1996 showcased her works with other Native American artists of the twentieth century, placing her as a unique, expressionist painter voicing real concerns, anguish, and anger. In her later paintings, Wa Wa Chaw used more earthy colors to create harmonious images of group scenes.

—Gregory Schaaf

WEST, Dick

Variant names: Wapah Nahyah
Tribal affiliations: Cheyenne
Painter

Born: Walter Richard West, near Darlington, Oklahoma, 8 September 1912. **Education:** Haskell Indian School, 1935; Bacone College, AA, 1938; University of Oklahoma, BFA, 1941, and MFA, 1950; mural techniques with Olaf Nordmark, 1941-42; graduate work, University of Redlands, Northeastern State University, University of Oklahoma, and University of Tulsa. **Military Service:** U.S. Navy, World War II. **Career:** Sculptor, painter, muralist—Bacone College, U.S. Post Office, Okemah, Oklahoma; designed official seal for the annual American Indian Exposition, Anadarko, Oklahoma, dustjacket cover for *The Cheyenne Way*, Karl Llewellyn and Hoebel Adamson, Norman, 1941, and a series of 50 medallions for the Franklin Mint, 1874-75; instructor and Director, Art Department, Bacone College, 1947 to 1970; Directory of Art, 1970-72, and Chairman of the Division of Humanities, 1972-77, Haskell Indian Nations University; Commissioner, Indian Arts and Crafts Board. **Awards:** Fellow, International Institute of Arts and Sciences, Zurich, Switzerland; President, Muscogee Art Guild; various honors at juried competitions, including those sponsored by the Denver Art Museum, the Cherokee National Museum, the Philbrook Art Center, and the Oklahoma State Fair; Honorary Degrees, Eastern Baptist College, St. David's, Pennsylvania, 1963; Baker University, Baldwin City, Kansas, 1977. **Died:** 3 May 1996.

Individual Exhibitions

1938	Bacone College, Bacone Oklahoma
1941	University of Oklahoma, Norman
1962	University of Redlands, Redlands, California
1963	Eastern Baptist College, St. David's Pennsylvania
1969	Muskogee Civic Center, Muskogee, Oklahoma
1973	Haskell Indian Nations University, Lawrence, Kansas
1984	Bacone College, Bacone, Oklahoma
1987	Southern Plains Indian Museum, Anadarko, Oklahoma
1989	*Red Earth Festival*, Myriad Plaza, Oklahoma City, Oklahoma
1992	University of Oklahoma, Norman
1993	Bacone College, Bacone, Oklahoma

Selected Group Exhibitions

1937	*American Indian Exposition and Congress*, Tulsa, Oklahoma
1947-65	*American Indian Paintings from the Permanent Collection*, Philbrook Museum of Art, Tulsa, Oklahoma (traveling)
1955	*An Exhibition of American Indian Painters*, James Graham and Sons, New York
1963	*Contemporary American Indian Art*, United States Department of State, Washington, D.C.
1965	*Second Annual Invitational Exhibition of American Paintings*, United States Department of State, Washington, D.C.
1972	*Trail of Tears Art Show*, Cherokee National Museum, Tahlequah, Oklahoma
	Contemporary Southern Plains Indian Paintings, sponsored by the Southern Plains Indian Museum and the Oklahoma Indian Arts and Crafts Co-operative, Anadarko, Oklahoma

Dick West. Courtesy of the West family.

1975   *Contemporary Indian Art Invitational*, Oregon State University, Corvalis (traveling)

1978   *100 Years of Native American Art*, Oklahoma Museum of Art, Oklahoma City

1979-80 *Native American Paintings*, organized by the Joslyn Art Museum, Mid-America Arts Alliance (traveling)

1979-85 *Oklahomans for Indian Opportunity*, The Galleria, Norman, Oklahoma

1980   *Native American Painting*, Mid-America Arts Alliance, touring

Native American Art at the Philbrook, Tulsa, Oklahoma

Plains Indians Paintings, Museum of Art, University of Oklahoma, Norman (traveling)

Bacone College Centennial, Bacone, Oklahoma (traveling)

1981   *Walk in Beauty, A National Invitational Native American Art Show*, Heard Museum, Phoenix, Arizona

1982   *Night of First Americans*, John F. Kennedy Center for the Performing Arts, Washington, D.C.

1982-83 *Contemporary Native American Indian Arts*, Smithsonian Institution, The Museum of Natural History, Washington, D.C.

1984-85 *Indianischer Kunstler*, organized by Philbrook Museum of Art, Tulsa, Oklahoma (touring exhibit, West Germany)

1991-92 *Shared Visions: Twentieth Century Native American Painting and Sculpture*, Heard Museum, Phoenix, Arizona (touring, international)

1992-93 *Visions of the People*, Minneapolis Institute of Arts, Minneapolis, Minnesota (traveling)

Collections

Bacone College, Bacone, Oklahoma; Bureau of Indian Affairs, Department of the Interior, Washington, D.C.; Denver Art Museum, Denver, Colorado; Eastern Baptist College, St. David's, Pennsylvania; Thomas Gilcrease Institute of American History and Art, Tulsa, Oklahoma; Indian Arts and Crafts Board, Department of the Interior, Anadarko, Oklahoma; Fred Jones, Jr., Museum of Art, University of Oklahoma, Norman; Joslyn Art Museum, Omaha, Nebraska; Kiva Museum of the American Indian, Boy Scouts of America, La Junta, Colorado; Museum of Northern Arizona, Flagstaff; Muskogee Art Guild, Muskogee, Oklahoma; National Gallery of Art, Washington, D.C.; National Museum of the American Indian, St. Augustine Center, Chicago, Illinois; Smithsonian Institution, Washington, D.C.; Philbrook Museum of Art, Tulsa, Oklahoma; Seminole Public Library, Seminole, Oklahoma; Southern Plains Indian Museum, Anadarko, Oklahoma.

Publications

On WEST: Books—*American Indian Painters,* by Oscar B. Jacobson and Jeanne d'Ucel, Nice, France, 1950; *A Pictorial History of the American Indian*, by Oliver LaFarge, New York, Crown Publishers, 1956; *Arts of the United States*, William H. Pierson, Jr.,

Dick West: *The Last Supper.* Courtesy of the West family.

and Martha Davidson, New York, McGraw-Hill 1960; *American Indian Painting of the Southwest and Plains Areas,* by Dorothy Dunn, Albuquerque, New Mexico, 1968; *The American Indian Speaks,* John R. Milton, editor, Vermillion, San Diego, 1969; *Indian Painters and White Patrons,* by J. J. Brody, Albuquerque, New Mexico, 1971; *Song from the Earth: American Indian Painting,* by Jamake Highwater, Boston, 1976; *100 Years of Native American Art* (exhibition catalog), by Arthur Silberman, Oklahoma City, 1978; *Pinturas Amerindas Contemporánes/E.U.A.,* by Lloyd Kiva New, Museo del Instituto de Artes Amerindios, 1979; "What is Indian Art?," by Jeanne O. Snodgrass-King, *Bacone College Centennial* (catalog), 1980; *American Indian Painting and Sculpture,* by Patricia Janis Broder, New York, Abbeville Press, 1981; *Magic Images,* by Edwin L. Wade and Rennard Strickland, Norman, Oklahoma, 1981; *Indianische Kunst im 20 Jahrhundert,* by Gerhard Hoffman, et al., Münich, Germany, 1984; *The Arts of the North American Indian: Native Traditions in Evolution,* by Edwin L. Wade, editor, New York, Hudson Hills Press, 1986; *Shared Visions: Native American Painters and Sculptors of the Twentieth Century,* by Margaret Archuleta and Renard Strickland, Phoenix, The Heard Museum, 1991; *Visions of the People: A Pictorial History of Plains Indian Life,* by Evan M. Maurer, Minneapolis Institute of Arts, 1992; *The Native Americans: An Illustrated History,* by Betty and Ian Ballentine, Atlanta, 1993. **Articles**—"Richard West, Sr. (1912-1996)," by Susan Shown Harjo, *Native Peoples,* Summer, 1996.

* * *

Perhaps no other American Indian artist was as well known, respected, and even beloved as Dick West, as a painter and teacher. He was extremely well known for his traditional paintings that paid particular attention to cultural authenticity regarding the lifeways of his Cheyenne people, in addition to his superb sense of color and craftsmanship. West is also remembered for his distinguished career as Director of the Art Department at Bacone College in Muskogee, Oklahoma. Anyone remotely familiar with or interested in American Indian painting is aware of the fact that from the 1940s through the 1960s he was on the cutting edge of Native American arts—a cutting edge that added vibrancy, fluidity, and new dimensions to the traditional (or flat style) of Indian painting. Few Indian artists have left a legacy equal to his.

Born Walter Richard West in Darlington, Oklahoma (within the old reservation boundaries of the Cheyenne and Arapaho tribes), he signed his artwork as Dick West or Wah-Pah-Nah-Yah (Lightfoot Runner). "His prime aim," according to Susan Shown Harjo, "was to show that American Indians, with a priceless heritage of history, legends, and color, could attain an important place in contemporary American art." Using an illustrative narrative style and careful details, West depicted historical social and religious activities of the Cheyenne as well as contemporary scenes.

West enjoyed an excellent art education at several institutions. After his first years at the Concho Indian School in Concho, Oklahoma (1917-1927), he went on to study at the famous Haskell Institute (1931-1936) and then to Bacone College (1936-1938) where he studied under Acee Blue Eagle, the founder of that college's art department. He became the first Native American student to earn a B.F.A. at the University of Oklahoma, where he attended from 1938-1941. In World War II from 1942 to 1946, West served in the United States Navy, and upon his discharge he returned to the University of Oklahoma, where he received an M.F.A. in 1950. Always keen to experience new learning opportunities in new mi-

lieux, he also studied special topics at various institutions: The University of Redlands (California), the University of Tulsa, Northeastern University, Tahlequah (Oklahoma), and the University of Kansas. One of the things for which West will be best remembered is his teaching career at Bacone College from 1947 to 1970. In 1980 Bacone honored West with the title of Professor Emeritus, elected him to the Alumni Hall of Fame in 1984, and in 1993 awarded him an Honorary Doctorate of Fine Arts. Upon his retirement from Bacone, West went to Haskell Indian Nations University, where from 1970 to 1972 he was Director of Art and ultimately became Chairman of the Division of Humanities (from 1972 to 1977). After Haskell, he was able to devote himself full-time to his art and to the role of "senior statesman" in the American Indian art world.

A deeply spiritual man who respected the wisdom of all religions, West was a practicing Baptist. He was motivated to create a series of religious paintings wherein the Universal Christ is depicted as a Plains Indian. His *Indian Christ in Gethsemane* hangs in the Bacone College Chapel along with others in the series: *The Madonna and Child, The Annunciation, The Last Supper, The Crucifixion,* and *The Ascension.*

After the death of his father on May 3, 1996, W. Richard West, Jr., Director of the National Museum of the American Indian, Washington, D.C., made this statement: "Dad enjoyed a life full of professional accomplishment as one of the Indian community's most outstanding artists. I will remember him most as a father who believed deeply in the beauty and worth of Cheyenne culture and who did so much through his art to preserve that culture. His commitment to Cheyenne values and traditions is his greatest contribution to his sons and to all others whose lives he touched and blessed."

—John Anson Warner

WHITE DEER, Gary

Variant names: Nukoa
Tribal affiliations: Choctaw
Painter

Born: Tulsa, Oklahoma, 17 December 1950. **Education:** Institute of American Indian Arts, 1968-1969; Haskell Indian Junior College, A.A., 1973. **Career:** Artist in residence, Indian City, near Anadarko, Oklahoma, 1973, and public schools, Sapula, Oklahoma, 1975-76; cultural leader among the Choctaw, including Choctaw Nation Dancers (head); helped develop cultural festivals in Oklahoma and Louisiana, and participates in workshops; panelist, Master Artist grants program, (Oklahoma) State Arts Council. **Awards:** Numerous, including American Indian and Cowboy Artists National Western Artist Exhibition, San Dimas, California (1978); American Indian Exposition, Anadarko, Oklahoma (1988); Five Civilized Tribes Museum, Muskogee, Oklahoma (1974-75, 1979, 1981, 1989-90); Philbrook Museum of Art, Tulsa (1975); Twin Cities Indian Market, St. Paul, Minnesota (1991-92); Tulsa Indian Art Festival (1992).

Individual Exhibitions

1992   *Paintings by Gary White Deer,* Southern Plains Indian Museum and Crafts Center, Anadarko, Oklahoma

Selected Group Exhibitions

1976-81 Ni-Wo-Di-Hi Galleries, Austin, Texas
1982   Cherokee National Museum, Muskogee, Oklahoma
1985   East Central State College, Ada, Oklahoma
1986   The Gilcrease Institute of American History and Art, Tulsa, Oklahoma
1987   Tulsa Indian Art Festival, Tulsa, Oklahoma
1990   Cherokee National Museum, Muskogee, Oklahoma
1991   Vereinhaus Glokenhof, Zurich, Switzerland
         Kingston, Jamaica
         The America House, Stuttgart, Germany
1993   Southern Plains Indian Museum and Crafts Center, Anadarko, Oklahoma

Collections

American Embassy, Paris, France; Choctaw Nation of Oklahoma; Thomas Gilcrease Institute of American History and Art, Tulsa, Oklahoma; Oklahoma State University, Stillwater, Oklahoma.

Publications

On WHITE DEER: Books—*Paintings by Gary White Deer* (catalog), Southern Plains Indian Museum and Crafts Center, Anadarko, Oklahoma, 1992. Film—"Indians of the Southeast," Part One of Six, *The Native Americans,* Turner Broadcasting, 1994.

*

Gary White Deer comments (1992):

I grew up watching my father paint within the genre of classic, old style Indian art. We were neighbors with Allan Houser at Inter-Mountain School in Brigham City, Utah, where he and my folks were working. This was in the early '50s. Allan Houser and my Dad were friends, and so they sometimes painted together. Those paintings my Dad did back then are still around, and their beautiful rhythms and colors still impact me, still influence my art.

When I attended the Institute of American Indian Arts in Santa Fe, I wasn't really serious about painting, but I remember that the main idea of the school seemed to be humanism over tribalism; that is, we were to become individualists. Abstract expression was the painting style most favored.

At Haskell Indian Junior College, the older tribal style my father had painted in was very much alive and well, and expressed wonderfully by Dr. Richard West. The main influence Dr. West had on me was an appreciation of the importance of visual tradition in Indian culture, and the need to portray cultural tradition correctly, while allowing for individual interpretation.

After Haskell, I became an "artist in residence" at Indian City, near Anadarko. This was 20 years ago, and the Indian art world was confined to about four major competitive shows, a few galleries and collectors. Also about this time I painted for a while with my wife's uncle, Robert Redbird. He introduced me to Southwest style painting and technique, and most importantly, showed me what would sell.

I am proud that I began painting at a time when Indian artists were also visually and culturally tribal people, who could portray accurately and with dignity the histories and cultures of their nations. (From *Paintings by Gary White Deer*.)

*   *   *

In very general terms, Gary White Deer is a modernist artist, but he does not embrace just one sort of modernist approach; his work can range from neo-realism and something close to abstraction and then to the Mexican/Southwest style somewhat reminiscent of the work of R. C. Gorman, Robert Redbird, and Bill Rabbit. Diversity and variety are the hallmarks of his work. In addition to his art, White Deer is very active as a cultural leader of his Choctaw people, increasingly emerging as a spokesperson for the revival of traditional Indian culture in America. Thus, his artistic career is wedded to his activities as a civic and cultural leader. He is a talented and versatile artist whose originals and prints are much sought after.

White Deer grew up in an artistic environment: his parents were employed for a time at the Inter-Mountain School in Brigham City, Utah, where his father, a traditional, flat style painter, was close friends with noted artist Allan Houser. White Deer studied for a year (1968-69) at the Institute of American Indian Arts (IAIA) in Santa Fe, New Mexico, but moved on to Haskell Indian Junior College in Lawrence, Kansas, where he influenced by Dick West. As White Deer puts it, "The main Dr. West had on me was an appreciation of the importance of visual tradition in Indian culture, and the need to portray cultural tradition correctly, while allowing for individual interpretation."

Upon graduating from Haskell in 1973 with an Associate in Arts degree, White Deer became an artist in residence at the Indian City establishment just south of Anadarko, Oklahoma. It was around this time that he worked with the famous Kiowa artist, Robert Redbird, who acquainted him with the Southwest style of painting known for its emphasis on massive figuration.

The variety of styles in White Deer's work is evidenced in the paintings exhibited in his show at the Southern Plains Indian Museum and Crafts Center in late 1992. Quite clearly, Redbird's influence can be seen in such southwestern oriented works as *Thoughts Flowing Like Eagles* (1987), while others, like *First Thunder* (1991), are more abstract. *Big Tree* (1988) has somewhat more realistic character, while *Money Isn't Everything* (1992) is a collage still dominated by realism, and in *The Untying of Creation* (1990) White Deer employs southwestern iconographic symbols in a collage-like arrangement, not unlike the paintings by David Chethlahe Paladin (Navajo), Helen Hardin (Santa Clara Pueblo), and Tony Da (San Ildefonso Pueblo).

From 1976 to 1981, White Deer had a professional relationship with a commercial gallery in Austin, Texas, resulting in a series of lithograph prints in large editions promoted and sold throughout North America and several foreign countries, which served to bring White Deer to international attention. In fact, one of the works, *Search for the Eagle's Way*, sold out 1,500 copies, and another print, *Holhkunna*, sold out 900 copies.

While being an active artist, White Deer has involved himself strongly in a variety of civic and cultural activities. He explains that "if one paints and then sells Indian traditions, one should also care about them enough to try and sustain them." White Deer has sung for and led Oklahoma Choctaw dances, including the "stomp" dance in the contemporary Cherokee style, played Choctaw and Creek stickball games, leads a Choctaw dance society called "Yellow Hill," named after an old Choctaw dance ground, and participates in the ceremonials of the Native American Church. Additionally, he has served as a Master of Ceremonies, Head Gourd dancer, coordinator, and occasionally, as a head dancer at Pow Wows, and coordinates the Annual Ada Pow Wow.

White Deer appeared on a discussion panel in one of a series of television/video programs, *The Native Americans*, produced by

Gary White Deer: *Wind Clan.* Courtesy of the artist.

Turner Broadcasting and issued in 1994. White Deer appeared in the first film, "Indians of the Southeast," where he spoke on the culture and history of the "Five Civilized Tribes" (of which the Choctaw is one) and to express his views on Indian cultural renewal.

—John Anson Warner

WHITEHORSE, Emmi

Tribal affiliations: Navajo
Painter

Born: Crownpoint, New Mexico, 1956. **Education:** Attended a government boarding school for Navajo girls; B.A. in painting in 1980, University of New Mexico; M.A. in printmaking with a minor in art history in 1982, University of New Mexico. **Career:** Studio artist in Bridgeport, Connecticut, 1982-87, and Santa Fe, New Mexico, 1987-.

Individual Exhibitions

1982	Sun Valley Center for Arts & Humanities, Sun Valley, Idaho
1984	Akmak Gallery, West Berlin
	Art Resources, Denver, Colorado
	Galleria del Cavallino, Venice
1985	A.I.C.A. Gallery, San Francisco, California
1987	A.I.C.A. Gallery, San Francisco, California
1988	Yuma Art Center, Yuma, Arizona
1989	Marilyn Butler Fine Art, Scottsdale, Arizona
1990	The Hartje Gallery, Frankfurt, Germany
	Lew Allen/Butler Fine Art, Santa Fe, New Mexico
	Thomas Riley Gallery, Chicago
1991	*Neeznaa* The Wheelright Museum, Santa Fe, New Mexico
	Karin Iserhagen Galerie, Basel, Switzerland
	Lew Allen Gallery, Santa Fe, New Mexico
	Hartje Gallery, Frankfurt, Germany
1992	Lew Allen Gallery, Santa Fe, New Mexico
	Jan Cicero Gallery, Chicago
	Will Thompson Gallery, Telluride, Colorado
	The Lowe Gallery, Atlanta, Georgia
1993	The Hartje Gallery, Frankfurt, Germany
	The Millicent Rogers Museum, Taos, New Mexico
	Lew Allen Gallery, Santa Fe, New Mexico
	Bentley/Tomlinson Gallery, Scottsdale, Arizona
1994	Horwitch Lew Allen Gallery, Santa Fe, New Mexico
	Lew Allen Gallery, Santa Fe, New Mexico
1995	L'Homme Art, Antwerp, Belgium
	The Hartje Gallery, Frankfurt, Germany
	Jan Maiden Contemporary Art, Columbus, Ohio
1996	Bentley Gallery, Scottsdale, Arizona

Selected Group Exhibitions

1979	Gallery Upstairs, Berkeley, California
	Downtown Center for the Arts, Albuquerque, New Mexico
	University of New Mexico, Albuquerque
1980	The University of North Dakota, Grand Forks
	The Southern Plains Museum, Anadarko, Oklahoma

	The Sioux Land Heritage Museum, Sioux Falls, South Dakota
	The Galleria del Cavalina, Venice
	The Wheelwright Museum, Santa Fe, New Mexico
1981	*Confluences of Configuration and Change,* (traveling)
	R. L. Nelson Gallery, University of California, Davis
	Museum of the Southwest, Midland, Texas
	The A.I.C.H. Gallery, New York
	The Brunnier Gallery, Iowa State University
	The Heard Museum, Phoenix
	Works on Paper, University of New Mexico, Albuquerque (traveling)
1982	*Modern Native American Abstraction,* The Philadelphia Art Alliance Gallery, Pennsylvania (traveling)
	Works on Paper, Santa Fe Festival of the Arts, Santa Fe, New Mexico
	The Aspen Institute at Baca, Crestone, Colorado
	Taos to Tucson, The Foundations Gallery, New York
	Native Women Artists, The A.I.C.H. Gallery, New York
1983	*The Southwest Scene,* The Brentwood Gallery, St. Louis, Missouri
	Native Artists of the Eighties, The Sacred Circle Gallery, Seattle, Washington
1984	*She Holds Her Own,* The Green County Council on the Arts, Catskill, New York
	Contemporary Native American Art Exhibition, Oklahoma State University, Stillwater
	Marilyn Butler Fine Art, Santa Fe, New Mexico
	Marilyn Butler Fine Art, Scottsdale, Arizona
1985	*Visage Transcended,* Traveling Mask show: The American Indian Contemporary Arts Gallery, San Francisco, California
	Eight Artists, The Southwest Museum, Los Angeles
	Women of Sweet Grass, Sage and Cedar, The A.I.C.H. Gallery, New York (traveling)
	Women of the American West, Bruce Museum, Greenwich, Connecticut
	Artists Under Thirty, The Silvermine Guild, New Canaan, Connecticut
1986	Stemmel Galleries, Reno, Nevada
1987	Fort Wayne Museum of Art, Indiana
	Read Stremmel Gallery, San Antonio, Texas
1988	Ann Reed Gallery, Sun Valley, Idaho
	Mask, the Old Pueblo Museum, Tucson
1989	*6 from Santa Fe,* Gibbes Museum of Art, Charleston, South Carolina
	Miller Gallery, Palm Desert, California
1990	*Primavera,* Tucson Museum of Art, Arizona
	Centro Culturah de la Raza, Balboa Park, San Diego
1991	*Presswork, the Art of Women Printmakers,* National Museum of Women in the Arts, Washington, D.C., (traveling)
1992	New Mexico State University, Las Cruces
1993	The Millicent Rogers Museum, Taos, New Mexico
1994	American Academy of Arts and Letters Purchase Exhibit, New York
1995	Westfalishces Museum, Münster, Germany

Collections

Albuquerque Museum, New Mexico; American Embassy, Rabat, Morocco; American Embassy, Tokyo; Arizona State University,

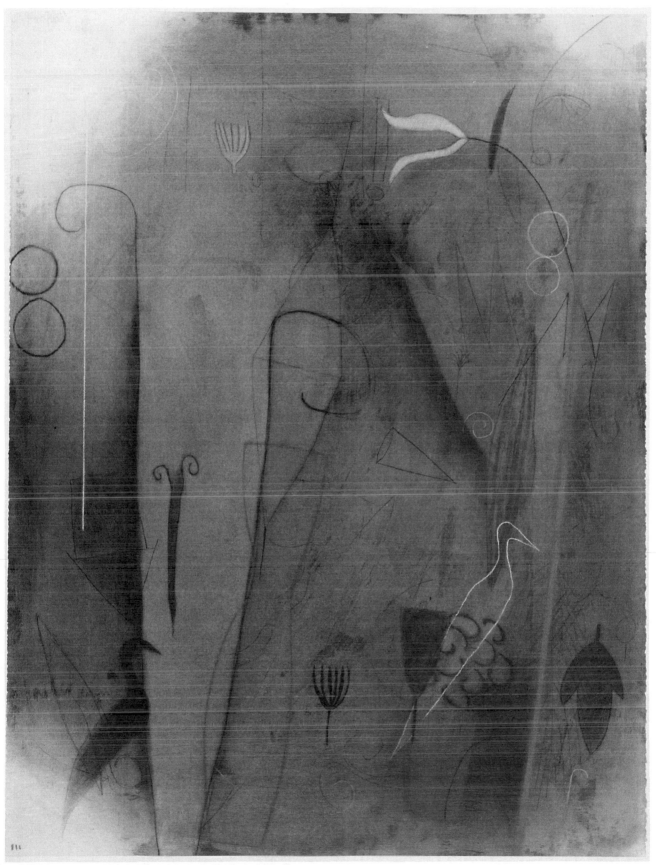

Emmi Whitehorse: #902 (untitled), 1991. Courtesy of the artist.

Tempe, Arizona; Art Bank/Art in Embassies, U.S. Department of State, Washington, D.C.; Gutenberg Buchergilde, Frankfurt, Germany; The Heard Museum, Phoenix; Joslyn Art Museum, Omaha, Nebraska; Mountain Bell, Denver, Colorado; Museum of Fine Arts, Santa Fe, New Mexico; St. Louis Museum, Missouri; State Capital Collection, State of New Mexico, Santa Fe; University of Arizona Museum of Art, Tucson; Wheelwright Museum, Santa Fe, New Mexico.

Publications

On WHITEHORSE: Books—*Emmi Whitehorse: Changing Woman* by W. Peterson, Santa Fe, New Mexico: Lew Allen/Butler Fine Art Gallery, 1990; *Neeznáá Emmi Whitehorse: Ten Years* by Lucy Lippard, Santa Fe, New Mexico: The Wheelwright Museum of the American Indian, 1990; *Mixed Blessings: New Art in a Multicultural America* by Lucy Lippard, New York, Pantheon Books, 1991; *Native Streams: Contemporary Native American Art* by Jan Cisero and Craig McDaniel, Jan Cicero Gallery, Chicago, Illinois, and Turman Art Gallery, Indiana State University, Terre Haute, Indiana, 1996. Articles—Interview with Larry Abbott, *Caliban 11*, University of Nebraska Press, 1992; "Shima: The Paintings of Emmi Whitehorse," Introduction to Wheelwright Museum Catalog, by Lucy R. Lippard, 1991; "Emmi Whitehorse," by Neery Melkonian, *Arts Magazine,* 1991; "Abshied von der edlen Rothaut," by N. Scott Momaday, *GEO Magazine* U.S.A. Southwest Special, April, 1989; "Frames of Reference: Native American Art in the Context of Modern and Post Modern Art", by Gerhard Hoffman, *Artspace Magazine*, Spring Issue, 1987; "Emmi Whitehorse, Kin' nah' zin,'" by Joseph Traugot, *Artspace Magazine*, Summer Issue, 1982; "Noble Savages and Wild Indians," by Jamake Highwater, *The New York Arts Journal*, January Issue, 1980.

*

Emmi Whitehorse comments:

My work deals with recreating worlds remembered. It is never-ending because I am constantly re-designing, re-placing, re-building it with personal images and concepts, always trying to bridge the future with the old—a compromise between the tradition and futurity.

My idea-material comes from the land, the environment in which I grew up. Also, each family member contributes to my imagery.

My choice of colors is not random but arbitrary and personal. My color usage often comes from colors my Grandmother uses in her weavings and also as a way of paying homage to her. She tends to be very abstract—sometimes using optical illusions but always balancing these with a delicacy of design.

I want to make use of these abstractions that I remembered, using it aesthetically to help create my work. This way, I'm closer to building that bridge between not only the new and the old, but also the two cultures in which I live. My hope is that my abstractions will help to change the regional art that is so stereotyped as "Indian Art" and be more readily accepted.

*   *   *

Whitehorse's art integrates her Navajo background with abstract shapes, forms, and color. Memories of her grandmother's weaving and shepherding and her own experiences at boarding school play an important part in the creation of her paintings. Many of the objects depicted are based on Navajo culture, such as arches that represent Navajo wedding baskets and comb/fork shapes that represent weaving objects that tighten yarn. Whitehorse paints with colors inspired by her native southwestern landscape. A sense of nature and geometry comes from her grandmother's weaving. Many of the shapes and objects provide symbolic and mythical meaning for the artist. Whitehorse's paintings give a sense of space where various shapes appear to be moving and floating. Early paintings include figures that are more geometric and pointed, often resembling the early petroglyphs found carved into the rock walls and canyons of the southwest.

Other forms found in her paintings came from her father's branding iron, and the gouges in wooden gates that record her family's sheep herds. Leaves, hands, feathers, plants, hooks, fish, houses, and silhouettes of human forms seem to represent the importance of personal identity and nature.

In later works these figures and shapes became more curved and with more open areas. Delicate lines are found throughout the paintings' surfaces. Some lines are curvy, others cross each other and some make separate shapes. Many of Whitehorse's paintings are expressed through various shades and tints of the primary colors. Other paintings are created with background shades and tints of analogous colors.

Whitehorse's work is often compared to that of the European artist Paul Klee because of her free-association imagery/fantasy and her individualistic approach to pictographic forms. Like Klee, Whitehorse uses shifting color planes and small pieces of paper collage. On the other hand critics such as Lucy Lippard feel that Whitehorse's compositional elements may be inspired by the Native American concept of balancing the four directions rather than the Western focus on top and bottom, as well as from Navajo sandpainting, which also influenced abstract-expressionist artists like Jackson Pollock.

As her painting career began in the early 1980s Whitehorse drew on her personal experiences and abstracted them. Her *Kin' Nan' Zin' (Standing Ruins)* series included geometric forms, prismatic planes, and atmospheric color that evoked childhood memories of the vast spaces on the Navajo reservation, the luminous sky, red earth, her grandmother's weaving, sheep, and ancient Anasazi sites. Some of the later works in the 80's that incorporated an indigenous identity were less abstract and included objects such as houses, stick-figures, leaves, horns, bowls, bells, flowers, and ladders. This approach is evident in the 1988 *Chaos in the Visitor's Dream.*

The female form is also evident in many of Whitehorse's paintings. The figures have been interpreted as goddesses or deities. The form is usually an incomplete torso with vase-shaped contours. Whitehorse refers to this figure as *White Shell Woman*, a mythic being in Navajo legends. Other silhouetted female forms are evident in Whitehorse's paintings, including bell-shaped women in full-length dresses. Although some critics associate them with *Changing Woman*, the central and most revered being in the Navajo cosmology, Whitehorse attributes a different source for her inspiration. According to Whitehorse, the white figure in a long dress depicts the type of so-called ideal woman, a fairytale princess, popular with young girls during Whitehorse's childhood years in a boarding school. Young Indian girls, caught in a conflict between traditional and white cultural expectations of women, often aspired to the somewhat unattainable goals of being a Miss America or high school prom queen. It should be noted that the Navajo culture is matrilineal and female energy is considered active, vital, creative and productive. *Changing Woman* represents regeneration, rejuvenation and renewal.

Two world views are ever-present in Emmi Whitehorse's art. There is the abstract, formalist world of balanced shapes and colors familiar to those who appreciate or espouse art for art's sake. And there is also the spiritual Navajo worldview that incorporates art into all aspects of life. Whitehorse could be described as a modernist concerned with the picture plane, but one who is inspired by the ancient surfaces of the southwest landscape. Like the land itself, her work is both layered and open, full of light, open, and active.

In the catalog accompanying her 1996 group exhibit, *Native Streams: Contemporary Native American Art*, Whitehorse describes her pictorial exploration of the land and everything related to it. She mentions her interest in unseen energy, the microcosms underneath ones feet, the growth that occurs in dark, damp places, and the magnification of nature in her work. In *Union II*, (1992, 51" x 78", oil/chalk/paper, canvas), Whitehorse employs visual symbols that are ambiguous and meant to be both illuminating and obscure. Memory, light, color, and visual symbology are the factors the artist mentions as aiding her artistic intentions, but perhaps most of all memory, "which comes back in bits and pieces."

—Phoebe Farris

WHITMAN, Richard Ray

Tribal affiliations: Yuchi
Photographer, filmmaker, and mixed media artist

Born: Claremore, Oklahoma, 14 May 1949. **Education:** A.A., Institute of American Indian Arts, Santa Fe, New Mexico, 1968-1970; California Institute of the Arts, Valencia, California, 1972; Oklahoma School of Photography, Oklahoma City, 1977. **Career:** Artist-in-Residence, Oklahoma State Arts Council; member of Makers, an artist cooperative founded in 1980; independent curator. **Awards:** Martin Luther King, Jr. Humanitarian Award, 1987.

Individual Exhibitions

1989   *Street Chiefs Series and Other Works*, International Hall of Photography, Oklahoma City, Oklahoma
1991   *Street Chiefs: Homeland Refugees*, Kings Gallery, St. Olaf College, Northfield, Minnesota
1996   *Red Mound: No Translation* (with Joe Dale Tate Nevaquaya), Living Arts Space, Tulsa, Oklahoma

Selected Group Exhibitions

1984   *Photographs by Native Americans of Oklahoma*, University of Oklahoma Museum of Art, Norman
1986   *We Are Always Turning Around on Purpose*, Amelie Wallace Gallery, The State University of New York, Old Westbury, New York
        Makers, Oklahoma City University, Oklahoma City
1987   *Eight Native American Artists*, Fort Wayne Museum of Art, Fort Wayne, Indiana
1988   *Beyond the Horse's Eye: Three Contemporary Native American Photographers*, American Indian Community House Gallery, New York
1990   *Language of the Lens*, The Heard Museum, Phoenix

The Decade Show, Museum of Contemporary Hispanic Art, The New Museum of Contemporary Art, and The Studio Museum in Harlem, New York
1991   *No Borders*, Native Indian/Inuit Photographers Association [NIIPA], Hamilton, Ontario
1992   *Green Acres: Neo-Colonialism in the U.S.*, Washington University Gallery of Art, St. Louis, Missouri
        Message Carriers, Photographic Resource Center, Boston University, Massachusetts
1993   *Indigenous Investigations* (with Hachivi Edgar Heap of Birds), The University of North Texas Art Gallery, Denton
        Through the Native Lens, Institute of American Indian Arts Museum, Santa Fe
        Indian Territories: 20th Century Native American Artists Dismantle 19th Century Euro-American Myths, Renee Fotouhi Fine Art East, East Hampton, New York
1994   *STAND: Four Artists Interpret the Native American Experience*, Bruce Art Gallery, Edinboro University of Pennsylvania, Edinboro
        First Nations: Four Native American Photographers, Impressions Gallery, York, England
1995   *Red Earth*, Institute of American Indian Arts Museum, Santa Fe
        Image and Self in Contemporary Native American Photoart, Hood Museum of Art, Dartmouth College, Hanover, New Hampshire
1996   *Native American Invitational and Masters Exhibition*, The Gilcrease Museum, Tulsa, Oklahoma
        Gifts of the Spirit: Works by Nineteenth-Century and Contemporary Native American Artists, The Peabody Essex Museum, Salem, Massachusetts
        Strong Hearts: Native American Visions and Voices, Ripley Center, The Smithsonian Institution, Washington, D.C.

Publications

By WHITMAN: Articles—Artist's statement, *Exposure*, Vol. 29, No. 1 (Fall); Artist's statement, *Image and Self in Contemporary Native American Photoart*, Hood Museum of Art, Dartmouth College, Hanover, New Hampshire, 1995. **Films**—*Carriers of the Light* (co-produced with Joe Dale Tate Nevaquaya and Pierre Lobstein), 1990; *Humanities Voice* (co-produced with Joe Dale Tate Nevaquaya and Pierre Lobstein), 1992; *The Grand Circle* (co-produced with Joe Dale Tate Nevaquaya and Pierre Lobstein), 1994. **Films as actor**—*War Party*, directed by Franc Roddam; Hemdale Productions, Los Angeles, California, 1987; *My Heroes Have Always Been Cowboys*, Samuel Goldwyn Company, Guthrie, Oklahoma, 1989; *Lakota Woman*, Turner Pictures (Turner Network Television), Atlanta, Georgia, 1994. **Other**—*Mazerunner: The Life and Art of T.C. Cannon* (poetry of T.C. Cannon read by Whitman; also created additional dialogue) produced and directed by Philip Albert; Oklahoma City, Oklahoma, 1993; *T.C. Cannon: He Stood in the Sun* by Joan Frederick (contributor of personal commentary about T.C. Cannon), Flagstaff, Arizona: Northland Publishing, 1995.

On WHITMAN: Books—*The Sweetgrass Lives On*, ed. by Jamake Highwater, New York: Lippincott and Crowell, 1980; "Richard Ray (Whitman)," in *Eight Native American Artists*, Fort Wayne Museum of Art, Fort Wayne, Indiana, 1987; *Mixed Blessings* by

Lucy Lippard, New York: Pantheon Books, 1990; *Reimaging America: The Arts of Social Change*, ed. by Hachivi Edgar Heap of Birds, Philadelphia: New Society Publishers, 1990; "Street Chiefs and Native Hosts: Richard Ray (Whitman) and Hachivi Edgar Heap of Birds Defend the Homeland," by W. Jackson Rushing, *Green Acres: Neo-Colonialism in the U.S.,* Washington University Gallery of Art, Washington University, St. Louis, Missouri, 1992; Artist's statement and interview with Sara-Jayne Parsons, in *Indigenous Investigations*, The University of North Texas Art Gallery, The University of North Texas, Denton, Texas, 1992. **Articles**—"A Curator's Perspective: Native Photographers Creating a Visual Native American History," by Theresa Harlan, *Exposure*, Vol. 29, No. 1, Fall 1993; *Aperture*, No. 139, Summer 1995; "Talking Heads," by Joan Frederick, *Oklahoma Today,* June-July, 1996. **Films**—*Five Portraits*, produced by Pierre Lobstein (includes Bob Haozous, Edgar Heap of Birds, Dan Lomahaftewa, Emmi Whitehorse, and Richard Ray Whitman), 1988.

*

Richard Ray Whitman comments:

My art and my Yuchi individuality have been about educating myself through my art process and my art-making, and it's helped me believe in my ideals, to trust in myself. I guess the question I am asked many times is, "do I consider myself a traditional Indian or a contemporary Indian?" Well, I consider myself both, but not at the same moment. It's not an either/or situation. Our traditions, and our experiences in contemporary life, are here at the same moment. Our ancestors left us a way; they brought it right up here, right up to this moment, to this very moment that I speak to you. From early on I've been interested in the power of expression in whatever form that takes. Maybe I'm still looking for my medium or my discipline, but I haven't really settled on anything particular, although I've been experimenting in video, incorporating image, text, and voice. I still consider myself a painter. There is nothing that will ever replace the feeling of being in front of a blank canvas or a blank sheet of paper or a blank space. It's just you and that space, and that is very organic. I don't think that feeling of unity, of communication with the medium, will ever be replaced. Sometimes when I take the photographic process to a certain point I pull back and

Richard Ray Whitman. Photograph by Jenny Woodruff; courtesy of the artist.

AIR

WATER

EARTH

FIRE

STATE(S) OF PERVASIVE INDIFFERENCE

Richard Ray Whitman: *Earth, Air, Fire, Water,* 1993. Courtesy of the artist.

then I pursue the writing some. Then, I'll run into a dead end and do video. But I'm always ready to come back to painting. I don't consider myself a mature artist, and I don't possess a single aesthetic philosophy. I'm constantly open to new ideas and ideologies. There's something new at every turn.

*　　*　　*

Richard Whitman's work is sometimes identified with other contemporary Native artists from Oklahoma, such as his brother, Joe Dale Tate Nevaquaya, Shan Goshorn, Hachivi Edgar Heap of Birds, and other members of the artist cooperative Makers, founded in 1980. Although much of Whitman's work derives from the specificity of his experience in Oklahoma and deals with the various tribes there, his work investigates the broader implications—not only of Indian experience in America but also issues of personal identity, social change, and cultural paradigms. His work abroad with other "marginalized" peoples furthers these concerns.

Whitman may be best known for his continuing series of photographs, *Street Chiefs*. Begun in 1973 after his return from the Wounded Knee demonstrations and continuing through the 1980s, and 90s, Whitman documented homeless urban Indians in Oklahoma and often exhibited the photographs with his poetry to complement the imagery. However, the photographs, meant to counter the romantic illustrations of Edward Curtis, should not be seen simply as a photorealistic documentation of poverty and a concern about homelessness. Rather, Whitman intends these works to be understood in the long history of the displacement of Native peoples in the building of America. He focuses on Oklahoma because as "Indian Territory" it became the dumping ground for tribes from the East, Southeast, and west of the Mississippi. The broader context for the photographs is the removal of Indian people from their homelands and the process of how Indian people became landless. Usually, the black and white *Street Chiefs* photographs portray one or two individuals in their "natural environments." Apart from the occasional inclusion of Whitman's poetry, the photographs are presented without commentary. The individuals are presented "as is," in the midst of their pain but also with their dignity and struggle to survive implicit. However, "Buy Oklahoma" (1986), from *Street Chiefs*, depicts a single figure beneath a Department of Agriculture billboard that proclaims "Buy Oklahoma" next to profile images of a cowboy and a head-dressed Indian. The juxtaposition between the billboard image and the reality of the street chief heightens the disparity between governmental policy and personal existence.

Whitman also recontextualizes his photographs into new work with new meanings. "Buy Oklahoma" is the central image in "History Lesson #4" from the *Homeland Series* (1989). This piece also includes some "Indian symbols" and some artifacts of the detritus of pop culture, like two children's toy headdresses. *Relocation Assimilation* (1989) places the photographs "Alley Allies" (1986) and "Street Chief #1" (1985) into a rectangular, wall-mounted box that contains, among other things, newspaper clippings and a statement by fellow artist, Hachivi Edgar Heap of Birds. The box format itself becomes a metaphor of the linear thinking of the dominant culture, while the language and images in the box push outward against this linear enclosure.

Whitman's experiments in the early 1990's with computer-generated prints on vellum have led to a series of large-scale images. *State(s) of Pervasive Indifference* (1993) portrays a young Native man wrapped in an American flag standing on the shoreline in Corpus Christi, Texas, in October, 1992, awaiting the arrival of a replica of one of Columbus' ships; *The Absence of Our Presence* (1993) refers ironically to the "Oklahoma Native America" tourist campaign initiated by the state; and *We Are the Evidence of the Western Hemisphere* (1993) depicts Carter Camp, one of the leaders at Wounded Knee, and the late James Whole Eagle (Whitman portrayed Camp in the film *Lakota Woman*). These photographs extend Whitman's concerns with issues of survival and identity.

These issues are also explored in Whitman's videos, most clearly in *The Grand Circle* (1994). For this film Whitman and his co-producers Nevaquaya and Lobstein mounted cameras on the dashboard and the rear panel of their car and drove through the Mound Culture areas of the Southeast along a route of Indian removal, criss-crossing rivers where Indian people were forced to traverse. These images are projected on a stationary skull in the center of the frame and from behind the eye sockets, while Nevaquaya's text revolves like a halo around the top of the skull. While many of the images and sounds are intended to be beyond identification, brief snippets—gunfire, military fife and drum marching music, crying—suggest the violence done to Indian people throughout the Southeast. That this violence continues is brought out through references to the School of the Americas, which was built over destroyed Mound Culture sites in Georgia.

In 1994, 1995 and 1996 Whitman and Nevaquaya conducted three to six week residencies in Marseille, France, where they worked with Comoran, Arabic, and Gypsy peoples on such topics as social and cultural analysis and the use of art as a mode of communication about the issues and concerns of diverse communities. This led to a group of Arabic and Gypsy students visiting a Native community in South Dakota in 1996.

—Larry Abbott

WILLIAMS Family, The

Tribal affiliations: Navajo
Potters

ROSE WILLIAMS. Born: Navajo Nation, Arizona, c. 1925. **Awards:** Numerous awards in competitions, including "Best of Show" award at the Navajo Nation Fair.

ALICE WILLIAMS CLING. Born: Alice Williams, Cow Springs, Navajo Nation, Arizona, 21 March 1946; daughter of Rose Williams. **Awards:** Numerous, including Santa Fe Indian Market and the Museum of Northern Arizona's Navajo Craftsman Exhibition.

SUSIE WILLIAMS CRANK. Born: Cow Springs, Navajo Nation, Arizona, 1950; daughter of Rose Williams.

LORRAINE WILLIAMS. Born: Sweetwater, Arizona, 1955. **Family:** Married George Williams, son of Rose Williams; two sons, two daughters. **Awards:** Numerous, including Museum of Northern Arizona's Navajo Craftsman Exhibition, the Santa Fe Indian Market, and the Gallup Intertribal Indian Ceremonial.

Selected Group Exhibitions

Rose Williams:

1988   *anii ánáádaalyaa'íí: Continuity and Innovation in Recent Navajo Art*, Wheelwright Museum of the American Indian, Santa Fe, New Mexico
1990   *Navajo Junction: Where Navajo potteries meet*, Arizona State Museum, University of Arizona, Tucson, Arizona
1993   *Leets'aa bi Diné Dáályé. It Is Called Navajo Pottery*, Phoebe A. Hearst Museum of Anthropology, University of California, Berkeley, California

Alice Williams Cling:

1978   Vice-Presidential Mansion, Washington, DC
1986   Navajo Nation Museum, Window Rock, Arizona
1987   Permanent installation, Navajo Nation Museum, Window Rock, Arizona
1988   *anii ánáádaalyaa'íí: Continuity and Innovation in Recent Navajo Art*, Wheelwright Museum of the American Indian, Santa Fe, New Mexico
1990   *Navajo Junction: where Navajo potteries meet*, Arizona State Museum, University of Arizona, Tucson, Arizona
1993   *Leets'aa bi Diné Dáályé: It Is Called Navajo Pottery*, Phoebe A. Hearst Museum of Anthropology, University of California, Berkeley, California
1994   *Contemporary Art of the Navajo Nation*, traveling exhibit organized by Cedar Rapids Museum of Art; Venues: Albuquerque Museum, Albuquerque, New Mexico ; the University Art Museum, State University of New York, Albany, New York; Museum of the Southwest, Midland, Texas.

Susie Williams Crank:

1993   *Leets'aa bi Diné Dáályé: It Is Called Navajo Pottery*, Phoebe A. Hearst Museum of Anthropology, University of California, Berkeley, California

Lorraine Williams:

1990   *Navajo Junction: where Navajo potteries meet*, Arizona State Museum, University of Arizona, Tucson, Arizona
1993   *Leets'aa bi Diné Dáályé: It Is Called Navajo Pottery*, Phoebe A. Hearst Museum of Anthropology, University of California, Berkeley, California
1994   *Contemporary Art of the Navajo Nation*, traveling exhibit organized by Cedar Rapids Museum of Art; Venues: Albuquerque Museum, Albuquerque, New Mexico ; the University Art Museum, State University of New York, Albany, New York; Museum of the Southwest, Midland, Texas.
1996-97 San Diego Museum of Man, California

Collections

Rose Williams: Amerind Foundation, Dragoon, Arizona; Arizona State Museum, University of Arizona, Tucson; California Academy of Sciences, San Francisco; Museum of Indian Arts & Culture, Museum of New Mexico, Santa Fe; Museum of Northern Arizona, Flag-

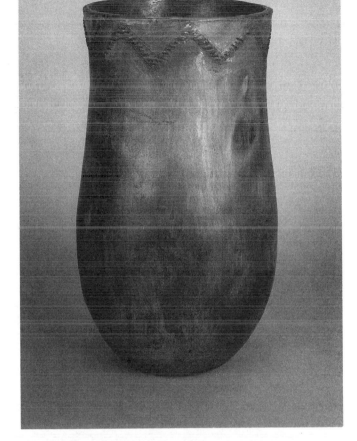

Rose Williams: Navajo pitch-coated jar, c. 1984. Photograph by Dong Lin; courtesy Russell P. Hartman collection.

staff; Navajo Nation Museum, Window Rock, Arizona; P. A. Hearst Museum of Anthropology, University of California, Berkeley; Wheelwright Museum of the American Indian, Santa Fe, New Mexico.

Alice Williams Cling: Amerind Foundation, Dragoon, Arizona; Arizona State Museum, University of Arizona, Tucson; California Academy of Sciences, San Francisco; Heard Museum, Phoenix, Arizona; Indian Arts and Crafts Board, U. S. Dept. of the Interior, Washington, D.C.; Museum of Indian Arts & Culture, Museum of New Mexico, Santa Fe; Museum of Northern Arizona, Flagstaff; Navajo Nation Museum, Window Rock, Arizona; P. A. Hearst Museum of Anthropology, University of California, Berkeley; St. Louis Art Museum, Missouri.

Susie Williams Crank: Amerind Foundation, Dragoon, Arizona; Arizona State Museum, University of Arizona, Tucson; Museum of Northern Arizona, Flagstaff; Navajo Nation Museum, Window Rock, Arizona; P. A. Hearst Museum of Anthropology, University of California, Berkeley.

Lorraine Williams: Amerind Foundation, Dragoon, Arizona; Arizona State Museum, University of Arizona, Tucson; Navajo Nation Museum, Window Rock, Arizona; San Diego Museum of Man, California.

Publications

On ROSE WILLIAMS: Books—*Navajo Pottery: Traditions and Innovations,* by Russell P. Hartman and Jan Musial, Flagstaff, Northland Press, 1987; *anii ánáádaalyaa'íí; Continuity and Innovation in Recent Navajo Art,* by Bruce Bernstein and Susan McGreevy, Santa Fe, NM: Wheelwright Museum, 1988; *The People Speak; Navajo Folk Art,* by Chuck and Jan Rosenak, Flagstaff, Northland Publishing Co., 1994; *Trading Post Guidebook,* by Patrick Eddington and Susan Makov, Flagstaff, Northland Publishing Co., 1995 **Articles**—"Techniques in Navajo Pottery Making," by Jan Bell, *Plateau* 58, no. 2, 1987; "Potters and their work," by H. Diane Wright and Jan Bell, *Plateau* 58, no. 2, 1987.

On ALICE WILLIAMS CLING: Books—*Navajo Pottery: Traditions and Innovations,* by Russell P. Hartman, Flagstaff, Northland Press, 1987; *anii ánáádaalyaa'íí; Continuity and Innovation in Recent Navajo Art*, exhibition catalog, by Bruce Bernstein and Susan McGreevy, Santa Fe, Wheelwright Museum, 1988; *Museum of American Folk Art Encyclopedia of Twentieth-Century American Folk Art and Artists*, by Chuck and Jan Rosenak, New York: Abbeville Press, 1990; *The People Speak; Navajo Folk Art,* by Chuck and Jan Rosenak, Flagstaff,

Northland Publishing Co., 1994; *Enduring Traditions; Art of the Navajo,* by Lois Essary Jacka, Flagstaff, Northland Publishing Co., 1994; *Trading Post Guidebook,* by Patrick Eddington and Susan Makov, Flagstaff, Northland Publishing Co., 1995; *Southwestern Pottery: Anasazi to Zuni,* by Allan Hayes and John Blom, Flagstaff, Northland Publishing Co., 1996. **Articles**—"Techniques in Navajo Pottery Making," by Jan Bell, *Plateau* 58, no. 2, 1987; "Potters and their work," by H. Diane Wright and Jan Bell, *Plateau* 58, no. 2, 1987; "Navajo Pottery; Contemporary Trends in a Traditional Craft," by H. Diane Wright, *American Indian Art* 12, no. 2, 1987.

On SUSIE WILLIAMS CRANK: Books: *Navajo Pottery: Traditions and Innovations,* by Russell P. Hartman and Jan Musial, Flagstaff, Northland Press, 1987; *The People Speak; Navajo Folk Art,* by Chuck and Jan Rosenak, Flagstaff, Northland Publishing Co., 1994; *Enduring Traditions; Art of the Navajo,* by Lois Essary Jacka, Flagstaff, Northland Publishing Co., 1994; *Southwestern Pottery: Anasazi to Zuni,* by Allan Hayes and John Blom, Flagstaff, Northland Publishing Co., 1996.

On LORRAINE WILLIAMS: Books—*Navajo Pottery: Traditions and Innovations,* by Russell P. Hartman and Jan Musial, Flagstaff,

Lorraine Williams: Navajo pitch-coated jar, 1991. Photograph by Dong Lin; courtesy Russell P. Hartman collection.

Northland Press, 1987; *The People Speak; Navajo Folk Art,* by Chuck and Jan Rosenak, Flagstaff, Northland Publishing Co., 1994; *Enduring Traditions; Art of the Navajo,* by Lois Essary Jacka, Flagstaff, Northland Publishing Co., 1994; *Ceremonial Indian Art, A Measure of Excellence, Volumes II & III,* by Laurance D. Linford, Gallup, NM: Inter-Tribal Indian Ceremonial Association, 1995; *Trading Post Guidebook,* by Patrick Eddington and Susan Makov, Flagstaff, Northland Publishing Co., 1995; *Southwestern Pottery: Anasazi to Zuni,* by Allan Hayes and John Blom, Flagstaff, Northland Publishing Co., 1996.

*   *   *

Among the many individuals involved in Navajo pottery making, members of the Williams family from the Shonto-Cow Springs area of the Navajo Reservation are especially recognized. Rose Williams and her daughters, Alice Williams Cling and Susie Williams Crank, and daughter-in-law, Lorraine Williams, have each produced a wide body of work and influenced many other contemporary Navajo potters. Together, they have set new standards of quality for the craft.

The personification of Navajo tradition and a respected elder in her community, Rose Williams has made pottery for more than 40 years. She has always made pottery for traditional use by her own people, a fact clearly reflected in her work, but today, much of her production is sold to non-Navajo collectors. Rose's specialty has become very large jars, sometimes measuring as high as 24 inches. Whether intended for cooking at a Navajo ceremony or for sale through a reservation trader or museum gallery, each piece is carefully smoothed and decorated with a simple clay band, known as a fillet, around the neck of a vessel, as prescribed by Navajo tradition. Her work has won numerous awards in competitions, including a coveted "Best of Show" award at the Navajo Nation Fair. Her picture and work have appeared in many publications, yet this petite grandmother who speaks only in her native Navajo language takes it all in stride. Her steadfast adherence to Navajo tradition and her willingness to teach others are perhaps her greatest contributions to Navajo pottery making, for without these, her children and the many other current potters could not expand the craft's boundaries in new directions.

Rose's eldest daughter, Alice Williams Cling, has long been counted among the top Navajo potters. Although she only began potting around 1976 when she was an adult, Alice has captured numerous awards, including those at Santa Fe's Indian Market and the Museum of Northern Arizona's Navajo Craftsman Exhibition. Exquisitely smoothed surfaces, minimal decoration, and classically proportioned vessel shapes have all become Alice Cling trademarks. Navajo pottery has always been noted for its overall crudeness, a reflection of its utilitarian roots. It was Alice who discovered something Pueblo potters have long known, i.e., to let a finished piece dry to a "leather-hard" stage before polishing it. She pioneered this technical innovation among Navajo potters and taught it to her mother and sisters. The result was Navajo pottery of a higher quality than had ever been seen before. The selective use of a red clay slip on her pots is another innovation adopted by Alice. Though not the first Navajo potter to employ this decorative technique, she was certainly the first to do so with consistent results. In some pieces, she has used a slip to accentuate certain areas of a pot, but currently she is more likely to slip the entire vessel.

Like her mother, Alice is very reserved, perhaps accounting for her minimalist's approach to decorating her work. Some of her

vessel shapes mimic 18th Century Navajo cooking jars, while others have a very modern feeling with tall, cylindrical necks. On some pieces, a neck starts out round at its base but is gradually transformed into a square shape as it rises. Rope-like handles, made by twisting together two or more clay coils, are truly wondrous creations. Many of Alice's pieces omit the traditional clay fillet entirely, concentrating solely upon the vessel's shape. On others, it may appear as a band of geometric shapes or an incised pattern that merely suggests its presence. Among Alice's body of work, her larger pieces best show her artistic abilities and creativity.

Susie Williams Crank has followed in her sister's steps, but her work is much lighter in weight than that of Alice, and is almost always covered with a satin finish of red clay slip. She experiments with many vessel forms, but especially favors those with full, round shapes, and wide jars with either very high or very low concave shoulders. She relies upon the shape to make the statement, seldom including any surface decoration other than the slip coating.

Lorraine Williams, Rose Williams' daughter-in-law, lives some distance from the other family members. Before marrying into the family, Lorraine had no pottery making background, other than having worked in a slip-cast ceramic ware plant on the Ute Reservation. Her pottery shows the characteristic smooth finish typical of work from this family, but it differs markedly from the work of other family members in its decoration. Lorraine produces a wide range of vessel shapes, treating each one like a canvas on which she incises a myriad of intricate designs, including Navajo rug patterns, figures taken from Navajo sand paintings, or floral motifs. These are then carefully painted with clay slips in many colors.

On vessels where Lorraine uses restraint in her design and selection of colors, the result is very pleasing. In other examples, however, the designs and colors become overly busy. An innovation that Lorraine has experimented with more than anyone else is the use of cut-outs, in which she cuts away portions of a vessel's wall to add an interesting effect or to accentuate an incised design. This is a technique requiring great skill to insure that the cut-out areas are not so large as to cause breakage during the firing process.

Lorraine is also an accomplished silver and goldsmith, but enjoys pottery making best. She has won major awards at the Museum of Northern Arizona's Navajo Craftsman Exhibition, the Santa Fe Indian Market, and the Gallup Intertribal Indian Ceremonial. Like her mother-in-law, she is passing on her knowledge and skills—to three of her 17 brothers and sisters.

—Russell P. Hartman

WILSON, Amanda
Variant names: Oymutee
Tribal affiliations: Concow Maidu
Basketweaver

Born: Butte County, California c. 1860s; native name means "The Sound a Quail Makes." **Family:** Married 1) Holai Lafonso, c. 1880s: two children; 2) Santa Wilson, c. 1900. **Career:** Basketweaver c. 1870 until her death, producing baskets for personal use, for local Maiduan, Pomoan, Patwin and Nomlaki peoples, and for non-Indian collectors; taught classes in basketweaving in Chico, California. **Died:** 1946 in Chico, California.

Amanda Wilson: Coiled acorn flour basket set, c. 1940. Courtesy Craig D. Bates.

Selected Group Exhibitions

Exhibition data during the artist's lifetime not available, as the artist kept no known records. Displays of her baskets after her death include numerous exhibitions throughout California by her nephew, Henry Kc'a'a'la Azbill (1896-1973). Baskets by Wilson have been exhibited without being identified as such at the Bidwell Mansion State Historic Site, Chico, California c. 1960-present. More recently exhibitions:

1991-93　*Objects of Myth and Memory*, Brooklyn Museum, New York (traveled to Oakland Museum, California; Heard Museum, Phoenix)
1995　Chico Museum, Chico, California
1996　*The Fine Art of California Basketry*, Crocker Art Museum, Sacramento, California

Collections

Bidwell State Historic Park, Chico, California; The Brooklyn Museum, New York; P.A. Hearst Museum of Anthropology, University of California, Berkeley.

Publications

On WILSON: Books—*Objects of Myth and Memory* by Diana Fane et. al, New York, 1991; *The Fine Art of California Basketry* by Brian Bibby, Sacramento, 1996. **Articles**—"Amanda Wilson: Maidu Weaver," by Craig Bates and Brian Bibby, *American Indian Art Magazine* 9(3):38-42,69, 1984; "Collecting Among the Chico Maidu: The Stewart Culin Collection at the Brooklyn Museum," by Craig D. Bates and Brian Bibby, *American Indian Art Magazine* 8(4):46-53, 1983; "Regional Variation in Coiled Maidu Basketry: Materials and Technology," by Craig D. Bates and Bruce Bernstein, *Journal of California and Great Basin Anthropology* 4(2):187-202, 1982.

*　　*　　*

Amanda Wilson was one of many traditional basket weavers of the Concow Maidu people, but her baskets are remarkable for the weaver's attention to detail, fine design sense, and the hallmark quail plume patterning she used in baskets. Wilson started weaving fine coiled baskets as a young child, using designs she would continue to employ for decades. At the time of her death, she was the last truly fine weaver among the Maiduan people of the Sacramento Valley.

Wilson preferred to use basket materials found in the Sacramento Valley, notably sedge root (for buff color), briar root (for black), and split redbud shoots (for red-brown). Wilson wove many baskets of fine presentation quality, as well as others for native use in cooking and preparing traditional foods. Many of her baskets show her distinctive arrangements of the Maidu "quail plume" pattern. It is possible that one of her Concow Maidu names, *Oymutee*, which translates "the sound a quail makes," explains, in part, her preference for this pattern. Wilson did not restrict herself to this pattern; she used other designs, including geometric forms. Wilson and her contemporaries recognized the designs by names that translate as "grapevine leaves" (a group of stacked triangles), "flicker quill headband" (a serrated-edged vertical band), "lightning" (a diagonal zigzag), "arrow" (a meandering, deeply serrated zigzag), and "ants road" (a narrow meandering horizontal band with serrated edges).

Wilson made numerous baskets for native use, both coiled and twined. She excelled in the production of twined burden baskets, cradlebaskets and seed beaters. Wilson's greatest production was in coiled baskets, however, and it was for her fine coiled baskets that she received the most recognition among both Native people and non-Indians.

Like many other Butte County weavers, Wilson often used an oval and slightly indented start in coiled baskets made for culinary purposes. She did not trim materials as meticulously as on other, finer baskets, and she would sometimes mix several distinct patterns in an asymmetric, yet intentional, fashion. Differing from those made for culinary use, the presentation baskets she made were more finely stitched (approximately twelve stitches and three coils per inch) and used very precisely arranged, symmetrical, and complex pattern combinations. Wilson's baskets closely resemble those of her contemporary Mary Azbill and, indeed, undocumented baskets by these women are often difficult, if not impossible, to differentiate.

Wilson did not limit her use of basketry patterns and forms to the traditional repertoire of designs and shapes she learned as a child. On one occasion, she wove a chalice-shaped basket for the local Presbyterian minister and used a Christian cross design. She wove another basket with a flame-like pattern for local landowner Annie K. Bidwell before 1909. That basket appears to have been inspired by Washoe basketry, particularly the work of Louisa Keyser (a.k.a., *Datsolalee*). While the flame-like patterns in Wilson's basket are not like those generally found in Maidu basketry, the basket's form and shape may have been inspired by photos of Keyser baskets on promotional brochures circulated by businessman Abe Cohen.

Wilson attempted to interest young people, both Indian and non-Indian, in weaving baskets, and she taught classes in Chico, California. It appears that none of her students went on to complete baskets or continue the fine basketmaking tradition of which Amanda Wilson was apparently the last practitioner.

—Craig Bates

WILSON, Lyle
Tribal affiliations: Kitamaat Haisla
Carver and printmaker

Born: Lyle Giles Wilson, Butedale, British Columbia, 1955. **Education:** Native Indian Teacher Education Programme, University of British Columbia 1976-79; Diploma in Printmaking, Emily Carr College of Art and Design, Vancouver, 1986; Bachelor of Education in Secondary Art Education, University of British Columbia, 1987. **Career:** Curatorial Assistant and artist in residence at the Museum of Anthropology, University of British Columbia, 1987-; sculptor and graphic artist. Commissions include: Animated Grizzly Bear transformation mask and dance costume for Expo 1992, Seville, Spain; 1992; Eagle and Beaver house-post, First Nations House of Learning, University of British Columbia, 1992; five high-relief panels, Canadian National Institute for the Blind, 1993; Eagle, Fish and Beaver totem (the three clans of Kitamaat), Canadian Consulate, Osaka, Japan, 1994; The Paddler totem, British Columbia Sports Hall of Fame, Vancouver, 1995.

Individual Exhibitions

1981   *International Works on Paper,* London Regional Art Gallery, London, Ontario
        Native American Arts '81, Philbrook Art Center, Tulsa, Oklahoma
1986   *What is Native American Art?,* Vancouver
1989   *Masks: An Exhibition of Northwest Coast Native Masks,* Inuit Gallery, Vancouver
1989   *When Worlds Collide,* UBC Museum of Anthropology (traveling)
1990   *Painted Drums of the Northwest Coast,* Inuit Gallery, Vancouver

Collections

Burnaby Art Gallery, Vancouver; Toronto Dominion Bank; Imperial Esse, Toronto; Royal British Columbia Museum, Vancouver; Museum of Anthropology, Faculty of Art Education, and First Nations House of Learning, University of British Columbia; Canada Council Art Bank, Ottawa.

Publications

By WILSON: Book—*Eulachon: A Fish to Cure Humanity,* with Allene Drake, UBC Museum of Anthropology, 1992 (also in French).

On WILSON: Books—*Visions: Contemporary Art in Canada,* Robert Bringhurst, editor, Vancouver, 1983; *Spirit Faces: Contemporary Masks of the Northwest Coast,* by Gary Wyatt, Vancouver, 1994. **Articles**—"Lyle Wilson: When Worlds Collide," by Karen Duffek, *UBC Museum of Anthropology Museum Notes,* No.28, 1989; "Northwest Coast Art: The Culture of the Land Claims," by Charlotte Townsend-Gault, *American Indian Quarterly,* Vol.18, 4, 1994.

*   *   *

Lyle Wilson. Photograph by Bill McLennan; courtesy of the artist.

Lyle Wilson is Haisla (sometimes known as Northern Kwakiutl), and works in one of the distinctive styles of the Northwest Coast that combines influences from both Kwakiutl and Tsimshian. His training as an educator and print-maker, together with his research experience at the Museum of Anthropology and encounters there with visitors from all over the world, have distinguished his cultural practice from the somewhat inward-turning tendency of many of the carvers who are maintaining the art forms of the coast. It has given Wilson a sense of the historical context of his work, a visual scholar's appreciation of the refinements of style, which, in his words, his predecessors "carried in their heads," and a sensitivity towards the complexity of what it means to be Haisla in the modern world.

When in art school at Emily Carr College of Art and Design, Wilson had encountered another tradition, that of critical modernism, and saw how he could apply it to a re-thinking of the norms of his own cultural tradition. He made a number of prints and etchings in which he experimented freely with the elements of the Haisla style. Wilson was among the first to break the mould and query tradition, as he did in *A Siren Called Tradition* (1980), showing that the style of the Northwest Coast is as valid a form of expression in the present as it had been in the past. *When Worlds Collide* (1979) took apart, literally deconstructed, the solid conglomerations of formlines, ovoids and U-forms that define the style, making the manoeuvre into a metaphor for the processes of change. *Ode to Billy Holm...Lalooska...Duane Pasco...& Jonathan Livingston Seagull* was important for disentangling a walking figure, liberated from pole, facade or robe, who could be a protagonist in the drama of disruption and alienation. Later Yuxweluptun (Lawrence Paul), also a student at Emily Carr, took Wilson's cue and developed an essentially modern alienated protagonist, at once recognizably of the Northwest Coast but detached, literally, from a cultural background.

The extent to which such experimentation can continue without losing its defining connection—not just to the forms but also the significance of the tradition—remains an open question that is hotly debated by artists, scholars and collectors. Wilson's response has been to study the tradition and take it forward. To this end he has been working with photographer Bill McLennan at the Museum of Anthropology since 1988 on the Image Recovery Project. This ongoing project uses infra-red photography to analyze historical Northwest Coast two-dimensional designs as found on the sides of cedar boxes and on house fronts. By literally clarifying painting that had become obscured by the patina of time and use, the process has revealed the individuality of the artists and a much greater degree of freedom than had previously been appreciated. It has shaken the prevailing view of the style as restricting and rule-bound. Wilson has made copies on both wood and paper that demonstrate the inventiveness of the originals. In doing so he maintains the tradition of learning by imitating while showing his respect for his predecessors ability to work without notations on paper or linear planning.

In 1992 Wilson carved a 12 foot house post of red cedar inlaid with yellow cedar, which with different figures, formally separated on both sides, showed the innovations possible within the genre. In 1995 he made it a personal project to carve a replica of a six foot house post (originally from Kitamaat, now in the collection of the Museum) and to do so through a process of hand-to-eye coordination. It clarifies how fully the masters of the past had internalized proportion, scale and relationships of part to whole and that the apprentice still has much to learn from the process of imitation and the mysterious connection between hand and brain. Wilson has replicated the old painting style as he has come to understand it more fully and is doing his part to transmit his learning to others.

Wilson made this pole to "give back" to the community school in Kitamaat. In explaining that it is "part of an age old tradition to give something back," he is making clear that there is an important part of him that "is Haisla." But as he also explains "there's probably no pure Haisla left, and what was it anyway? There are so many influences in me I can hardly claim to be a real Haisla."

And yet there are many instances of this "giving back." Wilson's work takes many forms and is made for many audiences. His work as co-curator of the exhibition, *Eulachon—A Fish to Cure Humanity* (1992), for the Museum, is consonant with his belief that culture consists of many shifting changing strands, some older, some newer, which cannot be easily disentangled.

—Charlotte Townsend-Gault

WOOD, Margaret

Tribal affiliations: Navajo; Seminole
Textile artist

Born: Parker, Arizona, 23 January 1950. **Family:** Married, two sons. **Education:** Arizona State University, Tempe, B.A., Elementary Education, 1971; University of Denver, Colorado, M.A. in Library Science, 1973. **Career:** Teacher, Window Rock School District, 1971-72; Director of Library Services, Navajo Community College, 1973-74; Librarian, Phoenix, Arizona, 1975-78; Intern/Lecturer, Heard Museum, Phoenix, Arizona, and Waverly Fabric Corporation, New York, 1986; Volunteer Executive Director for Atlatl (service organization for Native American arts), 1990-92; Education Consultant, Creighton Elementary School District, 1991-92; operates own business Native American Fashions, Inc. **Awards:** Heard Museum Guild Indian Fair Market, Heard Museum, Phoenix, 1977, Honorable Mention (Quilting Division), and 1993, Best of Division-Quilting.

Individual Exhibitions

1993   *Wall Hangings and Quilts by Margaret Wood*, Wheelwright Museum of the American Indian, Santa Fe, New Mexico
1995   *Margaret Wood: New Works: Art Quilts*, MARS Artspace, Phoenix, Arizona

Selected Group Exhibitions

1992   *Expanded Visions: Contemporary Native American Crafts*, California Craft Museum, San Francisco, California
1993   *Our Elder's Voices*, Mesa Southwest Museum, Mesa, Arizona
        Year of the American Craft Show, Joanne Rapp Gallery/ The Hand and the Spirit, Scottsdale, Arizona
        Maintaining Cultural Roots: Personal Expressions by Women, Tempe Arts Center, Tempe, Arizona
        Alter-Native: Offerings to Our Heritage, MARS Artspace, Scottsdale, Arizona
        MARS at Dinnerware/Dinnerware at MARS, Dinnerware Artists' Cooperative Gallery, Tucson, Arizona
1994   *Southwest Quilts*, Tohono Chul Park, Tucson, Arizona
        MARS Artspace at 1708 Gallery, 1708 Gallery, Richmond, Virginia
        Native America: Reflecting Contemporary Realities, The Museum at Warm Springs, Warm Springs, Oregon
1995   *Native America: Reflecting Contemporary Realities*, Hunter Museum of Art, Chattanooga, Tennessee
1996   *Singing our Songs: Women, Art, Healing*, American Indian Community House Gallery/Museum, New York, New York

Collections

Wheelwright Museum of the American Indian, Santa Fe, New Mexico

Publications

By WOOD: Book—*Native American Fashions: Adaptations of Traditional Designs*, New York, 1981. **Article**—"Sewing it Together: Native American and Hawaiian Quilting Traditions, *Akwe:kon Journal*, Fall/Winter 1994.

On WOOD: Books—*Quilts, A Living Tradition*, by Robert Shaw, New York, 1995. **Articles**—"Alter-Native: Offerings to Our Heritage," *PHX Downtown*, February 1993; "Margaret Wood's quilts, soft sculptures open new show," *The Santa Fe New Mexican's Weekly Arts & Entertainment Magazine*, 2 July 1993; "In Profile: Margaret Wood, *Native Peoples Magazine*, Vol. 9, no. 2, 1996.

*

Margaret Wood comments:

My work in quilts and clothing is based upon centuries of Native American fiber and arts tradition. In accordance with a long history of embracing new materials and decorative ideas, I consider my work a continuation of the evolution of Native American fashion and decorative work.

*   *   *

The quilt is perhaps one of the most personal, and least prominent, art forms in North America. Functionally, they are designed to keep us warm, and safe, while we are at our most vulnerable—while we are asleep. Margaret Wood looks to her own and other native cultures to find symbols, icons, and subtle cultural images for her soft sculptures and wall hung quilts. Based on the traditional technique of quilting, most of Wood's pieces present Native historical themes and images in a progressive and contemporary manner.

Preferring to work in series of a minimum of four pieces, symbolically representing the sacred four directions, Wood connects and presents her pieces in innovative ways. Her *Bag Series* draws from common containers used to carry everyday items and personal treasures, particularly by the more nomadic of the North American tribes. In this series, she uses subjects connected by function, such as pipe, saddle and tobacco bags. The sources of these containers come from an array of tribes as diverse as the Sioux, Crow, Cheyenne, and Apache Nations. Each piece is an actual bag with an opening at the top, but these wall hangings are as big as nine feet high by three feet wide. Intricate and simple patterns, derived from original motifs and designs show Wood's innate skills for using line and color.

Another group, the *Parfleche Series*, is based on rawhide storage bags painted with precise and strict geometric designs that were used frequently by the Plains Indians. In her *Spirit Series*, Wood uses Southwest Native American symbols, each of which is significant to her personally.

One of her most interesting wall hanging groups is the *Mosaic Series*. Wood created this as a tribute to revolutionary Hopi jeweler Charles Loloma, who expanded on traditionally accepted Indian Style of jewelry making. The series was based on four pieces of Loloma's work—a necklace, bracelet, earring, and ring, which Wood transformed into large, elaborate soft sculptures.

Wood nearly always begins with a piece she has either obtained or seen in a museum collection. One of her intentions is to get people to think about the original piece that inspired her quilt. She wants people to take a fresh and different approach to considering the talent, skill, and effort that was needed to create the original piece, and as a result, gain a sense of the nature and life of that person.

In 1991, after formally shifting her working emphasis from clothing design to wall hangings and quilts, she began creating pieces inspired by the quilts her mother made (which could all be hung) when Wood was a child. The work is slow and labor intensive. Though each piece is carefully planned, they rarely turn out as she intended. While the original concept of quilts as art is rooted in the home and on the bed, Wood is a leader in a movement that has firmly placed the modern quilt on the walls of galleries and museums around the world.

—Vesta Giles

WOODY, Elizabeth

Tribal affiliations: Warm Springs Yakima; Wasco; Navajo
Photographer and mixed media artist

Born: Ganado, Arizona, 26 December 1959. **Education:** Institute of American Indian Arts, A.A., 1983; Evergreen State College, B.A. 1991; also studied at Portland State University. **Career:** Studio Manager, Lillian Pitt Masks, Portland, Oregon, 1985-94; professor of creative writing, Institute of American Indian Arts, 1994-96; program assistant, Ecotrust, Portland, Oregon, 1996-. **Awards:** Brandywine Visiting Artists Fellowship, 1988; American Book Award, Before Columbus Foundation, 1990; Medicine Pathways for the Future Fellowship/Kellogg Fellowship, American Indian Ambassadors Program, 1993;

William Stafford Memorial Poetry Award, 1995.
Selected Group Exhibitions

1986	*Governor's Oregon American Indian Art Show*, State Capitol Building, Salem, Oregon
1988	*Native American Artists*, Greystone Gallery, Portland, Oregon
	Coyote Show, Frame Design Gallery, Bend, Oregon
	Contemporary Native American Art, Howard University, Washington, D.C.
1989	*Native Proof: Contemporary Native American Prints*, American Indian Community House Gallery, New York, and American Indian Contemporary Arts, San Francisco
1990	*Spirit and Ancestor: Contemporary Native American Art*, Maryhill Museum, Maryhill, Washington
1992	*For the Seventh Generation: Native American Artists Counter the Quincentenary*, Golden Artist Colors Gallery, Columbus, New York
	Decolonizing the Mind: End of a 500 Year Era, Center for the Contemporary Arts, Seattle, Washington
	By Our Hand: An Exhibition of Poetry by Native Americans, Hopkins Hall Gallery, Ohio State University, Columbus
	Oregon Folklife Master-Apprenticeship Exhibition, Oregon Governor's Office, Salem

Elizabeth Woody. Photograph by Joe Cantrell; courtesy of the artist.

Earth Fire Water: Native American Artists with Naoaki
    Sakamoto, Clatsop Community College Gallery,
    Astoria, Oregon
The Submuloc Show/Columbus Wohs, Atlatl, Phoenix
1993   Toi Te Ao-Aotearou, World Celebration of Indigenous Art
    and History, Te Taumata Gallery, Auckland, New Zealand
    Lillian Pitt and E. A. Woody, Washington State Univer-
    sity, Pullman
    North American Indian Contemporary Containers, Or-
    egon School of Arts and Crafts, Portland
    Spirits Keep Whistling Us Home: Contemporary Plateau
    Women's Art, Sacred Circle Gallery, Seattle, Washington
1994   Institute of American Indian Arts Biennial Faculty Exhibition,
    Institute of American Indian Arts Museum, Santa Fe
    Archives, Tula Foundation Gallery, Atlanta, Georgia (com-
    missioned installation, collaboration with Joe Feddersen)
    Reflex Portfolio: Seven Native American Artists, produced
    with the Elizabeth Tapper Printmaking Studio
1995   Volume I: Book Arts by Native American Artists, Ameri-
    can Indian Community House, New York

Publications

By WOODY: Books—Hand into Stone, New York: Contact II Press,
1988; Luminaries of the Humble, University of Arizona Press, 1994;
Seven Hands, Seven Hearts, Portland: Eighth Mountain Press, 1994.
Anthologies—Dancing on the Rim of the World, edited by Andrea
Lerner, introduction by Elizabeth Woody and Gloria Bird, University
of Arizona Press, 1990; "By Our Hand, Through the Memory, the
House Is More Than Form," in A Circle of Nations: Voices and Visions
of American Indians, edited by John Gattuso, Hillsboro, Oregon: Be-
yond Words Publishers, 1993; "The Girlfriends," in Re-inventing the
Enemy's Language, edited by Joy Harjo and Gloria Bird, New York:
W. W. Norton, New York, 1997; Between Species: Women and Ani-
mals, edited by Brenda Peterson, Deena Metzger, and Linda Hogan,
New York: Ballantine Books; Everything Matters, edited by Brian
Swann and Arnold Krupat, New York: Random House; Speaking for
the Generations: Native Essays for the Land and the People, edited by
Simon Ortiz, University of Arizona Press, 1997. **Stories**—
"HomeCooking," in Talking Leaves, edited by Craig Lesley, New York:
Laurel Books, 1991. **Essays**—"Skins 4/4: An Analysis of Color" (with
Joe Feddersen) in For the Seventh Generation: Native American Artists
Counter the Quincentenary, Columbus, New York, Columbus, New
York: Golden Artist Colors Gallery, 1992; "Histories Are Open to
Interpretation" (with Joe Feddersen) in The Submuloc Show/Colum-
bus Wohs, Phoenix: Atlatl, 1992; "Personal Connection of the Irrevo-
cable in Memory" in The Spirit of Native America, San Francisco:
American Indian Contemporary Arts, 1993.

On WOODY: Books—"Autobiography," We, the Human Beings,
College of Wooster Art Museum, 1992; 20th Century Native American Art: Essays on History and Criticism, edited by Jackson Rushing, London: Routledge, 1997. **Articles**—"Elizabeth Woody," The
Canadian Journal of Native Studies 15, no. 1, 1995.

Collections

Brandywine Workshop, Philadelphia; Cheney Cowles Museum,
Cheney, Washington; Portland Art Museum, Portland, Oregon.

*

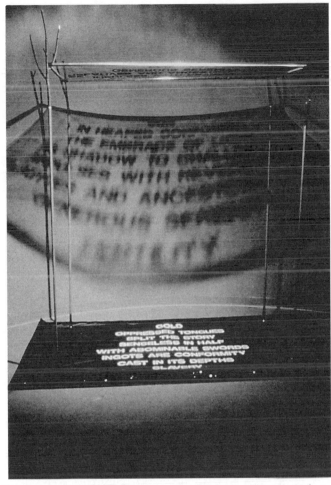

Elizabeth Woody: *Histories Are Open to Interpretation*,
collaborative piece with Joe Fedderson, 1992. Photograph by
Joe Cantrell; courtesy of the artist.

Elizabeth Woody comments:

   I don't know if I actually step into the political mode when I
write poetry. It's just that those are the terms of the language I have
to use for other people to understand what I have witnessed, because that's the common language, the political language. The English language, I think, is very limited in that way, whereas Native
language speakers have said to me that things are much more understandable and that associations and answers are easier to find in the
language because it's much more inclusive and collaborative.

*   *   *

   Elizabeth Woody's imagery comes in large measure from personal and family stories, from the petroglyphs in the Columbia
River Gorge, notably Tsagaglallal (She-Who-Watches), and from
the environment and history of the Columbia River Plateau region,
especially Celilo Falls, a central image in much of her poetry and
visual art. She works in numerous media, including photography,
paper, pastels, clay, beads, handweaving, leather, and cloth, and
often utilizes found and discarded materials from both natural and
man-made sources. She has collaborated on four projects with another Pacific Northwest artist, Joe Feddersen (Colville Confeder-

ated Tribes). These collaborations become interplays between two individual aesthetics and offer each artist new approaches to familiar materials.

Woody's first book of poems, *Hand into Stone*, explored the history and oral narratives of her people and her family. In "She-Who-Watches . . . The Names Are Prayer," Woody traces the destruction of Celilo Falls in 1956 to the pain and loss endured by the people who relied on the Columbia River for a way of life. "Hand into Stone" reflects on the poet's relationship with her grandmother and the continuity of generations.

These themes are continued in *Luminaries of the Humble*. In "Waterways Endeavor to Translate Silence from Currents," the poet again writes of the loss of Celilo Falls, the changes to the Columbia River, and the attendant loss of the sustenance provided there, not only through fishing for salmon but also in the relationships which were maintained through time and ritual. Only beneath the surface of the water and in the bones excavated by anthropologists do the songs of the ancestors remain. "Straight and Clear" is a prose poem that details the removal of bones from Memaloose Island, a traditional burial site in the Columbia River. Woody contrasts the destructive needs of contemporary non-Indian society with the lives of those connected to the earth and whose ancestors' bones have been desecrated.

Woody's collaborations with Joe Feddersen often extend the concerns found in her poems. *Inheritance Obscured by Neglect: Waterways Endeavor to Translate Silence from Currents* was a collaborative broadside done for *Reflex Magazine*. *Inheritance Obscured by Neglect*, a title of a piece of Feddersen's, became the departure point for this collaboration. There are three bands, or levels of photographs: the bottom photo, a historical document, shows a pile of skulls, the middle photo is of rounded rocks, and the top one is of water (Feddersen took the other two photos). The text of the poem is superimposed over the photographs. The images refer to the destruction of Memaloose Island and the removal of the bones from the burial site to the Smithsonian.

"Translation of Blood Quantum," from *Luminaries of the Humble*, is an expression of self-determination and tribal sovereignty. She writes of the inherent freedom and reciprocal relationships with nature that exist above and beyond any governmental intervention or control. The focus on blood quantum as the signifier of tribal or Indian identity reduces the totality of the individual into one component. This issue is also explored in "Skins 4/4: An Analysis of Color," one of her collaborations with Feddersen. Consisting of four photographs by Woody of hands partially covered by Mylar sheets, and playing off Josef Albers' *Homage to the Square*, the piece suggests that governmental efforts to enforce blood quantum classifications (especially through Public Law 101-644 for the identification of artists) is actually an attempt to ignore treaty obligations and to undermine the sovereignty of Indian nations. The use of the translucent Mylar partially obscures personal history, as represented in the hands. An excerpt of "Translation of Blood Quantum" was also used in their most recent collaboration, *Archives: Response to Static Form for Imparting Story/History*, done for the TULA Foundation (Atlanta, Georgia) in 1994.

In her writing and art Elizabeth Woody may deal with so-called political issues, but at base her work derives from a spiritual sense of the world. For Woody, the destruction of Celilo Falls, for example, and the desecration of Memaloose Island affect the spirit of a people. Her work describes the contours of this spirit.

—Larry Abbott

YOUNG MAN, Alfred

Variant names: Eagle Chief
Tribal affiliations: Plains Cree
Painter

Born: Browning, Montana, 12 April 1948; registered member of the Chippewa/Cree, Rocky Boy Reservation, Montana. **Education:** Institute of American Indian Arts, 1963-66, High School Diploma, 1966-68, Post-Graduate Diploma; The Slade School of Fine Arts, University College, London, England, BFA, 1968-72; University of Montana, MA, 1972-73; Northern Montana College, 1974-75, Teacher's Certificate; television specialist training, Total Community Education, Flathead Valley Community College, 1977-85; Rutgers University, Ph.D. studies, 1989. **Career:** Art Teacher, Rocky Boy Elementary School District #87, 1973-74; Remedial Reading and Art Instructor, 1975; Media Specialist and Instructor in Educational Television, Flathead Valley Community College, 1976-77; Native American Studies Department, University of Lethbridge, Assistant Professor, 1977-1992, Associate Professor, 1992-present; Canada Faculty Exchange Program, Department of Art, University of Lethbridge/Leeds University, 1985, University of Lethbridge/Hokkai Gakuen University, Sapporo, Hokkaido, Japan, 1992; manuscript/book reviewer for *American Indian Culture and Research Journal, American Indian Quarterly*, and *Prairie Forum: The Journal of the Canadian Research Center*.

Individual Exhibitions

1972   Long Gallery, University College London, London, England
1973   Museum of the Plains Indian, Browning, Montana
       University of Montana, Missoula

Selected Group Exhibitions

1965-68 Institute of American Indian Arts, Santa Fe, New Mexico
1972   *Richard Roney-Dougal and Alfred Young Man*, Long Gallery, University College, London, England
       Contemporary Indian Artists of Montana/Wyoming/Idaho, Museum of the Plains Indian, Browning, Montana
1974   Ellensburg Annual Northwest Coast Indian Art Exhibition, Ellensburg, Washington
1975   *Institute of American Indian Arts Alumni Exhibition*, Amon Carter Museum, Fort Worth, Texas
1975   *Three-Man Exhibition* (with Kevin Red Star and Neil Parsons), D. Q., University of California, Davis
1978   *One With the Earth*, Southern Alberta Art Gallery, Lethbridge (traveling)
1979   *Pintura Amerindia Contemporanea* (traveling, South America)

1980   *Three-Man Exhibition* (with George Longfish and Linda Lomahaftewa), University of Lethbridge Art Gallery, Lethbridge, Alberta
1981-82 *Confluences of Tradition and Change*, (traveling) Richard L. Nelson Gallery and C.N. Gorman Museum, University of California, Davis; Museum of the Southwest, Midland, Texas, Gallery of the American Indian Community House, New York; Brunnier Gallery, Iowa State University
1982   *Challenge of Spilyay*, Yakima Cultural Center, Yakima, Washington
       New Works by a New Generation, Regina, Saskatchewan
1984   *No Beads, No Trinkets*, American Indian Art Exchange, Seattle, Washington and Palais de nations, United Nations, Geneva, Switzerland
1986   Beall Park Art Center, Montana State University, Bozeman, Montana
       In the Spirit of the Lubicons, Wallace Gallery, Calgary, Alberta
1990   *Radicals and Renegades: American Indian Protest Art*, Institute of American Indian Arts, Santa Fe, New Mexico
1992   *Creativity Is Our Tradition*, Institute of American Indian Arts Museum, Santa Fe, New Mexico

Collections

American Indian Studies Department, University of California, Long Beach; Department of Indian and Northern Development, Ottawa, Ontario; Indian Association of Alberta, Edmonton; Indian Studies Department, Montana State University, Bozeman, Montana; Institute of American Indian Arts Museum, Santa Fe; Peigan Band Administration, Brocket, Alberta; Rocky Boy Elementary School, Rocky Boy, Montana; Universiade Collection of Native Art, Edmonton, Alberta; University of Lethbridge, Lethbridge, Alberta.

Publications

By YOUNG MAN: Books—*Networking: National Native Indian Artists Symposium IV* (editor), Lethbridge, Alberta, 1988; *A Dominican Experience: Three Aboriginal Artists of Canada in the Dominican Republic* (editor), Om niiak Native Arts Group, Ottawa, 1989; *Visions of Power*, exhibition catalog co-authored with Bryce Kanbara and Ingo Hessel, Toronto, York Quay Gallery/Leo Kamen Gallery, 1991; *Indigena: Contemporary Native Perspectives*, with McMaster, Martin, Crammer-Webster, Sioui Wendayete, Todd, and Keeshig-Tobias. Ottawa, 1992. **Articles**—"Token and Taboo: Academia vs Native Art," *Fuse Magazine*, vol. 11, no. 6, Toronto, July 1988; "Issues and Trends in Contemporary Native Art," *Parallelogramme Magazine*, vol. 13, no. 3, Toronto, February/March 1988; "The Savage Civilian: The Work of Rebecca

Belmore," (abridged) *Between Views*, exhibition catalog; Banff, Alberta: Walter Phillips Gallery, June-September 1991; "The Metaphysics of North American Indian Art," *Canadian Music: Issues of Hegemony and Identity*, Beverly Diamond and Robert Witmer (eds.) Toronto: Canadian Scholars' Press Inc., 1994; "An Historical Overview and Perception of Native Art, Culture, and The Role of the Native Curator: Non-fiction Story," (abridged) *New Territories 350/ 500 Years After*, Montreal: Vision Planetaire, June 1992; "Teaching North American Indian Art in Native American Studies," *Gakuen Ronshu: The Journal of Hokkai-Gakuen University*, no. 73, Sapporo-shi, Hokkaido, Japan, September 1992; "The co-Existence of non-Contemporary Realities," *Remote Control*, vol. 3, no. 2, Thunder Bay, Ontario: Definitely Superior Art Gallery, 1993; "Challenge to the Status Quo," *Talking Stick: First Nations Arts Magazine*, vol. 1, no. 2, Winter 1994. "To: John Bentley Mays/ From: Alfred Young Man," *Talking Stick: First Nations Arts Magazine*, vol. 1, no. 2, Summer 1994; "First Nations Art, 'Canada', and the CIA: A Short Non-fiction Story," *Studies In Critical Practices*, 1994.

On YOUNG MAN: Books—*Indian Painters and White Patrons*, by J. J. Brody, University of New Mexico Press, Albuquerque,

Alfred Young Man. Courtesy of the artist.

New Mexico, 1971; *Contemporary Indian Artists of Montana/Wyoming/Idaho*, exhibition catalog; Museum of the Plains Indian and Crafts Center, Browning, Montana, 1972; *The Institute of American Indian Arts Alumni Exhibition*, exhibition catalog, Santa Fe, New Mexico, 1973; *Song From the Earth*, by Jamake Highwater, Boston, 1976; *Chippewa and Cree: a bibliography of books, newspapers, articles, government documents and other printed and written matter in various libraries of the United States and Canada*, Rocky Boy, Montana, 1976; *Pintura Amerindia Contemporanea/ E.U.A.*, exhibition catalog, Santiago, Chile (Spanish only), 1979; *The Sweetgrass Lives On: 50 contemporary North American Indian Artists*, by Jamake Highwater, New York, 1980; *Confluences of Tradition and Change*, exhibition catalog; D.Q. University, University of California, Davis, 1981; *Pathways to Self-Determination: Canadian Indians and the Canadian State*, by Leroy Little Bear, Menno Boldt, and J. Anthony Long (eds.), University of Toronto Press, 1984; *Radicals and Renegades: American Indian Protest Art*, exhibition catalog, Institute of American Indian Arts Museum, Santa Fe, 1990; *Creativity Is Our Tradition: Three Decades of Contemporary Art at the Institute of American Indian Arts*, Santa Fe, 1992; *Land Spirit Power: First Nations at the National Gallery of Canada* by Diana Nemiroff, Robert Houle, Charlotte Townsend-Gault, Ottawa, 1992; *Creativity Is Our Tradition: Three Decades of Contemporary Indian Art at the Institute of American Indian Arts*, Rick Hill, editor, Santa Fe, Institute of American Indian Art, 1992; "More Totems and Taboos: Cultivating Alternative Approaches to First Nations Arts and Artists," by M. L. Vanessa Vogel, *Mandate Study 1990-93: An Investigation of Issues Surrounding the Exhibition, Collection and Interpretation of Contemporary Art by First Nations Artists*. Thunder Bay, Ontario, 1993; "The Fourth World and Fourth World Art," by Nelson H. H. Grabum, *In the Shadow of the Sun: Perspectives on Contemporary Native Art*, Canadian Museum of Civilization, Canadian Ethnology Service, Ottawa, 1993. **Articles**—"Face to Face: The Herald's Joanne Helmer Chats with Alfred Young Man on Nicaragua," *The Lethbridge Herald*, October 27 & 29, 1984; "Indian Artists Shrug Off Stereotypes To Express Defiant Spirits," The Arts Section. *The Albuquerque Journal*, 4 November 1990; "Contemporary Native Art: A Bibliography" by Larry Abbott, *The American Indian Quarterly*, vol. 18, no. 3, Summer 1994; "Ideology & Native American Nationalism: A Case Study," by John Anson Warner, *Journal of Inquiry and Research*, No. 59, January, 1994; "New Visions in Canadian Plains Painting," by John Anson Warner, *American Indian Art Magazine*, Spring 1995. **Film**—"Nicaragua: interview with Alfred Young Man," *The Bland Approach*, Terry Bland, CATV-12, Cablenet, Lethbridge (30 min.), 1984; *The Primal Mind*, PBS-TV, with Jamake Highwater, 1986; *North American Indian Art*, CATV-12 Cablenet, Lethbridge, Alberta, (interviewed, 60 min.), 1987; *Between Two Worlds*, CFRN-TV, Edmonton (interviewed, 60 min.), 1987; *Against the Grain*, CFAC-TV, Lethbridge (interviewed - 30 min.), 1988; *Ottawa: Inside Out* with Denise Rudniki, CBC-TV, (interviewed, 20 min.), 1994.

*

Alfred Young Man comments:
I'm an Indian artist and I do Indian art. Now, tell me that Indian art doesn't exist!

*   *   *

Alfred Young Man: *Astounding Stories,* **1978. Collection of the Center for Native American Studies, Montana State University; courtesy of the artist.**

Alfred Young Man, a Plains Cree Indian artist and an important thinker on subjects pertaining to Native American affairs, was one of the original students at the Institute of American Indian Arts (IAIA) in Santa Fe, New Mexico. His celebrity as a painter has always been associated with the critically oriented modernist works that he produced during and after his matriculation at IAIA (1963-1968). Young Man was an active painter until the late 1970s, when his productivity dropped off. Since 1977 he has been on the faculty of the University of Lethbridge in Lethbridge, Alberta, Canada, teaching Native American Studies. In the 1980s and 1990s he has become known more as a teacher/writer/scholar than as a painter. Whether or not he will resume the artistic productivity of his earlier years is unknown. In any case, he enjoys a current reputation for trenchant and critical studies of Native American arts, history, culture, and Indian-white relations. He is controversial and sometimes confrontational in his intellectual style.

Young Man was raised by his Cree family in the East Glacier township of northern Montana (near Glacier National Park) and had many searing and traumatic experiences at a B.I.A. boarding school in Cut Bank, Montana. His most fruitful educational experience came when he was one of the initial students admitted to art studies at IAIA. He says that he was always interested in art and that the curriculum at IAIA "naturally" appealed to him. He recollects that he was most influenced not by the faculty but by such fellow students as Kevin Red Star (Crow), T. C. Cannon (Caddo/Kiowa/Choctaw), Earl Eder (Yanktonai Sioux), and David Montana (Tohono O'odham, Papago). Together, they shared experiences, ideas, and recreational activities. Young Man views his paintings as realist in nature, but, quite clearly, his style shows traces of many modernist and post-modernist art movements (including abstract expressionism).

Young Man remained at IAIA for several years: he pursued his high school diploma there (1963-1966) and earned a post-graduate diploma as well (1966-1968). The ethos of this era at IAIA nurtured a type of art that purported to be socially relevant in its portrayal of Indian alienation from the bourgeois values of a materialistic and capitalistic white society. There is no question that Young Man had been well prepared by his experiences as a youth for this kind of artistic protest. Certainly in the 1960s Young Man produced some of his most important canvases: *I'd Love My Mother Even if She Was Black, Brown or White* (1968), *Three Creeks, a Ute and a Negro* (1968), *Family of Mine* (1967), *Portrait of My Family* (1967), and *Six White Men and One Indian* (1969). Rick Hill expresses this opinion about Young Man's years at IAIA: "Alfred Young Man produced some of his most powerful paintings as a student at IAIA. The work challenged people's thinking about Indians and race relations in general. Further, it calls into question the disparity between Indian images of the past and Young Man's portrayal of Indian life now." In a sense, Young Man never surpassed his work at IAIA although he did continue to be relatively productive right into the late 1970s: *The Vacation* (1977), *Collage* (1972), and *Peyote Vision* (1974) are among his most important works.

As an academic in a Native Studies Department at Lethbridge, Young Man has embraced a version of what I call 'Indian Nationalist' ideology (I know that he reproaches me for the use of this label but I cannot help it since I believe that the evidence can speak for itself). Indian Nationalist ideology most commonly incorporates four principles: (1) A definition of Indians as victims with an explication of that fundamental status in society; (2) Tribute paid to the "superior" values of traditional Native cultures; (3) Condemnation offered against white society, which is indicted for its consumerism, materialism, exploitation, militarism, and indifference to environmental concerns (i.e., harmony with nature and a love of mother earth); and (4) A claim that Indians must improve themselves in a separate condition from white society, where they can enjoy some degree of sovereignty and autonomy.

In regard to this ideological stance, I do not think it is difficult at all to situate Young Man within it. In his words, "From personal experience he [Young Man] knew there was virtually nothing more irritating and ultimately frustrating than to be told that you do not exist. He had been told all his life by educators, anthropologists, historians, politicians and Hollywood dreamers that his identity was not his own. It was rather, 'given' to him gratis Indian Affairs, anthropology, television, the movies, and the Christian clergy thing. Some Indian names like Calf Robe, Bruised Head, Big Head, Wolf Tail, Cat Face, and a hundred others were in reality piss-poor English translations of the real item. He was told that he lived in two worlds. He and his kind were said to live with a split psyche. What a dilemma! What crap! (from *First Nations Art, "Canada", and the CIA: A Short Non-Fiction Story*, 1994).

I have also suggested before (1985) that Young Man sees his art as wedded to a nationalist ideology. In the following passage by Young Man, I believe that this point, too, is clearly articulated: "Contemporary artists of Native ancestry in 'Canada' such as Joan Cardinal-Schubert, Ron Noganosh, Mike MacDonald, Carl Beam, Bob Boyer, and Edward Poitras produce art works which are rife with political and social commentary relative to such political phenomenon. Such philosophies have long been the basis upon which my own art work is produced.

In recent years Young Man has been busy with teaching, academic work, writing, and curating Indian art exhibitions. While he does not appear anymore to be very active as a painter, he nevertheless seems to have found a vocation in the world of ideas.

—John Anson Warner

YUXWELUPTUN

Variant names: Lawrence Paul
Tribal affiliations: Coast Salish; Okanagan
Carver, painter, mixed media artist, and installation artist

Born: Kamloops, British Columbia, 1957. **Education:** Graduated with honors from Emily Carr College of Art and Design, Vancouver, British Columbia, 1983.

Individual Exhibitions

1985-86	*Lawrence Paul*, The Bent Box Gallery, Vancouver
1986	*Art Off Main*, Downtown East Side Festival, Vancouver
1987	*Yuxweluptun*, National Native Indian Artists Symposium, Sir Alexander Galt Gallery, Lethbridge, Alberta
1995	*Man of Masks*, Gallery of Tribal Art, Vancouver
	Yuxweluptun: Born to Live and Die on Your Colonialist Reservations, Morris and Helen Belkin Art Gallery, University of British Columbia, Vancouver

Selected Group Exhibitions

1984	Warehouse Show, Vancouver
1985	Second Annual Juried Art Exhibition, Robson Square Media Centre, Vancouver
1986	*What Is Native American Art?*, Philbrook Art Centre, Tulsa
1987	*The Third Biennial of Native American Fine Arts*, Heard Museum, Phoenix
1988	*Spirits for the Lubicon*, Wallace Gallery, Calgary
	In the Shadow of the Sun, Canadian Museum of Civilisation, Hull, Quebec (traveling)
1989	*Native Artists from the Northwest Coast*, Volkerkundemuseum der Universitat Zurich
	Native American Expressions of Surrealism, Sacred Circle Gallery, Seattle
	Documents Northwest: The Poncho Series, Crossed Cultures, Seattle Art Museum
1991	*Lost Illusions: Recent Landscape Art*, Vancouver Art Gallery
1992	*Indigena: Contemporary Native Perspectives*, Canadian Museum of Civilization, Hull, Quebec (traveling)
	Land, Spirit, Power: First Nations at the National Gallery of Canada, Ottawa (traveling)
	New Territories: 350/500 Years After, Atelier Vision Planetaire, Montreal
1993	*Inherent Rights, Vision Rights*, Canadian Embassy, Paris
	Northwest Native American and First Nations Peoples' Art, Western Art Gallery, University of Washington, Seattle
	Legacy of Survival: The Arts of the Shuswap (Secwepemc) and Contemporary Canadian Native Art, Kamloops Art Gallery, Kamloops, British Columbia
1994	*Toponimias*, Fundacion la Caixa de Madrid, Madrid
	Art and Virtual Environments, Walter Phillips Gallery, Banff Centre for the Arts, Banff, Alberta
1996-97	*Emily Carr and Yuxweluptun*, Vancouver Art Gallery

Publications

By YUXWELUPTUN: Articles—"Lawrence Paul," in *Indigena: Contemporary Native Perspectives*, Hull, Quebec, 1992; "Lawrence

Paul Yuxweluptun," in *Land, Spirit, Power: First Nations at the National Gallery of Canada* (Ottawa), 1992.

On YUXWELUPTUN: Books—"Lawrence Paul," by Peter Gerber and Vanina Katz-Lahaigue, *Native Artists from the Northwest Coast*, Zurich: Switzerland, 1989; "Painting and the Social History of British Columbia," by Robert Linsley, *Vancouver Anthology*, Stan Douglas, editor, Vancouver: British Columbia, 1991. **Articles**—"Having Voices and Using Them: First Nations Artists and Native 'Art,'" by Charlotte Townsend-Gault, *Artsmagazine* LXV:6 (New York), 1991; "Postmodern Parody: a Political Strategy in Contemporary Canadian Native Art," by Allan J. Ryan, *Art Journal* 51 (New York), 1992; "Impurity and Danger," by Charlotte Townsend-Gault, *Current Anthropology* 34:1 (Chicago) 1993; "Translation or Perversion? Showing First Nations Art in Canada," by Charlotte Townsend-Gault, *Cultural Studies* 9:1 (London) 1995; "The Cul-

ture of the Land Claims," by Charlotte Townsend-Gault, *American Indian Quarterly* 18:4 (Nebraska) 1994.

*

Yuxweluptun comments (1992):

"I am concerned with the colonial mentality that is directly responsible for the toxicological disaster ... The European ethos—your utilitarian, imperious, imperialistic power and your capitalistic value of authoritarianism (has) destroyed First Nations' ancestral sacred lands in fewer than five hundred years." (From *Indigena: Contemporary Native Perspectives*)

*   *   *

Yuxweluptun, who regards the name 'Lawrence Paul' as his "white man's alias," has gone further than any other artist from the

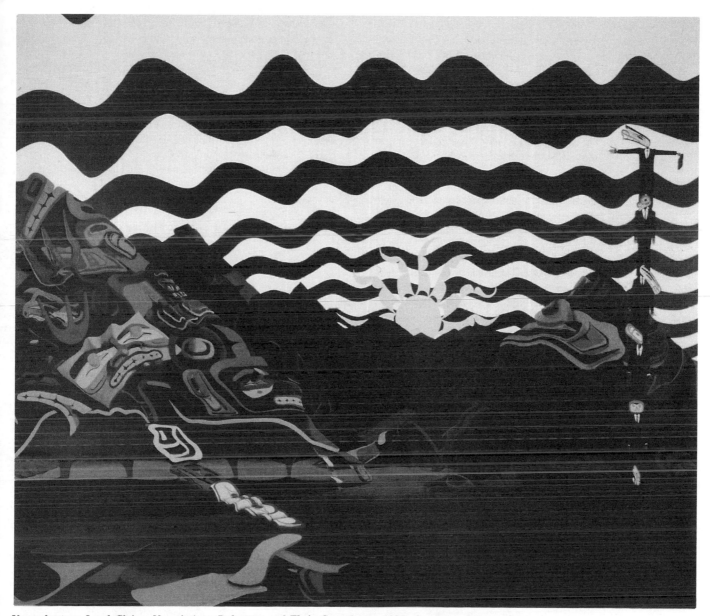

Yuxweluptun: *Land Claims Negotiations Delegates and Their Consultants*, 1995. Courtesy of the artist.

Northwest Coast in finding ways to adapt his inherited visual modes to the exigencies of contemporary art. Although there are precedents in the early work of Lyle Wilson and Ki-ke-in (Ron Hamilton) for liberating a masked, two-dimensional, human figure from dependence on the carved milieu of pole, settee or spindle whorl, Yuxweluptun has developed his own hybrid vocabulary in the years since leaving art college. In his increasingly large canvases, with titles such as *Severing Aboriginal Birth Rights and Extinguishment Policy* (1986), *Red Man Watching White Man Trying to Fix Hole in Sky* (1990) and *Scorched Earth, Clear-Cut Logging on Native Sovereign Lands, Shaman Coming to Fix* (1991), he shows how the idioms and cosmology of his Coast Salish culture can be a serious and inevitable vehicle for topical thought and social inquiry, and at the same time make an excoriating critique of systemic racism.

The reason often advanced for the persistence of the cultures of the Northwest Coast, and the strength of their traditions, is that it was the last part of what was to become Canada to be systematically colonized. Despite the subsequent catastrophic population decline, language loss and, in 1884, the outlawing of the most significant cultural practices, including the potlatch (a ban which was only withdrawn in 1951), many forms of cultural expression persist and flourish. Thus, Yuxweluptun, who grew up an 'urban Indian' in Vancouver, was as a teenager initiated into the ceremonial life of his father's Coast Salish people. He inherited rights to the Sxwayxwey from his father when he was 14; at 17 he became a Blackface dancer. Ceremonial aspects remain an important part of his life and belief, as is his knowledge of the land, learned while hunting and fishing.

Yuxweluptun is unusual amongst First Nations artists on the coast in having received an institutional art training. Most of his peers are apprenticed and practice in what, for want of a more nuanced word, is still described as the traditional way, as carvers. Consequently, his work defines and occupies a zone of productive conflict where new ways of being a Native artist in this region are worked out, and where the resulting canvases intervene in, upset and alter the direction of the discourse of advanced art. The local version of this discourse was initiated by Emily Carr. In the 1920s Carr brought modernist influence to bear on the European landscape tradition and found a pictorial language for the coastal forests of BC and their inhabitants. Where most non-natives were ignorant or prejudiced or both about the latter, Carr showed that the Canadian 'wilderness' had never been an unpopulated place. There is a sense in which Yuxweluptun is a successor to Carr, even as he knowingly appropriates her modes and re-appropriates her subject—native figures in the landscape. An historically significant installation at the Vancouver Art Gallery in 1997 juxtaposes their paintings in a dialogue that is simultaneously trans-generational, trans-ethnic and trans aesthetic.

Yuxweluptun's work has been controversial within the native community, where for some his art comes dangerously close to revealing secrets, the private knowledge specific to a Coast Salish community. There is also a feeling, not directed at Yuxweluptun alone, that too much pushing at the borders of traditional forms of expression, already victims of persecution, neglect and abandonment, could result in their diminishment. His reply is that if a form cannot be developed and changed it is fit only for a museum—"an Indian morgue," in his own words. Accordingly, he set out to claim a space in virtual reality, being determined to use this technology in its early stages to represent his people rather than allow them to be represented, yet again, by other people in ways over which they have no control. *Inherent Rights, Vision Rights* (1991), made under the aegis of the Computer Applications and Research Programme at the Banff Centre, makes possible a nighttime walk to a Salish longhouse where the central fire crackles loudly and masked dancers swirl around the observer.

Much of his work has been rooted in this conflation of cultural form and political act, as early paintings like *Red Man! Dance me on Sovereignty* (1985) shows clearly. It has, for example, allowed him to take a stand against the various inroads made by white society into his culture's integrity, for example with the religious wars still being waged on reservations: "All denominations are still missionising. Aren't they satisfied that in many places they have totally eradicated the culture?" It is the central theme of *Throwing their Culture Away* (1988).

Yuxweluptun has long been familiar with native British Columbian politics. His parents were involved with the North American Indian Brotherhood, his father headed the Union of B.C. Chiefs, while his mother was closely involved with the Indian Home-makers Association in B.C. His father, Ben Paul, an astute politician, has been called one of the most perceptive anthropologists of the white man on the Coast. As a boy Yuxweluptun travelled with them all over the province; their hope was that he would become a politician. Now his father sees that he is concerned with the same politics as himself, if "in different ways." It is a politics that leads to an uncompromising address to the non-native audience. His combative exhortations and in-your-face, cyber-punk techniques are, like his politics, rooted in the land.

Over the years the knowing, in-your-face deployment of cartoon-derived and kitsch effects has not diminished, although the borrowings from surrealism, especially from the work of Salvador Dali, have been modified. The sometimes gauche composition, as he mimics the grand, post-Renaissance landscape tradition, and passages of awkward, if not bad, painting, may be deliberate devices to skirt the pretension of the idea that there is such a thing as correct painting. Elements that persist are the trees, dense masses of green rendered in formlines and ovoids, the masked humans/spirits who are the protagonists of most paintings, and the artist's anger at the depredations of his land, which shapes his powerful, and increasingly popular, polemical paintings.

—Charlotte Townsend-Gault

ZOTOM, Paul

Variant names: Podaladalte
Tribal affiliations: Kiowa
Painter

Born: c. 1853; Kiowa name means Snake Head; baptized Paul Caryl Zotom, c. 1880, and also known as Zo Tom. **Education:** Hampton Institute, Hampton, Virginia. **Military Service:** Warrior; taken prisoner from Fort Sill, Oklahoma, to Fort Marion, St. Augustine, Florida, c. 1875. **Career:** Warrior; studied in Virginia and New York, late 1870s; baptized and ordained as a deacon, Episcopal church; established a mission in Oklahoma; commissioned for model tipi coverings by anthropologist James Mooney and for a series of buckskin shield covers; later in life he became a medicine man and member of the peyote religion.

Selected Group Exhibitions

1978   *100 Years of Native American Painting*, Oklahoma Museum of Art, Oklahoma City, Oklahoma

1979-80 *Native American Painting*, Mid-America Art Alliance, organized by the Joslyn Museum, Omaha, Nebraska (traveling)

1983 *Plains Indian Painting and Drawing of the 19th Century*, Colorado Springs Fine Arts Center, Colorado Springs, Colorado

1984-85 *Indianascher Kunstler* (traveling, Germany), organized by the Philbrook Museum, Tulsa, Oklahoma

1992 *Native American Heritage: A Survey of Native American Art*, Minneapolis Institute of Art, Minneapolis, Minnesota

1992-93 *Visions of the People*, Minneapolis Institute of Art, Minneapolis, Minnesota

1993 *Beyond the Prison Gates: The Fort Marion Experience and its Artistic Legacy*, organized by the National Cowboy Hall of Fame and Western Heritage Center, Oklahoma City, Oklahoma

Collections

Bienecke Rare Book and Manuscript Library, Yale University, New Haven, Connecticut; College Museum and Huntington Library, Hampton Institute, Hampton, Virginia; Colorado Springs Fine Arts Center, Colorado Springs, Colorado; Museum of the American Indian, New York.

Publications

On ZOTOM. Books—*Plains Indian Art from Fort Marion*, Karen Daniels Peterson, editor, Norman, University of Oklahoma Press, 1971; *Song From the Earth*, by Jamake Highwater, Boston, New York Graphic Society, 1976; *Great North American Indians: Profiles in Life and Leadership*, New York, Van Nostrand Reinhold Company, 1977; *100 Years of Native American Painting*, Oklahoma City, Oklahoma Museum of Art, 1978; *Native American Painting*, by Frederick Schmid and Patrick T. Houlihan, Kansas City, Mid-America Art Alliance, 1980; *Native American Painting: Selections from the Museum of the American Indian*, by David M. Fawcett and Lee A. Callander, New York, Museum of the American Indian, 1982; *Plains Indian Painting and Drawing of the 19th Century*, by Jonathan Batkin, Colorado Springs, Colorado Springs Fine Arts Center, 1983; *Indianascher Kunstler*, by Gerhard Hoffman, Munich, 1984; *Native Land: Sagas of the Indian Americas*, by Jamake Highwater, Boston, Little, Brown & Company, 1986; *Visions of the People*, by Evan M. Maurer, Minneapolis Institute of Art, 1992.

*   *   *

Paul Zotom was one of the southern Plains Indian warriors taken prisoner in 1875 at the end of the Red River War. These warriors became known as ledger artists because of their experiences drawing on ledger paper given to them while in captivity. While many of the ledger drawings are similar to narrative hide painting, a distinctive style was established by each individual artist. Ledger art is often considered in the study of evolving Native American painting styles and in the motivational shifts of Native American artists. However, a focus on these interests often overlooks the powerful emotional impact of the drawings.

On the Parapet of Fort Marion Next Day After Arrival (c. 1876) is typical of the narrative scenes created by Zotom documenting the experiences on the way to and after the arrival at Fort Marion. In the catalog to the exhibit, *100 Years of Native American Painting* (1978), Arthur Silberman points out the demoralizing effect of the journey and imprisonment and its expression in the work by Zotom. During the trip to the prison, one man was killed while trying to escape and another committed suicide. The prisoners were manacled and chained on the day after their arrival and were taken to the parapet of the fort. Silberman calls Zotom's portrait of the event "a poignant scene rendered with great skill and sensitivity... What Zotom portrays a year or two later is not an historic event but a recollection of a state of mind—the mood of those terrible days."

Jamake Highwater, in *Song from the Earth: American Indian Painting* (1976) notes that Zotom's works were more than mere documentation of events: "(He) filled an entire ledger book with curiously distant and rather sorrowfully remote landscapes describing his journey to prison and his life there. These are among the most charming and disarming of the ledger drawings. They express, like the drawings of children in Nazi concentration camps, an innocent response to tragedy, which makes the depicted events more tragic."

Zotom's experience illustrates an important change for artists that was a result of the Fort Marion experience. Warriors became conscious of their value as individual artists. They were celebrated in the press and given a great deal of attention. While he was imprisoned, Zotom was prolific in his art, but as far as is presently known, he did not create ledger drawings to any great degree following his release, though he did work as an artist. Zotom contributed, with Silverhorn and Ohettoint, to James Mooney's study of Kiowa tipis and shields, painting model tipis for Mooney in the late 1890s. Zotom also served as a mentor to several younger Kiowa artists who were part of the Indian Painting Renaissance of the early twentieth century.

—Kevin Smith

Metropolitan State University
Library Services
St. Paul, MN 55106

A SELECTED BIBLIOGRAPHY
ON NATIVE NORTH AMERICAN ARTISTS

Abbott, Lawrence. *I Stand in the Center of the Good.* Lincoln: University of Nebraska Press, 1994.

Alexander, Hartley Burr. *Pueblo Indian Painting.* Nice, France: C. Szwedzicki, 1932.

———. *Sioux Indian Painting.* Nice, France: C. Szwedzicki, 1938.

Amiotte, Arthur. *One Hundred Years of the Art of the Oglalas and Their Relatives.* Pine Ridge, South Dakota. Red Cloud Indian School, Heritage Center, Inc., 1988.

Archuleta, Margaret and Rennard Strickland. *Shared Visions: Native American Painting and Sculpture.* Phoenix: The Heard Museum, 1991.

Ballantine, Betty and Ian: *The Native Americans: An Illustrated History.* Atlanta: Turner Publishing, 1993.

Bates, Craig D. and Martha J. Lee. *Tradition and Innovation: A Basket History of the Indians of the Yosemite-Mono Lake Area.* Yosemite: National Park Service, 1990.

Berlo, Janet Catherine, editor, *The Early Years of Native American Art History.* Seattle: University of Washington Press, 1992.

———. *Plains Indian Drawings, 1865-1935: Pages from a Visionary History.* New York: Abrams, 1996.

Bernstein, Bruce and W. Jackson Rushing. *Modern by Tradition: American Indian Painting in the Studio Style.* Santa Fe: Museum of New Mexico, 1996.

Bibby, Brian. *The Fine Art of California Indian Basketry.* Sacramento: Crocker Art Museum and Heyday Books, 1996.

Blackboy, Cecil, et. al. *Painted Tipis by Contemporary Plains Indian Artists.* Anadarko, Oklahoma: Oklahoma Indian Arts and Crafts Cooperative, 1973.

Blodgett, Jean. *The Coming and Going of the Shaman: Eskimo Shamanism and Art.* Winnipeg: Winnipeg Art Gallery, 1978.

Blue Eagle, Acee. *Oklahoma Indian Painting, Poetry.* Tulsa: Acorn Publishing Company, 1959.

Broder, Patricia Janis. *American Indian Painting and Sculpture.* New York: Abbeville Press, 1981.

Brody, J. J. *Indian Painters and White Patrons.* Albuquerque: University of New Mexico Press, 1971.

———. *A Bridge across Cultures: Pueblo Painters in Santa Fe, 1910-1932.* Santa Fe: Wheelwright Museum of the American Indian, 1992.

Brown, Stephen. *The Spirit Within: Northwest Coast Native Art from the John H. Hauberg Collection.* Seattle: Seattle Art Museum, 1995.

Cardinal-Schubert, Joane. *Time for Dialogue.* Calgary: Calgary Aboriginal Awareness Society, 1992.

Coe, Ralph T. *Lost and Found Traditions: Native American Art 1965-85.* Seattle: University of Washington Press, 1986.

Cohodas, Marvin. *Degikup: Washoe Fancy Basketry 1895-1935.* Vancouver: The Fine Arts Gallery of the University of British Columbia, 1979.

Conn, Richard. *Circles of the World: Traditional Art of the Plains Indians.* Denver: Denver Art Museum; Seattle: University of Washington Press, Seattle, 1982.

Dawdy, Doris Ostrander. *Annotated Bibliography of American Indian Painting.* New York: Museum of the American Indian, 1968.

Dickason, Olive Patricia. *Indian Arts in Canada.* Ottawa: Department of Indian Affairs and Northern Development, 1972.

Dillingham, Rick. *Fourteen Families in Pueblo Pottery.* Santa Fe: 1994.

Dockstader, Frederick J. *Indian Art of the Americas.* New York: Museum of the American Indian, 1973.

Douglas, Frederic and Rene D. Harnoncourt. *Indian Art of the United States.* New York: Museum of Modern Art, 1941.

Driscoll, Bernadette. *Inuit Myths, Legends and Songs.* Winnipeg, Winnipeg Art Gallery, 1982.

Duff, Wilson, Bill Holm, and Bill Reid. *Art of the Raven.* Vancouver: University of British Columbia Press, 1967.

Dunn, Dorothy. *American Indian Painting of the Southwest and Plains Areas.* Albuquerque: University of New Mexico Press, 1968.

Ellison, Rosemary. *Contemporary Southern Plains Indian Painting;* Anadarko, Oklahoma: Oklahoma Indian Arts and Crafts Cooperative, 1972.

Fane, Diana, Ira Jacknix, and Lise M. Breen. *Objects of Myth and Memory: American Indian Art at The Brooklyn Museum.* Brooklyn: The Brooklyn Museum; Seattle: University of Washington Press, 1991.

Fawcett, David and Lee A. Callander. *Native American Painting: Selections from the Museum of the American Indian.* New York: Museum of the American Indian, 1982.

Feder, Norman. *American Indian Art.* New York: Abradale/Abrams, 1995.

Gonyea, Raymond, editor, *Spirit of the Earth: An Exhibition of Contemporary Native American Art.* New York: International Native American Council of Arts, 1982.

Gully, Anne, editor, *Watchful Eyes: Native American Women Artists.* Phoenix: The Heard Museum, 1994.

Hanson, James A. *Spirits in the Art from the Plains and Southwest Indian Cultures.* Santa Fe: Nedra Matteuccis, 1994.

Harjo, Joy, editor, *Reinventing Ourselves in the Enemy's Language.* Tucson: University of Arizona Press, 1993.

Hartman, Russell P. *Navajo Pottery: Traditions and Innovations.* Flagstaff: Northland Press, 1987.

Highwater, Jamake. *Song from the Earth: American Indian Painting.* Boston: New York Graphic Society, 1976.

———. *The Sweet Grass Lives On.* New York: Lippincott and Crowell, 1980.

———. *Arts of the Indian Americas.* New York: Harper & Row, 1983.

Hill, Rick. *Creativity Is Our Tradition: Three Decades of Contemporary Indian Art.* Santa Fe: Institute of American Indian Arts Museum, 1992.

Hill, Rick and Tom Hill. *Creations Journey: Native American Identity and Belief.* Washington, D.C.: Smithsonian Institution Press, 1994.

Hoffmann, Gerhard, et. al. *Indianische Kunst im 20 Jahrhundert.* Munich, Germany, 1984.

———. *Zeitgenoosische Kunst der Indianer und Eskimos Kanada.* Ottawa: Canadian Museum of Civilization, 1988.

Holm, Bill. *Northwest Coast Indian Art: An Analysis of Form.* Seattle: University of Washington Press, 1965.

Horse Capture, George P., et. al. *Robes of Splendor: Native North American Painted Buffalo Hides.* New York: New Press, 1993.

Houle, Robert. *New Work by a New Generation.* Regina, Saskatchewan: Norman Mackenzie Art Gallery, 1992.

Houlihan, Patrick T. *One Thousand Years of Southwestern Indian Ceramic Art.* New York: ACA American Indian Arts, 1982.

Houston, James. *Cape Dorset: A Decade of Eskimo Prints and Recent Sculptures.* Ottawa: National Gallery of Canada, 1967.

Jacka, Jerry and Lois. *Beyond Tradition: Contemporary Indian Art and Its Evolution.* Flagstaff: Northland Press, 1988.

———. *Enduring Traditions: Art of the Navajo.* Flagstaff: Northland Press, 1994.

Jacknix, Ira. *Carving Traditions of Northwest California.* Berkeley: University of California Press, 1995.

Jackson, Marion and Judith M. Nasby. *Contemporary Inuit Drawings.* Guelph, Ontario: McDonald Stewart Art Center, 1987.

Jacobson, Oscar B. *Kiowa Indian Art.* Nice, France: C. Szwedzicki, 1929.

———. *Indian Artists from Oklahoma.* Norman: University of Oklahoma Press, 1964.

Jacobson, Oscar B. and Jeanne D'Ucel. *American Indian Painters.* Nice, France: C. Szwedzicki, 1950.

Jensen, Doreen and Polly Sargent, editors, *Robes of Power: Totem Poles on Cloth.* Vancouver: The University of British Columbia Press, 1986.

Johannsen, Christian B. and John P. Ferguson, editors, *Iroquois Arts: A Directory of a People and Their Work.* Warnerville, New York: Association for the Advancement of Native North American Arts and Crafts, 1983.

Jonaitis, Aldona. *From the Land of the Totem Poles: The Northwest Coast Art Collection at the American Museum of Natural History.* Seattle: University of Washington Press, 1991.

———. *Chiefly Feasts: The Enduring Kwakiutl Potlach.* Seattle: University of Washington Press, 1991.

Jones, Ruthe Blalock. *Keepers of the Culture: Contemporary Southeastern Indian Artists.* Anniston, Alabama: Anniston Museum of Natural History, 1982.

Kabotie, Fred. *Designs from the Ancient Mimbrenos, with a Hopi Interpretation.* San Francisco: Grabhorn Press, 1949.

Katz, Jane B. *This Song Remembers: Self-Portraits of Native Americans in the Arts.* Boston: Houghton Mifflin Company, 1980.

LaFarge, Oliver. *A Pictorial History of the American Indian.* New York: Crown Publishers, 1956.

LaPena, Frank, and Janice Driesbach, editors, *The Extension of Tradition.* Sacramento: The Crocker Art Museum, 1985.

Latock, Barbara, editor, *Inuit Myths, Legends and Songs.* Winnipeg: Winnipeg Art Gallery, 1982.

Leroux, Odette, Marion Jackson, and Minnie Aodla, editors, *Inuit Women Artists: Voices from Cape Dorset.* Vancouver and Toronto: Douglas & McIntyre; Hull, Quebec: Canadian Museum of Civilization, 1994.

Lester, Patrick D. *The Biographical Directory of Native American Painters.* Norman: University of Oklahoma Press, 1995.

Lippard, Lucy R. *Mixed Blessings: New Art in a Multicultural Media.* New York: Pantheon Books, 1990.

Longfish, George and Joan Rondell. *Contemporary Native American Art: Contradictions in Indian Territory.* Stillwater: Oklahoma State University Press, 1983.

MacNair, Peter L., Alan L. Hoover, and Kevin Neary. *The Legacy: Continuing Traditions of Canadian Northwest Coast Art.* Victoria: British Columbia Provincial Museum, 1990.

Mather, Christine. *Native America: Arts, Traditions and Celebrations.* New York: Clarkson Potter, 1990.

Maurer, Evan M. *The Native American Heritage: A Survey of Native American Indian Art.* Lincoln: University of Nebraska Press, 1977.

———. *Visions of the People: A Pictorial History of Plains Indian Life.* Minneapolis: Minneapolis Institute of Arts, 1992.

McMaster, Gerald, et. al. *In the Shadow of the Sun: Perspectives on Contemporary Native Art.* Hull, Quebec: Canadian Museum of Civilization, 1993.

McMaster, Gerald, and Lee-Ann Martin. *Indigina: Contemporary Native Perspectives in Canadian Art.* Toronto: Craftsman House, 1994.

Monthan, Doris and Guy. *Art and Indian Individualists.* Flagstaff: Northland Press, 1975.

Moss, Kathlyn and Alice Scherer. *The New Beadwork.* New York: 1992.

Native Streams: Contemporary Native American Art. Chicago: Jan Cisero Gallery; Terre Haute: Turman Art Gallery, Indianapolis State University, 1996.

New, Lloyd Kiva. *American Indian Art in the 1980s.* Niagara Falls: Native American Center for the Living Arts, 1981.

Penney, David. *Art of the American Indian Frontier.* Seattle: University of Washington Press, 1993.

Penney, David and George C. Longfish. *Native American Art.* New York: H. L. Levin, 1994.

Podedworny, Carol: *Woodlands: Contemporary Art of the Anishnabe.* Thunder Bay, Ontario: Thunder Bay Art Gallery, 1989.

Ray, Dorothy J. *Aleut and Eskimo Art.* Seattle: University of Washington Press, 1981.

———. *A Legacy of Arctic Art.* Seattle: University of Washington Press, 1996.

Roberts, Carla, editor, *The Submuloc Show/Columbus Wohs.* Phoenix: Atlatl, 1992.

Roch, Ernst, editor, *Arts of the Eskimo: Prints.* Toronto: Oxford University Press, 1974.

Roosevelt, Anna C. and James G. E. Smith, editors, *The Ancestors: Native Artisans of the Americas.* New York: Museum of the American Indian, 1979.

Rushing, W. Jackson. *Native American Art and the New York Avant Garde: A History of Cultural Primitivism.* Austin: University of Texas Press, 1995.

———. *20th Century Native American Art: Essays on History and Criticism.* New York: Routledge, 1997.

Schiffer, Nancy N. *Navajo Arts and Crafts.* West Chester, Pennsylvania: Schiffer Publishing Ltd., 1992.

Seidelman, Harold and James Turner. *The Inuit Imagination: Arctic Myth and Sculpture.* Vancouver and Toronto: Douglas & McIntyre, 1993.

Silberman, Arthur. *100 Years of Native American Art.* Oklahoma City: Oklahoma Museum of Art, 1978.

Sloan, John and Oliver La Farge. *Introduction to American Indian Art.* New York: The Exposition of Indian Tribal Arts, Inc., 2 vols., 1931.

Smith, Jaune Quick-To-See. *Women of Sweetgrass, Cedar and Sage: Contemporary American Art by Native American Women.* New York: American Indian Community House, 1985.

Snodgrass, Jeanne. *American Indian Painters: A Biographical Directory.* New York: Museum of the American Indian, 1968.

Swinton, George. *Sculpture of the Eskimo.* Toronto: McClelland and Stewart, 1972.

Tanner, Clara Lee. *Southwest Indian Painting: A Changing Art.* Tucson: University of Arizona Press, 1973.

This Path We Travel. Washington, D.C.: National Museum of the American Indian, Smithsonian Institution, 1994.

Traugott, Joseph. *Appropriation and Transformation.* Albuquerque: University of New Mexico Press, 1990.

Trimble, Stephen. *Talking with the Clay: The Art of Pueblo Pottery.* Santa Fe: School of American Research Press, 1987.

Wade, Edwin L. and Rennard Strickland. *Magic Images: Contemporary Native American Indian Art.* Norman: University of Oklahoma Press, 1981.

Wade, Edwin L., editor, *The Arts of the North American Indian: Native Traditions in Evolution.* New York: Hudson Hills Press, 1986.

Warner, John Anson. *The Life and Art of the North American Indian*. New York: Crescent Books, 1975.

West, Richard W. *Treasures of the National Museum of the American Indian*. New York: Abbeville Press, 1996.

Wyckoff, Lydia, editor, *Vision + Voices: Native American Painting from the Philbrook Museum of Art*. Tulsa, Oklahoma, 1996.

Zurko, Kathleen McManus *We, The Human Beings*. Wooster, Ohio: College of Wooster Art Museum, 1992.

NAME INDEX

A

B

C

TRIBE INDEX

ACOMA PUEBLO
Wolf Robe Hunt
Lucy Lewis

ALEUT
Alvin Amason
John Hoover
Bill Prokopiof

ANISHNABE
Frank Big Bear
Jeffrey Chapman

APACHE
Carm Little Turtle

Cahuilla Apache
Bill Soza

Chiricahua Apache
Bob Haozous
Allan Houser

Jicarilla Apache
Darren Vigil Grey

Warm Springs Apache
Allan Houser

ARAPAHO
Mirac Creepingbear
Hachivi Edgar Heap of Birds
Charles Pratt
Carl Sweezy

ASSINIBOINE
Douglas Hyde

BEOTHUK
Mike MacDonald

BLACKFEET (U.S. designation)
King Kuka
Neil Parsons
Victor Pepion
Gary Schildt
Kathryn Stewart
Susan Stewart

BLACKFOOT (Canadian designation)
Faye HeavyShield
Gerald Tailfeathers

BLOOD
Gerald Tailfeathers

CADDO
T. C. Cannon

CAYUSE
P. Y. Minthorn

CHEROKEE
Marty Averett
Sara Bates
Jimalee Burton
Cecil Dick
Joan Hill
Lloyd Kiva New
Joanna Osburn-Bigfeather
Dana Tiger
Joseph Waano-Gano
Kay WalkingStick

CHEYENNE
Archie Blackowl
Bennie Buffalo
Hachivi Edgar Heap of Birds
Charles Pratt
Bently Spang
Dick West

CHIPPEWA
Earl Biss
David Bradley
Patrick DesJarlait
James Havard
Douglas Hyde
Alex Janvier
Glen La Fontaine
George Morrison

CHOCTAW
Marcus Amerman
Marty Averett
T. C. Cannon
James Havard
Dan V. Lomahaftewa
Linda Lomahaftewa
Gary White Deer

COCHITÍ PUEBLO
Helen Cordero
Joe Herrera
Diego Romero
Mateo Romero

COLVILLE
Joe Feddersen

COMANCHE
Blackbear Bosin
Rance Hood
Kay Miller
Leonard Riddles

COUSHATTA
Marty Averett

CREE (distinct from Plains Cree)
Kenny Baird
Rebecca Baird
Jackson Beardy

Goyce Kakegamic
Joshim Kakegamic
Glen La Fontaine
Jane Ash Poitras
Carl Ray
Jaune Quick-to-See Smith

CREEK
Fred Beaver
Acee Blue Eagle
Jimalee Burton
Doug Coffin
Anita Fields
Minisa Crumbo Halsey
Joan Hill
Bobby C. Martin
Solomon McCombs
Dana Tiger
Jerome Tiger
Hulleah Tsinhnahjinnie

CROW
Earl Biss
Kevin Red Star
Kathryn Stewart
Susan Stewart

DELAWARE
Parker Boyiddle
Ruthe Blalock Jones
Tom Poolaw

HAIDA
Robert Davidson
Freda Diesing
Charles Edenshaw
Bill Reid

Kaigani Haida
Dorothy Grant

HAISLA
Arthur Renwick

Kitamaat Haisla
Lyle Wilson

HOPI
David Dawangyumptewa
Preston Duwyenie
Fred Kabotie
Michael Kabotie
Charles Loloma
Otellie Loloma
Dan V. Lomahaftewa
Linda Lomahaftewa
Milland Dawa Lomakema
Preston Monongye
Waldo Mootzka
Raymond Naha
Dan Namingha

Nampeyo
Otis Polelonema
Polingaysi Qoyawayma
Dextra Quotskuyva
Ramona Sakiestewa
Bruce Timeche

HUPA
George Blake
Nathan Hale Olney, Jr.

INUIT
Manasie Akpaliapik
Abraham Anghik
Luke Anguhadluq
Ruth Annaqtussi Tulurialik
Barnabus Arnasungaaq
Davidialuk Alasuaq Amittu
Mark Emerak
Johnny Inukpuk
Helen Kalvak
Karoo Ashevak
John Kavik
Kenojuak Ashevak
Zacharias Kunuk
Victoria Mamnguksualuk
Jessie Oonark
Osuitok Ipeelee
John Pangnark
Josie Papialook
David Ruben Piqtoukun
Pitseolak
Abraham Pov
Pudlo
Joe Talirunnilik
John Tiktak
Mark Tungilik
Ovilu Tunnillie
Lucy Tasseor Tutsweetok
Marion Tuu'luuq
Judas Ullulaq

INUPIAQ
Melvin Olanna
Joseph Senungetuk

INUPIAT
Larry Ahvakana
Susie Bevins

IROQUOIS
Freddie Alexcee

ISLETA PUEBLO
Tony Jojola

JÉMEZ PUEBLO
José Rey Toledo

KAROK
Vivien Hailstone
Brian Tripp

KIOWA
Spencer Asah
James Auchiah
Dennis Belindo
Blackbear Bosin
Parker Boyiddle
T. C. Cannon
Sherman Chaddlesone
Mirac Creepingbear
Jack Hokeah
Al Momaday
Stephen Mopope
Tom Poolaw
James Silverhorn
Lois Smoky
Herman Toppah
Monroe Tsatoke
Darren Vigil Grey
Paul Zotom

KOOTENAI
Corwin Clairmont

KWAKIUTL
Douglas Cranmer
Richard Hunt
Tony Hunt
Mungo Martin
David Neel
Willie Seaweed
Lloyd Wadhams

LAKOTA

Hunkpapa Lakota
Joseph No Two Horns

Oglala Lakota
Arthur Amiotte
Amos Bad Heart Bull
Colleen Cutschall
Standing Bear

Yanktonai Lakota
Herman Red Elk

LUISEÑO
James Luna
Fritz Scholder
Wa Wa Chaw

MAIDU
Harry Fonseca

Concow Maidu
Mary Azbill
Frank Day
Frank Tuttle
Amanda Wilson

MALISEET
Lance Belanger

MÉTIS
Bob Boyer
Douglas Cardinal
Jim Logan
Kay Miller
Edward Poitras
Rick Rivet

MICMAC
Peter Clair
Mike MacDonald
Teresa Marshall
Leonard Paul
Luke Simon

MIWOK
Lucy Telles

Coast Miwok
Julia Parker
Leanna Tom

MOHAWK
Patricia Deadman
Richard Glazer Danay
Stan Hill
Shelly Niro
Bill Powless

NAVAJO
Elizabeth Abeyta
Narciso Abeyta
Tony Abeyta
Frank Austin
Beatien Yazz
Harrison Begay
Dennis Belindo
Big Lefthanded
Robert Chee
Lorenzo Clayton
Grey Cohoe
Mamie Deschillie
William B. Franklin
Louise Goodman
Carl N. Gorman
R. C. Gorman
Conrad House
Charlie Lee
Christine McHorse
Gerald Nailor
David Chethlahe Paladin
Ida Sahmie
Quincy Tahoma
Andy Tsinahjinnie
Hulleah Tsinhnahjinnie
Faye Tso
Emmi Whitehorse
The Williams Family
Margaret Wood
Elizabeth Woody
David Dawangyumptewa

NEZ PERCÉ
Douglas Hyde
P. Y. Minthorn

NISHGA
Larry McNeil

NOMTIPOM
Frank LaPeña

NUU-CHAH-NULTH
Art Thompson
Joe David
Ki-Ke-In

OJIBWAY
Ahmoo Angeconeb
Carl Beam
Jackson Beardy
Rebecca Belmore
Benjamin Chee Chee
Blake Debassige
Robert Houle
Glenna Matoush
Norval Morrisseau
Ron Noganosh
Daphne Odjig
Arthur Shilling
Roy Thomas

OKANAGAN
Joe Feddersen
Yuxweluptun

ONEIDA
David General

OSAGE
Norman Akers
Anita Fields
Yeffe Kimball

PAIUTE
The Dick Family
Jean LaMarr

Mono Lake Paiute
Carrie Bethel
Nellie Charlie
Tina Charlie
Lucy Telles
Leanna Tom

PATWIN
Mabel McKay

PAWNEE
Norman Akers
Acee Blue Eagle
Mirac Creepingbear

PEIGAN
Joane Cardinal-Schubert

PEORIA
Ruthe Blalock Jones

PIT RIVER
Jean LaMarr

PLAINS CREE
George Littlechild
Gerald McMaster
Allen Sapp
Alfred Young Man

POMO
Elsie Allen
Mary Benson
William Benson
Mabel McKay

Kashia Pomo
Julia Parker

POTAWATOMI
Doug Coffin
Woody Crumbo
Minisa Crumbo Halsey

SAC FOX
Duane Slick

SAHTU
Rick Rivet

SALISH
Corwin Clairmont
Jaune Quick-to-See Smith

Coast Salish
Susan Point
Yuxweluptun

SAN ILDEFONSO PUEBLO
Gilbert Atencio
Awa Tsireh
Popovi Da
Tony Da
Luis Gonzalez
Crescencio Martínez
Julian Martínez
Maria Martínez
Oqwa Pi
Tonita Peña
José D. Roybal
Soqween
Romando Vigil

SAN JUAN PUEBLO
Lorencita Atencio Bird
Rose Gonzales
Geronima Cruz Montoya

GEOGRAPHIC INDEX

CANADA

Alberta
Kenny Baird
Rebecca Baird
Douglas Cardinal
Joane Cardinal-Schubert
Faye HeavyShield
Alex Janvier
George Littlechild
Jane Ash Poitras
Gerald Tailfeathers

British Columbia
Freddie Alexcee
Dempsey Bob
Douglas Cranmer
Joe David
Freda Diesing
Charles Edenshaw
Walter Harris
Richard Hunt
Tony Hunt
Ki-Ke-In
Jim Logan
Mungo Martin
David Neel
Susan Point
Bill Reid
Arthur Renwick
Willie Seaweed
Art Thompson
Lloyd Wadhams
Lyle Wilson
Yuxweluptun

Manitoba
Jackson Beardy
Robert Houle
Lucy Tasseor Tutsweetok

New Brunswick
Lance Belanger
Peter Clair
Luke Simon

Northwest Territories
Manasie Akpaliapik
Abraham Anghik
Luke Anguhadluq
Ruth Annaqtussi Tulurialik
Barnabus Arnasungaaq
Mark Emerak
Helen Kalvak
Karoo Ashevak
John Kavik
Kenojuak Ashevak
Zacharias Kunuk
Victoria Mamnguksualuk
Jessie Oonark
Osuitok Ipeelee
John Pangnark

Josie Papialook
David Ruben Piqtoukun
Pitseolak
Pudlo
Rick Rivet
John Tiktak
Mark Tungilik
Ovilu Tunnillie
Marion Tuu'luuq
Judas Ullulaq

Nova Scotia
Mike MacDonald
Teresa Marshall
Leonard Paul

Ontario
Ahmoo Angeconeb
Carl Beam
Rebecca Belmore
Vincent Bomberry
Benjamin Chee Chee
Patricia Deadman
Blake Debassige
David General
Stan Hill
Goyce Kakegamic
Joshim Kakegamic
George Longfish
Glenna Matoush
Norval Morrisseau
Ron Noganosh
Daphne Odjig
Bill Powless
Carl Ray
Arthur Shilling
Roy Thomas

Quebec
Davidialuk Alasuaq Amittu
Johnny Inukpuk
Abraham Pov

Saskatchewan
Bob Boyer
Dana Claxton
Mary Longman
Gerald McMaster
Edward Poitras
Allen Sapp

MEXICO

Nuevo León
Domingo Cisneros

UNITED KINGDOM

Suffolk
Joanna Osburn-Bigfeather

UNITED STATES

Alaska
Larry Ahvakana
Alvin Amason
Susie Bevins
Robert Davidson
Dorothy Grant
John Hoover
Edna Davis Jackson
Nathan Jackson
Larry McNeil
Melvin Olanna
Bill Prokopiof
James Schoppert
Joseph Senungetuk

Arizona
Marcus Amerman
Frank Austin
Beatien Yazz
Harrison Begay
Dennis Belindo
Michael Chiago
David Dawangyumptewa
Preston Duwyenie
William B. Franklin
Louise Goodman
Carl N. Gorman
R. C. Gorman
Fred Kabotie
Michael Kabotie
Charlie Lee
Charles Loloma
Otellie Loloma
Dan V. Lomahaftewa
Linda Lomahaftewa
Milland Dawa Lomakema
Mario Martínez
Christine McHorse
Waldo Mootzka
Raymond Naha
Dan Namingha
Nampeyo
David Chethlahe Paladin
Otis Polelonema
Polingaysi Qoyawayma
Dextra Quotskuyva
Ida Sahmie
Quincy Tahoma
Bruce Timeche
Hulleah Tsinhnahjinnie
Faye Tso
The Williams Family
Margaret Wood
Elizabeth Woody

California
Elsie Allen
Mary Azbill
Mary Benson

William Benson
Carrie Bethel
George Blake
David Bradley
Nellie Charlie
Tina Charlie
Frank Day
The Dick Family
Harry Fonseca
Vivien Hailstone
Jean LaMarr
Frank LaPeña
Carm Little Turtle
James Luna
Mabel McKay
Preston Monongye
Julia Parker
Diego Romero
Mateo Romero
Preston Singletary
Bill Soza
Kathryn Stewart
Susan Stewart
Lucy Telles
Leanna Tom
Brian Tripp
Frank Tuttle
Wa Wa Chaw
Amanda Wilson

Colorado
Gilbert Atencio

Iowa
Charles Pushetonequa
Duane Slick

Kansas
Doug Coffin
Hachivi Edgar Heap of Birds

Minnesota
Frank Big Bear
Jeffrey Chapman
Patrick DesJarlait
George Morrison
Fritz Scholder

Montana
Corwin Clairmont
King Kuka
Neil Parsons
Victor Pepion
Herman Red Elk
Kevin Red Star
Gary Schildt
Jaune Quick-to-See Smith
Bently Spang
Alfred Young Man

Nebraska
Laurie Houseman-Whitehawk

MEDIUM INDEX

Architecture
Douglas Cardinal

Basketweaving
Elsie Allen
Mary Azbill
Mary Benson
William Benson
Carrie Bethel
Nellie Charlie
Tina Charlie
Peter Clair
The Dick Family
Vivien Hailstone
Rick Hill
Edna Davis Jackson
Louisa Keyser
Sarah Jim Mayo
Mabel McKay
Julia Parker
Lois Smoky
Lucy Telles
Leanna Tom
Brian Tripp
Amanda Wilson

Beads
Marcus Amerman

Buttons
Freda Diesing
Dorothy Grant

Carving
Manasie Akpaliapik
Freddie Alexcee
Barnabus Arnasungaaq
Rick Bartow
Susie Bevins
George Blake
Dempsey Bob
Jessie Cornplanter
Douglas Cranmer
Joe David
Robert Davidson
Blake Debassige
Freda Diesing
Charles Edenshaw
Walter Harris
Rick Hill
Stan Hill
Richard Hunt
Tony Hunt
Johnny Inukpuk
Nathan Jackson
John Kavik
Kenojuak Ashevak
Ki-Ke-In
Mungo Martin
David Neel
Joseph No Two Horns
Osuitok Ipeelee

Josie Papialook
David Ruben Piqtoukun
Susan Point
Pudlo
Bill Reid
James Schoppert
Willie Seaweed
Joseph Senungetuk
Art Thompson
Mark Tungilik
Lucy Tasseor Tutsweetok
Judas Ullulaq
Lloyd Wadhams
Lyle Wilson
Yuxweluptun

Ceramics
Elizabeth Abcyta
George Blake
Acee Blue Eagle
Mamie Deschillie
Anita Fields
R. C. Gorman
John Kavik
Otellie Loloma
Nora Naranjo-Morse
Joanna Osburn-Bigfeather
Lillian Pitt
Diego Romero
Luke Simon
Roger J. Tsabetsaye

Design
Frank Austin
Dorothy Grant
Gerald Nailor

Drafting
Amos Bad Heart Bull
Laurie Houseman-Whitehawk

Drawing
Arthur Amiotte
Luke Anguhadluq
Ruth Annaqtussi Tulurialik
Amos Bad Heart Bull
Frank Big Bear
Big Lefthanded
Benjamin Chee Chee
Davidialuk Alasuaq Amittu
Mark Emerak
R. C. Gorman
Sharol Graves
Hachivi Edgar Heap of Birds
Fred Kabotie
Helen Kalvak
John Kavik
Kenojuak Ashevak
Victoria Mamnguksualuk
Norval Morrisseau
Joseph No Two Horns

Nathan Hale Olney, Jr.
Jessie Oonark
Josie Papialook
Pitseolak
Bill Powless
Pudlo
Herman Red Elk
Standing Bear
Joe Talirunnilik
Ovilu Tunnillie

Filmmaking
Dana Claxton
Zacharias Kunuk
Shelly Niro
Bill Reid
Richard Ray Whitman

Glassblowing
Tony Jojola
Preston Singletary

Graphic
Blake Debassige
Walter Harris
Helen Kalvak
Ki-Ke-In
Ron Noganosh

Illustration
Jackson Beardy
Beatien Yazz
Harrison Begay
Michael Chiago
Jessie Cornplanter
Joan Hill
Rance Hood
Ki-Ke-In
Yeffe Kimball
Jack Malotte
Waldo Mootzka
Norval Morrisseau
Gerald Nailor
Bill Reid

Installation
Kenny Baird
Rebecca Baird
Sara Bates
Lance Belanger
Rebecca Belmore
Bob Boyer
Joane Cardinal-Schubert
Domingo Cisneros
Peter Clair
Colleen Cutschall
Bob Haozous
Faye HeavyShield
Robert Houle
Conrad House
James Luna

Teresa Marshall
Gerald McMaster
Ron Noganosh
Edward Poitras
Arthur Renwick
Bently Spang
Maxx Stevens
Susan Stewart
Charlene Teters
Hulleah Tsinhnahjinnie
Yuxweluptun

Jewelry
William Benson
Robert Davidson
Freda Diesing
Preston Duwyenie
Vivien Hailstone
Walter Harris
Richard Hunt
Tony Hunt
Wolf Robe Hunt
Rod Kaskalla
Ki-Ke-In
Charles Loloma
Otellie Loloma
Preston Monongye
Melvin Olanna
David Chethlahe Paladin
Susan Point
Roger J. Tsabetsaye
Ovilu Tunnillie
Lloyd Wadhams
Denise Wallace

Masks
Rick Bartow
Larry Beck
Susie Bevins
Joe Feddersen
Richard Hunt
Tony Hunt
Willie Seaweed

Mixed Media
Larry Ahvakana
Alvin Amason
Arthur Amiotte
Carl Beam
Domingo Cisneros
Corwin Clairmont
Doug Coffin
Anita Fields
Harry Fonseca
Ted Garner
Sharol Graves
Bob Haozous
Faye HeavyShield
Robert Houle
Conrad House
Edna Davis Jackson

Jean LaMarr
Frank LaPeña
Jim Logan
Mary Longman
Truman Lowe
James Luna
Teresa Marshall
Gerald McMaster
P. Y. Minthorn
David Neel
Joanna Osburn-Bigfeather
Jane Ash Poitras
Bill Prokopiof
Ernest Smith
Maxx Stevens
Brian Tripp
Richard Ray Whitman
Elizabeth Woody
Yuxweluptun

Murals
Fred Kabotie

Painting
Narciso Abeyta
Tony Abeyta
Norman Akers
Freddie Alexcee
Alvin Amason
Marcus Amerman
Arthur Amiotte
Ahmoo Angeconeb
Ruth Annaqtussi Tulurialik
Spencer Asah
Lorencita Atencio Bird
Gilbert Atencio
James Auchiah
Marty Averett
Awa Tsireh
Rebecca Baird
Rick Bartow
Carl Beam
Jackson Beardy
Beatien Yazz
Fred Beaver
Harrison Begay
Dennis Belindo
Frank Big Bear
Big Lefthanded
Earl Biss
Archie Blackowl
George Blake
Acee Blue Eagle
Blackbear Bosin
Bob Boyer
Parker Boyiddle
David Bradley
Bennie Buffalo
Jimalee Burton
T. C. Cannon
Joane Cardinal-Schubert

Sherman Chaddlesone
Jeffrey Chapman
Benjamin Chee Chee
Robert Chee
Michael Chiago
Corwin Clairmont
Lorenzo Clayton
Grey Cohoe
Helen Cordero
Jessie Cornplanter
Mirac Creepingbear
Woody Crumbo
Colleen Cutschall
Tony Da
David Dawangyumptewa
Frank Day
Blake Debassige
Patrick DesJarlait
Cecil Dick
Harry Fonseca
William B. Franklin
Richard Glazer Danay
Luis Gonzalez
Carl N. Gorman
R. C. Gorman
Sharol Graves
Hachivi Edgar Heap of Birds
Minisa Crumbo Halsey
Helen Hardin
Walter Harris
James Havard
Joe Herrera
Velino Shije Herrera
Joan Hill
Rick Hill
Jack Hokeah
Rance Hood
Robert Houle
Laurie Houseman-Whitehawk
Allan Houser
Oscar Howe
Richard Hunt
Wolf Robe Hunt
Alex Janvier
G. Peter Jemison
Ruthe Blalock Jones
Fred Kabotie
Michael Kabotie
Kai Sa
Goyce Kakegamic
Joshim Kakegamic
John Kavik
Ki-Ke-In
Yeffe Kimball
King Kuka
Jean LaMarr
Frank LaPeña
Calvin Larvie
James Lavadour
Charlie Lee
George Littlechild

Jim Logan
Charles Loloma
Otellie Loloma
Otellie Loloma
Dan V. Lomahaftewa
Linda Lomahaftewa
Milland Dawa Lomakema
George Longfish
Albert Looking Elk
C. F. Lovato
Jack Malotte
Bobby C. Martin
Crescencio Martínez
Julian Martínez
Maria Martínez
Mario Martínez
Glenna Matoush
Solomon McCombs
Gerald McMaster
Rafael Medina
Kay Miller
P. Y. Minthorn
Vicente Mirabal
Al Momaday
Preston Monongye
Geronima Cruz Montoya
Waldo Mootzka
Stephen Mopope
George Morrison
Norval Morrisseau
Raymond Naha
Gerald Nailor
Dan Namingha
Shelly Niro
Joseph No Two Horns
Daphne Odjig
Nathan Hale Olney, Jr.
Oqwa Pi
David Chethlahe Paladin
Neil Parsons
Leonard Paul
Tonita Peña
Victor Pepion
Susan Point
Otis Polelonema
Tom Poolaw
Pop Chalee
Bill Powless
Charles Pushetonequa
Polingaysi Qoyawayma
Carl Ray
Herman Red Elk
Kevin Red Star
Leonard Riddles
Rick Rivet
Mateo Romero
José D. Roybal
Ida Sahmie
Allen Sapp
Gary Schildt
Fritz Scholder

Willie Seaweed
Arthur Shilling
James Silverhorn
Luke Simon
Duane Slick
Ernest Smith
Jaune Quick-to-See Smith
Lois Smoky
Soqween
Bill Soza
Ernest Spybuck
Standing Bear
Kathryn Stewart
Susan Stewart
Patrick Swazo Hinds
Carl Sweezy
Quincy Tahoma
Gerald Tailfeathers
Roy Thomas
Dana Tiger
Jerome Tiger
Bruce Timeche
José Rey Toledo
Herman Toppah
Brian Tripp
Roger J. Tsabetsaye
Monroe Tsatoke
Andy Tsinahjinnie
Faye Tso
Frank Tuttle
Pablita Velarde
Romando Vigil
Darren Vigil Grey
Joseph Waano-Gano
Kay WalkingStick
Antowine Warrior
Wa Wa Chaw
Dick West
Gary White Deer
Emmi Whitehorse
Alfred Young Man
Yuxweluptun
Paul Zotom

Performance
Rebecca Belmore
Dana Claxton
James Luna
Duane Slick
Susan Stewart
Charlene Teters

Photography
Corwin Clairmont
Patricia Deadman
Joe Feddersen
Rick Hill
Laurie Houseman-Whitehawk
Frank LaPeña
Carm Little Turtle
James Luna

Mike MacDonald
Gerald McMaster
Larry McNeil
David Neel
Shelly Niro
Ron Noganosh
Arthur Renwick
Hulleah Tsinhnahjinnie
Richard Ray Whitman
Elizabeth Woody

Pottery
Awa Tsireh
Popovi Da
Tony Da
Preston Duwyenie
Jody Folwell
Rose Gonzales
Louise Goodman
Lela Gutiérrez
Van Gutiérrez
Lucy Lewis
Charles Loloma
Joseph Lonewolf
C. F. Lovato
Julian Martínez
Maria Martínez
Christine McHorse
Grace Medicine Flower
Trinidad Medina
Nampeyo
Nora Naranjo-Morse
Dextra Quotskuyva
Diego Romero
Roxanne Swentzell
Margaret Tafoya
Faye Tso
The Williams Family

Printmaking
Ahmoo Angeconeb
Carl Beam
David Bradley
Joane Cardinal-Schubert
Corwin Clairmont
Woody Crumbo
Joe David
Davidialuk Alasuaq Amittu
Robert Davidson
Blake Debassige
Freda Diesing
Mark Emerak
Hachivi Edgar Heap of Birds
Walter Harris
Tony Hunt
Goyce Kakegamic
Joshim Kakegamic
Kenojuak Ashevak
Ki-Ke-In
Jean LaMarr
James Lavadour
Jack Malotte

Victoria Mamnguksualuk
Bobby C. Martin
Norval Morrisseau
Jessie Oonark
Osuitok Ipeelee
Leonard Paul
Pitseolak
Jane Ash Poitras
Pudlo
Carl Ray
Joseph Senungetuk
Susan Stewart
Joe Talirunnilik
Art Thompson
Lloyd Wadhams
Lyle Wilson

Sculpture
Elizabeth Abeyta
Larry Ahvakana
Alvin Amason
Abraham Anghik
Luke Anguhadluq
Rebecca Baird
Carl Beam
Larry Beck
Acee Blue Eagle
Vincent Bomberry
Parker Boyiddle
David Bradley
Jeffrey Chapman
Doug Coffin
Davidialuk Alasuaq Amittu
Joe Feddersen
Anita Fields
Ted Garner
David General
Richard Glazer Danay
R. C. Gorman
Bob Haozous
Faye HeavyShield
Rance Hood
John Hoover
Allan Houser
Douglas Hyde
Edna Davis Jackson
Karoo Ashevak
King Kuka
Zacharias Kunuk
Glen La Fontaine
Truman Lowe
Victoria Mamnguksualuk
Glenna Matoush
George Morrison
Melvin Olanna
Joanna Osburn-Bigfeather
Osuitok Ipeelee
John Pangnark
Lillian Pitt
Susan Point
Edward Poitras

Abraham Pov
Charles Pratt
Bill Prokopiof
Bill Reid
Gary Schildt
Bently Spang
Roxanne Swentzell
Gerald Tailfeathers
Joe Talirunnilik
John Tiktak
Brian Tripp
Ovilu Tunnillie
Antowine Warrior

Silversmithing
Awa Tsireh

Textiles
Arthur Amiotte
Frank Austin
Edna Davis Jackson

Yeffe Kimball
C. F. Lovato
Lloyd Kiva New
Ramona Sakiestewa
Marion Tuu'luuq
Joseph Waano-Gano
Margaret Wood

Video
Kenny Baird
Hachivi Edgar Heap of Birds
Zacharias Kunuk
James Luna
Mike MacDonald
Susan Stewart

Weaving
Lorencita Atencio Bird
Dorothy Grant
Victoria Mamnguksualuk
Jessie Oonark

INDEX TO ILLUSTRATIONS

NOTES ON
ADVISERS and CONTRIBUTORS_____

ABBOTT, Larry. Essayist. Author of *I Stand in the Center of Good: Interviews with Contemporary Native American Artists;* contributor to *American Indian Quarterly, The Canadian Journal of Native Studies, Indian Artist,* and *Akwe:kon Journal.* **Essays:** Fonseca; Hachivi Edgar Heap of Birds; Joe Herrera; Little Turtle; Morrison; Namingha; Stevens; Tuttle; Whitman; Woody.

ARCHULETA, Margaret. Advisor. Curator of fine arts, Heard Museum, Phoenix, Arizona. Co-author with Rennard Strickland of *Shared Visions: Native American Painting and Sculpture in the Twentieth Century;* contributor to *Native Steams: Contemporary Native American Art* and the Heard Museum website.

BATES, Craig D. Essayist. Curator of ethnography, Yosemite National Park, California. Co-author of *Tradition and Innovation: A Basket History of the Indians of the Yosemite-Mono Lake Area.* **Essays:** Azbill; Bethel; Nellie and Tina Charlie; Parker; Telles.

BEAR, Perry. Essayist. Freelance writer, editor, and researcher specializing in the arts, literature, myth, and travel/cartography. **Essays:** Narciso Abeyta; Atencio Bird; Tony Da; Dawangyumptewa; Luis and Rose Gonzalez; Karoo Ashevak; Kimball; Kuka; Rafael Medina; Oqwa Pi; Pepion; Polelonema; Pratt; Roybal; Tsinahjinnie.

BERLO, Janet Catherine. Advisor and essayist. Susan B. Anthony Chair of Gender Studies and Art History, University of Rochester, Rochester, New York. Author of *Plains Indians Drawings, 1865-1935,* and *The Early Years of Native American Art History.* **Essays:** Amiotte; Anghik; Bad Heart Bull; Diesing; Emerak; Houseman-Whitehawk; Kalvak; Mamnguksualuk; No Two Horns; Piqtoukun; Standing Bear; Wallace.

BERNSTEIN, Bruce. Essayist. Director, Museum of American Indian Arts and Culture, Santa Fe, New Mexico; curator of over fifty exhibitions; member of board of directors, Southwestern Association for Indian Arts (SWAIA). Author of material on Native American art, including co-author of *Modern by Tradition: American Indian Painting in the Studio Style.* **Essays:** Begay; Popovi Da; Crescencio Martinez; Julian and Maria Martinez; Trinidad Medina; Tafoya; Toledo.

BURRETT, Deborah. Essayist. Ph.D candidate, Carleton University, with an emphasis on First Nations art. **Essays:** Cisneros; Longfish; Noganosh.

CAMPBELL, James D. Essayist. National director of Vis* Art Copyright, Inc., the copyright agency for visual arts in Canada; independent curator. Author of over 50 books and catalogues, including *Depth Makers: Selected Art Writings.* **Essays:** Havard; HeavyShield; Reid.

CHAMPAGNE, Duane. Advisor. Director, American Indian Studies Center, University of California, Los Angeles. Editor of the *American Indian Culture and Research Journal;* author of *The Native North American Almanac.*

CLARK, Janet. Advisor. Curator, Thunder Bay Art Gallery, Thunder Bay, Ontario; also curator of numerous exhibitions. Compiler, *Epogan: Recent Work by Peter J. Clair.*

COMPLO, Jennifer. Essayist. Associate curator, Eiteljorg Museum of American Indians and Western Art, Indianapolis, Indiana. **Essays:** Bates; Clairmont; Lowe.

COOLEY, Lisa. Essayist. MA in Native American Art History, University of Oklahoma; founder, The Artist's Right Hand, a company providing consulting and administrative services for artists, Santa Fe, New Mexico. **Essays:** Averett; Boyiddle; Poolaw.

CUTLER, Lori. Essayist. Director, Canadian Inuit Art Information Centre, Indian and Northern Affairs Canada, Ottawa, Ontario. **Essays:** Arnasungaaq; Ullulaq.

CUTSCHALL, Colleen. Advisor, essayist, and entrant. Artist; associate professor and coordinator of visual arts, Brandon University, Brandon, Manitoba; contributor to numerous books and journals. See her entry for further details. **Essay:** Cardinal-Schubert.

DOBKINS, Rebecca. Essayist. Anthropologist; instructor at several universities in the United States. Author of *Memory and Imagination: The Legacy of Maidu Indian Artist Frank Day.* **Essays:** Day; LaPena.

DUBIN, Margaret. Essayist. Ph.D candidate at the University of California, Berkeley. Author of numerous essays and articles on contemporary artists for journals and newspapers. **Essays:** Amason; Jojola; LaMarr; Logan; Dan and Linda Lomahaftewa; Mario Martinez; McNeil; Miller; Sakiestewa; Singletary; Slick; Spang.

DUNCAN, Kate. Essayist. Associate professor of Native American art history, Arizona State University and University of Washington. **Essays:** Beck; Olana; Senungetuk.

FARRIS, Phoebe. Essayist. Associate professor of art and design and women's studies, Purdue University. Frequent contributor to journals; editor of *Voices of Color: Art and Society in the Americas* and *Women Artists of Color: A Bio-Critical Sourcebook to 20th Century Artists in the Americas.* Guest curator and consultant to galleries and museums. **Essays:** Hardin; Whitehorse.

GAGNON, Louis. Essayist. Conservateur d'art inuit. Contributor to exhibitions, catalogues and journals focusing on Inuit art. **Essays:** Davidialuk; Inukpuk; Pov; Talirunnilik.

GILES, Vesta. Essayist. Vancouver-based freelance writer; contributor to books, including *Canadian Artists,* and to journals, including *Indian Artist,* and newspapers. **Essays:** Akpaliapik; Bomberry; Clair; Cutschall; General; Grant; La Fontaine; Garner; Longman; MacDonald; Malotte; Matoush; Olney; Osuitok Ipeelee; Paul; Pitt; Point; Prokopiof; Renwick; Rivet; Simon; Wadhams; White; Wood.

HAGER, Barbara. Essayist. Regular contributor to several national magazines and newspapers in Canada; author of *Honour Song,* a collection of profiles of prominent aboriginal Canadians. **Essay:** Mungo Martin.

HARTMAN, Russell. Essayist. Anthropologist with the California Academy of Sciences. Author of books, including *Navajo Pottery: Traditions and Innovations.* **Essays:** Beatien Yazz; Cannon; Chee; Deschillie; Goodman; Carl and R.C. Gorman; Charles Loloma; Keyser; McHorse; Nailor; Sahmie; Tso; Williams family.

HESSEL, Ingo. Essayist. Production and special projects coordinator, Canadian Inuit Art Information Centre, Indian and Northern

Affairs Canada, Ottawa, Ontario. Contributor to *Visions of Power: Contemporary Art by First Nations, Inuit and Japanese Canadians*, and other books, catalogues, and journals. **Essays:** Kavik; Pangnark; Tiktak; Tutsweetok.

HILL, Rick. Advisor and essayist. Author of guest preface, and entrant. Assistant professor of American studies, State University of New York at Buffalo. Special assistant for the National Museum of the American Indian, Smithsonian Institution, Washington, D.C.; former museum director, Institute of American Indian Arts, Santa Fe, New Mexico. He lives on the Tuscarora Reservation near Niagara Falls and continues to exhibit his paintings and fine art photography. Co-author of *Creation's Journey: Native American Identity and Belief* (see entry for further details). **Essays:** Coffin; Stan Hill; House; Hyde; Soza.

HOFFMANN, Gerhard and Gisela. Essayists. Both written extensively on art and artists. Gerhard edited *Indianische Kunst im 20 Jahrhundert* and *Im Schatten der Sonne: Zeitgenoessische Kunst der Indianer und Eskimos in Kanada* and important German exhibitions of Native American, First Nations, and Inuit art; contributor to *The Arts of the North American Indian: Native Traditions in Evolution,* edited by Edwin L. Wade. **Essays:** Tony Abeyta; Atencio; Biss; Buffalo; Clayton; Cohoe; Cordero; David; Franklin; Houser; Jemison; Lomakema; Lonewolf; Momaday; Mootzka; Pop Chalee; Red Star; Scholder; Silverhorn; Sweezy; Tahoma; Vigil.

JACKSON, Marion. Essayist. Professor of art history, Wayne State University; curator of exhibitions of Inuit art. Author and editor of numerous articles and catalogues, including *Contemporary Inuit Drawings* (with Judith Nasby) and *Qamanittuaq: Where the River Widens: Drawings by Baker Lake Artists* (with Judith Nasby and William Noah). **Essays:** Anguhadluq; Annaqtussi Tulurialik; Kenojuak Ashevak; Oonark; Papialuk; Pitseolak.

JANTZER-WHITE, Marilee. Essayist. Instructor in the Art History Department, University of California, Los Angeles. Contributor to journals and magazines. **Essays:** Big Bear; Chapman; DesJarlait.

LALONDE, Christine. Essayist. Curatorial assistant for Inuit art, National Gallery of Canada. Essayist, including articles for *Inuit Art Quarterly* and other publications. **Essays:** Kunuk; Tungilik; Tuu'luuq.

LaFRAMBOISE, C. J. Essayist. Museum director, Chippewa Heritage Center, Belcourt, North Dakota; freelance writer. **Essays:** Amerman; Duweynie.

LEROUX, Odette. Advisor. Curator of Inuit art, Canadian Ethnology Service, Hull, Quebec. Co-editor of *Inuit Women Artists: Voices from Cape Dorset.* Essayist; contributor to journals and catalogues, including *In the Shadow of the Sun: Perspectives on Contemporary Native Art.*

McMASTER, Gerald. Advisor and entrant. Artist; curator of Contemporary Indian Art, Canadian Museum of Civilization, Hull, Quebec. Author and co-editor of *Indigena: Contemporary Native Perspectives* and *In the Shadow of the Sun: Perspectives on Contemporary Native Art.* See entry for further details.

MITHLO, Nancy Marie. Essayist. Cultural anthropologist; instructor, University of New Mexico; lecturer. Writer on contemporary Native American artists with work represented in *Creativity Is Our Tradition: Three Decades of Native American Art* and *Indian Artist,* and other periodicals. **Essays:** Diego and Mateo Romero; Charlene Teters.

PENNEY, David. Advisor. Curator of Native American art, Detroit Institute of Arts. Author of *Art of the American Indian Frontier;* co-author with George Longfish of *Native American Art.*

PHILLIPS, Ruth. Essayist. Art historian specializing in the historical and contemporary arts of the Woodlands region. Director, Museum of Anthropology and professor of art history and anthropology, University of British Columbia. Curator of exhibitions. Author of books, including *Trading Identities: Native Souvenir Arts from Northeastern North America, 1700-1900.* **Essays:** Debassige; Morrisseau.

PODEDWORNY, Carol. Essayist. Curator. Author of essays and catalogues, including several for the Thunder Bay Art Gallery, such as *Woodlands: Contemporary Art of the Anishnabe;* editor. **Essays:** Angeconeb; Kenny and Rebecca Baird; Beardy; Belanger; Boyer; Chee Chee; Deadman; Janvier; Odjig; Edward Poitras; Sapp; Tailfeathers.

POTTER, Kristin. Essayist. Law school student and MA in art history, University of New Mexico. **Essays:** Bartow; Bevins; Bob; Feddersen; Graves; Marshall; Pudlo; Schoppert; Tunnillie.

REDCORN, Marla. Essayist. Assistant curator, Gilcrease Museum, Tulsa. Author and editor; contributor to *Visions + Voices: Native American Painting from the Philbrook Museum of Art.* **Essays:** Chaddlesone; Creepingbear; Smoky.

ROBERTS, Lisa. Essayist. Ph.D candidate at the University of Illinois; former assistant curator of Native American art, Detroit Institute of Arts; lecturer and writer. **Essays:** Awa Tsireh; Velino Shije Herrera; Fred Kabotie; Looking Elk; Luna; Pena; Quick-To-See-Smith; Velarde; WalkingStick.

ROBERTS, Carla. Advisor. Executive director, Atlatl, a national service organization for Native American arts based in Phoenix, Arizona. Editor, including *The Submuloc Show/Columbus Wohs.*

RUSHING, W. Jackson. Advisor and author of the introduction. Associate professor of art history, University of Missouri, St. Louis. Author and editor of numerous journal articles, exhibition catalogues and books on twentieth century art, including *20th Century Native American Art: Essays on History and Criticism* and *Native American Art and The New York Avant Garde: A History of Cultural Primitivism.*

RYAN, Allen. Essayist. Cultural anthropologist specializing in the use of humor. Contributor to numerous journals and catalogues, including *The Cowboy/Indian Show* and *House Made of Stars.* **Essays:** Haozous; Littlechild; Powless.

SCHAAF, Gregory. Essayist. Historian for various Indian nations; director, Center for Indigenous Arts & Cultures, Santa Fe, New Mexico. Author of books, including *Honoring the Weavers* and *Ancient Ancestors of the Southwest;* essayist. **Essays:** Allen;

Austin; Bensons; Blake; Burton; Cornplanter; Guiterrez; Kai-Sa; Larvie; Lee; Otellie Loloma; Lovato; Mayo; McKay; Monogye; Montoya; Naha; Nampeyo; New; Pushtanequa; Quotskuyua; Red Elk; Schildt; Smith; Swazo Hinds; Swentzel; Timeche; Toppah; Tripp; Vigil Grey; Waano-Gano; Wa Wa Chaw.

SCHEVIL, Margot Blum. Essayist. Research associate, Phoebe Hearst Museum of Anthropology, Berkeley, California. Author of essays, articles, and books, including *The Pollen Path: A Collection of Navajo Myths Retold.* **Essay:** Hailstone.

SCHWARTZ, Allan. Advisor. Head librarian, Institute of American Indian Arts, Santa Fe, New Mexico; coordinator of contributions from administrators at the Institute toward this publication.

SMITH, Kevin Warren. Essayist. Visual artist, musician, curator of exhibits, primarily of Indian artists of Oklahoma, and curator of education, Gilcrease Museum, Tulsa, Oklahoma. **Essays:** Akers; Beaver; Blackowl; Bosin; Crumbo; Cecil Dick; Halsey; Joan Hill; Howe; Wolf Robe Hunt; Jones; Bobby C. Martin; McCombs; Spybuck; Dana and Jerome Tiger; Zotom.

SPANG, Bently. Essayist and entrant. Artist; executive director, Montana Indian Contemporary Arts; curator; panelist at symposia and conferences. See entry for more details. **Essays:** Rick Hill; Kathryn and Susan Stewart.

STOREY, Ann. Essayist. Ph.D candidate in art history, University of Washington specializing in the confluence of Native American and European cultures at the time of contact; manager of art organizations; curator of several exhibitions on contemporary Native American art. **Essays:** Ahvakana; Hoover; Edna Davis Jackson; Parsons.

TOWNSEND-GAULT, Charlotte. Essayist. Social anthropologist; assistant professor of art history, University of British Columbia. Author of numerous essays on Native art for such journals as *Arts Magazine, Current Anthropology, Cultural Studies,* and *American Indian Quarterly.* **Essays:** Belmore; Claxton; Ki-ke-in; Neel; Yuxweluptun.

TREVELYN, Amy. Essayist. Professor of art history, Gettysburg College, Gettysburg, Pennsylvania; curator; essayist, editor and author of exhibition catalogues, including *Why Do You Call Us Indians?* **Essays:** Beam; Houle; Goyce and Josh Kakegamic; McMaster; Ray.

VIGIL, Jennifer. Advisor and essayist. Ph.D. candidate in art history with an emphasis on contemporary Native American art, University of Iowa; curator; writer. **Essays:** Elizabeth Abeyta; Fields; Folwell; Lewis; Minthorn; Naranjo-Morse; Niro; Jane Ash Poitras; Tsinajinnie.

WARNER, John Anson. Essayist. Professor at institutions in Canada, the United States, and Japan. Author of *The Life and Art of the American Indian*; contributor to books, including *The Arts of the North American Indian: Native Traditions in Evolution,* and periodicals, including *American Indian Art* and *Southwest Art.* **Essays:** Asah; Auchiah; Belindo; Cranmer; Davidson; Glazer Danay; Harris; Hokeah; Hood; Richard and Tony Hunt; Nathan Jackson; Mopope; Riddles; Seaweed; Tsatoke; Thomas; Thompson; Warrior; West; White Deer; Wilson; Young Man.

WHITE, Mary. Advisor. Head librarian, American Indian Studies Center, University of California, Berkeley; previously head librarian, Institute of American Indian Arts.

WRIGHT, Robin. Essayist. Curator of Northwestern Art, Burke Museum, University of Washington. **Essay:** Edenshaw.

YOUNG MAN, Alfred. Advisor and entrant. Artist; associate professor, Native American Studies Department, University of Lethbridge, Alberta. Manuscript/book reviewer for *American Indian Culture and Research Journal, American Indian Quarterly,* and *Prairie Forum: The Journal of the Canadian Research Center.* Author of numerous essays on political, cultural, and social issues. See entry for further details.

ZASTROW, Leona. Essayist. Educator, including elementary and secondary schools on the Gila River Reservation in Arizona; administrator of community curriculum planning and school outreach programs; president of Educational Planning for Individuals and Communities (EPIC), Inc. **Essays:** Bradley; Chiago; Kaskalla; Medicine Flower.

Metropolitan State University
Library Services
St. Paul. MN 55106